America's
TEST KITCHEN

WELCOME TO
AMERICA'S TEST KITCHEN

THIS BOOK HAS BEEN TESTED, WRITTEN, AND edited by the folks at America's Test Kitchen, a very real 2,500-square-foot kitchen located just outside of Boston. It is the home of *Cook's Illustrated* magazine and *Cook's Country* magazine and is the Monday-through-Friday destination for more than two dozen test cooks, editors, food scientists, tasters, and cookware specialists. Our mission is to test recipes over and over again until we understand how and why they work and until we arrive at the "best" version.

We start the process of testing a recipe with a complete lack of conviction, which means that we accept no claim, no theory, no technique, and no recipe at face value. We simply assemble as many variations as possible, test a half dozen of the most promising, and taste the results blind. We then construct our own hybrid recipe and continue to test it, varying ingredients, techniques, and cooking times until we reach a consensus. The result, we hope, is the best version of a particular recipe, but we realize that only you can be the final judge of our success

(or failure). As we like to say in the test kitchen, "We make the mistakes, so you don't have to."

All of this would not be possible without a belief that good cooking, much like good music, is indeed based on a foundation of objective technique. Some people like spicy foods and others don't, but there is a right way to sauté, there is a best way to cook a pot roast, and there are measurable scientific principles involved in producing perfectly beaten, stable egg whites. This is our ultimate goal: to investigate the fundamental principles of cooking so that you become a better cook. It is as simple as that.

You can watch us work (in our actual test kitchen) by tuning in to *America's Test Kitchen* (www.americastestkitchen.com) on public television or by subscribing to *Cook's Illustrated* magazine (www.cooksillustrated.com) or *Cook's Country* magazine (www.cookscountry.com), which are each published every other month. We welcome you into our kitchen, where you can stand by our side as we test our way to the "best" recipes in America.

THE BEST INTERNATIONAL RECIPE

A BEST RECIPE CLASSIC

THE BEST INTERNATIONAL RECIPE

A BEST RECIPE CLASSIC

BY THE EDITORS OF

COOK'S ILLUSTRATED

PHOTOGRAPHY

DANIEL J. VAN ACKERE AND CARL TREMBLAY

ILLUSTRATIONS

JOHN BURGOYNE

AMERICA'S TEST KITCHEN

BROOKLINE, MASSACHUSETTS

America's Test Kitchen
17 Station Street
Brookline, MA 02445

ISBN-13: 978-1-933615-17-2
ISBN-10: 1-933615-17-6

Library of Congress Cataloging-in-Publication Data
The Editors of Cook's Illustrated

The Best International Recipe
A Home Cook's Guide to the Best Recipes in the World

1st Edition
ISBN-13: 978-1-933615-17-2
ISBN-10: 1-933615-17-6
(hardcover): U.S. $35 CAN $41.50
1. Cooking. 1. Title
2007

Manufactured in the United States of America

10 9 8 7 6 5 4 3 2 1

Distributed by America's Test Kitchen, 17 Station Street, Brookline, MA 02445

Senior Editor: Lori Galvin
Senior Food Editor: Julia Collin Davison
Associate Editors: Elizabeth Wray Emery, Rachel Toomey, and Sarah Wilson
Test Cooks: Suzannah McFerran, Bryan Roof, and Megan Wycoff
Series Designer: Amy Klee
Designers: Tiffani Beckwith and Matthew Warnick
Staff Photographer: Daniel J. van Ackere
Additional Photography: Carl Tremblay
Food Styling: Mary Jane Sawyer
Illustrator: John Burgoyne
Director of Production: Guy Rochford
Senior Production Manager: Jessica Lindheimer Quirk
Color and Imaging Specialist: Andrew Mannone
Copyeditor: Cheryl Redmond
Proofreader: Debra Hudak
Indexer: Elizabeth Parson

Pictured on front of jacket: Panna Cotta (page 322)

Pictured on back of jacket: Chicken in a Pot (page 181), Spanish Shellfish Stew (page 232), Salerno-Style Spaghetti with Fried Eggs and Bread Crumbs (page 293), Chinese Barbecued Pork (page 534), Mexican Street Corn (page 13) and Pad Thai (page 480)

Pictured with chapter openers: 1. Mexico—Steak Fajitas (page 23), 2. Latin America and the Caribbean—Latino-Style Chicken and Rice (page 59), 3. British Isles and Ireland—Fish and Chips (page 94), 4. Central Europe and Scandinavia—Creamy Dill Cucumber Salad (page 115), 5. France—Pots de Crème au Chocolat (page 209), 6. Spain and Portugal—Classic Gazpacho (page 229), 7. Italy—Parmesan Risotto (page 274), 8. Greece and Turkey—Baklava (page 370), 9. Russia and Eastern Europe—Beef Stroganoff (page 395), 10. Africa and the Middle East—Middle Eastern–Style Lamb Pita Sandwich (page 428), 11. India—Saffron Chicken and Rice with Yogurt Sauce (page 449), 12. Southeast Asia—Vietnamese Spring Roll (page 473), 13. China—Pork and Cabbage Dumplings (page 498), 14. Japan and Korea—Chicken Teriyaki (page 548)

CONTENTS

PREFACE

OUR FAMILY TRAVELS A LOT DURING MARCH, when our kids all get a two-week school vacation. We have been to Ecuador, Vietnam, Belize, and Morocco, as well as to more conventional destinations in Europe. Most of these are hiking trips—we bring our boots and bandanas—and our goal is to find out a bit about how regular, everyday folks live in other parts of the world.

The culinary benefit of this travel is finding out firsthand what families really make for dinner, not what some fancy food magazine chooses for its cover. If you were to read about the cuisine of Morocco in a cookbook or epicurean publication, you would certainly encounter tagine and couscous (two recipes that can be made here at home with modest variations), but only by walking through the streets of Marrakech would you encounter the fabulous coconut cookies sold by street vendors or the flat breakfast bread baked in a tagine pot that we were served in a small riad (guest house) in Fez. Simply put, real home cooking from around the world is a whole lot more interesting and relevant to American home cooks than gourmet recipes from afar.

That was our intention in creating this book: to provide cooks in this country with recipes that make sense for home cooks, not hoary chestnuts or restaurant dishes that don't travel well. Sure, lots of these recipes will seem familiar—in those cases, we have worked hard through extensive testing to make them foolproof and well-adapted to the American kitchen. But others are both practical and new to an American audience. You have probably never tried Italy's garlicky spaghetti with bread crumbs and fried eggs or the delicious version of shepherd's pie made in Chile. Or, one of my favorites and a simple recipe to boot, the smoky, uniquely flavored street corn sold in Mexico that is easily replicated here in America by slathering whole ears of corn with a mayonnaise and cheese mixture and then running them under the broiler.

Of course, the banes of most international cookbooks are hard-to-find ingredients and over-the-top techniques. Real Mexican cooking, for example, is based on the availability of a host of pantry staples and common ingredients that American home cooks would be hard-pressed to find, much less keep on hand. So the job of our test kitchen is to translate these recipes, preserving their intent and basic character while helping them make a smooth transition to American shores.

Our favorite family vacation destination was Morocco. We landed in Marrakech and then drove two days over the Atlas Mountains down into the Sahara, where we spent four days hiking with four camels, a 70-year-old camel driver named Hussein, a cook, and our guide, Mohammed. The first morning in the desert, I awoke to find a rug spread out on the sand, with a small table perched in the middle. We sat cross-legged, drank excellent coffee, and enjoyed a stack of paper-thin crêpes that we spread with jam, rolled up, and consumed like large edible cigars. Here we were, seemingly in the middle of nowhere, enjoying a French classic that had been adapted to desert travel. A great example of a recipe that knows no boundaries.

This book, then, is an attempt at travel with a backpack rather than a large expense account. This is a busman's holiday in which we set out to find exactly the type of food that we prefer to cook at home: practical, straightforward, and foolproof. We intended to avoid the tourist traps, the group tours, the overpriced four-star meals, and the foods that are best left behind, since they make sense only for another culture in another part of the world.

So we offer this book to you as a trek of sorts, a simple walking expedition to far parts of the world where you will, we hope, enjoy the type of foods that every good cook wants to bring home. This collection of recipes represents the simple pleasures of home cooking, the sort of food that you can enjoy no matter where you live.

Christopher Kimball
Founder and Editor,
Cook's Illustrated and *Cook's Country*
Host, *America's Test Kitchen*

A Note on Conversions

SOME SAY COOKING IS A SCIENCE AND AN art. We would say that geography has a hand in it, too. Flour milled in the United Kingdom and elsewhere will feel and taste different from flour milled in the United States. So we cannot promise that the loaf of bread you bake in Canada or England will taste the same as a loaf baked in the States, but we can offer guidelines for converting weights and measures. We also recommend that you rely on your instincts when making our recipes. Refer to the visual cues provided. If the bread dough hasn't "come together in a ball," as described, you may need to add more flour—even if the recipe doesn't tell you so. You be the judge. For more information on conversions and ingredient equivalents, visit our Web site at www.cooksillustrated.com and type "conversion chart" in the search box.

The recipes in this book were developed using standard U.S. measures following U.S. government guidelines. The charts below offer equivalents for U.S., metric, and Imperial (U.K.) measures. All conversions are approximate and have been rounded up or down to the nearest whole number. For example:

1 teaspoon = 4.9292 milliliters, rounded up to 5 milliliters

1 ounce = 28.3495 grams, rounded down to 28 grams

Volume Conversions

U.S.	METRIC
1 teaspoon	5 milliliters
2 teaspoons	10 milliliters
1 tablespoon	15 milliliters
2 tablespoons	30 milliliters
¼ cup	59 milliliters
⅓ cup	79 milliliters
½ cup	118 milliliters
¾ cup	177 milliliters
1 cup	237 milliliters
1¼ cups	296 milliliters
1½ cups	355 milliliters
2 cups	473 milliliters
2½ cups	592 milliliters
3 cups	710 milliliters
4 cups (1 quart)	0.946 liter
1.06 quarts	1 liter
4 quarts (1 gallon)	3.8 liters

Weight Conversions

OUNCES	GRAMS
½	14
¾	21
1	28
1½	43
2	57
2½	71
3	85
3½	99
4	113
4½	128
5	142
6	170
7	198
8	227
9	255
10	283
12	340
16 (1 pound)	454

Conversions for Ingredients Commonly Used in Baking

Baking is an exacting science. Because measuring by weight is far more accurate than measuring by volume, and thus more likely to achieve reliable results, in our recipes we provide ounce measures in addition to cup measures for many ingredients. Refer to the chart below to convert these measures into grams.

INGREDIENT	OUNCES	GRAMS
I cup all-purpose flour*	5	142
I cup whole wheat flour	5½	156
I cup granulated (white) sugar	7	198
I cup packed brown sugar (light or dark)	7	198
I cup confectioners' sugar	4	113
I cup cocoa powder	3	85
Butter†		
4 tablespoons (½ stick, or ¼ cup)	2	57
8 tablespoons (I stick, or ½ cup)	4	113
16 tablespoons (2 sticks, or I cup)	8	227

* U.S. all-purpose flour, the most frequently used flour in this book, does not contain leaveners, as some European flours do. These leavened flours are called self-rising or self-raising. If you are using self-rising flour, take this into consideration before adding leavening to a recipe.

† In the United States, butter is sold both salted and unsalted. We generally recommend unsalted butter. If you are using salted butter, take this into consideration before adding salt to a recipe.

Oven Temperatures

FAHRENHEIT	CELSIUS	GAS MARK (IMPERIAL)
225	105	¼
250	120	½
275	130	I
300	150	2
325	165	3
350	180	4
375	190	5
400	200	6
425	220	7
450	230	8
475	245	9

Converting Temperatures from an Instant-Read Thermometer

We include doneness temperatures in many of our recipes, such as those for poultry, meat, and bread. We recommend an instant-read thermometer for the job. Refer to the table at left to convert Fahrenheit degrees to Celsius. Or, for temperatures not represented in the chart, use this simple formula:

Subtract 32 degrees from the Fahrenheit reading, then divide the result by 1.8 to find the Celsius reading.

EXAMPLE:

"Roast until the juices run clear when the chicken is cut with a paring knife or the thickest part of the breast registers 160 degrees on an instant-read thermometer." To convert:

160° F − 32 = 128°
128° ÷ 1.8 = 71° C (rounded down from 71.11)

1

MEXICO

MELTED CHEESE WITH POBLANO AND CHORIZO

Queso Fundido

SPANISH FOR "MELTED CHEESE," QUESO FUNDIDO is a hearty table dip of melted Mexican cheese topped with roasted poblano peppers and crispy chorizo sausage. Hot from the oven, it bubbles in an earthenware dish ready to be scooped up with warm tortillas. Its simplicity makes it well suited to both the restaurants and *fondas* (small local cafés) surrounding the numerous open-air markets of Mexico. As with so many of the dishes in Mexico, recipes vary by region. Since just about the only constant is the cheese, duplicating the flavor and characteristic "gooeyness" of an authentic queso fundido would be our starting point.

Authentic queso fundido is made with *queso asadero,* a firm cheese similar to mozzarella from the Toluca region of northern Mexico. Queso asadero literally translates to "grilling cheese," and is prized for its melting ability and salty tang. After searching for this cheese in local grocery stores and specialty cheese shops, we turned to Latin American markets, where at last we found it. But for those who don't have access to Latin American markets, could another cheese do? To find out, we researched other queso fundido recipes and learned that another cheese, quesadilla melting cheese, is often substituted for queso asadero. Unfortunately, this cheese did not

have the melting ability we had expected. Sure, it was gooey right out of the oven, but after five minutes it began to stiffen and set up. This cheese also lacked the mild, slightly tangy flavor we were looking for, so we began testing a variety of other cheeses, hoping to find one with the desired melting qualities. We set up a side-by-side test of five other cheeses—Monterey Jack, colby, mozzarella, Gouda, and fontina. All the cheeses were cubed and melted in a 375-degree oven for roughly 8 to 10 minutes. Among all the cheeses, Monterey Jack was the clear winner in both flavor and consistency.

We next wondered if shredding the cheese, rather than cubing it, would improve the cheese's texture even more. To find out, we cubed one batch, hand-shredded another, and purchased a preshredded variety, and put them to work in our recipe. All the cheeses melted at roughly the same rate, but the results were different for each. The hand-shredded cheese released much more of its oil than the cubed cheese, and the preshredded cheese, which is usually coated with an anticaking agent like cornstarch to prevent clumping, seized up almost instantly once out of the oven. Cubing the cheese was by far the winning method. It melted evenly and retained its oil because the large chunks melted slowly, which in turn, allowed it to stay melted and fluid for longer. The shredded cheese melted far too quickly, so that by the time the last shreds had melted the rest of the cheese had overcooked. During this test we also began to notice the importance of removing

---

PANTRY SPOTLIGHT

MEXICAN CHEESES

Cheese adds richness and flavor to many Mexican dishes. Many Mexican cheeses can be found in Latin American markets, but if you don't have such markets in your area, you might turn to your supermarket. The cheese sections of supermarkets across the country have expanded dramatically in recent years, increasing the likelihood of your finding Mexican cheese among the usual offerings of American cheddar, French Brie, Italian mascarpone, and the like. Here are descriptions of the Mexican cheeses used in this chapter and acceptable substitutes for them.

Queso Fresco is a fresh cow's milk cheese with a moist, crumbly texture and a lightly salty, milky flavor. Queso fresco does

not melt and it is usually sprinkled on bean dishes or stuffed into quesadillas or enchiladas. If you don't have queso fresco, farmer's cheese or feta make good substitutes.

Queso Añejado is aged queso fresco. It has a salty, sharp flavor, and a dry, crumbly texture. Also known as cotija and queso seco ("dry cheese"), queso añejado is ideal for sprinkling on finished dishes. Substitutes include Parmesan, Romano, and ricotta salata.

Queso Asadero, or grilling cheese, is a semisoft melting cheese similar to mozzarella from the Toluca region of northern Mexico. Prized for its melting ability, it is often used for Queso Fundido (page 3). Monterey Jack is an acceptable substitute.

CHORIZO SAUSAGE

Mexican chorizo is a bright, earthy-flavored fresh sausage made from ground pork, chiles, paprika, garlic, onions, and a hefty shot of vinegar. It is uncured and must be cooked thoroughly before consumption. It can be hard to find outside of Latin specialty markets, although Spanish chorizo can be substituted. Note that there are some differences between Spanish and Mexican chorizo. For starters, Spanish chorizo is cured (fully cooked) and comes in hot and mild varieties. Mexican and Spanish sausage can also differ in appearance. Our research indicated that Mexican chorizo is made from ground pork and crumbles easily and Spanish is made from large pieces of pork and being quite coarse, requires additional chopping. That said, a shopping trip revealed some Mexican sausage that appeared to have been made from chopped pork. Textural issues aside, we had good results in the test kitchen with both Mexican and Spanish chorizo sausage with the exception of one brand of Spanish sausage—Wellshire. Tasters remarked that its flavor reminded them of kielbasa, thus tasting out of place in our Mexican dishes.

the cheese from the oven as soon as it was melted. This meant not necessarily allowing it to bubble and brown around the edges, but pulling it out as soon as the last chunk had flattened. If the cheese began to overcook, it would release its oil, which would pool across the top of the cheese.

With the basics down, our cheese just needed its traditional garnish of poblanos and chorizo. Queso fundido is, by its nature, a relatively quick dish. But when we came to the issue of poblanos, things had the potential to slow down. Most of the recipes we researched called for roasted poblanos, a process that involves not only roasting, but also peeling them. In an effort to keep the process simple, we tried sautéing the poblano. Quickly sautéing the poblano with the chorizo and onion left the poblano slightly bitter and a bit too crunchy for our otherwise smooth cheese dip. So we decided to crank up the heat. This time we began by cooking the chorizo for one minute in a hot skillet to render the fat. Then we added a thinly sliced poblano and continued cooking over high heat until the skin of the pepper turned spotty brown. Next we added the onion. When the onion had softened and browned, we drained the

mixture on paper towels to prevent the topping from turning the cheese oily. We then spooned the hot chorizo mixture over the cubed cheese and tossed the whole thing in the oven. And in about 10 minutes, we had our queso fundido—velvety smooth and spicy—ready to be scooped with warm soft tortillas.

Melted Cheese with Poblano and Chorizo
Queso Fundido
SERVES 6 TO 8

Don't substitute preshredded Monterey Jack cheese; it is coated with anticaking agents that will cause the melted cheese to harden as soon as it is removed from the oven. Take care not to overcook the cheese or it will begin to leach oil.

6	(8-inch) flour or corn tortillas, cut into quarters
1	teaspoon vegetable oil
4	ounces chorizo sausage, chopped medium
1	medium poblano chile, stemmed, seeded, and sliced into thin strips
½	small onion, sliced thin
8	ounces Monterey Jack cheese or queso asadero, cut into ½-inch cubes

1. Adjust an oven rack to the lower-middle position and heat the oven to 375 degrees. Wrap the tortillas in foil; set aside.

2. Heat the oil in a 12-inch nonstick skillet over high heat until shimmering. Add the chorizo and cook until it begins to render a little fat, about 1 minute. Add the poblano and cook until it turns spotty brown, about 2 minutes. Add the onion and continue to cook until both the chorizo and vegetables are well browned, about 3 minutes. Transfer the chorizo mixture to a paper towel–lined plate to drain.

3. Spread the cheese evenly into an 8- or 9-inch shallow casserole or pie dish, then sprinkle with the chorizo mixture. Transfer the dish to the oven along with the tortilla packet and bake until the cheese is just melted and the tortillas are warm, 8 to 10 minutes. Serve immediately.

GUACAMOLE

UNLIKE MOST AMERICAN VERSIONS OF guacamole, which take an everything-but-the kitchen-sink approach to the ingredients, guacamole in Mexico is a simple affair. Usually no more than a roughly mashed mixture of avocados, lime juice, and salt, guacamole is often eaten with grilled meats, tacos, and enchiladas. The dish has long been a staple of the Mexican diet. Unfortunately, guacamole has traveled a long road, and the journey has not necessarily been kind. The guacamole we are served in restaurants, and even in the homes of friends, often sacrifices the singular, extraordinary character of the avocado—the culinary equivalent of velvet—by adding too many other flavorings. Even worse, the texture of the dip is usually reduced to an utterly smooth, listless puree.

We wanted our guacamole to be different. We wanted to highlight the dense, buttery texture and loamy, nutty flavor of the avocado. Any additions needed to provide bright counterpoints to the avocado without overwhelming it. Just as important, we wanted a chunky, rather than perfectly smooth, consistency.

We knew that good guacamole starts with good (i.e., ripe) avocados, and when making guacamole, we prefer the rough-skinned Hass avocado for its creamy texture and nutty flavor. Avoid larger varieties with smooth, green skin; their flesh tends to be watery and less flavorful. Assuming you have ripe avocados, how should you handle and mix them with the other ingredients? Most guacamole recipes direct you to mash all the avocados, and some recipes go so far as to puree them in a blender or food processor. After making dozens of batches, we came to believe that neither pureeing nor simple mashing was the way to go. Properly ripened avocados break down very easily when stirred, and we were aiming for a chunky texture. To get it, we ended up mashing two of our three diced avocados in our recipe lightly with a fork and mixing it with most of the other ingredients, then mixing the remaining diced avocado into the base using a very light hand. The mixing action breaks down the cubes somewhat, making for a chunky, yet cohesive dip.

Other problems we encountered in most recipes were an overabundance of onion or garlic and a dearth of acidic seasoning. After extensive testing with various amounts of onion, tasters found that 2 tablespoons of finely minced or grated onion gave the guacamole a nice spike without an overwhelming onion flavor. Garlic was also welcome if used with restraint; one clove was just enough. After trying various amounts of jalapeño chiles, tasters gave thumbs up to just one small chile. We also tried fresh lemon and lime juice. The acid was absolutely necessary, not only for flavor but also to help preserve the mixture's green color. Tasters preferred 2 tablespoons of lime juice (lemon tasted out of place).

Guacamole

MAKES 2½ TO 3 CUPS

Very ripe Hass avocados are key to this recipe. To minimize the risk of discoloration, prepare the minced ingredients first so they are ready to mix with the avocados as soon as they are cut. Like our Tomato Salsa (page 7) and Tomatillo Salsa (page 9), our guacamole makes a great accompaniment to a variety of Mexican dishes, as well as a dip for tortilla chips.

- 3 medium ripe Hass avocados, halved, pitted, and cut into ½-inch cubes
  Salt
- 2 tablespoons minced red onion
- ¼ cup minced fresh cilantro leaves
- 2 tablespoons juice from 1 lime
- 1 small jalapeño chile, seeds and ribs removed, chile minced
- 1 medium garlic clove, minced or pressed through a garlic press (about 1 teaspoon)

TESTING AVOCADOS FOR RIPENESS

A soft avocado is sometimes bruised rather than truly ripe. To be sure, flick the small stem of the avocado. If it comes off easily and you can see green underneath it, the avocado is ripe. If the stem does not come off or if you see brown underneath it, the avocado is not ripe.

PITTING AN AVOCADO

1. Start by slicing around the pit and through both ends with a chef's knife. With your hands, twist the avocado to separate the two halves.

2. Stick the blade of the chef's knife sharply into the pit. Lift the knife, twisting the blade to loosen and remove the pit.

3. Don't pull the pit off the knife with your hands. Instead, use a large wooden spoon to pry the pit safely off the knife.

Mash two of the avocados and ¼ teaspoon salt to a relatively smooth puree using a fork in a medium bowl. Gently fold in the remaining diced avocado and all of the remaining ingredients. Season with salt to taste and serve. (The guacamole can be covered with plastic wrap, pressed directly onto the surface of the mixture, and refrigerated for up to 1 day; return to room temperature, then remove the plastic wrap just before serving.)

DICING AN AVOCADO

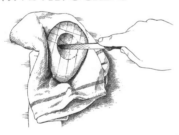

1. Use a dish towel to hold the avocado steady. Make ½-inch cross-hatch incisions in the flesh of each avocado half with a dinner knife, cutting down to but not through the skin.

2. Separate the diced flesh from the skin using a spoon inserted between the skin and the flesh and gently scoop out the avocado cubes.

TOMATO SALSA

Salsa Cruda

ALMOST EVERYONE'S FIRST EXPOSURE TO Mexican cuisine can be brought back to one simple condiment: *salsa cruda*. A chunky concoction of tomatoes, chiles, garlic, and onions, salsa is as big in Mexico as ketchup is in the U.S., and fewer recipes could be easier to make. Sweet, juicy tomatoes, bold onions, and bright cilantro embody the flavors of Mexican cuisine. But here in the U.S. even in the midst of tomato season, those backyard, farm-stand, and supermarket tomatoes sometimes lack the necessary flavor and juiciness. Complicating matters, salsa's popularity has opened the door to versions employing ingredients that are extravagant (smoked paprika) and extraneous (canned tomato juice), relegating fresh tomatoes to a minor role. One such recipe had us fishing around in water for minuscule pieces of tomato, while another used four different chiles but only one measly tomato. We wanted a fresh, chunky Mexican-style salsa that would emphasize the tomatoes; the other traditional flavors—lime, garlic, onion, chile, and cilantro—would have supporting roles. We also wanted to get the texture just right for scooping up and balancing on a tortilla chip.

Simply combining salsa ingredients in one bowl for mixing and serving turned out to be a bad idea. The tomatoes exuded so much juice that the other ingredients were submerged in liquid within minutes. The first step, then, was to solve the problem of watery salsa. Tomatoes are often peeled and seeded to remove excess moisture. Peeling, however, removed the structure that kept the diced tomatoes intact, resulting in a salsa that was too mushy. Seeding diminished the tomatoes' flavor, and tasters did not mind the presence of seeds. So much for peeling and seeding.

Here in the test kitchen we often salt tomatoes to concentrate flavor and extract liquid. This technique was promising, but because much more surface area was exposed when the tomatoes were

CUTTING TOMATOES FOR SALSA

1. Cut each cored tomato in half through the equator.

2. Cut each half into ⅜-inch-thick slices.

3. Stack two slices, cut them into ⅜-inch strips, then into ⅜-inch dice.

diced, the salt penetrated too deeply and broke them down too much. We were left with mealy, mushy tomatoes, and the salsa was just as watery as before. Dicing the tomatoes larger to expose less surface area was out of the question; the tomato pieces would be too large to balance on a tortilla chip. Taking round slices of tomatoes, salting them, and then dicing them after they had drained was just too much work.

Frustrated, we diced a few tomatoes, threw them into a colander without salting them, and walked away. Thirty minutes later, to our surprise, a few tablespoons of liquid had drained out; after a few shakes of the colander, the tomatoes were chunky and relatively dry. We found that in fewer than 30 minutes, not enough liquid had drained out, whereas more time didn't produce enough additional juice to justify the wait. Overall, we found that really ripe tomatoes exude more juice than less ripe supermarket tomatoes. This simple technique, with minimal tomato prep, had accomplished a major feat: It put all tomatoes, regardless of origin, ripeness, or juiciness, on a level—and dry—playing field.

With the main technique established, we fixed the spotlight on the supporting ingredients. We preferred red onions over white, yellow, and sweet onions for color and flavor. Jalapeño chiles were chosen over serrano, habanero, and poblano chiles because of their wide availability, slight vegetal flavor, and moderate heat. Lime juice tasted more authentic (and better) than red wine vinegar, rice vinegar, or lemon juice. Olive oil, while included at the beginning of the recipe testing process, was rejected later on when tasters found it dulled the other flavors.

We also investigated the best way to combine the ingredients and settled on the simplest technique. Marinating the tomatoes, onion, garlic, and chile in lime juice resulted in dull, washed-out flavors and involved extra bowls and work. We tried letting the drained tomatoes, onion, chiles, garlic, and cilantro sit for a bit before adding the lime juice, sugar, and salt. Now the flavors of the chile and onion stole the show. It was much more efficient to chop the chile, onion, garlic, and cilantro and layer each ingredient on top of the tomatoes while they drained in the colander. Once the tomatoes were finished draining, the chile, onion, garlic, cilantro, and tomatoes needed just a few stirs before being immediately finished with the lime juice, sugar, and salt, and then served.

Tomato Salsa
Salsa Cruda
MAKES ABOUT 3 CUPS

Heat varies from jalapeño to jalapeño and much of the heat resides in the ribs and seeds; we suggest mincing the seeds separately from the flesh, then adding them to taste. The amount of sugar and lime juice to use depends on the ripeness of the tomatoes. The salsa tastes best the same day it's made; it can be made 2 to 3 hours in advance, but hold off adding the salt, lime juice, and sugar until just before serving. The salsa is perfect for tortilla chips, but it's also a nice accompaniment to any Mexican dish including enchiladas (page 20), tacos (page 31), and simple grilled meats and fish.

1½	pounds firm, ripe tomatoes, cut into ⅜-inch dice (about 3 cups)
1	large jalapeño chile, seeds and ribs removed (seeds minced and reserved), chile minced
½	cup minced red onion
1	small garlic clove, minced or pressed through a garlic press (about ½ teaspoon)
¼	cup minced fresh cilantro leaves
½	teaspoon salt
	Pinch ground black pepper
2–6	teaspoons juice from 1 lime
	Sugar

1. Set a large colander in a large bowl. Place the tomatoes in the colander and let them drain for 30 minutes. As the tomatoes drain, layer the jalapeño, onion, garlic, and cilantro on top. Shake the colander to drain off the excess tomato juice; discard the juice and wipe out the bowl.

2. Transfer the contents of the colander to the now-empty bowl. Add the salt, pepper, and 2 teaspoons of the lime juice and toss to combine. Season with the minced jalapeño seeds, sugar, and additional lime juice to taste and serve.

Margaritas
MAKES ABOUT 1 QUART,
SERVING 4 TO 6

Margaritas are perhaps Mexico's best-known cocktail. For best flavor, we recommend steeping the zest and juice for the full 24 hours, although the margaritas will still be great if the mixture is steeped only for 4 hours. If you're in a rush and need to serve margaritas immediately, omit the zest and skip the steeping process altogether. For the tequila, we recommend tequila labeled "reposado," which is typically made from 100 percent agave and aged in oak casks for 2 to 12 months, which lends it a golden color and mellow flavor. If you cannot find superfine sugar, you can obtain a close approximation by processing regular granulated sugar in a food processor for 30 to 40 seconds.

4	teaspoons grated zest plus ½ cup juice from 4 limes
4	teaspoons grated zest plus ½ cup juice from 3 lemons
¼	cup superfine sugar (see note)
	Pinch salt
1	cup 100 percent agave tequila, preferably reposado (see note)
1	cup triple sec
2	cups crushed ice

1. Combine the lime zest and juice, lemon zest and juice, sugar, salt, tequila, and triple sec in a large liquid measuring cup. Cover with plastic wrap and refrigerate until the flavors meld, 4 to 24 hours.

2. Divide 1 cup of the crushed ice between 4 to 6 margarita or double old-fashioned glasses. Strain the margarita mixture into a 1-quart pitcher or cocktail shaker and add the remaining 1 cup crushed ice. Stir or shake until thoroughly combined and chilled, 20 to 60 seconds. Strain the margarita mixture into the ice-filled glasses and serve immediately.

INGREDIENTS: Tortilla Chips

A trip to the snack aisle suggests that tortilla chips may have surpassed potato chips as America's favorite snack food. So how do you pick the best of the bunch? Despite being made from just a handful of ingredients—cornmeal, oil, and salt—we found great variation in flavor among the different samples that we tried. As a general rule, we favored thin, delicate chips made from finely ground cornmeal. As far as salt went, the chips with a higher salt content generally fared better than lower salt. So what were our favorites? Our favorite widely available tortilla chips were Tostitos 100 Percent White Corn Restaurant Style Tortilla Chips. Doritos Toasted Corn Tortilla Chips also finished on top, praised for their fresh flavor and crisp texture; unfortunately, they are only available on the West Coast.

THE BEST TORTILLA CHIPS

Tostitos 100 Percent White Corn Restaurant Style Tortilla Chips have a fresh flavor and crisp texture that put them ahead of other brands.

PANTRY SPOTLIGHT

TOMATILLOS

Tomatillos give our Tomatillo Salsa its distinctive tart flavor and green color. Tomatillos resemble small green tomatoes (about the size of a walnut) and are covered by a thin papery husk. The husk should be dry and the fruit should be firm. Tomatillos are carried by some supermarkets and many Latin American markets.

TOMATILLO SALSA

Salsa Verde

SALSA VERDE IS PERHAPS MORE COMMON on the authentic Mexican table than tomato-based salsa cruda. Literally translated to mean "green sauce," salsa verde can either be chunky or smooth, cooked or raw, depending on individual taste. Instead of tomatoes, salsa verde relies on tomatillos, paper-skinned green tomato-like fruit with a tart, pineapple flavor. While a few salsa verde recipes use raw tomatillos, most cook the tomatillos either by boiling or roasting. Cooking softens the fruit, which can be quite firm, and mellows their acidity.

Many of the recipes we researched steered us in the direction of boiling tomatillos. We boiled the tomatillos until they were soft but still held their shape, about eight minutes, and then shocked them in cold water to stop the cooking. We then combined them with the traditional salsa verde seasoning—jalapeño, onion, garlic, cilantro, lime juice, and salt—in the bowl of a food processor. Using quick one-second pulses, we pureed the salsa to a chunky consistency. The result was clean and fruity. We also tried making the salsa with canned tomatillos. The flavor and color were not as bright, but they are an acceptable substitute if fresh cannot be had.

We next decided to try a roasted version, but simple roasting didn't give our tomatillos any flavorful char, so we turned to our broiler for help. After husking and washing the tomatillos, we combined them with jalapeño and onion then tossed the vegetables with oil to coat. We transferred the vegetables to a foil-lined baking sheet and set them under the broiler until charred. After a whir in the food processor with seasonings, we tasted the roasted salsa side by side against our boiled version.

We liked the smoky flavor that the roasting added to the salsa, so decided to offer it as a variation. For this roasted variation, fresh tomatillos are essential. We tried canned and they simply turned to mush.

Tomatillo Salsa
Salsa Verde
MAKES 2 ¼ CUPS

The outer husk of a fresh tomatillo should be dry, the tomatillo itself should be bright green, with a fresh, fruity smell. While fresh tomatillos are preferred for this recipe, canned ones will work as well; substitute two 13-ounce cans tomatillos, drained, and skip step 1. Serve this salsa with grilled meats or fish, tamales, fajitas, or simply as a dip for tortilla chips.

    Salt
- 1 pound fresh tomatillos (about 8), husked and washed
- ½ small onion, chopped coarse
- 1 medium jalapeño chile, seeds and ribs removed (seeds minced and reserved), chile minced
- 1 medium garlic clove, minced or pressed through a garlic press (about 1 teaspoon)
- ½ cup packed fresh cilantro leaves
- 1 tablespoon juice from 1 lime

1. Bring 2 quarts of water to a boil in a large saucepan. Fill a medium bowl with ice water. Stir in 2 teaspoons salt and the tomatillos into the boiling water and cook until the color of the tomatillos dulls slightly and they are tender but not mushy, 8 to 10 minutes. Drain the tomatillos, transfer to the ice water, and let cool, about 5 minutes.

2. Drain the tomatillos (no need to pat dry) and transfer to a food processor. Add the remaining ingredients and ½ teaspoon salt and process until roughly chopped, about 7 pulses. Season with the reserved minced jalapeño seeds and salt to taste and serve. (The salsa can be refrigerated in an airtight container for up to 5 days; return to room temperature and season with salt and lime juice to taste before serving.)

➤ VARIATION
Roasted Tomatillo Salsa
MAKES 1 ¼ CUPS
Canned tomatillos cannot be substituted in this recipe. This variation makes less salsa because the tomatillos release some of their liquid during the roasting.

- 1 pound fresh tomatillos (about 8), husked and washed
- ½ small onion, chopped coarse
- 1 medium jalapeño chile, seeds and ribs removed (seeds minced and reserved), chile halved lengthwise
- 1 medium garlic clove, peeled
- 1 teaspoon olive oil
- ½ cup packed fresh cilantro leaves
- 1 tablespoon juice from 1 lime
    Salt

1. Adjust an oven rack 5 inches from the broiling element and turn on the broiler. Toss the tomatillos, onion, jalapeño, and garlic with the oil and spread out over a foil-lined baking sheet. Broil, shaking the pan occasionally, until the vegetables are well charred, 10 to 12 minutes. Remove the vegetables from the oven and allow them to cool slightly, about 5 minutes.

2. Transfer the broiled vegetables to a food processor. Add the cilantro, lime juice, and ¼ teaspoon salt, and process until coarsely chopped, about 7 pulses. Season with the minced jalapeño seeds and salt to taste and serve. (The salsa can be refrigerated in an airtight container for up to 5 days; return to room temperature and season with salt and lime juice to taste before serving.)

DRUNKEN BEANS
Frijoles Borrachas

IT'S HARD TO IMAGINE MEXICAN CUISINE without beans. Beans are typically served as a side dish at almost every meal, usually in a heady mixture simmered with chiles, garlic, and large chunks of pork or sausage. One of the most popular bean dishes, drunken beans or *frijoles borrachas,* combines slow-cooked pinto beans with chiles, salt pork, fresh cilantro, and as its name implies, a generous splash of Mexican beer. The malty flavor in the beer gives the beans the distinctive flavor and intoxicating aroma that makes this dish so addictive.

To start, we tested canned beans versus dried. Our test quickly revealed that in this dish, dried beans are superior in flavor and texture to canned beans. Next we turned to determining the background flavor of our beans. This was less complicated than it sounds, and it simply boiled down to which kind of pork we were going to use as well as the basic aromatics. We started with salt pork and bacon and preferred the clean, salty flavor and richness of salt pork, although you can substitute slab bacon if salt pork is unavailable. Onions and garlic were a given; we sautéed them along with the pork to deepen their flavor and add a rounded flavor base to the beans.

Chiles were next up on our list. We first tried roasted poblanos, but their subtle flavor was lost in the flavor of the beans. So next we tried fresh jalapeños, along with canned chipotles in adobo sauce (smoked jalapeños packed in a vinegary tomato sauce). Tasters liked the clean taste of the fresh jalapeños paired with the smokiness of the chipotles. A squeeze of fresh lime and some fresh cilantro brightened the earthy flavor of the beans, and heightened the chile flavor.

Finally, we focused our attention on the beer. We tested various Mexican beers and liked the chocolaty flavor of the dark Mexican beers, such as Negro Modelo. Lighter beers turned out milder, blander-tasting beans. Note that Mexican dark beers are not as bitter as dark European stouts (like Guinness)—Mexican beers have a smoother, milder flavor that works well in this recipe.

Drunken Beans
Frijoles Borrachas
SERVES 8 TO 10 AS A SIDE DISH

If you don't have time to soak the beans overnight (or forgot) see our quick soak instructions on page 12. Vary the spiciness of the beans by adding more or less chipotle. If you can't find salt pork, we suggest replacing it with slab bacon; if you substitute sliced bacon, mince it as fine as possible to prevent it from having a shredded, flabby texture. Newcastle Brown Ale or Sam Adams Boston Lager can be used in place of Mexican beer. You can also substitute nonalcoholic beer such as O'Doul's Amber or Kaliber, but the final flavor will not be as deep and complex.

1	pound pinto beans, rinsed, picked over, and soaked overnight or quick-soaked (see page 12)
4	ounces salt pork, cut into ½-inch cubes
1	medium onion, minced
	Salt
3	medium garlic cloves, minced or pressed through a garlic press (about 1 tablespoon)
6	cups water
1	cup dark Mexican beer, such as Negro Modelo (see note)
1	jalapeño chile, seeds and ribs removed, chile minced
1–2	teaspoons minced chipotle chile in adobo sauce
¼	cup minced fresh cilantro leaves
2	limes, cut into wedges (for serving)

1. Drain the beans, discarding the soaking liquid; set aside. Cook the salt pork in a large Dutch oven over medium heat until lightly browned and rendered, about 5 minutes. Add the onion and ½ teaspoon salt and cook until lightly browned, 5 to 7 minutes. Stir in the garlic and cook until fragrant, about 30 seconds. Stir in the drained beans, water, and beer and bring to a boil. Reduce to a simmer and cook, uncovered, stirring occasionally, until the beans are tender, 1 to 1½ hours.

2. When the beans are tender, stir in the jalapeño and chipotle and simmer to blend the flavors, about 10 minutes. Season with salt to taste, sprinkle with the cilantro, and serve with the lime wedges.

SORTING DRIED BEANS WITH EASE

It is important to rinse and pick over dried beans to remove any stones or debris before cooking. To make this task easier, sort dried beans on a white plate or cutting board. The neutral background makes any unwanted matter easy to spot and discard.

REFRIED BEANS

Frijoles Refritos

AUTHENTIC REFRIED BEANS, OR *FRIJOLES refritos,* are leftover stewed beans cooked in a generous amount of lard until they are softened enough to mash. They are served garnished with toppings like sharp, crumbly cheese, scallions, bacon, and jalapeño chiles. The texture is lush and the flavor unbeatably rich and satisfying; no survey of Mexican cooking would be complete without this classic dish.

Determining the type of beans—canned or dried—was the first hurdle to overcome. Because the dish typically relies on leftover beans, and we were making ours from scratch, the convenience of canned beans makes sense. Plus, because the beans are mashed, the sometimes inferior texture of canned beans isn't an issue. Some tasters, however, prefer red dried beans, so we leave the choice up to you.

With our cooked beans in hand, we turned to various mashing procedures uncovered in our research. Most often, the beans are mashed in a pan with a wooden spoon or potato masher. The method was labor-intensive and yielded mediocre results. Even with overcooked beans, the chunky mash was punctuated with bits of tough, leathery bean skin. Clearly, we needed more force than that generated by a potato masher and an arm—like a food processor or blender. The food processor did a miraculous job. We drained the beans, put 2 cups of them in the workbowl with water to aid in pureeing, and processed the beans until smooth—about 30 seconds. The skins virtually disappeared, and the resulting puree was silky smooth. We then added the remaining cup of beans and pulsed until the mixture was just slightly chunky.

With our beans pureed, it was time to fry them. We tried corn, canola, vegetable, and olive oil, bacon fat and lard, but bacon fat won for its full flavor and rich texture. Three slices of bacon, which yield 1 tablespoon of bacon fat, was just enough. Olive oil was deemed a suitable alternative, although its flavor is mild in comparison. We tried every quantity from a scant tablespoon (unnoticeable) to ½ cup (overkill) for ½ pound of beans and settled on 3 tablespoons.

Our last task was to choose seasonings that would deepen the flavor of the otherwise mild-tasting beans. Onions, which are traditional, added depth and body as well as sweetness. Jalapeño chiles brought a hint of heat and a vegetal edge that tasters liked. Cumin, garlic, cilantro, and lime juice rounded out the seasonings. And everyone loved meaty bits of crisp bacon sprinkled over the beans just before serving.

Refried Beans

Frijoles Refritos

SERVES 4 TO 6

For the beans, you can use two 15-ounce cans of drained and rinsed beans, or simmer 8 ounces of dried pinto beans (see soaking instructions on page 12) in 3 quarts of water until tender, 1 to 2 hours (reserve ¾ cup of the cooking water). You can also use leftover Drunken Beans (page 10); remove and discard the salt pork before pureeing in step 1. Three tablespoons of olive oil can be substituted for the bacon, although the flavor will not be as rich and flavorful.

- 3 cups cooked pinto beans (see note)
- ¾ cup low-sodium chicken broth, or reserved bean cooking water
- ½ teaspoon salt
- 3 ounces (about 3 slices) bacon, chopped fine (see note)
- 1 small onion, minced
- 1 large jalapeño chile, seeds and ribs removed, chile minced
- ½ teaspoon ground cumin
- 2 medium garlic cloves, minced or pressed through a garlic press (about 2 teaspoons)
- 2 tablespoons minced fresh cilantro leaves
- 2 teaspoons juice from 1 lime

1. Puree 2 cups of the beans, broth, and salt in a food processor, stopping to scrape down the sides of the bowl as needed, until smooth, about 15 seconds Add the remaining 1 cup beans and pulse until the mixture is slightly chunky, about 10 pulses; set aside.

2. Cook the bacon in a 12-inch nonstick skillet over medium heat until browned and crisp and most of the fat has rendered, 5 to 8 minutes.

Transfer the bacon to a paper towel–lined plate, leaving the fat in the pan (you should have about 1 tablespoon of fat).

3. Add the onion, jalapeño, and cumin to the fat left in the skillet, return to medium-high heat, and cook until the onion is softened, 5 to 7 minutes. Stir in the garlic and cook until fragrant, about 30 seconds. Stir in the pureed beans, reduce the heat to medium, and cook until the beans are thick and creamy and the flavors have melded, about 4 to 6 minutes. Off the heat, stir in the cilantro and lime juice and season with salt to taste. Sprinkle with the reserved bacon and serve.

INGREDIENTS:
Supermarket Refried Beans

Traditional frijoles refritos start with dried pinto beans that are cooked, "fried well" in lard, then mashed. It's not rocket science, but it is time-consuming, so many cooks opt for a store-bought version instead. We sampled six brands of refried beans to determine if any were worth a spot on our Mexican table. Only two brands, Old El Paso Traditional and Ortega, use lard (the rest use vegetable oil), but to our tasters, lard offered no advantage in flavor or texture. Texture, however, turned out to be key—Spackle is still Spackle, even if it contains garlic and onions. Even the best-tasting brands left us disappointed by inferior texture. We can't recommend anything we tasted. And whatever you do, steer clear of dehydrated, instant refried beans. These were consistently stale and unappealing.

STREET CORN
Elote

IN MEXICO, STREET VENDORS SELL CORN on the cob from carts like vendors in the U.S. sell hotdogs. It comes either grilled *(elote asado)* or boiled *(elote cocido)* and both versions are popular. The corn is served coated with either melted butter, chili powder, and lime juice or with a creamy, cheesy mixture consisting of *crema* (a tangy cultured sour cream) or mayonnaise mixed with chili powder and garlic. The mixture is slathered over the corn and then sprinkled with a crumbly Mexican cheese such as queso anejo or queso fresco. The cheese-coated corn piqued our interest, so we set out to duplicate this Mexican market delicacy in our test kitchen. First, we focused on the cooking method for the corn and turned to grilling.

Utilizing the test kitchen's method for grilling corn, where all but the last layer of husk is removed, we grilled the corn turning the ears every few minutes until lightly charred and the kernels were crisp-tender. We removed the corn and brushed the ears with the spiced mayonnaise mixture, which we then sprinkled with cheese. (After some debate, we decided to forgo crema in favor of mayonnaise—easier to find and almost as traditional in Mexico as crema.) As for the cheese, we tried queso fresco, a crumbly white cheese, which can be found in Latin markets and some supermarkets; if you can't find it in your area, crumbled farmer's cheese or

---

CORE TECHNIQUE

SOAKING BEANS

Here in the test kitchen, we've found that many beans benefit from being soaked before cooking, such as the pinto beans in Drunken Beans (page 10), the cannellini beans in Tuscan White Bean and Bread Soup (page 267), and the flageolets in Cassoulet (page 187). The soaking allows the dried beans to absorb water and hydrate evenly, resulting in a creamy, evenly cooked final texture when cooked. Don't worry if you don't have time to soak the beans (or forgot)—we've come up with a "quick-soak" method that works nearly as well (we still slightly prefer the overnight soak if given a choice).

Overnight Soaking Method: Pick through and rinse the beans, then place in a large bowl and cover by several inches of water (about 5 cups of water for 1 pound of beans). Let sit at room temperature for 12 to 24 hours. Drain, discarding the soaking liquid, and cook the beans as directed.

Quick Soaking Method: Pick through and rinse the beans, then place in a saucepan and cover with 1 inch of water. Bring the beans to a boil and cook for 2 minutes. Remove the saucepan from the heat, cover, and let the beans steep for 1 hour. Drain, discarding the liquid, and cook the beans as directed.

feta makes a reasonable substitute. Tasters raved about this corn, as every bite was rewarded with a mouthful of creamy chili flavor. However, they commented that the cheese, which was merely sprinkled on top, tended to fall off when eaten. As we wondered if it was possible to melt the cheese onto the corn during the cooking process, we also decided to rethink our cooking method. We ended up making two decisions: first we mixed the cheese in with the mayonnaise, and second, we set aside our grill in favor of our broiler.

This time we fully husked the corn, drizzled it with a tablespoon of olive oil, and transferred it to a foil-lined baking sheet. Caramelizing the corn under the broiler took longer than on the grill, about 10 minutes per side. When the corn was nicely browned, we slathered on the cheese and mayonnaise mixture, and put it back under the broiler for one minute. This final minute under the broiler made a real difference. The mayonnaise began to lightly brown and bubble and the cheese melted just enough to stick to the corn. A squeeze of lime was all the corn needed at that point to send it over the top, and when compared to the grilled corn, tasters actually preferred the flavor of the broiled corn.

Street Corn

Elote

SERVES 6

If possible, leave the stalks of the corn attached; they make nice handles when cooking and eating.

6	large ears fresh corn, husks and silk removed
1	tablespoon olive oil
½	cup mayonnaise
2	tablespoons minced fresh cilantro leaves
1	tablespoon juice from 1 lime
1	medium garlic clove, minced or pressed through a garlic press (about 1 teaspoon)
1	teaspoon chili powder
	Salt
1	ounce queso fresco, farmer's cheese, or feta, crumbled (about ¼ cup)
	Ground black pepper
1	lime, cut into wedges (for serving)

1. Adjust an oven rack 5 inches from the broiler element and heat the broiler. Brush the corn on all sides with the olive oil and transfer to a foil-lined baking sheet. Broil the corn until well browned on one side, about 10 minutes. Turn the corn over and broil until browned on the opposite side, about 10 minutes longer.

2. While the corn broils, stir the mayonnaise, cilantro, lime juice, garlic, chili powder, and ¼ teaspoon salt together until uniform. Stir in the cheese and set aside.

3. Remove the corn from the oven and brush the corn on all sides with the mayonnaise mixture. Return to the broiler and broil the coated corn until the cheese coating is warm and slightly browned on top, about 1 minute. Season with salt and pepper to taste, and serve with the lime wedges and any remaining mayonnaise mixture.

MEXICAN RICE

Arroz a la Mexicana

IN MEXICO, RICE PILAF, OR *ARROZ A LA Mexicana,* often serves as a separate course, in the manner that Italians serve pasta; on the American table, it makes a unique side dish. Mexican rice is a red-hued mixture of rice with onions, garlic, tomatoes, chiles, and fresh herbs that gets its complex, nutty flavor from its golden-fried rice grains. It's a basic dish with a remarkably short ingredient list, yet we often find it vexing. Variable ingredient quantities and cooking techniques produced disparate results when we put a selection of recipes from respected Mexican cookbook authors to the test. Two of these recipes turned out soupy and greasy. These super soggy, oily versions were clearly off-track. Other recipes seemed misguided in terms of ingredient amounts. Some had just a hint of garlic, others tasted of tomato and nothing else, and one was overtaken by pungent cilantro.

To our thinking, the perfect version of this dish should exhibit clean, balanced flavors and tender, perfectly cooked rice. It should be rich but not oily, moist but not watery.

The liquid traditionally used in this dish is a mixture of chicken broth and pureed fresh tomatoes (plus a little salt); experiments with a variety of ratios helped us to settle on equal parts of each. With too much tomato puree, the rice tasted like warm gazpacho; with too little, its flavor waned.

Each and every recipe we consulted called for fresh tomatoes, and when we pitted rice made with canned tomatoes against rice made with fresh, the reason for using the latter crystallized for us. Batches made with fresh tomatoes tasted, well, fresh. Those made with canned tomatoes tasted overcooked and too tomatoey; the rice should be scented with tomatoes, not overtaken by them. To capture the one benefit of canned tomatoes—an intense, tomato-red color—we stirred in an untraditional ingredient: tomato paste. It gave the rice an appealing red hue while adding a little flavor at the same time.

The usual method for making Mexican rice is to sauté rinsed long-grain white rice in oil before adding the cooking liquid. Rice that was rinsed produced more distinct, separate grains when compared with unrinsed rice. While some recipes call for only a quick sauté, cooking the rice until it was golden brown proved crucial in providing a mild, toasted flavor and satisfying texture. As for the amount of oil, we experimented with a wide range, from 3 tablespoons to 1¼ cups. When we essentially deep-fried the rice in copious amounts of oil, as more than one recipe suggested, the rice was much too oily; even straining off excess oil from the rice, as directed, didn't help, and it was a messy process. Insubstantial amounts of oil made rice that was dry and lacking richness. One-third of a cup seemed just right—this rice was rich but not greasy.

We had questions about whether to sauté other components of the recipe, such as the aromatics and the tomato pulp. We tried multiple permutations and landed on a compromise technique of sautéing a generous amount of garlic and jalapeños, then mixing in a raw puree of tomato and onion. This technique produced the balanced yet fresh flavor we were after; it also allowed us to process the onion in the food processor along with the tomatoes rather than having to chop it by hand.

We were having trouble achieving properly cooked rice on the stovetop. The grains inevitably scorched and then turned soupy when we attempted a rescue with extra broth. In the past, we've converted rice recipes from finicky to infallible by baking the rice, and testing proved that this recipe would be no exception. Still, as we baked batch after batch of rice, we were frustrated by cooking times that were inconsistent. Most batches contained a smattering of crunchy grains mixed in with the tender ones. Prolonged cooking didn't solve the problem; what did was stirring the rice partway through cooking to reincorporate the tomato mixture, which had been settling on top of the pilaf. With this practice in place, every last grain cooked evenly.

While many traditional recipes consider fresh cilantro and minced jalapeño optional, in our book they are mandatory. The raw herbs and pungent chiles complement the richer tones of the cooked tomatoes, garlic, and onions. When a little something still seemed missing from the rice, we thought to offer wedges of lime. A squeeze of acidity illuminated the flavor even further.

Mexican Rice
Arroz a la Mexicana
SERVES 6 TO 8

Use an ovensafe pot about 12 inches in diameter so that the rice cooks evenly and in the time indicated. The pot's depth is less important than its diameter; we've successfully used both a straight-sided sauté pan and a Dutch oven. Whichever type of pot you use, it should have a tight-fitting, ovensafe lid. Vegetable broth can be substituted for the chicken broth. Because the spiciness of jalapeños varies from chile to chile, we try to control the heat by removing the ribs and seeds (the source of most of the heat) from those chiles that are cooked in the rice.

2 medium, ripe tomatoes (about 12 ounces),
   cored and quartered
1 medium white onion, peeled, trimmed,
   and quartered
3 medium jalapeño chiles, 2 halved with ribs
   and seeds removed, 1 minced with ribs and
   seeds
⅓ cup vegetable oil
2 cups long-grain white rice, rinsed
4 medium garlic cloves, minced or pressed
   through a garlic press (about 4 teaspoons)
2 cups low-sodium chicken broth
1 tablespoon tomato paste
1½ teaspoons salt
½ cup minced fresh cilantro leaves
1 lime, cut into wedges (for serving)

1. Adjust an oven rack to the middle position and heat the oven to 350 degrees. Process the tomatoes and onion in a food processor until smooth and thoroughly pureed, about 15 seconds, scraping down the bowl if necessary. Transfer the mixture to a liquid measuring cup; you should have 2 cups (if necessary, spoon off and discard any excess).

2. Heat the oil in a large, heavy-bottomed, oven-safe straight-sided sauté pan or Dutch oven (with a tight-fitting lid) over medium-high heat for 1 to 2 minutes. Drop 3 or 4 grains of the rinsed rice in the oil; if the grains sizzle, the oil is ready. Add the rice and cook, stirring frequently, until the rice is light golden and translucent, 6 to 8 minutes. Reduce the heat to medium, stir in the garlic and seeded minced jalapeños, and cook, stirring constantly, until fragrant, about 1½ minutes.

3. Stir in the pureed tomatoes and onion, chicken broth, tomato paste, and salt. Increase the heat to medium-high and bring to a boil. Cover, transfer to the oven, and bake until the liquid is absorbed and the rice is tender, 30 to 35 minutes, stirring well halfway through the cooking time.

4. Stir in the cilantro and reserved minced jalapeño with ribs and seeds to taste. Serve immediately with the lime wedges.

➤ VARIATION

Mexican Rice with Charred Tomatoes, Chiles, and Onion

In this variation, the vegetables are charred in a cast-iron skillet, which gives the finished dish a deeper color and a slightly toasty, smoky flavor. A cast-iron skillet works best for toasting the vegetables; a traditional or even a nonstick skillet will be left with burnt spots that are difficult to remove, even with vigorous scrubbing.

2 medium ripe tomatoes (about 12 ounces),
   cored
1 medium white onion, peeled and halved
6 medium garlic cloves, unpeeled
3 medium jalapeño chiles, 2 halved with ribs and
   seeds removed, 1 minced with ribs and seeds
2 cups long-grain white rice, rinsed
⅓ cup canola oil
2 cups low-sodium chicken broth
1 tablespoon tomato paste
1½ teaspoons salt
½ cup minced fresh cilantro leaves
1 lime, cut into wedges (for serving)

1. Heat a large cast-iron skillet over medium-high heat for about 2 minutes. Add the tomatoes, onion, garlic, and halved chiles and toast the vegetables, using tongs to turn them frequently, until softened and almost completely blackened, about 10 minutes for the tomatoes and 15 to 20 minutes for the other vegetables. When cool enough to handle, trim the root ends from the onion and halve each piece. Remove the skins from the garlic and mince. Mince the jalapeños.

2. Adjust an oven rack to the middle position and heat the oven to 350 degrees. Process the toasted tomato and onion in a food processor until smooth and thoroughly pureed, about 15 seconds, scraping down the bowl if necessary. Transfer the mixture to a liquid measuring cup; you should have 2 cups (if necessary, spoon off any excess so that the volume equals 2 cups).

3. Follow the recipe for Mexican Rice from step 2, adding the toasted minced jalapeños and garlic in step 3 along with the pureed tomato mixture.

TORTILLA SOUP

Sopa de Tortilla

A MEAL IN A BOWL, THIS SPICY CHICKEN-tomato broth overflowing with garnishes (fried tortilla strips, crumbled cheese, diced avocado, and lime wedges) always satisfies with intensely rich flavors and contrasting textures. In essence, it's a turbo-charged, south-of-the border chicken soup. But in rounding up recipes, our enthusiasm began to fade. Queso añejado? Epazote? Crema? Authentic recipes called for at least one, if not several, uniquely Mexican ingredients, none of which we were going to find at our local market. In addition, this recipe demanded a major investment of time; making homemade chicken stock and frying tortilla strips seemed beyond the pale for a weeknight soup.

Just to get our bearings, we did make a few of these authentic recipes (after a long hunt for ingredients). They tasted great, but the preparation was arduous at best. Yet when we cooked up a few "Americanized" recipes, we ended up with watery brews of store-bought chicken broth and canned tomatoes topped with stodgy, off-the-shelf tortilla chips. Quick, but definitely not what we would call great-tasting.

We started anew and broke the soup down into its three classic components: a flavor base made with fresh tomatoes, garlic, onion, and chiles; chicken stock; and an array of garnishes, including fried tortilla strips. We zeroed in on the flavor base first, recalling that the best of the soups we had made called for a basic Mexican cooking technique in which the vegetables are charred on a comal, or griddle, then pureed and fried to create a concentrated paste that flavors the soup.

Without a comal in the test kitchen, we used a cast-iron skillet for charring, and the results were superb, even with mediocre supermarket tomatoes. The downside was that it took 25 attentive minutes to complete the task. We wondered if we could skip charring altogether by adding smoke-flavored dried chiles to a puree of raw tomatoes, onion, and garlic. (We used guajillo chiles, which are often used to spice up tortilla soup.) The answer was yes, but toasting and grinding these hard-to-find chiles didn't bring us any closer to a quick and easy recipe. Chipotle chiles (smoked jalapeños) seemed like a more practical choice. Canned in a vinegary tomato mixture called adobo sauce, chipotles pack heat, roasted smoky flavor, and, more important, convenience. We also found that aggressively frying the raw tomatoes, onion, and chipotle puree over high heat forced all of the water out of the mixture and further concentrated its flavor.

With the vegetable charring step eliminated, we moved on to the chicken stock. Yes, the test kitchen does have an excellent recipe for homemade stock,

---

SHOPPING NOTES : Tortilla Soup

Tortilla soup gets its complex layers of flavor from a wide variety of sometimes hard-to-find ingredients. In our research, we found we were able to approximate these flavors with common ingredients.

Cilantro and oregano replicate the pungent flavor of fresh epazote better than dried epazote does.

Monterey Jack doesn't crumble like queso añejado, but it melts better than other choices, such as feta.

Sour cream is milder than cultured Mexican cream, but it's close enough.

but we were hoping to move this recipe into the express lane. The obvious alternative was to "doctor" low-sodium store-bought chicken broth, especially since this soup is awash with so many other vibrant flavors. We tried cooking chicken in store-bought broth bolstered with onion and garlic, reasoning that the chicken would release and take on flavor while it poached. (We chose bone-in chicken as it has more flavor than boneless.) Split chicken breasts poached in just 20 minutes and could then be shredded and stirred back into the soup before serving. (Rich-flavored chicken thighs are an equally good choice but, if poorly trimmed, they can make the soup greasy.) Cooked this way, the chicken retained its juiciness and tender texture and the broth was nicely flavored.

Every authentic recipe for tortilla soup calls for fresh epazote, a common Mexican herb that imparts a heady, distinctive flavor and fragrance to the broth. Unfortunately, while epazote is widely available in the American Southwest, it is virtually nonexistent in other parts of the country. Still, we managed to track some down for testing purposes. Its wild, pungent flavor is difficult to describe, but after careful tasting we decided that it most closely resembles fresh cilantro, mint, and oregano. Using a broth steeped with epazote as a control, we sampled broths made with each of these herbs. The winner was a pairing of strong, warm oregano with pungent cilantro. It was not identical to the flavor of epazote, but it scored highly for its intensity and complexity. We now had deeply flavored broth that when stirred together with the tomato mixture made for a soup that was starting to taste like the real thing.

Flour tortillas, whether fried or oven-baked, tasted fine on their own but quickly disintegrated in hot soup. That left us with corn tortillas. The classic preparation is frying, but cooking up two or three batches of corn tortilla strips took more time and attention than we wanted to muster. Tasters flatly rejected the notion of raw corn tortillas—a recommendation we found in more than one recipe—as they rapidly turned gummy and unpalatable when added to the hot soup. Corn tortillas require some sort of crisping. After much testing,

we came across a technique in a low-fat cookbook that was both fast and easy: Lightly oiled tortilla strips are simply toasted in the oven. The result? Chips that are just as crisp, less greasy, and much less trouble to prepare than their fried cousins.

As for the garnishes, we worked through the list one ingredient at a time. Lime added sharp, fresh notes to an already complex bowl, as did cilantro leaves and minced jalapeño. Avocado was another no-brainer. Thick, tart Mexican crema (a mildly tangy, cultured cream) is normally swirled into individual soup bowls, too. If it's unavailable, sour cream is a natural stand-in. Crumbled queso añejado (the test kitchen favorite) is sharp and rich, but may be hard to find for some. If you can't find it, use Monterey Jack, which melts nicely.

Tortilla Soup
Sopa de Tortilla
SERVES 6

If you desire a soup with mild spiciness, trim the ribs and seeds from the jalapeño (or omit the jalapeño altogether) and use the minimum amount of chipotle in adobo sauce. Look for thin corn tortillas—we found that thicker tortillas baked up chewy rather than crisp. Or, if you're inclined, make your own tortillas (see page 32).

2	bone-in, skin-on split chicken breasts (about 1½ pounds) or 4 bone-in, skin-on chicken thighs (about 1¼ pounds), skinned and trimmed
8	cups low-sodium chicken broth
1	very large white onion (about 1 pound), root end trimmed, quartered, and peeled
4	medium garlic cloves, peeled
2	large sprigs fresh epazote, or 8 to 10 sprigs fresh cilantro plus 1 sprig fresh oregano
	Salt
8	(6-inch) corn tortillas, cut into ½-inch-wide strips
2	tablespoons vegetable oil
2	medium tomatoes, cored and quartered
½	medium jalapeño chile, seeds and ribs removed if desired (see note)
1½–4	teaspoons minced chipotle chile in adobo sauce

GARNISHES

1 lime, cut into wedges
1 ripe Hass avocado, halved, pitted, and diced fine (see the illustrations on page 5)
8 ounces queso añejado, crumbled, or Monterey Jack cheese, diced fine
Cilantro leaves
Minced jalapeño chile
Mexican crema or sour cream

1. Bring the chicken, broth, 2 onion quarters, 2 garlic cloves, epazote (or cilantro and oregano), and ½ teaspoon salt to a boil over medium-high heat in a large saucepan. Reduce the heat to low, cover, and simmer until the chicken is just cooked through, about 20 minutes. Using tongs, transfer the chicken to a large plate. Pour the broth through a fine-mesh strainer, discarding the solids. When the chicken is cool enough to handle, shred into bite-sized pieces, discarding the bones.

2. Meanwhile, adjust an oven rack to the middle position and heat the oven to 425 degrees. Toss the tortilla strips with 1 tablespoon of the oil, spread them out over a rimmed baking sheet and bake, stirring occasionally, until crisp and dark golden, about 14 minutes. Season with salt and transfer to a paper towel–lined plate.

3. Puree the tomatoes, 2 remaining onion quarters, 2 remaining garlic cloves, jalapeño, 1½ teaspoons of the chipotle, and ⅛ teaspoon salt in a food processor until smooth. Heat the remaining tablespoon of oil in a large Dutch oven over high heat until shimmering. Add the pureed mixture and cook, stirring frequently, until the mixture has darkened in color, about 10 minutes. Stir in the strained broth and bring to a boil, then reduce the heat to low and simmer to blend the flavors, about 15 minutes. (Up to this point, the soup can be cooled and refrigerated for up to 4 days. Return to a simmer before continuing.)

4. Stir in the remaining chipotle to taste. Add the shredded chicken and simmer until heated through, about 5 minutes. Place some tortilla strips in the bottom of individual bowls, ladle the soup over the top, and serve, passing the garnishes separately.

CHICKEN ENCHILADAS

ON THE STREETS OF MEXICO ENCHILADAS are finger food. You're likely to find them sold by street vendors as chile-doused tortillas that have been lightly fried and topped with root vegetables and cheese. Heartier, fork-and-knife enchiladas are found in Mexico's cafeterias, the country's version of the American-style diner. Regardless of the style, enchiladas are quite possibly the most popular Mexican casserole in the world; a softened tortilla rolled around a savory, cheesy filling (often with chicken) and baked in a spicy chili sauce. Chicken enchiladas are a complete meal that offers a rich and complex combination of flavors, textures, and ingredients. The problem with preparing enchiladas at home is that traditional cooking methods require a whole day of preparation. Could we simplify the process, yet retain the authentic flavor of the real thing?

We began by preparing five simplified recipes, hoping to uncover valuable tips and techniques. All of them produced disappointing results. Mushy tortillas, bland or bitter sauces, uninspired fillings, too much cheese, and lackluster flavor left tasters yearning for something tastier and more authentic.

A side-by-side tasting of corn and wheat flour tortillas came out clearly in favor of the corn, with its more substantial texture. Tasters also preferred the small 6-inch tortillas, with 8-inch tortillas a close second. These sizes provided the best ratio of tortilla to filling to sauce, and both sizes fit neatly into a 9-inch-wide baking dish. Although ingredients and size mattered, we were happy to discover that brand didn't. Given the big flavors from the sauce and filling, flavor differences between various brands of tortillas (which are rather bland tasting anyway) were not important in the final dish.

Our next task was to figure out how to treat the tortillas so that they would be soft and pliable to roll and toothsome to eat. The traditional approach is to dip each tortilla in hot oil (to create a moisture barrier) and then in the sauce (to add flavor) prior to assembly. Although this technique works well, it is time-consuming, tedious, and messy. We tried rolling chilled corn tortillas straight from the package, but they were tough and cracked easily. Heating a stack of tortillas in the microwave also proved disappointing. The tortillas were soft, but the resulting enchiladas were mushy. Next we tried wrapping the tortillas in foil and steaming them on a plate over boiling water. These tortillas were also easy to roll but were wet and soggy when baked.

Thinking back to the traditional first step of dipping the tortilla in oil gave us an idea. Using the modern-day convenience of oil in a spray can, we placed the tortillas in a single layer on a baking sheet, sprayed both sides lightly with vegetable oil, and warmed them in a moderate oven. This proved to be the shortcut we were hoping to find. The oil-sprayed, oven-warmed tortillas were pliable, and their texture after being filled, rolled, and baked was nearly perfect.

Because red chili sauce is the most common sauce used in enchiladas, we decided to prepare a half dozen traditional recipes. The flavors were spicy and complex, the textures smooth and somewhat thick, the colors deep orange-red. The problem was that whole dried chiles played a central role in all of these sauces. Not only are whole chiles difficult to find in some areas, but they require substantial preparation time, including toasting, seeding, stemming, rehydrating, and processing in a blender. Store-bought chili powder would have to be part of the solution.

The obvious question was how to augment the flavor of the chili powder available in the supermarket. Our first thought was to heat the chili powder in oil, a process that intensifies flavors. We began by sautéing onions and garlic and then added the chili powder to the pan. This indeed produced a fuller, deeper flavor. We enhanced the flavor by adding ground cumin, coriander, and oregano—ingredients often found in authentic red chili sauces—as well as cayenne pepper for more heat. Tasters gave this combo a thumbs-up.

Many traditional recipes incorporate tomatoes for substance and flavor. With a nod toward convenience, we explored canned tomato products first. We tried adding diced tomatoes and then pureeing the mixture. The texture was too thick

and too tomatoey. Tomato sauce turned out to be a better option.

Focusing on flavor next, we prepared a batch with 2 teaspoons of sugar, which succeeded in expanding and enriching the flavor of the spices. Two teaspoons of lime juice constituted the final flavor adjustment, adding just enough acidity to activate the taste buds and enliven the sauce.

Next, we tackled the filling, starting with how to cook the chicken. We tried the common method of poaching, but tasters said this chicken was dry and bland. We tried roasting both white and dark meat, which was extremely time-consuming, although tasters really liked the dark meat. Obsessed with speed and flavor, we had an idea. Why not use boneless, skinless thighs and cook them right in the sauce? Cutting the thighs into thin strips across the grain, we added them to the pan after the spices were fragrant. The chicken cooked in less than 10 minutes, and it was nicely seasoned. Cooking the chicken in the sauce also lent the sauce a wonderful richness. To separate the chicken from the sauce, we poured the contents of the pot through a medium-mesh strainer.

With the chicken cooked and ready for the filling, we needed to add just a few complementary ingredients. Cheese topped our list. Queso fresco, the traditional choice, is a young, unripened cheese with a creamy color, a mild, slightly salty flavor, and

CORE TECHNIQUE

ROLLING TORTILLAS

Straight from the refrigerator, a corn tortilla is too stiff to roll and will tear at the edges (left). Spraying the tortilla with oil and heating it for 2 to 4 minutes in a 300-degree oven will make the tortilla pliable and easy to manage (right).

COOL AND STIFF   WARM AND PLIABLE

a crumbly texture. Because it is not readily available in the United States, we tried farmer's cheese. Tasters liked this cheese for its creamy texture and mellow flavor. But it was Monterey Jack and sharp white cheddar that made the top of the list. The Jack is mellow, while the cheddar adds a sharp, distinctive flavor that tasters preferred. (Cheese, we discovered, also helps to bind the filling ingredients.)

Looking for more heat, we taste-tested the addition of fresh jalapeños, chipotles in adobo sauce, and pickled jalapeños. The fresh jalapeños were too mild. Chipotles added a distinctive, warm heat and smoky flavor that some tasters enjoyed but that most found too spicy and assertive. Everyone was surprised to find that the very convenient pickled jalapeños (sold in both cans and jars) were the favorite. The vinegar pickling solution added spicy, bright, and sour notes to the filling.

Some recipes suggest filling and rolling one enchilada at a time, but we much preferred the efficiency offered by the assembly-line approach. We spread the oil-sprayed, oven-warmed tortillas on the countertop and spread ⅓ cup of filling down the center of each. We rolled them tightly and placed them seam side down, side by side, along the length of a 13 by 9-inch baking dish that had a little sauce in it. We then poured the rest of the sauce over the enchiladas and sprinkled them with a bit of extra cheese. We experimented with oven temperatures and times before settling on 400 degrees for 20 minutes, at which point the enchiladas were hot and ready to be served.

Enchiladas are traditionally eaten with an array of raw, salad-like garnishes. Tasters passed on chopped tomatoes, saying they did not add much flavor or texture. Raw onions were considered "too harsh." Sour cream and avocado were chosen for their cooling qualities, and romaine lettuce was favored for its "fresh, crispy crunch." Finally, lime wedges squeezed over the enchiladas were welcome as well.

Start to finish, our chicken enchiladas now took less than an hour and a half to make: 20 minutes for the sauce, 15 for the filling, 30 to assemble and bake, and 10 to prep the toppings. Not bad for a dish with authentic Mexican flavor.

Chicken Enchiladas
SERVES 4 TO 6

If you prefer, Monterey Jack can be used instead of cheddar or, for a mellower flavor and creamier texture, try substituting an equal amount of farmer's cheese. Be sure to cool the chicken before filling the tortillas, or the hot filling will make the enchiladas soggy. You can also substitute 1 cup shredded Shepherd-Style Spicy Pork (page 31), or Slow-Fried Pork (page 35) for the chicken; add it to the sauce and simmer as directed in step 1.

1½	tablespoons vegetable oil
1	medium onion, minced
3	medium garlic cloves, minced or pressed through a garlic press (about 1 tablespoon)
3	tablespoons chili powder
2	teaspoons ground coriander
2	teaspoons ground cumin
½	teaspoon salt
2	teaspoons sugar
4	boneless, skinless chicken thighs (about 12 ounces), trimmed and cut into ¼-inch-wide strips
2	(8-ounce) cans tomato sauce
¾	cup water
½	cup coarsely chopped fresh cilantro leaves
1	(4-ounce) can pickled jalapeños, drained and chopped (about ¼ cup)
10	ounces sharp cheddar cheese, shredded (about 2½ cups)
10	(6-inch) corn tortillas

GARNISHES
Sour cream
Diced avocado
Shredded romaine lettuce leaves
Lime wedges

1. Heat the oil in a large saucepan over medium-high heat until shimmering. Add the onion and cook until softened and lightly browned, 5 to 7 minutes. Stir in the garlic, chili powder, coriander, cumin, salt, and sugar and cook, stirring constantly, until fragrant, about 30 seconds. Stir in the chicken and coat thoroughly with the spices, about 30 seconds.

2. Stir in the tomato sauce and water and bring to a simmer. Reduce the heat to medium-low and continue to simmer, stirring occasionally, until the chicken is cooked through and flavors have melded, 8 to 10 minutes.

3. Adjust oven rack to the lower-middle position and heat the oven to 300 degrees. Pour the mixture through a medium-mesh strainer into a medium bowl, pressing on the strained chicken mixture to extract as much sauce as possible; set the strained sauce aside. Transfer the chicken mixture to a large plate and freeze for 10 minutes to cool; when cool, combine the chicken with the cilantro, jalapeños, and 2 cups of the cheddar in a medium bowl.

4. Following the illustrations on the right, smear the entire bottom of a 13 by 9-inch baking dish with ¾ cup of the chile sauce; set aside. Spray both sides of the tortillas with vegetable oil spray. Spread 5 of the tortillas over a baking sheet. Bake until tortillas are soft and pliable, 2 to 4 minutes. Transfer the tortillas to clean work surface. Drop a heaping ⅓ cup of the filling onto each warm, softened tortilla, and roll up tightly. Arrange the enchiladas, seam-side down, in the prepared baking dish. Repeat with the remaining tortillas (toasting and filling the tortillas, and arranging the enchiladas in the baking dish). Increase the oven temperature to 400 degrees. Pour the remaining chili sauce over the top of the enchiladas. Use the back of a spoon to spread the sauce so it coats the top of each tortilla. Sprinkle the remaining ½ cup cheddar down the center of the enchiladas.

5. Cover the baking dish with foil. Bake the enchiladas on the lower-middle rack until they are heated through and the cheese is melted, 20 to 25 minutes. Uncover and serve immediately, passing the garnishes separately.

➤ VARIATIONS

Cheese Enchiladas

Queso fresco is a slightly salty, fresh Mexican cheese, also known as queso blanco. If unavailable, substitute 6 ounces of farmer's cheese or feta.

Follow the recipe for Chicken Enchiladas, omitting the chicken and cheddar. Add 2 red bell peppers, finely chopped, with the onion in step 1 and

ASSEMBLING ENCHILADAS

1. Place the tortillas on 2 baking sheets. Spray both sides lightly with cooking spray. Bake, one sheet at a time, until the tortillas are soft and pliable, 2 to 4 minutes.

2. Place the warm tortillas on a work surface. Place a heaping ⅓ cup filling down the center of each tortilla.

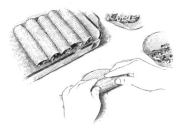

3. Smear the bottom of the baking dish with ¾ cup sauce. Roll each tortilla tightly. Place them in a baking dish, side by side, seam side down.

4. Pour the sauce over the top of the enchiladas. Use the back of a spoon to spread the sauce so it coats the top of each tortilla.

5. Sprinkle the remaining ½ cup cheese down the center of the enchiladas.

cook until softened, about 8 minutes. Add 6 ounces shredded Monterey Jack Cheese (about 2 cups) and 4 ounces crumbled queso fresco (about 1 cup) with the cilantro and jalapeños in step 3.

Beef Enchiladas

Follow the recipe for Chicken Enchiladas, substituting 1 pound boneless beef chuck steak, trimmed and sliced very thin, for the chicken. Increase the amount of water to 1¼ cups, and simmer the beef in step 2 until it is tender, about 45 minutes.

FAJITAS

FAJITAS—FLOUR TORTILLAS WRAPPED AROUND thin slices of charred beef—hail from Northern Mexico. Fajitas have become so popular across the U.S. that you'd be hard-pressed to find a Mexican restaurant from New York to California that doesn't serve them. Fajitas were originally made with skirt steak (a fatty cut with lots of flavor), but they are now made most often with flank steak. Like other steaks cut from the chest and side of the cow, flank has a rich, full, beefy flavor. Also, because it is thin, it cooks relatively quickly. Because flank steaks are typically too long to fit in a pan, grilling suits this cut—perfect for fajitas.

Although fajitas often include grilled peppers and onions—along with other condiments as desired—the dish is really about the steak, so that's where we focused our testing. Grilling flank steak may appear to be a pretty straightforward procedure, but we still had some questions about what was exactly the best way to go about it. We had two very simple goals: creating a good sear on the outside of this thin cut before it overcooked on the inside, and keeping it tender. We wondered whether the meat should be marinated or rubbed with spices, how hot the fire should be, and how long the meat should be cooked.

Virtually every recipe we found for flank steak called for marinating it. Most sources championed the marinade as a means of tenderizing the meat as well as adding flavor. We found that marinating the steak with a lot of acid for an extended period of time (more than two hours) eventually made this thin cut mushy and unappealing. If we omitted the acid, we could flavor the meat, but this took at least 12 hours. Once the steaks were cooked and sliced thin across the grain, there was virtually no difference in tenderness between those that had been marinated and those that had not. As for spice rubs, we couldn't find any profound difference in flavor the longer they were on the meat, and all the steaks developed an almost identical dark brown crust when cooked. And if we wanted our steak cooked more than medium-rare the spices began to burn. In the end, tasters found that a quick drizzle of lime juice added just before cooking contributed as much flavor as a 12-hour marinade. Another

PREPPING BELL PEPPERS FOR GRILLING

Remove and discard a ¼-inch-thick slice from the top and bottom of each pepper. Reach into the pepper and pull out the seeds in a single bunch. Slice down one side of the pepper, then lay it flat, skin side down, in a long strip. Slice a sharp knife along the inside of the pepper to remove the white ribs and any remaining seeds. The flattened and cleaned pepper is now ready for grilling.

PREPPING ONIONS FOR GRILLING

Impale ½-inch-thick slices of onion all the way through from side to side with a thin metal skewer. If using longer skewers, thread two slices on each skewer. The skewered onion slices remain intact as they grill, so that no rings can fall onto the coals. As a plus, the onions are easily flipped with tongs.

sprinkling after the meat was cooked further enhanced the fresh lime flavor.

Every source we checked was in the same camp when it came to cooking flank steak, and it is the right camp. Flank steak should be cooked over high heat for a short period of time. We tried lower heat and longer cooking times, but inevitably the meat ended up being tough. Because flank steak is too thin to be checked with a meat thermometer, you must resort to the most basic method of checking for doneness: Cut into the meat to see if it is done to your liking. Remember that carry-over heat will continue to cook the steak after it comes off the grill. So if you want the steak medium-rare, take it off the heat when it tests rare, and so on.

Most sources were also in agreement when it came to letting the steak rest after cooking. During cooking, the heat drives the juices to the center of the meat. This phenomenon is particularly noticeable with high-heat cooking. If you cut the meat right after it comes off the heat, much more of the juice spills out than if you allow the meat to rest, during which time the juices become evenly distributed throughout the meat once again. This is common wisdom among cooks, but to be sure it was correct, we cooked two more flank steaks, sliced one up immediately after it came off the fire, and allowed the second to rest for five minutes before slicing it. Not only did the first steak exude almost twice as much juice when sliced as the second, it also looked grayer and was not as tender. So in this case, conventional wisdom prevails: Give your steak a rest.

With our steak resting we moved on to the vegetables and tortillas. To make things easier we skewered our onion slices to keep them from falling apart on the grill. Our bell peppers were sliced open to increase their surface area, and to make them easier to handle. As the coals began to cool, we grilled our tortillas, giving them a smoky flavor with beautifully charred edges.

From there, we turned back to our steak, slicing it against the grain for tenderness. We packed our warm tortillas with the steak, peppers and onions, and topped the fajitas with a healthy dollop of salsa and guacamole and a squeeze of fresh lime.

Charcoal-Grilled Steak Fajitas
SERVES 8

Flank steaks are quite thin, so you will have to rely on timing, touch, and the nick-and-peek method rather than instant-read thermometer to determine doneness. Skirt steak can be substituted for flank steak, but because it's even thinner than flank steak, cook it just on the hot side of the grill, about 5 to 7 minutes, flipping the steak halfway through cooking. Instead of grilling the tortillas, you can wrap them in a clean, damp dish towel and warm them in a microwave on high for about 3 minutes; keep the tortillas wrapped until serving time. In addition to the condiments listed below, sour cream and shredded Monterey Jack are also good options.

1	(2½-pound) flank steak (see note)
¼	cup juice from 2 limes
	Salt and ground black pepper
1	very large red onion, peeled, sliced into ½-inch-thick rounds, and skewered (see the illustration on page 22)
3	medium red, yellow, and/or green bell peppers, stemmed, seeded, and flattened (see the illustration on page 22)
16	(10- to 12-inch) flour tortillas
1	lime, cut into wedges (for serving)
	Tomato Salsa (page 7) and/or Tomatillo Salsa (page 9)
	Guacamole (page 4)

1. Light a large chimney starter filled with charcoal (about 6 quarts) and allow to burn until all the charcoal is covered with a layer of fine gray ash.

2. Meanwhile, sprinkle both sides of the steak with 3 tablespoons of the lime juice, and season generously with salt and pepper.

3. Build a hot fire by spreading the coals over just two-thirds of the grill bottom (confining the coals to a smaller space makes for a hotter fire). Set the cooking grate in place, cover the grill with the lid, and let the grate heat up, about 5 minutes. The grill is ready when the coals are hot; you can hold your hand 5 inches above the cooking grate for just 2 seconds. Scrape the cooking grate clean with a grill brush.

4. Grill the steak over the coals until well seared and dark brown on the bottom, 5 to 7 minutes. Flip the steak over and continue to grill, sliding the steak to the cooler side of the grill if it begins to char, until the center of the steak is just slightly more rare than you desire, 2 to 6 minutes. (Check the center of the steak by nicking it with the tip of a knife and peeking inside.) Transfer the steak to a cutting board, tent loosely with foil, and let rest for 5 minutes.

5. While the steak rests, grill the onion and peppers over the coals, turning them occasionally, until the onions are lightly charred and the peppers are streaked with dark grill marks, 6 to 10 minutes. As the vegetables finish cooking (they might not all finish at the same time), transfer them to a plate and cover with foil to keep warm.

6. Using the remaining heat over the coals, grill both sides of the tortillas until just warmed, 10 to 20 seconds per side (do not overgrill or they will dry out and become brittle). Wrap the grilled tortillas in a clean kitchen towel to keep them soft and warm.

7. Slice the peppers and onions into thin strips; set aside. Slice the steak thin on the bias across the grain. Arrange the sliced meat and vegetables on a large platter, and sprinkle with the remaining lime juice and season with salt and pepper to taste. Serve immediately with the warm tortillas, passing the lime wedges, salsa(s), and guacamole, separately.

INGREDIENTS: Flour Tortillas

It's no surprise that the best flour tortillas are freshly made to order. But those of us without a local tortilleria must make do with the packaged offerings at the local supermarket. To find out which ones taste best, we rounded up every flour tortilla we could find. Tasters immediately zeroed in on texture, which varied dramatically from "doughy and stale" to "thin and flaky." The thinner brands were the hands down winners, with tasters choosing thin, flaky Tyson Mexican Original Flour Tortillas, Fajita Style as their clear favorite. Most brands had a mild, pleasantly wheaty flavor, but two of the doughier brands, Olé and La Banderita (both made by the same company), were panned for off, sour notes. Our advice is simple: Get the thinnest tortillas you can find at your local market.

➤ VARIATION
Gas-Grilled Steak Fajitas
Heat the grill with all the burners set to high and the lid down until very hot, about 15 minutes. Scrape the cooking grate clean with a grill brush. Leave all the burners on high. Follow the recipe for Charcoal-Grilled Steak Fajitas, grilling the steak, vegetables, and tortillas as directed in steps 4, 5 and 6, with the lid down.

SEARED SHRIMP
Camarones a la Plancha

CAMARONES A LA PLANCHA, OR GRIDDLE-SEARED shrimp, is a popular item throughout coastal Mexico. This dish of fresh shrimp seared on a hot griddle, topped with a mixture of tomatoes, chiles, cilantro, and lime juice, captures the essence of classic Mexican ingredients. When we thought of seafood in Mexico, this dish immediately came to mind as a must-have. But without a plancha of our own, we wondered if we could match the flavor of the authentic version.

Griddle-searing shrimp produces the ultimate combination of a well-caramelized exterior and a moist, tender interior. If executed properly, this cooking method also preserves the shrimp's plumpness and trademark briny sweetness. In the absence of a plancha, the shrimp were best cooked in a 12-inch skillet; its large surface area kept the shrimp from overcrowding the pan and steaming— a surefire way to prevent caramelization. In the past, tasters have preferred peeled and deveined shrimp for their flavor and ease, so we used those. Peeled shrimp are easier to eat and unpeeled shrimp fail to pick up the delicious caramelized flavor that pan-searing provides.

To achieve the perfect sear, oil was the ideal cooking medium, favored over both a dry pan (which made the shrimp leathery and metallic tasting) and butter (which tended to burn). To further increase the caramelization of the shrimp, we seasoned them with sugar in addition to salt and pepper. This promoted browning and accentuated the shrimp's natural sweetness, nicely set off by their inherent sea-saltiness. Even in a 12-inch skillet, 1½ pounds of shrimp must be cooked in two batches or they will steam instead of sear. The trick was to develop a technique that neither overcooked the shrimp nor let half of them turn cold while the other half finished cooking. To prevent overcooking, we seared the shrimp on one side, and then removed them to a platter while we cooked the second batch. After the second batch was seared and removed to the platter, we started the sauce. (Later, we'd return all the shrimp to the pan with the sauce to heat through and finish cooking.)

For our sauce, we began with the usual suspects—chopped fresh tomatoes, onions, garlic, jalapeño, lime juice, and cilantro. Done in the same pan as the shrimp (to pick up the flavor from the cooked shrimp), the mixture was cooked until the tomatoes broke down slightly and their water was released. Unfortunately, this made a sauce that was too loose, and tasters complained of the raw texture of the onions. Tasters also agreed that for a dish with such pizzazz it needed a more assertive flavor. We revisited our recipe and made some changes.

To reduce the amount of excess liquid in the sauce, we seeded the tomatoes. For one batch we even tried draining them in a colander to further reduce their liquid content, but the resulting sauce was a bit dry. To fix the texture of the onions, we switched to soft-textured scallions. We used the scallion whites in our sauce and the green tops for garnish to fortify the onion flavor. To add the smokiness redolent of a hot plancha, we replaced the fresh jalapeño with chipotle chiles in adobo. This gave us the flavor we were after with a hint of spiciness. We also adjusted the length of time that we cooked the sauce. Instead of giving the tomatoes a chance to release their liquid, we simply warmed the sauce through in the hot pan and added the shrimp to finish cooking. The shrimp were cooked through in about a minute, and we transferred the whole dish to a platter and garnished it with the scallion greens and freshly diced avocado. The shrimp was terrific by itself with a squeeze of lime, and even better served over steamed rice to catch the juices.

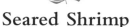

Seared Shrimp
Camarones a la Plancha
SERVES 4

The cooking times below are for extra-large shrimp. If this size is not available in your market, buy large shrimp and shorten the cooking time slightly.

3	medium tomatoes (about 1 pound), cored, seeded, and cut into ½-inch pieces
6	scallions, white and green parts separated, each sliced thin
¼	cup minced fresh cilantro leaves
3	medium garlic cloves, minced or pressed through a garlic press (about 1 tablespoon)
1–2	teaspoons minced chipotle in adobo
	Salt
1½	pounds extra-large shrimp (21 to 25 per pound), peeled and deveined
¼	teaspoon ground black pepper
⅛	teaspoon sugar
2	tablespoons vegetable oil
1	tablespoon juice from 1 lime
1	medium ripe avocado, halved, pitted, and diced (see the illustrations on page 5)
1	lime, cut into wedges (for serving)

1. Toss the tomatoes, scallion whites, cilantro, garlic, chipotle, and ¾ teaspoon salt together in a bowl; set aside.

2. Toss the shrimp with ¼ teaspoon salt, pepper, and sugar in a medium bowl. Heat 1 tablespoon of the oil in a 12-inch skillet over high heat until just smoking. Add half of the shrimp to the pan in a single layer and cook, without moving, until spotty brown on one side, about 1 minute. Transfer the shrimp to a large bowl (they will be underdone). Repeat with the remaining oil and shrimp; transfer to the bowl.

3. Return the skillet to high heat, add the tomato mixture and lime juice and cook until the tomatoes soften slightly, about 1 minute. Stir in the reserved shrimp and cook until the shrimp are cooked through and hot, about 1 minute. Transfer the shrimp to a large platter and sprinkle with the scallion greens and avocado. Serve immediately with the lime wedges.

Burritos

MAKES 4

At their most simple, authentic burritos are warm, soft flour tortillas wrapped tightly around a salt- and lime-marinated beef jerky called machacado along with a few vegetables. When burritos are rolled and fried, they're called chimichangas, or when they're rolled thin and fried, chivichangas. The Tex-Mex version of burritos—one most Americans are familiar with—is a little more substantial and along with sliced beef, pork, or chicken, includes rice, beans, and cheese. Note that leftover Slow-Fried Pork (page 35) or the pork from Shepherd-Style Spicy Pork Tacos (page 31) makes an excellent filling for burritos.

Adjust an oven rack to the middle position and heat the oven to 450 degrees. Line a baking sheet with foil and spray a second large sheet of foil with vegetable oil spray; set aside. Heat and roughly mash 1 (15.5-ounce) can pinto beans, drained and rinsed; set aside. Combine 1 cup hot cooked rice with 2 cups cooked beef, pork, or chicken, sliced thin, 1 cup shredded cheddar cheese, and ¼ cup minced fresh cilantro leaves. Place 4 (10-inch) flour tortillas on a clean work surface. Following the illustrations on the right, spread one-quarter of the bean mixture down the center of each tortilla, then mound the rice mixture on the beans, and fold the tortillas into burritos. Transfer the burritos, seam side down, to the prepared baking sheet and cover with the foil. Bake until heated through, 5 to 10 minutes. Serve immediately.

HOW TO ROLL A TIGHT BURRITO

1. Mound the filling about 1½ inches from the bottom of each tortilla, leaving a 2-inch border at the ends.

2. Roll the bottom edge of the tortilla up over the filling to cover it completely (the filling will begin to roll and tumble forward a little). Using the tortilla for leverage, press the filling back onto itself into a tight, compact log.

3. Fold the sides of the tortilla over the filling. Continue to roll the burrito into a tidy bundle. Place on a foil-lined baking sheet, seam side down. If the ends come unfolded, simply tuck them under the burrito.

FRESH CORN AND CHEESE TAMALES

TAMALES ARE SMALL, MOIST CORN CAKES filled with cheese, shredded chicken, or pork. On the Mexican table they can either be served as breakfast, or they can be the main course at dinner served alongside hearty dishes such as beans and carnitas. Served mostly during the holidays, tamales are time-consuming to prepare, with families gathering together in the kitchen to pitch in. With this

in mind, we set out to simplify the process without sacrificing the tamales' subtle but hearty flavor and light texture.

We began with the masa, the corn dough that comprises the bulk of the tamale. Masa is a dough that is made from corn kernels that have been cooked with slaked lime (which makes the corn easier to grind), and then ground to a flour. This flour is then mixed with water to form the masa. While masa can sometimes be purchased at Latin markets and tortilla factories, most people don't have access to it. So we turned to the next best thing, masa harina. Masa harina is the dried flour made from masa. It has a milder corn taste than masa, but is widely available in most grocery stores. The texture of masa harina by itself is too fine, and the flavor a bit bland, so we tried adding several variations of ground corn to supplement both texture and flavor. In two separate tests, we added cornmeal and grits (a coarser version of cornmeal) to the masa harina. The cornmeal mixture was soft and light with a true corn flavor, but its texture reminded everyone of corn muffins. The grits mixture, however, had a more granular texture similar to authentic tamales and sacrificed none of the flavor. Masa harina supplemented with grits won out.

With the base of our tamales coming together, we next found in our research that fresh corn is often incorporated into the tamale dough and thought the addition would provide some welcome texture to the dough and reinforce its corn flavor. We experimented with varying amounts of corn kernels before arriving at 1 cup, just enough to add sweetness and texture without overwhelming the tamale. We also tried frozen sweet corn kernels. Tasters had a hard time distinguishing fresh from frozen and, given their relative ease of preparation and year round availability, we decided to call for frozen kernels in our recipe.

Some recipes, we discovered, used baking powder in their dough, which helps to lighten the heavy dough. We also learned another trick to help lighten the dough: the mixing method. Instead of stirring the ingredients together by hand, we found that whipping the dry ingredients with the fat in a food processor creates air pockets in the dough that swell when steamed, creating a feathery, light tamale.

As for the fat, lard (supplemented with some butter) is traditional, but we wanted to see how other, more accessible fats, would fare. We tried tamales made with vegetable shortening, vegetable oil, and butter. The tamales made with vegetable shortening and vegetable oil didn't score well with tasters, who commented that the tamales tasted artificial and processed. The all-butter version was acceptable, although it lent the tamales an untraditional buttery flavor. We prefer the traditional lard and butter combination but leave the choice up to you.

SHOPPING NOTES: Tamales

Here are the three key ingredients we find essential to making moist, full-flavored tamales.

Masa Harina is the flour made from masa. Masa is made from dried corn kernels cooked in water with slaked lime until tender. The wet corn kernels are then ground to a flour, and mixed with water to form the dough, masa. Masa can be hard to find in the U.S., so we use masa harina, supplemented with grits to approximate the flavor and texture of masa.

Lard is rendered pork fat. Lard may be filtered, bleached, hydrogenated, or emulsified during processing, which extends its shelf life and mellows its flavor. Much of the lard found in grocery stores has undergone one or more of these processes, and its flavor is noticeably more nutty than fresh lard. Freshly rendered lard has a soft texture and more assertive pork flavor that is especially desirable in Mexican cooking. Fresh lard may be found in specialty Latin American markets and through mail-order sources.

Corn Husks are the once-fresh wrappers of field corn. They are sold dry in some grocery stores and many specialty markets. Corn husks are essential when making tamales; they impart an earthy, woodsy flavor. Look for large corn husks without signs of bugs or tears. Dried corn husks must be rehydrated in boiling water for 10 minutes before using to increase their flexibility and to clean and sterilize them. During the season when fresh corn is available and plentiful, fresh corn husks may be used, and they only require a quick blanch in boiling water before using.

With the tamale dough down, we could now focus on fillings. First, we developed a cheese-filled tamale with Monterey Jack. In an attempt to add a touch of flavor, we added ¼ cup of salsa (we used a salsa verde, which is traditional) to the cheese mixture and began stuffing the tamales. But as we assembled the tamales the salsa began to leak, making for a messy job. As we reconsidered our options, one taster suggested using pickled jalapeños in place of the salsa. Substituting a couple of tablespoons of minced pickled jalapeños was a success. The cheese mixture was much easier to handle and the pickled jalapeños added a piquant edge to the mild cheese. With the dough and filling squared away, we turned our attention to wrapping and folding the tamales.

Tamales are usually wrapped in dried corn husks, although in the tropical regions of coastal Mexico it is not uncommon to see them wrapped in banana leaves. Dried husks, which are more consistent in size and have a slightly sturdier texture than fresh, come in packets that often look like a single husk, but in fact produce at least five husks when rehydrated. Corn husks can be found in some grocery stores and most Latin American markets. And while we tried substituting corn husks with parchment paper and aluminum foil, the results weren't the same. To rehydrate the dried husks, we simply submerged them in boiling water for ten minutes with an occasional flip and stir.

When it came time to fold the tamales (see "Making Tamales" on page 29) most of the recipes we found required tying, a process we felt we could do without by simply folding the tamales and then placing them seam side facing the edges in a steamer basket. Once cooked, the tamales are firm to the touch and peel easily away from the husks. At last, we unwrapped them to reveal warm moist corn cakes filled with gooey cheese. With our cheese-filled tamale down, we turned to developing a variation with shredded chicken and cheese that is hearty and satisfying. This variation is also easy to prepare when you have leftover chicken on hand.

Corn and Cheese Tamales

MAKES 12 TAMALES, SERVES 4 TO 6 AS A
LIGHT MAIN COURSE

Be sure to use quick grits, not instant—instant grits are processed further and will adversely affect the texture and flavor of the tamales. You can substitute 1 cup fresh corn kernels (cut from about 1½ cobs), for frozen, if desired. You can also substitute 4 tablespoons (½ stick) unsalted butter for the lard if desired; the flavor, however, will have an untraditional, buttery flavor. Serve the tamales with Tomatillo Salsa (page 9); the tart salsa pairs perfectly with the tamales' sweet corn flavor.

¾	cup quick (not instant) grits
1	cup boiling water
¾	cup masa harina (see page 27)
15	large dried corn husks (see page 27)
1	cup frozen corn, thawed
4	tablespoons (½ stick) unsalted butter, cut into ½-inch cubes and softened
¼	cup (2 ounces) lard, softened (see page 27)
1	tablespoon sugar
1½	teaspoons baking powder
½	teaspoon salt
6	ounces Monterey Jack cheese, shredded (about 1½ cups)
1–2	tablespoons minced pickled jalapeños

PREVENTING SCORCHED PANS

When using just a little bit of water and a steamer basket, it's easy to let the pot run dry, causing a potentially dangerous situation. When steaming foods that take a long time to cook, such as tamales, here's how to figure out when the pot needs more water.

Before cooking, place a few glass marbles in the bottom of the pan. Add the water and the steamer basket, cover, and cook as usual. When the water level drops too low, the marbles will begin to rattle around, and the racket will remind you to add more water.

1. Place the grits in a medium bowl, whisk in the boiling water, and let stand until most of the water is absorbed, about 10 minutes. Stir in the masa harina to form a dough, cover, and let cool to room temperature, about 20 minutes.

2. Meanwhile, bring 2 quarts of water to a boil in a large pot. Stir in the corn husks, cover, and simmer until softened and flexible, about 10 minutes. Drain and set aside.

3. Process the masa dough, corn, butter, lard, sugar, baking powder, and salt together in a food processor until the mixture is light, sticky, and very smooth, about 1 minute, stopping to scrape down the sides of the bowl as needed.

4. In a small bowl, toss the cheese with the pickled jalapeños. Working with one husk at a time, spoon a scant ¼ cup of the dough into the center of each husk, following the illustrations on the right. Nestle a heaping tablespoon of the cheese-jalapeño mixture into the center of the dough and, using the sides of the husk, push the dough around the cheese to encase it completely. Fold the sides then the bottom of the husk over the filling, and lay seam side down on a large platter.

5. Fit a large Dutch oven with a steamer basket. Fill the pot with water until it just touches the bottom of the basket and bring to a boil. Following the illustration on the right, gently lay the tamales into the basket, seam side facing the edge of the steamer, with the open ends facing up. Cover and steam, checking the water level often and adding additional water as needed, until the tamales easily come free from the husks, about 1 hour. Transfer the tamales to a large platter and serve hot.

➤ VARIATION

Chicken Tamales

For instructions on how to cook and shred chicken for the filling, see page 30. You can also substitute 1 cup shredded Shepherd-Style Spicy Pork (page 31) or Slow-Fried Pork (page 35) for the chicken.

Follow the recipe for Fresh Corn and Cheese Tamales, reducing the amount of Monterey Jack to 2 ounces (about ½ cup) and adding 1 cup shredded cooked chicken to the cheese and jalapeño mixture in step 4.

MAKING TAMALES

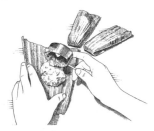

1. With the tapering end of the husk facing you, place a scant ¼ cup of the dough onto the center of the husk, leaving at least a 1 ½-inch border of husk at the tapered end.

2. Nestle a heaping tablespoon of the cheese-jalapeño mixture into the center of the dough and, using the sides of the husk, push the dough around the cheese mixture to encase it completely.

3. Fold the two long sides of the corn husk in over the corn mixture.

4. Fold the tapered end up, leaving the top open.

5. Meanwhile, line the steamer with husks. Stand the tamales up in a row, seam side facing the side of the steamer.

Shredded Cooked Chicken

MAKES ABOUT 1 CUP

Sometimes you just need a little bit of cooked chicken for a filling, as with our Chicken Tamales (page 29) or Chicken and Avocado Corn Cakes (page 48). Of course these recipes are great for using up leftover chicken, but if you don't have any on hand, here's how to quickly cook a chicken breast to yield moist, tender meat. This recipe will yield 1 cup of shredded chicken, but it can be doubled or tripled as needed; use a larger skillet and additional water to cover the bottom of the skillet.

1   boneless, skinless chicken breast
    (6 to 8 ounces), trimmed
    Salt and ground black pepper
1   tablespoon vegetable oil
⅓   cup water

1. Pat the chicken dry with paper towels and season with salt and pepper. Heat the oil in an 8-inch nonstick skillet over medium-high heat until just smoking. Add the chicken and cook until browned on one side, about 3 minutes.

2. Flip the chicken over, add the water, and cover. Reduce the heat to medium and continue to cook until the thickest part of the chicken registers 160 degrees on an instant-read thermometer, 5 to 7 minutes longer. Transfer to a carving board and cool slightly, then shred as desired.

SHEPHERD-STYLE SPICY PORK TACOS

Tacos al Pastor

TAQUERIAS THROUGHOUT MEXICO ARE FAMOUS for their *tacos al pastor* (shepherd-style tacos). They are small tacos made with chile-rubbed pork, chopped onions, a sprig or two of cilantro, and a squeeze of fresh lime. In Mexico, the pork is roasted on a vertical spit nestled against a wood-burning fire. The pork is topped with slices of fresh pineapple, and juice from the pineapple trickle down and caramelize, forming a dark crust on the meat's exterior. Sometimes a small piece of this roasted pineapple will end up in your taco. The earthy flavor of chiles permeates the meat, and the fruitiness of the pineapple lends a subtle sweetness. The tacos are quite small, usually only a few bites each; typically three tacos or more make a serving.

We wanted to duplicate this chile-flavored taco in our kitchen, but without the vertical spit or wood-burning fire. We wanted tender, moist meat, aggressively flavored and just spicy enough to be noticed without being overwhelming. The sweetness of the pineapple had to linger in the background, not be pronounced enough to be identified. It was going to be a long road for this simple taco, but the journey, as we would learn, would be well worth it.

Reviewing recipes for tacos al pastor, we found that most either used pork loin and shoulder (or butt, as it is also known), so we started there. Of the two, the shoulder seemed like the logical choice, as it is known for its melt-in-your-mouth tenderness after a long slow cooking, while pork loin tends to get dry when cooked for an extended period of time without ever getting tender. In order to get the pork shoulder to that "melting" point, we turned to braising, a covered cooking process that uses a minimal amount of liquid. The low moist heat from braising breaks down the connective tissue within the meat, and it literally falls apart when done. Several rounds of testing led us to an oven temperature of 350 degrees, just low enough to allow the meat to become tender while encouraging a soft crust to form. Pork shoulder is available bone-in or boneless, and since we would be shredding the meat postcooking, we chose to use a boneless shoulder.

After choosing our cut of pork we turned to the second most critical part of the recipe, our chile sauce. Many of the recipes we found called for a hard-to-find mixture of dried chiles and a laundry list of spices. We tried some of these recipes, but were left wondering where all of our effort had gone. We first decided to simplify the chiles, choosing anchos and chipotles, two varieties that are now very common in grocery stores throughout the country. The anchos lent the earthiness we were looking for, while the chipotles provided that smoky, open-fire flavor and heat. Dried chiles, which are rough and unbalanced straight from the package, need to be toasted and rehydrated to smooth out their flavor (see "Chiles 101" on page 37). After toasting them in the oven and rehydrating them in hot tap water, we combined them in a blender with an array of herbs and spices including cinnamon, allspice, cumin, cloves, oregano, and cilantro in varying amounts. As we tasted batch after batch of chile sauce, it became apparent that we were overcomplicating our sauce. So we decided to utilize what we thought were the key spices and omit the rest. We finally settled on cumin and cloves, which in conjunction with our chiles and garlic added both sweet and savory notes to our chile sauce.

Through our research, we found that pineapple juice also played a major role in many al pastor chile sauces. We added about ¾ cup pineapple juice to our chile sauce. The sweetness mellowed the heat from the chiles and helped form a crust on the meat. But before rubbing the pork with the sauce, we divided the sauce in half. Half would be used as a rub, while the other half would contain 2 tablespoons of vinegar and be used as a sauce for the finished pork. We found that adding vinegar to the sauce added brightness and helped distinguish the individual zest of the ingredients. Without the vinegar, the sauce tasted flat against the meat and did little to perk up the flavor.

With our sauce complete, we questioned whether we were missing the taco truck by not utilizing it as a marinade. After deciding that it was an avenue that we had to explore, we marinated one pork butt in the chile sauce for 24 hours and rubbed another with the sauce just before going into the oven. To our surprise, we preferred the pork rubbed just before cooking, as its chile aroma was fresher and more pronounced, and the pineapple's sweet-tart flavor more distinct. We shredded the pork in the baking dish incorporating the cooking liquid in the bottom of the pan, and tossed it with some of the remaining sauce to which vinegar had been added. We could tell

we were getting closer, but we needed to further examine our cooking technique.

Keeping in line with traditional tacos al pastor, we added pineapple slices to our braising pork. We first tried sandwiching our pork shoulder with pineapple slices, but this turned out to be too much pineapple flavor. We switched to simply placing the pineapple slices on top, but this just steamed the pineapple. Finally we placed two slices beneath the pork, and got the results we were after. In contact with the baking dish, the pineapple caramelized and lent a subtle flavor to the meat.

When the meat was done, we shredded it in the pan, breaking the pineapple pieces up throughout. The pineapple pieces added a fresh note to the pork as we packed it into steaming corn tortillas. We garnished the tacos with onions, cilantro, and fresh lime juice, and passed the extra sauce around. From start to finish, our tacos al pastor took little effort, but packed a deep authentic flavor.

Shepherd-Style Spicy Pork Tacos
Tacos al Pastor
SERVES 4 TO 6

These small tacos are made with soft corn tortillas and a modest amount of shredded meat. This meat also tastes great in place of the chicken in the tamales (page 29) and enchiladas (page 20), or as a filling for burritos (page 26). The bulk of this sauce is made of chiles, so substituting dried chili powder will not work here. We recommend wearing gloves when handling the toasted chiles as they are very spicy and might make your skin burn. We use a small baking dish here to prevent the roast pork drippings from burning; if using a larger dish, you may need to add water during roasting.

PORK

3	ancho chiles, brushed clean
2	dried chipotle chiles, brushed clean
I	(6-ounce can) pineapple juice
4	medium garlic cloves, peeled
2	slices pineapple (fresh or canned)
I ½	teaspoons salt
¼	teaspoon ground cumin

¼ teaspoon ground black pepper

⅛ teaspoon ground cloves

I (3-pound) boneless pork shoulder roast
(Boston butt)

2 tablespoons white vinegar

TACOS

I2 (6-inch) corn tortillas, warmed (see note
at right)
Fresh cilantro sprigs
Minced white or red onion
Sour cream
Lime wedges

1. FOR THE PORK: Adjust an oven rack to the middle position and heat the oven to 350 degrees. Place the ancho and chipotle chiles on a baking sheet and toast in the oven until fragrant and puffed, about 6 minutes. Remove the chiles from the oven and cool (leave the oven on). When cool enough to handle, seed and stem the chiles, then transfer to a medium bowl. Cover with hot tap water (about 3 cups) and soak, stirring occasionally, until softened, but not mushy, about 20 minutes.

2. Drain the chiles and transfer to a blender, discarding the water. Add the pineapple juice, garlic, salt, cumin, pepper, and cloves, and puree until smooth, 30 to 60 seconds (you should have about 1 cup).

3. Lay the pineapple slices in the bottom of an 8-inch square baking dish. Place the pork roast on top of the pineapple slices, and coat evenly with ½ cup of the pureed chile mixture. Cover the dish tightly with aluminum foil and roast in the oven until the pork is tender and falls apart when prodded with a fork, about 2½ hours.

4. Remove the pork from the oven, loosen the foil, and let rest for 15 minutes. Using two forks, shred the pork and pineapple in the dish, discarding any large pieces of fat or gristle. Stir the vinegar into the remaining ½ cup pureed chile mixture, then stir into the shredded pork to taste.

5. FOR THE TACOS: Spoon a small amount of the shredded pork into the center of each warm tortilla and serve with any remaining chile mixture, cilantro, onion, sour cream, and lime wedges.

CORN TORTILLAS

CORN TORTILLAS ARE THE UNIVERSAL accompaniment for food all throughout Mexico and are often referred to as the "bread" of Mexico. (Flour tortillas, though very popular in the U.S., are only eaten in the northern parts of Mexico—you won't find them much in the rest of the country.) Unless you live near a specialty shop that sells fresh tortillas, you have to make do with the supermarket variety, but their texture and comparison pales in comparison. You can, however, make your own fresh tortillas at home. Most of the recipes we researched were similar—masa harina and water are kneaded together to form a dough, then pressed into thin tortillas (either by hand or with a tortilla press) and toasted in a dry skillet. We tested the few discrepancies we noted in our researched recipes, including whether to add salt (yes), a little oil (yes), a little flour (no), and how long to rest the dough before pressing the tortillas (five minutes). Although you can press the dough into tortillas by hand or by using a heavy skillet, we found it difficult to get them uniformly thin without lots of practice. We prefer to use a tortilla press; you can find them at specialty shops and through mail-order sources.

~

Corn Tortillas

MAKES TWELVE 6-INCH TORTILLAS

The dough should be very wet; if it is too dry, the tortillas will be crisp and brittle. If the dough becomes too dry to work with, knead in additional water. Using two skillets to toast the tortillas in step 4 saves time. Don't skip the final steaming step; it's crucial for attaining a soft tortilla texture. To reheat tortillas quickly we found it best to use the microwave. Simply stack the tortillas on a plate, sprinkle them with a little water, cover them with microwave-safe plastic wrap, and microwave on high until warm and soft, 1 to 2 minutes—this method can also be used to heat store-bought tortillas.

2 cups masa harina (see page 27)

I teaspoon vegetable oil

¼ teaspoon salt

2 cups warm water

1. Cut twenty-four 8-inch squares of parchment paper; set aside.

2. Mix the masa, oil, and salt together in a medium bowl. Stir in 1¼ cups of the water with a rubber spatula to form a soft dough. Using your hands, knead the dough in the bowl, adding additional water as needed until the dough is very soft and has the texture of a very wet cookie dough (nearly too wet to handle). Cover and set the dough aside for 5 minutes.

3. TO PRESS THE TORTILLAS: Pinch off a 3-tablespoon-sized piece of dough, and roll into a ball. Lay one square of the parchment on the bottom of the press, place the ball of dough in the middle, and lay the second piece of parchment over the top. Press the ball gently into a ⅛-inch-thick tortilla (5 to 6 inches in diameter). Remove the parchment-encased tortilla from the press and set aside; repeat with the remaining dough and parchment squares. (The tortillas can be held, covered, at room temperature for up to 4 hours before cooking.)

4. TO COOK THE TORTILLAS: Line a baking sheet with two clean damp dish cloths; set side. Heat an 8 or 10-inch nonstick skillet (or griddle) over medium-high heat until hot, about 2 minutes. Working with one tortilla at a time, gently peel off the parchment, one side at a time, and lay the tortilla in the dry skillet. Cook, without moving, until the tortilla moves freely when the pan is shaken, about 30 seconds. Flip the tortilla over and cook until the edges curl and the bottom is spotty brown, 30 to 60 seconds. Flip the tortilla back over and continue to cook until the first side is spotty brown, 30 to 60 seconds. Lay the toasted tortilla between the damp dish cloths; repeat with the remaining tortillas. (The tortillas can be transferred to a zipper-lock bag and refrigerated for up to 5 days.)

➤ VARIATION

Chipotle Corn Tortillas

Chipotle chiles give these tortillas a spicy bite.

Follow the recipe for Corn Tortillas, adding 1 tablespoon minced chipotle chile in adobo sauce to the masa before adding the water in step 2.

MAKING CORN TORTILLAS

1. Roll the dough into balls (about 3 tablespoons of dough each).

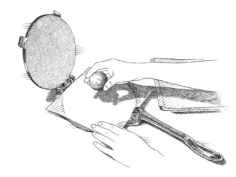

2. Line the bottom of the tortilla press with a sheet of parchment paper, and lay a ball of dough in the center.

3. Top with another sheet of parchment paper and press the dough into a 5 or 6-inch round tortilla; set the parchment-encased tortilla aside and repeat with the remaining dough.

4. To cook: Toast the tortillas, one at a time, in a hot, dry skillet, without moving, until the tortilla moves freely when the skillet is shaken, about 30 seconds. Flip and cook the second side until the edges curl and the underside is spotty brown, 30 to 60 seconds.

Slow-Fried Pork

Carnitas

SPANISH FOR "LITTLE MEATS," CARNITAS ARE popular street fare in Mexico. The meat—typically pork—is slowly fried in a large pot filled with vegetable oil or lard until it's meltingly tender with crispy, caramelized edges. The meat is then shredded and can be eaten on its own or stuffed into tacos or burritos. The deep flavor of this dish belies its simplicity, and we were determined to duplicate this Mexican classic in our kitchen.

With the exception of a few recipes calling for country-style pork ribs, all of our research directed us toward pork butt. Inexpensive yet flavorful, pork butt favors long, slow cooking and aggressive seasoning.

In our research, we found two methods for making carnitas. The first was simmering the pork in water until the water had evaporated and the pork had rendered its fat. Once the water was gone the pork fried in its rendered fat. The second was cooking the pork in low-temperature oil until the pork was fall-apart tender and brown, then draining the pork of the excess oil. We tried both methods and found simmering the pork in water to be more variable than cooking in oil. One cook's "simmer" might be another cook's "boil," thus the water might evaporate before the pork was sufficiently tender. Furthermore, the amount of fat on the pork dictated the amount of fat that would be rendered, and we sometimes found ourselves adding extra oil to the pan to fry the pork. Flavorwise, this pork was bland. The pork slow-cooked in oil was very good and we thought we were done, until a third method was brought to our attention.

This third method involves cooking the pork in oil supplemented with a small amount of water. We were curious to see what adding water would do, so we began by adding ¼ cup of water to 4 cups of oil. Using a thermometer, we monitored the temperature of the oil and water mixture and noticed that the water actually prevented the temperature of the oil from rising. These results were compounded as the amount of water was increased in subsequent tests. As we learned, this happens because the water requires heat to evaporate, heat that would normally be directed toward increasing the temperature of the oil, and as the water evaporates it takes heat with it. Eventually, as more and more water evaporates, heat is redirected back to the oil and the temperature of the oil will begin to increase. As it turns out, the cooling of the oil is beneficial because collagen breakdown within the pork is actually accelerated at low temperatures. But too much water throws off the cooking time, texture, and flavor of the pork. We tested this theory with ¼ cup of water all the way up to 1½ cups of water and found that ¼ cup of water was enough to promote collagen breakdown, encourage adequate browning, and yield great roasted flavor at the same time. But while we were ending up with great results on the stovetop, we had to constantly monitor the temperature of the oil. We needed to find an easier way to get the results we were after, so we turned to the oven.

In the oven, we were able to experiment with various cooking temperatures with greater accuracy (not to mention the added bonus of not having to constantly stand over a pot of hot oil). After bringing the oil to a simmer on the stovetop, we transferred the pot to a low, 300-degree oven to start. But at this temperature the pork took too long to cook, just barely browning by the time it was tender, and when we finally pulled it from the oven it had almost completely dried out. We attempted several more tests, increasing the oven temperature in 25-degree increments each time. Temperatures that were too low resulted in dry meat that was underbrowned, and too-high temperatures resulted in overly browned meat that was too tough to chew. We finally zeroed in on 375 degrees. At this oven temperature, we were able to maintain an oil temperature around 230 degrees until the water had evaporated, which allowed ample time for collagen breakdown, leaving us with pork that had browned almost exactly when it reached fork-tenderness.

With our water amount and oven temperature in order, we shifted focus to flavoring the pork. We experimented with adding various ingredients, such as citrus fruit and spices, to the oil. Oranges, halved and juiced and added to the oil, didn't come through in the pork, so we tried limes. The acid of the lime cut through the rich flavor of the meat and added just a hint of tanginess to the pork. In addition we added cinnamon sticks and bay leaves to the oil, and seasoned the pork with salt and cumin before placing it in the pot. We also uncovered one interesting substitute for the water in some recipes: Coca-Cola. Coke-braised carnitas are popular in Southern California, and when we tried this twist the results were worthy enough for us to include cola as a possible alternative to the water. The change in flavor was minor, but the phosphoric acid in the cola acted as a tenderizer, and the sugar further browned the pork, giving the crust a noticeable sweetness.

When the pork was done, we drained it in a colander to remove the excess fat, and then shredded it using a couple of forks. We served the carnitas wrapped in corn tortillas loaded with minced onion, cilantro, fresh lime juice, and a dollop of sour cream—tasters couldn't get enough.

Slow-Fried Pork

Carnitas

SERVES 4 TO 6

Although we suggest serving carnitas with warm corn tortillas here taco-style, you can also use them as a filling for tamales (page 29), enchiladas (page 20), or burritos (page 26). Vegetable oil can be substituted for the peanut oil, but we prefer peanut for its richer flavor. Do not save the oil after using; it will go rancid quickly. Coca-Cola doesn't flavor the pork significantly, but it does give the meat sweet, crisp, caramelized edges.

CARNITAS

1	(3-pound) boneless pork shoulder roast (Boston butt), trimmed and cut into 2-inch chunks
1	teaspoon ground cumin
	Salt
4	cups peanut oil (see note)
¼	cup water or Coca-Cola (see note)
2	cinnamon sticks
2	bay leaves
1	lime, halved
	Ground black pepper

TORTILLAS AND GARNISHES

12	(6-inch) corn tortillas, warmed (see note on page 32)
	Fresh cilantro sprigs
	Sour cream
	Minced white or red onion
	Lime wedges

1. Adjust an oven rack to the lower-middle position and heat the oven to 375 degrees. Pat the pork dry with paper towels, season with the cumin and 1 teaspoon salt, and transfer to a large Dutch oven. Add the oil, water, cinnamon, and bay leaves. Juice the lime directly into the pot, then add the spent lime halves.

2. Bring the mixture to a simmer over medium-high heat, then transfer to the oven and cook, uncovered, until the edges of the pork are well browned and the meat falls apart when prodded with a fork, about 2½ hours.

3. Remove the pot from the oven and, using a slotted spoon, transfer the pork to a colander set over a bowl; let drain about 10 minutes (discard the oil). Shred the pork using two forks and season with salt and pepper to taste. Serve with warm corn tortillas, cilantro, sour cream, onion, and lime wedges.

CORE TECHNIQUE

SLOW-FRYING

Tender shreds of pork with crispy edges are the hallmark of truly great carnitas. In our research, we found the most effective and fail-safe method for preparing the pork is slow-frying the pork in oil, supplemented with a small amount of water. The water helps prevent the oil temperature from rising, ensuring a gentle slow cooking, much like poaching, but with the added flavor and richness of frying. The results? Browned, flavorful, fork-tender pork. And while we initially tried this method on the stovetop, further testing revealed that transferring the pot to the oven was a convenient, foolproof way to ensure even cooking. Initially, we were skeptical of placing a pot of uncovered simmering oil in the oven, but because the temperature is so low, the oil remains inside the pot, not splattered all over the oven.

Chiles 101

CHILES, BOTH FRESH AND DRIED, ARE THE BACKBONE OF REGIONAL MEXICAN CUISINE, WITH THEIR unique flavors that range from mild and fresh, to acidic and spicy, to rich and deeply toasted. Some chiles are used for their spicy heat, while others with a more mild flavor are used to provide subtle background notes. You should use caution when working with chiles because the compound that makes them taste spicy, called capsaicin, can easily be rubbed off onto your hands (and then onto whatever you touch), causing a mild to very strong burning sensation. We recommend wearing disposable latex gloves and washing your hands thoroughly with soap and water when done handling chiles. As an added precaution, your cutting board and knife should be washed to prevent transferring the chiles' heat to other foods.

FRESH CHILES

WHEN SHOPPING FOR FRESH CHILES, LOOK FOR THOSE WITH BRIGHT COLORS AND TIGHT, UNBLEMISHED skin. Note that much of the heat in a chile lies in the seeds and ribs; you can omit the seeds or add them to a dish as desired to help control the spice levels. We sometimes add some of the seeds with the chiles and reserve the remaining seeds to adjust spiciness just before serving.

CHILE	APPEARANCE AND FLAVOR	HEAT	SUBSTITUTIONS
POBLANO	Thick-skinned peppers that vary in color from green to reddish-brown with a crisp bell pepper flavor	Mild	Bell pepper, Anaheim
ANAHEIM	Large, yellow-green to red in color with a tangy, mild flavor	Medium	Poblano
JALAPEÑO	Green or red in color with a bright, rich chile flavor	Medium to Hot	Serrano
SERRANO	Small green chiles similar in flavor to jalapeños	Hot	Jalapeño

SEEDING FRESH CHILES

Using a knife to remove the seeds and ribs from a hot chile pepper takes a very steady hand. Fortunately, there is a safer and equally effective alternative.

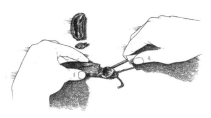

1. Cut the pepper in half lengthwise with a knife.

2. Starting opposite the stem end, run the edge of a small melon baller scoop down the inside of the pepper, scraping up seeds and ribs.

3. Cut off the core with the scoop.

DRIED CHILES

DRIED CHILES NEED TO BE TOASTED BEFORE USING IN ORDER TO BRING OUT THEIR LATENT FLAVORS. We find the oven to be the most reliable toasting method (see instructions below). After toasting, you need to stem and seed the chiles (wearing gloves). Then, depending on what dish you're making, the chiles can be rehydrated in hot water, torn into small pieces, or ground to a powder. By rehydrating the toasted chiles in hot water, you mellow their flavor, which is appropriate for sauces that are mild or are served raw, such as the sauce for our Shepherd–Style Spicy Pork Tacos (page 31). By tearing the toasted chiles into small pieces, you can add them directly to a soup or sauce for a more potent flavor that is appropriate for dishes such as Chicken Mole (page 40). Grinding the toasted chiles to a powder gives you a fresher tasting chile powder than what you'd find in the supermarket.

CHILE	APPEARANCE AND FLAVOR	HEAT	SUBSTITUTIONS
CALIFORNIA CHILE (DRIED ANAHEIM CHILE)	Similar in appearance to New Mexico chiles, but with a more mild flavor	Mild	New Mexico, ancho, guajillo
NEW MEXICO	Smooth, shiny, brick-red skin, with a crisp, slightly acidic, earthy flavor	Mild	Ancho, California chile
ANCHO (DRIED POBLANO PEPPER)	Dark mahogany red with wrinkly skin and a sweet, raisiny flavor	Medium	Mulato, pasilla, New Mexico, California chile
CASCABEL	Small, round chiles with seeds that rattle when shaken. Reddish-brown color with a deep, nutty flavor	Medium	Guajillo
GUAJILLO	Long, shiny, smooth skin with a reddish-brown color, and a bright, fruity, earthy flavor	Medium	Cascabels, New Mexico, California chile
MULATO (SMOKED POBLANO)	Similar in appearance to the ancho but darker with a sweet, earthy, smoky flavor	Medium	Ancho
CHIPOTLE (SMOKED JALAPEÑO PEPPER, DRIED OR CANNED IN ADOBO SAUCE)	Brick-red to brown, with a smoky, chocolate flavor	Hot	Morita
PASILLA (DRIED CHILACA CHILE)	Long, wrinkled, purplish, dark brown, with a rich grapey, herby flavor	Hot	Ancho, mulato

PREPARING DRIED CHILES

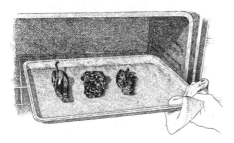

1. Clean the chiles of any visible dirt with a damp paper towel, then lay on a baking sheet and toast in a 350-degree oven until fragrant and puffed, about 6 minutes.

2. Let the chiles cool, then wearing gloves to protect your skin, break open the chile and brush out seeds. (The seeds can be reserved to add extra heat to dishes.) Remove the stem.

3. If rehydrating the chiles (this will mellow their flavor), transfer the toasted, seeded, and stemmed chiles to a large bowl and cover with boiling water. Let sit, stirring occasionally, until the chiles are softened but not mushy, about 20 minutes.

CHICKEN MOLE

MOLE, FROM THE AZTEC WORD FOR "SAUCE," is a rich blend of chiles, nuts, spices, fruit, and sometimes chocolate, and is considered the national dish of Mexico—either paired with chicken or turkey or ladled over enchiladas, rice, or potatoes. The popular moles, *mole rojo* (red mole) and *mole poblano*, are distinguished from other moles by their inclusion of chocolate and are the style of mole you're apt to find on most restaurant menus. An authentic mole has complex layers of flavor, but these exotic flavors come with a price: an extensive list of ingredients and a notoriously long and complicated cooking method. Our goal was to translate mole for American home cooks without sacrificing the dish's traditional flavor. As is often done in Mexico, we wanted our mole with chicken for a dish home cooks north of the border would welcome into their repertoire.

We began by testing three red and two poblano mole recipes uncovered in our research, and after three days of shopping, we finally found all of the ingredients to start cooking—a daunting start. Moles are generally made by individually sautéing each ingredient (garlic, nuts, chiles, etc.) in an ample amount of oil. This step acts to toast each item, bringing it to its peak of flavor. Next, all the ingredients are brought together in a large pot with the addition of broth or water and simmered to set the flavors. The mixture is then pureed smooth, and returned to the pot to continue cooking until the flavors meld—depending on the mole and the number of ingredients, this could take as long as three hours.

All of the moles we tried tasted a bit different from one another—some were sweeter, others were a bit spicy, and a few had a thicker consistency—but they all featured deep, rich, exotic flavors and took far too long to prepare. To simplify things, we cobbled together a working recipe—sautéing some basic aromatics (onion and garlic), then adding the remaining ingredients such as nuts, seeds, dried fruit, and chocolate. (We skipped cooking each ingredient individually, deeming the method too fussy.) At this point, the mixture was simmered with added chicken broth, and then pureed. With this as our starting point, we would test variables.

Dried chiles are a key ingredient in mole so we thought it would be an appropriate place for us to start. Most authentic mole recipes call for several (up to five or six) different types of chiles (such as mulatos, guajillos, pasillas, ancho, and chipotle; see page 37 for more information), but these chiles are to add flavor only, and are in no way meant to bring heat to the sauce. We sought out and tested all of these chiles in various sauces, and were pleased to find that we could come up with a delicious mole using just two of the most common: anchos and chipotles. Two ancho chiles laid down a full, mild, base of chile flavor while just half a chipotle added a more intense chile flavor and a hint of heat.

Our next step was to determine how to prep the ancho chiles before adding them to the sauce. Traditional moles often rely on pan-toasting the chiles to release more of their flavor, but we found this method required constant attention to keep the chiles from scorching (we burned a few batches before getting the hang of it ourselves). Rather, we found a more foolproof toasting method by using the oven. After about six minutes in a 350-degree oven, the chiles become fragrant and puffed—a clear indication that they are perfectly toasted but not burned. Traditional recipes often toast the chiles with a little oil, but we found no difference in flavor between chiles that were oven-toasted with and without oil. Removing seeds and stems from the chiles (neither is used in the sauce) is easiest to do after toasting.

Our final chile question was how to prep the chiles after toasting and we had three options: rehydrate the chiles in water, grind the chiles to a powder, or tear the chiles into small pieces. Rehydrating (or softening) the chiles in water is a method touted by many recipes; the soaked chiles are then drained before being added to the sauce. We didn't like this method because it produced a washed-out flavor. We tried increasing the amount of chiles to compensate for this lost flavor, but we still missed the assertive, warm flavor of the un-rehydrated chiles. And adding the chile-soaking water to the mole gave the sauce a bitter, off-flavor. Grinding the chiles to a powder didn't work because it made the sauce taste grainy. Rather, we found it easiest to break the chiles up into small pieces and add them right to the simmering sauce. This way, the chiles rehydrate and leach their flavor right into the sauce, rather than into water that gets poured down the drain.

Next, we moved on to the nut and seed components of the mole. Most recipes called for some combination of toasted almonds, pumpkin seeds, peanuts, and sesame seeds. We tested sauces made with each seed and nut on its own to determine their individual flavors, then came up with our own favorite combination. In the end, we liked the rich, creamy flavors of toasted almonds and sesame seeds, but not so much the overpowering flavor of peanuts, or the acrid flavor of pumpkin seeds. Most recipes call for finely ground almonds, but we didn't like their gritty texture in the otherwise smooth puree; straining the sauce was an option, but we found that this also strained out some of their flavor. Rather, we solved this problem by substituting almond butter for the ground almonds, and were pleasantly surprised to find that the butter also gave the sauce a luxurious, velvety texture. We also thought we'd try peanut butter, since it's more available, but its assertive flavor overpowered the subtleties of the mole.

Up to now we had been using semisweet chocolate in the sauce, but wondered if different chocolate types, including authentic Mexican chocolate, might make a difference. After testing various amounts of chocolate, we determined that 1 ounce is just enough to add flavor without overpowering the sauce. We pitted cocoa powder, unsweetened, semisweet, bittersweet, and Mexican chocolate against one another. (Mexican chocolate contains cinnamon and sometimes almonds and vanilla.) Only the unsweetened chocolate and cocoa powder stood out as tasting bitter, while the semisweet, bittersweet, and Mexican chocolates all worked well.

Our mole had begun to come together, but we noticed that it was still missing some of the complexity of the more elaborate recipes. Adding some spices, including cinnamon and cloves, along with some raisins helped our sauce flavor take a leap forward. Until now we had been simply using water as the liquid base for the sauce, but found that chicken broth tasted richer and better. Adding canned, diced tomatoes also helped round out the flavor and deepen the sauce's color.

Finally, we took a closer look at the cooking method. Rather than just sautéing the basic aromatics (onions and garlic) we found it beneficial to sauté the chiles, chocolate, and spices too. Sautéing drew out and deepened their flavors significantly. As for simmering times, we found no reason to simmer the sauce for longer than 10 minutes. This was enough time to concentrate the flavors and reduce it to the appropriate thickness while still leaving it fluid enough for the blender to do its work and turn our mole into a velvety liquid.

As the construction of our mole finally came to an end, we turned our attention to incorporating the chicken into the dish. Using a variety of bone-in chicken pieces, we left the skin on and seared the pieces until nicely browned on both sides. We then transferred the chicken to a baking dish and topped it liberally with our sauce. When tasters tried the chicken, they overwhelmingly commented that the skin was soggy. Anticipating that this would be an issue that would arise time and again, we decided to remove the skin from the chicken before cooking. Furthermore, we decided to omit the step of searing the chicken because we felt that the sauce was assertive enough to overpower any of the subtle caramelized flavors achieved from browning the chicken. So in the end, we simply skinned the chicken, seasoned it with salt and pepper, topped it with mole and placed it in a 400-degree oven until the center of the chicken breasts registered 160 degrees, or the thighs/drumsticks registered 170 degrees, 35 to 45 minutes.

Chicken Mole

SERVES 4 TO 6

Ancho chiles are poblano chiles that have been dried and chipotle chiles are jalapeño chiles that have been dried. For more information about chile varieties, see page 37. We recommend wearing gloves when handling the toasted chiles; they are very spicy and might burn your skin. The flavor of mole made with whole ancho chiles is superior to ground ancho powder, but if necessary, substitute 2 tablespoons ground ancho powder for the fresh; skip step 1 and add the powder with the cinnamon in step 2. Feel free to substitute ½ teaspoon ground chipotle powder or ½ teaspoon minced chipotles in adobo sauce, for the chipotle chile (we noted little difference in flavor) and add with the cinnamon in step 2.

2	ancho chiles (see note), brushed clean
½	chipotle chile (see note), brushed clean
3	tablespoons vegetable oil
I	medium onion, minced
½	teaspoon ground cinnamon
⅛	teaspoon ground cloves
I	ounce bittersweet, semisweet, or Mexican chocolate, chopped coarse
2	medium garlic cloves, minced or pressed through a garlic press (about 2 teaspoons)
2	cups low-sodium chicken broth
I	(14.5-ounce) can diced tomatoes, drained
¼	cup raisins
2	tablespoons sesame seeds, toasted, plus extra for garnish
¼	cup almond butter
	Salt and ground black pepper
	Sugar
3½	pounds bone-in chicken pieces (split breasts, legs, and/or thighs), skin removed

1. Adjust an oven rack to the middle position and heat the oven to 350 degrees. Place the ancho and chipotle chiles on a baking sheet and toast in the oven until fragrant and puffed, about 6 minutes. Remove the chiles from the oven and let cool (leave the oven on). When cool enough to handle, seed and stem the chiles, and break into small pieces.

2. Heat the oil in a large skillet over medium heat until shimmering. Add the onion and cook until softened, 5 to 7 minutes. Stir in the toasted chile pieces, cinnamon, cloves, and chocolate and cook until the spices are fragrant and the chocolate is melted and bubbly, about 2 minutes. Stir in the garlic and cook until fragrant, about 30 seconds. Stir in the broth, tomatoes, raisins, sesame seeds, and almond butter and cook, stirring occasionally, until slightly thickened and measures about 2½ cups, about 10 minutes. Transfer the chile mixture to a blender (or food processor) and process until smooth, about 20 seconds. Season with salt, pepper, and sugar to taste. (Up to this point, the sauce can be cooled and refrigerated for up to 3 days. Loosen the sauce with water as needed before continuing with the recipe.)

3. Adjust the oven temperature to 400 degrees. Pat the chicken pieces dry and season with salt and pepper. Arrange the chicken in a single layer in a shallow baking dish and cover with the mole sauce, turning the chicken to coat evenly. Bake, uncovered, until an instant-read thermometer inserted into the center of a chicken breast registers 160 degrees, or into a thigh or drumstick registers 170 degrees, 35 to 45 minutes.

4. Remove the chicken from the oven, cover loosely with foil, and let rest in the sauce for 5 to 10 minutes. Transfer the chicken to a large serving platter or individual serving plates, spoon the sauce over top, and sprinkle with sesame seeds before serving.

2

LATIN AMERICA AND THE CARIBBEAN

EMPANADAS

PREVALENT THROUGHOUT LATIN AMERICA and Spain, empanadas are filled pastries similar to turnovers. (The word "empanada" actually comes from the Spanish verb *empanar*, which translates as "to bake in pastry.") A selection of cookbooks—including some from Chile, Mexico, Argentina, Spain, and Colombia—yielded a dizzying number of empanada recipes. And although the dough recipes were all pretty similar, the filling variations were endless. Depending on the country of origin or the preferences of the person making them, savory empanadas might contain seafood, beef, chicken, cheese, or vegetables, while a sweet version might be filled with sweet potatoes or fruit. We decided to focus our attention first on the dough and then narrow down our filling choices.

To make empanadas, lard or vegetable shortening (such as Crisco) is typically warmed until liquid and then mixed with flour (and sometimes water) to form a dough. This method for adding fat to flour was unfamiliar to us, so we were curious about the results. Tasters complained that the dough made their fingers greasy, which was a surprise, considering the ratio of fat to flour was an average of 1 to 3—moderate for pastry dough. There were also complaints that the pastry was bland and tough. We knew we would have to try a different approach.

We found great results using a classic pie dough preparation, which cuts cold fat into the flour. The mixture is then combined with ice water by hand until a dough forms. This method produces a pastry that bakes up with tender flakiness. Our tasters preferred butter to vegetable shortening for improved flavor.

As we discovered early on in our research, there are many styles of fillings for empanadas, and many of them call for hard-to-find Latin American ingredients. Wanting to make our empanada recipe accessible to the American home cook, we decided to keep things simple with a basic beef and cheese filling. Most recipes we found for beef empanadas called for ground beef. Rounding up as many types of ground beef as we could find in our local markets, we made batches of empanadas using ground round, chuck, and sirloin with varying degrees of leanness. Ground round was dry with an off, livery flavor, and tasters were not impressed with the dull flavor of the sirloin. In the end, we agreed that 85 percent lean ground chuck had the best beef flavor and moisture content.

We started by sautéing aromatics (minced onion and garlic), then adding the beef and cooking it until well done. We then cooled the mixture and folded in shredded cheese. According to our research, the ideal beef empanada filling is wet and the crumbled meat should be enveloped in a thick sauce. Ours was moist but still a bit on the crumbly side. We found we could achieve the ideal saucy texture by adding a modest amount of low-sodium beef broth (¾ cup) after cooking the beef partway. The broth simmered with the beef mixture and reduced to a consistency that was moist, but not runny.

With the basics in place, we now focused our attention on boosting the filling's flavor. One tablespoon of tomato paste did much to heighten the beefiness of the filling, while fresh oregano added a nice layer of complexity. For spices, tasters approved of a combination of cumin, cloves, and cayenne. And a small amount of sugar added a good note of sweetness to the savory filling. Finally, tasters decided that a neutral melting cheese, such as Monterey Jack, was best. We also decided to create a variation using ground turkey, raisins, and olives, a classic Chilean combination (see page 44).

These empanadas do take time to make, but they can be prepared ahead of time with great results. You can make these meat-filled pastries three days in advance and refrigerate them, and they keep beautifully in the freezer for up to a month. When they're ready to go into the oven, brush them with a little egg wash. The egg gives the baked pastry a great shine and golden brown color—an attractive invitation to dig in.

Empanadas

MAKES 48 MINI EMPANADAS

If your kitchen is very warm, refrigerate all of the dough ingredients for 30 minutes before making the dough (see page 205 for more tips on working with tart and pie doughs). There should be plenty of dough to cut out and make 48 empanadas without having to reroll any dough scraps; we found the rerolled scraps of dough to be very tough.

3¾ cups (18¾ ounces) unbleached all-purpose flour, plus extra for the work surface

1 tablespoon sugar

1½ teaspoons salt

12 tablespoons (1½ sticks) unsalted butter, cut into ½-inch cubes and chilled

1¼ cups ice water

1 recipe empanada filling (see pages 43–44), chilled

1 large egg, beaten

1. Process the flour, sugar, and salt together in a food processor until combined, about 6 pulses. Scatter the butter pieces over the flour mixture and pulse until the mixture resembles coarse cornmeal with butter bits no larger than small peas, about 16 pulses.

2. Transfer the flour mixture to a large mixing bowl. Working with ¼ cup of water at a time, sprinkle the water over the flour mixture and stir it in using a rubber spatula, pressing the mixture against the side of the bowl to form a dough, until no small bits of flour remain (you may not need to use all of the water).

3. Turn the dough out onto a clean work surface and divide it into 2 equal pieces. Press each dough half into a cohesive ball then flatten the ball into a 6-inch disk. Wrap each disk in plastic and refrigerate until firm, about 2 hours or up to 2 days.

4. Line 2 baking sheets with parchment paper; set aside. Remove 1 disk of dough from the refrigerator. Roll the dough out on a lightly floured work surface into an 18-inch circle about ⅛ inch thick. Using a 3-inch round biscuit cutter, cut out 24 rounds and transfer them to a prepared baking sheet, discarding the dough scraps. Cover the dough rounds with plastic wrap and refrigerate while you repeat with the remaining disk of dough and prepared baking sheet.

5. Working with the first batch of dough rounds, follow the illustrations on page 44 to fill, shape, and seal the empanadas using roughly 1 teaspoon of the chilled filling per empanada. Crimp the edges of the empanadas using a fork, and arrange them on a fresh parchment paper–lined baking sheet. Wrap the baking sheet tightly with plastic wrap, and refrigerate while making a second batch of empanadas using the remaining dough rounds and filling. (The empanadas can be refrigerated for up to 3 days, or frozen for up to 1 month. After the empanadas are completely frozen, about 8 hours, they can be transferred to a zipper-lock bag to save space in the freezer. Transfer back to a parchment paper–lined baking sheet before baking.)

6. Adjust the oven racks to the upper- and lower-middle positions and heat the oven to 425 degrees. Brush the empanadas with the egg and bake until golden brown, about 20 minutes, switching and rotating the trays halfway through the baking time. (If frozen, increase the baking time to 25 minutes.) Cool for 5 minutes before serving.

Beef and Cheese Empanada Filling

ENOUGH FOR ABOUT 48 MINI EMPANADAS

The filling can be made while the empanada dough rests in the refrigerator.

1 tablespoon olive oil

1 medium onion, minced

1 tablespoon tomato paste

2 medium garlic cloves, minced or pressed through a garlic press (about 2 teaspoons)

1 teaspoon minced fresh oregano leaves, or ¼ teaspoon dried

1 teaspoon ground cumin

Pinch ground cloves

Pinch cayenne pepper

½ pound (85 percent lean) ground chuck

¾ cup low-sodium beef broth

1 teaspoon sugar

Salt and ground black pepper

2 ounces Monterey Jack cheese, shredded (about ½ cup)

MAKING EMPANADAS

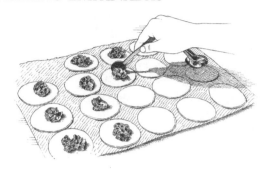

1. Place about 1 teaspoon of the filling in the center of each dough round and moisten the edge of the dough round with water, using either your finger or a pastry brush.

2. Fold the dough in half over the filling, making a half-moon shape.

3. Pinch the seam along the edge to close.

4. Using a dinner fork, crimp the sealed edge to secure.

1. Heat the oil in a 12-inch nonstick skillet over medium-high heat until just shimmering. Add the onion and cook until softened, 5 to 7 minutes. Stir in the tomato paste, garlic, oregano, cumin, cloves, and cayenne and cook until fragrant, about 30 seconds. Stir in the beef and cook, breaking up the meat with a wooden spoon, until no longer pink, about 4 minutes.

2. Stir in the broth, reduce the heat to low, and simmer until the mixture is moist but not wet, about 8 minutes. Off the heat, stir in the sugar and season with salt and pepper to taste. Transfer the mixture to a medium bowl, cover with plastic wrap, and refrigerate until completely cool, about 1 hour. Stir in the cheese and continue to chill until needed. (The filling can be refrigerated for up to 2 days.)

Turkey Empanada Filling with Raisins and Olives

ENOUGH FOR ABOUT 48 MINI EMPANADAS

The filling can be made while the empanada dough rests in the refrigerator. Ground pork or 85 percent lean ground beef can be substituted for the turkey. The combination of raisins and olives with ground meat and onions is classic in Chile, where it is called pino.

1	tablespoon olive oil
1	medium onion, minced
1	tablespoon tomato paste
2	medium garlic cloves, minced or pressed through a garlic press (about 2 teaspoons)
2	teaspoons paprika
1	teaspoon minced fresh thyme leaves, or ¼ teaspoon dried
	Ground black pepper
½	pound (93 percent lean) ground turkey
¾	cup low-sodium beef broth
⅓	cup raisins, chopped fine
⅓	cup brine-cured green olives, pitted and chopped (see the illustration on page 291)
1	teaspoon sugar
	Salt

1. Heat the oil in a 12-inch nonstick skillet over medium-high heat until just shimmering. Add the

onion and cook until softened, 5 to 7 minutes. Stir in the tomato paste, garlic, paprika, thyme, and ⅛ teaspoon pepper. Cook until fragrant, about 30 seconds. Stir in the turkey and cook, breaking up the meat with a wooden spoon, until no longer pink, about 4 minutes.

2. Stir in the broth and raisins, reduce the heat to low, and simmer until the mixture is moist but not wet, about 8 minutes. Off the heat, stir in the olives and sugar and season with salt and pepper to taste. Transfer the mixture to a medium bowl, cover with plastic wrap, and refrigerate until completely cool, about 1 hour. (The filling can be refrigerated for up to 2 days.)

VENEZUELAN STUFFED CORN CAKES

Arepas

AREPAS ARE A TYPE OF CORN CAKE POPULAR in Venezuela and Colombia, although variations exist in other Latin countries, and in recent years they have even made their way to cosmopolitan areas in the United States. Although the arepas in Venezuela and Colombia are very similar—both have a polenta-like texture and subtle corn flavor—they are typically served in different ways. Venezuelan-style arepas are split open and stuffed with a filling—anything from meat and cheese to eggs, corn, beans, and even fish—much like a sandwich. In Colombia, arepas tend to be eaten more like bread, simply spread with butter or topped with cheese, though sometimes they are stuffed and fried to be eaten as more of a meal.

Our research led us to believe that arepas originated in northern Venezuela; however, some of our Colombian friends have a different point of view. Rivalry aside, we decided to develop a recipe for Venezuelan arepas. After all, many sources actually refer to arepas as the "hamburger" of Venezuela, where they are sold at fast-food-like joints called *areparias*. The idea of sandwich-style arepas appealed greatly to us, so we decided we would focus our attention there.

Arepas are made using a flour called *masarepa* (also called *harina precocida* and *masa al instante*), which is a precooked white or yellow cornmeal. Both white and yellow masarepa can be found at many large supermarkets in the U.S., but the white variety, or *masarepa blanca*, is most often used in Venezuela, so we chose to use it in our recipe. Water, salt, and sometimes eggs, milk, or cheese are added to the flour to make a dough, and the arepas are then shaped into rounds that are typically anywhere from ¼ to 1 inch thick. The shaped arepas are browned on a griddle until a crust is formed, and then transferred to the oven to bake.

To develop our recipe, we began with the arepas themselves—we would worry about the fillings later. We started by testing several of the arepa recipes that we found in our research. Many of them recommended using equal parts masarepa and hot water; however, we found that this ratio produced a dry and crumbly arepa. We were working with 2 cups of masarepa, so we made batches of arepas using 2½ and 3 cups of warm water and compared them side by side. The arepas made with 3 cups of water were difficult to shape because the dough was so wet, and they fell apart when we cooked them. The batch made with 2½ cups of water was much better—these arepas were easy to shape, cooked up nicely, and were moist and tender—though some tasters thought they were a little dense. We remedied that by adding just 1 teaspoon of baking powder—not a traditional ingredient, but welcomed nonetheless for the subtle lightness that it gave to the arepas. To bring out the corn flavor, we also added a generous 1 teaspoon salt to the dough. Eggs, cheese, and herbs seemed excessive, especially since we were going to be adding a filling, so we left them out.

Now we were ready to fine-tune the shaping and cooking process. We got the shaping right pretty quickly—3-inch rounds about ½ inch thick were our favorite size. Any thinner, and they were difficult to split open and stuff; any thicker, and the ratio of cake to filling was too high, which also made the arepas messy and difficult to eat.

The cooking technique was also fairly straightforward. Instead of using a grill or griddle like many recipes do, we simplified the process and browned our arepas in a nonstick skillet with a little vegetable oil. Once they were golden and a crust had formed on both sides, we transferred them to a baking sheet and into a 400-degree oven to bake through in the center. The arepas were now ready to be split open and stuffed, so it was time for us to turn our attention to the fillings.

Arepas can be stuffed with a wide range of ingredients—even deli meats and leftovers are used. Off the bat, we decided to limit our fillings to simple ingredients that could be easily combined. We created three fillings: cheese; chicken and avocado; and black bean and cheese. We used the typical additions of scallions, cilantro, lime juice, and a little chili powder to provide a balanced flavor base for all three and then worked in the main ingredients.

For the cheese filling, we achieved the perfect textural balance by supplementing Monterey Jack with creamy queso fresco. To make the chicken and avocado filling, a classic combination called *reina pepiada* in Venezuela, we bound tender shredded chicken together with rich chunks of avocado. The bean and cheese filling, known as *dominó* in Venezuela, got its velvety texture not only from the cheese, but also by mashing the beans. We could fit a generous 3 tablespoons of filling into each arepa, which is plenty, considering that one arepa is perfect for a snack or light lunch, and two are a suitable dinner portion.

Venezuelan Stuffed Corn Cakes
Arepas
MAKES 8 CORN CAKES
Masarepa, a precooked corn flour that is also called harina precocida and masa al instante, is available in specialty Latin markets, and often in the Latin American aisle at supermarkets. While we had the best results with masarepa, we found that white cornmeal can be substituted. Arepas are a great way to use up leftovers—they can be stuffed with almost anything, like Refried Beans (page 11), the filling for Shepherd-Style Spicy Pork Tacos (page 31), and Slow-Fried Pork (page 35). Serve with Mojo Sauce (page 76), if desired.

2	cups (10 ounces) masarepa blanca
I	teaspoon salt
I	teaspoon baking powder
2½	cups warm water
¼	cup vegetable oil
I	recipe corn cake filling (below and page 48)

1. Adjust an oven rack to the middle position and heat the oven to 400 degrees. Whisk the masarepa, salt, and baking powder together in a medium bowl. Gradually add the water and stir to form a dough. Using a generous ⅓ cup of dough, form eight 3-inch rounds, each about ½ inch thick.

2. Heat 2 tablespoons of the oil in a 12-inch nonstick skillet over medium-high heat until shimmering. Add 4 of the arepas and cook until golden on both sides, about 4 minutes total. Transfer to a parchment paper–lined baking sheet and repeat with the remaining 2 tablespoons oil and the remaining 4 arepas. (The arepas can be refrigerated for up to 3 days, or frozen for up to 1 month in a zipper-lock bag).

3. Bake until the arepas sound hollow when tapped on the bottom, about 10 minutes. (If frozen, increase the baking time to 20 minutes.) Split the hot arepas open using a paring knife or 2 forks as if they were English muffins, and stuff each with a generous 3 tablespoons of the filling. Serve immediately.

Cheese Corn Cake Filling
MAKES ENOUGH FOR 8 CORN CAKES
The filling can be made while the arepas are in the oven. If you can't find queso fresco, either feta or farmer's cheese makes a good substitute.

8	ounces Monterey Jack cheese, shredded (about 2 cups)
4	ounces queso fresco, crumbled (about I cup) (see note)
2	tablespoons minced fresh cilantro leaves
2	scallions, sliced thin
I	tablespoon juice from I lime
¼	teaspoon chili powder
	Salt and ground black pepper

PANTRY SPOTLIGHT

CORN PRODUCTS

Corn is a cereal grain that is a staple food in many countries—some varieties are available fresh, while others are processed in many different ways. Here in the test kitchen, we know it's easy to get mixed up about the different forms that the grain can take, so we decided to provide some clarity on the subject.

Cornmeal, available either white or yellow, is made from dried corn that is milled into a fine, medium, or coarse grind. Small manufacturers often choose not to degerm, or remove all the germ, resulting in cornmeal with flecks that are both lighter and darker than the predominant color. Cornmeal is used in quick breads and baked goods, to dredge seafood and poultry for frying, and to make polenta (we prefer coarsely ground yellow cornmeal for making Italian polenta).

Hominy is made from dried corn kernels that have been soaked (or cooked) in an alkali solution (commonly lime-water or calcium hydroxide) to remove the germ and hull. It is used in soups, stews, breads, and casseroles and commonly available dried and canned.

Grits are a coarse meal that is made from ground dried hominy—they are popularly made into a porridge in the Southern United States. They are available both quick cooking and instant; here in the test kitchen we prefer the quick cooking for their grittier texture.

Masa is a dough made from hominy that is finely ground. It is used in Latin America to make tortillas, tamales, and pupusas. (Often fat, in the form of lard, is added to the masa.)

Masa harina is a fine flour made from dried masa. Water can be added to masa harina to make a dough, and subsequently tortillas, tamales, and pupusas. Maseca is a widely available brand of masa harina.

Masarepa, also called harina precocida and masa al instante, is a precooked corn flour prepared from starchier large kernel white corn (as opposed to the small kernel yellow corn familiar to Americans). The germ is removed from the kernels during processing and the kernels are dried and ground to a fine flour. Water is added to the flour to make dough for arepas.

Mix all the ingredients together and season with salt and pepper to taste. Cover with plastic wrap and refrigerate until needed. (The filling can be refrigerated for up to 2 days.)

Chicken and Avocado Corn Cake Filling

MAKES ENOUGH FOR 8 CORN CAKES

The filling can be made while the arepas are in the oven.

1	cup cooked chicken, shredded into bite-sized pieces (see page 69)
1	medium ripe avocado, halved, pitted, and cut into ½-inch chunks (see page 5)
2	tablespoons minced fresh cilantro leaves
2	scallions, sliced thin
1	tablespoon juice from 1 lime
¼	teaspoon chili powder
	Salt and ground black pepper

Mix all the ingredients together and season with salt and pepper to taste. Cover with plastic wrap and refrigerate until needed. (The filling can be refrigerated for up to 2 days.)

Black Bean and Cheese Corn Cake Filling

MAKES ENOUGH FOR 8 CORN CAKES

The filling can be made while the arepas are in the oven.

1	(15-ounce) can black beans, rinsed
4	ounces Monterey Jack cheese, shredded (about 1 cup)
2	tablespoons minced fresh cilantro leaves
2	scallions, sliced thin
1	tablespoon juice from 1 lime
¼	teaspoon chili powder
	Salt and ground black pepper

Using a potato masher or fork, mash the beans in a medium bowl until most are broken. Stir in the remaining ingredients and season with salt and pepper to taste. Cover with plastic wrap and refrigerate until needed. (The filling can be refrigerated for up to 2 days.)

CEVICHE

CEVICHE, CONSIDERED THE NATIONAL DISH of Peru (most food historians agree that it was first served in northern Peru), is a simple seafood dish that is also served in many other seafaring regions around the world. Rather than using heat to cook the seafood, a traditional ceviche uses acidic juices, such as lime or lemon juice, to do the "cooking." (The acidic liquid denatures protein in much the same way that heat does.) The result is a refreshing, summery dish that highlights the flavors of the fresh seafood and seasonal local flavors. Our questions surrounding this dish were simple: What kind of acidic liquid works best? What kind of seafood should we use? And finally, did we want to do as some modern recipes suggest and cook the seafood first, rather than letting the acid do all the work?

Starting with the ceviche's acidic medium, we tested several liquids based on recipes we researched including lime juice, lemon juice, white wine vinegar, and cider vinegar, as well as various combinations of these. The vinegars turned out to be bad both on their own and in combination with the fresh juices—they added harsh, stale flavors to the otherwise fresh-tasting dish. Tasters preferred the flavor of lime to lemon when the juices were used on their own, but neither was perfect. The lime juice was too sour and bitter, while the lemon was a tad bland. An equal ratio of lime to lemon juice was a nice compromise with a well-rounded, balanced flavor. Unfortunately, the lime-lemon combination still tasted a little generic to some tasters who missed the traditional lime flavor. To remedy this, we simply added a little lime zest, which helped bring the lime flavor to the foreground without making the ceviche taste overly tart. For the sake of saving time, we tried using bottled lime and lemon juice—and ruled this option out. The sweet, artificial flavor of these juices ruined the flavor of the seafood.

Next, we tested the types of seafood most commonly used for ceviche—shrimp (fresh and frozen) and scallops, as well as a variety of fish. The shrimp and scallops worked great. Taking a closer look at using fish, we tested several representative types including salmon, tuna, halibut, striped bass, cod, monkfish, and sole. Cod and monkfish made barely acceptable ceviche; the cod turned mealy and began to shred at the edges, while the monkfish was chewy and took forever to prepare. The striped bass was better, but its texture was slightly tough. Somewhat surprisingly, the tuna and salmon turned out to be among the favorites; although they are not often used in ceviche, we liked how they retained their distinctive flavors and tender textures (however, the tuna did turn an odd, bluish color). The halibut, sea bass, and sole also worked well; their mild flavors melded nicely with the other ingredients and they had a clean, bright, white appearance. More important than fish type, however, is the freshness of the fish; frozen or old fish will not stand up in this dish where freshness rules. If you can't find fresh fish, leave it out.

As we tested the various types of seafood, we also tested different ways to prepare it. Some of the modern recipes we found cook the seafood first, then toss it with the acidic juices, but we found this method unnecessarily complicated and it produced a less flavorful ceviche. Working with raw fish, we then looked at the two most popular methods for making ceviche: dicing the seafood into cubes and tossing it with the acidic juice in a bowl, or slicing the seafood thin, shingling it over a plate, and sprinkling it with the acidic juice. Dicing the seafood into 1-inch pieces and tossing it with the acid was certainly easy, but tasters didn't like how unevenly the diced seafood "cooked." The outside was cooked long before the inside and the resulting texture was very unappealing. We tried dicing the seafood smaller so the pieces would cook more evenly, but now the pieces melded together a little too much, which tasters didn't like. Slicing the seafood solved both problems. The pieces were now distinct and also cooked through at an even rate. The slices layered on a plate also made for a very attractive presentation. However, we now found it necessary to cover the fish completely with the lime-lemon juice in order for the seafood to cook evenly (and just sprinkling the fish with the juice was messy and made serving and eating difficult).

By combining the two methods we had the ideal ceviche technique. Slicing the seafood (all types, including shrimp and scallops) into ⅓-inch-thick, bite-sized pieces, then tossing them in a bowl with the lime-lemon juice was simple to do, easy to serve and eat, and ensured that all of the seafood would be evenly cooked. The bonus of this method is that all of the seafood types will cook at the same rate so that they can be combined if desired. Regardless of seafood type, it only took 45 to 60 minutes to cook the seafood in the fresh juice.

As for additional flavors, we noted that most traditional recipes are pretty simple, using only the seafood and lime juice, along with salt and maybe a minced hot chile pepper. But we found this simple ceviche just a little too plain, and liked the addition of garlic, scallions, cilantro, and a pinch of sugar. Various regions add other ingredients such as bell peppers, celery, oranges, tomatoes, and avocados and we found that all of them provided a welcome color, crunch, and flavor to the ceviche, both on their own and in combination with one another.

Lastly, we noted that some recipes serve the seafood in the acidic liquid, while others drain it away before serving. We found draining to be a pretty crucial step, or else the puckering tartness of the lime and lemon juices overwhelmed all the other flavors. Stirring in a little oil before serving is also a crucial step before serving to help meld the flavors and add some depth. Traditionally, ceviche is a casual dish most often served from a large, family-style serving bowl or over some lettuce leaves, but here in the test kitchen, we think it's exotic and elegant enough to be portioned into chilled martini glasses and served at a fancier affair.

Ceviche

SERVES 6 AS AN APPETIZER

Fresh seafood and freshly squeezed lime and lemon juice are essential for this dish. Be sure to pat all of the seafood dry with paper towels so that any moisture does not water down the marinade. Our favorite fish for this dish include salmon, tuna, halibut, sea bass, and sole. Slicing the seafood into pieces no thicker than ⅓ inch is important for even cooking; super-thin fish fillets (such as sole, flounder, or tilapia) are the easiest to use, as they require the least amount of prep. Heat is not used to cook the fish in this dish—the acid in the citrus juice firms it and makes it opaque.

1   pound extra-large shrimp (21 to 25 per
     pound), large sea scallops, skinless fish fillets,
     or a combination
1   teaspoon grated zest from 1 lime
½   cup juice from 4 limes
½   cup juice from 4 lemons
1   small red bell pepper, stemmed, seeded, and
     chopped fine
1   small jalapeño chile, stemmed, seeded, and
     minced
1   medium garlic clove, minced or pressed
     through a garlic press (about 1 teaspoon)
     Salt
¼   cup extra-virgin olive oil
4   scallions, sliced thin
3   tablespoons minced fresh cilantro leaves
½   teaspoon sugar
     Ground black pepper

1. If using shrimp, peel them completely, devein, and slice each shrimp in half lengthwise using a paring knife (through the deveined groove in the back). If using scallops, remove the side tendon (following the illustration on page 232) and slice into ⅓-inch-thick rounds. If using fish, remove any bones and slice into 1-inch squares about ⅓ inch thick.

2. Stir the lime zest, lime juice, lemon juice, bell pepper, jalapeño, garlic, and ½ teaspoon salt together in a medium bowl. Gently stir in the seafood, cover with plastic wrap, and refrigerate until the seafood is firm, opaque, and appears cooked, 45 to 60 minutes, stirring halfway through the marinating time.

3. Place the mixture in a fine-mesh strainer, leaving it a little wet, then return to the bowl. Gently stir in the oil, scallions, cilantro, and sugar. Season with salt and pepper to taste before serving.

➤ VARIATIONS
Ceviche with Celery and Orange
If the celery has leaves attached, mince them and add them with the cilantro for extra flavor.

Follow the recipe for Ceviche, substituting 2 medium ribs celery, minced, for the red pepper and adding 1 tablespoon grated orange zest with the lime zest in step 2. Gently fold in 2 large oranges, peeled, quartered, and sliced crosswise into ¼-inch-thick pieces (see the illustrations below) before serving.

Ceviche with Tomatoes and Avocados
Add the avocado just before serving to prevent it from breaking down and coating everything with its green color.

Follow the recipe for Ceviche, adding 1 cup cherry tomatoes, quartered, with the scallions in step 3. Gently stir in 1 ripe avocado, pitted and diced fine (see the illustrations on page 5), before serving.

CUTTING CITRUS
Here is how to cut up any citrus fruit into bite-sized pieces that don't fall apart when tossing or serving.

1. Cut away the rind and pith from the orange using a paring knife.

2. Quarter the peeled orange, then slice each quarter crosswise in ¼-inch-thick pieces.

CARIBBEAN RUM COCKTAILS

SUGARCANE IS A MAIN CROP AND MAJOR EXPORT FOR THE CARIBBEAN AND SOUTH AMERICA, so it is only natural that rum, a spirit made from sugarcane by-products, goes hand in hand with the culture and cuisine. Each island in the Caribbean has its own style of rum (there are light, dark, and spiced rums, and they vary in body, age, and alcohol content) and each island has a rum cocktail that it claims as its national drink. Below are recipes for some of our favorites.

Mojitos
SERVES 6

This Cuban cocktail has become increasingly popular in the United States in recent years. We like to use superfine sugar here because it dissolves more readily. If you cannot find superfine sugar, you can obtain a close approximation by processing regular granulated sugar in a food processor for about 30 seconds.

1	cup packed fresh mint leaves
¾	cup superfine sugar, plus extra to taste
3	cups carbonated water
1½	cups light rum
1	cup juice from 8 limes
	Pinch salt

Using a wooden spoon, muddle (crush) the mint and sugar in a pitcher until the sugar has dissolved. Stir in the water, rum, lime juice, and salt and season with additional sugar to taste. Pour the mixture over ice and serve.

Planter's Punch
SERVES 8 TO 10

This Jamaican punch is perfect for serving a crowd.

4	cups orange juice
4	cups pineapple juice
2	cups light or dark rum
⅓	cup juice from 3 limes
2	tablespoons grenadine
	Pinch salt

Stir all of the ingredients together in a large bowl. Refrigerate until chilled, at least 30 minutes or up to 4 hours. Serve over ice.

Strawberry Daiquiris
SERVES 6

This drink was popularized in the Cuban mining town of Daiquiri.

4	cups frozen strawberries, slightly thawed
2	cups crushed ice
1	cup light or dark rum
½	cup triple sec
⅓	cup juice from 3 limes, plus extra to taste
½	cup sugar
	Pinch salt

Puree all the ingredients in a blender until smooth, season with additional lime juice to taste, and serve immediately.

Piña Coladas
SERVES 6

Piña coladas hail from Puerto Rico. Cream of coconut is often found in the soda and drink-mix aisle at the grocery store. Be sure not to substitute coconut milk.

6	cups crushed ice
1	(14-ounce) can crushed pineapple, drained
1½	cups dark rum
1	cup cream of coconut
¼	cup juice from 2 limes
¼	cup sugar
	Pinch salt

Puree all the ingredients in a blender until smooth and serve immediately.

TWICE-FRIED PLANTAINS

Tostones

PLANTAINS ARE A VARIETY OF BANANA THAT are a mainstay of Latin and Caribbean cuisines, which can be attributed to the fact that they grow abundantly in tropical climates. Eaten both ripe and unripe (or "green"), plantains are firmer and less sweet than bananas, with a mild, earthy flavor. Unlike bananas, plantains are rarely eaten unless cooked, due to their starchy nature.

We started by researching different preparations for plantains, and we quickly discovered that preparation varies from country to country. To complicate matters even more, the same dish can have several different names, depending on its origin. In our research, we found that Latin cultures treat plantains much like we do potatoes—they are baked, roasted, boiled, mashed, and fried. After sampling a few of these preparations, we all had a clear favorite. No big surprise, but the fried plantains were gobbled up as fast as they came out of the oil.

Called *tostones* in Cuba, the Dominican Republic, and Puerto Rico, and *patacones* in Colombia, Panama, and Venezuela, these fried plantains are much like french fries in that they are fried twice. First, the plantains are sliced into rounds and par-fried at a relatively low temperature to soften them, then the rounds are pressed flat. Just before serving, the plantains are quick-fried at a higher temperature until nicely browned and crispy. At their best, tostones should have a tender interior and a nice crunch on the outside. They should be well-seasoned and taste of earthy plantain, with just a hint of the oil in which they were fried, and their coloring should be a deep golden. Armed with a bushel of plantains, we set out to achieve the ideal tostones.

Good tostones require the right plantains, and the best plantains for the job are the green, unripe ones—not the ripe, sweeter, softer ones. The green plantains are firm and starchy and thus hold up well in the hot oil. Ripe plantains, by contrast, are too soft for frying and won't crisp well. We found that slicing the plantains into ¾-inch rounds was perfect—when flattened they were about ¼ inch thick, which was just thick enough to allow the exterior to crisp up nicely during the second frying, while the interior remained soft and tender. While many Latin cooks use the traditional tool, called a *tostonera*, to flatten the plantains after the first frying, we found that the flat side of a spatula or a meat pounder worked just as well.

What is the right fat for making perfect tostones? To find out, we experimented with lard, vegetable shortening, vegetable oil, corn oil, and peanut oil. Lard and shortening make great tostones, but we figured that many cooks don't have these ingredients on hand. We moved on to vegetable oil. It rebounded well from temperature fluctuations and held up very well in subsequent frying, and the tostones tasted fantastic. Tostones fried in peanut and corn oil were also good.

Now it was time to get down to the frying, which actually means double-frying. Most Latin cookbook recipes call for an initial frying at 350 degrees and a final frying at 375 to 400 degrees. But we found these temperatures to be far too aggressive. We prefer an initial frying at 325 degrees, with the final frying at 350 degrees. Lower temperatures allow for easier monitoring; with higher temperatures, the tostones can quickly overcook.

With flawlessly crisp exteriors, and moist and tender interiors, all the tostones needed was a little seasoning. A large percentage of traditional recipes call for dipping the plantains in salted water after the first frying and before the second. Intrigued by this technique, we gave it a try. While the tostones were well seasoned, we found the extra step to be superfluous. Adding anything with extra moisture to hot oil made us nervous (even when we blotted them dry, they were still damp), the plantains took longer to crisp, and the ones that were simply seasoned with salt after the second frying turned out just as good. A little Mojo Sauce (page 76) on the side makes these the perfect snack or accompaniment to any Latin meal.

Twice-Fried Plantains

Tostones

MAKES ABOUT 32 PIECES

Green plantains are plantains that are not yet ripe. This recipe will not work with ripe plantains—they are much softer and less starchy than green plantains, and will become mushy in the hot oil. The oil will bubble up when you add the plantains, so be sure that you have at least 3 inches of room at the top of the pot. Serve with Mojo Sauce (page 76).

2   quarts vegetable oil
3   green plantains, peeled and sliced into
     ¾-inch rounds
     Salt

1. Heat the oil to 325 degrees in a large Dutch oven over medium heat. Add half of the plantains, increase the heat to medium-high, and cook, stirring often, until the plantains are light golden, 6 to 8 minutes. Using a wire mesh spider or slotted spoon, transfer the plantains to a thick paper bag or triple thickness of paper towels to drain. Return the oil to 325 degrees, and repeat with the remaining plantains; transfer to the bag.

2. While the plantains are still warm, flatten them to a ¼-inch thickness using the flat side of a sturdy spatula or meat pounder. (The flattened plantains can stand at room temperature for up to 2 hours or be wrapped in paper towels, sealed in a zipper-lock bag, and frozen up to 1 month.)

3. When ready to serve the tostones, reheat the oil to 350 degrees. Add half of the flattened plantains to the hot oil and fry, stirring often, until golden brown and crispy, 2 to 5 minutes. Transfer the plantains to a fresh paper bag or paper towels to drain and season with salt to taste; repeat with the remaining plantains. Serve immediately.

EQUIPMENT: Candy/Deep-Fry Thermometers

Candy thermometers are designed for stovetop recipes where close monitoring of temperature is key—especially candy making and deep-frying. The thermometer stays in the liquid during cooking. But which brand is best? To find out, we brought 13 models into the test kitchen and made multiple batches of caramel and our Twice-Fried Plantains (above).

Thermometers with the simplest style—a plain glass tube—worked fine, but they are also fragile and the gradations were hard to read. What's more, a few models had a tendency to slide down and touch the bottom of the pan, giving a false reading. Similar thermometers with a metal "foot" to keep the thermometer off the pan bottom didn't work in a small (shallow) batch of caramel or oil and were also hard to read. Dial-face thermometers required as much as 2½ inches of liquid—a rarity when making candies.

The best of the bunch were the digital models, which have easy-to-read consoles and alarm features that warn the cook when the caramel is done or the oil is hot enough. But they tend to be top-heavy, with a precarious grip on the saucepan. Testers wanted something similar to our favorite thermometer for roasts, the Polder Digital Cooking Timer/Thermometer in which a long wire separates the "brains" from the business end. We'd use the Polder for candy or frying but couldn't find a way to secure the probe to the side of the pot. Then we found the CDN Digital Cooking Thermometer and Timer. It's similar to the Polder but comes with a mounting clip that lets you attach the probe to your pan. An on/off switch would be nice (to save batteries over time), but it still gets our top recommendation for its clip-on ease.

THE BEST CANDY/DEEP-FRY THERMOMETER

The CDN Digital Cooking Thermometer and Timer ($24.95) is our top choice for candy making and deep-frying.

CUBAN-STYLE BLACK BEANS

Frijoles Negros

CUBAN CUISINE, FOR THE MOST PART, IS an amalgamation of Spanish, African, Caribbean, and even Chinese cuisines. Over the years, Cuban cooking has become a melting pot of these cultures and has evolved into what is known as Cuban Creole cuisine. At the heart of a typical Cuban meal (and Latin meals in general) are black beans. They are served as a side dish at almost every meal, often made into soup, and are flavorful and substantial enough to serve as a main course when served with white rice (a dish that is known as *Moros y Cristianos*, probably alluding to a time when the Moors controlled the Iberian Peninsula—the black beans symbolize the Moors and the white rice represents the Christians). We wanted to create a recipe for full-flavored, creamy beans that could stand up by themselves as a side dish, or make a satisfying meal when served with white rice.

We started our research by cooking several basic bean recipes culled from Latin American and Caribbean cookbooks. While we were focused on flavor, we also wanted to pay close attention to texture. The perfect black beans should be tender without being mushy, with just enough resistance to make a satisfying chew. We also hoped to find a way to get the beans to retain their black color—all too often, black beans develop an unappealing drab gray hue once cooked.

Focusing first on the texture of the beans, we discovered that it was important to cook the beans in enough water; too little water and the beans on top cooked more slowly than the beans underneath, and the whole pot took forever to cook. Twelve cups of water proved to be a sufficient amount to cook 1 pound of beans. We usually prefer beans that have been soaked before being cooked and figured this would be the case with our black beans as well. Just to be sure we compared beans that had been soaked overnight with a batch of unsoaked beans. We also tried a batch using a "quick-soak" method in which the beans were brought to a boil, briefly simmered, and then covered for one hour off the heat.

We found that the quick-soak method caused a large percentage of the beans to burst during cooking. This reduced the firm texture we were after, so we nixed that method. Contrary to our expectations, overnight soaking decreased the cooking time by only about half an hour and didn't improve the texture. Because soaking the night before is simply one more thing to remember to do, and the texture of unsoaked beans is great, we decided not to soak the black beans.

Next, to test the theory that salting toughens the skin of beans and lengthens cooking time, we tested beans salted at the end of cooking against those salted three-quarters of the way through, as well as against beans salted at the beginning. In a blind taste test, we couldn't tell the difference between the skins, but only the beans salted from the beginning were seasoned enough for our taste. And we found that 1 teaspoon was just the right amount.

Now that we had discovered how to cook beans to achieve the texture we wanted, it was time to determine the best way to build layers of flavor onto this base without drowning the earthy flavor of the beans. We first tried adding pork to our beans—a typical addition in many of the recipes we researched, meat gives the beans a necessary depth of flavor. We tested cooking beans with a ham hock, bacon, ham, and pork loin. We liked all four, and each gave the beans a slightly different flavor. Bacon and ham produced an assertive flavor, while pork loin was the subtlest of the pork choices. We ultimately decided to go with the ham hock, which provided a smooth background flavor.

In many Latin recipes, a *sofrito* (the Latin American answer to the French *mirepoix* of carrots, onions, and celery) is added to the cooked beans for flavor. Chopped vegetables—usually onion, garlic, and green bell pepper—are sautéed in olive oil until soft and then stirred into the beans. This mixture adds another layer of fresh flavor to the beans without overwhelming them.

To thicken the sauce, some recipes suggest pureeing the sofrito with some of the beans, while others call for mashing some beans with the sofrito. We found that pureeing intensified the flavor of the vegetables too much, overwhelming the beans. Simply mashing some beans and the sofrito by hand gets the job done.

We then ran several experiments with additional flavorings. We tested to see whether sugar was necessary and found that we didn't like the added sweetness. For an acidic component, we tested red wine vinegar against balsamic and cider vinegars, as well as lime and lemon juices. Lime juice was the best fit, and when we paired it with a sprinkling of cilantro, we knew we had the taste of tradition.

We were finally satisfied, save for the beans' unappealing grayish brown color. We knew there had to be a way to keep the beans black, and with great determination we set out to find it. It was our science editor who suggested that we try adding a little baking soda to the beans. The coating of black beans contains colored pigments that change color with changes in pH: the addition of an acidic component to the beans would make them lighter, whereas the alkaline nature of baking soda causes the beans to retain their dark color. We experimented by adding various amounts of baking soda to the beans both during and after cooking. A mere ⅛ teaspoon produced great-tasting beans (there was no soapy aftertaste, as was the case with larger quantities) with a darker, more appetizing color than unadulterated beans. Problem solved.

Cuban-Style Black Beans

Frijoles Negros

SERVES 6

The baking soda preserves the beans' attractive dark hue; without it, the beans will turn a muddy, grayish color. Don't use a nonstick skillet for the sofrito because the nonstick surface will get scratched up when mashing the beans in step 3. Serve with sour cream, minced red onion, and hot sauce. To create the classic Cuban dish, Moros y Christianos, serve with Simple Steamed White Rice (page 516).

BEANS

12 cups water, plus extra as needed

1 pound (about 2½ cups) dried black beans, rinsed and picked over

1 smoked ham hock

2 bay leaves

1 teaspoon salt

⅛ teaspoon baking soda

SOFRITO

2 tablespoons extra-virgin olive oil

1 medium onion, minced

1 small green bell pepper, stemmed, seeded, and minced

Salt

9 medium garlic cloves, minced or pressed through a garlic press (about 3 tablespoons)

2 teaspoons dried oregano

1½ teaspoons ground cumin

1 tablespoon juice from 1 lime

½ cup minced fresh cilantro leaves

Ground black pepper

1. FOR THE BEANS: Combine the water, beans, ham hock, bay leaves, salt, and baking soda in a large Dutch oven and bring to a boil over medium-high heat, skimming any impurities that rise to the surface. Reduce the heat to low and simmer, partially covered, until the beans are tender, 1½ to 2 hours. Discard the bay leaves. Remove the ham hock and set aside to cool; when cool enough to handle, remove the meat, discarding the bone and skin, and shred it into bite-sized pieces.

2. FOR THE SOFRITO: As the beans finish cooking, heat the oil in a 12-inch skillet over medium heat until shimmering. Add the onion, bell pepper, and ½ teaspoon salt and cook until the vegetables are softened, 8 to 10 minutes. Stir in the garlic, oregano, and cumin and cook until fragrant, about 30 seconds; set aside until needed.

3. TO FINISH THE DISH: Transfer 1 cup of the beans and 2 cups of the cooking liquid into the skillet with the sofrito. Mash the beans with a potato masher or fork until smooth. Simmer over medium heat, scraping up any browned bits, until the liquid is reduced and thickened, about 6 minutes.

4. Stir the sofrito-bean mixture and shredded ham into the pot of beans, bring to a simmer, and cook until the beans are creamy and the liquid thickens to a sauce consistency, 15 to 20 minutes. Stir in the lime juice and cilantro, season with salt and pepper to taste, and serve. (The beans can be refrigerated in an airtight container for up to 3 days; reheat over medium-low heat, adding water as needed to adjust the sauce consistency.)

TROPICAL FRUITS

TROPICAL REGIONS OF THE WORLD PRODUCE FRUITS THAT ARE DIFFERENT THAN THOSE FROM any other climate. Many of these fruits are unique to Latin America or Southeast Asia, while others grow in both places. The cuisines of these regions are shaped greatly by the fruits that abound. Many of these fruits, like bananas, pineapples, and mangos, are popular and widely available in the United States, while others, such as plantains, passion fruit, prickly pear, Cape gooseberry, and cherimoya, are much less common. While in the United States we eat most of our fruits ripe, many Latin American and Southeast Asian cuisines also use some of them—like plantains, mangos, and papayas—unripe, or "green."

Street vendors in the Caribbean and Latin America sell these fruits in various forms; most popularly as fruit shakes called *batidos* or *licuados,* as sorbet, or simply as is, to be eaten out of hand. In homes, families turn them into salsas and salads, and it is not uncommon to find these fruits grilled, baked, or even fried. We wanted to try some authentic Latin American and Caribbean preparations of these fruits, so we culled together some recipes, and developed our own versions using some of our favorite widely available tropical fruits.

We developed a refreshing fruit shake (batido) recipe and found that any ripe tropical fruit tasted great. To feature mango in its best light, we made a simple, fresh-tasting salad with avocado, chile, cilantro, and lime juice (see opposite page)—the perfect accompaniment to grilled meat or fish. Lastly, we created a recipe using the most ubiquitous tropical fruit, bananas. We baked the bananas with butter and brown sugar until softened and caramelized. When served with vanilla ice cream, this makes an excellent quick and easy dessert.

Fruit Shakes
Batidos
SERVES 4

You can make this drink using almost any tropical fruit you like—pineapple, banana, mango, papaya, guava, and passion fruit are our favorites. Drained canned fruit and frozen fruit can be substituted for the fresh; if using frozen fruit, do not thaw and substitute water for the ice.

3½	cups ripe fruit, cut into 1-inch chunks (see note)
2	cups ice
1½	cups cold milk
1	tablespoon sugar, plus extra to taste
½	teaspoon vanilla extract
	Pinch salt

Puree the ingredients in a blender until smooth and frothy, 20 to 30 seconds. Season with additional sugar to taste and serve immediately.

Baked Bananas
Platanitos Asados
SERVES 8

Very ripe plantains (the skin will be almost black) can be substituted for the bananas; do not, however, use very ripe bananas or they will become too mushy in the oven. Serve with sour cream or vanilla ice cream.

8	ripe bananas, peeled
½	cup light or dark brown sugar
4	tablespoons (½ stick) unsalted butter, cut into ½-inch cubes

1. Adjust an oven rack to the middle position and heat the oven to 350 degrees. Arrange the bananas in a 13 by 9-inch baking dish. Sprinkle with the sugar and dot with the butter. Cover with aluminum foil and bake for 30 minutes.

2. Uncover and continue to bake until the bananas are softened and golden brown, about 30 minutes more, flipping the bananas using a wide spatula or 2 spoons halfway through the baking time. Serve immediately.

Mango and Avocado Salad
Ensalada de Aguacate y Mango
SERVES 6

This salad is often made with unripe mango, which is harder and more tart than ripe mango; if using an unripe mango, cut it into thin matchsticks rather than large chunks. If you like your food spicy, add the ribs and seeds from the jalapeño.

2   large ripe mangos, peeled, pitted, and cut into 1-inch chunks
2   medium ripe avocados, halved, pitted, and cut into 1-inch chunks (see page 5)
¼   cup juice from 2 limes
¼   cup minced red onion
¼   cup minced fresh cilantro leaves
1   small jalapeño chile, stemmed, seeded, and minced (see note)
Salt and ground black pepper

Mix all of the ingredients together and season with salt and pepper to taste. Cover with plastic wrap and refrigerate until chilled, at least 1 hour and up to 24 hours.

EQUIPMENT: Mango Splitters

Removing the flesh from a mango in tidy pieces can challenge even a seasoned pro's knife skills. When we came across Oxo's mango splitter, we gave it a whirl. Similar to an apple corer—it's pressed down onto the fruit like a two-handed (ultra-sharp) cookie cutter—this gadget has a central hole shaped to match the narrow contours of a mango pit. At first, we had a terrible time balancing the mango for the initial cut, but once we trimmed the bottom flat, the splitter plunged through the fruit easily and cleanly. Try as we might, we couldn't round up a mango too small or large, and the mango splitter never left extra fruit on the pit by overestimating the pit's size.

THE BEST MANGO SPLITTER

The Oxo Mango Splitter ($11.95) is one of those rare kitchen gadgets that works.

PREPARING MANGOS

Because of their odd shape and slippery texture, mangos are notoriously difficult to peel. Here's how we handle this task. This method ensures long, attractive strips of fruit.

1. Remove a thin slice from one end of the mango so that it sits flat on a work surface.

2. Hold the mango cut side down and remove the skin with a sharp paring knife in thin strips, working from top to bottom.

3. Cut down along the side of the flat pit to remove the flesh from one side of the mango. Do the same on the other side of the pit.

4. Trim around the pit to remove any remaining flesh. The mango flesh can now be chopped or sliced as desired.

LATINO-STYLE CHICKEN AND RICE

Arroz con Pollo

THE BOLD-FLAVORED COUSIN OF AMERICAN-style chicken and rice, *arroz con pollo* (literally, "rice with chicken") is Latino comfort food at its most basic. Here in the test kitchen, we've had plenty of great versions: moist, tender chicken nestled in rice rich with peppers, onions, herbs, and deep chicken flavor—a satisfying one-dish meal.

Like most staples, however, arroz con pollo runs the gamut from the incredible to the merely edible, depending on how much time and effort you're willing to spend. The traditional method is to stew marinated chicken slowly with aromatic herbs and vegetables, creating a rich broth in which the rice is cooked once the chicken is fall-off-the-bone tender—terrific, yes, but also time-consuming. Quick versions speed things up by cooking the rice and chicken (often boneless) separately, then combining them just before serving. The trade-off is rice that's devoid of chicken flavor. Our goal was to split the difference: to streamline the more time-consuming, traditional recipes for arroz con pollo without sacrificing great taste.

If we wanted chicken-infused rice, it was clear the chicken and the rice would have to spend some time together. But how long was long enough? A few of the "quick" recipes we found called for simmering the chicken and rice together, chopping the chicken into small pieces that would be done in sync with the rice, in about half an hour. Was this our streamlined solution? The timing was right, but the results were not. The white meat and dark meat cooked unevenly, the skin was flabby, and, after 30 minutes, flavor infusion was minimal. Worse, the hacked-up chicken, replete with jagged bones, was wholly unappealing.

Regrouping, we decided to start with a traditional recipe and adjust things from there. We began, as we do with so many of our Spanish-influenced Latin dishes, with a sofrito, a mixture of chopped onions and green peppers sautéed in olive oil. Once the vegetables softened, we added the chicken and a few cups of water, turned the burner to low, and let the chicken poach for an hour. Removing the chicken, we added the rice to the pot, and 30 minutes later the rice had absorbed every drop of the rich broth the chicken had left behind. We added the chicken back to rewarm for 10 minutes, then lifted the lid. Now this was chicken-infused rice!

Unfortunately, it was also a two-hour project—and we hadn't even factored in the traditional marinade yet. What's more, while the dark meat was moist and tender, the leaner white meat was in bad shape. We recalled a recipe from our research that called for only thighs. Opting for all thighs meant uniform cooking times and shopping convenience (one big "value" pack).

A new problem emerged: thighs are laden with fat, and this made the dish greasy. Removing the skin helped, but the meat near the surface dried out and the flavor suffered. The answer was to trim away any visible pockets of waxy yellow fat and most of the skin, leaving just enough to protect the meat. We also replaced most of the water we were adding with an equal amount of store-bought chicken broth, which made up for lost chicken flavor. After stewing for almost an hour, the skin was pretty flabby, so we removed it while the rice finished cooking. To make the chicken even more appealing, we took the additional step of removing the meat from the bones.

With the chicken resolved, we moved on to the rice. The two traditional rice choices for arroz con pollo are long grain and medium grain. While both were fine, tasters preferred the creamier texture of medium-grain rice. But medium-grain rice was not without its problems. The grains had a tendency to split and release too much starch, making the overall texture of the dish pasty. Giving the rice a stir partway through cooking helped keep any one layer from overcooking, as did removing the pot from the direct heat of the stovetop to the diffuse heat of the oven.

Traditionally, arroz con pollo has an orange hue that comes from infusing oil with achiote, a tropical seed also used for coloring cheddar cheese. Achiote is hard to find, so we experimented with substitutions. Turmeric and saffron looked right but tasted wrong—too much like curry or paella.

(Achiote has no distinct flavor.) The solution was adding 8 ounces of canned tomato sauce along with the broth.

A common method for infusing this dish with more flavor is to marinate the chicken for a few hours or even overnight. A nice idea, but we were hoping to make this a weeknight dish. Instead, we tried a quick, 15-minute marinade with garlic, oregano, and white vinegar. The results were a step in the right direction. Tossing the chicken with olive oil, vinegar, and cilantro after pulling it off the bone—a postcooking "marinade"—gave it the additional boost it needed. Capers, red pepper flakes, pimentos, and briny olives rounded out the flavors.

All of our efforts at streamlining this dish had brought the cooking time down to 90 minutes—an hour to stew the chicken and half an hour to cook the rice—a far cry from the half-day affair we'd faced at the start. But was this the best we could do? To shave off still more time, we tried adding the rice to the pot when the chicken still had half an hour to go. The chicken was fine, but the rice near the chicken pieces cooked unevenly. The solution to this problem was easy: Instead of giving the rice only one stir during cooking, we gave it a second stir to redistribute the ingredients. Now both the rice and the chicken were perfectly cooked in just over an hour. We finally had a rich, flavorful dish that tasted authentic in a fraction of the time.

Latino-Style Chicken and Rice
Arroz con Pollo
SERVES 4 TO 6

To keep the dish from becoming greasy, it is important to remove excess fat from the chicken thighs and trim the skin. To use long-grain rice instead of medium-grain, increase the water to ¾ cup in step 3. When removing the chicken from the bone in step 5, we found it better to use two spoons rather than two forks; forks tend to shred the meat, while spoons pull it apart in chunks.

6   medium garlic cloves, minced or pressed
    through a garlic press (about 2 tablespoons)
5   teaspoons distilled white vinegar
    Salt and ground black pepper
½   teaspoon dried oregano
8   bone-in, skin-on chicken thighs (3½ to
    4 pounds), trimmed
2   tablespoons olive oil
1   medium onion, minced
1   small green bell pepper, stemmed, seeded,
    and chopped fine
¼   teaspoon red pepper flakes
¼   cup minced fresh cilantro leaves
1¾ cups low-sodium chicken broth
1   (8-ounce) can tomato sauce
½   cup water
3   cups medium-grain rice
½   cup green manzanilla olives, pitted and halved
    (see the illustration on page 291)
1   tablespoon capers, rinsed
½   cup jarred whole pimientos, drained and cut
    into 2 by ¼-inch strips
1   lemon, cut into wedges (for serving)

1. Adjust an oven rack to the middle position and heat the oven to 350 degrees. Combine the garlic, 3 teaspoons of the vinegar, 1 teaspoon salt, ½ teaspoon black pepper, and oregano in a large bowl. Add the chicken, coat it evenly with the marinade, and set aside for 15 minutes.

2. Heat 1 tablespoon of the oil in a Dutch oven over medium heat until shimmering. Add the onion, bell pepper, and red pepper flakes and cook, stirring occasionally, until the vegetables begin to soften, 5 to 7 minutes. Stir in 2 tablespoons of the cilantro.

3. Push the vegetables to the sides of the pot and increase the heat to medium-high. Add the chicken to the center of the pot, skin side down. Cook until the outer layer of meat becomes opaque, 2 to 4 minutes per side, reducing the heat if the chicken begins to brown. Stir in the broth, tomato sauce, and ¼ cup of the water. Bring to a simmer, cover, reduce the heat to medium-low, and simmer for 20 minutes.

4. Stir in the rice, olives, capers, and ¾ teaspoon salt and bring to a simmer. Cover, transfer to the oven, and cook, stirring every 10 minutes, until the thickest part of the chicken registers 175 degrees on an instant-read thermometer, about 30 minutes.

If after 20 minutes of cooking the rice appears dry and the bottom of the pot begins to scorch, stir in the remaining ¼ cup water.

5. Transfer the chicken to a plate and set the Dutch oven aside, covered. Pull the meat off the bones into large chunks using 2 spoons, discarding the skin and bones. Place the chicken in a large bowl and toss with the remaining tablespoon olive oil, remaining 2 teaspoons vinegar, remaining 2 tablespoons cilantro, and the pimientos. Season with salt and pepper to taste. Place the chicken on top of the rice, cover, and let stand until warmed through, about 5 minutes. Serve immediately with the lemon wedges.

➤ VARIATION

Latino-Style Chicken and Rice with Breast Meat

Follow the recipe for Latino-Style Chicken and Rice, substituting 4 whole bone-in, skin-on chicken breasts (3½ to 4 pounds), trimmed of excess skin and fat and cut in half crosswise, for the chicken thighs. Using tongs, remove the chicken from the pot in step 3 when it registers 160 degrees on an instant-read thermometer (after about 20 minutes). Transfer the chicken to a large plate, wrap tightly with foil, and set aside. In step 4, cook the rice mixture until the rice has absorbed all the liquid and is tender but still holds its shape, about 30 minutes.

PANTRY SPOTLIGHT

MEDIUM-GRAIN RICE

For arroz con pollo, we prefer the sticky-yet-firm consistency of medium-grain rice. Although there are widely available brands that hail from many places, we found that Hispanic brands of rice, such as Goya, had the best texture for this dish.

CHILEAN SHEPHERD'S PIE

Pastel de Choclo

PASTEL DE CHOCLO, A SHEPHERD'S PIE–STYLE preparation of meat and onions that is richly flavored with olives, hard-cooked eggs, and raisins, topped with a corn puree, and baked in a clay dish until a golden crust is formed, is the national dish of Chile. Pastel de choclo might sound somewhat unusual to American sensibilities; however, in Chile, it is a source of great pride and a staple on restaurant menus and in home kitchens alike.

Our research turned up evidence that this dish represents a melding of the cuisines of the native population (the Mapuche) and the Spanish conquistadors. The combination of sweet and savory ingredients, such as raisins with meat and onions, is evidence of the Spanish influence, as is the addition of cumin and olives. The corn, or choclo, is native to the Americas.

All pastel de choclo recipes, and many other Chilean dishes (like empanadas), use *pino*, a sautéed mixture of ground meat, onions, and spices flavored with hard-cooked egg, olives, and raisins. According to our research, the ideal pino is moist and the crumbled meat should be coated in a rich sauce.

We came across several pino variations in our research, and one difference was that some used ground beef while others called for ground lamb. In the test kitchen, tasters favored ground beef and found that the lamb was too strongly flavored for this dish—it overpowered the other ingredients. As with our empanada recipe, we favored 85 percent lean ground chuck for its beefy flavor and moisture content. The beef paired nicely with generous amounts of onions, cumin, and hot paprika.

While many recipes stir the eggs, olives, and raisins into the meat, others layer them on top. We preferred the distinction of these ingredients when layered over the meat. We thinly sliced the hard-cooked eggs and instead of putting whole pitted olives into the mix, we halved them so they were closer in size to the raisins and evenly distributed.

With the details of the pino resolved, we were ready to move on to the corn topping, but there was one matter of concern that we simply couldn't ignore—a large percentage of the recipes in our research also add cooked chicken to the pie. Though it seemed unnecessary with all the other ingredients, we thought we should at least consider it. We tested breasts and thighs, both bone-in, skin-on and boneless, skinless. The bones and skins made the dish difficult to eat, but boneless pieces of chicken were welcomed for their textural contrast and mild flavor. Shredding the chicken into bite-sized pieces made it more appealing and even easier to eat. Thighs were preferred over the breasts, which tasters complained were too lean and dry tasting.

Having made the chicken an integral part of the dish, we now had to figure out how to limit the number of pans we used—we didn't want to be left with a sink full of dishes to wash. Our solution was to first cook the chicken in a large skillet, and while it rested, we quickly wiped the skillet clean using paper towels and used it to make the pino.

At last we were ready to start on the corn topping. In Chile, the corn is different than the corn here—it is bigger (the kernels can be as large as a dime), starchier, and less sweet. In order to make the corn palatable and suitable for the topping, it is grated and cooked with quite a bit of sugar and milk or cream. Working with the sweet, small cobs available to us, we tried to mimic the mixture made with choclo.

We wanted a rich topping with good corn flavor that was thick enough to sit on top of the filling, and dry enough to form a crust in the oven. We found recipes that start by boiling the corn on the cob, then cutting the kernels off the cob and mixing them with a creamy sauce. This technique, however, loses much of the sweet, delicate corn flavor to the cooking water. We quickly rejected this method in favor of recipes that simmer the corn kernels (which are first cut free from the cobs) directly in the milk or cream. This technique releases their sugary, summery flavor into the sauce, which is where you want it to be.

Simply simmering fresh corn kernels in dairy, however, wasn't enough. It produced a thin, lumpy mixture that lacked the thickened, spoonable texture we desired. Scraping the pulp out of the spent cobs helped a bit, but we wanted the sauce a little thicker. Flour and cornstarch just made the sauce gummy and overwhelmed the flavor of the corn. We then tried the technique used for choclo of grating a few of the ears, which broke down some of the kernels into smaller pieces. This did the trick. By grating some of the raw kernels off the cob, we were able to release more of the corn's natural thickener. We found that grating about half of the corn in our recipe, and leaving the other kernels whole, thickened the sauce sufficiently and also provided some texture.

While many recipes cook the corn in milk, we found that cream was more stable (the milk curdled over high heat), and it added a pleasant richness. Aside from salt and pepper, all the creamed corn needed was a touch of basil for color and freshness.

While the traditional vessel for pastel de choclo is a clay pot from the artisan village of Pomaire near Santiago, we found that any crock or ovenproof bowl with at least a 2½-quart capacity works well. We have also seen recipes that call for baking the pastel de choclo in individual pots, which is great for dinner parties, making the dish a little less rustic. A sprinkling of sugar over the top, and 30 minutes in a 450-degree oven, yielded a casserole that had a beautiful golden brown crust.

Chilean Shepherd's Pie
Pastel de Choclo
SERVES 6

The amount of sugar you use will vary depending on the sweetness of the corn. Be sure to adjust the heat as the cream and corn cook, and stir the mixture frequently to prevent the bottom from burning. For a less rustic presentation, this dish can be assembled in six 2-cup ovenproof bowls or ramekins; the baking time for these smaller bowls will be shorter, about 15 to 20 minutes or until the tops are browned. If you don't have hot paprika, substitute ½ teaspoon regular paprika mixed with ⅛ teaspoon cayenne pepper.

10   medium ears fresh corn, husks and silk removed
1   cup heavy cream
      Salt and ground black pepper
¼   cup chopped fresh basil leaves
6   boneless, skinless chicken thighs (about 1½ pounds), trimmed
2   tablespoons olive oil
½   cup water
4   medium onions, minced (about 4 cups)
1   tablespoon ground cumin
½   teaspoon hot paprika
1   pound (85 percent lean) ground beef
4   hard-cooked eggs, sliced thin (see page 63)
¾   cup kalamata olives, pitted and halved (see the illustration on page 291)
½   cup raisins
1–2   teaspoons sugar

1. Adjust an oven rack to the middle position and heat the oven to 450 degrees. Following the illustrations on the right, cut the kernels from 5 ears of the corn into a medium bowl; set the cobs aside. Using the large holes of a box grater, grate the kernels from the remaining 5 ears of corn into the bowl; set the cobs aside. Using the back of a butter knife, scrape the milk and pulp from all of the cobs into the bowl.

2. Bring the corn kernel and pulp mixture, cream, ½ teaspoon salt, and ¼ teaspoon pepper to a simmer in a medium saucepan over medium-low heat. Cook, stirring often, until the mixture is thickened, about 15 minutes. Stir in the basil, season with salt and pepper to taste, and set aside.

3. Meanwhile, pat the chicken dry with paper towels and season with salt and pepper. Heat 2 teaspoons of the oil in a 12-inch nonstick skillet over medium-high heat until just smoking. Add the chicken and cook until browned on one side, about 3 minutes. Flip the chicken over, add the water, and cover. Reduce the heat to medium and continue to cook until the thickest part of the chicken registers 175 degrees on an instant-read thermometer, about 10 minutes longer. Transfer to a carving board and cool slightly, then shred into bite-sized pieces.

4. Wipe out the skillet with paper towels. Add the remaining 4 teaspoons oil, onions, cumin, paprika, and ½ teaspoon salt to the skillet. Cook over medium heat until the onions are softened, 8 to 10 minutes. Add the beef and cook, breaking up the meat with a wooden spoon, until no longer pink, about 4 minutes. Season with salt and pepper to taste.

5. Spread the beef in a casserole dish that has at least a 2½-quart capacity (measuring roughly 11 by 7 inches with 2½-inch sides). Layer the eggs, olives, and raisins over the beef, then arrange the shredded chicken on top. Cover the chicken with the corn mixture, sprinkle with the sugar, and bake until the corn is golden brown and forms a crust, 30 to 35 minutes. Let rest for 15 minutes before serving.

WORKING WITH FRESH CORN

1. To cut the kernels off a cob without having them fly all over the kitchen counter, hold the cob on its end inside a large wide bowl and use a paring knife to cut off the kernels.

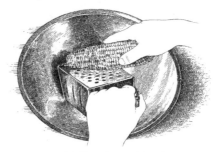

2. To grate the kernels off a cob, simply hold a box grater over a large wide bowl and use the large grating holes.

3. To scrap the milk and pulp from a corncob, firmly scrape the cob using the back of a knife (we like to use a butter knife).

HARD-COOKED EGGS

BECAUSE SO MANY HARD-COOKED (OR hard-boiled) egg recipes leave us with either cracked shells or green-tinged, sulfurous yolks (a common side effect of overcooked eggs), we wanted to develop a foolproof cooking method. The method below yields eggs with tender whites and perfectly cooked yolks every time.

Hard-Cooked Eggs

MAKES 6 EGGS

You can easily scale this recipe up or down as desired; alter the pot size as needed, but do not alter the cooking time. Fresher eggs will have more centered yolks when cooked, while older eggs will produce off-centered yolks.

6 large eggs

Place the eggs in a medium saucepan, cover with 1 inch of water, and bring to a boil over high heat. As soon as the water reaches a boil, remove the pan from the heat, cover, and let sit for 10 minutes. Transfer the eggs to an ice-water bath, chill for 5 minutes, then peel.

PEELING EGGS FAST

1. After draining the hot water from the pot used to cook the eggs, shake the pot back and forth to crack the shells.

2. Add enough ice water to cover the eggs and cool. The water seeps under the broken shells, allowing them to be slipped off without a struggle.

BRAZILIAN BLACK BEAN AND PORK STEW
Feijoada

FEIJOADA, A BLACK BEAN AND PORK STEW, has been the center of Brazilian family life for centuries, and today it has become so popular it is considered one of Brazil's national dishes. Feijoada was originally created by the African slaves who cooked on the plantations and would use up every last bit of the pig—including the feet, ears, tail, and snout. Today, on Saturday mornings, families and friends gather to prepare this rich dish, laden with pork, and serve it for lunch, buffet style, with the beans in a crock and the meats sliced on a platter, surrounded by various other traditional side dishes including white rice, sliced orange segments, sautéed kale, toasted manioc flour (see page 66), and hot sauce (see page 66). We wanted a feijoada with creamy flavorful beans with an intense smoky pork flavor, and meat that was tender and juicy. Recipes in hand, we headed into the kitchen with the intention of translating this Brazilian classic.

Many of the recipes we researched had the meat and beans stewing together for hours and hours. While these recipes tried to take into account the cooking time of the various meats (such as shoulders, ribs, tenderloins, and sausage) as well as the beans, the resulting dish was overcooked meat, mushy beans, and too much liquid. We realized the key to this recipe was going to be getting the timing right so that the beans and meat would all finish cooking together. We decided to strip the recipe down to the basics and start with the beans.

From our testing for Cuban-Style Black Beans (see page 54), we had a jump start on the best way to cook them. We found that there was no need to soak the black beans, as they cooked evenly from their dried state in just two hours. A mere teaspoon of salt added to the beans in the beginning of cooking—rather than at the end—does not toughen the skin as many cooks claim, but gave us well-seasoned beans. Some onion and garlic complemented the earthy flavor of the beans, while adding a small amount of baking soda to the beans at the beginning of cooking produced a darker, more appealing color. Now that we knew how to achieve perfectly cooked, flavorful beans we focused on the meat.

From the outset we decided that although many authentic recipes call for a combination of pig ears, tails, and feet, we would not include those in our feijoada. Our consensus was that the offal parts of the pig are difficult to find, take a fair amount of soaking, and take much too long to cook. After poring through a number of recipes for feijoada, it seemed one could use any number of combinations of pork and/or beef. Ingredient lists included *carne seca* (dried, jerky-like beef), slab bacon, spareribs, pork loins, and numerous varieties of sausages, ham hocks, and salt pork. We ultimately chose a combination of pork products that maintained some tradition, but that could easily be found and seemed more approachable to cook—we went with a ham hock to flavor the beans in the beginning of cooking, pork spareribs, linguiça sausage, and pork tenderloins.

The challenge now was to figure out how to layer the meat in with the beans so the flavors melded while getting all the elements of the stew to cook at the right rate. We wanted ribs that were tender and melted off the bone, sausage that was moist rather than dried out, and pork tenderloin that was juicy and tender rather than tough.

We had found that the beans would take about two hours to cook. Knowing that the ribs and sausage would take longer than the tenderloin, we added the ribs to the beans first, then the sausage, and finally the tenderloin. After a few more tests we found that the ribs and sausage took about one hour to cook, so we were able to add them to the beans together, after the beans had been cooking for about one hour and were just beginning to soften. The tenderloin only needed 20 to 30 minutes to cook to stay nice and juicy, so we added the tenderloin to the pot about 40 minutes after the ribs and sausage. However, with all this meat, real estate was now at a premium in the pot. The ham hock, used to add depth and flavor to the beans as they started cooking, crowded out the rest of the meat. Could we get the same flavor using chopped bacon rather than the large ham hock? Tasters agreed that although the bacon resulted in

a slightly stronger flavor, it got the job done and enabled us to comfortably layer all the meat in the pot. We cut the ribs into four-rib sections because they were easier to handle and fit better in the pot. We also decided to use baby back ribs instead of spare ribs because they were smaller and more consistent in size. We arrived at a layering method of nestling the ribs and sausage in the beans and submerging them almost completely. We found that stirring them once or twice during cooking, and flipping over any pieces of meat that were only partially submerged, resulted in more even cooking. Finally, we simply rested the tenderloins on top of the beans, so that they would sink in slightly as they cooked. The tenderloins were, in effect, steamed, and they remained tender and juicy. We were satisfied with the cooking of the meat, except for its extremely unappealing gray color.

Although none of the recipes called for browning the meat first, we decided to try it. We browned the meat in a large skillet, which required a few batches because of the large amount of meat. Tasters were pleased with the results. The meat had a nice rich brown crust, and the browning added another layer of flavor. And because the beans needed an hour head start anyway, we could brown the meat while the beans simmered. Wanting to take advantage of the flavorful brown bits left in the pan from browning the meat, we decided to deglaze the pan with a little water and add that to the simmering beans. The last challenge was figuring out how much liquid to add to the beans so that the texture and consistency of the finished dish was to our liking.

We found that although we had settled on the correct amount of water to use for cooking the beans alone, when we added the meat, we ended up with too much liquid. As it turned out, the meat was releasing liquid into the pot as it cooked, resulting in a brothy, thin consistency rather than the thick and creamy texture that we were after. We had started with 12 cups of water and after a few tests, were able to reduce it to 10½ cups, but no further. (Using less water just didn't give us enough cooking liquid to evenly cook both the beans and meats at the same time.) This helped, but the final texture of the beans was still a bit on the watery side. Mashing some of the beans to thicken the liquid worked very well, and gave the sauce a nice, creamy consistency, but it still wasn't enough; the beans were still a bit soupy. Finally, we realized that it was necessary to simply remove some the cooking liquid before mashing the beans, adding it back only as needed to adjust the beans to the desired consistency. We had finally arrived at a truly great feijoada—the beans were flavorful, rich, and creamy, with a variety of pork all cooked to perfection. A true labor of love, to be sure, but well worth the effort.

Brazilian Black Bean and Pork Stew

Feijoada

SERVES 8 TO 10

The baking soda added to the beans helps preserve their dark hue; without it, the beans will turn a muddy, grayish color. If the drippings look as though they are going to burn at any time when browning the meats in steps 2 or 3, simply add some of the water to the skillet, scrape the drippings up, and transfer them to the simmering beans; wipe the skillet dry between batches and continue to brown the meats as directed. This Brazilian dish is traditionally served with Simple Steamed White Rice (page 516), orange segments, toasted manioc flour, called farofa (see page 66), and a hot sauce called molho apimentado (see page 66).

4	ounces (about 4 slices) bacon, minced
1	medium onion, minced
4	medium garlic cloves, minced or pressed through a garlic press (about 4 teaspoons)
10½	cups water
2	pounds (about 4½ cups) dried black beans, rinsed and picked over
2	bay leaves
⅛	teaspoon baking soda
	Salt
2	pounds pork tenderloin (about 2 small), trimmed and cut in half widthwise
2	racks baby back ribs (2½ to 3 pounds each), trimmed and each rack cut into 3 pieces
	Ground black pepper
¼	cup vegetable oil
1	pound linguiça sausage, cut into 6-inch lengths

1. Cook the bacon in a heavy-bottomed, 12-quart stockpot over medium heat until partly rendered and lightly browned, about 5 minutes. Stir in the onion and cook until the onion is softened, 5 to 7 minutes. Stir in the garlic and cook until fragrant, about 30 seconds. Stir in 10 cups of the water, beans, bay leaves, baking soda, and 1 teaspoon salt and bring to a boil over high heat, skimming any impurities that rise to the surface. Reduce the heat to low, cover, and cook, stirring occasionally, until the beans begin to soften, about 1 hour.

2. Meanwhile, pat the pork tenderloins and ribs dry with paper towels and season with salt and pepper. Heat 1 tablespoon of the oil in a 12-inch skillet over medium-high heat until just smoking. Brown the tenderloin pieces on all sides, 8 to 10 minutes, reducing the heat if the pan begins to scorch. Transfer the tenderloins to a plate and set aside. Add ¼ cup of the water to the skillet, return to low heat, and scrape up the browned bits; add the water and bits to the simmering beans.

3. Wipe the skillet dry, add 1 tablespoon more of the oil, and return to medium-high heat until just smoking. Brown 2 of the rib pieces, on the meat side only, about 5 minutes, reducing the heat if the pan begins to scorch. Transfer the browned ribs to a plate, and repeat twice more with the remaining 2 tablespoons oil and 4 rib pieces. After all of the ribs are browned, add the remaining ¼ cup water to the skillet, return to low heat, and scrape up the browned bits; add the water and bits to the simmering beans.

4. After the beans have cooked for 1 hour, nestle the linguiça and browned ribs into the beans, submerging them as much as possible. Continue to cook the beans over low heat, covered, until the beans are soft, about 40 minutes, stirring thoroughly about halfway through the cooking time.

5. Gently lay the browned pork tenderloins on top of the beans (it's OK if they sink in a little) and continue to cook, covered, until the beans are tender and the centers of the tenderloins register 145 degrees on an instant-read thermometer, 20 to 30 minutes longer.

6. Using tongs, transfer the tenderloins, ribs, and linguiça to a large carving board and tent with aluminum foil. Discard the bay leaves. Remove 1 cup of the bean cooking liquid and reserve. Transfer

2 cups of the beans and ½ cup more of the bean cooking liquid to a bowl and mash smooth with a potato masher or fork, then return to the pot. Add the reserved cooking liquid back to the beans as needed to adjust their consistency to a loose but not soupy consistency.

7. Slice the pork tenderloin into ½-inch-thick slices. Cut the linguiça into ¾-inch pieces. Slice the ribs between each bone into single rib portions. Arrange the meats on a large, warmed serving platter. Season the beans with salt and pepper to taste, then serve with the meats.

BRAZILIAN ACCOMPANIMENTS

WHILE RESEARCHING RECIPES FOR BRAZILIAN BLACK BEAN AND PORK STEW (PAGE 65), WE found a constant reference to two traditional accompaniments: a toasted meal that is sprinkled over the beans called *farofa* and a salsa-like sauce called *molho apimentado*. Giving both of these accompaniments a whirl, we quickly fell in love with the exotic texture of the farofa, and spicy, fresh flavor of the molho appimentado. Although these accompaniments are distinctly Brazilian, they would taste great with any number of Latin American dishes, including Cuban-Style Black Beans (page 55) and Shredded Beef with Bell Peppers and Onions (page 68).

Brazilian Hot Sauce
Molho Apimentado
MAKES ABOUT 3 CUPS

Malagueta chiles, small hot Brazilian peppers, are traditionally used in this dish; however, we found a jalapeño chile to be a suitable (and easier-to-find) alternative.

2 medium firm, ripe tomatoes, cored, seeded, and chopped fine
1 large onion, minced
1 small green bell pepper, stemmed, seeded, and chopped fine
1 malagueta or jalapeño chile, stemmed, seeded, and minced
⅓ cup white wine vinegar
3 tablespoons extra-virgin olive oil
1 tablespoon minced fresh cilantro leaves
½ teaspoon salt

Combine all of the ingredients in a bowl and let stand at room temperature until the flavors meld, about 30 minutes, before serving. (The hot sauce can be stored in an airtight container in the refrigerator for up to 2 days.)

Brazilian Toasted Manioc Flour
Farofa
MAKES 1 CUP

Manioc flour or meal can be found in most Latin American specialty stores in a variety of textures ranging from fine to coarse (much like cornmeal); finely ground is most common but any type will work.

2 tablespoons unsalted butter
1 cup manioc flour

Melt the butter in a 10-inch skillet over medium heat. Add the manioc flour and cook, stirring frequently, until golden brown, 5 to 7 minutes. Transfer to a bowl and cool about 5 minutes before serving. (The toasted flour can be stored in an airtight container in the refrigerator for up to 5 days.)

SHREDDED BEEF WITH BELL PEPPERS AND ONIONS

Ropa Vieja

CUBANS HAVE INHERITED AN EXTRAORDI-narily varied culture with vibrant culinary influences that has resulted in a cuisine rich in flavors. Over the years, the blending of techniques and ingredients from the different cultures has evolved into what many describe as Cuban Creole cuisine. We have found that the food, in general, is not as spicy as other Caribbean cuisines and is more European in style. As we discovered when researching our recipe for Cuban-Style Black Beans (page 55), a Spanish-style sofrito of onions, garlic, and green bell peppers is used as the base for many of their dishes.

Ropa vieja, which translates to "old clothes," is a good example of a classic Cuban Creole dish. It is a simple preparation of shredded beef with peppers and onions simmered in a flavorful sauce. The name aptly describes the look and feel of the dish, as well as the "secondhand" beef traditionally used as the base. The beef is first used to make a broth, which was a staple in old Cuban households. The beef is shredded and used, along with some of the reduced beef broth, to make ropa vieja. However, because long simmered beef broth is not a staple in most American households, we set out to develop a recipe for ropa vieja that would capture the flavors of the dish yet save some time along the way.

The first decision was what type of beef to use. Most recipes call for either a beef brisket or a skirt steak. When we tasted these side by side, tasters were unanimous in their opinion: skirt steak was the clear winner. They found the skirt steak to be more tender and succulent. It shredded easily and some described it as less chewy than the brisket. The skirt steak had the added benefit of a shorter cooking time. Because skirt steak can be hard to find, we tested flank steak as well. It was a touch less tender, but a good substitute. With our meat decision made, we now turned to the broth and cooking method.

In our research, we found that the authentic recipes called for making a large batch of beef broth from the meat and then simmering the beef in a flavorful sauce with onions and peppers. However, after a few long days in the kitchen making beef broth, we were left with gallons of extra broth and pounds of gray, overcooked beef. We wondered if there was a different way to approach this dish. Since we didn't need all that extra broth, could we simply braise the meat? This turned out to be a perfect solution. Braising requires just enough liquid to barely cover the meat, so when the meat was finished cooking, we had all the liquid (broth) we needed to use in the finished dish. Using our standard method for braising, we browned the meat and set it off to the side, leaving the browned bits (fond) in the pan to make a flavorful braising liquid. We added some minced onion and tomato paste to the pan, which lightly caramelized, adding another layer of flavor. We then stirred in some water and returned the meat to the pan to slowly simmer while the onions dissolved into the broth.

The browning of the meat transformed it from a dull gray to a rich brown. However, while we got what we were looking for in color and a bit more flavor, this extra step took longer than we wanted since we had to brown the meat in batches. Because the meat was shredded in the finished dish anyway, could we get away with browning half of the meat and still capture enough color and flavor? Tasters agreed that browning half the meat was all we needed. They were also pleased with the braising method; it produced a broth with more body and depth, which no longer needed to be reduced (as the broth did) to concentrate the flavor before being added to the finished dish.

However, after a few more tests of braising the meat on the stovetop, we found that there was inconsistency in the amount of liquid that evaporated during the cooking time, yielding varying amounts of broth. We decided to try braising the meat in the oven in hopes that a more even cooking temperature would yield more consistent amounts of broth. This indeed solved our problem—the liquid stayed at a low simmer in a 325-degree oven, and each time we ended up with about two cups of liquid when the meat was finished cooking. This was just the amount of broth we needed for our sauce. With our method in place, we now turned to the flavors in the sauce and finishing the dish.

The recipes we researched all called for sautéing onions, green peppers, and garlic together with cumin and oregano, then adding some wine, tomato sauce, the reserved broth, and olives and simmering the sauce to let the flavors combine. The shredded beef is tossed in at the end to heat through. In our initial tests, tasters thought the tomato sauce imparted an overcooked tomato flavor. We were after a fresher and brighter taste. We then tried canned crushed tomatoes, canned diced tomatoes, and canned whole tomatoes. The crushed tomatoes varied significantly in taste and quality, depending on the brand. The diced tomatoes were a bit too chunky in the sauce and did not have enough time to cook down. The whole tomatoes presented the same problem. We found that crushing the diced tomatoes in the food processor with a few quick pulses, before adding them to the sauce, was the best way to get the texture and fresh taste we were looking for.

Finally, we experimented with the peppers. Green peppers are a staple in the dish but we tried adding some red peppers to offset the sometimes bitter taste that green peppers impart. Tasters liked the red peppers and found they added a pleasant sweetness. With a splash of vinegar at the end to brighten the flavor and a handful of chopped parsley, we now had a ropa vieja to savor.

Shredded Beef with Bell Peppers and Onions
Ropa Vieja
SERVES 8

We slightly prefer skirt steak to flank steak because it has a more tender texture but it can be difficult to find. To shorten the cooking time a bit, only half of the meat is browned in step 1. Serve with plain white rice.

MEAT

2½	pounds skirt or flank steak, cut into 3-inch pieces
	Salt and ground black pepper
2	tablespoons vegetable oil
1	medium onion, minced
2	tablespoons tomato paste
2½	cups water, plus extra as needed
2	bay leaves

PEPPERS AND SAUCE

1	(14.5-ounce) can diced tomatoes
2	tablespoons vegetable oil
2	large red bell peppers, stemmed, seeded, and sliced into thin strips
2	large green bell peppers, stemmed, seeded, and sliced into thin strips
1	medium onion, halved and sliced thin
½	teaspoon salt
3	medium garlic cloves, minced or pressed through a garlic press (about 1 tablespoon)
1	teaspoon dried oregano
¾	teaspoon ground cumin
½	cup dry white wine
½	cup pimiento-stuffed green olives, rinsed and halved
2	tablespoons fresh minced parsley leaves
1–3	tablespoons white wine vinegar
	Ground black pepper

1. FOR THE MEAT: Adjust an oven rack to the middle position and heat the oven to 325 degrees. Pat the meat dry with paper towels and season with salt and pepper. Heat the oil in a large Dutch oven over medium-high heat until just smoking. Brown half of the meat on both sides, about 5 minutes per side, reducing the heat if the pan begins to scorch. Transfer the meat to a plate; set aside.

2. Add the onion to the fat left in the pot and cook over medium heat until softened and browned, 7 to 10 minutes. Stir in the tomato paste and cook until slightly browned, about 1 minute. Stir in the water, scraping up any browned bits. Add the bay leaves, browned meat with any accumulated

juices, and remaining unbrowned meat and bring to a boil. Reduce to a simmer, cover, and transfer the pot to the oven. Cook until the meat is tender and a fork inserted into the center of the largest piece meets little resistance, 2 to 2½ hours.

3. Transfer the meat to a platter and cool slightly; when cool enough to handle, shred into small pieces using 2 forks (see the illustrations below). Pour the broth into a liquid measuring cup and let settle for 5 minutes. Spoon off and discard any fat that accumulates at the top of the broth; you should have about 2 cups of broth (if short, add water).

4. FOR THE PEPPERS AND SAUCE: Pulse the tomatoes and their juice in a food processor until crushed, about 7 pulses, and set aside. Add the oil to the Dutch oven and heat over medium-high heat until shimmering. Add the peppers, onion, and salt and cook until the vegetables are softened and lightly browned, 8 to 10 minutes. Stir in the garlic, oregano, and cumin and cook until fragrant, about 1 minute. Stir in the wine, scraping up any browned bits. Stir in the tomatoes, olives, and 2 cups reserved broth, bring to a simmer, and cook until the peppers are soft and the liquid has reduced slightly, 12 to 15 minutes.

5. Stir in the shredded meat and continue to cook until the meat is heated through and the flavors have combined, about 5 minutes. Stir in the parsley and 1 tablespoon of the vinegar, adding the remaining 2 tablespoons vinegar to taste. Season with salt and pepper to taste before serving.

SHREDDING BEEF AND CHICKEN

Hold one fork in each hand, with the tines facing down. Insert the tines into the beef and gently pull the forks away from each other, breaking the meat apart and into long thin strands.

JAMAICAN JERK CHICKEN

THE JAMAICAN STYLE OF COOKING KNOWN as jerk can be traced back to the native inhabitants of the island, the Carib-Arawak Indians, who cooked animals over green wood, which added a distinctive smoky flavor to the meat. The Indians also "jerked" the animals before cooking them, which meant making deep slashes in the meat and stuffing the resulting holes with herbs and spices to season it. From this seemingly primitive technique, Jamaican jerk—along with reggae music and Bob Marley—has evolved into one of Jamaica's most famous exports. A dish of hot chiles, warm spices, and smoky grilled meat accompanied by an ice-cold Red Stripe beer is our vision of island paradise.

More traditionally made with pork, today jerk is made increasingly with chicken and fish. Wanting to develop a recipe with chicken, we gathered some recipes from a variety of cookbooks and headed into the kitchen. While Jamaican jerk seasoning can be found in almost any supermarket spice aisle, it often tastes dusty and stale and barely penetrates the meat. After just one test, we knew we would be making a paste instead of simply using dried spices for the jerk seasoning. The challenges would be creating a jerk paste that was well balanced—not too spicy, too harsh, or too bland—and figuring out how to apply the paste so that it flavored the chicken, not just the skin.

We began by making our jerk paste with Scotch bonnets, the most popular hot chile of Jamaica, which we liked for their great flavor and slow, steady heat. We then added some allspice, garlic, thyme, and scallions. To temper the heat and spice, we added vegetable oil and dark, smoky molasses, both of which had the added benefit of making the paste smoother and more cohesive—perfect for adhering to the chicken.

In our research, we found that many recipes call for marinating the chicken for days—a step we wanted to skip. After much trial and error with "quick" marinating techniques, we realized that if we wanted the jerk seasonings to flavor the meat more quickly, we would have to rub the paste directly on the meat. This technique produced dramatic results, cutting the marinating time from 24 hours to two. Now we were ready to fire up the grill.

To keep the skin from burning before the meat near the bone was cooked through, we built a two-level fire on the grill. We began by placing the chicken skin side down over the hot part of the grill (with more coals) to crisp the skin. This caused the jerk paste on the exterior of the bird to char slightly—just enough to create an authentic smoky flavor. After flipping the chicken to cook it skin side up for a few minutes, we slid the chicken pieces over to the cooler side of the grill (with fewer coals) to finish cooking.

When serving the chicken, we passed around some lime wedges and a grilled fruit salsa (see page 71), an accompaniment common to Jamaican cuisine that we thought would complement the chicken nicely. The tart flavor of the lime along with the sweetness of the salsa mingled with the jerk beautifully, providing the perfect finishing touch.

Grilled Jamaican Jerk Chicken with Grilled Banana Salsa
SERVES 4

This recipe is pretty spicy; for a milder version, use the lesser amount of Scotch bonnets and discard the seeds and ribs before processing the chiles. If you cannot find Scotch bonnets, substitute an equal amount of habaneros or 4 to 6 jalapeños. Wear disposable latex gloves when handling the chiles, as Scotch bonnets are particularly potent and can cause a burning sensation (for more information on handling chiles, see page 37). For more information on setting up a grill, see page 366. This recipe can easily be doubled, but you may have to grill the chicken in two batches. Start to grill the onions and bananas for the salsa after the chicken has been moved to the cooler side of the grill in step 3.

1	bunch scallions, chopped coarse
¼	cup vegetable oil
2	tablespoons light or dark molasses
2–3	Scotch bonnet chiles, stemmed (and seeded if desired; see note)
3	medium garlic cloves, peeled
1	tablespoon dried thyme
2	teaspoons ground allspice
2	teaspoons salt
3	pounds bone-in, skin-on chicken pieces (split breasts, drumsticks, and/or thighs)
1	recipe Grilled Banana Salsa (page 71)
1	lime, cut into wedges (for serving)

1. Puree the scallions, oil, molasses, chiles, garlic, thyme, allspice, and salt in a food processor or blender until almost smooth, about 15 seconds. Wearing latex gloves and working with one piece of chicken at a time, slide your fingers between the skin and meat to loosen the skin, then rub 1 tablespoon of the spice mixture under the skin of each piece and transfer the chicken to a 1-gallon zipper-lock bag. Pour the remaining spice mixture over the chicken, seal the bag, and turn the bag so that the chicken pieces are covered with the mixture. Refrigerate for at least 2 hours or up to 36 hours.

2. Light a large chimney starter filled with charcoal (about 6 quarts) and allow to burn until all the charcoal is covered with a layer of fine gray ash. Build a hot fire by spreading the coals evenly over about two-thirds of the grill bottom (confining the coals to a smaller space makes for a hotter fire). Set the cooking grate in place, cover the grill with the lid, and let the grate heat up, about 5 minutes. The grill is ready when the coals are hot; you can hold your hand 5 inches above the cooking grate for just 2 seconds. Scrape the cooking grate clean with a grill brush.

3. Remove the chicken from the marinade and lay skin side down directly over the hot coals. Grill the chicken on both sides until well browned, 3 to 5 minutes per side. Slide the chicken to the cooler side of the grill (without coals) and continue to grill, uncovered, turning occasionally, until

the chicken is very dark and fully cooked, about 15 minutes for the breasts (until they register 160 degrees on an instant-read thermometer), or 22 minutes for the thighs and drumsticks (until they register 170 degrees). (If using both types of chicken, the breasts will need to be removed from the grill a few minutes before the thighs and drumsticks.)

4. Transfer the chicken to a platter and let rest for 10 minutes. Serve with the Grilled Banana Salsa and lime wedges.

➤ VARIATION

Gas-Grilled Jamaican Jerk Chicken

Heat the grill with all the burners set to high and the lid down until very hot, about 15 minutes. Scrape the cooking grate clean with a grill brush. Leave one burner on high and turn the other burners to low. Follow the recipe for Grilled Jamaican Jerk Chicken, grilling the chicken as directed in step 3, with the lid down. Serve immediately with the salsa and lime wedges.

Grilled Banana Salsa

MAKES ABOUT 3 CUPS

Grill the bananas and red onions after the chicken has been moved to the cool side of the grill and assemble the salsa while the cooked chicken rests. We like the starchy sweetness of bananas here, but other thickly sliced, sweet tropical fruits such as mangos, papayas, or even pineapple will work as well. This salsa also tastes great with grilled pork, seafood, and poultry.

3   firm but ripe bananas, peeled and halved
    lengthwise
1   large red onion, peeled and sliced into
    ½-inch-thick rounds
2   tablespoons vegetable oil
½   teaspoon ground cumin
    Salt and ground black pepper
2   tablespoons juice from 1 lime
2   tablespoons minced fresh mint leaves
1   tablespoon light brown sugar
1   tablespoon dark rum (optional)

1. Brush the banana halves and onion rounds with the oil and season with the cumin and salt and pepper to taste. Lay the onion directly over the hot coals and grill on both sides until well browned, 3 to 4 minutes per side. Transfer the onion to the cooler part of the grill and cook until softened, about 4 minutes. Lay the bananas directly over the hot coals and grill on both sides until browned in spots, about 2 minutes per side. Transfer the onion and bananas to a cutting board and cool slightly.

2. Coarsely chop the grilled bananas and onion, then toss with the lime juice, mint, brown sugar, and rum (if using) in a medium bowl. Season with salt and pepper to taste and serve. (The salsa can be refrigerated in an airtight container for up to 2 days. Bring to room temperature before serving.)

CUBAN-STYLE ROAST PORK

Lechón Asado

CITRUSY, GARLICKY ROASTED MEATS ARE popular in the Caribbean. One of the best examples is *lechón asado*, or roast pork marinated in a flavorful mixture of citrus, garlic, olive oil, and spices. Tradition calls for a whole pig cooked on a spit over a wood fire, but many modern versions use a suckling pig, fresh ham, or pork shoulder instead—and some recipes even bring the meat indoors to be roasted in the oven.

Our goal was to create a foolproof recipe for this bold-flavored dish, complete with crackling-crisp skin, tender meat, and bracing garlic-citrus sauce. We wanted a recipe that could be made outdoors (great for large summer parties) as well as a variation that could be made indoors (for city dwellers and winter months). After testing half a dozen recipes in various cookbooks, we realized we had our work cut out for us. Burnt skin that peeled off, chewy meat so dry even the sauce couldn't save it, and marinades that failed to impart much flavor were common problems. This recipe is a project, so if the texture and flavor aren't great, why bother?

Whether roasted on the grill or in the oven, Cuban-style roast pork has a texture somewhere between that of a juicy, sliceable American pork roast (which we prefer cooked to about 145 degrees) and fall-apart-when-you-touch-it pulled pork (cooked to almost 200 degrees). The best authentic recipes we sampled called for an internal temperature of around 190 degrees, at which point the collagen and fat had mostly broken down and rendered but not quite to the extent they would in pulled pork. As for the cut, we went with the picnic shoulder (often simply labeled "pork shoulder"), an inexpensive, fatty, bone-in cut that comes with a generous amount of skin attached; the crispy skin, after all, is a hallmark of this dish. (See "Picking the Perfect Pork Roast" below.)

The recipes we found for Cuban pork were a varied lot, but most followed the same sequence: Infuse the raw pork with flavor (with a marinade or wet paste), cook several hours on the grill using indirect heat, cut or slice into small pieces, then toss with a traditional mojo sauce, a garlicky vinaigrette that often serves double duty as a marinade. We would deal with flavor infusion later. First, we wanted to figure out the best way to cook the pork.

After letting the pork sit overnight in a working marinade of citrus juice, garlic, and olive oil, we proceeded to cook it over indirect heat, banking the coals on either side of the grill and placing the roast in between. Hours later, the interior had reached our target 190 degrees, but getting

there was tedious. To keep the roast from turning too dark, we had to rotate it every 30 minutes or so—that's seven or eight times per session. Add that to the number of times we had to refuel to keep the charcoal from dying out, and the grill lid was lying on the ground almost as much as it was covering the pork.

There had to be a better way. We tried a modified two-level fire, banking all the coals on one side of the grill and cooking the pork over the side without the coals. This was an improvement, but we were still refueling too often. What if we started out with higher heat, then let the fire slowly die out? Unfortunately, ramping up the 4 quarts of coal we'd been using to a full chimney (6 quarts) brought the initial temperature of the grill to a scorching 450 degrees, giving us pork that was more Cajun-blackened than Cuban-roasted.

Discouraged, we wondered whether we should throw in the towel and focus solely on an oven method instead. After all, traditional Cuban-style roast pork was originally cooked outdoors more out of necessity than in the interest of flavor development. But after pitting a pork shoulder cooked on the grill (with all its requisite choreography) against one simply tossed into the oven, the answer was clear. While the oven version was tasty (we included the recipe as an alternative), the grill version was the clear favorite for its delicious charred flavor.

The oven experiment had given us an idea. If tasters wanted grilled flavor, why not simply start

PICKING THE PERFECT PORK ROAST

What's the best cut for Cuban-style pork? We tried them all. Widely available Boston butt (the upper portion of the front leg) was an attractive option thanks to its high fat content. But it comes with no skin attached, and the crisp, flavorful skin is one of the highlights of this dish. Fresh ham (from the rear leg) has skin but is usually too lean. We settled on the picnic shoulder (also called pork shoulder), a flavorful cut from the lower portion of the front leg that almost always comes bone-in—and with a fair share of fat and rind to boot.

BOSTON BUTT
Fatty but skinless

FRESH HAM
Great skin but too lean

PICNIC SHOULDER
Our choice: great skin, great fat

THREE STEPS TO ENSURING JUICY, FLAVORFUL ROAST PORK

Bland meat, dry interior, and flavorless crust are three common problems with grill-roasted pork which each demands its own, customized solution. For the bland meat and dry interior, we combined a traditional brine (salt, sugar, and water) with a citrus marinade. And, to ratchet up the flavor of the crust, we coated the exterior with a potent garlic-citrus paste just before cooking. The result? Juicy meat infused with flavor.

| I. BRINE | 2. MARINADE | 3. PASTE |

out on the grill, then move the roast inside to finish? If we planned things right, maybe we could skip refueling altogether. Sure enough, starting with a two-thirds-full chimney allowed the pork to cook for almost three full hours before the coals died down. When we transferred the roast to a 325-degree oven, its internal temperature was around 130 degrees. Three hours later, out came a 190-degree pork roast with plenty of grilled flavor—and we'd used just one chimney of charcoal!

Our recipe had gone from five charcoal replenishments to no charcoal replenishments, but we still had to fiddle with the roast every half-hour or so to keep the side closest to the coals from burning. Unwilling to leave well enough alone, we wondered if we could somehow protect the pork so that we could avoid the half-hourly rotations. Covering the roast completely with aluminum foil created a steam effect, which wreaked havoc on the crispiness of the skin. This roast needed dry heat. The solution was a foil "shield" (see page 75), which allowed the heat to circulate around the meat yet kept it from turning black. More important, we had cut out the fuss—now the grill stayed closed for the entire session.

Half the recipes we had collected called for marinating the pork shoulder overnight (or even for two or three days); the other half went with a coating of wet paste. Each method had its advantages. The marinade penetrated deep into the meat,

while the paste held fast to the exterior of the pork throughout cooking, yielding an assertively flavored crust (the marinade just slipped off). For the best of both worlds, we opted for a combination.

Unfortunately, the wimpy marinade we were using—two or three fresh-squeezed oranges, plus a few minced garlic cloves—just wasn't cutting it. We gradually increased the citrus and garlic until we were up to two heads of garlic and almost two dozen oranges. (With this more powerful formula, we found that we could get away with marinating the pork for just 12 hours rather than two or three days.) Our research turned up many traditional recipes that used bitter orange juice, called *naranja agria*. We got our hands on a few cans, and it produced a great marinade, plus it saved us from having to juice all of those oranges.

As for the exterior paste, the usual blend of mashed garlic, salt, pepper, oregano, cumin, olive oil, and naranja agria, plus a shot of white vinegar for extra kick (basically, the components of a mojo sauce), worked just fine. Cutting fairly wide slits all over the pork proved to be the most effective method for trapping the paste's flavors.

We now had a solid (and fuss-free) cooking method and a great two-pronged technique for infusing flavor. The only problem remaining was an inconsistent texture. The sections of the meat closest to the crust (and, thus, near the exterior layer of fat) always came out moist and tender, but the leaner interior was less predictable. On a bad day, it could turn out so dry that even a generous slathering of mojo sauce barely saved it.

The test kitchen often relies on the magic of brining (soaking in a solution of salt, water, and sometimes sugar) to remedy lean-meat texture problems, but we were already spending 12 hours soaking the pork in a marinade. The answer was simple: We took the test kitchen's basic formula for a brine, replaced some of the water with orange juice, and created a hybrid brine-marinade. We compensated for the diluted flavor (courtesy of the added water) by upping the soaking time from 12 hours to between 18 and 24 hours. The result was flavorful meat that came out tender even close to the bone.

Most large cuts of meat benefit from resting after cooking, which allows the juices to redistribute evenly throughout the meat. Our Cuban pork roast was no exception. Compared side by side, a roast rested for 30 minutes was much juicier than one we sliced into immediately after cooking. Even more interesting is what happened when the roast rested for an entire hour: As expected, the exterior and the portions bordering knobs of fat were delicious, but now the lean interior portions were every bit as moist. Patience really is a virtue.

All the pork needed now was a final splash of mojo sauce, which could be quickly mixed and cooled to room temperature while the pork rested. Made with many of the same ingredients used in the brine and paste, the mojo provided another bright, fresh hit of flavor. As we took bites of the tangy, garlicky pork and sips from an icy mojito, we knew our efforts had been worth it: this dish had finally gotten its mojo back.

Cuban-Style Grill-Roasted Pork
Lechón Asado
SERVES 8 TO 10

Letting the cooked roast rest for a full hour before serving will yield noticeably more tender meat. This roast has a crispy skin that should be served along with the meat. Top the meat with Mojo Sauce (page 76). Traditional accompaniments include black beans (see page 55), rice (see page 516), and fried plantains (see page 53).

PORK AND BRINE
- 1   bone-in, skin-on pork picnic shoulder (7 to 8 pounds)
- 3   cups sugar
- 2   cups table salt, 4 cups Diamond Crystal Kosher salt, or 3 cups Morton Kosher salt
- 2   medium garlic heads, unpeeled cloves separated and crushed
- 4   cups orange juice

GARLIC-CITRUS PASTE
- 12   medium garlic cloves, peeled and coarsely chopped (about ¼ cup)
- 2   tablespoons ground cumin
- 2   tablespoons dried oregano
- 1   tablespoon salt
- 1½   teaspoons ground black pepper
- 6   tablespoons orange juice
- 2   tablespoons distilled white vinegar
- 2   tablespoons olive oil

1. **FOR THE PORK AND BRINE:** Cut 1-inch-deep slits (about 1 inch long) all over the roast, spaced about 2 inches apart. Dissolve the sugar and salt in 6 quarts cold water in a stockpot or large bucket. Stir in the garlic and orange juice, submerge the pork in the brine, and refrigerate for 18 to 24 hours.

2. **FOR THE GARLIC-CITRUS PASTE:** Pulse the garlic, cumin, oregano, salt, and pepper together in a food processor to a coarse paste, about 10 pulses. With the machine running, add the orange juice, vinegar, and oil through the feed tube and process until smooth, about 20 seconds. Remove the pork from the brine, rinse under cool running water, and pat dry with paper towels. Rub the paste all over the pork and into the slits. Refrigerate until ready to grill.

3. Light a large chimney starter filled two-thirds full with charcoal (about 4 quarts) and allow to burn until all the charcoal is covered with a layer of fine gray ash. Build a hot fire by spreading the coals evenly over one-half of the grill bottom (confining the coals to a smaller space creates hotter and cooler spots necessary for grill-roasting). Set the cooking grate in place, cover the grill with the lid, and let the grate heat up, about 5 minutes. Scrape the cooking grate clean with a grill brush.

4. Place the roast, skin side up, on the cool side of the grill and shield with foil following the illustrations below. Cover and grill-roast until the grill temperature falls to 225 degrees, 2 to 3 hours (the coals will be gray and partially disintegrated).

5. After 1¾ hours of grill-roasting, adjust an oven rack to the lower-middle position and heat the oven to 325 degrees. When the grill temperature has fallen to 225 degrees, remove the foil and transfer the roast to a wire rack set over a rimmed baking sheet (or roasting pan). Roast the pork in the oven until the skin is browned and crisp and the thickest part of the meat registers 190 degrees on an instant-read thermometer, 2 to 3 hours.

6. FOR SERVING: Transfer the roast to a carving board and let rest for 1 hour. Remove the skin in one

large piece. Scrape off and discard the top layer of fat, then cut the pork away from the bone in 3 or 4 large pieces. Slice each piece against the grain into ¼-inch slices. To serve the skin, scrape the excess fat from the underside and cut into strips. Serve immediately.

➤ VARIATIONS

Cuban-Style Grill-Roasted Pork on a Gas Grill

The trick to making Cuban-Style Roast Pork on a gas grill is to maintain a constant grill temperature of 325 degrees; be prepared to monitor the grill temperature and adjust the burners as needed to maintain this temperature throughout the 6-hour cooking time.

Follow the recipe for Cuban-Style Grill-Roasted Pork through step 2. Heat the grill with all the burners set to high and the lid down until very hot, about 15 minutes. Scrape the cooking grate clean with a grill brush. Leave one burner (the primary burner) on medium-high and turn the other burners off. Place the roast, skin side up, on the cool side of the grill and shield with foil following the illustrations on the left. Cover, adjust the primary burner as needed to maintain a grill temperature of 325 degrees, and grill-roast the pork until the skin is browned and crisp and the thickest part of the meat registers 190 degrees on an instant-read thermometer, about 6 hours, rotating the meat and removing the foil shield halfway through the cooking time. Follow the resting and slicing instructions from step 6.

Cuban-Style Oven-Roasted Pork

Follow the recipe for Cuban-Style Grill-Roasted Pork through step 2. Adjust an oven rack to the lower-middle position and heat the oven to 325 degrees. Place the pork, skin side down, on a wire rack set over a rimmed baking sheet (or in a roasting pan) and roast for 3 hours. Flip the roast skin side up and continue to roast until the thickest part of the meat registers 190 degrees on an instant-read thermometer, about 3 hours longer, lightly tenting the roast with foil if the skin begins to get too dark. Follow the resting and slicing instructions from step 6.

BUILDING A FOIL "SHIELD"

By protecting the pork roast with an aluminum foil shield, we kept it from getting too dark on the side closest to the heat—no rotation required.

1. Make two ½-inch folds on the long side of an 18-inch length of foil to form a reinforced edge. Place the foil on the center of the cooking grate, with the reinforced edge over the hot side of the grill. Position the roast, skin side up, over the cool side of the grill so that it covers about a third of the foil.

2. Lift and bend the edges of the foil to shield the sides of the roast, tucking in the edges.

Mojo Sauce

MAKES ABOUT 1 CUP

The sauce can be refrigerated in an airtight container for up to 1 day. If chilled, bring to room temperature before serving. Serve with Venezuelan Stuffed Corn Cakes (page 46), Twice-Fried Plantains (page 53), or Cuban-Style Grill-Roasted Pork (page 74).

4	medium garlic cloves, minced or pressed through a garlic press (about 4 teaspoons)
1	teaspoon salt
½	cup olive oil
½	teaspoon ground cumin
¼	cup distilled white vinegar
¼	cup orange juice
¼	teaspoon dried oregano
⅛	teaspoon ground black pepper

1. Place the minced garlic on a cutting board and sprinkle with the salt. Using the flat side of a chef's knife, drag the garlic and salt back and forth across the cutting board in small circular motions until the garlic is ground into a smooth paste.

2. Heat the oil in a medium saucepan over medium heat until shimmering. Stir in the garlic paste and cumin and cook until fragrant, about 30 seconds. Remove the pan from the heat and whisk in the remaining ingredients. Transfer to a bowl and cool to room temperature. Whisk the sauce to recombine before serving.

EASIER CITRUS PRESSING

A citrus press can be a handy tool, but using one to press the juice from several lemons or oranges can be a pain. Try cutting the fruit into quarters rather than halves. Juicing a quarter is not only easier than juicing a half, but it also yields more juice.

GRILLED ARGENTINE-STYLE SHORT RIBS

Asado de Tira

IF THERE IS ONE FOOD THAT EPITOMIZES THE cuisine of Argentina, without a doubt it is beef. Argentina boasts the highest consumption rate of beef of any country, which isn't surprising considering Argentine beef is reported to be the most flavorful and tender beef in the world. The country is full of fertile grasslands, known as the *pampas*, which are the ideal setting for cattle to graze. Cattle were introduced to the country by Spanish conquistadors as early as the sixteenth century, and cattle ranching has grown to become a huge part of the cuisine and the culture.

If beef is the food that represents Argentina, grilling is the cooking medium. Traditionally, meat was grilled over open flames by *gauchos*, or cowboys, who roamed the pampas; however, today, grilled meat can be found in the cities and pampas alike, served simply with just a drizzle of chimichurri—a zesty vinaigrette-like sauce of parsley and garlic. We wanted to try our hand at traditional Argentine grilled beef, and our research turned up several cuts of meat, from flank steak to skirt steak to porterhouses, and even short ribs. We decided to give the short ribs a try, and since we know them as a braising cut rather than a grilling cut, we figured we were in for a real challenge—but surely those gauchos know a few things about beef and wouldn't grill a short rib if it wasn't worthwhile.

Short ribs are just what their name says they are: short ribs cut from any location along the length of the cow's ribs. They can come from the lower belly section or higher up toward the back, from the shoulder (or chuck) area or the forward mid-section. Regardless of which rib section they're cut from, short ribs can be butchered in one of two ways: English-style or flanken-style (see the photos on page 555). Most likely you will see English-style short ribs—single ribs surrounded by a thick, blocky chunk of meat. Flanken-style short ribs, which are much less common, are sliced across the bones, so that each piece is a cross section of several bones surrounded by meat.

Since English-style short ribs are far more widely available than flanken-style, we started our initial grilling tests with them. We pitted three grilling methods against one another, but none worked perfectly. Grilling them directly over a bed of hot coals (as we would a regular steak), we merely burned the exterior before the thick middle portion of the meat was cooked through. Grilling over a more moderate fire worked a little better, but we still found the interior to be tough by the time the exterior was properly seared. Using a grill-roasting method in which the coals are banked on one side of the grill while the ribs lie on the opposite side, we hoped that the more gentle, indirect heat would solve our problems, but no such luck. After just half an hour of grill-roasting, the meat became dry and stringy. Worse, there were several layers of unrendered fat throughout each rib that were flabby and unappealing.

Undaunted, we then tried simmering the ribs on the stovetop and finishing them on the grill. This method is tedious. First, you have to make a flavorful liquid for the meat to stew in, and then you have to cook the ribs down in the liquid for a few hours to make them tender. Finally, you have to finish by grilling the ribs until crisped and browned, which takes only eight minutes or so—not enough time to give them much smoke flavor.

At this point, we wondered if it wasn't a butchering issue. Following the lead of some Asian recipes we've seen, we tried cutting down the ribs further before cooking. In effect, the meat is butterflied several times (slit crosswise and opened up like a book) until it is quite thin (between ¼ and ½ inch thick). Giving this a whirl, we threw the thinly cut short ribs over a hot grill and presto! This was the meat we were looking for—tender with just a slight chew, a crisp crust, and fully rendered fat. The only drawback is that you have to butcher the meat yourself, but it's not too difficult.

We then decided to see how flanken-style ribs would fare on the grill, so we cooked them directly over hot coals—and they worked well. The only trick here is the shopping. Not only are they hard to find, but much like the English-style ribs, they need to be sliced very thin. But unlike the English-style ribs, they can only be sliced thin by a butcher because cutting through the thick bones requires a special piece of equipment (a band saw).

Regardless of what type of ribs you use, you'll need to build a fire that is hot enough to sear the meat. The meat is thin and cooks extremely quickly, making it impossible to go for medium-rare or even medium meat. You just want to have good caramelization to add a layer of sweet flavor on the surface of the ribs. We found that a medium-hot fire (using a full chimney starter of charcoal) sears the meat in about five minutes.

PREPARING ENGLISH-STYLE RIBS

Getting flanken-style short ribs thin enough to grill requires the help of a butcher, but you can prepare English-style short ribs yourself.

1. With a paring or boning knife, trim the surface fat and silver skin from each rib.

2. Right above the bone, make a cut into the meat. Continue cutting almost, but not quite all the way, through the meat. Open the meat onto a cutting board, as you would open a book.

3. Make another cut into the meat, parallel to the board, making the lower half of the section of meat that you are slicing about ¼ inch thick, cutting almost, but not all the way, through to the end of the meat.

4. Repeat step 3 as needed, 1 or 2 more times, until the meat is about ¼ inch thick throughout. You should have a bone connected to a long strip of meat about ¼ inch thick.

All that was left to do was work out the details of the chimichurri. Parsley and garlic were givens, and tasters liked a heavy hand with both—1 cup minced fresh parsley and five garlic cloves. For more bite we added minced red onion, a little salt for adding seasoning, and red pepper flakes to heat things up. Extra-virgin olive oil was favored over both regular olive oil and vegetable oil, since it was able to stand up to the boldness of the other ingredients. For the acid, we settled on red wine vinegar, which was smooth, but not overshadowed by the other ingredients. To round things out and keep all the ingredients from tasting harsh, we added a little water. Now we had the perfect sauce to complement our authentic Argentine grilled meat!

Grilled Argentine-Style Short Ribs with Parsley and Garlic Sauce

Asado de Tira con Chimichurri

SERVES 4

Purchase English-style ribs with a good amount of meat on the bones; there should be at least 1 inch of meat above the bone. If you choose flanken-style ribs, you will need a butcher to cut them thin enough for this recipe. Keep a squirt bottle handy to douse any flare-ups caused by this fatty cut of meat. The chimichurri has the consistency of a loose, fresh salsa and tastes great with grilled beef, pork, poultry, and seafood.

CHIMICHURRI SAUCE

I	cup minced fresh parsley leaves
½	cup extra-virgin olive oil
¼	cup finely minced red onion
¼	cup red wine vinegar
2	tablespoons water
5	medium garlic cloves, minced or pressed through a garlic press (about 5 teaspoons)
I	teaspoon salt
¼	teaspoon red pepper flakes

SHORT RIBS

3	pounds English-style short ribs, prepared following the illustrations on page 77 or 2½ pounds flanken-style short ribs, about ¼ inch thick (see note) Salt and ground black pepper

1. FOR THE CHIMICHURRI SAUCE: Combine all of the ingredients and let stand at room temperature until the flavors meld, about 30 minutes, before serving. (The sauce can be refrigerated in an airtight container for up to 2 days.)

2. FOR THE SHORT RIBS: Light a large chimney starter filled with charcoal (about 6 quarts) and allow to burn until all the charcoal is covered with a layer of fine gray ash. Build a hot fire by spreading the coals evenly over about two-thirds of the grill bottom (confining the coals to a smaller space makes for a hotter fire). Set the cooking grate in place, cover the grill with the lid, and let the grate heat up, about 5 minutes. The grill is ready when the coals are hot; you can hold your hand 5 inches above the cooking grate for just 2 seconds. Scrape the cooking grate clean with a grill brush.

3. Pat the ribs dry with paper towels and season with salt and pepper. Lay half of the ribs directly over the hot coals. Grill, uncovered, until deeply browned, 2 to 2½ minutes per side. Transfer the ribs to a serving platter and cover with foil. Repeat with the second batch of ribs. Drizzle the sauce over the meat and serve immediately.

➤ VARIATION

Gas-Grilled Argentine-Style Short Ribs with Parsley and Garlic Sauce

Heat the grill with all the burners set to high and the lid down until very hot, about 15 minutes. Scrape the cooking grate clean with a grill brush. Follow the recipe for Grilled Argentine-Style Short Ribs with Parsley and Garlic Sauce, grilling the beef as directed in step 3 of the recipe, with the lid down.

RICE PUDDING

Arroz con Leche

RICE PUDDING IS A POPULAR DESSERT IN many cultures throughout the world, and especially in Latin America and the Caribbean, where it is known as arroz con leche in Spanish-speaking countries, and arroz doce or arroz de leite in Brazil (where Portuguese is the language). Popularly sold by street venders in small paper cups, or made by families at home, it is a mainstay of Latin American and Caribbean cuisines. Many versions exist, but one thing remains constant—at its best, rice pudding is simple and lightly sweet and it tastes of its primary component: rice. At its worst, the rice flavor is lost to cloying sweetness, condensed dairy, and a pasty, leaden consistency.

Right from the start, we agreed on the qualities of an ideal rice pudding: intact, tender grains bound loosely in a subtly sweet, milky sauce. We were looking for a straightforward stovetop rice pudding, in which both the texture and the flavor of the main ingredient would stand out.

We turned our attention to the cooking medium and method first. For our first experiment, we prepared and tasted eight existing recipes for rice pudding, each using a different combination of water, milk, and cream and each with varying ratios of rice to liquid. The tasting revealed that cooking the rice in milk or cream obscured the rice flavor, while cooking the rice in water emphasized it. The most appealing balance of rice flavor and satisfying yet not too rich consistency was achieved when we cooked 1 cup of rice in 2 cups of water until it was absorbed and then added equal parts (2½ cups each) of whole milk and half-and-half to make the pudding. Whole milk alone made the pudding too thin, but the milk and half-and-half together imparted just the right degree of richness. Eggs, butter, whipped cream, and heavy cream—on their own or in combination—overpowered the flavor of the rice.

We also tried a couple of variations in the cooking method, such as covering the pot or not and using a double boiler. The double boiler lengthened the cooking time by 25 minutes and turned out a pudding that was gummy and too sweet. By far, the best results came from cooking the rice and water in a covered pot, then simmering the cooked rice and dairy mixture uncovered. This technique gave us just what we wanted—distinct, tender grains of rice in a smooth sauce that tasted of milk rather than reduced cream. We found we could cut 10 minutes off the total cooking time by simmering the rice in the water and dairy mixture together from the start, but this approach sacrificed the texture of the grains and resulted in a pudding that our tasters described as overly dense and sweet.

Now it was time to try different kinds of rice. We tested the readily available varieties: supermarket brands of long- and medium-grain white (such as Goya, which distributes both of these types nationally), Arborio (a superstarchy Italian medium-grain white used to make risotto), and basmati (an aromatic long-grain white).

All rice contains two types of starch, called amylose and amylopectin, but they are present in different concentrations in different kinds of rice. Arborio, with its high level of amylopectin, made a stiff, gritty pudding. On the other end of the starch scale, long-grain rice, which is high in amylose, cooked up separate and fluffy. But the puddings made with long-grain rice were a little too thin for our liking, and the flavor of the basmati rice was too perfumey, overwhelming the milk. Medium-grain rice, which has a high proportion of amylopectin (but less than Arborio), cooked up a little more moist and sticky than long-grain rice. This type proved ideal for our pudding, which had a creamy texture and tasted distinctly of rice and milk. As a final test, we made a pudding with cooked rice that had been refrigerated overnight. Unfortunately, the result was liquidy and grainy, without discernible rice flavor.

Lastly, we wanted to add a few complementary flavorings, while at the same time keeping with tradition. Most of the recipes we came across in our research scented the rice with cinnamon and also added raisins. We liked the addition of both—the cinnamon added warmth and depth and the plump raisins added contrast and color to the creamy white rice.

Rice Pudding

Arroz con Leche

SERVES 6 TO 8

We prefer pudding made from medium-grain rice, but long-grain rice works too. Using a heavy-bottomed saucepan here is key to prevent the bottom from burning.

2	cups water
1	cup medium-grain rice
¼	teaspoon salt
2½	cups whole milk
2½	cups half-and-half
⅔	cup (4⅔ ounces) sugar
½	cup raisins
1½	teaspoons vanilla extract
1	teaspoon ground cinnamon

1. Bring the water to a boil in a large, heavy-bottomed saucepan. Stir in the rice and salt, cover, and simmer over low heat, stirring once or twice, until the water is almost fully absorbed, 15 to 20 minutes.

2. Stir in the milk, half-and-half, and sugar. Increase the heat to medium-high and bring to a simmer, then reduce the heat to maintain a simmer. Cook, uncovered and stirring frequently, until the mixture starts to thicken, about 30 minutes. Reduce the heat to low and continue to cook, stirring every couple of minutes to prevent sticking and scorching, until a spoon is just able to stand up in the pudding, about 15 minutes longer.

3. Remove from the heat and stir in the raisins, vanilla, and cinnamon. Serve warm, at room temperature, or chilled. (To store, press plastic wrap directly on the surface of the pudding and refrigerate for up to 2 days. If serving at room temperature or chilled, stir in up to 1 cup warm milk, 2 tablespoons at a time, as needed to loosen before serving.)

➤ VARIATION

Coconut Rice Pudding

This version is popular in Puerto Rico. To toast the coconut, spread it out on a baking sheet and toast it in a 325-degree oven, stirring often, until light golden, 10 to 15 minutes.

Follow the recipe for Rice Pudding, substituting coconut milk for the whole milk and garnishing with 1 cup of shredded sweetened coconut, toasted, before serving.

EQUIPMENT: **Large Saucepans**

A large saucepan is an essential piece of cookware. In the test kitchen, we use our large saucepans for making rice and oatmeal; blanching vegetables; and cooking small amounts of pasta, soup, stew, and all manner of sauces. Which begs an obvious question: does the brand of pan matter? In order to answer this question, we tested eight models, all between 3.3 and 4 quarts in size.

The tests we performed were based on common cooking tasks and designed to highlight specific characteristics of the pans' performance. To determine the relative cooking speed of each saucepan, we sautéed onions over medium heat. Cooking white rice provided a good indication of a pan's ability to heat evenly. Making pastry cream showed us how user friendly the pan was—was it shaped such that a whisk could reach into the corners without trouble, and could we pour liquid from it neatly?

We found that the most important quality for a saucepan is even and slow heating. The best pans for slow and steady cooking were either very heavy or had relatively thick bottoms. An aluminum core throughout the pan also ensures even heating

and minimal scorching. Finally, we liked pans with long handles; a few of the pans we tested had small handles on either side, which tend to get hot quickly and can be difficult to hold with one hand while scraping out the contents with the other.

So which pan should you buy? With its heft and aluminum core, the All-Clad saucepan excelled at every test; but it was also the most expensive. The Pinzon, though lighter than the All-Clad, has a thicker-than-average bottom and performed well in most tests. At a fraction of the cost, it is our best buy.

THE BEST LARGE SAUCEPAN

The All-Clad Stainless 4-Quart Saucepan (left) took top honors but at $184, it is pricey. The Pinzon 3.5-Quart Stainless Steel Sauce Pan (right) costs about $20 and is our best buy.

3

BRITISH ISLES AND IRELAND

SMOKED SALMON AND LEEK TART

MORE THAN A BAGEL AND CREAM CHEESE sidekick, smoked salmon is found in many dishes throughout the British Isles, from egg dishes like quiches and scrambled eggs to pastas and even pizza. Scots utilize their abundance of smoked salmon in several ways, but perhaps one of the tastiest is the smoked salmon and leek tart. The tart is similar to quiche in that the filling is built on a custard base, but it differs from quiche in the amount of custard—the tart contains just enough to bind the ingredients together, so the end result is a bit lighter than quiche, with the flavor of salmon at the fore. Each bite contains a trio of flavors and textures: flaky pastry, creamy custard, and briny, rich salmon. We set out to develop our own interpretation of this Scottish favorite.

We tried several tarts based on our research of Scottish cuisine. They ranged from the extremely simple and disappointingly flavorless to the horrendously complicated and confusing. Some tarts added various cheeses to the custard for richness and flavor (or replaced the custard altogether with cheese) while others stuck to a simple egg and cream custard. Some recipes folded the salmon into the custard and others arranged the salmon across the top of the tart. Leeks and onions and herbs were a common thread among the many versions, while the crusts couldn't have been more varied. We chose to start our testing from the ground up, with the pastry crust.

We love the flavor of an all-butter crust, but getting an all-butter dough into a tart shell in one piece is time-consuming and stressful—and often requires patching torn dough back together while going in and out of the refrigerator to keep the dough from getting too soft and difficult to handle. We wanted to cut out the steps of rolling out and repeatedly chilling the dough, so we turned to testing pat-in-the-pan–style crusts.

We tried several recipes, which included everything from shortening to eggs and even cream cheese, but they all produced crusts that were too cookie-like and crumbly—and more importantly, the intense butter flavor we wanted in this tart was lost. Simply patting our all-butter dough didn't

work either. The pieces of cold butter that typically get smeared in the dough during rolling remained in chunks that melted in the oven, leaving unsightly holes and cracks in their place. We then had the idea of cutting the butter completely into the flour. (Up to this point, we'd been partially cutting in the butter.) We used a food processor to speed things up and ensure that the butter was evenly cut throughout. This worked like a charm—the dough was firm enough to press into the pan and baked evenly as a traditional rolled tart dough. Even better, it tasted as buttery as we'd imagined.

In our testing of fillings, no one liked the tarts that either omitted the custard in favor of a cheese filling or enriched the custard with cheese—these tarts were simply too rich and lacked the delicacy of the simple custard tarts. Thus, we focused on getting our custard base just right. We started out by experimenting with various ratios of eggs and cream to yield a custard light enough to let the other ingredients shine through, but still bind them all together. We tried four eggs and 1 cup of cream, but that turned out to be too much custard for our crust—and too rich as well. When we reduced the eggs to three and swapped in ¾ cup half-and-half for the cream, some tasters commented that the tart tasted too eggy. We finally settled on two eggs and ½ cup of half-and-half. With the addition of some fresh dill, the custard was flavorful and delicate.

CORE TECHNIQUE

PAT-IN-THE-PAN–STYLE TART CRUSTS

Working with pastry dough can be a race against the clock. Why? Once the butter in the dough softens—which doesn't take very long at all—the dough becomes unmanageable, making rolling and fitting the dough nearly impossible. Sure, you can re-chill the dough, but we wondered if there was a better way for those of us who aren't as smooth and quick as a practiced pastry chef. We found our answer in a pat-in-the-pan–style pastry crust—no rolling or fitting required. In our testing, we found that cutting the butter almost completely into the flour made a cohesive dough that was easy to pat into the pan. And because the butter was evenly distributed, the crust baked as evenly as one prepared the traditional way, but without the hassle of rolling and fitting.

Moving along, we shifted our focus to the leeks. We found that a quick sauté in a hot pan left us with brown, bitter leeks that were stringy and tough. Experimenting with the opposite end of the spectrum, we tried cooking them slowly over low heat. This was a marked improvement in both texture and taste, but some bits and pieces were still getting too brown, so we covered the pan to sweat the leeks. Sweating allowed the leeks to cook to a meltingly tender state with deep, sweet flavor.

Next, we focused on incorporating the salmon into the tart. Many of the recipes we researched folded the salmon into the custard. We found this method to be incredibly disappointing. The once subtle flavor of the salmon turned unpleasantly fishy, overwhelming the other flavors in the filling. Not good at all. Placing the salmon over the custard didn't work well either. The salmon sunk down into the custard, again throwing all the flavors off balance. And the pieces of salmon that didn't become immersed in custard turned dry and chewy, once baked. We then wondered whether we should even be cooking the smoked salmon. After all, the smoking process "cooks" the salmon.

With this notion in mind, we went back to our library and thumbed through more smoked salmon tart recipes. We then came across one that added the smoked salmon to the tart after baking. The recipe was an odd man out among all the other recipes, but seemed worth trying. We set the salmon aside while the leek custard cooked in the tart crust. Once cooled, we spooned the chopped salmon over the custard filling. (We first tried laying slices of salmon over the top, but the long slices proved unwieldy when we cut into the tart, flopping away from the custard.) Tasters now raved about the distinct flavorful contrast between the delicate custard and the rich smoky salmon, a contrast that previously had been lost when the salmon was incorporated into the custard.

Some final touches brought our recipe to completion: tossing the salmon with a bit of olive oil (to keep things moist) and minced chives for some fresh onion flavor—a nice counterpoint to the cooked leeks in the custard. At last, we'd come up with a perfect slice of Scotland.

Smoked Salmon and Leek Tart

SERVES 8 AS AN APPETIZER,
OR 6 AS A MAIN COURSE

You will need a 9-inch fluted tart pan with a removable bottom for this recipe. Buy smoked salmon that looks bright and glossy and avoid salmon that looks milky and dry. This tart can be served chilled or at room temperature—it makes an excellent choice for brunch.

CRUST

1¼	cups (6¼ ounces) unbleached all-purpose flour
1	tablespoon sugar
½	teaspoon salt
8	tablespoons (1 stick) unsalted butter, cut into ½-inch cubes and chilled
3	tablespoons ice water

FILLING

1	tablespoon unsalted butter
1	pound leeks, white and light green parts only, halved lengthwise, sliced thin, and rinsed thoroughly (see the illustrations on page 86)
	Salt
2	large eggs
½	cup half-and-half
1	tablespoon minced fresh dill leaves
	Ground black pepper
6	ounces thinly sliced smoked salmon, cut into ¼-inch pieces
1	tablespoon extra-virgin olive oil
1	tablespoon minced fresh chives
1	lemon, cut into wedges (for serving)

1. FOR THE CRUST: Spray a 9-inch tart pan with a removable bottom with vegetable oil spray; set aside. Pulse the flour, sugar, and salt together in a food processor until combined, about 4 pulses. Scatter the butter pieces over the flour mixture and pulse until the mixture resembles coarse sand, about 15 pulses. Add 2 tablespoons of the ice water and continue to process until large clumps of dough form and no powdery bits remain, about 5 seconds. If the dough doesn't clump, add the remaining tablespoon water and pulse to incorporate, about 4 pulses.

TART DOUGH: NO ROLLING REQUIRED

1. Sprinkle walnut-sized clumps of dough evenly into the tart pan.

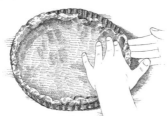

2. Working outward from the center, press the dough into an even layer, sealing any cracks.

3. Working around the edge, press the dough firmly into the corners of the pan with your index finger.

4. Go around the edge once more, pressing the dough up the sides and into the fluted ridges.

5. Use your thumb to level off the top edge. Use this excess dough to patch any holes.

2. Following the illustrations on the left, tear the dough into walnut-sized pieces, then pat it into the prepared tart pan. Lay plastic wrap over the dough and smooth out any bumps or shallow areas using your fingertips. Place the tart shell on a large plate and freeze until firm, about 30 minutes. Meanwhile, adjust an oven rack to the middle position and heat the oven to 375 degrees.

3. Place the frozen tart shell on a baking sheet. Gently press a piece of extra-wide heavy-duty aluminum foil that has been sprayed with vegetable oil spray against the dough and over the edges of the tart pan. Fill the shell with pie weights and bake until the top edge of the dough just starts to color and the surface of dough under the foil no longer looks wet, about 30 minutes.

4. Remove the shell from the oven and carefully remove the foil and weights. Return the baking sheet with the tart shell to the oven and continue to bake, uncovered, until golden brown, 5 to 10 minutes. Set the baking sheet with the tart shell on a wire rack to cool while making the filling. (Do not turn off the oven.)

5. FOR THE FILLING: While the crust is baking, melt the butter in a 10-inch skillet over medium heat. Add the leeks and ½ teaspoon salt and cook, covered, stirring occasionally, until the leeks are softened, about 10 minutes. Remove the pan from the heat, remove the lid, and let the leeks cool for 5 minutes.

6. Whisk the eggs, half-and-half, dill, and ¼ teaspoon ground black pepper together in a large bowl. Stir in the leeks until just incorporated. Spread the leek mixture over the bottom of the baked crust. Bake the tart on the baking sheet until the filling has set and the center feels firm to the touch, 20 to 25 minutes. Set the baking sheet with the tart shell on a wire rack and cool to room temperature, about 2 hours.

7. Toss the salmon with the olive oil and chives and season with salt and pepper to taste. Sprinkle the salmon evenly over the cooled tart. Slice the tart into wedges and serve with the lemon wedges.

COLCANNON SOUP

COLCANNON SOUP IS BASED ON THE traditional mashed potato dish of Ireland and Western Scotland containing cabbage or kale with leeks and onions—the whole flavored with meaty bacon. We couldn't imagine a more hearty pottage so we headed into the test kitchen to develop the ultimate version.

In our research we uncovered several variations of colcannon soup, each using a different variety of cabbage. Some soups used excessive amounts of cream and butter, while others supplemented this richness with bacon. Still others mashed potatoes in the pot for added texture and thickness. It seemed there were many tricks of the colcannon trade for us to wade through so we started from the ground up. Picking up some of the recurring themes of these many recipes, we cobbled together a working recipe and proceeded from there.

We began by sautéing the leeks, onions, and cabbage in rendered bacon fat. Starting with two slices of bacon, our soup had only a slight smokiness, and tasters agreed that the soup would be well served by increasing the bacon. At four slices the bacon began to overpower the other ingredients, but three slices gave us just the right amount of richness.

Some recipes use either leeks or onions in colcannon. Tasters liked the pungency of a soup made with just onions, but its flavor was a bit one-dimensional. Adding leeks to the pot improved

matters. The sweet leeks offset the sharpness of the onions and lent the soup some welcome texture.

While we found green cabbage to be the most frequently used cabbage in colcannon, we also tested savoy and napa cabbages. And sticking with traditional variations of colcannon soup we found, we also included curly kale. We sweated the cabbages and kale in four soups for a side-by-side comparison. The savoy cabbage all but disappeared in the soup, offering minimal flavor and even less texture—some tasters even asked if the soup contained cabbage! Napa cabbage was a little better, as its flavor came through more than the savoy, but its textural contribution, too, was hard to distinguish. The humble green cabbage, noticeably crisp when raw, gave us the texture we were looking for in our soup. It also offered a pleasant flavor supported by the leeks and onions, and was the clear favorite among tasters.

The batch we prepared with kale was good enough for a variation. The texture of the greens held up well in the soup and their earthy flavor had tasters reaching for a second bowl.

Moving on, we focused on the potatoes. Prior soup testing in the test kitchen had led us to the conclusion that the most appropriate potatoes for soup were waxy, low-starch potatoes such as red potatoes. Red potatoes hold their shape through cooking, and the fact that we needn't peel them prior to use made the soup preparation that much quicker.

As our soup began to take shape we noticed that the final product was more brothy than we had anticipated or desired. We tried mashing some of the potatoes in the pot in hopes of thickening the soup (a trick we had seen in our research), but were met with a mealy, still-too-thin soup. We then decided to thicken the soup with a roux (a mix of flour and fat, in this case, bacon fat). This gave us the thickening power we needed, and ½ cup of cream stirred in off the heat gave the soup a comforting, velvety texture (tasters preferred heavy cream over half-and-half).

A few minor adjustments were still required to brighten the soup and distinguish the many layers of flavor. White wine, added to the pan after we added the flour, cut through the richness of the

HANDLING KALE

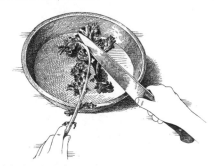

Hold each leaf at the base of the stem over a bowl filled with water and use a sharp knife to slash the leafy portion from either side of the thick stem. Discard the stems, and then wash and dry the leaves. Chop as directed.

soup; the rendered bacon pieces garnished the finished dish and brought the smoky undertones full circle; and a sprinkling of minced chives helped to fortify the bite of the onions and the mellow undertones of the leeks. At last we had a flavorful bowl of soup sporting the rich and layered flavors of a favorite Irish potato dish.

Colcannon Soup

SERVES 4 AS A MAIN COURSE

Other herbs, such as dill or parsley, can be substituted for the chives. A good quality chicken broth is essential to the delicate flavor of this recipe. See page 241 for our recommendations.

3	ounces (about 3 slices) bacon, cut into ½-inch pieces
1	medium onion, minced
1	pound leeks, white and light green parts only, halved lengthwise, sliced thin, and rinsed thoroughly (see the illustrations on the right)
8	ounces green cabbage (about ½ medium head), cored and chopped medium (about 4 cups)
2	medium garlic cloves, minced or pressed through a garlic press (about 2 teaspoons)
2	tablespoons unbleached all-purpose flour
½	cup white wine
4	cups low-sodium chicken broth
12	ounces red potatoes (about 3 medium), cut into ¾-inch chunks
½	cup heavy cream
	Salt and ground black pepper
2	tablespoons minced fresh chives

1. Cook the bacon in a large Dutch oven over medium-low heat until the fat is rendered and the bacon is crisp, 5 to 7 minutes. Transfer the bacon to a paper towel–lined plate, leaving the rendered fat in the pot.

2. Add the onion, leeks, and cabbage to the bacon fat in the Dutch oven and stir to coat. Cover and cook over medium heat until the vegetables are tender, about 10 minutes. Stir in the garlic and cook until fragrant, about 30 seconds. Stir in the flour and cook for about 1 minute.

3. Stir in the wine, scraping up any browned bits, and simmer until it has thickened slightly, about 2 minutes. Stir in the chicken broth and potatoes and bring to a boil. Reduce the heat to a simmer and cook until the potatoes are tender, about 15 minutes.

4. Off the heat, stir in the heavy cream and season with salt and pepper to taste. Portion the soup into individual serving bowls and, before serving, sprinkle with the reserved crumbled bacon and chives.

VARIATION

Colcannon Soup with Kale

Follow the recipe for Colcannon Soup, substituting 1 medium bunch kale (about 1 pound), thick stems trimmed and leaves chopped medium (about 4 cups), for the green cabbage.

PREPARING LEEKS

1. Trim and discard the roots and the dark green leaves.

2. Slice the trimmed leek in half lengthwise, then cut into ½-inch pieces.

3. Rinse the cut leeks thoroughly to remove dirt and sand.

GUINNESS BEEF STEW

A GREAT BEEF STEW REQUIRES LONG HOURS of slow and steady moist-heat cooking to tenderize the meat and marry the flavors of the vegetables and broth. We were determined to develop a robust and flavorful beef stew rich with the malty flavor of Guinness with a minimum of fuss.

First we focused on which cut of beef would work best. We quickly ruled out top and bottom round as too lean because they yielded dry, tough meat when stewed. Our next options were beef chuck and prepackaged beef chunks labeled "stew beef" at the supermarket. The chuck roast, which we cut up ourselves, was flavorful, tender, and juicy. After a few hours of cooking, the "stew beef" meat was either stringy and chewy or just plain bland. The reason for this is simple. Prepackaged stewing beef is often made up of irregularly shaped end pieces from different cuts of meat that can't be sold as steaks or roasts. As a result, they may vary in texture and size and so cook inconsistently, giving you little control over the quality of your final stew.

So with chuck roast as our cut of choice, we began examining a few recipes. Some of the recipes we found simply dumped the beef and vegetables into a pot and skipped the step of browning the beef and sautéing the vegetables first. All the recipes that had skipped this browning step were lackluster, to say the least. The broths were either pale and pasty or flavorless, with the viscosity of dishwater, and the beef in these recipes ranged from tough and dry to tender but flavorless. While we recognized that beef stew has the reputation of being a one-step, one-pot meal, in our estimation these dump-and-cook recipes weren't worth the bother or the expense. We knew that there had to be a better approach. Searing meat takes only minutes and builds the flavor foundation of the stew by leaving caramelized bits on the skillet bottom that can then be incorporated into the stew by a quick deglazing—in our case, with broth and beer. This adds both flavor and valuable color to the stew.

Satisfied that we had a solid beginning for the stew, we turned our attention to the vegetables. Any Irish stew worth its salt contains onions, carrots, and potatoes, and we decided to tackle the potatoes first. We were after a stew that was packed with tender but substantial chunks of potatoes. Russets broke apart by the time the meat was tender and left the stew with a grainy texture. We switched to waxy red potatoes, but ran into a similar problem, this time with crumbly potatoes. We tried adding them whole to the stew and then cutting them up just before serving, but thought this was too much work for a humble stew. The solution? We added cut potatoes to the stew during the final hour of cooking. This worked perfectly, and we found that they cooked through and retained their creaminess and integrity just as the meat was done. This same technique also worked well with the carrots.

Next we focused on the Guinness. With its characteristic malty flavor, Guinness can turn a sauce or stew bitter if used in excess. So we started with three 12-ounce bottles and then gradually worked our way down to just one. The only problem was that the bitterness of the stout still overshadowed the flavors of the root vegetables and the beef. To counteract the bitterness, we tried adding molasses to the stew but found its flavor too strong. Brown sugar proved to be a better choice, adding just enough caramelized sweetness to offset the strong stout. A splash of Guinness at the end of cooking brought the flavor of beer to the surface without dominating the stew. To augment the Guinness and give the stew the right amount of

---

PANTRY SPOTLIGHT

GUINNESS

When shopping for Guinness to make the Guinness Beef Stew, you'll find two options: Guinness Extra Stout (left) and Guinness Draught (right). Straight from the bottle, both beers have their merits. Some tasters praised the "mature, assertive" stout flavors of Guinness Extra Stout while others lauded the "silky smooth" creaminess of the Guinness Draught. But when cooked in the stew, Guinness Draught was the clear winner. Tasters preferred the "clean, toasted taste" of the stew made with Guinness Draught while the stew made with Guinness Extra Stout (although still acceptable) had a slightly "tannic, bitter" aftertaste.

liquid, we added beef broth, but found its flavor left a tinny aftertaste. Switching to chicken broth gave us the meaty flavor we were seeking. To add more complexity to the broth we added rosemary, thyme, and bay leaves in our initial tests. Rosemary tasted far too strong and turned bitter after 2½ hours of cooking, imparting a medicinal flavor to the stew, but thyme and bay leaves held up well and gave us the right degree of herbal flavor.

Our last challenge was to thicken the stew. With a covered pot, moisture from the meat and vegetables is released during the long cooking time and trapped in the enclosed environment. The potatoes lent some of their starch, but the stew still needed further thickening. Previous testing had

shown us that stews thickened with cornstarch had an unappealing slippery texture, and tasters generally preferred stews thickened with flour. After a few attempts, we finally landed on 3 tablespoons of flour mixed into the sautéed onions and garlic to thicken the stew to the proper consistency. Once we brought the stew to a simmer on the stovetop, we transferred it to the oven to gently cook through for one hour.

The resulting stew was a hearty concoction of tender meat, potatoes, and carrots with a full, beefy flavor. The Guinness rounded out the stew with a its slight hint of malt. After much testing, we had achieved a beef stew redolent of the Irish kitchen and one of our favorite stouts.

EQUIPMENT: Dutch Ovens

A large Dutch oven is one of the most useful pieces of cookware you can own, and it's virtually essential to preparing braised dishes and stews. By definition, a Dutch oven is nothing more than a wide, deep pot with a cover. Originally, they were constructed of heavyweight cast iron and designed to be set directly in an open fire and buried beneath coals. An entire meal could be cooked in this fashion, from soup to roast and even dessert. We have come far from those early days, and now that every household has an oven, Dutch ovens are primarily used for dishes that start on the stovetop and finish in moderate heat in the oven. As for the curious name, it traces back hundreds of years to a time when the highest-quality cast iron came from Holland. While you can still find a cast-iron Dutch oven close to the original style (which held its own in testing), we wanted to find the very best and put a dozen models of varying prices and construction through their paces.

First off, we found that a Dutch oven should have a capacity of at least 6 quarts to be useful. Eight quarts is even better. As we cooked in the pots, we came to prefer wider, shallower Dutch ovens because it's easier to see and reach inside them, and they offer more bottom surface area to accommodate larger batches of meat for browning. This reduces the number of batches required to brown a given quantity of meat and therefore reduces the chances of burning the flavorful pan drippings. Ideally, the diameter of a Dutch oven is twice as great as its height.

We also preferred pots with a light-colored interior finish, such as stainless steel or enameled cast iron. It is easier to judge

the caramelization of the drippings at a glance in these pots. Dark finishes can mask the color of the drippings, which may burn before you realize it. Our favorite pot is the 8-quart All-Clad Stainless Stockpot (despite the name, this pot is a Dutch oven). The 7-quart Le Creuset Round French Oven, which is made of enameled cast iron, also tested well. These pots are quite expensive, costing in excess of $200, even on sale. A less expensive alternative is the Chefmate Round Enameled Cast Iron Casserole for Target, costing an affordable $39.99, and the Mario Batali Italian Essentials Pot by Copco, a little pricier at $99.99. The old school–style 7-quart Lodge Dutch Oven, which is made from cast iron and retails for $39.99 is extremely heavy (a whopping 17 pounds), making it a bit hard to maneuver. It must be seasoned (wiped with oil) regularly, and the dark interior finish is not ideal, but it does brown food quite well.

THE BEST DUTCH OVENS

Our favorite pot is the 8-quart All-Clad Stainless Stockpot (left). Despite the name, this pot is a Dutch oven. Expect to spend over $200 for this piece of cookware. A less expensive alternative is the Chefmate Round Enameled Cast Iron Casserole for Target (right), which costs about $39.99. Although, the cooking surface in this pot is smaller and its capacity is 5 quarts, it has steady, even heating and a tight-fitting lid that retains moisture well.

Guinness Beef Stew

SERVES 6 TO 8

There is a lot of fat and gristle to trim away from a chuck roast, so don't be surprised if you trim off up to 1½ pounds. We prefer the flavor of Guinness Draught in this stew (with Guinness Extra Stout a close second), but you can substitute another brand of stout or a dark ale, such as Rogue Chocolate Stout or Newcastle Brown Ale.

1	boneless beef chuck roast (3 to 3½ pounds), trimmed and cut into 1½-inch chunks
	Salt and ground black pepper
3	tablespoons vegetable oil
2	medium onions, minced
1	tablespoon tomato paste
2	medium garlic cloves, minced or pressed through a garlic press (about 2 teaspoons)
3	tablespoons unbleached all-purpose flour
1½	cups low-sodium chicken broth
1	(12-ounce) bottle (about 1½ cups) Guinness Draught (see note)
1	tablespoon minced fresh thyme leaves, or 1 teaspoon dried
2	bay leaves
1	tablespoon dark brown sugar
1½	pounds Red Bliss potatoes (about 5 medium), scrubbed and cut into 1½-inch chunks
1	pound carrots, parsnips, or a combination, peeled and cut into 1-inch chunks
2	tablespoon minced fresh parsley leaves

1. Adjust an oven rack to the lower-middle position and heat the oven to 325 degrees. Pat the beef dry with paper towels and season with salt and pepper. Heat 1 tablespoon of the oil in a large Dutch oven over medium-high heat until just smoking. Add half of the meat and cook, stirring occasionally, until well browned, 7 to 10 minutes, reducing the heat if the pot begins to scorch. Transfer the browned beef to a medium bowl. Repeat with 1 more tablespoon oil and the remaining beef; transfer the meat to the bowl.

2. Add the remaining tablespoon oil to the pot and return to medium heat until shimmering. Add the onions and ¼ teaspoon salt and cook, stirring occasionally, until softened, 5 to 7 minutes. Stir in the tomato paste and garlic and cook until fragrant, about 30 seconds. Stir in the flour and cook for about 1 minute.

3. Stir in the broth and 1¼ cups of the beer, scraping up any browned bits. Stir in the thyme, bay leaves, brown sugar, and browned beef with any accumulated juices. Bring to a simmer, cover, and transfer to the oven for 1 hour.

4. Stir the potatoes and carrots into the stew and continue to cook in the oven, covered, until the beef and vegetables are tender, about 1 hour. Discard the bay leaves, stir in the remaining ¼ cup beer, and season with salt and pepper to taste. Stir in the parsley before serving.

MEAT AND ONION TURNOVERS

Forfar Bridies

INDIVIDUAL PASTRY TURNOVERS FILLED WITH minced beef and onions are popular across the United Kingdom. Eaten out of hand—no fork and knife required—they make a perfect option for lunch or with a salad, a light supper. In fact, coal miners often packed meat pies for lunch. In Scotland, the pies are called Forfar bridies, supposedly in honor of a bride and her wedding party from the town of Forfar at the turn of the nineteenth century. In England's Cornwall, they're called Cornish pasties and the filling often includes potatoes, turnips, or other root vegetables along with meat. Originally, the turnovers sported a thick, braided edge, which was used as a handle by coal miners, who weren't able to come out of the mines to wash up before eating. The turnover's edges, covered with coal dust, could simply be discarded. So what makes a good meat turnover? The pastry should be sturdy enough to contain the filling, but not heavy. And the filling should be well seasoned and moist, not dry or greasy. We set out to develop the best recipe for this simple, but hearty treat.

We started with our dough. We first tried our classic pie dough, cutting cold fat into flour and adding ice water until a dough formed. This method produces a pastry that bakes up with tender flakiness. Too tender, it turned out for these hand-sized turnovers. The pies crumbled in our hands as we tried to eat them. We needed a sturdier dough. Upon reviewing several recipes for meat turnovers, we found that indeed there was a difference. Classic pie dough contains about 2 parts flour to 1 part fat. And one round of pie dough usually contains a small amount of water—a few tablespoons. But the pastry doughs in the meat turnover recipes all used less fat and more water—a lot more water. We cut back on our fat, increased the water, and came out with a dough that was sturdy without being heavy. We then went back to refine the flavor of the dough, which is found in the fat. We tried different combinations of butter and vegetable shortening, and finally decided on an all-butter crust. Tasters preferred the flavor of butter with the meat filling, finding that the dough made with shortening was a bit greasy and heavy. With our crust down, we moved on to the filling.

We began our filling testing with the meat. We made batches of turnovers using 85 percent ground beef and 90 percent ground beef. While both batches had good beef flavor and moisture content, the 85 percent was deemed a bit too greasy for tasters, so we settled on 90 percent ground beef.

With the beef basics in place, we were able to focus our attention on boosting the flavor of the filling. We started by sautéing aromatics (minced onion and garlic) in vegetable oil, then we added the beef and cooked it until browned. We drained the mixture of the fat, fearing it would make our pastry soggy, then added the spices, a combination of nutmeg and dry mustard, followed by fresh thyme and a shot of Worcestershire sauce—all traditional seasonings. This wasn't a bad first attempt, but it wasn't great. Tasters remarked that the filling needed more flavor and moisture.

For our next attempt, we substituted butter for the vegetable oil, increased the garlic from one clove to three, and upped the thyme from 2 teaspoons to 1 tablespoon. We also fiddled with our method. For starters, we would not drain the beef of fat. We began by melting the butter, then added the beef, onion, garlic, and thyme (which was previously added toward the end of cooking) and cooked the mixture all together until browned. Not only did the mixture stay moist, but the flavors melded together better. When the beef was cooked through, we added the spices and the Worcestershire sauce as before. We had made some ground, but despite our efforts, the filling was still dry. The ideal filling should contain meat moistened with enough gravy to bind it together, but not as much as is found in a stew—after all, these turnovers are meant to be eaten out of hand.

Realizing that adding a small amount of sauce to the mixture was the only way to improve matters, we adjusted our recipe again. After browning the

CUTTING AND FILLING MEAT AND ONION TURNOVERS

1. Line 2 baking sheets with parchment. Roll 1 disk of dough into a 15-inch square on a lightly floured work surface. Using a 6-inch bowl or plate as a guide, cut out 4 rounds with a paring knife. Transfer the rounds to a parchment–lined baking sheet. Repeat with the second disk of dough.

2. Place a generous ¼ cup of the cooled filling in the center of each round. Wet the edges of the round with water and fold the dough in half over the filling, pressing with your thumb to seal the dough.

3. Crimp the sealed edge of the turnover with your thumb and forefinger.

beef mixture, we stirred in a tablespoon of flour along with the spices (the flour made a quick roux with the beef fat and butter), followed by ¼ cup of beer. We'd tried both chicken and beef broths, but they were just too bland. And wine tasted out of place. Beer, with its hoppy flavor and mild acidity, perfectly complemented the meaty mixture. In addition, we poured in ¼ cup heavy cream—an untraditional ingredient, but one that contributed richness, flavor, and a velvety texture. Our sauce coated the beef just as we'd hoped, without leaving it soupy.

Shaping and filling the turnovers proved to be an easy task. We cut out rounds of dough using a plate as a template (you can also use a bowl with an equal diameter). After spooning the filling into the center of the rounds, we simply folded the dough over, using water to help seal the pastry and crimped the edges.

A brush of egg wash, and a couple of adjustments to the oven temperature were all we needed to give these meat turnovers a crispy, golden crust. The filling was rich, moist, and piping hot—and tasters were lining up for seconds.

Meat and Onion Turnovers
Forfar Bridies
MAKES 8 TURNOVERS

If your kitchen is very warm, refrigerate all of the dough ingredients for 30 minutes before making the dough. There should be plenty of dough to cut out and make 8 turnovers without having to reroll any dough scraps; we found the rerolled scraps of dough to be very tough. These turnovers are as good at room temperature as they are hot out of the oven.

PASTRY

3¾	cups (18¾ ounces) unbleached all-purpose flour, plus extra for the work surface
1	tablespoon sugar
1½	teaspoons salt
12	tablespoons (1½ sticks) unsalted butter, cut into ½-inch cubes and chilled
1¼	cups ice water

MEAT FILLING

2	tablespoons unsalted butter
1	pound (90 percent lean) ground beef
1	medium onion, minced
3	medium garlic cloves, minced or pressed through a garlic press (about 1 tablespoon)
1	tablespoon minced fresh thyme leaves
	Salt and ground black pepper
1	teaspoon dried mustard
¼	teaspoon ground nutmeg
1	tablespoon unbleached all-purpose flour
¼	cup dark beer, such as Newcastle Brown Ale
¼	cup heavy cream
2	teaspoons Worcestershire sauce
1	large egg, beaten

1. FOR THE PASTRY: Process the flour, sugar, and salt together in a food processor until combined, about 4 pulses. Scatter the butter pieces over the flour mixture and pulse until the mixture resembles coarse cornmeal with butter bits no larger than small peas, about 16 pulses.

2. Transfer the flour mixture to a large mixing bowl. Working with ¼ cup of water at a time, sprinkle the water over the flour mixture and stir it in using a rubber spatula, pressing the mixture against the side of the bowl to form a dough, until no small bits of flour remain (you may not need to use all of the water).

3. Turn the dough out onto a clean work surface and divide it into 2 equal pieces. Press each dough half into a cohesive ball then flatten the ball into a 6-inch disk. Wrap each disk in plastic and refrigerate until firm, about 1 hour.

4. FOR THE FILLING: Melt the butter in a 12-inch skillet over medium-high heat. Add the ground beef, onion, garlic, and thyme, and season with salt and pepper. Cook, breaking the meat up with a wooden spoon, until the meat is no longer pink, about 5 minutes. Stir in the mustard, nutmeg, and flour and cook until fragrant, about 1 minute. Stir in the beer and bring to a simmer. Stir in the cream and simmer until the thickened, about 1 minute. Off the heat, stir in the Worcestershire sauce and season with salt and pepper to taste.

Transfer the beef mixture to a bowl and place it in the refrigerator to cool.

5. Line 2 baking sheets with parchment paper; set aside. Remove 1 disk of dough from the refrigerator. Roll the dough out on a lightly floured work surface into a 15-inch square about ⅛ inch thick. Following the illustrations on page 90, cut out four 6-inch rounds with a paring knife using a bowl or plate as a template. Transfer the rounds to a prepared baking sheet, discarding the dough scraps. Cover the dough rounds with plastic wrap and refrigerate; repeat with the remaining round of dough and prepared baking sheet.

6. Adjust an oven rack to the middle position and heat the oven to 425 degrees. Working with the first batch of dough rounds, follow the illustrations on page 90 to fill, shape, seal, and crimp the pies using a generous ¼ cup of the chilled filling per pie; repeat with the remaining dough rounds and filling. Brush the pies with the egg and arrange on a single baking sheet lined with a fresh sheet of parchment paper. Bake until golden brown, 25 to 30 minutes, rotating the tray halfway through the baking time. Cool for 5 minutes, or cool to room temperature, before serving. (Once cooled, the baked turnovers can be refrigerated in a zipper-lock bag for up to 2 days; return to room temperature before serving.)

FISH AND CHIPS

TAKE A TRIP TO LONDON AND YOU'LL INEVITABLY join the throngs queuing up at the storefront shops for England's most famous fast food: batter-dipped fried fish, dumped onto a mound of fried potatoes and doused with malt vinegar. But when the food arrives, your attitude about fried fish and chips will be forever changed. Unlike any fried fish platter you've ever ordered from a seaside shack (usually smallish strips dredged in seasoned flour), these are large pieces of thick cod that are moist, delicate, and still steaming inside a crisp and tender coating. And, unlike fast-food fries, the "chips" are cut thick and served up crispy, with soft interiors.

With fish-and-chip shops on every corner, most Britons wouldn't bother with the hassle and mess of deep-frying fish at home. But if we wanted to re-create the taste of an authentic London experience stateside, we had no other choice, given the thick, bready versions found in American pubs. Along the way, we needed to figure out some way to fry enough fish and potatoes for four in one pot of oil, yet get everything on the table at once. A few recipes suggested frying the potatoes in batches before cooking the fish, but by the time the food got to the table, everything was tired and greasy, including us.

Unsure how to resolve this logistical challenge, we decided to focus first on developing a recipe for a batter that would perform two important functions. First, protection: A piece of plain fish dropped into hot oil overcooks almost instantly. While a coating of flour or bread crumbs provides a modicum of defense, a wet batter is the best defense of all because it completely coats the delicate fish, allowing it to steam gently in its own moisture. Second, taste: The batter must form an appetizing coating that provides textural contrast with the moist fish.

In the bulk of the cookbook recipes we surveyed, the batter (usually a 50/50 mix of flour and beer) excelled at the first task and flunked the second. The fish came out moist, but the coatings were bready and thick. Worse, as the fried fish drained on paper towels, it continued to produce steam. The thick coating trapped and absorbed the moisture, and minutes later the soggy crust was falling off the fish. We tried thinning the batter with more beer, so that less steam would be trapped, but that brought on new problems. The liquid in the batter itself began to boil almost immediately upon hitting the oil, and the coating failed to survive this initial explosion of steam.

If we couldn't thin the batter, perhaps we could simply adjust its structure. The obvious culprit behind the bready texture was gluten, the protein that gives bread its structure and is produced when any wheat flour is mixed with water. What if we replaced some of the all-purpose flour with a starch that doesn't develop gluten? Sure enough, testing various amounts and combinations of rice flour, corn meal, and cornstarch led us to a 3 to 1 ratio of flour to cornstarch. It was our best batter yet: a thinner (but not wetter) mixture that survived the hot oil and fried up light and crisp. Finally, a tea-spoon of baking powder created tiny bubbles in the batter, giving the coating a lighter, airier texture. (The bubbles in the beer accomplished a similar effect; the baking powder simply enhanced it.)

One problem lingered: While the texture of the coating was great, it had a tendency to puff away from the fish as it fried, ultimately flaking off in large pieces with the first bite. We had been dry-ing the fish well and dredging the pieces in flour before battering—basic deep-frying techniques meant to stop this from happening—but it was still a problem. Then we recalled that when chicken is deep-fried the pieces are usually dredged twice to create a sturdy, crunchy coating. We tried spreading extra flour on a baking sheet and, after dredging and battering each piece, we gently coated the fish with flour again. Success! The resulting coating had a slightly crumbly, irregular texture that clung tightly to the fish. A bit of cayenne for spice and paprika for color finished the deal. Now for the chips.

A recipe developed years ago in the test kitchen confirmed what any restaurant line cook knows well: The best fries are cooked twice. They're "blanched" in relatively low-temperature oil, to cook the centers evenly, then finished in hotter oil just before serving to crisp the outsides to a golden brown. Because we were trying to re-create thicker, English-style "chips," we presumed that initial blanching step would be even more vital. Our plan was to blanch the fries, turn up the heat on the oil and fry the fish, then keep the fish warm while we finished cooking the fries.

Not much went right with this plan. To serve four people, we had to cook a fairly large batch of potatoes, and that meant blanching them off in two batches. All in all, we spent almost an hour hovering over a pot of bubbling oil, after which the kitchen was a splattered mess and we had no appetite left for fried anything. Even if we could stand it, the oil couldn't. Frying oil degrades with each use, absorbing water from the food and losing its ability to make things crisp.

Recently, a colleague had developed a recipe for skillet potatoes (see Potatoes Lyonnaise on page 160), which involved first parcooking sliced potatoes in a microwave oven. Could we parcook the fries this way as well, to get rid of most of the excess water before the potatoes hit the oil? Yes, but if microwaved too long (until completely tender), the thick fries began to crumble and fall apart. They would have to finish blanching in the oil, but only for a few minutes. With this head start, the total fry-ing time was cut by more than half, which meant that the oil was still in fine shape to fry the fish.

The blanched, cooled fries went back into the oil while the fried fish spent five minutes draining on paper towels. The fries emerged hot and crispy just a few minutes later. This patchwork method—alter-nating the fish and the fries—was both quick and easy, and it resulted in fish and chips that were done in perfect sync. Finally, we had a recipe to keep us satisfied until our next trip across the Atlantic.

PREPARING POTATOES FOR FISH AND CHIPS

  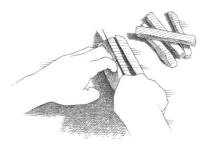

1. Trim each end. Carefully cut a thin slice from one side. Rotate the potato, and repeat with the remaining sides.

2. Cut each potato lengthwise into ½-inch slices.

3. Cut each potato slice into ½-inch batons.

Fish and Chips

SERVES 4

It's fish and chips, not fish then chips. To avoid the latter, we crafted a careful sequence of steps that also minimizes kitchen mess. The oil will bubble up when you add the fries, so be sure you have at least 5 inches of room at the top of the pot. Any beer (even nonalcoholic beers) will work in this recipe, with the exception of dark stouts and porters. If you have room in your refrigerator, air-dry the fish pieces, uncovered, on a wire rack set over a rimmed baking sheet while you prepare the batter and parcook the potatoes. Otherwise, make sure to pat the fish dry just before dredging and battering. Serve with traditional malt vinegar or tartar sauce.

3	pounds russet potatoes (about 4 large), peeled, ends and sides squared off, and cut lengthwise into ½-inch by ½-inch batons following the illustrations on page 93
3	quarts plus ¼ cup peanut, canola, or vegetable oil
1½	cups unbleached all-purpose flour
½	cup cornstarch
½	teaspoon cayenne pepper
½	teaspoon paprika
2	teaspoons salt
⅛	teaspoon ground black pepper
I	teaspoon baking powder
1½	cups (12 ounces) cold beer
1½	pounds cod or other thick white fish fillet, cut into six 3-ounce pieces about I inch thick, dried well (see note)

1. Toss the potatoes with ¼ cup of the oil in a large microwave-proof bowl, cover tightly with plastic wrap, and microwave on high power until the potatoes are partially translucent and pliable but still offer some resistance when pierced with the tip of a paring knife, 6 to 8 minutes, tossing them halfway through cooking. Being careful of the scalding steam, carefully remove the plastic wrap and drain the potatoes into a large mesh strainer. Rinse the potatoes well under cold running water. Spread the potatoes onto clean, dry kitchen towels and gently pat dry. Let the potatoes cool to room temperature, at least 10 minutes or up to 1 hour.

2. Meanwhile, whisk the flour, cornstarch, cayenne, paprika, salt, and pepper together in a large bowl; transfer ¾ cup of the flour mixture to a rimmed baking sheet. Whisk the baking powder into the bowl and set aside.

3. When the potatoes are cool, heat 2 more quarts of oil over medium heat in a large Dutch oven to 350 degrees. Add half of the potatoes, increase the heat to high, and cook, stirring often, until the potatoes turn light golden and just begin to brown at the corners, 3 to 5 minutes. Using a wire mesh spider or slotted spoon, transfer the potatoes to a thick paper bag or triple thickness of paper towels to drain. Return the oil to 350 degrees and repeat with the remaining potatoes; transfer to the bag to drain.

4. Add the remaining quart of oil to the pot and return to 375 degrees over medium-high heat. Meanwhile, dredge the fish through the flour mixture on the baking sheet, shaking off any excess, and transfer to a wire rack. Whisk 1¼ cups of the beer into the bowl of flour mixture until just combined (the mixture will be lumpy). Whisk in the remaining beer, 1 tablespoon at a time, until the batter falls from the whisk in a thin, steady stream and leaves a faint trail across the surface of the batter. Working with 1 piece of fish at a time, use tongs to dip the fish into the batter, let the excess batter run off, then return the fish to the baking sheet with flour mixture and turn to coat thoroughly. Repeat with the remaining fish, keeping the pieces in a single layer on the baking sheet.

5. When the oil reaches 375 degrees, increase the heat to high and add the battered fish using tongs, gently shaking off any excess flour. Fry the fish, stirring occasionally to prevent sticking, until golden brown, 6 to 8 minutes. Transfer the fried fish to a brown paper bag or triple thickness of paper towels to drain.

6. Return the oil to 375 degrees over high heat, add the potatoes, and fry until golden brown and crisp, about 3 minutes. Transfer the potatoes to a fresh paper bag or paper towels to drain. Season with salt to taste and serve immediately with the fish.

ROASTED RACK OF LAMB WITH WHISKEY SAUCE

LAMB AND WHISKEY ARE A NATURAL PAIRING; the slightly bracing, smoky flavor of whiskey is a perfect counterpoint to rich, ultra-tender rack of lamb. Like other simple but immensely satisfying dishes (roast chicken comes to mind), there's nothing to cooking lamb, except that there's no disguising imperfection. You want the meat to be perfectly pink and juicy, the outside intensely browned to boost flavor and provide contrasting texture, and the fat to be well enough rendered to encase the meat in a thin, crisp, brittle shell. And the accompanying sauce should heighten the flavor of the lamb and not disguise it.

With all of this in mind, we set out to find a foolproof way to roast this extravagant cut and build a whiskey sauce using its drippings. A traditional jus is easy to make from pan drippings if your butcher gives you bones from butchering and trimming the rack. But you don't get bones if you buy a rack from a supermarket or one that's been vacuum-sealed, and two racks on their own, cooked only to medium-rare, just don't produce enough jus for four people. We had to figure out a new way to make the sauce.

Starting with the lamb, we explored several cooking methods. Since good exterior caramelization is critical to the taste of any roasted meat, we needed to find out whether the rack would brown adequately in the oven or would need to first be browned on top of the stove. We hoped for the former; we like the ease of simply sliding the rack into the oven. So we decided to test four racks that had been trimmed and frenched (rib bones cleaned of meat and fat for an attractive presentation) at four different temperatures in a preheated oven: 425 degrees, 475 degrees, 500 degrees, and, finally, 200 degrees.

Unfortunately, none of the high oven temperatures gave us the quality of crust we were looking for, even when we preheated the roasting pan.

We knew that the conditions of our remaining test—roasting at 200 degrees—would not make for a nicely browned lamb; the meat wouldn't form a crust at such a low temperature. So we started this test by searing the fat side of the rack in a little vegetable oil in a skillet on top of the stove to get a crust before putting it in a 200-degree oven. The slow-roast technique was a bust: the meat was no more tender than when cooked at a high heat, it had a funny, murky taste and mushy texture that we didn't like, and it took much too long to cook. But the searing technique was terrific. The only refinement we needed was to find a way to brown the strip of eye meat that lies below the bones on the bony side of the rack. After some experimentation we came up with the system of leaning two racks upright one against the other in the pan; this allowed us to brown all parts of the meat before roasting.

Now we went back to testing oven temperatures. Once the racks were seared, we roasted them at 350, 425, and 475 degrees. We ended up taking the middle road. At 425 degrees, the lamb tasted at least as good as (if not better than) it did when cooked at a lower temperature, and there was more room for error than when it cooked at a higher heat.

But now we were running into an unexpected problem. Surprisingly, the racks we were cooking were too fatty. They looked great when they came out of the oven, but once carved the chops were covered with a layer of fat that was browned only on the exterior. Some chops also had a second layer of internal fat, separated by a thin piece of meat, called the cap, that didn't get browned at all. We didn't want to forfeit this little flap of meat (particularly at the price we paid for it), but there seemed no help for it: We needed to get rid of some of the fat. So we trimmed the flap and all the fat underneath it, leaving only a minimal amount at the top of the eye and covering the bones to give the cut its characteristic rounded shape.

The meat tasted great, needing only one final adjustment: We removed the silver skin that we had exposed in trimming the fat. (The silver skin is the pearlescent membrane found on certain cuts of meat. It is very tough and, if not removed, can cause meat to curl during cooking.)

Satisfied with our roasting technique, we were now ready to work on our whiskey sauce. We wanted the sauce to be ready just as soon as the lamb was done, so that we weren't starting from scratch with the pan drippings at the last minute. First we made a separate jus (a very concentrated, reduced stock made with meat, onions, carrots, garlic, and a little water), using lamb stew pieces on the bone bought separately at the supermarket. The jus tasted good, but making it was too much work; we didn't want to complicate a simple meal. So we went back to the pan drippings. If we transferred the rack to a second pan after browning on top of the stove, we could make a pan sauce while the lamb roasted. As it turned out, we got the best results by preheating the roasting pan in the oven so that it was hot when the lamb hit it.

We began our pan sauce by pouring off all but 2 teaspoons of the rendered lamb fat from the pan. To the fat we added two minced shallots and a couple of sprigs of rosemary. We cooked the shallots until lightly browned and added two minced garlic cloves. Next, we added ¼ cup of whiskey to deglaze the pan and scrape up the browned bits from the bottom of the pan. We chose to use Scotch whiskey for its smokiness and delicate sweetness. Once the whiskey had reduced to a mere tablespoon, we added 2½ cups of chicken broth, reduced the mixture to about ⅔ cup, whisked in 2 tablespoons of butter, and tasted.

This first run of sauce turned out flat, with little whiskey flavor and a thinner consistency than we had hoped for. So for subsequent tests we experimented with beef broth to give the sauce more meatiness, but tasters ultimately preferred chicken broth because it allowed the flavor of the lamb to come through. Next, we played with whiskey amounts, adding as much as 1 cup (think Molotov cocktail), and finally settling on ½ cup, with a tablespoon added at the end to fortify the whiskey flavor. To thicken the sauce, we added a teaspoon of flour to the shallots and garlic about 1 minute before stirring in the whiskey. This gave

the sauce body and allowed it to stick to the lamb when spooned over top. Finally, to brighten the sauce we finished it with a squeeze of fresh lemon and chopped parsley. The improved sauce matched perfectly with the lamb, and most importantly, the sauce was ready just as the lamb finished resting.

PREPARING RACK OF LAMB

1. Using a boning or paring knife, scrape the ribs clean of any scraps of meat or fat.

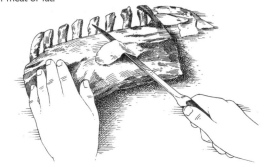

2. Trim off the outer layer of fat, the flap of meat underneath it, and the fat underneath that flap.

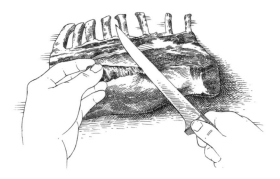

3. Remove the silver skin by sliding the boning knife between the silver skin and the flesh.

Roasted Rack of Lamb with Whiskey Sauce

SERVES 4

Have your butcher french the racks (remove excess fat from the rib bones) for you; inevitably, the ribs will need some cleaning up, but at least the bulk of the work will be done (see page 96 for more information on cleaning lamb racks). So that the timing of the lamb and whiskey sauce match up, have all the ingredients for the sauce ready before cooking the lamb. We preferred Scotch whiskey for its smokiness, but Irish or American whiskey can be substituted. Note that the whiskey may flame in step 5; simply remove the skillet from the heat and gently shake the skillet back and forth until the flames subside before continuing with the recipe as directed.

2	(8- or 9-rib) racks of lamb (1¼ to 1½ pounds each), rib bones frenched and meat trimmed of fat and silver skin
	Salt and ground black pepper
2	tablespoons vegetable oil
2	medium shallots, minced
2	sprigs fresh rosemary
2	medium garlic cloves, minced or pressed through a garlic press (about 2 teaspoons)
1	teaspoon unbleached all-purpose flour
½	cup plus 1 tablespoon Scotch whiskey
2½	cups low-sodium chicken broth
2	tablespoons unsalted butter, cut into 2 pieces
2	tablespoons minced fresh parsley leaves
1	teaspoon juice from 1 lemon

1. Adjust an oven rack to the lower-middle position, place a roasting pan lined with aluminum foil on the rack, and heat the oven to 425 degrees.

2. Pat the lamb dry with paper towels and season with salt and pepper. Heat the oil in a 12-inch skillet over medium high heat until just smoking. Place the lamb racks, meat side down, in the center of the skillet with the ribs facing outward. Cook until well browned, about 4 minutes. Using tongs, stand the racks up in the skillet, leaning them against each other for support, and brown the bottoms, about 2 minutes.

3. Transfer the lamb to the roasting pan in the oven and roast until an instant-read thermometer inserted into the center of each rack registers about 125 degrees for medium-rare or 130 degrees for medium, 12 to 15 minutes. Transfer the lamb to a carving board, tent loosely with aluminum foil, and let rest for 5 to 10 minutes.

4. While the lamb is roasting and resting, pour off all but 2 teaspoons of the fat left in the skillet and return to medium heat until shimmering. Add the shallots and rosemary and cook until the shallots are softened, about 2 minutes. Stir in the garlic and cook until fragrant, about 30 seconds. Stir in the flour and cook for 1 minute.

5. Off the heat, add the ½ cup whiskey and let sit about a minute. (The mixture will bubble.) Carefully return the skillet to medium heat and simmer until the whiskey almost completely evaporates, 3 to 5 minutes. (Note that there is a slight chance that the whiskey may begin to flame; simply remove the skillet from the heat and gently shake the skillet back and forth until the flames subside before continuing.) Stir in the chicken broth and continue to simmer until the mixture is slightly thickened and measures about ⅔ cup, 8 to 10 minutes.

6. Discard the rosemary sprigs and stir in any accumulated lamb juices. Turn the heat to low and whisk in the butter, one piece at a time. Off the heat, stir in the remaining tablespoon of whiskey, parsley, and lemon juice and season with salt and pepper to taste; transfer the sauce to a bowl or sauce boat. Cut the lamb racks into individual chops by slicing between each rib. Serve immediately with the whiskey sauce.

BROWNING RACKS OF LAMB

To achieve a good crust on a rack of lamb, brown it on both sides on top of the stove before placing it in the oven in a preheated roasting pan. Start by placing 2 racks in a hot pan with the meat in the center and the ribs facing outward (left). After the meat is browned, stand the racks up in the pan and lean them against each other to brown the bottoms (right).

SHEPHERD'S PIE

NOTHING MORE THAN A RICH LAMB STEW blanketed under a mashed-potato crust, shepherd's pie is a hearty casserole originally from northern Britain. Popular on the American table, it is best eaten on a blustery winter day while sidled up to a roaring fire. It's arguably America's favorite lamb dish.

Shepherd's pie was a meal traditionally made on Monday with Sunday night's leftovers—the remnants of the roast, vegetables, and mashed potatoes. In this day and age, few of us have such delicious Sunday dinners, much less leftovers, so we aimed to create an assertively flavored, but simple to prepare shepherd's pie from scratch.

Our first step was to figure out which cut of lamb worked best. To save on prep time, we hoped to use ground lamb. Shepherd's pie made with ground lamb was pretty good, but a bit bland, so we had to figure out how to heighten the flavor. We added a bit of tomato paste to bring out the sweeter meaty tones and then a dash of Worcestershire sauce to bring forth the lamb's more subtle flavors.

With the basic lamb flavors adequately elevated, we turned to choosing vegetables to complement the lamb. This proved easy. Sautéed onions added sweetness and depth, while a touch of garlic added a little zest. And sweet carrots and frozen peas—characteristic of many British-style meat stews—brought bright color to an otherwise drab-looking dish.

For herbs, we wanted big flavors strong enough to stand up to the lamb's richness. Rosemary and thyme are traditional lamb flavorings, and they tasted great in this instance. Fresh, not dried, herbs provided the best flavor.

As for the liquid in the stew, we settled on chicken broth enriched with red wine. Beef broth clashed with the lamb's earthy flavors, while chicken broth was neutral. After testing a variety of red wines, we liked a medium-bodied red wine best, such as a Côtes du Rhône, because it is well rounded and low in tannins—traits that allow it to marry well with the rich flavors in the dish.

With the stew assembled and cooked, we were ready to top it off with a mashed-potato crust. We quickly found out that simple mashed potatoes would not do; they crumbled and broke down while baking. We started our adjustments by reducing the amount of butter and dairy we usually add to mashed potatoes, so that when we placed them on top of the lamb sauce they would stay there instead of sinking into the lamb mixture. Also, we found that using heavy cream, rather than milk, produced a sturdier, less weepy, mashed-potato topping.

Assembling was as easy as pouring the filling into a deep-dish pie plate. A large rubber spatula was the best tool for spreading the potatoes evenly across the top of the stew. We found that it was important to completely cover the stew and seal the edges of the dish with the potato topping; otherwise the stew sometimes bubbled out of the dish.

Because the lamb is already tender when it goes into the casserole, the baking time is short. Once the potato crust begins to turn golden brown, the shepherd's pie is ready to come out of the oven.

Shepherd's Pie

SERVES 4 TO 6

You will need to use a shallow casserole dish with a 2- to 2½-quart capacity, such as an 11 by 7-inch baking dish, an oval casserole, or a 9- or 10-inch deep-dish pie plate (carefully measure its volume first; some pie plates are not deep enough). The lamb drippings intensify the lamb flavor, but if you prefer a less intense lamb flavor you can substitute 2 tablespoons of vegetable oil for the reserved lamb drippings in step 2. To add a little color, sprinkle the dish with some minced parsley before serving.

1½	pounds ground lamb
1	medium onion, minced
2	medium carrots, peeled and sliced ¼ inch thick
	Salt
2	medium garlic cloves, minced or pressed through a garlic press (about 2 teaspoons)
1	tablespoon tomato paste

¼   cup unbleached all-purpose flour

1¾   cups low-sodium chicken broth

¼   cup dry red wine

1   teaspoon Worcestershire sauce

1   teaspoon minced fresh thyme leaves,
      or ¼ teaspoon dried

1   teaspoon minced fresh rosemary leaves,
      or ¼ teaspoon dried

1   cup frozen peas, thawed
      Ground black pepper

2   pounds russet potatoes (about 4 medium),
      peeled and sliced ¾ inch thick

2   tablespoons unsalted butter, softened

½   cup heavy cream, warmed

1. Adjust an oven rack to the middle position and heat the oven to 450 degrees. Cook the lamb in a Dutch oven over medium-high heat, breaking the meat up with a wooden spoon, until the meat is no longer pink and the fat has rendered, about 5 minutes. Drain the lamb in a fine-mesh strainer set over a bowl to reserve the drippings.

2. Return 2 tablespoons of the reserved lamb drippings to the pot and heat over medium-low heat until shimmering. Add the onion, carrots, and ½ teaspoon salt and cook until softened and lightly browned, 7 to 10 minutes. Stir in the garlic and tomato paste and cook until fragrant, about 30 seconds. Stir in the flour and cook until incorporated, about 1 minute. Whisk in the chicken broth and wine, scraping up any browned bits, until the sauce is smooth. Stir in the reserved lamb, Worcestershire, thyme, and rosemary and cook until the mixture begins to thicken, about 2 minutes. Off the heat, stir in the peas and season with salt and pepper to taste. Transfer the mixture into a 2- to 2½-quart baking dish and set aside.

3. Meanwhile, cover the potatoes by 1 inch of water in a large saucepan and add 1 tablespoon salt. Bring to a boil, then reduce to a simmer and cook until the potatoes are tender and a fork can be slipped easily into the center, 10 to 12 minutes. Drain the potatoes, return them to the saucepan over low heat, and mash them to a smooth consistency. Stir in the butter and cream and season with salt and pepper to taste.

4. Following the illustrations below, dollop the mashed potatoes over the lamb filling and smooth into an even layer, making sure they attach to the edges of the casserole dish. (You should not see any filling.) Place the baking dish on a foil-lined baking sheet and bake until the edges are bubbling and the top is lightly browned, about 30 minutes. Cool for 10 minutes before serving.

MAKING A SHEPHERD'S PIE

1. Place the filling in a 2- to 2½-quart shallow casserole dish or pie plate, then drop spoonfuls of the mashed potatoes around the perimeter of the dish.

2. Use a rubber spatula to spread the potatoes out, attaching them to the rim of the pie plate. It's important to seal the edges this way to help prevent the filling from bubbling out of the plate in the oven.

3. Drop the remaining mashed potatoes in the center of the pie plate and then smooth the top with a spatula. Because the topping rises so high, we recommend baking the pie on a rimmed baking sheet (lined with aluminum foil for easy cleanup) to catch any leaks.

IRISH SODA BREAD

AUTHENTIC IRISH SODA BREAD HAS A TENDER, dense crumb and a rough-textured, crunchy crust. It is versatile enough to be served with butter and jam at breakfast, for sandwiches at lunch, or alongside the evening meal.

As we looked over a multitude of recipes for soda bread, we found that they fell into two categories. The American versions contained eggs, butter, and sugar in varying amounts along with caraway seeds, raisins, and many other flavorings. But most Irish cookbooks combined only four ingredients: flour (white and/or whole-wheat), baking soda, salt, and buttermilk.

We decided to begin our investigations with the flour. Because of Ireland's climate, the wheat grown there is a "soft," or low-protein, variety. While not suitable for strong European-style yeast breads, this flour is perfect for chemically leavened breads. This is basically because flour with a lower protein content produces a finer crumb and more tender product, key for breads that don't have the light texture provided when yeast is used as the leavener.

After suffering through several tough, heavy loaves made with unbleached all-purpose flour, we started exploring different proportions of cake flour—a low-protein flour—as well as all-purpose flour. And, in fact, the bread did become more tender

and a little lighter with the addition of some cake flour. As the ratio of cake to all-purpose exceeded 1 to 1, however, the bread became much more compact and heavy, with an undesirable mouthfeel: 1 cup of cake flour to 3 cups of unbleached all-purpose flour proved best.

Because the liquid to dry ingredient ratio is important in determining dough texture and bread moistness, we decided to test buttermilk next. (We also knew that the amount of this acidic liquid would have a direct effect on the amount of baking soda we would be able to use. As mentioned when discussing other recipes, baking soda reacts with acids such as those in buttermilk to provide leavening; however, if there is too much soda, some remains intact in the bread, giving it a slightly metallic taste.) As it turned out, bread made with 1¾ or 1⅔ cups of buttermilk produced bread that was doughy, almost gummy. With 1½ cups, the dough was firmer yet still moist—and the resulting bread was no longer doughy. (If you don't have buttermilk on hand, yogurt can be substituted for an equally delicious bread with a slightly rougher crust and lighter texture.)

With the amount of buttermilk decided upon, we were now ready to explore the amount and type of leavener used. After trying various combinations of baking soda, baking powder, and cream of tartar, we found that 1½ teaspoons of soda, combined with an equal amount of cream of tartar, provided just the right amount of lift for a bread that was light but not airy. Relying on the acidity of cream of tartar (rather than the acidity in the buttermilk) to react with the baking soda allows the tangy buttermilk flavor to come through.

Unfortunately, the flavor of these basic loaves was mediocre at best, lacking depth and dimension, and they were also a bit tough. Traditionally, very small amounts of sugar and/or butter are sometimes added to soda bread, so, starting with sugar, we baked loaves with 1 and with 2 tablespoons. Two tablespoons of sugar added just the flavor balance that was needed without making the bread sweet. It was only with the introduction of butter, though, that the loaves began to lose their toughness and become outstanding. After trying loaves with from 1 to 4 tablespoons of unsalted butter, 2

SCIENCE: A Light Hand

While testing the various ingredients in our Classic Irish Soda Bread, we discovered that the way the dough is handled while you are mixing it is as crucial as the amount and type of leavener used. Because baking soda begins reacting immediately with cream of tartar and does not provide the big second rise you get with double-acting baking powder, it is important to mix the dough quickly and not too vigorously. If you mix too slowly or too enthusiastically, too much carbon dioxide will be formed and will dissipate during the mixing process; not enough will then be produced during baking to provide the proper rise. Extended kneading also overdevelops the gluten in the flour, toughening the bread. It's no wonder that in Ireland a baker who produces a superior loaf of soda bread is traditionally said to have "a light hand," a great compliment.

tablespoons proved a clear winner. This bread was tender but not crumbly, compact but not heavy. More than two tablespoons of butter began to shift the flavor balance of the bread and add unnecessary richness.

We were getting very close to our goal, but the crust was still too hard, thick, and crumbly. In our research, we came upon various techniques for modifying the crust. Some dealt with the way the bread was baked, while others concentrated on how the bread was treated after baking. Trying to inhibit the formation of a thick crust by covering the bread with a bowl during the first 30 minutes of baking helped some, but the resulting bread took longer to bake and was pale and uneven in color. Using a large flowerpot and clay dish to simulate a cloche (a covered earthenware dish specifically designed for baking bread) again gave us a bread that didn't color well, even when we preheated the dish and buttered the dough.

But the next test, which, by no coincidence, closely simulated historical cooking methods for Irish soda bread, was a breakthrough. Baking the loaf in a well-buttered Dutch oven or cast-iron pot, covered only for the first 30 minutes, produced a well-risen loaf with an even, golden crust that was thin and crisp yet still had a bit of chew.

We realized, however, that not everyone has a cast-iron pot available, so we explored ways of softening the crust after baking. Wrapping the bread in a clean tea towel as soon as it emerged from the oven helped soften the crust, while a slightly damp tea towel softened it even more. The best technique, though, was to brush the warm loaf with some melted butter. This gave it an attractive sheen as well as a delicious, buttery crust with just enough crunch. Although we liked the crust of the bread baked in the Dutch oven a little better, the ease of baking it on a baking sheet made the loaf brushed with butter a more practical option.

Finally, make sure that you cool the bread for at least 30 to 40 minutes before serving. If cut when too hot, the bread will be dense and slightly doughy.

INGREDIENTS: Farmhouse Cheddars

Farmhouse cheddar cheese is the centerpiece to a ploughman's or farmer's lunch, a pub favorite that also includes bread (Irish soda bread is great) along with pickles for a simple, hearty lunch. Great farmhouse cheddar is hard, fine-textured, and flaky, with a sharp, tangy edge that's a little sweet, nutty, slightly bitter, and herbaceous. These various flavors come together to create a well-balanced, complex, and rewarding taste experience. Farmhouse cheddar is made by small creameries that start with unpasteurized milk, hand-cheddar the curd (cut the curd by hand and drain it), and then wrap and age the cheese in a cloth. To see just how good these cheeses really are, we organized a tasting, rounding up three farmhouse cheddars from England and one from Vermont. We also included Cabot, our top-ranked supermarket cheddar, for comparison. We tested the cheeses on their own and melted in grilled cheese sandwiches.

With a price range of about $11 to $19 per pound, farmhouse cheddars are not cheap, nor are they widely available. But if you live near a specialty foods or cheese store, we strongly recommend that you try them. Even in the grilled cheese sandwich, all four of the farmhouse cheddars topped Cabot. Whereas Cabot was merely "mellow" and "bland," the farmhouse brands were described as "honey-like," "grassy," and "laced with horseradish." Overall, the farmhouse brands provided a more exciting and enjoyable cheddar experience.

THE BEST FARMHOUSE CHEDDARS

Keen's Farmhouse Cheddar (above) from Somerset, England, was tangy, nutty, and rich at $17.95 for 1 pound, and was the clear favorite among tasters. Burrough's Farmhouse Cheddar, also from Somerset, England, was a close second with its balanced, sharp, and intense flavors for $18.95 per pound. Montgomery's Farmhouse Cheddar hailing from, you guessed it, Somerset, England, was herbaceous, earthy, and sharp and retailed for $17.95 per pound. The outsider, Shelburne Farms Farmhouse Cheddar from Shelburne, Vermont, was $10.95 per pound and delivered a nutty, delicate taste with a texture and flavor similar to Parmigiano-Reggiano.

Classic Irish Soda Bread
MAKES I LOAF

Once cooled, this bread is a great accompaniment to soups or stews, and leftovers make fine toast. With their flavorful grains and additions, the variations can stand alone.

3	cups (15 ounces) lower-protein unbleached all-purpose flour, such as Gold Medal or Pillsbury, plus extra for work surface
I	cup (4 ounces) plain cake flour
2	tablespoons sugar
I½	teaspoons baking soda
I½	teaspoons cream of tartar
I½	teaspoons salt
2	tablespoons unsalted butter, softened, plus I tablespoon melted butter for crust
I½	cups buttermilk

1. Adjust an oven rack to the upper-middle position and heat the oven to 400 degrees. Whisk the flours, sugar, baking soda, cream of tartar, and salt together in a large bowl. Work the softened butter into the dry ingredients with a fork or your fingertips until the texture resembles coarse crumbs.

2. Add the buttermilk and stir with a fork just until the dough begins to come together. Turn out onto a flour-coated work surface; knead just until the dough becomes cohesive and bumpy, 12 to 14 turns. (Do not knead until the dough is smooth or the bread will be tough.)

3. Pat the dough into a round about 6 inches in diameter and 2 inches high; place on a greased or parchment-lined baking sheet. Score the dough by cutting a cross shape on the top of the loaf. (See the illustration below.)

4. Bake until the loaf is golden brown and a skewer inserted into the center comes out clean or the internal temperature reaches 180 degrees, 40 to 45 minutes. Remove the loaf from the oven and brush the surface with the melted butter; cool to room temperature, 30 to 40 minutes.

➤ VARIATIONS
Irish Brown Soda Bread
Unlike the Classic Irish Soda Bread dough, which is dry, this dough is extremely sticky.

I¾	cups (8¾ ounces) lower-protein unbleached all-purpose flour, such as Gold Medal or Pillsbury, plus extra for work surface
I¼	cups (6⅞ ounces) whole wheat flour
½	cup (2 ounces) plain cake flour
½	cup toasted wheat germ
3	tablespoons brown sugar
I½	teaspoons baking soda
I½	teaspoons cream of tartar
I½	teaspoons salt
2	tablespoons unsalted butter, softened, plus I tablespoon melted butter for crust
I½	cups buttermilk

1. Adjust an oven rack to the upper-middle position and heat the oven to 400 degrees. Whisk the flours, wheat germ, brown sugar, baking soda, cream of tartar, and salt together in a large bowl. Work the softened butter into the dry ingredients with a fork or your fingertips until the texture resembles coarse crumbs.

2. Add the buttermilk and stir with a fork just until the dough begins to come together. Turn out onto a flour-coated work surface; knead just until the dough becomes cohesive and bumpy, 12 to 14 turns. (Do not knead until the dough is smooth or the bread will be tough.)

SCORING SODA BREAD

Use a serrated knife to cut a cross shape in the top of the dough. Each score should be 5 inches long and ¾ inch deep.

3. Pat the dough into a round about 6 inches in diameter and 2 inches high; place on a greased or parchment-lined baking sheet. Score the dough by cutting a cross shape on the top of the loaf. (See the illustration on page 102.)

4. Bake until the loaf is golden brown and a skewer inserted into the center comes out clean or the internal temperature reaches 190 degrees, 45 to 55 minutes. Remove the loaf from the oven and brush the surface with the melted butter; cool to room temperature, 30 to 40 minutes.

Oatmeal-Walnut Soda Bread

Most of the oats should be soaked in the buttermilk for an hour before proceeding with this recipe.

2½	cups (7½ ounces) old-fashioned rolled oats
1¾	cups buttermilk
1	cup walnuts
2	cups (10 ounces) lower-protein unbleached all-purpose flour, such as Gold Medal or Pillsbury, plus extra for work surface
½	cup (2 ounces) plain cake flour
½	cup (2¾ ounces) whole wheat flour
¼	cup packed (1¾ ounces) brown sugar
1½	teaspoons baking soda
1½	teaspoons cream of tartar
1½	teaspoons salt
2	tablespoons unsalted butter, softened, plus 1 tablespoon melted butter for crust

1. Place 2 cups of the oats in a medium bowl. Add the buttermilk and soak for 1 hour.

2. Adjust an oven rack to the upper-middle position and heat the oven to 400 degrees. Spread the walnuts on a baking sheet and toast them until fragrant, 5 to 10 minutes. Cool and chop coarsely.

3. Whisk the flours, the remaining ½ cup oats, brown sugar, baking soda, cream of tartar, and salt together in a large bowl. Work the softened butter into the dry ingredients with a fork or your fingertips until the texture resembles coarse crumbs.

4. Add the buttermilk-soaked oats and nuts and stir with a fork just until the dough begins to come together. Turn out onto a flour-coated work surface; knead just until the dough becomes cohesive

and bumpy, 12 to 14 turns. (Do not knead until the dough is smooth or the bread will be tough.)

5. Pat the dough into a round about 6 inches in diameter and 2 inches high; place on a greased or parchment-lined baking sheet. Score the dough by cutting a cross shape on the top of the loaf. (See the illustration on page 102.)

6. Bake until the loaf is golden brown and a skewer inserted into the center comes out clean or the internal temperature reaches 190 degrees, 45 to 55 minutes. Remove the loaf from the oven and brush the surface with the melted butter; cool to room temperature, 30 to 40 minutes.

American-Style Soda Bread with Raisins and Caraway Seeds

Additional sugar and an egg create a sweeter, richer bread.

3	cups (15 ounces) lower-protein unbleached all-purpose flour, such as Gold Medal or Pillsbury, plus extra for the work surface
1	cup (4 ounces) plain cake flour
¼	cup (1¾ ounces) sugar
1½	teaspoons baking soda
1½	teaspoons cream of tartar
1½	teaspoons salt
4	tablespoons (½ stick) unsalted butter, softened, plus 1 tablespoon melted butter for crust
1¼	cups buttermilk
1	large egg, lightly beaten
1	cup raisins
1	tablespoon caraway seeds

1. Adjust an oven rack to the upper-middle position and heat the oven to 400 degrees. Whisk the flours, sugar, baking soda, cream of tartar, and salt together in a large bowl. Work the softened butter into the dry ingredients with a fork or your fingertips until the mixture resembles coarse crumbs.

2. Combine the buttermilk and egg with a fork. Add the buttermilk-egg mixture, raisins, and caraway seeds and stir with a fork just until the dough begins to come together. Turn out onto a flour-coated work surface; knead just until the

dough becomes cohesive and bumpy, 12 to 14 turns. (Do not knead until the dough is smooth or the bread will be tough.)

3. Pat the dough into a round about 6 inches in diameter and 2 inches high; place on a greased or parchment-lined baking sheet. Score the dough by cutting a cross shape on the top of the loaf. (See the illustration on page 102.)

4. Bake, covering bread with aluminum foil if it is browning too much, until the loaf is golden brown and a skewer inserted into the center comes out clean or the internal temperature reaches 170 degrees, 40 to 45 minutes. Remove the loaf from the oven and brush the surface with the melted butter; cool to room temperature, 30 to 40 minutes.

SCONES

SCONES IN AMERICA—UNLIKE THEIR MORE diminutive British counterparts—have the reputation of being thick, heavy, dry bricks. To enhance their appeal, they are often disguised under a sugary shellac of achingly sweet glaze or filled with chopped ginger, chopped fruit, or chocolate chips. Despite these feeble attempts to dress them up, it is no secret that today's coffeehouse confections are a far cry from what a scone should be: tender and flaky, like a slightly sweetened biscuit.

We started our testing by focusing on the flour. We made a composite recipe with bread flour, with all-purpose flour, and with cake flour. The differences in outcome were astonishing. The scones made with bread flour were heavy and tough. The scones made with all-purpose flour were lighter and much more flavorful. Cake flour produced scones that were doughy in the center, with a raw taste and poor texture. Subsequent tests revealed that a lower-protein all-purpose flour, such as Gold Medal or Pillsbury, is better than a higher-protein flour, such as King Arthur.

After trying scones made with butter and with lard, we decided we preferred the rich flavor of butter. (If we made scones commercially, we might reconsider, because day-old scones made with lard hold up better. The preservative effects of different fats, along with lower cost, may be why store-bought scones are often made with margarine or other hydrogenated fats.) Although the amount of solid fat can be varied, we found 5 tablespoons of butter to 2 cups flour to be just right. More butter and the scones will almost melt in the oven. Less butter and the baked scones will be dry and tough.

The choice of liquid can also profoundly affect the flavor of a scone. We tested various liquids and found that cream made the best scones that were tender yet still light. Scones made with milk were bland and dry. Buttermilk gave scones plenty of flavor, but the scone was too flaky and biscuit-like. Scones made with cream were moister and more flavorful than the others.

We tried adding an egg to the dough. We found that it made the scones very cakey. Many tasters liked the effect of the egg. Since the addition of egg helps the scone hold onto moisture and remain fresher longer, we decided to use the egg in a variation called Cakey Scones.

In traditional recipes, one to two tablespoons of sugar is enough to sweeten an entire batch of scones. American scones tend to be far sweeter than the British versions, which are usually served with sweet toppings such as jam. Americans seem to eat their scones like muffins, without anything more than a smear of butter, so the sweetness is baked in. We prefer the British approach but decided to increase the sugar slightly to three tablespoons.

Finally, scones are often glazed to enhance their appearance and add sweetness. We tried brushing the dough with a beaten egg as well as with heavy cream just before baking. Scones brushed with egg can become too dark in the oven. We preferred the more delicate look of scones brushed with cream and then dusted with a little granulated sugar.

Scones can be mixed by hand or with a food processor. (The processor is used to cut fat into flour; minimal hand mixing is required afterward.) We found the food processor to be more reliable than mixing entirely by hand, which can overheat the butter and cause it to soften. Once the dough comes together, we prefer to pat it out onto a floured surface, and then cut it into eight wedges. We find this method easier than using a rolling pin.

Cream Scones with Currants

MAKES 8

The most traditional sweet biscuit-like texture is obtained by using both butter and heavy cream. If you prefer a more cake-like texture, or want the scones to stay fresher longer, try the Cakey Scones variation. The easiest and most reliable approach to mixing the butter into the dry ingredients is to use a food processor fitted with the metal blade. Resist the urge to eat the scones hot out of the oven. Letting them cool for at least 10 minutes firms them up and improves their texture.

2	cups (10 ounces) lower-protein unbleached all-purpose flour, such as Gold Medal or Pillsbury
1	tablespoon baking powder
3	tablespoons sugar
½	teaspoon salt
5	tablespoons cold unsalted butter, cut into ¼-inch cubes
½	cup currants
1	cup heavy cream

1. Adjust an oven rack to the middle position and heat the oven to 425 degrees.

2. Place the flour, baking powder, sugar, and salt in a large bowl or the workbowl of a food processor fitted with the metal blade. Whisk together or process with six 1-second pulses.

3. If making by hand, use two knives, a pastry blender, or your fingertips and quickly cut in the butter until the mixture resembles coarse meal with a few slightly larger butter lumps. If using a food processor, remove the cover and distribute the butter evenly over the dry ingredients. Cover and process with twelve 1-second pulses. Add the currants and quickly mix in or pulse one more time. Transfer the dough to a large bowl.

4. Stir in the heavy cream with a rubber spatula or fork until the dough begins to form, about 30 seconds.

5. Transfer the dough and all dry flour bits to a countertop and knead the dough by hand just until it comes together into a rough, slightly sticky ball, 5 to 10 seconds. Gently pat the dough into a ¾-inch-thick circle and using a bench scraper or chef's knife cut the scones into 8 wedges. Place the wedges on an ungreased baking sheet.

6. Bake until the scone tops are light brown, 12 to 15 minutes. Cool on a wire rack for at least 10 minutes. Serve warm or at room temperature.

VARIATIONS

Glazed Scones

A light cream and sugar glaze gives these scones an attractive sheen and a sweeter flavor. If baking the scones immediately after making the dough, brush the dough just before cutting it into wedges.

Follow the recipe for Cream Scones, brushing the tops of the scones with 1 tablespoon heavy cream and then sprinkling them with 1 tablespoon sugar just before baking them.

Cakey Scones

An egg changes the texture and color and helps these scones stay fresher longer, up to 2 days in an airtight container.

Follow the recipe for Cream Scones, reducing the butter to 4 tablespoons and the cream to ¾ cup. Add 1 large egg, lightly beaten, to the dough along with the cream.

Ginger Scones

Follow the recipe for Cream Scones, substituting ½ cup chopped crystallized ginger for the currants.

Cranberry-Orange Scones

Follow the recipe for Cream Scones, adding 1 teaspoon grated orange zest with the butter and substituting ¾ cup dried cranberries for the currants.

Lemon-Blueberry Scones

Mix the dough by hand after adding the blueberries to keep them plump and whole.

Follow the recipe for Cream Scones, adding 1 teaspoon grated lemon zest with the butter and substituting ½ cup fresh or frozen (not thawed) blueberries for the currants.

OATMEAL SCONES

OATMEAL SCONES CAN BE CONSIDERED THE black sheep of the scone family. Unlike the more feathery white-flour scone, oatmeal scones have the reputation of being dry oddities you might find at a health food market, where texture and taste are not primary concerns.

The first few recipes we tried confirmed our worst fears about oatmeal scones. There were the lean, mean, whole-wheat-flour oatmeal scones, which were gritty and dense, and the dried-fruit-laden oatmeal scones, which were thick like a cookie. Although tasters had different preferences when it came to texture, all agreed on the need for a stronger oat flavor. Our goal, then, was to pack the chewy nuttiness of oats into a moist and tender breakfast pastry, one that wouldn't require a fire hose to wash down the crumbs.

The first hurdle was deciding what type of oats to use. Because they take at least 30 minutes to cook, we quickly ruled out steel-cut oats for this recipe—the baking time of these scones would not be long enough to cook the oats through. The most familiar type seemed to be rolled oats, but we still had two choices: whole (old-fashioned) and quick-cooking. This was not such an easy decision, as each had qualities to recommend it. The flavor of the whole rolled oats was deeper and nuttier (a few tasters even asked if there was peanut butter in the scones) and the smaller, flaked quick-cooking oats had a softer texture, which was considered more palatable by some. We finally decided that either would do.

Next we had to figure out how to pack in the most oat flavor without sacrificing the texture of the scones. We were sure we could achieve this by simply processing the oats into the flour. But instead, the texture was horrible, very gluey and dense. We even tried adding real oat flour (found mostly in health foods stores) along with the all-purpose flour, but the same gumminess resulted. Waving our white flag, we attributed this failure to the fact that oat flour does not have any gluten. Without gluten, it had nothing to contribute to the structure of our scones, adding only dead weight and a leaden texture. Leaving the oats intact, we found that equal parts oats and flour provided good flavor and a decent texture. (Most of the test recipes called for much smaller proportions of oats, thus their wimpy oat flavor.) But we were still yearning for a nuttier taste, so we took a hint from one of the test recipes and toasted the oats before mixing them with the flour.

We kept the sugar content to a minimum—just enough to tenderize the scones while enhancing the oat flavor. We tried all granulated sugar, all light brown sugar, and a combination of the two. Some tasters liked the deep robust flavor of the brown sugar, but most preferred the lighter texture and cleaner flavor created by the granulated sugar alone.

With the addition of oats we ended up with less flour in our scones. Hence, we found just 2 teaspoons of baking powder to be an adequate leavener.

Moving on to the butter, we quickly realized why so many oatmeal scones are so dry: They don't have nearly enough fat. A lean oatmeal scone is simply not worth eating, so we used 10 tablespoons of butter, which adds flavor as well as tenderness. We used a mixture of milk and heavy cream for a rich oatmeal scone that doesn't double as a paperweight. (Using all half-and-half works just as well.) A single egg also contributed to a nice richness and airy crumb. As with any biscuit or scone recipe, we found it important not to overwork the dough. It should be mixed just until the ingredients come together.

We baked the scones ranging from 350 all the way up to 425 degrees, and every 25-degree increment in between. The best of the lot were those baked at 425 degrees, but they were not ideal. We tried pushing the oven temperature to 450 degrees (a bit of a gamble, as the sugar in the recipe might burn) and were rewarded. These scones had a dramatic rise and a deep golden brown crust. In such high heat, the cold butter melted quickly and produced steam, which created the light texture we were looking for. The intensity of the rise also gave the scones a cracked, craggy, rustic look that was enhanced when we added a sugar topping. The higher temperature also meant that the scones spent less time in the oven, which kept them from drying out.

Oatmeal Scones

MAKES 8 SCONES

We prefer to use an all-purpose flour with a lower protein level such as Pillsbury or Gold Medal, but if you are using King Arthur flour (which has a higher level of protein) add 1 to 2 tablespoons milk. Half-and-half is a suitable substitute for the milk-cream combination. Once baked, these scones will keep for up to 3 days in an airtight container at room temperature.

1½	cups (4½ ounces) old-fashioned rolled oats or quick-cooking oats
¼	cup whole milk
¼	cup heavy cream
1	large egg
1½	cups (7½ ounces) unbleached all-purpose flour (see note)
⅓	cup (2⅓ ounces) sugar, plus 1 tablespoon for sprinkling
2	teaspoons baking powder
½	teaspoon salt
10	tablespoons (1¼ sticks) cold unsalted butter, cut into ¼-inch cubes

1. Adjust an oven rack to the middle position and heat the oven to 375 degrees. Spread the oats out evenly over a baking sheet and toast them in the oven until they are fragrant and lightly browned, 7 to 9 minutes; cool on a wire rack. When the oats are cooled, measure out 2 tablespoons (for dusting the work surface) and set aside. Whisk the milk, cream, and egg in a large measuring cup until incorporated; remove 1 tablespoon to a small bowl and reserve for glazing.

2. Increase the oven temperature to 450 degrees. Line a baking sheet with parchment paper; set aside. Process the flour, sugar, baking powder, and salt together in a food processor until combined, about 4 pulses. Scatter the butter pieces over the flour mixture and pulse until the mixture resembles coarse cornmeal, 12 to 14 pulses. Transfer the mixture to a medium bowl and stir in the cooled oats. Using a rubber spatula, stir in the milk mixture until large clumps form. Using your hands, gently knead the mixture in the bowl until the dough forms a cohesive mass.

3. Dust the work surface with half of the reserved oats, turn the dough out onto the work surface, and dust the top with the remaining oats. Gently pat the dough into a circle about 1 inch thick. Using a bench scraper or chef's knife, cut the dough into 8 wedges and set on the parchment-lined baking sheet, spacing them about 2 inches apart. Brush the tops with the reserved milk-egg mixture and sprinkle with 1 tablespoon sugar. Bake until golden brown, 12 to 14 minutes. Set the baking sheet with the scones on a wire rack and let cool for 5 minutes, then transfer the scones directly to the rack and let cool to room temperature, about 30 minutes, before serving.

➤ VARIATIONS

Cinnamon-Raisin Oatmeal Scones
Follow the recipe for Oatmeal Scones, adding ¼ teaspoon ground cinnamon to the flour mixture and ½ cup golden raisins to the flour-butter mixture with the oats in step 2.

Apricot-Almond Oatmeal Scones
Follow the recipe for Oatmeal Scones, reducing the oats to 1 cup (3 ounces). Toast ½ cup slivered almonds with the oats in step 1 and add ½ cup chopped dried apricots to the flour-butter mixture with the oats and nuts in step 2.

Oatmeal Scones with Dried Cherries and Hazelnuts
Follow the recipe for Oatmeal Scones, reducing the oats to 1¼ cups (3¾ ounces). Toast ¼ cup coarsely chopped skinned hazelnuts with the oats in step 1 and add ½ cup chopped dried cherries to the flour-butter mixture with the oats and nuts in step 2.

Glazed Maple-Pecan Oatmeal Scones
Follow the recipe for Oatmeal Scones, toasting ½ cup coarsely chopped pecans with the oats in step 1. Omit the sugar and whisk ¼ cup maple syrup into the milk-egg mixture (before removing 1 tablespoon for brushing the scones). When the scones are cool, whisk 3 tablespoons maple syrup with ½ cup confectioners' sugar to make a glaze, drizzle it over the scones, and let set before serving, about 15 minutes.

STICKY TOFFEE PUDDING CAKE

CLASSICALLY BRITISH, STICKY TOFFEE PUDDING cake is a member of the pudding family, a hodge-podge of steamed and baked desserts that sport such colorful names as cabinet pudding, dock pudding, and roly-poly. Most "pudds" haven't traveled far beyond Britain's shores, but sticky toffee pudding cake is an exception. Flavored with dates and dark brown sugar, it is a simple, moist cake with a straightforward, earthy flavor. It's unapologetically sweet, and many of the versions we have tried have been sickeningly saccharine. Other versions possessed the bland floury flavor of undercooked pancakes. And as for texture, they ranged from stiff and pound-cakey to completely mushy. Our goal was to make a sticky toffee pudding cake that packed a full date flavor and had a tolerable sweetness level and a moist, tender crumb.

There's nothing complicated about this pudding cake; no separated eggs, sifted flour, or whipped anything. It is a simple batter of flour, butter, sweetener, and eggs to which dates are added. Very few recipes we found varied from a basic mixing technique—dry and wet ingredients are mixed separately and then combined—not dissimilar to the quick bread method. Flavors and baking methods, however, varied greatly. That said, we picked our favorite recipe from our initial survey and commenced testing.

The dates have the largest impact on flavor so we opted to start there. Most recipes call for dried dates, the ones sold next to the raisins; unlike fresh dates, they are inexpensive and available year-round. Traditionally, the dried dates are chopped and soaked in hot water laced with baking soda before mixing them into the batter. The alkalinity of the baking soda softens the dates' tough, papery skins and, as a bonus, helps to darken the pudding's color—more a matter of aesthetics than flavor. Skeptics that we are, we prepared batches of the pudding without soaking the dates and found their skins fibrous enough to detract from the pudding's tender texture. And the color was lighter than we desired. Back to tradition we went.

As for incorporating the dates into the batter, many recipes recommended coarsely chopping them and stirring them in. This worked, but it produced a mild date flavor, because the dates failed to fully permeate the cake. A better option, we found, was to process a portion of the dates with the sugar and leave the remainder coarsely chopped. The flavor surpassed that of the previous batches, and the texture was better as well—moister and softer.

Traditionally, sticky toffee pudding cake is sweetened with treacle, a syrup by-product of sugar production. It is similar to molasses in flavor but usually milder and without the bitter bite of most varieties of molasses. We tried molasses in our recipe but found it too assertive, even when cut with granulated sugar. Brown sugar proved a better substitute, buttressing the dates' mild flavor rather than overpowering it. Tasters' reactions were split down the middle between light and dark brown sugar, some appreciating the robustness of the dark, others preferring the subtlety of the light. We leave the decision up to you. As for auxiliary flavors, vanilla was a welcome addition, but tasters deemed everything else superfluous.

Sticky toffee pudding cake can either be baked in a large casserole or baking dish or divvied up into ramekins for individual servings. In either case, we found a water bath essential to a moist, tender texture. Without the temperature-taming water bath, the cake cooked too quickly and acquired a texture similar to quick bread. It was tasty but not the delicate dessert we sought. Surprisingly, there was a notable difference in texture between cakes in individual ramekins and a single cake in a large baking dish. The former had a lighter, more delicate texture than the latter, which was cakier and sturdier. The latter was more convenient, however, so we opted to include it as a variation.

The sugar and dates in the cake itself are only part of the "sticky" in the title; the rest comes from a toffee sauce that coats the cake. In all the recipes we found, the sauce was a simple blend of butter, brown sugar or treacle, and cream simmered until blended. After testing a few versions, we tweaked ratios of sugar and butter for a lighter-tasting, smoother sauce and added a splash of rum, a not uncommon flavoring, which cut through the sticky richness.

Individual Sticky Toffee Pudding Cakes

SERVES 8

While sticky toffee pudding cake is traditionally served with Crème Anglaise (page 202), vanilla ice cream also makes a nice accompaniment. To make the pudding cakes ahead of time, simply cover and refrigerate the unbaked batter (either in the mixing bowl or portioned into ramekins) for up to 24 hours; continue to bake as directed in step 4. The toffee sauce can be cooked up to 2 days ahead of time; reheat on medium-high heat in the microwave, stirring often, until hot, about 3 minutes.

PUDDING CAKES

Unsalted butter, for the ramekins

1¼   cups (6¼ ounces) unbleached all-purpose flour, plus extra for the ramekins

½   teaspoon baking powder

½   teaspoon salt

1¼   cups pitted dates, cut crosswise into ¼-inch slices

½   teaspoon baking soda

¾   cup warm water

¾   cup packed (5¼ ounces) light or dark brown sugar

2   large eggs

1½   teaspoons vanilla extract

4   tablespoons (½ stick) unsalted butter, melted

TOFFEE SAUCE

8   tablespoons (1 stick) unsalted butter

1   cup packed (7 ounces) light or dark brown sugar

⅔   cup heavy cream

1   tablespoon rum

1. FOR THE PUDDING CAKES: Adjust an oven rack to the middle position and heat the oven to 350 degrees. Butter and flour eight 4-ounce ramekins, then line the bottom of each with a round of parchment paper cut to fit. Place a kitchen towel on the bottom of large baking dish or roasting pan and arrange the ramekins on the towel. Bring a kettle of water to boil over high heat.

2. Whisk the flour, baking powder, and salt together in a medium bowl; set aside. Combine half the dates with the baking soda and water in a glass measuring cup (the dates should be completely submerged) and set aside to soften, about 5 minutes. Transfer the dates to a medium bowl, reserving the soaking liquid.

3. Process the remaining dates and brown sugar until just blended, about 5 pulses. Add the reserved soaking liquid, eggs, and vanilla and process until smooth, about 5 seconds. With the food processor running, pour the melted butter through the feed tube in a steady stream. Transfer this mixture to the bowl with the softened dates.

4. Gently stir the flour mixture into the date mixture until just combined. Divide the batter evenly among the prepared ramekins. Place the baking dish with ramekins on an oven rack. With great care, pour the boiling water into the baking dish, without splashing any water into the ramekins, until the water reaches two-thirds the height of the ramekins. Cover the pan tightly with aluminum foil, crimping the edges to seal. Bake the cakes until puffed and small holes appear on their surface, about 40 minutes.

5. FOR THE TOFFEE SAUCE: While the cakes bake, melt the butter in a medium saucepan over medium heat. Whisk in the brown sugar until smooth. Continue to cook, stirring occasionally, until the sugar is dissolved and the mixture looks puffy, 3 to 4 minutes. Slowly whisk in the cream and rum, reduce the heat to medium-low, and simmer until frothy, about 3 minutes. Remove from the heat, cover to keep warm, and set aside.

6. When the cakes are done, transfer the ramekins to a wire rack immediately and let cool for 10 minutes. Using a skewer or toothpick poke holes all over the tops of the cakes, then pour 1 tablespoon of toffee sauce over each cake and let it soak in.

7. TO SERVE: Run a paring knife around the edges of the ramekins to loosen the cakes. Invert each ramekin onto a plate or shallow bowl, remove the ramekin, and peel off the parchment paper lining. Pour the remaining toffee sauce evenly over the cakes and serve immediately.

➤ VARIATION
Large Sticky Toffee Pudding Cake

If you don't have individual ramekins, you can bake the pudding cake in an 8-inch square baking dish. The texture will be a bit more cakey.

Follow the recipe for Individual Sticky Toffee Pudding Cakes, substituting an 8-inch square baking dish, buttered and floured, for the ramekins. Bake as directed, until the outer 2 inches develop small holes and the center has puffed and is firm to the touch, about 40 minutes. Cool and glaze as directed. To serve, cut the cake into squares and pour the toffee sauce over the top before serving.

SUMMER PUDDING

SUMMER PUDDING DOESN'T FIT THE RICH, creamy, silky pudding archetype. In this classic English dessert, ripe, fragrant, lightly sweetened berries are gently cooked to coax out their juices, which are used to soak and soften slices of bread to make them meld with the fruit. This mélange of berries and bread is usually weighted down with heavy cans, then chilled overnight until it is a cohesive-enough mass to be unmolded.

We have always been intrigued by this "pudding," drawn in by its rustic, unaffected appeal. Unfortunately, many summer puddings are too sweet and the bread often seems to stand apart from the fruit, as if it were just a casing. We wanted sweet-tart berries and bread that melded right into them.

In a typical summer pudding, berries fill a bowl or mold of some sort that has been neatly lined with crustless bread. Some recipes say to line the bowl with full slices, laying them flat against the bottom and sides of the bowl. Others have you cutting the slices down into triangles and rectangles and arranging them such that, when unmolded, they form an attractive pattern. Well, trimming the crusts is easy, but trimming the bread to fit the bowl, then lining the bowl with the trimmed pieces, is a bit fussy. After making a couple of puddings, we quickly grew tired of this technique; it seemed to undermine the simplicity of the dessert.

We came across a couple of recipes that called for layering the bread right in with the berries instead of using it to line the bowl. Not only is this bread-on-the-inside method easier, but a summer pudding made in this fashion looks spectacular—the berries on the outside are brilliant jewels. Meanwhile, the layers of bread on the inside almost melt into the fruit.

Our next adjustment to this recipe was to lose the bowl as a mold. We switched instead to a loaf pan. Its rectangular shape requires less trimming of bread slices, and, once unmolded, the pudding better retains its shape. When we tried making individual summer puddings in ramekins, we found that individual servings transform this humble dessert into an elegant one. The individual puddings are also easily served: You simply unmold them onto a plate; there's no slicing or scooping involved.

With the form set, we moved on to the ingredients. For the 4 pints of berries we were using, ¾ cup of sugar was a good amount of sweetener. Lemon juice, we found, perked up the berry flavors and rounded them out. The berries need a gentle cooking to make their texture more yielding, more pudding-like, if you will. But don't worry—five minutes is all it takes, not even long enough to heat up the kitchen.

So far, we had been using a mix of strawberries, raspberries, blueberries, and blackberries and were pleased with the variety of flavors, textures, and colors.

The next obvious ingredient to investigate was the bread. We tried six different kinds as well as pound cake (for which we were secretly rooting). Hearty, coarse-textured sandwich bread and a rustic French loaf were too tough and tasted fermented and yeasty. Soft, pillowy sandwich bread became soggy and lifeless when soaked with juice. The pound cake, imbued with berry juice, turned into wet sand and had the textural appeal of sawdust. A good-quality white sandwich bread with a medium texture, somewhere between Wonder Bread and Pepperidge Farm, was good, but there were two very clear winners: challah and potato bread. Their even, tight-crumbed, tender texture and light sweetness were a perfect match for the berries. But challah is usually sold in unsliced braided loaves and therefore makes for irregular slices. We decided to sidestep this complication and go with potato bread, which comes in convenient bagged and sliced loaves, like sandwich bread.

Most summer pudding recipes call for stale bread, and for good reason. Fresh bread, when soaked with those berry juices, turns to mush. You might not think this would be so noticeable with the bread layered between all those berries, but every single taster remarked that the pudding made with fresh bread was soggy and gummy. On the other hand, stale bread absorbs some of the juices and melds with the berries while maintaining some structural integrity. We found that simply leaving slices out overnight until they were dry to the touch but still somewhat pliable resulted in bread that was easy to cut and also tasted good in the pudding.

Summer pudding must be weighted as it chills, to ensure the juices evenly distribute throughout for a cohesive pudding. But how long does the pudding need to chill? We made several and chilled them with and without weights for four hours and up to 30 hours. The pudding chilled for four hours contained bread that was barely soaked through and the berries barely clung together. At eight hours, the pudding was at its peak: The berries tasted fresh and held together, while the bread melted right into them. Twenty-four hours and the pudding was still good, though a hairsbreadth duller in color and flavor. After 30 hours, the pudding was well past its prime in flavor and texture.

Individual Summer Berry Puddings

SERVES 6

Stale the bread for this recipe by leaving it out overnight; it should be dry to the touch but not brittle. Otherwise, put the slices in a single layer on a rack in a 200-degree oven for 50 to 60 minutes, turning them once halfway through. For this recipe, you will need six 6-ounce ramekins and a round cookie cutter of slightly smaller diameter than the ramekins. Challah is the second choice for bread but will probably need to be cut into slices about ½ inch thick. If both potato bread and challah are unavailable, use a good-quality white sandwich bread with a dense, soft texture. Summer pudding can be made up to 24 hours before serving; any longer and the berries begin to lose their freshness.

ASSEMBLING SUMMER BERRY PUDDINGS

1. Cut out rounds of bread with a cookie cutter.

2. With a slotted spoon, place about ¼ cup of fruit into the bottoms of greased 6-ounce ramekins that have been placed on a baking sheet.

3. Lightly soak a round of bread in the fruit juices and place on top of the fruit in each ramekin. Divide the remaining fruit among the ramekins (about ½ cup more per ramekin).

4. Lightly soak a round of bread and place on top of the fruit in each ramekin; it should sit above the lip of the ramekin. Pour any remaining juices over the bread layer and cover the ramekins loosely with plastic wrap.

5. Place a second baking sheet on top, then weight with several heavy cans.

2   pints strawberries, hulled and sliced

1   pint raspberries

½   pint blueberries

½   pint blackberries

¾   cup (5¼ ounces) sugar

2   tablespoons juice from 1 lemon

12   slices stale potato bread, challah, or other good-quality white bread (see note)

1. Heat the strawberries, raspberries, blueberries, blackberries, and sugar in a large nonreactive saucepan over medium heat, stirring occasionally, until the berries begin to release their juice and the sugar has dissolved, about 5 minutes. Off the heat, stir in the lemon juice. Let cool to room temperature.

2. While the berries are cooling, use a cookie cutter to cut out 12 bread rounds that are slightly smaller in diameter than the ramekins (see illustration 1 on page 111).

3. Coat six 6-ounce ramekins with vegetable oil spray and place on a rimmed baking sheet. Following illustrations 2 through 6 on page 111, assemble, cover, and weight the summer puddings and refrigerate for at least 8 hours or up to 24 hours.

4. Remove the weights, baking sheet, and plastic wrap. Run a paring knife around the perimeter of each ramekin, unmold into individual bowls, and serve immediately with whipped cream, if desired.

➤ VARIATION

Large Summer Berry Pudding
SERVES 6 TO 8

To ensure that this larger pudding unmolds in one piece, use a greased loaf pan lined with plastic wrap. Because there is no need to cut out rounds for this version, you will need only about 8 bread slices, depending on their size.

Follow the recipe for Individual Summer Berry Puddings through step 1. While the berries are cooling, remove the crusts from the bread slices and trim so the slices will fit in a single layer in a 9 by 5-inch loaf pan. (You will need about 2 slices per layer and a total of 3 layers.) Coat the loaf pan with vegetable oil spray and line with plastic wrap. Make sure the wrap lies flat against the surface of the pan, leaving no air space. Place the loaf pan on a rimmed baking sheet and use a slotted spoon to place about 2 cups of fruit in the bottom of the pan. Lightly soak enough bread slices for 1 layer in the fruit juices and place on top of the fruit. Repeat with 2 more layers of fruit and bread. Top with the remaining juices, cover loosely with a second sheet of plastic wrap, and weight with a another loaf pan and 2 or 3 heavy cans; refrigerate for at least 8 hours or up to 24 hours. To unmold, remove the weights, loaf pan, and outer plastic wrap and invert the loaf onto a serving platter. Lift off the pan, remove the plastic wrap lining, slice, and serve.

ASSEMBLING A LARGE SUMMER BERRY PUDDING

1. Remove the crusts from the bread slices and trim the slices to fit in a single layer in a loaf pan. You will need 3 layers. Remove the bread from the pan.

2. Line the greased loaf pan with plastic wrap. Spread about 2 cups of fruit over the bottom.

3. Lightly soak 1 layer of bread slices in the fruit juices and place on top of the fruit. Repeat 2 more times. Top with the remaining juices, cover loosely with a second sheet of plastic wrap, and weight with another loaf pan and 2 or 3 heavy cans.

4

CENTRAL EUROPE AND SCANDINAVIA

SCANDINAVIAN CUCUMBER SALADS

Gurksallader

CUCUMBER SALADS ACCOMPANY MEALS across Scandinavia. The two styles most often served, and the two for which we wanted to develop recipes, are a cucumber salad with a creamy dill dressing and a cucumber salad with a sweet and tart vinaigrette.

The cucumber salads we find here in the United States typically turn soft and watery upon standing, and the dressing becomes diluted to near tastelessness by the cucumber water. In order to prevent such a limp, watery mess, many Scandinavian recipes salt the cucumbers before assembling the salad. Salt creates a higher concentration of ions (tiny, charged particles) at the surface of the vegetable than exists within its cells. To equalize the concentration levels, the water within the cells is drawn out through permeable cell walls. In the case of cucumbers, this leaves them wilted, yet very crunchy.

For maximum crispness, some recipes we found in our research press the cucumbers after salting them. To find out if pressing salted cucumbers really squeezes out more liquid (thus making the cucumbers crunchier), we trimmed and seeded six cucumbers to a weight of 8 ounces each, sliced them on the bias, and tossed each cucumber with ½ teaspoon of salt in its own colander set over a bowl. Three batches had zipper-lock freezer bags filled with water placed on top; no additional weight was added to the other three. Then we left them all to drain, measuring the liquid each had released after 30 minutes and after one, two, three, and 12 hours. At each time point, the weighted cucumbers had released about 1 tablespoon more liquid than the unweighted cucumbers. So weighting the cucumbers is worthwhile, especially if you only have an hour to salt them. (It should be noted that the cucumbers don't need to be weighted for any more than 3 hours—there was no difference in the amount of liquid released by cucumbers weighted for 3 hours and those that were weighted for a longer period of time.)

But how would weighted versus unweighted cucumbers perform in salads with different types of dressings? We mixed one batch each of the weighted and unweighted cucumbers with three types of sauces—creamy, oil-based, and water-based—and allowed each to sit at room temperature for one hour. This is where the true value of the weighted cucumbers became obvious; tasters unanimously preferred the salads made with pressed cucumbers for their superior crunch and potent dressings.

As for the amount of salt, some recipes simply use the quantity with which you would normally season the cucumber, while others say you should use more, up to 2 tablespoons per cucumber, and then rinse off the excess before further use. We tried salting cucumbers with 2 tablespoons of salt, and they gave up about 1 tablespoon more liquid within the first hour than those tossed with ½ teaspoon had. But they also required rinsing and blotting dry with paper towels, and they still tasted much too salty in the salads. We decided to forgo the extra salt. Many cucumber salads also include thinly sliced onion and we decided to toss the onion in with the cucumbers during salting—this helped tame the harsh bite of the raw onion.

With the method of salting and weighting the cucumbers determined, we turned our attention to the dressings for the two salads. We started by looking at the creamy dill dressing, with the basic ingredients typically consisting of a cream of some sort, an acid, and dill. We tried heavy cream, sour cream, and yogurt as the base. The heavy cream was far too watery for an already wet vegetable such as cucumbers, and left little of the silky texture we were after. The yogurt was also too thin to provide the requisite richness, but the sour cream proved ideal. The sour cream provided the creamy, thick texture we sought and also added a tangy flavor that tasters appreciated. For the acid, we liked cider vinegar because of its subtle fruity notes and tart flavor. To balance the flavors of this dressing all that was needed was a little sugar and pepper and, of course, fresh dill. After draining the salted and pressed cucumbers and onion, we added the dressing and tossed to coat. Happy with the results, we moved on to the sweet and tart salad.

The primary ingredients in our vinaigrette style cucumber salad are vinegar and sugar. Since all of the recipes we found called for white sugar, the only real question was what type of vinegar to use. We tested white vinegar, white wine vinegar, and cider vinegar. The favorite in this dressing was white vinegar, because of its neutral flavor. We settled on ½ cup of vinegar, enough to dress three medium cucumbers.

The amount of sugar to add was a bit of a question since we had seen anywhere from 2 tablespoons to 1 cup. Anything less than ¼ cup was not sweet enough, making a puckery vinaigrette, but if we added much more our dressing tasted like dessert. Six tablespoons proved ideal for a good balance of sweet and tart.

To make sure that the sugar fully dissolved, we brought the vinegar and sugar to a boil together, and then set it aside to cool to room temperature while we salted the cucumbers. Combining the cucumbers, thinly sliced onion, and fresh dill, along with the vinaigrette, gave us a perfectly light and tangy cucumber salad.

With two great Scandinavian cucumber salads full of flavor and crunch, the only decision left to make was which one to eat first.

Creamy Dill Cucumber Salad
Krämig Dill-Och Gurksallad
SERVES 4
Salting and draining the onion along with the cucumbers in this recipe helps mellow its bite.

3	medium cucumbers, peeled, halved, seeded, and sliced ¼ inch thick
½	medium onion, sliced very thin
	Salt
I	cup sour cream
¼	cup minced fresh dill
3	tablespoons cider vinegar
I	teaspoon sugar
	Ground black or white pepper

1. Toss the cucumbers, onion, and 1½ teaspoons salt together in a strainer or colander. Following the illustrations on page 116, place a water-filled 1-gallon zipper-lock bag on top and let the cucumbers drain for at least 1 hour, or up to 3 hours.

2. Whisk the sour cream, dill, vinegar, sugar, and ¼ teaspoon pepper together in a medium bowl. Add the drained cucumbers and onion and toss to coat. Refrigerate the salad until chilled, at least 1 hour or up to 6 hours. Season with salt and pepper to taste before serving.

➤ VARIATION
Sweet and Tart Cucumber Salad
For a milder flavor, substitute an equal amount of parsley for the dill.

3	medium cucumbers, peeled, halved, seeded, and sliced ¼ inch thick
I	medium onion, sliced very thin
	Salt
½	cup distilled white vinegar
6	tablespoons sugar
I	tablespoon minced fresh dill (see note)
	Ground black or white pepper

PANTRY SPOTLIGHT

WHITE PEPPER

In Germany and the surrounding countries, white pepper is often used for seasoning in place of black pepper. The berries used to make white pepper are the same as those used to make black pepper, but they are harvested at a riper stage. The hulls are then removed and with them goes some of the characteristic heat of black pepper. Compared to black pepper its flavor is a bit sharper, yet less spicy, with fragrant, citrusy overtones. While freshly ground white pepper is more fragrant than preground, we don't use white pepper frequently enough in the test kitchen to justify purchasing a pepper mill for the sole purpose of grinding it, nor can we be bothered emptying and then refilling the black pepper mill. Instead, we opt for preground white pepper, replenishing the stock when the pepper loses its fragrance. Equal amounts of ground white pepper can be substituted for the black pepper in many of the recipes in this chapter, if desired.

1. Toss the cucumbers, onion, and 1½ teaspoons salt together in a strainer or colander. Following the illustrations below, place a water-filled 1-gallon zipper-lock bag on top and let the cucumbers drain for at least 1 hour, or up to 3 hours.

2. Bring the vinegar and sugar to a boil in a small nonreactive saucepan over medium heat, stirring often, until the sugar dissolves. Pour the vinegar mixture into a medium bowl and cool to room temperature.

3. Add the drained cucumbers and onion and the dill to the cooled vinegar mixture and toss to coat. Refrigerate the salad until chilled, at least 1 hour or up to 6 hours. Season with salt and pepper to taste before serving.

SALTING CUCUMBERS

1. Peel each cucumber and halve lengthwise. Use a small spoon to remove the seeds and surrounding liquid from each cucumber half.

2. Place the cucumber halves flat side down on a work surface and slice them on the diagonal into ¼-inch-thick pieces.

3. Toss the cucumbers, onion, and salt in a colander set in a bowl. Place a water-filled 1-gallon zipper-lock bag on top of the cucumbers to weigh them down. Drain for at least 1 hour and up to 3 hours.

GERMAN POTATO SALAD

Kartoffelsalat

GERMAN POTATO SALAD, SERVED HOT OR warm, is pungently tangy from its vinegar dressing and packed with bacon flavor. It can be a welcome change of pace from the cold comfort of mayonnaise-based American-style potato salad, and so we set our sights on developing a truly great version.

Turning our attention first to the potatoes, we tested both red and Yukon golds. We preferred the red potatoes—their low starch content prevents them from falling apart easily, a problem with higher starch potatoes. They also have a relatively mild flavor, which would allow the dressing to take center stage. We decided to cut the potatoes before boiling, thus dramatically reducing their cooking time (and omitting the hassle of cutting hot potatoes). Using heavily salted water ensured that the potatoes were well seasoned.

Rendered bacon fat forms the foundation of the salad's deeply flavorful dressing. (Vegetable and olive oils were tested and flatly rejected.) We did, however, try some bacon-based dressings that were on the greasy side, so we aimed to find just the right level of richness without adding unnecessary fat. We adjusted the amount of bacon fat (and crumbled bacon pieces) until tasters were satisfied with the ratios. Half a pound of bacon yielded enough pieces of bacon for 2 pounds of potatoes. However, the amount of bacon fat rendered—⅓ cup—was too much for the dressing, so we skimmed off enough fat to leave us with ¼ cup bacon fat.

Choosing the right vinegar to balance the bacon fat was also key. Along with cider vinegar, we tested white wine, red wine, and distilled white vinegar (the usual choice in most German recipes). Tasters preferred the neutral flavor and clean acidity of the distilled white vinegar, which allowed the meaty bacon flavor to shine through. One cup of vinegar made the right quantity of dressing to moisten the potatoes (and we found that the hot potatoes soaked up an amazing amount of dressing), but now tasters' palates were assaulted with a harsh, unbalanced dressing. Not wanting to add more bacon fat back into the equation, we diluted the vinegar's sharpness with some of the potato cooking water, a trick in many of the German potato salad recipes we researched.

Sautéed onion was a must (raw onion was too harsh), and after trying red, white, and yellow onions, we found that you really can't go wrong with any of them. Mustard appears in some German potato salad recipes and after starting out with salads made with no mustard, tasters were receptive to its addition. We first tried Dijon (both smooth and whole grain varieties), but tasters weren't crazy about the wine flavor that it added. Brown mustard didn't make much of a flavor impact on our dressing, but whole grain German-style mustard proved

the best bet. Dotted with flecks of whole mustard seeds, the salad now had both the right flavor and a rustic appearance. A half-teaspoon of sugar offset the tartness of the vinegar and mustard, and some chopped parsley added freshness.

The salad is usually combined by mixing the dressing and potatoes in a big serving bowl. We found, though, that the potatoes lost most of their heat that way. Instead, we dumped the potatoes right into the skillet where the vinaigrette was waiting, giving them a quick toss right in the hot pan before piling the whole thing into a serving dish. This was German potato salad at its best—warm chunks of tangy, well-seasoned potato and meaty bits of bacon.

SAUERKRAUT

TRADITIONAL GERMAN SAUERKRAUT (LITERALLY SOUR CABBAGE) IS MADE BY SALTING AND PRESSING green cabbage over the course of several days; as the salt and pressure draw the moisture out of the cabbage, the cabbage wilts and ferments into sauerkraut. The sauerkraut is then sautéed with aromatics (and often bacon), and served alongside other German favorites such as pork chops, pork knuckle, and bratwurst. While making homemade sauerkraut from raw cabbage is a time-consuming endeavor, the sauerkraut you buy at the supermarket can taste lackluster served as is. Here is how to cook up the store-bought variety.

Warm Sauerkraut with Bacon and Apples
Krautsafat mit Speck und Äpfeln
SERVES 6
Try to buy fresh sauerkraut sold at the delicatessen or in vacuum-sealed packages rather than canned or jarred cooked sauerkraut. Rinsing the sauerkraut before cooking dramatically improves the flavors of this dish. Juniper berries lend the sauerkraut a subtle piney flavor, but try to pick them out before serving, or at least avoid biting into one, as they're not meant to be eaten.

- 2 tablespoons unsalted butter
- 1 small onion, halved and sliced thin
- 10 whole juniper berries
- 3 medium bay leaves
-   Salt
- 2 pounds packaged sauerkraut, well rinsed and drained
- 1 medium Granny Smith apple, peeled and grated on the large holes of a box grater
- 3 ounces (about 3 slices) bacon
- 1 tablespoon brown sugar
- 1¾ cups low-sodium chicken broth
-   Ground black pepper

Melt 1 tablespoon of the butter in a 12-inch skillet over medium-high heat. Add the onion, juniper berries, bay leaves, and ¼ teaspoon salt and cook, stirring frequently, until the onion is softened, 3 to 5 minutes. Stir in the sauerkraut, apple, bacon, brown sugar, and broth, increase the heat to medium-high, and bring to a simmer. Reduce to medium-low and continue to simmer until the liquid is almost evaporated, about 20 minutes. Remove the bacon and bay leaves, stir in the remaining tablespoon of butter, and season with salt and pepper to taste.

German Potato Salad

Kartoffelsalat

SERVES 4 TO 6

Unlike a nonstick skillet, a traditional skillet will allow the bacon to form caramelized bits on the pan bottom. This will result in a richer-tasting dressing and a more flavorful salad.

2 pounds red potatoes (about 6 medium), scrubbed and cut into 1-inch chunks
   Salt
8 ounces (about 8 slices) bacon, sliced crosswise into ½-inch-thick pieces
1 medium onion, minced
½ teaspoon sugar
½ cup distilled white vinegar
1 tablespoon whole grain mustard
¼ teaspoon ground black pepper
¼ cup minced fresh parsley leaves

1. Place the potatoes and 1 tablespoon salt in a Dutch oven and cover with 1 inch cold water. Bring to a boil over high heat, reduce the heat to medium-low, and simmer until the potatoes are tender (a thin-bladed paring knife can be slipped in and out of the potatoes with little resistance), about 10 minutes. Reserve ½ cup of the potato cooking water, then drain the potatoes. Return the potatoes to the pot and cover to keep warm.

2. While the potatoes are cooking, fry the bacon in a large skillet over medium heat, stirring occasionally, until browned and crisp, about 5 minutes. With a slotted spoon, transfer the bacon to a paper towel–lined plate, and pour off all but ¼ cup of the bacon grease.

3. Add the onion to the fat left in the skillet and cook, stirring occasionally, over medium heat until softened and beginning to brown, 5 to 7 minutes. Stir in the sugar until dissolved, about 30 seconds. Add the vinegar and reserved potato cooking water, bring to a simmer, and cook until the mixture is reduced to about 1 cup, about 3 minutes. Off the heat, whisk in the mustard and pepper.

4. Add the potatoes, parsley, and bacon to the skillet and toss to combine. Season with salt and pepper to taste then transfer to a medium serving bowl and serve warm.

SWEET AND SOUR RED CABBAGE

Süsse-Saurer Rotkohl

CABBAGE HAS LONG BEEN A STAPLE OF BOTH the German and Austrian diet. It is prepared in a variety of ways, but one of the simplest dishes (and one of our favorites) is red cabbage braised with sweet and sour flavorings. Though this is a simple recipe, it is one that requires a careful balancing act between the sweet and sour elements. We hoped to strike that balance and develop an ideal side dish to accompany a hearty main course of roast meat.

Most of the recipes we researched seemed strikingly similar: they included shredded cabbage, onions, some sort of liquid such as broth, wine, or juice, and a few seasonings. But once we got into the kitchen and prepared these recipes, the similarities among them ended. Some of the braised cabbage dishes tasted raw and oddly seasoned while others were overcooked and had an overpowering aroma. We needed to break this recipe down to the basics and start from the ground up.

Starting with the cabbage, we found the pre-shredded variety to be useless because it was either shredded much too thin or the shreds were uneven within the package, resulting in uneven cooking—some bites were fine, while others were raw or overcooked. Shredding your own cabbage by hand isn't difficult and you can make the task even easier by using a food processor.

Next, we examined the cooking method. Braising is a cooking method in which liquid is added to the pot and covered to create a gentle, moist heat environment. Some recipes we looked at covered the pot from the outset and others did not. The uncovered cabbage took longer to cook, looked slightly bleached out at the edges, and had less flavor compared to the cabbage that was cooked underneath a lid. Finally, we tested cooking times. When the cabbage was cooked for less than 30 minutes it tasted raw and crunchy, while cabbage cooked for an hour tasted mushy and overcooked. The ultimate braising time proved to be 30 to 40 minutes, at which point the cabbage was softened but retained a slight bite.

Taking a closer look at the braising liquids from the recipes we researched, we tried them all: orange juice, chicken broth, vinegar, apple cider, red wine, and even port. Tasting them side by side, we picked the sweet and fruity (but not overwhelmingly so) apple cider as our favorite. Just 1½ cups of cider was plenty to provide some steam to help the cabbage wilt and braise, without leaving a lot in the bottom of the pan at the end to make the cooked cabbage too wet. A final douse of vinegar before serving helped perk up the flavors and balance the sweet with a little tart.

With the basics down, we turned to refining the flavors in our cabbage. Tasters complained that the cabbage was a little lean tasting, so we decided to add some bacon, which lent a smoky depth and richness to the finished dish. Sugar helped to pump up the flavor further, and brown sugar added a bit more flavor than white. Moving on to the spices, we tried everything from peppercorns and juniper berries to pumpkin pie spice and finally settled on a combination of cinnamon, caraway seeds, allspice, bay leaves, and thyme. At last, we had found the perfect balance of sweet and tart.

Sweet and Sour Red Cabbage
Süsse-Saurer Rotkohl
SERVES 8 TO 10

Typically this dish is served as an accompaniment to duck, pork, or beef. This cabbage tastes even better the next day.

4	ounces (about 4 slices) bacon, chopped fine
I	medium onion, minced
I	cinnamon stick, or ¼ teaspoon ground cinnamon
½	teaspoon caraway seeds
¼	teaspoon ground allspice
	Salt
I	large head red cabbage (2 pounds), cored and sliced ¼ inch thick
I½	cups apple cider
2	sprigs fresh thyme, or ½ teaspoon dried
3	bay leaves
3	tablespoons light brown sugar
3	tablespoons cider vinegar
	Ground black pepper

SHREDDING CABBAGE

1. Cut the cabbage into quarters and cut away the hard piece of core attached to each quarter.

2. Separate the cored cabbage into stacks of leaves that flatten when pressed lightly.

3a. Use a chef's knife to cut each stack diagonally (this ensures long pieces) into thin shreds.

3b. Or roll the stacked leaves crosswise to fit them into the feed tube of a food processor fitted with the shredding disk.

1. Cook the bacon in a large Dutch oven over medium heat until just beginning to render its fat, about 2 minutes. Add the onion, cinnamon, caraway seeds, allspice, and ¼ teaspoon salt and continue to cook until the onion is browned and softened, about 10 minutes.

2. Add the cabbage, cider, thyme, bay leaves, 1 tablespoon of the sugar, and ½ teaspoon salt. Cover and cook, stirring often, until the cabbage is wilted and tender, 30 to 40 minutes.

3. Discard the cinnamon stick, thyme sprigs, and bay leaves. Add the vinegar and remaining 2 tablespoons sugar. Season with salt and pepper to taste and serve. (The cabbage can be refrigerated for up to 4 days; reheat in the microwave on high power, stirring once, 3 to 5 minutes.)

SPÄTZLE

SOME CLAIM THAT THIS DISH WAS NAMED spätzle because the noodles look like fat-bodied little sparrows (*Spatz* in southern German dialect). Others maintain that the name is derived from the Italian word for cutting into pieces, *spezzare*. Whichever the case, spätzle is now so common that it can be found in the pasta aisle of grocery stores in Germany, Austria, Switzerland, France, and Italy. Spätzle is typically served buttered as a side dish to roast chicken, pork, or other hearty meat dishes.

We began by preparing four spätzle recipes representing the varying styles uncovered in our research. All of the recipes called for the same basic ingredients—eggs, flour, milk or water, and salt—but their ratios of flour, eggs, and liquid differed wildly; the resulting batters ranged from thick and muffin-like to thin and pancake-like. Out of the four recipes we tried, only one of them had a decent flavor, while the others tasted bland. As for texture, none hit the mark—all were dry, rubbery, and oddly spongy. We wanted a spätzle with a firm texture and rich, wheaty, eggy flavor.

Based on this initial testing, we began to look more closely at the variables. Since spätzle is essentially just egg pasta, we started by testing the egg

amount. We had been using three eggs, but most of the other recipes we found used many more. Would additional eggs provide additional flavor or help firm up the texture? Testing a range of egg amounts from two to six, we were very surprised to find that the extra eggs had a minimal impact on the spätzle's texture, but dramatic impact on its flavor. The more eggs we added to the batter, the more one-dimensional and off-tasting the spätzle became. Using just two eggs in the batter produced the best-tasting spätzle with well-balanced—not overwhelmingly eggy—flavor.

Next we moved on to the liquid component. We tested making spätzle with milk, water, and a combination of the two. The spätzle made with just water was gummy and tasted bland, while the milk and water combo was better but still tasted a bit lean. In addition, these spätzle didn't brown as well as the ones made with all milk batter, which produced richly flavored, plump spätzle. We tested the difference between whole milk, low-fat, and nonfat milk, and found that whole milk was the hands-down winner.

Next we took a look at the idea of resting the batter before cooking. Would it make any difference to the final flavor or texture, and if so, what was the ideal resting time? Making five batches of batter, we cooked one batch immediately and compared it to the other batches, which we let

MAKING SPÄTZLE

If you don't own a spätzle press, improvise with this method: Spread ¼–⅓ cup of the batter out thinly and evenly over a small cutting board. Holding the board over the pot of water and using a chef's knife, slice and scrape the batter into the water in 2-inch long shreds.

rest for 15, 30, 45, and 60 minutes before cooking. Although the flavors were identical for all five batches, the textures were dramatically different. The unrested batter produced spätzle that were soft and spongy, while the 45- and 60-minute rested batters produced spätzle that were increasingly tough. The 15- and 30-minute rested batters produced spätzle with the perfect delicate yet toothsome texture we were looking for. (And better yet, this is roughly the same amount of time it takes for the cooking water to come to a boil.)

While spätzle batter is very easy to make, the challenge has always been the shaping and boiling of the noodles. Typically the batter is spread on a long and narrow cutting board, which is held over a pot of boiling water, and then the batter is sliced off into the water. Several recipes suggested pushing the batter through a colander, among other tricks. We found that these suggestions all made disasters, and left us frustrated. Luckily, you can easily purchase a spätzle maker—we tried several but our favorite was the press, since it was so quick and easy. If you don't have a spätzle maker, then we recommend making it the old-fashioned way (by slicing and scraping the batter into the water from a cutting board), which was much easier, and less messy, than the other options we tried. Once

the spätzle floats to the top of the boiling water it is cooked, and you can remove it to a strainer. The result is a simple yet hearty rustic noodle dish— a perfect accompaniment to roast meat or, when layered with cheese and onion, a meal in itself.

~≍~

Spätzle

SERVES 6 AS A SIDE DISH

We don't recommend substituting low-fat or nonfat milk in this recipe. If you don't have a spätzle maker, you can make rustic-looking spätzle by cutting it into the water from a cutting board (see the illustration on page 120). This recipe makes plain spätzle, which is typically eaten with a roast or a hearty meat dish (such as Sautéed Pork Chops with Onions and Apples, page 133).

2	cups (10 ounces) unbleached all-purpose flour
	Salt
¼	teaspoon ground black pepper
¼	teaspoon freshly grated nutmeg
1	cup whole milk
2	large eggs

1. Whisk the flour, ½ teaspoon salt, pepper, and nutmeg together in a large bowl. In a separate bowl, whisk the milk and eggs together. Slowly stir the milk mixture into the flour mixture until combined, then whisk briefly until smooth. Cover the bowl with plastic wrap and let the batter rest for 15 to 30 minutes (do not let the batter rest any longer).

2. While the batter rests, bring 3 quarts of water to boil in a large pot and stir in 1 tablespoon salt.

3. Process about ½ cup of the batter into the water using a spätzle maker (see the illustration on page 120 for how to make spätzle using a cutting board). Boil the spätzle until it floats, about 1 minute. Using a slotted spoon (or small strainer), transfer the spätzle to a large plate and cover with foil to keep warm. Repeat three more times with the remaining batter. Serve immediately.

SPÄTZLE PRESS

While you can make spätzle by hand, we prefer to use a spätzle press. The Kull Spätzle Press ($45) is easy to use and consistent in producing uniform spätzle. Simply portion about ½ cup of the batter into the hopper, and press the handles together to extrude the spätzle directly into the water.

➤ VARIATIONS
Buttered Spätzle
SERVES 6 AS A SIDE DISH

These spätzle make a nice accompaniment to chicken and fish dishes, and can be dressed up with a sprinkling of minced parsley leaves.

3	tablespoons unsalted butter
I	shallot, minced
I	recipe Spätzle (page 121)
	Salt and ground black pepper

Melt the butter in a 12-inch nonstick skillet over medium heat. Add the shallot and cook until softened but not browned, about 3 minutes. Increase the heat to medium-high, add the spätzle, and cook, stirring often, until the spätzle is golden and crisp at the edges, 5 to 7 minutes. Season with salt and pepper to taste and serve immediately.

Spätzle with Cheese
SERVES 4 AS A MAIN COURSE

This dish is fairly substantial with layers of cheese and onions, and makes a nice, simple supper when served with a salad.

2	tablespoons vegetable oil
2	medium onions, halved and sliced thin
	Salt
	Unsalted butter, for the baking dish
I	recipe Spätzle (page 121)
	Ground black pepper
8	ounces Gruyère cheese, grated (about 2 cups)

1. Adjust an oven rack to the upper-middle position and heat the oven to 375 degrees. Heat the oil in a 12-inch nonstick skillet over medium heat until shimmering. Add the onions and ½ teaspoon salt, cover, and cook, stirring occasionally, until the onions are softened and watery, about 10 minutes. Uncover and continue to cook, stirring often, until the onions are dry and golden, about 10 minutes longer; set aside off the heat.

2. Butter a 13 by 9-inch baking dish and spread half of the cooked spätzle into an even layer. Season the spätzle with salt and pepper to taste, then sprinkle with half of the onions and half of the Gruyère. Spread the remaining spätzle over the top, season again with salt and pepper to taste, and sprinkle with the remaining onions and remaining Gruyère. Bake until the cheese is melted and the top is golden, about 20 minutes. Serve immediately.

GERMAN BACON AND ONION TART
Flammeküeche

LEGEND HOLDS THAT *FLAMMEKÜECHE* (LITERALLY "baked in flames"), or *tarte flambé* as it is known in France, originated hundreds of years ago with peasant farmers in the Alsace region of France and the neighboring Baden-Württemberg region of Germany. These farmers would gather together and bake bread in communal wood-burning ovens. At these small gatherings they made this tart, composed of a cracker-like crust topped with fromage blanc (a soft farmers cheese) or crème fraîche, caramelized onions, and lardons (fatty thick bacon), to test the temperature of the oven. At the peak of its heat, when ready for bread baking, the ovens would be able to bake Flammeküeche in one or two minutes.

These "pizzas" are so popular in France and Germany that several different brands can be found in the freezer section of grocery stores. In Germany, flammeküeche-style tarts are made with everything from pretzels to croissants, and are sold as snack food in train stations everywhere. We knew that this pizza-like dish would also be a big hit in American homes, so we set out to develop an authentic recipe using appropriate substitutes for the less-common ingredients.

We began by baking several tarts from recipes uncovered in our research and, not surprisingly, found that a good crust was key. Some of the crusts we encountered were flaky and delicate, similar to pie crust, while others had a thick, bready crust. Then there were the crusts we liked best—these crusts were similar to pizza but ultra thin and crisp. With a clear picture of what we wanted, we turned to our existing recipe for thin-crust pizza dough as a starting point.

Our thin-crust pizza dough is made in the food processor and requires a 24-hour resting period in the refrigerator to allow the dough to ferment and relax. But we wondered if we could get away with a shorter resting period. We baked tarts with dough that hadn't rested as well as with dough that had rested for one, two, and all the way up to 24 hours to see what the differences were. The dough that hadn't rested and the one-hour dough were tough to eat and hard to roll out. We liked the 24-hour dough best, but only a slight bit better than the two-hour dough. Because we wanted a recipe that could be made in one day, we decided on a two-hour resting period. The dough was easy to work with and had all of the crunch and flavor we had come to expect.

We knew that we had to roll the crust out thinner than we did for pizza to achieve the proper Flammeküeche crust. The only instrument for the task of achieving a crust as thin as a credit card or thinner is a rolling pin. We dusted a large sheet of parchment paper lightly with flour and placed the dough on top. We then placed an 18-inch piece of plastic wrap directly on the surface of the dough to prevent the dough from sticking and tearing as we rolled. The tackiness of the dough against the parchment prevents the dough from springing and shrinking back, eliminating the need for excess flouring when rolling out the dough.

Wanting the cracker-like simplicity of a rich burnished crust, we knew that we would need every bit of conventional oven heat we could get in the five to seven minutes or so it would take to bake. That meant a 500-degree oven and a pizza stone (an essential piece of equipment) with an hour's head start to preheat. (Though we tested a slightly lower oven heat as well, the extra minutes the Flammeküeche needed to brown left the finished crust more tough than crisp.) While it wasn't as hot as the ovens this dish was invented in, it turned out a very crisp crust nonetheless.

With the crust ready we turned to another key ingredient: the lardons. We purchased whole-slab bacon, thick-sliced bacon, and regularly sliced bacon. We prepared our working recipe with all three to determine which worked best. The regularly sliced bacon was quickly eliminated for being too insubstantial. The slab bacon was favored for its meatiness, but it can be hard to find. The thick-sliced bacon lent a similar flavor to the dish as the slab bacon and is heartier than the regular bacon, so it is our first choice.

Next we moved on to the dairy component of this dish. Some recipes call for fromage blanc, others swear by crème fraîche, and some recipes combine the two. Crème fraîche is our favorite, but since it can be somewhat hard to find, we tested some alternatives, including sour cream, pureed cottage cheese, and a combination of the two. Some tasters liked the thicker texture of the cottage cheese, but all agreed that it was too bland. We thought we had a winner with a sour cream–cottage cheese mix until we tasted the sour cream alone. It had a more pronounced flavor, and tasters preferred the creamy texture. (That said, if you can find crème fraîche, we recommend using it.)

As for the caramelized onions, recipes called for diced onions, thinly sliced onions, and thickly sliced onions. We tried all three and liked the thinly sliced onions best since they added texture, but were not so large that we were eating chunks of onion. The next question was how much caramelization was necessary. We've seen everything from pale to deep golden-brown. We opted for something in the middle; we wanted the onions to just begin to turn golden, so that they would have a nice sweet flavor. We covered the skillet for the first 10 minutes while the onions cooked and released their moisture. Then we removed the cover and continued to cook the onions until they began to turn golden. We found that a moderate, steady heat provided us with the most flavor and a meltingly tender texture.

German Bacon and Onion Tart

Flammeküeche

SERVES 4 AS A MAIN COURSE,
OR 6 AS AN APPETIZER

For the lightest, crispest crust, use an unbleached all-purpose flour with a protein content no higher than 10.5 percent, such as Gold Medal or Pillsbury. Serve the tart with a salad for dinner, or cut it into small pieces and serve as an appetizer. This tart tastes great with Gewürztraminer (a German white wine).

TART DOUGH

2	cups (10 ounces) unbleached all-purpose flour, plus extra as needed
½	teaspoon instant yeast
½	teaspoon honey
½	teaspoon salt
¾	cup plus 2 tablespoons warm water (100 to 105 degrees)
¼	cup vegetable oil

TOPPING

1	cup crème fraîche or sour cream
	Salt and ground black or white pepper
½	teaspoon freshly grated nutmeg
8	ounces (about 6 slices) thick-cut bacon, cut crosswise into ¼-inch-wide strips
4	medium onions, halved and sliced thin (about 4 cups)

1. FOR THE TART DOUGH: Combine the flour, yeast, honey, and salt in a food processor. With the machine running, add the water through the feed tube, followed by the vegetable oil. Continue to process until the dough forms a ball, about 30 seconds.

2. Turn the dough out onto the counter and knead by hand for 30 seconds, adding extra flour if the dough is sticky. Wrap the dough in plastic wrap and refrigerate for 2 hours, or up to 2 days.

3. Adjust an oven rack to the lowest position, set a baking stone on the rack, and heat the oven to 500 degrees; let the baking stone heat for 1 hour.

4. FOR THE TOPPING: Meanwhile, mix the crème fraîche, 1 teaspoon salt, ½ teaspoon pepper, and nutmeg together, cover with plastic wrap, and refrigerate until needed.

5. Cook the bacon in a 12-inch nonstick skillet over medium heat until browned and most of the fat has rendered, about 10 minutes. Transfer the bacon to a paper towel–lined plate, leaving the fat in the skillet. Add the onions and ½ teaspoon salt to the fat left in the skillet, cover, and cook over medium heat, stirring occasionally, until the onions are softened and have released their juices, about 10 minutes. Uncover and continue to cook, stirring often, until the onions begin to brown, about 6 minutes; set aside off the heat.

6. TO ASSEMBLE AND BAKE: Remove the dough from the refrigerator. Divide it into two equal pieces, forming each piece into a ball. Place one ball on a lightly floured sheet of parchment paper and cover with one large sheet of plastic wrap (or two small overlapping pieces). Using a rolling pin, roll the dough into a 15 by 9-inch oval. Slide the parchment paper with the dough onto an inverted baking sheet.

7. Spread half of the crème fraîche mixture over the dough, leaving a ½-inch border at the edge. Scatter half of the onion mixture and half of the bacon over the top. Slide the parchment with the tart onto the heated baking stone. Bake until the edges of the tart are golden brown and the parchment releases from the tart bottom, 5 to 7 minutes. While the first tart bakes, roll out and assemble the second tart on a sheet of parchment paper using the remaining dough and topping. Cut the baked tarts into about 6 pieces and serve immediately.

SLICING ONIONS THIN

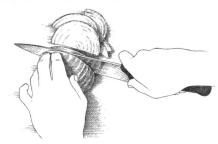

To slice an onion thin, halve it pole to pole, peel it, set it on a cut side, and then slice crosswise.

FONDUE, TAKEN FROM THE FRENCH WORD *fondre* meaning "to melt," was created out of necessity. On particularly frosty winter days, cooks skipped the trip into town for provisions and instead transformed leftover cheese rinds and stale bread into a hearty meal. A fondue pot is very useful for keeping the fondue warm and fluid, but you can substitute any heavy-bottomed pan; when the cheese mixture cools and congeals, simply place the pot over medium heat until the fondue is warm again (you may need to whisk in additional wine to loosen the consistency).

Swiss Fondue

SERVES 4 AS A MAIN COURSE,
OR 6 AS AN APPETIZER

Using high-quality cheese will make a big difference in flavor. Besides bread cubes, fondue is often served with boiled fingerling potatoes, cubed ham, cornichons, pickled carrots, and pickled cauliflower.

1	medium garlic clove, peeled and sliced in half lengthwise
1¾	cups dry white wine
	Salt
8	ounces Gruyère cheese, grated
8	ounces Emmentaler cheese, grated
1½	tablespoons cornstarch
⅛	teaspoon freshly grated nutmeg
	Ground black or white pepper
1	baguette, cut into 1-inch cubes

Thoroughly rub the inside of a medium saucepan with the cut sides of the garlic clove, then discard the garlic. Add the white wine and 1 teaspoon salt to the saucepan and bring to a simmer over medium heat. Meanwhile, toss the cheeses with the cornstarch. When the wine is simmering, slowly whisk in the cheese mixture, one handful at a time, and let melt completely. Stir in the nutmeg and season with salt and pepper to taste. Transfer to a fondue pot and serve immediately with the bread.

POACHED SALMON
Pochierter Lachs

ACROSS SCANDINAVIA AND NORTHERN Germany, salmon is an integral part of the diet. It is served many ways—cured, baked, pan-seared, and smoked—but often it is poached. Poached salmon can be served either hot or cold, making it a versatile dish for many different occasions. We wanted to develop a simple recipe for poached salmon and create a couple of sauces to accompany it.

We began our testing with the poaching liquid. This is usually a mixture of water, an acid (vinegar, wine, or lemon juice), aromatics (carrots, onion, and celery), herbs, and spices. First, we wanted to determine if the acid was even necessary. Omitting the aromatics, herbs, and spices, we poached the salmon in plain salted water as well as water spiked with three different acids: vinegar, wine, and lemon juice. The plain salted water produced fish that paradoxically tasted overly rich and flat at the same time. The cider vinegar produced a cleaner flavor, but the fish was still a bit dull tasting. The wine really livened up the flavor but also lent a mild bitterness to the dish. The lemon juice brightened the flavor of the salmon, but wasn't quite sturdy enough on its own. A mix of white wine and lemon juice however, was perfect, producing clean, brightly flavored fish.

Having settled on a lemon-wine combination as our acid, we put the aromatics, spices, and herbs back into the equation. We tried various combinations of carrot, onion, and celery. Carrots and onions lent a welcome sweetness, but celery overpowered some of the other flavors, so we chose to leave it out.

Moving on to the herbs, we tried parsley, thyme, and bay leaves. We settled on thyme as the preferred herb because its flavor remained fresh even after a lengthy simmering time. We also added garlic and peppercorns to the poaching liquid because they gave the fish a subtle flavor boost, while salt proved essential to heightening the overall flavor of the dish.

Finally we tested the amount of time the poaching liquid needed to simmer before cooking the fish. We found that 20 to 30 minutes was sufficient time for the wine and lemon juice to mellow and the vegetables to soften and infuse their flavor into the liquid. Any less and the liquid can taste harsh and unbalanced.

Up to this point we had been cooking the fish at a gentle sub-simmer with essentially no bubbling of the poaching liquid. We tested this technique against two other methods: boiling the poaching liquid with the fish in it and bringing the liquid to a boil, adding the fish, then turning off the heat. Not surprisingly, the boiled version tasted watery, as if the flavors of the fish had been boiled away. The fish also cooked unevenly, with a 30-degree difference between the center and outside of the fish. Turning off the heat after submerging the fish was not that much better—it took much too long to cook because once the fish was added, the temperature of the broth cooled dramatically. Based on this testing, our original method of poaching the fish in a sub-simmer for about six minutes proved ideal.

With our method firmly in place, all we had left to do was develop a variation that called for serving the salmon chilled (a preparation particularly popular in Sweden) and then decide on sauces that would complement each version. For our warm poached salmon we decided on a mustard hollandaise. Hollandaise, though typically associated with French cuisine, is frequently used in German cuisine and the addition of mustard gives the sauce a welcome brightness that offsets the salmon's rich flavor. For our cold poached variation, we went with a simple sour cream sauce lightly seasoned with dill and lemon.

Poached Salmon with Mustard Hollandaise

Pochierter Lachs mit Semf-Hollandaise
SERVES 6

Skin-on or skinless salmon can be used here. If using skin-on salmon, you may want to remove the skin, which peels off easily, before serving. Poaching the salmon very gently is key; when the salmon is cooking in step 3, the broth should have no or very few bubbles. Any leftover poaching liquid can be strained and refrigerated for up to 1 week and reused for poaching, or frozen for up to 1 month.

SALMON AND POACHING LIQUID

1	cup dry white wine or vermouth
1	large carrot, peeled and chopped medium
1	small onion, chopped medium
3	sprigs fresh thyme
2	medium garlic cloves, peeled
2	teaspoons whole black or white peppercorns
	Salt
1	lemon, halved
6	salmon fillets (6 ounces each), 1¼ inches thick, pinbones removed
	Ground black or white pepper

HOLLANDAISE

3	large egg yolks
2	tablespoons whole grain mustard
16	tablespoons (2 sticks) unsalted butter, melted and still warm
7	teaspoons hot water
	Salt and ground black or white pepper
	Lemon juice from 1 lemon
2	tablespoons minced fresh tarragon, dill, or parsley leaves

1. FOR THE POACHING LIQUID: Combine 6 cups of water, the wine, carrot, onion, thyme sprigs, garlic, peppercorns, and 1 teaspoon salt in a large Dutch oven. Squeeze all the juice from the lemon into the pot and add the spent lemon halves. Bring to a simmer and cook, partially covered, until the broth is flavorful, 20 to 30 minutes.

2. FOR THE HOLLANDAISE: Meanwhile, process the egg yolks and mustard together in a blender until smooth and frothy, about 10 seconds. With the blender running, very slowly drizzle in half of the butter until the mixture is quite thick, about 1½ minutes. Blend in 2 teaspoons of the hot water, then continue to slowly blend in the remaining butter, about 1 minute. Blend in additional hot water, 1 teaspoon at a time, as needed until the sauce smoothly coats the back of a spoon. Transfer to a microwave-safe bowl, cover tightly with plastic wrap, and set aside.

3. FOR THE SALMON: Remove the lemon halves from the poaching broth and discard. Season the salmon with salt and pepper and gently slip the

salmon into the broth. Arrange the salmon so that all the pieces are submerged (some pieces may overlap). Return to a gentle sub-simmer, cover, and cook until the fish flakes apart easily when prodded with a fork or paring knife, 6 to 10 minutes.

4. Using a slotted spoon or spatula, gently transfer the fish to a large platter. Remove and discard any poaching aromatics that may have clung to the fish. Microwave the hollandaise on medium-low power until hot, stirring often, 2 to 4 minutes. Season with salt, pepper, and lemon juice to taste. Portion the fish onto individual plates and pour the hollandaise over the top. Sprinkle with the tarragon and serve immediately.

➤ VARIATION
Cold Poached Salmon with Dill–Sour Cream Sauce

The sauce for this Swedish dish can be made and refrigerated up to 2 days in advance.

SALMON AND POACHING LIQUID
1	cup dry white wine or vermouth
1	large carrot, peeled and chopped medium
1	small onion, chopped medium
3	sprigs fresh thyme
2	medium garlic cloves, peeled
2	teaspoons whole black or white peppercorns
	Salt
1	lemon, halved
6	salmon fillets (6 ounces each), 1¼ inches thick, pinbones removed
	Ground black or white pepper

SAUCE
1	cup sour cream
1	shallot, minced
1	tablespoon minced fresh dill
1½	teaspoons juice from 1 lemon
	Salt and ground black or white pepper
1	lemon, cut into wedges (for serving)

1. FOR THE POACHING LIQUID: Combine 6 cups of water, the wine, carrot, onion, thyme sprigs, garlic, peppercorns, and 1 teaspoon salt in a large Dutch oven. Squeeze all the juice from the lemon

into the pot and add the spent lemon halves. Bring to a simmer and cook, partially covered, until the broth is flavorful, 20 to 30 minutes.

2. FOR THE SALMON: Remove the lemon halves from the poaching broth and discard. Season the salmon with salt and pepper and gently slip the salmon into the broth. Arrange the salmon so that all the pieces are submerged (some pieces may overlap). Return to a gentle sub-simmer, cover, and cook until the fish flakes apart easily when prodded with a fork or paring knife, 6 to 10 minutes.

3. Using a slotted spoon or spatula, gently transfer the fish to a large platter. Remove and discard any poaching aromatics that may have clung to the fish. Cover the salmon with plastic wrap and poke several vent holes in the plastic. Refrigerate until chilled, at least 1 hour or up to 2 days.

4. FOR THE SAUCE: Mix the sour cream, shallot, dill, and lemon juice together and season with salt and pepper to taste. Cover and refrigerate until the flavors have blended, at least 10 minutes or up to 6 hours.

5. To serve, gently brush any solidified poaching liquid off the salmon. Portion the fish onto individual plates, dollop the sauce over the top, and serve with the lemon wedges.

WIENER SCHNITZEL

WIENER SCHNITZEL, OR "VIENNESE CUTLET," is one of the most celebrated and recognized Austrian dishes. It has been said that cooking proper Wiener schnitzel takes years of practice. Large, sweet tasting veal cutlets (schnitzel) are pounded incredibly thin and then breaded using ultra-fine bread crumbs. Fried to a crisp, buttery light gold, the coating magically wrinkles as it cooks to form a dramatic, rumpled appearance. Although this recipe requires far more attention than a simple breaded veal cutlet, we wondered if we could skip the requisite years of practice and uncover the secrets of authentic Wiener schnitzel in the test kitchen.

Focusing first on the veal itself, we found some recipes that use schnitzel cut from the loin as opposed to being cut from the round, which is more common. But with loin cutlets costing an astonishing $27 per pound at our local market, they were quickly eliminated from our testing. Working with cutlets from the round, we found that flavor depends largely on freshness. Fresh veal has a bright, rosy pink color while veal that's been around for a while has a dull or slightly gray hue.

Buying cutlets big enough for Wiener schnitzel can be a tricky business. Most butchers slice cutlets as thin as possible, usually weighing in around two ounces. But we wanted them to be twice as big and found it best to either cut them ourselves from a large piece of veal round or special order 4-ounce veal cutlets from a trusted butcher. Pounded thin, the 4-ounce cutlets become quite large, and it is customary to serve just one per person.

Moving on to the coating, we found that the fresh bread crumbs we usually prefer for breading were not quite right. Their texture was too coarse and by the time they reached the ideal crispness they were much too dark in color. Using dried bread crumbs made it easier to achieve a crisp texture and light golden color; however, store-bought dried bread crumbs tasted bland and stale. Instead, we decided to make our own by processing fresh slices of sandwich bread into crumbs using the food processor and then drying them out in the oven before processing them again to a uniform, superfine consistency.

The standard method for adhering the crumbs

BUYING VEAL CUTLETS

Veal cutlets should be cut from the top round. Most supermarkets use the leg or sirloin and do not butcher the meat properly, cutting it with the grain, not across the grain, as is best. Look for cutlets in which no linear striation is evident. The linear striation in the cutlet on the left is an indication that the veal has been cut with the grain and will be tough. Instead, the cutlet should have a smooth surface, like the cutlet on the right, in which no lines are evident. If your market doesn't offer cutlets that look this, consider cutting your own cutlets from a piece of top round, following the illustrations on page 129.

to the cutlet includes three steps: the veal is dredged first in flour, then egg, and finally bread crumbs. A few of the recipes we researched skipped the flouring step or replaced it with an additional layer of bread crumbs. We tried breading cutlets using each of these techniques and determined that the standard method with flour worked best. We also found it important that both the flour and egg layers be as thin as possible to prevent the coating from being too thick or lumpy.

Next, we tested cooking the cutlets in oil versus butter. Tasters liked the flavor of the butter but preferred the ultra-crisp texture of the schnitzel fried in oil. By using a combination of oil and a little butter we struck the perfect balance. Heating the oil and butter until very hot (375 degrees) proved essential in preventing the crust from becoming soggy. At this high temperature, the schnitzels cook through in only 2 to 3 minutes. This quick cooking time was essential—because the schnitzels are so large, only two can be cooked at the same time which means that they need to be cooked in batches, and we didn't want the first batch cooling off before the second batch was finished.

Last, we fussed with various techniques to encourage the breading to wrinkle into its hallmark texture. Using enough oil and butter so that the schnitzels actually floated in the skillet proved key. Shaking the pan constantly as they cooked, a method recommended by some recipes, also proved worthwhile. Finding that these tricks did a nice job of wrinkling the first batch, we were disappointed when the second batch turned out completely flat (although the cutlets tasted fine). Using fresh oil and butter to cook the second batch was the only way around this problem. Since this approach takes longer than reusing the oil and butter from the first batch, we now found it necessary to keep the first batch warm in a low oven.

Requiring just a brief blotting with paper towels to remove any excess oil before being served, authentic Wiener schnitzel can be on your table in just about 30 minutes. Served simply with wedges of lemon, these veal cutlets make a great meal any night of the week.

Wiener Schnitzel

SERVES 4

Using fresh oil and butter for cooking the second batch of schnitzel is only necessary if you desire the authentic, wrinkled texture on the finished cutlets. To ensure ample room for the schnitzels as they fry, use a 12-inch skillet. We prefer frying in a nonstick pan for easier cleanup; however, a traditional skillet can be used. Do not trim the crusts off the bread slices, or they will not yield enough crumbs. See page 128 for information about buying veal cutlets.

8	slices high-quality white bread, torn into large pieces
½	cup unbleached all-purpose flour
2	large eggs
1½	cups plus 1 tablespoon vegetable oil
4	veal cutlets cut from the round, ½ inch thick (about 4 ounces each)
	Salt and ground black pepper
4	tablespoons (½ stick) unsalted butter
1	lemon, cut into wedges (for serving)

1. Adjust an oven rack to the middle position and heat the oven to 300 degrees. Process the bread in a food processor to very fine crumbs, about 30 seconds. Transfer the crumbs to a rimmed baking sheet and bake, stirring occasionally, until dried but not browned, 15 to 20 minutes. Process the crumbs again in the food processor until finely ground, 5 to 10 seconds.

2. Lower the oven temperature to 200 degrees and set a paper towel–lined plate on the middle rack. Spread the bread crumbs in a shallow dish. Spread the flour in a second shallow dish. Beat the eggs with 1 tablespoon of the oil in a third shallow dish.

3. Place the cutlets between two sheets of parchment or waxed paper and pound to a thickness of ⅛ to ¼ inch. Season the cutlets with salt and pepper. Working with one cutlet at a time, dredge the cutlets thoroughly in the flour, shaking off the excess, then coat with the egg, allowing the excess to drip back into the dish to ensure a very thin coating, and finally coat evenly with bread crumbs, pressing on the crumbs to adhere. Place the breaded cutlets in a single layer on a wire rack set over a baking sheet; let the coating dry for 5 minutes.

4. Heat ¾ cup of the oil and 2 tablespoons of the butter in a 12-inch skillet over high heat until it registers 375 degrees on an instant-read thermometer (or the edge of a cutlet bubbles vigorously when dipped into the oil), 2 to 4 minutes. Lay 2 cutlets, without overlapping them, in the skillet and cook, continuously shaking the pan gently, until wrinkled and a light golden brown on both sides, 1 to 1½ minutes per side.

5. Set the cutlets on the warm paper towel–lined plate and flip the cutlets several times to blot up any excess oil. Return the plate to the warm oven. Discard the oil in the skillet and wipe the skillet clean using tongs and a wad of paper towels. Repeat step 4 using the remaining ¾ cup oil, 2 tablespoons butter, and the now-clean skillet to cook the remaining cutlets. Serve immediately with the lemon wedges.

CUTTING VEAL CUTLETS

1. With a boning knife, remove the silver skin, the white membrane that covers the meat in places, from a piece of veal top round. Discard the skin.

2. Using a long, inflexible slicing knife, cut the round on the bias across the grain into cutlets ½ inch thick.

GRAVLAX

GRAVLAX—SALT-AND-SUGAR CURED SALMON—IS A SCANDINAVIAN STAPLE. THE ABUNDANCE of salmon and the need to store food for the cold winter months naturally led to preserving fish in this manner. The salt draws liquid from the fish and cures it, while the sugar serves to counter the harshness of the salt. But because a traditional cure has little or no liquid, the fish can develop oversalted areas that are too dry and even a bit tough. In our recipe, a wet brine of red onion juice helps avoid this problem by ensuring that the salt is evenly distributed throughout the salmon. Serve with toasted rye bread and Creamy Dill Cucumber Salad (page 115).

Gravlax

SERVES 10 TO 12

Don't buy a larger side of salmon; it won't fit well in the bag.

3   medium red onions, peeled and quartered
1   cup kosher salt
¾   cup sugar
1   teaspoon ground black pepper
2   cups coarsely chopped fresh dill (both stems and leaves)
1   (3- to 4-pound) whole side of salmon, skinned, excess fat and brown flesh removed, and pinbones removed with tweezers
1   cup minced fresh dill

1. Process the onions in a food processor until liquefied, about 4 minutes. Strain the mixture through a fine-mesh strainer to extract 2 cups of liquid, then stir in the salt and sugar until dissolved. Stir in the pepper and coarsely chopped dill.

2. Place the salmon diagonally in a 2-gallon zipper-lock bag and add the onion mixture. Seal the bag, removing any excess air, and lay the fish skin side up on a rimmed baking sheet. Place a second baking sheet on top and set about 7 pounds of weight (such as heavy cans or bricks) on top. Refrigerate the weighted fish until very firm, 12 to 18 hours.

3. Remove the salmon from the bag and pat dry with paper towels, removing any dill stems. (The salmon can be wrapped in parchment paper then plastic wrap and refrigerated for up to 1 week.) Before serving, sprinkle the minced dill over the top and sides of the salmon and slice very thin on the bias.

SWEDISH MEATBALLS

Köttbullar

TYPICALLY FOUND ON A BUFFET TABLE OR served as a hot appetizer, Swedish meatballs are one of the best-known Swedish culinary specialties. Norway, Denmark, and Finland all have their own versions, but it is the Swedish meatball that Americans are most familiar with. These mild-flavored mini meatballs are made with a combination of meats (typically beef, pork, and/or veal) and served in a creamy and mildly sweet sauce. For many of us, however, their mention brings to mind dreadful lead sinkers swimming in condensed cream of mushroom "gravy" in a chafing dish.

Wanting to rectify this disappointing American rendition of a classic Swedish dish, we set out in search of the real thing.

Examining several authentic Swedish recipes, we were surprised to find how similar they were to an Italian meatball recipe. Most used a combination of ground pork and beef, added bread that had been soaked in some sort of dairy for tenderness, and pan-fried the meatballs in a skillet. Using our own Italian-style meatball recipe as the basis for our testing, we simply stripped out the Italian flavors of garlic and Parmesan and added a pinch of nutmeg and allspice (typical additions to the Swedish meatball) for our first test. With a tender texture and delicate flavor, these meatballs only needed a few improvements, according to our tasters. Besides finding their size a bit too large, we needed to find a replacement for the buttermilk in which the bread was soaked—its tangy flavor was overpowering the delicate Swedish seasonings. Replacing the original ½ cup of buttermilk in our Italian meatballs with ¼ cup of heavy cream gave our meatballs the desired mild flavor and cohesive texture characteristic of Swedish meatballs. Reducing the size of the meatballs to a more appropriate size was easy. Using a generous tablespoon measurement, we found our working recipe yielded roughly 30 meatballs.

Onion is a customary addition to Swedish meatballs and we tried several ways of incorporating it into the meat mixture. Adding raw minced onion produced a stinky, steamed onion flavor and the bits of onion ruined the smooth texture of the meatballs. Sautéing the minced onion (a method found in many recipes we researched) before adding it to the meat mixture tasted good; however, it was an extra step we thought we could eliminate. Grating raw onion against the large holes of a box grater quickly broke the onion down to a mild-tasting, pulpy mush that was easily incorporated into the ground meat. This method was the clear winner.

Most authentic recipes use the pan drippings left over from frying the meatballs to make an accompanying creamy sauce with a slightly sweet flavor. This sauce is usually made with chicken broth and either sour cream or heavy cream. We first tried reducing broth in the pan with the drippings, then whisking in some sour cream and herbs. This, however, produced a watery, hollow-tasting sauce. Lightly thickening the broth with some flour and butter (a roux) produced a better consistency, while some bay leaves and brown sugar boosted the flavor of the sauce. Tasters liked sauces finished with either sour cream or heavy cream. With just a brief window in which to serve the sour cream sauce before it separated (thus taking on an ugly curdled appearance), we chose to go with the heavy cream. Seasoned with a sprinkling of fresh dill and a squeeze of lemon juice, our sauce was complete—and a perfect complement to our Swedish meatballs.

Swedish Meatballs
Köttbullar
SERVES 4 TO 6

Though these meatballs and sauce are often served as an appetizer, they also make a great main course when served with egg noodles or mashed potatoes. To serve as an appetizer, keep the meatballs and sauce warm in a chafing dish. Over time, the sauce will thicken but it can be thinned with a little milk or water.

MEATBALLS

2	slices high-quality white sandwich bread, crusts discarded and bread quartered
¼	cup heavy cream
8	ounces (85 percent lean) ground beef
8	ounces ground pork
I	large egg yolk
I	small onion, grated on the large holes of a box grater
⅛	teaspoon freshly grated nutmeg
⅛	teaspoon ground allspice
	Salt and ground black pepper
I–I½	cups vegetable oil

SAUCE

I	tablespoon unsalted butter
I	tablespoon unbleached all-purpose flour
I¾	cups low-sodium chicken broth
I	tablespoon dark brown sugar
2	bay leaves
½	cup heavy cream
2	tablespoons juice from I lemon
I	tablespoon minced fresh dill or parsley leaves
	Salt and ground black pepper

1. FOR THE MEATBALLS: In a large bowl, mash the bread and cream together to form a smooth paste. Add the ground meats, egg yolk, onion, nutmeg, allspice, ½ teaspoon salt, and ¼ teaspoon pepper and mix until uniform. Shape the mixture into 1-inch-round meatballs (1 generous tablespoon per meatball; you should have about 30 meatballs).

2. Measure ¼ inch of oil into a 10- to 12-inch sauté pan and heat over medium-high heat; test the temperature of the oil with the edge of a

meatball. When the oil sizzles, add the meatballs in a single layer and fry, turning as needed, until lightly browned on all sides, 7 to 10 minutes. Adjust the heat as needed to keep the oil sizzling but not smoking. Transfer the browned meatballs to a paper towel–lined plate and set aside.

3. FOR THE SAUCE: Discard the oil in the pan but leave behind any browned bits. Add the butter and melt over medium-high heat. Stir in the flour and cook for 30 seconds. Stir in the broth, sugar, and bay leaves and bring to a simmer, scraping up the browned bits. Cook until the sauce thickens, about 5 minutes.

4. Stir in the cream and meatballs and simmer, turning them occasionally, until heated through, about 5 minutes. Off the heat, discard the bay leaves, stir in the lemon juice and dill, and season with salt and pepper to taste.

PORK CHOPS WITH ONIONS AND APPLES

Schweinekoteletts mit Äpfeln und Zwiebeln

THE MOST POPULAR MEAT IN GERMANY WOULD have to be pork. The majority of German sausages are made with pork, and it is served in hundreds of different styles from roasted pork with cracklings in Bavaria to blood sausage with apples and onions in the north. We wanted a simple German pork dish that could be prepared on a weeknight, and braised pork chops with an apple and onion pan sauce fit the bill perfectly.

We gathered several recipes, and the cooking process seemed straightforward enough: Brown the chops and then brown the onions and apples, return everything to the pan, and braise until tender. But initial recipe tests produced bland, dry pork and near-tasteless gravies with woeful consistencies ranging from pasty to processed to gelatinous to watery.

Poor texture and shallow flavor had robbed the pork chops of their savory-sweet glory. To get this recipe right, we knew we'd have to identify the best chop (the one closest to the German cut) and the best way to cook it. And the gravy was no less important. We wanted a heady, multidimensional flavor, bold onion presence, and a satiny, just-thick-enough texture.

Some of the recipes we looked at specified sirloin chops, which are cut from the rear end of the loin. Our tasters found this cut a little dry, and in any case it's often unavailable. Blade chops, cut from the far front end of the loin, were juicier, but they suffer the same spotty availability. Of the two remaining types of chops, center-cut loin and rib, we found the latter to be the juiciest and most flavorful because it has a bit more fat.

We tried chops of varying thickness as the recipes we looked at called for a range. We tried chops as thick as 1½ inches and as thin as ½ inch and were surprised when tasters unanimously chose the thin ½-inch chops. Apparently thick chops overwhelmed the gravy, which tasters felt should share equal billing with the meat. Thin chops also picked up more onion flavor during cooking. While we were at it we tried boneless chops, but they turned out dry, so we decided to stick with bone-in for optimum juiciness.

Next we set about determining the ideal cooking time. Although we prefer to slightly undercook pork to ensure tenderness, this was one instance in which further cooking was necessary, because we wanted to infuse the meat with the flavor of the gravy and onions. After their initial browning, the chops registered a rosy 140 degrees on an instant-read thermometer. They were cooked through and tender, but since they had yet to be smothered, they had none of the onion flavor we were after. Fifteen minutes of braising in the gravy boosted the flavor but toughened the chops, which now registered almost 200 degrees. At that temperature, the meat fibers have contracted and expelled moisture, but the fat and connective tissue between the fibers, called collagen, have not had a chance to melt fully and turn into gelatin. It is this gelatin that makes braised meats especially rich and tender. Another 15 minutes of braising solved the problem. At this point, the chops registered 210 degrees, and the extra time allowed the fat and collagen to melt completely, so the meat was tender and succulent in addition to being oniony from the gravy.

This recipe typically has a gravy that builds on the flavor of the browned pork chops. Water produced weak, thin gravy, but chicken broth improved the picture, adding much-needed flavor. Several of the recipes we had found called for apple cider to highlight the apple flavors. We tried cider and were very pleased with the results, especially since the pork itself added meaty tones, balancing the sauce.

Flour is typically used to thicken a liquid into a gravy. We added it in three different ways, flouring the chops, flouring the onions, and making a roux. Flouring the chops before browning turned their exteriors gummy and left the gravy with a chalky texture. Flouring the onions left the gravy tasting of raw flour. The roux (a mixture of flour and fat—in this case, vegetable oil) occasioned the use of an extra pan, but the results were fantastic. These results were made even better by substituting bacon fat (we would reserve the bacon for sprinkling over the finished dish) for the vegetable oil and by cooking the roux for five minutes to a light brown color. The sweet/salty/smoky bacon flavor underscored and deepened all the other flavors, and browning the roux imparted a rich, toasty flavor to the dish.

The onions and apples are the essential flavors of the gravy. We tried them minced, chopped, cut into wedges, and sliced both thick and thin. A thin-sliced onion cooked to a melting texture was our favorite. Apples cut in ⅜-inch wedges held together the best in the sauce. We tried different quantities of onions and apples and found that for four pork chops, one onion and two apples worked best. We tried simply softening the onions until they were translucent rather than cooking them until their edges browned, a technique that accentuated their natural sweetness and also allowed us to cook the onions and apples together without the apples turning to mush.

The onions and the apples cook in the same pan used to brown the chops. We wanted to make sure that the onions released enough moisture to help dissolve (or deglaze) the flavorful, sticky, brown fond left in the pan by the chops, so we salted them lightly. The heat and salt worked together to jump start the breakdown of the onions' cell walls, which set their juices flowing. We also added 2 tablespoons of water to the pan for insurance.

Our last flavor tweak was an unusual one. We eliminated the salt we'd been using to season the chops themselves. Tasters agreed that the salt added to the onions and apples, along with the naturally salty bacon, adequately seasoned the dish. At last we had a classic German pork dish with a pleasing contrast of flavors and textures to satisfy most any appetite.

Sautéed Pork Chops with Onions and Apples
Schweinekoteletts mit Äpfeln und Zwiebeln
SERVES 4

These pork chops taste great with Spätzle (page 121) to soak up the rich gravy. If your pork chops are much thicker or thinner, you will need to adjust the cooking time accordingly.

3   ounces (about 3 slices) bacon, chopped medium
2   tablespoons vegetable oil, plus extra as needed
2   tablespoons unbleached all-purpose flour
1¾ cups apple cider
4   bone-in, rib-end pork chops, ½ to ¾ inch thick
    Ground black pepper
1   medium onion, halved and sliced thin
2   medium Granny Smith apples, peeled, cored, and cut into ⅜-inch wedges
2   tablespoons water
    Salt
1   medium garlic clove, minced or pressed through a garlic press (about 1 teaspoon)
1   teaspoon minced fresh thyme leaves
2   bay leaves
1   tablespoon minced fresh parsley leaves (optional)

1. Fry the bacon in a small saucepan over medium heat until crisp, 8 to 10 minutes. Using a slotted spoon, transfer the bacon to a paper towel–lined plate, leaving the fat in the saucepan (you should have 2 tablespoons bacon fat; if not, supplement with vegetable oil).

2. Return the saucepan with the bacon fat to medium-low heat and gradually whisk in the flour until smooth. Cook, whisking frequently, until the mixture is light brown (the color of peanut butter), about 5 minutes. Slowly whisk in the apple cider. Increase the heat to medium-high and bring to a boil, stirring occasionally; cover and set aside off the heat.

3. Pat the pork chops dry with paper towels and season with pepper. Heat 1 tablespoon of the oil in a 12-inch skillet over high heat until smoking. Brown the chops until deep golden on both sides, about 3 minutes per side. Transfer the chops to a large plate and set aside.

4. Add the onion, apples, water, ½ teaspoon salt, and the remaining tablespoon oil to the now-empty skillet and return to medium heat. Using a wooden spoon, scrape up any browned bits and cook, stirring frequently, until the onion is softened, 5 to 7 minutes. Stir in the garlic and thyme and cook until fragrant, about 30 seconds.

5. Return the chops to the skillet in single layer along with any accumulated juices and the cider sauce. Cover the chops with the onions and add the bay leaves. Cover the skillet, reduce the heat to low, and simmer until the pork is tender and a paring knife inserted into the chops meets very little resistance, about 30 minutes.

6. Transfer the chops to a warmed serving platter and tent with foil. Increase the heat to medium-high and simmer the sauce rapidly, stirring frequently, until thickened to a gravy-like consistency, about 5 minutes. Discard the bay leaves, stir in the parsley (if using), and season with salt and pepper to taste. Cover the chops with the sauce, sprinkle with the reserved bacon, and serve immediately.

CHRISTMAS SPICE COOKIES

Lebkuchen

GERMANS LOVE THEIR CHRISTMAS COOKIES. So much so that many of the favorites are sold October through March, and are a highlight of outdoor Christmas markets. We wanted to include a recipe for one of the most popular German Christmas cookies, *lebkuchen*, which is often translated into English as gingerbread cookies—an odd translation considering they have no ginger, though they do have a cakey texture that is distantly similar to gingerbread cookies. These chocolate- or sugar-glazed cookies are essentially spice-nut cookies, which are chock-full of ground nuts and flavored with a healthy dose of lemon and orange zest.

After a bit of searching, we gathered together three recipes from German cookbooks along with two that were sent to us from German friends. The recipes varied wildly. Some called for ground hazelnuts, others for chunks of walnuts or almond slices. The differences didn't stop there—the egg amounts ranged from one to eight eggs and the flour from 2 tablespoons to 2 cups. Some recipes included butter while others did not, and the spices called for varied both in amounts and types. We hoped that at least one of these recipes would give us the lebkuchen we sought, but the resulting cookies were all disappointing. They were runny, hard, sticky, or cakey, and none had balanced flavors. We even began to wonder if this was a truly great cookie worthy of our attention.

At this point we knew we would have to start from scratch. Back at the drawing board, we looked at even more lebkuchen recipes and slowly began to find more consistency: They had little flour, loads of nuts, little to no butter, a fairly high amount of eggs, and generous doses of lemon and orange zest. Using these rough guidelines as a starting point, we cobbled together a working recipe and began to test the variables.

We began by testing cookies made with almonds, hazelnuts, walnuts, and a combination of these nuts. The walnut flavor was too subtle in combination with the orange and lemon zest, while the almonds had nice full flavor—but they were too oily on their own. The hazelnuts were preferred for their strong nutty flavor and were a nice complement to the citrus zest. But tasters also felt that the hazelnuts were a bit too strong by themselves, so we tried a mix of half almonds and half hazelnuts and were delighted with the resulting balance of flavors. We tested the difference between skin-on (unblanched) and skinless (blanched) nuts and found little difference in flavor, but a big difference in color; the skins added a rich, dark color to the cookie.

We had been grinding the nuts as fine as possible in the food processor, but were still unhappy with the coarse, grainy texture they added to the cookie. To achieve a finer grind, we found it necessary to add some sugar to the nuts in the food processor, and then let them process for 45 seconds. The result was a fine nut powder, which made a more delicate cookie.

Next we looked at the egg amounts, and were surprised to find that many traditional German recipes called for five or more eggs. Testing everything from eight all the way down to three eggs, we noted a big change in both the cookies' texture and flavor. Too many eggs dulled the spice flavor and turned the cookies into sticky cakes, while too few eggs made the cookies tough and biscuit-like. Four eggs was the perfect amount, producing a cakey cookie with crisp edges.

Up to this point, we had been using 2 cups of dark brown sugar in our recipe, but tasters felt that the cookies were a bit too sweet and sticky. Lowering the amount of sugar from 2 cups to 1½ cups helped with the sweetness level, but we then wondered if the type of sugar—light brown, dark brown, or white—would make a difference. Testing the three sugars on their own and in combination with one another, we found the best flavor and texture in a combination of white and light brown sugar. The light brown sugar added a mild molasses flavor to the spices, while the white sugar helped the citrus and spice flavors shine through and prevented the cookies from becoming too sticky.

Like most recipes we had researched, we had been using a modest amount of flour and lots of nuts—⅓ cup of flour to 18 ounces of nuts. Adding more flour and reducing the amount of nuts in various batches, we had increasingly great results until we struck a perfect ratio of 1½ cups of flour to 12 ounces of nuts.

Many recipes we found for this cookie don't add butter; instead, the dough depends solely on the fat from the ground nuts. We found, however, that a little butter is a good thing and without it, the cookies take on a doorstop-like texture. Testing batches with various amount of butter from 4 tablespoons to 1½ sticks, we found the ideal amount to be 6 tablespoons. More butter made the cookies greasy, while less made the cookies too tough.

Finally we turned our attention to finessing the other flavors essential to this cookie. We fussed with a variety of spice combinations and amounts until we landed on a mixture of freshly grated orange and lemon zest, cocoa powder, vanilla, cinnamon, cardamom, and nutmeg. In Germany, lebkuchen is rarely served plain, but is instead topped with a sugar or chocolate glaze. To make a quick sugar glaze we mixed confectioners' sugar with milk, and for an easy chocolate glaze we simply melted semisweet chocolate. The glazes are brushed or spooned onto the baked, cooled cookies and allowed to set before serving (the chocolate requires some refrigeration to set). Just to make sure we had these

CORE TECHNIQUE

TOASTING NUTS AND SEEDS

The best way to maximize the flavor of nuts and seeds is to toast them, no matter if you are baking with them, using them in a sauce, or sprinkling them over a salad or pasta.

To toast a small amount of nuts or seeds (less than 1 cup), put them in a dry skillet over medium heat and cook, shaking the pan often, until fragrant and lightly browned, 3 to 8 minutes. To toast large quantities of nuts, spread the nuts in a single layer on a rimmed baking sheet (or two baking sheets if necessary) and toast in a 350-degree oven, shaking the pan often, until fragrant and lightly browned, 5 to 10 minutes. Be sure to watch the nuts closely as they toast—they can go from golden to burnt very quickly.

cookies right, we held a tasting and pitted our recipe against some imported German lebkuchen. Not only did tasters agreed that our recipe was an authentic representation, but there was no doubt as to whether these cookies were worthy of our attention—they had become a real test kitchen favorite.

Christmas Spice Cookies
Lebkuchen
MAKES 30 COOKIES

If using a standing mixer in step 2, use the paddle attachment. The cookie dough will be very sticky, and the final cookie will have a soft, chewy, and slightly cakey texture. Testing the cookies for doneness can be a bit tricky; we found it easiest to check the edges of the cookies for firmness (they should be set), and the tops for cracking (there should be lots of tiny cracks).

COOKIES

6	ounces unblanched hazelnuts, toasted and cooled (about 1¼ cups)
6	ounces unblanched whole almonds, toasted and cooled (about 1 cup)
¾	cup (5¼ ounces) granulated sugar
1½	teaspoons ground cinnamon
½	teaspoons ground cardamom
½	teaspoon freshly grated nutmeg
3	tablespoons grated zest from 3 oranges
2	tablespoons grated zest from 2 lemons
1½	cups (7½ ounces) unbleached all-purpose flour
2	tablespoons Dutch-processed cocoa
½	teaspoon salt
6	tablespoons (¾ stick) unsalted butter, softened
¾	cup packed (5¼ ounces) light brown sugar
4	large eggs
1	teaspoon vanilla extract

GLAZE

1¾	cups (7 ounces) confectioners' sugar
¼	cup whole milk

1. FOR THE COOKIES: Adjust two oven racks to the upper and lower-middle positions and heat the oven to 350 degrees. Line two baking sheets with parchment paper. Process the toasted nuts, granulated sugar, cinnamon, cardamom, and nutmeg in a food processor to a fine meal, 30 to 60 seconds, stopping and scraping down the sides as needed. Add the orange and lemon zest and continue to process until combined, about 15 seconds; set aside.

2. In a small bowl, whisk the flour, cocoa, and salt together; set aside. In a large bowl, beat the butter and brown sugar together using an electric mixer at medium speed until light and fluffy, about 2 minutes, scraping down the sides of the bowl as needed. Add the eggs and vanilla and continue to mix until incorporated. Add the flour mixture and continue to mix until combined, about 1 minute. Add the ground nut mixture and continue to mix until evenly combined (the bowl will be very full).

3. Using two greased soupspoons (or a greased 1¾-inch spring-loaded ice cream scoop), portion 2-tablespoon-sized mounds of dough, spaced about 1½ inches apart, onto the baking sheets (each sheet should hold about 10 cookies and you should have enough dough left for another sheet of cookies).

4. Bake the cookies until the edges are firm and the tops are puffed with tiny cracks, 13 to 18 minutes, switching and rotating the sheets halfway through the baking time. Set the cookies aside to cool on the baking sheets until set, about 5 minutes, then transfer the cookies to a wire rack to cool completely. Reline one of the baking sheets with parchment paper, portion out the remaining dough into cookies, and bake as directed.

5. FOR THE GLAZE: When the cookies are cool, whisk the confectioners' sugar and milk together in a medium bowl until smooth and incorporated. (If the glaze begins to dry out as it sits, add water, 1 teaspoon at a time, to loosen.) Using a pastry brush, brush a thin layer of the glaze over the tops of the cookies, and let sit until the glaze has set, about 10 minutes.

➤ VARIATION
Christmas Spice Cookies with Chocolate Glaze

You will need 10 ounces of semisweet chocolate. The two-stage melting process for the chocolate helps ensure that it is the proper consistency.

Follow the recipe for Christmas Spice Cookies, omitting the glaze. When the cookies are cool, melt 8 ounces semisweet chocolate in the microwave on medium power, stirring several times, until smooth, about 3 minutes. Stir in an additional 2 ounces finely chopped semisweet chocolate until melted. (If the chocolate does not melt entirely, heat an additional 30 seconds at medium power.) Working with one cookie at a time, dollop about 1 teaspoon of chocolate onto the center of a cookie then use the back of the spoon to spread the chocolate into an even layer. Refrigerate the cookies until the chocolate sets, about 15 minutes.

RASPBERRY-NUT TART

Linzertorte

LINZERTORTE IS THOUGHT TO BE THE OLDEST tart in the world, at least according to its hometown of Linz, Austria. Whatever its age, this torte has proved to be a timeless classic, with its buttery nut crust and sweet raspberry jam filling.

But while the ingredients for Linzertorte couldn't be easier to prepare—a food processor makes quick work of the rich, nutty crust and the raspberry jam filling is store-bought—the process of transforming these two components into a finished tart can drive perfectionists (like us) over the edge. You can make a homely but still delicious Linzertorte with only modest effort, but for the holidays, we think it should look its best.

A Linzertorte is more crust than filling, so we started there. Walnuts made for a bitter, soft crust but tasters liked a combination of hazelnuts and almonds. Toasting the nuts was worth the extra step, but skinning the hazelnuts—a messy and irksome process—was not. As bizarre as it may sound, a hard-cooked egg yolk is standard in many classic recipes. Several sources credited this unlikely ingredient

MULLED SPICED WINE
Glögg

GLÖGG IS A SCANDINAVIAN MULLED WINE drink similar to other drinks served in Europe. It is traditionally served during the Christmas season. The warm drink usually consists of red wine simmered with spices, citrus zest, and sometimes a splash of a stronger spirit such as cognac. The mixture is heated, but not allowed to boil so the alcohol does not evaporate.

Mulled Spice Wine
Glögg
MAKES ABOUT 1½ QUARTS, SERVING 8

Any $10 bottle of medium- to full-bodied red wine will work here. Be sure to rid the orange zest of any white pith or it will make the drink bitter.

3	cinnamon sticks
10	whole cloves
10	black peppercorns
1	teaspoon (about 25) allspice berries
2	(750 ml) bottles medium- or full-bodied red wine
4	(2-inch-long) strips zest from 1 orange (see illustrations on page 346)
½	cup sugar plus extra to taste
2–4	tablespoons brandy

1. Toast the cinnamon, cloves, peppercorns, and allspice in a medium heavy-bottomed nonreactive saucepan over medium-high heat until fragrant, about 2 minutes. Add the wine, orange zest, and ½ cup sugar, cover partially, and bring to simmer, stirring occasionally to dissolve the sugar. Reduce the heat to low and simmer for 1 hour or until the wine is infused (do not boil, or cook for longer than 1 hour).

2. Strain the wine through a fine-mesh strainer, discarding the solids, and return to the saucepan. Stir in the brandy and additional sugar to taste. Serve warm. (If the wine cools, it can be reheated in the microwave or in a saucepan on the stovetop.)

with creating a supremely tender dough, but dough made with a cooked yolk was frail and crumbly. Instead, a single raw egg moistened and bound the dough nicely. Of the traditional spice choices, tasters endorsed cinnamon and allspice but rejected cloves. So far, this was smooth sailing.

Rolling the dough (and getting it into the pan) is where this recipe hit a snag. The standard method of rolling out the dough and gingerly fitting it into a tart pan was futile, as the delicate dough cracked and split. Patting the dough in place by hand yielded an uneven and unattractive crust.

After much consideration (and failure), we hit upon an unconventional but reliable method. We took a portion of the dough and rolled it out directly on the surface of the removable bottom disk of the tart pan, stopping just shy of the edges. We then dropped the tart pan bottom into the fluted ring and pressed the dough by hand just to the edges. To form the sidewalls, we took pieces of the remaining dough, rolled them into ropes, and gently pressed them partway up the walls of the tart pan. Success! As for the traditional lattice top, our attempt to sidestep rolling out dough and cutting strips was a failure; we tried crosshatching ropes of dough, but they looked odd. The best that could be done was to roll out the rather sticky dough between sheets of parchment paper or plastic wrap, cut the strips, and then chill them thoroughly. And forget about weaving the strips as you would if making a pie. Linzertorte dough lacks the resilience necessary for that kind of manipulation. Instead, by placing the strips one by one in precise order over the jam-filled tart, we found we could mimic the effect of a basket-weave design.

Yet our Linzertorte was still falling short of perfection. Beneath the layer of jam, the bottom crust was soft and slightly floury, as if underbaked. Adjustments in oven temperature were of no avail. We were forced to take more drastic measures and decided to prebake the unfilled pastry.

Although this worked, it was yet another step, one that required pie weights and foil. We reconsidered for a moment. The bottom crust posed the problem, not the sides. So we threw together another dough, lined only the bottom of the tart pan—stopping short of creating the walls—and prebaked the bottom crust without pie weights.

The crust was now fully baked and crisp. Once cooled, it was easy enough to use the remaining dough to form the sides of the tart shell. After a quick slick with jam and the arrangement of the lattice strips, we were ready to bake the tart. We brushed the dough with cream and sprinkled it with coarse turbinado sugar before baking. Served with a final flourish of whipped cream, this tart finally delivered on the promise of its rich heritage.

Raspberry-Nut Tart
Linzertorte
SERVES 10 TO 12

The tart dough can be made in advance, wrapped in plastic wrap, and refrigerated for up to 48 hours; let it soften at room temperature until malleable, about 1 hour, before using. Study the illustrations before forming the lattice top; once the strips have been put in place they cannot be repositioned because of the stickiness of the raspberry filling. Don't worry if the lattice strips tear or crack—any breaks will be almost unnoticeable once the tart is baked. The baked tart will hold well at room temperature for a day or so. Serve with lightly sweetened whipped cream flavored with kirsch (cherry liqueur) or framboise (raspberry liqueur).

5	ounces unblanched hazelnuts, toasted and cooled (about 1 cup)
2	ounces blanched whole almonds, toasted and cooled (about 1/3 cup)
1/2	cup plus 2 tablespoons granulated sugar
1/2	teaspoon salt
1	teaspoon grated zest from 1 lemon
1/2	teaspoon ground cinnamon
1/8	teaspoon ground allspice
1 1/2	cups (7 1/2 ounces) unbleached all-purpose flour
12	tablespoons (1 1/2 sticks) unsalted butter, cut into 1/2-inch cubes and chilled
1	large egg
1	teaspoon vanilla extract
1 1/4	cups raspberry preserves (13 1/2 ounces)
1	tablespoon juice from 1 lemon
1	tablespoon heavy cream
1 1/2	teaspoons turbinado or Demerara sugar (optional)

1. Adjust an oven rack to the lower-middle position and heat the oven to 350 degrees. Spray the inside of an 11-inch tart pan with a removable bottom with vegetable oil spray. Separate the bottom from the sides of the tart pan. Line the bottom with a piece of parchment paper that has been trimmed to fit and spray the parchment with vegetable oil; set aside.

2. Pulse the toasted nuts, granulated sugar, and salt in a food processor until very finely ground, about 18 pulses. Add the lemon zest, cinnamon, and allspice and pulse to combine. Add the flour and pulse to combine. Scatter the butter pieces over the mixture and pulse until the mixture resembles coarse meal, 12 to 15 pulses.

3. In a small bowl, use a fork to combine the egg and vanilla. With the machine running, pour the egg mixture through the feed tube and continue to process until the dough forms a large ball, about 10 seconds.

4. Transfer the dough to the counter and press into a cohesive mound. Divide the dough into 2 pieces, one piece slightly larger than other (the larger piece should weigh about 15 ounces and the smaller piece about 13 ounces). Flatten each piece into a 5-inch disk.

5. Following the illustrations below, place the smaller disk of dough in the center of the tart pan bottom, cover with plastic wrap, and roll out until just shy of the pan edges. Remove the plastic wrap, drop the pan bottom into fluted ring, and press the dough flush to the sides of the pan using your fingers. Using a dinner fork, poke holes uniformly in the dough and set the tart pan on the baking sheet and bake until beginning to brown around the edges, 15 to 18 minutes. Set the baking sheet on a wire rack and cool to room temperature.

6. Following the illustrations, pinch 4 Ping-Pong-ball-sized pieces from the larger disk of dough, and roll into ⅜-inch-diameter ropes. Lay the ropes around the edge of the cooled tart, connecting the rope ends, until the rim of the tart pan has been lined. Using your fingers, gently press the rope into fluted sides of tart pan, creating walls about ⅝ inch high (walls should not be as high as the rim of tart pan). Set the tart pan aside on a baking sheet.

7. Reshape the remaining dough into a disk and roll between two large, greased sheets of parchment into a 12-inch round about ⅛ inch thick (if the

FORMING THE CRUST

The Linzertorte dough is so delicate that we found it best to prebake just the bottom crust and add the sides later.

1. Roll out the small disk of dough on a parchment-lined tart pan bottom.

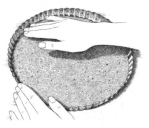

2. Drop the pan bottom into the fluted ring and press the dough to the edges. Set the tart pan on a baking sheet and bake.

3. Roll the balls of dough into ⅜-inch-thick ropes for the tart edges.

4. Once the tart bottom has cooled, line the edges with ropes of dough and press the ropes against the pan to form neat sides.

dough becomes too sticky and soft, refrigerate or freeze it until firm and workable). Peel off the top layer of parchment. Using a greased ruler, cut the dough into ¾-inch-wide strips (you will need 10 strips). Slide the parchment with the dough onto a baking sheet, cover loosely with parchment, and freeze until firm but not stiff, about 20 minutes (or refrigerate until firm, about 40 minutes).

8. While the lattice strips chill, stir the raspberry preserves and lemon juice together and spread the mixture evenly into the tart shell. Remove the dough strips from the freezer, loosen the parchment on the top, then invert and loosen the other piece of parchment. Following the illustrations below use two of the longest dough strips to create a big X in the center of the tart. Continue to lay the remaining strips around the tart to form a lattice. Press the ends of the strips against the rim of tart pan to trim.

MAKING A LATTICE TOP

Linzertorte dough is too soft to weave, but you can still create the illusion of a woven crust with this method.

1. Crisscross 2 long strips of dough to form an "X" over the center of the tart. Place 4 short strips around the edges, parallel to the central strips.

2. Place I strip between each edge strip and central strip.

3. Press the excess dough against the rim of the pan to trim.

9. Gently brush the lattice strips with the heavy cream and sprinkle with the turbinado sugar (if using). Bake the tart (still on the baking sheet) until deep golden brown, about 50 minutes. Let the tart cool on the baking sheet on a wire rack to room temperature, about 2 hours. Remove the outer tart pan ring. Slide a thin metal spatula between the parchment paper and bottom crust to loosen. Slide the tart onto a serving platter, cut into wedges, and serve.

CHOCOLATE TORTE WITH APRICOT JAM
Sacher Torte

A CREATION OF EARLY 19TH-CENTURY VIENNA, the Sacher torte is a chocolate layer cake flavored with apricot jam or glaze and coated with a thin, rich layer of chocolate. Despite the dessert's simplicity, we found countless different recipes—everything from the cake to the filling and icing was called into question. With our heads spinning from the different avenues to explore, we went into the test kitchen determined to make this elegant, flavorful dessert live up to its refined reputation.

We began our testing at square one by baking and tasting a variety of chocolate cakes. Devil's food cake and American chocolate butter cakes were quickly ruled out for this dessert as either too sweet or too rich. We tried sponge cakes, including our recipe for génoise, a French-style sponge cake. Some were laced with finely ground nuts—a traditional touch we found in several recipes. Tasters much preferred the génoise. Relatively light in texture, the cake had just the right amount of chocolate flavor and richness. Easy to make, the cake delivered a delicate chocolate flavor and light texture that readily absorbed the flavor of the apricot jam and complemented the sleek chocolate glaze.

As for the apricot flavoring, some recipes claim that the cake should simply be coated in an apricot glaze made from apricot jam that has been simmered with additional sugar until syrupy and strained of any chunky pieces. Others claim that a layer of raw apricot jam sandwiched between layers of cake, in addition to the coating of glaze, is the more authentic version. In the test kitchen, we tasted both versions and much preferred the additional layer of jam in the center of the cake. Tasters found the more pronounced apricot flavor a better accent to the cake's rich chocolate coating. Some tasters felt that the chunky bits of fruit marred the cake's texture, so we opted to process the jam in a food processor until relatively smooth. Briefly heating the jam made it easier to spread onto the cake.

For the smooth chocolate topping, we tried a variety of different chocolate glazes. Most were variations on ganache, a mixture of melted chocolate and cream, often with butter added. Although delicious in their own right, these coatings were too thick and creamy for our Sacher torte—they were more akin to frosting than glaze. We then tried adding corn syrup to the chocolate and cream and the result was just right. Adding the corn syrup gave the glaze a sleek, shiny appearance and a smooth, pourable consistency.

Its long and famous history would suggest that this cake is for adventurous pastry experts alone. But in reality the cake requires few ingredients and, with store-bought apricot jam and an easy chocolate glaze, it's simple to make, too.

Chocolate Torte with Apricot Jam

Sacher Torte

SERVES 8 TO 10

This cake stores very well in an airtight container in the refrigerator for up to 48 hours. The cake texture becomes slightly more dense and the overall flavor more intense after at least 6 hours in the refrigerator. Bring the cake to room temperature before serving with whipped cream.

CAKE

4   tablespoons (½ stick) unsalted butter
¾   cup (3¾ ounces) unbleached all-purpose flour
¼   cup (¾ ounce) Dutch-processed cocoa
½   teaspoon salt
6   large eggs
1   cup (7 ounces) sugar
1   teaspoon vanilla extract

APRICOT FILLING

1   (18-ounce) jar apricot jam (about 1⅓ cups)

CHOCOLATE GLAZE

½   cup heavy cream
2   tablespoons light corn syrup
4   ounces semisweet or bittersweet chocolate, chopped
½   teaspoon vanilla extract

1. FOR THE CAKE: Adjust an oven rack to the middle position and heat the oven to 350 degrees. Line the bottom of a 9-inch springform pan with a circle of parchment paper.

2. Melt the butter in a small saucepan over low heat. Remove from the heat and set aside. Sift the flour, cocoa, and salt together onto a large piece of parchment paper; set aside.

3. Whisk together the eggs and sugar in the bowl of a standing mixer until combined. Place the bowl over a pan of barely simmering water, making sure that the water does not touch the bottom of the bowl, and heat the egg mixture, whisking constantly, until warm to the touch, about 110 degrees on an instant-read thermometer. Remove from the heat and beat at medium-high speed until the eggs are pale, cream-colored, voluminous, and form a thick ribbon of tiny billowy bubbles that falls from the whisk and rests on top of the batter for several seconds when the whisk is held about 4 inches above the egg mixture (this should take 6 to 8 minutes). Beat in the vanilla. Turn off the mixer, transfer 1 cup of the egg mixture to a medium bowl, and stir in the melted butter until combined; set aside. Grab the two ends of the sheet of parchment paper (holding the flour mixture) to form a funnel and, with the mixer running at the lowest speed, slowly sprinkle the flour mixture into the batter until just barely incorporated. Add the melted butter mixture back to the batter in the standing mixer bowl and, with the mixer still running at the lowest speed, mix gently to incorporate, being careful not to deflate the batter.

4. Immediately push the batter from the bowl into the prepared springform pan with a rubber spatula, holding the bowl close to the bottom of the pan. Smooth the top with a spatula. Bake until

the cake is deep brown and springs back lightly when pressed with a finger, about 35 minutes. Transfer the pan to a wire rack and cool completely. When the cake is cool, run the blade of a thin metal spatula around the inside circumference of the springform pan to loosen the cake from the sides of the pan and remove. Invert the cake onto a plate or baking sheet, remove the pan bottom and parchment paper, and reinvert the cake onto the rack. Split in half following the illustrations on the right and set aside.

5. FOR THE FILLING: Process the apricot jam in a food processor until smooth, about 10 seconds. Transfer to a small saucepan and bring to a simmer, stirring constantly, over medium heat. Remove from the heat and set aside.

6. FOR THE GLAZE: Bring the cream and corn syrup to a full simmer over medium heat in a medium saucepan. Off the heat, add the chocolate; cover and let stand for 8 minutes. (If the chocolate has not completely melted, return the saucepan to low heat and stir constantly until melted.) Add the vanilla; stir very gently until the mixture is smooth. Cool until tepid so that a spoonful drizzled back into the pan mounds slightly. (The glaze can be refrigerated to speed up the cooling process, stirring every few minutes to ensure even cooling.)

7. TO ASSEMBLE THE TORTE: Invert the top layer of the cake onto a cardboard round cut just larger than the diameter of the cake. Using a spatula, spread ½ cup of the apricot jam evenly over the cake. Invert the second layer of cake over the first. Place the cake and cardboard round on a wire rack that has been set on a large rimmed baking sheet. Pour the remaining apricot jam on the top of the cake and, using an offset spatula, spread the jam over the edges and along the sides of the cake. Allow the excess jam to fall off the sides of the cake onto the baking sheet. Refrigerate the cake on the wire rack set on the baking sheet until the apricot jam is set, about 30 minutes.

8. Pour the chocolate glaze on top of the cake. Using a spatula, spread the glaze evenly over the top of the cake and spread it along the sides of the cake. Refrigerate the cake, still on the rack set over the baking sheet, until set, at least 1 hour and up to 48 hours. Transfer the cake to a large platter and serve.

LEVELING AND SPLITTING A CAKE

1. If the cake has mounded in the center, it should be leveled before being split. Gently press an outstretched hand on its surface and, holding a serrated knife parallel to the work surface, use a steady sawing motion to begin cutting at the same level as the cake's lowest point, slicing off the mound.

2. To cut into even layers, measure the height of the cake with a ruler and cut a small incision into the side with a paring knife to mark the desired thickness of your layers. Repeat every 3 to 4 inches around the circumference of the cake.

3. With a long serrated knife held parallel to the work surface, score the cake: With an outstretched palm gently pressed on the surface, slowly spin the cake away from you while pulling the knife toward you. The goal is to connect the incisions and score the cake, not to slice it.

4. Following the markings on the cake, cut deeper and deeper in the same manner. Gradually move the knife closer to the cake's center with each rotation. When the knife progresses past the cake's center, the cut is complete. Carefully slide the knife out and separate the layers.

5

FRANCE

OYSTERS WITH MIGNONETTE SAUCE

Huîtres Mignonette

A SIMPLE YET SATISFYING FIRST COURSE IN France is half a dozen oysters served with a bracingly bright sauce called *sauce mignonette*. Sauce mignonette, or mignonette as it's generally referred to, is a trio of strongly flavored ingredients: crushed black peppercorns, minced shallots, and red wine vinegar. The key to this sauce is twofold: you need to crack the peppercorns by hand (crushing them using the bottom of a pot or a rolling pin) and you need to allow the mignonette to sit for at least one hour, but ideally overnight, so that the flavors can marry.

While this is a simple first course, with a total of four ingredients, there are some rules that cannot be overlooked. The oysters must be ice cold and they should be served nestled in a bed of crushed ice to maintain a chilled temperature. They should also be opened as carefully as possible, in order to preserve as much of the brine (or liquor) that surrounds the oyster meat.

Oysters on the Half Shell with Mignonette Sauce

Huîtres Mignonette
SERVES 6

Serve the sauce in a small bowl with a small serving spoon, so guests can drizzle the sauce, as desired, over the oysters before eating.

3	tablespoons black peppercorns, crushed coarse
1	medium shallot, minced (about 3 tablespoons)
⅔	cup red wine vinegar
36	fresh oysters, shucked

Stir the peppercorns, shallot, and vinegar together in a small serving bowl and let sit for 1 hour. (The sauce can be covered and refrigerated for up to 3 days.) Serve with the freshly shucked oysters.

SHUCKING OYSTERS

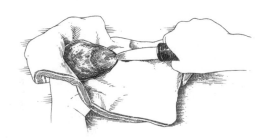

1. Start by holding the oyster cupped side down in a kitchen towel. Keep the oyster flat as you work to keep the flavorful juices from spilling out of the shell. Locate the hinge with the tip of the knife.

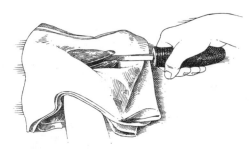

2. Push between the edges of the shells, wiggling back and forth to pry them open.

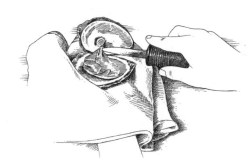

3. Detach the meat from the top shell and discard the shell.

4. To make eating easier, sever the muscle that holds the meat of the oyster to the bottom shell. As you do all of this, work over a bowl to catch the flavorful oyster liquor that is released.

PÂTÉ

A SLICE OF RICH, MEATY PÂTÉ EATEN ON ITS own or spread on a crust of bread can be an ethereal experience. Yet this dish has very humble beginnings. Traditionally made with the leftover scraps of meat and fat from butchering the family pig, pâtés and their close relatives, terrines, have slowly been elevated to an art form over the years, making use of top-grade ingredients like truffles and foie gras (the rich and luxurious fattened liver of a goose or duck). Pâtés and terrines can be as simple and coarse as chopped chicken liver and as extravagant and delicate as a molded *terrine de foie gras*.

There is, however, a bit of confusion when it comes to the terms pâté and terrine: A pâté traditionally (and strictly speaking) refers only to a pastry shell filled with meat, fish, vegetables, or fruit, prepared in a mold, baked in the oven, and served in thick slices, either hot or cold. *Pâté en terrine* (or simply terrine) is a meat, game, or fish preparation put into a terrine dish (a deep, rectangular dish) lined with bacon and cooked in the oven. A terrine is always served cold. Today the terms pâté and terrine are used interchangeably so the French now call the authentic pâté (the one baked in the crust) *pâté en croute*. Modern pâtés and terrines can be made with coarsely ground or chopped meats (such as country pâté, or pâté de campagne) or with pureed meats, for a finer textured pâté. These molded and baked terrines, while delicious, can be terribly labor-intensive.

So for those of us who love the flavor, though not the work, of homemade pâté, there is a range of pâtés that are very approachable for the home cook. A liver mousse, for example, is a simple pâté that can be made with the liver of duck, pork, or chicken. With a simple mousse pâté, the meat and aromatics are sautéed first, then pureed and placed in a mold (or a bowl), then chilled until ready to eat. These mousse pâtés typically also contain whipped cream or butter to lighten their flavor and texture—perfect for smearing on bread or a cracker.

Chicken Liver Pâté
Pâté de Foie de Poulet
MAKES ABOUT 2 CUPS

It is important to cook the livers until just rosy in the center in order to avoid the telltale chalky flavor that results from overcooking. The exposed surface of the pâté tends to oxidize quickly, discoloring and developing a slight metallic flavor. We found that pressing plastic wrap flush against the surface of the pâté minimizes this effect, and any remaining discoloration can be easily scraped away before serving. Serve with toasted slices of baguette, toast points, or crackers. Because livers are highly perishable (as are all organ meats), this pâté should be consumed within two days of preparation.

8	tablespoons (1 stick) unsalted butter
3	large shallots, sliced (about ¾ cup)
1	tablespoon minced fresh thyme leaves
	Salt
1	pound chicken livers, rinsed and patted dry, fat and connective tissue removed
¾	cup dry vermouth
2	teaspoons brandy
	Ground black pepper

1. Melt the butter in a 12-inch skillet over medium-high heat. Add the shallots, thyme, and ¼ teaspoon salt and cook until the shallots are lightly browned, about 5 minutes. Add the chicken livers and cook, stirring constantly, about 1 minute. Add the vermouth and simmer until the livers are cooked but still have a rosy interior, 4 to 6 minutes.

2. Using a slotted spoon, transfer the livers to a food processor, leaving the liquid in the skillet. Continue to simmer the liquid over medium-high heat until slightly syrupy, about 2 minutes, then add to the processor.

3. Add the brandy to the processor and process the mixture until very smooth, about 2 minutes, stopping to scrape down the sides of the bowl as needed. Season with salt and pepper to taste, then transfer to a clean serving bowl and smooth the top. Press plastic wrap flush to the surface of the pâté and refrigerate until firm, at least 6 hours or up to 2 days. Let soften at room temperature for 30 minutes before serving.

CHEESE PUFFS

Gougères

GOUGÈRES, CHEESE-FLAVORED CREAM PUFFS, hail from Burgundy and are an ideal hors d'oeuvre paired with a glass of the region's famous red wine. Made from the French pastry dough *pâte à choux*, a perfect gougère has a crisp caramel-colored exterior that yields to a tender, slightly moist interior. It should taste nutty from the browned cheese and a little eggy—not unlike the soft, custardy interior of a popover. Unfortunately, most versions we've had are either dry and brittle or devoid of flavor and soggy. What is the trick to a perfect gougère?

To start, we needed to have a better understanding of the base. Pâte à choux is the most basic French pastry. It has both sweet and savory applications and is most familiar when filled with pastry cream to make éclairs. Beware the pitfalls of bad pâte à choux. The dough will spread on the baking sheet if too soft, and it may not rise properly. It may bake up lopsided, it can collapse after baking, and, finally (the most common problem), it can turn soggy as it cools. We decided to start by developing a technique and recipe for pâte à choux, then we'd move on to incorporating the cheese for the best gougères.

The traditional technique of making pâte à choux is to bring water or milk, salt, and butter to a boil in a saucepan. When the mixture reaches a rolling boil, flour is stirred in to make a paste, the saucepan is returned to low heat, and the paste is cooked, all the while being stirred to stimulate the development of gluten, the protein that gives bread doughs elasticity and provides for a better, stronger rise in the oven. Then the dough is removed from the heat and eggs are beaten in one by one. The pâte à choux is then ready to be piped onto a baking sheet and baked.

To determine how long the paste really needs to be cooked on the stovetop, we made four batches and cooked each to a different degree—from not at all up to five minutes—over low heat. The uncooked batch and the one cooked for only a minute failed to attain much height when we baked them. The batches made from paste cooked for three and five minutes, however, both baked into voluminous puffs. Because none of the tasters could detect a significant difference between these two, we opted for three minutes of cooking. Since stovetops undoubtedly vary, we took the temperature of the paste and used this as an additional measure of doneness.

The traditional method of introducing the eggs is to do so gradually, stirring vigorously after each addition. If added all at once, the eggs splash about and require the patience of Job and the arm of Hercules to incorporate them into the dough. We discovered, however, that all of this grunt work was entirely unnecessary when we transferred the cooked paste to either a standing mixer or a food processor. The eggs incorporated swiftly, with a minimal amount of effort. Best of all, both machines produced pastry superior to one made by hand—the puffs rose higher and were lighter and airier. It was the food processor, though, that became our machine of choice, because it brought the paste together with mercurial speed. We let the hot paste whirl around for a few seconds to cool it slightly, then, with the machine running, we added the eggs in a steady stream. Pâte à choux has never come together more quickly and easily.

With the technique set, we focused next on the ingredients, beginning with the liquid. Pastry made exclusively with milk was gloriously golden but disappointingly soft; one made with only water was light and crisp but ashen and wan. Neither appealed. With equal parts milk and water, the pastry browned nicely, but its texture remained slightly soft. Three parts water to one part milk made a pastry that both colored and crisped agreeably.

Whole eggs are the most common option in pâte à choux, but we found that two whole eggs with an additional egg white yielded the most delicate texture, richest flavor, and golden color.

Butter is added to pâte à choux not only for flavor but also for texture; the fat helps to keep the dough tender. We tried amounts ranging from 3 to 5 tablespoons and found that the latter yielded the richest flavor and most delicately crisp texture.

Finally, we tackled the flour. After attempts with bread and pastry flour proved insignificant, we decided to stick with all-purpose flour. Its moderate level of protein developed just the right amount of gluten.

The next step was placing shapely portions of dough on a baking sheet. While some recipes suggest that a pastry bag can be sidestepped and the pâte à choux simply dropped onto the baking sheet like cookie dough, we had no success with this technique; the baked puffs were uneven and unattractive. Turning to a pastry bag fitted with a plain tip, we piped the neatest, roundest mounds possible onto a greased and parchment paper–lined baking sheet. Some recipes suggested using the back of a teaspoon dipped in water to smooth the surface and even out the shape of the mounds, and this technique proved useful.

With our pâte à choux recipe in order, we added varying amounts of Gruyère cheese (the traditional cheese used in these puffs) until we found the perfect amount: 3 ounces. The proper baking of pâte à choux is as key to the pastry's success as are proper preparation and ingredients. If the puffs are soft and underdone but removed from the oven because they are brown, they will collapse before your very eyes. The puffs are leavened by steam pushing up from the interior so, as you might imagine, they require a blast of heat to get them going. With a little experimentation, we hit upon the right temperature and time combination: 425 degrees for 15 minutes, then down to 375 degrees for another 8 to 13 minutes.

After being baked, the pastry may be crisp externally, but the inside remains moist with residual steam. If this steam is not released, the moisture will be absorbed into the pastry, making it soggy. This means that, immediately following baking, the puffs must be slit to release steam and returned to a turned-off, propped-open oven where they can dry out for about 45 minutes to ensure crispness. Once dry and crisp and finally cooled, the puffs can stay at room temperature for a day or be stored in a zipper-lock bag and thrown into the freezer for a month or so. Just a brief warm-up in the oven to rejuvenate them and they are ready to serve.

Cheese Puffs
Gougères
MAKES SIXTEEN 3-INCH PUFFS

If Gruyère is unavailable, Swiss or Emmentaler cheese may be substituted. Coating the pan with nonstick cooking spray then lining it with parchment paper ensures that the parchment will stay in place when piping out the sticky cheese puff dough in step 4. Serve as an hors d'oeuvre or as an accompaniment to soup or salad.

2	large eggs
1	large egg white
6	tablespoons water
5	tablespoons unsalted butter, cut into ½-inch cubes
2	tablespoons whole milk
¼	teaspoon salt
½	cup (2½ ounces) unbleached all-purpose flour, sifted
3	ounces Gruyère cheese, shredded (about ¾ cup)
	Pinch cayenne pepper

1. Adjust an oven rack to the middle position and heat the oven to 425 degrees. Spray a large baking sheet with nonstick cooking spray and line it with parchment paper; set aside. Fit a large pastry bag with a ½-inch plain tip; set aside. Beat the eggs and egg white together with a fork in a small liquid measuring cup; you should have ½ cup (discard any excess).

2. Bring the water, butter, milk, and salt to a boil in a small saucepan over medium heat, stirring occasionally, until the butter is melted. Immediately remove the saucepan from the heat and stir in the flour until well combined and the mixture forms a dough that clears the sides of the pan, about 45 seconds. Return the saucepan to low heat and cook, stirring constantly using a smearing motion, until the mixture is slightly shiny, looks like wet sand, and tiny beads of fat appear on the bottom of the saucepan, about 3 minutes (the mixture should register 175 to 180 degrees on an instant-read thermometer).

3. Immediately transfer the mixture to a food processor and process with the feed tube open for 10 seconds to cool slightly. With the machine running, gradually add the eggs in a steady stream. When all the eggs have been added, scrape down the sides of the bowl, add the cheese and cayenne and continue to process for 30 seconds until a smooth, thick, sticky paste forms.

4. Following the illustrations on page 214, fill the prepared pastry bag with the paste. Twisting the top of the bag to apply pressure, push the paste toward the bag tip and pipe onto the prepared baking sheet into sixteen 2-inch mounds, spaced about 1 inch apart. Use the back of a teaspoon dipped in a bowl of cold water to even out the shape and smooth the surface of the piped mounds.

5. Bake for 15 minutes, then without opening the oven door, reduce the oven temperature to 375 degrees and continue to bake until no longer soft and squishy, but fairly firm and golden brown, 8 to 13 minutes longer.

6. Remove the baking sheet from the oven and with a paring knife cut a ¾-inch slit into the side of each puff to release the steam. Return the puffs to the oven, turn the oven off, and prop the oven door open with the handle of a wooden spoon. Let the pastry dry until the center is just moist (not wet) and the surface is crisp, about 45 minutes. Serve warm. (The puffs can be cooled completely and stored at room temperature for up to 24 hours, or frozen in a zipper-lock bag for up to 1 month. Before serving, crisp them in a 300-degree oven for 5 minutes if room temperature, or 8 minutes if frozen.)

➤ VARIATION
Gougères Ring
MAKES ONE 12-INCH RING

This variation makes a nice presentation. Although the puffs bake into each other, they can easily be pulled apart at the table.

Follow the recipe for Cheese Puffs, piping the paste in step 4 into 2-inch mounds, arranged in a ring with the sides of the puffs just touching each other. Bake and dry as directed in steps 5 and 6. (The puffs will bake into each other but will still remain distinct.)

PROVENÇAL VEGETABLE SOUP
Soupe au Pistou

DURING THE SUMMER MONTHS IN THE SOUTH of France, there is one soup that reigns supreme and it is *soupe au pistou*—a summer vegetable soup with a delicate broth that is intensified by a dollop of garlicky pistou—the French equivalent of Italy's pesto. The recipe for this soup reads like the offerings at a Provençal farmers market in August: basil, garlic, haricot verts (slim green beans), zucchini, and a white bean known as *coco de Mollans*. It's no wonder that soupe au pistou works so well—as they say, what grows together, goes together.

When this soup is good, you get the sense that not only can you see summer in the bowl, but you can taste it as well. Unfortunately, we've had our share of bad versions. Overcooked vegetables and the wrong proportions, as well as too much garlic in the pistou, can ruin not only the flavor of this soup, but the texture as well. Our goal was to develop a recipe to guarantee the perfect balance of all the elements in this classic Provençal soup.

Every soup needs a base, a broth in which to simmer (in this case) the vegetables. To make a good summer soup, these tender vegetables would need the support of a broth that was rich and multidimensional, not characterized by any single, distinctive flavor. We started our testing by making a vegetable stock. Herbs, garlic, and vegetables such as onion, carrot, celery, tomato, and fennel were simmered in water, then strained out before fresh vegetables were added to create the soup. The resulting broth had the pleasant flavor of fresh vegetables, but once we swirled in the pistou, the delicate flavors became overwhelmed by the pistou's heady garlic, basil, and cheese.

These early steps quickly taught us something about the inherent nature of a vegetable soup that has a flavorful condiment like pistou stirred in—the pistou and vegetables are dominant, with the broth acting as a canvas to show them off. In other words, we needn't labor over a delicate broth whose flavor would be obscured by stronger flavors. So instead of homemade stock, we focused on testing store-bought broths. Beef broth didn't make any sense in a vegetable soup, so we omitted it from the lineup, but chicken broth, while not perfect, was promising, with a mellow and sturdy character. We also tested vegetable broth, which we liked even more, although its flavors were a bit potent. But when we mixed the vegetable broth with water (a 1 to 1 ratio), we were able to achieve an excellent balance of flavors.

Now we could focus on the stars of this soup: summer vegetables. Not wanting to clutter the soup with any vegetables that weren't essential, we steered toward a simple, clean soup filled only with vegetables of the season. Leeks, green beans, and zucchini all made the cut quickly. Their tender flavors, different shapes, and varying shades of green made for a balanced summer lineup.

Next we turned to traditional white beans to give the soup some heft. Typically, fresh white beans are used, but fresh beans can be difficult to find. Instead we tested both canned and dried white beans (cannellini or navy beans). Both canned and dried were great in this dish, but the canned white beans won out for sheer convenience. Pasta is also a traditional accompaniment to the summer vegetables, and we chose orecchiette pasta for its easy-to-spoon shape, but any small pasta or thin strand pasta broken into 2-inch pieces will work. We added carrots, celery, and garlic to give the soup an aromatic quality. Finally, tomatoes were chosen to add a modicum of acid as well as a dash of color. Since the flavor and texture of fresh tomatoes is often a gamble (after all, we don't live in Provence), we chose canned tomatoes, which we often use in the test kitchen for soups, stews, and sauces. For texture, we settled on whole tomatoes rather than diced—diced tomatoes turned to mush too quickly. We seeded the tomatoes to prevent any bitterness from spoiling the clean flavors of the soup. And finally, we diced and rinsed the tomatoes—rinsing them ensures a clear, not murky, broth.

Our vegetables chosen, we turned to perfecting the technique. For this recipe, timing is everything. Ideally, all the vegetables and pasta should be finished cooking at once, then served immediately before any of them overcooks. To do that we simply added the elements that cook the longest first and staggered the addition of the rest based on their required cooking times.

We started by cooking the leeks, carrots, and celery slowly over medium heat. Once they were soft, we added the garlic for 30 seconds, just long enough to bloom the flavor. To this we added the liquid, 6 cups each of broth and water, allowing the mixture to simmer for a few minutes—this doctoring method fortified our vegetable broth into a well-rounded base. Now it was time to add the pasta and vegetables. Since the pasta needs the longest amount of time to cook, we added that first. After a few minutes we added the haricots verts. Last, we tossed in the white beans, tomatoes, and zucchini, all of which needed only a couple of minutes to heat through and turn tender.

Now, it was time to tackle the pistou. Although it's traditionally made by mashing fresh basil, garlic, and olive oil together in a mortar and pestle, our first task was to update this technique for modern kitchens. Turning to the food processor, we made the pistou in seconds. While cheese is sometimes added to the finished soup, we decided to simplify things and add it directly into the pistou. With our condiment prepared, we were ready to serve the soup. Some recipes call for pouring the soup over the pistou in a large serving bowl, then ladling portions out. But we wanted tasters to be able to appreciate the variety of vegetables in this soup before the pistou made our clear broth cloudy. So we ladled the soup into individual serving bowls, then topped each with a dollop of pistou, leaving it up each person to stir it in as desired. This soup looked just like summer—and tasted like it too.

TRIMMING ENDS FROM GREEN BEANS

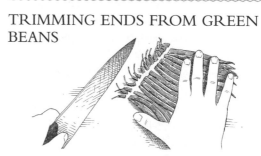

Instead of trimming the end from one green bean at a time, line up the beans on a cutting board and trim all of the ends with just one slice.

Provençal Vegetable Soup

Soupe au Pistou

SERVES 6 AS A MAIN COURSE

If you cannot find haricots verts (thin green beans), substitute regular green beans and cook them for an extra minute or two. You can substitute any small pasta shape or thin strand pasta broken into 2-inch lengths for the orecchiette (the cooking times might alter slightly). Rinsing the canned tomatoes after they've been drained and chopped prevents the soup from looking murky. The pistou can't be made more than a few hours ahead or its color will dull.

PISTOU

- ¾ cup packed fresh basil leaves
- ½ cup olive oil
- 1½ ounces Parmesan, grated (about ¾ cup)
- 2 medium garlic cloves, minced or pressed through a garlic press (about 2 teaspoons)
- ⅛ teaspoon ground black pepper

SOUP

- 2 tablespoons olive oil
- 1 large leek (about 8 ounces), white and light green part only, halved lengthwise, and sliced ½ inch thick
- 2 celery ribs, cut into ½-inch pieces
- 2 medium carrots, peeled and sliced ¼ inch thick
  Salt
- 4 medium garlic cloves, minced or pressed through a garlic press (about 4 teaspoons)
- 6 cups low-sodium vegetable broth
- 6 cups water
- 1 cup orecchiette pasta (see note)
- 1 pound haricot verts, trimmed and cut into ½-inch pieces (see note)
- 1 medium zucchini, quartered lengthwise and sliced ¼ inch thick
- 1 (15-ounce) can cannellini or navy beans, drained and rinsed
- 1 (14.5-ounce) can whole tomatoes, drained, seeded, chopped medium, and rinsed
  Ground black pepper

1. FOR THE PISTOU: Process all of the ingredients together in a food processor until pureed and smooth, about 10 seconds; set aside.

2. FOR THE SOUP: Heat the oil in a large Dutch oven over medium heat until shimmering. Add the leek, celery, carrots, and ½ teaspoon salt and cook, stirring occasionally, until softened, 8 to 10 minutes.

3. Stir in the garlic and cook until fragrant, about 30 seconds. Stir in the broth and water and bring to a simmer. Stir in the pasta and simmer until slightly softened, about 5 minutes. Stir in the haricots verts and simmer until bright green but still crunchy, about 3 minutes. Stir in the zucchini, cannellini beans, and tomatoes and simmer until all the vegetables are tender, about 3 minutes longer.

4. Season with salt and pepper to taste. Ladle the soup into individual serving bowls and garnish each with a generous tablespoon of the pistou before serving.

FRENCH ONION SOUP

Soupe à l'Oignon Gratinée

THE ORIGINS OF *SOUPE À L'OIGNON GRATINÉE* are often disputed; some think the soup hails from Lyon where onions grow plentifully, while others believe it's an invention of Parisian restaurants. And the third possibility—and the most likely—is that the soup was born out of necessity from a peasant's larder: water is added to onions, topped with stale bread and cheese, and voilà, you have soup.

Pedigree aside, we do know that French onion soup should have a dark, rich broth, intensely flavored by an abundance of slow-cooked onions, and covered by a crusty slice of French bread that is broth-soaked beneath and cheesy on top. We had developed a recipe that fit this description perfectly, using an abundance of caramelized onions and a mix of chicken and beef broths, so we thought we knew all there was to know about French onion soup. That was, until a friend from France, Henri Pinon, visited the test kitchen and set us straight.

Henri reviewed our recipe and, with a wave of his hand, said our recipe was fine, but he knew of a better way. This we had to see, so we stepped back and watched Henri prepare his soup. He began by caramelizing sliced onions in oil until they became quite dark, then he deglazed them with water to stop them from sticking or burning, scraping up all the browned bits (the fond) that had accumulated on the bottom of the pot. So far so good—his recipe was similar to the test kitchen's. But then he did something we hadn't seen before. He repeated this caramelization process (cooking the onions, deglazing, and scraping) multiple times over the course of a couple of hours, until the onions were a deep mahogany brown we never thought possible. And remember, he was only using oil, onions, and water. Finally, he added 8 cups of water and finished the soup with a bit of white wine—no stock at all!

We tasted the soup and were amazed by the layers of onion flavor—the result of the repeated building of fond and deglazing. We're quite familiar with building a fond and deglazing, but we'd never repeated the technique over and over like this. This simple soup tasted rich and deep and more oniony than the test kitchen's version. We decided at that point to revisit our recipe and see if we could incorporate some of his technique.

While we loved the results of Henri's technique, we knew most home cooks wouldn't want to spend three plus hours making onion soup, so we needed to make some modifications. First, we had to start with the onions. We had used red onions in the past, but really liked Henri's soup using yellow onions. Preparing batches of soup using Henri's technique, one with red onions and one with yellow onions, we tasted them side by side. Both red and yellow onions yielded a good onion soup, but the red onions gave the soup a murky color. The yellow onions had the right balance—intensely oniony, sweet but not cloying, with subtle complexity and nuance and a rich, clear broth.

Now to the heart and soul of this dish—caramelization, the procedure in which the onions are cooked slowly until the melting sugars in the onions burn slightly, thus causing browning. Caramelization is a two-step process: First, the moisture is cooked out of the onions. Then, with the moisture gone, the onions begin to brown and caramelize. Browning happens quickly following the evaporation of moisture, but the whole process can take anywhere from 10 minutes to two hours, depending on the degree of caramelization desired—at least that's what we thought. Henri's slow method for the entire process took even longer; at least three hours. We wanted a compromise in cooking time and looked for a way to jump-start the caramelization process.

We found our jump start in how we cooked the moisture out of the onions. First, we found that adding salt to the onions as they began to cook helped draw out some of the water. Second, we found that covering the pot for this initial cooking time encouraged the onions to sweat and soften, losing volume (and moisture) in much less time than if we had left the pot uncovered. Encouraged by our efforts, we now focused on the actual caramelization of the onions.

We tended the pot for the next 30 minutes, stirring frequently, until the onions were dark brown and very soft, but they hadn't yet achieved that completely broken-down texture and deep, dark brown color we remembered from Henri's version. We increased the cooking times in 10-minute increments, watching subtle changes take place in

---

CORE TECHNIQUE

INCREASING THE POWER OF FOND

Fond, the browned bits left clinging to the pan after sautéing meat or aromatics, contribute a great base of flavor to sauces, soups, and stews. In our French Onion Soup, we took the method of creating fond one step further. Here, the fond results from caramelized onions. Once the fond has been created, we deglaze the pan and allow the liquid to evaporate. But instead of continuing with the recipe, we repeat the process again and again— caramelizing and deglazing, allowing for multiple layers of fond. The result? A broth with an intensely oniony flavor.

the onions' appearance the longer they cooked. Each time the onion fond built up on the bottom of the pan and became dark brown, we deglazed it with a little water, scraping the bottom clean again. This process happened three times before, with careful scrutiny, we decided these onions were ready to be made into soup. They were very dark brown and so soft as to form a paste.

Adding the water and wine, we simmered the soup for just 10 minutes and it was rich and flavorful, but we wondered if we could make it even better. Taking a cue from the test kitchen's original recipe, we veered from Henri's method to test store-bought broths. Testing beef, chicken, and vegetable broths side by side and then a combination of broths (chicken and beef, chicken and vegetable, etc.) we found that none were quite right. All chicken broth made our soup taste too chickeny and the combination of chicken and beef (which we used in our original recipe) didn't taste right using this new method. Finally, we found that diluting chicken broth with water (slightly more water than broth) produced a broth that heightened the flavor of the onions, yet didn't mask it. And instead of finishing the soup with white wine, as we did in the original, we found that dry sherry was a better fit, deepening the soup's rich, earthy flavors.

With our soup just right, it was time to focus on the bread and cheese. Some recipes call for placing the bread in the bottom of the bowl and ladling the soup over it. We disagree. We opt to set the bread on top, so that only the bottom of the slice is moistened with broth while its top is crusted with cheese. The bread can then physically support the cheese and prevent it from sinking into the soup. To keep as much cheese as possible on the surface, we found it best to use two slices of bread to fill the mouth of the bowl completely. A baguette can be cut on the bias as necessary to secure the closest fit in the bowl and should be dried out in the oven until toasted, which helps to delay the soggy bread factor. Traditionally, French onion soup is topped with Swiss, Gruyère, or Emmentaler. Swiss was passable, but both Gruyère and Emmentaler melted to perfection and were sweet, nutty, and faintly tangy.

The final coup that weakens knees and makes French onion soup irresistible is a browned, bubbly, molten cheese crust. The quickest way to brown the cheese is to set the bowls on a baking sheet under the broiler, making heat-safe bowls essential—this is no soup for fine china. Bowls or crocks with handles also make maneuvering easier. In the end, we found that this is in no way a fast soup, but it needn't be an all-day affair either.

French Onion Soup
Soupe à l'Oignon Gratinée
SERVES 6

Be patient while caramelizing the onions; the process is slow (it takes about 2 hours) but the resulting soup, which comes together quickly after caramelization, is well worth the effort. You can substitute Swiss for Emmentaler or Gruyère cheese. Use broiler-safe bowls and make sure the rim of the bowls is 4 to 5 inches from the heating element in order to obtain good browning. If your bowls are not broiler-safe (or if you are unsure) set the oven temperature to 500 degrees and bake the soup (rather than broil) in step 6 until the cheese is melted.

3	tablespoons unsalted butter
5	medium yellow onions (about 3 pounds), halved and sliced thin
	Salt
4¾	cups water, plus extra as needed
4	cups low-sodium chicken broth
8	sprigs fresh thyme, tied together with kitchen twine
I	bay leaf
¼	cup dry sherry
	Ground black pepper
I	baguette, sliced on the bias into ¾-inch-thick slices
8	ounces Gruyère or Emmentaler cheese, shredded (about 2½ cups) (see note)

1. Melt the butter in a large Dutch oven over medium heat. Stir in the onions and 1 teaspoon salt, cover, and cook until the onions are wet and slightly wilted, about 10 minutes. Uncover and continue to cook, stirring occasionally, until the

liquid cooks off and the onions are translucent, about 20 minutes.

2. Reduce the heat to low and continue to cook the onions, frequently scraping up any browned bits on the bottom of the pot, until deep brown and very soft, 40 to 60 minutes.

3. Continue to cook the onions, stirring every 5 minutes, until a dark crust covers the bottom of the pan, about 10 minutes. Stir in ¼ cup of water, scrape up the crust, and continue to cook until another dark crust forms, 2 to 3 minutes; repeat this process 2 more times.

4. Stir in the chicken broth, remaining 4 cups water, thyme, and bay leaf, scraping up any final bits of the browned crust. Bring to a simmer and cook for 10 minutes. Remove and discard the thyme and bay leaf. Off the heat, stir in the sherry and season with salt and pepper to taste.

5. Meanwhile, adjust an oven rack to the middle position and heat the oven to 325 degrees. Arrange the baguette slices in a single layer on a baking sheet and bake until the bread is dry, crisp, and very lightly colored at the edges, about 10 minutes; set aside.

6. To serve: Adjust an oven rack 6 inches from the broiler element and heat the broiler. Set individual broiler-safe soup bowls or crocks on a baking sheet and fill each with about 1¾ cups of soup. Top each bowl with 2 baguette slices and sprinkle evenly with the Gruyère. Broil until well browned and bubbly, 5 to 10 minutes. Cool 5 minutes before serving.

SALAD WITH BACON AND POACHED EGG

Salade Lyonnaise

IT'S NOT OFTEN THAT A SALAD CAN BE BOTH refined and immensely satisfying—salade Lyonnaise is one. It starts with frisée (a mildly bitter curly lettuce), which is often mixed with other lettuces in order to obtain a variety of textures and flavors. Lardons (French-style bacon) are cooked until the fat renders; the meat is tossed into the salad as a garnish and the fat forms the flavorful base of the vinaigrette. Bread slices are cut into croutons, seasoned, and crisped. Perched on top of the salad is the pièce de résistance—a poached egg, still warm and runny in the center—which, when broken, helps mingle together all the flavors.

Salade Lyonnaise has gradually gained popularity in American restaurants over the last decade and has appeared on menus in many guises. Sometimes cheese is added, often nuts accompany the cheese, and we've even seen it served with pan-roasted sweetbreads. But operating on the belief that simpler is oftentimes better, we returned to tradition to develop a recipe that would marry these flavors in a traditional way, yet at the same time make it feasible for the home cook.

The most obvious starting point was the lettuce. Frisée comes in small, tight heads attached at the core. It is a member of the chicory family and has delicately slender, curly leaves with a slightly bitter flavor. While frisée is delicious on its own, we came across a handful of recipes for salade Lyonnaise in our research that mixed the frisée with other lettuces for a contrast in color and flavor. We tried dandelion greens and mâche, which both work well with frisée. And because these greens can sometimes be hard to find, we looked for an alternative and found one in mesclun mix (a combination of young greens, which typically includes dandelion greens, mâche, radicchio, and frisée).

With our lettuces decided, we turned to the croutons. We started with white sandwich bread, cut into cubes (white sandwich bread makes consistently sized croutons and is usually on hand). From here we had two choices: brown and crisp them in a sauté pan or bake them in the oven. The sauté pan yielded perfect croutons, but needed a lot of attention to prevent burning. The croutons made in the oven were low maintenance and yielded perfectly browned and crispy croutons.

Next we focused our attention on the bacon. Traditionally the bacon is cut into lardons (thin strips) from a slab, then fried to render the fat (later used for the vinaigrette). We found it difficult to find slab bacon in our supermarket and decided to use sliced bacon instead. First we cut the slices into thin strips, but by the time their fat had rendered they were more like jarred bacon bits than the meaty, chewy-crisp bursts of smoky bacon that make this salad so good. Instead, we turned to thick-cut bacon, cut the slices into ½-inch dice, and fried them to the point where they were just getting crispy, yet still had a slight chew and enough presence that they didn't get lost with the other flavors.

With our bacon rendered and set aside, we developed the vinaigrette. What gives the vinaigrette in a salade Lyonnaise its distinctive flavor is the rendered bacon fat left over from frying the bacon. As shallots are traditional in this dressing, we started by softening them in the bacon fat over medium-low heat. Once the shallots were cooked, we poured in red wine vinegar—the traditional choice, although sherry vinegar is also quite good in this salad. (It's worthwhile to note that this vinaigrette is a bit more acidic than most; the acidity is necessary to cut through the richness contributed by the bacon fat, olive oil, and poached egg.) Adding the vinegar to the pan allowed us to scrape up the browned bits left behind from cooking the bacon. Along with the vinegar, we added some Dijon mustard. We finished our meaty, acidic dressing with olive oil. Once we tossed the lettuces in the warm vinaigrette, we portioned it onto six individual serving plates sprinkling the bacon and croutons evenly over them.

With our salad near completion, we set about poaching the eggs. We knew from past test kitchen findings that adding a bit of white distilled vinegar to the poaching water prevents the eggs from feathering out and becoming ragged-looking. The tricky part, however, is poaching six eggs at the same time. We found a simple solution, one that requires only a few extra dishes. Two eggs are cracked into each of three tea cups then gently lowered into the water. This method allows all six eggs to be slipped into the water at the same time. To remove each of the six eggs from the water without overcooking, we carefully and quickly removed each egg onto a plate using a slotted spoon—this took only 30 seconds. From there we gently slid an egg onto each salad—the crowning touch to an enduring French favorite.

Salad with Bacon and Poached Egg

Salade Lyonnaise

SERVES 6

Mesclun mix can be substituted for the dandelion greens and mâche. Timing is key here; the salad should be dressed just moments before poaching the eggs. If the salad is dressed too early it will wilt, but if the poached eggs sit for too long the yolks will overcook and solidify. Serve this main course salad for lunch or a light supper.

CROUTONS

4   slices high-quality white sandwich bread, cut into ½-inch cubes
I   tablespoon olive oil
Salt and ground black pepper

SALAD

6   ounces frisée (about 2 small heads), torn into bite-sized pieces
3   ounces dandelion greens (see note)
3   ounces mâche (see note)
4½ ounces thick-cut bacon (about 4 slices), cut into ½-inch pieces
I   medium shallot, minced (about 3 tablespoons)
⅓   cup red wine vinegar
I   tablespoon Dijon mustard or whole grain mustard
⅓   cup olive oil

EGGS

Salt
2   tablespoons distilled white vinegar
6   large eggs

1. FOR THE CROUTONS: Adjust an oven rack to the upper-middle position and heat the oven to 400 degrees. Toss the bread cubes with the olive oil, ½ teaspoon salt, and ⅛ teaspoon pepper and spread out over a rimmed baking sheet. Bake until the croutons are golden brown and crisp, 8 to 10 minutes; set aside.

2. FOR THE SALAD: Toss the lettuces together in a large bowl; set aside. Cook the bacon in an 8-inch skillet over medium-high heat until golden brown

and crisp, but still chewy, 4 to 6 minutes. Transfer the bacon to a paper towel–lined plate, leaving the rendered fat in the skillet. Add the shallot to the fat in the skillet and cook over medium heat until softened, 2 to 4 minutes. Stir in the vinegar and mustard, scraping up any browned bits and cook until slightly thickened, about 2 minutes. Off the heat, stir in the oil and set aside.

3. **For the eggs:** Fill a 12–inch nonstick skillet nearly to the rim with water. Add 1 teaspoon salt and the vinegar to the water and bring to a boil over high heat. Meanwhile, following the illustration below, crack 2 eggs each into 3 small tea cups with handles. When the water boils, turn off the heat and immediately lower the lips of the cups into the water at once and tip the eggs into the water. Cover and poach the eggs off the heat until the whites are cooked but the yolks are still runny in the center, about 5 minutes.

4. **To assemble the salad:** While the eggs poach, drizzle the vinaigrette over the greens and toss thoroughly to coat. Divide the greens among 6 individual serving plates and sprinkle the bacon and croutons evenly over the top. Using a slotted spoon, quickly and carefully transfer the eggs, 1 at a time, to a large, clean plate, pausing briefly to let the water drain back into the skillet. Once all of the eggs have been transferred, use your fingers to gently slide 1 egg onto the top of each salad. Serve immediately.

POACHING EGGS

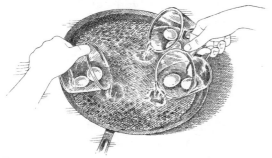

To slip 6 eggs into simmering water at the same time, crack the eggs into 3 small cups with handles (2 eggs per cup). Lower the lips of all the cups just into the water at the same time and tip the eggs simultaneously into the pan.

INGREDIENTS: Dijon Mustard

Mustard history dates back at least 3,000 years to ancient Egyptian, Roman, Greek, and Asian civilizations, and was used not only as a condiment, but for medicinal purposes as well. The original mustards were made from grinding the mustard seeds (either black or brown) into a thick paste with vinegar. A chemical reaction would occur when oils in the ground mustard were mixed with liquid to create mustard's telltale bite (place a whole mustard seed on your tongue and it won't taste like mustard).

Yet it wasn't until 1856 in the town of Dijon, France (in the Burgundy region), that the famous Dijon mustard was created by a gentleman named Jean Naigeon. Monsieur Naigeon substituted verjus (a sour juice made from unripe grapes) for the usual vinegar, resulting in a smoother-tasting condiment.

Today Dijon mustard can be made anywhere in the world and still be considered authentic as long as it follows the original recipe established in Dijon—it must be prepared from brown or black ground mustard seeds, the seed coats must be filtered out, and no coloring agents, stabilizing agents, or fillers may be used. The one major difference in modern Dijon mustards is that they are usually made with vinegar (less harsh than the type originally used) or wine rather than verjus.

THE BEST SUPERMARKET DIJON MUSTARDS

The winners of our supermarket brand Dijon mustard tasting include Roland Extra Strong Dijon Mustard (left), an American brand manufactured in France, widely praised for its excellent flavor balance, having acidity, salt, and heat in pleasing proportions to one another. Grey Poupon Dijon Mustard (center) is manufactured stateside by Nabisco in accordance with the original recipe from Dijon. Tasters praised its "well-rounded flavor," "nice balance," and "creamy texture." Delouis Fils Moutarde de Dijon (right), made in France, exhibited a multidimensional, deep, well-balanced flavor that was described as "straightforward" and "tangy."

MUSSELS IN WHITE WINE WITH PARSLEY

Moules à la Marinière

MOULES MARINIÈRE CONTAINS JUST A FEW simple ingredients: mussels, shallots, parsley, wine, and butter, all cooked together—but the effect is astonishing. The deeply flavorful broth is a mingling of wine, aromatics, and the briny mussel liquor that seeps out as the mussels steam open. Ideally there should be some crusty bread on the table in order to mop up every last drop—we've often heard that the mussels are an obstacle one gets through to reach the broth. But then, we'd argue the mussels are just as delicious.

Loosely translated, *marinière* means bargeman's wife and *moules marinière* translates to the simplest cooking method for this humble bivalve—sauté the shallots, add wine and herbs, drop in the mussels, and steam. Once the mussels open, enrich the broth with butter and perhaps some cream. Is this all it takes or is there a secret to truly great moules marinière? We were ready to find out.

We started with the mussels. Although in the U.S. mussels are more often enjoyed in restaurants, they are readily available at many supermarkets. They require very little prep and are easy (and quick) to cook. Most mussels are now farmed

DEBEARDING MUSSELS

Mussels contain a weedy beard protruding from the crack between the two shells. It's fairly small and can be difficult to tug out of place. We have found the easiest way to perform this task is to trap the beard between the side of a small paring knife and your thumb and pull to remove it. The flat surface of the knife gives you some leverage to extract the pesky beard.

either on ropes or along seabeds. (You may also see "wild" mussels at the market. These mussels are caught the old-fashioned way—by dredging along the sea floor. In our tests, we found them extremely muddy and not worth the bother.) Rope-cultured mussels can be as much as twice the cost of wild or bottom-cultured mussels, but we found them to be free of grit in our testing and since mussels are generally inexpensive (no more than a few dollars a pound), we think clean mussels are worth the extra money. Look for tags, usually attached to the bag containing the mussels, that indicate how and where the mussels have been grown.

When shopping, look for tightly closed mussels (avoid any that are gaping, which may be dying or dead and should not be eaten). Store mussels in a bowl in the refrigerator and use within a day or two. (Do not store in a sealed container, as this will cause them to die.) Mussels may need scrubbing as well as debearding, which simply means pulling off the weedy protrusion attached to the mussel (see the illustration below). Note that debearding mussels should be done just before you are ready to cook them.

The steaming liquid for the mussels is typically white wine. But in the test kitchen, where we don't like to leave any stone unturned, we thought we'd see how fish stock would fare. The stock turned out to be bland in comparison to the bright acidity of the wine, which is necessary to offset the briny mussels. While it is possible to steam 6 pounds of bivalves in less than a cup of liquid (naturally, the pot must be tightly sealed), we like to have extra broth for dunking bread or for saucing rice. We settled on using 2 cups of white wine to cook 6 pounds of mussels. We also made some refinements to the cooking broth. A generous dose of garlic (six cloves), as well as three whole shallots and a bay leaf, further emboldened the broth's flavors.

Once the mussels have steamed opened, expelling their own liquid into the wine mixture, the mussels are removed. It's at this point that a dairy ingredient is added to the broth for richness. We tested the usual suspects uncovered in our research: butter, cream, sour cream, and crème fraîche. The butter was essential to add richness to the broth and

6 tablespoons was the perfect amount, balancing the acid and enriching the mussel liquor. The sour cream and crème fraîche were eliminated immediately because the tanginess altered the flavor of the broth too much. Heavy cream alone deadened the flavors of this broth, but added to the broth finished with butter, the balance was just right. A mere ¼ cup was all it took to round out the flavors, but some tasters liked it even richer, using up to ½ cup of heavy cream. Finally, we added minced parsley and reunited the finished broth with the mussels. Now all we needed was some crusty bread or rice to fully enjoy the dish.

Mussels in White Wine with Parsley

Moules à la Marinière

SERVES 6

Any type of mussel will work here; littlenecks or cherrystone clams can also be substituted (large clams will require 9 to 10 minutes of steaming time). This recipe is easy to scale up or down in order to serve any number of people; figure about 1 pound of mussels per person as an appetizer. Serve with crusty bread, garlic toasts, or rice.

6	tablespoons (¾ stick) unsalted butter
3	medium shallots, minced (about 9 tablespoons)
6	medium garlic cloves, minced or pressed through a garlic press (about 2 tablespoons)
2	cups dry white wine
I	bay leaf
6	pounds mussels, scrubbed and debearded if necessary (see the illustration on page 156)
¼	cup heavy cream
½	cup minced fresh parsley leaves
	Salt and ground black pepper

1. Melt 2 tablespoons of the butter in a large Dutch oven over medium-high heat. Add the shallots and cook until softened, about 2 minutes. Stir in the garlic and cook until fragrant, about 30 seconds. Stir in the wine and bay leaf and simmer until the flavors have blended, about 3 minutes.

2. Increase the heat to high and add the mussels. Cover and cook, stirring occasionally, until the mussels open, 4 to 9 minutes.

3. Using a slotted spoon, transfer the mussels to a large serving bowl, leaving the liquid in the pot; discard any mussels that have not opened. Remove and discard the bay leaf. Stir the remaining 4 tablespoons butter and the cream into the broth and simmer over medium-high heat until the butter is melted and the liquid is slightly thickened, about 2 minutes. Stir in the parsley and season with salt and pepper to taste. Pour the sauce over the mussels and serve immediately.

➤ VARIATIONS

Steamed Mussels with Saffron

Saffron lends its distinctive flavor and orange hue to this variation.

Follow the recipe for Mussels in White Wine with Parsley, omitting the garlic and parsley, and adding a generous pinch of saffron threads to the pot with the shallots in step 1.

Steamed Mussels with Tomatoes

Follow the recipe for Mussels in White Wine with Parsley, adding ½ cup finely diced fresh tomato with the parsley in step 3.

GARLIC AND CHEESE MASHED POTATOES

Aligot

ALIGOT IS TO MASHED POTATOES AS PÂTÉ IS to meatloaf. The basic idea is the same, but variations on technique and flavor additions transform the dish into something extraordinary. Originating in southwest France, aligot is a mixture of mashed potatoes rich with a local fresh cow's milk cheese, called *tome de Cantal*. This dish is so well loved that festivals are built around it. Take a bite and you'll know why. Seeing aligot prepared at one of these festivals is something to behold. With the mashed potatoes finished and bubbling over a flame, the cheese is added in great handfuls while a wooden spoon or paddle stirs without interruption. The result is smooth, elastic, satiny potatoes that can stretch high into the air. Everyone cheers when the spoon is lifted. In the U.S. aligot has popped up in French restaurants as a popular side dish. Taking the hot fires, cauldrons, and wooden paddles out of the equation, we set out to recreate this dish for the American home kitchen.

With a fistful of recipes in hand, we started our testing. The potatoes were first. Russets are traditionally used and with their higher starch content yielded a smoother, more elastic aligot than either Red Bliss or Yukon Gold potatoes. We've found in past test kitchen recipes that the best-tasting mashed potatoes are made by boiling potatoes in their skins, peeling, then ricing to yield a tender, smooth puree. We pitted this method against the simpler, more authentic version of peeling, chopping, and boiling the potatoes and found that once all the cheese is added, the extra effort of boiling the potatoes in their skins is lost in the overall flavor of the dish. So, peel, slice, and boil it would be. At this point, we also wanted to consider the mashing method.

These potatoes aren't your standard fluffy mashed spuds. They're more refined, like a potato puree. Mashing the potatoes by hand wouldn't produce the super smooth potatoes we needed. We could use a ricer, but even better was a food processor, because we were able to incorporate the dairy ingredients evenly and swiftly. It should be noted that overworking the potatoes will turn the puree gummy, so be sure to process just until smooth.

Next we focused our attention on building flavor. Not all aligot recipes include garlic, but most do and tasters preferred the aromatic flavor addition. We found a couple of ways in which the garlic is added—either drop a couple of peeled cloves into the potato boiling water (which takes some of the bite out of the garlic) or mince it raw and stir it into the mashed potatoes. Tasters preferred the latter, as the garlic flavor was washed out when boiled with the potatoes.

Traditional recipes call for the use of butter and crème fraîche. Crème fraîche is a matured, thickened cream with a tangy flavor and sour cream makes a good substitute. We decided to test both, as well as heavy cream, which we thought would also work well. The crème fraîche and sour cream were unanimously preferred to the heavy cream. The tanginess added a depth of flavor that heavy cream couldn't provide. Crème fraîche won out over the sour cream for richness, but it can be hard to find in the average supermarket. The bottom line: if you can find it, use crème fraîche; if not, use sour cream. As for the butter, the test kitchen's mashed potato recipe contains 10 tablespoons per 2 pounds of potatoes. After testing various amounts, we settled on 8 tablespoons.

We put off the trickiest ingredient for last: the cheese. Traditionally aligot is made with Cantal, a young cow's-milk cheese that is virtually impossible to find stateside. We needed to come up with a substitution, hopefully one that didn't require access to a fine cheese chop. After carefully tasting the Cantal cheese, we determined that the flavor was most like a sharp cheddar with a hint of an assertive, nutty Swiss like Gruyère. We added a combination of sharp cheddar and Gruyère to the potatoes and picked up our forks for a tasting. The flavor was there, but the stringy, elastic nature of the potatoes was not, so we added some mozzarella to the mix. With this combination we had the right flavor profile and the ability to stretch this aligot to impressive heights. That said, we learned a few tricks the hard way along this journey—the most important being not to heat the aligot too long once the cheese has been added. The longer the cheese is cooked, the closer it becomes to losing its elasticity and becoming brittle. The flavor doesn't suffer, but the show won't win you any oohs and ahhs.

MAKING ALIGOT

Once the cheese is added to the mashed potatoes, the mixture should be stirred vigorously until the cheese is melted and the mixture is smooth and elastic.

Garlic and Cheese Mashed Potatoes

Aligot

SERVES 4 TO 6

The finished potatoes should have a smooth and elastic texture and form long ribbons when you lift the spoon up from the pot. Cantal cheese is traditional in this dish—if you can find it, substitute 14 ounces (3½ cups shredded) for the cheddar, mozzarella, and Gruyère. Over-processing the potatoes in the food processor in step 2 will turn them gummy—have the ingredients ready and work quickly. Don't overcook the potatoes for too long in step 3; if over-cooked, the cheese will turn brittle and ruin the smooth supple texture of the dish.

2   pounds russet potatoes (about 4 medium), peeled and sliced ¾ inch thick
     Salt
8   tablespoons (1 stick) unsalted butter, cut into ½-inch pieces
3   medium garlic cloves, minced or pressed through a garlic press (about 1 tablespoon)
1   cup crème fraîche or sour cream
6   ounces cheddar cheese, shredded (about 1¼ cups)
4   ounces mozzarella cheese, shredded (about 1 cup)
4   ounces Gruyère cheese, shredded (about 1 cup)
     Ground black pepper

1. Cover the potatoes by 1 inch of water in a large saucepan and add 1 tablespoon salt. Bring to a boil, then reduce to a simmer and cook until the potatoes are tender and a fork can be slipped easily into the center, 10 to 12 minutes. Reserve ¼ cup of the cooking water, then drain the potatoes into a colander. Wipe the saucepan dry and set aside.

2. Pulse the cooked potatoes, reserved cooking water, butter, garlic, and 1½ teaspoons salt together in a food processor until the butter is melted and incorporated, about 5 pulses. Add the crème fraîche and continue to process until the potatoes are smooth and creamy, about 20 seconds. Meanwhile, toss the cheeses together in a medium bowl until evenly combined and set aside.

3. Transfer the potato mixture back to the saucepan and cook over medium heat, slowly stirring in the cheese, one handful at a time, until all the cheese is incorporated. Continue to cook the cheese and potatoes, beating them vigorously and constantly with a wooden spoon, until all the cheese is melted and the mixture is smooth and elastic, 4 to 6 minutes. Season with salt and pepper to taste and serve immediately.

POTATOES LYONNAISE

Pommes de Terre à la Lyonnaise

ONE OF THE HALLMARK DISHES OF FRANCE'S premier gastronomic city, Lyon, *pommes de terre à la Lyonnaise* (aka potatoes Lyonnaise) is a study in simple elegance. Although originally conceived as a dish of economy (an easy way to use up leftover boiled potatoes), it has come to represent the best of classic French bistro cuisine: buttery, browned potato slices interwoven with strands of sweet, caramelized onion and fresh, grassy parsley—a simple yet complex four-ingredient skillet potato dish.

The reality, however, is often far removed from that buttery, earthy ideal. Most versions we tested were greasy and heavy rather than rich and complex. A few were so bad—with sodden spuds and waterlogged onions—that we were reminded how often the simplest dishes are the most difficult. Our goal was to re-create this bistro favorite for the home cook.

Having no leftover cooked potatoes on hand (the case with most home cooks), we wondered if we could proceed with raw spuds without precooking. Starting with a large skillet, we sautéed the raw slices over fairly high heat and got dismal results: The exteriors had cooked to a near-blackened crisp before the interiors got even remotely tender. Over moderate heat, however, the potatoes took forever to develop a nice, browned crust. Cooking the potatoes covered got us closer to what we wanted. Still, they were too dry. Some sort of parcooking would have to be a first step.

Borrowing a technique used in the test kitchen for an American short-order classic, home fries, we began by microwaving the ¼-inch-thick slices of potato in a tablespoon of melted butter until barely tender. This gave them the head start they needed. The time it took the potatoes to brown was now also sufficient to cook them through. Using just one more tablespoon of butter (most classic recipes call for 4 to 6 tablespoons), a simple brown-and-flip approach, and medium-high heat, we cooked the potatoes in less than 15 minutes. Great color and cooking method, but the russet potatoes we'd been using often came out mealy. In a spud-to-spud taste test, creamy, golden-fleshed, medium-starch Yukon Gold potatoes beat out the high-starch russets and the "rubbery," low-starch Red Bliss by a comfortable margin.

Potatoes Lyonnaise would just be sautéed potatoes if not for the addition of onions, the definitive ingredient of dishes prepared à la Lyonnaise. For sweet, concentrated flavor, the onions would have to be cooked separately from the potatoes. Cooking them all the way through over medium-high heat dried them out. Covering the skillet and cooking on medium once they had released some moisture created an environment of gentle, moist heat. Deglazing the pan with a small amount of water gave them the chance to cook in their own flavorful juices.

To put the steps together in an efficient manner was easy. While the onions cooked, the potatoes began their warm-up in the microwave. Once the onions finished cooking and were removed to a nearby bowl, the potatoes had a turn in the pan. To meld the flavors, we added the onions back into the pan and briefly sautéed the two together. Now we had an updated version of a French classic that was good enough (and quick enough) to make even without leftover potatoes.

Potatoes Lyonnaise
Pommes de Terre à la Lyonnaise
SERVES 4

Be sure to leave the potatoes uncovered and toss them halfway through microwaving in step 1; by leaving the potatoes uncovered the potatoes will dry out a bit and brown better in the skillet. If using a lightweight skillet, you may need to stir the potatoes more frequently to prevent burning.

3   tablespoons unsalted butter
2   pounds Yukon Gold potatoes (about 4 medium), peeled and sliced ¼ inch thick
1   large onion (about 14 ounces), halved and sliced ¼ inch thick
     Salt
2   tablespoons water
     Ground black pepper
1   tablespoon minced fresh parsley leaves

1. Microwave 1 tablespoon of the butter in a large microwave-safe bowl on high power until melted, about 45 seconds. Add the potatoes, toss to coat with butter, and continue to microwave, uncovered, on high power until the potatoes just start to turn tender, about 6 minutes, tossing halfway through the cooking time. Toss again, then set aside until needed.

2. Meanwhile, melt 1 more tablespoon butter in a heavy-bottomed 12-inch nonstick skillet over medium-high heat. Add the onion and ¼ teaspoon salt and cook, stirring occasionally, until the onions begin to soften, about 3 minutes. Reduce the heat to medium, cover, and cook, stirring occasionally, until the onions are light brown and soft, about 12 minutes longer, adding the water and scraping up any browned bits as the pan gets dry halfway through the cooking time. Transfer the onions to a bowl, cover, and set aside.

3. Add the remaining tablespoon butter to the skillet and melt over medium-high heat. Add the potatoes and distribute them evenly in the skillet. Cook, without stirring, until browned on the bottom, about 3 minutes. Using a rubber spatula, gently stir the potatoes and continue to cook, stirring every 2 to 3 minutes, until the potatoes are well browned and tender when pierced with the tip of a paring knife, 8 to 10 minutes.

4. Season the potatoes with salt and pepper to taste, then gently stir in the onions. Continue to cook over medium-high heat until the onions are heated through, 1 to 2 minutes. Transfer to a large plate, sprinkle with the parsley, and serve immediately.

ZUCCHINI AND TOMATO TIAN

Tian de Courgettes aux Tomates

HAILING FROM PROVENCE AND NAMED FOR the region's popular terracotta dishes, this combination of summer vegetables is perfumed with olive oil and thyme and crusted with Gruyère cheese. The trick to a great tian is finding how to ensure perfectly cooked vegetables; mushy or undercooked vegetables will not do.

In our research, we found a couple of ways to prepare tian. In one method, the vegetables are simply layered and baked. The other lines the dish with caramelized onions (and sometimes garlic) and then places the vegetables on top. After trying versions of both styles, tasters unanimously opted for the dish with caramelized onions. And off the bat, we chose the vegetables: tomatoes and squash (yellow summer squash and zucchini squash) and thought we might later include potatoes for a variation.

The obvious starting point with this dish is the first layer—the onions. Using yellow onions (which we know from past test kitchen tests caramelize well and have great flavor), we diced and sliced onions and started cooking. Tasters preferred the way the sliced onions looked, but didn't notice any difference in flavor between them and diced onions. We found that by using a nonstick pan and keeping the heat level to medium, we got softened, caramelized onions in just 12 to 15 minutes. We also added some minced garlic toward the end of cooking, to achieve a full aromatic flavor.

Next we focused on the vegetables. We chose plum tomatoes because their diameter most closely resembled that of the squash and we sought out squash that were all about the same size. (Size is important to evenly cooked and attractive rows of vegetables in the finished dish.) Our first challenge was slicing the vegetables to the right thickness. Vegetables sliced ½ inch thick took too long to cook and vegetables sliced ⅛ inch thick cooked too quickly, turning mushy in the process. Right in between—¼ inch thick—turned out to be just right. With our sharpest knife in one hand and

EQUIPMENT: Gratin Dishes

By their very definition, gratins—dishes that are topped with bread crumbs or cheese and butter and browned under a broiler—require a special dish to ensure the crispiest crust possible. Those dishes are usually oval, with a large surface area and low sides. Gratin dishes, like any highly specialized kitchen tool, can cost a lot more than their generic counterparts. But are they really necessary? Will a shallow casserole or baking dish yield the same results? We gathered eight possible options, ranging from a $7 Pyrex casserole dish to the $160 All-Clad stainless au gratin dish. We learned that size does matter and that looks aren't everything.

We tested gratin dishes using our vegetable tian recipe, which requires a final bake in the oven to brown the cheese that is sprinkled on top. Dishes with smaller surface areas, such as the 59-square-inch Corning Ware 2½ quart oval dish ($19.99), made for a thick layer of cheese that never got a chance to fully brown. Larger dishes, like the 117-square-inch Pyrex 3-quart casserole dish ($7), caused the cheese to be scattered so widely that it never formed a cohesive topping.

Another factor that affected our gratin was the depth of the dish. The Corning Ware 4-quart oval roaster ($21.99) had 4-inch-high sides that cast a shadow over the topping, never quite giving it a chance to brown at the edges. We found 1- to 2-inch sides (the most common height) to be ideal.

Of the eight dishes tested, we found two standouts: the Pyrex 2-quart casserole dish ($7) and the All-Clad stainless oval au gratin dish ($160). While we swooned over the sleek design of the All-Clad, we concede that the humbly designed Pyrex 2-quart produces similar results for a small fraction of the cost.

THE BEST GRATIN DISHES

The Pyrex 2-quart Casserole Dish (top) performed admirably in tests and is our best buy at just $7. If you're seeking something a little sleeker to put on your table, the All-Clad Stainless au Gratin (bottom) also performed well but comes with a hefty price, $160.

a ruler in the other hand we started slicing. Five minutes later we had barely accumulated enough slices to get the first row finished.

Putting our knife aside, we turned to a mandoline (a compact, hand-operated machine that ensures evenly thin, or thick, slices; see "Mandolines and V-Slicers" on page 163). With this handy gadget we were able to slice the vegetables perfectly in seconds. (You can also use a food processor fitted with a ¼-inch-thick slicing blade, although, because of the quickness of the machine, there is less control.) Now it was a matter of assembling the sliced vegetables. Alternating the slices and keeping them fairly tightly shingled was easy and we managed to cover the entire baking dish quickly. We sprinkled fresh thyme over the dish, drizzled the vegetables with olive oil, and from there it went into the oven.

Baking a tian is usually a two-step process. First the assembled dish (minus the cheese) goes into the oven until the vegetables are cooked. Then the tian is sprinkled with shredded cheese and cooked again until the whole tian is bubbling and the cheese has browned. Initially, we had trouble with the first step because the vegetables took so long to cook through that by the time the cheese was done in the second step, the vegetables had overcooked and turned dull in color. Partially cooking the vegetables this way didn't work any better—and even worse, the vegetables turned dry and chewy. Following the advice of a few recipes, we next tried covering the baking dish with foil on the first go-round. The foil traps the heat and thus partially

MAKING A VEGETABLE TIAN

Alternately shingle the vegetables—zucchini, yellow squash, and tomatoes—tightly on top of the onions in tidy, attractive rows.

steams the vegetables. When the tian emerged, the vegetables were only partially cooked but they still contained moisture, which, it turns out, is key. Because the vegetables were still moist, for the second go-round we slid the dish back into the oven uncovered, after adding the cheese. We checked the tian every five minutes and found that 25 minutes produced a perfect tian—soft, caramelized onions, bright, tender vegetables and a browned and bubbling crust from the cheese.

For a heartier cool-weather variation, we incorporated potatoes into the dish and added crisp bacon to the onion layer. While bacon is not traditional in Provence, we found no complaints among tasters.

Zucchini and Tomato Tian with Caramelized Onions
Tian de Courgettes aux Tomates
SERVES 6

Try to buy squash and tomatoes that have roughly the same diameter. Slicing the vegetables ¼ inch thick is crucial for the success of this dish; use a mandoline, a V-slicer (see page 163 for more information), or a food processor fitted with a ¼-inch-thick slicing blade. You can also slice them carefully by hand using a very sharp knife. An ovensafe Provençal-style gratin dish can be substituted for the 13 by 9-inch baking dish, as long as it's of similar size.

¼	cup extra-virgin olive oil
3	medium yellow onions, halved and sliced ¼ inch thick (about 3 cups)
	Salt
2	medium garlic cloves, minced or pressed through a garlic press (about 2 teaspoons)
I	pound zucchini, trimmed and sliced ¼ inch thick
I	pound yellow squash, trimmed and sliced ¼ inch thick
I	pound plum tomatoes, cored and sliced ¼ inch thick
I	teaspoon minced fresh thyme leaves
	Ground black pepper
2	ounces Gruyère cheese, shredded (about ½ cup)

EQUIPMENT: Mandolines and V-Slicers

What's cheaper than a food processor and faster (if not also sharper) than a chef's knife? A mandoline. This hand-operated slicing machine comes in two basic styles: the classic stainless-steel model, supported by legs, and the plastic hand-held model, often called a V-slicer. We put both types of machines—ranging in price from $5.99 to $169—to the test. To determine the winners, we sliced melons, cut carrots into julienne (matchstick pieces), cut potatoes into batonets (long, skinny, french-fry pieces), and sliced potatoes into thin rounds. Then we evaluated three aspects of the mandolines: ease of use, including degree of effort, adjustment ease, grip/handle comfort, and safety; quality, including sturdiness and uniformity/cleanliness of slices; and cleanup.

Of the five plastic models we tested, three of them were good choices. The Progressive Mandoline ($27.99) was easy to use and clean, whereas the New Benriner ($32.95) scored highest in comfort and durability. Although the safety guard that holds the food on the Pyrex Kitchen Slicer ($5.99) did not glide easily, it's easy to overlook this flaw given the low price, making it our best buy.

We also tested two classic stainless-steel mandolines. The deBuyer mandoline from Williams-Sonoma ($169) was controversial. Shorter testers had difficulty gaining leverage to cut consistently; some melon slices were ⅛ inch thicker on one side. However, the safety mechanism, sturdiness, and adjustment mechanism were lauded by taller testers. With some practice, all testers were able to produce perfect slices, julienne, and batonets

with the Bron Coucke mandoline ($99). This machine has fewer parts to clean and switch out than its plastic counterparts and requires less effort to operate once the user becomes familiar with it. Still, the quality comes at an awfully high price.

THE BEST V-SLICER

Plastic mandolines (also called V-slicers) may not be as sturdy as stainless-steel versions, but their quality far exceeds the minimal dollar investment. At a mere $5.99, the Pyrex Kitchen Slicer is our best buy.

THE BEST CLASSIC MANDOLINE

Of the two stainless-steel mandolines tested, we preferred this model made by Bron Coucke. Note, however, that it costs 10 times more than a good V-slicer.

---

1. Adjust an oven rack to the middle position and heat the oven to 375 degrees. Brush a 13 by 9-inch baking dish with 1 tablespoon of the oil; set aside.

2. Heat 2 more tablespoons of the oil in a 12-inch nonstick skillet over medium heat until shimmering. Add the onions and ½ teaspoon salt and cook until softened and lightly browned, 12 to 15 minutes. Stir in the garlic and cook until fragrant, about 30 seconds. Spread the onion mixture onto the bottom of the prepared baking dish.

3. Following the illustration on page 162, alternately shingle the sliced zucchini, yellow squash, and tomatoes into a single layer of 4 tightly fit rows on top of the onions. Sprinkle with the remaining 1 tablespoon oil and thyme and season with salt and pepper to taste. Cover the dish with aluminum

foil and bake until the vegetables are tender, about 30 minutes.

4. Remove the foil, sprinkle the cheese over the top, and continue to bake until bubbling around the edge and lightly browned on top, 20 to 30 minutes. Let rest for 10 minutes before serving.

➤ VARIATION

Zucchini, Tomato, and Potato Tian

Follow the recipe for Zucchini and Tomato Tian with Caramelized Onions, substituting 1 pound russet potatoes, peeled and sliced ¼ inch thick, for the yellow squash. Substitute 3 slices thick-cut bacon, sliced into thin strips, for the 2 tablespoons oil in step 2; cook the bacon over medium heat until the fat has rendered, about 5 minutes, before adding the onions and continue to cook as directed.

BRAISED LEEKS

Poireaux Braisé

OFTEN CALLED THE ASPARAGUS OF THE POOR in France, leeks are an underrated vegetable here in the United States, usually reserved for soup or building a flavor base for other dishes. But their unique, onion-like sweetness makes them a delicious side dish and in France they are often braised, which enhances their delicate flavor. Looking like giant scallions, leeks are related to both garlic and onion, though their flavor and fragrance are milder and more subtle. Smaller leeks are more tender than the larger ones, but it is the larger, more mature leek that lends itself so well to braising.

Braiser, the French verb and cooking term meaning "to braise," is to brown food in fat, then cook it in a covered casserole with a small amount of liquid until tender. We usually associate this term with meat—braising turns tougher cuts of meat tender—but braising also works well with vegetables that are either too fibrous to eat raw or, more typically, with hearty vegetables such as leeks, fennel, or endive that won't fall apart when cooked and obtain a different (and more interesting) flavor profile, as well as a tender, creamy texture. At their best, braised leeks are sweet and tender, with their layers held together by the root, making it easy to remove them from the pan and gracefully lay them across a serving platter. The caramelization they obtain from browning adds a depth of flavor to this elegant vegetable side dish and the effort is minimal.

Unfortunately, as with just about every simple dish, bad versions abound. Leeks that have been cooked too long until mushy or caramelized too aggressively, leaving behind a bitter flavor, are common. We set out to avoid these pitfalls while turning this humble vegetable into an elegant side dish.

Our first action was to better acquaint ourselves with the best leeks for braising. After all, most of us have little experience with braising this vegetable (occasionally we use it to provide aromatic flavor to our dishes in lieu of onions or garlic). Leeks come in all sizes, but in most stores they are bundled together without regard to size. To ensure even cooking times, we made our own bundles of same-size leeks. We also tried to buy the leeks with the longest white stems, the most tender and useable part of a leek; the white parts can vary from 4 up to 8 inches so it pays to be discriminating when selecting them.

Don't be fooled by supermarkets that sell leeks that are already trimmed down to the lighter base part. While this may seem like a good deal because you aren't paying for the upper leaves, which are discarded anyway, the truth is that the actual purpose of this procedure is to trim away aging leaves and make tough, old leeks look fresher to the unwary consumer. The bottom line: hand select your leeks and try to find a store that sells them untrimmed. Once you get them home, trimming is essential because it is the only way to expose the many layers of the leek and clean it properly. Instead of following the often-recommended technique of slicing off the leaves right where they lighten into the white base of the leek, we found we could move about 2 inches upward into the leaves, to the point at which the light green part turns dark green, without any ill effect.

The next step is to clean the leeks. Since leeks grow underground, during the process of pushing upward they collect dirt between their layers. We've come across leeks that had only a few grains of dirt between the layers, but we've also found leeks with mud jammed in the crevices. We found that the best way to clean the leeks for this recipe is to halve them lengthwise, leaving the root end intact, but trimming off the dangling roots. Under running water, gently pull the layers apart to wash away the dirt nestled inside (see the illustration on page 166). Once cleaned, the halved leeks are ready to be braised.

Next we focused on technique. Since braises usually start with browning, we followed suit. We browned both the cut side and the rounded side of all our leek halves and proceeded with the braise. The resulting braise was flavorful, but handling the leeks so much made them much more vulnerable to falling apart and we wanted them to remain whole for a nice presentation. Next we tried browning the leeks on the cut side only, pouring the braising liquid over the leeks once browned. We didn't handle or turn the leeks at all as they cooked; we simply checked a couple of them along the way to make sure they were golden brown. Most tasters noticed a slight difference between leeks that were browned on both sides versus only one, although the leeks that weren't turned were in much better shape at the end of the braise. To compensate for only browning one side, we tried sprinkling a little sugar into the pan before adding the leeks to help the caramelization and this worked—the leeks caramelized to a deeper brown, which resulted in a sauce with richer flavor.

We continued our testing by exploring braising liquids. Water, a common choice, had few supporters among our tasters. Cream was too rich and cider too seasonal for a year-round recipe. White wine made the dish too acidic, and while chicken broth tasted deep and round, it obscured the flavor of the leeks. The ideal balance turned out to be a mixture of equal parts white wine and chicken broth, which produced deep yet brightly flavored leeks that retained a hint of oniony flavor—something we wanted to preserve. We added some fresh thyme leaves for more flavor and then, making the most of the braising liquid, we reduced it to make a light sauce after the leeks finished cooking.

To finish the sauce, we removed the lid as soon as the leeks were cooked and turned up the heat. This method yielded a rich sauce, but the delicate leeks suffered in the blast of high heat necessary to reduce the braising liquid. We backed up, removed the leeks once they were finished cooking, and tented them with foil to keep them warm. With the leeks safely on the serving platter, we were able to crank up the heat and reduce the braising liquid, which came together in just a couple of minutes. A tablespoon of butter and a little lemon juice rounded out the flavors of the sauce and minced parsley added color. Less than 30 minutes of effort turned these humble leeks into an elegant and satisfying side dish.

Braised Leeks
Poireaux Braisé
SERVES 4

We prefer to use large leeks for this recipe; the diameter of each leek should be about 1 inch and you should trim it to be about 6 inches in length in order to fit easily in the skillet. When prepping the leeks, be sure to trim only the dangling roots from the root end, leaving the rest of the root intact to hold the layers together. The leeks can fall apart easily when cooking if not handled gently. To check the browning progress, grasp the root ends gingerly with tongs and peek underneath the cut side. You will need a skillet with a tight-fitting lid for this recipe. We found a nonstick skillet works best here, but a traditional skillet can be used.

3	tablespoons unsalted butter
½	teaspoon sugar
	Salt
4	large leeks, white and light green parts only, root ends trimmed (see note) and halved lengthwise
¼	cup dry white wine
¼	cup low-sodium chicken broth
½	teaspoon minced fresh thyme leaves
1	tablespoon minced fresh parsley leaves (optional)
1	teaspoon juice from 1 lemon
	Ground black pepper

1. Melt 2 tablespoons of the butter in a 12-inch nonstick skillet over medium-high heat. Sprinkle the sugar and ¼ teaspoon salt evenly over the bottom of the skillet and add the leeks, cut side down, in a single layer. Cook, shaking the skillet occasionally, until golden brown, about 5 minutes, adjusting the heat as needed if browning too quickly.

2. Add the wine, broth, and thyme. Reduce the heat to low, cover, and simmer until the leeks lose their vibrant color, turn translucent, and a paring knife inserted into the root end meets little resistance, about 10 minutes.

3. Gently transfer the leeks to a warmed serving platter, leaving the liquid in the skillet; cover the

leeks and set aside. Return the liquid to a simmer over medium-high heat and cook until it has a syrupy sauce consistency, 1 to 2 minutes. Off the heat, whisk in the remaining tablespoon butter, parsley (if using), and lemon juice and season with salt and pepper to taste. Spoon the sauce over the leeks and serve immediately.

➤ VARIATIONS

Braised Endive

Both red and green endive work well here.

Follow the recipe for Braised Leeks, increasing the amount of sugar to 1 teaspoon and reducing the amount of lemon juice to ½ teaspoon. Substitute 4 heads endive, trimmed and halved lengthwise, for the leeks; increase the covered cooking time in step 2 to 12 to 15 minutes.

Braised Fennel

Don't core the fennel bulb before cutting it into wedges; the core will help hold the layers of fennel together during cooking.

Follow the recipe for Braised Leeks, substituting 2 fennel bulbs, trimmed of stalks, halved, and each half cut into 4 wedges, for the leeks; increase the browning time in step 1 to about 10 minutes and the covered cooking time in step 2 to 15 to 18 minutes.

CLEANING LEEKS

When braising leeks, we like to cut the leeks lengthwise in half, but we always find dirt nestled between the layers. To clean them, hold the leek under cold, running water, carefully pulling the leaves apart to allow the dirt to wash away. Then gently pat dry with a paper towel.

CHEESE SOUFFLÉ
Soufflé au Fromage

SOUFFLÉ AU FROMAGE—LIGHT-AS-AIR EGGS and tangy Gruyère cheese married together and baked to unfathomable heights—this was one dish we wanted in our recipe repertoire. Yet we've all fallen victim to a soufflé's fickle behavior (its potential to collapse as it emerges from the oven) and therefore felt that in order to pull off a foolproof recipe for cheese soufflé we first needed to understand the basics behind how soufflés work.

According to food historians, modern soufflés (both sweet and savory) are a product of 18th century French cuisine, a relatively recent contribution to France's culinary history. Essentially, a soufflé is simply a sauce into which stiffly beaten egg whites are incorporated. It is then turned into a mold and baked in the oven until it puffs up and the top browns.

But what is a perfect soufflé? It is a soufflé that has a crusty exterior packed with flavor, a dramatic rise above the rim, an airy but substantial outer layer, and a rich, moist center. A great soufflé must also convey a true mouthful of flavor—in a cheese soufflé, the cheese high notes should be clear and strong.

Our first consideration in testing was what to use as the "base," the mixture that gives substance and flavor to the soufflé, as opposed to the airiness and lift provided by the whipped egg whites. The base can be a béchamel (a classic French sauce made with equal amounts of butter and flour, whisked with milk over heat) or a bouillie (flour cooked with milk until thickened). After trying several versions of each of these options, we found that we consistently preferred the béchamel base. It provided the soufflé with good cheese flavor and a puffed yet substantial texture. By contrast, the versions made with a bouillie were all too dense and pudding-like for our tasters' palates.

With our base figured out, we turned our attention to the cheese. Traditionally this soufflé is made with Gruyère cheese, but some tasters mentioned that they don't always have Gruyère on hand and wondered if cheddar or Swiss could stand in. To address this issue, we tested a host of cheeses; cheddar, Swiss, and Gouda all worked fine, due to their similarity in flavor and meltability to Gruyère. Even softer cheeses like goat cheese or blue cheese fared well when mixed into a basic soufflé recipe, although their higher moisture content prevented the soufflé from rising as high. When all was said and done, tasters still preferred the flavor of the soufflé made with Gruyère, although in a pinch, cheddar, Swiss, or Gouda can be substituted.

Now we turned our attention to the quantity of cheese. We started with 5 ounces. The resulting soufflé had strong cheese flavor, but not much rise, most likely because we had added too much cheese and it was weighing the soufflé down. We tested varying amounts lower than 5 ounces to get a better texture and a higher rise and decided that 4 ounces was perfect to provide strong cheese flavor and an impressively tall soufflé.

Some recipes we came across in our research also coated the soufflé dish with a dusting of cheese (and sprinkled the cheese over the soufflé as well). After greasing our soufflé dish with butter, we added Parmesan to coat it and after pouring in the soufflé, sprinkled more Parmesan on top. The addition was a success—the Parmesan helped to give the soufflé an attractive golden brown color and by virtue of its salty nature, it heightened the flavor of the Gruyère.

We now moved on to check other variables, including oven temperature, a water bath, and the soufflé dish itself. For many sturdier recipes a 25-degree variance in oven temperature is not crucial to the outcome of the item, but it had a dramatic impact on our soufflé. Our initial oven temperature was 350 degrees, but to be sure this temperature was optimum, we tested both 325 and 400 degrees as well. The higher oven temperature resulted in an overcooked exterior and an undercooked interior, while the lower temperature did not brown the exterior enough to provide good flavor and also produced a texture that was too even, given that we were looking for a loose center at the point at which the exterior was nicely cooked. We decided to stick with 350 degrees.

One factor we found to be of surprising importance was the baking dish. We tried using a standard casserole dish for one of the tests, and the soufflé rose right out of the dish onto the floor of the oven! The problem was that the dish did not have the perfectly straight sides of a soufflé dish. It pays to make sure that you are using a real soufflé dish (a round ceramic dish with tall straight sides) to ensure the highest rise in a soufflé.

We also tested the theory that a chilled soufflé dish improves the rise (we had tested this method with chocolate soufflé and surprisingly it worked) but we discovered that it made little difference with a cheese soufflé.

Given that many egg-based dishes are baked in a water bath (the baking dish is placed in a larger pan with hot water for a more gentle heat), we decided to give this a try. Unfortunately, it was an awful idea—the outer crust of the soufflé turned out wet, with a gelatin-like appearance, and the soufflé did not rise well.

During the course of all this testing, we found that a cheese soufflé will give you three indications of when it is done: you can smell the cheese, it stops rising, and only the very center of the top jiggles when gently shaken. Of course, these are all imprecise methods. If you have an instant-read thermometer, slide it through the side of the top—it should measure 170 degrees. If you don't have a thermometer, simply take two large spoons, pull open the top of the soufflé, and peek inside. If

SOUFFLÉ DISHES

We tried baking our soufflé in a variety of baking dishes, but only a soufflé dish with its straight sides guaranteed that our soufflé rose evenly and stayed in the dish, not all over the bottom of our oven. Soufflé dishes are relatively inexpensive and can be found in a variety of cookware stores.

the center is still soupy, simply put the dish back in the oven. Much to our surprise, and as heretical as it may sound, this probing in no way harmed the soufflé—it lost no volume and no one noticed the spot where the spoons went in. While our soufflé strongly held its shape for a couple of minutes after we took it out of the oven, it does eventually deflate, so to maximize the oohs and aahs at your table, have everyone seated before serving.

DISCERNING PROPERLY BEATEN EGG WHITES

1. Underbeaten egg whites are foamy and soft. They will turn a batter watery and produce a finished baked good that looks flat.

2. Overbeaten egg whites look dry and grainy and will begin to separate. They will not fold in easily with other batter ingredients, will clump up in the batter, and produce a finished baked good that looks spotty and sunken.

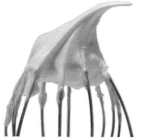

3. Properly beaten egg whites look creamy and glossy. They will hold a stiff peak yet fold in easily with other batter ingredients, will give the batter a billowy texture, and will produce a finished baked good that has uniformly lofted texture.

Cheese Soufflé

Soufflé au Fromage

SERVES 3 TO 4

Cheddar, Swiss, or Gouda cheese can be substituted for the Gruyère. You will need a 2-quart soufflé dish for this recipe.

3	tablespoons unsalted butter, cut into ½-inch chunks, plus extra for coating the dish
½	ounce Parmesan cheese, grated (about ¼ cup)
3	tablespoons unbleached all-purpose flour
1	cup whole milk
4	ounces Gruyère cheese, shredded (about 1 cup)
½	teaspoon salt
¼	teaspoon ground black pepper
	Pinch freshly ground nutmeg
3	large eggs, separated
¼	teaspoon cream of tartar

1. Adjust an oven rack to the middle position and heat the oven to 350 degrees. Thoroughly butter the inside of a 2-quart soufflé dish, then coat evenly with 2 tablespoons of the Parmesan; set aside.

2. Melt the butter in a medium saucepan over medium heat. Stir in the flour and cook until golden, about 1 minute. Slowly whisk in the milk. Bring to a simmer and cook, whisking constantly, until thickened and smooth, about 1 minute. Off the heat, whisk in the Gruyère, salt, pepper, and nutmeg. Transfer the mixture to a large bowl. Whisk in the egg yolks until completely incorporated and set aside.

3. Using an electric mixer, whip the egg whites in a separate bowl on medium-low speed until they are opaque and frothy, about 30 seconds. Add the cream of tartar, increase the speed to medium-high, and continue to whip, watching carefully, until they are thick and form stiff peaks, about 2½ minutes.

4. Working with one-quarter of the whipped egg whites at a time, gently fold them into the yolk mixture until almost no white streaks remain (a few streaks are okay). Gently pour the mixture into the prepared soufflé dish and sprinkle with the remaining 2 tablespoons Parmesan.

5. Bake until the top is nicely browned, the center jiggles slightly, and an instant-read thermometer inserted through the top side registers 170 degrees, 25 to 30 minutes. Serve immediately.

➤ VARIATION

Cheese Soufflé with Shallots and Herbs
Flecks of herbs add flavor and color to this variation.

Follow the recipe for Soufflé au Fromage, cooking 1 small minced shallot in the butter in step 2 until softened, about 2 minutes, before stirring the flour. Stir 1 tablespoon minced fresh chives, 1 tablespoon minced fresh parsley leaves, and 1½ teaspoons minced fresh tarragon leaves into the yolk mixture at the end of step 2.

SAUTÉED SOLE WITH BROWNED BUTTER AND LEMON

Sole Meunière

SOLE MEUNIÈRE IS A DECEPTIVELY EASY French restaurant dish that ought to serve as a model recipe for home cooking. The term *meunière* means "miller's wife" or "female owner of a mill" and refers simply to the fillets being dredged lightly in flour (no need for eggs or bread crumbs) before being cooked on the stovetop until a golden crust forms. This allows the inside to remain moist and flavorful. And even better, this method, when executed properly, is easy.

Sole meunière features a browned butter sauce seasoned with lemon and parsley, which is poured over the fish just before serving. What could be simpler or more delicious? That's what we thought, too, before we cooked a few test batches to get a handle on the technique for making this dish. What we got were plates of pale, soggy fillets in pools of greasy sauce—that is, if the fish hadn't stuck to the pan or fallen apart as we tried to plate it. Despite these failures (or maybe because of them), two things did become clear. The simplicity of this dish makes it imperative that everything be prepared

and cooked just so, and the delicious flavor of this dish made it worthwhile to fix these problems.

Taking a closer look at our initial meunière recipes, it was no wonder that we had found little success at the stove. Some recipes called for almost two sticks of butter for two pounds of fish. Who wants to eat fish literally swimming in fat? We certainly didn't. Other recipes resulted in fish that were soggy and white—they never browned. It was time to go back to basics.

Whole Dover sole—a variety of white flatfish—is the most authentic choice for preparing fish à la meunière, but it is hard to come by even in the best of fish markets and prohibitively expensive when it can be had. We settled instead on a filleted white flatfish that would be available in most markets, thinking that sole or flounder would be the options. That said, we soon became aware of a veritable parade of choices—gray sole, lemon sole, yellowtail flounder, southern flounder, summer flounder, winter flounder, petrale sole, rex sole, rock sole, and starry flounder. After cooking 20 pounds of flatfish, we discovered that variety didn't much matter (tasters approved of them all); what counted was the thickness of the fillet and its freshness. If the fillet was thinner than ⅜ inch, it was nearly impossible to brown it without overcooking it. Fillets that were ⅜ inch thick or slightly more were perfect. Those that weighed 5 to 6 ounces each fit easily in a large skillet. Fillets weighing 7 to 10 ounces were also acceptable, although they required cutting and trimming.

Small things can make a big difference when it comes to cooking fish. For one, a thin coat of flour speeds up the browning, which is a particularly useful thing to know when you've got thin fillets that cook quickly. Straight from the fishmonger's wrapping paper, fillets are typically wet. They must be patted dry or the flour will become thick and gluey. Simply dredging the dried fillets in flour presented problems. Excess flour fell off the fish and into the pan, where it burned. Shaking off the extra flour before cooking solves this problem. Still, even after a quick shake, the fillets cooked up with blotchy brown crusts that did nothing for the flavor.

CORE TECHNIQUE

SAUTÉING DELICATE FISH FILLETS

Sautéing delicate fish fillets such as sole or flounder can be tricky because the tender fish is apt to stick to the pan and break apart. Some recipes coat the fillets with egg and flour, which does create a barrier against sticking, but its thick texture and rich flavor overwhelm the fish. Other recipes dredge the fish in flour, but the flour tends to stick in some places and not others, resulting in "bald" spots and uneven browning. We found the solution in a simple method. We sprinkle the fillets with salt and pepper and let them stand for five minutes. The salt draws out moisture in the fish, creating a thin, moist sheen—just enough for the flour to evenly adhere to. This method produces a crust thin enough to protect the fish without overwhelming the fillets' texture or flavor.

We then tried a technique used by Julia Child, who recommends seasoning the fillets with salt and pepper and letting them sit before dredging. After five minutes, the fillets had begun to glisten with moisture. We dredged them with flour, shook off the excess, and cooked them. "Perfectly seasoned and evenly coated" was the thumbs-up response from tasters. Why does letting the seasoned fish rest for five minutes make such a difference? The salt extracts water from the fish, not so much as to make it wet but just enough to give it a thin coating of moisture that helps to ensure a perfectly even coating of flour. Without "bald spots" in the coating, the fish browns uniformly and tastes better.

The technique of pan-frying necessitates a heavy skillet and a good amount of fat. Food is cooked in a single layer and you must wait patiently for it to brown, turning it once and then waiting again. The temptation is to lift the food and take a peek, but it is essential to resist the impulse. For maximum browning (and to keep the fish from falling apart), the fish must be left undisturbed as it cooks.

We found that traditional skillets did not work well. No matter how much fat we used, the fish had a tendency to stick. A nonstick skillet, on the other hand, worked well every time, producing beautifully browned fillets without sticking. A 12-inch skillet is a must, we discovered, and even then only two fillets would fit at a time without overlapping. We wanted our recipe to serve four, but using two skillets side by side seemed unreasonable. Instead, we chose to cook the fish in two batches, using a warmed plate in a preheated 200-degree oven to keep the first batch hot.

Clarified butter (butter with the milk solids removed) is the traditional fat used by the French. Not only does clarified butter lend a rich flavor to the fish, but it has a higher smoking point (and thus burns less easily) than whole butter. Clarifying butter is easy, but it is too lengthy a process for a quick midweek entrée. Would tasters notice its absence? We cooked one batch with canola oil and another with clarified butter, and even the least discerning tasters noticed the difference. Whole butter burned, but a mixture of oil and butter, a classic combination, did the trick.

Next we experimented with the amount of fat. Although recipes ranged from 1 to 6 tablespoons (for two fillets), we found that 2 tablespoons were ample, especially in a nonstick skillet. At this point, because we were using so little fat, we were technically sautéing rather than pan-frying. We began by cooking the fillets over low heat, but the results were mediocre at best; the fillets did not brown but instead poached in the fat, and the taste was

FLIPPING FISH FILLETS

To turn fish fillets without breaking them, use 2 spatulas; a regular model and an extra-wide version especially designed for fish work best. Using the regular spatula, gently lift the long side of the fillet. Then, supporting the fillet with the extra-wide spatula, flip it so that the browned side faces up.

lackluster. High heat turned out to be equally problematic. By the time the interior of each fillet had cooked, some of the exterior had scorched, resulting in a bitter and unappealing taste. Our next try was a winner. We heated the pan over high heat, then lowered the heat to medium-high as soon as we added the fish. The exterior browned beautifully, while the inside remained succulent.

For fillets that were the ideal thickness of ⅜ inch, three minutes on the first side and about two minutes on the second side achieved both a flavorful, nutty-tasting exterior and a moist, delicate interior. Because the side that is cooked first is the most attractive, we found it best to stick to the hard-and-fast rule of cooking for three minutes on the first side and then adjusting the time for the second side. (With flatfish, the side of the fillet that is cooked first also matters—it should be the side that was cut from the bones, not the skin side.) The question was, how could we tell when a thin fillet was done? Restaurant chefs press the fillets with their fingers—a reliable technique but one that requires practice. Observation eventually indicated that the fillet was done when opaque. Because the fish continues to cook off the heat of the stovetop (and in the gentle heat of the preheated oven), it is imperative to remove it slightly before it's fully done. Instead of using the tip of a knife, a method that tends to damage the fillet, we found that a toothpick inserted into a thick edge worked well.

One last cooking consideration remained to be resolved. Traditionally, the sauce served with meunière is beurre noisette, or browned butter, with lemon and parsley added. Crucial to the flavor of the sauce, which adds a rich nuttiness to the fish, is proper browning of the milk solids in the butter, a task not easily accomplished in a nonstick skillet. The problem is that the dark surface of the pan makes it nearly impossible to judge the color of the butter. The solution was simple: we browned the butter in a medium stainless steel skillet; its shiny bottom made it easy to monitor the color. We then added lemon juice to the browned butter, sprinkled the fish with parsley, and poured the sauce over the fish.

Sautéed Sole with Browned Butter and Lemon
Sole Meunière
SERVES 4

Try to purchase fillets that are of similar size, and avoid those that weigh less than 5 ounces because they will cook too quickly. A nonstick skillet ensures that the fillets will release from the pan, but for the sauce a traditional skillet is preferable because its light-colored surface will allow you to monitor the color of the butter as it browns. Laying the fish in the skillet "bone" side down is beneficial for browning, though not crucial; see page 172 for more information.

FISH

4	sole or flounder fillets (5 to 6 ounces each and ⅜ inch thick)
	Salt and ground black pepper
½	cup unbleached all-purpose flour
2	tablespoons vegetable oil
2	tablespoons unsalted butter, cut into 2 pieces

BROWNED BUTTER

4	tablespoons (½ stick) unsalted butter, cut into 4 pieces
1	tablespoon minced fresh parsley leaves
1½	tablespoons juice from 1 lemon
1	lemon, cut into wedges (for serving)

1. FOR THE FISH: Adjust the oven racks to the lower- and upper-middle positions, set 4 heatproof dinner plates on the racks, and heat the oven to 200 degrees. Pat the fish dry with paper towels and season both sides with salt and pepper; let stand until the fillets are glistening with moisture, about 5 minutes.

2. Spread the flour into a wide, shallow dish. Coat both sides of the fillets with flour, shake off the excess, and lay in a single layer on a baking sheet. Heat 1 tablespoon of the oil in a 12-inch nonstick skillet over high heat until shimmering. Add 1 tablespoon of the butter and swirl to melt and coat the pan bottom. Carefully place 2 fillets in the skillet, "bone" side down, and immediately reduce the heat to medium-high, and cook, without moving the fish, until the edges of the fillets are opaque and the bottom is golden brown, about 3 minutes.

171

3. Following the illustration on page 170, use 2 spatulas to gently flip the fillets, then continue to cook on the second side until the thickest part of the fillet easily separates into flakes when a toothpick is inserted, about 2 minutes longer. Transfer each of the fillets to a heated dinner plate in the oven. Wipe out the skillet and repeat with the remaining 1 tablespoon oil, 1 tablespoon butter, and the remaining fillets; transfer each fillet to a plate in oven.

4. FOR THE BROWNED BUTTER: While the fillets rest in the oven, melt the butter in a 10-inch skillet over medium-high heat and cook, swirling the pan constantly, until the butter is golden brown and has a nutty aroma, 2 to 3 minutes. Off the heat, stir in the lemon juice and season with salt and pepper to taste. Remove the fillets from the oven, spoon the sauce over each fillet, and sprinkle with the parsley. Serve immediately with the lemon wedges.

➤ VARIATIONS

Sautéed Sole with Toasted Slivered Almonds

Follow the recipe for Sautéed Sole with Browned Butter and Lemon, adding ¼ cup slivered almonds to the skillet when the butter has melted in step 4.

Sautéed Sole with Capers

Follow the recipe for Sautéed Sole with Browned Butter and Lemon, adding 2 tablespoons rinsed capers to the butter with the lemon juice in step 4.

ANATOMY OF A FLATFISH FILLET

Flatfish fillets have two distinct sides, and the order in which they are cooked can make a difference. The side of the fillet that was facing the bones in the fish browns best and makes the most attractive presentation on the plate. The side of the fillet that was facing the skin is darker and doesn't brown as well. When cooking, start the fillets bone side down, then flip them once a nice crust has formed. When the fillets are cooked through, slide them, bone side up, onto heated dinner plates.

BONE SIDE
Rounded indentations run along the length of the fillet on this side.

SKIN SIDE
The fillet is darker and flatter.

PAN-SEARED SALMON WITH BRAISED LENTILS
Saumon avec Lentilles du Puy

SALMON WITH LENTILS HAS BEEN A CLASSIC pairing in homes and restaurants across France for centuries, putting to good use their famous lentilles du Puy and the salmon fished from their shores. For good reason, this match of earthy lentils and assertively flavored salmon has become something of a restaurant darling here in America in recent years, appearing on hundreds of menus in one variation or another. Our goal was to re-create this pairing for the home cook, including with it a leafy green used often in French cooking, Swiss chard, for a complete meal.

We started our testing with the lentils, looking for a way to cook them so that they were infused with flavor but not overpowered by any one ingredient. We knew we'd want to build a flavor base in the skillet and then add the lentils and water and broth. Experimenting with a variety of aromatics, including garlic, shallots, scallions, and onions, we settled on the latter for their sweetness and body. The other options proved too assertive. Much of the flavor in the lentils, however, was to come from an unexpected ingredient: chard stems. Chard is an unusual green in that the stems are as desirable as the leaves. Chard stems possess an earthy, beetlike flavor that betrays the fact that chard is, in fact, a relative of beets, bred for its leaves instead of its roots. From the outset, we had decided that the stems would be braised with the lentils and the more delicate leaves would be cooked separately. Since chard stems are at their best sautéed in butter, that is how we prepared them, cooking them with the onions. Fresh thyme sprigs complemented the other flavors in the braised lentils and chicken stock provided a neutral yet rich backdrop.

With the lentils simmering away in the saucepan, we addressed the leaves of the Swiss chard. Our intention was to wilt them much as we do spinach or any other leafy green, by putting the chopped greens in a hot pan with some butter and cooking them until they are tender. We normally favor the addition of garlic and lemon to sautéed greens, but in this case we let them stand alone, simply seasoned with salt and the butter in which they were cooked. Once cooked, they went into a bowl, covered, to wait for the fish to cook and for the final assembly of the recipe.

Turning our attention to pan-searing the salmon, we gave the skillet a quick wipe with paper towels and patted the salmon dry carefully, seasoning it liberally with salt and freshly ground black pepper. We found that a modest amount of oil—just 1 tablespoon—was enough to brown the fish and crisp the skin.

With all the components cooked and ready to go, it was time to assemble the meal. As we were placing the lentils and chard on the plates, we realized it would be just as easy to wilt the chard in the cooked lentils omitting one extra step (plus the need to wipe out the skillet). When folded into the braised lentils the sliced leaves wilted perfectly. As a finishing touch, we stirred a tablespoon of butter into the lentils, which added just the right amount of richness. Now all we had to do was place a mound of lentils and chard on each plate, then top with the salmon.

REMOVING PINBONES FROM SALMON

1. Using the tips of your fingers, gently rub the surface of the salmon to locate any pinbones.

2. If you feel any bones, use a pair of needle-nose pliers or tweezers to pull them out.

Inspired by our success, we decided to try another classic French pairing: lentils and sausage. Following the format of our salmon recipe we simply swapped the sausage for the salmon—an easy substitution that created a very different dish (though the sausage requires some preparation).

When this dish is ordered in France, it usually comes to the table with the sausage nestled in the lentils, but cooking the sausage in the lentils made for a very greasy dish. Instead we browned the sausages first in a sauté pan, then added them to the lentils just before serving (of course, you could just place them on top of the mound of lentils and chard). Either way, this dish was easy, authentic, and delicious.

Pan-Seared Salmon with Braised Lentils

Saumon avec Lentilles du Puy

SERVES 4

You can use either skin-on or skinless salmon here; some tasters loved the crisp, cooked salmon skin. Puy lentils, sometimes called French green lentils, are our first choice for this recipe, but brown, black, or regular green lentils can be substituted; note that cooking times may vary depending on the type of lentils used. Lentils lose flavor with age, and because most packaged lentils do not have expiration dates, try to buy them from a store that specializes in natural foods and grains.

3	tablespoons unsalted butter
1	small onion, minced
1	bunch Swiss chard (10 to 12 ounces), stems and leaves separated (see page 174), stems chopped medium and leaves sliced thin
2	medium garlic cloves, minced or pressed through a garlic press (about 2 teaspoons)
4	sprigs fresh thyme
	Salt
1	cup lentilles du Puy (about 7 ounces), picked over and rinsed
1¾	cups low-sodium chicken broth
	Ground black pepper
4	center-cut salmon fillets (about 6 ounces each), pinbones removed
1	tablespoon vegetable oil

173

1. Melt 2 tablespoons of the butter in a large saucepan over medium-high heat. Add the onion, chard stems, garlic, thyme, and ¼ teaspoon of salt and cook, stirring frequently, until the vegetables soften and begin to brown, about 5 minutes. Stir in the lentils and broth and bring to a boil. Reduce the heat to low, cover, and cook until the lentils are tender, 40 to 50 minutes.

2. Uncover and continue to cook, stirring often, until most of the excess liquid has evaporated, about 2 minutes. Remove from the heat, discard the thyme, and season with salt and pepper to taste; cover to keep warm and set aside.

3. Pat the salmon dry with paper towels and season with salt and pepper. Heat the oil in a large 12-inch nonstick skillet over medium-high heat until just smoking. Place the fillets in the skillet, flesh side down, and cook without moving until well browned, 2½ to 3 minutes. Gently flip the fish and continue to cook until the fish is opaque and just firm, 2½ to 3 minutes longer. Transfer the fish to a clean plate, tent loosely with foil, and let rest for 5 minutes.

4. While the salmon rests, return the saucepan of lentils to medium-high heat and cook until hot, about 4 minutes. Stir in the chard leaves and the remaining 1 tablespoon butter and cook, stirring constantly, until the chard is wilted and incorporated, 1½ to 2 minutes. Spoon a small pile of lentils in the center of 4 individual serving plates and rest a piece of salmon on top. Serve immediately.

➤ VARIATION

Lentils with Sausage

Sausages are a bistro favorite in France, and make for a hearty dinner when served with the lentils.

Follow the recipe for Pan-Seared Salmon with Braised Lentils, substituting 1½ pounds sausage links (about 6 links) for the salmon; brown the sausage on all sides in step 3, about 7 minutes. When browned, pour ½ cup of water over the sausages in the skillet, cover, reduce the heat to medium, and cook until no longer pink in the center, 10 to 15 minutes. Transfer the cooked sausages to a cutting board, tent loosely with foil, and let rest while cooking the chard leaves in step 4. To serve, slice the sausages on the bias and rest on top of the lentils.

SEPARATING CHARD STEMS AND LEAVES

Hold each leaf at the base of the stem over a bowl filled with water. Use a sharp knife to slash the leafy portion from either side of the thick stem. The cutting motion here is the same you would use with a machete. This technique also works well with kale and mustard greens.

BROILED SCALLOPS WITH CREAMY MUSHROOM SAUCE

Coquilles St. Jacques Bonne Femme

BONNE FEMME IS FRENCH FOR "GOOD WIFE" or "good woman" and refers to dishes that are prepared simply and served family style, often in the casserole dish or pan in which they are cooked. Scallops and sole in France are often served à la bonne femme, which usually means that they are topped with a simple white wine or cream sauce with slivers of mushroom and then placed under the broiler to gratinée, or brown. What could be better or easier? It seemed to us that this simple dish could be a weeknight meal or a dinner party dish.

We were stumped, however, as soon as we started researching this recipe and ways in which to cook the scallops. At first we were misled by its name—that is until we realized that in most French cookbooks, scallops are called coquilles St. Jacques, which many of us think of as a dish containing scallops and a cream-wine sauce, topped with bread crumbs and placed under the broiler to brown. After further digging, we realized quite simply that coquilles St. Jacques is both the legendary dish and how the French tend to refer to the shellfish itself. In the case of our recipe, coquilles St. Jacques means simply scallops and coquilles

St. Jacques bonne femme means scallops prepared with a simple white wine, mushroom, and cream sauce. Now that we understood the nomenclature and the humble origins of this recipe, we set out to create the best version of it in the most straightforward way possible.

We started our testing by first considering the choice of scallop. There are three main varieties of scallops: sea, bay, and calico. Sea scallops, which are the largest of the three (usually at least an inch in diameter and often much bigger), are available year-round throughout the country and are the best choice for most recipes. Small, cork-shaped bay scallops (about half an inch in diameter) are harvested in a small area from Cape Cod to Long Island. Bay scallops are seasonal—available from late fall through midwinter—and are very expensive, up to $20 a pound. They are delicious but nearly impossible to find unless you live by the water in the Northeast or have access to an exceptional seafood market. Calico scallops (so named because of their splotchy shells) are small like bay scallops and harvested in the southern United States and around the world. They are inexpensive (often priced at just a few dollars a pound) but generally not very good. Our recommendation is to stick with sea scallops.

So what should you be aware of when buying sea scallops? Look first at their color. Scallops are naturally ivory or pinkish tan; processing (dipping them in a phosphate and water mixture to extend shelf life) turns them bright white. Processed scallops are slippery and swollen and usually sitting in a milky white liquid at the store. You should look for unprocessed scallops (also called dry scallops), which are sticky and flabby; they will taste fresher than processed scallops and will develop a nice crust when browned because they are not pumped with water. If they are surrounded by any liquid (and often they are not), the juices are clear, not white. When in doubt, simply ask your fishmonger, although usually good markets will label unprocessed scallops as dry. Sometimes they are sold cut up, but we found that they can lose moisture when handled this way and are best purchased whole.

With the scallop issue resolved, we were now ready to begin our testing for scallops bonne femme. The traditional method for making them in France is to place the scallops in a single layer in a buttered baking dish (one that can be put in the oven as well as under the broiler) and parbake them while making a mushroom sauce on the stovetop. The sauce is spooned over the scallops, which are then put under the broiler or in the oven until bubbly and browned. We started our testing with the sauce. A classic bonne femme sauce starts with white wine and heavy cream cooked together until thickened. Mushrooms are added and cooked until they have released their moisture and the sauce has again cooked down to a thickened state. In our first attempt at making this dish, we added the sauce to the scallops, cooking them together under the broiler. This yielded overcooked scallops and a broken and thin cream sauce. Clearly we'd need to focus on the scallops and the sauce separately and nail down our cooking times.

Focusing on cooking the scallops first, one thing was clear: to preserve their creamy and delicate texture, we'd have to cook them to medium-rare, which means the scallops are hot all the way through but the centers still retain some translucence. As scallops cook, the soft flesh firms and you can see an opaqueness that slowly creeps toward the center. The scallop is medium-rare when the sides have firmed up and all but about the middle third of the scallop has turned opaque. This will take somewhere between four and seven minutes under the broiler, depending upon the size of your scallops and the power of your broiler. Vigilance is the name of the game here—one minute too long and your scallops will be tough, your dish ruined. Through our testing we found that extra-large scallops (about 2 inches in diameter and 1 inch thick) took about seven minutes to parcook while smaller scallops (about 1 inch in diameter and ½ inch thick) took only four minutes.

Now to marry the sauce with the parcooked scallops. We whipped up a simple sauce but this time broiled the scallops until they were opaque but not cooked all the way through. At this point, we poured our creamy mushroom sauce over the scallops and browned them under the broiler. This worked fine, but somehow the dish didn't feel silky or rich enough. It was time to focus on the sauce.

Up to this point we'd been working with the classic bonne femme trio of mushrooms, white wine, and heavy cream, but we felt this sauce needed more flavor. Many traditional recipes use fish fumet (homemade fish stock) but that was too time-consuming for us, so we added a modest ½ cup chicken broth, which helped round out the flavors. Fresh thyme added herbal notes and a bit of color, and we also added some lemon juice to brighten the sauce. Our crowning touch was a tip we had picked up from an old French cookbook, which reserved some of the heavy cream and whipped it to stiff peaks. Once the rest of the sauce is reduced, it is quickly cooled to room temperature and the whipped cream is gently folded into it. When the sauce is spooned over the scallops, it doesn't run down the sides and onto the plate, rather it clings to the scallops, giving the overall dish a luxurious richness.

Broiled Scallops with Creamy Mushroom Sauce

Coquilles St. Jacques Bonne Femme

SERVES 4

The cooking time of the scallops will depend on the strength of your broiler and the size of the scallops; we found that extra-large scallops (about 2 inches diameter and 1 inch thick) took about 7 minutes while smaller scallops (about 1 inch diameter and ½ inch thick) took only 4 minutes. These scallops can also be cooked in individual baking dishes and adjust the oven rack so that the rims are 6 inches from the heating element.

```
2    cups heavy cream
1    cup dry white wine
½    cup low-sodium chicken broth
1    pound white button mushrooms, wiped clean
     and sliced thin
1    large shallot, minced (about ¼ cup)
1    teaspoon minced fresh thyme leaves
     Salt and ground black pepper
1    teaspoon juice from 1 lemon
     Unsalted butter, for the baking dish
1¼   pounds large sea scallops (about 16 scallops),
     tendons removed (see the illustration on
     page 232)
```

1. Bring 1½ cups of the heavy cream, the white wine, chicken broth, mushrooms, shallot, thyme, ½ teaspoon salt, and pepper to taste to a boil in a 12-inch nonstick skillet over high heat. Reduce to a simmer and cook until the mixture has thickened and measures between 2 and 2½ cups, 20 to 25 minutes; add the lemon juice off the heat. Transfer the mixture to a large bowl and let cool slightly.

2. Meanwhile, adjust an oven rack 6 inches from the broiler element and heat the broiler. Thoroughly butter the inside of a 2-quart broiler-safe baking dish; set aside. Using an electric mixer, whip the remaining ½ cup heavy cream on medium-low speed until small bubbles form, about 30 seconds. Increase the speed to medium-high and continue to whip the mixture until it thickens and forms stiff peaks, about 1 minute longer; set aside.

3. Pat the scallops dry with paper towels, season with salt and pepper, and arrange in a single layer in the prepared baking dish. Broil the scallops until the exterior looks opaque but the interior remains translucent, 4 to 7 minutes (see note).

4. While the scallops cook, gently fold the whipped cream into the cooled mushroom sauce until almost no white streaks remain (a few streaks are okay). Spoon the sauce over broiled scallops and continue to broil until the sauce is nicely browned and the scallops are cooked through, about 1 minute. Serve immediately.

PAN-SEARED DUCK BREASTS

Magrets de Canard Poêle

OF ALL THE CLASSIC FRENCH DISHES THAT have made it across the Atlantic, there is one in particular that hasn't caught on quite the way the others have—pan-seared duck breasts. Perhaps it is the excessive amount of fat between the skin and the meat that scares people away, or perhaps there aren't enough recipes. We don't know, but here in the test kitchen it's one of our favorites and we couldn't have dreamed up a more perfect place to develop a recipe for duck than in the middle of our chapter on France.

Magret is the French word for duck breast—the leanest portion of the duck. It is usually served pink with a well-rendered and crispy skin. Duck pairs especially well with fruit (think duck à l'orange) as well as more assertive sauces like a green peppercorn sauce, a classic dish found on menus all across France.

There are two ways to cook duck breasts: as part of a whole roasted duck or as boneless fillets. Because the meat in the legs is considerably tougher than the breast, any attempt to roast a duck without overcooking the breast meat is impossible. Your only path out of that mess is to slow-roast the whole duck for two to three hours until most of the fat has rendered from the skin and the meat is more akin to duck confit (see page 188) than roasted duck. While confit is delicious, we like our duck breasts cooked medium rare with perfectly rendered skin, and there's only one way to do that: remove the breasts from the bone and cook them on their own. With scores of duck breasts in hand, we went to work to test the best method for achieving the trifecta of perfectly cooked duck breasts: pink, tender meat covered by a well-rendered, thin layer of fat and crispy, golden skin.

Depending on the variety of duck, an entire breast can weigh anywhere from 12 to 20 ounces. The most commonly available size is 12 ounces, which splits neatly into two breast halves, each weighing about 6 ounces—an ideal amount for one person. Duck breast meat is firm and flavorful and tastes best when cooked to medium-rare, or about 125 degrees measured on an instant-read thermometer (its final resting temperature being 130 degrees). Although health experts recommend cooking all poultry, including duck, to at least 160 degrees, we found that eating duck breast cooked this long is akin to eating a well-done steak.

The technique of cooking the breast is tricky, however, as the thick layer of skin and fat needs some serious attention during the cooking process. The skin on a duck breast adds flavor and a pleasantly crisp texture when prepared correctly, but our initial tests proved that cooking a piece of meat

with so much fat has some pitfalls.

We focused on one cooking method that we felt held the most promise: sautéing (we eliminated broiling because the skin was prone to spontaneous combustion and ruled out grilling because of the flare-ups). We started by removing the excess fat (the fat that hangs off the meat itself) to avoid even more rendered fat in the pan, and turned our attention to the heat level. We put the meat into the sauté pan skin side down for half the time and then flipped it to finish cooking. We did this at multiple heat levels: high, medium, and medium-low. The duck breasts cooked over high heat turned a deep mahogany brown quickly, but didn't render enough fat before we had to flip them to prevent burning the skin. The duck finished cooking in a matter of minutes and tasters were not impressed with the resulting flabby skin. The duck breasts cooked at medium heat fared much better, and the fat was rendered before the skin turned a desirable golden color, but after flipping them, the meat overcooked very quickly and the skin was still too flabby. We finally came close to success when we cooked the breasts over medium-low heat—it wasn't perfect but we were within striking distance.

With the heat set at medium-low, we turned to a method we had read about in various recipes where the skin is scored to allow extra fat to melt away from the skin. When we scored the skin, we found that it cooked up crisper and with very little chewiness. The balance between the skin and the meat was just about perfect, but starting the duck at so low a temperature was still taking too long and leading to dry, overcooked meat. Our solution? We set a dry pan over medium heat for three minutes, then we lowered the heat to medium-low before adding the duck breasts skin side down. They sizzled at first, but then started rendering fat immediately, shaving minutes off the cooking time.

We stumbled upon one last trick. We let one batch go skin side down too long. Thinking that we had ruined them, we turned them back over and finished cooking the duck for a few minutes. To our surprise, the meat was perfectly cooked and the skin even crisper than before. Upon reflection, it makes sense to cook duck breast longer on the skin side; we just needed to cook it almost entirely on the skin side before flipping it to the delicate flesh side. The skin acts as a sort of insulator for the meat, allowing the breast to be cooked skin side down for as long as it takes to properly render the fat and brown. Once flipped it takes literally two minutes to cook the duck to rare, an additional one to two minutes to get it up to medium rare, and the result is meat that is sweet, tender and moist.

Now for the finishing touches. As with other meat, it is important to let duck rest before cutting into it so that it holds onto its juices better. To properly carve the duck, we recommend cutting the breast on the diagonal into ½-inch-thick slices, and for a nice presentation you can then fan the slices out over a plate. You can serve the duck breast whole, but this presentation works especially well with sauces and is attractive.

With our perfectly rendered and cooked duck breasts resting on a cutting board, we set out to create a couple of simple pan sauces that we could whip together quickly. The first sauce was a creamy green peppercorn sauce that we got underway by first sautéing some diced shallots in the same pan in which we cooked the duck (be sure to pour off all but 1 tablespoon of the rendered fat or you'll be deep frying the shallots instead). To this we added some port for sweetness and acidity and green peppercorns for a bright, assertive flavor. Chicken broth and heavy cream rounded out and finished this classic sauce. Our second sauce was

SCORING DUCK BREASTS

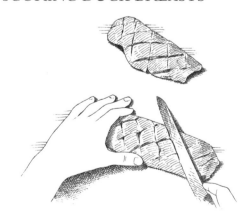

To render the most fat and yield the crispiest duck skin, score the skin with a serrated knife in a diagonal pattern, being careful not to cut into the meat.

built around dried cherries, which, like green peppercorns, are a classic pairing for duck in France. Because the cherries are so sweet, we used red wine to temper their sweetness with acidity, finishing the sauce with chicken broth and cold butter. Four perfectly cooked duck breasts, two simple sauces, one perfectly French meal.

Pan-Seared Duck Breasts with Green Peppercorn Sauce
Magret de Canard au Poivre Vert
SERVES 4

Cooking the duck skin side down over moderate heat is key in order to render the fat and crisp the skin; adjust the stove temperature as needed to maintain a constant but gentle simmer during this cooking time. Both a traditional and nonstick skillet will work here, but a nonstick skillet makes for easier cleanup. We prefer to cook duck breasts to medium-rare; however, you can cook them to your desired level of doneness in step 2 (see the information on testing meat for doneness on page 190).

4	boneless duck breast halves (about 6 ounces each), skin scored on the diagonal (see the illustration on the left)
	Salt and ground black pepper
2	medium shallots, minced (about ⅓ cup)
¾	cup ruby port
2	tablespoons dried green peppercorns, crushed
I	cup low-sodium chicken broth
½	cup heavy cream
I	teaspoon lemon juice from I lemon

1. Pat the duck breasts dry with paper towels and season with salt and pepper. Heat a 12-inch nonstick skillet over medium heat until hot, about 3 minutes. Add the duck breasts, skin side down, lower the heat to medium-low, and cook until the fat begins to render, about 5 minutes. Continue to cook, adjusting the heat as needed for the fat to maintain a constant but gentle simmer, until most of the fat has rendered and the skin is deep golden and crisp, 20 to 25 minutes longer.

2. Flip the duck breasts over and continue to cook until the center of the breasts are medium-rare and measure 125 degrees on an instant-read

EQUIPMENT: Instant-Read Thermometers

In the test kitchen we use an instant-read thermometer to determine when meat, poultry, and even bread are optimally cooked. We also use it to check the temperature of sugar syrup when making meringues, caramel sauce, and candy and to test the temperature of oil when frying. Our favorite instant-read thermometer is the ThermoWorks Super-Fast Thermapen, a test kitchen workhorse that quickly provides accurate readings across a broad range of temperatures. But at $85, the Thermapen isn't cheap. And in the past, the only inexpensive instant-read thermometers available were mediocre dial-face models. Dial-face thermometers are hard to read, and their sensors are in the wrong place—more than an inch up the stem. In contrast, digital instant-read thermometers have their sensors on the very tip of their probe, making them easy to use in both shallow liquids and deep roasts.

But in recent years, cheaper digital instant-read thermometers have become available. Could any of them approach the performance of our trusty Thermapen? We purchased eight digital instant-read thermometers, all priced under $25, and put them through their paces in the kitchen.

Three of the models we tested (Cooper-Atkins, CDN Candy, and Polder 363-90) weren't perfectly accurate in boiling water and/or ice water. What's more, none of the offenders featured a calibrating function.

In our next test—taking the temperature of hot oil (where you want a reading as soon as possible), testers' hands became uncomfortably hot with the slower models. Fast response time proved to be an especially important factor in our ratings.

Does the size of the thermometer make a difference? Bigger is better, but only to a point. With its mammoth 8¼-inch probe, the CDN Candy thermometer had no trouble finding the center

of our biggest roast, but it was cumbersome with smaller items. At the other end of the spectrum, the probes on the CDN Q2-450, Cooper-Atkins, and Polder 371 were too short (just 2¾ inches) to reach the center of a big roast. The ideal probe length is 4 to 5 inches.

Some of the thermometers include "extra" features—such as auto shut-off and minimum/maximum temperature memory—but these were deemed nonessential. Testers did value thermometers that could be calibrated. They also liked thermometers that registered a wide range of temperatures, from below zero (for frozen items) to 400 degrees.

What did we find? None of our cheap contenders could match the speed, temperature range, or accuracy of the Thermapen, but the CDN DTQ450 came pretty close, and for a fraction of the price.

THE BEST INSTANT-READ THERMOMETERS

The ThermoWorks Super-Fast Thermapen 211-476 (left) is fast, accurate, and easy to use. The Thermapen also has the widest temperature range (-58 to 572 degrees), but note its hefty price tag—$85. The CDN ProAccurate Quick Tip Digital Cooking Thermometer DTQ450 (right) was not quite as fast as the mighty Thermapen, but fast enough and its low price, $17.95, puts it in reach of most cooks.

---

thermometer, 2 to 5 minutes. Transfer the duck to a carving board, tent loosely with foil, and let rest while making the sauce (the duck temperature will rise to 130 degrees before serving).

3. Pour off all but 1 tablespoon of the fat left in the skillet. Add the shallots and cook over medium-high heat until softened, 2 to 3 minutes. Add the port and green peppercorns and cook until the liquid has reduced to a syrupy consistency, about 4 minutes. Add the chicken broth and cream and cook until the sauce has thickened and measures about 1 cup, about 5 minutes. Off the heat, stir in the lemon juice and season with salt and pepper

to taste; transfer the sauce to a bowl or gravy boat. Slice the duck breasts thin and serve, passing the sauce separately or pouring it over the duck.

> VARIATION

Pan-Seared Duck Breasts with Dried Cherry Sauce

Follow the recipe for Pan-Seared Duck Breasts with Green Peppercorn Sauce, substituting ¾ cup dry red wine for the port and ¼ cup dried cherries for the peppercorns. Omit the cream and whisk 2 tablespoons cold, unsalted butter into the sauce just before removing it from the heat.

CHICKEN IN A POT

Poulet en Cocotte

POULET EN COCOTTE (CHICKEN IN A POT) IS A casserole method for roasting chicken that produces unbelievably moist meat. Casserole-roasting is a common way of cooking in France that originated as a means to protect the Sunday roast from unpredictable oven temperatures. In years past, ovens had no real thermostat, just a knob that regulated the flow of gas, and dry-roasting a bird could lead to an inedible dinner. Roasting in a casserole protected the roast from variable conditions in the oven. And for people with tiny ovens, or no ovens at all, a heavy, tight-lidded casserole on the stovetop became the oven-surrogate. Ovens and stovetops have come a long way since then, but the method of cooking a chicken in a tightly closed pot remains a popular and delicious way to prepare chicken today.

Our test kitchen has seen literally hundreds of roasted birds emerge from our ovens, so we thought we knew a thing or two about the perfect roasted bird. One look at a recipe for casserole-roasted chicken, where the chicken is left to roast in a closed pot had us scratching our heads. What about the skin? How does it get crisp? Our resident Francophile shook his head as he'd heard this argument before, "Where did Americans get the idea that chicken skin has to be crisp?" The goal of this dish, he explained, is to have moist, succulent meat and well-rendered skin. It won't be crisp and it won't be golden brown, but it will be delicious.

Skeptical, we entered the test kitchen with a half dozen recipes directing us toward a technique that was as foreign to us as an oven with no thermostat.

First we needed to understand a bit more about this dish. What we did know is that roasting typically occurs in a dry-air oven environment, but casserole-roasting occurs under moister, less brutal conditions, as little moisture from the chicken can escape the vessel. To really get a handle on this technique, we started with a couple of roasting chickens—one cooked in the pot, the other in a roasting pan using our favorite method. The skin of the "dry-roasted" chicken was a beautiful golden brown compared to that of the "moist-roasted" chicken, but the tasters' opinions took a 180-degree turn when we tasted the meat. The chicken roasted in the closed pot was unbelievably moist, so moist in fact that no one cared that the skin wasn't golden brown. Excited by this new method of roasting chicken, we started our testing in earnest, using only the most basic recipe in order to focus on the technique of casserole-roasting chicken.

Many of the recipes we came across in our research use a roasting chicken (a bird that weighs about 5 pounds), a size slightly larger than we normally use in the test kitchen. Since we wanted this recipe to feed at least four people, we went with the larger bird. We pulled out every large pot with a lid that we could find and started. An hour later, a group of very different looking chickens emerged from the ovens, coming together to tell one story: a heavy pot with a tight-fitting lid is essential to this recipe. Copper pots are fine, but often their lids are ill-fitting and too thin to reflect heat back into the pot, and cast iron reacts with acids (wine, onions, shallots, garlic), which wouldn't work for us as we planned on building a sauce to go with our chicken once it was cooked. Our preferred vessel is enameled cast iron, which distributes heat evenly across its bottom surface, and whose heavy lid radiates the interior heat back into it.

With the proper cooking vessel in order, we tested oven temperatures from 325 degrees all the way up to 475 degrees. The chicken cooked at the highest heat emerged from the oven with an impressive golden-colored skin and unfortunately

---

CORE TECHNIQUE

FASTER, MOISTER ROAST CHICKEN

We like a well-seasoned roast chicken with a crackling crisp crust from time to time, but were intrigued when we heard about a French method for baking roast chicken in a covered pot—a method which results in super moist chicken in less time than it takes to roast a chicken conventionally (normally 1½ hours). We tried this method, piling the chicken and aromatics into a covered Dutch oven and sliding it into the oven. In just an hour, we had the moistest roast chicken we'd ever tasted, along with enough rich pan juices to make a quick, flavorful sauce. And the absence of a golden brown skin? No one missed it with this faster, moister chicken.

TUCKING POULTRY WINGS

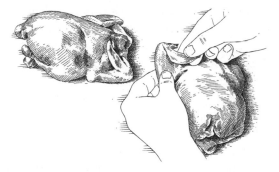

No matter if you're cooking a big turkey, medium-sized chicken, or a tiny game hen, tucking the wings back behind the neck before cooking is an important step. Doing this prevents the tips of the wings from burning, and keeps the wings from lying on top of the breast meat so that the skin covering the breast can brown evenly. To boot, it makes for a tidy presentation after the bird is cooked.

the driest meat. Slightly lower temperatures—450 degrees and 425 degrees—weren't much better and tasters all agreed that the meat was too dry to justify this alternate cooking method.

On the opposite end of this test, 325 degrees was too low; while the meat was moist and succulent, the skin was virtually without color and still quite flabby. The temperature was not high enough to render the fat in the skin while the chicken slowly cooked and it just took too long, logging over 1½ hours in the oven. The perfect temperature was 375 degrees for just 1 hour; tasters were very enthusiastic about the moist meat and well-rendered skin. We also noted that because the pot is covered, it traps the heat inside, thus speeding cooking time—a very nice bonus.

With our temperature decided, we tested how necessary it is to flip the bird during roasting. Up to this point we had just been leaving the chicken on its back, not bothering to flip it at all, so that we could test other factors. However, the test kitchen's time-tested roasting method says to flip the chicken twice during cooking to ensure even cooking so that the thighs cook at the same rate as the breasts. We tested no flips, one flip (breast to back), and two flips (wing, wing, back) and tasters could not detect a difference in the flavor or the texture of the meat. Zero flips it was—this recipe just kept getting better.

We had noticed in our previous tests that once the chicken emerges from the oven and is moved to a carving board to rest, there is a plethora of juices and fat left in the pot with which to make a sauce. At first we just skimmed the fat, added some white wine and chicken broth, and reduced the liquid until it had thickened to the desired consistency, but it needed something more. We sliced shallots and peeled garlic and roasted them with the chicken, scattering them around the roasting bird. By the time the bird was finished, the shallots and garlic were soft, caramelized, and sweet—just the flavor boost our sauce needed. We added thyme and bay leaves and finished the sauce with some cold butter whisked in at the end. The sauce with the caramelized shallots and garlic was just right. We spooned the sauce over our portions of sliced chicken and dug in. This chicken truly was a revelation—more moist and well-seasoned than any chicken we'd ever eaten before. And the skin? We'd almost forgotten about it. True it wasn't the mahogany crisp cloak of a dry-roasted bird, but it was thin and perfectly rendered, which was just fine by us.

Chicken in a Pot
Poulet en Cocotte
SERVES 4
We recommend using a large Dutch oven with a tight-fitting lid, but any appropriately sized pot with a lid will work.

1	whole roasting chicken (4½ to 5 pounds), giblets discarded and wings tucked (see the illustration above)
	Salt and ground black pepper
1	tablespoon olive oil
2	large shallots, halved and sliced thin (about ½ cup)
6	medium garlic cloves, peeled and trimmed
½	cup dry white wine
½	cup low-sodium chicken broth
2	bay leaves
1	teaspoon minced fresh thyme leaves
2	tablespoons unsalted butter, cut into 2 pieces and chilled

1. Adjust an oven rack to the lower middle position and heat the oven to 375 degrees. Pat the chicken dry with paper towels and season with salt and pepper. Add the oil, shallots, and garlic cloves to a large Dutch oven, and lay the chicken on top, breast side up. Cover and bake until an instant-read thermometer registers 160 degrees in the center of the breast, about 1 hour.

2. Tip the chicken to drain the juices from the cavity into the pot. Transfer the chicken to a carving board, tent loosely with foil, and let rest while finishing the sauce. Pour all the cooking juices into a fat separator and set aside to settle, about 3 minutes. Pour the defatted juices back into the pot and stir in the wine, broth, bay leaves, and thyme. Bring to a boil over medium-high heat, and cook until the liquid has reduced to about 1 cup, 5 to 10 minutes.

3. Off the heat, remove the bay leaves, whisk in the butter, and season with salt and pepper to taste; transfer the sauce to a bowl or gravy boat. Carve the chicken and serve, passing the sauce separately.

Chicken Fricassee

Fricassée de Poulet

THE NAME OF THIS DISH COMES FROM AN old French word, *fricasser* (to fry), but the dish fricassée is a bit confusing. It is often mistaken for a sauté (where no liquid is included in the cooking) or for a stew (where the meat is simmered in liquid for the entire process). But in a fricassee the meat, usually chicken, is sautéed in butter or sometimes oil before being stewed with vegetables. The chicken, carved into pieces before cooking, is served surrounded by the vegetables along with a pan sauce bound with egg yolks and cream. In other words, it's exactly in between the two, neither sauté nor stew—it's a fricassee. The end result is like a thick, chunky stew. When made properly, this dish is meaty, rich, and satisfying. Unfortunately, we've had versions where the sauce is thin and insipid and the chicken is dry despite all the liquid it is cooked in. For such a simple dish, this has a lot of room for improvement.

Taking a first glance at our array of authentic fricassee recipes, we noticed a few things they had in common. First, they all use a whole chicken cut into pieces. Second, the recipe starts by browning the chicken in fat, then adding liquid to finish the dish as a stew. Finally, the resulting sauce is finished with an egg yolk liaison, or beaten egg yolks with heavy cream. For this dish, these three characteristics had to be put to the test first.

We first addressed the issue of the chicken itself. Since we like a choice of white or dark meat, we prefer chicken parts (such as thighs or breasts). You can use skinless chicken parts if you like, but we suggest chicken parts with the skin on, as the skin helps to contribute flavor to the sauce from the browning process.

Next we focused on technique. With the basic model in place (brown the chicken in butter or oil, then add liquid and cook), we started by browning our chicken in vegetable oil, as early tests revealed the chicken burned in places when browned in butter. We next tested the stewing liquid. Many traditional French recipes simmer the chicken in equal amounts of chicken stock and white wine. Tasters judged this sauce too acidic, a result of the generous amount of wine, we reasoned. For our next version we cut out the wine and used only chicken broth, but the sauce tasted too flat. A bit of wine was definitely in order. Adding the wine back in incremental amounts, we found that ½ cup of dry white wine with 1½ cups of chicken broth yielded the right balance of meaty richness and bright flavors. To this liquid base, we added our vegetable garnish. We tested carrots, celery, mushrooms, pearl onions, yellow onions, shallots, garlic, and all combinations of the above. Our favorite combination was pearl onions and mushrooms with a little minced garlic, thyme, and bay leaves added for flavor.

With our flavors in place, it was time to get our timing down. We browned two batches of chicken first, one batch lightly and the other to a deep golden brown on both sides. The more the caramelization in the pan, the richer the sauce, so browning to a deep golden brown is our preference. Once the chicken was nicely browned, we removed it from the pan to cook our garnish. We had planned to caramelize the onions before adding the mushrooms, but with 30 minutes already gone by, we decided to save time by cooking the two vegetables together. From there we added our aromatic flavorings, deglazed the pan with white wine, then added the chicken broth. We were now ready to return the chicken to finish cooking.

With the chicken pieces nestled in the stewing liquid, we started our timer. Twenty minutes later the breast meat was perfectly cooked but the thighs were still undercooked and tough. Another 20 minutes later, the thighs were approaching perfect while the breasts were dry and overcooked. We were going to have to stagger the time the meat went into the pan if we wanted a perfect fricassee. Simple enough; once our stewing liquid was simmering and ready for the chicken, we added only the thighs and cooked them, covered for 40 minutes. At that point we added the breast meat and cooked the entire dish for an additional 20 minutes. All the meat was perfectly cooked and it was time to finish the sauce.

Traditional recipes call for egg yolks and cream to finish this sauce, but we didn't want an extremely rich sauce, and trying to prevent the egg yolks from curdling in the pan seemed too fussy for this simple meal. We omitted the eggs and focused on the cream, adding various amounts to find the perfect balance of richness and meatiness. Tasters were stuck between ⅓ cup and ½ cup cream, some citing the more generous amount as too rich, while others felt it was just right. We went with ⅓ cup, knowing we could always add more if necessary. Either way, this chicken fricassee was everything we wanted it to be: rich and deeply flavored. It's essential to serve the fricassee over rice or noodles, or to offer crusty bread to soak up the delicious sauce.

Chicken Fricassee
Fricassée de Poulet
SERVES 4

If using both chicken breasts and thighs/drumsticks, we recommend cutting the breast pieces in half so that each person can have some white meat and dark meat. The breasts and thighs/drumsticks do not cook at the same time; if using both, note that the breast pieces are added partway through the cooking time.

4	pounds bone-in, skin-on chicken parts (split breasts cut in half, drumsticks, and/or thighs)
	Salt and ground black pepper
2	tablespoons vegetable oil
2	tablespoons unsalted butter
1	medium onion, minced
10	ounces white button mushrooms, brushed clean and quartered
2	medium garlic cloves, minced or pressed through a garlic press (about 2 teaspoons)
2	teaspoons minced fresh thyme leaves
2	tablespoons unbleached all-purpose flour
½	cup dry white wine
1½	cups low-sodium chicken broth
2	bay leaves
⅓	cup heavy cream
2	teaspoons juice from 1 lemon
2	tablespoons minced fresh parsley leaves

1. Pat the chicken dry with paper towels and season with salt and pepper. Heat the oil in a large Dutch oven over medium-high heat until just smoking. Brown half of the chicken on both sides, 5 to 8 minutes per side, reducing the heat if the pan begins to scorch. Transfer the chicken to a plate, leaving the fat in the pot. Return the pot with fat to medium-high heat and repeat with the remaining chicken; transfer the chicken to the plate, and discard all of the fat.

2. Add the butter to the pot and return to medium heat until melted. Add the onion, mushrooms, and ¼ teaspoon salt and cook, stirring occasionally, until lightly browned, about 10 minutes. Stir in the garlic and thyme and cook until fragrant, about 30 seconds. Stir in the flour and cook for 1 minute. Stir in the wine, scraping up any browned bits. Stir in the broth and bay leaves.

3. Nestle the chicken, along with any accumulated juices, into the pot and bring to a simmer. Cover, turn the heat to medium-low, and simmer until the chicken is fully cooked and tender, about 20 minutes for the breasts (160 degrees on an instant-read thermometer), or 1 hour for the thighs and drumsticks. (If using both types of chicken, simmer the thighs and drumsticks for 40 minutes before adding the breasts.)

4. Transfer the chicken to a serving dish, tent loosely with foil, and let rest while finishing the sauce. Skim as much fat as possible off the surface of the sauce, stir in the cream, return to a simmer, and cook until the sauce has thickened and measures about 1½ cups, 15 to 20 minutes. Remove and discard the bay leaves. Stir in the lemon juice and season with salt and pepper to taste. Spoon the sauce over the chicken, sprinkle with the parsley, and serve.

CHICKEN BRAISED IN RED WINE

Coq au Vin

THIS CLASSIC FRICASSEE OF CUT-UP CHICKEN is cooked in a red wine sauce and finished with a garnish of bacon, tiny glazed pearl onions, and sautéed mushrooms. At its best, coq au vin is hugely tasty, the acidity of the wine rounded out by rich, salty bacon and sweet, caramelized onions and mushrooms. The chicken acts like a sponge, soaking up those same dark, compelling flavors. We set about creating a recipe that would satisfy our appetite for a really great coq au vin.

We started out by cooking and tasting a number of recipes from French cookbooks. We noticed that the recipes fell into two categories: those that were simple and rustic in character, and ones that were a bit more complicated, but promised a more refined dish. The recipes in the first category were versions of a straightforward brown fricassee. Tasting these simpler versions, we recognized them as the serviceable renditions of recent memory: The sauces were good but not extraordinary; the chicken tasted mostly like chicken.

We moved on to testing a handful of much more complicated recipes. One of them, also a brown fricassee, was a two-day affair with a much more elaborate sauce. The recipe began by combining red wine with veal stock and browned vegetables and reducing this mixture by about half. The chicken was then browned and the pan deglazed with the reduced wine mixture. Once the chicken was

cooked, the sauce was strained, bound first with *beurre manié* (a paste of mashed butter and flour), and then with a bit of chicken liver pureed with heavy cream, and finished with flambéed cognac.

Although this particular recipe was built on the same basic model as the others, this dish was in a whole different league. It was what a good coq au vin ought to be—the sauce was beautifully textured, clean-flavored, and rich without being heavy or murky. The chicken was drenched in flavor. Though we were able to make it in just one day instead of two, the recipe unquestionably demanded more time, more last-minute fussing, and a lot more dishes.

In trying to simplify this recipe, two techniques stood out when we compared it with the others. First, our working recipe bound the sauce differently, using beurre manié and chicken liver rather than sprinkling the meat or vegetables with flour at the beginning. This recipe also used all chicken legs instead of both legs and breasts, which is traditional.

We first tested a coq au vin bound with beurre manié and compared it with one in which the vegetables were sprinkled with flour. We liked the streamlined method of sprinkling the flour over the vegetables to give the sauce some viscosity, but felt the richness of the butter in the beurre manié was missing in this leaner sauce. To solve that, we whisked cold butter into the finished sauce, which rounded out the flavors with the added benefit of thickening the sauce.

Traditionally coq au vin makes use of an entire bird, so when we tasted the version that used legs

CLEANING MUSHROOMS

Mushrooms, with their hard-to-reach spots, can be difficult to clean. We like to use a clean, soft-bristled toothbrush. It provides a comfortable handle, and the small head slips easily under the gills to capture every stray bit of dirt. You can also use a damp paper towel to wipe away the dirt.

only, many tasters missed the white meat. Other tasters felt all dark meat made sense for gauging the cooking time since white and dark meats cook at a different rate. The bottom line: use the cuts you like. As long as the thighs get a head start cooking before the breasts are added to the pot, the end result is just as good either way.

Having determined that the flour sprinkled on the vegetables and the sauce finished with butter were two important keys to the success of this dish, we ran some final tests to find out if the addition of cognac, chicken liver, or tomato paste improved the sauce enough to merit the extra trouble. Only tomato paste made the cut, as it's easy to whisk in and added the extra flavor and body.

Chicken Braised in Red Wine
Coq au Vin
SERVES 4

Regular bacon can be substituted for the thick-cut. Use any $10 bottle of fruity, medium-bodied red wine such a Pinot Noir, Côtes du Rhône, or Zinfandel. If using both chicken breasts and thighs/drumsticks, we recommend cutting the breast pieces in half so that each person can have some white meat and dark meat. The breasts and thighs/drumsticks do not cook at the same time; if using both, note that the breast pieces are added partway through the cooking time. Serve with egg noodles.

6 ounces thick-cut bacon (about 5 slices), chopped medium
Vegetable oil, as needed
4 pounds bone-in, skin-on chicken pieces (split breasts cut in half, drumsticks, and/or thighs)
Salt and ground black pepper
5 ounces frozen pearl onions, thawed (about 2 cups)
10 ounces white button mushrooms, wiped clean and quartered
2 medium garlic cloves, minced or pressed through a garlic press (about 2 teaspoons)
1 tablespoon tomato paste
3 tablespoons unbleached all-purpose flour
1 (750-ml) bottle medium-bodied red wine (about 3 cups, see note)
2½ cups low-sodium chicken broth
1 teaspoon minced fresh thyme leaves, or ¼ teaspoon dried
2 bay leaves
2 tablespoons unsalted butter, cut into 2 pieces, chilled
2 tablespoons minced fresh parsley leaves

1. Fry the bacon in a large Dutch oven over medium heat until crisp, 5 to 7 minutes. Transfer the bacon to a paper towel–lined plate, leaving the fat in the pot (you should have about 2 tablespoons fat; if necessary add some vegetable oil).

2. Pat the chicken dry with paper towels and season with salt and pepper. Return the pot with the bacon fat to medium-high heat until shimmering. Brown half of the chicken on both sides, 5 to 8 minutes per side, reducing the heat if the pan begins to scorch. Transfer the chicken to a plate, leaving the fat in the pot. Return the pot with fat to medium-high heat and repeat with the remaining chicken; transfer the chicken to the plate.

3. Pour off all but 1 tablespoon of the fat in the pot (or add vegetable oil if needed). Add the pearl onions and mushrooms and cook over medium heat, stirring occasionally, until lightly browned, about 10 minutes. Stir in the garlic and tomato paste and cook until fragrant, about 30 seconds. Stir in the flour and cook for 1 minute. Stir the wine, broth thyme, and bay leaves, scraping up any browned bits.

4. Nestle the chicken, along with any accumulated juices, into the pot and bring to a simmer. Cover, turn the heat to medium-low, and simmer until the chicken is fully cooked and tender, about 20 minutes for the breasts (160 degrees on an instant-read thermometer), or 1 hour for the thighs and drumsticks. (If using both types of chicken, simmer the thighs and drumsticks for 40 minutes before adding the breasts.)

5. Transfer the chicken to a serving dish, tent loosely with foil, and let rest while finishing the sauce. Skim as much fat as possible off the surface of the sauce and return to a simmer until the sauce is thickened and measures about 2 cups, about 20 minutes. Off the heat, whisk in the butter and season with salt and pepper to taste. Pour the sauce over the chicken, sprinkle with the reserved bacon and parsley, and serve.

CASSOULET

CASSOULET IS PERHAPS FRANCE'S MOST revered stew. Hailing from the Languedoc region, the dish typically is composed of garlicky white beans, pork sausage, duck confit, and a variety of other meats such as lamb and pork loin—the whole capped with a buttery bread crumb topping. Unlike a simple beef stew, which requires just one type of meat, a cassoulet contains a host of meats, all of which meld together into one rich and hearty meal. While this classic French peasant dish can be replicated at restaurants, it is usually not regarded as a dish for the casual home cook. The time investment alone is impractical and it can be difficult to achieve a perfect balance of flavors. On more than one occasion we have eaten cassoulets that were overwhelmed by salt or swimming in fat, most often because of the confit and sausages. But we love this dish so much that we decided it would be worth the effort to try to streamline it without compromising its fundamental nature.

We started our testing with the duck confit—an essential component of cassoulet. You can purchase confit by mail order or in some specialty shops, but we wanted to also try our hand at making our own. The method is as follows: duck legs are placed in a large container, sprinkled heavily with salt, and cured for 24 to 48 hours. The salt draws the juices out, which both preserves and tenderizes the meat. After this sojourn in salt, the meat is slowly simmered in its own fat, so that the flavor of the fat penetrates the spaces previously occupied by the juices. The finished confit may be used immediately or stored in an airtight container. We felt we could cut this time down considerably—after all, the salt cure used to be for preserving, which we can now do in our modern refrigerators. We wanted to salt the duck just long enough to allow the salt to penetrate the meat, in order to make the flavors more pronounced. A couple of hours wasn't long enough, but overnight was perfect. With an overnight salt cure and two hours in a moderately low oven, our duck confit was ready.

Our next test involved figuring out which meats to use and how to avoid the issue of slow-roasting. We knew that we wanted to be true to the original recipe and use either fresh pork or lamb. We decided to try stewing the meat in liquid on top of the stove. This method yielded great results in terms of tenderness, but the meat had none of the depth of flavor that occurs with roasting. Searing the meat first took care of that problem. Because we were now stewing the meat, we needed to use cuts that were appropriate for this method. We tried pork loin, the choice in so many cassoulet recipes, but the loin became waterlogged and tasteless during stewing. We also tried pork butt, which is actually part of the shoulder. This cut, which has more internal fat than the center loin, retained the moisture and flavor that was lost with the other cut. To facilitate quicker cooking, we cut the roast into 1-inch pieces. We did similar tests with the lamb. Lamb shoulder is the best cut for stewing, but it can be difficult to find in markets. Instead we turned to thick lamb shoulder chops, cut into 1-inch pieces. Finally, perfectly tender meat without the effort of roasting. Either lamb or pork works here, but for our cassoulet, we decided to go with the less expensive and readily available pork butt.

Next we focused on the topping. Tradition dictates fresh bread crumbs, but tasters disliked the way they made the meaty broth in the cassoulet gritty. Our solution? Croutons. We buttered and seasoned cubes of bread and baked them in the oven until golden brown and crisp. Once added to the cassoulet, the bottoms soaked up the meaty juices while the tops stayed buttery and crisp.

Now for the heart and soul of this dish—the beans. In all the discussions over what ingredients should go into a cassoulet, everyone agreed on at least one thing: the dish must be made with white, kidney-shaped beans. The two kinds of white beans from this region in France are the *tarbais* (a large flat bean with a kidney shape) and the *lingot* (smaller and rounder). Which of these beans to use is a debate of great importance to the French, but since neither bean is available stateside, we needed to find a close facsimile. Our criteria were that the beans would retain their shape and add a soft texture to the dish. Canned beans fell apart quickly, so we opted for dried beans. We tested four varieties, and the winner was the pale green flageolet bean. These small, French kidney-shaped beans have a creamy, tender texture and delicate flavor that perfectly enhanced the cassoulet. (Flageolets can be hard to find outside of specialty markets and gourmet shops, in which case cannellini and navy beans can be substituted.) An overnight soak in water left these swollen beans ready to cook. For the beans to be their most flavorful, we decided to add them early on after the pork had browned, so the beans could soften and cook through as the pork stewed.

The traditional sausage used in cassoulet is garlic pork sausage, one that we had much difficulty finding in our markets. After ruling out the use of this hard-to-find sausage (and not willing to take the time to make our own) we found garlic chicken sausage or sweet Italian sausage (without fennel seed if possible) to be the best substitutes for the rich, salty garlic pork sausages. We browned these while the beans were cooking (although you can brown them in the same pot as the beans as a first step—just remove the browned sausages before adding the beans) in order to render as much as the fat as possible and obtain a rich golden color. Once the sausages were browned, we set them aside to await the assembly of the cassoulet.

We started with the beans and braised pork, adding them to our baking dish in great spoonfuls. Into this mixture we nestled the browned sausages and then arranged the duck confit legs on top in order to allow the skin to crisp and brown during the baking process. We decided to hold off adding the croutons to prevent them from burning, so after the cassoulet had cooked for 50 minutes, we sprinkled the croutons on top and 10 minutes later our cassoulet emerged from the oven browned, bubbling, and perfect. This isn't a quick dish, but with a little time management, the process moves swiftly. At last we had it: a homemade cassoulet that was worthy of its reputation.

Cassoulet
SERVES 6

You can either buy duck confit at some high-end butcher shops, specialty shops, or online (try www.dartagnan.com or www.hudsonvalleyfoiegras.com) or make it yourself (see the recipe on page 189). Note that duck confit is covered in a thick coating of fat, which must be scraped off prior to heating in this recipe. Many supermarkets limit their sausage varieties to Italian hot or sweet (both of which contain fennel and other Italian seasonings). We urge you to seek out simpler garlic pork sausage (sometimes called Irish sausage). That said, you can substitute other types of sausage, but note that the flavor and texture of the finished dish will not be as authentic. For a more attractive presentation and easier serving, divide the cooked beans and pork into 6 individual ovenproof 2-cup capacity serving bowls after step 1; add the sausage and duck as directed in step 2 and bake on a rimmed baking sheet. Season this dish sparingly with salt, as many of its components are already well seasoned.

PORK AND BEANS

2	pounds dried flageolet beans (or cannellini or navy beans) rinsed, picked over, and soaked overnight or quick-soaked (see page 12 for soaking instructions)
1	tablespoon vegetable oil
1	pound boneless pork shoulder (Boston butt), trimmed and cut into 1-inch chunks
1	medium onion, minced
9	medium garlic cloves, minced or pressed through a garlic press (about 3 tablespoons)
2	tablespoons minced fresh thyme leaves, or 2 teaspoons dried
	Salt
1	cup dry white wine
1	tablespoon tomato paste
10	cups low-sodium chicken broth, plus extra as needed
1	(28-ounce) can diced tomatoes, drained

CASSOULET

5	slices high-quality white sandwich bread, cut into ½-inch cubes

3 tablespoons unsalted butter, melted
   Salt and ground black pepper
6 (4- to 6-inch long) garlic pork sausage links
   (about 1 pound, see note)
6 confit duck legs, scraped clean of confit fat
   (see note)

1. FOR THE PORK AND BEANS: Drain the beans, discarding the soaking liquid; set aside. Heat the oil in a large Dutch oven set over medium-high heat until just smoking. Add the pork and cook, stirring occasionally, until well browned, about 10 minutes, reducing the heat if the pan begins to scorch. Stir in the onion, garlic, thyme, and ½ teaspoon salt and cook until the onion begins to soften, about 3 minutes. Stir in the wine and tomato paste, scraping up any browned bits. Stir in the drained beans, chicken broth, and tomatoes, and bring to a boil. Reduce to a gentle simmer and cook uncovered, stirring occasionally, until the beans and pork are just tender, about 1 hour.

2. FOR THE CASSOULET: Meanwhile, adjust an oven rack to the middle position and heat the oven to 400 degrees. Toss the bread cubes with the butter, ¼ teaspoon salt, and ⅛ teaspoon pepper, and spread out over a rimmed baking sheet. Bake until light golden and crisp, about 15 minutes; set aside (leave the oven on). Brown the sausages in a 12-inch nonstick skillet over medium heat until golden on all sides, 5 to 8 minutes; transfer to a paper towel–lined plate and set aside.

3. When the beans are just tender, the level of the broth and beans should be equal; if necessary add more broth. Nestle the sausages into the bean mixture, and lay the duck legs, skin side up, on top of the beans (the duck skin should be exposed; do not nestle into the beans). Bake, uncovered, until the duck skin is golden and crisp, and the casserole is bubbling around the edges, about 50 minutes. Sprinkle the croutons over the top and continue to bake until they form a crust, about 10 minutes longer. Let the cassoulet rest and absorb some of the liquid, 15 to 20 minutes, before serving in shallow wide bowls.

DUCK CONFIT

ORIGINALLY, DUCK OR GOOSE CONFIT CAME about before the days of refrigeration as a means to preserve the meat in order to last the family through the long winter months—confit translates as "to conserve." It started with a salt cure (salt staves off bacteria, ensuring a longer shelf life) for up to 48 hours and then the duck was very slowly simmered in its own fat until meltingly tender. From there it was packed in a special earthenware urn, the fat was poured over the meat until covered (as bacteria cannot grow in fat), and the urn was buried deep into the ground to stay cool until the confit legs were plucked from the urn for a meal. Why legs? Dark meat takes well to slow cooking, where white meat does not.

Food preservation has come a long way since then. These days, the duck legs are salted for flavor, not for curing. We had done some testing along these lines in the past and found that salting meat does not dry it out; instead, it actually helps the meat retain moisture. It's simply a matter of timing. Meat naturally contains some salt and lots of water that coexist in a happy balance, but sprinkling salt on its surface throws off the balance. The water in the meat immediately starts moving toward the saltier surface to restore equilibrium. Once that happens, the exterior salt has pulled so much water to the surface that it alters the balance of the salt concentration. To restore equilibrium again, the water simply changes direction, flowing back into the meat, this time bringing the dissolved salt with it. Essentially, it's a brine without the water. It takes as much as eight hours for this entire process to happen. (Once equilibrium is restored, the balance remains indefinitely; however, the salt continues to tenderize the meat so if you let it rest too long you end up with mushy meat.) With this knowledge and a couple of tests, we found an overnight cure with salt was the perfect amount of time to properly season the duck legs before they are cooked. Some thyme leaves and dried bay leaves added to the cure gave a hint of aromatics to the flavor of the duck.

As for the cooking method, there's only one kind of fat we recommend cooking the duck in— its own. Most duck confit recipes we researched cooked the duck slowly in a moderately low oven, and we agree with this advice. The oven makes it easy to maintain a consistent moderate temperature with zero hot spots (as opposed to cooking it on the stovetop). After testing a variety of oven temperatures, we found that cooking the legs for two hours at 300 degrees yielded the texture we were looking for. The only tricky part of this method is getting the baking dish of duck legs and hot fat to and from the oven without spilling it. Our recommendation—use a baking dish that fits the duck legs snugly in one layer, but has tall sides, and place it on a rimmed baking sheet.

Duck Confit

MAKES 6 CONFIT DUCK LEGS

Duck fat can be found at high-end butcher shops, specialty shops, or online (try www.dartagnan.com or www.hudson-valleyfoiegras.com). The duck fat is crucial here for texture and flavor; however, if you are a little short, you can substitute vegetable oil. The duck fat can be reused again and again for up to a year if stored properly; to store, simply remelt the fat, strain it through a fine-mesh strainer, and refrigerate in an airtight container (discard the fat when it develops an off-smell).

6	duck legs, trimmed of excess fat
1	tablespoon kosher salt
¼	teaspoon ground black pepper
10	sprigs fresh thyme
4	bay leaves, crumbled
6–8	cups duck fat, melted (see note)

1. Sprinkle the duck legs evenly with the salt and pepper. Toss the legs with the thyme and bay leaves in a large bowl, cover tightly with plastic wrap, and refrigerate for 8 to 24 hours.

2. Adjust an oven rack to the middle position and heat the oven to 300 degrees. Lay the legs, skin side up, in a single layer in a large baking dish, and sprinkle the thyme and bay leaves over top. Place the dish on a rimmed baking sheet. Melt the duck

fat in a medium saucepan over medium heat until liquefied, 5 to 10 minutes. Pour the melted duck fat over the legs until they are just covered. Bake, without moving the duck, until the skin has rendered most of its fat, the meat is completely tender, and the leg bones twist easily away from the meat, about 2 hours (the oil will be bubbling gently).

3. Being very careful of the hot fat, transfer the dish to a wire rack and let cool completely, about 2 hours. (At this point, the duck legs, if encased completely in fat, can be wrapped with plastic wrap and refrigerated for up to 1 month; if necessary transfer the cooled legs to a smaller container and pour the cooled fat over the top to cover completely. For Cassoulet, remove the legs from the fat, scrape off as much of the fat as possible, and use as directed on page 187.)

4. To serve the legs on their own, remove them from the fat and scrape off as much of the fat as possible. Lay the duck legs, skin side down, in a 12-inch nonstick skillet and cook gently over medium-low heat until the skin is crisp, 8 to 10 minutes. Gently flip the legs over and continue to cook until the legs are heated through, 4 to 6 minutes. Serve immediately.

PORK TENDERLOIN MEDALLIONS WITH CIDER SAUCE

Médaillons Filet Mignon de Porc au Cidre

FRENCH PORK PRODUCTS ARE RARELY imported into the United States and because of France's different method of butchering, cuts of meat often don't have exact American equivalents or recognizable translations. But there is one cut we can always identify, whether in French or English, and that is the tenderloin of pork—the leanest, most tender cut of the animal. With only two tenderloins from each pig, each weighing an average of 1 to 1¼ pounds (pretty small when you consider the average pig weighs a few hundred pounds), it's no wonder this cut of meat is special.

With its wide availability in American super-markets, no bones, and minimal fat, pork tender-loin has plenty going for it. When cooked properly, it has a tenderness rivaling that of beef tender-loin, the deluxe roast that gives us filet mignon. Medallions are simply small, round, tender cuts of meat, like beef, pork, or veal, most appropriately cut from the tenderloin.

On the downside, this ultra-lean cut has an ultra-mild flavor that needs a major boost. Long mari-nades and hybrid searing-roasting techniques (the latter providing flavorful browning) help remedy such deficiencies, but they also take the home cook a long way from the realm of the no-fuss meal.

With a cut of meat so tender and small, we knew it would cook fast. We set out to develop a recipe for a fast weeknight dinner, making use of only a small arsenal of tools at our disposal to enhance flavor and ensure juiciness. Skillets and quick pan sauces were in; brining, marinating, and heating a grill or oven were out.

The first problem was the tenderloin's oblong, tapered shape. Vacuum-sealed individually or in sets of two, the tenderloins looked like neatly packed, identically sized sausages. Once unpacked, however, it became clear that they vary greatly in length (from 9 inches to 14 inches) and shape. And

when packed in pairs, the two loins were almost guaranteed to be substantially different in weight, making it tricky to portion them out into equal servings. Tucking the tail end under the thicker section, then tying it into an evenly shaped roast, fixed that problem. But cooking the tenderloins whole (either pan-roasting or sautéing) took too much time—more than 30 minutes.

Slicing the tenderloins into thin medallions made for uniform thickness, but some pieces were nearly 3 inches wide while others were barely an inch. Attempts to cheat nature with creative bias slicing proved unreliable and tedious. What about cutting the smaller parts thicker and pounding them to equal width? More consistent, yes, but thanks to the expanded surface area, they required sautéing in several batches.

Overcooking was an even bigger problem with these sliced medallions. We wanted to get as much browning on the exterior as possible to provide textural contrast with the tender interior, and to improve flavor. But with such thin slices, we had only two choices: overcooked medallions with a pronounced, flavorful sear or wan, gray disks. Neither was an acceptable compromise.

To get adequate browning without overcook-ing the interior, we next tried increasing the

CHECKING MEAT DONENESS WITH AN INSTANT-READ THERMOMETER

An instant-read thermometer is your best bet for checking the doneness of meat and poultry. See our testing of instant-read thermometers on page 179. The chart below presents ideal serving temperatures. Since the temperature of meat will continue to rise as its rests, it should be taken off the heat just before it reaches the desired temperature. (This phenomenon doesn't occur with poultry and fish.) These tempera-tures (in degrees Fahrenheit) reflect our opinions regarding optimal flavor and juiciness. The U.S. Department of Agriculture recommends cooking beef, lamb, veal steaks and roasts, and fish to 145 degrees, pork and all ground meat to 160 degrees, and poultry to 180 degrees to eliminate potential food-borne pathogens.

	RARE	MEDIUM-RARE	MEDIUM	WELL-DONE
FISH	110°F	120°F	140°F	*
RED MEAT (BEEF, LAMB, VEAL)	125°F	130°F	140°F	160°F**
PORK	*	*	145°F	160°F**
POULTRY (WHITE MEAT)	*	*	*	160°F to 165°F
POULTRY (DARK MEAT)	*	*	*	175°F
DUCK	125°F	130°F	140°F	160°F

*Not recommended
**Recommended only for ground meat dishes, such as meat loaf

thickness of the medallions by increments—first half an inch, then ¾ inch, 1 inch, and so on—until they began to resemble miniature versions of beef tenderloin filets. At 2 inches thick, our "pork mignons" developed a dark brown sear before the interiors had cooked through. At 1½ inches, the interior was cooked through but still juicy and the top and bottom surfaces were beautifully browned. These rounds also offered the advantage of fitting into a 12-inch skillet in one batch. Treating pork tenderloin like beef tenderloin was really doing the trick! Several tasters objected to leaving the sides unbrowned, so we stood the medallions on their sides (using tongs) during the searing process.

Cutting the pork into 1½-inch pieces left odd bits from both ends of the tenderloin, and even the slices from the central section were problematic, making for oblong pieces that would flop over and "flatten" awkwardly during cooking rather than maintaining their tidy cylindrical shape. To limit the number of odd pieces, we scored the section near the tail, creating a small flap of meat that folded underneath the larger half to yield the right-sized medallion (see the illustrations on page 192). To prevent the pork from flopping over, we took another cue from beef tenderloin and tied the meat with twine, which gave it much better structure. (Blanched bacon, wrapped around the thick medallions and fastened with toothpicks, was another effective method that also gave the dish a smoky flavor, see the illustrations on page 193.)

At this point, our pork tenderloin medallions were juicy and nicely browned—and they could all be cooked in just one batch. But we wanted to boost the flavor even more. Unwilling to revisit the notion of a marinade, we decided to take advantage of the deep fond (the browned bits) left in the skillet by coming up with a few easy pan sauces to make while the medallions were given a five-minute rest, which allowed the juices to redistribute evenly.

Following the test kitchen's usual method for pan sauces, we cooked aromatics in the hot skillet until fragrant, deglazed the skillet with broth, then reduced the broth along with other flavorful ingredients. Given how mild pork tenderloin can be, we gravitated toward bold flavors. Raiding the pantry for staple items, we created a complex sauce inspired by the famous apple cider of Normandy. With a mix of diced apples, apple cider, apple brandy, cinnamon, shallots, and thyme, we were almost there, but the sauce wasn't thickening as much as we wanted during the pork's five-minute resting period. The solution was to cook most of the ingredients in a saucepan beforehand, then pour the reduced liquid into the skillet to finish. This time the sauce turned silky and clung perfectly to the tender pieces of pork.

Pork Tenderloin Medallions with Cider Sauce

Médaillons de Filet Mignon de Porc au Cidre

SERVE 4 TO 6

We prefer natural pork to enhanced pork (pork that has been injected with a salt solution to increase moistness and flavor), though both will work in this recipe. Begin checking the doneness of smaller medallions 1 or 2 minutes early; they may need to be taken out of the pan a little sooner than the time specified. For more information on testing meat for doneness, see the opposite page.

SAUCE
1½	cups apple cider
1	cup low-sodium chicken broth
2	teaspoons cider vinegar
1	cinnamon stick
4	tablespoons (½ stick) unsalted butter, cut into 4 pieces
2	large shallots, minced (about ½ cup)
1	tart apple, such as Granny Smith, cored, peeled, and diced small
¼	cup Calvados or apple-flavored brandy
1	teaspoon minced fresh thyme leaves
	Salt and ground black pepper

PORK
2	pork tenderloins (1 to 1¼ pounds each), trimmed of fat and silver skin
	Salt and ground black pepper
2	tablespoons vegetable oil

1. **FOR THE SAUCE:** Simmer the cider, broth, vinegar, and cinnamon stick together in a medium saucepan over medium-high heat until the liquid measures 1 cup, 10 to 12 minutes. Discard the cinnamon stick and reserve the cider mixture until ready to finish the sauce.

2. **FOR THE PORK:** Meanwhile, cut the tenderloins crosswise into 1½-inch-thick medallions. Following the illustrations below, tie each medallion around the perimeter with kitchen twine and tie the thinner end pieces together. Pat the medallions dry with paper towels and season with salt and pepper.

3. Heat the oil in 12-inch skillet over medium-high heat until shimmering. Brown the medallions on both cut sides, 3 to 5 minutes per side. Reduce the heat to medium. Using tongs, stand each medallion on its side and cook, turning pieces as necessary, until sides are well browned and internal temperature registers 145 to 150 degrees on an instant-read thermometer, 8 to 12 minutes. Transfer the medallions to a platter, tent with aluminum foil, and let rest while finishing the sauce

4. To finish the sauce, pour off any fat left in the skillet, add 1 tablespoon of the butter and melt over medium heat. Add the shallots and apple and cook until softened and beginning to brown, 1 to 2 minutes. Off the heat, add the Calvados. Return the skillet to medium heat and cook, scraping up any browned bits, for about 1 minute. Add the reserved cider mixture, any accumulated pork juices, and thyme, increase the heat to medium-high, and simmer until thickened and measures to 1¼ cups, 3 to 4 minutes. Off the heat, whisk in the remaining 3 tablespoons butter, and season with salt and pepper to taste; transfer the sauce to a bowl or gravy boat. Serve the pork, passing the sauce separately or pouring it over the top.

> VARIATION

Bacon-Wrapped Pork Tenderloin Medallions

Using bacon in place of twine adds a meaty, smoky dimension to the medallions.

Place 12 to 14 slices bacon (1 slice for each pork medallion), slightly overlapping, in a microwave-safe pie plate and cover with plastic wrap. Cook in the microwave on high power until the slices shrink and release about ½ cup fat but are neither browned nor crisp, 1 to 3 minutes. Transfer the bacon to paper towels until cool, 2 to 3 minutes. Follow the recipe for Pork Tenderloin Medallions with Cider Sauce, wrapping 1 piece of bacon around the perimeter of each medallion in place of the kitchen twine in step 2; secure the ends of each bacon strip where they overlap using 2 toothpicks at an angle, following the illustration on page 193. Season the pork with pepper (do not salt) and cook as directed in step 3 (the time required for searing the sides with the bacon may be slightly longer).

TURNING THE END PIECE INTO A MEDALLION

After cutting the tenderloins into symmetrical 1½-inch medallions, you will inevitably have a few irregularly shaped pieces left over. The tapered end pieces can be scored, folded, and tied into medallions (as shown here). Tie any remaining smaller pieces together into a medallion shape, making sure top and bottom surfaces are flat.

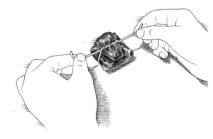

1. Score the tenderloin's tapered end piece.

2. Fold in half at the incision.

3. Tie the medallion with twine, making sure the top and bottom surfaces are flat.

TRICKS FOR TYING PORK MEDALLIONS

Thick medallions allow for more browning, but they can flop over in the pan. To prevent this, tie each piece with twine or a strip of parcooked bacon secured with two toothpicks.

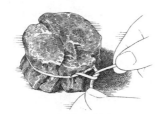

BUTCHER'S TWINE

BACON "TWINE"

PROVENÇAL BEEF STEW

Daube Provençal

DAUBE PROVENÇAL, ALSO KNOW AS DAUBE Niçoise, is a stewed beef dish from the city of Nice (considered the capital of Provence) that makes use of many of its local ingredients. It is traditionally cooked in an earthenware pot called a daubière (hence the name) and nestled into the fireplace surrounded by the burning embers to cook long and slow, transforming chunks of beef, red wine, and aromatics (such as garlic, olives, anchovies, oranges, dried mushrooms, and tomatoes) into a rich, deep, and flavorful stew.

But few of these ingredients made it into the large stack of "authentic" recipes we uncovered in our research. When tested, many of these recipes were one-note wonders—beef stew with olives or beef stew with oranges. One exception to this early testing was a recipe from Julia Child, which included most of the flavors we wanted. Although not without problems, her version inspired us to follow suit and led to our main challenge with

this recipe: we would have to find a way to turn these strong, independent flavors of Provence into a robust but cohesive stew.

Over the years, the test kitchen has developed countless beef stews as well as a reliable set of techniques to turn tough beef into tender stew: Brown the beef (to ensure the richest, meatiest flavor); add the aromatic vegetables; sprinkle some flour in the pan (to thicken the braising liquid); deglaze with the predominant cooking liquid; add the meat back to the pot; and, finally, cover and cook in a low to medium oven until tender. Our choice of meat for stew is cut from the chuck, or shoulder, which is notoriously tough (the meat softens nicely during long, slow cooking) but also flavorful. While various chuck cuts are appropriate for this recipe, we found that the chuck-eye roast offered the best flavor and texture.

Most beef stews have a personality-defining ingredient, like the wine in beef Burgundy or the beer in carbonnade. In contrast, daube Provençal relies on a complex blend of ingredients, which we methodically began to test. Tasters loved the earthiness of dried cèpes (the mushroom known more commonly by its Italian name, porcini). Niçoise olives lent a briny and authentic local flavor, and tomatoes brought brightness and texture. Orange peel contributed a subtle floral element, while herbs, particularly thyme and bay leaves, are a natural addition in anything from Provence.

Tasters weren't enthusiastic about every authentic ingredient we tried. When we broached the subject of anchovies, some tasters claimed that these pungent fish have no place in beef stew. When we made our stew without the anchovies, tasters claimed the stew lacked depth of flavor. Over the next couple of days, we quietly added the anchovies back in one at a time and stopped at three fillets, at which point tasters praised the rich, earthy flavors of the dish and noticed a complexity that had been missing without them. (They never knew the secret.)

Pig's trotters, a standard ingredient in many older recipes, contribute body to the sauce in the form of gelatin and flavor from the pork meat and fat. But the protests against a foot in the stew were too much, and this time we caved in. As a compromise, we substituted salt pork, a salt-cured cut from the pig's belly, and adjusted the amount of salt in the stew to accommodate it. Several tasters still protested the extra fat on principle, but a side-by-side comparison made it clear that salt pork, like anchovies, added a richness of flavor that was unmistakably absent when it was not included. In any case, the salt pork was added in a single piece that we removed and discarded just before serving, once the pork had given up its flavor to the stew.

We had been following the French technique of adding a small amount of flour in the form of a roux, a butter and flour thickener, but up to this point we weren't satisfied with the consistency of the sauce. The butter sometimes ended up floating to the top of the stew, making it look greasy, and the sauce was still too thin. We returned to our established technique and omitted the step of making a roux. Instead, we sprinkled flour into the pot to cook with the vegetables and tomato paste. We also increased the amount of flour to ⅓ cup, which is a little more than most recipes contain. The result was immediately noticeable. The extra flour created a braising liquid that thickened to the consistency of a luxurious sauce.

What started as a key ingredient in daube Provençal, the red wine, had now been relegated to a mere afterthought, barely discernible amid the other ingredients. Our recipe contained a half bottle. Could we add more? Conservatively, we began adding more wine, careful not to sacrifice the integrity of the other flavors. In the end, we discovered that this stew was bold enough to accommodate an entire bottle—at least in theory. The wine tasted a bit raw. So we put the stew back into the oven for additional 15-minute increments until the total cooking time approached three hours. The resulting sauce was gorgeous, with rich round flavors and a velvety texture.

What was good for the sauce wasn't so good for the meat. We had been cutting the chuck roast into 1-inch cubes, a standard size for beef stew. But with the longer cooking time, the meat was drying out and losing its distinct character. By cutting the chuck roast into 2-inch pieces, we were able to keep the longer braising time and create a truly complex sauce. The beef was now tender and flavorful, and the larger pieces added to the rustic quality of this dish—an ideal rendition of a Provençal classic.

SHOPPING NOTES: Provençal Beef Stew

A variety of bold, rich ingredients work in harmony to give this Provençal stew its distinctive bright flavors.

Salt Pork is cured (but not smoked) and gives the stew richness and flavor. Buy a piece that's at least 75 percent meat, with a minimum of fat.

Olives, such as tiny, briny niçoise olives lend briny zest. Cook some of the olives with the stew, then add more just before serving to maximize their impact.

Anchovies add earthiness to this dish—don't leave them out! Meaty Ortiz anchovies (in olive oil) won a test kitchen tasting.

Tomatoes add sweetness and acidity to this stew. Progresso whole peeled tomatoes were the winner of a test kitchen tasting.

Red Wine such as a bold Cabernet gives the stew depth. Simmer for at least 2½ hours to cook off the raw flavors.

Provençal Beef Stew

Daube Provençal

SERVES 6

We tie the salt pork with twine in order to make it easy to identify after cooking; otherwise, it looks exactly like a piece of stew meat. Cabernet Sauvignon is our favorite wine for this recipe, but Côtes du Rhône and Zinfandel also work. If niçoise olives are not available, kalamata olives, though not authentic, can be substituted. Because the tomatoes are added just before serving, it is preferable to use canned whole tomatoes and dice them yourself—they are more tender than canned diced tomatoes. Serve this French beef stew with egg noodles or boiled potatoes.

3½	pounds boneless beef chuck-eye roast, trimmed and cut into 2-inch chunks
	Salt and ground black pepper
3	tablespoons olive oil
2	medium onions, halved and sliced ⅛ inch thick (about 4 cups)
¾	ounce dried porcini mushrooms, rehydrated, liquid strained, and mushrooms minced (see page 283 for more information)
⅓	cup unbleached all-purpose flour
2	tablespoons tomato paste
I	(750-ml) bottle bold red wine (about 3 cups; see note)
1½	cup low-sodium chicken broth
I	cup water
I	pound carrots (about 6 medium), peeled and sliced I inch thick
5	ounces salt pork, rind removed, tied tightly with butcher's twine for identification purposes
4	(3-inch long) strips orange zest from one orange, cut into thin matchsticks
I	cup pitted niçoise olives, patted dry and chopped coarse
4	medium garlic cloves, peeled and sliced thin
3	anchovy fillets, rinsed and minced (about I teaspoon)
5	sprigs thyme, tied together with kitchen twine
2	bay leaves
I	(14.5-ounce) can whole tomatoes, drained and cut into ½-inch pieces
2	tablespoons minced fresh parsley leaves

1. Adjust an oven rack to lower-middle position and heat the oven to 325 degrees. Pat the beef dry with paper towels, and season with salt and pepper. Heat 1 tablespoon of the oil in a large Dutch oven over medium-high heat until just smoking. Add half of the meat and cook, stirring occasionally, until well browned, 7 to 10 minutes, reducing the heat if the pot begins to scorch. Transfer the browned beef to a medium bowl. Repeat with 1 more tablespoon oil and the remaining beef; transfer the meat to the bowl.

2. Add one more tablespoon of the oil to the pot and return to medium heat until shimmering. Add the onions, porcini, and 1 teaspoon salt, and cook until softened, 5 to 7 minutes. Stir in the flour and tomato paste and cook, stirring constantly, for 1 minute. Slowly whisk in the wine, scraping up any browned bits. Whisk in the broth and water until smooth.

3. Stir in the browned meat with any accumulated juices, carrots, salt pork, orange zest, ½ of the olives, garlic, anchovies, thyme bundle, and bay leaves. Bring to a simmer, and arrange the meat so it is completely covered by the liquid. Cover the pot partially (the lid should be just off center to leave about 1 inch open), transfer to the oven, and cook until a fork inserted in the beef meets little resistance and the sauce is thickened and glossy, 2½ to 3 hours.

4. Remove and discard the salt pork (easily identified by the string), thyme bundle, and bay leaves. Stir in the tomatoes and the remaining ½ cup olives, cover, and set aside to heat through, about 5 minutes. Using a spoon, skim the excess fat from the surface of the stew. Stir in the parsley before serving.

PAN-SEARED STEAK

Steak Poêle

WE'VE ORDERED OUR FAIR SHARE OF STEAKS in restaurants across the U.S., and cooked scores of them at home, but the idea of a juicy, flavorful steak is oftentimes better than the reality. Flavorless or shoe-leather tough meat are just two of the pitfalls we find. Also, we know how restaurants get a perfect sear—one steak in the pan at a time—but how do we translate this to an easy weeknight meal, with four steaks in one pan? Since we don't regularly dine in Parisian bistros, or cook one steak at a time, we set out to recreate bistro steak for four in our own kitchen.

In the test kitchen, we have established a fool-proof method for pan-searing steaks, and we didn't find it necessary to stray from this technique (get the pan and the oil very hot until just smoking, then lay the steaks in the pan to cook undisturbed until well browned before flipping). We did, however, have questions about the steak choice. In France, bistro steaks are often prepared with a cut called entrecôte (literally, "between the ribs") or from less expensive cuts like a culotte (skirt steak) or onglet (hanger steak). You won't find an entrecôte in American supermarkets, but it's similar to our rib-eye steak—both are cut from the same area as a prime rib. The one big difference is that entrecôte steaks are quite thin, usually just ½ to ¾ inch thick (skirt or hangar steaks are also quite thin). With a home stove and four steaks in a single pan, we found that thicker rib-eyes gave us more time to get a nice sear on the meat without over-cooking the middle.

Oftentimes, rib-eyes are sold in 1-pound steaks, which posed two problems. First, this is far too much meat for one serving and second, it's impossible to fit four large steaks in a sauté pan. We fixed the problem by cutting two of the steaks in half (either vertically or horizontally), to make four 8-ounce portions—a perfect size for one (see the photos). If we cut them down the center to make four small, thick steaks, we had no problem searing all the meat together. If cut horizontally in half, it was a tighter squeeze and, depending on the size of

the sauté pan, we were in some cases forced to cook the steaks in two batches to avoid crowding the pan. Either way, these steaks were ample and thick enough to get a beautiful sear on both sides before the center of the meat was cooked.

We had finally created a recipe that could almost rival the Parisian bistro meals we remembered. The only hitch: The steaks were a little bland. Maybe French beef is better? Then we recalled that most bistros spoon a flavored butter or a simple pan sauce over the steak. Flavored butters are a cinch to prepare—simply mix minced shallot, garlic, and herbs into softened butter. And with all the fond leftover in the pan after cooking the steak, pan sauces aren't much more difficult. Gathering some French ingredients from our pantry, we started our sauce by adding minced shallots to the now-empty sauté pan. To that we added chicken broth, cognac and rehydrated cèpes (or porcinis as they are more commonly known). Once the sauce was reduced we stirred in cold butter until the sauce was enriched and thickened. A little garlic and parsley added the right aromatic flavors.

A classic bistro sauce is the bordelaise, a long-

ONE STEAK BECOMES TWO

In order to fit four steaks into a skillet at the same time, it is necessary to buy two 1-pound steaks and cut them in half according to their thickness. If your steaks are 1¼ to 1¾ inches thick, cut them in half vertically into small, thick steaks. If your steaks are thicker than 1¾ inches thick, cut them in half horizontally into two thinner steaks.

THIN STEAK
Cut in half vertically

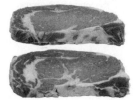

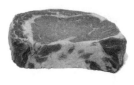

THICK STEAK
Cut in half horizontally

simmered red wine sauce that starts with a red wine reduction and veal stock. We love the flavor of this sauce with steak, but knew we needed to update and streamline this time-consuming sauce. Treating it like our other pan sauce, we started with minced shallots in the sauté pan. As the shallots cooked and let off some liquid, we deglazed the fond left behind in the pan. To this we added a generous amount of red wine and some chicken broth (veal stock is just too much work for a simple pan sauce) and continued to simmer it until it reached the right consistency.

Our final sauce was a mustard cream sauce using Dijon mustard (see our tasting of Dijon mustard on page 155). Again we started with minced shallots in the pan then added white wine (since Dijon is made with white wine, this was a natural addition to this sauce). We decided to use whole grain mustard as tasters preferred the appearance of the sauce and the textural contrast of the whole grains, but plain Dijon will also work. To this we added cream to temper Dijon's bite and some fresh tarragon, a natural pairing.

Pan-Seared Steak

Steak Poêle

SERVES 4

A 12-inch skillet is essential for cooking four steaks at once. The times and temperatures given in the recipe are for medium-rare; if you like your steaks more or less done, you will need to alter the cooking times accordingly. See page 190 for more information on testing meat for doneness.

BUTTER

4	tablespoons (½ stick) unsalted butter, softened
½	medium shallot, minced (about 1½ tablespoons)
1	garlic clove, minced or pressed through a garlic press (about 1 teaspoon)
1	tablespoon minced fresh parsley leaves
1	tablespoon minced fresh chives
¼	teaspoon salt
¼	teaspoon ground black pepper

STEAK

2	boneless strip or rib-eye steaks (1 pound each), cut in half (see the photos on page 196) Salt and ground black pepper
1	tablespoon vegetable oil

1. FOR THE BUTTER: Stir all of the ingredients together and set aside.

2. FOR THE STEAK: Pat the steaks dry with paper towels and season with salt and pepper. Heat the oil in a 12-inch skillet over medium-high heat until just smoking. Lay the steaks in the pan, leaving as much space as possible between them, and cook, without moving, until well browned, about 4 minutes.

3. Flip the steaks and continue to cook until an instant-read thermometer inserted in the center registers 130 degrees for medium-rare, 3 to 7 minutes. Transfer the steaks to a large plate, tent with aluminum foil, and let to rest for 15 minutes. Spoon a portion of the butter over each steak and serve immediately.

PAN SAUCES

PAN SAUCES CAN BE A MODERN INTERPRETATION of the long simmered sauces found in restaurants and in French cookbooks. The beauty of pan sauces is that they can come together in a matter of minutes, often in the amount of time it takes for the cooked meat to rest. The other benefit of a pan sauce is making use of the fond, or browned bits that have accumulated in the bottom of the sauté pan. With canned broth and fond, anyone can have a good pan sauce to accompany their dinner.

Here are some of our favorite pan sauces for steaks. Simply follow the recipe for Bistro Steak, replacing the herb butter with one of the sauces below while the steaks rest in step 3. The sauces are made in the same skillet that the steaks are cooked in. Be sure not to wash the skillet after cooking the steaks—those remaining browned bits add important flavor to all of these sauces.

CORE TECHNIQUE

KEYS TO PERFECT PAN SAUCES

1. Deglaze the fond

Making the sauce in the same skillet that was used to cook the meat is crucial for the sauce's flavor; those leftover browned bits stuck on the skillet bottom (aka fond) add a deep and meaty flavor. When the liquid—usually a combination of broth and wine or something stronger, like cognac—is added to the skillet, it will sizzle and steam vigorously. If using lots of alcohol, we suggest adding it to the skillet off the heat to prevent it from flaming.

2. Reduce

Reducing the broth and wine is important in order to bring the flavors of the sauce together, soften the alcohol flavor, and thicken the liquid into a sauce. Knowing when to stop reducing the sauce is the hard part; if you over reduce the sauce, just add a little water or broth. Measuring the reduced liquid is the most accurate way to check how far the sauce has been reduced; most recipes specify an exact reduction amount, but some will give a more general visual cue, such as reduced by one half.

3. Return the meat juices to the skillet

As the meat rests, it will likely release juices, which should be added back to the sauce for flavor. If there is a lot of juice and it thins out the sauce, let the sauce simmer an additional minute or two to restore its proper consistency. Some sauces also contain cream or butter, which is stirred in at this point to enrich and thicken the sauce.

Red Wine Sauce
Sauce Bordelaise
MAKES ABOUT ¾ CUP, ENOUGH FOR 4 STEAKS
Use any $10 bottle of fruity, medium-bodied red wine such a Pinot Noir, Côtes du Rhône, or Zinfandel.

	Vegetable oil, as needed
1	medium shallot, minced (about 3 tablespoons)
¾	cup low-sodium chicken broth
½	cup dry red wine
2	teaspoons brown sugar
3	tablespoons unsalted butter, cut into 3 pieces and chilled
1	teaspoon minced fresh thyme leaves
	Salt and ground black pepper

1. After transferring the steaks to a large plate, pour off all but 1 tablespoon of the fat left the skillet (or add oil if needed). Add the shallot to the fat left in the skillet and cook over medium heat until softened, about 2 minutes. Stir in the broth, wine, and sugar, scraping up any browned bits. Simmer until the sauce has thickened and measures about ½ cup, 3 to 5 minutes.

2. Stir in any accumulated steak juices. Turn the heat to low and whisk in the butter, 1 piece at a time. Off the heat, stir in the thyme and season with salt and pepper to taste; transfer the sauce to a bowl or gravy boat. Serve the steak, passing the sauce separately or pouring it over the top.

Mushroom-Cognac Sauce
Sauce aux Champignons à la Crème et Cognac
MAKES ABOUT ¾ CUP, ENOUGH FOR 4 STEAKS
Because the sauce comes together very quickly, we suggest prepping the dried mushrooms before cooking the steaks (see page 283 for more information).

	Vegetable oil, as needed
1	medium shallot, minced (about 3 tablespoons)
2	medium garlic cloves, minced or pressed through a garlic press (about 2 teaspoons)
½	cup cognac
½	cup low-sodium chicken broth

½ ounce dried porcini or cèpe mushrooms, rehydrated, liquid strained and reserved, and mushrooms minced (see note)

3 tablespoons unsalted butter, cut into 3 pieces and chilled

1 tablespoon minced fresh parsley leaves
Salt and ground black pepper

1. After transferring the steaks to a large plate, pour off all but 1 tablespoon of the fat from the skillet (or add oil if needed). Add the shallot to the fat left in the skillet and cook over medium heat until softened, about 2 minutes. Stir in the garlic and cook until fragrant, about 30 seconds. Stir in the cognac, broth, and porcini rehydrating liquid and mushrooms, scraping up any browned bits. Simmer until the sauce has thickened and measures about ½ cup, 3 to 5 minutes.

2. Stir in any accumulated meat juices. Turn the heat to low and whisk in the butter, 1 piece at a time. Off the heat, stir in the parsley and season with salt and pepper to taste; transfer the sauce to a bowl or gravy boat. Serve the steak, passing the sauce separately or pouring it over the top.

Mustard-Cream Sauce

Sauce Dijon

MAKES ¾ CUP SAUCE, ENOUGH FOR 4 STEAKS
We prefer the texture and flavor of whole grain mustard here, however regular Dijon mustard can be substituted.

Vegetable oil, as needed

1 medium shallot, minced (about 3 tablespoons)

2 tablespoons dry white wine

½ cup low-sodium chicken broth

6 tablespoons heavy cream

3 tablespoons whole grain Dijon mustard

1 tablespoon minced fresh tarragon leaves
Salt and ground black pepper

1. After transferring the steaks to a large plate, pour off all but 1 tablespoon of the fat from the skillet (or add oil if needed). Add the shallot to the fat left in the skillet and cook over medium heat until softened, about 2 minutes. Stir in the wine and broth, scraping up any browned bits. Simmer

until the sauce has thickened and measures about ¼ cup, 3 to 5 minutes.

2. Stir in the cream and any accumulated meat juices and return to a brief simmer. Off the heat, stir in the mustard and tarragon and season with salt and pepper to taste; transfer the sauce to a bowl or gravy boat. Serve the steak, passing the sauce separately or pouring it over the top.

WINE-POACHED PEARS

Poires Pochées au Vin

THERE IS A CLASSIC FRENCH DESSERT CALLED Poire Belle Helene, which made its first appearance in restaurants along the Grands Boulevards of Paris in 1865 and quickly became popular. It owes its name to Hélène, the principal character in the Offenbach operetta, "La Belle Hélène," which debuted in December of the preceding year. The dish is composed of pears poached in vanilla syrup, served with chocolate sauce and vanilla ice cream. We wanted to include a recipe for poached pears in this chapter, and though this dessert is still popular and delicious today, we wanted something a little more modern and less rich. Omitting the chocolate sauce and ice cream, we set out to develop a recipe for poached pears that were soft and tender, infused with aromatics, and served chilled with the poaching liquid as the sauce.

Poaching is a particularly apt way to cook fruit. Unlike other cooking methods, poaching allows the shape, texture, and inherent flavor of the fruit to remain intact, while improving its tenderness and enhancing rather than masking its flavor. We tested poaching pears in varying states of ripeness. Perfectly ripe fruit poached quickly and easily. But we found that poaching is also a perfect remedy for underripe or bland fruit, rendering it immediately edible. Rock-hard pears, however, never attained a tender texture no matter how long they simmered, and if the pears were too ripe, they were difficult to handle and easily cooked to mush. Moderately ripe pears, then, became our favorites to work with; the pears should give slightly when pressed with a finger.

We next focused our attention on which pear

to use—we immediately narrowed it down to the readily available pear varieties: Bosc, d'Anjou, Comice, and Bartlett. The favorites were the Bartlett, for its floral, honeyed notes, and the Bosc, because it tasted like a sweet, ripe pear should taste. The other two varieties were unremarkable in flavor and the least attractive in appearance, as they experienced some discoloration during poaching.

With pear varieties selected, we went about trying to bolster their flavor by testing different poaching mediums. Most of the recipes we came across in our research poached the pears in either a simple syrup of sugar and water or a sugar-sweetened white wine, but we were curious about other poaching liquids. We tried several different sugar-laced poaching mediums including water, juice, wine, and combinations of the three. The pears poached with water tasted flat and dull (perhaps that's why the pears of La Belle Hélène were served with chocolate sauce and ice cream), while the fruit juice added a generic-tasting "fruit" flavor with the pear. The wine-poached pears, however, were bright and spirited—the unanimous winner. Cutting the wine with another liquid was not necessary—it simply watered down the bright wine flavor. In order to have enough liquid to poach six pears, we found it necessary to use an entire 750-ml bottle (about 3 cups). Even with an entire bottle of wine it's a tight squeeze to cover six pears; turning the pears a few times as they poach is important.

Working with both red and white wine, we liked the flavor of each in its own right. Tasters noted milder, floral flavors in the pears poached in white wine, which lent itself to additional poaching aromatics such as herbs and lemon. The deep, robust flavor of red wine, on the other hand, paired well with black peppercorns and whole cloves. Regardless of the wine type, we liked the added flavor of cinnamon and vanilla in the poaching liquid as well as the resulting sauce.

Depending on the ripeness of the pears, poaching them can take anywhere from 10 to 20 minutes. Poaching the pears covered at a gentle simmer is important for even cooking. Once the pears are tender, recipes often recommend that they be allowed to cool in the poaching liquid. This, we found, was good advice. If the pears were plucked from the hot poaching liquid, the syrup did not have a chance to be absorbed into the flesh of the fruit and this resulted in a drier texture. If left to cool in the liquid, the pears absorbed some syrup, took on a candied translucency, and became plump, sweet, and spicy.

We next turned our attention to how to prepare the pears. Readying pears for poaching is rarely more than a matter of peeling and coring, though we still had to make one last decision—halved or whole? We tested the difference between poaching pears that were cored then either halved or left whole (if whole, they were cored through the bottom). Although the whole pears made for a very attractive presentation, we had trouble cooking

CORING PEARS

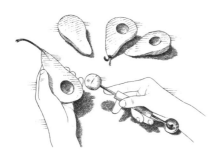

1. Using a melon baller or teaspoon measuring spoon, scoop out the seed and core in the center of each pear half.

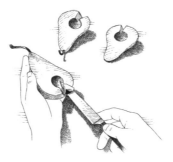

2. Using the tip of a paring knife, cut out the blossom end (bottom) of each pear half.

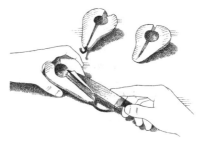

3. Then remove the thin fibrous core and stem by making a V-shaped incision along both sides of the core, leaving the stem attached if desired.

them evenly. Often, the bottom of the pear (around the cored area) would turn mushy and fall apart before the top end was even tender. Cutting the pears in half helped to even out the cooking times dramatically (and they still looked quite pretty).

Finally, we tested sugar amounts. Most of the recipes for poached pears that we researched make super sweet poaching liquids. After extensive testing, however, we chose a light syrup made with just ¾ cup of sugar to 3 cups of wine. This light syrup does not have the consistency of syrup made with more sugar, but it also is not cloyingly sweet. The downside of a light syrup is that it is too thin to use as a sauce when chilled. To fix this, we removed the pears from the syrup after poaching, and turned up the heat to boil the liquid and reduce and thicken it to a saucy consistency. We then poured the hot, thickened syrup over the pears and allowed it to cool. Once cooled, it napped the pear in a thin coat of syrup that was so flavorful, we never missed the chocolate sauce and ice cream.

White Wine–Poached Pears with Lemon and Herbs
Poires Pochées à la Citronelle
SERVES 6

For the best texture, try to buy pears that are neither fully ripe nor rock hard; choose those that yield just slightly when pressed. Use a vegetable peeler to peel strips of zest, but take care to avoid the bitter pith beneath the skin. For the white wine, we recommend a medium-bodied dry white wine such as Sauvignon Blanc or Chardonnay. Serve with Crème Anglaise (page 202) if desired.

1	(750-ml) bottle dry white wine (about 3 cups)
¾	cup (5¼ ounces) sugar
6	strips zest from 1 lemon
5	sprigs fresh mint
3	sprigs fresh thyme
1	vanilla bean, halved lengthwise, seeds scraped out and reserved (see the illustrations)
½	cinnamon stick
⅛	teaspoon salt
2	tablespoons juice from 1 lemon
6	ripe but firm pears (about 8 ounces each), preferably Bosc or Bartlett

1. Bring the wine, sugar, lemon zest, mint, thyme, vanilla seeds and pod, cinnamon, and salt to a simmer in a large saucepan over medium heat and cook, stirring occasionally, until sugar dissolves completely, about 5 minutes; cover and set aside until needed.

2. Meanwhile, fill a large bowl with water and add the lemon juice. Peel, halve, and core the pears following the illustrations on page 200, adding them to the lemon water to prevent browning.

3. Drain the pears, discarding the lemon water, and add to the wine mixture. Bring to a boil over high heat, then reduce the heat to low, cover, and simmer until pears are tender and a toothpick or skewer can be inserted into pear with very little resistance, 10 to 20 minutes, gently turning the pears over every 5 or so minutes.

4. Using a slotted spoon, transfer the fruit to a shallow casserole dish. Return the syrup to medium heat and simmer until it is slightly thickened and measures 1¼ to 1½ cups, about 15 minutes. Strain the syrup through a fine-mesh strainer, then pour over the pears, discarding the strained solids. Refrigerate the pears until well chilled, at least 2 hours or up to 3 days. To serve, spoon portions of fruit and syrup into individual bowls.

SCIENCE: Ripening Pears

In developing our recipe for Wine-Poached Pears we discovered that the ripeness of the pears affects the poaching time. Ideally, the pears should be ripe, but still firm. But getting those ripe-but-firm pears from the grocery store turned out to be difficult. We wondered why. According to the Pear Bureau Northwest, pears are an uncommon type of fruit that do not ripen successfully on the tree. They must be harvested at maturity, but before they ripen, lest their texture turn gritty and granular. This explains why virtually all pears at the grocery store are rock-hard. We tested three methods for ripening: at room temperature, in a paper bag on the counter, and in the refrigerator.

The pears went into their respective corners on a Monday, and we tasted them each day to gauge their ripeness. By the end of the week, there was a clear loser. The pears kept in the fridge were only slightly riper and softer than when purchased. Those stored in a bag and those put in a basket on the counter ripened at the same speed; by Friday they were both ready for poaching.

> VARIATION

Red Wine–Poached Pears with Black Pepper and Cloves

We skip the lemon water bath for the pears in this variation for two reasons: the flavor of lemon and red wine clash in our opinion, and (unlike white wine) the color of the red wine will mask any browning that occurs as the pears are being prepped in step 2. For the red wine, choose a dry medium-bodied red, such as a Côtes du Rhône, Pinot Noir, or Merlot.

Follow the recipe for White Wine–Poached Pears with Lemon and Herbs, replacing the white wine with red wine (see note), omitting the lemon zest in step 1 and lemon water bath in step 2. Add 25 black peppercorns and 3 whole cloves to the saucepan with the wine in step 1.

REMOVING SEEDS FROM A VANILLA BEAN

1. Use a small, sharp knife to cut the vanilla bean in half lengthwise.

2. Place the knife at one end of one bean half and press down to flatten the bean as you move the knife away from you and catch the seeds on the edge of the blade. Add the seeds as well as the pods to the liquid ingredients.

CRÈME ANGLAISE

CRÈME ANGLAISE IS A THIN, CUSTARDY SAUCE SERVED WITH A VARIETY OF DESSERTS. Often paired with chocolate desserts to undercut chocolate's sweet, slightly bitter flavor, it also makes an excellent accompaniment to Poached Pears (page 201) and Sticky Toffee Pudding Cakes (page 109). The sauce is traditionally thickened with just egg yolks, but we added a pinch of cornstarch for extra insurance.

Crème Anglaise

MAKES ABOUT 2 CUPS

Don't overcook the mixture in step 2, or the eggs will curdle and the sauce will be very lumpy. The sauce will keep, covered and refrigerated, for 2 days.

2 cups heavy cream
1 vanilla bean, halved lengthwise, seeds scraped out and reserved (see page 201)
4 large egg yolks
½ cup (3½ ounces) sugar
½ teaspoon cornstarch
Pinch salt

1. Bring the cream and vanilla seeds and pod to a simmer in a medium saucepan over medium-high heat. When the cream reaches a simmer, reduce the heat to medium-low.

2. In a medium bowl, whisk the egg yolks, sugar, cornstarch, and salt together. Slowly whisk ½ cup of the hot cream into the yolk mixture, then slowly whisk the tempered yolk mixture into the hot cream. Continue to cook over medium-low heat, stirring constantly, until the sauce has thickened and reaches 180 degrees on an instant-read thermometer, about 5 minutes.

3. Immediately pour the crème anglaise through a fine-mesh strainer into a medium bowl. Press plastic wrap directly against the surface of the sauce to prevent a skin from forming, and refrigerate until chilled, about 2 hours, before serving.

FREE-FORM SUMMER FRUIT TART

Galette aux Fruits

WITH A PLETHORA OF BERRIES IN FRENCH farmers markets each summer, it's no wonder the fruit tart is practically their national dessert. The delicate *fraises des bois* (small, ultra-sweet strawberries), *myrtilles* (bilberries, like wild blueberries), *framboises* (raspberries), and *mûres* (blackberries), all brimming with flavor, are ripe for the picking, and ready to eat. But while these berries are perfect nestled atop pastry cream in a tart, sometimes it's a nice change to gently bake them in a tart, to bring out their flavor even more.

The most flavorful desserts are often the simplest ones. Such is the case with this tart. Given the simplicity of the dessert—fresh fruit placed unceremoniously on top of pastry—we wanted to make an easy-to-work-with pastry that would be tender, flaky, and flavorful.

We began our testing by making a variety of doughs, all of which we found too firm or too bland. We wanted a relatively soft dough that would be easy to roll out and would provide a delicate but flavorful contrast to the fruit, so we tested different liquid and fat ingredients. Although vegetable shortening made the dough tender, it added no flavor and therefore was rejected. Butter alone worked best. We tried adding eggs—whole eggs and egg yolks, alone or in combination—and found that although the eggs contributed to the tenderness of the dough, they did not add as much flavor as we wanted. We then tried heavy cream, buttermilk, yogurt, sour cream, and cream cheese. The heavy cream made the dough too tender, the cream cheese was too overpowering, but the buttermilk, yogurt, and sour cream worked well. Of the three, our favorite was sour cream in combination with a couple tablespoons of water. The sour cream added just the right amount of richness and tang without detracting from the fruit flavors. We found that 2 teaspoons of sugar was ideal. Any more produced a dough too delicate and tender for our purposes. Any

less and the dough was too firm.

At this point, tasters gave high marks to our tart dough. But something was missing. Following the lead of a similar tart dough recipe we found, we replaced ¼ cup of the flour with cornmeal and were pleased with the results. The cornmeal played a supporting, not dominant, role that made the dough even more flaky and tender. It also added a subtle earthy component to the buttery flavor of the tart pastry. We were surprised that although tasters much preferred this pastry to the one without the cornmeal, they could not immediately identify the difference in ingredients.

We tried our tart dough with a variety of fruit fillings and found that 3 cups of prepared fruit worked best. We liked tarts made with a mixture of berries, such as strawberries, blueberries, blackberries, and raspberries, along with pitted, sliced stone fruit, such as peaches, nectarines, plums, and apricots. Tasting the fruit before assembling the tart helped us determine how much sugar to toss with the fruit. We found that 3 tablespoons sugar tossed with the fruit and 2 tablespoons butter slivered over the top generally gave the right amount of sweetness and flavor. If, however, the fruit you are using is especially tart or underripe, add up to 2 additional tablespoons of sugar to the fruit.

Shaping the tart couldn't be easier. After the dough is rolled into a 13-inch circle, 3 cups of fresh fruit is placed on top, leaving a 2½-inch border. Once sprinkled with sugar and dotted with slivers of butter, the fruit is partially covered by the tart pastry as you lift up and fold over the edges of the dough. As you pick up an edge of the circle of dough and place it over the fruit, the dough will pleat naturally. There is no need to force the dough into a particular shape. The pastry will cover the edges of the fruit and leave the center exposed. Brush the edges of the pastry with water and then sprinkle them with sugar to create a crisp, sweet surface once the tart is baked. Tasters liked the tart served warm or at room temperature—a dollop of whipped cream or France's tangy version, called crème fraîche, is also welcome.

Free-Form Summer Fruit Tart

Galette aux Fruits

SERVES 6

For more information on working with tart dough, see page 205. We prefer a tart made with a mix of stone fruits and berries (our favorite combinations are plums and raspberries, peaches and blueberries, and apricots and blackberries), but you can use only one type of fruit if you prefer. Peeling the stone fruit (even the peaches) is not necessary. Taste the fruit before adding sugar to it; use the lesser amount if the fruit is very sweet, more if it is tart. Once baked, the tart is best eaten warm, or within 3 or 4 hours, although leftovers do reheat well in a 350-degree oven. Excellent accompaniments are vanilla ice cream or lightly sweetened whipped cream or crème fraîche.

DOUGH

2	tablespoons sour cream
2	tablespoons ice water
I	cup (5 ounces) unbleached all-purpose flour
¼	cup (about 1⅓ ounces) fine stone-ground yellow cornmeal
2	teaspoons sugar
½	teaspoon salt
7	tablespoons unsalted butter, cut into ½-inch pieces and chilled

FILLING

I	pound (3 cups) fresh mixed berries and/or pitted stone fruit cut into ¼-inch slices
4–6	tablespoons sugar
2	tablespoons unsalted butter, cut into ¼-inch pieces

1. FOR THE DOUGH: Stir together the sour cream and water in a small liquid measuring cup. Set aside in the refrigerator to keep cold until needed.

2. Pulse the flour, cornmeal, sugar, and salt together in a food processor until combined, about 4 pulses. Scatter half of the butter pieces over the flour mixture and pulse until the butter is the size of small peas, about 4 pulses. Scatter the remaining butter over the flour mixture and pulse until most of the butter is incorporated and some pea-sized bits remain, about 4 pulses. Continue to pulse, adding the sour cream mixture through the feed tube, until the dough just comes together around the blade, 4 to 6 pulses. Turn the dough onto a large sheet of plastic wrap, flatten into a 6-inch disk, wrap tightly, and refrigerate for at least 1 hour, or up to 2 days.

3. When ready to assemble and bake the tart, adjust an oven rack to the middle position and heat the oven to 400 degrees. Remove the dough from the refrigerator and unwrap. Roll the dough between 2 large sheets of lightly floured parchment paper into a 13-inch round. Slide the dough, still between the parchment, onto a baking sheet and refrigerate until firm, about 20 minutes.

4. FOR THE FILLING: Remove the dough and baking sheet from the refrigerator and peel off the top sheet of parchment paper. Toss the fruit with 3 to 5 tablespoons of the sugar as needed to sweeten. Pile the fruit in the center of the dough, leaving a 2½-inch border of dough around the edge. Dot the butter over the fruit. Fold the edges of the dough over the fruit following the illustration on page 205. (If the dough is sticking to the parchment, run a bench scraper or thin metal spatula under the pastry to loosen it from the paper.) Using a pastry brush, brush the edges of the dough with water and sprinkle with the remaining tablespoon sugar.

5. Bake until the crust is golden brown and crisp and the fruit is bubbling, about 40 minutes. Place the baking sheet on a wire rack and allow the tart to cool for 10 minutes. Using a large offset spatula, transfer the tart to the wire rack to cool an additional 10 minutes. The tart may be served warm or at room temperature.

➤ VARIATION

Individual Summer Fruit Tartlets

If your baking sheet is too small to fit six tartlets, arrange them on two trays and bake on the upper- and lower-middle oven racks, switching and rotating the trays halfway through the baking time.

Follow the instructions for Free-Form Summer Fruit Tart, dividing and rolling the dough out into six 6-inch rounds between small sheets of parchment paper in step 3; chill the dough rounds with parchment as directed. When assembling the tarts in step 4, lay the dough rounds with parchment on the counter, remove the top sheets of parchment, and pile ½ cup sweetened fruit in the center of each round, leaving a 1½-inch border of dough. Divide the butter among the tartlets, then fold the dough over the fruit, brush the top with water, and sprinkle with sugar as directed. Transfer the tartlets to a large baking sheet, trimming the parchment bottoms as needed to fit on the baking sheet. Bake and cool as directed in step 5, reducing the baking time to 30 minutes.

CORE TECHNIQUE

TIPS FOR ROLLING TART DOUGH

While we offer a sturdy pat-in-the-pan dough on page 84 that requires no rolling and fitting, there are some delicate tart doughs where rolling cannot be avoided. Here are some tips for making the task easier.

1. Chill it

After making the dough, it needs at least I hour of chilling time in order to become cold and firm but malleable. The dough can, however, be made up to 2 days ahead of time.

2. Roll when malleable

If the dough is chilled for longer than I hour, it will probably be very cold and hard. Let it stand at room temperature 15 to 20 minutes until it is firm but malleable before rolling it out. If the dough ever becomes too soft when rolling out, simply return it to the refrigerator for a few minutes until it is firm enough to continue rolling.

3. Use parchment paper

Rolling the dough out between 2 sheets of floured parchment paper is our favorite method because it allows us to flip the dough over and rotate it easily.

4. Sprinkle with flour

Sprinkling flour between the dough and parchment is important because the grains of flour act like little ball bearings that allow the dough to roll over the parchment rather than stick to it. Re-flour the parchment as needed while rolling out the dough by gently peeling back the parchment (one sheet at a time) and sprinkling the dough with flour. If the dough sticks to the parchment, use a bench scraper to help loosen it.

5. Bake on parchment paper

Leaving the dough encased between the parchment sheets after it is rolled out makes transferring it between the counter, refrigerator, and oven much easier. Don't worry about removing the bottom layer of parchment before baking— the parchment will release itself from the tart during baking.

SHAPING A FREE-FORM TART

1. Place the fruit in the center of the rolled-out dough, leaving a 2½-inch border.

2. Fold the dough border up over the filling, using the underlying parchment to lift and pleat the dough to fit snugly.

UPSIDE-DOWN APPLE TART

Tarte Tatin

IN THE LATE 19TH CENTURY, TWO FRENCH sisters owned and ran l'Hotel Tatin in the Loire Valley of France. The elder sister, Stéphanie, managed the kitchen—she was a particularly fine cook but was often distracted by the bustle of kitchen. Her specialty was a standard apple tart, buttery pastry and sweetened apples. One day during the midday scramble, Stéphanie mistakenly placed her tart in the oven upside down. Once it was baked, she realized her mistake, but decided to carry on and simply flipped the dessert right side up. The result: a bed of buttery pastry cradling the most amazing caramelized apples anyone had ever encountered. Thus, a simple French apple tart became tarte Tatin.

Over the years, the method for this upside-down tart have been refined into a two-step process that begins on the stovetop. The apples, neatly arranged in a tarte Tatin pan or a skillet, are boiled in a buttery caramel sauce over ferociously high

PREPARING TARTE TATIN

1. Place the first apple quarter cut side down and with an end touching the skillet wall. As you continue to arrange the apples, lift each quarter on its edge while placing the next apple quarter on its edge, so that the apples stand straight up. Fill the skillet middle with the remaining quarters, cutting them in half, if necessary, to fill the space.

2. Return the skillet to high heat; cook until the juices turn from butterscotch to a rich amber color, 10 to 12 minutes. Remove the skillet from the heat and, using a fork or the tip of a paring knife, turn the apples onto the uncaramelized sides.

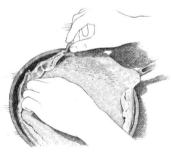

3. Slide the prepared dough off the baking sheet over the skillet and, taking care not to burn your fingers, tuck the dough edges gently up against the skillet wall. Bake and cool as directed.

4. Place a heatproof serving platter over the skillet and hold it tightly against the skillet. Invert the skillet and platter and set the platter on the counter. Lift the skillet up off the platter, leaving the tart behind.

heat until they absorb the syrup and become virtually candied. These syrup-soaked apples are then covered with a circle of pastry, and the tart, skillet and all is slid into the oven. After baking, the tart is flipped over, revealing concentric circles of apples glazed with a golden caramel. It can be served with whipped cream or vanilla ice cream or with a tangy topping that offsets the sweetness of the caramel, such as crème fraîche.

When tarte Tatin first came to this country, all sorts of recipes for it appeared. Some were based on traditional French formulas, but others were highly Americanized. The latter, generally speaking, simply do not work. These unsuccessful recipes vary, but most of them exhibit one of two serious flaws. One of these mistakes is using sliced or chopped apples, which makes a wet, loose tart that sprawls and collapses when inverted. The second common error in Americanized recipes is the decision to caramelize the apples on top of the stove after the tart has been completely baked. Caramelizing a fully baked tart is simply impossible. If the tart turns out juicy, it will not caramelize at all, and if it bakes up dry, it will burn. And you won't even know which disaster is about to befall you because you cannot see what the apples are doing underneath the crust.

Tarte Tatin is typically made with apple quarters. Some recipes, however, call for apple halves, and we found this idea intriguing. When made with apple quarters, tarte Tatin can sometimes seem a little light on fruit because the apples lose juice and shrink when caramelized. When we tried using halved apples, though, we encountered a new set of problems.

In our first experiments, we had trouble getting the caramel to penetrate all the way through such large pieces of apple. While we eventually resolved this problem simply by cooking the apples longer, we were still not enthralled by the results. Our tarte Tatin now struck us as pulpy and mushy, and there seemed to be too much fruit in relation to crust. Worse, we found that if the skillet was just a tad too small—or the apples unusually juicy—the caramel overflowed the pan during the caramelization process, making a horrible mess.

In the end, we abandoned the apple halves, but these experiments nonetheless proved useful since they gave us an idea of how to refine the original method using quarters. When you make a tarte Tatin with halved apples, the apples rest on the outer peeled surface so that the full cut side faces up. Apple quarters, by contrast, tend to flop over onto a cut side, but we reasoned that if we tipped each apple quarter onto its cut edge and held it there while we laid the next quarter in place, we could fit more fruit in the skillet. It turned out that we were able to cram an entire extra apple into the skillet this way, with very good results. The tart looked fuller and tasted fruitier, but it did not suffer from apple overload or overflow onto the stove.

The only problem now was that the apples, because they were almost perpendicular to the skillet, caramelized only on the skillet side, leaving the other side pale and sour. One recipe we found solved this problem by flipping the apples over during the caramelization process. This maneuver sounded tricky to us, but, as the recipe promised, it was easily accomplished by spearing the quarters with a table fork or the tip of a paring knife. Even though the caramelized side of the apples is very soft, the side facing up remains firm enough not to tear when the apples are speared and flipped. Furthermore, even if the skillet doesn't have a non-stick coating, the apple quarters never stick.

We have always used Granny Smith apples for tarte Tatin, but many recipes recommend Golden Delicious, and one recipe that we had on hand specified, of all things, Red Delicious, which, it was claimed, gave the tart a pretty look because of the elongated shape. We tested both Golden and Red Delicious as well as Gala and Fuji apples. The results were surprising. We had expected most of the apples to fall apart, but all held their shape quite well. Flavor, however, was another story. The Golden Delicious apples were acceptable, if barely, but the rest were tasteless. We tried adding lemon juice to augment the flavor of the insipid apples, but did not find this to be an effective remedy. You need to start with apples that are flavorful to begin with, and if supermarket apples are your only option, we think it is safest to stick with Granny Smiths.

Finally, there is the matter of the crust. A crust for tarte Tatin needs extra durability and strength, and so bakers of tarte Tatin usually make the crust with an egg. Egg pastry does not have to be sweetened, but it is indisputably more delicious when it is, and therein lies the problem. Sugar makes pastry dough sticky, crumbly, and generally difficult to handle, and it also tends to fuse the spacers—the little bits of butter that make pastry flaky—leaving the baked crust crunchy, cookie-like, and a little hard. After struggling with these problems for years, we finally discovered that the solution was to use confectioners' sugar rather than regular granulated. Granulated sugar is too coarse to dissolve well in dough. It remains in individual grains, then melts into tiny droplets of sticky syrup that wreak havoc. Confectioners' sugar, by contrast, simply disappears, sweetening the dough without causing any problems. It makes a superbly flaky egg pastry, worthy of the dessert masterpiece called tarte Tatin.

Upside-Down Apple Tart

Tarte Tatin

SERVES 8

If the caramel isn't cooked to a rich amber color in step 4, the apples will look pale and dull rather than shiny and appealingly caramelized. We recommend using a nonstick skillet, but any heavy-bottomed, 12-inch ovenproof skillet will do.

PASTRY

1 ⅓	cups (6 ⅔ ounces) unbleached all-purpose flour, plus extra for the work surface
¼	cup (1 ounce) confectioners' sugar
½	teaspoon salt
8	tablespoons (1 stick) unsalted butter, cut into ¼ inch pieces and chilled
1	large egg, lightly beaten and chilled

APPLES

8	tablespoons (1 stick) unsalted butter
¾	cup (5 ¼ ounces) granulated sugar
6	large Granny Smith apples (about 3 pounds), peeled, quartered, and cored

TOPPING

1	cup heavy cream, cold
½	cup sour cream, cold

1. **FOR THE PASTRY:** Pulse the flour, sugar, and salt in a food processor until combined. Scatter the butter pieces over the flour mixture and pulse until the mixture resembles cornmeal, 7 to 12 pulses. Turn the mixture into a medium bowl, add the egg, and stir with a fork until little balls form. Press the balls together with the back of the fork, then gather the dough into a ball. Turn the dough onto a large sheet of plastic wrap, flatten into a 6-inch disk, wrap tightly, and refrigerate at least 1 hour, or up to 2 days.

2. Remove the dough from the refrigerator and unwrap. Roll the dough between 2 large sheets of lightly floured parchment paper into a 14-inch round. Flour a rimless baking sheet and slide the dough onto the sheet. Cover with a piece of parchment and refrigerate while preparing the apples.

3. **FOR THE APPLES:** Adjust an oven rack to the upper-middle position and heat the oven to 375 degrees. Melt the butter in a 12-inch ovenproof skillet, then remove from the heat and sprinkle evenly with the sugar. Following the illustrations on page 206, arrange the apples in the skillet by placing the first apple quarter, cut side down and with an end touching the skillet wall. As you continue to arrange the apples, lift each quarter on its edge while placing the next apple quarter on its edge, so that the apple quarters stand straight up. Fill the skillet middle with the remaining quarters, placing them cut side down, cutting the quarters in half, if necessary, to fill the space.

4. Return the skillet to high heat and cook until the juices turn to a rich amber color, 10 to 12 minutes. Remove the skillet from the heat and, using a fork or the tip of a paring knife, turn the apples onto their uncaramelized sides. Return the skillet to the high heat and cook until the second side of the apples turn brown, about 5 minutes longer.

5. Remove the skillet from the heat. Remove the dough and baking sheet from the refrigerator and peel off the top sheet of parchment paper. Slide the prepared dough off the baking sheet onto the apple filling and, taking care not to burn your fingers, tuck the dough edges gently up against the skillet wall.

6. Bake until the crust is golden brown, 25 to 30 minutes. Set the skillet on a wire rack and let cool for about 25 minutes. Loosen the edges with a knife, place a serving plate on top of the skillet, and, holding the plate and skillet together firmly, invert the tart onto the serving plate. Scrape out any apples that stick to the skillet and put them back into place. (The tart can be kept for several hours at room temperature, but unmold it onto a dish that can withstand mild heat. Before serving, warm the tart for 10 minutes in a 200-degree oven.)

7. **FOR THE TOPPING:** Using an electric mixer, whip the heavy cream and sour cream together on medium-high speed until the mixture thickens and forms soft peaks, about 1 minute. Slice the tart into wedges, dollop with the topping, and serve.

POTS DE CRÈME AU CHOCOLAT

LITERALLY TRANSLATED, *POTS DE CRÈME* means pots of cream, but cream in this case refers to custard, a word the French simply don't have a translation for. Once we tasted our first pots de crème, we understood exactly why tiny Limoges china pots were commissioned especially for this exotic pudding-like dessert. The custard is so remarkably rich, so intensely flavored that just a small amount satisfies. When properly made, this rich custard boasts a satiny texture and intense chocolate flavor, but we've had other versions that are no better than cafeteria pudding. We set out to develop a recipe for this dessert that was not only authentic, but foolproof.

We started with a handful of authentic recipes. Not surprisingly, the ingredients were more or less the same across the board: chocolate, eggs, sugar, and cream (or other such dairy). The difference lay in the ratio of ingredients and the way the custard was cooked. Most of the recipes employed the usual treatment for baked custard: a hot water bath and a moderately low oven. But two out of the 20 or so recipes we found employed an unconventional method in which the custard is cooked on the stovetop in a saucepan, then poured into ramekins. Very interesting.

The downfall of the other recipes was that they

required a large roasting pan that accommodated all the ramekins and a hot water bath that threatened to splash the custards every time the pan was moved. In addition, the individual custards didn't always cook at the same rate, which meant going in and out of the oven multiple times to gauge doneness and plucking hot ramekins from the water bath only to have them drip onto their neighbors. We wanted the simpler recipe that would be as user-friendly as possible.

Using the standard baked custard method for the time being, we went to work on ingredients. We started with the dairy. To serve eight, a chocolate pot de crème recipe requires about 2 cups of milk, half-and-half, or heavy cream. The richest recipes use heavy cream exclusively, but most call for a combination of cream and milk. We tested it all, in different ratios, and decided that 1½ cups of cream and ¾ cup of half-and-half had just the right amount of richness and body. Next up, eggs, which enrich and help thicken the custard. Yolks are the norm. We experimented with as many as eight and as few as four. Five was the right number to make a luxurious custard. This is fewer than what many recipes call for, but we wanted to use a lot of chocolate, and we knew that would also help the custard to set up.

Intensity of flavor was key, so we passed over milk chocolate and semisweet chocolate because we knew they'd be too mild. Cocoa powder and unsweetened chocolate were too gritty, so we focused our testing on bittersweet chocolate. With only 4 ounces of this dark chocolate, the pots de crème were too milky; with a whole pound, they were unpalatably rich. Our tastes tended toward a recipe made with 12 ounces—incredibly thick and chocolaty—but since most tasters couldn't abide the heavy texture, we went with 10 ounces. With only one exception, this was at least 50 percent more chocolate than in any other recipe that we encountered.

It was now time to settle the matter of cooking method. Using the same ingredients, we made two versions of pots de crème. We baked one in a moderately low oven in a water bath, covered with foil to prevent the surface of the custards from drying out; the other we made on the stovetop in the style of a stirred custard, or crème anglaise in the culinary vernacular. It was unequivocal. The crème anglaise method was immensely easier than the traditional (and cumbersome) baking method—and the results were close to identical. (The baked custards were ever so slightly firmer and more set than the stirred ones, but tasters weren't the least bit concerned.) What wasn't identical was the hassle factor: The crème anglaise method was easy and reliable. The eggs, sugar, and dairy are cooked on the stovetop, the resulting custard is poured over the chocolate, then the mixture is gently whisked until combined. The only equipment required is a saucepan and a heatproof spatula; no roasting pan and no water bath. To boot, when cooked on the stovetop the pots de crème were finished in a fraction of the time they took to bake. To our delight, we had not only made this refined French classic foolproof, we'd simplified it as well.

Pots de Crème au Chocolat
SERVES 8

We prefer pots de crème made with 60 percent cocoa bittersweet chocolate (our favorite brands are Ghirardelli, Callebaut, Valrhona, and El Rey), but 70 percent bittersweet chocolate can also be used. If using a 70 percent bittersweet chocolate (we like Lindt, El Rey, and Valrhona), reduce the amount of chocolate to 8 ounces. A tablespoon of strong brewed coffee may be substituted for the instant espresso and water. Covered tightly with plastic wrap, the pots de crème will keep for up to 3 days in the refrigerator, but the whipped cream must be made just before serving.

POTS DE CRÈME

10	ounces bittersweet chocolate (see note), chopped fine
5	large egg yolks
5	tablespoons (1¼ ounces) sugar
¼	teaspoon salt
1½	cups heavy cream
¾	cup half-and-half
1	tablespoon vanilla extract
½	teaspoon instant espresso
1	tablespoon water

WHIPPED CREAM AND GARNISH

½   **cup heavy cream, cold**
2   **teaspoons sugar**
½   **teaspoon vanilla extract**
       Cocoa for dusting (optional)
       Chocolate shavings for sprinkling (optional)

1. FOR THE POTS DE CRÈME: Place the chocolate in a medium heatproof bowl; set a fine-mesh strainer over the bowl and set aside.

2. Whisk the yolks, sugar, and salt together in a medium bowl until combined, then whisk in the heavy cream and half-and-half. Transfer the mixture to a medium saucepan. Cook the mixture over medium-low heat, stirring constantly and scraping the bottom of the pot with a wooden spoon, until it is thickened and silky and registers 175 to 180 degrees on an instant-read thermometer, 8 to 12 minutes. (Do not let the custard overcook or simmer.)

3. Immediately pour the custard through the strainer over the chocolate. Let the mixture stand to melt the chocolate, about 5 minutes. Whisk gently until smooth, then whisk in the vanilla and espresso. Divide the mixture evenly among eight 5-ounce ramekins. Gently tap the ramekins against the counter to remove any air bubbles.

4. Cool the pots de crème to room temperature, then cover with plastic wrap and refrigerate until chilled, at least 4 hours or up to 72 hours. Before serving, let the pots de crème stand at room temperature for 20 to 30 minutes.

5. FOR THE WHIPPED CREAM AND GARNISH: Using an electric mixer, whip the cream, sugar, and vanilla on medium-low speed until small bubbles form, about 30 seconds. Increase the speed to medium-high and continue to whip the mixture thickens and forms stiff peaks, about 1 minute; set aside. Dollop each pot de crème with about 2 tablespoons of whipped cream and garnish with cocoa or chocolate shavings, if desired.

CRÈME BRÛLÉE

CRÈME BRÛLÉE IS A CLASSIC FRENCH DISH of smooth custard with a caramelized sugar topping. A proper crème brûlée should have a crackle-crisp bittersweet sugar crust over a chilly custard of balanced egginess, creaminess, and sweetness. But the majority of crème brûlées the test kitchen sampled revealed a trio of problems with this showstopper dessert: The custard is tepid, not cold; the texture is leaden, not ethereal; and the flavors are muted and dull. And if the topping isn't a paltry sugar crust, it's one so thick it requires a pickax. We set out to fix these problems and create the perfect crème brûlée.

First we sought to settle the issue of eggs. Firmer custard, like that in crème caramel, is made with whole eggs, which help the custard to achieve a clean-cutting quality. Crème brûlée is richer and softer—with a pudding-like, spoon-clinging texture—in part because of the exclusive use of yolks. With 4 cups of heavy cream as the dairy ingredient for the moment, we went to work. The custard refused to set at all with as few as six yolks; with eight (a common number for the amount of cream) it was better, but still rather slurpy. With 10, however, we struck gold. The custard had a lovely lilting texture, an elegant mouthfeel, a glossy, luminescent look, and the richest flavor.

We ventured to make crème brûlées with different kinds of cream. Half-and-half (with a fat content of about 10 percent) was far too lean, and the custard was watery and lightweight. With whipping cream (about 30 percent fat), the custard was improved but still a bit loose. Heavy cream (about 36 percent fat) was the ticket. The custard was thick but not overbearing, luxurious but not death-defying.

We tested various sugar quantities, from ½ cup to ¾ cup. Two-thirds cup was the winner; with more sugar the crème brûlée was too saccharine, and with less the simple egg and cream flavors tasted muted and dull. We also found that a pinch of salt heightened flavors and that a vanilla bean was superior to extract.

With the proportions in place, we attempted to find the best cooking technique for the custard. Custard made with icebox-cold eggs and cream can go into the oven, but nearly all recipes instruct the cook to scald the cream before gradually whisking it into the yolks. When compared, a started-cold custard and a scalded-cream custard displayed startling differences. The former had a silkier, smoother texture. Custard research explained that eggs respond favorably to cooking at a slow, gentle pace. If heated quickly, they set only just shortly before they enter the overcooked zone, leaving a very narrow window between just right and overdone. If heated gently, however, they begin to thicken the custard at a lower temperature and continue to do so gradually until it, too, eventually overcooks. In other words, the scalded-cream method is more likely to produce custard with an overcooked—hence inferior—texture.

The downside to starting with cold ingredients is that unless the cream is heated, it is impossible to extract flavor from a vanilla bean. Also, if the cream is heated, the sugar can go into the pot for easy dissolution. Otherwise, the sugar must be vigorously beaten with the yolks to encourage it to dissolve. When we did this, the resulting custard was very frothy and baked up with a dry, soap-foam-like surface. Scalding cream and sugar, steeping with vanilla, and then refrigerating until cold seemed an overwrought process, so we tested a hybrid technique. We heated only half the cream with the sugar and the vanilla bean. After a 15-minute steeping off the heat to extract flavor from the vanilla bean, we added the remaining cold cream to bring the temperature down before whisking it into the yolks. This hybrid technique created a custard with a fineness equal to the one started cold—and it baked in less time, too.

Next we investigated oven temperatures. At 325 degrees, the custards puffed and browned on the surface. Too hot. At 300 degrees, they fared beautifully. As for the water bath (or bain-marie, which prevents the periphery of a custard from overcooking while the center saunters to the finish line),

we used a large baking dish that held the ramekins comfortably. (The ramekins must not touch and should be at least ½ inch away from the sides of the dish.) We lined the bottom with a kitchen towel to protect the bottoms of the ramekins from the heat of the dish and to stabilize them.

The golden rule of custards is that they must not be overcooked lest they lose their smooth, silken texture and become grainy and curdled. Judging doneness by gently shaking the custards or by slipping a paring knife into them was not reliable. An instant-read thermometer tells you exactly when the custards must come out of the oven: between 170 and 175 degrees. If you do not have a thermometer, look at the center of the custard. It should be barely set—shaky but not sloshy. The custard will continue to cook from residual heat once out of the oven. A deep chill then helps to solidify things. If your oven has a history of uneven heating, the custards may finish at different rates, so it is advisable to check each one separately rather than take the whole lot out at once.

For the crackly caramel crust, we tried brown sugar, regular granulated sugar, and turbinado and Demerara sugars (the latter two are coarse light brown sugars). Because brown sugar is moist and lumpy, recipes often recommend drying it in a

MAKING THE "BRÛLÉE"

Carefully ignite the torch, then lower it until the end of the flame is about 1 inch from the sprinkled sugar. Hold the flame in place until you see the sugar melt and burn to a caramel color, then move along to the next patch of unburnt sugar repeating the process until the entire custard has a deep golden crust.

low oven and crushing it to break up lumps. We found that it just isn't worth the effort. Turbinado and Demerara sugar were superior to granulated only because their coarseness makes them easy to distribute evenly over the custards.

There are a few approaches to caramelizing the sugar. The broiler is almost guaranteed to fail; the heat is uneven and inadequate. A salamander—a long-handled iron plate that is heated and held just above the sugar—is hardly practical since these plates are hard to come by. A torch accomplishes the task efficiently. A hardware-store propane torch is the tool of choice, but a small butane kitchen torch, available in cookware stores, can do the job, just at a more leisurely pace.

While being "brûléed," the custard is unavoidably warmed a bit. In standard round ramekins, usually only the upper third of the custard is affected. But in shallow dishes (our favorite for their higher ratio of crust to custard), the custard can be completely warmed through. In our opinion, a warm custard can ruin an otherwise perfect crème brûlée. To remedy this problem, we refrigerated the finished crème brûlées, and the crust maintained its crackly texture for up to 45 minutes. Beneath the shattering sugar crust lay an interplay of creamy, cold, sweet, bitter, smooth, and crackly—perfect crème brûlée.

Crème Brûlée
SERVES 8

Don't separate the eggs until the cream has finished steeping; otherwise, a dry film will form on the yolks. We prefer the deeper flavor and speckles of seeds from a vanilla bean, but 2 teaspoons of extract can be substituted; whisk the extract into the yolks in step 4. The best way to judge doneness is with a digital instant-read thermometer. The custards, especially if baked in shallow fluted dishes, will not be deep enough to provide an accurate reading with a dial-face thermometer. You will need either a kitchen torch or a hardware-store propane torch for caramelizing the sugar. We recommend using turbinado or Demerara sugar for the crust, but regular granulated sugar will work too; use only 1 scant teaspoon on each ramekin or 1 teaspoon on each shallow fluted dish.

4	cups heavy cream, chilled
⅔	cup (4⅔ ounces) granulated sugar
	Pinch salt
1	vanilla bean, halved lengthwise, seeds scraped out and reserved (see page 201)
10	large egg yolks (see note)
8–12	teaspoons turbinado or Demerara sugar (see note)

1. Adjust an oven rack to the lower-middle position and heat the oven to 300 degrees.

2. Combine 2 cups of the cream, the sugar, salt, vanilla seeds and pod together in a medium saucepan and bring to a boil over medium heat, stirring occasionally to dissolve the sugar. Remove the pan from heat and let steep to infuse the flavors, about 15 minutes.

3. Meanwhile, place a kitchen towel on the bottom of large baking dish or roasting pan and arrange eight 4- to 5-ounce ramekins (or shallow fluted dishes) on the towel. Bring a kettle of water to a boil over high heat.

4. After the cream has steeped, stir in the remaining 2 cups of cream to cool down the mixture. Whisk the yolks together in a large bowl until uniform. Whisk about 1 cup of the cream mixture into the yolks until loosened and combined; repeat with another 1 cup of the cream. Add the remaining cream and whisk until evenly colored and thoroughly combined. Strain through a fine-mesh strainer into a 2-quart measuring cup or pitcher; discard the solids in the strainer. Pour or ladle the mixture evenly into the ramekins.

5. Gently place the baking dish with ramekins on the oven rack. With great care, pour the boiling water into the baking dish, without splashing any water into the ramekins, until the water reaches two-thirds the height of the ramekins. Bake until the centers of the custards are just barely set and are no longer sloshy, and an instant-read thermometer inserted in the centers registers 170 to 175 degrees, 30 to 35 minutes (25 to 30 minutes for shallow fluted dishes). Begin checking the temperature about 5 minutes before the recommended time.

6. Transfer the ramekins to a wire rack and cool to room temperature, about 2 hours. Set the

ramekins on a rimmed baking sheet, cover tightly with plastic wrap, and refrigerate until cold, at least 4 hours or up to 4 days.

7. Uncover the ramekins; if condensation has collected on the custards, place a paper towel on the surface to soak up the moisture. Sprinkle each with about 1 teaspoon turbinado sugar (1½ teaspoons for shallow fluted dishes); tilt and tap each ramekin for even coverage. Following the illustration on page 211, ignite the torch and caramelize the sugar. Refrigerate the ramekins, uncovered, to rechill, 30 to 45 minutes (but no longer).

➤ VARIATIONS

Espresso Crème Brûlée

Place ¼ cup espresso beans in a zipper-lock bag and crush lightly with a rolling pin or meat pounder until coarsely cracked. Follow the recipe for Crème Brûlée, substituting the cracked espresso beans for the vanilla bean and whisking 1 teaspoon vanilla extract into the yolks in step 4 before adding the cream.

Tea-Infused Crème Brûlée

Knot together the strings of 10 bags of Irish Breakfast tea. Follow the recipe for Crème Brûlée, substituting the tea bags for the vanilla bean; after steeping, squeeze the bags with tongs or press into a mesh strainer to extract all the liquid. Whisk 1 teaspoon vanilla extract into the yolks in step 4 before adding the cream.

A SURE GRIP FOR TONGS

We recommend the use of tongs to remove ramekins of custard from a water bath. Cooks who worry about the ramekins slipping in the tongs can try this tip: Slip rubber bands around each of the 2 tong pincers, and the sticky rubber will provide a surer grip.

FRENCH-STYLE MACAROONS

Macarons

TWO LIGHT-AS-AIR, MERINGUE-Y ALMOND cookies sandwiched together with a sweet cream filling, macarons melt in the mouth. Originally created in Venice during the Renaissance these cookies made their way to France and today are famous throughout the country. Once a rare find in the United States, macaroons have become increasingly popular. They can be found at many of the finer bakeries or on a petits fours tray delivered with your bill at a fancy restaurant. They're becoming so popular, in fact, that those bakeries that do make them are having a tough time baking enough to meet demands. We wanted to develop a home-cook-friendly recipe that could rival those in any upscale restaurant or Parisian patisserie.

These cookies are typically made simply with almond flour, egg whites, and sugar—once the batter is prepared, it is piped through a pastry bag onto a parchment paper–lined baking sheet and left to dry until a skin forms. (This step of allowing the batter to dry may seem a bit odd, but the skin that forms is crucial to ensuring a macaroon with an attractive smooth surface. When we skipped this step in early tests, the cookies baked up cracked and craggy-looking.) After the cookies are baked and cooked, they are filled and ready to serve. The goal is to achieve a very light, crisp crust and moist, chewy interior.

Using a basic working recipe, cobbled together from a couple of recipes that we found in our research, we started by testing the amount of sugar. Many of the recipes we reviewed use an equal amount of sugar to almond flour. (Almond flour is made from very finely ground skinless almonds, sold in some specialty stores. You can make your own by grinding skinless slivered almonds in a food processor, but the result won't be as fine as purchased almond flour.) Tasters found these macaroons cloyingly sweet and felt that a reduction in the amount of sugar would be a good place to start with this recipe. We tested only those amounts lower than the 3¾ cups we started with, maintaining the amount of almond flour. We found 3⅓ cups of sugar just right—any lower and the structure of the cookie became brittle and fell apart.

While on the topic of sugar, we tested different kinds. We immediately ruled out brown sugar for its higher moisture content and focused on three white sugars: granulated, superfine, and confectioners'. The superfine sugar was unpredictable—half the cookies we baked came out of the oven cracked and unevenly baked. The granulated sugar was better, but tasters found the confectioners' sugar gave the smoothest texture with a pure almond flavor.

Next we focused on eggs. We were currently using five egg whites beaten into a meringue (these cookies get no egg yolks) and wondered how more or less eggs would affect these cookies—after all, the egg whites are the only moisture added to this batter and therefore play a significant role in the cookies' texture. A batter made with four egg whites was thick and difficult to pipe—once cooked they were very heavy. Six egg whites made a very loose batter and cookies that baked up dry and flaky. Five whites turned out to be just right—light, yet moist. We added a modest 5 teaspoons of granulated sugar (additional confectioners' sugar wasn't enough) and a pinch of cream of tartar to give our meringue a bit more structure.

With our sugar and egg whites in order, we turned our attention to the almond flour. Up to this point we had been mixing our almond flour and confectioners' sugar together in a bowl, then folding in the whipped egg whites. In the course of researching this dessert, we found a recipe that calls for processing the two dry ingredients together in a food processor to help break the almond flour up further. We wondered if this would make a difference so we tested it. These cookies came out smoother than any others so far. Some recipes for macaroons also include food coloring to give the cookies a pretty pastel tint, but we found that this batter was so finicky, any additional liquid, even a few drops, upset the balance, so we opted not to tint our macaroons.

With our basic cookie batter in order, we tested flavor enhancements (obviously almond is the primary flavor of this cookie). Almond extract added to the batter was tested first, as a logical addition to these cookies, but the almond flavor was too potent. Vanilla extract was a perfect flavor addition and 1 tablespoon did the trick. We also tried using a vanilla bean, as we liked the look of the black specks in these cookies, but ultimately went with the extract as more convenient.

For the cookies' filling, we tested buttercream frosting, fruit preserves, ganache, and melted chocolate (all of which we've seen used to fill macaroons) and while tasters liked all of the options, the buttercream was preferred for its rich flavor and creamy texture. While there are easier ways to build a buttercream frosting—some are just butter and confectioners' sugar—we needed a light and stable buttercream that would stay sandwiched between

PIPING MACAROONS

This method for piping macaroons can also be used to pipe Cheese Puffs (page 147).

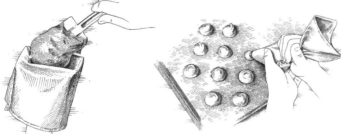

1. Fill a pastry bag with the batter and push the batter to the bottom of the bag using your hands or a rubber spatula; twist the top of the bag to seal.

2. Pipe the paste or batter onto the parchment-lined baking sheets into 2-inch mounds, spaced about 1 inch apart.

3. Use the back of a teaspoon or your finger dipped in cold water to even out the shape and smooth the surface of the piped mounds.

our cookies. To achieve this, we made an old-fashioned buttercream that relies on eggs for body, stability, and richness. We started by mixing the eggs, sugar, and salt in a bowl set over simmering water (at this point flavorings, such as vanilla can also be added). Once the sugar was melted and the mixture warm, we removed the bowl from the heat and beat the mixture until it turned light and airy. We then added butter and continued to beat until the mixture became soft, supple, and very creamy. This lush buttercream was the perfect accent to our crisp, light cookies.

French-Style Macaroons

Macarons

MAKES 20 SANDWICH COOKIES

If you can't find almond flour (sold in well-stocked grocery stores and specialty stores), substitute 11 ounces of slivered almonds, processed to a fine flour in a food processor; continue to process with the sugar as directed in step 1. Allow the piped cookies to stand as directed to allow a skin to form in step 4—this skin prevents the cookies from cracking the oven, ensuring a smooth finished cookie. You should be able to portion all 40 cookies between 2 standard-sized baking sheets. If not, use 3 sheets. Note that you must bake only 1 sheet at a time for the cookies to bake evenly. Instead of using buttercream for the filling, you can substitute 4 ounces of bittersweet chocolate, melted and cooled, or 1¼ cups of fruit preserves, pureed until smooth. For more information on whipping egg whites, see page 168.

3¾	cups (15 ounces) almond flour
3⅓	cups (13⅓ ounces) confectioners' sugar
⅛	teaspoon salt
5	large egg whites, at room temperature
	Pinch of cream of tartar
5	teaspoons granulated sugar
I	tablespoon vanilla extract
2	cups Vanilla Buttercream Frosting, Coffee Buttercream Frosting, or Orange Buttercream Frosting (recipes on page 216)

1. Spray 2 large baking sheets with nonstick cooking spray and line with parchment paper; set aside. Fit a large pastry bag with a ½-inch plain tip; set aside. Process half of the almond flour, confectioners' sugar, and salt together in a food processor until the mixture is very finely ground, about 20 seconds. Transfer to a bowl and repeat with the remaining almond flour and confectioners sugar; stir together and set aside.

2. Using an electric mixer, whip the egg whites on medium-low speed until they are opaque and frothy, about 30 seconds. Add the cream of tartar, increase the speed to medium-high, and continue to whip, watching carefully, until they are white, thick, voluminous, and the consistency of shaving cream, about 90 seconds. Slowly sprinkle in the granulated sugar and continue to whip until stiff peaks form and the sugar is incorporated, about 60 seconds.

3. Transfer the egg whites to a large bowl in order to accommodate the remaining ingredients. Gently fold one quarter of the almond flour mixture into the whites, followed by the vanilla. Gradually fold in the remaining almond mixture until a thick, gloppy batter forms.

4. Following the illustrations on page 214, fill the prepared pastry bag with the batter. Twisting the top of the bag to apply pressure, push the batter toward the bag tip and pipe onto the prepared baking sheets into forty 2-inch mounds, spaced about 1-inch apart. Use the back of a teaspoon or your finger dipped in a bowl of cold water to even out the shape and smooth the surface of the piped mounds. Let the macaroons rest at room temperature until the tops are dry and a smooth skin has formed, 1 to 2 hours.

5. Thirty minutes before baking, adjust an oven rack to the middle position and heat the oven to 325 degrees. Bake the cookies, 1 sheet at a time, until lightly browned, about 20 minutes, rotating the tray halfway through the baking time. Directly after baking, carefully slide the parchment with cookies onto a wire rack and cool completely. (The unfilled cookies can be stored in an airtight container at room temperature for up to 3 days, or frozen for up to 3 weeks; if frozen, let thaw at room temperature for 2 hours before filling.)

6. TO FILL THE COOKIES: Spread about 1 tablespoon of the buttercream over the flat sides of half the cookies and gently cover with the flat sides of the remaining cookies to form sandwiches; serve.

Vanilla Buttercream Frosting

MAKES ABOUT 2 CUPS

After adding half the butter to the mixture in step 2, the buttercream may look curdled; it will smooth out with additional butter.

2	large eggs
½	cup (3½ ounces) sugar
1	teaspoons vanilla extract
	Pinch salt
16	tablespoons (2 sticks) unsalted butter, softened but still cool, each stick cut into quarters

1. Combine the eggs, sugar, vanilla, and salt in the bowl of a standing mixer; place the bowl over a pan of simmering water (do not let the bottom of the bowl touch the water). Whisking gently but constantly, heat the mixture until it is thin and foamy and registers 160 degrees on an instant-read thermometer.

2. Remove the bowl from the water. Beat the egg mixture at medium-high speed until light, airy, and cooled to room temperature, about 5 minutes. Reduce the speed to medium and add the butter, 1 piece at a time (it may look curdled halfway through). Once all the butter is added, increase the speed to high and beat 1 minute, until light, fluffy, and thoroughly combined. (The buttercream can be covered and refrigerated for up to 5 days).

➤ VARIATIONS

Coffee Buttercream Frosting

Dissolve 2 tablespoons instant espresso in 1 table-spoon warm water. Follow the recipe for Vanilla Buttercream Frosting, omitting the vanilla and beating the dissolved coffee into the buttercream after the butter has been added.

Orange Buttercream Frosting

Follow the recipe for Vanilla Buttercream Frosting, omitting the vanilla and beating ½ tea-spoon orange extract into the buttercream after the butter has been added.

GAUGING SOFTENED BUTTER

Proper butter temperature is as crucial in a simple sugar cookie as it is in buttercream. You can, of course, use an instant-read thermometer to gauge properly softened butter, which should be between 65 and 70 degrees (about room temperature), or you can rely on a few helpful hints below.

 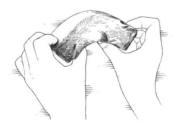 

1. When you unwrap the butter, the wrapper should have a creamy residue on the inside. If there's no residue, the butter is probably too cold.

2. The stick of butter should bend with little resistance and without cracking or breaking.

3. The butter should give slightly when pressed but it should still hold its shape.

6

SPAIN AND PORTUGAL

TAPAS

TAPEO IS THE SPANISH CUSTOM OF GATHERING before a meal for a glass of sherry and a sampling of snacks called *tapas*, which comes from the verb *tapar*, to cover, and originated with a bartender's habit of placing a little plate or slice of bread on top of a glass to keep the flies out. Soon some olives, almonds, or ham could be found on the plate and while restaurants today are better at keeping the flies at bay, *el tapeo* has evolved into the custom of traveling from bar to bar to taste the specialties of each. These small plates range from very simple to very elaborate, varying as much as the cooks who make them. Portugal has a similar tradition to tapas called *acepipes*. For the American cook, tapas make ideal party food and we set out to develop several of the most popular.

STUFFED MUSHROOMS
Champiñones Rellenas

WE'VE MADE OUR FAIR SHARE OF STUFFED mushrooms in the test kitchen and they almost always contain a bread-based stuffing with multiple ingredients. Tapas-style mushrooms on the other hand, are a simple affair—just a few well-chosen ingredients nestled inside each mushroom cap.

We started with the mushrooms. Taking a cue from prior tests on stuffed mushrooms, we chose white or cremini mushroom caps between 1½ and 2 inches in diameter. To intensify their flavor prior to stuffing, we roasted the mushrooms with olive oil, salt, and pepper. Once roasted, the mushrooms shrank to just the right size to hold enough filling for a two-bite tapa.

With our mushrooms down, we turned to our fillings. For our first filling, we chose the cheese for which Spain is most famous: Manchego (see right). A sheep's milk cheese from La Mancha, Manchego is a semi-firm, nutty cheese that works well with the earthy flavors of mushrooms. We topped the shredded cheese with strips of sweet roasted bell pepper. After filling the mushrooms, we slid them back into the oven for an additional 10 minutes until the cheese was bubbling. Garnished with minced parsley, these mushrooms were ready to serve.

For a second cheese-filled mushroom, we chose Spain's blue cheese, queso de Cabrales. A combination of goat, cow, and sheep's milk, this is a strongly flavored cheese, with earthy, salty flavors.

For a final mushroom filling, we chose Spain's popular sausage, chorizo, a cured pork sausage with a spicy heat. A slice of this sausage makes the perfect-sized disk to fit inside the mushroom cap. Because chorizo has a strong flavor that blooms further once heated, the only other ingredient needed was minced parsley for a bit of freshness and color.

PANTRY SPOTLIGHT

SPANISH CHEESES

While Spanish cheeses are not as widely available stateside as are French cheeses, they play as important a role in the recipes and customs of Spanish cuisine. Among the more widely available and better known cheeses are Manchego and queso de Cabrales.

Manchego, a sheep's milk cheese, is sold at three stages of maturation (*fresco,* aged for 60 days; *semicurado,* aged for two to four months; and *curado,* aged for more than six months). The majority of the Manchego available to us in the United States is semicurado; it has an ivory-yellow color and a rind (often dark brown or black) marked with cross-hatches. It tastes slightly sharp and full-flavored with a mild nuttiness.

Queso de Cabrales is a densely streaked blue cheese from Asturias in northern Spain, (there are over 30 officially registered varieties of cheese in this region). Cabrales is made from three different milks: unpasteurized cow's milk is mixed with varying quantities of goat's and sheep's milk. It obtains its characteristic blue veining in the limestone caves typical of the region where it matures for three to six months. It has a sharp, salty "blue" flavor and a moist, crumbly texture.

Stuffed Mushrooms with Roasted Red Peppers and Manchego

Champiñones Rellenas

MAKES 24 MUSHROOMS

Be sure to buy mushrooms with caps that measure between 1½ and 2 inches in diameter; they will shrink substantially as they roast. See page 409 for instructions on how to roast your own peppers. If you have a good amount of mushroom stems left over, consider saving them for another use, such as in Mushroom Pierogi (page 384) or Mushroom Ravioli (page 283).

24	(1½- to 2-inch-wide) white or cremini mushroom caps, wiped clean and stems removed completely
2	tablespoons extra-virgin olive oil
¼	teaspoon salt
⅛	teaspoon ground black pepper
2	ounces Manchego cheese, shredded (about ½ cup)
1	jarred roasted red pepper (about 4 ounces), rinsed, patted dry, and sliced into thin strips about 2 inches long (about ½ cup)
2	tablespoons minced fresh parsley leaves

1. Adjust an oven rack to the lower-middle position and heat the oven to 450 degrees. Line a baking sheet with aluminum foil. Toss the mushroom caps with the oil, salt, and pepper and lay gill side down on the prepared baking sheet. Roast the mushrooms until they release their juices and shrink, about 25 minutes.

2. Remove the caps from the oven and let them cool slightly. When cool enough to handle, flip the caps over, fill with the cheese, and place a few strips of roasted red pepper on top. (At this point, the stuffed mushrooms can be covered and refrigerated for up to 2 days before continuing with the recipe, but note you may need to cook the mushrooms an extra few minutes.)

3. Bake until the mushrooms are hot and the cheese is melted and bubbling, about 10 minutes. Transfer the mushrooms to a serving platter, sprinkle with the parsley, and let sit for 5 minutes before serving.

➤ VARIATIONS

Cabrales Stuffed Mushrooms

Cabrales is a strongly flavored blue cheese; feel free to substitute any other strongly flavored blue cheese, such as Stilton.

Follow the recipe for Stuffed Mushrooms with Roasted Red Peppers and Manchego, substituting 2 ounces Cabrales blue cheese, crumbled (about ½ cup), for the roasted red pepper and Manchego cheese.

Chorizo Stuffed Mushrooms

Use Spanish-style chorizo here, which is cured and sliceable, rather than Mexican-style chorizo, which is more crumbly (and often raw).

Follow the recipe for Mushrooms Stuffed with Roasted Red Peppers and Manchego, substituting 4 ounces chorizo, sliced into ¼-inch-thick disks, for the roasted bell pepper and Manchego, and increasing the baking time in step 3 until the chorizo is hot, about 20 minutes.

INGREDIENTS:
Jarred Roasted Red Peppers

Roasting your own peppers isn't difficult, but when you're in a rush, why bother—especially when you can buy peppers already roasted? And in the case of our Stuffed Mushrooms with Roasted Red Peppers and Manchego, using jarred roasted red peppers helps you pull together a tapa in short order. But are all brands of jarred roasted red bell peppers created equal? To find out, we collected six brands from local supermarkets. The top two brands, Divina and Greek Gourmet, were preferred for their "soft and tender texture" (Divina) and "refreshing," "piquant," "smoky" flavor (Greek Gourmet). The other brands were marked down for their lack of "roasty flavor" and for the unpleasantly overpowering flavor of the brines. These peppers tasted as if they'd been "buried under brine and acid." The conclusion? Tasters preferred peppers with a full, smoky, roasted flavor, a brine that was spicy but not too sweet, and a tender texture. Look for our winning brands, Divina and Greek Gourmet, in well-stocked supermarkets or specialty markets.

SALT COD FRITTERS
Pastéis de Bacalhau

FRITTERS, OR *PASTÉIS*, ARE SMALL DEEP-FRIED savory cakes made with meat, fish, or vegetables. Salt cod fritters are among Portugal and Spain's best loved fritters. But too often these fritters can taste overly fishy or salty. And some are fried so poorly that the cakes turn leaden and greasy. We aimed to replicate the perfect cod fritter—a golden-crusted cake of light creamy cod and mashed potato bound with béchamel, a creamy white sauce.

We started with the salt cod. Salting was developed long ago as a means of preserving foods. Modern processing of salt cod includes removing and salting the fillets immediately after being caught, then hanging them in the sun to dry. The salting process rids the fish of excess moisture, intensifying its flavor and giving it a firm, pleasantly chewy texture. In order to cook with salt cod, it must first be rinsed of excess salt then left to sit in clear water until it has both rehydrated and desalinated. This usually takes about 24 hours.

We tested a quick-soak method, similar to one we use for dried beans, where we rinsed the salt cod then brought it up to a boil, changed the water, and brought it to a boil again, but the method did not rid the fish of enough salt. Instead, we reverted to traditional means—soaking the cod in cool water for 24 hours, changing the water twice. It has soaked long enough once you can easily break apart the fish with your fingers.

Next we tested potatoes. We tried waxy new potatoes, russets, and Yukon Gold potatoes. The low-starch waxy potatoes were simply too granular to ensure the creamy consistency we wanted. Although both starchier russets and Yukon Golds worked well, tasters preferred russets for their superior texture and flavor.

With the two primary ingredients in order, we turned our attention to the creamy sauce that binds this mixture together—the béchamel, a classic milk sauce thickened with a roux (butter and flour). We wanted enough béchamel to help bind the fish and potato together and prevent the mixture from drying out. At the same time, we wanted to avoid a soggy, wet mixture. With ½ stick butter, ¼ cup flour, and ½ cup milk, we had just enough béchamel for our fritters. We also incorporated garlic to infuse the sauce with flavor. Preparing béchamel is not difficult. Simply melt the butter, whisk in the flour, then follow by whisking in milk. Once smooth and thickened, the sauce is done.

At this point, our fritters were nearly there but tasted a little lean. Some recipes add olive oil and we gave that a whirl—¼ cup olive oil gave us the richness and flavor the fritters lacked. We also added an egg for further richness and structure and 2 tablespoons of chopped parsley for freshness. And for lift, we added ⅛ teaspoon baking powder. Now it was time to start frying.

Although frying can be tricky, it's not difficult if you take a few precautions. To prevent fried foods from absorbing the oil during frying, you must keep the interior of the foods, specifically the water contained in the foods, above the boiling point (212 degrees). When above the boiling point, the outward pressure of the escaping water vapor keeps oil from soaking into the food. If the frying oil is not hot enough, on the other hand, it will seep into the food, making it greasy. The key is to get the oil hot enough at the start (we found 375 degrees works well with our fritters) to maintain a temperature during cooking that will keep the moisture in the food, in essence, boiling. After about six minutes in hot oil, our fritters were golden brown and light, not greasy. Since the fritters must be fried in two batches for even cooking, we kept the first batch warm in a low oven, while we fried the second batch. Some tasters liked them with just a squeeze of lemon while others thought a dip in Garlic Mayonnaise (page 225) or Romesco Sauce (page 225) was essential.

~~~

Salt Cod Fritters
Pastéis de Bacalhau
MAKES ABOUT 24 FRITTERS
Look for salt cod in fish markets and some well-stocked supermarkets. It is shelf stable and typically packaged in a wooden box or plastic bag. Be sure to change the water when soaking the salt cod as directed in step 1, or the fritters will taste unpalatably salty. Serve with Garlic Mayonnaise (page 225) or Romesco Sauce (page 225).

I	pound salt cod, checked for bones and rinsed thoroughly
12	ounces russet potatoes (about 2 small), peeled and cut into 1-inch chunks
4	tablespoons (½ stick) unsalted butter
3	medium garlic cloves, minced or pressed through a garlic press (about 1 tablespoon)
¼	cup unbleached all-purpose flour
½	cup whole or low-fat milk
¼	cup extra-virgin olive oil
I	large egg, lightly beaten
⅛	teaspoon baking powder
2	tablespoons minced fresh parsley leaves
⅛	teaspoon salt
⅛	teaspoon ground back pepper
4–6	cups vegetable oil (for frying)
I	lemon, cut into wedges (for serving)

1. Submerge the salt cod in a large bowl of cool water; cover and refrigerate until the cod is soft enough to break apart easily with your fingers, about 24 hours, changing the water twice to rid the fish of excess salt.

2. Drain the salt cod, discarding the water. Place the salt cod and potato in a large saucepan and cover by 2 inches of water. Bring to a boil, then reduce to a simmer and cook until the cod and potatoes are tender, 15 to 20 minutes.

3. Meanwhile, melt the butter in a small saucepan over medium heat. Add the garlic and cook until fragrant, about 30 seconds. Whisk in the flour and cook for 1 minute. Slowly whisk in the milk and cook, whisking constantly, until the béchamel is thickened and smooth, about 3 minutes. Set aside to cool slightly.

4. Drain the cod and potatoes thoroughly, then transfer to a large bowl. Using a fork, mash the cod and potatoes into small pieces. Stir in the béchamel, olive oil, egg, baking powder, parsley, salt, and pepper until well incorporated and the mixture has a creamy consistency. (At this point, the mixture can be refrigerated in an airtight container for up to 2 days. Let stand for 30 minutes before frying.)

5. Adjust an oven rack to the middle position, place a large paper towel–lined plate on the rack, and heat the oven to 200 degrees. Measure 3 inches of vegetable oil into a large Dutch oven and heat to 375 degrees. (Use an instant-read thermometer that registers high temperatures or clip a candy/deep-fat thermometer onto the side of the pan.) Using two spoons, carefully scoop 12 golf ball–sized fritters into the hot oil. Fry, stirring to prevent them from sticking, until golden, about 6 minutes. Transfer the fritters to the plate in the oven using a wire spider or slotted spoon. Return the oil to 375 degrees and repeat with the remaining cod mixture. Serve immediately with the lemon wedges.

COCKTAIL MEATBALLS IN TOMATO-SAFFRON SAUCE
Albondigas al Azafrán

ALBONDIGAS TRANSLATE SIMPLY AS MEATBALLS and feature in many traditional Spanish dishes. When made and served for tapas, they're bite-sized and often served from a *cazuela* (Spanish-style baking dish) swimming in a flavorful saffron-infused sauce. Our goal was to recreate this dish for the American table.

Our first focus was the meatballs. After reviewing several recipes, we noticed that the meatballs aren't much different from Italian meatballs. The basics are very similar—a combination of ground meat (we like beef and pork), along with egg yolk (for richness and structure), bread mixed with milk to form a paste (for tenderness), and seasonings like salt, pepper, and parsley.

While cheese is not traditional in these meatballs, tasters felt that the addition might improve things, so we added a little grated Manchego cheese (for more information, see page 218). In lieu of Manchego, Parmesan also works well. Because these meatballs are meant to be consumed in one bite, we made them quite small—just 1 teaspoon of meatball mixture to make ½-inch-round meatballs. After browning the meatballs in a nonstick skillet (to prevent the meatballs from sticking and breaking apart), we removed them from the pan to prepare the sauce.

Making use of the fond (the browned bits left behind in the pan), we started by cooking the *sofri-git*, or onion and tomato, in the now-empty pan, carefully scraping up the browned bits. We next added chicken broth and white wine to the pan, along with the aromatics. At this point, the sauce was plenty flavorful, and we added the meatballs back and cooked them through.

The Spanish often employ the use of a *picada*, a paste made from ground bread, almonds, and sometimes garlic and herbs, to flavor and thicken soups, stews, and sauces. For our sauce, we chose a combination of ground almonds, parsley, garlic, saffron, and paprika. Once the meatballs were cooked through, we stirred in the picada to infuse the sauce with vibrant flavor and an enticing aroma. And while we don't keep a stash of cazuelas on hand for serving, any shallow serving platter or gratin dish can be used.

Cocktail Meatballs in Tomato-Saffron Sauce
Albondigas al Azafrán
MAKES 35 TO 40 SMALL MEATBALLS

We like to use a nonstick skillet in this recipe because it prevents the tender meatballs from sticking to the pan and breaking apart. Serve with toothpicks or cocktail forks.

MEATBALLS

2 slices high-quality white sandwich bread, torn into small pieces
⅓ cup whole milk
8 ounces (85 percent lean) ground beef
8 ounces ground pork
½ ounce Manchego or Parmesan cheese, grated (about ¼ cup)
2 tablespoons minced fresh parsley leaves
1 large egg yolk
1 medium garlic clove, minced or pressed through a garlic press (about 1 teaspoon)
¾ teaspoon salt
⅛ teaspoon ground black pepper
2 tablespoons olive oil

SAUCE

1 small onion, minced
1 small tomato, cored, seeded, and chopped medium
1 cup low-sodium chicken broth
½ cup dry white wine
2 bay leaves

PICADA

1 tablespoon minced fresh parsley leaves
1 tablespoon finely chopped almonds
2 medium garlic cloves, minced or pressed through a garlic press (about 2 teaspoons)
¼ teaspoon saffron threads, crumbled
¼ teaspoon paprika
Salt and ground black pepper

1. FOR THE MEATBALLS: In a large bowl, mash the bread and milk together to form a smooth paste. Add the ground meats, Manchego, parsley, egg yolk, garlic, salt, and pepper to the mashed bread and mix until uniform. Shape the mixture into ½-inch-round meatballs (1 teaspoon per meatball; you should have 35 to 40 meatballs).

2. Heat the oil in a 12-inch nonstick skillet over medium-high heat until shimmering. Add half of the meatballs and brown on all sides, about 10 minutes, reducing the heat if the oil begins to smoke. Transfer the meatballs to a paper towel–lined plate and repeat with the remaining meatballs. Discard all but 1 tablespoon of the oil left in the skillet.

3. FOR THE SAUCE: Add the onion to the oil left in the skillet and cook over medium heat, scraping up any browned bits, until very soft and lightly browned, 6 to 9 minutes. Stir in the tomato and cook for 1 minute. Stir in the broth, wine, and bay leaves, then carefully return the meatballs to the skillet. Cover and simmer until the meatballs are just cooked through, 5 to 10 minutes.

4. FOR THE PICADA: While the meatballs cook, mash together the parsley, almonds, garlic, saffron, paprika, ⅛ teaspoon salt, and a pinch pepper. When the meatballs are cooked, remove and discard the bay leaves. Stir the picada into the sauce and season with salt and pepper to taste. Transfer the meatballs and sauce to a serving dish and serve immediately.

JAMÓN SERRANO

Jamón Serrano, or Serrano ham, is frequently found on the tapas table. This rich, earthy, sweet and salty air-cured ham is produced in several towns in the Andalusian mountain region. Jamón Serrano always comes from white pigs that have been fattened intensively (unlike Spain's other air-cured ham, the coveted *jamón Ibérico*, which comes from the black-bristled, boar-like Ibérico pig). Once slaughtered, the haunches (called jamón Serrano) and shoulder hams (called *paleta*) are salted with coarse-grain sea salt and air-cured for at least 12 months, and in extreme cases as long as 32 months. Jamón Serrano is very similar to Italy's *prosciutto di Parma* in texture and flavor. Like its Italian neighbor, jamón Serrano is served very thinly sliced and eaten on its own, yet it also is cooked with any number of meat and fish dishes. Costing as much as $25 per pound and available only in specialty markets, jamòn Serrano is a delicacy to be savored.

SIZZLING SHRIMP IN GARLIC SAUCE
Gambas al Ajillo

EVEN IF YOU CAN'T SMELL *GAMBAS AL AJILLO* approaching the table, you can usually hear it. It arrives in a *cazuela* (Spanish-style baking dish), still sizzling as the juices from the briny pink shrimp mingle with the hot, spicy garlic oil. Often served with crusty bread to sop up the garlic oil once the shrimp have been finished off, this dish is among Spain's most popular tapas. We knew we'd need to make a few alterations in this dish for the home cook. Because few households have a stash of cazuelas in their pantry, we needed to find an alternate cooking vessel. And we needed to determine just the right cooking technique so our shrimp were plump and flavorful.

We began with the baking dish. We knew that we wanted a dish that could hold all the shrimp in one to two layers, and if it could go from oven to table, even better. A gratin dish (roughly 11 by 7 inches) is perfectly suited for this recipe, but we also found that an ovenproof skillet works well.

We started with some flavorful extra-virgin olive oil and found 1 cup was perfect to cook 1½ pounds of shrimp—any more and the finished oil lacked the intense flavor obtained from cooking this amount of shrimp; any less and there was not nearly enough oil in which to dip the bread.

With the oil in our baking dish, we added various amounts of freshly minced garlic until we found 2 tablespoons (or six medium cloves) just right. Dried chiles are usually added to the oil, but we found hot pepper flakes a more convenient alternative and 2 tablespoons added plenty of heat. Last we added a generous 2 tablespoons of minced parsley for color and freshness. With our flavorful cooking oil in order, we turned our attention to cooking the shrimp.

Traditionally, this dish is served with small shrimp, but tasters preferred large shrimp. (Also, in early tests, we found that smaller shrimp cooked through more quickly and thus were apt to overcook.) Cooking the shrimp is a swift process. Once the garlic oil was prepared, we dropped in the shrimp and returned the dish to the oven. We started with a hot 450 degrees and worked our way up to 500 degrees, which produced just what we'd hoped—sweet, tender shrimp with an alluring sizzle.

Sizzling Shrimp in Garlic Sauce
Gambas al Ajillo
SERVES 6 TO 8 AS A FIRST COURSE

We use large shrimp (31 to 40 per pound) in this recipe. If using extra-large shrimp, extend the cooking time slightly—we don't advise using smaller shrimp, as they cook through too quickly. This dish is best presented straight from the oven while still sizzling, so have everything prepped before you start cooking, and have a trivet set on the table for the hot dish. Serve with crusty bread to dip in the flavorful oil.

1	cup extra-virgin olive oil
6	medium garlic cloves, minced or pressed through a garlic press (about 2 tablespoons)
2	bay leaves
2	tablespoons red pepper flakes
2	tablespoons minced fresh parsley leaves
1½	pounds large shrimp (31 to 40 per pound), peeled and deveined
	Salt and ground black pepper

1. Adjust an oven rack to the middle position and heat the oven to 500 degrees. Pour the oil into a shallow casserole dish that measures roughly 11 by 7 inches. Add the garlic, bay leaves, pepper flakes, and parsley and bake until the garlic is fragrant and sizzling, 2 to 4 minutes.

2. Add the shrimp to the sizzling oil and continue to bake, stirring once, until the shrimp are just cooked through, 2 to 3 minutes. Remove and discard the bay leaves. Season with salt and pepper to taste and serve immediately from the baking dish.

SPANISH TORTILLA

A SPANISH TORTILLA IS A SAVORY, VELVETY potato and egg cake similar to an omelet or frittata. Served in wedges, it is, perhaps, Spain's most recognizable tapa. Along with potatoes and eggs, the tortilla also typically contains lots of olive oil for flavor and moisture. The best tortillas are firm enough to cut into wedges, but still tender—never tough. But we've encountered both dry and greasy tortillas, so it would be one of our goals to carefully consider both the technique for preparing the tortilla and the amount of oil required.

We started with the potatoes. Starchy, creamy potatoes are universally called for in this dish, so we immediately began testing with russets and Yukon Golds. The russets ended up edging out the Yukon Golds for their creamier texture. We knew we wanted the potatoes thinly sliced as is traditional and found that ⅛-inch-thick slices worked perfectly. Along with the potatoes, onions are commonly found in this dish. Yellow Spanish onions are typically used, but we found that Vidalias and other similar mild, sweet onions also work well.

We next focused our attention on cooking technique. Many recipes start by frying the potatoes and onions in up to 2 cups of olive oil, which seemed excessive to us. Our hunch was confirmed when we found ourselves pouring off excess oil from our finished tortilla. We tested lesser amounts and found that ½ cup was enough to cook the potatoes and onions and add richness and flavor to the finished tortilla.

Next, beaten eggs are added to the potato mixture. Some recipes finish cooking the tortilla on the stovetop, but flipping the tortilla to finish cooking the top proved cumbersome. Instead, we turned to a technique we use for frittatas—cooking the tortilla just until the eggs are set (about 1 minute) then transferring the tortilla to the oven to finish cooking through (about 9 minutes). Once the tortilla was puffed and had started to pull away from the sides of the skillet, it was ready. Obviously, a nonstick skillet is essential to guarantee easy release of the tortilla. While the tortilla is usually cooled and served at room temperature, it can also be served hot from the skillet—the choice is up to you.

Spanish Tortilla

MAKES ONE 10-INCH TORTILLA,
SERVES 6 TO 8

We like to use russet potatoes here for their earthy flavor; however, Yukon Gold potatoes can be substituted. Using a 10-inch nonstick skillet here is important; do not use a smaller or larger skillet, because the cooking times will not apply. For a deeply golden brown crust that is traditional in southern parts of Spain, see the Spanish Tortilla with a Golden Crust variation. The tortilla can be served warm or at room temperature. Serve with Garlic Mayonnaise (page 225) or Romesco Sauce (page 225).

½	cup extra-virgin olive oil
1	pound russet potatoes (about 3 medium), peeled and sliced into ⅛-inch-thick rounds
1	medium onion, halved and sliced ⅛ inch thick
	Salt
10	large eggs
¼	teaspoon ground black pepper

1. Adjust an oven rack to the middle position and heat the oven to 425 degrees. Heat the oil in a 10-inch ovenproof nonstick skillet over medium heat until shimmering. Add the potatoes, onion, and ½ teaspoon salt and stir to coat thoroughly. Cover and cook, stirring occasionally, until the potatoes and onion are soft, 8 to 10 minutes.

2. Whisk the eggs, pepper, and 1 teaspoon salt together until uniformly yellow. Pour the eggs over the potatoes, stir gently to combine, and continue to cook until the eggs begin to set, about 1 minute.

3. Transfer the skillet to the oven and bake until the eggs are cooked, the top is puffed, and the edges have pulled away slightly from the sides of the pan, about 9 minutes. Use a rubber spatula to loosen the tortilla from the skillet, then carefully slide it onto a carving board. Slice into wedges and serve. (The tortilla can also be made up to 4 hours in advance and served at room temperature.)

➤ VARIATION

Spanish Tortilla with a Golden Crust

This extra step is not necessary, but does make for an attractive presentation and is common in southern Spain.

Follow the recipe for Spanish Tortilla, returning the finished tortilla in the skillet to medium-high on the stovetop until lightly browned on the bottom, about 1 minute, using a spatula to peek at the crust as it cooks. To unmold the tortilla so that the browned side faces up, simply slide the tortilla onto a large plate, then place a serving platter over the top, and, firmly grasping both plates, flip the tortilla onto the serving platter, browned side up.

SPANISH DIPPING SAUCES

ALLIOLI AND ROMESCO ARE TWO OF SPAIN'S most popular dipping sauces. Allioli is an emulsion of garlic, olive oil, and eggs that is very similar to the garlicky French mayonnaise *aioli*. A food processor, rather than hand-whisking, makes quick work of this sauce. Romesco is a bright red, nut-thickened sauce that gets its color from the dried sweet piquant romesco pepper. We use red bell peppers in place of hard-to-find romesco peppers, along with traditional ingredients like tomatoes, garlic, almonds, sherry vinegar, and olive oil. Authentic versions are ground together in a mortar and pestle, but we prefer the more contemporary food processor. Both sauces can be served with crudités or see individual recipes for further serving suggestions.

Garlic Mayonnaise
Allioli
MAKES ABOUT I CUP

This finished sauce contains raw eggs. Extra-virgin olive oil is too strong to be used alone here; if you do not have regular olive oil, use equal parts extra-virgin olive oil and vegetable oil. We use ground white pepper because it's not visible in the finished allioli, but black pepper can be substituted. Serve as a dipping sauce with crudités or use as a sandwich spread—tasters particularly liked slices of Spanish Tortilla (page 224) spread with allioli and slipped between pieces of crusty bread.

2	large egg yolks
4	teaspoons juice from I lemon
I	medium garlic clove, minced or pressed through a garlic press (about I teaspoon)
⅛	teaspoon sugar
	Salt and ground white pepper (see note)
¾	cup olive oil

Process the yolks, lemon juice, garlic, sugar, ¼ teaspoon salt, and ⅛ teaspoon pepper together in a food processor until combined, about 10 seconds. With the machine running, gradually add the oil through the feed tube in a slow, steady stream, about 30 seconds. Scrape down the sides of the bowl with a rubber spatula and process for 5 seconds longer. Season with salt and pepper to taste. (The allioli can be refrigerated in an airtight container for up to 3 days.)

Romesco Sauce
MAKES ABOUT 2 CUPS

If you like, roast your own red peppers (see page 409) and substitute 3 whole roasted peppers for the jarred peppers. For our tasting of jarred roasted red peppers, see page 219. We like to serve Romesco Sauce with Salt Cod Fritters (page 220) and Spanish Tortilla (page 224). Romesco sauce is also excellent spooned over grilled or broiled chicken and fish, or used as a dipping sauce for crudités.

1   slice high-quality white sandwich bread

3   tablespoons slivered almonds, toasted
     (see page 135)

1   (12-ounce) jar roasted red peppers (about
     1 ¾ cups), drained, rinsed, and patted dry
     (see note)

1   small ripe tomato, cored, seeded, and
     chopped medium

2   tablespoons extra-virgin olive oil

4½   teaspoons sherry vinegar

1   medium garlic clove, minced or pressed
     through a garlic press (about 1 teaspoon)

¼   teaspoon cayenne pepper
     Salt and ground black pepper

Toast the bread in a toaster at the lowest setting until the surface is dry but not browned. Slice the bread into rough ½-inch pieces (you should have about ½ cup). Process the bread pieces and almonds in a food processor until the bread and nuts are finely ground, 10 to 15 seconds. Add the red peppers, tomato, oil, vinegar, garlic, cayenne, and ½ teaspoon salt and continue to process until the mixture has a mayonnaise-like texture, 20 to 30 seconds. Season with salt and pepper to taste. (The sauce can be refrigerated in an airtight container for up to 3 days.)

SANGRÍA

SANGRÍA, SPAIN'S WELL-KNOWN PARTY drink, is often consumed without much thought, but there's no reason why it can't be better than the sweet concoctions served in most punch bowls. Working to find the right ingredient proportions for a standard 750-milliliter bottle of wine, we started by testing the other building blocks of sangría: orange and lemon slices, juice, sugar, and orange-flavored liqueur.

After tinkering with various proportions of cut-up fruit, we settled on a ratio of two oranges to one lemon. We tried limes, too, but found them too bitter. We did note that two sliced oranges and one sliced lemon in the pitcher made it difficult to pour the sangría, so we opted to squeeze the juice from one of the oranges. We also tried peeling the fruit, on the theory that the zest and pith might be contributing some bitterness, but without them, the sangría tasted too winey and a bit flat. Last, we tried mashing the fruit and the sugar together gently in the pitcher before adding the liquids. This improved the sangría by releasing some juice from the fruit and oils from the zest.

We wondered whether the type of sugar was important, since granulated, superfine, and a simple syrup of sugar dissolved in water all appeared in recipes. The flavor difference turned out to be infinitesimal, as did any difference in the smoothness of the drink, as each one dissolved completely. What did matter was the amount of sugar—¼ cup gave the punch a pleasant, but not cloying, sweetness.

The orange liqueur that is part of all sangría recipes also provides some sweetness and fruitiness. We tried expensive brands such as Cointreau, Curaçao, and Grand Marnier, as well as the more pedestrian triple sec, which was the surprise winner for its bold, sweet flavor. One-quarter cup of triple sec was just right; less, or none, made for a bland and one-dimensional sangría.

With the basic formula down, we turned to the choice of wine. Across the board, bartenders, wine merchants, and Spanish restaurateurs all advised us to keep it cheap. They argued that the addition of sugar and fruit would throw off the balance of the wine, so why spend a lot on something carefully crafted and pricey? Our tests so far had been done with a discount liquor store's house-label Merlot, a medium-bodied wine that cost a whopping $4.49 a bottle. Other wines we had tried included Beaujolais-Villages, which tasters thought too fruity and light; Zinfandel, which tasted bright and acidic; jug Burgundy, which was somewhat richer and rounder; and Rioja, which tasters found a bit flat and dull. We tried a more expensive Merlot (priced at $16.99), but only one taster out of five preferred the sangría made from it. Our advice, then, is to use cheap wine whose character you know and can live with. Fruity, pleasant Merlot is a good choice.

A number of recipes suggested preparing the sangría ahead of time and letting it rest in the refrigerator before serving. When all was said and done, we came to consider the resting time essential. After tasting an eight-hour-old sangría, a freshly made batch seemed harsh and edgy. Rest assured, though, if you can't stand the anticipation, two hours of refrigeration serves the purpose adequately.

Sangría

SERVES 4

The longer sangría sits before drinking, the more smooth and mellow it will taste. A full day is best, but if that's impossible, give it an absolute minimum of two hours to sit. Use large, heavy, juicy oranges and lemons for the best flavor. Doubling or tripling the recipe is fine, but you'll have to switch to a large punch bowl in place of the pitcher. We tried several inexpensive wines, and tasters thought most of them performed well in this recipe. A fruity Merlot is an especially good choice.

2	large juice oranges, washed; one orange sliced, remaining orange juiced
1	large lemon, washed and sliced
¼	cup sugar
¼	cup triple sec
1	(750-milliliter) bottle inexpensive, fruity, medium-bodied red wine, chilled (see note)

1. Add the sliced orange and lemon and sugar to a large pitcher; mash gently with a wooden spoon until the fruit releases some juice but is not totally crushed, and the sugar dissolves, about 1 minute. Stir in the orange juice, triple sec, and wine; refrigerate for at least 2 hours and up to 8 hours.

2. Before serving, add 6 to 8 ice cubes and stir briskly to distribute the settled fruit and pulp; serve immediately.

Gazpacho

GAZPACHO WAS FIRST DEVELOPED AS PEASANT fare and included simply bread, olive oil, garlic, salt, and vinegar. After tomatoes and bell peppers arrived in Spain from America, they too became part of the mix and are now viewed as essential to this ice-cold, uncooked vegetable soup. (For information on the more simple style of gazpacho, white gazpacho, see page 230.) Gazpacho is often referred to as "liquid salad" in its native Spain. That slang name may be more apt on these shores, though, as many American gazpacho recipes instruct the cook to simply puree all the vegetables together in the blender. The resulting mixture is more like a thin vegetable porridge with an anonymous vegetal flavor, whereas we were looking for a soup with clearly flavored, distinct pieces of vegetable in a bracing tomato broth. With our preference for a chunky-style soup established, we had to figure out the best method for preparing the vegetables and seasoning this refreshing Spanish classic.

Although it was a breeze to use, the blender broke the vegetables down beyond recognition. The food processor performed somewhat better, especially when we processed each vegetable separately. This method had distinct pros and cons. On the pro side were ease and the fact that the vegetables released some juice as they broke down, which helped flavor the soup. The con was that no matter how we finessed the pulse feature, the vegetable pieces were neither neatly chopped nor consistently sized. This was especially true of the tomatoes, which broke down to a pulp. The texture of the resulting soup was more along the lines of vegetable slush, which might be acceptable given the ease of preparation, but was still not ideal. On balance, the food processor is a decent option, especially if you favor speed and convenience, so we've included a variation using it.

Needless to say, we preferred the old-fashioned, purist method of hand chopping the vegetables. It does involve some extra work, but it went much more swiftly than we'd imagined, and the benefits to the gazpacho's texture were dazzling. Because the pieces were consistent in size and shape, they not only retained their individual flavors but also set off the tomato broth beautifully, adding immeasurably to the whole. This was just what we were after.

One last procedural issue we investigated was the resting time. Gazpacho is best served ice-cold, and the chilling time also allows the flavors to develop and meld. We found that four hours was the minimum time required for the soup to chill and the flavors to blossom.

Several of the key ingredients and seasonings also bore some exploration. Tomatoes are a star player here, and we preferred beefsteak to plum because they were larger, juicier, and easier to chop. Gazpacho is truly a dish to make only when local tomatoes are plentiful. We made several batches using handsome supermarket tomatoes, but the flavor paled in comparison to those batches made with perfectly ripe, local, farm-stand tomatoes. We considered skinning and seeding them, but not a single taster complained when we didn't, so we skipped the extra steps.

When it came to peppers, we preferred red to green for their sweeter flavor. But red was less popular in the onion department; tasters rejected red onions, as well as plain yellow, as too sharp. Instead, they favored sweet onions, such as Vidalia or Maui, and shallots equally. We did note, however, that any onion was overpowering if used in the quantities recommended in most recipes (especially in the leftovers the next day), and the same was true of garlic, so we dramatically reduced the quantity of both. To ensure thorough seasoning of the whole mixture, we marinated the vegetables briefly in the garlic, salt, pepper, and vinegar before adding the bulk of the liquid. These batches had more balanced flavors than the batches that were seasoned after all the ingredients were combined.

The liquid component was also critical. Most recipes called for tomato juice, which we sampled both straight and mixed in various amounts with water and canned low-sodium chicken broth. The winning ratio was 5 cups of tomato juice thinned with 1 cup of water to make the 6-cup total we needed. The water cut the viscosity of the juice just enough to make it brothy and light, but not downright thin. Given our preference for ice-cold

DICING THE VEGETABLES FOR GAZPACHO

TOMATOES

1. Core the tomatoes, halve them pole to pole, and working over a bowl to catch all the juices, scoop out (and reserve) the inner pulp and seeds with a dinner spoon. Cut the pulp into ¼-inch dice.

2. Cut the empty tomato halves into ¼-inch slices. Turn the slices 90 degrees and cut into even ¼-inch pieces.

PEPPERS

1. Slice a ¾-inch section off both the tip and stem ends of the peppers. Make one slice through the wall of each pepper, lay the pepper skin side down on a board, and open the flesh, exposing the seeds and membranes.

2. Cut away and discard the seeds and membranes. Cut the flesh into ¼-inch strips. Turn the strips 90 degrees and cut them into even ¼-inch pieces. Also, cut the tips and tops into even ¼-inch dice.

CUCUMBERS

1. Cut a ¾-inch section off both ends of the cucumbers. Halve the cucumbers lengthwise and scoop out the seeds with a dinner spoon. Cut each seeded half lengthwise into ¼-inch strips.

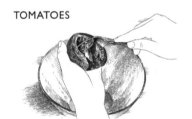

2. Turn the strips 90 degrees and cut into even ¼-inch pieces.

gazpacho, we decided to add ice cubes instead of straight water. The ice cubes helped chill the soup while providing water as they melted. We also conducted a blind tasting of tomato juices in which Welch's showed very well.

Finally, a word about the two primary seasonings, vinegar and olive oil. Spain is a noted producer of sherry, so it follows that sherry vinegar is a popular choice for gazpacho. When we tasted it, along with champagne, red wine, and white wine vinegars, the sherry vinegar was our favorite by far, adding not only acidity but also richness and depth. If you find that your stock of sherry vinegar has run dry, white wine vinegar was the runner-up and can be substituted. The oil contributes both flavor and richness to this simple soup, and only extra-virgin will do. Liquid or not, would you dress a beautiful summer salad with anything less?

Classic Gazpacho
MAKES 3 QUARTS, SERVING 8 TO 10

This recipe makes a large quantity because the leftovers are so good, but it can easily be halved if you prefer. We prefer to use Welch's tomato juice here. Traditionally, the same vegetables used in the soup are also used as a garnish. If that appeals to you, cut additional vegetables while you prepare those called for in the recipe. Other garnish possibilities include croutons (see page 154), chopped black olives, chopped hard-cooked eggs (see recipe on page 63), and finely diced avocado.

3   medium ripe beefsteak tomatoes (about 1½ pounds), cored and cut into ¼-inch cubes
2   medium red bell peppers (about 1 pound), cored, seeded, and cut into ¼-inch cubes
2   small cucumbers (about 1 pound), one peeled and the other with skin on, both seeded and cut into ¼-inch cubes
½   small sweet onion, such as Vidalia, Maui, or Walla Walla, or 2 large shallots, minced (about ½ cup)
⅓   cup sherry vinegar
2   medium garlic cloves, minced or pressed through a garlic press (about 2 teaspoons)
    Salt and ground black pepper

5   cups tomato juice (see note)
1   teaspoon hot sauce (optional)
8   ice cubes
    Extra-virgin olive oil, for serving

1. Combine the tomatoes, bell peppers, cucumbers, onion, vinegar, garlic, 2 teaspoons salt, and black pepper to taste in a large (at least 4-quart) nonreactive bowl. Let stand until the vegetables just begin to release their juices, about 5 minutes. Stir in the tomato juice, hot sauce (if using), and ice cubes. Cover tightly and refrigerate to blend the flavors, at least 4 hours or up to 2 days.

2. Season with salt and pepper to taste and remove and discard any unmelted ice cubes. Serve cold, drizzling each portion with about 1 teaspoon extra-virgin olive oil and topping with the desired garnishes (see note).

➤ VARIATIONS
Quick Food Processor Gazpacho
Follow the recipe for Classic Gazpacho, using the same ingredients and quantities. Core and quarter the tomatoes and process them in a food processor until broken down into ¼- to ¾-inch pieces, about 12 pulses; transfer to a large bowl. Cut the cored and seeded peppers and seeded cucumbers into rough 1-inch pieces and process them separately until broken down into ¼- to ¾-inch pieces, about 12 pulses; add to the bowl with the tomatoes. Mince the garlic as instructed, then add to the bowl with the vegetables along with salt, vinegar, and ground black pepper to taste; continue with the recipe as directed.

Spicy Gazpacho with Chipotle Chiles and Lime
A garnish of finely diced ripe avocado is a must with this variation.

Follow the recipe for Classic or Quick Food Processor Gazpacho, omitting the optional hot pepper sauce and adding 2½ tablespoons minced canned chipotle chiles in adobo sauce, ¼ cup minced fresh cilantro leaves, 6 tablespoons lime juice, and 2 teaspoons grated lime zest along with the tomato juice and ice cubes.

WHITE GAZPACHO

Ajo Blanco

WHEN AMERICANS HEAR THE WORD GAZPACHO they invariably think tomatoes, but in Spain, gazpacho is often made without tomatoes or any vegetables at all. Traditional white gazpacho, *ajo blanco*, contains seven ingredients: blanched almonds, olive oil, vinegar or lemon juice, garlic, bread, salt, and water. These ingredients are pureed, chilled, and garnished with halved, and sometimes skinned, green grapes. Some variations include pine nuts in addition to the almonds, egg yolks or whites for texture and frothiness, and melon or diced green apple for a garnish. But for the most part, white gazpacho recipes are fairly consistent, at least in terms of the ingredients.

To get a handle on this subject, we prepared three recipes from our library that exhibited the greatest variation. The resulting soups elicited a mix of reactions from tasters. Many complained about the gritty and gummy texture of the soups and predominant flavors of vinegar and garlic. Some tasters suggested it wasn't worth continuing with recipe development. Still, other staffers insisted that white gazpacho, as they had tasted it in Spain, could be delicious.

Our goal here was clear: The soup needed to have a balanced acidity and sweetness, a smooth and creamy texture, and a refreshing spiciness. We started development from the ground up.

Several gazpacho recipes we had found during our research work use *verjus*, unfermented wine grape juice, for body and flavor. We have used verjus in the past and love it for its pleasant fruitiness, muted acidity, and dynamic flavor. We sensed that it was perfect for the job, and our hunch paid off, at least in part. White gazpacho made with verjus was outstanding: bright, strong, and fully flavored, without any cloying sweetness. The garlic flavor was piercing and clean.

Unfortunately, this test was only partly helpful. Verjus can be extraordinarily hard to find, so it was out of the question to call for it in our final recipe, but we could use it for inspiration. To approximate the flavor, we decided to puree and strain green grapes for their juice and to add a touch of lemon juice to balance out the sweetness. While far from the unique flavor of verjus, our homemade grape juice was a good substitute.

It was important for us to keep in mind that grapes vary in ripeness, their tartness inconsistent. Our initial testing was with very unripe grapes, so we added only a little lemon juice. We bought ripe, sweet grapes for subsequent testing and increased the amount of lemon juice to approximate the desired tartness. The soup should be a bit tart but not sour.

For the almonds, we ended up choosing blanched slivered almonds. We lightly toasted one batch, but tasters found the toasted flavor overpowering, so we skipped this step.

Our recipe was beginning to take shape. The bread was the last major issue to examine. While most recipes suggest a hearty country loaf as the best thickening agent, we wondered how other choices would perform. Sourdough bread was too strong and disrupted the delicate sweet and sour flavor of the gazpacho. Baguettes were wasteful; after the crust was removed and discarded there was very little bread left. We were happy with the results from a pullman-style sandwich loaf, such as Pepperidge Farm. The bread is mild-flavored and has a tight crumb, which easily broke down into the gazpacho. Since this bread is so readily available, we decided to use it in our final recipe.

At this point, we realized that processing the bread too long caused the gumminess tasters had so disliked in our early tests. If the bread is fully incorporated into the soup, the texture becomes gummy. We found that adding soaked bread to the blender and pulsing it 10 times was just enough to combine and disperse some of the bread's starch. While not all of the bread was incorporated into the gazpacho, it added just enough starch to slightly thicken the soup.

After processing the bread, the soup was strained to attain a palatable consistency. We found that a fine-mesh strainer was crucial to achieving a silky smooth texture. We were surprised by the amount of solids (bread, almond, and grape) left after blending. If these solids were left in the gazpacho, the texture was grainy and unpleasant. The ideal white gazpacho should have the thickness and texture of heavy cream.

The traditional garnish for white gazpacho is halved green grapes. Because we included grapes in the soup itself, we looked for some alternatives. We found several traditional recipes with tart green apple or melon garnishes. Tasters liked the apple but were indifferent about the melon. The pale cream color of apple subtly accented the soup's slight green hue. A few threads of mint further emphasized the green. And a few crisp, garlicky croutons added a pleasing contrast to this silky soup.

White Gazpacho
Ajo Blanco
MAKES ABOUT 6 CUPS, SERVING 4 TO 6

Using the right amount of bread here is crucial; bread slices can vary in size depending on the brand, so we found it best to weigh the bread rather than count slices. Texture is a major consideration when preparing this refreshing soup. Don't overprocess the bread, and be sure to pass the soup through a fine-mesh strainer. Also, don't skimp on the garnishes here because they add important flavor and texture. Chop the apples for the garnish just before serving so they don't turn brown.

SOUP

4	ounces high-quality white sandwich bread (4 to 5 slices), crusts discarded and torn into ½-inch pieces
4½	cups ice water (roughly half water, half ice)
8	ounces slivered almonds (about 2 cups)
8	ounces seedless green grapes, washed and stemmed (about 2 cups)
3	medium garlic cloves, minced or pressed through a garlic press (about 1 tablespoon)
4	teaspoons juice from 1 lemon, plus extra to taste
	Salt
⅛	teaspoon cayenne pepper
2	tablespoons extra-virgin olive oil

GARNISH

2	cups croutons (see page 154)
1	small Granny Smith apple, peeled, cored, and chopped fine
1	tablespoon coarsely chopped fresh mint leaves

1. Combine the bread and 1½ cups of the ice water in a medium bowl and set aside for several minutes to soften.

2. Meanwhile, process the almonds, grapes, garlic, lemon juice, 1¼ teaspoons salt, cayenne, and remaining 3 cups of ice water in a blender until the mixture is completely liquefied, about 3 minutes (depending on the size of the blender, you may have to do this in two batches).

3. Add the bread mixture and olive oil and pulse until the mixture looks frothy and a bit lumpy, about 10 pulses. (Do not overprocess; the mixture will not be smooth.) Strain the pureed mixture through a fine-mesh strainer set over a medium bowl, pressing on the solids to extract all of the liquid. Discard the solids.

4. Season the soup with salt and lemon juice to taste. Cover tightly and refrigerate to blend the flavors, at least 2 hours or up to 2 days. Serve cold, garnishing each portion with croutons, apple, and mint.

SPANISH SHELLFISH STEW
Zarzuela

FIND A COUNTRY WITH A COASTLINE AND you will find fish stew in the culinary repertoire. Less well-known than France's *bouillabaisse* and Italy's *cioppino* is Spain's version of shellfish stew, *zarzuela*. Chock-full of shellfish like lobsters, clams, and mussels, this tomato-based stew is seasoned with saffron and paprika and thickened with a *picada*, a flavorful mixture of ground almonds, bread crumbs, and olive oil. Unlike most fish stews, zarzuela contains no fish stock—instead the shellfish release their rich liquors into the pot as they cook. The shells, too, serve to fortify the flavorful broth. We liked the idea of a stew that didn't rely on a finicky stock and set about mastering this popular Spanish dish.

We gathered together several recipes for zarzuela and started cooking. Like many Spanish recipes, zarzuela starts with a *sofrito* of onions, garlic, and

REMOVING TENDONS FROM SCALLOPS

The small, rough-textured, crescent-shaped tendon that attaches the scallop to the shell will toughen when cooked. Use your fingers to peel the tendon away from the side of each scallop before cooking.

red bell peppers, cooked until softened. Paprika, saffron, red pepper flakes, and bay leaves join the sofrito to form a distinctly Spanish flavor base. Tomatoes and dry white wine are then added to the pot to form the liquid base of the broth. Fresh tomatoes are available for such a brief time in the U.S. that we immediately reached for canned. We looked at both whole and diced tomatoes. Although we had to chop the whole tomatoes, their flavor and texture in this stew were preferable to canned diced tomatoes. Some recipes also include brandy in addition to white wine. After making the broth with and without, tasters favored the depth of flavor that brandy lent to the dish.

With our broth and flavoring settled, it was now time to turn our attention to the shellfish. Typically, the dish includes lobster, shrimp, scallops, mussels, and clams. After some discussion, we decided to omit lobster from the lineup in our master recipe, as lobster can be difficult for the home cook to tackle. Instead, we'd offer lobster as a variation. Looking at the shellfish remaining, we knew we'd have to do some fiddling to make up for the lack of flavorful lobster.

Knowing that shells contribute significant flavor to dishes, and given that we had decided to peel our shrimp before adding them to the stew (for easier eating), we thought we'd use the shrimp shells to enrich the broth's flavor. We sautéed the

shells in a touch of olive oil and then steeped them in the wine. We chose to do this at the outset of cooking, so the shells would have plenty of time to infuse the wine. A quick strain of the wine to remove the shells and we had a terrific flavor boost for our broth.

The final challenge was producing a stew with perfectly cooked shellfish. Since each of the different shellfish was a different size, requiring a different cooking time, we knew we'd have to stagger the time when we added each variety. After some trial and error, we determined that the clams should be added to the stew first, followed by the mussels and scallops, and finally the shrimp.

A picada is stirred into the shellfish stew at the end to add both body and flavor. Most picadas contain ground almonds and fried bread ground into crumbs. We found that fried bread (which required a significant amount of oil) turned our stew greasy. Instead we toasted fresh bread crumbs with a little olive oil. We also tossed in the almonds with the bread crumbs, so they too toasted, intensifying their flavor. Stirring the picada into the shellfish stew once the shellfish was cooked thickened the broth perfectly, and its rich, mellow flavor rounded out the bold stew. All that was left to do was sprinkle the dish with a handful of chopped fresh parsley and a squeeze of lemon for a bright fresh finish to this Spanish favorite.

Spanish Shellfish Stew
Zarzuela
SERVES 4

Be sure to buy shrimp with their shells on and reserve the shells when cleaning the shrimp; they add important flavor to the cooking liquid in step 2. We like Sauvignon Blanc or any non-oaky Chardonnay in this recipe. Any small clams, such as littlenecks work well, but avoid large clams which will not only take up more room in the pot, but will exude more liquid than desired, diluting the broth. The cooking time of the scallops will depend on their size; we used extra-large scallops (about 2 inches in diameter and 1 inch thick), but if your scallops are smaller (about 1 inch in diameter and ½ inch thick), they will cook more quickly and should be added to the pot with the shrimp.

PICADA

¼ cup slivered almonds (about 1 ounce)

2 slices high-quality white sandwich bread, torn into quarters

2 tablespoons extra-virgin olive oil

⅛ teaspoon salt

Pinch ground black pepper

STEW

¼ cup olive oil

16 extra-large shrimp (21 to 25 per pound), peeled, deveined, and shells reserved

1½ cups dry white wine (see note)

1 medium onion, minced

1 medium red bell pepper, stemmed, seeded, and chopped fine

Salt

3 medium garlic cloves, minced or pressed through a garlic press (about 1 tablespoon)

1 teaspoon sweet paprika

¼ teaspoon saffron threads, crumbled

⅛ teaspoon red pepper flakes

2 bay leaves

2 tablespoons brandy

1 (28-ounce) can whole tomatoes, tomatoes chopped medium and juice reserved

16 littleneck clams (about 1½ pounds), scrubbed (see note)

16 mussels (about 8 ounces), scrubbed and debearded if necessary (see the illustration on page 156)

8 large sea scallops (about 8 ounces), tendons removed (see the illustration on page 232)

1 tablespoon minced fresh parsley leaves

Ground black pepper

1 teaspoon juice from 1 lemon, plus extra to taste

1. FOR THE PICADA: Adjust an oven rack to the middle position and heat the oven to 375 degrees. Pulse the nuts in a food processor to fine crumbs, about 15 pulses. Add the bread, olive oil, salt, and pepper and continue to pulse the bread to coarse crumbs, about 10 pulses. Spread the mixture out evenly over a rimmed baking sheet and toast, stirring often, until golden brown, about 10 minutes; set aside to cool.

2. FOR THE STEW: Heat 1 tablespoon of the oil in a medium saucepan over medium heat until shimmering. Add the reserved shrimp shells and cook until pink, about 5 minutes. Off the heat, stir in the wine, cover, and let steep until ready to use.

3. Heat the remaining 3 tablespoons oil in a large Dutch oven over medium heat until shimmering. Add the onion, bell pepper, and ¼ teaspoon salt and cook until the onion is softened and lightly browned, 7 to 10 minutes. Stir in the garlic, paprika, saffron, pepper flakes, and bay leaves and cook until fragrant, about 30 seconds. Stir in the brandy and simmer for 30 seconds. Stir in the tomatoes with their juice and cook until slightly thickened, 5 to 7 minutes.

4. Strain the wine mixture into the Dutch oven through a fine-mesh strainer, pressing on the shrimp shells to extract as much liquid as possible; discard the shells. Continue to simmer until the flavors have melded, 3 to 5 minutes. (At this point, the broth can be cooled and refrigerated in an airtight container for up to 1 day. Bring the broth to a simmer in a covered large Dutch oven over medium heat before continuing.)

5. Increase the heat to medium high, add the clams, cover, and cook, stirring occasionally, until the first few clams begin to open, about 5 minutes. Add the mussels and scallops, cover, and continue to cook until most of the clams have opened, about 3 minutes longer. Add the shrimp, cover, and continue to cook until the shrimp are pink and cooked through and the clams and mussels have opened, about 2 minutes longer.

6. Discard the bay leaves and any mussels or clams that have not opened. Stir in the picada and parsley and season with salt, pepper, and lemon juice to taste. Serve immediately.

➤ VARIATION

Spanish Shellfish Stew with Lobster

In Spain, this stew is made with langostinos, or prawns. Fresh prawns are difficult to find stateside, so we chose to use lobster instead. You will need to kill and break down the lobsters before cooking. This is much easier to do when the lobsters have been chilled in the freezer for 15 to 20 minutes (do not overfreeze); expect some residual movement in the lobster pieces for a short while afterward.

233

Follow the recipe for Spanish Shellfish Stew, reducing the amount of clams, mussels, and shrimp to 12 each. Remove the claws, tail, and legs from 2 (1¼- to 1½-pound) lobsters following the illustrations below. Add the lobster legs to the pot with the shrimp shells in step 2. In step 5, add the lobster claws to the pot with the clams and add the lobster tails to the pot with the mussels and scallops; cook as directed.

PREPARING LOBSTER

1. Freeze the lobsters for 15 to 20 minutes (do not overfreeze). Holding the lobster firmly with a kitchen towel, firmly drive the tip of a large heavy-duty chef's knife through the back of the upper portion of the lobster's head, then swing the knife down through the head to sever.

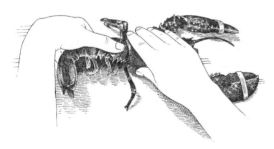

2. Using your hands, twist the tail free from the body.

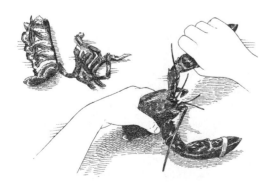

3. Using your hands, twist the legs free from the body and, finally, twist the claws free from the body.

CLAMS AND CHORIZO
Amêijoas na Cataplana

AMÊIJOAS NA CATAPLANA, OR CLAMS AND chorizo, is a classic combination of two of Portugal's prized ingredients—spicy pork sausage and plump clams—steamed in a spicy tomato broth. Sometimes called *cataplana* for short (which refers to the hinged, clam-shaped vessel in which the dish is traditionally cooked), the dish makes a hearty supper served with crusty bread to soak up the flavorful broth. But just because something is simple doesn't mean it is always prepared well. This was obvious after we tested a handful of authentic cataplana recipes. Many recipes included a plethora of ingredients such as bell peppers and mushrooms, which muddied the flavors of the dish. We wanted to pare this dish back to its simple roots to highlight the briny clams and spicy sausage.

To start, we steamed two batches of clams available in our area: soft-shell clams (better known as steamers) and littlenecks. We quickly ruled out the steamers, agreeing their shells were too brittle and prone to breaking apart in the broth. The littlenecks were perfect—plump and flavorful.

We turned to the sausage next. Most recipes called for a dried sausage such as chorizo, a spicy cured sausage, or linguiça (a garlicky Portuguese sausage). After testing batches made side by side, we found that we preferred the spicy meatiness of the chorizo. (Chorizo comes in two varieties, Mexican and Spanish; in keeping with tradition we chose Spanish. For more information on both varieties of chorizo, see page 3.) We found that ½ pound sausage added abundant flavor to the dish but didn't overpower the clams. We also preferred our sausage cut into larger pieces than most recipes suggested, agreeing they added more textural contrast than sausage diced small.

Our next step was to address the broth. Off the bat we included onion and garlic, traditional ingredients in the dish's aromatic base. Tomatoes, the base of the broth, were up next. Canned whole tomatoes worked well with a modicum of additional effort to cut them into pieces, and they held up better than canned diced tomatoes. To finish the broth, we added white wine for acidity; ¾ cup was

SCRUBBING CLAMS

Use a soft brush, sometimes sold in kitchen shops as a vegetable brush, to scrub away any bits of sand trapped in the shell.

enough to brighten the flavors of the dish without leaving an alcohol aftertaste. Finally, a number of recipes we found in our research added freshly minced parsley just before serving—2 tablespoons was just enough to give this dish a bright color and some herbal lift.

Clams and Chorizo
Amêijoas na Cataplana
SERVES 4

Tasters preferred Spanish-style chorizo (see page 3 for more information on chorizo) to Portuguese linguiça sausage in this recipe, but linguiça can be substituted if desired. Serve with garlic toasts or crusty bread to sop up the heady broth.

1	tablespoon extra-virgin olive oil
½	pound chorizo sausage, sliced in half lengthwise, then sliced crosswise into ½-inch-wide pieces
1	medium onion, minced
3	medium garlic cloves, minced or pressed through a garlic press (about 1 tablespoon)
1	(28-ounce) can whole tomatoes, tomatoes chopped medium and juice reserved
¾	cup dry white wine
4	pounds littleneck clams, scrubbed (see the illustration above)
2	tablespoons minced fresh parsley leaves

1. Heat the oil in a large Dutch oven over medium heat until shimmering. Add the chorizo and cook, stirring occasionally, until browned and slightly rendered, about 4 minutes. Transfer the chorizo to a paper towel–lined plate, leaving the fat in the pot.

2. Add the onion to the fat in the pot and cook over medium-high heat until softened, 5 to 7 minutes. Stir in the garlic and cook until fragrant, about 30 seconds. Stir in the tomatoes with their juice and wine and simmer until thickened slightly, about 3 minutes.

3. Increase the heat to high and stir in the clams and reserved chorizo. Cover and cook, stirring once, until the clams have opened, 4 to 8 minutes.

4. Use a slotted spoon to transfer the clams and chorizo to a large serving bowl or individual bowls; discard any clams that haven't opened. Stir the parsley into the broth, then pour the broth over the clams and serve.

PAELLA

DESPITE ITS CURRENT REPUTATION AS A colorful Spanish restaurant staple, *paella* hasn't always been categorized as a party food. Developed just outside the region of Valencia, Spain, by agricultural workers as a means of cooking large quantities of rice, traditional paella was anything but fancy. Cooked in flat-bottomed pans over an open wood fire and flavored with local, easy-to-find ingredients such as snails, rabbit, and green beans, this utilitarian dish was a far cry from what we know as paella today. Paella has evolved into a big production piece with a commanding list of ingredients, ranging from artichokes, green beans, broad beans, bell peppers, peas, and pork to chorizo, chicken, lobster, scallops, calamari, fish, mussels, clams, and shrimp. We set out to create a simpler, less daunting recipe for the home cook that could be made in a reasonable amount of time, with a manageable number of ingredients, and without a special paella pan.

While none of the recipes we found in our research were perfect, some did offer important clues. One was that if the rice and proteins were to cook uniformly, they had to be arranged in a not-too-thick, relatively even layer. Crowding or mounding the ingredients in a pile was a surefire route to disaster, as a recipe for eight made in a 12-inch skillet quickly proved. So what was the best paella pan replacement? A Dutch oven held the same amount of ingredients as a 14- to 15-inch paella pan, fit perfectly on the stovetop, and offered the best distribution and retention of heat.

Looking over various recipes, there seemed to be five key steps: browning the sturdier proteins, sautéing the aromatics, toasting the rice, adding liquid to steam the rice, and, last, cooking the seafood. As for proteins, we quickly ruled out lobster (too much work), diced pork (sausage would be enough), fish (flakes too easily and gets lost in the rice), and rabbit and snails (too unconventional). We were left with chorizo, chicken, shrimp (preferred over scallops or calamari), and mussels (favored over clams).

We began by browning the chicken and chorizo, which would give the meat a head start and lend necessary flavor to the fat used to sauté the onion and garlic later on. While many recipes call for bone-in, skin-on chicken pieces, to save time we opted for boneless, skinless thighs (richer in flavor and less prone to drying out than breasts). We seared both sides of some halved chicken thighs in olive oil, not cooking them all the way through to make sure they would be tender and juicy once added back in with the rice to complete cooking.

Spanish cuisine uses the trio of onions, tomatoes, and garlic—called *sofrito*—as the building block for its rice dishes. We began by sautéing one finely diced onion until soft and stirring in a large dose (2 tablespoons) of minced garlic. Traditionally, the final ingredient, tomato, is added in seeded, grated form. To avoid the mess (as well as skinned fingers), we used a can of drained diced tomatoes instead, mincing the pieces for a similarly fine consistency and cooking the resulting pulp until thick and slightly darkened.

With the sofrito complete, we could now focus on the rice. Long-grain rice seemed out of place (a paella is not supposed to be light and fluffy) and medium-grain rice didn't seem quite right. Out of the short-grain varieties, Valencia was preferred for its creamy but still distinct grains, with Italian Arborio following closely behind (see "Pantry Spotlight: Valencia Rice," page 237). One cup of rice was nowhere near enough for a small crowd; 2 cups was just right. Once the rice was sautéed in the sofrito just long enough to become slightly toasted and coated with the flavorful base, it was time to add the liquid. For its clean, full-bodied flavor, tasters preferred rice cooked in straight chicken broth to clam juice or a combination of the two. Replacing some of the broth with a bit of white wine provided an additional layer of flavor.

PANTRY SPOTLIGHT

SAFFRON

Cultivated from the crocus flower, saffron is a delicate red thread pulled from the stigma (the female part of the crocus) by hand at harvest each October. Because each flower yields only 3 stigmas, it can take the *mondadoras* (petal strippers) up to 200 hours to yield only 1 pound of saffron—thus explaining why it is the most expensive spice in the world. Once harvested, the saffron threads are roasted over a gentle charcoal or gas fire to dry and then stored in a dark place free of humidity.

Saffron is available in two forms—threads and powder. Conventional wisdom says that deep, dark red threads are better than yellow or orange threads. We held a small tasting of broths infused with different saffron samples and the threads with considerable spots of yellow and orange did in fact yield the weakest-colored and flattest-tasting broths. The reddest threads yielded intensely flavorful broths.

Conventional wisdom also cautions against the use of powdered saffron. Some sources say that inferior threads are used to produce the powder and that coloring agents may be added. While this may be true, we found powdered saffron purchased from a reputable source to be just as flavorful and fragrant as even the highest-quality threads. (Note that you will need about one-third to one-half the volume measurement of threads.)

In conclusion, when shopping for saffron, look for dark red threads without any interspersion of yellow or orange threads. Or, to save money, choose a good-quality powdered saffron.

POWDERED SAFFRON   SAFFRON THREADS

Saffron gives paella its brilliant color and adds a distinctive earthy flavor. Most recipes call for steeping the saffron threads in a pot of simmering liquid, but, to save time and keep this a one-pot dish, we added cold liquid along with ½ teaspoon of saffron and 2 bay leaves (as well as the browned chicken and chorizo) to the rice and brought everything to a boil. After a few quick stirs to make sure the saffron was distributed evenly, we covered the pot and turned things down to a simmer, leaving the paella untouched until the rice had soaked up most of the liquid. But this all-stovetop steaming method had a major flaw. While the rice in the middle of the pot was cooked perfectly, grains along the edges were partially undercooked. Our solution was simple: transfer the pot to the oven to finish cooking. Once the rice came up to a simmer, we placed the pot in a 350-degree oven and 15 minutes later the grains had evenly absorbed nearly all of the liquid. Once the seafood was added and the rice given more time to cook, there wasn't a raw grain to be seen.

With the rice nearly done, the quick-cooking seafood was ready to make its appearance. The mussels, placed in the pot hinged-end down so that they could open readily, cooked in about 10 minutes.

EQUIPMENT: Paella Pans

Paella pans are simply shallow round pans with looped handles on either side. While we use a Dutch oven for our paella recipe, using a paella pan makes for an attractive tableside presentation. While these pans can be quite expensive, we did find cheaper alternatives, all of which worked well. So, unless you plan on making paella frequently, choose a cheaper pan. Of those we tested, we liked La Ideal Enameled Steel 13.25-inch Paella Pan, which has a very reasonable price of just $29.99. As an added bonus, this enameled pan doesn't need to be seasoned as do the more traditional cast-iron paella pans.

THE BEST PAELLA PAN

The La Ideal Enameled Steel 13.25 inch Paella Pan came out on top among the competition and is reasonably priced ($29.99).

When the shrimp were added raw along with the mussels, they were perfectly juicy but bland. The solution? We briefly marinated the raw shrimp in olive oil, salt, pepper, and minced garlic to boost the flavor.

Now all the paella lacked was vegetables. Peas and bell pepper were the most vibrant, least fussy choices. We chose to scatter the peas over the rice toward the end of cooking which allowed them to retain their bright green hue. In paella, bell pepper often gets lost when mixed with the sofrito or when stirred into the rice. Wanting to showcase it, we decided to use strips of sautéed red bell pepper as a garnish.

At this point, we could easily have called it a day, but several people demanded *soccarat,* the crusty brown layer of rice that develops on the bottom of a perfectly cooked batch of paella. Curious to see if we could get this to work in a Dutch oven, we waited until the dish was completely cooked and then removed the lid and put the pot back on the stove. After only about five minutes, a spoon inserted into the depths of the rice revealed nicely caramelized grains. Before we let anyone dig in, we allowed the paella to rest, covered, so the rice could continue to firm up and absorb excess moisture. After adding a garnish of parsley and lemon, we were done. Our final recipe had all the flavor and sparkle of this world-famous Spanish dish minus the absurdly hefty workload.

Paella

SERVES 6

This recipe is for making paella in a Dutch oven; the Dutch oven should be 11 to 12 inches in diameter with at least a 6-quart capacity. With minor modifications, it can also be made in a paella pan (see the variation "Paella Using a Paella Pan or Skillet"). Spanish chorizo is the sausage of choice for paella, but Mexican chorizo or linguiça is an acceptable substitute (see page 3 for more information on chorizo). Soccarat, a layer of crusty browned rice that forms on the bottom of the pan, is a traditional part of paella. We have provided instructions to develop soccarat in step 6; if you prefer, skip this step and go directly from step 5 to 7.

I	pound extra-large shrimp (21 to 25 per pound), peeled and deveined
	Olive oil
9	medium garlic cloves, minced or pressed through a garlic press (about 3 tablespoons)
	Salt and ground black pepper
I	pound boneless, skinless chicken thighs, trimmed and halved crosswise
I	red bell pepper, stemmed, seeded, and cut into ½-inch-wide strips
8	ounces Spanish chorizo, sliced ½ inch thick on the bias
I	medium onion, minced
I	(14.5-ounce) can diced tomatoes, drained, minced, and drained again
3	cups low-sodium chicken broth
2	cups Valencia or Arborio rice
⅓	cup dry white wine
½	teaspoon saffron threads, crumbled
2	bay leaves
12	mussels (about 6 ounces), scrubbed and debearded if necessary (see the illustration on page 156)
½	cup frozen peas, thawed
2	tablespoons minced fresh parsley leaves
I	lemon, cut into wedges (for serving)

1. Adjust an oven rack to the lower-middle position and heat the oven to 350 degrees. Toss the shrimp with 1 tablespoon oil, 1 teaspoon of the garlic, ¼ teaspoon salt, and ¼ teaspoon pepper in a medium bowl; cover with plastic wrap and refrigerate until needed. Season the chicken thighs with salt and pepper and set aside.

2. Heat 2 teaspoons oil in a large Dutch oven over medium-high heat until shimmering. Add the bell pepper and cook, stirring occasionally, until the skin begins to blister and turn spotty black, 3 to 4 minutes. Transfer the pepper to a small plate and set aside.

3. Add 1 teaspoon oil to the now-empty Dutch oven and heat until shimmering. Brown the chicken on both sides, 6 to 8 minutes, then transfer to a clean plate. Reduce the heat to medium, add the chorizo, and cook, stirring frequently, until deeply browned and the fat begins to render, 4 to 5 minutes. Transfer the chorizo to the bowl with the chicken and set aside.

4. Add enough oil to the fat in the Dutch oven to equal 2 tablespoons, add the onion, and cook over medium heat, stirring frequently, until softened, 5 to 7 minutes. Stir in the remaining 8 teaspoons garlic and cook until fragrant, about 30 seconds. Stir in the tomatoes and cook until the mixture begins to darken and thicken slightly, about 3 minutes. Stir in the chicken broth, rice, wine, saffron, bay leaves, and ½ teaspoon salt. Return the chicken and chorizo to the pot, increase the heat to medium-high, and bring to boil. Cover the pot, transfer to the oven, and cook until the rice absorbs almost all of the liquid, about 15 minutes.

5. Remove the pot from the oven, scatter the shrimp over the rice, insert the mussels into the rice (hinged side down so they stand upright), arrange the bell pepper strips in a pinwheel pattern, and scatter the peas over the top. Cover, return to the oven, and cook until the shrimp are opaque and the mussels have opened, 10 to 12 minutes.

6. OPTIONAL: If soccarat is desired, set the Dutch oven, uncovered, over medium-high heat for about 5 minutes, rotating the pot 180 degrees halfway through for even browning.

7. Let the paella stand, covered, for about 5 minutes. Discard the bay leaves and any mussels that have not opened. Sprinkle with the parsley and serve with lemon wedges.

Paella Using a Paella Pan or Skillet

A paella pan makes for an attractive and impressive presentation. Use one that is 14 to 15 inches in diameter. A 14-inch ovensafe skillet will work as well, but do not attempt to use anything smaller because the contents will simply not fit.

Follow the recipe for Paella, increasing the chicken broth to 3¼ cups and the wine to ½ cup. Before placing the pan in the oven, cover tightly with foil. For soccarat, cook the paella, uncovered, over medium-high heat for about 3 minutes, rotating the pan 180 degrees halfway through for even browning.

SKILLET-BAKED RICE WITH CHICKEN AND LEMONY MEATBALLS

Arroz con Costra

THIS BAKED RICE DISH IS SPAIN'S ANSWER TO a skillet supper. An array of meats such as chicken and pork mingle with lemony meatballs and chickpeas amid red pepper–infused rice, topped off with an egg crust. This dish might sound odd, but its variety of textures and layers of flavor is ultimately very satisfying. With so many ingredients, especially the choice of meat (some recipes include rabbit, chicken, pork, sausages, and meatballs), we knew we had to narrow them down to a manageable few. And keeping in mind that this is a one-pan meal, we aimed to streamline the recipe where possible, without compromising flavor or texture.

To narrow things down, we cooked several batches using various combinations of meat. We felt rabbit wasn't worth the bother and chose chicken instead. Meatballs were a must—any batch made without them elicited thumbs-down from tasters. With these two decided, we felt that the dish had plenty of heft, so pork and sausages were struck from the list. As a compromise, we chose to use ground pork in our meatballs and add bacon to the dish to further reinforce the rich pork flavor that is traditional.

For the meatballs, we combined ground pork with bread moistened with milk to ensure tenderness. We also added an egg for richness and structure. With the basic mixture in order, we turned our attention to flavor. Some recipes for this dish include ground almonds in the meatballs and tasters loved the richness and texture they added. And lemon, in the form of grated lemon zest, added a citrusy kick that truly made these meatballs stand out. Minced fresh parsley was the only herb necessary for a hit of freshness.

With the meatball mixture formed into 1-inch balls ready to be browned, we next turned our attention to the chicken, bacon, and chickpeas. For convenience and ease, we chose boneless, skinless chicken breasts and canned chickpeas. Many authentic recipes call for slab bacon cut into chunks, but with the limited availability of slab bacon in our supermarkets we opted for thick-cut sliced bacon, cut into medium-small dice. With our meats (and meatballs) prepped and assembled, it was time to start cooking. First, we cooked the bacon and then browned the chicken in its rendered fat. The meatballs were browned next. We then removed all the meat to a plate while we worked on the rice.

Bomba and *Calasparra* are medium-grain Spanish rices traditional to this dish, although you can use another medium-grain rice. (Long-grain rice can also be used, although the dish's texture won't be as creamy.) We added the rice to the skillet, along a garlicky red pepper puree (whirred together in a blender), which provided just enough liquid to scrape the fond from the bottom of the skillet. We then added more chicken broth to the skillet and nestled the browned meats and chickpeas into the rice, so that the whole dish could finish cooking together. At this point, we transferred the skillet to the oven for gentle, even cooking.

The final element to the dish, the egg crust, is somewhat like a souffléed omelet. Once the rice had absorbed the liquid, we removed the skillet from the oven and poured a mixture of whisked eggs and milk evenly over the top of the dish. Once back in the oven, the egg mixture puffs slightly and turns golden brown. At last we had produced a skillet supper worth writing home about.

Skillet-Baked Rice with Chicken and Lemony Meatballs

Arroz con Costra

SERVES 6

Spanish medium-grain rices such as Bomba or Calasparra are traditional in this dish, but you can substitute another medium-grain rice. Or, use an equal amount of long-grain rice, although the dish will be less creamy. A 12-inch skillet is essential to this recipe.

MEATBALLS

1	slice high-quality white sandwich bread, torn into small pieces
1	tablespoon milk
8	ounces ground pork
¼	cup slivered almonds, chopped fine
3	tablespoons minced fresh parsley leaves
1	large egg
1	tablespoon grated zest from 1 lemon
	Salt and ground black pepper

RICE

6	tablespoons olive oil
3	medium garlic cloves, peeled
4	cups low-sodium chicken broth
1	jarred roasted red pepper (about 4 ounces), rinsed and patted dry (about ½ cup)
4	ounces thick-cut bacon (about 3 slices), cut into ½-inch cubes
12	ounces boneless, skinless chicken breasts, cut into 1-inch chunks
	Salt and ground black pepper
2	cups medium-grain rice (see note)
1	cup canned chickpeas, drained and rinsed

EGG CRUST

7	large eggs
¼	cup whole milk
	Salt

1. FOR THE MEATBALLS: In a large bowl, mash the bread and milk together to form a smooth paste. Add the ground pork, almonds, parsley, egg, lemon zest, ½ teaspoon salt, and ¼ teaspoon pepper and mix until uniform. Shape the mixture into 1-inch-round meatballs (1 generous tablespoon per meatball; you

should have about 18 meatballs). Refrigerate the meatballs on a large platter or baking sheet until needed. (The meatballs can be prepared up to this point, covered, and refrigerated for up to 2 days.)

2. FOR THE RICE: Heat the oil and garlic cloves in a 12-inch ovenproof skillet over low heat until the garlic cloves are fragrant and softened, about 3 minutes. Using a slotted spoon, transfer the garlic to a blender (or food processor) leaving the oil in the skillet. Add ½ cup of the chicken broth and the roasted red peppers to the blender, and process until smooth, about 20 seconds; set aside.

3. Add the bacon to the skillet and cook until rendered and browned, 4 to 6 minutes. Transfer to a medium bowl, leaving the fat behind in the skillet.

4. Pat the chicken dry with paper towels and season with salt and pepper. Heat the fat left in the skillet over high heat until shimmering and brown the chicken on both all sides, about 5 to 8 minutes. Using a slotted spoon, transfer the chicken to the bowl with the bacon, leaving the fat in the skillet.

5. Adjust an oven rack to the middle position and heat the oven to 350 degrees. Add the meatballs to the fat left in the skillet and cook over medium-high heat until browned on all sides, 7 to 10 minutes. Using a slotted spoon, transfer the meatballs to the bowl with the chicken.

6. Add the rice and red pepper puree to the skillet and cook over medium heat, scraping up any browned bits, until the liquid reduces and the rice starts to look creamy, 2 to 3 minutes. Stir in the remaining 3½ cups broth, bring to a simmer, and cook, stirring often, until the rice swells and the liquid thickens, about 5 minutes. Stir in the reserved chicken, meatballs, bacon, and the chickpeas and return to a simmer, stirring often. Transfer the skillet to the oven (do not cover) and continue to cook, until the liquid is absorbed, 8 to 10 minutes.

7. FOR THE EGG CRUST: Meanwhile, whisk the eggs, milk, and 1 teaspoon salt together in a medium bowl. When the rice has absorbed most of the liquid in the skillet, pour the egg mixture evenly over the rice. Increase the oven temperature to 500 degrees and continue to bake until the top is browned, about 10 minutes. Remove the skillet from the oven and let it sit for 10 minutes before serving.

BRAISED CHICKEN WITH ALMONDS AND PINE NUTS

Pollo en Pepitoria

POLLO EN PEPITORIA IS A HEARTY BRAISED chicken dish flavored with a mixture of sherry, ground almonds, garlic, and saffron. It is said to date back to 13th-century Hispanic-Moorish cooking, but despite its long history, this dish was a newcomer to the test kitchen. Intrigued by its surprising combination of flavors, we set out to make the best pollo en pepitoria this side of the Atlantic.

Most authentic recipes start with a whole chicken, but we wanted our version of this recipe to be a bit simpler so we opted for quicker cooking, more convenient chicken parts. Using chicken parts also allowed us to customize the dish depending on if we wanted white meat or dark. We chose bone-in, skin-on parts. Just a little trimming of excess fat and skin was all the preparation the chicken pieces needed.

To begin, we browned the chicken in a Dutch oven to develop a fond—the base of the flavorful sauce. While the chicken rested on a plate, we cooked an onion in the pan, adding tomatoes once the onion had softened. Next, we added chicken broth and wine to the mix. In our research, we found that some recipes call for a dry white wine while others call for a dry (or "fino") sherry. We tested them both, side by side, and tasters unanimously chose the sauce with sherry—its deep, earthy flavor made this dish unique. Another ingredient important to the dish is a pinch of ground cinnamon. It adds a depth of flavor that isn't obvious, but is missed when omitted from the recipe. Once the broth and wine were added and the fond was scraped from the bottom of the pan, we placed the chicken back in the pan and covered it,

---

INGREDIENTS: Supermarket Chicken Broth

Most cooks today simply don't have the time to make homemade chicken broth. And it can take nearly as long just to choose from the confusing array of offerings in the supermarket: Alongside the standard metal cans of broth and the dehydrated bouillon powders sit dozens of broths sporting "aseptic" packaging (resealable paper cartons) and glass jars filled with "base" (chicken broth reduced to a concentrated paste). So which options are best? We recommend choosing a mass-produced, lower-sodium brand and checking the label for evidence of mirepoix ingredients (carrots, celery, onion, and herbs). In a tasting of all the widely available brands, Swanson Certified Organic was a clear winner. And if you don't mind adding water, Better Than Bouillon Chicken Base came in a very close second and was the favorite of several tasters. Swanson's less expensive "Natural Goodness" Chicken Broth was just about as good as the winner, though some tasters thought it tasted "overly roasted."

THE BEST CHICKEN BROTHS

SWANSON CERTIFIED ORGANIC FREE RANGE CHICKEN BROTH
Swanson's newest broth won tasters over with "very chickeny, straightforward, and honest flavors," a hearty aroma, and restrained "hints of roastiness."

BETTER THAN BOUILLON CHICKEN BASE
We're not ready to switch to a concentrated base for all our broth needs (you have to add water), but the 18-month refrigerator shelf life means it's a good replacement for dehydrated bouillon.

SWANSON "NATURAL GOODNESS" CHICKEN BROTH
Swanson's standard low-sodium broth was full of chicken flavor, but several tasters noted an out-of-place overly roasted flavor.

to finish cooking. When the chicken was done, we tented it with foil while we finished the sauce.

The last element to go into the skillet was the picada. A combination of ground almonds, pine nuts, parsley, and saffron, picada adds unmistakable body and flavor to the sauce. (For more about picada, see below.) For further texture and richness, we added a minced hard-cooked egg to the sauce as well. Once the sauce returned to a simmer, we cooked it until thickened, which took just a couple of minutes, then poured it directly over the chicken and we had a juicy, flavorful chicken dish easy enough to serve during the week and special enough for company.

Braised Chicken with Almonds and Pine Nuts

Pollo en Pepitoria

SERVES 4

Be sure to choose a sherry labeled "fino" which means it's dry. The picada is most easily ground into a paste in a food processor or in a mortar and pestle, but it can also be chopped by hand. Rice makes a good accompaniment to this dish.

PICADA

2	tablespoons chopped almonds
2	tablespoons chopped pine nuts
2	medium garlic cloves, minced or pressed through a garlic press (about 2 teaspoons)
1	tablespoon minced fresh parsley leaves
1/8	teaspoon saffron threads, crumbled
1	hard-cooked egg (page 63), minced

CHICKEN AND SAUCE

4	pounds bone-in, skin-on chicken pieces (split breasts cut in half, drumsticks, and/or thighs)
	Salt and ground black pepper
1	tablespoon olive oil, plus extra as needed
1	small onion, minced
1	small tomato, cored, seeded, and chopped medium
1/2	cup low-sodium chicken broth
1/2	cup dry sherry
	Pinch ground cinnamon

1. **FOR THE PICADA:** Process the nuts, garlic, parsley, and saffron in a food processor until paste-like, 12 to 15 seconds. Stir in the egg and set aside.

2. **FOR THE CHICKEN:** Pat the chicken dry with paper towels and season with salt and pepper. Heat the oil in a large Dutch oven over medium-high heat until just smoking. Brown half of the chicken on both sides, 5 to 8 minutes per side, reducing the heat if the pan begins to scorch. Transfer the chicken to a plate, leaving the fat in the pot. Return the pot with the fat to medium-high heat and repeat with the remaining chicken; transfer the chicken to the plate.

3. Pour off all but 1 tablespoon of the fat in the pot (or add olive oil if needed). Add the onion and cook over medium heat until softened, 5 to 7 minutes. Stir in the tomato, broth, sherry, and cinnamon, scraping up any browned bits.

4. Nestle the chicken, along with any accumulated juices, into the pot and bring to a simmer. Cover, turn the heat to medium-low, and simmer until the chicken is fully cooked and tender, about 20 minutes for the breasts (160 degrees on an instant-read thermometer) or 1 hour for the thighs and drumsticks. (If using both types of chicken, simmer the thighs and drumsticks for 40 minutes before adding the breasts.)

5. Transfer the chicken to a serving dish, tent loosely with foil, and let rest while finishing the sauce. Stir the picada into the sauce and return to a simmer until the sauce is thickened, 3 to 5 minutes. Pour the sauce over the chicken and serve.

CORE TECHNIQUE

THICKENING SAUCES AND STEWS

Many Spanish recipes are finished with a *picada*, a paste stirred into the sauce or stew as a thickening and flavoring agent. A picada is made up of ingredients such as bread crumbs, ground nuts (typically almonds), olive oil, garlic, herbs and/or spices all pounded together with a mortar and pestle (or more commonly these days with a food processor). Picadas are used to thicken all sorts of sauces such as Cocktail Meatballs in Tomato-Saffron Sauce (page 222), Spanish Shellfish Stew (page 232), and Braised Chicken with Almonds and Pine Nuts (at left).

FLAN

FLAN IS A DECEPTIVELY SIMPLE, CLASSIC Spanish dessert. Made with just a few ingredients that are readily available (sugar, eggs, and milk), it is similar in construction and flavor to other baked custards from around the world. This dessert is slightly lighter than a standard baked custard, with an ultra-creamy and tender texture. It also sports a thin sweet caramel that pools over the custard once unmolded. The perfect flan is mellow in flavor, neither too sweet nor too eggy. It should also be firm enough to unmold on a serving plate without collapsing. These would be our goals in developing an exemplary flan.

Eggs are integral to flan, so we started there. Not all recipes found in our research agreed on the number of eggs or the proportion of egg yolks to egg whites. Here's what we found when we started baking: Too many whites produced a custard that was almost solid and rubbery; too few egg whites, on the other hand, and our custard collapsed—egg whites, we discovered, give the custard structure. Egg yolks provide richness—too few and the flan tasted lean and too many left the flan tasting, well, too eggy. After much tinkering, we came up with what we consider the ideal ratio: 2 whites to 5 yolks. The resulting custard was tender yet not overly rich and firm enough to unmold easily.

Next we looked at the milk. We made our initial custard using whole milk, but it tasted too thin and the egg flavor dominated. Next we augmented the milk with heavy cream but the flan's richness seemed out of place and too close to its French neighbor, crème caramel. We reviewed recipes from Spanish and Latin American cookbooks and found that some include sweetened condensed milk, which is rich and creamy, without the intense fat of heavy cream. This made sense, so we swapped in some sweetened condensed milk for the whole milk. The resulting flan was more in line with the best flan we've eaten, but still a bit too rich. This was easily fixed by changing to 2 percent milk. We also enjoyed an extra bonus from the condensed milk—because it's sweetened, it made our dessert sweet enough so that we didn't need to include sugar.

Refining the flavors of the flan was easy. We tested varying amounts of vanilla, which received so-so remarks, but when we added grated lemon zest, a traditional flavoring in this dessert, tasters loved the citrus undertones. A mere ¼ teaspoon was all this dessert needed.

Finally, the crowning touch—the caramel. There are basically two methods of making caramel. In the dry method, you use only sugar, cooking it slowly until it melts and caramelizes. The wet method uses a combination of water and sugar. The sugar begins to dissolve in the water, then the mixture is simmered until the water evaporates and the sugar caramelizes. The dry method can be tricky to pull off, so we opted for the wet as a way of increasing the margin of success for the home cook.

While some recipes instruct you to pour the caramel in the mold (we use a cake pan) and then tilt the pan to coat the sides, we ended up burning our fingers. (A bowl of ice water nearby saved the day.) Because caramel is hot enough to cause serious burns, we rethought this method. Instead, we decided to coat only the bottom of the mold, reasoning that the caramel sinks to the bottom of the mold while baking anyway. When

SCIENCE:
The "Magic" of Sweetened Condensed Milk

These days, convenience food products are everywhere, but the trend is hardly new. Back in 1856, American home cooks began taking advantage of sweetened condensed milk, a shelf-stable dairy product based on discoveries made centuries earlier by cooks in India and Latin America. Packed with calories and nutrients, this "magical" product has been credited with everything from reducing the infant mortality rate to nourishing Civil War soldiers. But today it's mostly about dessert-making and convenience. Just pop open a can. Thick and rich, we use sweetened condensed milk to give our Flan (page 244) creamy flavor without the fatty richness of heavy cream.

Sweetened condensed milk is made commercially by flash-heating fresh milk and evaporating it, using a specialized vacuum drier (that's the "condensed" part). Once granulated sugar is added, the preservation process begins. The water-hungry granulated sugar and the natural sugar in the milk (lactose) pull in moisture from bacteria, killing them off in the process. The result is milk thickened to a gooey syrup—an ideal consistency for many desserts, such as our flan.

we unmolded the custard, the caramel still poured evenly over the top. This easier and safer method is our top choice.

How you bake flan and how long you bake it can make the difference between a great dessert and a mediocre, or even disappointing, one. After considerable experimentation, we determined that baking the custards at 350 degrees in a bain-marie, or water bath, to maintain an even, gentle heating environment, produced custards that were creamy and smooth. This involves simply placing the mold in a larger baking pan, then filling the baking pan with boiling water until it reaches partway up the sides of the pan of custard. We also found that lining the baking pan first with a towel further ensures that the bottom of the custard won't overcook.

Flan

SERVES 6

We prefer to use low-fat milk in this recipe, although any type of milk (even nonfat) can be used, resulting in varying degrees of richness. Note that the custard will look barely set once it reaches its doneness temperature of between 170 and 175 degrees, but it will firm up as it chills in the refrigerator. Be careful when working with the hot caramel in step 1.

½	cup (3½ ounces) sugar
2	tablespoons water
2	large eggs
3	large egg yolks
¼	teaspoon grated zest from 1 lemon
1	(14-ounce) can sweetened condensed milk
1½	cups low-fat milk (see note)

1. Adjust an oven rack to the middle position and heat the oven to 350 degrees. Place a kitchen towel in the bottom of a large baking dish or roasting pan and place a 9-inch cake pan in the center. Bring the sugar and water to a boil in a small saucepan, swirling the pan gently, until the sugar has dissolved, about 3 minutes. Reduce to a simmer and cook, gently swirling the pan occasionally, until the mixture has caramelized to a deep, dark mahogany color, 7 to 10 minutes. Following the illustration on the right, carefully pour the caramel into the cake pan and cool slightly until hardened.

2. Bring a kettle or large saucepan of water to a boil over high heat. Meanwhile, whisk the whole eggs and egg yolks together in a medium bowl until thoroughly combined, about 1 minute. Whisk in the zest, sweetened condensed milk, and low-fat milk. Pour the mixture into the cake pan and gently place the roasting pan on the oven rack. Being careful not to splash any water inside the pan of custard, pour the boiling water into the roasting pan until the water reaches halfway up the side of the cake pan. Bake until the center of the custard is just barely set, is no longer sloshy, and an instant-read thermometer inserted in the center registers 170 to 175 degrees, 30 to 40 minutes (start checking the temperature after 25 minutes).

3. Carefully remove the roasting pan from the oven and carefully transfer the cake pan to a wire rack and let cool to room temperature, about 2 hours. Wrap the cake pan with plastic wrap and refrigerate the custard until completely chilled, at least 2 hours and up to 24 hours.

4. Run a knife around the cake pan to loosen the custard. Invert a large serving platter over the top of the cake pan, and grasping both the cake pan and platter, gently flip the custard onto the platter, drizzling any extra caramel sauce over the top (some caramel will remain stuck in the pan). Serve immediately.

POURING CARAMEL FOR FLAN

Caramel is extremely hot and can cause serious burns, so care should be taken during this step. Before making the caramel, ready your water bath by placing a kitchen towel in the bottom of a large baking dish or roasting pan. Place a 9-inch cake pan in the center. Once the caramel is ready, carefully and slowly pour the caramel into the pan, being careful not to splash caramel onto yourself or outside of the cake pan.

VENEZUELAN CORN CAKES STUFFED WITH CHICKEN AND AVOCADO   **PAGE 46**

FISH AND CHIPS **PAGE 94**

SPANISH SHELLFISH STEW **PAGE 232**

CHINESE BARBECUED PORK   **PAGE 534**

SALERNO-STYLE SPAGHETTI WITH FRIED EGGS AND BREAD CRUMBS **PAGE 293**

MOROCCAN CHICKEN TAGINE WITH CHICKPEAS AND APRICOTS   **PAGE 424**

SESAME NOODLES WITH SWEET PEPPER AND CUCUMBER   **PAGE 508**

251

TANDOORI CHICKEN   **PAGE 457**

GARLIC-LEMON POTATOES **PAGE 352**

253

SICHUAN GREEN BEANS   **PAGE 505**

PROVENÇAL BEEF STEW **PAGE 195**

TORTILLA SOUP **PAGE 17**

MEXICAN STREET CORN **PAGE 13**

257

TIRAMISÙ   **PAGE 327**

FRENCH-STYLE MACAROONS **PAGE 215**

LINZERTORTE **PAGE 138**

7

ITALY

VEGETABLE TARTS

Torta alle Verdure

PIZZA MAY BE THE DISH THAT WENT ON TO international stardom, but there are numerous lesser-known savory Italian *tortas* (tarts) and pies equally deserving of the spotlight. One of these is a vegetable tart, a simple tart with an emphasis on seasonal vegetables while the other basic components—cheese and crust—play supporting roles. These tarts vary in style and ingredients: some have just a bottom crust, some have no crust at all, and others are completely encased in crust. Fillings may contain a thick, egg-based custard or just one type of cheese, but these tarts all have one thing in common: a commitment to seasonal freshness. With that in mind, we set out to develop a recipe for a vegetable tart that we could make any time of year.

But what was our ideal tart given this vast landscape? After spending many hours at the stove testing a variety of recipes, we found ourselves pining for simplicity. We were drawn to the tarts that were more delicate, used less filling, and whose vegetables were clearly discernable. Our ideal tart would feature a single vegetable and have a flavorful, cracker-like pie crust.

Focusing first on the crust, we liked the appearance of a traditional tart shell and knew it needed to be sturdy enough to support the toppings. Puff pastry was too delicate for our purposes and we wanted something with more flavor than regular pie dough. We learned that olive oil crusts are traditional in many regions of Italy, and so we eagerly decided to explore this idea. We tried out a few recipes we found and the results were disappointing. Overall these initial crusts ranged from greasy and tough to dry and crumbly. All of them were extremely difficult to roll out, and none of them were able to support a filling. But the olive oil added a terrific flavor so we pressed on.

Cobbling together our own recipe, we tossed out the idea of a rolled out crust and took a good look at our favorite press-in butter tart crust (used in the Smoked Salmon Tart on page 83). Swapping olive oil for the butter, our first attempt at an olive oil press-in crust fared little better than the first few recipes we had tried. It was greasy and crumbly with a texture that was much too delicate—more akin to a shortbread than a sturdy tart dough—but patting the tart dough into the pan was a welcome reprieve from the hassles of rolling it out. Also, this dough had a little sugar in it and tasters liked how the sweetness balanced the assertive flavor of the olive oil.

To make the crust sturdier, we tested various amounts of oil. Adding more oil made the dough more tender and delicate, while using less made it stronger. When we added too little oil, however, the dough became tough and a bit chewy. Six tablespoons of oil (compared to the eight tablespoons we had been using) proved to be ideal.

Parbaking the crust before adding any filling helped ensure that the crust baked evenly. To prevent the crust from shrinking as it baked, we found it important to freeze the shell first and then bake it using pie weights. At the recommendation of one test cook, we also decided to sprinkle a thin layer of Parmesan over the tart shell. Not only did this add good flavor and texture, but the Parmesan added a layer of protection from the watery vegetable topping, ensuring that our crust would be crisp and sliceable, not soggy.

With the crust in place, we turned our attention to the filling. Following the direction of several recipes we liked, we landed on the idea of having a thin, creamy layer of cheese over the bottom of the tart (on top of the Parmesan crust), which would then be topped with a layer of vegetables. We tried shredded whole milk mozzarella, fresh mozzarella, and ricotta mixed with a little mozzarella and Parmesan. The two mozzarella-only versions yielded tough, unappealing, rubbery layers of cheese that congealed when cooled. The ricotta mixture, however, was a hit. Tasters liked the ricotta's creamy texture in combination with the nutty flavor of the Parmesan and the binding quality of the mozzarella. Both whole milk or part-skim ricotta worked fine, but the part-skim ricotta prevented the filling from tasting overly rich, allowing the other flavors to shine.

It was now time to tackle the vegetables and we knew our biggest challenge was still ahead of us: finding a way to keep the tart shell crisp given most vegetables' high water content. Getting rid of excess moisture would be the key to success. Starting with tomatoes (the most common vegetable we found in our research), we tested the difference between using beefsteak and plum. As we suspected, the beefsteak tomatoes contained much more water than the plum tomatoes and the resulting tart was a soggy, waterlogged mess. But even the plum tomatoes exuded too much liquid and made the top of the tart slick with moisture. To fix this, we sliced the plum tomatoes and salted them, allowing them to drain on paper towels for 30 minutes. Blotting the salted tomatoes dry before layering them on the tart produced a beautiful tart with just a slightly glossy sheen of moisture. The added bonus of the salting step was that it intensified the flavor of the tomatoes.

Since tomatoes are at their best only a short time during the year, we looked for other vegetables we could use when tomatoes aren't in season. Starting with zucchini, we were able to make a successful transition with relative ease. Zucchini release as much water, if not more, than tomatoes. We tried salting and blotting them, just as we had with the tomatoes and this worked well.

Next we tried eggplant and artichokes, but both were disappointments. Tasters felt that the eggplant tart didn't look nearly as attractive as our previous tarts, the texture of the eggplant was too similar to that of the ricotta, and the flavors were muddled. The artichokes, although a staple ingredient in many Italian tarts, were just too heavy and weighed the delicate tart down. Finally, we tried mushrooms. Knowing that moisture would again be a problem, we decided to cook the mushrooms first quickly in a skillet so they could release their water. To give them a slight flavor boost, we added a touch of garlic and thyme as they sautéed—perfect. Zucchini in spring and early summer, tomatoes in late summer and early fall, and mushrooms in the winter—we now had a tart for all seasons.

INGREDIENTS: Parmesan Cheese

When it comes to Parmesan cheese, there's a wide range of options—everything from the whitish powder in plastic containers to imported cheese that costs up to $17 a pound. You can buy cheese that has been grated, or you can pick out a whole hunk and grate it yourself. We wondered if the authentic Parmigiano-Reggiano imported from Italy would be that much better when tasted side by side with a domestic Parmesan at half the price.

The samples in our tasting included five pregrated Parmesan cheeses (domestic and imported), three wedges of domestic Parmesan, a wedge of Grana Padano (an Italian grating cheese considered a Parmesan type), one of Reggianito (another Parmesan-type cheese from Argentina), and two of Parmigiano-Reggiano. All of the cheeses were tasted grated, at room temperature.

All of the cheeses in the tasting except the Parmigiano-Reggiano were extremely salty. In fact, Parmigiano-Reggiano contains about two-thirds less sodium than other Parmesans. This is because the wheels of Parmigiano-Reggiano are so large that they do not become as saturated with salt during the brining process that is one of the final steps in making the cheese. (The average wheel is about 9 inches high and 16 to 18 inches in diameter and weighs 75 to 90 pounds; domestic Parmesan wheels average 24 pounds.)

One domestic Parmesan scored well enough to be recommended—BelGioioso. The other less expensive options paled in comparison with the real thing. The pregrated cheeses received especially low ratings and harsh comments from our panel. Most were much too salty and marred by odd off-flavors. Most everyone agreed that these poor imitations could actually ruin a dish.

THE BEST PARMESANS

Nothing compares with real Parmigiano-Reggiano (left). If you can, buy a piece freshly cut from a large wheel (look for the pin-dot writing on the rind—it should spell out some portion of the words Parmigiano-Reggiano). Expect to spend $12 to $17 per pound. Priced at just $9 per pound, domestically made BelGioioso Parmesan (right) is surprisingly good and it is our best buy.

Tomato Tart

Torta di Pomodoro

SERVES 6 TO 8

Use a 9-inch fluted metal tart pan with a removable bottom for this recipe. The filling in this tart is relatively thin, so press the dough only ¾ inch up the sides of the tart pan. We preferred the light flavor of part-skim ricotta here, but whole milk ricotta can be substituted; do not use fat-free ricotta.

CRUST

1¼	cups (6¼ ounces) unbleached all-purpose flour
1	tablespoon sugar
½	teaspoon salt
6	tablespoons extra-virgin olive oil
3	tablespoons ice water
1	ounce Parmesan, grated (about ½ cup)

FILLING

3	medium plum tomatoes, cored and sliced ¼ inch thick
	Salt
2	tablespoons plus 1 teaspoon extra-virgin olive oil
1	medium garlic clove, minced or pressed through a garlic press (about 1 teaspoon)
½	cup part-skim ricotta
1	ounce Parmesan, grated (about ½ cup)
1	ounce mozzarella, shredded (about ¼ cup)
	Ground black pepper
2	tablespoons shredded fresh basil leaves (see page 298)

1. FOR THE CRUST: Spray a 9-inch tart pan with a removable bottom with vegetable oil spray; set aside. Pulse the flour, sugar, and salt together in a food processor until combined, about 4 pulses. Drizzle the oil over the flour mixture and pulse until the mixture resembles coarse sand, about 12 pulses. Add 2 tablespoons of the ice water and continue to process until some of the dough begins to clump into large pieces and no powdery bits remain, about 5 seconds. If powdery bits of flour remain, add the remaining tablespoon water and pulse to incorporate, about 4 pulses. (The dough should have many little Grape-Nut-sized crumbs with a few large clumps.)

2. Dump all but ⅓ cup of the dough crumbs into the prepared tart pan and, using your hands, press the crumbs into an even layer over the tart pan bottom. Sprinkle the remaining ⅓ cup crumbs around the edge of the tart pan and press into a tidy crust edge, about ¾ inch up the sides of the pan (the dough will be very malleable and feel a little greasy). Lay plastic wrap over the dough and smooth out any bumps or shallow areas using your palm. Place the tart pan on a large plate and freeze the dough until firm, about 30 minutes. Meanwhile, adjust an oven rack to the middle position and heat the oven to 375 degrees.

3. Place the frozen tart shell (still in the tart pan) on a baking sheet. Gently press a piece of extra-wide heavy-duty aluminum foil that has been sprayed with vegetable oil spray against the dough and over the edges of the tart pan. Fill the shell with pie weights and bake until the top edge of the dough just starts to color and the surface of the dough under the foil no longer looks wet, about 30 minutes.

4. Remove the tart shell from the oven and carefully remove the foil and weights. Sprinkle the Parmesan evenly over the bottom of the tart shell, then return to the oven and continue to bake until the cheese is golden brown, 5 to 10 minutes. Set the baking sheet with the tart shell on a wire rack to cool slightly, about 10 minutes. (At this point the cooled shell can be wrapped tightly in plastic wrap and held at room temperature for up to 1 day.) Increase the oven temperature to 425 degrees.

5. FOR THE FILLING: Meanwhile, spread the tomatoes out over several layers of paper towels. Sprinkle with ½ teaspoon salt and let drain for 30 minutes; gently blot the tops of the tomatoes dry with paper towels before using. In a small bowl, whisk 2 tablespoons of the olive oil and the garlic together; set aside. In a separate bowl, mix the ricotta, Parmesan, mozzarella, and remaining 1 teaspoon olive oil together and season with salt and pepper to taste.

6. Spread the ricotta mixture evenly over the bottom of the cooled tart shell. Shingle the tomatoes attractively on top of the ricotta in concentric

circles, starting at the outside edge. Drizzle the garlic and olive oil mixture evenly over the tomatoes. Bake the tart until the cheese is bubbling and the tomatoes are slightly wilted, 20 to 25 minutes.

7. Let the tart cool slightly on a wire rack for 5 minutes, then sprinkle with the basil. Remove the tart from the tart pan and transfer to a serving platter or cutting board. Cut into wedges and serve. (The finished tart can also be held at room temperature for up to 1 hour before serving.)

➤ VARIATIONS

Zucchini Tart

Follow the recipe for Tomato Tart, substituting 1 large zucchini (about 8 ounces), sliced into ¼-inch-thick rounds, for the tomatoes; salt, drain, and blot the zucchini dry as directed in step 5.

Mushroom Tart

Heat 1 tablespoon olive oil in a 12-inch nonstick skillet over medium-high heat until shimmering. Add 1 pound white button mushrooms, wiped clean and sliced thin, and ½ teaspoon salt and cook until their moisture has released and they are lightly browned, about 15 minutes. Stir in 1 minced garlic clove and 2 teaspoons minced fresh thyme leaves and cook until fragrant, about 1 minute longer. Follow the recipe for Tomato Tart, substituting the sautéed mushrooms for the salted tomatoes in step 6; sprinkle them evenly over the tart, drizzle with the garlic oil, and bake as directed.

TUSCAN WHITE BEAN AND BREAD SOUP

Ribollita

RIBOLLITA, WHICH MEANS "REBOILED," IS A homey, classic dish from the Tuscany region of Italy made from leftover white bean soup. Slices of day-old rustic bread are submerged in the rewarmed soup until softened and then the mixture is blended or mashed until it becomes stew-like. (True ribollita connoisseurs say that it must be thick enough to eat with a fork.) But as with many meals made from leftovers—such as corned beef hash made with leftovers from a boiled dinner or fried rice made from yesterday's side dish—the secondary meal has as much (if not more) appeal than the original dish. Such is the case with ribollita, and many modern recipes no longer make reference to the original white bean soup, but rather spell out how to make ribollita from scratch.

Ribollita has been known to spark enthusiastic debate between Tuscan cooks and trattorias alike, each declaring their version as the best. Inspired by the passionate opinions surrounding this soup, we did some careful research in hopes of getting this dish just right. After poring over many recipes, we found only four ingredients that appeared consistently in every one: white beans, kale, day-old rustic Tuscan bread, and good-quality extra-virgin olive oil. The other ingredients—such as herbs, aromatics, vegetables, and cheeses—were all debatable.

After testing a few of these recipes, several problems quickly became obvious. The broths were sorely lacking in flavor, the beans were mushy, and the bread was an unappealing, sloppy mess. Furthermore, this soup is meant to be incredibly thick, which was not the case in these watered-down versions. When we let one ribollita sit overnight, as called for in many recipes, the soup thickened considerably. It was now more reminiscent of a stew than a soup because the beans and bread had absorbed nearly all the liquid. However, we were not particularly fond of this two-day affair. Could we find a way to make flavorful ribollita that could be prepared and eaten the same day?

Starting with the beans, we wanted them to be creamy on the inside but still firm enough to hold their shape. Based on past experience, we figured that our ideal texture would only be attainable by starting out with dried beans that were then soaked overnight, followed by some careful simmering. But after spending hours trying to achieve just the right texture, we started to realize that ribollita, unlike other bean soups, is not about perfectly cooked beans. In fact, ribollita (again, meaning "reboiled") is meant to have very soft, slightly broken down beans, which help to thicken the broth.

INGREDIENTS: Balsamic Vinegar

Balsamic vinegar, with its big, sweet, caramel flavor, is one of Italy's most famous food products and is currently the best-selling vinegar in the U.S. We mix it in salad dressing; drizzle it on meat, fish, and vegetables; and add it to sauces, soups, and desserts.

But the array of options can be overwhelming. Traditional aged balsamic vinegar, produced in the Emilia-Romagna region of Italy, can cost $200 per bottle. You can also walk into any supermarket in America and fork over $2 or $3 for a big bottle of balsamic. So what are the differences and which should you choose?

It turns out there are two kinds of balsamic vinegar and they're made by entirely different processes. The traditional technique takes a minimum of 12 years and begins with late-harvest grapes (usually white Trebbiano). The sweet, raisiny juice, skin, and seeds, called grape must, is boiled in open vats until reduced to about half its original volume. This concentrated must is added to the largest of a battery of wooden barrels, which are kept in uninsulated attics in this region where the summers are hot and the winters frosty. The battery comprises barrels of different woods—including oak, cherry, juniper, and mulberry—and sizes. The barrels aren't sealed; they have cloth-covered openings on top to allow evaporation. Each year, before the vinegar maker adds the new must to the largest barrel, he transfers some of its ever-more concentrated contents to the next largest, and so on down the line, before finally removing a liter or two of the oldest vinegar from the smallest barrel.

What's more, all this can only happen in two provinces of Emilia-Romagna: Modena and Reggio Emilia, an area designated as a government-protected denomination of origin or DOP. Each province has its own consortium of experts who approve the balsamic before sealing it in its official 3-ounce bottle (an inverted tulip shape for Reggio Emilia; a ball with a neck for Modena). If you want a guarantee that you're getting true balsamic vinegar, look for the word tradizionale and these distinctive bottles—and be prepared to pay dearly.

Commercial balsamic vinegar can be made in as little as a few hours. With no law defining balsamic vinegar in the United States, manufacturers supply the huge demand any way they can, coloring and sweetening wine vinegar and calling it "balsamic vinegar of Modena."

Tasted straight from the bottle, there was no contest between supermarket and traditional balsamics. Even the best of the commercial bunch—while similarly sweet, brown, and viscous—couldn't compete with the complex, rich flavor of true balsamic vinegar. With notes of honey, fig, raisin, caramel, and wood; a smooth, lingering taste; and an aroma like fine port, traditional balsamic is good enough to sip like liqueur.

But you don't need to take out a loan to keep balsamic vinegar in your pantry. The test kitchen made a vinaigrette and a pan sauce with both a 25-year-old traditional balsamic from Reggio Emilia and the top supermarket brand from our taste tests—and frankly, the traditional stuff did not justify its price tag. So don't waste your money on pricey traditional balsamic vinegar if you're going to toss it on salad or cook with it.

THE BEST SUPERMARKET BALSAMIC VINEGAR

Lucini Gran Riserva is sweet and thick (both characteristics of traditional balsamic), but also acidic, which prevents the vinegar from tasting excessively sweet. At about $2 per ounce, it's our top choice for everyday use or cooking.

THE BEST GOURMET BALSAMIC VINEGARS

The $60-per-ounce traditional balsamic vinegar Cavalli Gold Seal (left) was tasters' favorite, but two reasonably priced gourmet brands, Oliviers & Co. Premium and Rubio (center and right), were nearly as good—and they cost just $3 to $4 per ounce. Pick one of these when you want to drizzle vinegar over a finished dish.

Not to mention that in ribollita, the beans are not meant to be the star ingredient, but rather share the spotlight with the kale, bread, and olive oil.

If perfectly cooked beans are not the point of this dish, could we save hours of soaking and simmering time by using canned beans? We did a side-by-side test of soups made with canned beans and soups made with freshly cooked dried beans, and tasters were surprised to find that they were happy with both versions. To further replicate the texture of day-old broken-down beans, we tried mashing half of the canned beans in a bowl before adding them to the soup. This worked wonders and gave the mixture a more stew-like, less brothy consistency—and to make it even easier we used a food processor.

Because we were no longer cooking our beans and creating a flavorful bean liquid, we looked for another way to boost flavor and decided to try adding some chicken broth to our soup. We tested a batch made with all water against one made with all chicken broth, as well as one made with half water, half broth. We preferred the batch made with half water and half broth; the chicken broth lent a subtle depth of flavor without overwhelming the other ingredients.

Adding carrots and tomatoes along with the kale made a big improvement in the overall flavor, as did a healthy dose of garlic. Adding a potato lent the dish a nice earthy flavor, but more importantly, it helped to thicken the broth yet a bit more. Rosemary is a traditional herb in many white bean soups and we liked the idea of it in our ribollita. We tried simmering the rosemary with everything else, but that produced a bitter, medicinal broth. Steeping it off the heat in the hot liquid for just a few minutes at the end of our recipe gave us just the right amount of bright, fresh rosemary flavor. To finish, we found that a generous drizzle of high-quality extra-virgin olive oil over each bowl before serving was invaluable.

Up to now, we had been simply placing a piece of day-old bread (good-quality artisanal or rustic bread) in the bottom of the soup bowl, then ladling the bean mixture over the top, but tasters weren't wowed by the bread's texture. The slices of bread merely turned into large, mushy chunks of slop. Drying the bread in the oven helped the bread maintain some of its structure, rather than turn completely to mush. And cutting the bread into cubes allowed us to distribute the bread more evenly throughout the soup, which helped to thicken the broth as well.

Tasters were adamant, however, that some of the bread needed to retain yet more of its texture and chew. The solution was simple: We just reserved some of the bread cubes to add to individual bowls of soup just before serving so they did not have a chance to break down. Finally, we had captured the flavors of this Tuscan soup in a fraction of the time that traditional recipes require.

Tuscan White Bean and Bread Soup

Ribollita

SERVES 8

We prefer to use a crusty loaf of ciabatta bread in this recipe, but any rustic, country-style bread will work; do not use sliced sandwich bread. Chard can be substituted for the kale. Serve with grated Parmesan cheese.

6	cups crusty, rustic bread cut into 1-inch chunks (about 7 ounces) (see note)
2	(15-ounce) cans cannellini beans, drained and rinsed
6	cups water
⅓	cup extra-virgin olive oil, plus extra for serving
3	medium carrots, peeled and chopped fine
1	onion, minced
1	large bunch kale (about 1 pound), thick stems and leaves separated, stems chopped fine, and leaves sliced into 1-inch-thick strips (see page 174)
	Salt
6	medium garlic cloves, minced or pressed through a garlic press (about 2 tablespoons)
1	(28-ounce) can diced tomatoes, drained
1	large russet potato (about 10 ounces), peeled and cut into ½-inch chunks
2	bay leaves
1	sprig fresh rosemary
	Ground black pepper
	Grated Parmesan cheese, for serving

1. Adjust an oven rack to the middle position and heat the oven to 300 degrees. Spread the bread cubes out over a rimmed baking sheet and bake until dried but not browned, about 30 minutes; set aside. Process half of the beans and ¼ cup of the water in a food processor until mostly smooth, about 12 pulses, stopping to scrape down the sides of the bowl as needed; set aside.

2. Heat the oil in a large Dutch oven over medium heat until shimmering. Add the carrots, onion, kale stems, and ½ teaspoon salt and cook until the vegetables are softened, 8 to 10 minutes.

3. Stir in the garlic and cook until fragrant, about 30 seconds. Stir in the tomatoes and cook until softened, about 2 minutes. Stir in the pureed beans, remaining whole beans, remaining water, kale leaves, potato, and bay leaves and bring to a simmer. Reduce the heat to low, partially cover, and simmer until the potato is tender, about 40 minutes.

4. Stir the rosemary sprig and 2 cups of the dried bread cubes into the soup, cover, and let stand off the heat until the bread is soggy and falling apart, 15 to 20 minutes.

5. Discard the rosemary sprig and bay leaves and stir to break up the bread pieces and thicken the soup. Season to taste with salt and pepper. Divide the remaining bread cubes among individual bowls and ladle the thickened soup over the top. Drizzle olive oil over the top of each portion and serve, passing the Parmesan cheese separately.

SICILIAN CHICKPEAS AND ESCAROLE

Minestra di Ceci

A SEEMINGLY ENDLESS VARIETY OF DISHES with beans and greens stewed together are found throughout southern Europe. They are a prime example of what Italians call *cucina povera*, or "cuisine of the poor," as they combine readily available, inexpensive (or free, in the case of wild greens) ingredients in a highly nutritious meal.

Sicily's beloved chickpeas (*ceci*) shine when paired with leafy escarole. Their sweetness and firm, chewy texture is complemented by the bitterness and supple smoothness of the wilted greens. Coated with a drizzle of extra-virgin olive oil and served with crusty bread, this dish makes an irresistible one-pot main course. However, like many cucina povera dishes, we discovered that it needed a little updating to suit our modern palates.

Chickpeas are the heart of this dish. While we normally prefer dried beans over canned, we have found that canned chickpeas are perfectly acceptable in some instances, as their texture and flavor are little compromised by the canning process. And admittedly, cooking dried chickpeas takes some effort; they must be soaked overnight and then take a minimum of 1½ hours to cook. When the beans were combined with the other assertive ingredients in this dish, tasters had a hard time telling if they were canned or dried.

Aromatics, such as onions, carrots, and garlic, are traditional flavorings for this dish. As is common throughout southern Italy, we lightly toasted the garlic in the olive oil prior to adding the other aromatics. Toasting mellowed the garlic's fierce bite to a nutty sweetness that contributed body and depth to the dish. We toasted red pepper flakes at the same time, as the heat activates their volatile oils for a deeper, roasted flavor—an improvement noted by tasters.

With the aromatics cooked, the beans and some liquid can be added to the pot. Although the escarole can be washed and shaken dry so the leaves are still damp, more liquid is needed for steaming it. Water was a bit bland and tasters preferred the flavor of chicken broth.

Raisins appear in numerous savory dishes throughout southern Italy. The savory use of dried fruit is a vestige of the Arab influence on Italian cooking. In this case, the raisins balance the dish, tying together the beans and greens and tempering the heat from the pepper flakes. The raisins are usually plumped so that their texture acts as a counterpoint to the beans; they literally burst in your mouth. For this reason, we found it best to add them to the pot along with the chickpeas and chicken broth.

Because the beans were already cooked through, the actual cooking time—outside of sautéing the aromatics—was just long enough to wilt the escarole and blend the flavors. After wrestling with wilting the escarole in a skillet, we discovered that a deep Dutch oven made for hassle-free cooking. We added all of the escarole at once and covered the pot so the escarole could cook in the trapped steam. As the escarole wilted, we stirred it into the chickpea mixture. Once all of the escarole had wilted, we found it necessary to simmer the dish uncovered briefly to concentrate the watery liquid shed by the greens. Parsley and lemon juice brightened the appearance and flavor of the final dish.

Sicilian Chickpeas and Escarole
Minestra di Ceci
SERVES 4 TO 6 AS A MAIN COURSE, OR
6 TO 8 AS A SIDE DISH

If you have problems locating escarole, substitute chicory, although its flavor is stronger. The overall sweetness of this dish stands up well to a fair amount of spiciness and you can adjust the amount of red pepper flakes to taste. For a vegetarian main course, substitute vegetable broth for the chicken broth and serve this dish with toasted, crusty bread or polenta (page 271). This is also an excellent side dish with roast pork or fish.

¼	cup extra-virgin olive oil, plus extra for serving
4	medium garlic cloves, sliced thin
¼	teaspoon red pepper flakes
1	medium onion, minced
1	carrot, peeled and chopped medium
	Salt
2	(15-ounce) cans chickpeas, drained and rinsed
⅓	cup raisins
1	cup low-sodium chicken broth
1	head escarole (about 1 pound), trimmed, cut into 1-inch lengths, washed and left damp
2	tablespoons minced fresh parsley leaves
2	teaspoons juice from 1 lemon
	Ground black pepper

1. Combine the oil, garlic, and red pepper flakes in a large Dutch oven over medium heat. As the oil begins to sizzle, shake the pan back and forth so that the garlic does not stick (stirring with a wooden spoon will cause the garlic to clump). Cook until the garlic turns very pale gold, 2 to 2½ minutes.

2. Stir in the onion, carrot, and ½ teaspoon salt and cook, stirring frequently, until the vegetables are softened and lightly browned, 7 to 8 minutes. Reduce the heat to medium and stir in the chickpeas, raisins, and broth.

3. Add the damp escarole, cover, and cook, stirring every 2 minutes, until the escarole has wilted, 8 to 10 minutes. Uncover, increase the heat to high, and continue to cook until the liquid is reduced to a light coating on the bottom of the pan, about 5 minutes. Off the heat, stir in the parsley and lemon juice and season with salt and pepper to taste. Serve immediately with extra-virgin olive oil for drizzling at the table.

POLENTA

POLENTA HAILS FROM THE NORTHERN regions of Italy and is simply coarse-ground cornmeal cooked in water to form a soft mush. Often served as a side dish to roasted meats, stews, and braises, it can also be served as a hearty first course or light entrée when topped with sautéed cherry tomatoes or sausage and Swiss chard. Ideally, its texture should be smooth, creamy, and soft, but still stiff enough to be eaten with a fork or hold its shape when dolloped onto a plate. The corn flavor should be dominant, complemented simply with a little butter or cheese.

Although making polenta sounds easy, the traditional Italian method for cooking it is a lot of work. The polenta must be slowly added to boiling salted water and stirred constantly (to prevent scorching) during the entire 30- to 40-minute cooking time. Within five minutes, you'll feel like you've been arm-wrestling Arnold Schwarzenegger. Thirty minutes of such constant stirring can seem like an eternity.

Of course, this assumes that you have avoided

the biggest pitfall of all, the seizing problem at the beginning of the cooking process. Cornmeal is a starch and starch thickens when mixed with water and heated. If this happens too quickly, the cornmeal seizes up into a solid, nearly immovable mass.

We tested adding cornmeal to cold water, using more water, using less water, and using different grinds of cornmeal, all to no avail. Yes, we learned to prevent seizing (add the cornmeal very slowly), but we still needed to stir constantly for at least 30 minutes to prevent scorching.

This testing did, however, reveal some important information about cornmeal—the type of cornmeal you use can make all the difference. Finely ground cornmeal, such as the Quaker brand sold in many supermarkets, is too powdery and makes gummy, gluey polenta. Stone-ground cornmeal also produced lousy polenta because the grind was so uneven. The best polenta is made with evenly ground, medium- to coarse-ground cornmeal—often packaged and sold as "polenta." We also discovered that a ratio of 4 parts water to 1 part cornmeal delivers the right consistency. As for salt, 1 teaspoon is the right amount for 1 cup of cornmeal.

At this point in our testing, we started to explore alternative cooking methods. The microwave was a bust, yielding sticky, raw-tasting polenta. The pressure cooker was even worse; the polenta took a long time to cook and then stuck firmly to the pot. We finally got good results when we prepared polenta in a double boiler. The polenta is cooked over simmering water so it cannot scorch or seize up the way it can when cooked over direct heat. It emerges with a soft, light texture and sweet corn flavor. There is only one drawback, and it is a big one: time.

While a double boiler produced undeniably rich, creamy polenta, the cooking time was prohibitively long. Even with the minimum attention that the technique required, 1½ hours of cooking was simply impractical. We wondered whether we could produce similar results by more conventional methods. The double boiler method proved to us that slow, very gentle heat was the key to unlocking

cornmeal's smooth texture, not vigilant stirring. Could we approximate a double boiler's low heat with a conventional saucepan?

Luckily, we could. A heavy-bottomed saucepan on the stove's lowest possible setting (or in conjunction with a flame tamer; see page 289) shielded the polenta from cooking too rapidly and allowed for the starches to be released and the flavor of the cornmeal to develop. Keeping the cover on the pot held in moisture and reduced the risk of scorching the polenta, even when we stirred infrequently rather than constantly. Within 30 minutes, a third

EQUIPMENT: Cheese Graters

Whether you are dusting a plate of pasta or grating a full cup of cheese to use in a recipe, a good grater should be efficient and easy to use. After grating more than 10 pounds of Parmesan, we concluded that success is dependent on a combination of sharp grating teeth, a comfortable handle or grip, and good leverage for pressing the cheese onto the grater.

Our favorite model was a flat grater based on a small, maneuverable woodworking tool called a rasp. Shaped like a ruler, but with lots and lots of tiny, sharp raised teeth, the Microplane Grater can grate large quantities of cheese smoothly and almost effortlessly. The black plastic handle, which we found more comfortable than any of the others, also earned high praise. Other flat graters also scored well. What about box graters? They can deliver good results and can do more than just grate hard cheese—but if grating hard cheese is the task at hand, a box grater is not our first choice.

THE BEST GRATER

The Microplane Grater has very sharp teeth and a solid handle, which together make grating cheese a breeze. This grater also makes quick work of ginger and citrus zest.

of the time it took in the double boiler, we had creamy polenta ready for the table. We did find, however, that with the slightly higher temperature, stirring was a more significant issue. When we left the polenta unheeded for more than seven minutes, it tended to stick to the pot bottom and corners, where it remained immovable until washing. Stirring vigorously every five minutes prevented such mishaps.

Simple Polenta

SERVES 6 AS A SIDE DISH

Be sure to use medium- or coarse-ground cornmeal or cornmeal labeled as "polenta;" finely ground cornmeal will cook up to a much different texture. If you do not have a heavy-bottomed saucepan, you may need to use a flame tamer to manage the heat (see page 289 for information on making one with aluminum foil). It's easy to tell whether you need a flame tamer or not; if the polenta bubbles or sputters at all after the first 10 minutes, the heat is too high and you need one. Properly heated polenta will do little more than release wisps of steam. When stirring the polenta, scrape the sides and bottom of the pot to ensure even cooking.

6	cups water
	Salt
1½	cups polenta or evenly ground medium- or coarse-ground cornmeal
1½	ounces Parmesan cheese, grated (about ¾ cup)
3	tablespoons unsalted butter, cut into large chunks
	Ground black pepper

1. Bring the water to a boil in a heavy-bottomed 4-quart saucepan over medium-high heat. Once boiling, add 1½ teaspoons salt and pour the polenta into the water in a very slow stream from a measuring cup, all the while stirring in a circular motion with a wooden spoon following the illustration on page 272.

2. Reduce the heat to the lowest possible setting and cover. Cook, vigorously stirring the polenta once every 5 minutes, making sure to scrape clean the bottom and corners of the pot, until the polenta has lost its raw cornmeal taste and becomes soft and smooth, about 30 minutes. Stir in the Parmesan and butter and season with salt and pepper to taste. Serve immediately.

➤ VARIATIONS

Polenta with Sautéed Cherry Tomatoes and Fresh Mozzarella

SERVES 4 AS A MAIN COURSE, OR 6 AS A SIDE DISH

We like to use cherry tomatoes here for their sweet flavor and firm, sturdy texture; if substituting regular tomatoes, be sure to seed them before cooking or the topping will be quite watery. Don't stir the cheese into the sautéed tomatoes or it will melt prematurely and turn rubbery.

1	recipe Simple Polenta (at left)
3	tablespoons olive oil
2	medium garlic cloves, peeled and sliced thin
	Pinch red pepper flakes
	Pinch sugar
2	pints cherry tomatoes, halved
	Salt and ground black pepper
6	ounces fresh mozzarella, cut into ⅓-inch cubes (about 1 cup)
2	tablespoons shredded fresh basil leaves (see page 298)

Follow the recipe for Simple Polenta. During the final 5 minutes of cooking the polenta, heat the oil, garlic, pepper flakes, and sugar in a 12-inch nonstick skillet over medium-high heat until fragrant and sizzling, about 1 minute. Stir in the tomatoes and cook until they just begin to wilt, about 1 minute; season with salt and pepper to taste and set the skillet aside off the heat. Spoon the polenta into individual serving bowls and top with the mozzarella. Spoon the tomato mixture with any accumulated juices over the top and sprinkle with the basil before serving.

Polenta with Sautéed Sausage and Chard

SERVES 4 AS A MAIN COURSE,
OR 6 AS A SIDE DISH

Both white- and red-stemmed chard will work here, but the red-stemmed chard will give the juices a bright red color.

1	recipe Simple Polenta (page 271)
2	tablespoons extra-virgin olive oil
8	ounces sweet or hot Italian sausage, casing removed
1	small onion, minced
1	small bunch Swiss chard, stems and leaves separated, stems chopped fine and leaves cut into 1-inch wide strips
3	medium garlic cloves, minced or pressed through a garlic press (about 1 tablespoon)
½	cup low-sodium chicken broth
	Salt and ground black pepper

Follow the recipe for Simple Polenta. During the final 10 minutes of cooking the polenta, heat the oil in a 12-inch nonstick over medium-high heat until shimmering. Add the sausage, onion, and chard stems and cook, breaking up the meat with a wooden spoon, until the meat begins to brown and the vegetables are softened, 5 to 7 minutes. Stir in the garlic and cook until fragrant, about 30 seconds. Stir in the chard leaves and broth and cook, tossing constantly with tongs, until the leaves are wilted and the mixture is slightly saucy, about 2 minutes. Season with salt and pepper to taste and set the skillet aside off the heat. Spoon the polenta into individual serving bowls, top with the sausage mixture along with any accumulated juices, and serve.

MAKING POLENTA

When the water comes to a boil, add the salt, then pour the polenta into the water in a very slow stream from a measuring cup, stirring in a circular motion with a wooden spoon to prevent clumping.

RISOTTO

PASTA IS OFTEN THOUGHT OF AS THE predominant starch in Italian cuisine, but Italy is also known for its rice—in fact, Italy is the leading grower/producer of rice in Europe. Risotto is a classic preparation of Italian rice in which the rice is simmered—along with judicious amounts of wine and broth—and stirred until the starch in the rice is transformed into a velvety, creamy sauce that coats the grains of rice, which are cooked to an al dente texture. Risotto is one of the highlights of Italian cooking and, unsurprisingly, the myths surrounding it abound. In the matter of cooking technique and equipment, everyone has a firm opinion, so we set out to separate fact from fiction and get to the heart of risotto.

Obviously, the rice is the key element to a texturally flawless risotto. When buying rice, it is imperative that you pay attention to the size of the grains. Rice can be classified as long-grain, medium-grain, or short-grain. Long-grain rice is about four times as long as it is wide. Medium-grain rice is twice as long as it is wide. Short-grain rice is round. In general, long-grain rice cooks up fluffy and separate, while medium- and short-grain rice tend to cling or become starchy.

We found that medium-grain rice is the best choice for risotto, in which we want some starchiness but not too much. But not all medium-grain rice is the same. In our kitchen tests, we found that the risotto technique may be used with non-Italian medium-grain rice, but the finished texture will pale in comparison to risotto made with Italian rice, which provides the best contrast between supple sauce and firm rice. We think Italian rice is a must.

Italian rice comes in four varieties: *superfino, fino, semifino,* and *commune.* The top two grades include Arborio (the most widely available), Carnaroli, and Vialone Nano. There are even more varieties, like Baldo and the quick-cooking Poseidone, but they can be difficult to find outside of Italy.

In a side-by-side taste test of Arborio, Carnaroli, and Vialone Nano, tasters were split evenly between the Arborio and Carnaroli; those liking firmer rice grains chose Arborio and those liking softer, creamier rice chose Carnaroli. Vialone was deemed too soft and had a pasty texture; the grains lacked a firm center.

Luckily, risotto is so popular that most markets carry at least one brand of Italian rice, generally Arborio. Because this rice is so widely available, we call for it in our recipes. If you like a softer, creamier rice and can find Carnaroli, buy it; it can be used in all the risotto recipes. In any case, do not be swayed by fancy "rustic" or gimmicky packaging with inflated price tags. We purchased Arborio from a variety of stores—from supermarkets to upscale Italian markets—and found little difference in the finished dish. However, do be wary of the rice's age because, like most grains, rice does go stale. Risotto made with rice past its prime turns mealy and chalky, loses its al dente core, and lacks the thick creaminess of fresh rice. To be on the safe side, we generally purchase rice in vacuum-packed bags, about one to two pounds at a time. Rice from bulk bins of unquestionable vintage is a dicey proposition.

Having good-quality rice is only half the battle; cooking is the rest. After countless batches with minute variations, we were certain about a few points. First, slowly cooking diced onions until they softened and yielded their juices was imperative to the dish's final flavor and texture, while their sweetness lent depth. The next step was sautéing the rice, which prompted its starches to turn translucent—a good visual clue for adding liquid. When we did not cook the rice prior to adding liquid, the risotto was mushy and chalky and the rice grains lacked their distinctive chew.

Once the rice was toasted, it was time to add the liquids. The wine must be added before the broth so that the boozy flavor has a chance to cook off. Otherwise, we found the alcohol punch was too much. Virtually all risottos are made with a light, dry white wine, although some regional specialties are made with red wine. Risotto made without wine lacks dimension and tastes bland, so don't skip this ingredient.

The recipes we researched offered a wide range of options for broth, from plain water to veal stock. Water didn't impress us and veal stock is rare in all but the best-provisioned professional kitchen. Straight beef broth and chicken broth proved too

INGREDIENTS: Truffle Oil

In addition to whole truffles (see page 275), there are lots of truffle products on the market, the most prevalent of which is truffle oil. We purchased more than 13 bottles of both black and white truffle oil (spending just shy of $400) and tasted the oils side by side to find out if all truffles oils were created equal.

To start, we learned that there are three basic techniques for making both black and white truffle oil. The most costly is called aromatization, in which fresh truffles are scattered around a small room filled with pans of oil. The aroma fills the space and, after a daily stir, the oil absorbs the truffle aroma in about six months. The second, more cost-effective method is to steep the truffles in oil (either olive or safflower), allowing their aroma to permeate the oil. The third, least desirable, way is to soak the truffles in some form of solvent, which is then added to the oil. We concluded that it was difficult to determine exactly which method had been used based on the unregulated wording of ingredient lists. On the bottles we tested, we found everything from just olive oil and truffles to oil, natural flavoring, aroma, and artificial flavoring.

The six black truffle oils almost all tasted of toxic chemicals with noxious aromas. Overall, we found the white truffle oils to be the most dependable source of truffle flavor without buying the truffles themselves. We were impressed by their pleasant, earthy, rich aromas—dramatically different from the foul aromas of black truffle oils. The overall winner of the tasting was Fondo di Alba ($28.99 for a 55ml bottle), an Italian oil made from olive oil and white truffles. It garnered remarks such as "well balanced," "incredibly fragrant," and "this is what truffle oil should taste like." Try drizzling it over any number of dishes, including eggs, pizza, bruschetta, plain pasta, simple steamed vegetables, and french fries. Once opened, the oil should be stored in the refrigerator and will keep for up to one month, after which it will begin to lose its potent flavor.

We spent more than $400 on truffle oils and found that overall white truffle oil is superior to black truffle oil. When buying white truffle oil, look for bottles that list only white truffles and either olive oil or safflower oil as the ingredients.

intense, but diluting chicken broth with roughly an equal amount of water was just right. The chicken broth added richness and depth without taking over.

Although contrary to conventional wisdom and the instructions in most cookbooks, we discovered that constant stirring is unnecessary. We added half the broth once the wine had cooked off and allowed the rice to simmer for about 10 minutes, or half the cooking time, with little attention. The rice floated freely, individual grains suspended by the bubbling broth. During this period, we stirred the rice infrequently—about every three minutes—to ensure that it was not sticking to the bottom of the pan. Once all the broth was absorbed by the rice, we added more, a scant half-cup at a time. For this period, stirring every minute or so was important; if we did not, the rice stuck to the bottom of the pan.

There is quite a bit of controversy surrounding the doneness of risotto. Some insist it should have a chalky, solid bite, while others feel it should be soft to the core. Tasters expressed individual preferences quite strongly, so you must taste as the rice nears completion and decide for yourself. Generally, we began tasting our rice after about 20 minutes of cooking; you can always cook it longer for a softer texture, but you can never bring back bite.

SHAVING PARMESAN

Sometimes, laying shavings of Parmesan over the top of a simple pasta dish, risotto, or polenta before serving is nicer than grated Parmesan. To quickly achieve paper-thin slices of Parmesan, employ your vegetable peeler. Run the peeler over a block of Parmesan and use a light touch for thin shavings.

For the final touch, Parmesan goes in at the very end to preserve its distinctive flavor and aroma. Grated cheese proved best, as it melted almost instantaneously. Because its taste is so prominent, the quality of the cheese is paramount. This is the perfect occasion for buying the authentic Parmesan freshly cut from the wheel, boldly displaying its branded trademark on the rind.

Parmesan Risotto

SERVES 6 AS A FIRST COURSE OR SIDE DISH

Don't worry if you have broth left over once the rice is finished cooking; different brands of rice all cook differently and we prefer to err on the side of slightly too much broth rather than too little. If you do use all the broth and the rice has not finished cooking, add hot water. This is risotto at its simplest and is appropriate as a first course or it can accompany a variety of meals, from grilled or braised meat to a mélange of roasted vegetables. Serve with Parmesan shavings (see below).

3½	cups low-sodium chicken broth
3	cups water
4	tablespoons (½ stick) unsalted butter
I	medium onion, minced
	Salt
2	cups Arborio rice
I	cup dry white wine
2	ounces Parmesan cheese, grated (about I cup)
	Ground black pepper

1. Bring the broth and water to a simmer in a medium saucepan over medium-high heat. Reduce the heat to the lowest possible setting to keep the broth warm.

2. Melt the butter in a medium saucepan over medium heat. Add the onion and ½ teaspoon salt and cook, stirring occasionally, until softened, 5 to 7 minutes. Add the rice and cook, stirring frequently, until the edges of the grains are transparent, about 4 minutes.

3. Add the wine and cook, stirring frequently, until the wine is completely absorbed by the rice, about 2 minutes. Add 3 cups of the warm broth

and simmer, stirring infrequently (about every 3 minutes), until the liquid is absorbed and the bottom of the pan is dry, 10 to 12 minutes.

4. Continue to cook, stirring frequently and adding more broth, ½ cup at a time, every 3 to 4 minutes as needed to keep the pan bottom from drying out, until the grains of rice are cooked through but still somewhat firm in the center, 10 to 12 minutes. Off the heat, stir in the Parmesan cheese, season with salt and pepper to taste, and serve immediately in warm shallow bowls.

➤ VARIATIONS

Saffron Risotto

Follow the recipe for Parmesan Risotto, crumbling ¼ teaspoon saffron threads into the pot with the rice in step 2.

Truffle Risotto

For more information on truffles and truffle oil, see below and page 273.

Follow the recipe for Parmesan Risotto, reducing the amount of Parmesan to 1 ounce (about ½ cup). Stir 2 teaspoons white truffle oil into the pot before adding the Parmesan in step 4. If desired, use a truffle shaver or vegetable peeler to shave whole truffles over the top before serving.

PANTRY SPOTLIGHT

TRUFFLES

Truffles are among the most expensive ingredients in the world. There are both white and black truffles but white truffles are very expensive and hard to find, while black truffles are a bit more affordable and easier to track down at a local gourmet shop. There are five species of black truffles and choosing the right one will make all the difference. Look for varieties called Périgord (French), Tricastin (Spanish), or Norcia (Umbrian). The other two varieties—the musky truffle and the Chinese truffle—are inferior in aroma and flavor and cost much less. Although truffles are harvested in both the summer and winter months, winter truffles are traditionally preferred for their intense flavor and heady aroma. Summer truffles, on the other hand, are harvested when they are immature and suffer dramatically in terms of flavor and fragrance. Generally, fresh truffles are shaved over finished dishes before serving.

FRESH EGG PASTA

Pasta all'uovo

FRESH AND DRIED PASTA BOTH HAVE A PLACE in the Italian kitchen. Fresh pasta has a softer and more delicate texture, while dried pasta is sturdier, with a pleasant chew. There are many simple, elegant sauces that taste best with fresh pasta, such as Sage and Hazelnut Browned Butter Sauce (page 282), and other dishes such as ravioli (see page 277) start with homemade pasta. Good fresh pasta can be difficult to come by, so we set out to develop our own recipe for foolproof fresh egg pasta. This meant figuring out the proper ratio of eggs to flour as well as the roles of salt and olive oil in the dough. Most recipes start with all-purpose flour, but we figured it was worth testing various kinds of flour. We also wanted to devise a kneading method that was quick and easy.

Before beginning to develop our pasta dough recipe, we wanted to settle on a basic technique. Pasta dough can be made three ways. Traditionally, the dough is made by hand on a clean counter. The flour is formed into a ring, the eggs are cracked into the center, and the flour is slowly worked into the eggs with a fork. When the eggs are no longer runny, hand-kneading begins. The whole process takes at least 20 minutes and requires a lot of hand strength.

Another option is an electric pasta maker that kneads the dough and cuts it into various shapes. Although these machines have some appeal, they are quite expensive. We find that a food processor makes pasta dough much more quickly than the old-fashioned hand method. As most cooks already own a food processor, we decided to use it as our mixing method.

Most recipes for fresh egg pasta start with three eggs and then add various amounts of flour. A three-egg dough will produce about one pound of fresh pasta, so this seemed like a good place to start our working recipe. We saw recipes that called for as little as ½ cup of flour per egg and others that called for as much as ¾ cup of flour per egg. After several tests, we settled on ⅔ cup of flour per egg or 2 cups of all-purpose flour for three eggs.

In most tests, this ratio produced perfect pasta dough without adjustments, but on a few occasions the dough was a bit dry. This seemed to happen on

ROLLING OUT PASTA DOUGH

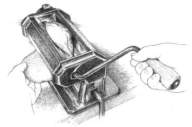  

1. Cut about one-fifth of the dough from the ball and flatten it into a disk. Run the disk through the rollers set to the widest position.

2. Bring the ends of the dough toward the middle and press down to seal.

3. Feed the open side of the pasta through the rollers. Repeat steps 1 and 2.

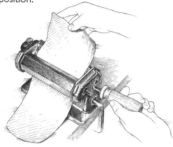  

4. Without folding again, run the pasta through the widest setting twice or until the dough is smooth. If the dough is at all sticky, lightly dust it with flour. Begin to roll the pasta thinner by putting it through the machine repeatedly, narrowing the setting each time.

5. Roll until the dough is thin and satiny, dusting with flour if sticky. You should be able to see the outline of your hand through the pasta. Lay the pasta on a clean kitchen towel and cover it with a damp cloth. Repeat with the other pieces of dough.

6. To make fettuccine, run each sheet through the wide cutter on the pasta machine. Each noodle will measure 1/8 to 1/4 inch across.

dry days, but it also could be that slight variations in egg size threw off the ratio. It was easy enough to add a little water to bring the dough together. The dough was almost never too wet.

Once the dough came together, we found it beneficial to knead it by hand for a minute or two. The motor on our food processor started to labor before the dough was smooth enough. Taking the dough out as soon as it came together prevented our food processor from overheating.

At this point, we had the basic recipe and method down, so it was time to start testing additional flavorings. We found no benefit from adding salt to the dough. If the pasta is cooked in salted water or stock, it will be well seasoned. Olive oil made the fresh pasta a bit slick and seems out of place in some recipes.

We had been using unbleached all-purpose flour in our tests. We then tested several brands of bleached all-purpose flour and found only minimal differences in the way each flour absorbed the egg. We could not detect any significant differences in flavor. On the other hand, high-protein bread flour and low-protein cake flour had disastrous effects. Bread flour produced a very tough dough that was hard to handle, while pasta made with cake flour was too soft and crumbly.

With our dough made, it was time to test rolling techniques. Many Italian sources tout the superiority of hand-rolled pasta. However, every time we rolled pasta dough with a pin, it was too thick. Although thick fettuccine is not an abomination, pasta for tortellini, with its doubled edges, must be thin. Perhaps after years of practice we could roll pasta thin enough, but for now we prefer a hand-cranked pasta machine. We tested the Imperia and Atlas pasta machines—the two major brands in Italy and widely available in cookware shops in the United States—and found them equally good at turning dough into thin, smooth, satiny sheets of pasta.

Fresh Egg Pasta

Pasta all'uovo

MAKES ABOUT 1 POUND

Although the food processor does most of the work, finish kneading this dough by hand. Keep pressing and folding the dough until it is extremely smooth. For cooking instructions for fresh pasta strands (such as fettuccine), see page 284.

2   cups (10 ounces) unbleached all-purpose flour
3   large eggs, beaten
     Water, as needed

1. Pulse the flour in a food processor to aerate it. Add the eggs and process until the dough forms a rough ball, about 30 seconds. (If the dough resembles small pebbles, add water, ½ teaspoon at a time; if the dough sticks to the side of the workbowl, add flour, 1 tablespoon at a time, and process until the dough forms a rough ball.)

2. Turn out the dough ball and small bits onto a dry work surface and knead by hand until the dough is smooth, 1 to 2 minutes. Cover with plastic wrap and set aside to relax for at least 15 minutes or up to 2 hours.

3. Cut the dough into 5 even pieces and, using a manual pasta machine, roll out the dough following the illustrations on page 276. Leave the pasta in sheets if making ravioli or cut the pasta sheets into long strands to make fettuccine.

RAVIOLI

HOMEMADE RAVIOLI IS SUPPLE AND TENDER, while supermarket ravioli tends to be tough and doughy. We wanted to develop a straightforward, easy-to-follow recipe for making great ravioli at home. Of course, making filled pasta strikes fear into many home cooks, who expect the job to be impossibly difficult and time-consuming.

After making countless batches of ravioli, we found that these fears are only partially warranted. Ravioli are not difficult to prepare, but they are time-consuming because each piece must be shaped by hand. And we don't make this statement lightly. We're certainly not averse to shortcuts and were more than willing to try the various ravioli-making gadgets sold in any well-stocked kitchen shop. Sadly, we must report that the gimmicks we tried for making quick ravioli don't really work.

In terms of ravioli gadgets, we first tried the attachments that can be fitted onto a manual pasta machine to turn out ravioli. It looks so easy. Take two sheets of pasta, some filling, and turn out hundreds of ravioli in minutes. Unfortunately, we had problems with the pasta sticking together and can't recommend these attachments. We threw away at least half the ravioli we made because they were misshapen or broken. Such waste just isn't acceptable.

Likewise, we were disappointed with the metal molds sometimes used by pasta shops. They seemed

PASTA DOUGH DONE RIGHT

Pasta dough can be a bit tricky to get just right. Higher-protein flour will absorb the eggs more readily than lower-protein flour and the resulting dough may be dry. During the summer, flour holds more moisture, so the dough may turn out a bit wet. Here's how to judge the consistency of the pasta dough and make adjustments in the food processor.

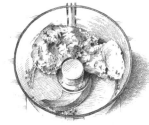

DRY DOUGH

If after 30 seconds of processing the dough resembles small pebbles, it is too dry. With the motor running, add ½ teaspoon water. Repeat one more time, if necessary.

WET DOUGH

If the dough sticks to the sides of the workbowl, it is too wet. Add 1 tablespoon flour at a time until the dough is no longer tacky.

PERFECT DOUGH

Dough with the right amount of moisture will come together in one large mass. To incorporate any small bits, turn the contents onto a floured surface and knead them together.

MAKING RAVIOLI

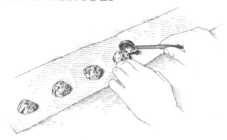

1. Use a pizza wheel or sharp knife to cut one fresh pasta sheet at a time into long rectangles measuring 4 inches across. Place small balls of filling (about 1 rounded teaspoon each) in a line 1 inch from the bottom of the pasta sheet. Leave 1¼ inches between the balls of filling.

2. Fold the top of the pasta over the filling and line it up with the bottom edge. Press the layers of dough together securely around each filling, sealing the bottom and the two open sides with your finger.

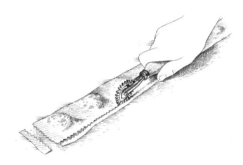

3. Use a fluted pastry wheel to cut along the two sides and bottom of the sealed pasta sheet.

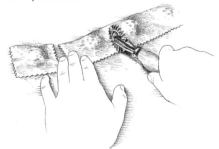

4. Run the pastry wheel between the balls of filling to cut out the ravioli.

more trouble than they are worth, as the pasta sheets must be cut precisely to fit in the molds. The other choice is to waste a lot of fresh pasta but, given the amount of time and effort it takes to make the pasta, that doesn't make much sense. In the end, we found that cutting and shaping the pasta dough by hand is the most straightforward and foolproof way to make ravioli pasta.

Because ravioli have doubled edges where the pasta is folded over the filling and sealed together, we found that the pasta sheets must be rolled as thin as possible. Otherwise, the edges may remain too chewy when the rest of the pasta is already cooked through. Use the last setting on a manual pasta machine for the best results.

The biggest problem most home cooks encounter when making ravioli is that the pasta sometimes opens up when they are boiled. There's nothing worse than seeing all the filling floating around the pot, so it's imperative to seal the edges of each piece of filled pasta properly. We tried brushing the edges of the dough with water and with lightly beaten egg, but both made the dough sticky and harder to handle. We had the best results when we used the pasta sheet as quickly as possible, when it was still moist and pliable. Pasta sheets that have been left out to dry (even for just 20 to 30 minutes) will be too brittle to manipulate. If your dough has become dry, brushing the edges lightly with water is best (eggs just make a sticky mess). Just be careful to brush the edges lightly, or the dough will become very tacky.

To guarantee that the pasta does not dry out, we recommend that you roll one sheet of dough at a time, then fill and shape it. Once the first batch of ravioli is made, start over again with another piece of pasta dough, running it through the pasta machine and then cutting and filling it as directed.

When boiling the ravioli, we found it necessary to cook the pasta in two batches to prevent the ravioli from sticking together. Transfer the first batch to a warmed pasta bowl, sauce it lightly, then cover it with foil so it will stay hot while the second batch cooks. If you prefer, bring two pots of water to a boil and divide the pasta between the two pots to cook it all at one time.

Most any finely chopped or ground meat, seafood, poultry, or vegetable can be turned into a filling for ravioli, but we focused on three we particularly like—a simple cheese filling, butternut squash, and mushroom. Regardless of what type of filling you use, however, the biggest trick is to not overstuff the ravioli, or they will burst apart as they cook. A generous teaspoon of filling per ravioli is plenty.

For the cheese ravioli, we liked a combination of ricotta, Parmesan, and basil for flavor, along with a little mozzarella and egg yolk for texture. Frozen spinach is a nice addition to this filling—just be sure to thoroughly squeeze out any excess liquid. This type of ravioli tasted best when paired with a light, simple tomato sauce; heavier sauces overpowered the delicate flavors.

Another classic ravioli filling is one made with either a puree of butternut squash or chopped mushrooms and both are often paired with a browned butter–sage sauce rather than a tomato-based sauce. Unlike the cheese fillings that require an egg yolk as a binder, these fillings only require a little oil and/or butter, along with a healthy handful of Parmesan, to hold together. The trick, however, is to cook both the squash and mushrooms first to drive off their natural moisture and concentrate their flavor before adding the remaining filling ingredients.

Given the amount of work involved, we wanted to be able to shape our ravioli in advance and then cook them as desired. (You don't want to be shaping ravioli while dinner guests wait.) We found it best to transfer shaped ravioli to a well-floured baking sheet (the flour helps prevent sticking). If you are not going to cook the pasta right away, cover it with a damp kitchen towel, wrap the tray with plastic wrap, and refrigerate for up to four hours. After four hours, we found the pasta dried out.

For longer storage, we discovered that the freezer is the best place for ravioli. Place the floured baking sheets with ravioli in the freezer until the pasta shapes are frozen solid, about two hours. Transfer the frozen pastas to a large zipper-lock plastic bag and freeze them for up to a month. Don't defrost frozen pasta; simply drop it into boiling water and add a minute or two to the cooking time.

Homemade Cheese Ravioli with Simple Tomato Sauce

SERVES 6 TO 8 AS A MAIN COURSE,
MAKES ABOUT 45 RAVIOLI

We like the clean, simple flavor of our homemade sauce here, but 4 cups of any simple tomato sauce can be substituted. Be sure to dust the counter and pasta dough liberally with flour to prevent sticking and keep the dough covered to prevent it from drying out.

SAUCE

3	(14.5-ounce) cans diced tomatoes
¼	cup olive oil
4	garlic cloves, minced or pressed through a garlic press (about 4 teaspoons)
⅛	teaspoon red pepper flakes
1	teaspoon sugar
	Salt
3	tablespoons shredded fresh basil leaves (see page 298)
	Ground black pepper

RAVIOLI

1	cup ricotta cheese
1	ounce Parmesan cheese, grated (½ cup), plus extra for serving
2	ounces mozzarella cheese, shredded (½ cup)
1	large egg yolk
2	tablespoons minced fresh basil or parsley leaves
	Salt and ground black pepper
	Flour, for dusting the baking sheets
1	recipe Fresh Egg Pasta (page 277), rested

1. FOR THE SAUCE: Pulse the tomatoes with their juice in a food processor to a coarse puree, about 15 seconds; set aside. Heat 2 tablespoons of the oil, garlic, and red pepper flakes in a large saucepan over medium heat until fragrant, about 1 minute. Stir in the pureed tomatoes, sugar, and ½ teaspoon salt, bring to a simmer, and cook until slightly thickened, 20 to 30 minutes. Off the heat, stir in the remaining 2 tablespoons oil and basil and season with salt and pepper to taste. Cover and set aside to keep warm until needed. (The sauce can be refrigerated for up to 2 days.)

2. FOR THE RAVIOLI: Mix the ricotta, Parmesan, mozzarella, egg yolk, and basil together and season with salt and pepper to taste; set aside. Dust 2 large rimmed baking sheets liberally with flour; set aside. Divide the pasta dough into 5 even pieces and cover with plastic wrap. Following illustrations 1–5 on page 276, unwrap 1 piece of dough at a time and roll out the dough using a pasta machine. Following the illustrations on page 278, use a pizza wheel or sharp knife to cut one pasta sheet at a time into long rectangles measuring 4 inches across. Place generous 1-teaspoon dollops of the filling over the bottom half of the dough, spaced about 1¼ inches apart. (If the edges of the dough seem dry, dab with water.) Fold the top of the pasta over the filling and press the layers of dough together securely around each filling to seal.

3. Use a fluted pastry wheel to cut the ravioli apart and trim the edges. Transfer the finished ravioli to a floured baking sheet, cover with a damp kitchen towel, and set aside. Repeat with the remaining pasta and filling. (The towel-covered baking sheets of ravioli can be wrapped with plastic wrap and refrigerated for up to 4 hours. The ravioli can also be frozen; when completely frozen, the ravioli can be transferred to a zipper-lock bag to save space in the freezer. Do not thaw before boiling.)

4. Bring 4 quarts of water to a boil in a large pot for the ravioli. Add 1 tablespoon salt and half of the ravioli. Cook, stirring often and lowering the heat if necessary to keep the water at a gentle boil, until the ravioli are tender, about 2 minutes (3 to 4 minutes if frozen). Using a slotted spoon or wire spider, transfer the cooked ravioli to a warm serving platter, spoon some of the sauce over the top, and cover with foil to keep warm. Return the water to a boil, cook the remaining ravioli, and transfer to the platter. Pour the remaining warm sauce over the ravioli, toss gently, and serve immediately, passing extra Parmesan cheese separately.

➤ VARIATION

Homemade Spinach and Cheese Ravioli with Simple Tomato Sauce

Follow the recipe for Homemade Cheese Ravioli with Simple Tomato Sauce, stirring 1 (10-ounce) package frozen spinach, thawed, thoroughly wrung dry, and chopped coarse, into the ricotta filling in step 2.

INGREDIENTS: Ricotta Cheese

Originally crafted from the whey by-product of Romano cheese making, ricotta cheese has garnered fame on its own as a white, cushiony filling for baked pasta dishes. As ricotta has gained global popularity, however, preservation methods used by many large-scale manufacturers have turned these once fluffy, buttery, sweet curds into chalky, sour spreads. Seeking at least one noble specimen, we sampled four nationally available brands of part-skim ricotta.

The three commercially processed brands—Dragone, Sargento, and Sorrento—consistently garnered unfavorable adjectives such as "rancid," "grainy," and "soggy." At the other end of the spectrum entirely sat the all-natural Calabro. Described as being "fresh" and "creamy" with "perfect" curds, it was the hands-down favorite.

All three commercial brands are packed with gums and other stabilizers to guarantee shelf-stability for weeks. Calabro's curds, on the other hand, are fresh-drawn from nothing other than Vermont farm whole milk, skim milk, a starter, and a sprinkle of salt. Granted, the latter's shelf life spans only a matter of days, but one spoonful should be enough to guarantee its quick disappearance from your fridge. If you can't find Calabro, read labels and look for another fresh ricotta without gums or stabilizers.

THE BEST RICOTTA CHEESE

When it comes to ricotta, choose a freshly made cheese without gums or stabilizers. We particularly like Calabro Ricotta, which is available nationwide.

Canned Tomato Products 101

CANNED TOMATO PRODUCTS ARE A PANTRY STAPLE, BUT WHICH ONES SHOULD YOU BUY? OVER THE years, we've taste tested nearly every type and brand of tomato product we could lay our hands on—including whole, diced, crushed, puree, and paste. Here's our opinion on what tastes best.

DICED TOMATOES

Good for: Rustic sauces with a chunky or coarse texture, long-cooked stews, or as a substitute for crushed tomatoes (the tomatoes are processed with their juice in a food processor).

What to buy: Sales of diced tomatoes dominate the canned tomato category. Overall, we prefer diced tomatoes packed in juice rather than those packed in puree because they have a fresher flavor. Our preferred brand, Muir Glen, garnered comments such as "sweet," "fresh tasting," and "most like fresh tomatoes."

THE BEST DICED TOMATOES

MUIR GLEN ORGANIC DICED TOMATOES

CRUSHED TOMATOES

Good for: Fresh-tasting, looser-textured sauces. (The texture of crushed tomatoes varies widely so if you can't find one of our recommended brands, we suggest crushing your own using canned diced tomatoes and a food processor for a consistent, reliable texture.)

What to buy: Crushed tomatoes have a wide range of textures. Some are thick as puree, while others are downright watery. Tasters picked Tuttorosso Crushed Tomatoes in Thick Puree with Basil as their favorite, declaring them to be "chunky, with dimensional flavor" and "very fresh-tasting." Do not confuse these with Tuttorosso's New World Style Crushed Tomatoes which rated quite poorly in our test. Tuttorosso isn't available everywhere, but Muir Glen Organic Crushed Tomatoes with Basil are available nationwide and came in a close second.

THE BEST CRUSHED TOMATOES

TUTTOROSSO CRUSHED TOMATOES IN THICK PUREE WITH BASIL

MUIR GLEN ORGANIC CRUSHED TOMATOES WITH BASIL

WHOLE TOMATOES

Good for: Dicing into bite-sized pieces and adding to dishes with a short simmering time or as a finishing ingredient added during the final few minutes of cooking.

What to buy: Whole tomatoes are peeled and packed in juice or puree. Overall, we found that those packed in juice have a livelier flavor. Our winning brand, Progresso, earned comments such as "bright, lively flavor" and "the perfect balance of acidic and fruity notes." Progresso sells whole tomatoes packed in juice and packed in puree, so be sure to read the fine print and buy the ones packed in juice.

THE BEST WHOLE TOMATOES

PROGRESSO ITALIAN-STYLE WHOLE PEELED TOMATOES WITH BASIL

TOMATO PUREE

Good for: Long-simmered, smooth, thick sauces with a deep, hearty flavor.

What to buy: We tasted eight brands of tomato puree, and although it was a very close call, Hunt's Tomato Puree edged out the other brands with tasters', comments including "nice and thick" and "tomatoey."

THE BEST TOMATO PUREE

HUNT'S TOMATO PUREE

TOMATO PASTE

Good for: Adding a slightly deeper, rounded flavor and color to nearly any soup, sauce, or stew.

What to buy: The only tomato paste packaged in a tube (invaluable for using and storing) and the only paste that contains a small amount of fat, Amore was the hands-down favorite. Tasters found its flavor to be "intense" and "fresh."

THE BEST TOMATO PASTE

AMORE

Squash Ravioli with Sage and Hazelnut Browned Butter Sauce

SERVES 6 TO 8, MAKES ABOUT 45 RAVIOLI

Do not use frozen squash here; its flavor is very bland and will be disappointing. Sliced or slivered almonds can be substituted for the hazelnuts.

RAVIOLI

1	pound butternut squash (about ½ medium), peeled, seeded, and cut into 1-inch chunks
4	tablespoons (½ stick) unsalted butter
1	tablespoon brown sugar
	Salt
	Pinch freshly grated nutmeg
2	ounces Parmesan cheese, grated (1 cup)
⅛	teaspoon ground black pepper
	Flour, for dusting the baking sheets
1	recipe Fresh Egg Pasta (page 277)

SAUCE

8	tablespoons (1 stick) unsalted butter, cut into 4 pieces
¼	cup coarsely chopped hazelnuts (about 1 ounce)
2	tablespoons minced fresh sage leaves
	Salt
2	teaspoons juice from 1 lemon
1	ounce Parmesan, shaved (see page 274)

1. FOR THE RAVIOLI: Place the squash in a large microwave-safe bowl. Cover the bowl tightly with plastic wrap and microwave on high until the squash is tender and easily pierced with a dinner fork, 10 to 15 minutes.

2. Carefully remove the plastic wrap (watch for scalding steam), drain the squash, and transfer to a food processor. Add the butter, sugar, ¼ teaspoon salt, and nutmeg and process until the mixture is smooth, 15 to 20 seconds, stopping to scrape down the sides of the bowl as needed. Transfer to a bowl, stir in the Parmesan and pepper, and refrigerate the filling until no longer warm, 15 to 25 minutes.

3. Dust 2 large rimmed baking sheets liberally with flour; set aside. Divide the pasta dough into 5 even pieces and cover with plastic wrap. Following illustrations 1–5 on page 276, unwrap 1 piece of dough at a time and roll out the dough using a pasta machine. Following the illustrations on page 278, use a pizza wheel or sharp knife to cut one pasta sheet at a time into long rectangles measuring 4 inches across. Place generous 1-teaspoon dollops of the filling over the bottom half of the dough, spaced about 1¼ inches apart. (If the edges of the dough seem dry, dab with water.) Fold the top of the pasta over the filling and press the layers of dough together securely around each filling to seal.

4. Use a fluted pastry wheel to cut the ravioli apart and trim the edges. Transfer the finished ravioli to a floured baking sheet, cover with a damp kitchen towel, and set aside. Repeat with the remaining pasta and filling. (The towel-covered baking sheets of ravioli can be wrapped with plastic wrap and refrigerated for up to 4 hours. The ravioli can also be frozen; when completely frozen, the ravioli can be transferred to a zipper-lock bag to save space in the freezer. Do not thaw before boiling.)

5. FOR THE SAUCE: Before cooking the ravioli, heat the butter, hazelnuts, sage, and ¼ teaspoon salt in a 10-inch skillet over medium-high heat and cook, swirling the pan constantly, until the butter is melted with golden brown color and nutty aroma, about 3 minutes. Off the heat, stir in the lemon juice; set aside.

6. Bring 4 quarts of water to a boil in a large pot for the ravioli. Add 1 tablespoon salt and half of the ravioli. Cook, stirring often and lowering the heat if necessary to keep the water at a gentle boil, until the ravioli are tender, about 2 minutes (3 to 4 minutes if frozen). Using a slotted spoon or wire spider, transfer the cooked ravioli to a warm serving platter, spoon some of the butter sauce over the top, and cover with foil to keep warm. Return the water to a boil, cook the remaining ravioli, and transfer to the platter. Swirl 2 tablespoons of the ravioli cooking water into the remaining butter sauce, then pour the sauce over the ravioli, top with the shaved Parmesan, and serve immediately.

➤ VARIATION

Mushroom Ravioli with Sage and Hazelnut Browned Butter Sauce

This variation tastes especially good when 1 teaspoon of white truffle oil is substituted for the lemon juice in the sauce (see page 273 for more information on truffle oil). The hazelnuts can be omitted from the sauce if desired.

1½	pounds white button mushrooms, wiped clean and quartered
2	tablespoons olive oil
2	medium shallots, minced (about ⅓ cup)
5	medium garlic cloves, minced or pressed through a garlic press (about 5 teaspoons)
1	ounce dried porcini mushrooms, rinsed and minced
	Salt
¼	cup heavy cream
2	ounces Parmesan cheese, grated (1 cup)
2	tablespoons minced fresh parsley leaves
	Ground black pepper

1. Pulse half of the white mushrooms in a food processor until finely chopped, about 15 pulses; transfer to a bowl and repeat with the remaining white mushrooms. Heat the oil in a 12-inch non-stick skillet over medium heat until shimmering. Add the shallot and garlic and cook until fragrant, about 30 seconds. Stir in the chopped white mushrooms, porcini mushrooms, and ½ teaspoon salt. Cover, turn the heat to medium-low, and cook, stirring occasionally, until the mushrooms are wet and wilted, about 10 minutes.

2. Uncover, increase the heat to high, and continue to cook until the mushroom liquid has evaporated and the mixture is clumpy and starting to brown, about 10 minutes. Stir in the cream and cook until the mixture is sticky and cohesive but not wet, about 1 minute. Transfer the mixture to a bowl, stir in the Parmesan and parsley, season with pepper to taste, and refrigerate the filling until no longer warm, 15 to 25 minutes. Follow the recipe for Squash Ravioli with Sage and Hazelnut Browned Butter Sauce, substituting the mushroom filling for the squash filling in step 3.

PANTRY SPOTLIGHT

PORCINI MUSHROOMS

Mushrooms are an important ingredient in Italian cuisine and porcini mushrooms (known as *cèpes* in France, *Steinpilz* in Germany, and *belyi grib* in Russia) are highly prized for their heady, woodsy flavor. Fresh porcini are available just a few weeks out of the year (you use them as you would any fresh mushroom), but luckily dried porcini are available year round and can be found at nearly any supermarket.

The drying process not only extends the shelf life of the porcini, but it also intensifies its flavor. Using just a small amount of dried porcini can add an incredibly deep, rich mushroom flavor. When using dried porcini, it is important to first rinse them of any dirt or sand. For recipes with longer cooking times, you can simply mince the dried porcini and add them to the pot near the beginning of the cooking time. For recipes with shorter cooking times, however, it is best to soften and rehydrate the dried porcini in warm water before chopping them and stirring them into the pot along with the rehydrating liquid (which should be strained of grit).

When buying porcini mushrooms, look for mushrooms that are large and thick (see top photo below) and either tan or brown. Avoid packages with lots of dust and crumbled bits (see middle photo below) and keep an eye out for small pinholes, telltale signs that worms got to the mushrooms (see bottom photo below). Eyeballing is good, but smelling the mushrooms (especially if sold loose) is also helpful to judge quality. Purchase dried porcini with an earthy (not musty or stale) aroma; mushrooms with no aroma at all are likely to have little or no flavor.

For best flavor, look for large thick tan or brown porcini.

Packages of porcini containing crumbled bits are of poor quality and should be avoided.

Avoid porcini mushrooms with small pinholes, which are a sign that they have been contaminated by worms.

Cooking Pasta 101

Cooking pasta seems simple—just boil water and wait—but cooking perfect pasta takes some finesse. Here's how we do it.

CHOOSING PASTA

You have two basic choices—dried or fresh. Dried pasta is made from high-protein durum wheat flour, so it cooks up springy and firm and is suitable for thick tomato and meat sauces as well as concentrated oil-based sauces. Fresh pasta is made from softer all-purpose flour and is quite delicate. Its rough, porous surface pairs well with dairy-based sauces.

DRIED SEMOLINA PASTA

No longer gummy and bland, American brands of semolina (which is coarsely ground durum wheat) pasta have improved so much that many bested their pricey Italian counterparts in our tasting.

➤ COOKING TIPS

When cooked to al dente, pasta retains some chew but is neither hard nor gummy at the center.

DRIED PASTA WINNER: RONZONI

FRESH EGG PASTA

While your best bet for fresh pasta is still homemade, there are a few serviceable supermarket options. Our favorite brand is found in the refrigerator case, sealed in spoilage-retardant packaging and made from pasteurized eggs.

➤ COOKING TIPS

Fresh pasta is easily overcooked, so test early. Drain the pasta a few minutes before it reaches al dente, return it to the empty pot, and then cook with the sauce for another minute or two. The underdone pasta will absorb flavor from the sauce and the starch from the pasta will help thicken the sauce.

FRESH PASTA WINNER: BUITONI

WHOLE WHEAT AND GRAIN PASTAS

Most of the whole wheat pastas we tried were gummy, grainy, or lacking in "wheaty" flavor, but there were a few that we really liked. Our favorite is made from a blend of whole wheat and regular flours. We were less thrilled about the alternative-grain pastas we tried. Made from rice, corn, quinoa, and spelt, these products were plagued by shaggy, mushy textures and off-flavors. If you're desperate to avoid wheat, try Tinkyáda Organic Brown Rice Pasta.

➤ COOKING TIPS

Cook and use as you would dried semolina pasta.

WHOLE WHEAT PASTA WINNER: RONZONI HEALTHY HARVEST

MATCHING PASTA SAUCES AND SHAPES

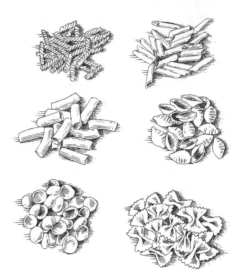

SHORT PASTAS

Short tubular or molded pasta shapes do an excellent job of trapping chunky sauces. Sauces with very large chunks are best with rigatoni or other large tubes. Sauces with small chunks make more sense with fusilli or penne. Clockwise from top right, the shapes shown are: penne, shells, farfalle, orecchiette, rigatoni, and fusilli.

STRAND PASTAS

Long strands are best with smooth sauces or sauces with very small chunks. In general, wider noodles, such as pappardelle and fettuccine, can support slightly chunkier sauces than can very thin noodles. Clockwise from top right, the shapes shown are: fettuccine, linguine, spaghetti, capellini, and pappardelle.

AT A GLANCE
COOKING PASTA
1. Add salt and pasta to water at a rolling boil.
2. Stir immediately to prevent sticking.
3. Cover and return to boil, stirring often.
4. Check early and often for doneness.
5. Reserve some cooking water and drain.
6. Sauce, season, and serve immediately.

THE SETUP

Pasta cooks quickly and should be served immediately, so have all the necessary ingredients and utensils assembled before you begin—as well as your family or dinner guests. As the Italians say, "People wait for pasta, not the other way around."

Water and Pot: You'll need 4 quarts of water to cook I pound of dried pasta. Any less and the noodles may stick. Pasta leaches starch as it cooks. Without plenty of water to dilute it, the starch coats the noodles, making them sticky.

The pot should be large, with at least a 6-quart capacity—to guard against boilovers. But forget expensive metal pots and fancy mesh inserts. A lightweight, inexpensive stockpot with sturdy handles and a lid does the job just fine.

Oil: Unless you're serving a butter- or cream-based sauce, keep some extra-virgin olive oil on hand for drizzling over the sauced pasta for a final burst of flavor. Just don't waste it in the cooking water: It won't prevent the pasta from sticking (not a problem if you use enough water), but it will prevent the sauce from coating the pasta.

Pasta: One pound of dried pasta generally serves four to six people as a main course, depending on whether the sauce is light (tomato sauce), rich (creamy Alfredo or hearty Bolognese), or bulked up with other ingredients such as vegetables or seafood.

Liquid Measuring Cup: In that last flurry of activity before saucing the pasta and getting dinner on the table, it's easy to forget to reserve some cooking water to thin the sauce, if needed. We often place a measuring cup in the colander as a reminder when we start to cook.

Colander: Once the pasta is drained, give the colander a shake or two, but don't shake the pasta bone-dry. The little bit of hot cooking water clinging to the pasta will help the sauce coat it.

Sauce: Don't drop the pasta into the water until the sauce is nearly ready. Smooth sauces and sauces with very small bits, such as garlic and oil, are best with long strands of pasta. Chunkier sauces are best matched with short tubular or molded shapes.

Salt: Properly seasoned cooking water is crucial for good flavor—use 1 tablespoon table salt (or 2 tablespoons kosher salt) per 4 quarts of water.

Serving Bowls and Ladle: We like to serve pasta in wide soup bowls, as the edge provides an easy place to twirl noodles on a fork. To warm, before serving the pasta (especially important with cream sauces, which cool quickly and congeal) add a few extra cups of water to the pasta pot. When it boils, ladle about ½ cup of boiling water into each bowl and let stand while the pasta cooks.

Pasta Fork: Of the countless items of pasta paraphernalia we've tested over the years, the only one we recommend is a pasta fork—a long-handled, perforated spoon with ridged teeth. The wood variety is clunky and prone to splitting, but the plastic and stainless-steel versions are great. Not essential—basic tongs work fine—but we're glad we bought one.

QUICK TIP
WARM THE SERVING BOWL

If you're using a large serving bowl, try placing it underneath the colander while draining the pasta. The hot water heats up the bowl, which keeps the pasta warm longer.

MARINARA SAUCE

MARINARA, MEANING "SAILOR STYLE" IS THE name given to a tomato-based pasta sauce that first became popular in the seafaring town of Naples. Compared to a fast and fresh tomato sauce, the flavor of a marinara is complex and rich, thanks to a long, slow simmering time. Unfortunately, this complexity of flavor comes at the price of hours in the kitchen. In our opinion, a long simmering time is important for some pasta sauces, such as Classic Bolognese (page 289). But for marinara, we wondered if we could achieve authentic, long-cooked flavor without spending all day in the kitchen—so we set our timer for one hour, hoping to create a multidimensional sauce that could be made on a weeknight.

To get started, we weeded through hundreds of marinara recipes to find a handful of recipes to get our feet wet. We tried some that were "quick" versions but also some that were cooked for longer than an hour. The differences were readily apparent. The quick sauces were generally thin and lacked depth of flavor. The long-cooked sauces got the complexity right, but most relied on an ambitious laundry list of ingredients to achieve it—not to mention a lot of time. The sauce we were after had to capture some of these robust flavors within the confines of fairly quick cooking.

Because prime fresh tomatoes are available for such a limited time during the year, we opted for canned. But canned tomatoes take up nearly half an aisle at the supermarket. Which variety should we choose? Crushed, pureed, and diced tomatoes offered the ultimate ease in sauce making: open can, dump contents into pan. But all three options have downsides. Pureed tomatoes go into the can already cooked, which imparts a stale, flat flavor to the final sauce. Crushed tomatoes are generally packed in tomato puree: same problem. With these, the sauces came out tasting like unremarkable homemade versions of the jarred spaghetti sauces sold at the supermarket. With canned diced tomatoes, the problem was texture, not flavor. In the past, we've learned that manufacturers treat diced tomatoes with calcium chloride to keep them from losing their shape and turning to mush. That's fine

for many dishes, but for recipes in which a smooth consistency is desired, calcium chloride does its job too well, making the tomatoes harder to break down—and the resulting sauces oddly granular.

The only choice left, then, was canned whole tomatoes. (While whole tomatoes are also treated with calcium chloride, the chemical has direct contact with a much smaller percentage of the tomato.) The big drawback of using whole tomatoes in a sauce is that they have to be cut up. Chopping them on a cutting board was a mess. The solution was to dump the tomatoes into a strainer over a bowl and then hand-crush them, removing the hard core and any stray bits of skin.

That's when we made the first of several decisions that would enable us to get long-simmered complexity in a short time. Most marinara recipes call for simply adding a can (or two) of tomatoes to the pot, juice and all—and some even call for throwing in a can of water. Now that we were separating the solids from the juice anyway, why not experiment with adding less of the reserved liquid? The trick worked: By adding only 2½ cups of the drained juice from two cans of whole tomatoes (rather than the full 3½ cups we had collected) and omitting the extra water, we managed to cut the simmering time by almost 20 minutes.

Up until now we had been following the standard marinara procedure of sautéing aromatics (onions and garlic) in olive oil in a saucepan before adding the tomatoes, liquid, and flavorings, then simmering. That's fine if you have all day, but we had only an hour. So we switched from a saucepan to a skillet, hoping the greater surface area would encourage faster evaporation and, thus, faster concentration of flavors.

It was faster, all right—down to just under an hour—but we felt that the sauce could use gutsier tomato flavor. Not only was the solution simple, but it was the key step in giving our quick sauce the complexity of a long-simmered one. Before adding the liquids and simmering, we sautéed the tomatoes until they glazed the bottom of the pan. Only then did we add the liquids, a normally routine step that, by essentially deglazing the pan, added crucial flavor to our sauce.

With the tomato flavor under control, it was time to develop more depth of flavor. Onions added a pleasant sweetness, but carrots, although sweet, also added an earthy flavor that diminished that of the tomatoes. Sugar, added at the end of cooking, proved to be the working solution to balance the flavors: too much and our sauce began to taste like it came out of a jar; too little and the acidity overwhelmed the other flavors. Tasters loved the robust, complex flavor of red wine and a mere ⅓ cup was just the right amount. But not just any bottle: Wines with a heavy oak flavor rated lower than those with little to no oak presence. (Chianti and Merlot scored particularly high marks.)

We now had a good marinara ready to ladle and serve in less than an hour. Could we further bolster the complexity without adding minutes? On a hunch, we tried reserving a few of the uncooked canned tomatoes and adding them near the end of cooking. When we served this sauce alongside the earlier version, tasters were unanimous in their preference for the new sauce; just six tomatoes pureed into the sauce at the end added enough brightness to complement the deeper profile of the cooked sauce.

So far the sauce had little flavor from herbs beyond oregano. Fresh basil, also added at the end, contributed a floral aroma that complemented the sauce's careful balance of sweet and acid. We adjusted the salt and pepper and added extra-virgin olive oil to round things out.

Marinara Sauce

MAKES 4 CUPS, ENOUGH TO SAUCE
1 POUND OF PASTA

Because canned tomatoes vary in acidity and saltiness, it's best to add salt, pepper, and sugar to taste just before serving. If you prefer a chunkier sauce, pulse just three or four times in the food processor in step 4.

2   (28-ounce) cans whole tomatoes
2   tablespoons olive oil
1   medium onion, minced
2   medium garlic cloves, minced or pressed
      through a garlic press (about 2 teaspoons)

½   teaspoon dried oregano
⅓   cup dry red wine, such as Chianti or Merlot
3   tablespoons chopped fresh basil leaves
1   tablespoon extra-virgin olive oil
      Salt and ground black pepper
1–2   teaspoons sugar, as needed (see note)

1. Pour the tomatoes into a strainer set over a large bowl. Open the tomatoes with your hands and remove and discard the fibrous cores. Let the tomatoes drain for about 5 minutes. Measure out and reserve ¾ cup tomatoes from the strainer; set the remaining tomatoes in the strainer aside. Reserve 2½ cups of the strained tomato juice, discarding any extra.

2. Heat the olive oil in a 12-inch skillet over medium heat until shimmering. Add the onion and cook until softened and golden around the edges, 6 to 8 minutes. Stir in the garlic and oregano and cook until fragrant, about 30 seconds. Stir in the tomatoes from the strainer and increase the heat to medium-high. Cook, stirring every minute, until the liquid has evaporated, the tomatoes begin to stick to the bottom of the pan, and a brown fond forms around the pan edges, 10 to 12 minutes.

3. Stir in the wine and cook until thick and syrupy, about 1 minute. Stir in the tomato juice, bring to a simmer, then reduce the heat to medium and cook, stirring occasionally and loosening any browned bits, until the sauce is thick, 8 to 10 minutes.

4. Transfer the sauce to a food processor, add the ¾ cup reserved tomatoes, and process until slightly chunky, about 8 long pulses. Return the sauce to the skillet, add the basil and extra-virgin olive oil, and season with salt, pepper, and sugar to taste. (The sauce can be cooled, transferred to an airtight container, and refrigerated for up to 2 days or frozen for up to 1 month. Add water as needed to thin out the sauce when reheating.)

➤ VARIATION
Spicy Marinara Sauce
Follow the recipe for Marinara Sauce, adding 1 teaspoon red pepper flakes with the garlic in step 2 and substituting ¼ cup minced parsley for the basil in step 4.

BOLOGNESE SAUCE

Ragù

BOLOGNESE IS A LONG-COOKED MEAT SAUCE that hails from the city of Bologna in the northern region of Emilia-Romagna—a region known for its meat and cheeses. Unlike other meat sauces in which tomatoes dominate (think jars of spaghetti sauce with flecks of meat in a sea of tomato puree), Bolognese sauce is about the meat, with the tomatoes in a supporting role. Bolognese also differs from many tomato-based meat sauces in that it contains dairy, usually butter, milk, and/or cream. The dairy gives the meat an especially sweet, appealing flavor.

Bolognese sauce is not hard to prepare (the hands-on work is less than 30 minutes), but it does require hours of slow simmering. The sauce must be worth the effort. Bolognese should be complex, with a good balance of flavors. The meat should be first and foremost, but there should be sweet, salty, and acidic flavors in the background.

All Bolognese recipes can be broken down into three steps. First, vegetables are sautéed in fat. Ground meat is then browned in the pan. The final step is the addition of liquids and slow simmering over very low heat.

After an initial round of testing in which we made five styles of Bolognese, we had a recipe we liked pretty well. We favored a combination of onions, carrots, and celery as the vegetables and we liked them sautéed in butter rather than oil. We also discovered that a combination of ground beef, veal, and pork made this sauce especially complex and rich-tasting. The veal adds finesse and delicacy to the sauce, while the pork makes it sweet.

Settling on the liquid element of the recipe, however, proved more difficult. The secret to a great Bolognese sauce is the sequential reduction of various liquids over the sautéed meat and vegetables. The idea is to build flavor and tenderize the meat, which toughens during the browning phase. Many recipes insist on a particular order for adding these liquids. The most common liquid choices we uncovered in our research were milk, cream, stock, wine, and tomatoes (fresh, canned whole, crushed, or paste). We ended up testing numerous combinations to find the perfect balance.

Liquids are treated in two ways. In the earlier part of the cooking process, liquids are added to the pan and simmered briskly until fully evaporated, the point being to impart flavor rather than to cook the meat and vegetables. Wine is always treated this way; if the wine is not evaporated, the sauce will be too alcoholic. Milk and cream are often but not always treated this way. Later, either stock or tomatoes are added in greater quantity and allowed to cook off very slowly. These liquids add flavor, but they also serve as the cooking medium for the sauce during the slow simmering phase.

We tested pouring wine over the browned meat first, followed by milk. We also tried them in the opposite order—milk first, then wine. We found that the meat cooked in milk first was softer and sweeter. As the bits of meat cook, they develop a hard crust that makes it more difficult for them to absorb liquid. Adding the milk first, when the meat is just barely cooked, works better. The milk penetrates more easily, tenderizing the meat and making it especially sweet.

We tried using cream instead of milk but felt that the sauce was too rich. Milk provides just enough dairy flavor to complement the meat flavor. (Some recipes finish the sauce with cream. We found that cream added just before the sauce was done was also overpowering.) So we settled on milk as the first liquid for the sauce. For the second liquid, we liked both white and red wine. White wine was a bit more delicate and is our choice for the basic recipe.

Then we moved on to the final element in most recipes, the cooking liquid. We did not like any of the recipes we tested with broth. As for tomato paste, we felt that it had little to offer; with none of the bright acidity of canned whole tomatoes and no fresh tomato flavor, it produced a dull sauce.

We tried tomatoes three more ways—fresh, canned whole, and canned crushed. Fresh tomatoes did nothing for the sauce and were a lot of work, as we found it necessary to peel them. (If not peeled, the skins would separate during the long cooking process and mar the texture of the sauce.) Crushed tomatoes were fine, but they were not as juicy (nor as consistent in terms of texture) as canned diced tomatoes that we crushed ourselves in the food processor.

Because Bolognese sauce simmers for quite a while, it's nice to use juicy crushed tomatoes to keep the pot from scorching.

Our recipe was finally taking shape, with all the ingredients in place. But we still wanted to know if it was necessary to cook Bolognese sauce over low heat and, if so, how long the sauce must simmer. When we tried to hurry the process by cooking over medium heat to evaporate the tomato juice more quickly, the meat was too firm and the flavors were not melded. Long simmering over the lowest possible heat—a few bubbles may rise to the surface of the sauce at one time, but it should not be simmering all over—is the only method that allows enough time for flavor to develop and for the meat to become tender.

As for the timing, we found that the sauce was too soupy after two hours on low heat and the meat was still pretty firm. At three hours, the meat was much softer, with a melt-in-the-mouth consistency. The sauce was dense and smooth at this point. We tried simmering the sauce for four hours but found no benefit—some batches even reduced too much and scorched a bit.

MAKING A FLAME TAMER

A flame tamer (or heat diffuser) is a metal disk that can be fitted over a burner (electric or gas) to reduce the heat transfer. This device is especially useful when trying to keep a pot at the barest simmer. If you don't own a flame tamer (it costs less than $10 and is stocked at most kitchenware stores), you can fashion one from aluminum foil. Take a long sheet of foil and shape it into a 1-inch-thick ring that will fit on your burner. Make sure that the ring is an even thickness so that a pot will rest flat on it. A foil ring elevates the pot slightly above the flame or electric coil, allowing you to keep a pot of Bolognese or polenta at the merest simmer.

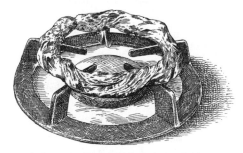

A homemade flame tamer made with aluminum foil keeps sauces, such as Bolognese, from simmering too briskly, even on a stovetop that runs fairly hot.

Classic Bolognese Sauce
Ragù
MAKES ABOUT 4 CUPS, ENOUGH TO SAUCE
1 POUND OF PASTA

Simmering this sauce very gently is key to its super silky texture; if your stovetop runs hot, use a flame tamer (see below). Meatloaf mix (a packaged combination of equal parts ground beef, veal, and pork) can be very fatty, so be sure to skim the fat from the surface of the sauce as it simmers. Don't substitute low-fat or skim milk here. When serving with pasta, toss the noodles with a few tablespoons of butter before tossing with the sauce.

3	tablespoons unsalted butter
¼	cup minced onion
¼	cup minced carrot
¼	cup minced celery
	Salt
1	pound meatloaf mix or ⅓ pound each ground beef chuck, ground veal, and ground pork
1½	cups whole milk
1½	cups dry white wine
3	(14.5-ounce) cans diced tomatoes, drained, with 1½ cups of the juice reserved

1. Melt the butter in a large Dutch oven over medium heat. Add the onion, carrot, celery, and 1 teaspoon salt and cook until softened, 6 to 8 minutes. Stir in the ground meat and cook, breaking up the meat with a wooden spoon, until no longer pink, about 3 minutes.

2. Stir in the milk, bring to a simmer, and cook until the milk has evaporated and only clear fat remains, about 25 minutes. Stir in the wine, bring to a simmer, and cook until it has evaporated, about 25 minutes.

3. Meanwhile, pulse the tomatoes in a food processor until slightly chunky, about 8 pulses. Add the tomatoes and reserved tomato juice to the pot and bring to a bare simmer. Cook gently over low heat until the liquid has evaporated, 3 to 3½ hours. Season with salt to taste and serve over buttered noodles. (The sauce can be cooled, transferred to an airtight container, and refrigerated for up to 2 days or frozen for up to 1 month. If frozen, thaw and reheat in a medium saucepan, covered, over medium-low heat until hot.)

PESTO

ITALIANS GENERALLY RESERVE THE TERM *pesto* for fresh sauces made with basil, but there are many other traditional, pesto-like purees that can be tossed with pasta—made with ingredients such as olives, herbs, arugula, and toasted nuts, to name a few. Regardless of what you call these super-flavorful, finely chopped, olive oil–based sauces, they are an easy way to make a quick meal.

Although pesto is traditionally made using a mortar and pestle, we found a food processor to be the fastest and most consistent method. Using high-quality extra-virgin olive oil and Parmesan (or Pecorino Romano) cheese is important, as is toasting the garlic in order to mellow and sweeten its otherwise harsh, hot flavor.

Each pesto recipe yields enough to sauce 1 pound of pasta. When draining the cooked pasta, reserve a portion of the pasta cooking water and stir a little of it into the pesto to loosen its consistency and bloom its flavor. Use additional pasta cooking water as needed to loosen the pasta once it has been tossed with the pesto. All of the pestos can be transferred to an airtight container, covered with a thin layer of oil (1 to 2 tablespoons), and refrigerated for up to four days or frozen for up to one month. If frozen, thaw before using.

Classic Basil Pesto

MAKES ABOUT ¾ CUP,
ENOUGH FOR 1 POUND OF PASTA

Pounding the basil releases its flavorful oils into the pesto more readily. Basil often darkens in pesto, but you can boost the color by adding the parsley.

- ¼ cup pine nuts, walnuts, or almonds
- 3 medium garlic cloves, unpeeled
- 2 cups packed fresh basil leaves
- 2 tablespoons packed fresh parsley leaves (optional)
- 7 tablespoons extra-virgin olive oil
  Salt
- ¼ cup finely grated Parmesan or Pecorino Romano cheese
  Ground black pepper

1. Toast the nuts in a small heavy skillet over medium heat, stirring frequently, until just golden and fragrant, about 5 minutes; set aside. Add the garlic to the empty skillet and toast over medium heat, shaking the pan occasionally, until fragrant and the color of the cloves deepens slightly, about 7 minutes. Let the garlic cool slightly, then peel and chop.

2. Place the basil and parsley (if using) in a heavy-duty 1-gallon zipper-lock bag. Pound the bag with the flat side of a meat pounder or rolling pin until all the leaves are bruised.

3. Process the nuts, garlic, herbs, oil, and ½ teaspoon salt in a food processor, stopping to scrape down the sides of the bowl as needed, until smooth, about 1 minute. Stir in the Parmesan and season with salt and pepper to taste.

Toasted Nut and Parsley Pesto

MAKES 1 CUP,
ENOUGH FOR 1 POUND OF PASTA

- 1 cup pecans, walnuts, pine nuts, whole blanched almonds, skinned hazelnuts, unsalted pistachios, or a combination
- 3 medium garlic cloves, unpeeled
- 7 tablespoons extra-virgin olive oil
- ½ cup packed fresh parsley leaves
  Salt
- 1 ounce Parmesan cheese, grated (about ½ cup)
  Ground black pepper

1. Toast the nuts in a small heavy skillet over medium heat, stirring frequently, until just golden and fragrant, about 5 minutes; set aside. Add the garlic to the empty skillet and toast over medium heat, shaking the pan occasionally, until fragrant and the color of the cloves deepens slightly, about 7 minutes. Let the garlic cool slightly, then peel and chop.

2. Process the nuts, garlic, oil, parsley, and ½ teaspoon salt in a food processor, stopping to scrape down the sides of the bowl as needed, until smooth, about 1½ minutes. Stir in the Parmesan and season with salt and pepper to taste.

Olive Pesto

MAKES 1½ CUPS,
ENOUGH FOR 1 POUND OF PASTA

This pesto is called olivada *in Italy. Use high-quality olives here. The anchovy adds flavor but not fishiness to the pesto.*

3	medium garlic cloves, unpeeled
1½	cups kalamata olives, pitted
6	tablespoons extra-virgin olive oil
1	medium shallot, chopped coarse (3 tablespoons)
8	large basil leaves
¼	cup packed fresh parsley leaves
1	anchovy fillet, rinsed and minced (optional)
1	tablespoon juice from 1 lemon
	Salt
1	ounce Parmesan cheese, grated (about ½ cup)
	Ground black pepper

1. Toast the garlic in a small heavy skillet over medium heat, shaking the pan occasionally, until fragrant and the color of the cloves deepens slightly, about 8 minutes. Let the garlic cool slightly, then peel and chop.

2. Process the garlic, olives, oil, shallot, basil, parsley, anchovy (if using), lemon juice, and ½ teaspoon salt in a food processor, stopping to scrape down the sides of the bowl as needed, until smooth, about 1 minute. Stir in the Parmesan and season with salt and pepper to taste.

PITTING OLIVES

Removing the pits from olives by hand is not an easy job. We found the following method to be the most expedient. Cover a cutting board with a clean kitchen towel and spread the olives on top, spacing them about 1 inch apart. Place a second clean towel over the olives. Using a mallet, pound the olives firmly for 10 to 15 seconds, being careful not to split the pits. Remove the top towel and, using your fingers, press the pit out of each olive.

EQUIPMENT: Food Processors

A food processor can make quick work out of any number of kitchen tasks, from slicing potatoes and shredding cheese to pureeing sauces and making pasta or tart doughs. After using a food processor repeatedly over the years, we have found two brands that have surpassed all others. The KitchenAid 12-Cup KFP750 ($249.99) and the 11-Cup Cuisinart Pro Custom 11 ($179.95) each have a large-capacity workbowl and powerful motor that excels at any kitchen task we throw at it. The KitchenAid was the hands-down winner with vegetable prep, but the Cuisinart performs all other tasks as well (or better) and costs far less.

THE BEST FOOD PROCESSORS

If vegetable prep is important to you, buy the KitchenAid 12-Cup food processor (left). Otherwise, the 11-Cup Cuisinart Pro Custom 11 (right) performed all other tasks as well as (or better than) its pricier competition.

SALERNO–STYLE PASTA WITH FRIED EGGS AND BREAD CRUMBS

PASTA WITH FRIED EGGS, SOMETIMES KNOWN as Salerno style (Salerno is a town that lies just south of Naples), is a perfect weeknight dinner—all you need are a few pantry staples to create a rustic, flavorful, and satisfying dish.

At first, we wondered why anyone would need a recipe for this dish. You simply toss some spaghetti with olive oil, a handful of freshly grated Parmesan, and a softly fried egg. As you toss the pasta, the soft yolk breaks apart, creating a savory sauce that clings beautifully to the pasta. Yet after a few tries, we realized we had a few things to learn. If the eggs sat for just a few extra minutes, the yolks hardened and we were unable to achieve the rich, silky sauce that is the hallmark of this dish. We knew that timing would be the key to success.

Because this dish is meant to be simple, relying on basic pantry staples, the recipes we researched all called for the same general ingredients: spaghetti, fried eggs, Parmesan, and extra-virgin olive oil. Beyond the basics were a few variations that included a selection of fresh herbs, bacon, caramelized onions, roasted red peppers, and savory accents such as capers and bread crumbs.

Knowing that the perfect fried egg was essential to the success of this dish, we turned our attention there first. We were after an egg with a white that is firm and a yolk that is slightly thick but still runny. We found a nonstick skillet to be a crucial piece of equipment if you hope to slide the eggs out of the pan unbroken. Preheating the pan to just the right temperature before cooking the eggs is also key. If you use a pan that is too cool, the egg white will spread out and become overcooked, rubbery, and tough. However, if the pan is too hot, the white will brown at the edges as soon as it hits the pan and end up tasting metallic. When the pan is heated just right, the white neither runs all over the place nor sputters and bubbles; instead, it just sizzles and sets up into a perfectly thick, restrained oval. In order to achieve this, we found it necessary to heat the skillet for five minutes over low heat.

We also found it important for the eggs to all hit the pan at the same time (we would need four eggs total). It takes only two to three minutes to cook each egg, so if you add the eggs to the pan as you crack them you'll wind up with unevenly cooked eggs. We found the easiest way to get the eggs into the pan at the same time was to crack them into small bowls, then tip the bowls into the hot skillet simultaneously (see the illustration on page 293). Covering the skillet as the eggs cooked helped trap the steam and cooked the top of the eggs without having to flip them over.

We now had perfectly cooked eggs, but how would we time their cooking with that of the pasta? Ideally, the pasta and eggs would be done at the same time, but trying to time perfectly al dente pasta with perfectly cooked eggs—which both have a short window for ideal doneness—was just too tricky. We would have to cook the eggs either just before the spaghetti was finished cooking or just after. We tried both ways and quickly realized that our perfectly cooked eggs began to deteriorate when they waited on the pasta—when we moved the eggs from the skillet to a plate they turned cold and rubbery within a minute, yet if we left them in the skillet they overcooked from the residual heat. It was much easier, therefore, to fry the eggs just after the spaghetti was drained (we gave the skillet for the eggs a head start by preheating it as the pasta finished cooking). To keep the pasta from sticking together or drying out while waiting on the eggs, we simply tossed it with the other ingredients along with a good dose of the pasta cooking water and held it in the pasta cooking pot with the lid on.

There was one remaining problem: after the eggs were tossed with the pasta, the sauce created by the yolks began to congeal in an incredibly short amount of time. Remembering that one of the initial recipes we tried topped each individual serving with one egg, we decided to give it a try. This was the winner. Each person was able to toss the egg into his or her own bowl, creating the sauce as it was being eaten, so there was no time for the sauce to harden in a serving bowl. Furthermore, it was an attractive presentation and added to the rustic appeal of the dish.

With our eggs cooked to perfection and our sequence and timing in place, we turned to the finishing flavors and textures. We decided to add some garlic for a flavor boost, yet because there were so few ingredients we had to be careful that the garlic didn't overpower the other flavors of the dish. We tried grating raw garlic, sautéing slivered garlic, and adding crushed whole cloves, but none compared to the flavor of caramelized garlic. This method involves slowly sautéing minced garlic with olive oil in a skillet until it turns golden and mellow, producing a garlic flavor far more complex than simple sautéed garlic. We found four cloves of garlic to be just the right amount.

Olive oil contributes complexity to this dish and extra-virgin olive oil is a must. A good quality

Parmesan cheese adds a nutty depth of flavor and is another important addition. We added a little parsley for freshness and a pinch of crushed red pepper flakes for a spicy kick. We were almost finished, but tasters requested a contrasting texture in this otherwise soft-textured dish of pasta and eggs, and toasted homemade bread crumbs seemed a natural fit. Tossing them into the pasta didn't work because they clumped together and became soggy very quickly. Instead, we found that sprinkling them on top of the pasta just before adding the eggs provided the perfect finish to this simple pantry dinner.

Salerno-Style Spaghetti with Fried Eggs and Bread Crumbs

SERVES 4

Timing is key here; the pasta should be drained just before cooking the eggs, but make sure the skillet preheats for 5 minutes before adding the eggs. A nonstick skillet is essential because it ensures an easy release of the eggs.

2	slices high-quality white sandwich bread, torn into quarters
10	tablespoons extra-virgin olive oil
	Salt and ground black pepper
4	medium garlic cloves, minced or pressed through a garlic press (about 4 teaspoons)
¼–½	teaspoon red pepper flakes
1	pound spaghetti
1	ounce Parmesan cheese, grated (about ½ cup), plus extra for serving
¼	cup minced fresh parsley leaves
4	large eggs, cracked into 2 small bowls (2 eggs per bowl)

1. Adjust an oven rack to the middle position and heat the oven to 375 degrees. Pulse the bread in a food processor to coarse crumbs, about 10 pulses. Toss the bread with 2 tablespoons of the oil and season with salt and pepper to taste. Spread the crumbs out over a rimmed baking sheet and bake, stirring often, until golden brown, 8 to 10 minutes; set aside.

2. Bring 4 quarts of water to a boil in a large pot for the pasta. Meanwhile, cook 3 tablespoons of the oil, garlic, pepper flakes, and ¼ teaspoon salt in a 12-inch nonstick skillet over low heat, stirring constantly, until the garlic foams, is sticky, and straw-colored, 8 to 10 minutes. Transfer the garlic mixture to a small bowl and set aside. Wipe the skillet clean with a wad of paper towels and set aside.

3. Stir 1 tablespoon salt and the pasta into the boiling water and cook, stirring often, until al dente. A minute or two before draining the pasta, return the skillet to low heat for 5 minutes (for the eggs). Reserve 1 cup of the pasta cooking water, then drain the pasta and return it to the pot. Stir in ½ cup of the reserved pasta cooking water, the garlic mixture, 3 tablespoons of the oil, Parmesan, parsley, and ¾ teaspoon salt and toss to combine. Cover and set aside to keep warm while cooking the eggs.

4. When the skillet is hot, add the remaining 2 tablespoons oil and swirl to coat the pan. Following the illustration below, quickly add the eggs to the skillet. Season the eggs with salt and pepper, cover, and cook until the whites are set but the yolks are still runny, 2 to 3 minutes. Uncover the eggs and remove from the heat.

5. Loosen the pasta with the reserved cooking water as needed, then divide it into 4 individual serving bowls. Sprinkle each bowl with 2 tablespoons of the bread crumbs. Carefully slide one fried egg on top in each bowl and serve immediately, passing extra Parmesan separately.

GETTING THE EGGS INTO THE PAN

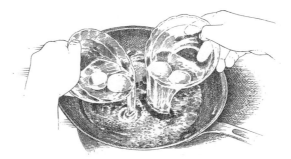

Crack the eggs into two small bowls, then add the eggs, sliding them into the hot skillet simultaneously from opposite sides of the pan.

PASTA WITH TOMATOES, BACON, AND ONION

Pasta all'Amatriciana

PASTA ALL'AMATRICIANA IS ARGUABLY ROME'S most famous dish. It starts with *bucatini*, an extra-long tube pasta that looks like a drinking straw. The sauce contains tomato, bacon, onion, dried chile, and Pecorino Romano cheese. Like most Roman cooking, this dish is bold and brash. The recipe comes from Amatrice, a town outside of Rome, but it has become a classic, like pesto and carbonara, available in restaurants from Milan to Los Angeles.

What makes Amatriciana so popular? First, most cooks have all the ingredients on hand. Second, the sauce can be made in the time it takes to boil the water and cook the pasta. Third, although the recipe is simple, the flavors are complex and perfectly balanced—acidity from the tomatoes, sweetness from the sautéed onions, heat from the dried chile, meatiness and salt from the bacon, and tangy dairy from

the cheese. Our goals in developing our version were to stay faithful to the traditional recipes but to use ingredients available to Americans. The biggest challenge was the bacon. Romans use *guanciale*, which is bacon made from pork jowls. In the rest of Italy, pancetta (bacon made from pork belly) is used. Since pancetta can be difficult to find, we wondered how American bacon would compare.

We began our testing by comparing pancetta, American bacon, Canadian bacon, Irish bacon (both of the latter are cured pork loin), and salt pork (unsmoked pork belly). Tasters preferred the pancetta, which was the meatiest. The pure pork and salt flavors of the pancetta worked best with the sauce and it is our first choice if you can find it. All three bacons were good, but most tasters felt that the smoke flavor and sweetness were distracting. The Canadian bacon and the Irish bacon (also called Irish back bacon) were meatier than the American bacon, although both were deemed a bit "hamlike." Regular American bacon was excessively fatty. If using it, you will need to drain off the rendered fat, an unnecessary step when using pancetta, Canadian bacon, or Irish bacon.

The only product not recommended is the salt pork. Although it comes from the belly and is not smoked, it is much too fatty to use in a pasta sauce (we do, however, like to use it as a pancetta substitute in other recipes, such as Beef in Barolo on page 319, where the extra fat is not an issue). Whatever kind of bacon you use, make sure it is sliced thick. When we used thinly sliced pancetta or regular American bacon, the meat nearly disappeared in the sauce.

Our next tests focused on technique. About half of the recipes we consulted called for sautéing the bacon and onion together, then building the tomato sauce on top of them. In the remaining recipes, the bacon was fried until crisp, removed from the pan, and then the onion was cooked in the bacon fat. Once the onion softened, it was time to make the tomato sauce. The crisped bacon was added back just before tossing the sauce with the pasta. When we simmered the bacon with the tomatoes, it lost its crisp texture. By the time the sauce was done, the bacon was leathery and lacking in flavor. We much preferred bacon that was fried and then removed

---

PANTRY SPOTLIGHT

PANCETTA

Pancetta and American bacon come from the same part of the pig—the belly—but the curing process is different. American bacon is cured with salt, sugar, and spices (the mix varies from producer to producer) and smoked. Pancetta is not smoked and the cure does not contain sugar—just salt, pepper, and usually cloves. After being cured for about two weeks, pancetta is rolled up tightly like a jelly roll, and packed into a casing. Pancetta often can be found at the deli counter where they will slice it to order. If you can't find pancetta, you can substitute an equal amount of bacon. If substituting bacon, make sure it is sliced as thick as the recipe requires; you may need to use slab bacon.

Pancetta is rolled tightly, packed in a casing, and then sliced thick or thin as desired.

from the pan. It was crisp and chewy when tossed with the pasta and retained its salty, meaty flavor.

The next issue was the tomato. Crushed tomatoes made the worst sauce—the tomato flavor was weak and the consistency of the sauce was too thin. We also missed the chunks of tomato, which give this sauce some character. Fresh tomatoes were good but tasters liked canned diced tomatoes even better because they were a tad juicier and they can be used any time of year. Whole tomatoes packed in juice—which must be diced by hand—were the best, offering a slightly softer texture than the canned diced tomatoes.

We tried simmering a small dried red chile in the sauce as an alternative to the red pepper flakes. The red pepper flakes won out, as they provide a more consistent heat level. Some Amatriciana recipes call for Parmesan cheese, although Pecorino Romano is traditional. We found the taste of Parmesan too subtle to stand up to the heat of the pepper flakes. Sharp, robust Pecorino Romano works better.

Pasta with Tomato, Bacon, and Onion

Pasta all'Amatriciana

SERVES 4

This dish is traditionally made with bucatini, also called perciatelli, which appear to be thick, round strands but are actually thin, extra-long tubes (like drinking straws). Linguine works fine, too. When buying pancetta, ask the butcher to slice it ¼ inch thick; if using bacon, buy slab bacon and cut it into ¼-inch-thick slices yourself.

2	tablespoons extra-virgin olive oil, plus extra as needed
6	ounces ¼-inch-thick sliced pancetta or bacon, cut into strips about ¼ inch wide
I	medium onion, minced
	Salt
⅛–¼	teaspoon red pepper flakes
I	(28-ounce) can whole tomatoes, tomatoes diced medium and juices reserved
	Salt
I	pound bucatini, perciatelli, or linguine
I	ounce Pecorino Romano cheese, grated (about ½ cup), plus extra for serving

1. Bring 4 quarts of water to a boil in a large pot for the pasta.

2. Meanwhile, heat the oil in a 12-inch skillet over medium heat until shimmering. Add the pancetta and cook until lightly browned and crisp, about 8 minutes. Transfer the pancetta to a paper towel–lined plate. Discard all but 4 tablespoons of fat left in the skillet (if necessary, add oil).

3. Add the onion and ¼ teaspoon salt to the fat left in the skillet and cook over medium heat until softened, 5 to 7 minutes. Stir in the red pepper flakes and cook until fragrant, about 30 seconds. Stir in the tomatoes with their juice and simmer until slightly thickened, about 10 minutes. Set aside, covered, off the heat to keep warm.

4. Stir 1 tablespoon salt and the pasta into the boiling water and cook, stirring often, until the pasta is al dente. Reserve 1 cup of the pasta cooking water, then drain the pasta and return it to the pot. Stir ⅓ cup of the reserved pasta cooking water, tomato sauce, pancetta, and Pecorino Romano into the pasta. Season with salt to taste and serve, adding the remaining reserved pasta cooking water as needed to loosen the sauce.

ORECCHIETTE WITH BROCCOLI RABE

Orecchiette alle Cime di Rapa

BROCCOLI RABE IS NATIVE TO THE Mediterranean region and although it was once a wild herb, it is now widely grown throughout southern Italy. Broccoli rabe looks much like long-stemmed broccoli, but has a spicy, bitter flavor that is commonly paired with sausage, garlic, and orecchiette (an ear-shaped pasta) for a simple and satisfying meal.

If you are not familiar with broccoli rabe, it can seem tricky to cook. Broccoli rabe contains thick stalks, tender leaves, and small florets. If all the stalks were removed, there would be little left to this plant. We had to devise a cooking method that would soften the stalks but keep the florets and leaves from becoming mushy.

We tested boiling and steaming and found that steaming is not ideal—it cooks this tough green unevenly. By the time the thick stalks softened, the tender florets were mushy. Boiling does a better job of cooking the various parts of this plant evenly, if only because it is faster and there is less time for the florets to become mushy. But the thick ends of each stalk never softened properly, even when boiled, so we decided they should be trimmed before cooking. The remaining portion of the stalks and the florets should be cut into bite-sized pieces (about 1½ inches long).

Using the same pot of water for boiling the broccoli rabe and the pasta made for a streamlined method; we simply boiled the broccoli rabe first, then removed it with a slotted spoon or spider, and then boiled the pasta. Vegetables are often

dunked into ice water after being quickly boiled to prevent any further cooking from residual heat (a process called blanching), but we found this step unnecessarily cumbersome for such a simple dish. Rather, we undercooked the broccoli rabe by a few seconds then let the residual heat finish cooking it through while the pasta boiled.

Sweet sausage is a classic pairing with broccoli rabe and pasta—its flavor helps to balance out the bitterness of the greens. We found it best to remove the sausage from its casing and break it into small, bite-sized pieces so that its flavor could be evenly distributed throughout the dish without having to use a large amount. A generous dose of sautéed garlic and pinch of spicy red pepper flakes also pumped up the flavor of the dish nicely.

As for the sauce, tasters preferred a combination of a little olive oil and cheese rather than a broth-based sauce to lightly coat the pasta. The additional flavors of the broth (we tried both chicken and vegetable broth) were unwelcome and overwhelmed this otherwise fresh tasting dish. Some recipes we found used a combination of butter and oil for the sauce, and tasters agreed that a little butter in the sauce tasted good; stirring the butter into the pasta with the sauce preserved its fresh, clean dairy flavor. When dealing with a simple olive oil–based sauce where only a small amount of oil is used, we noted that it important to reserve some of the pasta water to help keep the finished dish from appearing dry. The pasta water has a seasoned flavor and slightly starchy consistency that is ideal at keeping the dish fresh and moist without adding any unwelcome flavors.

PREPARING BROCCOLI RABE

1. The thick stalk ends of broccoli rabe should be trimmed and discarded. Use a sharp knife to cut off the thickest part (usually the bottom 2 inches) of each stalk.

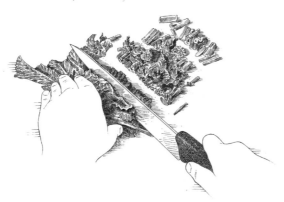

2. Cut the remaining stalks and florets into bite-sized pieces about 1½ inches long.

Orecchiette with Sausage and Broccoli Rabe
Orecchiette alle Cime di Rapa
SERVES 4

Ziti or penne can be substituted for the orecchiette. If you prefer to use broccoli instead of broccoli rabe, use 2 pounds cut into 1-inch florets and increase the boiling time to 2 minutes in step 3. A wire spider comes in handy when cooking the broccoli rabe; see page 433 for more information.

2 tablespoons extra-virgin olive oil

8 ounces sweet Italian sausage, casings
   removed

6 garlic cloves, minced or pressed through a
   garlic press (about 2 tablespoons)

¼–½ teaspoon red pepper flakes
   Salt

1 bunch broccoli rabe (about 1 pound), ends
   trimmed and cut into 1½-inch lengths (see
   the illustrations on page 296)

1 pound orecchiette

2 ounces Parmesan or Asiago cheese, grated
   (about 1 cup)

2 tablespoon unsalted butter
   Ground black pepper

1. Bring 4 quarts of water to a boil in a large pot for the pasta.

2. Meanwhile, heat the oil in a 12-inch nonstick skillet over medium-high heat until shimmering. Add the sausage and cook until lightly browned, breaking the meat up with a wooden spoon, about 5 minutes. Stir in the garlic and red pepper flakes and cook until fragrant, about 30 seconds; set aside off the heat.

3. Stir 1 tablespoon salt and the broccoli rabe into the boiling water and cook, stirring often, until the broccoli rabe stems are crisp-tender, about 1½ minutes (do not overcook). Using a slotted spoon or wire spider, transfer the broccoli rabe to the skillet with the sausage mixture and set aside.

4. Return the water to a boil, stir in the pasta, and cook, stirring often, until the pasta is al dente. Reserve 1 cup of the pasta cooking water, then drain the orecchiette and return it to the pot. Stir in ⅓ cup of the pasta cooking water, sausage–broccoli rabe mixture, Parmesan, and butter until well combined. Add the remaining reserved pasta cooking water as needed to loosen the sauce. Season with salt and pepper to taste and serve.

➤ VARIATION

Orecchiette with Broccoli Rabe and White Beans

Follow the recipe for Orecchiette with Sausage and Broccoli Rabe, omitting the sausage (if desired) and increasing the oil to ¼ cup. Heat the oil in a 12-inch skillet until shimmering, add 1 (15-ounce) can canellini beans, drained and rinsed, 1 minced shallot, ½ teaspoon coarsely chopped fennel seeds, ¼ teaspoon dried oregano, and the garlic and pepper flakes. Cook until the beans are warmed through, about 2 minutes; set aside and continue with the recipe as directed.

INGREDIENTS: Canned White Beans

In developing our recipe for Orecchiette with Broccoli Rabe and White Beans, we tested four widely available brands of canned white beans such as cannellini, navy beans, and great Northern beans. We tasted each contender twice: straight from the can (after being drained and rinsed and prepared in our pasta recipe. We had two clear winners. Westbrae great Northern beans had the best flavor and texture—described as "earthy" and "creamy" by our tasters. Progresso cannellini beans were well-liked for being "plump" and "sweet." Eden navy beans were small and broken and rejected by our tasters. Goya cannellini beans received mixed scores. Their flavor received high marks, but tasters were put off by their "weird" gray color and "tough" skins.

THE BEST CANNED WHITE BEANS

Westbrae Organic Great Northern Beans (left) and Progresso Cannellini Beans (right) are the test kitchen's top picks for both flavor and texture.

SPAGHETTI WITH LEMON

Spaghetti al Limone

SPAGHETTI AL LIMONE (SPAGHETTI WITH LEMON) is a great example of simple Italian cooking at its best—a few basic ingredients are combined to create a boldly flavored, satisfying meal. In researching various recipes for this dish, we found the

SHREDDING BASIL

To shred basil or other leafy herbs and greens, simply stack several leaves on top of one another, roll them up, and slice. In the case of basil, we have found that rolling the leaves from tip to tail minimizes bruising and browning.

ingredients varied only slightly. Lemon juice, lemon zest, pasta, and Parmesan cheese were essentials, while extra-virgin olive oil, butter, heavy cream, and basil were the variables.

To get a sense of what this dish should be, we tested three basic recipes—the first using extra-virgin olive oil, the second using butter, and the third using a combination of heavy cream and butter. The version with just butter tasted a bit bland (although tasters did enjoy the butter flavor) while the version made with butter and cream was much too heavy, overpowering the bright lemon flavor. The pasta also absorbed the cream quickly and reminded us of an Alfredo sauce. Tasters unanimously declared extra-virgin olive oil the winner—it complemented the lemon flavor beautifully. An added benefit of using oil was that the sauce did not need to be cooked; instead the oil and lemon juice form a simple vinaigrette that can be tossed with the warm pasta just before serving.

But what is the ideal ratio of lemon to olive oil? In our first few tests we used an equal amount of lemon juice and oil, but the tart citrus flavor was much too strong, and left tasters puckering their lips. Reducing the amount of lemon juice in small increments, we found that ⅓ cup lemon juice to ½ cup extra-virgin olive oil provided the best balance. Two teaspoons of lemon zest boosted the lemon flavor without adding acidity.

Even with the lemon juice, zest, and olive oil amounts figured out, some tasters still felt that the sauce was a little unbalanced. Our first instinct was to add some pasta cooking water to see if it would mellow the flavor. This worked fine at keeping the sauce fluid over the pasta, but it did little for the flavor. Remembering that we liked the flavor of butter in our original tests, we wondered if a little butter might enrich the lemon flavor. We added a pat of butter to the warm pasta and it was just what we were looking for—the butter took the edge off the lemon and rounded out the flavor of the sauce.

The Parmesan cheese we simply stirred in with the olive oil and lemon juice; it thickened the sauce slightly and contributed a warm nutty flavor that tasters appreciated. They also liked a sprinkling of basil. We then wondered if garlic had a place in our dish—we had seen it in a couple of the recipes we researched and thought we should give it a try. Wanting to stick with our working recipe which required no cooking of the sauce, we decided to make a paste from the garlic by adding a little salt—a technique often used when adding garlic to a vinaigrette that helps mellow its pungent flavor slightly. The addition of just one clove prepared in this manner went a long way. Tasters loved the flavor it imparted; it gave depth to the lemon flavor without competing with it. We now had a dish that is easy enough to prepare for a quick weeknight meal, yet still elegant enough to serve to company.

Spaghetti with Lemon and Basil
Spaghetti al Limone e Basilico
SERVES 4 TO 6

Because this recipe is so simple, it is important to use high-quality extra-virgin olive oil, fresh-squeezed lemon juice, and fresh basil here.

½	cup extra-virgin olive oil
⅓	cup juice from 2 lemons
2	teaspoons grated zest from 1 lemon
1	small garlic clove, minced to a paste (see the illustration on page 299)
	Salt
2	ounces Parmesan cheese, grated (about 1 cup)
	Ground black pepper
1	pound spaghetti
2	tablespoons unsalted butter, softened
¼	cup shredded fresh basil leaves (see the illustration above)

1. Bring 4 quarts of water to a boil in a large pot. Meanwhile, whisk the olive oil, lemon juice, lemon zest, garlic, and ½ teaspoon salt together in a small bowl, then stir in the Parmesan cheese until thick and creamy; set aside.

2. Add 1 tablespoon salt and the spaghetti into the boiling water and cook, stirring often, until the pasta is al dente. Reserve ½ cup of the pasta cooking water, then drain the pasta and return to the pot. Stir in the olive oil mixture, butter, and basil and toss to coat. Season with salt and pepper to taste and serve, adding the reserved pasta cooking water as needed to loosen the sauce.

MINCING GARLIC TO A PASTE

Adding a little salt to garlic when mincing it does two things: it breaks down the garlic into a paste and helps mellow the garlic's pungent flavor—especially nice if it is being used raw in a vinaigrette or other application. If possible use kosher or coarse salt, as the larger crystals do a better job of breaking down the garlic than fine table salt.

1. Mince the garlic as you normally would on a cutting board. Sprinkle the minced garlic with a pinch of salt.

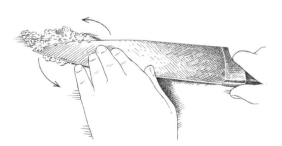

2. Drag the side of a chef's knife over the garlic-salt mixture to form a fine paste. Continue to mince and drag the knife as necessary until the paste is smooth.

CREAMY BAKED FOUR-CHEESE PASTA

Pasta ai Quattro Formaggi

IN ITALIAN, AL FORNO MEANS "FROM THE oven," so logically, *pasta al forno* means "pasta from the oven." Here in the test kitchen, we are all familiar with al forno pastas—lasagna, baked ziti, and even baked macaroni and cheese are among the most popular versions in this country. In our research through authentic Italian cookbooks, however, we came across an array of pasta al forno recipes, with various pasta shapes, sauces, and flavorings—in Italy, when it comes to pasta al forno, it seems as though the sky is the limit.

We decided to marry the pasta al forno technique with the flavors of *pasta ai quattro formaggi*, the classic Italian pasta dish with four cheeses and heavy cream. This combination of baked pasta and a creamy cheese sauce is a great example of simple Italian cooking. Our goal was to discover how to make this dish a great one, delivering a pasta dinner that was silky smooth and rich, with a golden brown crust on top.

Of course, we found that the cheese was the first issue in terms of both flavor and texture. We were committed to Italian cheeses, but this barely diminished our choices—the recipes we found called for varying combinations and amounts. Recipes contained anywhere from 1 cup to 6½ cups of cheese for 1 pound of pasta, and the selection of cheeses was just as dizzying: Asiago, fontina, Taleggio, Pecorino Romano, mascarpone, mozzarella, Gorgonzola, Parmesan, and ricotta all turned up in our research. However, some initial testing reduced the scope quickly: Mascarpone and ricotta added neither flavor nor texture, and Asiago was bland. Pasta tossed with mozzarella was gooey and greasy, whereas Taleggio was not only difficult to obtain but also made the pasta too rich and gluey. Tasters favored a combination of Italian fontina (which is creamier and better-tasting than versions of this cheese made elsewhere), Gorgonzola, Pecorino Romano, and Parmesan.

With our winning cheese combination settled upon, we turned our attention to incorporating it into the other ingredients of the dish. Both heating the cheeses and cream together and adding the cheeses separately to the hot pasta produced nasty messes. Each attempt caused the cheeses to curdle, separate, and/or turn greasy. Some recipes solve this problem by starting with a white sauce—a balsamella or béchamel—which is made by cooking butter and flour together (to make a roux) then whisking in milk or cream, followed by the cheese. The flour in the sauce works as a type of binder that helps prevent the cheese from separating. This approach worked great, and we found that basing the sauce on cream was better than basing it on milk. Unlike milk, cream thickens and stabilizes on its own as it simmers and reduces, and therefore a sauce made with cream requires less flour than one was made with milk. And the less flour you use in the sauce, the silkier the texture of the final dish.

In order to sauce 1 pound of pasta well, the béchamel needed to yield about 3 cups. Not wanting to load up the sauce with 3 cups of heavy cream, we borrowed a technique we use in many of our other pasta recipes, and added some of the pasta cooking water to the sauce. Combining 1½ cups of the pasta cooking water with 1½ cups of cream yielded a creamy, light-tasting sauce.

Yet we were still bothered by the notion of stirring the cheeses into the béchamel. In theory, the less the cheeses are cooked, the more flavor you'll get from them. With this in mind, we tried mixing the cheeses into the hot pasta with the hot béchamel just before going into the oven. This worked wonderfully and the final dish was the most flavorful yet.

Tubular pasta shapes and large shells allow the sauce to coat the pasta inside and out and are the best choice here. Many al forno recipes suggest cooking the pasta fully and then baking it for 30 minutes, but we found this method resulted in mushy pasta. To keep the pasta from overcooking in the oven, we found it necessary to undercook it by a few minutes, and then minimize the baking time.

Just 15 minutes in a 500-degree oven (in a shallow baking dish so it heats more quickly) is enough to turn the pasta and sauce into pasta al forno—the beautifully browned top contrasts nicely with the creamy pasta and helps balance the richness of the sauce.

Creamy Baked Four-Cheese Pasta
Pasta ai Quattro Formaggi
SERVES 4 TO 6

If you do not like the flavor of blue cheese such as Gorgonzola, omit it and increase the fontina to 7 ounces. Under-boiling the pasta in step 1 is important, or it will overcook in the oven and taste mushy. Be careful when seasoning the sauce with salt in step 2, as the cheeses tend to be quite salty. If you choose to use shell pasta, be sure to buy the large variety and not the jumbo size.

	Salt
I	pound penne, ziti, or large shells
2	tablespoons unsalted butter
2	tablespoons unbleached all-purpose flour
2	medium garlic cloves, minced or pressed through a garlic press (about 2 teaspoons)
I½	cups heavy cream
	Ground black pepper
4	ounces Italian fontina cheese, shredded (about I ⅓ cups)
3	ounces Gorgonzola cheese, crumbled (about ¾ cup)
2	ounces Parmesan cheese, grated (about I cup)
I	ounce Pecorino Romano cheese, grated (about ½ cup)

1. Adjust an oven rack to the middle position and heat the oven to 500 degrees. Bring 4 quarts of water to a boil in a large pot. Stir 1 tablespoon salt and the pasta into the boiling water and cook, stirring often, until just softened and shy of being al dente, about 7 minutes. Reserve 1½ cups of the pasta cooking water, then drain the pasta and return it to the pot; cover the pot to keep warm.

2. Melt the butter in a small saucepan over medium-low heat. Add the flour and cook, stirring constantly, until golden, about 1 minute. Stir in the garlic and cook until fragrant, about 30 seconds. Slowly whisk in the cream and reserved pasta cooking water. Bring to a simmer and cook, whisking often, until slightly thickened, about 1 minute. Season with salt and pepper to taste.

3. Pour the sauce over the pasta and stir in the fontina, Gorgonzola, ½ cup of the Parmesan, and the Pecorino. Transfer to a 13 by 9-inch baking dish and sprinkle with the remaining ½ cup Parmesan. Bake until the top is golden brown, about 15 minutes. Serve immediately.

Ricotta Gnocchi

WHEN IT COMES TO GNOCCHI, THE TYPE most familiar in the U.S. is made with potato. But in our research of this dish, we found a potato-less version of gnocchi—ricotta gnocchi, which hails from Florence. Intrigued, we took a closer look at this version. Described as pillowy and tender, this dish sounded elegant and we became eager to develop our own version.

Reviewing a wide swath of recipes revealed that, like many Italian dishes, this Florentine specialty doesn't require a long list of ingredients, just ricotta, eggs, flour, Parmesan cheese, salt, pepper, and sometimes herbs or spinach. The technique is quite simple, too. The dough is simply rolled out into ropes, cut into small pieces, and boiled. Even the two Italian names for ricotta gnocchi sound forgiving: *malfatti* (badly made), referring to their sometimes less-than-model-perfect appearance, and *gnudi* (naked), because they resemble ravioli without their pasta jackets.

We knew the success of this dish would hinge on its most prominent ingredient: ricotta cheese. Most recipes called for a whole pound. Tasters preferred whole-milk ricotta to the leaner, less flavorful part-skim variety. We began by forming a basic dough, combining a pound of ricotta with an egg, 1 cup of flour, ¼ cup of Parmesan cheese, and some salt and pepper. Instead of the pillowy bundles we'd been hoping for, we got leaden, floury blobs lacking in cheese flavor. More Parmesan helped ramp up the cheese flavor, but to lighten the texture we needed to use less flour. However, when we cut back on the flour, the dough was too sticky and unworkable.

When a fellow test cook commented on the wateriness of supermarket ricotta (in Italy, ricotta is creamy and dry, but American supermarket brands are curdy and wet), we saw an opportunity. In the test kitchen, we often thicken yogurt by draining it in the refrigerator. What if we drained the ricotta? Sure enough, the result was a slightly drier dough that had more structure. Now we could work on cutting back the flour.

Taking baby steps, we reduced the amount of flour to ¾ cup, which made the gnocchi slightly less gummy. At ½ cup, they were even better, but still not perfect. Any less flour and the dough became a batter that was overly sticky. We couldn't remove any more moisture from the ricotta, so we tried swapping in potato starch and cornstarch for some of the flour, but they just made the gnocchi gluey and slimy.

We then remembered a recipe found in our research that we'd tried and dismissed for its use of an unexpected ingredient: fresh bread crumbs. Could this simple addition—one that's often coupled with milk or egg to add tenderness to meat loaf—absorb more of the moisture in the dough and allow us to add less flour? These gnocchi were a little better, but

TWO KINDS OF GNOCCHI

RICOTTA GNOCCHI   POTATO GNOCCHI

The more familiar potato gnocchi (right) have a texture that's between pasta and dumpling. The ricotta cheese version (left) are more delicate, with a texture like ravioli without the pasta jackets.

not enough to justify the extra effort. But we weren't ready to give up. What if we toasted the crumbs? For our next test, we made a dough with just 6 tablespoons of flour and ½ cup of homemade dried bread crumbs. The resulting gnocchi held together and had the perfect combination of tenderness and structure. (Hoping for a shortcut, we tried substituting store-bought bread crumbs, but they gave the gnocchi a stale taste.)

But there was one element still missing from this balancing act—proper technique. We wondered if chilling the dough would help matters even further. We tested various chilling times and found that just 15 minutes in the refrigerator helped the dough stiffen and become more workable. Rolling it out afterward by hand wasn't difficult, provided we did so gently and worked with a little bit at a time.

The gnocchi were ready to be simmered. By the time they floated to the surface, they needed just two more minutes in the water before being scooped out with a slotted spoon. One last step remained: tossing the tender little dumplings in a simple sauce of browned butter, minced shallots, and sage. When we set the platter of gnocchi in front of tasters, it took all of five minutes before the last piece disappeared. We guess they weren't so "badly made" after all.

Ricotta Gnocchi with Browned Butter and Sage Sauce

SERVES 4 TO 6 AS A FIRST COURSE, OR 2 TO 3 AS A MAIN DISH

We recommend using Calabro whole milk ricotta, although other brands and part-skim cheese will work in this recipe. After the dough has been refrigerated for 15 minutes, it should be slightly tacky to the touch and a few moist crumbs should adhere to your fingers (see the photo on page 303). If the dough seems too wet, stir in additional flour 1 tablespoon at a time until the proper consistency is achieved. When rolling the gnocchi, use just enough flour to keep the dough from sticking to your hands and work surface; using too much flour will result in tough gnocchi. The gnocchi can be rolled, cut, and refrigerated for up to 24 hours. To freeze the uncooked gnocchi, place the baking sheet in the freezer

until the gnocchi are firm (about 1 hour), then transfer them to a zipper-lock bag and store them for up to 1 month. Thaw frozen gnocchi overnight in the refrigerator or at room temperature for 1 hour before cooking as directed. To prevent the gnocchi from cooling too quickly, warm the serving platter or serving bowls in a 200-degree oven.

GNOCCHI
- 1 (15- or 16-ounce) container whole milk ricotta cheese (see note)
- 2 large slices white sandwich bread, crusts removed and bread torn into quarters
- 1 large egg
- 2 tablespoons minced fresh basil leaves
- 2 tablespoons minced fresh parsley leaves
  Table salt
- ¼ teaspoon ground black pepper
- 1 ounce Parmesan cheese, grated (about ½ cup)
- 6 tablespoons all-purpose flour, plus extra for the work surface

BROWNED BUTTER AND SAGE SAUCE
- 4 tablespoons (½ stick) unsalted butter, cut into 4 pieces
- ⅛ teaspoon salt
- 1 small shallot, minced (about 2 tablespoons)
- 2 teaspoons minced fresh sage leaves
- 1 teaspoon juice from 1 lemon

1. FOR THE GNOCCHI: Line a fine-mesh strainer set over a deep container or bowl with 3 paper coffee filters or a triple layer of paper towels. Place the ricotta in the lined strainer, cover, and refrigerate for 1 hour. Adjust an oven rack to the middle position and heat the oven to 300 degrees.

2. Process the bread in a food processor until finely ground, about 10 seconds. Spread the crumbs on a rimmed baking sheet and bake until dry and just beginning to turn golden, about 10 minutes, stirring once during baking time. Let cool to room temperature. (You should have about ½ cup crumbs.)

3. Transfer the drained ricotta to a food processor and pulse until the curds break down into a fine, grainy consistency, about 8 pulses. Using a rubber

spatula, combine the ricotta, egg, basil, parsley, ½ teaspoon salt, and pepper in a large bowl. Add the Parmesan, flour, and bread crumbs; stir until well combined. Refrigerate the dough for 15 minutes.

4. Lightly dust a work surface with flour. With floured hands, roll a lemon-sized piece of dough into a ¾-inch-thick rope, rolling from the center of the dough outward. Cut the rope into ¾-inch-long pieces and transfer to a parchment paper–lined rimmed baking sheet. Repeat with the remaining dough, dusting the surface with flour as needed.

5. FOR THE SAUCE: Melt the butter and salt in a 12-inch skillet over medium-high heat, swirling occasionally, until the butter is browned and releases a nutty aroma, about 1½ minutes. Off the heat, add the shallot and sage, stirring until the shallot is fragrant, about 1 minute. Stir in the lemon juice; cover to keep warm.

6. TO COOK THE GNOCCHI: Bring 4 quarts of water to a boil in a large pot or Dutch oven over high heat. Add 1 tablespoon salt. Reduce the heat so that the water is simmering, then gently drop half of the gnocchi into the water and cook until all the pieces float to the surface. Continue to simmer until the gnocchi are cooked through, about 2 minutes longer, adjusting the heat to maintain a gentle simmer. Using a slotted spoon, scoop the gnocchi from the water, allowing the excess water to drain from the spoon; transfer the gnocchi to the skillet with the sauce and cover to keep warm. Repeat the cooking process with the remaining gnocchi. Using a rubber spatula, gently toss the gnocchi with the sauce until uniformly coated. Transfer the gnocchi to a warmed serving platter or divide among warmed individual bowls and serve immediately.

CORE TECHNIQUE

SIMMER, DON'T BOIL GNOCCHI

Most pasta should be cooked at a full boil, but if gnocchi are cooked at a full boil they can fall apart from the vigorous churning. Once the water comes to a boil, reduce the heat, add the gnocchi, and make sure the water just simmers.

➤ VARIATION

Ricotta Gnocchi with Tomato-Cream Sauce

SERVES 4 TO 6 AS A FIRST COURSE, OR 2 TO 3 AS A MAIN DISH

1	(14.5-ounce) can diced tomatoes
1	tablespoon extra-virgin olive oil
1	medium garlic clove, minced or pressed through a garlic press (about 1 teaspoon)
¼	teaspoon salt
⅛	teaspoon sugar
2	tablespoons chopped fresh basil leaves
2	tablespoons heavy cream

1. Follow the recipe for Ricotta Gnocchi with Browned Butter and Sage Sauce through step 4, omitting the sauce.

2. Process the tomatoes with their juice in a food processor until smooth, about 15 seconds. Heat the oil in a 12-inch nonstick skillet over medium heat until shimmering. Add the garlic and cook until fragrant but not brown, about 20 seconds. Stir in the tomatoes, salt, and sugar. Simmer until thickened slightly, 5 to 6 minutes. Remove the pan from the heat and stir in the basil and cream. Cover to keep warm.

3. To cook and finish the gnocchi, follow the recipe from step 6.

PROPER DOUGH CONSISTENCY

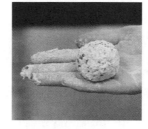 

JUST RIGHT   **TOO SOFT**

Gnocchi dough should be moist and slightly tacky to the touch. When the proper consistency is achieved, a few crumbs should stick to your finger (left). If the dough is too wet and a lot of crumbs stick to your finger (right), stir in an additional 1 tablespoon of flour.

LASAGNA WITH MEATBALLS

Lasagna di Carnivale alla Napoletana

IN ITALY, CARNIVALE IS A FESTIVAL THAT takes place just before Lent, the period of time before Easter during which Roman Catholics do not eat meat. Traditionally, Carnivale was a time to consume all of the meat that remained in the village before the fast, but these days, it is a great public celebration that entails dressing up in costumes, wearing decorative masks, and partying all day and night. In Naples, a city in southern Italy, a lasagna with tiny meatballs, tomato sauce, and mozzarella cheese is traditionally made to celebrate Carnivale. Appropriately, it is called *lasagna di Carnivale*.

We have eaten more than our share of lasagna, which are often nothing more than mushy noodles swimming in a sea of red sauce and cheese. We wanted to try the Neapolitan style of lasagna, with its distinct layers, moderate amount of deeply flavored sauce, and tender meatballs, but we would never make it at home—it contains 25 ingredients and takes an entire day to prepare. Starting from the true Italian premise that less sauce and more pasta is better, we wanted to devise a recipe with these classic tastes but without the backbreaking labor.

Our first task was to make sense of the cheese component. Various Italian recipes call for mozzarella, ricotta (sometimes mixed with whole eggs or egg yolks), and/or a hard grating cheese (usually Parmesan, but sometimes Pecorino Romano). After trying the various combinations, we realized that ricotta was responsible for what we call "lasagna meltdown"—the loss of shape and distinct layering. Even with the addition of whole eggs or yolks as a thickener, we found that ricotta is too watery to use in lasagna that includes meatballs, and usually leads to a sloppy mess.

Mozzarella provides plenty of creaminess, and its stringiness binds the layers to each other and helps keep them from slipping apart when served. Fresh mozzarella, however, has too much moisture to be effective. When it melts, it releases so much liquid that the lasagna becomes mushy and watery.

In addition, the delicate flavor of expensive fresh mozzarella is lost in the baking. After a few disastrous attempts with fresh mozzarella, we turned to its shrink-wrapped cousin, whole milk mozzarella, and had much better results. We also found that a small amount of either Parmesan or Pecorino Romano provides a pleasantly sharp contrast to the somewhat mild mozzarella.

With the cheese question resolved, we next focused on the meatballs. Here again we looked to traditional Italian recipes for inspiration, then tried to simplify. We seasoned ground beef with herbs, cheese, egg yolks, and bread crumbs. However, instead of rolling out real meatballs, which would be too large to rest snugly between the layers of pasta, we pinched off small bits of the mixture. We tried pinching them off directly into hot oil, which worked fine, but required us to stand over the oil frying for upwards of four batches. Instead, we placed the meatballs on a baking sheet and after just eight minutes in a 450-degree oven, they were done.

Since our aim was to simplify matters, we decided to add the meatballs to a quick-cooking tomato sauce made with crushed tomatoes. Many traditional recipes simmer whole tomatoes or tomato puree for hours to make a rich, complex sauce. However, since lasagna has so many competing elements, we found that little was gained by this lengthy process. Simmering canned, crushed tomatoes just long enough to make a sauce—about 10 minutes—was sufficient.

Next we focused our attention on the choice of noodles and layering tricks. Here in the test kitchen, we often make lasagna with no-boil noodles. They really simplify the process and produce great results, so we thought we would give them a try here. We made our working recipe with no-boil noodles, only to find out that they did not work—they emerged from the oven with a tough, cardboard-like texture. Thinking that soaking the noodles in hot water would help them to soften, we gave it a try. No luck. Our lightly sauced lasagna simply did not have enough moisture for the noodles to absorb and become tender as the lasagna cooked. This type of lasagna requires a more traditional type of noodle.

Many Italian lasagna recipes call for fresh pasta. Tasters liked the thinness of the fresh noodles, but voted unanimously against making them from scratch—after all, we were trying to simplify our lasagna-making process, not complicate it. We then tried several brands of fresh pasta from our local markets but they varied dramatically, not only in thickness and dimensions, but also in quality. Traditional dried lasagna noodles—the type that require being boiled before assembling the lasagna—turned out to be our favorite, in part because they were the most reliable, but also because tasters were happiest with the lasagna they produced. The only key to working with these noodles is boiling them until soft and then rinsing them with cold water; this stops them from cooking further and becoming mushy, and also rinses away some of the starch, preventing them from sticking together.

In terms of the actual layering procedure, we found it helpful to grease the baking pan with cooking spray. We then spread a small amount of tomato sauce (without any meatballs) over the pan to moisten the bottom layer of pasta, and added the first layer of noodles. After that, we spread the sauce and meatballs evenly over the noodles, covered them with shredded mozzarella, then sprinkled on grated Parmesan. We then built more layers by this same process. We realized that the tomato sauce and meatballs tended to dry out when not covered by pasta, so the final layer we covered only with the two cheeses, which brown during baking to give an attractive appearance.

After just 20 minutes in a 400-degree oven, the lasagna was ready to eat (although we do recommend letting it cool for 5 minutes before serving). This lasagna is certainly just as satisfying as traditional Neapolitan versions, and quicker to assemble. The best part is that you don't have to wait for Carnivale to enjoy it!

Lasagna with Meatballs
Lasagna di Carnivale alla Napoletana
SERVES 8

Do not substitute no-boil noodles; they do not work in this dish. The size of the noodles will depend on the brand; if the noodles are short (such as DeCecco) you will layer them crosswise in the dish, but if they are long (such as Barilla and Ronzoni) you will layer them lengthwise in the dish. Regardless of which brand of noodle you are using, there should be 3 noodles per layer.

MEATBALLS AND SAUCE
- 1   pound (85 percent lean) ground beef
- 2   ounces Parmesan or Pecorino Romano cheese, grated (about 1 cup)
- ½   cup store-bought plain dried bread crumbs
- 2   large eggs, lightly beaten
- ½   cup minced fresh basil or parsley leaves
  Salt and ground black pepper
- 3   tablespoons olive oil
- 2   medium garlic cloves, minced or pressed through a garlic press (about 2 teaspoons)
- 1   (28-ounce) can crushed tomatoes

NOODLES AND CHEESE
- 1   tablespoon salt
- 12   dried lasagna noodles (see note)
- 1   pound whole milk mozzarella cheese, shredded (about 4 cups)
- 4   ounces Parmesan or Pecorino Romano cheese, grated (about 2 cups)

1. FOR THE MEATBALLS AND SAUCE: Adjust an oven rack to the middle position and heat the oven to 450 degrees. Spray a rimmed baking sheet with vegetable oil spray; set aside. Mix the beef, cheese, bread crumbs, eggs, 5 tablespoons of the basil, 1 teaspoon salt, and ½ teaspoon pepper together until uniform. Pinch off scant 1 teaspoon–sized pieces of the mixture (about the size of a small grape), roll into small balls, and arrange on the prepared baking sheet. Bake the meatballs until just cooked through and lightly browned, 8 to 10 minutes. Transfer the meatballs to a paper towel–lined platter and set aside.

2. Heat the oil and garlic in a medium saucepan over medium heat until the garlic starts to sizzle, about 2 minutes. Stir in the tomatoes, bring to a simmer, and cook until the sauce thickens slightly, 10 to 15 minutes. Off the heat, stir in the remaining 3 tablespoons basil and season with salt and pepper to taste. Stir the meatballs into the sauce and cover to keep warm until needed.

3. **FOR THE NOODLES AND CHEESE:** Meanwhile, bring 4 quarts of water to a boil in a large pot. Stir the salt and noodles into the boiling water and cook, stirring often, until the pasta is al dente. Drain the noodles and rinse them under cold water until cool. Spread the noodles out in a single layer over clean kitchen towels. (Do not use paper towels; they will stick to the pasta.)

4. Spray a 13 by 9-inch baking dish with vegetable oil spray. Smear 3 tablespoons of the tomato sauce (without any meatballs) over the bottom of the pan. Line the pan with a layer of pasta, making sure that the noodles touch but do not overlap. Spread about 1½ cups of the tomato sauce with meatballs evenly over the pasta. Sprinkle evenly with 1 cup of the mozzarella and ½ cup of the Parmesan. Repeat the layering of pasta, tomato sauce with meatballs, and cheeses 2 more times. For the fourth and final layer, cover the pasta with the remaining 1 cup mozzarella and sprinkle with the remaining ½ cup Parmesan. (At this point, the lasagna can wrapped tightly with plastic wrap and refrigerated for up to 2 days; let the lasagna sit on the counter for 1 hour before baking.)

5. Adjust an oven rack to the middle position and heat the oven to 400 degrees. Bake until the cheese on top turns golden brown in spots and the sauce is bubbling, 20 to 25 minutes. Let the lasagna rest for 5 to 10 minutes before cutting and serving.

CHICKEN UNDER A BRICK

Pollo al Mattone

THE POINT OF COOKING A CHICKEN UNDER a brick is not simply to impress your friends and family (although it does look cool), but rather to achieve a stunningly crisp skin. After the chicken is butterflied and pounded flat, it is pressed into a hot pan under the weight of a brick (which, for reasons of hygiene, is usually wrapped in foil). The brick helps keep the chicken flat as it cooks, forcing all of the skin to make contact with the pan. Typically marinated with garlic and rosemary, this flavorful

chicken cooks in about 45 minutes.

After trying a few recipes, however, we noted two big problems. The beautiful, crisp skin often turned soggy or greasy as the chicken finished cooking and the marinade burned in the hot pan, making the chicken taste scorched. We also took notice of a few problems that could be immediately rectified. First, the weight of two bricks (or heavy cans) is much better than just one. Second, the bricks offered a more even distribution of weight when placed on a baking sheet or cast-iron skillet. Finally, we found that chickens much larger than 3 pounds were difficult to fit into a 12-inch skillet.

To start, we set the rosemary and garlic marinade aside and focused on the cooking method. Using two unmarinated butterflied chickens, we tested the difference between pounding the chicken to an even thickness using a mallet versus simply pressing the chicken flat by hand. When pounded with a mallet, the super-flat chicken cooked evenly and more of the skin was able to make contact with the pan and turn crisp. By comparison, only portions of skin on the chicken flattened by hand were nicely browned.

We cooked these chickens according to most of the recipes we researched: skin side down first with bricks on top, then flipped over to cook the underside, replacing the bricks to help keep the chicken flat. We found, however, that this method didn't work so well. After the chickens were flipped and the weight was replaced on top, the skin (which was now crisp and delicate) tore in places and began to steam, turning shaggy and flaccid. We then tried not replacing the bricks after the chicken was flipped, but the skin still turned rubbery from the steam and splattering oil.

Next, we tried cooking the underside of the chicken first, finishing with the breast side down, but this didn't work either. By the time the chicken was ready to flip, the pan was loaded with grease and nasty burnt bits were pressed into the skin, making it spotty and slightly bitter. We then decided to try a different approach altogether. We cooked the chicken skin side down, underneath the weights, until it had a beautiful color. We then removed the bricks, flipped the bird over, and finished it in a hot oven. The hot, dry air of the oven ensured that the skin remained crisp as the chicken finished cooking through.

With the method in place, we moved our attention to adding back the marinade. Marinating the chicken before cooking did us little good—the herbs and garlic that stuck to the skin burned as they were pressed into the hot pan under the weight of the brick. Instead, we discovered we could simply brush the marinade onto the chicken before it went into the oven. The flavors of the marinade remained fresh and potent while the heat of the oven fused the marinade to the skin instantly, without ruining the skin's crisp texture. Tasters preferred a simple olive oil–based marinade flavored with garlic, rosemary, or oregano, hot red pepper flakes, and black pepper. Emerging from the oven fragrant and stunningly gorgeous, the chicken simply needs to rest for 5 to 10 minutes, allowing the juices to redistribute before serving.

Finally, we tried moving our recipe to the grill based on the recommendation of a few cookbooks. The flavor from grilling was a welcome variation to our skillet method, but it did require some slight modifications. With a charcoal grill, we found it important not to place any coals directly underneath the chicken or flare-ups would incinerate the skin. Banking the coals off to either side of the grill, we successfully cooked the chicken in the middle of the grill with no coals burning directly beneath it. On a gas grill, flare-ups are less common, and cooking directly over medium-low burners worked great. Also, unlike the skillet-cooked chicken, which is flipped skin side up after 25 minutes and finished in the oven, the grilled chicken can be cooked completely on the grill with the lid down—the lid traps the heat much like the oven. The bonus of this adapted grilling method is that the chicken doesn't need to be flipped at any point during the cooking; it can remain skin side down for the entire grilling time. Although we found the bricks crucial for the skillet-cooked chicken (they press the skin flush to the skillet for ultimate browning), we found them to be optional on the grill; because the chicken is grilled skin side down for the entire time, the skin becomes completely golden and crisp without using the bricks.

Chicken Under a Brick
Pollo al Mattone
SERVES 3 TO 4

Our favorite weights are a small baking sheet (it should fit inside the 12-inch skillet) and two bricks. You can also use other heavy items such as a Dutch oven or cast-iron pan loaded with several heavy cans (the weights are not necessary if grilling; see the variations). Be careful when removing the skillet from the oven as the handle will be very hot. If you can only find a larger chicken (3½ to 4 pounds), use one of the grill variations (you may need to add several minutes to the cooking time).

1	small whole chicken (3 pounds), butterflied and pounded flat following the illustrations on page 308
	Salt and ground black pepper
1	tablespoon vegetable oil
¼	cup extra-virgin olive oil
1	medium garlic clove, minced or pressed through a garlic press (about 1 teaspoon)
½	teaspoon minced fresh rosemary or oregano leaves
	Pinch red pepper flakes

1. Adjust an oven rack to the lowest position and heat the oven to 450 degrees. Pat the chicken dry with paper towels and season with salt and pepper.

2. Heat the vegetable oil in an ovensafe 12-inch skillet over medium-high heat until just smoking. Place the chicken skin side down in the skillet and turn the heat down to medium. Place a small baking sheet (or plate) and two bricks (or heavy cans) on top of the chicken and cook, checking every 5 minutes or so (to ensure the chicken is cooking evenly), until evenly browned, about 25 minutes. (After 20 minutes, the chicken should be fairly crisp and golden; if it is not, turn the heat up to medium-high and continue to cook until well browned.)

3. Meanwhile, mix the olive oil, garlic, rosemary, pepper flakes, ⅛ teaspoon salt, and ⅛ teaspoon black pepper together; set aside.

4. Remove the skillet from the heat and remove the baking sheet with bricks. Using tongs, carefully

flip the chicken skin side up. (If more than 3 tablespoons fat have collected in the skillet, transfer the chicken to a clean plate and pour most of the fat out of the skillet. Return the chicken to the skillet skin side up and continue.)

5. Brush the skin with the marinade and transfer the skillet to the oven. Cook until the thickest part of the thigh registers 170 to 175 degrees on an instant-read thermometer, 7 to 10 minutes. Being careful of the hot skillet handle, transfer the chicken to a carving board and let rest for 10 minutes. Carve and serve.

➤ VARIATIONS

Chicken Under a Brick on a Charcoal Grill

See page 366 for more information on grilling. The chicken in this variation is not flipped during cooking but is cooked skin side down for the entire time. Weighing the chicken down with bricks is not necessary on the grill but you can use them if desired.

Follow the recipe for Chicken Under a Brick, lighting a large chimney starter full of charcoal (about 6 quarts) and allowing it to burn until all the charcoal is covered with a layer of fine gray ash. Build a grill-roasting fire by banking the coals on either side of the grill, leaving the center of the grill without any coals. Set the cooking grate in place, cover the grill with the lid, and let the grate heat up, about 5 minutes. Scrape the cooking grate clean with a grill brush. Lay the chicken skin side down in the center of the grill with no coals underneath. Cover, fully open the lid vents, and grill-roast until an instant-read thermometer inserted into the thickest part of the thigh registers 170 to 175 degrees, 30 to 40 minutes. Transfer the chicken, skin side up, to a carving board, drizzle with the oil mixture, then rest, carve, and serve as directed.

Chicken Under a Brick on a Gas Grill

See page 366 for more information on grilling. The chicken in this variation is not flipped during cooking but is cooked skin side down for the entire time. Weighing the chicken down with bricks is not necessary on the grill but you can use them if desired.

Follow the recipe for Chicken Under a Brick, heating the grill with all the burners set to high and the lid down until very hot, about 15 minutes. Scrape the cooking grate clean with a grill brush. Turn all the burners to medium-low, and position the chicken skin side down on the center of the grill grate. Cover and grill-roast until an instant-read thermometer inserted into the thickest part of the thigh registers 170 to 175 degrees, 30 to 40 minutes. Transfer the chicken, skin side up, to a carving board, drizzle with the oil mixture, then rest, carve, and serve as directed.

BUTTERFLYING A CHICKEN

1. With the breast side down and the tail of the chicken facing you, use the poultry shears to cut along one side of the backbone down its entire length.

2. With the breast side still down, turn the neck end to face you. Cut along the other side of the backbone and remove it.

3. Turn the chicken breast side up; open the chicken out on the work surface. Use the palm of your hand to flatten it. Cover the chicken with plastic wrap and gently pound flat with a mallet.

SAUTÉED VEAL CUTLETS WITH PROSCIUTTO AND SAGE

Saltimbocca alla Romana

ITS NAME LITERALLY MEANING "JUMP IN THE mouth," *saltimbocca* is a simple variation on a basic veal scaloppine. Thinly sliced pieces of prosciutto and leaves of sage are pressed into veal cutlets and secured with a toothpick before the cutlets are quickly sautéed and served with a light pan sauce. The simple combination of these three flavors is so good that the cutlets jump into your mouth.

Though simple, this dish is not without its pitfalls. The biggest problem is that the cutlets are so thin that it is difficult for them to acquire a brown crust without overcooking. Also, we noted that many cutlets buckle and turn tough as they cook, while others remain flat and tender.

Beginning our testing at the meat counter, we found most packaged veal cutlets are inaccurately butchered. Proper veal scaloppine should be cut from the top round, the upper portion of the leg, which is lean and has no muscle separation. The packaged cutlets we found were obviously cut from the shoulder and other parts of the animal, resulting in shaggy, fatty pieces that fell apart and cooked unevenly. Cutting your own cutlets is important and luckily it is easy to do. Many recipes also pound the cutlets to an even thickness, and

MAKING SALTIMBOCCA

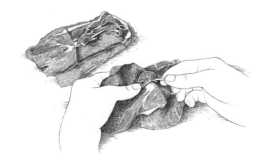

Using a toothpick as if it were a stickpin, secure the sage and prosciutto to the cutlet by poking the toothpick down through the three layers, then back out again. The toothpick should be parallel to the cutlet and as flat as possible.

PANTRY SPOTLIGHT

PROSCIUTTO

Prosciutto is a ham that has been salted, pressed, and air-dried in the Italian fashion and, unlike many other regional cured hams produced around the world, it is not smoked. As a signature product for more than two thousand years, Italian prosciutto is legally protected and tightly monitored by Italian law—all aspects of prosciutto production, from the pigpen to the aging house, are strictly regulated and controlled. And although prosciutto is now produced in various parts of the world, the best versions still come from two regions of Italy: Parma and San Daniele. We tasted a variety of domestic and Italian prosciuttos side by side, and there was no comparison. The domestic prosciutto tasted harsh, salty, and rubbery while the authentic prosciutto had a balanced, complex flavor and silky texture. As an antipasto, prosciutto is customarily served raw (or *crudo*, in Italian) in paper-thin slices, or wrapped around slices of melon or wedges of figs.

we agree that pounding is a good idea. Tasters preferred the lightly pounded cutlets for their delicate texture and uniform thinness.

Next, we focused on how to get a crust on the cutlets without overcooking them. Using a hot pan, we were surprised to find that pounded cutlets cooked in just two minutes or less—about one minute per side. When cooked for any longer, the meat turned dry and stringy. In an effort to get some sort of brown crust within that short cooking time, we tried flouring the cutlets. Compared to cutlets that were unfloured, the floured pieces browned in spots and had a crisp exterior that nicely contrasted with the soft interior. The flour also acted as a barrier that helped protect the delicate meat as it cooked.

A 12-inch skillet was the obvious choice for a pan, as it could fit a recipe's worth of cutlets into just two batches. Nonstick made for goof-proof cooking and easy cleanup, but it also prevented the build up of fond. Fond is the bits of meat that stick to the pan during cooking and lend indescribable depth and body to pan sauces. Not willing to sacrifice flavor for the sake of convenience, we chose a traditional skillet.

Having figured out how to buy and cook veal cutlets properly, it was easy to add prosciutto and sage to our basic sautéed cutlet recipe. Although many recipes pound the prosciutto and sage into the cutlets, we found this didn't work very well. The pounding simply tore the thin prosciutto and fragile sage to shaggy pieces. Instead, we simply pressed the tacky prosciutto into the already pounded cutlet with our hands. Laying the sage leaf on top of the prosciutto, we secured the trio with a toothpick.

All the saltimbocca recipes we found paired the cutlets with a quick pan sauce using the fond left in the pan. When making such a sauce, we found it best to hold the sautéed meat in a warm oven because the cutlets tend to cool off fast. Making a straightforward pan sauce using shallot, lemon juice, parsley, butter, and broth, we noted that adding a little wine helped to round out the other flavors. Authentic recipes we researched called for either white wine or Marsala, but tasters far preferred the flavor of the white wine, finding the Marsala a bit overpowering and sweet. Finished with a white wine pan sauce, saltimbocca is both incredibly simple and elegant.

CUTTING VEAL CUTLETS

1. With a boning knife, remove the silver skin (the white membrane that covers the meat in places) from a piece of veal top round.

2. Once the silver skin has been removed, use a long, inflexible slicing knife to cut slices—on the bias and against the grain—that are between ¼ and ½ inch thick.

Sautéed Veal Cutlets with Prosciutto and Sage
Saltimbocca alla Romana
SERVES 4

See below for information on cutting your own cutlets. Be sure to use large cutlets that will each serve one person (about 6 ounces each). If the cutlets are on the small side, consider serving 1½ to 2 cutlets per person; you will need to cook them in additional batches with extra oil in step 1. See page 198 for more information on making pan sauces.

4	large, ½-inch-thick veal cutlets (about 1½ pounds; see note)
4	thin prosciutto slices (about 3 ounces)
4	large fresh sage leaves
	Salt and ground black pepper
⅓	cup unbleached all-purpose flour
3	tablespoons extra-virgin olive oil
1	large shallot, minced (4 tablespoons)
¾	cup low-sodium chicken broth
½	cup dry white wine
3	tablespoons unsalted butter, cut into 2 pieces
1	tablespoon minced fresh parsley leaves
1	teaspoon juice from 1 lemon

1. Adjust an oven rack to the middle position and heat the oven to 200 degrees. Place the cutlets between 2 sheets of parchment or wax paper and pound to a thickness of ¼ inch. Place 1 slice of prosciutto on top of each cutlet and lay 1 sage leaf in the center, pressing them into the veal with the palm of your hand. Secure the prosciutto and sage with a toothpick following the illustration on page 309. Season the cutlets with salt and pepper. Measure the flour into a shallow dish or pie plate, then dredge the cutlets in the flour and shake to remove the excess.

2. Heat 1 tablespoon of the oil in a heavy-bottomed 12-inch skillet over medium-high heat until just smoking. Lay 2 of the cutlets, prosciutto side down, in the skillet, making sure they do not overlap, and cook without moving until lightly browned, about 1 minute. Flip the cutlets over and continue to cook until the meat feels firm when pressed, 30 to 60 seconds. Transfer the cutlets to a clean plate, cover with foil, and transfer to the

warm oven. Repeat with 1 more tablespoon of the oil and the remaining cutlets; transfer to the plate in the oven.

3. Add the remaining tablespoon oil and the shallot to the skillet, return to medium heat, and cook until softened, about 2 minutes. Stir in the broth and wine and cook, scraping up the browned bits, until slightly thickened, about 8 minutes. Reduce the heat to low, stir in any accumulated juices from the cutlets, then whisk in the butter, 1 piece at a time. Off the heat, stir in the parsley and lemon juice and season with salt and pepper to taste. Arrange the cutlets, prosciutto side up, on a large platter or individual plates and pour the sauce over the top. Serve immediately.

➤ VARIATION

Sautéed Chicken Cutlets with Prosciutto and Sage

Follow the recipe for Sautéed Veal Cutlets with Prosciutto and Sage, substituting 4 large, ½-inch-thick chicken cutlets (about 1½ pounds) for the veal cutlets.

SLICING CHICKEN BREASTS INTO CUTLETS

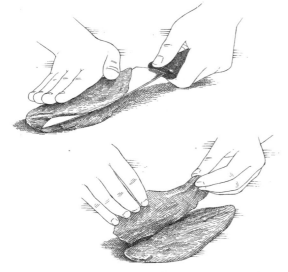

Lay the chicken breast flat on a cutting board, smooth side facing up. Rest one hand on top of the chicken and using a sharp chef's knife, carefully slice the chicken in half horizontally to yield two thin cutlets between ⅜ and ½ inch thick.

ITALIAN BRAISED VEAL SHANKS
Osso Buco

OSSO BUCO IS A WELL-KNOWN MILANESE dish of braised veal shanks. The ingredients are simple: veal shanks (which are browned), aromatics (onions, carrots, and celery, all sautéed), and liquids (a blend of wine, broth, and tomatoes). The shank is a robust cut of meat and the bone adds tremendous flavor to the stewing liquid. The resulting dish should be rich in flavor and color and somewhat brothy but not stewy. Our goals for this dish were straightforward—we wanted to perfect (and simplify, if possible) the cooking technique while extracting the most flavor from its simple ingredients.

Most recipes we reviewed called for shanks from the upper portion of the hind leg, cut into pieces between 1 and 1½ inches thick. We found that purchasing shanks is tricky, even when we special-ordered them. From one market, we received stunning shanks with a lovely pinkish blush, which were ideal except for the weight. Each shank weighed between 12 and 16 ounces—too large for individual servings. Part of the appeal of osso buco is receiving an individual shank as a portion. At another market, the shanks were generally in the ideal weight range, but the butchering job was less than perfect. In the same package, shank widths varied from 1 to 2½ inches and were occasionally cut on an extreme bias, making tying difficult (see the explanation below) and searing uneven.

The first step, then, is to shop carefully. We found a thickness of 1½ inches and a weight of 8 ounces ideal. Make sure all the shanks you buy are close to these specifications. Each shank should have two nicely cut, flat sides to facilitate browning.

Preparing the meat for braising was the next challenge. Most recipes called for tying the shanks and dredging them in flour before searing. We found that tying a piece of butcher's twine around the equator of each shank does prevent the meat from falling apart and makes for a more attractive presentation. When we skipped this step, the meat fell off the bone and floated about in the pot.

Flouring the meat, however, was another matter. Tasters felt that the meat floured before searing was gummy and lacked depth. The flour on the meat browns rather than the meat itself and the flour coating may peel off during the long braising time.

To develop the best flavor in the shanks, we seasoned them generously with salt and pepper and seared them until a thick, golden brown crust formed. We seared the shanks in two batches (even if they could all fit in the pan at the same time) so that we could deglaze the pan twice with wine, thereby enriching the braising liquid doubly.

The most difficult part of developing this recipe was attaining an ideal braising liquid and sauce. Braising, by design, is a relatively inexact cooking method because the rate at which the liquid reduces can vary greatly. Some of the initial recipes we tried yielded far too much liquid, which was thin in flavor and texture. In other cases, the liquid nearly evaporated by the time the meat was tender. We needed to create a foolproof, flavorful braising liquid and cooking technique that produced a rich sauce in a suitable volume and did not need a lot of last-minute fussing.

We experimented with numerous techniques to attain our ideal liquid, including reductions before braising and after braising (with the aromatics and without) and a reduction of the wine to a syrup during the deglazing process. In the end, we settled on the easiest method: natural reduction in the oven. The seal on most Dutch ovens is not perfectly tight, so the liquid reduces as the osso buco cooks. We found further simmering on the stovetop unnecessary as long as we started with the right amount of liquid in the pot.

The braising liquid traditionally begins with meat (beef or veal) stock and then white wine and tomatoes are added. As few cooks have homemade stock on hand and store-bought beef broth is often unappealing, we knew that store-bought chicken broth would be our likely starting point. Two cups seemed the right amount and tests confirmed this. To enrich the flavor of the broth, we used a hefty amount of diced onion, carrot, and celery. Tasters liked the large amount of garlic in one recipe, so

we finely minced five cloves and added them to the pot prior to the broth. We rounded out the flavors with a couple of bay leaves.

A few recipes we found called for an entire bottle of wine, but when we tried this amount it completely overpowered the other flavors with its acidity. Some testers also felt that the meat was tougher than previous batches with less wine. We scaled the wine back to 2½ cups, about two-thirds of a bottle, and were happy with the results. More than half of the wine is used to deglaze the pot between searing batches of veal shanks and thus the final dish is not as alcoholic or liquidy as it might seem.

With the wine and broth amounts settled, we needed to figure out how to best incorporate tomatoes. Most tasters did not like too much tomato because they felt it easily overwhelmed the other flavors. Fresh tomatoes are always a gamble outside of the summer months, so we chose canned diced tomatoes, thoroughly strained of their juice. This approach worked out well and one small can was just the right amount.

We still needed to determine the ideal braising time. Several sources suggested cooking the veal shanks until they were almost the consistency of pulled pork. Tasters loved the flavor of veal cooked this way, but it was less than attractive. We wanted compact meat firmly attached to the bone, so we cooked the meat just until it was fork-tender but still clinging to the bone. Two hours in the oven produced veal that was meltingly soft but still attached to the bone. With some of the larger shanks, the cooking time extended to about 2½ hours.

We experimented with oven temperature and found that 325 degrees reduced the braising liquid to the right consistency and did not harm the texture of the meat. While beef stews are best cooked at 300 degrees, veal shanks have so much collagen and connective tissue that they can be braised at a slightly higher temperature.

Just before serving, osso buco is typically sprinkled with gremolata, a mixture of minced garlic, parsley, and lemon zest. We were surprised to find variations on this classic trio. A number of recipes included orange zest mixed with lemon zest or on its own. Other recipes included anchovies. We tested three gremolatas: one traditional, one with equal amounts of orange zest and lemon zest, and one with anchovies. Tasters liked all three but favored the traditional version.

In some recipes the gremolata is used as a garnish and in others it is added to the pot just before serving. We chose a compromise approach, stirring half the gremolata into the pot and letting it stand for five minutes so that the flavors of the garlic, lemon, and parsley permeated the dish. We sprinkled the remaining gremolata on individual servings for a hit of freshness.

Italian Braised Veal Shanks

Osso Buco
SERVES 6

To keep the meat attached to the bone during the long simmering process, tie a piece of twine around the thickest portion of each shank before it is browned. The zest in the gremolata should be a bit more coarse than usual; we like to use a vegetable peeler or paring knife to remove the zest (without any white pith) from a single lemon, then mince it with a chef's knife. Osso buco is traditionally served with saffron risotto (see page 275), however, polenta (see page 277) is an excellent option as well.

OSSO BUCO

- 6 (1½-inch-thick) veal shanks (8 to 10 ounces each), tied around the equator with butcher's twine
  Salt and ground black pepper
- 6 tablespoons vegetable oil
- 2½ cups dry white wine
- 2 medium onions, cut into ½-inch pieces (about 2 cups)
- 2 medium carrots, peeled and cut into ½-inch pieces (about 1½ cups)
- 2 medium celery ribs, cut into ½-inch pieces (about 1 cup)
- 6 medium garlic cloves, minced or pressed through a garlic press (about 2 tablespoons)
- 2 cups low-sodium chicken broth
- 1 (14.5-ounce) can diced tomatoes, drained
- 2 bay leaves

GREMOLATA

- 3 medium garlic cloves, minced or pressed through a garlic press (about 1 tablespoon)
- 2 teaspoons minced lemon zest (see note)
- ¼ cup minced fresh parsley leaves

1. FOR THE OSSO BUCO: Adjust an oven rack to the lower-middle position and heat the oven to 325 degrees.

2. Pat the shanks dry with paper towels and season with salt and pepper. Heat 2 tablespoons of the oil in a large Dutch oven over medium-high heat until shimmering. Brown half of the shanks on both sides, about 5 minutes per side, reducing the heat if the pan begins to scorch; transfer to a bowl and set aside. Off the heat, add ½ cup of the wine to the Dutch oven, scraping up the browned bits, then pour into the bowl with the browned shanks. Return the pot to medium-high heat, and repeat with 2 more tablespoons of the oil and the remaining shanks. Add another ½ cup of the wine and transfer to the bowl.

3. Add the remaining 2 tablespoons oil to the pot and return to medium heat until shimmering. Add the onions, carrots, and celery and cook, stirring occasionally, until soft and lightly browned, about 9 minutes. Stir in the garlic and cook until lightly browned, about 1 minute. Stir in the remaining 1½ cups wine, broth, tomatoes, and bay leaves. Add the browned shanks with any accumulated juices, increase the heat to high, and bring to a simmer. Cover the pot, transfer to the oven, and cook until the meat is easily pierced with a fork but not falling off the bone, about 2 hours. (At this point, the osso buco can be refrigerated for up to 2 days. Return to a simmer over medium-low heat before continuing.)

4. FOR THE GREMOLATA: Combine the garlic, lemon zest, and parsley in a small bowl.

5. When the shanks are cooked, remove the pot from the oven, remove the bay leaves, and stir in half of the gremolata. Season with salt and pepper to taste and let stand, uncovered, for 5 minutes. Remove the shanks from the pot, cut off the twine, and place the veal shanks in 6 individual serving bowls. Ladle some braising liquid over each shank and sprinkle with the remaining gremolata. Serve.

TUSCAN PORK ROAST

Arista di Maiale

TUSCAN-STYLE ROAST PORK IS A SIMPLE DISH of roasted pork loin served boneless, sliced thick, and often accompanied by pan juices. The meat is succulent, the crust crisp, and the roast is infused with the local flavors of rosemary and garlic (rosemary grows as tall as hedges in Tuscany). It's great hot from the oven or cold sliced in sandwiches, and it is surprisingly inexpensive. This is a roast that can be a showpiece for a special occasion or a family meal with leftovers.

But for such a simple roast, problems abound. The meat can be dry, tough, and unevenly cooked; the crust can be nonexistent, resulting in a pale and unappealing dish; and the rosemary and garlic flavors can be either too bland or too harsh. Our research revealed that there is no consensus on the cut of meat, the best way to flavor the pork, or the oven temperature at which to roast it.

We began by testing the cut of meat. Recipes called for a wide range of choices, the most popular being a boneless center-cut pork loin. Preparing and tasting 12 recipes convinced us to use a bone-in loin. These roasts had a richer pork flavor and were noticeably juicier. The boneless loins, in comparison, failed on the taste test, but we noted that they

TWO CENTER-CUT PORK ROASTS

Both the rib roast (right) and loin roast (left) can be labeled "center-cut roast" at the market, but they are not the same. The meat on the pork rib roast includes a protective cap of fat and muscle and is marbled with more fat than the loin roast. The marbling (threads of intramuscular fat) and the fat in the cap melt during cooking and flavor the meat as well as ensure its juiciness. The loin roast has less marbling, lacks a protective cap of fat and muscle, and does not have as many rib bones, so the meat is more likely to dry out in the oven. For these reasons, we recommend a rib roast, not a loin roast.

were easier to carve. We also observed that because we cooked the boneless roasts on a rack, the meat on the bottom roasted rather than steamed. With this information in hand, we hoped to find a bone-in choice that would also give us what we liked about the boneless option.

We quickly eliminated the blade roast and the sirloin roast, both of which are composed of many separate muscles and fatty deposits. Tests showed that these cuts were difficult to cook evenly, flavor well, and carve.

Both the rib roast and the loin roast seemed worthy candidates. Each of these roasts consists largely of the same single, uniformly shaped muscle, so we prepared them side by side. The meat on the rib roast includes a protective cap of fat and muscle and is marbled with more fat than the loin roast. The marbling (threads of intramuscular fat) and the fat in the cap melt during cooking and flavor the meat as well as ensure juiciness. The loin roast has less marbling, lacks a protective cap of fat and muscle, and does not have as many rib bones. We were happy to discover that the rib roast provided not just the tastiest meat, but also a natural, built-in cooking rack—the rib bones.

Purchasing a rib roast requires an understanding of the distinction between the rib roast and the loin roast because sometimes these roasts are labeled exactly the same: "center-cut, bone-in roast." If you are looking in a meat case, refer to the photographs below, or simply ask your butcher.

With the cut of meat decided, we turned our attention to the traditional Tuscan flavors. Rosemary, garlic, and olive oil are strong characters, and we were determined to harness and marry their flavors so that the roast would be perfumed with their essence. We identified the classic approaches and began testing.

Stuffing slivers of garlic, with or without rosemary, into slits on the outside of the roast failed to impress. The flavors did not permeate deeply (even when we refrigerated the loin overnight before cooking) and the garlic and rosemary were not pleasant to eat. Garlic and rosemary rubbed on the outside tended to burn and become bitter. Rosemary sprigs tied to the outside looked appealing, but the flavor did not penetrate and the crust did not brown evenly. In an attempt to flavor the center of the meat, some recipes call for creating a hole in the middle of the loin and then stuffing it, while other recipes have you slit open the loin and spread a rosemary garlic mixture on the inside. These approaches held promise, but the garlic was often undercooked and harsh and the rosemary overpowering.

We were convinced that putting a paste in the center of the meat was the answer. Making the paste by hand with the help of a garlic press gave us the best results. Equal parts rosemary and garlic was most pleasing, and tests showed that including olive oil helps heat and cook the garlic and rosemary paste, which facilitates the infusion of flavor.

We were on our twenty-sixth roast and still having problems using the paste to infuse the meat with flavor. Our search for creative solutions led us to remove the meat from the bone, cut it open in the center, and open it like a book, a technique called butterflying. We placed the paste in the cut and then tied the roast back together. This roast was very flavorful, but there was too much paste, which was overpowering and unpleasant to eat. We tried another butterflied loin with the intention of spreading less of the paste into the cut when the naked bones gave us an idea. We slathered the bones with two-thirds of the paste and spread the rest in the cut, then tied the meat back onto the bones. Now the rosemary and garlic flavors infused the meat, but the paste stayed on the bones when the roast was sliced and served. The bonus of deconstructing the roast to apply the paste was that carving was no longer an issue. By simply cutting the twine after cooking, the bone-in roast was now as easy to slice and serve as the boneless roasts we had tried at the beginning. Our search for flavor had served up convenience as well.

PREPARING A TUSCAN PORK ROAST

1. Position the loin so that the rib bones are perpendicular to the cutting board. Using a sharp knife and starting from the far end working toward you, separate the meat from the rib bones by pressing—almost scraping—the knife along the rib bones.

2. Use a series of small, easy strokes to cut all along the bones, following the rib bones along the curve to the backbone until the meat is free of the bones. You will have a compact eye of the loin, with a small flap attached to the side.

3. Slice through the center of the entire length of the eye, stopping 1 inch shy of the edge.

4. Open the eye up so it is spread flat like butterfly wings and rub one third of the garlic-rosemary paste in an even layer on one side of the cut, leaving ½ inch on each end bare.

5. Spread the remaining paste evenly along the bones from where the meat was cut, leaving ½ inch on each end bare. Fold the eye back together and secure the meat on the bones exactly from where it was cut.

6. Use seven lengths of butcher's twine to tie the meat back onto the bones.

315

We now had a very good-tasting roast, but we were looking for the best. We wanted to address the fact that pigs are bred leaner these days, and less fat means less flavor and less moisture. We decided to try brining, soaking the pork (both the meat and the bones) in a saltwater solution. Brining causes the protein cells within the meat to unravel and thus capture and retain both moisture and seasoning. Sure enough, tests confirmed that this technique produced a roast that was better seasoned and juicer. We added rosemary and garlic to the brine along with brown sugar for depth and caramelization. This created a terrific and aromatic roast, with complex flavors that were both strong and savory.

We were in the home stretch and ready to experiment with roasting methods. Our goal—a crispy and flavorful crust combined with tender, moist meat—was in sight.

Roasting at a constant temperature was not ideal. A low temperature (325 degrees or lower) produced the best meat, while high heat (400 degrees or higher) produced the best crust. A moderate oven temperature produced neither delectable meat nor an appealing crust. We resisted dividing the cooking between the stovetop and the oven, trying every imaginable combination of high heat and low heat in the oven instead. But this approach also failed. The high heat dried out the meat or even worse; occasionally, the high heat resulted in billows of smoke pouring out of the oven from the pork fat.

The answer came easily once we let go of our resolve to limit cooking to the oven. By searing the roast on the stovetop and then finishing it in the oven, we found a fail-safe method for producing an excellent crust and perfectly cooked meat. A constant 325-degree oven subsequent to stovetop searing gave us the best results. As we usually do in the test kitchen, we aimed for a final internal temperature of 150 degrees, at which point the meat would be fully cooked yet retain a slightly rosy hue inside. (This means you need to pull the roast from the oven when it reaches 140 degrees—after resting, the temperature will rise about 10 degrees.)

Finally, we had developed a recipe for a Tuscan-style roast pork loin that lives up to its reputation.

Tuscan-Style Roast Pork Loin with Garlic and Rosemary
Arista di Maiale
SERVES 6 TO 8

The roasting time is determined in part by the shape of the roast; a long, thin roast will cook faster than a roast with a large circumference. Though not traditionally served, the ribs are rich with flavor. If you'd like to serve them or enjoy them yourself, after untying the roast and removing the loin scrape the excess garlic-rosemary paste from the ribs, set the ribs on a rimmed baking sheet, and put them in a 375-degree oven for about 20 minutes or until they are brown and crisp.

ROAST

2	cups kosher salt or 1 cup table salt
2	cups packed dark brown sugar
10	large garlic cloves, lightly crushed and peeled
5	sprigs fresh rosemary
1	bone-in, center-cut 4-pound pork rib roast with chine bone cracked, preferably from the rib end (see page 314), prepared according to illustrations 1 and 2 on page 315

GARLIC-ROSEMARY PASTE AND JUS

8	medium garlic cloves, minced to a paste (about 1½ tablespoons) (see page 299)
1½	tablespoons coarsely chopped fresh rosemary
1	tablespoon extra-virgin olive oil
	Salt and ground black pepper
1	cup dry white wine
1	large shallot, minced
1½	teaspoons minced fresh rosemary
1¾	cups low-sodium chicken broth
2	tablespoons unsalted butter

1. FOR THE ROAST: Dissolve the salt and brown sugar in 1½ quarts of hot tap water in a large stockpot or clean bucket. Stir in the garlic and rosemary. Add 2½ quarts of cold water and submerge the meat and bones in the brine. Refrigerate until fully seasoned, about 3 hours. Rinse the meat and ribs under cold water and dry thoroughly with paper towels.

2. FOR THE PASTE AND JUS: While the roast brines, mix the garlic, chopped rosemary, olive oil, ⅛ teaspoon salt and 1 teaspoon pepper in a small bowl to form a paste; set aside.

3. When the roast is out of the brine, adjust an oven rack to the middle position and heat the oven to 325 degrees. Heat a heavy-bottomed 12-inch skillet over medium heat until hot. Place the roast, fat side down, in the skillet and cook until well browned, about 8 minutes. Transfer the roast, browned side up, to a rimmed baking sheet and set aside. Pour off the fat from the skillet and add the wine. Increase the heat to high and bring to a boil, scraping the skillet with a wooden spoon until the browned bits are loosened. Set the skillet aside.

4. Make a lengthwise incision in the pork loin and rub with one-third of the garlic-rosemary paste (see illustration 4 on page 315). Rub the remaining paste on the cut side of the ribs where the meat was attached (see illustration 5). Tie the meat to the ribs (see illustration 6); sprinkle the browned side of the roast with 1 teaspoon pepper. Pour the reserved wine and browned bits from the skillet into the roasting pan. Roast, basting the loin with the pan drippings every 20 minutes, until the center of the loin registers about 140 degrees on an instant-read thermometer, 65 to 80 minutes. (If the wine evaporates, add ½ cup water to the roasting pan to prevent scorching.) Transfer the roast to a carving board and tent loosely with foil. Let stand until the center of the loin registers about 150 degrees on an instant-read thermometer, about 15 minutes.

5. While the roast rests, spoon most of the fat from the roasting pan and place the pan over 2 burners at high heat. Add the shallot and minced rosemary. Scrape up the browned bits with a wooden spoon and boil the liquid until reduced by half and the shallot has softened, about 2 minutes. Add the chicken broth and continue to cook, stirring occasionally, until reduced by half, about 8 minutes. Add any accumulated pork juices and cook 1 minute longer. Off the heat, whisk in the butter 1 tablespoon at a time. Strain the jus into a gravy boat or small bowl.

6. Cut the twine on the roast and remove the meat from the bones. Set the meat, browned side up, on a board and cut it into ¼-inch-thick slices. Serve immediately, passing the jus separately.

BEEF IN BAROLO

Brasato al Barolo

BEEF IN BAROLO IS AN ELEGANT DISH (reminiscent of Beef Bourguignon) with the focus centered on the rich, complex flavors of a great red wine and a tender beef roast. Barolo is a wine made from the Nebbiolo grape in the northern region of Piedmont and is known for its hearty aromas of oak, licorice, plum, roses, and violets. As the meat slowly cooks in the Barolo, the flavors meld and mellow, emerging from the oven with a heady aroma and potent flavor.

The problem, however, is that Barolo is a tannic, full-bodied, and expensive wine that produces harsh, astringent-tasting beef if not handled correctly. And strangely, most recipes we researched pair this expensive wine (most bottles start at a whopping $30) with a tough, cheap cut of pot roast meat. Given the investment (of wine and time), we needed to be seriously impressed with this dish in order to consider it a worthwhile endeavor.

Prior test kitchen efforts to perfect pot roast revealed chuck roast as the overwhelming favorite cut of meat for its moistness and flavor. Initial tests of several beef in Barolo recipes confirmed these results. A boneless chuck-eye roast braised entirely in Barolo was mostly tender and rich in flavor. In contrast, a boneless sirloin yielded what one taster called "insanely dry" meat and a watery, raw-tasting wine sauce. Perhaps it would be wiser to stick with a chuck roast after all. But which one?

In a side-by-side comparison of three classic chuck roasts—a boneless chuck-eye roast, a seven-bone roast, and a top-blade roast—tasters praised each for being moist, tender, and beefy. In the end, the decision boiled down to aesthetics and convenience. The center of the top-blade roast sported an unappealing strip of partially melted connective tissue that was reminiscent of meat-flavored gummy bears. The seven-bone roast was hard to carve and even harder to find in the supermarket. The chuck-eye roast won by default.

Our recipe was beginning to take shape, but after four long hours of braising, the meat was precariously close to being shredded and overdone and contained unsightly pockets of squishy fat and connective tissue. While this might be acceptable in a more rustic pot roast, beef in Barolo demands a more refined presentation. The fat would have to go.

We wondered what would happen if we split the large cylindrical roast into two sleeker halves. Dividing the roast into two fairly equal pieces was easy, as the seam of fat that runs down the center of the roast acts as a built-in guide. We trimmed the obvious wads of fat from each lobe, leaving a thin layer of fat cap, and seasoned and tied each piece to keep it from falling apart during braising. With less extraneous fat and a shortened cooking time (the meat was now done in three hours), these two roasts were definitely better than one.

Following Italian custom, we began this recipe by searing the roasts in olive oil rather than vegetable oil, but the sauce needed pizzazz. We remembered seeing pancetta in some of the recipes we had come across and decided to brown the meat in the fat rendered from this Italian bacon instead, reserving the crisp pieces for later on. This helped immensely in developing flavor. (If you have trouble finding pancetta, salt pork also does the trick.) Putting the browned roast aside, we then sautéed a hefty quantity of onions, carrots, and celery, adding a tablespoon of tomato paste to create a nice, deep roasted flavor. After stirring in minced garlic, a small amount of sugar, and a tablespoon of flour to help thicken the sauce during the final reduction, we were ready to add the wine.

Barolo is hailed as Italy's "king of wines and wine of kings" and the price alone makes it the "wine of kings." Unlike its lighter, fruitier Italian counterparts, such as Chianti, which are often better off quaffed from a glass than used in vigorous cooking, Barolo is very hardy and can carry the day, even after being simmered for hours. We found that several other, cheaper "big reds" can be substituted but if you are willing to spend the money this dish calls out for its namesake. Fortunately we also found an inexpensive Barolo that performed admirably. (See "Barolo and Barolo Substitutes" at right.)

As expected, the same qualities in Barolo that give this dish its characteristically robust flavor also presented some issues when cooking. This "king" was more out-of-control despot than temperate monarch—harsh and generally disliked. First, we focused on how and when to add the wine. Should it be reduced first to concentrate its flavors, added in two parts (at the beginning and the end), or simply dumped in with the meat? Much to our surprise and delight, dumping the whole bottle into the pot turned out to be the best option.

But we still needed to find an ingredient to counterbalance the harsh flavors in this big wine. Broth did not work; neither did water. Eventually, we discovered that diced tomatoes, drained of their juice, did the trick. The meaty tomatoes produced

INGREDIENTS:
Barolo and Barolo Substitutes

We tasted four bottles of Barolo, ranging in price from $11 to $40, in our Beef in Barolo recipe, and were happy to find that the least expensive bottle worked just fine. The only problem is that, although Barolo is widely available, inexpensive Barolo can be hard to find.

If you can't find a cheap Barolo, we found a few, moderately priced wine-cabinet staples that can be substituted. It takes a potent wine to withstand three hours in the oven and still have much character, and although neither a Chianti, a Merlot, nor a Côtes du Rhône were up to the task (they tasted flat), a Cabernet Sauvignon (our favorite Barolo stand-in) and a red Zinfandel (our second favorite stand-in) will do the job nicely.

BAROLO
If you can find a cheap bottle of Barolo (around $10), use it.

GOOD STAND-INS
If you can't find a cheap Barolo, choose a $10 bottle of either Cabernet Sauvignon or red Zinfandel.

the balance of sweet, salty, and hearty flavors this dish needed.

We then gently placed the beef back into the pot along with a few fresh herbs, brought everything back up to a simmer, covered the pot with foil to prevent moisture loss, replaced the lid, and let the beef braise in a 300-degree oven for three hours. (When given less time, the meat was too resilient; given more, it fell apart like pulled pork.) Flipping the meat every 45 minutes helped to achieve perfect tenderness without dry patches, as did lining the pot with foil underneath the lid to prevent the liquid from evaporating as it cooked.

Once the meat was tender, we removed it from the pot to rest while we concentrated on the sauce, which we felt ought to be a far cry from the typical pot roast liquid. After all, why use Barolo to start with if the sauce isn't grand? After skimming off the top layer of fat to remove as much grease as possible, we reduced the liquid over high heat to concentrate and intensify the multiple layers of flavor. Pureeing the liquid, vegetables, and herbs yielded a weak sauce that eventually separated into watery and mealy components. Straining the vegetables proved to be key. Boiled down to 1½ cups, the sauce was dark and lustrous, with the body and finesse of something you might serve over a fine steak.

Worth the expense and effort? You bet. And you don't need to dip into a savings account to put this dish on the table.

Beef Braised in Barolo
Brasato al Barolo
SERVES 6

Purchase pancetta that is cut to order, about ¼ inch thick; for more information on pancetta and possible substitutes, see page 294. Laying a sheet of aluminum foil underneath the lid of the pot helps to ensure the lid has a tight fit, preventing the liquid from evaporating and leaving the roast bare during cooking. Serve this stew with Simple Polenta (page 271) or mashed potatoes.

1	boneless chuck-eye roast (about 3½ pounds), prepared according to the illustrations below
	Salt and ground black pepper
4	ounces pancetta, cut into ¼-inch cubes
2	medium onions, chopped medium
2	medium carrots, peeled and chopped medium
2	medium celery ribs, chopped medium
1	tablespoon tomato paste
3	medium garlic cloves, minced or pressed through a garlic press (about 1 tablespoon)
½	teaspoon sugar
1	tablespoon unbleached all-purpose flour
1	(750 milliliter) bottle Barolo wine (about 3 cups, see page 318)
1	(14.5 ounces) can diced tomatoes, drained
10	sprigs fresh parsley
1	sprig fresh rosemary
1	teaspoon minced fresh thyme leaves

PREPARING A CHUCK-EYE ROAST

1. Pull the roast apart at its major seams (delineated by lines of fat and silver skin) into two halves. Use a knife as necessary.

2. With a paring knife, remove large knobs of fat from each piece, leaving a thin layer of fat on the meat.

3. Tie three pieces of kitchen twine around each piece of meat to keep it from falling apart.

1. Adjust an oven rack to the middle position and heat the oven to 300 degrees. Pat the beef pieces dry with paper towels and season with salt and pepper. Cook the pancetta in a large Dutch oven over medium heat, stirring occasionally, until browned and crisp, about 8 minutes. Using a slotted spoon, transfer the pancetta to a paper towel–lined plate leaving the fat in the pot; set aside.

2. Pour off all but 2 tablespoons of the fat left in the pot, and return to medium-high heat until just smoking. Brown the beef pieces well on all sides, about 8 minutes, reducing the heat if the pot begins to scorch. Transfer the beef to a large plate; set aside.

3. Add the onions, carrots, celery, and tomato paste to the fat left in the pot, and cook over medium until the vegetables begin to soften and brown, about 6 minutes. Stir in the garlic, sugar, flour, and reserved pancetta, and cook until combined and fragrant, about 30 seconds. Stir in the wine and tomatoes, scraping up any browned bits.

4. Add the parsley, rosemary, and browned roasts with any accumulated juices to pot. Bring to a boil, cover with a large sheet of aluminum foil, then cover tightly with the lid. Transfer the pot to the oven and cook, turning the beef every 45 minutes, until a dinner fork easily slips in and out of the meat, about 3 hours. (At this point, the meat can be refrigerated in the sauce for up to 2 days. Before continuing, skim the fat congealed from the surface and gently reheat in a covered pot over medium heat, turning the meat once or twice, until heated through, about 45 minutes.)

5. Transfer the beef roasts to a cutting board and tent with foil to keep warm. Allow the braising liquid to settle about 5 minutes, then skim any fat off the surface using a wide spoon. Stir in the thyme, bring to a boil, and cook, whisking vigorously to help the vegetables break down, until the mixture is thickened and measures about 3½ cups, about 18 minutes. Strain the liquid through large fine-mesh strainer, pressing on the solids to extract as much liquid as possible (you should have about 1½ cups of strained sauce; if necessary, return the strained sauce to the Dutch oven and reduce to 1½ cups). Discard the solids in the strainer, and season the sauce with salt and pepper to taste.

6. Remove and discard the kitchen twine from the meat. Slice the meat against grain into ½-inch-thick slices, and portion the meat between individual warmed bowls or plates. Pour about ¼ cup of the sauce over each portion and serve immediately.

PANNA COTTA
THOUGH ITS NAME IS LYRICAL, THE LITERAL translation of panna cotta—"cooked cream"—does nothing to suggest its ethereal qualities. In fact, panna cotta is not cooked at all. Neither is it complicated with eggs, as is a custard. Instead, sugar and gelatin are melted in cream and milk, and the whole is then turned into individual ramekins and chilled. It calls for few ingredients, comes together quickly, and forms a rich but neutral backdrop for any number of accompaniments: strawberry coulis, fresh raspberries, light caramel, chocolate sauce.

That said, we've certainly had our share of sub-par versions that run the gamut from watery and flat-tasting to chewy and tough. With such a simple and short ingredient list, it was clear that a great panna cotta required a careful balancing act. Our mission, therefore, was to determine the correct proportions for the four main ingredients: cream, milk, sugar, and gelatin.

We began by preparing five recipes from well-known Italian cookbooks. Each of them used similar ingredients in varying proportions and dealt with the ingredients in much the same way. Two called for confectioners' sugar (favored in Italian desserts), while the others used granulated sugar. Two simmered the cream; the others merely warmed it. One recipe whipped half the cream and folded it into the base. Procedurally, the recipes were extremely straightforward.

On tasting the recipes, it was clear they fell into two groups. Those with higher proportions of milk were slippery and translucent, their flavor elusive and flat. Those with more cream had a rich texture and a creamier, more rounded flavor. What united these recipes most noticeably, however, was a slightly rubbery chew—the result of too much gelatin.

Focusing on the gelatin first, we began to build a working recipe around a single packet, thinking that would simplify matters. The next step was to establish the correct proportion of liquid for this amount of gelatin. Starting with a 3-1 ratio of cream to milk (a ratio we found in many recipes) for a total of 4 cups liquid, we made batch after batch of panna cotta.

After making several panna cotta recipes, we were surprised to find textural inconsistencies between batches that should have been identical. Upon closer inspection, we realized that the amount of gelatin in a packet is not at all consistent but varies widely from one packet to another. In fact, in two packages of gelatin (each containing four packets), we found eight different weights. Realizing we would have to measure the gelatin by the teaspoonful, we pressed on. Starting with 2 teaspoons of gelatin, we gradually increased the amount in increments of ⅛ teaspoon, all the way up to 3 teaspoons. We found that 2½ teaspoons produced a firm enough yet still fragile finished texture after 4 hours. Now we wanted to see how long panna cotta with this amount of gelatin would hold in the refrigerator before becoming tough and unappealing. Each day, we unmolded a panna cotta, carefully jiggled it on the plate, and tested it for firmness and flavor. After one day the gelatin had tightened noticeably from its first taste (after just four hours), yet tasters all agreed this firmer version was still within the range of acceptability. Each day after that, we followed the same pattern, and each day the texture and flavor of the panna cotta remained exactly the same. That is, until day six, at which point tasters thought this creamy dessert developed a rubbery texture and tasted "off."

Pleased with our large window for storage, and with the ratios of the main ingredients determined, we moved on to fine-tuning our technique. Because cold temperatures hasten gelatin's firming action it seemed reasonable to keep most of the liquid cold. Why heat all the milk and cream when we needed just enough hot liquid to melt the gelatin and sugar? We gave the milk this assignment, pouring it into a saucepan, sprinkling the gelatin over it, and then giving the gelatin 10 minutes to swell and absorb the liquid before heating. We then heated the mixture just enough to melt the gelatin (it sustains damage at high temperatures) and added the sugar off the heat to dissolve.

To do its job, melted gelatin must be mixed with the other recipe ingredients while its molecules have enough heat energy to move through the mixture. By combining ingredients hastily in the past, we had often precipitated gelatin seizures, causing the melted gelatin to harden into chewy strings, which ruined the texture of the dessert. So we stirred the cold cream slowly into the milk to temper it.

Several test cooks in the kitchen have learned to stir gelatin-based desserts over an ice bath—allowing the gelatin to thicken somewhat under gentle agitation—before refrigerating them to set. This process is supposed to produce a finer finished texture. Hoping to avoid this step in a recipe that was otherwise so easy, we presented tasters with side-by-side creams, one stirred first over ice and one simply refrigerated. They unanimously preferred the texture of the panna cotta chilled over ice, describing it as lighter, creamier, and smoother. Given the stellar results, the extra 10 minutes required did not seem unreasonable.

All our panna cotta needed now was a subtle flavor accent and a vanilla bean was just the thing. Lemon zest and juice were also bright additions, so we decided to use them in a variation. With a simple technique and an elegant presentation, we now had an ideal version of this Italian classic.

REJUVENATING DRY VANILLA BEANS

Instead of throwing away a vanilla bean that has dried out after prolonged storage, try this technique to restore its moisture. Place the dry bean in a closed container overnight with a fresh piece of white bread. The moisture from the bread should soften the bean enough to let you split it and scrape out the seeds.

Panna Cotta

SERVES 8

Do not substitute low-fat or nonfat milk here. If your vanilla bean is shriveled and dried out you will want to use a slightly longer piece; 2 teaspoons of vanilla extract can be substituted for the vanilla bean seeds. Though panna cotta is traditionally unmolded onto individual plates for serving, it can also be served in the ramekins (or use wine glasses). Serve panna cotta very cold with Berry Coulis (page 323) or lightly sweetened berries.

1	cup whole milk
2½	teaspoons unflavored gelatin
1	(2-inch) piece vanilla bean, halved lengthwise (see page 201)
3	cups heavy cream
6	tablespoons (3½ ounces) sugar
	Pinch salt

1. Pour the milk into a medium saucepan. Sprinkle the gelatin evenly over the milk and let stand to hydrate, about 10 minutes.

2. Meanwhile, scrape the seeds from the vanilla bean following the illustrations on page 201. Combine the vanilla seeds and pod and cream in a large measuring cup; set aside. Set eight 4-ounce ramekins on a baking sheet and set aside. Make a large bowl of ice water using 2 trays of ice cubes and 4 cups cold water; set aside.

3. Heat the milk and gelatin mixture over high heat, stirring constantly, until the gelatin is dissolved and the mixture registers 135 degrees on an instant-read thermometer, about 1½ minutes. Off the heat, stir in the sugar and salt until dissolved, about 1 minute. Stirring constantly, slowly add the cream and vanilla mixture.

4. Transfer the mixture to a medium bowl and set the bowl gently into the ice water. Let the mixture chill, stirring frequently, until it has thickened to the consistency of eggnog and registers 50 degrees on an instant-read thermometer, about 10 minutes.

5. Strain the mixture into a pitcher, then pour it evenly into the ramekins. Cover each ramekin with plastic wrap, making sure that the plastic does not mar the surface of the cream, and refrigerate until just set and chilled, at least 4 hours or up to 5 days.

6. Unwrap the panna cotta and run a paring knife between the custard and the side of the ramekin in 1 smooth stroke. (If the shape of your ramekin makes this difficult, quickly dip the ramekin into a hot water bath to loosen the custard.) Flip the ramekins upside down onto individual serving plates. Shake the ramekins gently to unmold the panna cotta; lift the ramekins from the plate.

➤ VARIATION

Lemon Panna Cotta

The easiest way to make chopped lemon zest is to peel off several strips of lemon zest, then chop them up; be sure that the zest is chopped quite coarse so that it can be easily strained out.

Follow the recipe for Panna Cotta, increasing the amount of gelatin to 2¾ teaspoons. Add 2 tablespoons coarsely chopped lemon zest to the cream with the vanilla seeds and pod in step 2. Stir ¼ cup fresh lemon juice into the thickened mixture before pouring it into the ramekins in step 5.

SCIENCE: How Gelatin Works

Gelatin is a flavorless, nearly colorless substance derived from the collagen in connective tissue and bones, extracted commercially and dehydrated. It works on the same principle as in a meat stew that you put in the fridge hot and remove the next day as a solid one-piece mosaic. When you reheat the stew, the collagen melts and the stew reverts to its liquid state. Commercial gelatin begins dry in granular or leaf form and must first be rehydrated in cool liquid—where it absorbs about three times its weight—then melted, and finally cooled. Gelatin has clout when cold. Depending on the length of cooling time and the concentration of the solution, gelatin molecules form anything from a web-like gel—in the case of panna cotta, for example—to a solid block that can be cut with a knife (as illustrated by cafeteria Jell-O cubes).

Berry Coulis

Salsa ai Frutti di Bosco

MAKES 1½ CUPS

Coulis is simply sweetened fruit pureed into a sauce, and it's an ideal accompaniment to a variety of desserts, such as Panna Cotta (page 322). Because the types of berries used as well as their ripeness will affect the sweetness of the coulis, the amount of sugar is variable. Start with 5 tablespoons, then add more to taste. Additional sugar should be stirred in immediately after straining, while the coulis is still warm, so that the sugar will readily dissolve.

12	ounces (2½ to 3 cups) fresh or thawed frozen raspberries, blueberries, blackberries, or sliced strawberries
¼	cup water, plus extra as needed for serving
5–7	tablespoons sugar
⅛	teaspoon salt
2	teaspoons juice from 1 lemon

1. Bring the berries, ¼ cup water, 5 tablespoons of the sugar, and salt to a simmer in a medium nonreactive saucepan over medium heat. Cook, stirring occasionally, until the sugar is dissolved and the berries are heated through, about 1 minute.

2. Transfer the mixture to a blender or food processor and puree until smooth, about 20 seconds. Strain through a fine-mesh strainer into a small bowl, pressing and stirring the puree with a rubber spatula to extract as much seedless puree as possible.

3. Stir in the lemon juice and season with the remaining sugar to taste. Serve or transfer to an airtight container and refrigerate for up to 4 days or freeze for up to 1 month. (If frozen, thaw the coulis overnight in the refrigerator and loosen with water as needed before serving.)

ALMOND CAKE

Torta di Mandorle

ALMONDS HAVE BEEN A CULINARY STAPLE in Mediterranean countries for centuries, used in place of flour for cakes and for thickening sauces. Found in many Italian desserts, almonds come in two forms: bitter and sweet. The bitter almond is the smaller of the two and has the typical almond taste, which is used to boost the flavor of products made with sweet almonds. It has to be heat-treated before use, however, as otherwise it is toxic. Bitter almonds are available in Europe but not in the United States. The sweet almond is what we find in our local supermarkets and is the star ingredient in almond cake, a simple Italian dessert. Like pound cake, almond cake is a versatile dessert that is as good plain as it is with a simple sauce, whipped cream, or fresh berries.

There are many types of almond cakes, some using marzipan (sweetened almond paste), and others using polenta, or cornmeal, to add texture. To get the lay of the land, we tasted several of these cakes side by side—both baking some recipes we found and ordering some cakes from reputable local Italian bakeries. Some of the cakes were downright unpalatable, with flavors so sickly sweet that we could barely choke them down, while others were so incredibly dense they required a serrated knife. There were a few, however, that offered a simple, coarse, pound cake–like texture and a clean, lightly sweetened almond flavor. These were the cakes that tasters homed in on as their favorites and although they had some serious textural and flavor problems of their own, they held promise.

Cobbling together a basic working recipe based on the few initial cakes we liked, we were first intrigued by the complete absence of flour in some. In fact, many of the recipes used only finely ground almonds as the base. Our first goal was to determine if we were going to add any flour to our cake, or let the almonds really speak for themselves. Testing different ratios of almonds (ground fine in a food processor) and all-purpose flour, we started with a batter made of half flour and half almonds. Tasters complained that the almond flavor was too faint and the cake too light. Working our way toward more almonds and less flour in ¼-cup increments, the cakes got progressively better. We finally settled on ¾ cup of flour and 3½ cups of almonds. Any more flour and the cake lost its appealing rustic texture, but any less and this cake was too moist and heavy. A final substitution of cake flour for the all-purpose flour gave our almond cake a welcome lightness without sacrificing pure almond flavor.

Next we focused our attention on the sugar. We already knew we wanted granulated sugar in this cake recipe, not only for its pure sweetness, but because we knew brown sugar would add moisture that this cake definitely didn't need (it already had plenty of moisture from the oil in the almonds). Our challenge was to figure out just how much sugar was necessary. Taking a cue from other similar recipes, we started with 1½ cups of sugar. We added some to the almonds when we ground them in the food processor—to prevent them from turning into nut butter—and just ½ cup did the trick. The remaining 1 cup was creamed with the butter before adding the other ingredients. The resulting cake was flavorful and the sugar really brought out the almond flavor, but the crust that formed was almost like candy. Reducing the sugar by ¼ cup worked perfectly.

We were making progress, but this cake needed a higher rise and so we looked to baking powder. Starting with ¼ teaspoon, we worked our way up to 1 teaspoon. One teaspoon was too much, giving the cake an unappealing metallic taste, while ¼ teaspoon was not enough to contribute much lift. We found that ½ teaspoon baking powder provided just the right lift and texture.

Most almond cakes that we found in our research called for three eggs, but that seemed like a lot for a single-layer cake. After testing one, two, and three eggs, we were surprised to find that three was exactly right after all—any less and the cake sagged in the middle. Now the cake had good structure, with a light spring and tender crumb.

Up to this point, our batter was coming together pretty easily, but the end result was thick and required a spatula to spread it into the pan. Taking a cue from past cake recipes, we started adding liquid to thin the batter out. Water worked great, making the batter pourable and the cake's texture was now also lighter. Unfortunately, a little too light—after all, we'd worked so hard to get the right balance of flavors it seemed counterintuitive to now water them down. But substituting milk for water satisfied all our tasters. This cake was finally where we wanted it to be.

Almond Cake
Torta di Mandorle
SERVES 8 TO 10

This cake has a dense, pound cake–like texture and tastes great when served with fresh berries and whipped cream or lightly sweetened mascarpone. Do not substitute low-fat or nonfat milk for the whole milk. Blanched almonds are almonds without their skin. Be careful not to overtoast the almonds or the cake will have a dry, crumbly texture. You can substitute 14 ounces (about 3 cups) whole blanched almonds for the slivered; increase their oven toasting time to 11 minutes and their processing time to 30 seconds in step 2.

14	ounces blanched, slivered almonds (about 3½ cups) (see note)
1¼	cups (8¾ ounces) sugar
	Pinch salt
¾	cup (3 ounces) cake flour
½	teaspoon baking powder
8	tablespoons (1 stick) unsalted butter, at room temperature
3	large eggs, at room temperature
½	cup whole milk

1. Adjust an oven rack to the middle position and heat the oven to 350 degrees. Spray a 9-inch springform pan with vegetable oil spray and line the bottom of the pan with parchment paper.

2. Spread the almonds out on a rimmed baking

sheet and toast in the oven until very lightly toasted and fragrant, 5 to 7 minutes (do not over-toast); cool completely. Process the almonds, ½ cup of the sugar, and the salt in a food processor until very finely ground, with a texture that resembles flour, 10 to 15 seconds. Add the flour and baking powder and pulse to incorporate, about 5 pulses; set aside.

3. Using an electric mixer, cream the butter and remaining ¾ cup sugar on medium speed until light and fluffy, 3 to 5 minutes. Add the eggs, 1 at a time, beating briefly after each addition to incorporate, about 1 minute. Add the ground almond mixture and beat until just incorporated, about 30 seconds. Add the milk and beat until just incorporated, about 30 seconds more.

4. Transfer the batter to the prepared pan and smooth the top. Bake until the cake is puffed and golden on top and a toothpick inserted at the center comes out clean, 30 to 40 minutes, rotating the pan halfway through the baking time.

5. Let the cake cool in the pan on a wire rack for 15 minutes, then remove the sides of the pan and let the cake cool to room temperature, about 2 hours before removing the cake pan bottom. (The fully cooled cake can be wrapped tightly with plastic wrap and stored at room temperature for up to 5 days or frozen for up to 1 month. If frozen, let the cake thaw completely at room temperature, 2 to 4 hours, then serve warm.)

6. The cake can be served at room temperature or warm. To serve warm, lay the cake on a baking sheet and warm in a 350-degree oven for 10 to 15 minutes.

Tiramisù

LIKE BALSAMIC VINEGAR OR POLENTA, TIRAMISÙ was virtually unheard of in the United States until about 20 years ago. Now, it's found everywhere from pizza parlors to chain restaurants. Unlike many Italian recipes, this one hasn't been bastardized, but that's not to say tiramisù is generally well made.

Despite its simplicity (tiramisù requires just a handful of ingredients and no cooking), there is a lot that can go wrong. If it's soggy and wet, or on the other hand dry and parched, or if it's dense and heavy, or too sweet, or too fiery with alcohol, it's not worth the caloric cost.

The name tiramisù translates to "pick me up," a reference to the invigorating qualities of the espresso, sugar, and alcohol that the dish contains. It's not an Old World dessert, but rather a 20th-century restaurant creation. Store-bought ladyfingers (sponge cake–like cookies) are dipped into alcohol-spiked espresso and are layered into a dish along with buttery mascarpone (a thick cultured cream) that has been enriched with sugar and raw eggs. The dish is dusted with cocoa or sprinkled with chocolate and served chilled.

A good tiramisù is a seamless union of flavors and textures—it's difficult to tell where cookie ends and cream begins, where bitter espresso gives over to the bite of alcohol, and whether unctuous or uplifting is the better adjective to describe it. It's quite easily made at home, so rather than lament the unworthy versions out there, we decided to make a batch…or two…or 40…to get to the bottom of a good one.

We sorted through the dozens of recipes that we gathered. The most complicated ones involved making a zabaglione, a frothy custard, as the base of the mascarpone filling (a zabaglione requires a double boiler, vigilance, and a lot of whisking). We made six recipes and determined that a zabaglione base was not worth the trouble.

Therefore, the mechanics of making the mascarpone filling became quite simple: Raw egg yolks and sugar would be combined and the spirits mixed in, followed by the mascarpone. From our early tests, we decided that a 13 by 9-inch dish was the right size, but that only 1 pound of mascarpone (the amount most recipes call for) was inadequate—the cookie to cream ratio was off and the tiramisù was slight in stature. Another ½ pound (one more container) and the amount of filling was generous, but not excessive.

With no yolks or too few, the filling's flavor wasn't as rich as tasters liked and its texture was heavy, a problem that plagued several of the recipes we initially tested. Six yolks made the filling silky and suave and the flavor rich and round. For those

ARRANGING LADY FINGERS

1. Arrange the soaked cookies in a single layer in the baking dish, breaking or trimming the ladyfingers as needed to fit neatly into the dish.

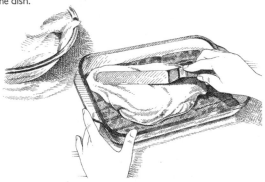

2. Spread half of the mascarpone mixture over the ladyfingers. Use a rubber spatula to spread the mixture to the sides and into the corners of the dish and smooth the surface.

3. Dust with 2 tablespoons of the cocoa and repeat the process.

wary of desserts made with raw eggs, we eventually created a slightly more involved variation that cooks the six yolks.

Next, we tested different amounts of sugar and decided that ⅔ cup provided the perfect amount of sweetness. We also added an ingredient—salt—that isn't found in most tiramisù recipes (we saw only one that calls for salt and it was only a pinch at that). Salt greatly heightened all the flavors and made the most remarkable difference.

Tiramisù recipes fall into three camps: those that call for the addition of whipped egg whites to the filling, those that call for the addition of whipped cream, and those that call for neither. Without whipped whites or whipped cream as a lightening agent, the filling was too heavy. Whipped egg whites watered down the flavor of the filling and made it too airy. Whipped cream lightened the texture without affecting the mascarpone's delicate flavor, at least when used in moderation. We found that ¾ cup of cream (half the amount in many other recipes) was sufficient.

To make tiramisù, ladyfingers are dipped into espresso spiked with alcohol so that the rather dry, bland cookies are moistened and absorb coffee flavor. Brewed espresso is not a practical option for many home cooks, so we tried three things in its stead: strong coffee made from espresso-roast coffee, espresso made from instant espresso granules, and a rather wicked potion made by dissolving instant espresso in strong brewed coffee. Though it wasn't very palatable straight from a cup, the latter tasted best in the tiramisù.

Tiramisù recipes don't bother to give detailed instructions about how to dip the ladyfingers, but we found that the dipping or soaking technique greatly affects the outcome. A quick in-and-out dip wasn't adequate for moistening the cookies and the result was a dry tiramisù. Fully submerging or otherwise saturating the ladyfingers yielded a wet, squishy tiramisù. Eventually, we did find a method that worked reliably. One at a time we'd drop each ladyfinger in the liquid so that it floated on the surface, then we'd quickly roll it over in the liquid to moisten the second side. The process should take just two to three seconds.

The only thing left to determine was the best spirit (Marsala, brandy, and rum are all common additions) with which to spike the filling and the coffee soaking mixture. Marsala gave the tiramisù syrupy, citrusy notes, and not much fire. Brandy gave it a lightly fruity, rather neutral flavor, but a good kick. Dark rum, with its caramel character, complemented the rich, deep, toasty qualities of the coffee and was the undisputed favorite. We started with a modest 4 tablespoons (divided equally between the filling and the coffee mixture), but that was far too weak. We ratcheted up the rum several times before hitting the ideal amount—9 tablespoons.

Components perfected, our tiramisù was assembled like any other. We arranged half of the dipped ladyfingers in the dish and spread half of the

---

CORE TECHNIQUE

SOAKING LADYFINGERS

The process of soaking the ladyfingers for tiramisù would seem to require no explanation, but this simple technique can make the difference between really great and truly awful tiramisù. Rather than fully submerge the ladyfingers in the espresso mixture (which results in a heavy, soggy tiramisù), drop the ladyfingers into the liquid one at a time and then quickly roll them over to moisten the second side. The whole process should take only two to three seconds.

PERFECTLY SOAKED LADYFINGER

OVERSOAKED LADYFINGER

---

mascarpone over them. We followed the lead of a few recipes and dusted this first mascarpone layer with cocoa. Then we repeated the layering and finished the tiramisù with more cocoa. (A sprinkling of grated chocolate was a nice addition.) The last detail: Tiramisù requires at least 6 hours in the fridge for the flavors and textures to meld.

Simple to prepare but grand enough to serve a large famiglia, tiramisù is an ideal holiday dessert as much as it is the perfect conclusion to an Italian feast. And, finally, this pick-me-up is no longer a letdown—it's worth every creamy, coffee-flavored, rum-spiked calorie.

Tiramisù

SERVES 10 TO 12

In a pinch, brandy and even Scotch can stand in for the dark rum. The test kitchen prefers tiramisù with a pronounced rum flavor; for a less potent rum flavor halve the amount of rum added to the coffee mixture in step 1. Do not allow the mascarpone to warm to room temperature before using it; it has a tendency to break if allowed to do so.

2½	cups strong brewed coffee, cooled to room temperature
1½	tablespoons instant espresso
9	tablespoons dark rum
6	large egg yolks
⅔	cup sugar
¼	teaspoon salt
1½	pounds mascarpone
¾	cup cold heavy cream
14	ounces (42 to 60, depending on the size) dried ladyfingers
3½	tablespoons cocoa, preferably Dutch-processed
¼	cup grated semisweet or bittersweet chocolate (optional)

1. Stir the coffee, instant espresso, and 5 tablespoons of the rum in a wide bowl or baking dish until the instant espresso dissolves; set aside.

2. In the bowl of a standing mixer fitted with the whisk attachment, beat the yolks at low speed until just combined. Add the sugar and salt and beat at medium-high speed until pale yellow, 1½ to 2 minutes, scraping down the bowl once or twice. Add the remaining 4 tablespoons rum and beat at medium speed until just combined, 20 to 30 seconds; scrape the bowl. Add the mascarpone and beat at medium speed until no lumps remain, 30 to 45 seconds, scraping down the bowl once or twice. Transfer the mixture to a large bowl and set aside.

3. In the now-empty mixer bowl (no need to clean the bowl), beat the cream at medium speed until frothy, 1 to 1½ minutes. Increase the speed to high and continue to beat until the cream holds stiff peaks, 1 to 1½ minutes longer. Using a rubber spatula, fold one-third of the whipped cream into the mascarpone mixture to lighten, then gently fold in the remaining whipped cream until no white streaks remain. Set the mascarpone mixture aside.

4. Working one at a time, drop half of the ladyfingers in the coffee mixture, roll them over, and transfer them to a 13 by 9-inch glass or ceramic baking dish. (Don't submerge the ladyfingers in the coffee mixture; the entire process should take no longer than 2 to 3 seconds for each cookie.) Arrange the soaked cookies in a single layer in the baking dish, breaking or trimming the ladyfingers as needed to fit neatly into the dish.

5. Spread half of the mascarpone mixture over the ladyfingers; use a rubber spatula to spread the mixture to the sides and into the corners of the dish and smooth the surface. Place 2 tablespoons of the cocoa in a fine-mesh strainer and dust the cocoa over the mascarpone.

6. Repeat the dipping and arrangement of the ladyfingers; spread the remaining mascarpone mixture over the ladyfingers and dust with the remaining 1½ tablespoons cocoa. Wipe the edges of the dish with a dry paper towel. Cover with plastic wrap and refrigerate until the flavors and textures have melded, 6 to 24 hours. Sprinkle with grated chocolate, if using; cut into pieces and serve chilled.

➤VARIATIONS

Tiramisù without Raw Eggs

The recipe involves cooking the yolks in a double boiler, which requires a little more effort and makes for a slightly thicker mascarpone filling, but the results are just as decadent as a traditional tiramisù. You will need an additional ⅓ cup of heavy cream.

Follow the recipe for Tiramisù through step 1. In step 2, add ⅓ cup heavy cream to the yolks after the salt and sugar; do not whisk in the remaining rum. Set the bowl with the yolks over a saucepan containing 1 inch gently simmering water; cook, constantly scraping along the bottom and sides of the bowl with a heatproof rubber spatula, until the mixture coats the back of a spoon and registers 160 degrees, 4 to 7 minutes. Remove from the heat and stir vigorously to cool slightly, then set aside to cool to room temperature, about 15 minutes. Whisk in the remaining 4 tablespoons rum until combined. Transfer the bowl to a standing mixer fitted with the whisk attachment, add the mascarpone, and beat at medium speed until no lumps remain, 30 to 45 seconds. Transfer the mixture to a large bowl and set aside. Continue with the recipe from step 3, using the full amount of cream specified (¾ cup).

Tiramisù with Sambuca and Lemon

Follow the recipe for Tiramisù, substituting 2 tablespoons sambuca for the dark rum in the coffee mixture in step 1; substituting 2 tablespoons sambuca for the dark rum in the mascarpone mixture in step 2; and adding 1¼ teaspoons grated and minced lemon zest to the egg mixture along with the mascarpone in step 2.

Tiramisù with Frangelico and Orange

Amaretto, an almond-flavored liqueur, can be substituted for the Frangelico.

Follow the recipe for Tiramisù, reducing the rum in the coffee mixture to 3 tablespoons and adding 3 tablespoons Frangelico in step 1; reducing the rum in the egg mixture to 2 tablespoons and adding 3 tablespoons Frangelico in step 2; and adding ½ teaspoon grated and minced orange zest to the egg mixture along with the mascarpone in step 2.

ESPRESSO

ITALIAN MEALS ALMOST ALWAYS END WITH espresso. Italians also drink espresso at breakfast and throughout the day, often standing up at cafés and downing a shot in a matter of seconds. Thanks to Starbucks and other coffee companies, Americans have discovered the joys of coffee Italian-style. In many American cities, a cappuccino is as easy to buy as a cup of regular joe, and even esoteric drinks, such as macchiato (see page 330), are now widely available.

Espresso professionals compare their brew to wine. In many respects, they are right: Espresso is an extremely complex beverage with more than 600 individual flavor components and there is tremendous variation among beans grown in different areas. But there is one clear difference between espresso and wine: Wine is ready to drink when you buy it, whereas making good espresso requires a good machine and proper technique. The type of beans, the roasting method, and the grinding process all make a difference, and even the best coffee can be easily ruined by bad form at home.

A properly made espresso features the characteristic light brown topping called *crema*. This foamy extraction adds a smoothness and creaminess not found in other coffee drinks. The presence of a well-defined crema (there should be enough crema to briefly trap sugar crystals sprinkled over the espresso) is a sign that the right coffee has been paired with the right extraction technique.

High-quality espresso starts with high-quality arabica beans. Most experts recommend buying a good espresso blend rather than varietals. Knowledgeable roasters create blends that accentuate the positive attributes of each bean. Few varietals are suited for the quick extraction process of espresso.

The key to buying beans for espresso at home is to find a store that sells good beans and then experiment to find a roast that suits your palate. Look for dark brown but not black beans that have an oily sheen; dry, cracked beans are well past their prime.

Ideally, you should buy a small quantity of fresh whole beans and grind them yourself as needed. Some experts prefer expensive burr grinders, but we've had decent luck with inexpensive blade grinders. For the best results, grind only small quantities (fill the grinder halfway) and wipe the container clean after each use to prevent a buildup of oils. To promote an even grind, hold the grinder securely and shake it as you grind, much as you might shake a martini. Beans for espresso should be ground quite fine.

Properly blending, roasting, and grinding coffee is half the battle; technique is equally important. Because lukewarm espresso is unappealing and will not hold crema, begin by preheating the filter holder, basket, and coffee cup—just run the machine without coffee, letting the water drip into the cup.

Then fill the filter basket (the correct amount, technically, is 7 grams of coffee for each cup) and lightly tamp the grounds. Some machines come with a special tool and others have a built-in tamper; you can also use the back of a small measuring cup. Tamping is important because if the grounds are loose, the water will run through them too quickly and the espresso will be watery. However, avoid overtamping, which can completely prevent the water from seeping through the grounds. The correct amount of tamping depends, to some extent, on the grind. Coffee that is slightly coarse should be firmly packed; coffee that is very fine should be lightly tamped.

Wipe the excess coffee from the rim of the basket to ensure a firm seal between the holder and the brew head, then slide the filter holder tightly into place. You are now ready to brew.

Turn on the pump and allow espresso to slowly flow out of the machine for about 20 seconds or until the coffee stream has turned light brown. Shut off the pump and allow the stream to finish dripping for several seconds. If the brew head continues to leak, remove the filter holder. (In any case, do not leave the filter holder in the machine when it's not in use, as this may weaken the brew head seal.)

Most people wonder which milk is best for frothing; some have had luck with low-fat milk, while others insist only whole milk does the job. But our tests showed that temperature and age are much more important than fat content. Skim, low-fat, and whole milk can all be steamed successfully, although skim milk produces drier foam and whole milk yields creamier foam. Because we prefer creamier froth, we use either 2 percent or whole milk. Half-and-half and light cream contain too much fat to froth. Regardless of the type of milk, we found that milk below 40 degrees froths much better than that which is warmer. Avoid pouring cold milk into a warm frothing container; you might even chill the container in the freezer for several minutes before frothing.

Frothing milk is more challenging than brewing espresso. With most of the machines we have tested over the years, we were able to make an excellent cup of espresso on the first try, but our initial attempts at frothing milk have been erratic. Although each machine has its own peculiarities, these general guidelines will help.

First, place fresh, cold milk in a narrow container; the most common vessel is made of stainless steel, but you can use a ceramic mug. Make sure the container is not more than one-third full. When the steam light goes on, open the steam valve briefly into an empty cup to let out any accumulated water. Place the steam valve into the milk, just below the surface, open the valve, and gently move the container in a circular fashion to steam and froth the milk. After about 20 seconds, there should be a nice head of froth on top of the steamed milk. When you're done, open the steam valve into an empty container to remove clogged milk, then wipe the wand to remove any milk particles before they harden. Enjoy!

ESPRESSO DRINKS

ALTHOUGH AMERICANS TEND TO THINK MORE IS BETTER, A SINGLE PORTION OF ESPRESSO contains just 1½ ounces of liquid and should be served in a warmed 2- to 3-ounce demitasse. Espresso can be sipped slowly or quaffed, Italian-style, in one or two gulps. If you want more coffee, make a lungo or doppio (see below).

Espresso Ristretto
A short or "restricted" espresso of about 1 ounce. To make this, simply cut short the flow of water when brewing this intense espresso.

Espresso Lungo
The opposite of a ristretto, this is made by adding an ounce or two of hot water (not from the brew head) to make a milder or "long" cup. When diluted with more hot water (at least 3 or 4 ounces), this drink is sometimes called an Americano.

Espresso Doppio
A "double"—3 ounces of espresso made by filling the 2-cup basket and letting the contents drip into one 4- or 5-ounce cup.

Espresso Macchiato
A single espresso "marked" with a tablespoon of frothed milk.

Espresso con Panna
A single shot of espresso with a small dollop of whipped cream.

Espresso Romano
Espresso served with lemon peel. Italians turn up their noses at this American invention and for good reason; the acidity in the lemon peel does not enhance the flavor of the espresso.

Espresso Corretto
A single espresso with a splash of brandy or other spirits.

Cappuccino
A single espresso topped with equal amounts of steamed milk and frothed milk and served in a 5- to 6-ounce cup. Europeans usually add plain or vanilla-scented sugar, but many Americans dust the top of the foam with cocoa powder, cinnamon, or nutmeg as well.

Caffé Latte
"Coffee with milk" (known as *café au lait* in French and *café con leche* in Spanish), made with a double shot of espresso, 5 or 6 ounces of steamed milk, and very little or no froth. Add more espresso or milk to strengthen or weaken the mix and serve in large bowl-shaped cups (about 9 or 10 ounces) or tall, wide-mouthed glasses.

Latte Macchiato
A tall glass of steamed milk (sometimes with froth) into which a single espresso is slowly poured to "mark" the milk with coffee.

Caffé Mocha
A single espresso flavored with ½ ounce of chocolate syrup and topped with 4 to 5 ounces of steamed milk and whipped cream. Dust with cocoa or shaved chocolate, if desired.

Mocha Latte
Latte with chocolate syrup added to the espresso, but no whipped cream or grated chocolate. Other syrups, especially almond, hazelnut, and orange, can be used in the same way.

8

GREECE AND TURKEY

MARINATED OLIVES

Elies Marinates

OLIVES ARE PREVALENT THROUGHOUT THE Mediterranean, but the number of Greek varieties of olives just might exceed that of any other country. In Greece, olives run the gamut in size from tiny pea size olives to those as big as a prune, and their colors range from green to black and every shade in between. They are commonly served as a *meze* (a small bite that can be served as an appetizer before a meal or as a snack with drinks), sometimes unadorned but often marinated. Here in the test kitchen, we quickly discovered that the mushy, bland marinated olives we find at the supermarket in this country are much different than the marinated olives in Greece; there, crocks are filled with beautiful firm, meaty olives fragrant with garlic, herbs, and spices and coated in olive oil. Inspired by the true Greek version, we set out in search of a recipe for great marinated olives.

We already knew that if you start with good olives (and that can be a big if) and good olive oil, it's pretty hard to make bad marinated olives. That said, some olive mixes are better than others, with more complex flavors. We wanted to make a mixture of marinated olives that would be easy to put together and full of the flavors of the Mediterranean. And since we knew they would have to marinate for several hours, they had to be worth the wait.

Good olives are the right place to begin, and that means olives with their pits and packed in brine. (Oil-cured olives can be added in small quantities, but in large quantities we find their flavors too potent for this dish.) Pitted olives generally have little flavor, and you can't expect marinating to make them taste better. Our tasters liked a mix of black and green olives. We tested half a dozen varieties of each color and didn't find a bad olive.

In addition to the olive oil, a typical marinade includes garlic, herbs (our tasters liked thyme best), and red pepper flakes (we found that more heat was more welcome and opted for a full teaspoon). We liked thinly sliced shallots as well; they softened in the marinade and added their gentle allium flavor to the mix. Grated orange zest (rather than the more traditional lemon zest) won tasters over with its fresh, lively citrus kick.

The real surprise was the addition of ouzo, a Greek liqueur that tastes like licorice. The heady anise flavor worked wonders on the olives and made the mix much more interesting.

The final issue to resolve was how long to marinate the olives. Tasters found that the olives required 12 hours to pick up sufficient flavor and were even better after a day or two. In fact, we held marinated olives in the refrigerator for a week and concluded that time only served to improve the flavor.

INGREDIENTS: Olives

Olives are grown throughout moderate climates like the Mediterranean basin and are technically the fruit of the olive tree. There are literally hundreds of varieties of olives found throughout the globe, but all can be categorized by two factors: their ripeness when picked and the manner in which they are cured. Green olives, picked before they are fully ripe, tend to have fruitier and somewhat lighter flavors, while ripe olives—which range in color from dark brown to purple or deep black—have deeper, more fully developed flavors.

Olives destined for the table (as opposed to those used for oil) must be cured to remove a bitter compound. Common types of curing include water, brine, dry (in salt), and oil. Some olives are cracked to hasten the curing process; others are left whole. Curing affects both flavor and texture. Brine-cured olives, the most commonly available style, tend to be plump and very moist; large Greek kalamatas and tiny French niçoises are both brine cured. Oil- and salt-cured olives, such as Moroccan-style olives, are wrinkled and shrunken and possess a very assertive, concentrated flavor. Canned (or jarred) pitted olives (which are not refrigerated and reside in the condiments aisles of supermarkets) should be avoided—we find they are devoid of flavor.

As for particular names, olives may be named after their type of cure, their place of origin, or their actual varietal name. The most important thing to remember about these little fruits is that they vary widely from batch to batch and year to year. Tasting is the only way to judge the quality of any particular batch.

Olives should be stored in the refrigerator in an airtight container. Salt-cured olives are best consumed within a month from the time of purchase; brine-cured olives will last indefinitely, as long as they are submerged in brine.

Marinated Olives

Elies Marinates

MAKES ABOUT 3 CUPS

These olives will keep in the refrigerator for at least a week and are perfect to have on hand for impromptu entertaining. (Be sure to remember to put out a small bowl for the pits.) Ouzo is an anise-flavored liqueur that is served as an aperitif throughout Greece; you can substitute Pernod.

1½	cups large brine-cured green olives with pits
1½	cups large brine-cured black olives with pits
3	medium shallots, halved and sliced thin
¼	cup extra-virgin olive oil
2	tablespoons ouzo (see note)
3	medium garlic cloves, peeled and crushed
1	teaspoon grated zest from 1 orange
1	teaspoon minced fresh thyme leaves
1	teaspoon red pepper flakes
¾	teaspoon salt
	Pinch cayenne pepper

Rinse the olives thoroughly, drain, and pat dry with paper towels. Toss the olives with the remaining ingredients, cover, and refrigerate for at least 12 hours or up to 1 week. Let the olives sit at room temperature for about 30 minutes before serving.

FETA CHEESE

FETA IS POSITIVELY GREECE'S MOST WELL-KNOWN cheese, although it is also a familiar presence on Turkish, Bulgarian, Romanian, and French tables. Greek feta is made from sheep's or goat's milk, or a mixture of the two. To make feta, the milk is curdled, shaped into a block, and steeped in brine. It is tangy and crumbly, yet moist and creamy, and can range from very soft to semihard. Feta is commonly served as a meze, although it just as frequently is found in salads, side dishes, entrées, and even desserts.

Here in the test kitchen, we wanted to develop some recipes using feta as a meze. In our research, we found three very different preparations for feta—marinated feta, whipped feta, and roasted or broiled feta—all of which can be served with warm pita bread or slices of baguette and a bowl of olives. We armed ourselves with pounds and pounds of feta to uncover the secrets of each one.

We started with marinated feta, which in Greece is often kept on hand to serve an unexpected guest. Marinating feta in an herb-infused oil is a great way to boost the briny cheese's flavor, but store-bought marinated feta is often overpriced and the flavors can be dull. We started by assembling a marinade based on some of the flavors we liked in our Marinated Olives (see left).

We gently heated the shallot, oregano, lemon zest, and red pepper flakes in olive oil, which created a nice, round, mellow shallot flavor that complemented the fragrant oregano, the citrusy bouquet of the fresh lemon zest, and the spicy heat from the red pepper flakes. Off the heat, we stirred in the feta cheese and allowed the mixture to cool. The residual heat of the oil softened the cheese just enough without melting it, and the cheese soaked up all the flavors from the oil. While the infused oil was spiked with great flavor, we found that after gently cooking for almost 20 minutes, the oil lost a bit of its own character. We found the addition of fresh oil to be a welcome flavor boost, and it really brought the flavors of the marinade together.

Next, we turned our attention to whipped feta, a dip or spread that is a classic on the meze table, especially in the northeastern region of Greece called Thessaloniki. It easy to make—all of the ingredients are processed in a food processor until smooth—but its flavor impact is huge. Aside from the feta, there are few ingredients required—olive oil, lemon juice, and something spicy to add heat are all this simple dish needs.

Since all of the recipes we researched called for a different ingredient to add the requisite heat, we had to figure out which one we liked best. We whipped up batches using fresh green chiles, red pepper flakes, and ground cayenne pepper. Tasters preferred the way that the ground cayenne was evenly incorporated into the dip, and the subtle background heat that it imparted. We found that the dip was a little loose after it came out of the food processor, but after some time in the refrigerator it set up to an ideal spread-like consistency. And before serving, we drizzled a little olive oil and sprinkled some cayenne pepper over the top.

Happy with our whipped feta, we moved on to develop a feta dish that would go in the oven. In our research we uncovered dozens of recipes for roasted, baked, or broiled feta, all of which start with slabs cut from the block of cheese. Some have a garnish of tomatoes or roasted red peppers and are served as a first course, while others are served simply on the meze table with just a drizzle of olive oil. To start off, we tested the three different cooking methods using plain, unadorned feta that we sliced into ½-inch-thick slabs.

We roasted one batch of feta in a 400-degree oven, baked the second in a foil packet, and the third we broiled. Tasters were more than happy to sample all three varieties, however, they had definite preferences. Roasting dried out the exterior of the feta before the inside was softened. Baking in a foil packet produced lusciously creamy feta, but tasters preferred the golden brown exterior of the feta that was broiled. The heat from the broiler browned the exterior of the feta, intensifying its flavor and adding a welcome contrast in texture to the soft and creamy interior.

With the technique resolved, we moved on to the garnishing options. Tasters thought sliced tomatoes and roasted red peppers were superfluous, but welcomed a dash of red pepper flakes, which added a nice hit of heat. A generous amount of extra-virgin olive oil was a given, and to prevent it from spattering in the oven, we drizzled it over the feta as it came out of the oven, along with a little parsley for color and freshness.

With our recipes finally complete, we now wondered: Does it make a difference what type of feta you use? Up to this point we had been using imported Greek feta (available at specialty stores) with great results, but wondered if supermarket feta would work just as well. The feta in the supermarket is almost certainly made by a large producer that uses pasteurized cow's milk rather than sheep's or goat's milk. At the supermarket we purchased two blocks, one sitting on a Styrofoam tray wrapped in plastic (as is much of the feta sold in the supermarket) and the other in a vacuum-sealed package that also contained a small amount of brine. (The Greek cheese we had been using came sitting in a puddle of brine in a plastic container.)

As we suspected, the Greek feta was preferred for its creaminess and pleasant milky flavor. Much to our surprise, however, the vacuum-sealed supermarket cheese fared pretty well in all of our recipes, aside from being a touch salty. Far from being dry and chalky, it was moist, creamy, fresh-tasting, and tangy—all the qualities one looks for in feta. Coming in a very distant third was the feta placed on a Styrofoam tray. It had a chalky consistency and was nearly flavorless.

What did we learn? Packaging feta cheese with some of the brine is the key to a moist texture. The quintessential feta should be creamy, tangy, supple, and moist, and you are not going to find these qualities in a block of cheese that has been left to sit high and dry on a Styrofoam tray. In the package of vacuum-sealed feta, we could see the moisture, and the cheese, when pressed, was somewhat soft and yielding rather than hard and crumbly.

The marinated feta holds well in the refrigerator for about one week, while the whipped feta can be refrigerated for up to two days. We found that it's best to let both come to room temperature before serving. As for the broiled feta, it is best served straight from the oven.

Marinated Feta Cheese with Lemon and Shallot
MAKES ABOUT 2 ½ CUPS

Serve with wedges of warm pita bread or slices of baguette. Even after the feta has been eaten, the remaining flavorful oil is great for dipping with bread.

1 ¼	cups extra-virgin olive oil
1	medium shallot, sliced thin
1	tablespoon minced fresh oregano leaves
1	teaspoon grated zest from 1 lemon
¼	teaspoon red pepper flakes
8	ounces feta cheese, cut into ½-inch cubes (about 2 cups)

1. Cook 1 cup of the oil, shallot, oregano, lemon zest, and pepper flakes in a small saucepan over low heat until the shallot is softened, about 18 minutes.

2. Remove the saucepan from the heat and gently stir in the feta. Cover and let sit until the mixture reaches room temperature, about 1½ hours.

3. Stir in the remaining ¼ cup oil and serve. (The mixture can be transferred to an airtight container and refrigerated for up to 1 week. Before serving, let sit at room temperature until the oil liquefies, about 1 hour.)

➤ VARIATION
Marinated Feta Cheese with Orange, Green Olives, and Garlic

Use high-quality brine-cured green olives here.

Follow the recipe for Marinated Feta Cheese with Lemon and Shallot, substituting 1 teaspoon grated orange zest for the lemon zest and 2 sliced garlic cloves for the shallot. Stir ½ cup coarsely chopped pitted green olives (about 4 ounces) into the oil with the feta.

Spicy Whipped Feta
Htipiti
MAKES ABOUT 2 CUPS

This may seem like a lot of feta at the start, but its volume condenses dramatically when processed. Serve with pita chips (see page 406), wedges of warm pita bread, or slices of baguette. Be sure to rinse the feta before using it in this recipe or the dip will be too salty.

I	pound feta cheese, crumbled (about 4 cups)
⅓	cup extra-virgin olive oil, plus extra for serving
I	tablespoon juice from I lemon
½	teaspoon cayenne pepper, plus extra for serving
¼	teaspoon ground black pepper

Process all of the ingredients together in a food processor until smooth, about 20 seconds. Transfer the mixture to a serving bowl, cover with plastic wrap, and refrigerate until firm, about 2 hours or up to 2 days. Drizzle with additional extra-virgin olive oil and sprinkle with additional cayenne before serving.

➤ VARIATION
Spicy Whipped Feta with Roasted Red Peppers

If substituting homemade roasted red peppers (see page 409), you will need 2 medium peppers.

Follow the recipe for Spicy Whipped Feta, adding 6 ounces jarred roasted red peppers (about 1 cup), drained, rinsed, and thoroughly patted dry with paper towels to the food processor with the other ingredients.

Broiled Feta
Saganaki
SERVES 8 TO 12

Broilers can vary in strength dramatically, so use our cooking times as guidelines and check the feta often as it cooks. Cutting the feta into ½-inch-thick slabs is crucial here; if sliced thinner, the cheese will crumble apart, but if sliced thicker, it will not heat through. Serve with wedges of warm pita bread or slices of baguette as a casual appetizer with cocktails. Or, for a more formal appetizer, try serving individual portions of the feta alongside a small salad.

2	blocks feta cheese (about 8 ounces each), sliced into ½-inch-thick slabs
¼	teaspoon red pepper flakes
¼	teaspoon ground black pepper
2	tablespoons extra-virgin olive oil
2	teaspoons minced fresh parsley leaves

Adjust an oven rack 4 inches from the broiler element and heat the broiler. Pat the feta dry with paper towels and place on a foil-lined baking sheet (or in a broiler-safe gratin dish). Sprinkle with the red pepper flakes and ground black pepper. Broil until the edges of the cheese are golden, 3 to 8 minutes. Drizzle with the oil and sprinkle with the parsley. Serve immediately.

CUCUMBER, GARLIC, AND YOGURT SAUCE

Tzatziki

IN GREECE, *TZATZIKI*—PART SALAD, PART sauce, part dip—has many uses. It is a regular on the meze table with pita chips and raw vegetables, dolloped on vegetable fritters and stuffed grape leaves, drizzled over gyros, eaten with rice, or served with roasted and grilled vegetables and meats. A combination of yogurt, cucumbers, herbs, oil, and garlic, tzatziki at its best is refreshing and cool yet rich and creamy all at the same time. Unfortunately, we have had more than our share of bad tzatziki. It can be bland and watery or overwhelmed with garlic.

Many of the recipes we found use plain supermarket yogurt, while others call for Greek yogurt, which is thicker and creamier (see page 337 for more information). We decided to try both, working with a basic recipe using peeled and diced cucumber, olive oil, dill, garlic, salt, and pepper.

The sauce made with the supermarket yogurt was much too thin and its flavors were diluted. Supermarket yogurt is much thinner than Greek yogurt and when combined with the cucumbers (which release a large quantity of water) the result was a diluted, watery sauce. The Greek yogurt, however, gave us exactly the results we wanted. Though it was too thick on its own, the addition of the cucumbers thinned the sauce to the perfect consistency, and the liquid they released only served to reinforce the sauce's cucumber flavor.

Next, we had to address how to prepare the cucumber. We knew that peeling was a given because we didn't want tough bits of dark green skin and seeding was also important, since the seeds are mostly all liquid; however, we weren't sure how to cut the cucumber. We have seen recipes that dice, slice, and shred the cucumber. Since we wanted to be able to serve this as a dip, slicing was out. Finely dicing worked better, but we found that getting the cucumber pieces small enough took a little more precision and effort than we wanted. Shredding the cucumbers on the large holes of a box grater worked best. The cucumber didn't disappear into the yogurt or make the sauce too chunky.

With the cucumbers resolved, all that was left to do was tweak the flavorings. Two tablespoons of extra-virgin olive oil proved to be the perfect amount—any less and the sauce tasted too lean, any more and its flavor began to overpower the yogurt. For the herbs, we liked both mint and dill. The choice is yours, and if you can't decide, use both. Determining how much garlic to use and whether it should be raw or cooked was a little trickier. After testing varying amounts, both raw and cooked, we settled on just one small clove of raw garlic—just enough to know it's there, but not so much that it wards off the evil eye, not to mention your friends.

~

Cucumber, Garlic, and Yogurt Sauce
Tzatziki
MAKES ABOUT 2 CUPS

Using Greek yogurt here is key; don't substitute regular plain yogurt or the sauce will be very watery. FAGE Total Classic Greek yogurt is the most widely available brand in this country. You can also make your own Greek-style thickened yogurt (see page 337) to use in place of the Greek yogurt. This sauce can be served simply with raw vegetables and pita wedges or as an accompaniment to Zucchini Fritters (page 339), Stuffed Eggplant (page 349), or Charcoal-Grilled Shish Kebabs (page 368).

- 1 medium cucumber, peeled, halved lengthwise, and seeded (see the illustrations on page 116)
- 1 cup Greek yogurt (see note)
- 2 tablespoons extra-virgin olive oil
- 2 tablespoons minced fresh mint and/or dill leaves
- 1 small garlic clove, minced or pressed through a garlic press (about ½ teaspoon)
  Salt and ground black pepper

Shred the cucumber on the large holes of a box grater. Whisk the yogurt, oil, mint, and garlic together in a medium bowl. Stir in the cucumbers and season with salt and pepper to taste. Cover and refrigerate until chilled, about 1 hour. (The sauce can be refrigerated for up to 2 days.)

GREEK-STYLE THICKENED YOGURT

GREEK YOGURT, OR YOGHURT, IS MUCH THICKER AND CREAMIER THAN THE YOGURT TYPICALLY found here in the United States. You can sometimes find Greek yogurt (sometimes called Middle Eastern or Mediterranean-style yogurt) in natural foods stores, specialty markets, and even regular supermarkets, but you can also make it at home. All you need is a fine-mesh strainer lined with a couple of basket-style coffee filters or cheesecloth. Draining the yogurt of its liquid (the whey) results in a thick, creamy, tangy yogurt. Serve the thickened yogurt as they do in Greece—drizzled with honey for breakfast, in Cucumber, Garlic, and Yogurt Sauce (page 336), or as a cool and refreshing side dish at any meal.

Greek-Style Thickened Yogurt

MAKES 1 CUP

Make sure the yogurt doesn't contain modified food starch, gelatin, or gums—they prevent the yogurt from draining. You can use whole, low-fat, or even nonfat yogurt to make the thickened yogurt, but whole milk yogurt tastes best.

16   ounces (2 cups) plain yogurt (see note)

1. Following the illustration on the right, line a fine-mesh strainer with 3 basket-style paper coffee filters or a double layer of cheesecloth. Set the strainer over a deep container (there should be enough room for a generous 1 cup liquid to drain without touching the strainer). Spoon the yogurt into the strainer, cover tightly with plastic wrap, and refrigerate until the yogurt has released about 1 cup liquid and has a creamy, thick texture, 10 to 12 hours (it can stay in the strainer for up to 2 days).

2. Transfer the yogurt to a clean container, discarding the drained liquid, and refrigerate for up to 1 week.

MAKING THICKENED YOGURT

Spoon the yogurt into a fine-mesh strainer lined with 3 paper coffee filters or a double layer of cheesecloth, cover, and refrigerate. After 10 to 12 hours, about 1 cup of the liquid will have drained out of the yogurt and the yogurt will have a creamy, thick consistency.

TURKISH NUT SAUCE

Tarator

TARATOR, A RICH, SMOOTH MIXTURE MADE FROM nuts, bread, water, olive oil, garlic, and lemon is served throughout Turkey as a dip with pita bread and vegetables, or as a sauce for fish, shellfish, and grilled meats. It is thick and creamy without the addition of any eggs or dairy—this dip relies on the combination of nuts, bread, and oil for its velvety texture. The best part about it, aside from being versatile and tasting so good, is that it is incredibly easy to make—all the ingredients are simply processed in a food processor or blender until smooth.

With such a simple preparation, our questions about this dip focused on the ingredients: mainly, which type of nut to use and whether or not they should be toasted. We thought we would tackle the type of nut first. Traditionally, tarator is made with hazelnuts, but our research turned up several versions that called for almonds, walnuts, and pine nuts. We made batches with all four nuts, and because we couldn't decide which we liked best, and they all worked in the recipe, we leave the choice up to you. Note that the flavor intensity of the sauce greatly depends on the type of nut used. For example, hazelnuts will produce a sauce with a much stronger flavor than pine nuts.

Because this sauce is so easy to make and it requires no cooking, we were hoping that we could save time and the dirtying of a skillet by forgoing the customary toasting step used in the test kitchen to draw out the flavor in nuts. After a side-by-side tasting, however, we concluded that toasting the nuts really was essential. It brought out the complexity of the nuts, and deepened the sauce's overall flavor.

Before we were finished with the recipe, we had to tweak the seasonings. A generous dose of lemon juice and a little garlic helped balance the richness of the nuts while a touch of cayenne pepper added welcome heat, giving us the perfect sauce for dipping or serving with kebabs of grilled meat.

Turkish Nut Sauce

Tarator

MAKES ABOUT 2 CUPS

Serve this Turkish sauce as a dip with pita chips (see page 406), wedges of warm pita bread, or raw vegetables. It also makes a nice accompaniment to almost any grilled meat or fish.

2	slices high-quality white sandwich bread, crusts removed and bread torn into pieces
½	cup water, plus extra as needed
1½	cups blanched almonds, blanched hazelnuts, pine nuts, or walnuts, toasted (see page 135)
6	tablespoons extra-virgin olive oil
3	tablespoons juice from 1 lemon, plus extra as needed
1	medium garlic clove, minced or pressed through a garlic press (about 1 teaspoon) Salt and ground black pepper
⅛	teaspoon cayenne pepper

Place the bread in a bowl and pour the water over it to moisten. Process the soaked bread, nuts, oil, lemon juice, garlic, ½ teaspoon salt, ¼ teaspoon pepper, and cayenne in a blender (or food processor) until smooth, about 20 seconds. Add additional water as needed until the sauce is just thicker than the consistency of heavy cream. Season with salt, pepper, and lemon juice to taste. Serve at room temperature. (The sauce can be refrigerated for up to 2 days; bring to room temperature before serving.)

ZUCCHINI FRITTERS

Kabak Mucveri

VEGETABLE FRITTERS, EATEN AS A MEZE OR side dish with a yogurt sauce, are popular throughout the Mediterranean and Middle East, where they are often made from leftover vegetables or when there is an abundance of a certain crop, such as zucchini, artichokes, eggplant, or okra. In our research, we found that a great number of Turkish fritter recipes call for zucchini, and we decided to follow this route because, come mid-summer, we are always looking for some new and interesting ways to use the copious amounts of zucchini available in grocery stores. The problem with moisture-rich vegetables like zucchini is that all too often they result in soggy, bland fritters. We wanted crisp, highly seasoned fritters and knew we would have to find a way to get rid of all that excess moisture.

We researched several recipes and found only small differences among ingredient lists and techniques. All the recipes called for some sort of binder (usually eggs, a starch, or a combination of the two) and seasonings. According to several recipes, salting and draining the zucchini before combining them with the other fritter ingredients is vital, yet other recipes omitted this step. Also, although all the recipes cooked the fritters in a skillet, they called for different amounts of oil.

We began by testing whether or not the zucchini should be salted. After shredding zucchini on the large holes of a box grater, we prepared it three ways before adding it to a basic fritter recipe: we tossed it with salt and set it aside in a fine-mesh strainer; spread it on paper towels and sprinkled it with salt; and left it unsalted. We tested each of these preparations letting the zucchini sit for 30 minutes and for 10 minutes. The 30-minute salting caused the zucchini to lose a substantial amount of liquid, resulting in crisp and relatively dry fritters, but the finished fritters were only marginally better than those made with zucchini that sat for just 10 minutes. In contrast, the fritters made with unsalted zucchini were soggy and not at all crisp. We concluded that salting for 10 minutes was essential. And we preferred salting the zucchini in a strainer, rather than on paper towels, so the moisture was able to drain off. After 10 minutes in a strainer, we placed the zucchini on paper towels, rolled the zucchini in the towels, and gave the roll a quick squeeze.

Next, we tested various binders, including all-purpose flour, potato starch, and cornstarch, both with and without egg. Tasters far preferred the consistent, unified texture of the fritters made with egg. As for the starch, the differences were noticeable but minimal, so we chose flour because it is what most cooks have on hand.

For seasonings, we looked to traditional recipes for direction. All of the recipes we came across in our research called for onions or scallions—our tasters preferred the more delicate allium flavor that scallions imparted. Dill was also quite common in traditional recipes, and we found that its freshness was welcomed here. Last, but certainly not least, we added crumbled feta cheese. Now, within every bite of crispy zucchini was a pocket of creamy, tangy, and salty feta cheese.

SHREDDING ZUCCHINI

1. Shred trimmed zucchini on the large holes of a box grater or in a food processor fitted with the shredding disk.

2. After salting and draining the zucchini, wrap it in paper towels and squeeze out excess liquid. Proceed immediately with the recipe.

Making enough fritters to serve four to six people required cooking them in two batches. We found it easy to wipe the used oil from a large nonstick skillet after the first batch and add fresh oil to the relatively clean pan for the second. (If we skipped this step, the burnt bits from the first batch of fritters stuck to the second batch.) As for the amount of oil, we noted that using too much was simply a waste, while using too little caused the fritters to cook unevenly and burn. Three tablespoons oil per batch struck the perfect balance between crisp fritters and economy.

Zucchini Fritters
Kabak Mucveri
MAKES 12 FRITTERS, SERVING 4 TO 6

Be sure to squeeze the zucchini until it is completely dry, or the fritters will fall apart in the skillet. Don't let the squeeze-dried zucchini sit on its own for too long or it will brown. These fritters are great warm or at room temperature, and can be served as a side dish or as a meze with cocktails. Serve with Cucumber, Garlic, and Yogurt Sauce (page 336).

1	pound zucchini (about 2 medium), trimmed
1	teaspoon salt
8	ounces feta cheese, crumbled (about 2 cups)
2	scallions, minced
2	tablespoons minced fresh dill
2	large eggs, lightly beaten
1	medium garlic clove, minced or pressed through a garlic press (about 1 teaspoon)
¼	teaspoon ground black pepper
¼	cup unbleached all-purpose flour
6	tablespoons olive oil
1	lemon, cut into wedges (for serving)

1. Adjust an oven rack to the middle position and heat the oven to 200 degrees. Following the illustration on the left, shred the zucchini on the large holes of a box grater or in a food processor fitted with the shredding disk. Toss the shredded zucchini with the salt and let it drain in a fine-mesh strainer set over a bowl for 10 minutes. Wrap the zucchini in paper towels and squeeze out the excess liquid.

2. Combine the dried zucchini, feta, scallions, dill, eggs, garlic, and pepper together in a medium bowl. Sprinkle the flour over the mixture and stir until uniformly incorporated.

3. Heat 3 tablespoons of the oil in a 12-inch nonstick skillet over medium heat until shimmering. Drop 2-tablespoon-sized portions of the batter into the pan, then use the back of a spoon to press the batter into 2-inch-wide fritters (you should fit about 6 fritters in the pan at a time). Fry until golden brown on both sides, 2 to 3 minutes per side.

4. Transfer the fritters to a paper towel–lined baking sheet and place in the oven to keep warm. Wipe the skillet clean with paper towels. Return the skillet to medium-high heat, add the remaining 3 tablespoons oil, and repeat with the remaining batter. Serve warm or at room temperature with the lemon wedges.

PHYLLO PIE WITH SPINACH AND FETA

Spanakopita

IN GREECE, TAVERNAS ARE SMALL, CASUAL restaurants serving up traditional local fare. Most tavernas, and certainly every Greek-American restaurant in this country, offer some version of spinach pie, called spanakopita, on their menu—*spanaki* meaning spinach and *pita* meaning pie. Not necessarily a "pie" as we traditionally think of it in this country, Greek spinach pie is made by layering sheets of phyllo dough (see page 344) in a baking dish with a tasty blend of spinach, onions, and tangy feta cheese, spiked with lemon, garlic, and herbs. The pie is then baked and cut into squares—each piece is the perfect marriage of crisp, flaky pastry and a savory filling.

On paper, spanakopita never fails to make the mouth water. Unfortunately, modern-day versions of this traditional Greek dish rarely taste as good as they sound. More often than not, the basic components of spanakopita don't so much combine as collide, working at cross-purposes to produce unimpressive results. A dense, stringy layer of overcooked spinach is not enhanced by a thin, shattered crust of dried-out pastry. Scattered chunks of salty feta cheese don't do much to round out the dish. To top it off, working with store-bought phyllo dough can test anyone's patience. Lots of labor and an often disappointing payoff—is spanakopita really worth it?

We wanted a spanakopita that lived up to its billing and didn't require an army of Greek grandmothers to prepare. We focused first on perfecting a spinach and feta filling with big, bold flavors. (This same filling can be used to make Phyllo Triangles with Spinach and Feta, page 342.) Since spanakopita means "spinach pie," we knew where to start—with the green stuff, and lots of it. Too many recipes we found skimped on the spinach, resulting in spanakopitas that are thin and greasy due to a disproportionate amount of phyllo. We wanted a thick layer of filling that would stand up to the pastry crust. Many recipes call for as much as two bags of fresh spinach, which needs to be washed, cooked, drained, chopped, and squeezed dry. As it turns out, tasters were equally pleased with filling made from frozen chopped spinach, which certainly is more convenient, as it only needs to be thawed and squeezed dry.

Tangy feta pairs perfectly with earthy spinach, but the marriage of flavors is ruined when big chunks of the salty cheese are found adrift in a sea of clumpy greens. Eggs are a standard ingredient in spanakopita recipes, and rightly so. They bind the filling ingredients together, add richness and flavor, and lighten the layer of spinach that would otherwise get dense and soggy when baked in the oven. By first crumbling the feta, then mixing it with the eggs, we were able to distribute the cheese more evenly throughout the pie.

Scallions, garlic, and herbs such as dill are traditional ingredients in spanakopita but are usually called for in such paltry amounts that their flavors simply disappear. We doubled the quantities of each, which allowed their presence to be known. Lemon juice and grated nutmeg were less commonly listed, but tasters approved of both. The flavors were now bright and clean, but the filling still seemed a little dry, and it lacked richness. A few recipes included ricotta cheese to tame the bite of the feta and our tasters agreed that it rounded out the flavors and gave the filling just the right creamy texture.

When spread into a 13 by 9-inch baking dish, our spinach filling stood a proud 1½ inches high, a marked improvement over the sad, sunken versions we had seen earlier in our testing. A filling this thick needed more than a few paper-thin sheets of pastry to hold it all together. We found that 16 sheets of phyllo (eight on top and eight on the bottom) made crusts that were substantial but still tender. More than that and the pastry was tough to bite through. We tried adding a middle layer of four sheets of phyllo and found that it helped the pie keep its shape after it was sliced.

Phyllo is famous for its crisp, flaky layers, but it was this quality that gave us the most trouble once the pie hit the hot oven. In every test, the papery layers curled and separated from each other as they baked. Cutting into the pie sent shattered pieces of phyllo everywhere.

Some dessert recipes involving phyllo advise sprinkling each layer with granulated sugar, which then melts in the oven and helps the pastry stick together. We didn't want a sweet crust, but would grated cheese work the same way? A small quantity of grated Parmesan dusted across each of the top layer's sheets worked wonders, yielding a cohesive crust that was tender but offered just the right amount of chew.

Lastly, we wondered about the lengthy baking times specified by most recipes—usually an hour in the oven at 350 degrees, until the phyllo is golden and crisp. The results? Our bright flavors were washed out and flat, the spinach was well on its way to being mushy and overcooked, and the phyllo was dried out and more prone to shattering. Increasing the temperature to 400 degrees and reducing the cooking time to about 35 minutes resulted in a filling and crust that were both done to perfection.

Phyllo pies are also often made with a meat filling, so we decided to make a variation using ground chicken, which was easy enough to do using the same basic method.

Phyllo Pie with Spinach and Feta
Spanakopita
SERVES 6 TO 8 AS A MAIN COURSE

Make sure that the phyllo is fully thawed before use; don't thaw it in the microwave, but let it sit in the refrigerator overnight or on the countertop for four to five hours. Clarified butter can be used instead of the olive oil (see page 371 for more information on clarified butter). For more information on working with phyllo, see page 344.

FILLING
- 1   pound feta cheese, crumbled into fine pieces (about 4 cups)
- 12 ounces whole milk ricotta cheese (about 1½ cups)
- 4   large eggs, lightly beaten
- 1   bunch scallions, sliced thin
- ⅓   cup minced fresh dill leaves
- 3   tablespoons juice from 1 lemon
- 2   medium garlic cloves, minced or pressed through a garlic press (about 2 teaspoons)
- 1   teaspoon freshly grated nutmeg
- ¾   teaspoon salt
- ⅛   teaspoon ground black pepper
- 3   (10-ounce) packages frozen chopped spinach, thawed and squeezed dry

PHYLLO LAYERS
- ¾   cup olive oil or clarified butter (see page 371)
- ½   pound (14 by 9-inch) phyllo, thawed (see note)
- 1   ounce Parmesan cheese, grated (about ½ cup)

1. **FOR THE FILLING:** Mix the feta, ricotta, eggs, scallions, dill, lemon juice, garlic, nutmeg, salt, and pepper together in a large bowl. Stir in the spinach until uniform. (The filling can be refrigerated in an airtight container for up to 24 hours.)

2. **FOR THE PHYLLO LAYERS:** Adjust an oven rack to the middle position and heat the oven to 400 degrees. Brush a 13 by 9-inch baking dish liberally with oil. Following the illustrations on page 342, lay 1 phyllo sheet in the bottom of the prepared dish, and brush thoroughly with oil. Repeat

with 7 more phyllo sheets, brushing each with oil. Spread half of the spinach mixture evenly into the dish. Cover with 4 more phyllo sheets, brushing each with oil.

3. Spread the remaining spinach mixture evenly into the dish. Cover with 7 more phyllo sheets, brushing each with oil and sprinkling each with about 1 tablespoon of Parmesan. Lay the final sheet of phyllo over the top and brush with oil (do not sprinkle the final layer with Parmesan).

4. Working from the center outward, use the palms of your hands to compress the layers and press out any air pockets. Using a sharp knife, lightly score the pie into serving squares but do not cut through more than the top 3 sheets of phyllo. Bake until the phyllo is golden and crisp, 30 to 35 minutes. Cool on a wire rack for at least 10 minutes or up to 2 hours before serving. (The pie can be wrapped tightly in plastic wrap and refrigerated for up to 4 days. Leftovers are best at room temperature or reheated in a 350-degree oven until crisp and heated through, about 25 minutes.)

➤ VARIATION

Phyllo Triangles with Spinach and Feta
SERVES 8 TO 10 AS AN APPETIZER

These triangle phyllo pastries are simply bite-sized versions of the larger phyllo pie; in Greece, these smaller versions are served as a meze or snack. The unbaked triangles freeze very well; freeze them on a parchment paper–lined baking sheet until firm, about 1 hour, then transfer them to a zipper-lock bag and freeze for up to 1 month. Do not thaw before baking; the baking times will remain the same.

Follow the recipe for Phyllo Pie with Spinach and Feta, cutting all of the filling ingredient amounts in half, doubling the amount of phyllo, and omitting the Parmesan. Adjust the oven racks to the upper- and lower-middle positions and heat the oven to 375 degrees. Following the illustrations on page 343, form the phyllo triangles, using a generous 1 tablespoon of filling per triangle. Spread the triangles out over 2 parchment paper–lined baking sheets. Bake the triangles until golden, about 20 minutes, switching and rotating the sheets halfway through the baking time.

ASSEMBLING PHYLLO PIES

1. Liberally oil a 13 by 9-inch baking dish. Place a sheet of phyllo in the baking dish.

2. Brush the phyllo lightly with oil. Repeat with 7 more sheets of phyllo, brushing each sheet with oil.

3. Spread half of the filling on top of the phyllo. Layer 4 pieces of phyllo on top of the filling, brushing each with oil. Spread the remaining filling over the top. Cover with 7 more sheets of phyllo, brushing each with oil and sprinkling each with 1 tablespoon of Parmesan.

4. Place 1 last piece of phyllo over the layer and brush with oil (do not sprinkle with Parmesan). Using a sharp knife, lightly score into serving squares, taking care not to cut through more than the top 3 pieces of phyllo.

Phyllo Pie with Chicken
Kotopita

SERVES 6 TO 8 AS A MAIN COURSE

Make sure that the phyllo is fully thawed before use; don't thaw it in the microwave, but let it sit in the refrigerator overnight or on the countertop for four to five hours. For more information on working with phyllo, see page 344. Make sure the feta and cooked ground chicken are broken into very small pieces before assembling with the pie.

FILLING

1	tablespoon olive oil
2	pounds ground chicken
8	ounces feta cheese, crumbled into fine pieces (about 2 cups)
3	large eggs, lightly beaten
1	bunch scallions, sliced thin
½	cup pitted kalamata olives, chopped
⅓	cup minced fresh mint leaves
3	tablespoons juice from 1 lemon
2	medium garlic cloves, minced or pressed through a garlic press (about 2 teaspoons)
1	teaspoon salt
¼	teaspoon ground black pepper
¼	teaspoon cayenne pepper

PHYLLO LAYERS

¾	cup olive oil or clarified butter (see page 371)
½	pound (14 by 9-inch) phyllo, thawed (see note)
1	ounce Parmesan cheese, grated (about ½ cup)

1. FOR THE FILLING: Heat the oil in a large skillet over medium heat until shimmering. Add the chicken and cook, breaking the meat into small pieces with a wooden spoon, until no longer pink, about 5 minutes. Transfer to a strainer and let drain, about 5 minutes. Break apart any large clumps of meat with your fingers.

2. Meanwhile, mix the feta, eggs, scallions, olives, mint, lemon juice, garlic, salt, pepper, and cayenne together in a large bowl. Stir in the drained chicken until uniform. (The filling can be refrigerated in an airtight container for up to 24 hours.)

3. FOR THE PHYLLO LAYERS: Adjust an oven rack to the middle position and heat the oven to 400 degrees. Brush a 13 by 9-inch baking dish liberally with oil. Following the illustrations on page 342, lay 1 phyllo sheet in the bottom of the prepared dish and brush thoroughly with oil. Repeat with 7 more phyllo sheets, brushing each with oil. Spread half of the chicken mixture evenly into the dish. Cover with 4 more phyllo sheets, brushing each with oil.

4. Spread the remaining chicken mixture evenly into the dish. Cover with 7 more phyllo sheets, brushing each with oil and sprinkling each with about 1 tablespoon of Parmesan. Lay the final sheet of phyllo over the top and brush with oil (do not sprinkle the final layer with Parmesan).

5. Working from the center outward, use the palms of your hands to compress the layers and press out any air pockets. Using a sharp knife, lightly score the pie into serving squares but do

MAKING PHYLLO TRIANGLES

1. With the short end near you, brush a phyllo sheet with oil, then top it with a second sheet. Cut the sheets lengthwise to make two 4½-inch strips and brush the top with oil.

2. Place a generous 1 tablespoon of filling on the bottom left-hand corner of each strip. Fold up the phyllo to form a right-angle triangle. Continue folding up and over, as if folding a flag, to the end of the strip.

3. Brush the triangle with oil and place seam side down on 2 parchment paper–lined baking sheets. Repeat with the remaining phyllo and filling. Bake as directed.

not cut through more than the top 3 sheets of phyllo. Bake until the phyllo is golden and crisp, 30 to 35 minutes. Cool on a wire rack for at least 10 minutes or up to 2 hours before serving. (The pie can be wrapped tightly in plastic wrap and refrigerated for up to 4 days. Leftovers are best at room temperature or reheated in a 350-degree oven until crisp and heated through, about 25 minutes.)

➤ VARIATION
Phyllo Triangles with Chicken
SERVES 8 TO 10 AS AN APPETIZER

These triangle phyllo pastries are simply bite-sized versions of the larger phyllo pie; in Greece, these smaller versions are served as a meze or snack. The unbaked triangles freeze very well; freeze them on a parchment paper–lined baking sheet until firm, about 1 hour, then transfer them to a zipper-lock bag and freeze for up to 1 month. Do not thaw before baking; the baking times will remain the same.

Follow the recipe for Phyllo Pie with Chicken, cutting all of the filling ingredient amounts in half, doubling the amount of phyllo, and omitting the Parmesan. Adjust the oven racks to the upper- and lower-middle positions and heat the oven to 375 degrees. Following the illustrations on page 343, form the phyllo triangles, using a generous 1 tablespoon of the filling per triangle. Spread the triangles out over 2 parchment paper–lined baking sheets. Bake the triangles until golden, about 20 minutes, switching and rotating the sheets halfway through the baking time.

INGREDIENTS: Phyllo

Phyllo can be found throughout Greece, Turkey, and the Middle East—it is easy to use, can be formed into myriad shapes, and works equally well in sweet and savory recipes. For all its versatility, though, phyllo is not without pitfalls. Unless you are overly ambitious and want to make phyllo from scratch—a feat that is rare these days—phyllo comes from the supermarket in very thin sheets that are either frozen or chilled.

The most important thing to know when working with the pastry is that it needs to be at room temperature when you use it. Most problems arise from hastily thawed phyllo; sheets that are still cold will crack along the folds or may be stuck together at the corners. If the package is frozen, it should be thawed slowly in the refrigerator for at least eight hours or overnight. (You can also thaw it on the countertop for four to five hours.)

Unless there is a Greek or Middle Eastern food shop in your area, it is best to buy phyllo from a busy supermarket, where the product is likely to move quickly and therefore be fresher. Some manufacturers date their phyllo, so you can tell if it is fresh. Even if there is no date on the package, you know that phyllo is good and fresh if you can bunch up a sheet in your hand and open it again without it cracking.

Almost every phyllo recipe calls for brushing each layer of pastry with some sort of fat. In sweet dishes such as Baklava (page 370), we use clarified butter; in savory dishes such as Phyllo Pie with Spinach and Feta (page 341), olive oil or clarified butter may be used. (For more information about clarified butter, see page 371.)

Phyllo doesn't need to be brushed excessively with fat, however. A teaspoon of butter or oil per sheet is adequate if used with care, although the best results in terms of flavor and crispness are usually had with a slightly more generous use of fat, about half a tablespoon per sheet.

The most popular brand of phyllo, Athens, is available in two sizes. Both are 1-pound packages, with the larger size containing 20 sheets measuring 14 by 18 inches and the smaller containing 40 sheets measuring 14 by 9 inches—exactly half the size of the larger sheets. We developed our recipes with the smaller sheets. If using the larger sheets, simply cut them in half widthwise to make 40 (14 by 9-inch) sheets. Extra sheets can be rewrapped and kept refrigerated for one week or refrozen for two months.

THE BEST PHYLLO DOUGH

Athens fillo dough is available in supermarkets nationwide in two sizes and yields crisp pastry every time.

VILLAGE SALAD

Salata Horiatiko

WE ARE ALL FAMILIAR WITH SOME VERSION of Greek salad, a pizza-parlor staple consisting of iceberg lettuce, chunks of green pepper, and a few pale wedges of tomato, sparsely dotted with cubes of feta and garnished with one forlorn olive of questionable origin. The accompanying dressing is usually loaded with musty dried herbs. It didn't take us long to realize that this is a far cry from what you will find in Greece, where the salad often comes to the table without lettuce—consisting instead of the freshest chopped vegetables in an herby vinaigrette with creamy crumbles of briny feta cheese and meaty, fruity olives. In Greece, this salad is known as *salata horiatiko,* which translates as village salad, but is also known as country or peasant salad.

We wanted to create our own version of this simple salad and we started with the vinaigrette, using ingredients ranging from vinegar and lemon juice to yogurt and mustard. Tasters thought that the yogurt-based dressing overwhelmed the salad and that the mustard and cider vinegar versions were one-dimensional. Lemon juice was harsh and distilled white vinegar was dull, but a dressing that combined lemon juice and red wine vinegar had the balanced flavor we were looking for, particularly when combined with extra-virgin olive oil. We knew right from the start that there was no place for dried herbs in this salad. Fresh herbs typically used in Greek cuisine include dill, oregano, parsley, mint, and basil. Tasters loved all of the herbs, but most of them lost their zip when mixed with the vinaigrette. Only oregano's bold flavor stood up well to the vinegar and lemon juice and was the clear favorite, while a small amount of garlic gave the dressing the final kick it needed.

Cucumbers and tomatoes are essential to this salad, and only the ripest tomatoes would do. Green and red bell peppers got a unanimous thumbs down. Onion was next. When the pungency of the raw onion sent some tasters running for breath mints, someone suggested soaking the onion in water to eliminate its caustic bite. We took that idea one step further: Why not marinate the onion in the vinaigrette? On a whim, we included some cucumber as well. The results were striking. The cucumber, which had been watery and bland just minutes before, was bright and flavorful, while the onion had lost its unpleasant potency.

We were now finished with the bulk of our recipe, but something was still missing. We returned to the mint and parsley that had been eliminated from the vinaigrette. We chose to add them back in, this time by simply mixing them with the tomatoes and then tossing this mixture together with the onion and cucumber marinating in the vinaigrette. A generous sprinkling of feta and kalamata olives finished the salad. One bite was all it took for tasters to nod their approval—we had a satisfying Greek salad, full of the bold flavors of the Mediterranean.

~

Village Salad
Salata Horiatiko
SERVES 6 TO 8

This salad, made without lettuce, is served throughout Greece, and is also known as country or peasant salad. It is particularly good in the summer, when fresh tomatoes are at their peak. For efficiency, prepare the other salad ingredients while the onion and cucumber marinate.

VINAIGRETTE

4½	teaspoons red wine vinegar
1	teaspoon juice from 1 lemon
2	teaspoons minced fresh oregano leaves
½	teaspoon salt
⅛	teaspoon ground black pepper
1	medium garlic clove, minced or pressed through a garlic press (about 1 teaspoon)
6	tablespoons extra-virgin olive oil

SALAD

½	medium red onion, sliced thin
2	medium cucumbers, peeled, halved lengthwise, seeded (see the illustration on page 116), and sliced ⅛ inch thick
6	medium tomatoes (about 2 pounds), cored, seeded, and sliced into ½-inch wedges
¼	cup loosely packed torn fresh parsley leaves
¼	cup loosely packed torn fresh mint leaves
20	large kalamata olives, pitted and quartered
5	ounces feta cheese, crumbled (about 1¼ cup)

1. FOR THE VINAIGRETTE: Whisk all of the ingredients together in a large bowl until combined.

2. FOR THE SALAD: Add the onion and cucumbers to the vinaigrette and toss to combine. Let stand for 20 minutes. Add the tomatoes, parsley, and mint and toss to coat with the dressing. Transfer the salad to a serving platter and sprinkle the olives and feta over the top. Serve immediately.

EGG-LEMON SOUP

Avgolemono

AVGOLEMONO, OR GREEK EGG-LEMON SOUP, IS a simple yet utterly satisfying dish—flavorful chicken broth is simmered with rice, accented with lemon, and then thickened with beaten eggs. The use of eggs to create viscosity in soup is not a technique that is uniquely Greek—the Chinese have egg drop soup, and the Italians have straciatella. In these soups, however, the eggs are allowed to coagulate and feather in the broth; in Greece, the eggs are used to yield very different results. The eggs act as a thickener to create a suave, creamy consistency. You can taste the eggs in the finished soup, but you can't see them.

For those who have never encountered it, this soup is the essence of simple home cooking, based on common pantry ingredients. With only four simple ingredients (chicken broth, eggs, lemon, and rice), egg-lemon soup would seem a cinch to make. Straightforward though it is, we did find issues to investigate. First, the texture must be rich and soft, not thin or frothy or pasty, all of which it sometimes is. Also, the soup should be free of tough bits of cooked egg, which would mar its luxurious texture. Finally, a full, lemony flavor—more than just acidity—should balance the savory flavor of the stock.

That eggs are responsible for the smooth texture of this soup was one point of accord found in all of the recipes we researched. There was considerable debate, however, over the number of eggs, whether to use them whole or separated, whether to whip separated whites to a foam, how long to beat the yolks, and whether to beat them by hand or with a blender or food processor.

Initial tests based on 2 quarts of broth and two eggs demonstrated that whole eggs produced better body than yolks alone but that the yolks produced a superior flavor. At the same time, we ruled out separating the eggs and whipping the whites as well as using a machine to beat yolks or whole eggs; both led to soups that were unappealingly foamy and aerated, with weak body and a pale color. The two-egg soup was a little too thin for us, though, so from there we tinkered with different numbers of eggs and extra yolks until we finally settled on two whole eggs plus two yolks as the foundation of our ideal texture and color.

Next we had to ponder even finer points concerning the eggs. First was their temperature. Some recipes warned that the eggs must be at room temperature if they are to marry successfully with the broth. While we had absolutely no problem thickening the soup with eggs right out of the refrigerator, we did find that eggs that sat at room temperature for 15 to 20 minutes yielded a marginally smoother soup. The upshot? Remove the eggs from the refrigerator ahead of time, but don't give it a second thought if you don't. Likewise, several recipes insisted on beating the eggs for up to five minutes before introducing the broth, but we found this extra effort unwarranted. Not only was it harder to do than beating them lightly and quickly, but it created undesirable foam and faded the color of the soup. Like whipping the eggs in a machine, longer beating added too much air.

REMOVING LARGE STRIPS OF CITRUS ZEST

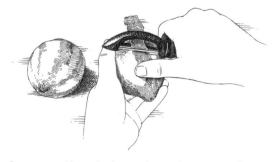

Run a vegetable peeler from pole to pole to remove long, wide strips of zest.

TEMPERING EGGS

Whisking constantly, trickle the hot broth mixture into the beaten eggs with a ladle.

The second point of agreement in the recipes we researched was how to add the eggs to the chicken broth, and this was by the method of tempering. This process consists of first beating the eggs lightly and then slowly beating in some of the hot broth. This mixture is then added to the remaining hot broth to finish the soup. The effect of tempering is to elevate the temperature of the eggs gradually so that they don't seize up and form curds in the soup. The added broth dilutes the eggs, raising the temperature at which coagulation occurs. Just to cover all the bases, we tried skipping the tempering process. Sure enough, we produced chunks of scrambled eggs floating in watery soup. Eggs normally coagulate at roughly 150 degrees, and simmering broth can approach 200 degrees.

One recipe offered a variation on the tempering technique. Rather than adding the broth to the eggs in a thin stream, this recipe called for adding all of the broth to the eggs ½ cup at a time. When we tried this method, the eggs didn't curdle, but the texture of the soup did suffer. The smoothest soups resulted from the tried-and-true method of trickling the broth in gradually.

The rice cooked in the broth also plays a role in the thickening process. Rice leaches some of its starch into the liquid as the grains swell and cook. Those loose starch molecules act to slightly increase the coagulation temperature of the eggs by becoming part of the network of denatured proteins that join together to do the work of thickening. The presence of the starch in the protein network provides some buffer against curdling the eggs should the soup overheat during the final cooking process. So, in this sense, the rice helps to stabilize the entire mixture.

With the texture just where we wanted it, we turned our attention to the flavor. In most of the soups we'd made so far, the lemon flavor was fleeting. It came and went on the palate in almost the same instant. We tried various amounts of lemon juice, but adding more than ¼ cup made the soup taste harsh. Extra acidity was not the answer. Though none of the recipes we consulted had mentioned it, we tried adding lemon zest—the yellow outermost part of the peel—to the equation. The addition of zest, simmered in the broth with the rice, was a success, giving the soup a refreshing tang and full lemon resonance. This flavor stayed with us. Adding bay leaves and a trace amount of spice to the stock brought even greater depth of flavor. Cardamom, in particular, added real finesse and was the perfect finishing touch.

Egg-Lemon Soup
Avgolemono
SERVES 6 TO 8

This is a classic soup served all over Greece. About 5 minutes of heating produces a soft, velvety texture—any longer and the soup begins to turn pasty. Scallions and/or fresh mint make simple and flavorful garnishes. Serve the soup immediately—it thickens to a gravy-like consistency when reheated.

2	quarts low-sodium chicken broth
½	cup long-grain white rice
12	(4-inch-long) strips zest from 2 lemons (see the illustration on page 346)
4	green cardamom pods, crushed, or 2 whole cloves
2	bay leaves
1½	teaspoons salt
2	large eggs, at room temperature
2	large egg yolks, at room temperature
¼	cup juice from 2 lemons
1	scallion, sliced thin, and/or 3 tablespoons chopped fresh mint leaves

1. Bring the broth to a boil in a large saucepan over high heat. Add the rice, lemon zest, cardamom, bay leaves, and salt. Reduce the heat to medium and simmer until the rice is tender, 16 to 20 minutes.

2. Remove and discard the bay leaves, cardamom, and lemon zest. Return the broth to a boil over high heat, then reduce the heat to low. Whisk the whole eggs, yolks, and lemon juice together in a medium bowl until combined.

3. Following the illustration on page 347, ladle about 2 cups of the hot broth and slowly whisk it into the eggs to temper, then slowly whisk the egg mixture back into the soup. Continue to cook the soup over low heat, stirring constantly, until slightly thickened, 4 to 5 minutes. Do not let the soup simmer or boil. Divide the soup among serving bowls, sprinkle with scallion and/or mint, and serve immediately.

STUFFED EGGPLANT

Imam Bayildi

STUFFED EGGPLANT, OR *IMAM BAYILDI*, IS one of the more well-known specialties of Turkish cuisine. Roughly translated as "the imam fainted," the story behind this dish is that a Turkish priest, or imam, sat down one night to a meal of stuffed eggplant cooked in olive oil and upon tasting the dish, promptly fainted. The question remains, however, as to whether he fainted because the eggplant tasted so good, or because of his wife's prolific use of the ever-so-expensive household staple, olive oil. Regardless of the impetus, stuffed eggplant has become a popular dish not only in Turkey, but in Greece and throughout the Middle East. We wanted to replicate this mythic vegetable dish.

At its best, stuffed eggplant consists of tender eggplant filled with onions and garlic and scented with warm spices and fruity olive oil. Unfortunately, many recipes we tried featured oil-saturated eggplant and bland, watery fillings. We wanted a stuffed eggplant recipe that would do justice to the imam's wife—one with creamy, earthy eggplant, and a hearty, flavorful filling that would make a satisfying side dish or an interesting vegetarian entrée.

We began our testing with the long, slender Japanese or Asian eggplants, but we quickly found that they did not have enough flesh, which made stuffing them difficult. Large (sometimes called globe) eggplants, on the other hand, had too much flesh. Not only did they take too long to cook, they also needed to be cut up before serving, which ruined the attractive presentation of eggplant halves. The smaller variety of eggplant—sometimes labeled Italian—however, worked great. Smaller than the globes, but not as thin as the Japanese eggplants, these were ideal for stuffing. (We had the best results with firm eggplants that weigh about 10 ounces each.) Their flesh cooks up creamy, with an earthy flavor that is not at all bitter—a trait often associated with eggplant.

With the type of eggplant resolved, we had to figure out the best cooking method. We started by cutting the eggplants in half lengthwise, as opposed to leaving them whole as many recipes do, under the logic that one half was the perfect serving for a side dish, and two halves made a suitable entrée portion. We started by sautéing the eggplants in a skillet on the stovetop in some olive oil. The cut sides of the eggplants caramelized beautifully, which intensified the flavor of the eggplant.

We found that flipping the eggplants in the skillet caused the skin to break, which prevented the eggplants from holding the filling. But by leaving them cut side down the entire time, the previously caramelized exterior became just plain burnt by the time the eggplants were tender. As a solution, after browning the eggplants (and without flipping them), we reduced the heat, covered the pan, and continued to cook the eggplant until tender. This part-sauté/part-steam combination method was almost seamless, except for the fact that we had to cook the eggplants in two batches because we couldn't fit them all into one skillet.

Hoping to avoid multiple batches, we borrowed a technique we have used for stuffed zucchini and turned to the oven. We brushed the eggplant halves with oil and seasoned them with salt and pepper, then we arranged them cut side down on a preheated baking sheet, and covered them with foil. After less than an hour in a 400-degree oven, the eggplant emerged golden brown and tender. Pleased with the results, we turned our attention to the filling.

We needed a filling that would transform the eggplant into a light meal or an elegant side dish, and one that could be easily prepared while the eggplant was in the oven. To start, we tried using a simple combination of onion, which we caramelized slightly, garlic, and grated Pecorino Romano cheese (a substitution for the Greek cheese typically used, *kefalotyri*, which is hard to find). Tasters liked the flavor but wanted something more substantial, a filling that would hold its own against the meaty eggplant.

We then tested fillings made with bread cubes and bread crumbs, ingredients we had seen in our research, but both resulted in a mushy texture. Next, we turned to vegetables. We came upon several recipes that called for green bell peppers, but tasters thought they were too bitter. The combination of diced tomatoes and toasted pine nuts, however, was a perfect fit. The tomatoes added substance without making the filling mushy or adding too much moisture, and also imparted a sweetness that was the perfect complement to the eggplant. The nuts, aside from imparting richness and flavor, also added a pleasant, lightly crunchy texture to the filling.

Now we just had to round out the flavors. We seasoned the filling with oregano, cinnamon, and a little cayenne for heat. After stirring in some red wine vinegar to brighten the overall flavor of the dish and balance the sweetness of the onions, we were ready to stuff the eggplants.

We simply opened up the center of each eggplant by pushing the flesh to the sides using two forks. We then mounded a generous amount (about ¼ cup) of filling into each opening, and sprinkled extra grated cheese over the top of each eggplant half. While many recipes then steam the stuffed eggplants or braise them in olive oil, we found that after just five minutes in a 400-degree oven, the eggplant and filling were heated through, without being laden with olive oil or mushy and water-logged. A sprinkling of fresh parsley for color and freshness was all it took to finish things off. Now we had a recipe for stuffed eggplant that tastes so good, it just might make you swoon.

Stuffed Eggplant
Imam Bayildi
SERVES 4 AS AN MAIN COURSE, OR 8 AS A SIDE DISH
This specific dish has origins in Turkey, although variations can be found throughout Greece and the entire Middle East. Serve with Cucumber, Garlic, and Yogurt Sauce (page 336) or Greek-Style Thickened Yogurt (page 337). This dish can be served hot or at room temperature.

4 Italian eggplants (about 10 ounces each), halved lengthwise
¼ cup olive oil
Salt and ground black pepper
1 medium onion, minced
3 medium garlic cloves, minced or pressed through a garlic press (about 1 tablespoon)
2 teaspoons minced fresh oregano leaves, or ½ teaspoon dried
¼ teaspoon ground cinnamon
⅛ teaspoon cayenne pepper
1 pound plum tomatoes (3 to 4 tomatoes), cored, seeded, and chopped medium
2 ounces Pecorino Romano cheese, grated (about 1 cup)
¼ cup pine nuts, toasted (see page 135)
1 tablespoon red wine vinegar
2 tablespoons minced fresh parsley leaves

1. Adjust two oven racks to the upper-middle and lowest positions, place a rimmed baking sheet on the lowest rack, and heat the oven to 400 degrees.

2. Brush the cut sides of the eggplant with 2 tablespoons of the oil and season with salt and pepper. Set the eggplant cut side down on the hot baking sheet and, using oven mitts, carefully cover with foil. Roast until the eggplant is golden brown and tender, 50 to 55 minutes. Carefully transfer the eggplant to a paper towel–lined baking sheet and let drain. Do not turn off the oven.

3. Meanwhile, heat the remaining 2 tablespoons oil in a 12-inch skillet over medium heat until shimmering. Add the onion and ½ teaspoon salt and cook until softened and browned, about 10 minutes. Stir in the garlic, oregano, cinnamon, and cayenne and cook until fragrant, about 30 seconds. Stir in the tomatoes, ¾ cup of the cheese, nuts, and vinegar and cook until warmed through, about 1 minute. Season with salt and pepper to taste and set aside.

4. Return the roasted eggplant cut side up to the rimmed baking sheet (or use a large casserole dish). Using two forks, gently push the flesh to the sides of each eggplant half to make room for the filling. Mound about ¼ cup of the filling into each eggplant. (At this point, the eggplants can be covered and refrigerated for up to 24 hours.)

5. Sprinkle with the remaining ¼ cup cheese and bake on the upper-middle rack until the cheese is melted, 5 to 10 minutes. (If refrigerated, increase the baking time to 8 to 12 minutes.) Sprinkle with the parsley and serve warm or at room temperature.

GARLIC-LEMON POTATOES

Patates sto Fourno

GARLIC-LEMON POTATOES ARE A STAPLE ON most taverna menus throughout Greece and are typically served alongside a simple roast chicken or a piece of grilled fish. Often cut in small cubes and either baked in the oven or sautéed on the stovetop, these popular potatoes are at once tangy with lemon, sharp with garlic, and earthy with oregano. Done well, the potatoes are crusty, well browned, and accented by a full (but not overpowering) lemon flavor and plenty of garlic bite. If things go wrong, though, the result is a soggy and sour side dish.

Most of the recipes we found revealed that the standard home-cooking technique for garlic-lemon potatoes is to cube raw potatoes, toss them in a baking dish with a mixture of lemon juice, garlic, oregano, and oil, add a little water, and then bake them until the water has evaporated and the

CUTTING POTATO WEDGES

Quarter each potato lengthwise into 4 evenly sized wedges, then slice each wedge in half lengthwise (each potato will yield 8 wedges).

potatoes have absorbed the flavors of the seasoning mixture. A number of recipes demanded what seemed to us an unreasonably long baking time of 90 minutes as well as constant monitoring and stirring of the potatoes near the end of cooking. As we discovered when we made the potatoes according to this traditional method, they didn't turn out even close to perfect anyway. The texture was downright soggy, and most tasters felt that the lemon flavor was harsh and acidic. Worse yet was the total absence of the crisp, browned crust that we desired. We decided our first task would be reducing the cooking time.

More research turned up two possible solutions: oven-roasting without the seasonings and stovetop cooking in a skillet. Oven-roasting the potatoes and then adding a lemon-garlic-herb mixture when they emerged from the oven was a huge improvement. These simple steps cut the cooking time in half, to 45 minutes, while also producing a flavorful, caramelized crust. The results we got from the skillet method were even better. With the intense heat of the hot pan over a medium-high flame, the potatoes developed a gorgeous, flavorful, mahogany brown crust in just 11 minutes. Although perfect on the outside, the potatoes were not completely cooked on the inside. After a number of tests, we found that simply covering the skillet and allowing the browned potatoes to cook for an additional 5 minutes gave them a tender and velvety interior. Now we had cut the cooking time down from 90 minutes to less than 20, and the results were crisp and flavorful.

We tested different skillets and found a heavy-bottomed, 12-inch nonstick model best suited to the task. The heavy construction translates to even heat distribution, which reduces the risk of burning and maximizes browning. And don't skimp on size—the large diameter provided enough space to arrange the potatoes in a single layer for optimal browning. Finally, while the nonstick finish made cleanup a breeze, it is not essential. We successfully cooked the potatoes in a conventional pan (without a nonstick coating), but the pan required a fair amount of elbow grease to clean. In the course of testing, we settled on using only four potatoes for the recipe (so as not to compromise the browning by crowding the pan) and we made sure the potatoes were evenly sized (so all the pieces would cook at the same rate).

In terms of the cooking medium, we liked the flavor of extra-virgin olive oil, though some butter was necessary to boost the flavor of the oil and promote browning. Because we liked the flavor of extra-virgin olive oil so much, we decided to add some additional oil to the cooked potatoes along with the seasonings.

We were surprised that few recipes specified what type of potato to use. Surely there would be differences between high-starch/low-moisture potatoes such as russets (commonly used for baking), medium-starch potatoes such as all-purpose or Yukon Gold, and low-starch/high-moisture potatoes such as Red Bliss, which are often used for roasting and boiling. After testing representatives from the three categories, our tasters flatly rejected russets because the pieces broke apart easily and were mealy. Yukon Golds were the favorite for their appealing blend of smooth, velvety texture, rich yellow hue, and buttery flavor—though Red Bliss potatoes, with their supple, creamy texture, took a close second. With regard to preparing the Yukon Golds, tasters preferred peeled potatoes cut into wedges about ¾ inch thick as opposed to thicker wedges, slices, or cubes.

Lemon, garlic, and oregano give this dish its character. Most of the recipes we consulted called for lemon juice, some as little as 2 tablespoons and others as much as ½ cup. Throughout our testing, tasters agreed that potatoes flavored with lemon juice alone tasted sharp, shallow, and acidic. So we tried adding some grated lemon zest to impart a deeper lemon flavor. Indeed it did; tasters responded well to batches made with a full 1 teaspoon of grated zest per 2 pounds of potatoes, along with a modest 2 tablespoons of juice for brightness and moderate acidity.

Garlic is another key flavoring. At first we thought that raw garlic might have too much bite for the dish, but tasters dismissed our attempts to tame the garlic flavor by toasting the whole cloves or cooking the minced garlic in oil until it

EQUIPMENT: Garlic Presses

A defiantly sticky and undeniably stinky job, hand-mincing garlic is a chore many cooks avoid by pressing the cloves through a garlic press. The question for us was not whether garlic presses work, but which of the many available models works best. After squeezing our way through 12 different models, the unanimous winner was Kuhn Rikon's 2315 Epicurean Garlic Press. Solidly constructed of stainless steel, it has an almost luxurious feel, with ergonomically curved handles that are comfortable to squeeze and a hopper that smoothly and automatically lifts out for cleaning as you open the handles. It passed all our kitchen tests with flying colors. At $35, however, it is also quite expensive. Also doing well in our tests was the Trudeau Garlic Press—with a solid construction, it is sturdy and easy to use, and is our best buy at a reasonable $11.99.

THE BEST GARLIC PRESSES

The Kuhn Rikon 2315 Epicurean Garlic Press (top) produces a very fine mince, good yield, and great paste consistency, making it the all-around winner. The Trudeau Garlic Press (bottom) is a solid and reliable choice for those looking to spend a little less and is our best buy.

was sweet and mellow. Judging the flavor of these batches too "docile" and "wimpy," they agreed that raw garlic was the way to go. One clove, two cloves, and even three cloves were deemed too weak. We were shocked when tasters chose the batch of potatoes with four cloves of minced raw garlic, describing it as "bright, fresh, and gutsy." Last, we replaced the dusty-tasting dried oregano used in so many recipes with fresh, and all the tasters approved.

The only thing left was to determine the optimum amount of time for the potatoes and seasonings to get acquainted. Testing showed that adding the lemon, garlic, and herbs to the pan midway through the potatoes' cooking time (or any earlier) not only diminished their flavor but also increased the risk of burning the garlic. Instead, we mixed the seasonings into the potatoes once they were fully cooked, which provided the strong hits of flavor that our tasters demanded.

Now these classic potatoes are so quick and easy to make at home, you don't have to go to Greece to enjoy them.

Garlic-Lemon Potatoes
Patates sto Fourno
SERVES 4

If your potatoes are larger than 8 ounces you may have to increase the covered cooking time by up to 4 minutes. You can also add ¼ cup of sliced sun-dried tomatoes to this dish.

2 tablespoons extra-virgin olive oil

1 tablespoon unsalted butter

4 medium Yukon Gold potatoes (7 to 8 ounces each; about 2 pounds total), peeled and cut lengthwise into 8 wedges (see the illustration on page 350)

2 tablespoons juice and 1 teaspoon grated zest from 1 lemon

2 tablespoons minced fresh oregano leaves

4 medium garlic cloves, minced or pressed through a garlic press (about 4 teaspoons)

1 teaspoon salt

½ teaspoon ground black pepper

2 tablespoons minced fresh parsley leaves (optional)

1. Heat 1 tablespoon of the oil and the butter in a 12-inch nonstick skillet over medium-high heat until the butter melts. Brown the potatoes on both cut sides, about 5 minutes per side. Turn the heat to medium-low, cover, and cook until the potatoes are tender when pierced with the tip of a paring knife, about 6 minutes.

2. While the potatoes cook, combine the remaining tablespoon oil, lemon juice and zest, oregano, garlic, salt, and pepper in a small bowl. When the potatoes are tender, add the garlic-lemon mixture and stir in carefully (so as not to break the potato wedges). Continue to cook, uncovered, until the seasoning mixture is heated through and fragrant, 1 to 2 minutes. Sprinkle the potatoes with parsley (if using) and serve immediately.

➤ VARIATION

Garlic-Lemon Potatoes with Olives and Feta
Follow the recipe for Garlic-Lemon Potatoes, sprinkling 3 ounces crumbled feta cheese (about ¾ cup) and ¼ cup sliced, pitted kalamata olives over the potatoes before serving.

BEANS AND GREENS
Gigantes Plaki

GIANT BEANS, APPROPRIATELY NAMED *GIGANTES*, are popular throughout Greece. Similar in size and texture to large lima beans, gigantes are about 1½ inches long, with a velvety, creamy texture and an earthy flavor. In Greece, they are used in a variety of ways, from soups and stews to salads and side dishes, to create rustic, full-flavored dishes.

Greens are ubiquitous in Greek cuisine as well, perhaps because they grow wild throughout the countryside. When it comes to greens, spinach, sorrel, chervil, and chard are among the heavy hitters, although there are hundreds of wild varieties unique to each region. Present at almost every meal, they may be simply boiled and dressed with olive oil and lemon, braised with aromatics, simmered in milk, baked in pies, or stirred into soups. We had visions of combining these two ingredients into a rich, hearty, satisfying side dish that could be served alongside a garlicky leg of lamb or with a piece of crusty bread as a light lunch or vegetarian main course.

We quickly outlined what we didn't want: mushy, broken-up beans and drab, bitter-tasting, murky-colored greens. We started with the greens, and set out to determine which type of green was best for our recipe and the best way to cook it. Here in the test kitchen, we cook a lot of greens, and generally, we follow a five-step approach for reducing the bitterness that many of them possess: blanch, shock (dunk in ice water), squeeze dry, chop, and sauté. The upside is that when handled this way, their color is vibrant, the bitterness is tamed, and the resulting greens are robust but not overpowering. The downside? The whole process demands precious time and multiple pieces of kitchen equipment. After sampling a variety of greens raw, two of them emerged as absolute standouts: spinach and chard. Tasters noted their appealing vegetal and mineral qualities but made not one mention of bitterness, giving us new hope for a straightforward cooking method.

We continued our cooking-method tests working with spinach, which tasters favored for its earthy taste, delicate, tender texture, and also for its wide availability and convenience—often it comes already cleaned. Sure enough, a simple sauté tasted great, but the quantity of raw spinach necessary for this recipe meant that we would have to cook it in three or four batches. The solution was a sauté and steam combination. We quickly wilted half of the spinach in a hot pan with olive oil and aromatic onions and garlic, and then squeezed in the remainder of the raw spinach. We covered the pan, and just two minutes later, bright green, tender, flavorful greens were ours.

For the beans, we found that dried large lima beans were the best substitute for the Greek gigantes, which can be difficult to find outside of specialty markets. (That said, if you can find gigantes, we recommend using them.) Many of the recipes we found for giant beans came with tips and warnings on how to achieve cooked beans with perfect texture. "Always soak the beans overnight to ensure even cooking" and "Never salt the beans

while they are cooking or they will become tough or split open" were not uncommon counsel. Surely these "rules" were established for a reason, right?

We decided to find out and started with rule number one: Always soak the beans. We cooked up three batches of beans. Prior to cooking, we soaked one batch overnight and another according to the "quick-soak" method (water and beans simmer for two minutes, then are placed off heat, covered, and allowed to sit in the water for one hour). We didn't presoak the third batch at all. The results were as we expected. Both batches that were soaked produced perfectly cooked, creamy, yet not soggy beans that retained their texture. The unsoaked beans, on the other hand, had an uneven texture and took a lot longer to cook; by the time half of the beans were tender, the other half had overcooked and disintegrated.

Now we could take on rule number two: Never salt the beans during cooking. Recipes that warned against salting stated that it would cause the outer shell of the bean to toughen. We tested beans cooked in salted water against unsalted beans and the salted beans were indeed slightly firmer on the outside. However, these beans were not any less cooked on the inside than the unsalted beans. In addition, the small amount of resistance that the salted beans had developed on the outside seemed to prevent them from bursting. The beans were now softly structured on the outside and tooth-tender on the inside.

So now that we had perfectly cooked beans and a foolproof method for cooking the spinach, we had to marry the two. After cooking the beans, we drained them and set them aside. In the same pan we then cooked the aromatics and the spinach, and stirred in the cooked beans. To finish up and round out the dish, we worked in flavorful ingredients. We added tomatoes, fresh dill, and a couple more tablespoons of fruity extra-virgin olive oil to enrich the dish, then we sprinkled tangy feta cheese over the top.

Tasters liked the dish as is, but we decided to take it yet one step further. We had seen a recipe in our research that bakes the beans and greens in a casserole with bread crumbs on top. There are few things we love more than golden brown, crispy, well-seasoned bread crumbs, so we transferred the casserole to a baking dish and sprinkled the bread crumbs (and feta) over the top. The dish emerged from the oven just 20 minutes later, and tasters were anxiously waiting to gobble it up.

Giant Beans with Spinach and Feta

Gigantes Plaki

SERVES 6 TO 8

Dried giant beans, called gigantes, can be found in Greek and Middle Eastern markets; alternatively, you can use dried large lima beans. If you don't have time to cook dried beans, you can substitute 2 (15-ounce) cans cannellini beans, rinsed, for the giant beans; skip step 1 and stir the canned beans into the spinach in step 4. This dish can double as a vegetarian entrée when served with crusty bread.

8	ounces (about 1¼ cups) dried giant beans or dried large lima beans, rinsed, picked over, and soaked overnight or quick-soaked (see page 12)
	Salt
2	slices high-quality white sandwich bread, quartered
6	tablespoons extra-virgin olive oil
2	medium onions, minced
3	medium garlic cloves, minced or pressed through a garlic press (about 1 tablespoon)
2	(10-ounce) bags spinach, stemmed and washed
2	(14.5-ounce) cans diced tomatoes, drained
¼	cup minced fresh dill leaves
	Ground black pepper
6	ounces feta cheese, crumbled (about 1½ cups)
1	lemon, cut into wedges (for serving)

1. Drain the beans, discarding the soaking liquid; set aside. Bring the beans, 2 quarts fresh water, and 1 teaspoon salt to a boil in a Dutch oven. Reduce to a simmer and cook until the beans are tender, 1 to 1½ hours, stirring occasionally.

2. Meanwhile, process the bread with 2 tablespoons of the oil in a food processor to coarse crumbs, about 5 pulses; set aside.

3. Adjust an oven rack to the middle position and heat the oven to 400 degrees. When the beans are tender, drain and discard the cooking liquid; set aside. Wipe out the Dutch oven, add 2 more tablespoons of the oil to the pot, and heat over medium heat until shimmering. Add the onions and ½ teaspoon salt and cook until softened, 5 to 7 minutes.

4. Stir in the garlic and cook until fragrant, about 30 seconds. Add half of the spinach, cover, and cook until beginning to wilt, about 2 minutes. Stir in the remaining spinach, cover, and continue to cook until wilted, about 2 minutes longer. Off the heat, gently stir in the drained beans, tomatoes, dill, and the remaining 2 tablespoons oil. Season with salt and pepper to taste and transfer to a 13 by 9-inch baking dish. (At this point, the dish can be covered and refrigerated for up to 24 hours.)

5. Sprinkle the feta, then the fresh bread crumbs evenly over the top. Bake until the bread crumbs are golden brown and the edges are bubbling, about 20 minutes. (If refrigerated, increase the baking time to 25 to 30 minutes.) Serve immediately with the lemon wedges.

LAYERED EGGPLANT AND LAMB CASSEROLE

Moussaka

MANY OF US ARE FAMILIAR WITH *MOUSSAKA*, a staple of fine Greek restaurants and diners alike, or some say a clichéd symbol of Greek food in America. Regardless, moussaka, a rich casserole of roasted eggplant, tomato sauce enriched with meat (usually ground lamb), and creamy béchamel, is a cornerstone of Greek cuisine. It is similar to lasagna in that it is a layered casserole, with sheets of eggplant instead of noodles sandwiching the filling and sauce. The problem, we find, is that often the eggplant is rife with oil and the filling and sauce are cloyingly rich yet disappointingly bland—nothing like the delicate, nuanced casserole that it should be. We wanted to make a version as close to authentic as we could get, and worth all of the effort.

Eggplant is the Achilles' heel of moussaka. Most of the recipes we found either pan-fried or roasted the eggplant before assembling the casserole. Fried eggplant was, across the board, greasy. The porous vegetable greedily soaked up oil from the pan, and then leached it into the moussaka once baked (with its rich lamb filling, additional fat is one thing moussaka never needs). We found that roasted eggplant wasn't nearly as greasy, requiring a minimum amount of oil to brown, and had a superior texture and flavor. The high heat of the oven effectively caramelized the eggplant, magnifying its sweetness and tempering its bitterness. So roasting it was.

Once the eggplant was cut and ready for the oven, we tossed it in a small amount of olive oil to promote browning and experimented with temperatures ranging between 375 and 500 degrees. Roasted too hot, the edges of the eggplant burned before the center cooked. Too low, and the slices took an eternity to brown and consequently turned mushy. We finally settled on 450 degrees for 45 minutes because the eggplant slices browned evenly without turning too soft. During this time, we set out to prepare the filling and béchamel.

But we were in for a rude surprise. We had cooked two baking sheets' worth of eggplant slices (from 4 pounds of eggplant), the most the oven could accommodate at one time. When we went to assemble the moussaka, we found that there were barely enough eggplant slices for two layers in an 8 by 8-inch baking dish, or just four dinner-sized servings. We wanted the recipe to serve double that. So, to fill a 13 by 9-inch baking dish, we would have to prepare a staggering 8 pounds of eggplant, requiring a minimum of two hours to roast it all (two batches of two baking sheets, the most home ovens will cook evenly). Coupling the extensive cooking time with the effort required for the filling and sauce, this was quickly becoming a long-winded recipe.

We decided to revisit how we were preparing the moussaka and whether or not there was a way to streamline things. Instead of slicing the eggplant into broad planks, we opted to cut it into chunky cubes, which allowed us to fit a little more eggplant onto each of the baking sheets. We placed these chunks of eggplant on the bottom of the casserole to be blanketed in filling, which was then capped with béchamel. Unconventional, perhaps, but it was a simple solution that minimized the work and time required.

The best lamb-and-tomato fillings we have tasted are rich, slightly sweet, and perfumed with cinnamon and oregano. Unlike ground beef that is sold with the fat content marked on the package, ground lamb is generally unmarked and almost always pretty fatty. We quickly realized that the meat needed to be browned and the excess fat drained off before we could add the filling's other ingredients. Removing the excess fat also removed much of the lamb's gaminess—a flavor with which some tasters took issue.

A good quantity of onions and garlic was a given, their sweetness and piquancy lending the filling a solid base of flavor. We experimented with the usual canned tomato products—whole, diced, and pureed—and preferred the latter. Both whole (chopped coarse) and diced tomatoes failed to break down to the thick, jammy consistency characteristic of our favorite moussaka fillings. To boost the fruity sweetness of the puree, we included a couple of tablespoons of tomato paste and sugar. Slowly simmered for about half an hour, the filling's excess moisture evaporated and the flavors blended. But the filling still tasted a bit flat and we realized that it needed some acidity—any tartness had been cooked out of the tomatoes. We easily settled on red wine as the best option because it provided a mildly acidic kick and a fruitiness that intensified the flavor of the tomatoes.

As for seasoning the filling, Greeks tend to include a fairly substantial amount of cinnamon. We found that too much cinnamon easily overpowered the dish's other flavors, so we settled on a modest ¾ teaspoon. And for herbs, oregano lent the right amount of freshness.

The béchamel for moussaka should form a thick blanket over the top, sealing in the filling. We quickly realized that this béchamel had to be significantly thicker than most of those that we had prepared for other casserole-type recipes. We increased the flour in the sauce incrementally until we attained a thick, velvety texture that sealed in the bubbling filling and browned attractively.

In classic recipes, the béchamel is often enriched with a crumbly aged cheese called myzithra. We found that myzithra's flavor, which is salty, drier, and richer-tasting than Greece's more common feta cheese, could be approximated with a healthy dose of Parmesan.

Baking the moussaka was a simple matter of watching the filling percolate beneath the béchamel. A moderately hot oven—400 degrees— quickly brought the moussaka up to temperature without burning the béchamel.

Layered Eggplant and Lamb Casserole
Moussaka
SERVES 6 TO 8

When buying eggplant, look for those that are glossy, feel firm, and are heavy for their size. Do not substitute low-fat or nonfat milk in the sauce.

4	pounds eggplant (about 4 medium), peeled and cut into ¾-inch cubes
3	tablespoons olive oil
	Salt and ground black pepper
2	pounds ground lamb
I	medium onion, minced
2	tablespoons tomato paste
4	medium garlic cloves, minced or pressed through a garlic press (about 4 teaspoons)
I	tablespoon minced fresh oregano leaves, or I teaspoon dried
I	teaspoon sugar
¾	teaspoon ground cinnamon
I	(28-ounce) can tomato puree
½	cup dry red wine
3	tablespoons unsalted butter
¼	cup unbleached all-purpose flour
2	cups whole milk
2	ounces Parmesan cheese, grated (about I cup)
	Pinch ground nutmeg

1. Adjust 2 oven racks to the upper- and lower-middle positions and heat the oven to 450 degrees. Line 2 rimmed baking sheets with aluminum foil and spray with vegetable oil spray (or use nonstick foil). Toss the eggplant with the oil, 1 teaspoon salt, and ¼ teaspoon pepper and spread the eggplant evenly over the prepared baking sheets. Bake until light golden brown, 40 to 50 minutes, switching and rotating the pans halfway though the roasting time. Set aside to cool. Leave the oven on, reducing the temperature to 400 degrees.

2. Meanwhile, cook the lamb in a large Dutch oven over medium-high heat, breaking the meat into small pieces with a wooden spoon, until no longer pink and the fat has rendered, about 5 minutes. Strain the lamb through a fine-mesh strainer, reserving the drippings.

3. Return 2 tablespoons of the reserved lamb drippings, onion, and ½ teaspoon salt to the pot and cook over medium heat until softened, 5 to 7 minutes. Stir in the tomato paste, garlic, oregano, sugar, and cinnamon and cook until fragrant, about 30 seconds. Stir in the drained lamb, tomato puree, and wine, increase the heat to high, and bring to a simmer. Reduce the heat to low, cover partially, and cook, stirring occasionally, until the juices have evaporated and the sauce has thickened, 25 to 30 minutes. Season with salt and pepper to taste.

4. While the lamb simmers, melt the butter in a medium saucepan over medium-high heat. Add the flour and cook, stirring constantly, for 1 minute. Gradually whisk in the milk. Bring to a simmer and cook, whisking often, until the sauce thickens and no longer tastes of flour, about 5 minutes. Off the heat, whisk in the Parmesan and nutmeg and season with salt and pepper to taste; cover and set aside.

5. Spread the roasted eggplant evenly into a 13 by 9-inch baking dish. Spread the lamb filling over the eggplant, then pour the béchamel evenly over the top. (At this point, the casserole can be covered and refrigerated for up to 2 days.)

6. Bake the casserole, uncovered, until the top is lightly golden, 25 to 35 minutes. (If refrigerated, cover the dish with foil and bake for 30 to 40 minutes, then uncover and continue to bake for 15 to 20 minutes). Let stand for 10 minutes before serving.

PASTA AND GROUND LAMB CASSEROLE

Pastitsio

EVERY GREEK COOKBOOK HAS A RECIPE FOR *pastitsio,* a layered casserole consisting of a ground meat and tomato sauce, pasta, a creamy béchamel, and a sprinkling of cheese. In Greek, the word pastitsio means "made from pasta." When well prepared, it is comfort food at its finest, but often recipes for pastitsio yield a mishmash of over-seasoned lamb filling, soggy, overcooked pasta, and thick, gluey béchamel. We aimed to make a pastitsio worthy of serving to our friends from Greece—one that would bring them back to their grandmother's kitchen.

We began by testing various interpretations of pastitsio. Some of the recipes called for ground beef or veal, while others called for ground lamb. Tests revealed that those made with beef were dry and those made with veal lacked depth of flavor. Lamb, on the other hand, was rich and moist and it contributed a gaminess that we have come to associate with Greek cuisine. We had learned in our moussaka recipe (see page 354), that ground lamb can be incredibly fat laden, making the casserole greasy. To remedy this, we browned the ground lamb and then drained the excess fat off before adding the other ingredients.

With the lamb cooking technique established, we turned to the aromatics. Onion and garlic were a given, but getting the spices set proved to be more of a puzzle. Several recipes called for showering the ground lamb with a whole array of spices, including cumin, coriander, cardamom, cinnamon, nutmeg, and cloves. But tasters found the abundance of spices overpowering. We aimed for a lighter touch, and the simple combination of cinnamon, oregano, and nutmeg did the trick.

Next, we had to decide on the type of tomato product to use. Diced tomatoes were acceptable, but tasters did not care for the overly assertive chunks of tomato, which did not blend with the other ingredients in the sauce. Tasters preferred the even distribution of crushed tomatoes, but felt that the tomato flavor was not quite bold enough. We fortified the crushed tomatoes with ¼ cup of

tomato paste, which provided the perfect backbone of flavor. After simmering the lamb and tomato mixture for only five minutes, our meat sauce was thickened slightly and intensely flavored. The addition of ½ cup of Pecorino Romano (a substitute for the Greek cheese *kefalotyri*, which is hard to find) enriched the sauce, while intensifying the flavor of the lamb.

With one major component of the dish resolved, we turned to the béchamel, a creamy sauce made from milk that is thickened with a roux (a paste made from flour and hot fat). There was one major problem with the recipes we had tested thus far: meager amounts of béchamel, which made the casserole dry. We began testing the sauce amount. Two, three, four, and even five cups of sauce produced dry casseroles. We were surprised by the amount of sauce required, but the pasta absorbed a good deal of the sauce in the oven, and we wanted a creamy casserole. Tasters were finally satisfied with the consistency of the casserole when we used six cups of béchamel!

Many of the recipes we came across called for the addition of eggs in the béchamel to help hold the sauce together during baking. We thought we would give this a try. To prevent the eggs from coagulating when we combined them with the sauce, we used a common kitchen technique called tempering, in which some of the hot milk mixture is whisked into the eggs before adding it to the rest of the béchamel. This prevented the eggs from scrambling immediately; however, we found that they scrambled as the casserole baked in the oven. To prevent this, we reduced the baking time from 50 minutes in a 350-degree oven to 30 minutes in a 400-degree oven. This allowed the top to brown while keeping the sauce smooth and creamy. We tested differing amounts of eggs and settled on just one egg to our six cups of sauce. Lastly, to enhance the flavor, we added sautéed onion, a healthy bit of garlic, Pecorino Romano cheese, and a touch of nutmeg.

Next it was time to test the pasta. While many recipes call for long pasta such as perciatelli or spaghetti, tasters complained that they were difficult to eat in a casserole. Instead, we turned to more manageable pasta shapes. We tested large and small elbow macaroni, penne, and ziti. The penne and ziti bulked up the size of the dish with unnecessary air pockets, thus eliminating the desired compact layers. They also produced a pasta-heavy casserole that didn't have the creaminess we were after. Large macaroni was a definite improvement, but we wanted each bite to combine all three elements of the casserole evenly. The smaller elbow macaroni maximized the structure of the casserole, and gave tasters multi-flavored bites with every spoonful. To keep the macaroni firm, we reduced the pasta boiling time to five minutes, leaving us with very al dente pasta that became completely tender in the oven.

Our final test concerned the cheese and topping. Tasters thought bread crumbs seemed out of place, but agreed that we needed a finishing touch. Once again, we turned to Pecorino Romano—a light sprinkling was all our pastitsio needed.

Pasta and Ground Lamb Casserole

Pastitsio

SERVES 6 TO 8

The baking dish is very full when it goes into the oven. Just in case it overflows, bake it on a foil-lined baking sheet. Do not substitute low-fat or nonfat milk in the sauce.

2	pounds ground lamb
2	medium onions, minced
	Salt
¼	cup tomato paste
9	garlic cloves, minced or pressed through a garlic press (about 3 tablespoons)
1	tablespoon minced fresh oregano leaves, or 1 teaspoon dried
1	teaspoon ground cinnamon
½	teaspoon fresh grated nutmeg
1	(28-ounce) can crushed tomatoes
3	ounces Pecorino Romano cheese, grated (about 1½ cups)
	Ground black pepper
12	ounces elbow macaroni (3 cups)
4	tablespoons (½ stick) unsalted butter
⅓	cup unbleached all-purpose flour
6	cups whole milk
1	large egg

1. Adjust an oven rack to the middle position and heat the oven to 400 degrees. Cook the lamb in a 12-inch skillet over medium-high heat, breaking the meat into small pieces with a wooden spoon, until no longer pink and the fat has rendered, about 5 minutes. Strain the lamb through a fine-mesh strainer, reserving the drippings.

2. Return 2 tablespoons of the reserved lamb drippings, 1 of the onions, and ½ teaspoon salt to the skillet and cook over medium heat until softened, 5 to 7 minutes. Stir in the tomato paste, 2 tablespoons of the garlic, oregano, cinnamon, and ¼ teaspoon of the nutmeg and cook until fragrant, about 30 seconds. Stir in the drained lamb and crushed tomatoes. Bring to a simmer and cook over medium-low heat until the sauce has thickened, about 5 minutes. Off the heat, stir in ½ cup of the cheese and season with salt and pepper to taste; set aside.

3. Meanwhile, bring 4 quarts water to a boil in a large Dutch oven. Stir in the macaroni and 1 tablespoon salt and cook, stirring often, until just al dente, about 5 minutes. Drain the pasta, rinse under cool water until cold, and leave in the colander.

4. Wipe out the Dutch oven, add the butter, and return to medium heat until melted. Add the remaining onion and ½ teaspoon salt and cook until softened, 5 to 7 minutes. Stir in the remaining tablespoon garlic and cook until fragrant, about 30 seconds. Stir in the flour and cook, stirring constantly, for 1 minute. Gradually whisk in the milk. Bring to a simmer and cook, whisking often, until the sauce thickens and no longer tastes of flour, about 10 minutes.

5. Off the heat, whisk in ½ cup of the cheese and the remaining ¼ teaspoon nutmeg. Season with salt and pepper to taste. Crack the egg into a small bowl. Following the illustration on page 347, whisk about ½ cup of the béchamel into the egg to temper, then slowly whisk the egg mixture back into sauce. Stir in the cooked macaroni until evenly coated with the sauce.

6. Spread half of the macaroni into a 13 by 9-inch baking dish, then spread the lamb mixture evenly over top. Spread remaining macaroni evenly over the lamb and sprinkle with the remaining ½ cup of the cheese. (At this point, the casserole can be covered and refrigerated for up to 2 days.)

7. Place the baking dish on a foil-lined baking sheet and bake until the edges are bubbling and the top is lightly golden, about 30 minutes. (If refrigerated, cover the dish with foil and bake for 30 to 40 minutes, then uncover and continue to bake for 15 to 20 minutes). Let stand for 10 minutes before serving.

CHICKEN IN WALNUT SAUCE

Circassian Chicken

CIRCASSIAN CHICKEN IS A DISH OF TENDER poached chicken served in a creamy walnut sauce and drizzled with bright red chile oil. Commonly prepared on special occasions, and often served at room temperature on the Turkish meze table with wedges of pita bread, this dish acquired its name for the historic region of Circassia, the area between the Black Sea, the Kuban River, and the Caucasus.

This dish allegedly got its name because the color of the sauce is reminiscent of the flaxen hair and fair complexions of the beautiful Circassian women in the sultan's harem during the Ottoman Empire. Pedigree aside, we were intrigued by the rich, nutty, flavors and presentation of this chicken dish and decided to develop our own version of this recipe.

We started with the chicken. Many recipes we found called for bone-in, skin-on chicken pieces, others used whole boneless, skinless chicken breasts, and some called for chunks of breast meat. Tasters immediately disregarded the chicken chunks because they were tough and dry and they did not readily absorb the sauce. Bone-in, skin-on chicken pieces, which were then shredded so they had more surface area to mingle with the sauce, worked much better, although tasters disliked the dark meat in the light-colored sauce. Our favorite were boneless, skinless chicken breasts—they were easier to shred without any skin and bones in the way, and they cooked more quickly than bone-in, skin-on chicken.

With the cut of chicken resolved, we questioned the cooking method. We found our answer in a half sautéing and half poaching method. Using a large skillet, we browned the chicken breasts on just one side. We then flipped the chicken over, added broth to the skillet, reduced the heat, and covered the skillet until the breasts were cooked through. This method yielded just what we were looking for: moist, well-seasoned chicken breasts. In addition, the sautéing step built fond (flavorful brown bits on the bottom of the skillet), which we then deglazed with the broth and used to add flavor to the sauce.

Many traditional versions of this sauce use a mortar and pestle to grind all the ingredients and make the sauce smooth, but we knew right away that we would be using a food processor or blender to speed up the process. Since this dish is mostly about the sauce and the sauce is all about walnuts—they provide the characteristic nutty flavor and creamy texture—fresh, high-quality nuts are crucial to this recipe. (A batch made using walnuts we found in the back of the cupboard yielded an overly bitter, off-tasting, and chalky sauce.) We tried making the sauce with both untoasted and toasted walnuts and tasters were unanimous in their preference for the bold, deep flavor of the toasted nuts.

For background flavor we found that the simple combination of sautéed onion and garlic, spiced with paprika for complexity and cayenne for a little heat, perfectly complemented the nuts. And the broth from cooking the chicken not only facilitated pureeing, it also added depth and chickeny flavor. To give the sauce the right viscosity, we borrowed a traditional Turkish technique in which bread is soaked in water or broth and then pureed with the other ingredients. After we stirred the chicken into the sauce, all that was left to do was work on the garnish.

Typically, this beige-colored dish is served on a platter and drizzled with brick red oil made from paprika and walnut or olive oil. We were bent on keeping with tradition and we tried different amounts of paprika and oil until we landed on a ratio of 1 teaspoon paprika to 1 tablespoon oil. To infuse the oil with the paprika, we heated it just until it sizzled. Most recipes that we came across do not strain the paprika from the oil; however, tasters thought it was chalky when left in so we opted to strain it (see below right for more information). We then drizzled the vibrant red oil over the dish and sprinkled it with a little parsley for even more color and a touch of freshness.

Chicken in Walnut Sauce
Circassian Chicken
SERVES 4 TO 6

This dish is served on special occasions in Turkey, and often as a meze with warm pita bread. While this dish is excellent warm, it is commonly served at room temperature. Be sure to use fresh, high-quality walnuts here.

2   pounds boneless, skinless chicken breasts
    Salt and ground black pepper
3   tablespoons olive oil
3   cups low-sodium chicken broth
2   slices high-quality white sandwich bread, crusts removed and bread torn into pieces
1   medium onion, minced
4   teaspoons sweet paprika
3   medium garlic cloves, minced or pressed through a garlic press (about 1 tablespoon)
½   teaspoon cayenne pepper
2   cups walnuts, toasted (see page 135)
2   tablespoons minced fresh parsley leaves
2   tablespoons Paprika Oil (at right), for drizzling

1. Pat the chicken dry with paper towels and season with salt and pepper. Heat 1 tablespoon of the oil in a 12-inch skillet over medium-high heat until just smoking. Add the chicken and cook until golden brown on the first side, about 4 minutes. Flip the chicken over, reduce the heat to medium-low, and add the broth. Cover and cook until the thickest part of the breast registers 160 degrees on an instant-read thermometer, about 5 minutes.

2. Transfer the chicken to a plate, tent with foil, and let rest for 5 minutes. Strain and reserve the broth. Pour ½ cup of the reserved broth over the bread to moisten; set aside.

3. Wipe out the skillet with paper towels. Add the remaining 2 tablespoons oil to the skillet and heat over medium heat until shimmering. Add the onion and ½ teaspoon salt and cook until softened, 5 to 7 minutes. Stir in the paprika, garlic, and cayenne and cook until fragrant, about 30 seconds.

4. Process the onion mixture, soaked bread, walnuts, and 2 cups of the reserved broth in a food processor (or blender) until smooth, about 20 seconds, scraping down the sides of the bowl. Add additional broth as needed until the sauce is just thicker than the consistency of heavy cream.

5. When the chicken is cool enough to handle, shred it into bite-sized pieces. Toss the chicken with the sauce and season with salt and pepper to taste. (To serve hot, transfer the sauce and chicken mixture to a large skillet and reheat over medium heat.) Sprinkle with the parsley and drizzle with the paprika oil before serving.

PAPRIKA OIL

PAPRIKA OIL POPPED UP IN SEVERAL Turkish recipes we researched including soups and stews, egg dishes, and Chicken in Walnut Sauce (at left). It is usually drizzled over the dish before serving, and we think it is an interesting way to add both color and flavor to a variety of dishes. Here's how to make it.

Paprika Oil
MAKES ¼ CUP

Don't overcook the oil and paprika mixture or it will turn dark and bitter.

¼   cup walnut or olive oil
4   teaspoons sweet or hot paprika

Cook the oil and paprika together in a small skillet over medium-low heat until the oil starts to sizzle, 3 to 4 minutes. Pour the oil through a small strainer lined with a coffee filter into a small bowl. Discard the solids and use the oil. (The oil can be refrigerated for up to 1 month.)

FLAMBÉED SHRIMP WITH TOMATOES, FETA CHEESE, AND OUZO

Garides Saganaki me Tomata, Feta, kai Ouzo

THE COMBINATION OF SHRIMP, TOMATOES, and feta cheese appears in home kitchens, tavernas, and restaurants all over Greece, under a proliferation of names and styles. Sometimes the shrimp are baked or simmered in a sauce, often they are fried in olive oil, and other times they are pan-seared. Whatever form this dish takes, there are a few things that remain constant—plump shrimp are complemented by sweet, fruity tomatoes and briny feta cheese, and there is always enough sauce left over to sop up with bread. With a basic idea of what this dish should be, we set out in the kitchen to figure out the specifics.

Starting with the shrimp, we quickly found that tasters preferred shrimp that were pan-seared because of the caramelized flavor this cooking method produced. Shrimp that were simply simmered in the sauce were bland, while those fried in oil were greasy. From there we uncovered a few important details for pan-searing. First, tasters unanimously favored shrimp that were peeled before being cooked. Peeled shrimp are easier to eat, and unpeeled shrimp fail to pick up the delicious caramelized flavor that pan-searing provides. Second, the shrimp were best cooked in a 12-inch skillet; its large surface area kept the shrimp from overcrowding the pan and steaming—a surefire way to prevent caramelization. Third, oil was the ideal cooking medium, preferred over both a dry pan (which made the shrimp leathery and metallic-tasting) and butter (which tended to burn).

But here we encountered a problem. We found that in the time it took for the shrimp to brown and caramelize properly, they turned out tough and overcooked. Looking for another way to promote browning in a shorter time frame, we thought to add a pinch of sugar to the shrimp. Not only did the sugar caramelize into a nice brown crust, it also accentuated the shrimp's natural sweetness and nicely set off their inherent sea-saltiness.

Even in a 12-inch skillet, 2 pounds of shrimp must be cooked in two batches, or they will steam instead of sear. The trick was to develop a technique that didn't overcook the shrimp. To prevent overcooking, we seared the shrimp on one side, removed the pan from the flame, gave them a quick flip, and transferred them to a bowl while we seared

INGREDIENTS: Frozen Shrimp

Even the most basic markets now sell several kinds of shrimp. We cooked more than 100 pounds to find out just what to look for (and avoid) at the supermarket.

FRESH OR FROZEN?

Because nearly all shrimp are frozen at sea, you have no way of knowing when those "fresh" shrimp in the fish case were thawed (unless you are on very personal terms with your fishmonger). We found that the flavor and texture of thawed shrimp deteriorate after a few days, so you're better off buying frozen.

PEELED OR UNPEELED?

If you think you can dodge some work by buying frozen shrimp that have been peeled, think again. Someone had to thaw those shrimp in order to remove their shells, and they can get pretty banged up when they are refrozen (compare the left and center photos below).

CHECK THE INGREDIENTS

Finally, check the ingredient list. Frozen shrimp are often treated or enhanced with additives such as sodium bisulfate, STP (sodium tripolyphosphate), or salt to prevent darkening (which occurs as the shrimp ages) or to counter "drip loss," the industry term referring to the amount of water in the shrimp that is lost as it thaws. We have found that treated shrimp have a strange translucency and an unpleasant texture and suggest that you avoid them (see the right photo below). Look for the bags of frozen shrimp that list shrimp as the only ingredient.

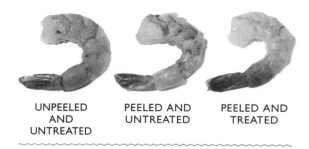

UNPEELED AND UNTREATED   PEELED AND UNTREATED   PEELED AND TREATED

the second batch, moved them to the bowl, then built the sauce. As soon as the sauce was finished cooking (the shrimp were now near room temperature), we tossed them back into the pan and let the residual heat work its magic. After about a minute, all of the shrimp were perfectly cooked and piping hot.

With the shrimp resolved, we turned our attention to the sauce. We wanted to limit the vegetables to a select few to keep preparation brief—nothing adds to prep time like cleaning and cutting a long list of vegetables. Onions seemed like a natural for depth and body. For the tomatoes, the canned diced variety kept things easy and flavorful; skinning, seeding, and chopping fresh tomatoes took too much time, and the bland flavor and mealy texture of fresh supermarket tomatoes simply couldn't match that of the canned. In addition, we could reserve a little of the juice from the diced tomatoes to add to the sauce, further emphasizing the tomato flavor.

As for flavoring the dish, a healthy dose of garlic and red pepper flakes gave the shrimp and sauce a welcome kick—we sautéed them briefly with the onions to allow their flavors to mellow just slightly. A handful of coarsely chopped fresh herbs seemed apropos as well, and after testing a slew of options, tasters favored a simple combination of oregano and parsley. The oregano lent the dish a decidedly Greek edge while the parsley—added just before serving—contributed a fresh hit of color.

Last, but certainly not least, was the feta cheese. While many recipes simmer the feta in the sauce so it breaks down, we preferred it crumbled and scattered over the finished dish so it melted slightly yet remained distinct. The cheese's salty, briny bite was a great foil to the sweetness of the shrimp and the fruitiness of the tomato. We normally shy away from combining cheese and fish, but in this instance, it was a perfect pairing. We were now finished with our dish, but a few tasters thought it was still missing a little something. A healthy shot of ouzo—a licorice flavored spirit popular throughout Greece—sprinkled over the finished dish and then flambéed was the perfect accent.

TWO WAYS TO FLAMBÉ

A. To flambé on a gas stove, add the ouzo to the pan, tilting the pan toward the flame to ignite it and then shaking the skillet.

B. To flambé on an electric stove, add the ouzo to the pan, wave a lit match over the pan until the ouzo ignites, and then shake the skillet.

Flambéed Shrimp with Tomatoes, Feta Cheese, and Ouzo

Garides Saganaki me Tomata, Feta, kai Ouzo

SERVES 4 TO 6

Serve this dish with warm pita bread or crusty bread to sop up the sauce. Ouzo is an anise-flavored liqueur that is served as an aperitif throughout Greece; Pernod can be substituted for the ouzo. When flambéing the ouzo, be sure to tie back any loose hair and roll up your sleeves.

¼	cup extra-virgin olive oil
2	pounds extra-large shrimp (21 to 25 per pound), peeled and deveined
	Salt and ground black pepper
⅛	teaspoon sugar
1	medium onion, minced
6	medium garlic cloves, minced or pressed through a garlic press (about 2 tablespoons)
1	tablespoon minced fresh oregano leaves, or ½ teaspoon dried
¼–½	teaspoon red pepper flakes

1   (28-ounce) can diced tomatoes, drained with
    ½ cup juice reserved

¼   cup ouzo

4   ounces feta cheese, crumbled (about 1 cup)

2   tablespoons minced fresh parsley leaves

1. Heat 1 tablespoon of the oil in a 12-inch skillet over high heat until just smoking. Meanwhile, pat the shrimp dry with paper towels and season with salt, pepper, and sugar. Add half of the shrimp to the skillet in a single layer and cook, without stirring, until the bottoms of the shrimp turn spotty brown, about 30 seconds. Off the heat, flip the shrimp over, then transfer to a medium bowl and repeat with 1 more tablespoon oil and the remaining shrimp.

2. Add the remaining 2 tablespoons oil, onion, and ½ teaspoon salt to the skillet and cook over medium heat until the onion is softened, 5 to 7 minutes. Stir in the garlic, oregano, and red pepper flakes and cook until fragrant, about 30 seconds. Stir in the tomatoes and ½ cup of their juice and cook until thickened slightly, about 2 minutes.

3. Stir the reserved shrimp and accumulated juices and ouzo into the skillet. Following the illustrations on page 362, ignite the ouzo and shake the skillet until the flames subside. Sprinkle with the feta and parsley before serving.

DEVEINING SHRIMP

Hold the shelled shrimp between your thumb and forefinger and cut down the length of its back, about ⅛ to ¼ inch deep, with a sharp paring knife. If the shrimp has a vein, it will be exposed and can be pulled out easily. Once you have freed the vein with the tip of a paring knife, just touch the knife to a paper towel and the vein will slip off the knife and stick to the towel.

OUZO

Ouzo is a licorice-flavored liqueur that is served as an aperitif throughout Greece in sidewalk cafes and special ouzo bars called *ouzeria* with meze. It is distilled from grapes, raisins, figs, and sugar, and then infused with various herbs and spices, such as coriander, anise, and mastic (a woodsy, musty, and vanilla-flavored spice made from the crystallized resinous sap of a tree in the pistachio family). Ouzo can vary greatly from bottle to bottle in terms of sweetness and complexity, as well as in color—it can range from clear liquid to black. We like to sip ouzo on its own, but it is also an excellent way to flavor dishes, such as Marinated Olives (page 333) and Flambéed Shrimp with Tomatoes, Ouzo, and Feta Cheese (page 362).

CHARCOAL-GRILLED SQUID

Kalamarakia

THE COUNTRY OF GREECE BOASTS OVER 8,000 miles of coastline and more than 220 inhabited islands, so it is no surprise that fresh seafood is a mainstay of the cuisine. After flipping through many Greek cookbooks, we were intrigued by the abundance of squid, an ingredient we rarely see here in this country unless it's batter-fried. Though squid is also fried in Greece, it is often prepared in myriad other ways, whether it be baked, stuffed, braised, sautéed, or grilled. We wanted to explore a way of cooking squid that would be new to us, and the idea of simple, crispy grilled squid tossed with a lemony vinaigrette appealed tremendously to our appetites.

Though grilling squid was new to us, we already knew a little something about the pitfalls of cooking this mollusk. We find that if lightly cooked, squid remains chewy but tender. However, if cooked for more than a few minutes, squid becomes tough and rubbery. Squid cooked 10 or 15 minutes is so tough it is nearly inedible. Yet, if braised in a tomato sauce or other liquid for a long time, squid will become tender again. This process may not take a full hour (a half hour will usually do), but the general rule holds true.

Since grilling squid for half an hour is not an option (it would be reduced to ashes), we knew that quick cooking was a must. After much testing, we found that squid cooks in as little as three minutes over a hot fire. In our tests, tasters consistently preferred smaller squid (no more than four inches long). These squid were more tender than larger specimens.

To promote maximum browning and even cooking, we found it best to slit the squid bodies lengthwise and then open the bodies to create a single rectangular piece of squid. These squid "steaks" lie flat on the grill, so there's no need to worry about the inside cooking more slowly than the exterior.

Small tentacles are delicious grilled. However, they tend to fall through the cooking grate.

Skewering them solved this problem. The tentacles taste best when quite crisp. Since they don't seem to toughen as quickly as the bodies, we found that they can be grilled for an extra minute or two without danger.

Most markets sell cleaned squid that can be ready to grill in just a few minutes. If you want to take the time, you can buy uncleaned squid. However, the cleaning process is tedious and time-consuming. While uncleaned squid may seem like a bargain at the market, there's a tremendous amount of waste (almost 50 percent), so by the time you have cleaned it, the difference in cost between cleaned and uncleaned squid is negligible.

After grilling, we sliced the squid bodies into strips and tossed them, along with the tentacles, with a simple vinaigrette made from extra-virgin olive oil and lemon juice, accented by parsley for freshness and a little bit of garlic for bite. As soon as we took one bite of the crispy, tender squid drenched in the zesty lemon vinaigrette, we got the feeling we had just been transported to a beachside taverna on a Greek island.

CLEANING AND PREPARING SQUID

1. Reach into the body with your fingers and grasp as much of the innards as you can. Gently pull out the heart and innards.

2. You may have to make a second attempt to remove the hard, plastic-like quill; it will come out easily once you find it.

3. Cut the tentacles just above the squid's eye. Be careful of the black ink, which does stain. Discard the innards.

4. Check the tentacles for a beak. Squeeze out and discard the beak if necessary. Reserve the tentacles.

5. The thin, membrane-like skin on the squid body is edible but can be easily peeled off for a white appearance.

6. Use a pair of kitchen shears to cut lengthwise down one side of the squid body. Open the squid and flatten into a single piece.

Charcoal-Grilled Squid with Lemon and Garlic

Kalamarakia

SERVES 4

Be sure to use small squid (with bodies 3 to 4 inches in length) because they cook more quickly and are more tender than large squid. Cleaned squid saves a great deal of time; we suggest using it if you can find it. If not, follow the illustrations on page 364, which show how to clean squid. It takes about 2¾ pounds of uncleaned squid to yield 1½ pounds of cleaned squid.

5   tablespoons extra-virgin olive oil
2   tablespoons juice from 1 lemon
2   teaspoons minced fresh parsley leaves
1   medium garlic clove, minced or pressed
    through a garlic press (about 1 teaspoon)
    Salt and ground black pepper
1½ pounds small squid, cleaned and prepared
    according to the illustrations on page 364
1   lemon, cut into wedges (for serving)

1. Light a large chimney starter filled with charcoal (about 6 quarts) and allow to burn until all the charcoal is covered with a layer of fine gray ash.

2. Meanwhile, combine 3 tablespoons of the oil, lemon juice, parsley, garlic, ½ teaspoon salt, and ¼ teaspoon pepper in a large bowl; set aside. Using scissors, butterfly the squid bodies following the illustrations on page 364. Pat the bodies and tentacles dry with paper towels, then toss with the remaining 2 tablespoons oil and season with salt and pepper. Thread the tentacles onto skewers.

3. Build a hot fire by spreading the coals evenly over ⅔ of the grill bottom (confining the coals to a smaller space makes for a hotter fire). Set the cooking grate in place, cover the grill with the lid, and let the grate heat up, about 5 minutes. Use a grill brush to scrape the cooking grate clean. The grill is ready when the coals are hot (you can hold your hand 5 inches above the cooking grate for just 2 seconds).

4. Lay the squid bodies and tentacle skewers directly over the hot coals. Grill the bodies on both sides until curled, opaque, and lightly browned on the edges, about 1½ minutes per side. Transfer the bodies to a large platter, but continue to grill the tentacles until the ends are brown and crisp, 1 to 2 minutes longer, flipping them as needed.

5. Transfer the bodies to a cutting board and slice them into thin strips. Remove the tentacles from the skewers. Toss the grilled squid with the vinaigrette and serve immediately with the lemon wedges.

➤ VARIATION

Gas-Grilled Squid with Lemon and Garlic
Heat the grill with all the burners set to high and the lid down until very hot, about 15 minutes. Scrape the cooking grate clean with a grill brush. Leave all the burners on high. Follow the recipe for Charcoal-Grilled Squid, grilling the squid as directed in step 4, with the lid down and adding 1 to 2 minutes to the cooking time.

EQUIPMENT: Skewers

There can't be much "performance" difference between one pointed stick and another, can there? Well, we thought the same thing when we started to test skewers. Once we surveyed the field, our attitude changed. It really is possible to buy bad skewers.

First of all, forget what most grilling books say: if you're cooking over very high heat, bamboo skewers will burn and break apart—no matter how long you soak them in water beforehand. We had better luck with metal skewers. They may cost more, but they're reusable and they can handle the heartiest kebabs without bending or breaking.

Not all metal skewers are created equal, however. We had a tough time flipping food on round skewers—the skewer itself turned just fine, but the food stayed in place. Flat skewers proved much more effective. Double-pronged skewers turned the food, but some were flimsy and most had a tendency to twist out of their parallel configuration. Other models were so bulky that they severed the meat in half.

Our choice: any flat, thin metal skewer will do. We particularly like Norpro's 12-inch stainless-steel skewers (six skewers for $10), which are just 3/16-inch thick.

BEST SKEWERS

We like flat, thin metal skewers for kebabs, like Norpro's 12-inch stainless-steel skewers, which are just 3/16-inch thick.

Grilling 101

GRILLING IS A VERSATILE TECHNIQUE THAT INVOLVES COOKING FOOD DIRECTLY OVER HEAT, WHETHER generated by charcoal or gas. The goal is to cook the food quickly over a lot of heat. We prefer the flavor that charcoal adds to grilled food; however, there is no disputing that a gas grill is easier to set up. We leave the choice of grill up to you, and we provide directions in our recipes for both charcoal and gas grills.

LIGHTING THE GRILL

For Charcoal: The easiest way we've found to light a charcoal fire is using a chimney starter (also called a flue starter). To use this simple device, fill the bottom section with crumpled newspaper, set the starter on the bottom grate, and fill the chimney with charcoal (a large starter holds about six quarts of charcoal briquettes, which is enough to make all the fires listed below). When the newspaper is lit, the flames ignite the charcoal. Once the coals are coated with an even layer of fine gray ash, they are ready to be turned out into the grill.

For Gas: To preheat a gas grill, turn all the burners on high with the lid down for 15 minutes.

CLEANING AND OILING A COOKING GRATE

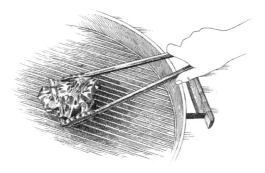

Oiling your cooking grate is a must for preventing fish, burgers, and other foods from sticking to the grill. But the cooking grate should be cleaned before it is oiled. Heat the cooking grate, then use a grill brush or fashion your own grill brush with a crumpled wad of aluminum foil and long-handled tongs.

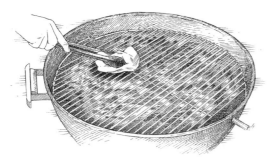

Once your cooking grate is clean, a slick of oil over the grate will further prevent food from sticking. Simply dip a wad of paper towels in vegetable oil, grasp the oiled towels with a pair of long-handled tongs, and rub the oil over the hot cooking grate.

GAUGING THE TEMPERATURE OF YOUR GRILL

Use the chart below to determine the intensity of the fire. We use the terms "hot fire," "medium-hot fire," and so forth in our grilling recipes. To take the temperature of the fire, hold your hand 5 inches above the cooking grate and count how many seconds you can comfortably leave it in place.

INTENSITY OF FIRE	TIME YOU CAN HOLD YOUR HAND 5 INCHES ABOVE GRATE
HOT	2 seconds
MEDIUM-HOT	3 to 4 seconds
MEDIUM	5 to 6 seconds
MEDIUM-LOW	7 seconds

PREVENTING FLARE-UPS FROM THE GRILL

Flare-ups are caused primarily by fats melting into the fire, but you don't need to let a grease fire get out of control and ruin your meal. As a precaution, keep a squirt bottle or plant mister filled with water near the grill. At the first sign of flames, try to pull foods to a cool part of the grill and douse the flames with water.

SHISH KEBABS

THE BACKYARD BARBECUE ALWAYS SEEMS so familiar, so American. But grilling is a technique that is used in almost every country around the globe. Shish kebab—which translates to "meat roasted on skewers or a spit"—is perhaps the most recognized dish from Turkey, and it is possibly their greatest "barbecue" dish.

Traditionally made with lamb, in recent years shish kebab has also come to include poultry, pork, and beef, as well as vegetables such as onions, bell peppers, mushrooms, and cherry tomatoes. Here in the test kitchen, we are fans of all types of meat kebabs as well as kebabs with vegetables. When done right, the meat is well browned and the vegetables are crisp and tender. Everything is perfumed with the flavor of smoke.

But timing can be tricky—a kebab's components cook at different rates and either the vegetables are still raw when the meat is cooked perfectly to medium-rare or the meat is long overdone by the time the vegetables have been cooked properly. Our efforts to resolve this dilemma led us to explore which vegetables serve the kebab best. Getting the grill temperature just right was another challenge. Too hot and the kebabs charred on the outside without being fully cooked; too cool and they cooked without the benefit of flavorful browning.

Many vegetables don't cook through by the time the meat reaches the right temperature. This can be particularly ugly if you're using eggplant, mushrooms, or zucchini. We tried precooking the vegetables, but they turned slimy and were difficult to skewer. We thought about cooking them separately alongside the meat on the grill, but that's just not kebabs. Other vegetables, such as cherry tomatoes, initially looked great on the skewer but had a hard time staying put once cooked.

As we worked our way through various vegetables, we came up with two that work well within the constraints of this particular cooking method. Red onions and bell peppers have a similar texture and cook through at about the same rate. When cut fairly small, these two vegetables were the perfect accompaniments to the meat, adding flavor and color to the kebab without demanding any special attention.

As for the meat, we found that beef, pork, lamb, and chicken all make great kebabs. But after some experimentation, we learned that not all cuts worked equally well. For beef, we prefer to use blade steak, a very flavorful (and inexpensive) cut, or top sirloin. With pork, boneless, center-cut pork chops work best because they have good flavor and very little fat. With lamb, the leg is our favorite cut, for both flavor and tenderness. Look for a small leg of lamb or a small roast, if possible. As for chicken kebabs, although white breast meat can be used, we prefer the juicier and more flavorful boneless, skinless thighs. (If you choose to cook both white and dark meats, do not mix them on the same skewer since they cook at different rates.)

What these handsome kebabs needed now was seasoning, so we tried a variety of spices, dry rubs, and marinades on the meat. Spice rubs tasted good but left the surface of the meat chalky and dry;

PREPARING ONIONS FOR KEBABS

1. Trim off the stem and root ends and cut the onion into quarters. Peel the 3 outer layers of the onion away from the core.

2. Working with the outer layers only, cut each quarter in half—from pole to pole—into 3 equal strips.

3. Cut each of the 12 strips crosswise into 3 pieces. You should have thirty-six 3-layer stacks of separate pieces of onion.

the kebabs just aren't on the fire long enough for their juices to mix with the dried spices and form a glaze. Marinades, on the other hand, added a layer of moisture that kept the kebabs from drying out on the grill while their flavors penetrated the meat.

Two hours in the marinade was sufficient time to achieve some flavor, but it took a good eight hours for these flavors to really sink in. Marinating for 12 hours, or overnight, was even better. Then we backtracked and decided to reserve a portion of the unused marinade, spike it with lemon juice, and pour it over the grilled meat before serving for a final hit of flavor.

Charcoal-Grilled Shish Kebabs
SERVES 6

For attractive skewers, use different colors of bell peppers. Serve with Cucumber, Garlic, and Yogurt Sauce (page 336) or Turkish Nut Sauce (page 338).

½	cup olive oil
10	large fresh mint leaves
1½	teaspoons chopped fresh rosemary
3	medium garlic cloves, peeled
2	tablespoons juice plus 1½ teaspoons grated zest from 1 lemon
1	teaspoon salt
⅛	teaspoon ground black pepper
2	pounds beef, pork, lamb, or chicken, trimmed and cut into 1½-inch chunks
1	large red onion, cut into ¾-inch cubes (see the illustrations on page 367)
3	medium bell peppers, cored, seeded, and cut into 1-inch pieces

1. Process the oil, mint, rosemary, garlic, lemon zest, salt, and pepper in a food processor until smooth, about 1 minute. Transfer ¼ cup of the marinade to an airtight container, stir in the lemon juice, and refrigerate until needed. Combine the remaining marinade and meat in a zipper-lock bag and refrigerate for at least 2 hours or up to 24 hours.

2. Light a large chimney starter filled with charcoal (about 6 quarts) and allow to burn until all the charcoal is covered with a layer of fine gray ash.

3. Meanwhile, using twelve 12-inch metal skewers, thread each with 1 piece of meat, an onion cube, and 2 pieces of pepper. Repeat this sequence two more times, placing a piece of meat on the end of each skewer.

4. Build a hot fire by spreading the coals evenly over ⅔ of the grill bottom (confining the coals to a smaller space makes for a hotter fire). Set the cooking grate in place, cover the grill with the lid, and let the grate heat up, about 5 minutes. Use a grill brush to scrape the cooking grate clean. The grill is ready when the coals are hot (you can hold your hand 5 inches above the cooking grate for just 2 seconds).

5. Lay the kebabs directly over the hot coals and grill, turning the skewers occasionally, until well browned all over and the beef or lamb is cooked to medium-rare, 7 to 8 minutes, or the chicken or pork is just cooked through, about 8 to 12 minutes. Transfer the kebabs to a serving platter, pour the reserved marinade over the top, and let rest for 5 to 10 minutes before serving.

➤ VARIATION
Gas-Grilled Shish Kebabs
Heat the grill with all burners set to high and the lid down until very hot, about 15 minutes. Scrape the cooking grate clean with a grill brush. Leave all the burners on high. Follow the recipe for Charcoal-Grilled Shish Kebabs, grilling the kebabs as directed in step 5, with the lid down.

BAKLAVA
BAKLAVA IS A CROSS-CULTURAL SWEETMEAT phenomenon. It is commonly regarded as a Greek pastry but accepted as Turkish in origin, and progenitors are said to be Assyrian. Yet the question remains unanswered as to why, in this country, in this modern age, baklava, so lavish with butter, sugar, and nuts, is so often a lamentable experience. Sad, soggy, punishingly sweet, and utterly lifeless specimens are ubiquitous. Extremely rare is baklava like you find in Greece and Turkey—crisp, flaky, buttery lozenges, light yet rich, filled with fragrant nuts and spices, and sweetened just assertively enough to pair

perfectly with a Turkish coffee (see page 372 for information on making Turkish coffee).

We opted to develop a Greek-style baklava, sweetened in part by honey and flavored with spices such as cinnamon and cloves.

Over the course of three days, we plodded through representative recipes to a disappointing end. Though the ground rules for all of the recipes were the same—buttered phyllo sheets are layered into a baking dish with nuts, the assemblage baked and then soaked in sugar syrup—the outcomes were vastly different. Some syrups were thin and watery, others viscous and chewy. The baklava was either over-spiced, it lacked cohesiveness, or had a moist, pasty nut filling that made the baklava heavy and soggy. Clearly, we had a challenge ahead of us.

Prepared phyllo is sold boxed in the supermarket freezer section (homemade phyllo was out of the question) and the phyllo sheets conveniently yield perfectly sized pieces for a straight-sided 13 by 9-inch baking pan. Phyllo has a reputation for being difficult to work with in its uncooked state. Indeed, the paper-thin sheets are quick to dry out and become brittle. Despite recipes' advice to use one or another protective covering, we found that during baklava assembly the phyllo was best kept under a sheet of plastic wrap, then covered with a damp kitchen towel as added insurance (for more information about phyllo see page 344).

Using a pound of very finely chopped nuts (about 4 cups), a full 1-pound box of phyllo (some recipes called for only ½ or ¾ pound), and a 13 by 9-inch baking pan, we started building the baklava. Pieces of baklava with only one thick, central layer of nuts tended to split in two (they lacked cohesion). With the nuts divided into two layers separated by several sheets of phyllo, the pieces held together better, but the baklava composed of three relatively thin nut layers (we reduced the nuts by 4 ounces) between four sections of phyllo had the superior structure. Our final recipe required nearly the entire pound of phyllo.

We immediately dismissed pecans as too sweet and too American. Hazelnuts need to be skinned and were not well liked by tasters. Most everyone also objected to an all-walnut filling (too harsh and bitter) or an all-almond filling (rather nondescript). Eight ounces of almonds and 4 ounces of walnuts (chopped very fine—almost ground—in a food processor) was a good blend. Toasting the nuts was unnecessary because the nuts cook thoroughly in the time it takes to bake the baklava. We tried various spice combinations and the winner consisted of 1¼ teaspoons warm, familiar ground cinnamon and ¼ teaspoon deep, rich ground cloves.

Must the butter be clarified, as many recipes suggested? (To learn more about clarified butter, see "Clarified Butter," page 371.) The surface of the baklava made with whole butter was splotchy brown, while that made with clarified butter colored uniformly. It also had a cleaner, sweeter flavor. And because the water had been extracted from the clarified butter, the phyllo layers were slightly flakier and crisper.

We tried, as one recipe suggested, buttering every other sheet of phyllo, but this resulted in a dry baklava that was chalky and gritty. Clearly, every sheet needed a coating of butter. Some recipes advocated dousing the assembled baklava with a half cup or more of melted butter, a step that we found absurdly excessive. Yet it turned out that this step was indeed essential to help prevent (though not eliminate) the curling of the uppermost phyllo sheets during baking. We, however, opted for a more modest 4 tablespoons of butter.

After assembly but before baking, the baklava must be cut into the familiar diamond-shaped pieces. Merely scoring the layers, as some recipes suggest, was a waste of time; the baklava needs to be fully cut. A serrated knife or a bread knife, used with a gentle sawing motion, made the easiest and cleanest cuts, but even with a good knife, this step does take a bit of patience (and perseverance).

A low 300-degree oven and a slow 75- to 90-minute baking time proved best. The top and bottom phyllo layers colored evenly and the nuts became golden and fragrant. Even with shorter baking times, higher temperatures tended to over-darken both the bottom pastry layer and the nuts.

Except for a few tablespoons of sugar mixed into the nut filling, the sugar in baklava is introduced after baking in the form of a syrup. The syrup is absorbed by the bottom layers of pastry and nuts, which become moist and cohesive.

Honey is an essential ingredient in a Greek-style baklava, but tasters found its flavor to be cloying and overpowering when used in large quantities. One-third of a cup of a mild-flavored honey such as orange blossom was the ideal amount; 1¼ cups of granulated sugar supplemented the sweetness.

The amount of water in the syrup determines its viscosity, a key factor in the moistness and crispness of the pastry. If the syrup is too thin and watery, the pastry becomes wet and soggy. If the syrup is too thick, the baklava resists absorption and the bottom layers are sticky and heavy. Three-quarters of a cup of water was the right amount, combined with 1 tablespoon of lemon juice to spruce up the flavor.

Taking full advantage of the fact that the syrup must be heated to dissolve the sugar, we tried infusing it with spices, a step common to most recipes. A few strips of lemon zest, a cinnamon stick, several cloves, and a pinch of salt were all welcome additions. They added a full, soft flavor and a rich, heady fragrance.

Finally, we needed to determine how to introduce the syrup to the baklava. Some recipes assert that for best absorption, room-temperature syrup must be poured over hot baklava as it emerges from the oven. Others take the opposing stance—that the baklava must be room temperature and the syrup hot. Hot baklava joined by cool syrup clearly gave the individual pieces superior cohesion, moistness, and texture. When pouring the syrup over the baklava, we poured the majority into the cuts so as not to soften the top layers of crisped pastry. We lightly drizzled the last couple of tablespoons of syrup over the entire surface, which gave the baklava a glistening sheen and a tackiness to which a nut garnish could adhere.

As if the process of making perfect baklava weren't arduous enough, it really should be left to stand overnight—the flavors meld and mellow and the texture becomes more unified. But take consolation in the thought that it holds for upward of a week (so long as humidity doesn't ruin its crispness) and that its lavishness allows for it to be consumed only one piece at a time.

Baklava

MAKES 32 TO 40 PIECES

Make sure that the phyllo is fully thawed before use; don't thaw it in the microwave, but let it sit it in the refrigerator overnight or on the countertop for four to five hours. For more information on working with phyllo dough, see page 344. A straight-sided traditional (not nonstick) metal baking pan works best for making baklava. If you don't have one, a glass baking dish will work. When assembling, use the nicest, most intact phyllo sheets for the bottom and top layers; use sheets with tears in the middle layers, where their imperfections will go unnoticed. If, after assembly, you have remaining clarified butter, store it in an airtight container in the refrigerator; it can be used for sautéing.

SUGAR SYRUP

1¼	cups sugar
¾	cup water
⅓	cup honey
1	4-inch-long strip zest from 1 lemon (see the illustration on page 346)
1	tablespoon juice from 1 lemon
1	cinnamon stick
5	whole cloves
⅛	teaspoon salt

NUT FILLING

8	ounces blanched slivered almonds (about 2½ cups)
4	ounces walnuts (about 1 cup)
1¼	teaspoons ground cinnamon
¼	teaspoon ground cloves
2	tablespoons sugar
⅛	teaspoon salt

PASTRY AND BUTTER

1½	cups (3 sticks) unsalted butter, clarified (see instructions on page 370), melted and cooled slightly (about 1 cup), plus more for buttering the pan
1	pound (14 by 9-inch) phyllo, thawed (see note)

1. **FOR THE SUGAR SYRUP:** Bring the syrup ingredients to a boil in a small saucepan over medium-high heat, stirring occasionally. Transfer to a 2-cup measuring cup, set aside to cool, then discard the spices and lemon zest. (The cooled syrup can be refrigerated in an airtight container up to 4 days.)

2. **FOR THE NUT FILLING:** Pulse the almonds and walnuts in a food processor until very finely chopped, about 25 pulses. Transfer the nuts to a medium bowl and reserve 1 tablespoon for garnish. Stir the cinnamon, cloves, sugar, and salt into the nuts.

3. **TO ASSEMBLE AND BAKE:** Adjust an oven rack to the lower-middle position and heat the oven to 300 degrees. Unwrap and unfold the phyllo and carefully smooth it with your hands to flatten. Cover with plastic wrap, then a damp kitchen towel. Butter a 13 by 9-inch baking pan.

4. Following the illustrations on page 372, place 1 phyllo sheet in the bottom of the prepared pan and brush with the butter until completely coated. Repeat with 7 more phyllo sheets, brushing each with butter. Evenly distribute about 1 cup of the nut filling over the phyllo. Cover the filling with 1 more phyllo sheet and dab with butter (the phyllo will slip if butter is brushed on). Repeat with 5 more phyllo sheets, brushing each with butter. Continue layering with 1 more cup nut filling, 6 sheets phyllo, and the remaining 1 cup nut filling. Finish with 8 to 10 sheets phyllo, brushing each except the final sheet with butter.

5. Working from the center outward, use the palms of your hands to compress the layers and press out any air pockets. Spoon 4 tablespoons of the butter on the top layer and brush to cover the surface. Use a serrated knife with a pointed tip in a gentle sawing motion to cut the baklava into diamonds, rotating the pan as necessary to complete the cuts. Bake until golden and crisped, about 1½ hours, rotating the baking pan halfway through baking.

6. Immediately after removing the baklava from the oven, pour the cooled syrup over the cut lines until about 2 tablespoons remain (the syrup will sizzle when it hits the hot pan). Drizzle the remaining syrup over the surface. Garnish the center of each piece with a pinch of the reserved ground nuts. Cool to room temperature on a wire rack, about 3 hours, then cover with foil and let stand at least 8 hours before serving. (Once cooled, the baklava can be served, but the flavor and texture improve if left to stand at least 8 hours. The baklava can be wrapped tightly in foil and kept at room temperature up to 10 days.)

SCIENCE: Clarified Butter

Butter has a lot of fat, but it also contains—in small amounts—proteins, carbohydrates, and minerals (the milk solids), as well as water, all of which are distributed throughout the fat in an emulsion. Usually these residual ingredients are welcome flavor bonuses, but in certain rare applications, such as baklava, these extras become more nuisance than nuance and should be removed in a process called clarifying.

To clarify butter, it is heated to break the emulsion, which causes its different components to separate according to density and chemical predisposition. White foam collects at the top; this consists of air that has been encapsulated by milk solids. Directly below the foam lies the butterfat; by law, the fat must make up 80 percent of the total content of the butter. Underneath the fat lies a thin layer that includes proteins and phospholipids. Finally, at the bottom lies the aqueous layer; this is predominantly water along with some dissolved material.

The simplest method of clarifying butter is to cut it into 1-inch chunks, then melt it in a small saucepan over medium-low heat, which takes about 10 minutes. Once taken off the heat, the butter is allowed to settle for 10 minutes and is then skimmed with a soupspoon to clarify it.

Butter can also be clarified using a microwave oven. Start by cutting the butter into 1-inch chunks, then place it in a microwave-safe bowl covered with plastic in the microwave at 50 percent power for about five minutes. Let the butter settle for 10 minutes, then skim off and discard the foam on the surface. Let the butter cool to room temperature, then cover it with plastic wrap and refrigerate until the fat solidifies, which takes at least four hours. The solidified butter can then be popped out of the bowl (where the water and solids will remain) and its damp bottom dried with paper towels.

ASSEMBLING BAKLAVA

1. Cover the phyllo to keep it moist.

2. Place 8 phyllo sheets in a buttered baking dish, brushing each sheet with butter.

3. Spread 1 cup of the nut filling over the bottom layer of phyllo. Place 6 phyllo sheets over the nut layer, brushing each sheet with butter. Spread another 1 cup nut filling over the phyllo.

4. Repeat with 6 more sheets buttered phyllo and the remaining 1 cup nut filling. Finish with 8 to 10 more sheets of buttered phyllo.

5. Using your hands, compress the layers to remove air pockets, working from the center outward.

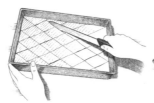

6. Cut the baklava into diamonds using a serrated knife, then bake.

7. Pour the syrup over the cut lines of the baked baklava.

8. Garnish each piece of baklava with chopped nuts.

TURKISH COFFEE
Türk Kahvesi

IN TURKEY, COFFEE IS MORE THAN JUST A caffeine fix—it is a ritual, shared in coffee-houses and homes among friends and family. Traditionally, Turkish coffee is made in a pot with a long-handle called an ibrik or cevze and it is served in demitasse cups. Very finely ground coffee (similar to espresso), sugar, and sometimes cardamom are boiled in water, in several stages, and then the mixture, grounds and all, is served. The thick, strong coffee is sipped, and when it's gone, the grounds left in the bottom of the cup are turned out onto the saucer, and fortunes are told using the patterns that they make.

We wanted to share in this ceremony here in the test kitchen. And while we didn't quite master the art of reading the future in the coffee grounds (you will have to consult with a Turkish expert for that), we were able to come up with a formula for a great cup of Turkish coffee using finely ground espresso and a small saucepan. (If you happen to have Turkish coffee and a Turkish coffee pot, you can use those instead.)

To MAKE TURKISH COFFEE: For four servings, bring 4 tablespoons finely ground espresso, 1 tablespoon sugar, and ½ cup cold water to a boil in a small saucepan over medium-high heat. When the coffee starts to rise in the pot, remove it from the heat, stir, and return it to the heat. Repeat this process two more times. After the last rising, spoon the foam into 4 demitasse cups and pour the coffee over the top. Serve immediately.

9

RUSSIA AND EASTERN EUROPE

EGGPLANT CAVIAR

Baklazhannaya Ikra

BAKLAZHANNAYA IKRA, EGGPLANT CAVIAR, IS a staple in both Russian and Georgian households and is traditionally known as poor man's caviar because the tiny seeds in the eggplant resemble caviar eggs. Similar to Baba Ghanoush (page 404), eggplant caviar is a savory spread served with hearty brown bread as an hors d'oeuvre. However, rather than the smoky eggplant flavor that is characteristic of baba ghanoush, it has a simple, earthy flavor that concentrates on the pure richness of the eggplant.

After poring over a number of recipes from Russian and Georgian cookbooks, we found the ingredient lists to be fairly consistent: eggplant, garlic, onion, olive oil, and either lemon juice or red wine vinegar, and finally, some type of tomato product. After a few batches of eggplant caviar we realized the key to success would be the cooking of the eggplant. We were after smooth and silky eggplant caviar, with balanced acidity, and one that allowed the eggplant to remain the star ingredient.

The authentic recipes we found either roasted the eggplant in the oven or cooked it on the stovetop. We started by testing three cooking methods: roasting, broiling, and sautéing diced eggplant. Tasters liked the effect of roasting versus broiling and sautéing. Broiling the eggplant charred the edges before the interior was done, and while sautéing was somewhat better, the method took far too long and the flavor seemed lackluster. Roasting, however, intensified the eggplant flavor and gave the vegetable a silky consistency. With roasting as our chosen method, we decided to dig a little deeper into the best way to roast the eggplant.

We had been roasting the eggplant whole; however, in our research we found that some recipes cut the eggplants in half lengthwise, scored the flesh side, and roasted them flesh side down. We did a side-by-side test of these two methods, and we roasted a diced eggplant to see if we could cut down on the cooking time. The diced eggplant did not work well; cooking toughened the edges, leaving chewy bits in the spread. Although eggplant roasted whole was fine, even better was the eggplant that was cut in half and scored. Eggplant prepared this way released its liquid more quickly during the roasting process and thereby concentrated the eggplant flavor. The slight caramelizing effect added a bit of depth, too. With a few more tests, we settled on cooking the eggplant in a 400-degree oven for about one hour until the skin was shriveled. We then scooped out the hot soft interior that now resembled pulp and let it drain to get rid of excess liquid.

Eggplant has a reputation for sometimes tasting bitter and recipes for other types of eggplant dishes call for removing the seeds. This was problematic for two reasons. First, the caviar-like seeds are what give this dish its name. Second, the eggplants we were using were packed with seeds—it would be incredibly wasteful to discard all of that flesh. When developing our baba ghanoush recipe, we compared versions made with and without the seeds and found that neither version was bitter, so there was no reason to discard the seeds. This was good news for our purposes here.

With our eggplant cooked to perfection, we now turned to the other flavoring ingredients in the dish. Many recipes we reviewed fold in raw garlic and onion, but we found their harsh bite out of place in this smooth, silky dip. Instead, we sautéed both to mellow their flavor.

SCORING AN EGGPLANT

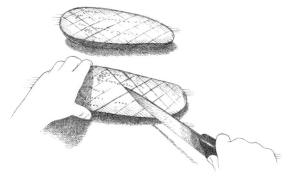

Using the tip of a chef's knife, score the cut side of each eggplant half in a 1-inch diamond pattern, about 1 inch deep.

Tomatoes also showed up as a flavoring in a number of recipes we consulted; they lent a sweet, meaty dimension of flavor to the eggplant. We tested fresh tomatoes against canned diced tomatoes. Even with out-of-season tomatoes, tasters preferred the fresh to canned. But one problem we found was that the mixture turned watery. We tried salting and draining the tomatoes, but this seemed like a lot of bother. We then thought of tomato paste. This was exactly what our eggplant needed—just 1 teaspoon of intensely flavored paste deepened and sweetened the eggplant flavor without harming the texture of the creamy, silky spread. And to finish, we stirred in some olive oil for further richness and fresh lemon juice and fresh dill to brighten the flavors. For a variation, we incorporated roasted red peppers, which are included in many Russian recipes, and which tasters enjoyed.

Eggplant Caviar

Baklazhannaya Ikra

MAKES ABOUT 1½ CUPS

Serve on small slices of brown bread or on top of Buckwheat Pancakes (page 377). Russian brown bread has a substantial texture and has a somewhat tangy flavor, much like German brown bread. If you are unable to find authentic Russian (or German) brown bread, cocktail pumpernickel is a good substitute.

1	large eggplant (about 1½ pounds), unpeeled and halved lengthwise
6	tablespoons extra-virgin olive oil
	Salt and ground black pepper
1	small onion, minced
3	medium garlic cloves, minced or pressed through a garlic press (about 1 tablespoon)
1	teaspoon tomato paste
1	tablespoon fresh juice from 1 lemon
1	teaspoon minced fresh dill

1. Adjust an oven rack to the middle position and heat the oven to 400 degrees. Line a rimmed baking sheet with foil. Following the illustration on page 374, score the cut sides of the eggplant about 1 inch deep. Drizzle the scored sides of the eggplant with 2 tablespoons of the olive oil and season with salt and pepper.

2. Lay the eggplant cut side down on the prepared baking sheet and roast until the eggplant is very soft, the skin is shriveled and shrunken, and a knife piercing the flesh meets no resistance, about 1 hour. Let the eggplant cool until able to handle, about 5 minutes.

3. Set a small colander over a bowl (or in the sink). Use a spoon to scoop the hot eggplant pulp out of the skins into the colander; discard the skins. Scrape up any eggplant that has stuck to the foil and add it to the colander. Let the pulp drain for 30 minutes. Transfer the eggplant pulp to a cutting board and chop coarse; transfer the chopped eggplant to a bowl and set aside.

4. Meanwhile, heat 2 more tablespoons of the oil in a 10-inch nonstick skillet over medium heat until shimmering. Add the onion and cook until softened, 5 to 7 minutes. Stir in the garlic and cook until fragrant, about 30 seconds. Stir in the tomato paste and cook until the mixture deepens in color slightly, about 3 minutes. Stir in the chopped eggplant and cook until warmed through, about 2 minutes longer.

5. Transfer the eggplant mixture to a serving bowl. Stir in the remaining 2 tablespoons olive oil and the lemon juice and season with salt and pepper to taste. Cover and refrigerate until chilled, at least 1 hour or up to 2 days. Stir in the dill and season again with salt and pepper before serving.

➤ VARIATION

Eggplant Caviar with Roasted Red Peppers

For more information on roasting red peppers see page 409. To pull this dip together even more quickly, use jarred roasted red peppers; see page 219 for information on our recommended brand.

Follow the recipe for Eggplant Caviar, adding ¼ cup roasted red peppers, drained, rinsed, and patted dry (if jarred), chopped fine, with the oil and lemon juice in step 5.

CAVIAR

CAVIAR IS RUSSIA'S PRIZED DELICACY, legendary worldwide, and a central part of Russian cuisine that has been enjoyed for centuries. Caviar can be most simply defined as any kind of slightly salted fish eggs, or roe. The caviar of gourmet reputation has traditionally been the roe of one of three species of sturgeon harvested from the rivers feeding into the Caspian Sea and the Black Sea: beluga sturgeon (beluga caviar), Russian sturgeon (osetra caviar), and stellate sturgeon (sevruga caviar).

Sadly, these prized fish have been pushed to the brink of extinction by a combination of overfishing, poaching, and pollution. Legal caviar from these waters is now either exorbitantly priced or unavailable. Beluga caviar from the Caspian Sea was formally banned by the United Nations in January of 2006, in an effort to save these fish from extinction. As a result, restaurateurs and caviar lovers have turned their attention to American caviar.

American fish roe can be labeled "caviar," with no other qualification, only if it comes from a sturgeon-related species. The four types of American sturgeon caviar that are most prevalent are paddlefish sturgeon, hackleback sturgeon, white sturgeon, and lake sturgeon. The most available and reasonably priced type of American caviar is paddlefish, which ranges in appearance from a light to dark steely gray.

It has a briny taste, which can be described as smooth and buttery, with a rich, clean flavor.

Several popular American fish roe offerings come from species entirely unrelated to sturgeon, including salmon, bowfin, whitefish, and lumpfish. Roe from these fish can be labeled "caviar" only if the name of the fish is included, as in "salmon caviar," and so on.

Each 1-ounce jar of caviar contains about 4 teaspoons of roe, serving two to three people. Caviar can be stored, unopened, in the refrigerator for up to four weeks; once opened, it should be used within three days. The best way to store opened caviar is to press a layer of plastic wrap directly on the eggs to prevent exposure to the air.

Caviar picks up metallic flavors very easily. Should it come in a tin container, don't store it in the tin if you have any leftovers (you can store it in either plastic or glass). Likewise, caviar should never be served in a metal bowl or with a metal spoon. Classic caviar spoons are made from mother of pearl, bone, or tortoise shell, but plastic works well too.

Serve caviar cold, in a bowl nestled on ice. It is traditionally served on top of blini (see page 377) with butter, or with toast points. Other nice accompaniments include sour cream or crème fraîche, minced red onion, sieved egg whites and yolks, capers, and chives.

BUCKWHEAT PANCAKES
Blini

BLINI COME FROM THE SLAVIC WORD *BLIN*, meaning a symbol of the sun. These round golden pancakes were traditionally served hot and slathered with as much butter as the pancake could absorb during an ancient festival to mark the beginning of spring. Traditionally, blini are cooked in a similar style to crêpes, in a 5 to 7-inch crêpe pan or skillet. They are then spread with a variety of fillings such as jam, caviar, smoked fish, or sour cream, then rolled up and served. We decided instead to focus on silver dollar–sized blini, called *oladi*. The small pancakes are topped with a spoonful of the same fillings and make an excellent hors d'oeuvre.

While many blini are yeasted, we wanted a less time-consuming version and found some recipes leavened with baking powder and baking soda. These were also favored by some of our tasters for their slightly sweet, less sour taste. In the West, buckwheat flour is associated with blini, but in Russia, buckwheat hasn't always been available and regular wheat flour (all-purpose flour), is often used. Tasters did like the distinctive flavor buckwheat flour lends the blini, so we developed our recipe with a combination of buckwheat and all-purpose flours. A note about buckwheat: it isn't actually wheat at all, but an herb, whose seeds are ground to make flour. Buckwheat flour can be found in natural foods stores and some well-stocked supermarkets. And if you don't have time to make blini from scratch or can't find buckwheat flour, we did sample some buckwheat pancake mixes. While not as flavorful or moist, these mixes were okay in a pinch.

Buckwheat Pancakes

Blini

MAKES ABOUT 60 SMALL PANCAKES

To make 8 larger-sized pancakes, use an 8-inch nonstick skillet in step 3 and add ¼ cup of the batter to the skillet at a time; the cooking times will be about the same. Try spreading these larger pancakes with jam and rolling them up for breakfast or brunch. Buckwheat flour can be found in natural foods stores and well-stocked supermarkets. A few traditional toppings for blini include caviar, chopped smoked fish such as smoked salmon, and sour cream.

½	cup (2½ ounces) unbleached all-purpose flour
½	cup (2½ ounces) buckwheat flour (see note)
I	tablespoon sugar
½	teaspoon salt
½	teaspoon baking powder
¼	teaspoon baking soda
¾	cup buttermilk
½	cup whole milk
I	large egg
2	tablespoons unsalted butter, melted and cooled, plus extra for cooking the blini

1. Adjust an oven rack to the middle position and heat the oven to 200 degrees. Line a rimmed baking sheet with foil, top with a wire rack, and spray the rack with vegetable oil spray; set aside.

2. Whisk the flours, sugar, salt, baking powder, and baking soda together in a medium bowl and set aside. In a separate bowl, whisk the buttermilk, milk, egg, and melted butter together. Whisk the buttermilk mixture into the flour mixture until just combined (do not overmix).

3. Using a pastry brush, brush the bottom and sides of a 12-inch nonstick skillet very lightly with melted butter; heat the skillet over medium heat. When the butter stops sizzling, add the batter in spots to the skillet using 1 scant tablespoon of batter per pancake (6 to 8 pancakes will fit at a time). Cook until large bubbles begin to appear, 1½ to 2 minutes. Flip the pancakes over and cook until golden on the second side, about 1½ minutes longer.

4. Transfer the pancakes to the prepared wire rack and keep warm, uncovered, in the oven. Repeat with additional butter and the remaining batter. Let cool slightly before topping and serving. (The pancakes can be frozen to for up to 1 week; let them cool to room temperature, wrap them in plastic wrap, and freeze. Thaw the frozen pancakes in the refrigerator for 24 hours, then spread out over a baking sheet and warm in a 350-degree oven for about 5 minutes before serving.)

WILD MUSHROOM AND BARLEY SOUP

Gribnoi Sup

MUSHROOMS PLAY A PROMINENT ROLE AT the Russian table. By the end of summer and into fall, the markets are brimming with handpicked wild mushrooms, where farmers sell what they have foraged. We thought that a hearty, rustic mushroom soup was a perfect way to highlight this staple ingredient.

In our research we found a wide range of mushroom soups in Russia, but the mushroom soups containing barley jumped out at us as especially appropriate for a nourishing cold-weather soup. Our aim was to create a mushroom-barley soup that was all about the headiness of mushrooms, with the barley lending a bit of texture and thickening power. In addition, we wanted our mushroom-barley soup to be able to stand on its own without leaning on a time-consuming homemade beef stock—a common ingredient in many recipes here in the United States. In Russia, when making mushroom soup, many traditionalists would say not to use stock at all, because it overwhelms the flavor of the mushrooms.

We started by analyzing the liquid component of the soup. Would certain types of broths distract us from the mushrooms and overwhelm their flavor? We started with a simple working recipe and did a side-by-side test using the following liquids: water and store-bought chicken, beef, and vegetable broths and combinations of each. Tasters were unanimous in their opinion that the soup made with all chicken broth trumped the rest. Chicken broth lent the soup a rich, hearty flavor and added to the meatiness of the barley. Most important, rather than detracting from the intense mushroom flavor, the chicken broth enhanced the mushrooms.

The ratio of barley to liquid was a quick decision. In recipes uncovered during our research, this ratio varied from 2 teaspoons to 2 tablespoons of barley per cup of liquid. Knowing that barley is a hearty grain, we ventured a guess that the lower barley-to-liquid ratio would be more appropriate. As it turned out, about 1 tablespoon per cup of liquid proved best. This provided just the right interchange between the barley and the soup, allowing a couple of nuggets to find their way into each spoonful without overwhelming the other ingredients.

With a working recipe coming together, we next turned to building flavor. We identified three different ingredients that might build flavor in this soup—tomato paste, wine, and dried porcini mushrooms, this last ingredient being extremely common in many Russian recipes. While some tasters found the flavor of the tomato paste comforting, other tasters argued that its flavor and color (a burnished orange-red) was too much like canned soup. On the wine front, red wine muddied the flavors of the soup rather than bringing them together, whereas white wine made the soup base too harsh. It was the addition of dried porcini mushrooms that won the crowd, providing a boost of mushroom essence and richness.

As for fresh mushrooms, the cornerstone of the soup, we had been using the supermarket staple white button mushrooms in all of our trials. With the soup basics in check, we decided to tinker with different mushroom varieties. In Russia, there is a large variety of wild mushrooms, some of which are difficult to find on a consistent basis, including chanterelles and fresh porcinis, or *belyi grib* in Russian. Not wanting to get too esoteric, we stuck to testing fresh mushroom varieties that are readily available in U.S. supermarkets—portobellos, cremini, and shiitakes. While the shiitakes developed an unwelcome texture, too chewy and similar to fat rubber bands due to the long cooking time of the soup, the cremini and the portobellos gave the soup bravado. And we liked white button mushrooms, too. Although any one mushroom can be used, we liked a combination of all three for added depth and textural contrast, but we leave the choice to you. More important was using a combination of dried and fresh mushrooms. The fresh mushrooms lent a meaty texture while the dried mushrooms gave the soup the intensity we sought. Tasters were now clutching their bowls of mushroom-barley soup, comforted by its earthy warmth, and helping themselves to seconds.

REMOVING GILLS FROM PORTOBELLO MUSHROOMS

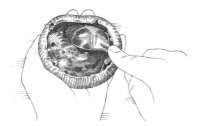

We found that it was necessary to remove the black gills from the portobello mushrooms because they make soup muddy in appearance. Using a soupspoon, scrape and discard the dark-colored gills from the underside of the mushroom.

Wild Mushroom and Barley Soup
Gribnoi Sup
SERVES 6

If using portobello mushrooms, scrape out and discard the dark-colored gills on the underside of the cap to prevent them from muddying the flavor of the soup (see left).

3   tablespoons vegetable oil
1   large onion, minced

½   ounce dried porcini mushrooms, rinsed
     and minced
     Salt
2   medium carrots, peeled and cut into
     ½-inch pieces
I   pound white, cremini, or portobello
     mushrooms, or a combination, wiped
     clean and sliced into ¼-inch-thick,
     bite-sized pieces (see note)
3   medium garlic cloves, minced or
     pressed through a garlic press (about
     I tablespoon)
9   cups low-sodium chicken broth
½   cup pearl barley
I   bay leaf
I   teaspoon minced fresh thyme leaves
     Ground black pepper

1. Heat the oil in a large Dutch oven over medium-high heat until shimmering. Add the onion, porcini mushrooms, and ½ teaspoon salt and cook until the onion is softened, 5 to 7 minutes. Stir in the carrots and continue to cook until the carrots begin to soften, 3 to 5 minutes. Stir in the fresh mushrooms and cook until they release their liquid, 8 to 10 minutes. Stir in the garlic and cook until fragrant, about 30 seconds.

2. Stir in the broth, barley, bay leaf, and thyme. Bring the soup to a boil, reduce the heat to low, cover, and simmer gently until the barley is tender, about 45 minutes. Discard the bay leaf and season with salt and pepper to taste before serving.

GREEN BEANS WITH CILANTRO SAUCE

Mtsvane Lobio Kindzis Satsebelit

IN RESEARCHING THE CUISINES OF RUSSIA and eastern Europe, we were surprised by the abundance of fresh herbs, olive oil, and nuts used in some recipes—a stark contrast to the rich stews and sour cream–based sauces that most of us associate with this region. This is especially true in Georgia, located just south of Russia, where these flavors

are quite common. Thousands of years ago, during the time of the Silk Road, when caravans traveled between Asia and Europe, cilantro, basil, tarragon, nuts, and olive oil—the flavors of the Mediterranean and the Middle East—left their stamp on the cuisine. As a result, you'll find that many Georgian dishes are enriched with an array of herbs, nuts, and olive oil.

One of our favorites is *kindzis satsebelit,* a sauce much like an Italian pesto that blends cilantro with other fresh herbs, walnuts, and olive oil. This thick, intensely flavored sauce is commonly used as a dip for vegetables or drizzled over grilled or roasted meats. We wanted to develop a recipe for this bright-tasting sauce to use as a dressing for tender green beans and create the perfect summertime side dish.

We started with the herbs. Many recipes that we came across in our research called for several herbs, with cilantro in the forefront and the others—basil, parsley, and/or tarragon—used in lesser quantities for background herbal flavor. We tested using a combination of all of the herbs, as well as just cilantro paired with one of the others, only to find that the addition of even just a second herb detracted from the bright, fresh cilantro flavor that we were after. We decided that we needed to say goodbye to the other herbs and focus on the cilantro.

We realized that we were going to need to use a lot of cilantro in our recipe—after all, it is so abundant in Georgia that it is sold by weight, rather than by the bunch as it is here in the United States. We found that two bunches of cilantro gave us vibrant cilantro flavor. Typically, with cilantro (and other herbs), we use just the leaves, but many Georgian recipes also include the stems. Cilantro stems are more tender than those of other herbs and they easily broke down in the food processor (the preferred method for making pesto that we borrowed for this recipe).

With the herbs resolved, we concentrated on fine-tuning the flavors in the sauce without disrupting the great herbal flavor that we had achieved. Nuts were a given and walnuts were the most common in the recipes that we researched. To bring out their flavor, we found that toasting them was essential. Unlike pesto, which relies on extra-virgin olive oil for flavor, this sauce was best made with regular olive oil because its milder flavor allowed the cilantro to really shine through. A single scallion brightened the green color of the sauce and added depth, in addition to two cloves of garlic. As with our pesto, we found that toasting the garlic mellowed and sweetened its otherwise harsh bite. Finally, a touch of lemon juice rounded out the flavors and helped to loosen the sauce to just the right consistency.

All that was left to do was marry the sauce with the green beans. To cook the beans, we borrowed a restaurant technique that is used to set the color in green vegetables, called "blanching and shocking." First, we boiled the beans in salted water until just tender (the blanching step) and then we quickly drained and cooled them in ice water to stop the cooking and set the vibrant green color (the shocking step). The beans were evenly cooked, with a sweet flavor and tender texture—the perfect match for our flavorful sauce. And with this light and flavorful dish down, we turned to creating a slightly heartier variation, in which we substituted slices of creamy red potatoes for a portion of the beans—tasters agreed it was a winning combination.

Green Beans with Cilantro Sauce

Mtsvane Lobio Kindzis Satsebelit

SERVES 6 TO 8

We prefer the mild flavor of regular olive oil in this sauce compared to the stronger flavor of extra-virgin olive oil. Don't worry about patting the beans dry with towels before tossing them with the sauce; any water that clings to the beans helps to thin out the sauce. This sauce is also good served with crudités or alongside grilled or roasted meat, chicken, or fish.

¼	cup walnuts
2	medium garlic cloves, unpeeled
2½	cups packed cilantro leaves and stems, tough stem ends trimmed (about 2 bunches)
½	cup olive oil (see note)
4	teaspoons juice from 1 lemon
1	scallion, sliced thin
	Salt and ground black pepper
2	pounds green beans, stem ends trimmed

1. Toast the walnuts in a small, heavy skillet over medium heat, stirring frequently, until just golden and fragrant, about 5 minutes; set aside. Add the garlic to the empty skillet and toast over medium heat, shaking the pan occasionally, until fragrant and the color of the cloves deepens slightly, about 7 minutes. Let the garlic cool slightly, then peel and chop.

2. Process the walnuts, garlic, cilantro, oil, lemon juice, scallion, ½ teaspoon salt, and ⅛ teaspoon pepper in a food processor, stopping to scrape down the sides of the bowl as needed, until smooth, about 1 minute. Add more salt and pepper to taste. (The sauce can be refrigerated in an airtight container for up to 2 days.)

3. Bring 3 quarts of water to a boil in a large saucepan or Dutch oven over high heat. Meanwhile, fill a large bowl with ice water; set aside. Add 1 tablespoon salt and the green beans to the boiling water and cook until crisp-tender, about 4 minutes. Drain the beans, transfer to the ice water, and let sit until chilled, about 2 minutes.

4. Drain the beans well, transfer to a serving bowl, and toss with the cilantro sauce. Season with salt and pepper to taste and serve. (The dressed beans can be refrigerated for up to 4 hours.)

> VARIATION

Green Beans and Potatoes with Cilantro Sauce

Handle the potato slices gently after they are cooked to prevent them from breaking apart. Note that the green beans are cut into pieces for this variation, so that they're easier to eat with a fork alongside the potato slices.

1. Follow the recipe for Green Beans with Cilantro Sauce through step 2. Scrub 1 pound red potatoes and cut into ¼-inch-thick slices. Place the potatoes and 1 tablespoon salt in a large saucepan and cover with 1 inch cold water. Bring to a boil over high heat, reduce the heat to medium-low, and simmer until the potatoes are tender (a thin-bladed paring knife can be slipped in and out of the potatoes with little resistance), about 5 minutes. Drain the potatoes and arrange in a single layer on a rimmed baking sheet. (Rinse out the saucepan to use for the green beans.) Brush both sides of the potato slices with half of the cilantro sauce and let cool to room temperature, about 30 minutes.

2. Proceed with step 3, using the same amount of water and salt, but reducing the amount of green beans to 1 pound and cutting them into 2-inch lengths. Cook until crisp-tender, 2 to 3 minutes. Drain and shock as directed. Toss the beans in a serving bowl with the remaining cilantro sauce and season with salt and pepper to taste. Gently fold in the potatoes and serve. (The dressed potatoes and green beans can be refrigerated for up to 4 hours.)

POLISH DUMPLINGS

Pierogi

SAVORY DUMPLINGS ARE SERVED THROUGH out Russia and eastern Europe and vary in wrapper, filling, and of course, name (*pierogi*, *pilmeni*, and *vareniki* are just a few). To narrow the field, we chose to focus on the classic Polish pierogi. Pierogi are made with any number of fillings, including sauerkraut, cheese, potatoes, mushrooms, and meat, encased in thin, pasta-style dough, boiled, and then sautéed briefly to finish. The pillowy dumplings are often served as a main course with strands of caramelized onion and sour cream—truly decadent and delicious. We couldn't wait to get into the kitchen to develop our own version.

To get the lay of the land, we prepared a few recipes from Polish cookbooks and, because we came across them in the supermarket, heated some frozen varieties. The supermarket pierogi were truly awful—the dough was dense and chewy and the fillings were hard to swallow. Some of the pierogi we made ourselves also suffered from heaviness and bland flavor. We aimed to develop a delicate, yet sturdy dough wrapped around a savory, satisfying filling. We decided to begin with the pierogi dough.

Pierogi dough is similar to pasta dough and because we had developed fresh pasta in past test kitchen tests, we knew that figuring out the proper ratio of eggs to flour would be key to a tender but sturdy wrapper. We started by testing three pierogi dough recipes found in researching the dumplings. Each recipe consisted of flour, eggs, water, and oil, although the ratios in each recipe varied. The dough that showed the most promise was the one made with 2 cups of flour and two eggs. This dough yielded a delicate but sturdy wrapper. The other doughs each contained higher proportions of flour to egg and as a result their texture turned out tough and a bit chewy. We therefore decided to base the recipe on a ratio of one egg for every cup of flour. We were next curious about using egg yolks versus whole eggs. We reasoned that fat-rich yolks might make the pierogi even more tender. We tested dough made with two egg yolks against dough made with two whole eggs. The dough made with two yolks was too tender while the dough made with two whole eggs was fine—and we thought we were finished. But then we tried the pierogi made with one egg and one yolk, and found the perfect balance between structure and tenderness. Now that we had our ratio of eggs to flour, we turned to the oil and water.

Some recipes we found included oil and some did not, so we tested one batch of dough made with oil and one without. The dough made with oil was a touch more tender and had a bit more flavor than the dough without, so we included it. As for water, we found that 4 to 6 tablespoons was enough to pull the dough together without making it heavy.

With our dough in place and ready to be filled, we turned to the fillings. We knew we wanted to develop a few filling options and with some more research settled on three: potato and cheese, mushroom, and ground meat. For the potato filling, we started with potato mashed with cheddar cheese and farmer's cheese. The cheese adds rich flavor and the fat in the cheese helps bind together the potatoes. Still, tasters found the filling a bit dry, so we added butter—just 2 tablespoons lent the filling moisture and further richness. Onions also added another welcome savory note.

Next, we moved on to the mushroom filling. We knew from experience that cooking the mushrooms properly was crucial to avoiding a wet soggy filling. Cooking the mushrooms over medium-low heat, covered, enabled them to release their juices. We then uncovered the pan and increased the heat, allowing the mushroom liquid to cook off rapidly, and enabling the mushrooms to brown slightly, adding a nice depth of flavor. We used a combination of fresh mushrooms and dried porcini for maximum, earthy flavor. Some onion and garlic boosted the mushroom flavor and a touch of sour cream, added once the mixture was cooked, lent some tangy richness and helped bind the filling together.

Finally we turned to the ground meat filling. The ingredients in most recipes were consistent: a combination of ground beef and pork, onions, and a few herbs. Pulling from some testing we had recently done for Chinese Pork and Cabbage Dumplings (page 498), we knew that ground pork and beef fillings have a tendency to form a dense, solid mass when shaped and cooked. To prevent the meat from compacting into a dense ball, we added lightly beaten egg whites to the meat mixture. The theory is that egg whites will puff up when cooked, almost like soufflé, incorporating tiny air bubbles into the otherwise compact ground meat. Sure enough, the outcome was perfect: We now had a light and tender filling.

A word about onions. We noted that we'd included sautéed onion in all three fillings. And we'd also caramelized onion to serve over the pierogi, as tradition dictates. But was it necessary to cook onions twice for an already involved recipe? We took a step back and decided that if we caramelized slightly more onion than needed for the garnish, we could use some for the filling and skip the step of hauling out an extra pan. Just ¼ cup caramelized onion, chopped fine, easily did the trick. (Note that the caramelized onion garnish requires just a brief rewarming before serving.)

When forming the pierogi, we found that it was easiest to roll out half the dough, punch out the circles, and then fill them right away. (When the dough sat for too long before being filled, it dried out, making sealing the dough more difficult.) If the dough didn't seal readily, we brushed a little bit of water along the edges before pressing them together. We used the tines of a fork to crimp the dough and make an attractive edge on the half moon–shaped dumplings.

Cooking pierogi is easy. Simply boil them in water, drain, and then sauté them in butter until golden brown. To serve, we spooned the caramelized onions over the warm pierogi, finished off with a dollop of sour cream. Tasters agreed this was comfort food worth the effort.

Polish Dumplings
Pierogi

MAKES 32 TO 34 DUMPLINGS, SERVING 4 TO 6

Assemble the pierogi within a few hours of preparing the dough—otherwise the dough will be too dry to work with. We found that the dough scraps can be rerolled out just once; further rerolling turns the pierogi very tough. The filling and assembly steps for pierogi are the same as for empanadas; see the illustrations on page 44. A wire spider comes in handy when boiling the pierogi; see page 433 for more information. If the caramelized onions cool off too much by the time you're serving the pierogi, reheat them in a microwave-safe bowl on 100 percent power for about 30 seconds.

PIEROGI DOUGH

2	cups (10 ounces) unbleached all-purpose flour, plus extra for the work surface
½	teaspoon salt
1	large whole egg
1	large egg yolk
1	tablespoon vegetable oil
4–6	tablespoons cold water
4	tablespoons (½ stick) unsalted butter, for sautéing the pierogi

CARAMELIZED ONIONS

4	tablespoons (½ stick) unsalted butter
3	large onions, halved and sliced thin
	Salt

1	recipe Filling for Polish Dumplings (pages 383–384)
	Sour cream (for serving)

1. FOR THE PIEROGI DOUGH: Pulse the flour and salt together in a food processor until combined, about 4 pulses. With the machine running, slowly add the whole egg, egg yolk, and oil through the feed tube until the mixture resembles wet sand, about 30 seconds. With the machine running, slowly add 4 tablespoons of the water until the dough forms a ball. If the dough doesn't ball up, add the remaining water, 1 tablespoon at a time, with the processor running until a dough ball forms (you may not use all the water). The dough

should feel very soft and malleable.

2. Transfer the dough to a lightly floured work surface and knead by hand until it firms slightly and becomes smooth, about 2 minutes. Cover with plastic wrap and set aside to relax for at least 15 minutes or up to 2 hours.

3. FOR THE CARAMELIZED ONIONS: Meanwhile, melt the butter in a 12-inch nonstick skillet over medium heat. Add the onions and ¼ teaspoon salt and cook until very soft and well browned, 15 to 20 minutes. Measure out ¼ cup of the onions, chop them fine, and reserve them for one of the fillings on pages 383–384. Cover the pan of caramelized onions to keep warm.

4. Dust a baking sheet liberally with flour; set aside. Divide the dough into 2 even pieces and cover with plastic wrap. Working with 1 piece of dough at a time, unwrap the dough and roll out on a lightly floured work surface into a 15-inch circle, about ¹⁄₁₆ inch thick. Using a 3-inch round biscuit cutter, cut out as many rounds as possible. Carefully gather up the dough scraps, wrap them in plastic wrap, and set aside. Following the illustrations on page 44, fill, shape, and crimp the pierogi using roughly 1 teaspoon of the filling per dough round; transfer to the prepared baking sheet and cover with a damp kitchen towel. Repeat with the remaining dough rounds.

5. Gently knead all of the dough scraps together into a ball and let relax for 5 to 10 minutes. Roll out, cut, and assemble additional pierogi, discarding any remaining dough scraps. (The towel-covered baking sheet of pierogi can be wrapped with plastic wrap and refrigerated for up to 4 hours. The pierogi can also be frozen for up to 1 month; when completely frozen, the pierogi can be transferred to a zipper-lock bag to save space in the freezer. Do not thaw before boiling.)

6. Bring 4 quarts of water to a boil in a large pot. Add 1 tablespoon of salt and half the pierogi. Cook, stirring often, until the edges feel al dente, 5 to 6 minutes (8 to 10 minutes if frozen). Using a wire spider or slotted spoon, transfer the pierogi to a colander and set aside. Return the water to a boil and cook the remaining pierogi.

7. While the second batch of dumplings is boiling, melt 2 tablespoons of the butter in a 12-inch nonstick skillet over medium-high heat. Add the first batch of boiled and drained pierogi and sauté until golden on both sides, 1 to 2 minutes per side. Transfer the browned pierogi to a platter and cover to keep warm. Drain and sauté the remaining pierogi using the remaining 2 tablespoons butter. Sprinkle the caramelized onions over the top and serve with sour cream.

Potato and Cheese Filling for Polish Dumplings
MAKES ABOUT 1 CUP, ENOUGH TO FILL 32 TO 34 DUMPLINGS

While we prefer the flavor and texture of farmer's cheese here, an equal amount of ricotta cheese can be substituted. Use either a food mill or a ricer to process the cooked potatoes for the filling; do not use a food processor or the filling will have a gummy texture. Rather than cooking onions separately for the filling, we incorporate some of the caramelized onions used to garnish the dumplings.

1	medium russet potato (about 9 ounces), peeled and sliced ¾ inch thick
	Salt
¼	cup reserved chopped caramelized onions (see step 3 at left)
1½	ounces cheddar cheese, shredded (about ⅓ cup)
1½	ounces farmer's cheese (about ¼ cup) (see note)
1	tablespoon unsalted butter
	Ground black pepper

1. Cover the potatoes by 1 inch of water in a large saucepan and add 1 tablespoon salt. Bring to a boil, then reduce to a simmer and cook until the potatoes are tender and a fork can be slipped easily into the center, 10 to 12 minutes. Drain the potatoes into a colander.

2. Set a food mill or ricer over a medium bowl and process the potatoes into the bowl. Add the caramelized onions. Stir in the cheeses and butter until incorporated and season with salt and pepper to taste. Cool slightly before filling the pierogi or cover with plastic wrap and refrigerate until needed, but no longer than 2 days.

Mushroom Filling for Polish Dumplings

MAKES ABOUT I CUP, ENOUGH TO FILL
32 TO 34 DUMPLINGS

For more information on using porcini mushrooms, see page 283. Rather than cooking onions separately for the filling, we incorporate some of the caramelized onions used to garnish the dumplings.

12	ounces white mushrooms, wiped clean and quartered
I	tablespoon unsalted butter
3	medium garlic cloves, minced or pressed through a garlic press (about I tablespoon)
½	ounce dried porcini mushrooms, rinsed and minced
	Salt
¼	cup reserved chopped caramelized onions (see step 3 on page 383)
2	tablespoons sour cream
I	tablespoon minced fresh parsley leaves
	Ground black pepper

1. Pulse the white mushrooms in a food processor until finely chopped, about 15 pulses; transfer to a bowl and set aside. Melt the butter in a 12-inch nonstick skillet over medium heat until shimmering. Add the garlic and cook until fragrant, about 30 seconds. Stir in the processed mushrooms, porcini mushrooms, and ¼ teaspoon salt. Cover, turn the heat to medium-low, and cook, stirring occasionally, until the mushrooms are wet and wilted, about 7 minutes.

2. Uncover, increase the heat to medium-high heat, and continue to cook until the mushroom liquid has evaporated and the mixture clumps and is starting to brown, about 7 minutes.

3. Add the reserved chopped caramelized onions. Stir in the sour cream and cook until the mixture is sticky and cohesive but not wet, about 30 seconds. Transfer the mixture to a bowl; cool slightly. Stir in the parsley and season with salt and pepper to taste before filling the pierogi or cover with plastic wrap and refrigerate until needed, but no longer than 2 days.

Meat Filling for Polish Dumplings

MAKES ABOUT I CUP, ENOUGH TO FILL
32 TO 34 DUMPLINGS

Rather than cooking onions separately for the filling, we incorporate some of the caramelized onions used to garnish the dumplings.

¼	pound (93 percent lean) ground beef
¼	pound ground pork
¼	cup reserved chopped caramelized onions (see step 3 on page 383)
2	tablespoons minced fresh parsley leaves
I	tablespoon minced fresh chives
I	large egg white, lightly beaten
¼	teaspoon salt
	Pinch ground black pepper

Mix all of the ingredients together in a medium bowl until uniformly combined. Use right away to fill pierogi or cover with plastic wrap and refrigerate until needed, but no longer than 2 days.

STUFFED CABBAGE ROLLS WITH SWEET AND SOUR TOMATO SAUCE

Galumpkis

STUFFED CABBAGE ROLLS ARE COMMON throughout eastern European countries and accordingly the dish goes by many names, from *galumpkis* in Poland and *golubtsy* in Russia to *holubtsi* in the Ukraine. In this country, they have become a staple on menus at Jewish-style delis. At their best, stuffed cabbage rolls are homey and satisfying, with their simply seasoned, melt-in-your-mouth meat filling that is encased in pliant, mildly sweet cabbage leaves and topped with a sweet and tangy tomato sauce.

Unfortunately, good versions of this dish can

be hard to find. We have all tasted our fair share of forgettable stuffed cabbage—dense, rubbery fillings; mushy, foul-smelling cabbage; and watery sauces. On top of these pitfalls, stuffed cabbage rolls can be time-consuming to make—the filling and sauce need to be cooked, the cabbage leaves must be separated, stuffed, and rolled, and then cooked for upward of 1 hour. Is the end result even worth the effort? We were determined to turn this classic around and streamline the recipe without compromising flavor.

We started with the cabbage. Most recipes in our research called for green cabbage, although we did find a few that used its crinkly-leaved cousin, savoy. Due to its wide availability, we stuck with green cabbage (savoy was hard to find in many of our local supermarkets).

Next, we had to determine the best way to separate the cabbage leaves from the head. Some recipes boil the head of cabbage in water until the leaves wilt, while others freeze the head of cabbage and then run it under warm water, which softens the leaves and causes them to fall away. Both methods worked, but we found that the former method was easier because it didn't require 24 hours of planning. And boiling the cabbage blanched the leaves, which softened their texture and mellowed the cabbage's flavor.

With the leaves ready for stuffing, we focused on the filling. Many recipes we tested used all ground beef, while others called for some combination of ground beef, ground pork, and/or ground veal. Tasters preferred the combination of beef, pork, and veal for its tenderness and flavor. And conveniently, most supermarkets sell this trio of meats prepackaged and labeled as "meatloaf mix."

All meat fillings need a starchy binder and, taking cues from other stuffed cabbage recipes, we added rice to ours. After testing various amounts, we settled on just ¼ cup, which we conveniently simmered in the cabbage cooking water until tender and rinsed it until cool before adding it to the meat. The rice broke up the monotony of an all-meat filling, giving it a lighter texture.

We needed to choose a liquid component that would add moisture and act as an additional binder. We tried both milk and heavy cream. Tasters favored the heavy cream, which added not only moisture, but richness. We also came across many recipes that included an egg, but we found the addition counteracted the work of the rice and cream, turning the filling dense and rubbery, so we left it out.

Since this meat filling is traditionally mildly flavored to counterbalance the tangy tomato sauce, we made an effort to use restraint with our seasonings. Onion, however, was a given. And after sampling raw, sautéed, and caramelized onions, tasters agreed that a small amount of raw onion (just half an onion) produced the best flavor profile, and it required no additional cooking. We grated the onion half on the large holes of a box grater, which produced fine pieces that were easily incorporated into the filling and didn't add the unwelcome crunch of chopped onion. Salt, pepper, and fresh parsley (or dill) were the only other embellishments that our filling needed before we rolled it up in the blanched cabbage leaves.

With the rolls ready to go, we still needed to figure out the details of the tomato sauce and the best cooking method for the cabbage rolls. Since the sauce provides the dish with much of its flavor, we turned our attention there first. After experimenting with different types of canned tomatoes, we established that we liked the texture of a sauce made with one large can (28 ounces) of tomato puree for body and one small can (14.5 ounces) of diced tomatoes for texture. Unfortunately, the flavor of the sauce made with tomato puree was reminiscent of canned tomato soup. Determined to improve the sauce's flavor without disturbing the perfect textural balance, we tried making our own tomato puree. We found success by processing two cans of diced tomatoes in a food processor until smooth. Our sauce now had the right texture and great fresh tomato flavor.

When we started to add the sweet and sour elements to the sauce, we discovered that some tasters liked the sauce on the sweeter side, while others preferred it to be more tangy. We resolved this by adding a set amount of brown sugar and cider vinegar and calling for seasoning to taste with extra sugar and vinegar. Similarly, some tasters insisted on the addition of raisins, while others didn't care for them. We decided to make them an optional ingredient. With the base of the sauce set, we looked to round out its flavors.

Clove is a common ingredient in these sauce recipes, but ground cloves tasted harsh, and fishing whole cloves out of the sauce before serving was simply too fussy. Instead, we studded the remaining onion half with cloves—a classical French technique called *oignon pique*—and simmered it in the sauce. The clove-studded onion added depth and spice to the sauce and it was easy to remove.

Lastly, we had to determine the best method for cooking the cabbage rolls. Up until this point, we had success by baking the cabbage rolls smothered in the sauce in the oven in a covered baking dish. But because we had seen many recipes that cooked the cabbage rolls in the sauce on the stovetop, we thought we would give this a try. Looking to streamline the recipe and limit the number of pans that we used, we found that the stovetop method was a bit easier. We simply arranged the cabbage rolls in the same Dutch oven that we had used for the cabbage and rice. We then poured the sauce over the top and brought the mixture to a simmer. At the same time, we noticed we hadn't used our entire head of cabbage, so we shredded that up, built a bed of cabbage in the pot to cushion the rolls, and then covered the rolls with the remaining shreds. The shredded cabbage not only guards against scorching, but it lends additional flavor and texture to the tangy sauce.

Looking to other stuffed cabbage recipes as a guide, we simmered the mixture for 1½ hours. The result was exactly what we were trying to avoid: an overcooked mess of mushy cabbage and dry filling. Fortunately, this problem was easy to remedy. We simply simmered the cabbage rolls in the sauce until the filling was cooked through and the cabbage was tender—this took just 45 minutes! We also found that simmering the mixture uncovered allowed the flavors of the sauce to meld and concentrate. With its tender and sweet cabbage, and bright sauce flavoring the modest meat filling, this dish is the ultimate in comfort food.

ASSEMBLING CABBAGE ROLLS

1. Cut out and discard the cabbage core, using a paring knife.

2. Using tongs, gently transfer the outer leaves of cabbage to a colander as they blanch.

3. Cut the thick rib from the base of the cabbage leaves and remove.

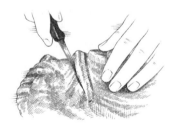

4. With the core end of the cabbage leaf facing you, arrange 2 tablespoons of the filling just above the area where the thick rib has been removed.

5. Fold the sides of the cabbage leaf over the filling.

6. Roll the bottom edge of the leaf up over the filling into a tight and tidy roll.

Stuffed Cabbage Rolls with Sweet and Sour Tomato Sauce

Galumpkis

SERVES 6 TO 8

Although some of the rolls may break apart while cooking, their flavor will not be affected. Plan on serving 2 to 3 rolls per person. If your supermarket does not have meatloaf mix, substitute 12 ounces each of ground pork and 80 percent lean ground beef.

1	medium head green cabbage (about 2 pounds), cored (see page 386)
	Salt
¼	cup long-grain white rice
1	medium onion, peeled and halved
8	whole cloves
1½	pounds ground meatloaf mix
½	cup heavy cream
2	tablespoons minced fresh dill or parsley leaves
	Ground black pepper
½	cup raisins (optional)
3	(14.5-ounce) cans diced tomatoes
1	cup water
3	tablespoons light brown sugar, plus extra to taste
2	tablespoons cider vinegar, plus extra to taste

1. Bring 4 quarts of water to a boil in a large Dutch oven over high heat. Add the cored head of cabbage and 1 tablespoon salt and cook until the outer cabbage leaves just begin to wilt, about 5 minutes, rotating the cabbage in the water every minute. Use tongs to gently remove the outer 20 leaves from the simmering head of cabbage, one at a time from the core end, as each wilts. Transfer the leaves to a colander and let cool. Remove the remaining blanched head of cabbage from the water and let it cool. Do not discard the water.

2. Return the water to a boil over high heat. Stir in the rice and boil until tender, about 13 minutes. Drain the rice through a fine-mesh strainer and rinse until cool; let the rice drain thoroughly.

3. Meanwhile, stud one onion half with the cloves; set aside. Grate the remaining onion half over the large holes of a box grater. In a medium bowl, combine the cooked rice, grated onion, ground meat, cream, dill, 1½ teaspoons salt, and ½ teaspoon pepper. Trim any tough ribs from the cabbage leaves and, following the illustrations on page 386, tightly roll a generous 2 tablespoons of the meat mixture into each leaf (you will have about 18 rolls). Finely chop the remaining blanched cabbage leaves and head.

4. Scatter half of the shredded cabbage leaves in the Dutch oven. Arrange the cabbage rolls, seam side down, on top of the shredded cabbage, fitting them in snugly to prevent unrolling. (If you are using a smaller pot, arrange the rolls in two layers.) Sprinkle the raisins (if using) and the remaining shredded cabbage over the rolls.

5. Process 2 cans of the tomatoes with their juice in a food processor until smooth, about 15 seconds. Transfer the processed tomatoes to a large bowl and stir in the remaining 1 can diced tomatoes with their juice, water, brown sugar, vinegar, and ½ teaspoon salt. Pour the tomato mixture over the cabbage, then nestle the clove-studded onion into the liquid, clove side facing down. Bring the mixture to a boil, then reduce to a simmer and cook, uncovered, until the cabbage is tender and the flavors of the sauce are concentrated, about 45 minutes.

6. Discard the clove-studded onion half. To serve, gently transfer the cabbage rolls to a serving dish (or individual plates) using a slotted spoon. Season the sauce with sugar, vinegar, salt, and pepper to taste. Spoon some of the sauce over the rolls and serve, passing the extra sauce separately. (The cooked cabbage rolls and sauce can be refrigerated separately in airtight containers for up to 2 days. To serve, reheat the sauce in a saucepan over medium-low heat and arrange the cabbage rolls in a 13 by 9-inch baking dish. Pour the warmed sauce over the rolls, wrap the dish tightly with foil, and reheat in a 400-degree oven until the rolls are hot throughout, about 30 minutes.)

CHICKEN PAPRIKASH

THIS HUNGARIAN SPECIALTY HAS BEEN popular in this country for decades. The chicken is succulent, the flavors mellow and a bit sweet, and the color a vibrant red. Sour cream makes the sauce comforting but not overly rich, while paprika gives the stew its characteristic appearance and flavor.

Chicken paprikash is a simple stew, but you wouldn't know it from all the recipes out there. Too many recipes have lengthy ingredient lists, and the resulting stews taste muddled. Our goal was to keep the focus on the main flavors—the chicken, the sour cream, and the paprika—with vegetables in the background. Another common problem with this dish is the sauce. In many versions, the sauce is thick and gluey. Ideally, the sauce will have the right consistency to coat egg noodles. A sauce that is too thick can't do this.

We began our tests by examining the chicken component. Almost all the recipes we found called

INGREDIENTS: Paprika

The brilliant red powder we call paprika comes from the dried pods (fruit) of the plant species *Capsicum annuum L.*, the clan of peppers that ranges from sweet bells to the very hottest chiles. Several varieties of Capsicum annuum L. are used to produce paprika; there is no one specific "paprika pepper." Pods differ in shape and size and vary in degree of potency. Some are round, others are elongated. Some show no pungency, others are fairly hot.

The best paprika is thought to come from Hungary and Spain. In the United States, California and Texas are the main producers. Most European paprika pods are set out to dry naturally in the sun, a process that takes up to 25 days. Domestically grown paprika pods are oven-dried in about 30 hours.

Paprikas can be hot, sweet, or somewhere in between. The differences in pungency, color, and flavor relate to the proportion of mesocarp (fruit wall), placenta (the white veins), and seeds that are ground together. Sweet paprika is made mostly from peppers' mesocarp, while hot paprika is a product of the placenta and seeds. The latter are ground to yield a spicy powder with an orange-brown color and, some spice experts say, poor flavor. It is almost as pungent as common chili powders and cayenne pepper.

The problem with all of this information is that except for allowing you to choose intelligently between sweet and hot paprika, it does you little practical good at the supermarket. In stores and catalogs we uncovered six choices: McCormick's (from California), Whole Foods organic (also California), Penzeys Hungary Sweet, Szeged Hungarian Hot, Pendery's Spanish, and Igo Basque Piment d'Espelette. The Pendery's Spanish paprika had the deepest red color. Tasters likened the color of the rest to "Crayola-orange," "saffron," or "brick."

Once the paprikas were incorporated into our Chicken Paprikash, there were equally diverse comments on flavor. Penzeys Hungary Sweet emerged as the overall favorite, hailed for its "roasty," "bold," and "balanced" flavor. The spice did not overpower the stew, but it had plenty of depth. Pendery's Spanish was the runner-up. It had an "earthy" quality and very rich flavor (though not as rich as our winner), with fruity notes. McCormick's finished in third place and was touted for its "lush," "big red pepper" flavor. Paprikash made with the other three paprikas received less favorable comments. Szeged Hungarian Hot was deemed intense and slightly bitter, the Whole Foods paprika was judged bland and uninteresting, and the Igo Basque Piment d'Espelette was so hot that it was hard to detect any flavor (tasters liked this paprika the least).

Our conclusion? Chicken paprikash is best flavored with Hungarian sweet paprika. Other sweet paprikas (from Spain or California) can deliver good results, but don't use hot paprika in this dish.

THE BEST PAPRIKA

Tasters enjoyed the robust but balanced flavor of Penzeys Hungary Sweet (left) and gave this paprika top scores. Pendery's Spanish (center) took second place, hailed for its deep color and rich flavor. McCormick's (right) earned third place in the tasting and is widely available in supermarkets.

for whole chicken, cut up into pieces, which makes sense. We had learned from experience with a variety of chicken stews that batches made entirely with white meat lacked the depth and character of those made with a blend of dark and white. But when we cooked the white and dark meat in the same way—simmered partially submerged in broth—the white meat turned dry and stringy.

Noting that the dark meat—drumsticks and thighs—take roughly one hour of simmering time to become tender, we found that the breasts (cut in half for easier serving), took only 20 minutes. Giving the dark meat a 40-minute head start in the pot took care of the different cooking times and ensured that all of the chicken was perfectly cooked and ready at the same time.

We focused on the paprika next. (For information about paprika, see page 388). Many recipes suggest seasoning the chicken with salt and paprika before browning. We tried this approach and were disappointed with the results. The wonderful paprika aroma that initially filled the kitchen soon turned to a smell of singed peppers. The flavor of the finished dish was bitter and the color had morphed from bright red to burnt sienna. We decided to season the chicken with salt and black pepper and add the paprika later.

With our chicken browned and reserved, we started to test various vegetable options, including onions, peppers, carrots, tomatoes, and mushrooms. Onions were a must—their pungent flavor balanced the sweetness of the paprika. Tasters found both red and green peppers to be welcome additions to the pot. They enhanced the natural sweetness of the paprika and worked well with the onions and chicken. Long strips of peppers looked out of place in this dish, so we cut each cleaned pepper in half before slicing it thin. These shorter strips softened a bit more in the pot and proved easier to eat. Tasters rejected carrots and mushrooms. Although tasty additions, neither seemed essential and so both were vetoed. Tomatoes, however, were deemed crucial to achieving a proper balance between the sweet and acidic components in this dish. Tasters responded favorably to the addition of canned diced tomatoes. We drained the tomatoes so that their juice did not overwhelm the flavors of the other vegetables.

With the vegetables in place, we focused on the seasonings. We found it best to add the paprika to the pot once the onions and peppers had softened. A quick sauté in oil brought out the full flavor of this spice. We tried adding some garlic with the paprika but found its flavor oddly out of place with the mellow sweet flavors in paprikash. Tasters felt that a little dried marjoram was a worthy addition. We also added some flour to the pot at this point to help thicken the stew. A tablespoon of flour provided just enough thickening power.

Although the drained tomatoes provide a little moisture, most paprikash recipes call for some wine to deglaze the pan. We found red wine too harsh; white wine worked better with the other flavors. Sour cream is the final component, added only when the chicken has completely stewed. It gives the sauce body and tang and has a thickening effect as well. Some sources we found in our research suggest using a combination of sour cream and heavy cream. Although we liked the effect that the heavy cream had on the consistency of the sauce (it was velvety and smooth), we missed the tang of recipes made with just sour cream. In the end, we decided to finish the stew with sour cream alone—⅓ cup. If sour cream is added directly to the pot it can curdle. Tempering the sour cream (stirring some of the hot liquid from the stew pot together with the sour cream in a small bowl, then adding the warmed mixture to the pot) will prevent curdling. Once the sour cream goes into the pot, the stew should be served promptly.

After adding this crucial finishing touch to the dish, we came across an unexpected problem: the sour cream dulled the flavor of the paprika. First we tried increasing the amount of paprika added to the pan for sautéing, but still, once the sour cream was added, the potency of the paprika was lost. Finally, we achieved great results by reserving some of the paprika and blending it with the sour cream. This method brought another dimension to the dish, giving it a more intense paprika flavor.

Chicken Paprikash

SERVES 4

Be sure to add the sour cream just before serving, especially if making the dish in advance. Rice or mashed potatoes are good accompaniments, but buttered egg noodles were the tasters' favorite. To serve four people, you'll need to boil about 8 ounces of dried noodles; toss the hot noodles with a tablespoon or two of butter before serving.

4	pounds bone-in, skin-on chicken pieces (split breasts cut in half, drumsticks, and/or thighs)
	Salt and ground black pepper
4	teaspoons vegetable oil, plus extra as needed
1	large onion, halved and sliced thin
1	large red bell pepper, stemmed, seeded, and sliced into ¼-inch-wide strips
1	large green bell pepper, stemmed, seeded, and sliced into ¼-inch-wide strips
3½	tablespoons sweet paprika (see page 388)
1	tablespoon unbleached all-purpose flour
1	(14.5-ounce) can diced tomatoes, drained
½	cup dry white wine
¼	teaspoon dried marjoram
⅓	cup sour cream
2	tablespoons minced fresh parsley leaves

1. Pat the chicken dry with paper towels and season with salt and pepper. Heat 2 teaspoons of the oil in a large Dutch oven over medium-high heat until shimmering. Brown half of the chicken on both sides, 5 to 8 minutes per side, reducing the heat if the pan begins to scorch. Transfer the chicken to a plate, leaving the fat in the pot. Return the pot with fat to medium-high heat and repeat with the remaining 2 teaspoons oil and chicken; transfer the chicken to the plate.

2. Pour off all but 1 tablespoon of the fat in the pot (or add more oil if needed). Add the onion and cook over medium heat, stirring occasionally, until softened, 5 to 7 minutes. Stir in the red and green bell peppers and cook, stirring occasionally, until the onion is browned and the peppers are softened, about 3 minutes. Stir in 3 tablespoons of the paprika and the flour and cook until fragrant, about 30 seconds. Stir in the tomatoes, wine, and marjoram, scraping up any browned bits.

3. Nestle the chicken, along with any accumulated juices, into the pot and bring to a simmer. Cover, turn the heat to medium-low, and simmer until the chicken is fully cooked and tender, about 20 minutes for the breasts (they should register 160 degrees on an instant-read thermometer) or 1 hour for the thighs and drumsticks. (If using both types of chicken, simmer the thighs and drumsticks for 40 minutes before adding the breasts.)

4. Transfer the chicken to a serving dish, tent loosely with foil, and let rest while finishing the sauce. Skim as much fat as possible off the surface of the sauce, return to a brief simmer over medium-high heat, then remove from the heat. Stir the remaining 1½ teaspoons paprika and a few tablespoons of the sauce into the sour cream to temper, then stir the sour cream mixture into the pot. Season the sauce with salt and pepper to taste. Pour the sauce and peppers over the chicken, sprinkle with the parsley, and serve.

CORE TECHNIQUE

FINISHING SAUCES AND STEWS

While butter and cream are often used to finish a sauce or stew in western Europe, sour cream is the preferred dairy in many Russian and eastern Europe dishes. The cool, creamy tang of sour cream is a perfect foil to eastern European spices like paprika in such dishes as Chicken Paprikash (at left) and Beef Goulash (page 392). Note that the sour cream should be tempered before being added to a hot dish to prevent curdling. Tempering means simply adding a bit of the stew's hot liquid to the sour cream to gently bring its temperature up. At this point, the tempered sour cream can be stirred into the stew and then the dish should be served promptly—it will curdle if later reheated. Even when tempered, sour cream can be finicky in a hot dish, so it's best to stick to full-fat sour cream for best texture and flavor.

BEEF GOULASH

THIS SIMPLE EASTERN EUROPEAN STEW HAS been around for centuries. The word goulash comes from the Hungarian *gulyas*, which means "herd of cattle." Originally, cattlemen seared and stewed beef until the liquid evaporated and then dried the meat in the sun. When needed, the meat was rehydrated with water and, depending on how much liquid was added, goulash stew or soup was created. Goulash stew—without the drying step—is the more popular, modern version and the one more familiar in the United States.

There are several versions of modern goulash stew. Beef, onions, garlic, and paprika are constants. Other possible ingredients include potatoes, tomatoes, and bell peppers. Our goal was to create a very simple stew with tender, flavorful beef and browned onions in an intensely flavored, rich sauce. The sauce would be thick and brownish red in color, both from the paprika and the good browning that the meat and onions would receive.

We found that chuck meat was the best choice because it cooks up tender and flavorful. Traditional recipes brown the beef in lard, and we found that the gentle pork flavor of good lard does add something to this dish. Given the fact that most cooks don't have lard on hand, we tried bacon fat as a substitute. Tasters reacted negatively to goulash made with bacon fat. They said the smoky flavor imparted by the bacon was at odds with this stew. Vegetable oil turned out to be a better choice. Although not as flavorful as lard, oil will suffice.

On a related subject, we discovered that leaving a little fat attached to the pieces of meat boosts flavor and helps compensate for the missing pork flavor if lard is not used. You will need to defat the stew before serving, but this is easily done with a spoon.

In these early tests, we found that browning the meat well is essential to flavor development in goulash. The hearty, rich flavor and color of goulash is dependent on browning the meat and onions and then deglazing the crusty, deep brown bits stuck to the bottom of the Dutch oven.

We found that adding a little salt with the onions caused them to release moisture and kept them from scorching. This moisture also helped to loosen the browned bits, a process that is completed once the liquid is added to the pan. Although onions are a must, the recipes we looked at were divided on the question of garlic. Tasters, however, were not. Everyone in the test kitchen liked garlic in this stew. Six cloves added depth and also balanced the sweetness of the paprika and onions. Once the garlic was fragrant, it was time for the paprika to go into the pot. Sweet Hungarian paprika (see page 388 for more details) is essential in this recipe. We added the flour (to thicken the stew) at the same time.

Recipes uncovered in our research used an assortment of liquids, including water, beef stock, and chicken stock. We found that water created a bland stew. Homemade beef stock was delicious in this dish but required a large investment of time. We wondered if we could substitute store-bought broth without compromising the flavor too much.

Store-bought beef broth tasted concentrated and somewhat off-flavored after the long cooking time and did not work in goulash. We had better results with chicken broth. It gave the stew good body and the chicken flavor faded behind the beef and spices. Some recipes also include wine in the mix, although authentic recipes do not. We tried varying amounts of red wine and tasters felt that its flavor was too overpowering. Goulash should be soft and mellow; while red wine added complexity, it also made the stew acidic and a bit harsh. A few sources suggested white wine, but tasters were again unimpressed, so we left it out. Our recipe was coming together—browned beef and onions, garlic and paprika for flavor, and chicken broth as the liquid.

We had two major issues to resolve—tomatoes and vegetables. We started with the tomatoes. Many goulash recipes contain tomato, although the original dish (which dates back several centuries before the arrival of tomatoes from the New World) certainly did not. We decided to make four batches of goulash—one with canned diced tomatoes, one with plain tomato sauce, one with tomato paste, and one with no tomato product. The diced tomatoes and tomato sauce proved to be too dominant and made the stew reminiscent of beef cacciatore. Tomato paste, however, blended into the background and enhanced other flavors in the dish. Compared with the stew made without any tomatoes, the version with tomato paste was more complex and appealing. In fact, the tomatoes functioned a bit like wine in terms of adding depth, but they were also much more subtle than wine and thus more in tune with the spirit of goulash.

Vegetables were easy to incorporate into the dish. Tasters liked large chunks of red and green bell peppers, especially when added to the stew near the end of the cooking time. When added earlier (just after the onions are browned is a common choice), the peppers become mushy and fell apart. We found that if they are added to the stew while it is in the oven, the peppers soften without turning mushy.

We tested carrots, cabbage, celery, and green beans (ingredients used in some of the recipes we had collected) but did not like any of them in goulash. Potatoes were a different story. Several recipes added them to the stew pot with the liquid so they would fall apart and thicken the stew. Although we did not like this approach, we did like potatoes simmered in the stew until tender. Adding the potatoes partway through the oven cooking time yielded this result, so we decided to include potatoes in a variation.

Many Hungarian goulash recipes do not include sour cream, which seems more popular in German and Austrian versions. But our tasters all felt that the sour cream mellowed and enriched this stew. To prevent the sour cream from curdling, we combined the sour cream with a little hot stewing liquid to temper it and then stirred the mixture back into the stew pot.

Goulash is traditionally served over buttered egg noodles or Spätzle (page 121). Egg noodles require almost no effort to cook and are our first choice. Mashed potatoes are not traditional, but they make an excellent accompaniment, too.

Beef Goulash

SERVES 6

Traditional beef goulash is a mellow-flavored stew with sweet overtones; add a pinch of hot paprika or cayenne pepper if you want a little kick. Beef fat adds good flavor to this sauce, so don't trim the meat too closely; when trimming the beef, remove the external fat from the roast but leave most of the internal fat intact. Serve with buttered egg noodles. To serve six people, you'll need to boil about 12 ounces of dried noodles; toss the hot noodles with a tablespoon or two of butter and a pinch of toasted caraway seeds before serving.

3½	pounds boneless beef chuck-eye roast, trimmed and cut into 1½-inch chunks
	Salt and ground black pepper
3	tablespoons vegetable oil or lard
4	large onions, minced (about 5 cups)
6	medium garlic cloves, minced or pressed through a garlic press (about 2 tablespoons)
5	tablespoons sweet paprika (see page 388)
¼	cup unbleached all-purpose flour
2	tablespoons tomato paste
3	cups low-sodium chicken broth
2	bay leaves
1	teaspoon dried marjoram
1	large red bell pepper, stemmed, seeded, and cut into ½-inch pieces
1	large green bell pepper, stemmed, seeded, and cut into ½-inch pieces
½	cup sour cream
¼	cup minced fresh parsley leaves

1. Adjust an oven rack to the lower-middle position and heat the oven to 325 degrees. Pat the beef dry with paper towels and season with salt and pepper. Heat 1 tablespoon of the oil in a large Dutch oven over medium-high heat until just smoking. Add half of the meat and cook, stirring occasionally, until well browned, 7 to 10 minutes, reducing the heat if the pot begins to scorch. Transfer the browned beef to a medium bowl. Repeat with 1 more tablespoon oil and the remaining beef; transfer the meat to the bowl.

2. Add the remaining 1 tablespoon oil to the pot and return to medium heat until shimmering. Add the onions and 1 teaspoon salt and cook until softened, 5 to 7 minutes. Stir in the garlic and cook until fragrant, about 30 seconds. Stir in the paprika, flour, and tomato paste and cook, stirring constantly, for 1 minute.

3. Slowly whisk in the broth, scraping up any browned bits. Stir in the browned meat with any accumulated juices, bay leaves, and marjoram. Bring to a simmer and arrange the meat so it is completely covered by the liquid. Cover the pot, transfer it to the oven, and cook for 1 hour and 20 minutes.

4. Stir the red and green bell peppers into the stew, cover, and continue to cook in the oven until a fork inserted in the beef meets little resistance, about 40 minutes longer. (At this point, the stew can be cooled to room temperature and refrigerated in an airtight container for up to 2 days. Reheat in a large Dutch oven over medium heat before continuing).

5. Remove the pot from the oven, and let rest for 5 to 10 minutes. Using a spoon, skim the excess fat from the surface of the stew. Remove and discard the bay leaves. Stir about ½ cup of the sauce into the sour cream to temper, then stir the sour cream mixture into the stew. Stir in the parsley, season with salt and pepper to taste, and serve.

➤ VARIATION

Beef Goulash with Potatoes and Caraway
With potatoes added, there's no need to serve this stew over noodles. Caraway seeds are a traditional addition to Hungarian goulash.

Follow the recipe for Beef Goulash, reducing the amount of beef to 3 pounds and adding 1 teaspoon caraway seeds with the paprika in step 2. Stir ¾ pound red potatoes, peeled and cut into 1-inch dice, into the stew after it has cooked in the oven for 1 hour. Continue with the recipe as directed.

BEEF STROGANOFF

IN THE UNITED STATES, BEEF STROGANOFF (most often cheap strips of beef and mushy noodles drowned in a gloppy sauce) is typically associated with banquet or cafeteria fare. This is a shame because in Russia, where the recipe originated, it is an elegant dish, originally created for nobility. Made properly, beef stroganoff is decadent, with tender succulent beef and a silky sauce. We set out to restore this dish to its original glory.

Beef, mushrooms, onions, and sour cream are classic ingredients in a stroganoff. Beyond that there are no standard seasonings. The meat that goes into a stroganoff is a tender cut like tenderloin rather than braising cuts such as chuck or brisket, which need time and patience to grow tender under a lid. We first set up a basic recipe using 1 pound of beef, 6 ounces of mushrooms, minced onions, 1 tablespoon of flour, 1 cup of chicken broth, and ½ cup of sour cream, then went off to test cuts of beef. Though we knew beef tenderloin was traditional in stroganoff, as we sliced up this incredibly tender and expensive cut of meat, we wondered why. If you spend a lot of money on filet, you do not necessarily want to smother it with gravy. Could we come up with a stroganoff that was equally tender and flavorful, yet inexpensive, while maintaining its allure?

We decided to change direction and try some cheaper cuts of beef. Because cheaper cuts of meat are generally tough, we knew we would have to move from a quick sauté to a short braise, because the moist heat breaks down the fibers and collagen in meat, making tough cuts tender. Sliced blade steaks shrank into unappetizing curls. We had better success with sirloin steak tips (aka flap meat); they were tender, but they transformed into an accordion shape as they cooked. We found that pounding the tips before cutting them into strips compressed the fibers of the meat and helped keep the strips neat and uniform as they cooked. Tasters were happy with the meat choice and were willing to put up with a slightly longer cooking time for a cheaper cut of beef that was equally, if not more, flavorful. Buying steak tips, however, can get a little

INGREDIENTS: Steak Tips

Steak tips can come from two different parts of the cow. One type comes from tender, expensive cuts in the middle of the back of the cow, such as the tenderloin. These tips are a superior cut, but not what we consider to be a true steak tip, which should be a more pedestrian cut that is magically transformed into a desirable dish through pounding and cooking. If the steak tips at your market cost $8 to $10 per pound, the meat likely comes from the tenderloin.

True steak tips come from various muscles in the sirloin and round and cost about $5 per pound. After tasting 50 pounds of these lower-priced steak tips cuts, tasters had a clear favorite: a single muscle that butchers call flap meat, with tips from this cut typically labeled "sirloin tips." A whole piece of flap meat weighs about 2½ pounds. One piece can range in thickness from ½ inch to 1½ inches and may be sold as cubes, strips, or small steaks. It has a rich, deep beefy flavor and a distinctive longitudinal grain.

We found that it's best to buy flap meat in steak form rather than cut into cubes or strips, which are often taken from nearby muscles in the hip and butt that are neither as tasty nor as tender. Because meat labeling is so haphazard, you must visually identify flap meat; buying it in steak form makes this easy.

CUBES

STEAKS   **STRIPS**

Steak tips can be cut from a half-dozen muscles and are sold in three basic forms: cubes, strips, and steaks. To make sure that you are buying the most flavorful cut (called flap meat sirloin tips by butchers and pictured above), buy whole steaks.

tricky; see page 394 for additional information.

Many recipes flour the meat to promote browning and thicken the sauce. But flouring left the sautéed meat lying in the sauce looking like swathed mummies. Adding a single tablespoon of flour to the pan after the meat had been sautéed worked far better. Since most beef stroganoff recipes feature strips of meat that appear to have been browned very little, if at all, we thought it would only be fair to try a batch of meat thrown in a skillet with no attention to browning. Sure enough, it looked just like the stroganoffs we had seen in hotel chafing dishes. Unfortunately, it tasted like them, too. Browning, we decided, would be essential.

We now turned to building the sauce. We knew that the fond, or browned bits left in the pan after sautéing, would be critical to a flavorful sauce and needed only to be lifted from the pan with a little liquid, or deglazed. Traditional recipes all called for homemade beef stock. Because making beef stock is so time-consuming, we wanted to try store-bought broth instead. From past experience, we knew that store-bought beef broth is not always the favored substitute, as its flavor can overwhelm the dish. Therefore, in subsequent tests, we tried using chicken broth and a combination of beef broth and chicken broth. Tasters felt that the chicken broth worked best. The flavors now boosted the meaty flavor, but did not overwhelm the dish. Next we decided to test red wine and brandy, which were common ingredients in many recipes. They were each nice additions, but for this dish tasters slightly preferred the brandy.

Aromatics were up next. We liked the bright flavor of the onions and increased the amount from ¼ cup to ½ cup for even more flavor. We also wanted the mushrooms to have a presence equal to the beef, so we decided to increase their amount from 6 ounces to 10 ounces.

Now came the laundry list of flavorings we found in many recipes from our research. There is an almost desperate "anything goes" feeling in some recipes for beef stroganoff. Different combinations of ingredients, such as prepared mustard, paprika, Worcestershire sauce, cider vinegar, tomato paste, brown sugar, and sherry, ultimately antagonized each other. Still, our impulse, like everyone else's, was to try all the seasonings to build complexity. Despite our desire to pump flavor into the sauce, the only survivors were 1 teaspoon of tomato paste and 1½ teaspoons of dark brown sugar.

For the final essential ingredient, we finished the dish with ⅔ cup of sour cream. However, as we learned in making our Chicken Paprikash (page 390) and Beef Goulash (page 392), we needed to proceed with caution. If sour cream is added directly to the pot it can curdle. Tempering the sour cream (stirring some of the hot liquid from the stew pot together with the sour cream in a small bowl, then adding the warmed mixture to the pot) will prevent curdling. Once the sour cream goes into the pot, the stew should be served promptly. We added a touch of lemon juice and a handful of parsley to complete the dish. This at last was stroganoff, recognizably retro, quite affordable, and, in the company of a bowl of hot, buttered noodles, pretty irresistible.

Beef Stroganoff

SERVES 4

For more information on buying flap meat sirloin steak tips, see page 394. In Russia this dish is often served over buttered boiled new potatoes, but buttered egg noodles are good too. To serve four people, you'll need to boil about 8 ounces of dried noodles; toss the hot noodles with a tablespoon or two of butter before serving.

1½	pounds flap meat sirloin steak tips
	Salt and ground black pepper
¼	cup vegetable oil
10	ounces white mushrooms, wiped clean and sliced thin
1	medium onion, minced
2	tablespoons unbleached all-purpose flour
1	teaspoon tomato paste
2	cups low-sodium chicken broth
⅓	cup brandy
1½	teaspoons dark brown sugar
⅔	cup sour cream
2	teaspoons juice from 1 lemon
1	tablespoon minced fresh parsley leaves

1. Using a meat pounder, pound the beef to an even ½-inch thickness. Slicing with the grain of the meat, slice the meat into 2-inch-wide strips. Slice each strip crosswise into ½-inch-wide pieces.

2. Pat the beef dry with paper towels and season with salt and pepper. Heat 1 tablespoon of the oil in a 12-inch skillet over medium-high heat until just smoking. Brown half of the beef until well browned on both sides, 6 to 8 minutes. Transfer to a medium bowl and repeat with 1 more tablespoon of the oil and the remaining beef.

3. Add the remaining 2 tablespoons oil to the skillet and return to medium-high heat until shimmering. Add the mushrooms, onion, and ½ teaspoon salt, and cook until the liquid from the mushrooms has evaporated, about 8 minutes. (If the pan begins to scorch, add the accumulated beef juices to the skillet.)

4. Stir in the flour and tomato paste and cook for 30 seconds. Gradually whisk in the broth. Stir in the brandy, sugar, and beef with any accumulated juices. Bring to a simmer and cook, uncovered, over low heat until the beef is tender and the sauce is thickened, 30 to 35 minutes.

5. Remove the skillet from the heat. Stir a few tablespoons of the sauce into the sour cream to temper, then stir the sour cream mixture into the skillet. Stir in the lemon juice and parsley and season with salt and pepper to taste before serving.

BLINTZES

Blinchiki

A BLINTZ IS A FILLED THIN PANCAKE, WHICH is very similar to a French crêpe. *Blinchiki*, as they are called in Russia, are crêpes rolled with either sweet or savory fillings and then browned in butter before serving. Our mission was to develop a recipe for crêpes filled with a sweet cheese filling, something that could be eaten for breakfast, brunch, or even teatime. Blintzes are often topped with a dollop of sour cream or a dusting of confectioners' sugar, and sometimes a sauce. Feeling indulgent, we decided to develop a cherry sauce because cherries are prevalent throughout Russia and eastern Europe and are integral to their cuisine.

Our goal was to develop perfect blintzes, tasty enough to eat right out of the pan, with a texture that was tender rather than rubbery. We wanted them to be thin and flexible enough to fold and roll, but sturdy enough to hold a filling. For a starting point, we turned to our archives, where over the years there has been significant testing to find the perfect crêpe recipe. As we played with a number of recipes, we found that a batter slightly thicker than heavy cream worked best, as the batter coated the pan easily, yielding thin delicate crêpes. Thinner batters bubbled significantly when they hit the pan, making holes, while thicker batters produced heavy, rubbery crêpes.

While working to achieve the right consistency, we ran a number of other tests trying to find the right balance of ingredients to produce the best texture and taste. We found that whole milk was superior to both low-fat and nonfat milk, both of which lacked the rich full flavor we were after. Finally, we played with the number of eggs and amount of butter. We arrived at two eggs, which produced a less rubbery texture and more appealing flavor—a batter made with three eggs was too eggy-tasting. On the butter front, more was definitely better. We tested blintzes made with from 1 to 4 tablespoons of melted butter. While the texture of the blintzes made with 1 tablespoon of butter was absolutely fine, the flavor was better with more. Four tablespoons made for a greasy batter, but 3 tablespoons of butter was perfect.

We now turned from the batter to the mixing process and resting time. We found that a hand-mixed batter left excess lumps, did not coat the pan as easily, and created crêpes with a spongy texture. We turned to the blender and food processor in hopes that they would prevent these problems and make the batter effortless to put together. Our theory proved correct. Mixing the batter in either machine was quick and easy and the resulting blintzes were slightly more tender. Many recipes called for the batter to rest for a minimum of two hours to allow the gluten to relax, ensuring tender crêpes.

We tested resting times at 30-minute intervals to find the shortest possible resting time needed to settle the foam and bring the batter to the proper thickness. The finished crêpes were noticeably more tender with the passing of each 30-minute interval up to the two-hour mark; after that, there was no difference. Nor could we find any appreciable difference in the finished blintzes when the batter sat, covered and refrigerated, overnight.

With our crêpes tasting delicious on their own, we focused on the sweet cheese filling. Farmer's cheese was the most common cheese used in the authentic Russian recipes. However, we decided to test a few others to make sure this would be the favorite. We tested farmer's cheese, cottage cheese, and ricotta. The cottage cheese was the least desirable; it produced soggy blintzes. The ricotta cheese was better, although some tasters commented that the filling was reminiscent of cannoli. The farmer's cheese was a huge hit; the flavor was creamy and rich. The cheese did need to be thinned slightly so we tested two options, heavy cream and sour cream. The heavy cream was a perfect match, adding a touch of richness and complementing the farmer's cheese. The sour cream imparted too much tang. With a bit of sugar to sweeten the cheese and a touch of vanilla, the filling was complete.

Finally we turned to the cherry sauce that would top our blintzes and bring the whole dish together. Sour cherries, which are grown in abundance in Russia and eastern Europe, have sufficient acidity to cook up well and become truly expressive with a touch of sugar. (Sweet cherries, like Bings, lose their flavor when cooked.) Sour cherries are classified in two groups, Montmorency and Morello. Most sour cherries grown in the U.S. are Montmorency.

Although we knew that fresh sour cherries would be transcendent in our sauce, they only appear in our markets for a brief period in July. We needed another option for the remaining 11 months of the year. Though sour cherries (the Montmorency cherry) are grown in relatively large quantities in Michigan, here in the Northeast our grocery shelves are mainly stocked with crayon-red canned gravy with lumps called "pie filling."

While frozen Michigan sour cherries maintained their color well, their flavor was left largely to the imagination. Both canned and jarred sour cherries from Michigan were mushy and developed an anemic pallor when cooked. At last we found jarred Morellos. Deep ruby red, plump, meaty, and tart, they delivered bracing flavor and a great texture right out of the jar.

Because jarred and canned cherries have been processed, they are already cooked, so the less heat they are exposed to thereafter, the better. We strained off the juices and set the cherries aside. We knew we wanted to use some of the reserved cherry juice to make the sauce, sweetened with some sugar. We then added a bit of red wine, a cinnamon stick, a pinch of salt and a whiff of almond extract. Red wine and cherries have a natural affinity; the cinnamon stick added a fragrant woody depth; and,

as it does with all fruits, salt performed its usual minor miracle. The almond extract brought the entire experience up a few notches. After a bit more research we decided to revisit the red wine, since it is not used that often in Russian cooking. We tested the sauce using water and lemon to replace the red wine. The sauce made with water was a bit boring, while the one made with lemon juice was a bit too tart. The red wine was clearly favored by all. We therefore opted to keep it in, although it is not traditional.

For the thickener, we resolved to use cornstarch. We wanted the sauce to be fairly thick, similar to compote, so as not to run all over the plate, creating soggy blintzes. When we spooned the Morello cherry sauce over the warm blintzes, and dusted them with confectioners' sugar, tasters smiled and devoured them one by one.

ASSEMBLING BLINTZES

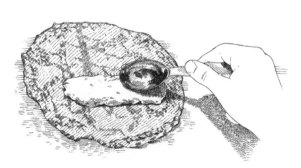

1. Spoon 1 generous tablespoon of the filling onto a crêpe, just off center, and spread it in a horizontal line.

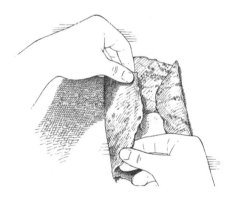

2. Fold the sides of the crêpe in toward the center.

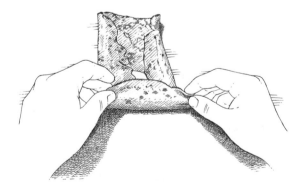

3. Fold up the bottom edge of the crêpe over the sides to encase the filling.

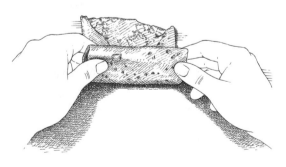

4. Continue to roll the crêpe into a tidy package. Repeat with remaining crêpes and filling.

397

Blintzes with Sweet Cheese Filling
Blinchiki

MAKES 16 TO 20 BLINTZES, SERVING 6 TO 8

While we prefer the flavor and texture of farmer's cheese here, an equal amount of ricotta cheese can be substituted. The filling, cherry sauce, and plate of crêpes can all be wrapped tightly in plastic wrap and refrigerated separately for up to three days; reheat the stack of cold crêpes for 10 seconds in a microwave on 50 percent power to soften before filling. Once filled and rolled, the blintzes can be covered and refrigerated for up to six hours before browning.

CRÊPES

1	cup (5 ounces) unbleached all-purpose flour
1	cup whole milk
6	tablespoons water
2	large eggs
3	tablespoons unsalted butter, melted, plus more for cooking the crêpes
2	tablespoons granulated sugar
1	teaspoon vanilla extract
¼	teaspoon salt

FILLING

12	ounces farmer's cheese (about 2 cups)
¼	cup heavy cream
3	tablespoons granulated sugar
2	tablespoons unsalted butter, melted and cooled
1	teaspoon vanilla extract

CHERRY SAUCE

¼	cup (1¾ ounces) granulated sugar
2½	teaspoons cornstarch
	Pinch salt
1	(24-ounce) jar Morello cherries, drained (about 2 cups cherries) with ½ cup juice reserved
¼	cup dry red wine
1	cinnamon stick
	Almond extract
2	tablespoons unsalted butter, for cooking the filled blintzes
	Confectioners' sugar, for dusting

1. **FOR THE CRÊPES:** Blend all of the ingredients together in a blender (or food processor) until smooth, about 4 seconds. Transfer the batter to a covered container and refrigerate for at least 2 hours or up to 2 days.

2. **FOR THE FILLING:** While the batter is resting, mix all of the filling ingredients together in a bowl. Cover and refrigerate until needed.

3. **FOR THE SAUCE:** Stir the granulated sugar, cornstarch, and salt together in a medium saucepan. Whisk in the reserved cherry juice and wine. Add the cinnamon stick and cook over medium-high heat, whisking frequently, until the mixture simmers and thickens, 3 to 5 minutes. Discard the cinnamon stick. Stir in the cherries and a drop of almond extract and return to a brief simmer; cover to keep warm and set aside.

4. Using a pastry brush, brush the bottom and sides of a 6- to 8-inch nonstick skillet (or crêpe pan) very lightly with melted butter. Gently stir the batter to recombine. When the butter stops sizzling, remove the pan from the heat, tilt the pan slightly and pour 2½ tablespoons of the batter (you can fill a ¼ cup measuring cup a little past the halfway mark) into the pan. As you pour the batter, rotate the pan to swirl the batter evenly over the face of the pan before returning it to the heat.

5. Cook the crêpe until the first side is spotty golden brown, 30 to 60 seconds. Use a thin spatula to flip the crêpe and continue to cook until the second side is just set, but not brown, about 15 seconds longer. Transfer the crêpe to a parchment paper–lined plate and let cool (you can stack the crêpes on top of each other). Repeat with the remaining batter, brushing the pan with butter as needed.

6. Working with 1 crêpe at a time, spoon 1 generous tablespoon of the cheese filling over the browned side and fold following the illustrations on page 397. Repeat with the remaining crêpes and filling.

7. **TO FINISH:** Melt 1 tablespoon of the butter in a 12-inch nonstick skillet over medium heat. Add half of the blintzes and cook until the first side is golden brown, about 1 minute. Gently flip the blintzes over and continue to cook until the second side is golden brown, about 1 minute longer.

Transfer the browned blintzes to a platter and cover with foil to keep warm. Repeat with the remaining 1 tablespoon butter and unbrowned blintzes.

8. Reheat the cherry sauce over medium heat if necessary. Dust the warm blintzes with confectioners' sugar, spoon some of the cherry sauce over the top, and serve, passing the remaining sauce separately.

Cinnamon and Walnut Sweet Bread

Babka

BABKA, A DIMINUTIVE OF THE POLISH WORD *baba*, meaning "grandmother," is a rich and decadent coffeecake-style bread that is traditionally reserved for Easter Sunday in eastern Europe. Made with eggs, sugar, and butter and filled with cinnamon, sugar, nuts, and sometimes raisins, traditional babka is characterized by its round shape (sometimes with a hole in the middle), caramelized exterior, butter-rich flavor, and gooey filling. Nowadays, in the United States, bakeries sell babkas any day of the week, and flavors and shapes have evolved from the classic to include various flavorings and shapes—we have even seen chocolate babka muffins. While we love these modern versions, we wanted to develop a recipe that paid homage to eastern European grandmothers.

Eaten on its own—good babka doesn't need butter or jam—babka is one of our favorite breads. But like anything, bad babka is truly bad: greasy and leaden as well as overly sticky, sweet, and dense, or worse, unpalatably dry and bready. Our goal was to develop a babka rich in flavor, tender in texture, and worth every calorie.

We decided to start with the dough and worry about the filling later. The first ingredient up for examination was the flour. We tried both all-purpose flour and bread flour. All-purpose flour was the clear winner, giving the babka a fluffier, more tender crumb. The babka made with bread flour was heavy and dense. Tasters quickly settled

on ½ cup sugar as the right amount for the dough, which made the bread sweet without it tasting cloying. A little vanilla extract added complexity to the dough.

One of the hallmarks of babka is its eggy flavor. Because we wanted our babka to be tender and rich, we started by using just yolks. To our surprise, the all-egg-yolk babka was dry and heavy. We tried various yolk and whole-egg combinations and found that the lightest, most tender babka was made with three whole eggs.

As for liquids, we tried water, milk, and sour cream. Sour cream produced the best results, giving the babka a richer flavor than either milk or water. We tried yeast amounts ranging from 1 teaspoon to 2 tablespoons and got the best results with 1 package (2¼ teaspoons) of yeast.

Babka just wouldn't be babka without butter—it is usually in the dough and in the filling. But how much should we add to the dough? We tried amounts as little as 4 tablespoons and as much as a whopping 20 tablespoons. As we expected, more butter made the bread taste better and gave it a richer texture. However, there was a limit. Sixteen tablespoons of butter did the trick; the loaves made with more than that became leaden and greasy.

Now that the butter amount was set, we needed to find the best way to incorporate it. Traditionally, the butter is softened and kneaded into the dough. We wanted to know what would happen if we added melted butter instead. Adding the butter in its liquid form made the dough greasy and wet, necessitating the addition of more flour, which resulted in a drier, tougher babka. Softened butter was a must.

On to the mixing method. Because there was so much butter in the dough, we found that kneading by hand was difficult. By the time the dough was fully kneaded, the heat from our hands had melted some of the butter, resulting in a heavy, greasy bread. The food processor failed to totally incorporate the butter, making it necessary to finish kneading the dough by hand (again, not the answer). We needed to find a method that would knead the dough thoroughly while allowing it to remain cool. The answer was to use a standing mixer with the dough hook. This evenly incorporated the butter while keeping the dough from over heating.

Babka is traditionally allowed to ferment in a cool place overnight. What would happen if the dough were allowed to rise in a warm place? We let one loaf rise at room temperature for two hours and put it up against another that had risen in the refrigerator overnight. The room-temperature babka had a strong yeasty flavor, oily texture, and uneven crumb; the refrigerator babka had a clean,

SHAPING BABKA

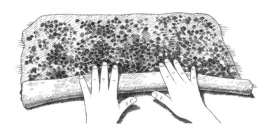

1. Sprinkle the filling evenly over the dough, leaving ½ inch at the far end, and roll up the dough into a long, taut cylinder, then brush the seam with water and pinch to secure.

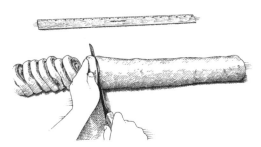

2. Dust the roll with flour and gently pat the roll into a uniform, 24-inch-long roll. Using a serrated knife, slice the roll into ¾-inch-thick slices (you should have about 32 slices; don't worry if your slices are slightly smaller or bigger and you yield a few more or less).

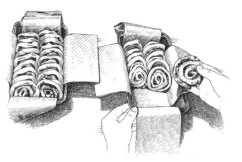

3. In each loaf pan, arrange the dough slices in 2 long rows (about 8 slices per row) that run the length of the pan. Cover the pans loosely with plastic wrap and let rise at room temperature.

mild flavor with a delicate, even texture. Allowing the dough to rise in the refrigerator accomplishes two things: The lower temperature keeps the butter from melting, and it lets the yeast develop slowly, resulting in a fine, tender crumb. After experimenting with fermentation times, we found that a stay of at least 10 hours in the refrigerator was necessary.

With our dough ready, we turned our attention to the filling, which came together easily. Cinnamon was a given and our tasters preferred a modest 2 teaspoons—after all, this was babka, not cinnamon rolls. Butter was also necessary to make the filling rich and moist. We tested granulated sugar as well as light and dark brown sugar in the filling. Granulated sugar was too dry and added little flavor. Dark brown sugar proved too wet and turned syrupy, like the filling for a sticky bun. And the strong molasses flavor detracted from the cinnamon. Light brown sugar proved the best sweetener, adding moisture and a lighter molasses flavor that complemented the cinnamon. Salt mixed with the cinnamon and sugar helped marry the flavors and sharpen the sugar's sweetness.

The variables in the babka filling are usually nuts and raisins. Nuts were unanimously accepted among tasters. We found that toasted and coarsely chopped walnuts tasted best. Untoasted nuts tasted bland and steamed. As for the raisins, tasters were split down the middle, so we decided to make them optional.

With the dough and filling resolved, we turned to shaping, which was a lot easier than we had expected. Instead of making one large babka in a Bundt or tube pan, we decided to stray from tradition and make two loaves. (This way we could eat one and freeze one.) The soft dough gracefully yielded to a light touch under the rolling pin as we rolled it out. We then sprinkled it with the filling and rolled it up slowly and tightly into a cylinder. Some babka recipes simply place the cylinder of dough into the pan, while others slice it into rounds and arrange them in the pan. We tested both methods and found that the loaf made with the slices of dough baked up with a golden brown, craggy, and crunchy top that tasters preferred to the smooth surface of the other loaf. The best tool for cutting the soft dough into rounds turned out to be a serrated knife, which lets you smoothly cut through soft dough without squeezing the filling out of place. We then arranged the slices in the loaf pans and set them aside to proof before putting them into the oven. (Egg wash and an extra sprinkling of cinnamon and sugar gave the loaves golden brown, crackly, and sweet tops.)

We knew we wanted an initial blast of high heat to give the loaves a proper rise and a nicely browned crust. To determine the best baking temperature, we tried baking the babka at temperatures ranging from 300 to 425 degrees. After much testing, we determined that placing the bread in a 450-degree oven, then immediately turning the temperature down to 350 degrees for the duration of the baking gave us an evenly baked bread with a uniformly browned exterior. Now for the most difficult part of the recipe—waiting for the babka to cool before eating it!

Cinnamon and Walnut Sweet Bread

Babka

MAKES TWO 9-INCH LOAVES

Because of all the butter in this dough, we don't recommend kneading it by hand or in a food processor. After mixing for the final 15 minutes, the dough should be very soft and slightly sticky, but not wet. You will know that you have added enough flour in step 2 if, when you touch the finished dough, it pulls away from your fingers. This is a rustic bread, so do not worry about slicing the raw dough in step 6 into perfect rounds or even if you are a few rounds short.

DOUGH

5½ cups (27½ ounces) unbleached all-purpose flour, plus extra for the work surface
1 package (2¼ teaspoons) instant or rapid-rise yeast
1 cup sour cream
½ cup (3½ ounces) granulated sugar
3 large eggs
¼ cup water
4 teaspoons vanilla extract
1 teaspoon salt
16 tablespoons (2 sticks) unsalted butter, cut into 16 pieces and softened but still cool

FILLING

1½ cups (10½ ounces) packed light or dark brown sugar
8 tablespoons (1 stick) unsalted butter, melted
1 cup walnuts, toasted and chopped coarse (see page 135)
1 cup raisins (optional)
2 teaspoons ground cinnamon
Pinch salt

GLAZE

1 tablespoon granulated sugar
¼ teaspoon ground cinnamon
1 large egg
1 tablespoon water

1. FOR THE DOUGH: In a medium bowl, whisk together 4½ cups of the flour and the yeast; set aside. In the bowl of a standing mixer, whisk together the sour cream, granulated sugar, eggs, water, vanilla, and salt. Add the flour mixture (do not stir in) and, using the dough hook, knead the mixture on low speed until the ingredients are evenly combined, about 3 minutes. Increase the mixer speed to medium-low and continue to knead until the dough becomes smooth, about 8 minutes longer, stopping to scrape down the sides of the bowl occasionally. (The dough will be very wet.)

2. With the mixer running on medium-low, slowly add the butter, 1 piece at a time, waiting about 15 seconds between additions. After the butter has been added, scrape down the sides of the bowl and continue to knead the dough on medium-low until the dough forms a very soft ball, about 15 minutes longer. Add the remaining 1 cup (5 ounces) flour, 2 tablespoons at a time, until the dough is no longer wet and it clears the sides but sticks to the bottom of the bowl. (You may not need all the flour; the dough should be very soft and sticky.)

3. Scrape the dough into a large, lightly oiled bowl. Cover with plastic wrap and refrigerate for 10 to 24 hours. (Because of the high butter content, the dough will rise only slightly.)

4. FOR THE FILLING: Mix all of the ingredients together; set aside. Spray two 9-inch loaf pans with vegetable oil spray, then line with overhanging

strips of parchment paper following the illustrations below. Spray the parchment paper with vegetable oil spray and set aside.

5. Turn the cold dough onto a lightly floured work surface. Use a rolling pin to roll the dough into an 18 by 24-inch rectangle, about 1/16-inch thick, with the long side facing you. Following the illustrations on page 400, sprinkle the filling evenly over the dough, leaving a 1/2-inch border at the far edge. Using both hands, roll the dough into a long, taut cylinder. Pinch the seam closed to secure.

6. Lightly dust the roll with flour and pat into a uniform, 24-inch-long cylinder. Using a serrated knife, slice the roll into 3/4-inch thick slices (you should have about 32 slices). Arrange the slices in 2 long rows in each of the prepared loaf pans (about 16 slices per pan). Loosely cover the pans with plastic wrap and let rise at room temperature until almost doubled in size, 2 to 2 1/2 hours.

7. FOR THE GLAZE AND TO BAKE: Adjust an oven rack to the lower-middle position and heat the oven to 450 degrees. Mix the granulated sugar and cinnamon together. In a separate bowl, beat the egg with the water. Brush the loaves gently with the egg mixture, then sprinkle with the cinnamon-sugar mixture. Place the loaf pans in the oven and reduce the temperature to 350 degrees. Bake the loaves until browned and an instant-read thermometer inserted into the side of the loaf reads 190 degrees, 50 to 60 minutes, rotating the pans halfway through the baking time. (If the tops of the loaves look like they are getting too dark, tent the pans loosely with foil.)

8. Transfer the loaf pans to a wire rack and let cool for 15 minutes. Using the overhanging parchment as a grip, remove the babka from the loaf pans. Let the loaves cool completely on the rack before slicing and serving. (The cooled loaves can be wrapped tightly in plastic wrap and stored at room temperature for up to 3 days or frozen for up to 1 month. If frozen, let thaw completely at room temperature, then refresh briefly in a 350-degree oven until lightly warmed before serving.)

QUICK RELEASE FOR BREAD

Because quick breads and sweet yeasted breads have a tendency to stick to the loaf pan, we like to spray the pan with vegetable oil spray and, for extra assurance, we also like to line the pan with a parchment "sling."

1. Make a sling for the loaf by laying long, wide strips of parchment paper across the length and width of the pan so that the paper overlaps the edges.

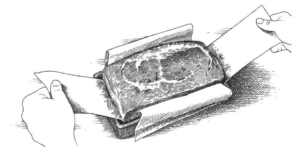

2. Use the overlap as a handy grip when it's time to remove the loaf from the pan.

10

AFRICA AND THE MIDDLE EAST

GRILL-ROASTED EGGPLANT DIP

Baba Ghanoush

THE DRIVING FORCE BEHIND *BABA GHANOUSH* is sultry, rich grill-roasted eggplant. The dip's beguiling creaminess and haunting flavor come from tahini (sesame paste) enhanced with a bit of garlic and brightened with both fresh lemon juice and parsley.

The traditional method for cooking the eggplant for baba ghanoush is to scorch it over a hot, smoky grill. There the purple fruit grows bruised and blackened, until its insides fairly slosh within their charred carapace. The hot, soft interior is scooped out with a spoon and the outer ruins discarded.

While eggplant cooked this much may sound woefully overcooked to some, we discovered that eggplant cooked any less tasted spongy-green and remained unmoved by seasonings. This finding elicited an important question: Can a decent baba ghanoush be made without a grill? Taking instruction from the hot grill fire we had used, we roasted a few large eggplants in a 500-degree oven. It took about 45 minutes to collapse the fruit and transform the insides to pulp. Though the baba ghanoushes we made with grill-roasted eggplants were superior flavorwise to those made with the oven-roasted eggplants, the latter were perfectly acceptable, so we offer oven-roasting as a variation.

Eggplant suffers from a reputation for bitterness. Most baba ghanoush recipes call for discarding the seeds (the supposed source of the bitterness), but the insides of the eggplants we were roasting were veritably paved with them. We thought it impractical and wasteful to jettison that amount of produce, so we performed side-by-side tests comparing versions of the dip with and without seeds. We found no tangible grounds for seed dismissal. The dip was not bitter. The seeds stayed.

Our research on this recipe disclosed that one variety of eggplant was sometimes favored over another. That prompted us to make baba ghanoush with standard large globe eggplants, with compact Italian eggplants, and with long, slender Japanese eggplants. The globe eggplants resulted in a baba ghanoush that was slightly more moist. By contrast, the Italian eggplants were drier and the Japanese eggplants were also quite dry. Tasters favored the moister globe eggplants—which are also easiest to find. It is important to note that the eggplant should not be too bulbous or it will not cook evenly.

The eggplant can be mashed with a fork, but we preferred to use the food processor to pulse the eggplant, leaving the texture slightly coarse. The food processor also makes it a cinch to incorporate the other ingredients.

As for the proportions of said ingredients, tests indicated that less was always more. Minced garlic gathers strength and can become aggressive when added in substantial amounts. Many recipes we reviewed also called for tahini in amounts that overwhelmed the eggplant. The same can be said for the amount of lemon juice: Too much will dash the smoky richness of the eggplant with astringent tartness.

If you're serving a crowd, the recipe can easily be doubled or tripled. Time does nothing to improve the flavor of baba ghanoush. An hour-long stay in the refrigerator for a light chilling is all that's needed.

Charcoal Grill-Roasted Eggplant Dip
Baba Ghanoush
MAKES ABOUT 2 CUPS

Tahini is a sesame paste that can be found in Middle Eastern markets as well as in the international food aisles of many supermarkets. When buying eggplants, select ones with shiny, taut, and unbruised skin and an even shape (eggplants with a bulbous shape won't cook evenly). Poking the eggplant before cooking prevents it from bursting. Baba ghanoush does not keep well, so make it the same day you plan to serve it. Pita Chips (page 406), fresh pita bread cut into wedges, black olives, tomato wedges, and cucumber slices are nice accompaniments.

- 2 pounds eggplant (about 2 large globe), poked all over with a fork
- 2 tablespoons tahini (see note)
- 1 tablespoon juice from 1 lemon
- 1 small garlic clove, minced or pressed through a garlic press (about ½ teaspoon)

Salt and ground black pepper

1 tablespoon extra-virgin olive oil

2 teaspoons minced fresh parsley leaves

1. Light a large chimney starter filled with charcoal (about 6 quarts) and allow to burn until all the charcoal is covered with a layer of fine gray ash. Build a hot fire by spreading the coals evenly over about two-thirds of the grill bottom (confining the coals to a smaller space makes for a hotter fire). Set the cooking grate in place, cover the grill with the lid, and let the grate heat up, about 5 minutes. The grill is ready when the coals are hot; you can hold your hand 5 inches above the cooking grate for just 2 seconds. Scrape the cooking grate clean with a grill brush.

2. Lay the whole eggplants directly over the hot coals and grill, turning the eggplants occasionally, until the skins darken and wrinkle on all sides and the eggplants are uniformly soft when pressed with tongs, about 25 minutes.

3. Transfer the eggplants to a rimmed baking sheet and let cool for 5 minutes. Set a small colander over a bowl or in the sink. Trim the top and bottom off each eggplant. Slit the eggplants lengthwise. Use a spoon to scoop the hot pulp from the skins into the colander (you should have about 2 cups packed pulp); discard the skins. Let the pulp drain for 3 minutes.

4. Process the drained pulp, tahini, lemon juice, garlic, ¼ teaspoon salt, and ¼ teaspoon pepper together in a food processor until the mixture has a coarse, chunky texture, about 8 pulses. Season with salt and pepper to taste. Transfer to a serving bowl, press plastic wrap flush to the surface of the dip, and refrigerate until lightly chilled, 45 to 60 minutes. To serve, use a spoon to make a trough in the center of the dip and spoon the olive oil into it. Sprinkle with the parsley and serve.

➤ VARIATIONS

Gas Grill–Roasted Eggplant Dip

Heat the grill with all the burners set to high and the lid down until very hot, about 15 minutes. Scrape the cooking grate clean with a grill brush. Leave all the burners on high. Follow the recipe for Charcoal Grill–Roasted Eggplant Dip, grilling the eggplant as directed in step 2, with the lid down.

Oven-Roasted Eggplant Dip

This version will not taste as smoky as the grilled versions; feel free to season with smoked salt (found in the spice aisle of many well-stocked supermarkets) to compensate if desired.

Adjust an oven rack to the middle position and heat the oven to 500 degrees. Line a rimmed baking sheet with foil, set the eggplants on the baking sheet, and roast, turning every 15 minutes, until the eggplants are uniformly soft when pressed with tongs, about 60 minutes. Follow the recipe for Charcoal Grill–Roasted Eggplant Dip, substituting the roasted eggplants for the grilled eggplants in step 3.

HUMMUS

THIS SIMPLE CHICKPEA PUREE, ALTHOUGH relatively new to the American diet, has been eaten since the time of Socrates and Plato—and with good reason. Unfortunately, many of us are more familiar with the packaged tubs of prepared hummus sold in supermarkets across the United States, which don't taste very good. We wanted to make a great homemade hummus, similar to versions we'd tasted in Middle Eastern restaurants.

We did some research and found that hummus actually has multiple interpretations. Across the Middle East and throughout the Mediterranean region, hummus varies by texture and flavor. What all versions have in common is only the combination of chickpeas and tahini (sesame paste). Tasting several batches of hummus side by side, tasters homed in on a hummus seasoned with lemon and garlic, with a smooth, stiff, dip-like texture that was far less oily than that of the other contenders.

We were impressed by the results obtained with canned chickpeas. Typically, the beans are packed in a slippery, water-based liquid and we found that the hummus tasted cleaner when we rinsed the chickpeas before pureeing them. We also noted that some of the thin skins would come off the beans if they were quickly towel-dried after rinsing, ensuring a smoother puree.

A 15-ounce can of chickpeas made a good-size batch of hummus, so we then moved our attention to the seasonings. We tried various amounts of

EASY HOMEMADE PITA CHIPS

PITA CHIPS ARE A NATURAL ACCOMPANIMENT TO MIDDLE-EASTERN SPREADS AND DIPS and, when made at home, they taste far better than the expensive bags of broken chips available at the grocery store. Although these addictively crunchy snacks are perfect for dipping, they are also good on their own and can be jazzed up with a range of herb and spice variations, a few of which are listed below.

Pita Chips

MAKES 48 CHIPS,
OR ENOUGH FOR 2 CUPS OF DIP

4   (8-inch) pita breads, split open and
    cut into wedges (see the illustrations
    below)
¼   cup olive oil
1   teaspoon salt

1. Adjust the oven racks to the upper- and lower-middle positions and heat the oven to 350 degrees. Spread the pita triangles, smooth side down, over 2 rimmed baking sheets. Brush the top of each chip lightly with oil and sprinkle with salt.

2. Bake the wedges until they begin to crisp and brown lightly, 6 to 8 minutes. Flip the chips smooth side up, switch and rotate the baking sheets in the oven, and continue to bake until the chips are fully toasted, 6 to 8 minutes longer.

3. Remove the baking sheets from the oven and cool the chips before serving. (The chips can be held in an airtight container for up to 3 days. If necessary, briefly re-crisp in a 350-degree oven for a few minutes before serving.)

➤ VARIATIONS
Garlic-Herb Pita Chips
Follow the recipe for Pita Chips, mixing 1½ teaspoons garlic powder and 2 tablespoons fresh minced thyme, basil, or oregano with the salt before sprinkling it over the chips in step 1.

Chili-Spiced Pita Chips
Follow the recipe for Pita Chips, mixing 1 tablespoon chili powder, ½ teaspoon garlic powder, and a pinch cayenne pepper with the salt before sprinkling it over the chips in step 1.

CUTTING PITA BREAD

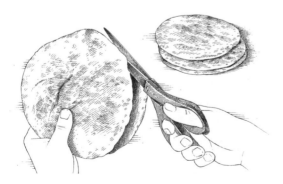

1. Using kitchen shears, cut around the perimeter of each pita bread to yield 2 thin rounds.

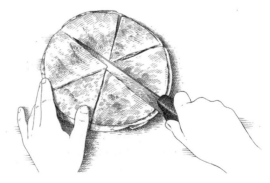

2. Stack the pita rounds and, using a chef's knife, cut them into 6 wedges each.

tahini and found that ¼ cup yielded a good balance of flavors. One clove of garlic along with a pinch of cayenne added just the right bite. Three tablespoons of lemon juice gave our dip some pleasant brightness.

Last but not least, we needed to address the texture. Extra-virgin olive oil was the obvious choice, but we soon discovered that the amount of oil needed to achieve a smooth yet sturdy consistency was overpowering in flavor. We corrected this by replacing half the oil with water, which brought all the flavors into line. We also refrigerated the hummus for 30 minutes or so to meld the flavors. At last, we had realized our goal: hummus that tasted far better than anything one could buy at the store.

Hummus

MAKES ABOUT 2 CUPS

Tahini is a sesame paste that can be found in Middle Eastern markets as well as in the international food aisles of many supermarkets. Garnish the hummus with a drizzle of extra-virgin olive oil, black olives, pomegranate seeds, ground cumin, or additional cayenne pepper. Serve hummus with Pita Chips (page 406), fresh pita bread cut into wedges, or crudités.

I	(15-ounce) can chickpeas, drained and rinsed
¼	cup tahini (see note)
¼	cup extra-virgin olive oil
¼	cup water
3	tablespoons juice from I lemon
I	medium garlic clove, minced or pressed through a garlic press (about I teaspoon)
¾	teaspoon salt
	Cayenne pepper

Process all of the ingredients, including cayenne to taste, together in a food processor until smooth, about 40 seconds, scraping down the sides of the bowl as needed. Transfer the hummus to a serving bowl, cover with plastic wrap, and chill until the flavors meld, at least 30 minutes. Serve cold. (The hummus can be refrigerated in an airtight container for up to 2 days.)

ROASTED RED PEPPER AND WALNUT DIP

Muhammara

MUHAMMARA, MADE FROM ROASTED RED peppers, walnuts, and pomegranate molasses, is a popular dip made throughout the eastern Mediterranean. In Arabic, the word muhammara means brick-colored, which is the exact hue of the dip. The proportion of the ingredients in muhammara varies from country to country and region to region. Here in the test kitchen, we wanted to develop our own version of this sweet, smoky, and savory dip that we could serve with pita chips or warm slices of baguette, or even use to enhance a simple piece of grilled chicken, fish, or lamb.

The first hurdle was the roasted peppers. There are good-quality jarred peppers available; however, since the roasted red peppers are the star of the show, we decided to roast our own (see the recipe on page 408). Freshly roasted sweet red bell peppers assume a whole new layer of complex, smoky flavor, which we knew would only better our dip.

After some trial and error, we found that the best way to roast bell peppers was to cut them and then broil them on a rack set about 3 inches from the broiler element for eight to 10 minutes. The peppers consistently achieved a meaty texture and rich flavor. In addition, peppers that have been cut open and roasted under the broiler are easier to peel than peppers roasted by any other method. The skin blackens and swells up like a balloon and lifts off in large sections.

Unless you have asbestos fingers, roasted peppers need time to cool before handling, and steaming during this time does make the charred skin a bit easier to peel off. The ideal steaming time is 15 minutes—any less and the peppers are still too hot to work with comfortably. Also, seeding the peppers before roasting makes it possible to peel the peppers without having to rinse them to wash away the seeds. If you are still tempted to rinse, notice the rich oils that cling to the peppers as you peel them. It seems silly to rinse away those oils since they'll add so much flavor to the dip.

Since our recipe called for pomegranate molasses (3 tablespoons), our next challenge was to find an alternative, since it can be difficult to locate outside Middle Eastern markets. We were successful making our own—we reduced store-bought pomegranate juice down to a syrup—but it took over one hour to get the right consistency. Wanting something quicker and seeking molasses' thick, syrupy texture and sweet-sour flavor, we tested a variety of pantry ingredients to come up with a substitute. In the end, we found that a combination of lemon juice, honey, and mild molasses worked well. Well-seasoned with Mediterranean hot red pepper or cayenne pepper, ground cumin, and salt, the dip required only a small amount of flavorful extra-virgin olive oil to help loosen its consistency and toasted walnuts to enrich it.

At this point, our dip tasted good, but it was still missing something. Taking a look at other recipes for muhammara, we quickly realized what it was—dried bread crumbs or crumbled wheat crackers. After testing batches made with various kinds of crumbs, we settled on a generic brand of plain wheat crackers from the supermarket because they contributed both flavor and substance to the mix, turning our red pepper and walnut dip into a fair replication of authentic muhammara. Last, we noted that the flavors needed time to meld—at least 30 minutes—before serving.

Roasted Red Pepper and Walnut Dip
Muhammara
MAKES ABOUT 2 CUPS

We prefer fresh roasted red peppers in this dip, but using jarred makes this dish come together quickly—the choice is up to you. When roasting the peppers, note that cooking times vary, depending on the broiler, so watch the peppers carefully as they roast. Pomegranate molasses can be found in Middle Eastern markets as well as in the international food aisles of many supermarkets; if you cannot find it, substitute 3 tablespoons lemon juice, 1 tablespoon mild molasses, and 1 teaspoon honey. Serve this dip with Pita Chips (page 406), fresh pita bread cut into wedges, or baguette slices.

1	recipe Roasted Red Bell Peppers (below) or 1 (12-ounce) jar roasted red peppers (about 4 peppers), drained
1	cup walnuts, toasted (see page 135)
¼	cup coarsely ground plain wheat crackers
3	tablespoons pomegranate molasses (see note)
2	tablespoons extra-virgin olive oil
¾	teaspoon salt
½	teaspoon ground cumin
¼–½	teaspoon cayenne pepper

Pulse the ingredients in a food processor until smooth, about 10 pulses. Transfer the mixture to a serving bowl, cover with plastic wrap, and chill until the flavors meld, at least 30 minutes; serve cold. (The spread can be refrigerated for up to 2 days.)

Roasted Red Bell Peppers
MAKES 4 ROASTED PEPPERS

Cooking times vary, depending on the broiler, so watch the peppers carefully as they roast. Increase the cooking time slightly if your peppers are just out of the refrigerator instead of at room temperature.

4	medium-to-large red bell peppers (6 to 9 ounces each), prepared according to illustrations 1–4 on page 409

1. Adjust an oven rack to be 2½ to 3½ inches from the broiler element and heat the broiler. (If necessary, set an upside-down rimmed baking sheet on the oven rack to get close to the broiler element; see illustration 5 on page 409.)

2. Spread the peppers out over a foil-lined baking sheet and broil until the skin is charred and puffed but the flesh is still firm, 8 to 10 minutes, rotating the pan halfway through the baking time.

3. Transfer the hot peppers to a bowl, cover with foil, and let steam until the skins peel off easily, 10 to 15 minutes. Peel and discard the skin and use as desired.

PREPARING BELL PEPPERS FOR ROASTING

1. Slice ¼ inch from the top and bottom of the bell pepper, then gently remove the stem from the top slice.

2. Pull the core out of the pepper.

3. Make a slit down one side of the pepper, then lay it flat, skin side down, in one long strip. Slide a sharp knife along the inside of the pepper and remove all ribs and seeds.

4. Arrange the strips of peppers and the tops and bottoms skin side up on a foil-lined baking sheet. Flatten the strips with the palm of your hand.

5. Adjust an oven rack to the top position. If the rack is more than 3 inches from the heating element, set a rimmed baking sheet, bottom up, on the rack under the baking sheet. Roast until the skin of the peppers is charred and puffed up like a balloon but the flesh is still firm.

6. Remove the baking sheet from the oven and steam the peppers in a covered bowl to make them easier to peel. The skin should come off in large strips.

CHICKPEA FRITTERS

Falafel

FALAFEL ARE SAVORY FRIED PATTIES MADE from ground chickpeas and/or fava beans and flavored with herbs and spices. Eaten all over the Middle East, falafel are commonly sold by street vendors in pita bread sandwiches or eaten as a meze or hors d'oeuvres. The best falafel have a moist, light interior and a well-browned, crisp crust. They are flavorful enough to eat on their own, but are improved twofold by a drizzle of their classic accompaniment, a zesty tahini sauce.

Unfortunately, we have all had our fair share of bad falafel—dry, dense, greasy, and devoid of flavor. Sampling versions from several local Middle Eastern restaurants and sandwich shops only confirmed this reality—we were hard pressed to find a falafel worth eating. We would have to develop a recipe of our own.

We started our research by sorting through Middle Eastern and vegetarian cookbooks. We learned that Egyptian-style falafel are made entirely from dried split fava beans, while Israeli-style are made with dried chickpeas, and every country in between uses some combination of the two. Unable to find dried split fava beans at our local markets, we chose Israeli-style falafel by process of elimination.

Anxious to get into the kitchen, we made several recipes that we had come across in our research. All of the recipes use dried chickpeas. In initial tests, we tried canned chickpeas, which were a disaster—they were simply too moist and made very mushy falafel.

We were surprised to find out that none of the recipes cooked the dried chickpeas, but rather soaked them in water overnight, ground them in the food processor with the other ingredients, then shaped and fried them. However, the similarities stopped there; sizes and shapes were all over the place. We decided to turn our focus to shaping the falafel and worry about the seasonings later.

In our initial tests we realized that size matters when it comes to falafel. Larger falafel took longer to cook through, making them as dry as sawdust on the inside, without enough of the contrasting outer crust. By contrast, smaller falafel (about 1 tablespoon each) had the perfect ratio of crispy crust to tender interior. Four or five fit nicely into a sandwich, and they were also just the right size—two bites—for an appetizer. We formed some into balls and some into disks. Tasters unanimously preferred the contrasting interior and exterior textures of the disks, which we shaped ½ inch thick and 1 inch wide.

With the size and shape resolved, we turned to the seasonings. While tasters welcomed the flavor of onion, it released moisture, which turned our falafel mushy. And draining the minced onion seemed like too much of a bother. Instead, we turned to scallions, which we liked for their flavor and for the bright green color. Fresh herbs reinforced the green color and tasters liked the complexity of cilantro and parsley over just a single herb. Garlic was a given, along with ground cumin, salt, and ground black pepper. Many recipes also season the falafel with ground cinnamon and our tasters favored the warm floral notes that it imparted. When it came to frying, deep-frying produced the most evenly browned falafel and 375 degrees was the perfect temperature. After just 4 to 5 minutes in the oil, the falafel were cooked through and beautifully browned.

All that was left to do was whip up the tahini sauce. We thinned the tahini with water and seasoned it simply with garlic, lemon juice, and salt. To make the sauce smooth and creamy, we processed all of the ingredients in a food processor (a blender will also work). While we like the falafel simply dipped into the sauce, it is also excellent served in pita bread or lavash with chopped vegetables and tahini sauce.

Chickpea Fritters
Falafel

MAKES 20 FALAFEL,
ENOUGH FOR 4 LARGE SANDWICHES

The chickpeas in this recipe must be soaked overnight; you cannot substitute canned beans or quick-soaked chickpeas because their texture will result in soggy falafel. A wire spider comes in handy here when cooking the falafel; see page 433 for more information. Serve the falafel in lavash or pita bread with lettuce, pickled vegetables, and chopped tomatoes or cucumbers or as an hors d'oeuvres with the tahini sauce as a dip.

TAHINI SAUCE

½	cup tahini
¼	cup juice from 2 lemons
½	cup water
2	medium garlic cloves, minced or pressed through a garlic press (about 2 teaspoons)
	Salt

FALAFEL

6	ounces dried chickpeas (1 cup) rinsed, picked over, and soaked overnight in water to cover by an inch (see page 12)
5	scallions, chopped coarse
½	cup packed fresh parsley leaves
½	cup packed fresh cilantro leaves
3	medium garlic cloves, minced or pressed through a garlic press (about 1 tablespoon)
1	teaspoon salt
½	teaspoon ground black pepper
¼	teaspoon ground cumin
⅛	teaspoon ground cinnamon
2	quarts vegetable oil, for frying

1. FOR THE TAHINI SAUCE: Process all of the ingredients in a food processor until smooth, about 20 seconds. Season with salt to taste and set aside. (The sauce can be refrigerated in an airtight container for up to 4 days. Bring to room temperature and stir to combine before serving.)

2. FOR THE FALAFEL: Adjust an oven rack to the middle position and heat the oven to 200 degrees. Drain the chickpeas, discarding the soaking liquid. Process all of the ingredients except for the oil in a

food processor until smooth, about 1 minute, scraping down the sides of the bowl as needed. Form the mixture into 1 tablespoon–sized disks, about ½ inch thick and 1 inch wide and arrange on a parchment paper–lined baking sheet. (The falafel can be refrigerated at this point for up to 2 hours.)

3. Heat the oil in a 5-quart large Dutch oven over medium-high heat to 375 degrees. (Use an instant-read thermometer that registers high temperatures or clip a candy/deep-fat thermometer onto the side of the pan.) Fry half of the falafel, stirring occasionally and adjusting the heat as needed to maintain 375 degrees, until deep brown, about 5 minutes. Transfer to a paper towel–lined baking sheet using a slotted spoon or wire spider and keep warm in the oven. Return the oil to 375 degrees and repeat with the remaining falafel. Serve immediately with the sauce.

PARSLEY AND BULGUR SALAD

Tabbouleh

IN ADDITION TO FINELY MINCED PARSLEY, A perfect tabbouleh includes morsels of bulgur (crushed, parboiled wheat) tossed in a penetrating, minty lemon dressing with bits of ripe tomato. In the U.S. bulgur is dominant, while in the Middle East, parsley makes up the bulk of the salad. While these principal ingredients remain the same, a variety of preparation techniques exist, each cook being convinced that his or her method produces the finest version. We set out to develop a recipe approachable to the American home cook.

Bulgur is available in three varieties: fine-, medium-, and coarse-grain. Of the three, coarse-grain is the most labor-intensive because it requires cooking to soften the grain. For this reason, we omitted it from testing and instead focused on fine and medium varieties. Tasters preferred the delicate fine-grain bulgur, but medium-grain works just as well. Next we moved on to the preparation of the bulgur.

We tried processing the bulgur in the five most common ways. First we rinsed the grain, combined it with the minced tomato, and set it aside to absorb the tomato juice. With this method, the bulgur remained unacceptably crunchy.

Next we marinated the bulgur in a lemon juice and olive oil dressing. This approach produced bulgur that was tasty but slightly heavy. The third method, soaking the grain in water until fluffy and then squeezing out the excess moisture, produced an equally acceptable—but equally heavy—nutty-flavored wheat.

Next we soaked the wheat in water for about five minutes, then drained the liquid and replaced it with the lemon–olive oil dressing. We discovered that the wheat's texture was good and the flavor superior to the other versions.

But the all-out winner came as a surprise. We first rinsed the bulgur, then mixed it with fresh lemon juice. We then set the mixture aside to allow the juice to be absorbed. When treated in this way, bulgur acquires a fresh and intense flavor.

To complete the dish, we combined the lemon-soaked bulgur with the parsley, finely chopped scallions, fresh mint, and tomatoes. Then we tossed it with the remaining dressing ingredients and let the mixture sit for an hour or so to blend the flavors before serving. We found that after five or six hours the scallions tend to become too strong and overpower the other flavors, so this dish should be served within a few hours.

The final question was the proportion of parsley to bulgur. Although some Middle-Eastern restaurateurs present a 9 to 1 ratio of parsley to bulgur, we find that the wholesome goodness of the wheat is lost unless it is in a more harmonious balance. We recommend that the finished dish contain 5 parts parsley to 3 or 4 parts wheat.

Parsley and Bulgur Salad

Tabbouleh

SERVES 4 TO 6

Fine-grain bulgur is best in this recipe, but medium-grain will work; avoid coarse-grain bulgur, which must be cooked. Middle Eastern cooks frequently serve this salad with crisp inner leaves of romaine lettuce, using them as spoons to scoop the salad from the serving dish.

½   cup fine-grain or medium-grain bulgur wheat
⅓   cup juice from 2 to 3 lemons
2   cups minced fresh parsley leaves (about
    2 bunches)
2   medium tomatoes (about 12 ounces), cored,
    seeded, and chopped medium
4   scallions, minced
2   tablespoons minced fresh mint leaves
⅓   cup extra-virgin olive oil
    Salt
⅛   teaspoon cayenne pepper (optional)

1. Rinse the bulgur thoroughly in a fine-mesh strainer under running water, then set aside to drain, about 5 minutes. Toss the bulgur with ¼ cup of the lemon juice in a large bowl and set aside until the grains are tender and fluffy, 20 to 40 minutes, depending on the age and type of the bulgur.

2. Stir in the parsley, tomatoes, scallions, and mint to combine. In a separate bowl whisk the remaining 4 teaspoons lemon juice, olive oil, ¼ teaspoon salt, and cayenne (if using) together, then pour over the bulgur mixture and toss to coat. Cover and refrigerate to let the flavors blend, 1 to 2 hours. (The salad can be refrigerated, reserving the scallions separately, in an airtight container for up to 24 hours. Add the scallions just before serving.) Season with salt to taste and serve.

PITA BREAD SALAD

Fattoush

IN ARABIC, *FATTOUSH* MEANS MOISTENED bread and it's also the name of a salad served all over the Middle East. Traditionally, fattoush consists of small bites of pita bread mixed with chopped vegetables and tossed with lemon, mint, and a fruity olive oil dressing. After making several of these traditional Middle Eastern salads, we noticed a few minor flaws. While the salads we tested were refreshing, they lacked the body and texture that we were after. The bread was overly moistened—soggy, in fact. We wanted our bread to be soft, but with a bit of chew.

We decided to tackle the issue of the bread first. We learned from our first tests that fresh pita bread was not well-suited for this salad. We had a hunch that historically this salad transpired as a way to use up stale pita bread; however, here in the test kitchen, we rarely have stale pita on hand. Toasting the bread in the oven seemed like the next best thing. A moderate oven (375 degrees) for just 7 minutes produced crisp bread—any longer and the bread became toasted and brittle and didn't soften in the salad. When we married the bread with vegetables and dressing, it was excellent—softened but not mushy and still with some texture and chew. We noticed that after the salad sat in the dressing for a few minutes, however, the vegetables released a great deal of liquid and the bread quickly fell apart. A new problem had evolved—vegetable selection was going to be trickier than we thought.

We immediately turned our attention to the vegetables. We wanted to select ingredients that would lend crispness to the salad without adding excess moisture. We found many recipes that called for romaine lettuce—tasters agreed with the addition. It added crunch without making the other ingredients soggy and it contributed body as well. Tomatoes were a given, but the variety proved to be important. We knew from our previous tests that traditional vine-ripened tomatoes had too many juices, but we found that halved cherry tomatoes contributed deep tomato flavor with much less liquid. Cucumbers were also a given, and by seeding them we were able to expel much of their moisture, thereby keeping the bread from becoming too soggy.

Our salad needed some bite and onions came to mind. We tried both thinly sliced red onion and scallions. Tasters complained that the red onion was too harsh, but the scallions added subtle onion flavor that complemented, but did not overpower, the other ingredients. To finish our pita bread salad, we needed a dressing.

We knew we wanted to stay with the traditional trio of olive oil, lemon, and mint, but we found that our normal ratio of 4 parts oil to 1 part acid resulted in a boring salad, short on brightness. We played with the ratio until settling on 2 parts oil to 1 part acid. While this might seem extreme, it gave the salad a tartness that tasters preferred. Finally, we added chopped mint and parsley. The only problem was that they were not evenly distributed throughout the chunky salad; with one bite you might get intense herb flavor and with the next you might not get any. To evenly distribute the mint and parsley throughout the vinaigrette, we threw all of the dressing ingredients in a blender and processed them until the herbs were finely minced. The salad made with this dressing was just right; the herby flavor was well dispersed and complemented the other ingredients without overpowering them.

Lastly, we wanted to develop a variation on the classic. Feta cheese naturally came to mind, as it is one of the more popular cheeses in the eastern Mediterranean. Feta's bright, fresh flavor melded well in the salad without making it too heavy. With the addition of the feta to the salad, briny kalamata olives made perfect sense. This variation, although not totally authentic, is incredibly satisfying nonetheless.

Pita Bread Salad

Fattoush

SERVES 6

This salad is a great way to use up stale pita bread, but the bread will still need to be toasted. Serve with grilled meat, poultry, or fish for a summer lunch or light dinner.

4	(8-inch) pita breads, torn into ½-inch pieces
½	cup extra-virgin olive oil
¼	cup packed fresh mint leaves
¼	cup packed fresh parsley leaves
¼	cup juice from 2 lemons
3	scallions, sliced thin
I	pint cherry tomatoes, halved
I	medium cucumber, peeled, seeded, and chopped medium
I	small head romaine lettuce, cut or torn into 1-inch pieces (about 6 cups loosely packed)

1. Adjust an oven rack to the middle position and heat the oven to 375 degrees. Spread the bread out over a rimmed baking sheet and bake until crisp but not brown, 7 to 10 minutes. Cool to room temperature.

2. Pulse the oil, mint, parsley, and lemon juice in a blender until the mint and parsley are finely chopped, about 20 pulses. Toss the cooled bread, herb dressing, scallions, tomatoes, cucumber, and lettuce together in a large bowl and serve.

➤ VARIATION

Pita Bread Salad with Olives and Feta
Follow the recipe for Pita Bread Salad, adding ½ cup kalamata olives, pitted and sliced, to the salad in step 2, and sprinkling the salad with 6 ounces feta cheese, crumbled (about 1½ cups), just before serving.

FENNEL SALAD

IN NORTH AFRICA AND OTHER REGIONS OF the Middle East and Mediterranean, the fennel plant is utilized in various forms—the seeds are used as a spice, the fronds as an herb, and the bulb, either cooked or raw, is eaten as a side dish or salad. Fennel has a delicate, sweet, light anise flavor and a delicious crunch that is similar to celery, only without the strings.

In North Africa, Algeria and Tunisia specifically, this vegetable is often paired with complementary flavors and used to make distinctive salads that are the perfect first course or side dish, particularly when served with roasted or grilled meats and fish—right up our alley. Our research turned up several recipes that featured fennel with oranges and olives and we decided to take this approach.

Sweet, juicy oranges and briny olives are the perfect match for crisp fennel. Although we found many recipes for this simple combination, we noted a few tricks in the preparation of both the fennel and the oranges. We liked the fennel best when it was sliced as thin as possible. A very sharp knife makes quick work of this task. Second, we noted the importance of cutting the oranges into bite-sized pieces; the trick is to avoid letting the orange segments fall apart as the salad is tossed. We achieved this by trimming the outer rind and bitter white pith from the oranges with a sharp knife, then breaking the oranges down into quarters. We trimmed the inner pith and seeds from inside each quarter, then cut crosswise through each quarter (across the segments). Cut this way, the segment borders and connective tissue helped keep the oranges from breaking down further as they were tossed in the salad (see the illustrations on page 50).

To finish the salad off, we added a small amount of potent oil-cured black olives, which are ubiquitous in the region, some fresh mint, good extra-virgin olive oil, salt, and black pepper. Because this dish is so simple, the quality of each ingredient, from the fennel to the oil must be the best.

Algerian-Style Fennel, Orange, and Olive Salad

SERVES 4 TO 6

Blood oranges, with their red skin and reddish-orange flesh, are traditional in this dish; use them if you can find them. While this bright and refreshing salad is great on its own, we think it is the perfect accompaniment to Moroccan-Spiced Roast Boneless Leg of Lamb (page 429) or Pan-Roasted Halibut Steaks with Chermoula (page 421).

2	medium fennel bulbs (about 2 pounds), trimmed of stalks, cored, and sliced thin (see the illustrations on the right)
3	large oranges, peeled, quartered, and cut into ¼-inch pieces (see the illustrations on page 50)
½	cup oil-cured black olives, pitted and sliced thin
¼	cup coarsely chopped fresh mint leaves
¼	cup extra-virgin olive oil
2	tablespoons juice from 1 lemon
	Salt and ground black pepper

Toss the fennel, oranges, olives, and mint together in a large bowl. Whisk the oil, lemon juice, ¼ teaspoon salt, and ⅛ teaspoon pepper together, then pour over the fennel mixture and toss to coat. Season with salt and pepper to taste and serve. (The salad can be refrigerated in an airtight container for 2 days.)

PREPARING FENNEL

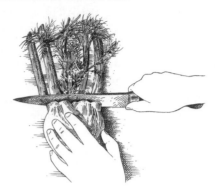

1. Cut off the stem and feathery fronds. (The fronds can be minced and used for a garnish.)

2. Trim a very thin slice from the base and remove any tough or blemished outer layers from the bulb.

3. Cut the bulb in half through the base. Use a small, sharp knife to remove the pyramid-shaped core.

4. Slice the fennel halves into thin strips.

COUSCOUS

ALTHOUGH COUSCOUS, THE NATIONAL DISH OF Morocco, looks like grain it is technically pasta—the tiny size is deceiving. It is made from semolina flour "rolled" with lightly salted water until minute balls form; these are then steamed and dried for long-term storage. In the United States, couscous has become a popular alternative to same-old starchy side dishes like white rice or noodles. And while we have tasted our fair share of couscous in restaurants, we really wanted to come up with the best way to make light, fluffy, and savory couscous at home, to serve alongside a flavorful tagine (see pages 423–424) or tender slices of roast lamb (see page 429).

Traditionally, couscous is cooked in a special pot called a *couscoussier*, which is essentially a stockpot fitted with a small-holed colander. The couscous sits in the colander and plumps in the steam produced by the pot's contents—stock, soup, or stew. While an ersatz couscoussier can be rigged with a saucepan and colander, a much easier method produces entirely acceptable couscous. Hot water or stock is poured over couscous in a bowl, which is then sealed with plastic wrap. Within minutes—12, to be exact—the couscous is tender and ready to eat.

The drawback to this technique is that the couscous tends to clump into tight balls that must be separated—a bothersome chore that inevitably leads to burned fingertips. We found the addition of a little oil or butter to the hydrating liquid helped but didn't completely rectify the situation. Borrowing a technique from rice pilaf, we tried toasting the raw couscous in a little butter before adding the liquid. The resulting couscous was our best batch yet; the grains were discrete and the flavor nutty.

With our couscous plumped and smooth, we were ready to address the couscous flavorings. Although it is not traditional to add aromatics to plain couscous, we reasoned that as we had already heated a skillet to toast the couscous, it would be easy enough to sauté aromatics. We found that just one small onion sautéed in butter lent the couscous both sweetness and a subtle sharpness. Garlic seemed too harsh and out of place.

For liquid, water was the easiest choice, but it made for a bland couscous, even with the onion. We then tried chicken broth, but it was too strong; the chicken flavor overpowered the mild couscous. A combination of chicken broth and water, however, worked fine, giving the couscous body and a pleasant richness. As a final touch, we chose to add a little lemon juice, which sharpened the seasonings.

We liked the simplicity of the dish—it was the perfect neutral accompaniment to a host of flavors—but some tasters wanted to jazz the couscous up a bit, so we developed a variation. Looking through cookbooks, we found that in North Africa, the line between sweet and savory dishes is fuzzy. Meats and vegetables are often combined with dried fruits, nuts, and warm spices generally reserved for sweets in European-style cooking. So couscous with almonds and raisins seemed far from extraordinary; in fact, it's a staple dish throughout Morocco and Algeria. Without altering our basic recipe too much, we added a pinch of saffron, with its alluring golden hue and distinct aroma, along with toasted sliced almonds and sautéed raisins.

Basic Couscous

MAKES 8 CUPS, SERVES 4 TO 6

For the fluffiest texture, use a large fork to fluff the grains; a spoon or spatula can mush its light texture. Specialty markets may carry couscous of varying sizes (such as large pearl Israeli-style couscous), but stick to the basic fine-grained variety, as the other sizes require different cooking methods. The simple flavors of this pilaf pair well with a wide variety of meat, poultry, and vegetable dishes including Moroccan Chicken Tagine with Olives and Lemon (page 423) or Pan-Roasted Halibut Steaks with Chermoula (page 421).

4	tablespoons (½ stick) unsalted butter
2	cups couscous
I	small onion, minced
	Salt
2	cups water
I¾	cups low-sodium chicken broth
I½	teaspoons juice from I lemon
	Ground black pepper

1. Melt 2 tablespoons of the butter in a large skillet over medium-high heat. Add the couscous and cook, stirring frequently, until some grains are just beginning to brown, about 3 minutes. Transfer the couscous to a large bowl.

2. Add the remaining 2 tablespoons butter, onion, and ¾ teaspoon salt to the skillet and cook, stirring occasionally, until softened, 5 to 7 minutes. Stir in the water and broth and bring to a boil.

3. Pour the boiling liquid over the toasted couscous, cover tightly with plastic wrap, and let sit until the couscous is tender, about 12 minutes. Remove the plastic wrap, fluff the grains with a fork, and gently stir in the lemon juice. Season with salt and pepper to taste and serve immediately.

➤ VARIATION

Saffron Couscous with Almonds and Raisins

Follow the recipe for Basic Couscous, adding a pinch of saffron threads, crumbled, and ¾ cup raisins with the onion in step 2. Stir ¾ cup sliced almonds, toasted, into the couscous with the lemon juice in step 3.

MOROCCAN-STYLE CARROT SALAD

CARROT SALADS IN THE U.S. ARE TYPICALLY mayonnaise-based, sweetened with raisins, and frankly a bit ho-hum. But not long ago, one of us had a carrot salad in a local Moroccan restaurant. The shredded carrots were tossed with orange slices and flavored with cumin, coriander, and cinnamon—all spices characteristic of North African cooking. This was not your mother's carrot salad.

In our research, we found a wide range of carrot salads from North Africa. The ingredients and procedures for the salads were all similar. Most recipes called for grated carrots tossed with olive oil, lemon juice, and North African spices. Many recipes specified additional flavors, such as olives, toasted almonds, orange flower water, and, yes, even raisins.

Our first question was how to cut the carrots.

Some recipes called for the carrots to be pared into thin ribbons with a vegetable peeler. While this made a pretty salad, the vinaigrette had nothing to cling to, so the carrots were rather bland. We, instead, turned to grating. We tried a couple methods of grating the carrots—with a box grater and with a food processor. We found the large holes on the box grater worked the best. The food processor grated the carrots too fine; the resulting salad didn't have enough body or texture and was watery. The carrot pieces from the box grater were a little larger.

Considering that we were going to add oranges to the salad, it seemed natural to build a vinaigrette around orange juice. The orange juice didn't provide enough acidity, however, resulting in a salad that was too sweet. A squeeze of lemon juice balanced the flavor. As for the oil, extra-virgin olive oil worked best. A touch of honey added a pleasing floral note.

Moving to the spices in the vinaigrette, we initially tried ½ teaspoon each of coriander, cumin, and cinnamon. This was entirely too overpowering; none of the spices stood out and the total amount gave the salad a grainy feeling. So we tried reducing the amount of spices and making one spice the dominant flavor. Tasters felt that cinnamon and coriander were too sweet to serve as dominant flavors, failing to provide enough contrast. Cumin, on the other hand, worked perfectly in the starring role. The musky aroma and slight nuttiness of the cumin complemented the sweetness of the carrots. With a hint of cinnamon (the coriander seemed redundant and was dropped) and a little heat provided by cayenne pepper, we finally had our dressing. Now all we had to do was to dress the carrots—or so we thought.

Several minutes after we dressed the salad, a pool of juice—water being expelled by the carrots—developed in the bowl. We explored several ways of getting rid of this liquid. We tried salting the carrots as we would cucumbers to rid them of unwanted juices, but this process required at least half an hour. We also tried squeezing the carrots in a towel after we grated them, but this resulted in a loss of flavor. We then turned to the idea of letting the carrots sit in a strainer for several minutes after being dressed. While this certainly got rid of the extra water, it also got rid of flavor. We finally settled on increasing the amount of spices in the vinaigrette; the carrots thus received an initial overdose of spices that would stand up to the inevitable excess of liquid. By straining some of the liquid from the salad, we reached a proper level of seasoning and our salad was complete.

Moroccan-Style Carrot Salad

SERVES 6

Make sure to segment the oranges over a small bowl to catch their juices; you will need 3 tablespoons of juice. For more heat, use the higher amount of cayenne. The flavor combinations in this slaw-like salad make it a natural to serve with Moroccan-Spiced Roast Boneless Leg of Lamb (page 429) and Basic Couscous (page 415).

I	pound carrots (about 6 medium), peeled and grated over the large holes of a box grater
2	medium seedless oranges, peeled and segmented (see the illustrations on the right), 3 tablespoons juice reserved
3	tablespoons minced fresh cilantro leaves
¼	cup extra-virgin olive oil
I	tablespoon juice from I lemon
I	teaspoon honey
¾	teaspoon ground cumin
½	teaspoon salt
⅛–¼	teaspoon cayenne pepper (see note)
⅛	teaspoon ground cinnamon

1. Toss the grated carrots, orange segments, and cilantro together in a large bowl. Whisk the reserved orange juice, oil, lemon juice, honey, cumin, salt, cayenne, and cinnamon together, then pour over the carrot mixture and toss to coat.

2. Let the salad sit until liquid starts to pool in the bottom of the bowl, about 3 minutes. Transfer the salad to a fine-mesh strainer set over a large bowl and let drain for 2 minutes. Transfer the salad to a serving bowl or platter, discard the strained juices, and serve. (The salad can be refrigerated in an airtight container for 2 days.)

SEGMENTING AN ORANGE

1. Start by slicing a ½-inch-thick piece off the top and bottom of the orange.

2. With the fruit resting flat against the work surface, use a very sharp paring knife to slice off the rind, including all of the bitter white pith. Try to follow the contours of the fruit as closely as possible.

3. Working over a bowl to catch the juices, slip the blade between a membrane and one section of fruit and slice to the center, separating one side of the section.

4. Turn the blade of the knife so that it is facing out and is lined up along the membrane on the opposite side of the section. Slide the blade from the center out along the membrane to free the section completely. Continue until all of the sections are removed.

WEST AFRICAN SWEET POTATO AND PEANUT SOUP

SWEET POTATOES ARE A DELICIOUS VEGETABLE unjustly relegated to side dish status in most American meals. In other parts of the world, however, sweet potatoes are used more widely, and they are the star of the meal in many African countries. One common preparation is a thick sweet potato soup flavored with protein-rich peanuts (commonly called groundnuts in Africa) and warm seasonings like cinnamon and cayenne. We were intrigued by this preparation and set about to create our own version.

During our initial research, we found dozens of recipes for sweet potato and peanut soup, many including a long list of spices and flavorings. After cooking and tasting a few, the test kitchen decided the simplest recipes did the best job of highlighting the mild flavor of the sweet potato. The best soups we tasted were smooth, creamy, and fragrant with pungent spices. Our task, then, was to combine sweet potatoes and peanuts with just a few complementary flavors.

The first step was choosing the proper sweet potatoes. The most common variety of sweet potato sold in American markets is the Beauregard. These possess the familiar dusty orange hue and mild flavor and they performed well in our kitchen tests in soup. Two other varieties of sweet potato, Jewel and Red Garnet (which are often sold erroneously as yams) also work well in the soup. Both have more intense color than the Beauregard.

With pounds and pounds of Beauregards at the ready, we began recipe development. Onions and garlic were a must, as they provided depth and richness. Just one onion did the trick and tasters favored the pungency and body conveyed by a healthy dose of minced garlic. After testing both butter and vegetable oil as cooking mediums, we favored butter because it gave the aromatics a sweeter, nuttier flavor.

Chicken broth seemed the best option for liquid, as it provided just enough richness without dominating the other flavors. We did find, however, that the best-flavored soup came from slightly diluting the chicken broth with water; the flavor of straight chicken broth competed with the sweet potatoes and peanuts.

Peanuts may sound eccentric in soup, but they paired surprisingly well with the sweet potatoes. While many recipes we found used whole peanuts, we liked the lushness imparted by peanut butter. Both creamy and chunky varieties worked fine; the soup is pureed in the end.

For spices, recipes offered dozens of choices. Many of them, like cinnamon, cloves, and cumin, muddied the sweet potato flavor. Coriander was almost a standard in our research recipes—and for good reason. Its slightly floral flavor and aroma perfectly complemented the sweet potato. Little used in most American cooking, coriander is the seed of the coriander plant, which, when used as a leafy herb, is called cilantro. A little coriander goes a long way. We started off the soup with upward of a teaspoon and, through subsequent tests, scaled the amount back to a scant half-teaspoon. We also added a little cayenne pepper to the soup. Some tasters enjoyed the soup downright spicy, while others felt too much heat ruined it; we leave the heat level to your discretion. Fresh cilantro was the ideal final touch. Its fresh bite reinforced the coriander and the flecks of green in the orange puree looked appealing.

West African Sweet Potato and Peanut Soup
SERVES 4 TO 6

Although this recipe was developed with standard sweet potatoes (called Beauregards), Jewel and Red Garnet sweet potatoes also work well. Do stick to the orange-fleshed varieties; white or purple-fleshed sweet potatoes, in conjunction with the peanut butter, would blend to an unappetizing color.

- 2 tablespoons unsalted butter
- 1 medium onion, minced
- 1 teaspoon light brown sugar
   Salt
- 3 medium garlic cloves, minced or pressed through a garlic press (about 1 tablespoon)

½ teaspoon ground coriander
⅛–¼ teaspoon cayenne pepper
3½ cups low-sodium chicken broth
2 cups water
2 pounds sweet potatoes (about 3 medium), peeled, quartered lengthwise, and sliced thin
3 tablespoons peanut butter
Ground black pepper
1 tablespoon minced fresh cilantro leaves

1. Melt the butter in a large Dutch oven over medium-high heat. Add the onion, brown sugar, and 1 teaspoon salt and cook, stirring frequently, until the onion is softened, 5 to 7 minutes. Stir in the garlic, coriander, and cayenne and cook until fragrant, about 30 seconds.

2. Add the broth, water, sweet potatoes, and peanut butter. Bring to a boil over high heat. Turn the heat to low and cook, partially covered, until the sweet potatoes are easily pierced with a knife, 25 to 30 minutes.

3. Working in batches, puree the soup in a blender (or food processor) until smooth, and then return to a clean saucepan. (At this point, the soup can be refrigerated for up to 2 days; reheat over medium-low heat.) Season with salt and pepper to taste, stir in the cilantro, and serve.

FISH WITH CHERMOULA

CHERMOULA IS A TRADITIONAL MOROCCAN fish marinade made with hefty amounts of cilantro, lemon, and garlic. In classic Moroccan cooking, a hearty white fish is marinated in the chermoula and then cooked on a bed of vegetables in a conical-shaped, earthenware vessel called a *tagine* (see page 422 for more information). In recent years, however, we have seen chermoula popping up on restaurant menus, where it is used as a sauce for sautéed or grilled fish. After making a traditional-style tagine using fish marinated in chermoula, we decided to follow the simpler, more modern approach—a straightforward recipe for fish that tipped our hat to Moroccan cuisine, but put our own twist on it

and better showcased the bright, zesty flavors of the chermoula.

We started with the fish. Right away we chose halibut, with its naturally lean, firm texture and clean, mild flavor. Halibut is often preferred braised rather than roasted or sautéed because this moist-heat cooking technique keeps the fish from drying out. The downside, however, is that braising does not develop as much flavor as other methods, producing fish the test kitchen considers lackluster. So we set out to discover a cooking method that not only added flavor but also produced a perfectly cooked, moist and tender piece of fish.

Before addressing the questions of technique, we took to the supermarkets and fishmongers to settle on the best cut of halibut with which to proceed. By virtue of availability, we settled on steaks rather than fillets. But steaks vary considerably in size depending on the weight of the particular fish, which typically ranges from 15 to 50 pounds but can reach up to 300 pounds.

After buying more than 40 pounds of halibut, our advice is this: Inspect the steaks in the fish case and choose the two that are closest in size. This approach ensures that the steaks will cook at the same rate, thus avoiding the problem of overcooking the smaller one. We found the best size steak for the home cook to be between 10 and 12 inches in length and roughly 1¼ inches thick (see "Three Kinds of Halibut Steak" on page 420). (We did test thinner and thicker steaks, adjusting the cooking time as necessary, and had success with both.) We also tried halibut steaks that we purchased frozen. The flavor matched that of the fresh fish, but tasters were disappointed in the mushy texture.

Keeping in mind that we wanted to brown the fish to develop flavor, we tested two different techniques: skillet-cooking on the stovetop and roasting in the oven. Neither was ideal. The skillet-seared fish browned nicely but became a little dry. The roasted sample was moist and evenly cooked, but it barely browned and thus had little flavor. To achieve intense, rich flavor, we chose a common restaurant technique and combined the methods.

First we seared the fish in a heavy-duty oven-proof skillet on the stovetop and then we put the whole thing—pan and fish—into the oven to finish cooking. This approach was an improvement, but we still had a problem. Our efforts to brown the fish sufficiently to enhance flavor usually caused it to overcook.

After much additional testing, we finally hit on the solution. Instead of sautéing the fish on both sides, we seared it on one side only, flipped it in the pan, and then placed it in the oven to finish with the seared side up. This worked beautifully, combining the enhanced flavor of browned fish with the moist interior that came from finishing in the oven's even heat. Finally, moist fish with great sautéed flavor.

Next we explored a few refinements. All home cooks know that fish sticks to the pan, and a non-stick skillet is the common solution to this problem. In this case, however, we feared that many nonstick skillets would not be truly oven-worthy, so we had to solve the sticking problem that came with the use of a traditional skillet. We knew that success would lie in a properly heated pan. All it took was a generous amount of olive oil (2 tablespoons) heated over high heat until just smoking. We then turned the heat to medium-high and immediately added the fish to the hot pan. The fish browned beautifully and sticking was not an issue.

Oven temperatures were up next for testing and we tried four settings: 425, 450, 475, and 500 degrees. Finding no discernible difference in the fish roasted at any of these temperatures, we opted for 425 degrees because it offered the greatest margin for error. (The slower the oven, the longer

TRIMMING CARTILAGE

Cutting off the cartilage at the ends of the steaks ensures that they will fit neatly in the pan and diminishes the likelihood that the small bones located there will end up on your dinner plate.

the window of time for doneness.) Timing was another key to moist, perfectly cooked fish. For the type and thickness of steaks we were using, we found that six minutes of oven time left the fish a bit underdone. At roughly nine minutes the flakes were opaque, but they had not sacrificed any moisture or tenderness.

With the fish seared and roasted properly, we needed to work on our chermoula sauce to accompany it. Wondering about the best way to make chermoula, we browsed our library and turned up several recipes. According to these recipes, chermoula is based on herbs—either cilantro or a mixture of cilantro and mint—which are processed with olive oil, lemon juice, and garlic and then flavored with various other spices.

We made two batches of the sauce, one using straight cilantro and the other using a combination of cilantro and mint. The majority of tasters

THREE KINDS OF HALIBUT STEAK

Most halibut steaks consist of four pieces of meat attached to a central bone (left). It is not uncommon, however, to encounter a steak with just two pieces, both located on the same side of the center bone (center). These steaks were cut from the center of the halibut, adjacent to the belly cavity. The belly, in effect, separates the two halves. We slightly preferred full steaks with four meat sections; each full steak serves two or three people. If you can find only the belly steaks, you will have to purchase four steaks instead of two to make the recipe. Avoid very small, boneless steaks (right) cut entirely free from the bone and each other. Most boneless steaks won't serve even one person.

FULL STEAK
4 sections

BELLY CUT
2 sections

BONELESS STEAK
1 section

preferred the sauce with just cilantro, feeling that in the other sauce the cilantro and mint were fighting for prominence. As with a basic vinaigrette, we determined that a ratio of 4 parts oil to 1 part acid (lemon juice) was the best balance for chermoula when tasted on its own, but when it was combined with the fish, tasters preferred a chermoula with a bit more lemon. Also, searching for a more pesto-like consistency, we upped the amount of cilantro from ½ cup (the amount called for in most recipes) to ¾ cup. The amount of garlic in the recipes we found varied from one clove up to a whopping six cloves; we settled on four cloves, feeling that the garlic should be assertive but not overpowering. For the spices, we chose cumin for its characteristic muskiness, paprika for smokiness, and cayenne for heat.

We spooned a little of the sauce on each piece of fish, and then passed the remainder at the table. Tasters raved about the way that the flavorful sauce complemented the moist, tender fish. We now had a recipe for a simple, yet interesting weeknight dinner in our repertoire.

Pan-Roasted Halibut Steaks with Chermoula

SERVES 4 TO 6

Even well-dried fish can cause the hot oil in the pan to splatter. You can minimize splattering by laying the halibut steaks in the pan gently and putting the edge closest to you in the pan first so the far edge falls away from you. Serve with Basic Couscous (page 415) and Moroccan-Style Carrot Salad (page 417). To prevent the fish from sticking to the bottom of the skillet, be sure to heat the pan over high heat in step 2 until the oil is just smoking.

CHERMOULA

¾	cup packed fresh cilantro leaves
½	cup extra-virgin olive oil
3	tablespoons juice from 1 large lemon
4	medium garlic cloves, minced or pressed through a garlic press (about 4 teaspoons)
1	teaspoon ground cumin
1	teaspoon paprika
¼	teaspoon cayenne pepper
¼	teaspoon salt

HALIBUT

2	(full) halibut steaks (see the photos on page 420), each about 1¼ inches thick and 10 to 12 inches long (about 2½ pounds total), trimmed of cartilage at both ends (see the illustration on page 420)
	Salt and ground black pepper
2	tablespoons olive oil

1. FOR THE CHERMOULA: Process all of the ingredients together in a food processor until smooth, about 20 seconds, stopping to scrape down the sides of the bowl as needed. Transfer to a serving bowl and set aside. (The chermoula can be refrigerated in an airtight container for up to 2 days.)

2. FOR THE HALIBUT: Adjust an oven rack to the middle position and heat the oven to 425 degrees. Pat the halibut dry with paper towels and season with salt and pepper. Heat the oil in a 12-inch ovenproof skillet over high heat until just smoking. Turn the heat to medium-high, carefully lay the steaks in the pan, and sear until spotty brown, about 4 minutes. Off the heat, flip the steaks over using two thin-bladed metal spatulas.

3. Transfer the skillet to the oven and roast the halibut until the flesh is opaque and the fish flakes apart when gently prodded with a paring knife, about 9 minutes. Transfer the steaks to a carving board and, following the illustration below, separate the skin and bones from the fish with a spatula. Spoon 1 tablespoon of the chermoula over each piece of fish and serve immediately, passing the remaining chermoula at the table.

SERVING HALIBUT STEAKS

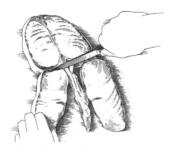

Remove the skin from the cooked steaks and separate each quadrant of meat from the bones by slipping a spatula or knife gently between them. Transfer the pieces to a warm serving platter.

MOROCCAN CHICKEN TAGINE WITH OLIVES AND LEMON

Djej Emshmel

TAGINES ARE A NORTH AFRICAN SPECIALTY —exotically spiced, assertively flavored stews slow-cooked in earthenware vessels of the same name. They can include all manner of meats, vegetables, and fruit, though our hands–down favorite combines chicken with briny olives and tart lemon.

While we love tagine, it's not a dish we ever thought was suited for American home cooking. Why? The few traditional recipes we had seen required time-consuming, labor-intensive cooking methods, a special pot (the tagine), and hard-to-find ingredients. We're usually game for a day in the kitchen or a hunt for exotica, but isn't tagine, at its most elemental level, just stew?

A little research proved that we weren't the first to take a stab at making tagine more accessible. While most of the recipes we tried lacked the depth of an authentic tagine, they did hold promise, proving that a Western cooking method (braising in a Dutch

EQUIPMENT: **Tagines**

Tagines (the cooking vessel, not the stew) have lately enjoyed a fashionable comeback in cookware catalogs and food magazines. A shallower take on the Dutch oven, a tagine has a distinctive conical lid that makes for a dramatic presentation at the dinner table. According to tradition, the conical shape helps cooking performance as well: as steam rises during cooking, it condenses in the tip of the relatively cool lid (it's farther from the heat source than most lids) and drips back into the stew, conserving water in the process. Less steam loss means you can start off with less liquid to begin with and thus end up with more concentrated flavors. Or so the story goes.

To put this theory to the test, we brought equal amounts of water to a simmer in three tagines—a traditional terra cotta model ($34) and modern versions from All-Clad ($199) and Le Creuset ($120)—put the lids on, and let the water "cook" over low heat. We included our favorite Dutch ovens (also All-Clad and Le Creuset; see page 88 for more information) for comparison. After one hour, we measured the water left in each of the pots, and it was clear that the tagine's conical shape was not such an advantage after all. The big losers—literally—were the All-Clad Dutch oven and the traditional terra cotta tagine, which lost 16 percent and 30 percent of their water, respectively. (By contrast, the others lost only 8 to 9 percent.) More important than the shape of the pot were the lid's weight and fit: the leaky All-Clad Dutch oven had the lightest lid, while the base and lid of the handmade terra cotta tagine simply didn't fit together as precisely as their machine-made counterparts.

What does all this loss mean when it's more than water cooking? Not much, said our tasters, after sampling five batches

of Moroccan chicken. Although the amount of liquid left behind in the stews varied, that variance translated to little discernible flavor difference. If you're a stickler for tradition, try to choose a tagine with a heavy, tight-fitting lid or be ready to add additional liquid if the sauce begins to dry out during cooking.

THE BEST TAGINES

TRADITIONAL
The handmade lid of this traditional terra cotta tagine ($34) lets steam leak out, but it made a decent tagine, it isn't very expensive, and it looks good on the table.

TOP TAGINE
All-Clad's tagine ($199) made a great Moroccan braise, but with such limited use, it's hard to say if its worth the hefty price tag.

A FINE OPTION
Le Creuset's Dutch oven ($230) produces a tasty tagine—and its usefulness doesn't stop there.

oven) was a serviceable substitution for stewing for hours in a tagine. We also discovered that the flavors we associated with Moroccan cooking weren't necessarily "exotic"—they were a strategic blending of ingredients we already had in our cupboard.

Almost all of the recipes we collected specified a whole chicken, broken down into pieces, and we soon found out why. Batches made entirely with white meat lacked the depth and character of those made with a blend of dark and white. But when we cooked the white and dark meat in the same way—simmered partially submerged in broth—the white meat turned dry and stringy.

Noting that the dark meat—drumsticks and thighs—take roughly one hour of simmering time to become tender, we found that the breasts (cut in half for easier serving), took only 20 minutes. Giving the dark meat a 40-minute head start in the pot took care of the different cooking times and ensured that all of the chicken was perfectly cooked and ready at the same time.

Some recipes called for rubbing the chicken with lemon and salt and letting the meat marinate before cooking; others employed salt alone or salt blended with spices. We found that adding spices at this point resulted in a muddy-flavored broth.

Some carrots, a large sliced onion, and a few minced garlic cloves rounded out the basic flavors of the stew and we finally felt ready to tackle the defining ingredients: spices, olives, and lemon. Many recipes called for a spice blend called *ras el hanout*, which translates loosely as "top of the shop" and may contain upward of 30 spices. We experimented with a broad range of spices until we landed on a blend that was short on ingredients but long on flavor. Cumin and ginger lent depth, cinnamon brought warmth that tempered a little cayenne heat, and citrusy coriander boosted the stew's lemon flavor. Paprika added sweetness but, perhaps more important, colored the broth a deep, attractive red. Thoroughly toasting the spices in hot oil brought out the full depth of their flavors.

Finding the right olive proved harder than we anticipated. Big, meaty, green Moroccan olives were the obvious choice for the stew, but they were a rarity at any of our local markets. Other meaty green olives, like Manzanilla, Cerignola, and Lucques, were either too mild or too assertive to match the other flavors in the stew. Greek "cracked" olives, however, tasted great and were easy to find. When we added the olives to the stew too soon, their flavor leached out into the braising liquid, rendering them bland and bitter. Stirring in the olives just a few minutes before serving proved a better approach, as they retained their piquant flavor and firm texture.

The lemon flavor in authentic tagines comes from preserved lemon, a long-cured Moroccan condiment that's hard to find outside of specialty stores. "Quick" preserved lemons can be produced at home in a few days, but we wanted to keep our recipe as simple as possible. Part tart citrus, part pickled brine, traditional preserved lemon has a unique flavor that's tough to imitate. So we chose not to try; instead, we aimed for a rich citrus backnote in the dish. We added a few broad ribbons of lemon zest along with the onions and the high heat coaxed out the zest's oils and mellowed them. Adding a lemon's worth of juice just before serving reinforced the bright flavor.

A spoonful of honey further balanced things and chopped cilantro leaves freshened the flavors, but we felt the stew still lacked a certain spark. A last-minute addition of raw garlic and finely chopped lemon zest seemed to clinch it, as the sharpness brought out the best in each of the stew's components.

Moroccan Chicken Tagine with Olives and Lemon
Djej Emshmel
SERVES 4

Use a vegetable peeler to remove wide strips of zest from the lemon before juicing it (see page 346); be sure to trim away the bitter-tasting white pith from the zest before using. The breasts and thighs/drumsticks do not cook in the same amount of time; if using both, note that the breast pieces are added partway through the cooking time. If cooking in an authentic tagine (see page 422), you may need to add additional liquid (water or broth) to the stew as it cooks to prevent the sauce from drying out. Serve with Basic Couscous (page 415).

5	medium garlic cloves, minced or pressed through a garlic press (about 5 teaspoons)
1¼	teaspoons sweet paprika
½	teaspoon ground cumin
¼	teaspoon cayenne pepper
¼	teaspoon ground ginger
¼	teaspoon ground coriander
¼	teaspoon ground cinnamon
3	(2-inch-long) strips lemon zest from 1 to 2 lemons (see page 346)
4	pounds bone-in, skin-on chicken pieces (split breasts cut in half, drumsticks, and/or thighs)
	Salt and ground black pepper
2	tablespoons olive oil
1	large onion, halved and sliced ¼ inch thick
2	medium carrots, peeled and cut crosswise into ½-inch-thick coins, very large pieces cut into half-moons (about 2 cups)
2	cups low-sodium chicken broth
1	tablespoon honey
1	cup Greek cracked green olives (see page 332), rinsed, pitted, and halved
2	tablespoons chopped fresh cilantro leaves
3	tablespoons juice from 1 to 2 lemons

1. Combine 4 teaspoons of the garlic, paprika, cumin, cayenne, ginger, coriander, and cinnamon together in a small bowl and set aside. Mince 1 strip of the lemon zest and mix with the remaining teaspoon of minced garlic in a separate small bowl; set aside.

2. Pat the chicken dry with paper towels and season with salt and pepper. Heat the oil in a large Dutch oven over medium-high heat until just smoking. Brown half of the chicken on both sides, 5 to 8 minutes per side, reducing the heat if the pan begins to scorch. Transfer the chicken to a plate, leaving the fat in the pot. Return the pot with the fat to medium-high heat and repeat with the remaining chicken; transfer the chicken to the plate.

3. Pour off all but 1 tablespoon of the fat left in the pot. Add the onion and the remaining 2 lemon zest strips and cook over medium heat, stirring occasionally, until softened, 5 to 7 minutes. Stir in the garlic-spice mixture and cook until fragrant, about 30 seconds. Stir in the carrots, broth, and honey, scraping up any browned bits.

4. Nestle the chicken, along with any accumulated juices, into the pot and bring to a simmer. Cover, turn the heat to medium-low, and simmer until the chicken is fully cooked and tender, about 20 minutes for the breasts (160 degrees on an instant-read thermometer) or 1 hour for the thighs and drumsticks. (If using both types of chicken, simmer the thighs and drumsticks for 40 minutes before adding the breasts.)

5. Transfer the chicken to a serving dish, tent loosely with foil, and let rest while finishing the sauce. Skim as much fat as possible off the surface of the sauce, add the olives, and return to a simmer until the sauce is thickened slightly and the carrots are tender, 4 to 6 minutes. Return the chicken to the pot. Stir in the garlic–lemon zest mixture, cilantro, and lemon juice. Season with salt and pepper to taste and serve immediately.

➤ VARIATIONS

Moroccan Chicken Tagine with Chickpeas and Apricots

Follow the recipe for Moroccan Chicken Tagine with Olives and Lemon, replacing 1 of the carrots with 1 cup dried apricots, halved, and replacing the olives with 1 (15-ounce) can chickpeas, drained and rinsed.

Moroccan Lamb Tagine with Olives and Lemon

Here we adapt our chicken tagine to use lamb, which is very popular in Morocco. If desired, the lamb can be pulled off the bone and shredded before it is returned to the pot in step 5.

Follow the recipe for Moroccan Chicken Tagine with Olives and Lemon, substituting 3½ to 4 pounds shoulder lamb chops, about 1 inch thick, for the chicken. Brown them as directed in step 2, and simmer them as directed in step 4 until tender, about 1 hour.

ETHIOPIAN-STYLE CHICKEN STEW

Doro Wat

WHEN WE THINK OF ETHIOPIAN FOOD, RICHLY flavored stews come to mind. Stews in Ethiopia are deeply flavored with warm spices and are traditionally served with *injera,* a type of flatbread that is made from a grain called teff and is used as a utensil to eat the stew. Our favorite of these Ethiopian stews is *doro wat,* a hearty chicken stew garnished with hard-cooked eggs. In this stew—and many others—the meat is cooked in a cardamom, garlic, ginger, and cinnamon-spiced butter called *nitter kibbeh* and seasoned with *berbere,* a spice blend typically consisting of hot red chiles, paprika, cloves, nutmeg, fenugreek, and cumin. While both the spiced butter and spice blend add complex, bold flavor to the stew, we were put off by the extra steps they required. We hoped to create a streamlined recipe for doro wat, one that had all the flavor of a traditional recipe without all of the fussy components.

We started our testing with an array of recipes from African cookbooks, only to discover that a chicken stew from Ethiopia is not unlike a chicken stew from any other country. The method is fairly standard—brown the chicken, sauté the aromatics, then add liquid and cook—it's just the seasonings and garnishes that differ.

We first addressed the issue of the chicken itself. For most of our chicken stews, we prefer chicken pieces with the skin on, and this one was no exception—the skin helps to contribute flavor to the sauce from the browning process and we like a choice of white or dark meat. Not surprisingly, we found that the breasts cooked in a third of the time as the thighs, so we would have to stagger the cooking. Once the liquid was simmering and ready for the chicken, we added only the thighs and cooked them for 40 minutes. At that point we added the breast meat and cooked the entire dish for an additional 20 minutes. All the meat was perfectly cooked and it was time to focus on the cooking liquid.

Although Ethiopian stews traditionally use water (and seasonings) as the liquid base, chicken broth and red wine have found their way into more contemporary recipes. After making a few batches of recipes with chicken broth and wine, tasters agreed that the combination gives the stew a nice acidity and depth of flavor. We did need to work on the balance of flavors, as the stewing liquid, once reduced, was a bit too assertive and salty for our tastes. This was easily remedied by diluting the mixture with some water. We found that 2 cups of red wine with 2 cups of chicken broth and 1½ cups water yielded the right balance of chickeny richness and bright flavors.

Now for the real challenge: mimicking the flavor of a traditional Ethiopian stew, but without the time-consuming preparations of spice mixes and spice butters. We were instantly able to slim down the list of spices by using chili powder, a mixture of spices that usually contains hot red chiles, cumin, oregano, garlic, and paprika. With the chili powder, we included what we deemed the other essential spices, cardamom, nutmeg, and fenugreek. (Fenugreek is a slightly bitter herb sold in whole seeds or ground.) We found that cooking the spices along with the aromatics—onion, ginger, and garlic—heightened their flavors. At this point a spiced butter seemed superfluous in the highly seasoned stew, but finishing the dish with plain butter gave it a rich lift. The final addition to the stew, tomato paste (another modern addition) promoted the dark color of the stew and added another layer of flavor.

Like several other recipes from around the world—Chilean Shepherd's Pie (page 61), Braised Chicken with Almonds and Pine Nuts (page 242), and Skillet-Baked Rice with Chicken and Lemony Meatballs (page 240)—this stew combines chicken and eggs in the same dish. In doro wat, the eggs are generally hard-cooked and left whole, so we did the same. Tasters liked how the sauce coated the eggs, contrasting their mild flavor with each bite.

With the stew finished, we developed a recipe for injera. Traditionally made from teff, a mild, nutty-flavored grain that is ground into flour, and a sourdough-like starter, the bread is prepared much like a crêpe or pancake—the batter is poured into a heated skillet and the pan is swirled to cover the bottom of the pan with the batter. The bread is cooked covered, so no flipping is necessary. The resulting bread has a tangy flavor and a spongy texture with lots of holes—it is tender, but sturdy enough to scoop up bites of stew. Rather than fussing with a sourdough starter, we obtained the characteristic holes in the bread by using a combination of baking powder and baking soda and we mimicked the sour flavor with lemon juice. While this bread isn't an essential component of the dish, we think it adds to the dining experience—no silverware required!

Ethiopian-Style Spicy Chicken Stew

Doro Wat

SERVES 4

The chicken breasts and thighs do not cook at the same time; note that the breast pieces are added partway through the cooking time. If desired, the chicken can be pulled off the bone and shredded before it is returned to the pot in step 4 (see the illustration on page 69). Fenugreek, a slightly bitter herb, can be found in the spice aisle of well-stocked supermarkets and specialty markets. The Ethiopian flatbread injera, though traditional, is not an essential part of this recipe. The stew can alternatively be served with white rice or noodles.

4	pounds bone-in, skin-on chicken pieces (split breasts cut in half, drumsticks, and/or thighs)
	Salt and ground black pepper
2	tablespoons vegetable oil
1	medium onion, minced
2	tablespoons tomato paste
3	medium garlic cloves, minced or pressed through a garlic press (about 1 tablespoon)
1	tablespoon minced or grated fresh ginger
1	tablespoon chili powder
½	teaspoon ground cardamom
½	teaspoon ground nutmeg
½	teaspoon ground fenugreek (see note)
3	tablespoons unbleached all-purpose flour
2	cups low-sodium chicken broth
2	cups dry red wine
1½	cups water
4	hard-cooked eggs (see page 63)
2	tablespoons unsalted butter, cut into 2 pieces and chilled
1	recipe Ethiopian Flatbread (recipe follows)

1. Pat the chicken dry with paper towels and season with salt and pepper. Heat the oil in a large Dutch oven over medium-high heat until just smoking. Brown half of the chicken on both sides, 5 to 8 minutes per side, reducing the heat if the pan begins to scorch. Transfer the chicken to a plate, leaving the fat in the pot. Return the pot with the fat to medium-high heat and repeat with the remaining chicken; transfer the chicken to the plate.

2. Pour off all but 1 tablespoon of the fat left in the pot. Add the onion and cook over medium heat, stirring occasionally, until softened, 5 to 7 minutes. Stir in the tomato paste, garlic, ginger, chili powder, cardamom, nutmeg, and fenugreek and cook until fragrant, about 30 seconds. Stir in the flour and cook for 1 minute. Stir in the broth, wine, and water, scraping up any browned bits.

3. Nestle the chicken, along with any accumulated juices, into the pot and bring to a simmer. Cover, turn the heat to medium-low, and simmer until the chicken is fully cooked and tender, about 20 minutes for the breasts (160 degrees on an instant-read thermometer) or 1 hour for the thighs and drumsticks. (If using both types of chicken, simmer the thighs and drumsticks for 40 minutes before adding the breasts.)

4. Transfer the chicken to a serving dish, tent loosely with foil, and let rest while finishing the sauce. Skim as much fat as possible off the surface of the sauce and return to a simmer until the sauce is thickened and measures about 3 cups, about 20 minutes. Stir in the eggs and cook until warmed through, about 1 minute. Off the heat, stir in the butter and season with salt and pepper to taste. Pour the sauce over the chicken and serve with the flatbread.

Ethiopian Flatbread

Injera

MAKES 4 FLATBREADS

Teff flour can be found at natural foods stores or African/Middle Eastern specialty stores. These flatbreads are soft and slightly spongy, as opposed to a pita bread which has a somewhat sturdy character. The bread is cooked covered, which makes flipping unnecessary.

2   cups (10 ounces) unbleached all-purpose flour
½   cup (2½ ounces) teff flour (see note) or whole wheat or rye flour
½   teaspoon salt
1   teaspoon baking powder
1   teaspoon baking soda
2   cups water
6   tablespoons juice from 2 lemons
2   teaspoons vegetable oil

1. Whisk the flours, salt, baking powder, and baking soda together in a medium bowl. Add the water and lemon juice and whisk until smooth. Heat ½ teaspoon of the vegetable oil in a 12-inch nonstick skillet over low heat. Pour ¾ cup of the batter into the skillet and swirl to coat the bottom of the pan. Cover and cook until small bubbles appear on the surface, the flatbread springs back when pressed, and the bottom is lightly browned, about 8 minutes.

2. Slide the flatbread onto a large plate, cover with plastic wrap, and repeat with the remaining oil and batter 3 more times. The flatbreads can be held at room temperature for up to 4 hours; they can be served warm or at room temperature. (The breads can be cooled, transferred to a zipper-lock bag, and refrigerated for up to 2 days. Wrap the breads with a damp towel and reheat in the microwave on high power until warm and softened, 30 to 60 seconds.)

MIDDLE EASTERN–STYLE LAMB PITA SANDWICHES

Kefta Kebab

WHETHER YOU CALL THEM KEFTA, KIBBE, kofta, or simply ground meat patties, lamb-based patties appear all over the Middle East. Generally sold by street vendors, the patties are stuffed into sandwiches with any number of toppings, from incendiary sauces and exotic pickles to a simple tahini or yogurt-based sauce and lettuce. We think these sandwiches are ideal for an unusual weeknight dinner. A Middle Eastern spice palette and subtly exotic lamb can turn an otherwise prosaic meatball sandwich into something special.

The sandwich comprises three parts: the meat patties, the garnishes, and the bread. The patty recipes we researched ran the gamut with respect to flavor and technique. Some included a long list of ingredients that necessitated a great deal of effort, while others kept the flavors simple and preparation brief. A quick taste test of extremes suggested we seek a comfortable medium. The simplest versions tasted bland, while the fancy versions buried the meat under a mass of spices and took entirely too long to assemble.

After looking at numerous ingredient lists, we broke down the patty into three components: the meat, the binding, and the seasoning. Unlike ground beef, ground lamb is normally available only in one unspecified fat content. You could ask your butcher to grind fresh meat for you, but we found it unnecessary, as surplus fat renders out. Much of lamb's somewhat gamey flavor is located in the fat; we found that leaner meat tasted milder, if this is a concern. (You can request leaner lamb from a butcher who can grind it to order.)

Many recipes we researched contained lots of spices. To reduce complexity, we added only cilantro, finely chopped onion, and minced garlic to the lamb before rolling the mixture into balls and flattening them into small disks.

Once the seasoned patties were cooked through, tasters thought their texture was too dense and dry. Taking a cue from some of our meatball recipes, we incorporated a modified panade (a paste of fresh bread crumbs and milk) to make the meat juicier. But now tasters found the patties a little too mushy. Our recipe called for pita pockets with tops that needed to be cut off before they could be filled. What if we replaced the white bread crumbs with crumbs from this drier bread? This gave the patties a sturdier structure along with fuller, more savory flavor—and no more waste. (We then warmed the pitas in the oven while we cooked the patties.)

Traditionally, the patties are grilled on skewers, but for the sake of convenience, we opted for pan-frying. Broiling would have been the logical indoor replacement for grilling, but we found pan-frying offered more control and the patties developed a crisper crust. All of the patties could fit into a large skillet at one time and were cooked through in less than 10 minutes. After a quick blot on paper towels, they were ready to eat.

Just because we had nicely warmed pitas and well-seasoned meat didn't mean we were finished. Yogurt-based sauces appear throughout the Middle East and were a perfect accompaniment, as the yogurt's sharpness cuts the lamb's richness. We added cilantro for brightness and cayenne pepper for spiciness. To add pungency and round out the yogurt's tang, we included minced garlic—just one clove, so as not to overwhelm the other flavors.

With all of our components ready, all we had to do now was put together the sandwich. Taking one warmed pita at a time, we spread a quarter of the sauce on one side before adding three lamb patties and filling the rest of the space with lettuce and tomatoes. A single bite confirmed that this was a great weeknight alternative to a cold cut sandwich or burger.

Middle Eastern–Style Lamb Pita Sandwiches

Kefta Kebab

SERVES 4

Although we prefer the richness of plain whole milk yogurt, low-fat yogurt can be substituted. Don't be concerned if the skillet appears crowded when cooking the patties, they will shrink slightly as they cook. The patties can be prepared through step 3 and refrigerated for up to a day or frozen up to a week before cooking as directed in step 4 (frozen patties should be thawed in the refrigerator before cooking).

YOGURT SAUCE

1	cup plain whole milk yogurt
1	tablespoon minced fresh cilantro or mint leaves
1	small garlic clove, minced or pressed through a garlic press (about ½ teaspoon)
	Salt
	Cayenne pepper

SANDWICHES

4	(8-inch) pita breads
½	medium onion, chopped coarse (about ½ cup)
4	teaspoons juice from 1 lemon
2	medium garlic cloves, minced or pressed through a garlic press (about 2 teaspoons)
½	teaspoon salt
¼	teaspoon ground black pepper
1	pound ground lamb
2	tablespoons minced fresh cilantro leaves
2	teaspoons vegetable oil
1	large tomato, sliced thin
2	cups shredded iceberg lettuce

1. FOR THE YOGURT SAUCE: Combine the yogurt, cilantro, and garlic in a small bowl; season with salt and cayenne to taste and set aside. (The sauce can be refrigerated in an airtight container for up to 2 days.)

2. FOR THE SANDWICHES: Adjust an oven rack to the middle position and heat the oven to 350 degrees. Trim the top quarter off of each piece of pita, reserving the trimmed pieces, then stack the pitas and tightly wrap them with foil. Tear the reserved pita trimmings into ½-inch pieces; you should have about ¾ cup.

3. Process the torn pita pieces, onion, lemon juice, garlic, salt, and pepper together in a food processor to a smooth, uniform paste, about 30 seconds, stopping to scrape down the sides of the bowl as needed. Transfer the onion mixture to a large bowl, add the lamb and cilantro and mix until uniform. Divide the mixture into 12 equal pieces (¼ cup each) and roll them into balls. Gently flatten the balls into round disks, about ½ inch thick and 2½ inches in diameter.

4. Place the foil-wrapped pitas directly on the oven rack and heat for 10 minutes. Meanwhile, heat the oil in a 12-inch nonstick skillet over medium-high heat until just smoking. Add the patties and cook until well browned and crusty, 3 to 4 minutes. Flip the patties, reduce the heat to medium, and cook until well browned and crusty on the second side, about 5 minutes longer. Transfer the patties to a paper towel–lined plate.

5. Spread ¼ cup of the sauce inside the warm pitas. Divide the patties evenly among the pitas and top with the tomato slices and shredded lettuce. Serve, passing the remaining sauce at the table.

MOROCCAN-SPICED LAMB

Mechoui

MECHOUI, A BERBER SPECIALTY, IS A SPIT-roasted whole lamb that is mopped frequently with butter and spices as it cooks, resulting in a crispy, well-seasoned crust and moist, tender meat. Obviously, spit-roasting a whole lamb in the test kitchen was out of the question. Instead, we set out to develop a recipe that showcased the flavors of the traditional dish using a cut of lamb and a technique that was well suited to the American home kitchen.

We started our testing with the easiest method and cut of lamb possible. Whole boneless legs can weigh 8 to 9 pounds—great for a crowd, but impractical for a typical dinner. More practical were boneless half legs, which weigh 3 to 4 pounds. We found the sirloin (top) to be more tender than the shank (lower) end, but both roast beautifully.

After settling on the half leg, we decided to experiment with oven temperatures. The best lamb was roasted at 400 degrees. But because we wanted a crisp crust, we cooked the lamb at 450 to 500 degrees to start and then reduced the temperature to 375 degrees to finish.

This oven-searing method brought us closest to our goal, but the exterior fat still smoked and gave the meat an unwanted gamey flavor. Taking a cue from our roasted rack of lamb recipes, we tried pan-searing the lamb on the stovetop before putting it into the oven to finish at 375 degrees. The results were perfect. The direct heat jump-started the cooking of the lamb's exterior, producing a crisp crust in a matter of minutes. The flesh, meanwhile, remained very tender, and although there was still a little smoke, the meat picked up none of the gamey flavor produced with oven-searing. Using a roasting rack allowed the lamb to cook evenly on all sides once transferred to the oven.

With our cooking method established, we were ready to test flavorings. We knew that it is traditional to baste the lamb with a zesty butter as it roasts and we wanted to follow suit. All of the recipes

we found seasoned the butter with garlic, cumin, and paprika and some recipes also added ground coriander—our tasters preferred the fresher flavor of cilantro. Dried thyme was the final addition to the butter, adding a deep, woodsy backbone.

Basting with this spiced butter promoted a tasty crust; however, we wanted more flavor to penetrate the interior of the roast. It was then that we decided to rub the lamb with some of the flavorful butter before rolling and tying the roast. The butter and spices melted into the meat as it roasted, resulting in a juicy, tender, well-seasoned roast. But some of the drippings, we noticed, tended to burn on the bottom of our dry roasting pan, so we added some chicken broth (just 1 cup) to the pan before roasting, which kept the drippings fluid. Before serving, we carved the roast into ½-inch slices and poured the flavorful pan drippings over the top. After our first bite we knew we had done it: Moroccan-spiced lamb with spit-roasted flavor, made in the comfort of our own kitchen.

Moroccan-Spiced Roast Boneless Leg of Lamb

Mechoui

SERVES 6

Be sure to remove any twine (or elastic netting) from the lamb before prepping it as directed. Remember to reserve the pan drippings to pour them over the sliced lamb before serving—they are extremely flavorful.

1	cup low-sodium chicken broth
1	boneless half leg of lamb (3½ to 4 pounds), trimmed of surface fat
½	cup packed fresh cilantro leaves
5	medium garlic cloves, minced or pressed through a garlic press (about 5 teaspoons)
2	teaspoons dried thyme leaves
2	teaspoons paprika
2	teaspoons ground cumin
	Salt and ground black pepper
8	tablespoons (1 stick) unsalted butter, softened
1	tablespoon olive oil

1. Adjust an oven rack to the lower-middle position and heat the oven to 375 degrees. Set a rack inside a large roasting pan, add the broth to the pan, and set aside. Following illustration 1 on the right, lay the lamb with the rough interior side facing up (which was against the bone), cover with plastic wrap, and pound to an even ¾-inch thickness.

2. Process the cilantro, garlic, thyme, paprika, cumin, 1 teaspoon salt, and ½ teaspoon pepper in a food processor until finely chopped. Add the butter and process until smooth, about 20 seconds.

3. Rub half of the butter mixture over the rough interior side of the lamb, leaving a 1-inch border around the edge. Following illustrations 2 and 3, roll and tie the lamb into a compact roast. Pat the roast dry with paper towels and season with salt and pepper.

4. Heat the oil in a 12-inch skillet over medium-high heat until just smoking. Brown the lamb until well browned on all sides, about 2 minutes per side, reducing the heat if the pan begins to scorch. Following illustration 4, use tongs to stand the roast on each end to brown, about 30 seconds per end. Melt the remaining butter mixture in a saucepan over low heat or in a microwave on 50 percent power for 1 minute; set aside.

5. Transfer the browned roast to the rack in the roasting pan and roast until an instant-read thermometer inserted into the thickest part registers 130 to 135 degrees (medium-rare), 45 to 55 minutes, basting with the reserved melted butter mixture every 10 minutes. Transfer the meat to a carving board, tent with foil, and let rest for 10 to 15 minutes. Cut into ½-inch slices, pour the pan drippings over the lamb and serve immediately.

PREPARING ROAST BONELESS LEG OF LAMB

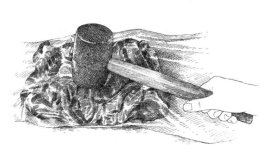

1. Cover the lamb with plastic wrap and pound to a uniform ¾-inch thickness.

2. Cover with the butter mixture, leaving a 1-inch border around the edge, then roll lengthwise into a tight cylinder.

3. Using kitchen twine, tie the roast into a neat package, by looping the twine around the roast at intervals and then down the length of the roast.

4. Holding the leg with tongs, sear the two ends until well browned.

11

INDIA

INDIAN-STYLE TURNOVERS

Samosas

MANY CUISINES FEATURE SOME VERSION OF meat- or vegetable-filled turnovers, and Indian cuisine is no exception. India's version is called *samosas* and they are ubiquitous throughout the country and are also a familiar sight on restaurant menus in the U.S. At their best, samosas contain a pungently spiced filling of either vegetables or meat (sometimes both), encompassed by a thin, crispy pastry shell. But restaurant versions available to us often fall far short of our expectations, offering bland fillings and a thick, doughy exterior. Our goal was to improve on this poorly interpreted classic with a recipe for making samosas at home.

We gathered a sampling of samosas from local restaurants as well as from a few recipes we found in cookbooks. The results were disappointing: bland, gloppy fillings of potato and beef with overcooked army-green peas strewn throughout were the norm. In addition, many of the crusts were excessively doughy in the corners and soft and bready where they covered the filling. It was clear we had our work cut out for us. After concocting a basic meat and potato filling, we decided to turn our attention first to the crust.

Our research uncovered a wide variety of crusts. Some used whole wheat flour while others used standard all-purpose flour. Some incorporated cold butter, much like a pie dough, while others used melted butter and/or vegetable oil. We even encountered some recipes that called for yogurt. With so many options and combinations, we kept it basic and moved forward with what seemed to be the most authentic ingredients.

Our first dough consisted of whole wheat flour, water, vegetable oil, and salt. The resulting crust was excessively bready and chewy and the earthy whole grain flavor competed with the filling. We switched to all-purpose flour, which was an improvement, yielding better flavor and slightly better texture, but the finished crust was still too bready. We then began experimenting with different fats in varying amounts. Our first test was to explore the advantages and disadvantages of cold butter processed into the flour. The pieces of butter left weak spots in the dough that gave way to the filling, punching holes in our finished samosas. The crust was also too flaky and delicate after frying to support the substantial filling.

We then experimented with melted butter and vegetable oil. Since there appeared to be no advantage to using butter, either in taste or texture, we decided to stick with oil. One tablespoon of oil did little to benefit the dough and left us with the same old bready crust that we had encountered in our previous tests. Two tablespoons of oil began to

---

INGREDIENTS: **Spices 101**

Spices define Indian cooking and their quality is of utmost importance: they can either ruin a dish or elevate it to another level. Rancid or stale spices impart a muddy, dull taste to foods, whereas fresh spices strengthen a dish's fragrant aroma and taste. All too often home cooks reach for old, stale bottles of spices that essentially have turned into expensive dust. Following a few simple rules and techniques can help you get the most from your spice rack.

In most cases, purchasing whole spices and grinding them is preferable to buying ground spices. Whole spices have a longer shelf life (about twice that of preground spices) and freshly ground spices have superior aroma and flavor. That said, there is no denying the convenience of purchasing preground spices. But whether whole or ground, spices should be bought in the smallest quantities available. Ethnic markets often have a high turnover of spices and are a great place to shop. It also pays to check the expiration date.

When storing spices, the biggest mistake cooks make is keeping them close to the stove. Heat, moisture, air, and light quickly shorten the shelf life of spices, leaving them dull; keep spices in a cool, dark, dry place, in a well-sealed container.

Toasting spices releases their volatile oils and aroma, intensifying their flavor and resulting in a mellow smokiness. To toast spices, put them in a small skillet without any oil and set the skillet over medium heat. Shake the skillet occasionally to prevent scorching and toast until they are fragrant, no more than 30 seconds for ground spices and 1 to 3 minutes for whole spices. Cool whole spices slightly before grinding. Whole spices toast at different rates so toast each spice individually or one spice may burn before another is fully toasted. In India, toasted, ground spices are often used in dry rubs for meat.

show promise; the crust was getting crisper and the dough was becoming easier to work with. Three tablespoons was the magic number. This dough was more forgiving and after frying it came out crispy and golden. Visiting the high end of the spectrum, 4 tablespoons of oil made the dough excessively greasy during rolling and during the stuffing process the dough began to tear.

But we wondered if we could make the dough even easier to work with. Based on a recipe we found during our initial research, we tried adding yogurt. By adding a mere 2 tablespoons of yogurt and subsequently decreasing the amount of water, we had a dough that was now incredibly light and elastic.

These turnovers are typically triangular in shape and after some experimentation, we found we could most easily replicate this traditional shape by cutting the dough into half moons and then forming a cone shape, leaving one end open. We then packed the filling into the opening and pinched the edges to seal the samosas. (Because we had created such an elastic dough, it was extremely forgiving when stuffed to the brim with filling.)

Although some recipes now call for baking samosas, they are traditionally fried and we saw no reason to change paths here—in our opinion, that is the only way to achieve the hallmark crispy, golden crust. Heating the oil to a temperature of 375 degrees proved ideal—any less and the oil cooled down too much when the samosas were added, resulting in pale, doughy crusts.

Many of the samosas we purchased from local restaurants contained both meat and potatoes, and our initial tests started with this basic combination. For the meat we experimented with both ground beef and lamb. After several tests, tasters unanimously decided that the combination of meat and potatoes was excessively heavy. The potatoes also dulled the rich flavor of the meat and so we decided to save them for an all-vegetable variation. In place of the potatoes we used peas, another classic component, and tasters enjoyed the sweetness and burst of color they added.

Though our filling was much improved, it was still excessively greasy. We switched from 85 percent lean to 90 percent lean ground meat, but tasters

EQUIPMENT: Spider Skimmers

If you peek into a restaurant kitchen, you'll see chefs working over steaming stockpots or vats of bubbling oil using shallow, woven wire baskets on long handles to retrieve blanched vegetables, ravioli, french fries, thin-skinned wontons, and samosas. Suffice it to say that most chefs wouldn't part with their "spiders," as they are called, which effortlessly scoop out multiple handfuls of food with one swoop and leave all the hot cooking oil, water, or broth behind.

But is one species of spider superior to the others? While cooking skinny french fries and plump cheese ravioli, we noted that several models trapped too much liquid and sharp wire edges snagged delicate ravioli wrappers. Wood handles soaked up oil and water, discoloring the wood and absorbing odors. One model, the Typhoon Extra-Large Wire Skimmer ($15), avoided all these flaws and is our clear favorite.

THE BEST SPIDER SKIMMER

The Typhoon Extra-Large Wire Skimmer sports a solid metal handle that won't soak up oil or odors and a uniform mesh face that lets liquid pass through with ease.

missed the texture of the fattier meat and the additional flavor it contributed. Our solution was to drain the meat after sautéing, reserving 2 tablespoons of fat to bloom our spices and sauté the rest of the ingredients.

Determining the right combination of spices for our filling was an even bigger challenge, given the vast array of choices in Indian cuisine. After much trial and error, we eventually settled on a mixture of ground spices, including coriander, cumin, cinnamon, nutmeg, cloves, and cayenne pepper. Preground spices were used largely for convenience and were bloomed (cooked in oil) for maximum flavor (see "Spices 101" on page 432).

After deciding on our spices, aromatics such as onions, tomato paste, garlic, and ginger were added to the mix, along with yogurt for its cooling, fresh counterpoint to the complex spice mixture. This combination of flavors and textures was a far cry from the bland, dense fillings we had sampled at the

FILLING SAMOSAS

1. Cut the dough into 12 equal pieces, and roll each piece into a 5-inch circle on a well-floured work surface. Working with 1 dough round at time, cut the dough evenly in half into 2 half-moon shapes.

2. Working with 1 half-moon piece of dough, moisten the straight side with a wet finger, then fold in half. Press to seal the seam on the straight side only and crimp with a fork to secure; leave the rounded edge open and unsealed.

3. Pick up the piece of dough and hold it gently in a cupped hand, with the open, unsealed edge facing up; gently open the dough into a cone shape. Fill the dough cone with 2 tablespoons of the filling and pack the filling in tightly in order to leave a ¼-inch rim at the top.

4. Moisten the inside rim of the cone with a wet finger, and pinch the top edge together to seal.

5. Lay the samosa on a flat surface and crimp all the edges with a fork to secure.

beginning of our tests, and our enthusiasm carried over to developing our potato filling.

For our potato filling we chose to use whole cumin, fennel, and mustard seeds for their added texture, which provided a welcome contrast to the soft potato filling. Fenugreek added a subtle bitter note and red pepper flakes provided some heat. Just as in the meat-filled samosas, we oil-bloomed these spices. Onions, garlic, and ginger were then added to the pan, followed by boiled, diced potatoes. The potatoes cooked until they began to brown around the edges, at which point the peas were stirred in and warmed through. The mixture was transferred to a bowl where it was finished with cilantro and lemon juice. We had successfully translated this Indian classic into an easy and accessible snack for any occasion.

Indian-Style Turnovers
Samosas
MAKES 24 TURNOVERS

We prefer whole milk yogurt here, though low-fat or nonfat yogurt can be substituted. We pack these samosas with a lot of filling; the dough is very elastic and will easily stretch around the filling without bursting. A wire spider comes in handy when frying the samosas; see page 433 for more information. Serve the samosas with Tamarind Chutney (page 442) or Cilantro-Mint Chutney (page 442).

- 2   cups (10 ounces) unbleached all-purpose flour, plus extra for the work surface
- ½   teaspoon salt
- 2   tablespoons plain whole milk yogurt
- 3   quarts plus 3 tablespoons vegetable oil
- 6   tablespoons cold water
- 1   recipe turnover filling (see pages 435–436), chilled

1. Pulse the flour and salt together in a food processor until combined, about 4 pulses. Drizzle the yogurt and 3 tablespoons of the oil over the flour mixture and process until the mixture resembles coarse cornmeal, about 5 seconds. With the machine running, slowly add 4 tablespoons of the water through the feed tube until the dough forms a ball. If the dough doesn't come together, add the remaining 2 tablespoons water, 1 tablespoon at a time, with

BLOOMING SPICES

The technique of cooking whole or ground spices in hot butter or oil for a few seconds is called "blooming" and is used at the start of many Indian recipes—it not only deepens the flavor of the spices, as toasting does (see "Spices 101" on page 432), but it also flavors the oil in which all the remaining ingredients will be cooked. To bloom spices, heat vegetable oil in a nonstick skillet (we prefer a nonstick skillet to prevent the spices from sticking and burning) over medium-high heat until shimmering (or if using butter, heat until the foaming subsides) and add all the spices together. Cook the spices while stirring or shaking the pan, until they become fragrant and their color turns a shade darker, about 10 seconds. This technique is particularly well suited to soups and curries. (Whole spices do not get ground after blooming, so they should be discarded—particularly large ones such as cardamom, cinnamon sticks, and cloves—if not being served whole in the finished dish.)

the processor running, until a dough ball forms. The dough should feel very soft and malleable.

2. Transfer the dough to a floured work surface and knead by hand until it firms slightly, about 2 minutes. Wrap the dough in plastic wrap and let rest for at least 20 minutes or refrigerate for up to 1 day.

3. Cut the dough into 12 equal pieces, and keep the pieces covered with a sheet of plastic wrap coated with vegetable oil spray to prevent them from drying out. Working with 1 piece of dough at a time, roll the dough into a 5-inch round using a rolling pin. Cut each dough round in half to form 24 half moons. Following the illustrations on page 434, shape, fill, and seal the samosas, using 2 tablespoons of filling per samosa.

4. Adjust an oven rack to the middle position and heat the oven to 200 degrees. Line a baking sheet with several layers of paper towels and set aside. Heat the remaining 3 quarts oil in a large Dutch oven over medium-high heat to 375 degrees. Add 8 of the samosas and fry until golden brown and bubbly, 2½ to 3 minutes, adjusting the heat as needed to maintain 375 degrees. Using a wire spider or slotted spoon, transfer the samosas to the prepared baking sheet and keep warm in the oven. Return the oil to 375 degrees and repeat with the remaining samosas in two batches. Serve.

Meat Turnover Filling

MAKES ENOUGH FOR 24 TURNOVERS

You can substitute low-fat or nonfat yogurt here—it might curdle a bit when cooked in step 3, but the curds will be nearly undetectable once inside the samosas.

SPICES

2	teaspoons ground coriander
2	teaspoons ground cumin
¾	teaspoon ground cinnamon
½	teaspoon ground nutmeg
¼	teaspoon ground cloves
¼	teaspoon cayenne pepper

BEEF FILLING

1	tablespoon vegetable oil
1½	pounds (85 percent) lean ground beef or lamb
1	large onion, minced
	Salt
5	medium garlic cloves, minced or pressed through a garlic press (about 5 teaspoons)
1	tablespoon minced or grated fresh ginger
2	teaspoons tomato paste
½	cup frozen peas, thawed
2	tablespoons plain whole milk yogurt
	Ground black pepper

1. Combine the spices in a small bowl and set aside. Heat the oil in a 12-inch nonstick skillet over medium-high heat until shimmering. Add the beef and cook, breaking up the meat with a wooden spoon, until the meat is no longer pink and all the liquid has cooked off, about 7 minutes. Drain the meat in a fine-mesh strainer set over a bowl to reserve the drippings.

2. Return 2 tablespoons of the reserved drippings to the skillet, add the spices, and sauté over medium-high heat until fragrant, about 10 seconds. Stir in the onion and 1 teaspoon salt and cook until softened, 5 to 7 minutes. Stir in the garlic, ginger, and tomato paste and cook until fragrant, about 30 seconds.

3. Stir in the drained meat, peas, and yogurt and cook until the mixture is cohesive and no longer wet, about 2 minutes. Transfer the mixture to a medium bowl, cover with plastic wrap, and

refrigerate until completely cool, about 1 hour. Season with salt and pepper to taste before using. (The filling can be refrigerated for up to 2 days.)

⌁

Potato Turnover Filling

MAKES ENOUGH FOR 24 TURNOVERS

We prefer the texture of whole fennel and cumin seeds in this filling; however, you can substitute ½ teaspoon ground fennel and ½ teaspoon ground cumin if desired.

SPICES
1	teaspoon fennel seeds
1	teaspoon cumin seeds
1	teaspoon brown mustard seeds
¼	teaspoon ground fenugreek
¼	teaspoon ground turmeric
⅛	teaspoon red pepper flakes

POTATO FILLING
2	pounds russet potatoes (about 4 medium), peeled and cut into 1-inch chunks
	Salt
3	tablespoons vegetable oil
1	medium onion, minced
3	medium garlic cloves, minced or pressed though a garlic press (about 1 tablespoon)
1½	teaspoons minced or grated fresh ginger
½	cup frozen peas, thawed
¼	cup minced fresh cilantro leaves
1½	teaspoons juice from 1 lemon
	Ground black pepper

1. Combine the spices in a small bowl and set aside. Cover the potatoes by 1 inch of water in a large saucepan and add 1 tablespoon salt. Bring to a boil, then reduce to a simmer and cook until the potatoes are tender and a fork can be slipped easily into the center, 12 to 15 minutes. Drain the potatoes and set aside to cool slightly.

2. Heat the oil in a 12-inch nonstick skillet over medium-high heat until shimmering. Add the spices and sauté until fragrant, about 10 seconds. Stir in the onion and 1 teaspoon salt and cook until softened, 5 to 7 minutes. Stir in the garlic and ginger and cook until fragrant, about 30 seconds. Stir in the cooled potatoes and cook until they begin

to brown around the edges, 5 to 7 minutes. Stir in the peas to combine.

3. Transfer the mixture to a medium bowl, cover with plastic wrap, and refrigerate until completely cool, about 1 hour. Stir in the cilantro and lemon juice and season with salt and pepper to taste before using. (The filling can be refrigerated for up to 2 days.)

MULLIGATAWNY

LITERALLY TRANSLATED TO MEAN "PEPPER water," *mulligatawny* is a pureed vegetable soup that is mildly spicy but not hot. The soup has a faint sweetness, usually from coconut, and is often seen garnished with chicken or lamb. At its best, mulligatawny is silky and elegant with potent yet balanced spices and aromatics. But very often this soup falls far short of expectations, with poorly incorporated, raw-tasting spices, and an overly thin base. We wanted to reclaim this soup's once velvety texture and deep, complex flavor.

We decided to start with the question of the liquid base. Our research indicated that chicken broth, lamb broth, beef broth, vegetable broth, and water were all possible choices. Tasters found vegetable broth too sweet and vegetal and beef broth too strong, even a bit sour. Lamb broth was overpowering and we ruled it out because of the work involved in making it. In the end, we decided that chicken broth was the ideal base for the wide range of spices and vegetables. Water made a tasty vegetarian soup that was not quite as rich as the versions made with chicken broth, but still acceptable.

Curry powder, a blend of spices sold in this country, is a central ingredient in most mulligatawny soups. (In India, cooks typically don't purchase spice blends but make their own, which are referred to generally as *masalas*.) After experimenting with several store-bought curry powders (which vary in their combination of spices), we found the end product to be muted and muddy-tasting, so we decided to make our own. After a little tinkering, we found great results with a blend of garam masala, cumin, coriander, and turmeric. We found it best to bloom the spices in butter. (For more information on blooming spices for the best flavor, see page 435.)

We focused next on the aromatics—garlic and ginger—and on the coconut. After testing various amounts of garlic and ginger, we noted that we liked equal amounts of both. As for the coconut, some recipes called for coconut milk, others for fresh coconut meat, and still others added dried coconut. The coconut milk gave the soup a silky consistency, but the flavor tended to dominate the dish. Fresh coconut was not flavorful enough and in any case was much too troublesome to prepare. Dried coconut was the best option, adding enough flavor to the soup without taking it over. Sweetened shredded coconut gave us the balance that we were looking for. We cooked the coconut with the onions to allow it to brown and develop its flavor before the rest of the ingredients were added.

With our aromatics and spices under control it was time to test the vegetables, which would give the soup flavor, bulk, and color when pureed. We tested onions, carrots, celery, cauliflower, spinach, and peas. Not surprisingly, we found that onions were a must in the soup. Carrots added color and sweetness and the celery provided a cool flavor that contrasted nicely with the hot spices. Cauliflower was rejected for the cabbage-like flavor it gave to the soup. Spinach and peas did little to enhance the soup's flavor. In addition, they imparted an undesirable color when pureed.

Several recipes suggested using pureed rice or lentils to thicken the soup and while tasters didn't oppose these flavors (in fact they liked the additional flavor of the lentils), they didn't like the thick, porridge-like texture they produced when pureed. After a bit more testing, we found that sprinkling a little flour over the sautéed aromatics (to make a roux) gave the soup a thickened yet velvety consistency—silky and substantial but not heavy. Although a few sources said that pureeing the soup was optional, we think that mulligatawny must be mostly smooth, perhaps punctuated by a small amount of lentils, chicken, or lamb.

Returning to the idea of adding lentils to the soup—leaving them whole rather than pureeing them as a thickener—we experimented with adding them after the soup was pureed and tested

PREPARING GINGER

You can prepare ginger for the recipes in this chapter in one of two ways: mincing or grating. Ginger is highly fibrous, so a sharp knife or grater is a must. Our first choice for grating ginger is a ceramic ginger grater (a shallow bowl with a raised center covered with small teeth), but we realize that most kitchens do not stock such a tool. A Microplane rasp grater had been our second choice, but recent tests have revealed a better substitute: the small holes of a box grater. The box grater works more like the ceramic grater, leaving behind a smoother, more refined puree of ginger, whereas the Microplane produces a coarser mixture of both fibers and puree. Just be sure to work with a large nub of ginger—and watch your knuckles.

MINCING GINGER

1. Slice the peeled knob of ginger into thin rounds, then fan the rounds out and cut them into thin, matchstick-like strips.

2. Chop the matchsticks crosswise into a fine mince.

GRATING GINGER

Peel a small section of a large piece of ginger. Grate the peeled portion, using the rest of the ginger as a handle to keep fingers safely away from the grater.

several lentil varieties. Chana dal, a smaller cousin to chickpeas, also known as yellow split peas, imparted an overly earthy, vegetal flavor that didn't meld with the flavor of the soup—not to mention that they took over an hour to cook. Red lentils all but disintegrated in the soup, leaving a grainy texture. We finally settled on standard brown lentils (or green French lentils), which held their shape when cooked and readily absorbed the surrounding flavors. A dollop of yogurt and shower of cilantro was all that we needed to finish this deeply flavorful and elegant soup. Traditionally, mulligatawny is served over basmati rice, although this version can certainly stand on its own as either a main course or an appetizer.

Mulligatawny

SERVES 8 AS AN APPETIZER, OR 4 TO 6 AS A MAIN COURSE

French green lentils (lentilles du Puy) will also work well here; the cooking time will remain the same. Do not use red lentils because they turn very soft when cooked and will disintegrate into the soup.

SPICES

2½	teaspoons garam masala
1½	teaspoons ground cumin
1½	teaspoons ground coriander
1	teaspoon ground turmeric

SOUP

3	tablespoons unsalted butter
2	medium onions, minced
½	cup sweetened shredded or flaked coconut
4	medium garlic cloves, minced or pressed through a garlic press (about 4 teaspoons)
4	teaspoons grated or minced fresh ginger
1	teaspoon tomato paste
¼	cup unbleached all-purpose flour
7	cups low-sodium chicken broth
2	medium carrots, peeled and chopped medium
1	celery rib, chopped medium
½	cup brown lentils, rinsed and picked over (see note)
	Salt and ground black pepper
2	tablespoons minced fresh cilantro leaves
	Plain yogurt (for serving)

1. Combine the spices in a small bowl and set aside. Melt the butter in a large Dutch oven over medium heat. Add the spices and sauté until fragrant, about 10 seconds. Add the onions and coconut and cook until softened, 5 to 7 minutes. Stir in the garlic, ginger, and tomato paste and cook until fragrant, about 30 seconds. Stir in the flour until evenly combined, about 1 minute. Gradually whisk in the chicken broth.

2. Stir in the carrots and celery, increase the heat to medium-high, and bring to a boil. Cover, reduce the heat to low, and simmer until the vegetables are tender, 20 to 25 minutes.

3. Puree the soup in a blender in batches until smooth and return to a clean pot. Add the lentils and return to a simmer over medium-high heat. Cover, reduce the heat to medium-low, and cook until the lentils are tender, about 40 minutes. (The soup can be refrigerated in an airtight container for up to 3 days; reheat over medium-low heat.)

4. Season with salt and pepper to taste. Ladle the soup into individual bowls, sprinkle with the cilantro, and dollop with yogurt before serving.

➤ VARIATIONS

Mulligatawny with Chicken

Follow the recipe for Mulligatawny, adding 1½ pounds boneless, skinless chicken breasts, trimmed, to the pot with the vegetables in step 2 and simmer until cooked through, 20 to 25 minutes. With tongs, transfer the cooked chicken to a carving board, cool slightly, and cut crosswise ¼-inch slices. Continue with the recipe, returning the sliced chicken to the pureed soup to reheat before seasoning in step 4.

Mulligatawny with Lamb

You will need to buy 2 pounds leg of lamb in order to yield approximately 1½ pounds of trimmed lamb for the soup.

Follow the recipe for Mulligatawny, adding 1½ pounds trimmed boneless leg of lamb, cut into 1 by 1½-inch chunks, to the soup along with the lentils in step 3; simmer until both the lentils and lamb are tender, 40 to 45 minutes.

INDIAN–STYLE FLATBREAD

Naan

SEVERAL SOUTH AND CENTRAL ASIAN cuisines—from Afghanistan down through Pakistan and India—prepare breads far different in style than American and European loaf breads. Generally flat or lightly puffed and round in shape, they are soft and chewy—more suited to tearing apart and dipping into stews and sauces than making into sandwiches or toast. Flatbreads of this style can be prepared quickly with a modicum of effort, as their flavor and texture are not dependent on a long, slow rise. We sought to replicate the flavor and texture of *naan*, a common Indian-style flatbread. Naan should be soft and tender yet chewy, with a slightly wheaty, mellow flavor. And it should be easy enough to prepare while dinner is cooking.

Flour is the main ingredient in naan, so it was our starting point. We tried a range of flour mixtures, from all whole wheat to all white, and from all-purpose to bread flour. We found the combination of whole wheat and bread flour to be the best. In our research, we found some recipes that called for chapati flour, a finely milled whole wheat flour that contributes a more delicate texture. We liked chapati flour but it can be hard to find, so we tried to replicate its texture by passing supermarket whole wheat flour through a fine sieve, which removed some of the rougher bran flakes. This step resulted in a more tender texture, meaning we could take advantage of the flavor of whole wheat flour without the heaviness.

Because we wanted a simple naan that didn't take hours to prepare (some recipes we found were lengthy and time-consuming), we were pleased to discover that 45 minutes to 1 hour was sufficient rising time. The bread is rolled or stretched rather thin and so it does not require a long rising time to develop the complex structure necessary to produce the large holes and crunchy, crisp crust that are important in many loaf-style breads. The yeast and short rising time still create the tiny air pockets and structure necessary to deliver a tender, chewy texture. After shaping, the breads need only a brief rest instead of a long proofing stage, which saves even more time.

We found that dividing the dough into eight pieces, shaping each piece into a ball, and then rolling and stretching it was the best way to manipulate the dough. Though this dough is more forgiving than most, a few minutes of rest between these steps helped to prevent the dough from shrinking back and wrinkling. Better yet, naan is intended to be rustic in appearance, so if the stretched dough is thinner in spots or a little uneven, it simply adds an interesting dimension to the cooked bread. (Another great discovery we made along the way was that the dough will keep in the refrigerator for a couple of days—simply let the dough come to room temperature and then proceed with the rolling and cooking.)

We were now ready to bake our bread. We tried simulating a tandoor oven (a coal-heated beehive-shaped oven that can reach extremely high temperatures) by placing a baking stone on the center rack of a 500-degree oven. We placed the dough on the hot stone, flipping it after a couple of minutes, and before we knew it the bread was done. However, the resulting bread was tough and dry, more like a cracker than the soft, chewy bread we wanted. It seemed that even though a tandoor oven reaches temperatures that far exceed our oven, our dough was actually drying out. So we sought out another method for cooking our naan.

Pan-grilling our bread on the stovetop seemed like a good way to mimic the intense heat of the tandoor without drying out the naan (the heat

ROUNDING DOUGH

With a cupped palm, roll each piece of dough into a smooth, taut ball (using the friction between the unfloured counter and the ball of dough), then loosely cover with greased plastic wrap and let rest before rolling out.

doesn't surround the bread as it does in the oven). After several attempts we found it best to heat the pan for 5 minutes over medium-high heat before cooking the bread. A cast-iron skillet is the best choice because of its ability to retain heat and cook evenly without burning, although any heavy-bottomed pan will do the job. (If not using a cast-iron pan, we recommend heating it for only two to three minutes.)

We discovered that when we fully cooked the bread on one side first, large, unwieldy bubbles formed on the surface. When we turned the bread over to cook the second side, it was "suspended" on the bubbles and didn't lie flat in the pan. As a result, the bread did not cook evenly. To solve that problem, we cooked the first side for 30 seconds, until only small bubbles appeared. At that point, we flipped the bread, cooked the other side for a couple of minutes, and then flipped it back to the first side to finish cooking. The result was an evenly cooked and evenly colored bread, ready to accompany most any meal.

Indian-Style Flatbread
Naan
MAKES EIGHT 6- TO 7-INCH BREADS

We slightly prefer the flavor of whole milk yogurt here, however low-fat or nonfat yogurt can be substituted. If the dough refuses to stay in a 6-inch round when rolling it out in step 5, cover and set it aside to let rest and relax for 5 to 10 minutes before trying again.

2½	cups (13¾ ounces) bread flour, plus extra as needed
¼	cup (1⅜ ounces) whole wheat flour, sifted before measuring to remove coarse flakes of bran
1	package (about 2¼ teaspoons) instant or rapid rise yeast
2	teaspoons sugar
	Salt
1	cup water, at room temperature
¼	cup plain whole milk yogurt
1	tablespoon olive oil, plus extra for the bowl
2	tablespoons sesame seeds (optional)
4	tablespoons (½ stick) unsalted butter, melted

1. Combine the flours, yeast, sugar, and 1½ teaspoons salt in the bowl of a standing mixer and mix with the paddle attachment until blended, about 15 seconds. Add the water, yogurt, and olive oil and mix on low speed until a shaggy dough forms, about 30 seconds.

2. Replace the paddle with the dough hook and knead the dough on medium speed until smooth and glossy, about 8 minutes, adding additional bread flour in 1-tablespoon increments, allowing 20 seconds between each addition, as needed for the dough to clear the sides of the bowl, but stick to the very bottom of the bowl. Transfer the dough to a clean work surface and lightly knead by hand for 1 minute.

3. Shape the dough into a large ball, transfer to a large, lightly oiled bowl, cover with plastic wrap, and place in a draft-free spot until the dough has doubled in size, 45 minutes to 1 hour. (At this point, the dough can be lightly punched down, wrapped tightly in plastic wrap, and refrigerated for up to 2 days.)

4. Turn the dough out onto a clean work surface, cut into 8 equal portions, and roll each portion into a round ball following the illustration on page 439. Set the balls aside on the counter (or a baking sheet), cover with greased plastic wrap, and let rest for 10 minutes.

5. Working with 1 ball of dough at a time, lay on a lightly floured work surface and roll into a 6-inch circle using a rolling pin (if the dough is sticky, sprinkle very lightly with flour). If using the sesame seeds, brush the tops of the dough rounds lightly with water, sprinkle each with 1 teaspoon seeds, and gently roll over with a rolling pin once or twice so the seeds adhere to the dough. Set the rounds aside on the floured counter (or a floured baking sheet) and cover with greased plastic wrap.

6. Heat a heavy 12-inch skillet (preferably cast iron) over medium-high heat until hot, 5 minutes. (If using a lighter pan, heat for only 2 to 3 minutes.) Working with 1 piece of dough at a time, lift the dough and gently stretch about 1 inch larger, and lay it in the skillet. Cook until small bubbles appear on the surface of the dough, about 30 seconds. Flip the bread and continue to cook until the bottom is speckled and deep golden brown in spots, about 2 minutes. Flip the bread over again and cook until

the bottom is speckled and deep golden brown in spots, 1 to 2 minutes longer.

7. Transfer the bread to a wire rack, brush lightly with butter, season with salt, and let cool for about 5 minutes. Repeat with the remaining dough rounds. Wrap the breads loosely in a clean kitchen towel and serve immediately. (The bread can be wrapped in foil and stored at room temperature for up to 2 days. Reheat in a 300-degree oven until warm, about 15 minutes.)

➤ VARIATION

Hand-Mixed Indian-Style Flatbread

Follow the recipe for Indian-Style Flatbread, whisking the flours, yeast, sugar, and 1½ teaspoons salt together in a large bowl. In a separate bowl, whisk the water, yogurt, and olive oil together. Using a wooden spoon, stir the water mixture into the flour mixture until a shaggy dough forms. Turn the dough out of the mixing bowl onto a very lightly floured work surface and knead by hand until smooth and elastic, 12 to 15 minutes. Add additional flour, 1 tablespoon at a time, as needed to prevent the dough from sticking to your hands (a little sticking is OK; do not add too much flour to the dough). Continue with step 3 as directed.

CHUTNEYS

CHUTNEYS ARE SPICY-SWEET CONDIMENTS that are served with all meals in India. They can have a salsa or jam-like consistency or they might simply be a coarse mix of dried fruit and nuts. Cooks in even the most humble homes would never dream of serving food without chutneys, no matter how simple. Whether they offer an unexpected blast of heat or cooling relief from the spicy cuisine, they are an integral part of every meal and add a welcome complexity to most any dish.

A staple of Indian cuisine for centuries, chutney was first exported to Europe in the 17th century. Soon after their export began, so too did the practice of commercialization and preservation. Today chutneys can be purchased at most supermarkets.

Chutneys can be made and eaten on the spot or they can be cooked and preserved for later consumption. Though they usually contain some form of chile, not all chutneys are spicy. They can represent a variety of tastes from sweet and sour to hot and spicy to cool and refreshing. Chutneys can be used as a sauce, they can take the place of a vegetable side dish, and they can even be used as a dip for flatbread.

Chutneys in the northern part of India are typically made using fresh herbs and fruit, whereas in the southern regions lentils and grated coconut are popular, with an array of combinations throughout the states in between. Chutneys in the North may either be cooked or simply tossed together like a fresh salsa, while chutneys from the South often resemble a dry paste pounded together with a mortar (*khal*) and pestle (*batta*). This pounding releases the flavor of the ingredients, creating extremely pungent and flavorful chutneys.

The following chutneys can accompany most any meal. The onion relish is great sprinkled over curries and rice pilaf. Cilantro-mint chutney and tamarind chutney make perfect dipping sauces for crispy samosas. And the mango chutney is well suited to tandoori chicken and lamb.

➤

Onion Relish

MAKES ABOUT 1 CUP

A regular yellow onion can be substituted for the sweet onion; however, you will need to increase the sugar to 1 teaspoon. Serve with any Indian dish, especially Chicken Curry (page 454), Saffron Chicken and Rice with Yogurt Sauce (page 449), or Tandoori Chicken (page 457).

1	sweet onion, such as Vidalia, Maui, or Walla Walla, minced
1	tablespoon juice from 1 lime
½	teaspoon sweet paprika
½	teaspoon sugar
⅛	teaspoon salt
	Pinch cayenne pepper

Combine all of the ingredients in a medium bowl and serve. (The relish can be refrigerated in an airtight container for up to 1 day.)

Cilantro-Mint Chutney

MAKES ABOUT 1 CUP

We prefer the flavor of whole milk yogurt here; however, low-fat or nonfat yogurt can be substituted. Serve with any Indian dish, including Indian-Style Turnovers (page 434), Chicken Curry (page 454), or Saffron Chicken and Rice with Yogurt Sauce (page 447).

2	cups tightly packed fresh cilantro leaves
1	cup tightly packed fresh mint leaves
1/3	cup plain whole milk yogurt
1/4	cup minced onion
1	tablespoon juice from 1 lime
1 1/2	teaspoons sugar
1/2	teaspoon ground cumin
1/4	teaspoon salt

Process all of the ingredients in a food processor until smooth, about 20 seconds, scraping down the sides of the bowl as needed and serve. (The chutney can be refrigerated in an airtight container for up to 1 day.)

Tamarind Chutney

MAKES ABOUT 1 CUP

You cannot substitute tamarind concentrate here; for more information on buying tamarind, see page 479. For an accurate measurement of boiling water, bring a full kettle of water to boil, then measure out the desired amount. Serve with Indian-Style Turnovers (page 434).

4	ounces tamarind paste or pulp (see note)
2	cups boiling water
1/2	cup packed light or dark brown sugar

1. Following the instructions on page 479, soak and rehydrate the tamarind paste in the boiling water until softened, about 30 minutes. Push the tamarind mixture through a fine-mesh strainer into a small saucepan, to remove the seeds and fibers and extract as much pulp as possible.

2. Stir in the sugar and bring to a boil. Reduce to a simmer and cook until the mixture is the consistency of maple syrup, about 15 minutes. Cool to room temperature before serving, about 1 hour. (The chutney can be refrigerated in an airtight container for up to 4 days.)

INGREDIENTS: Mango Chutney

Mango chutney (sometimes called Major Grey's chutney) is a welcome accompaniment to many curries and roasted meats. The name "Major Grey" is based on a fictional British soldier who supposedly enjoyed the sweet-and-sour punch of chutneys so much that he bottled his own. The name is not copyrighted and any bottled chutney can carry it.

Classic preparations cook unripe green mangos with sugar, vinegar, and aromatic spices. But high levels of fructose corn syrup and caramel color cloud many store-bought varieties and any natural mango flavors are often overshadowed by these additives.

Many of the supermarket brands we tested were sickeningly sweet, with insipid, weak flavor. Tasters disliked the unnatural mango flavor in Crosse and Blackwell Major Grey's Chutney. A substantial dollop of ginger oil spiced Patak's Sweet Mango

Chutney so heavily that tasters were torn; some appreciated the pungent, perfumed zing, while others complained about the ginger overload. Tasters liked the balanced sweetness and acidity of both Sharwood's Major Grey Mango Chutney and The Silver Palate Mango Chutney. In the end, the addition of lemon juice and peel gave The Silver Palate Mango Chutney a tangy boost that made it our favorite.

THE BEST MANGO CHUTNEY
A good mango chutney, like this one from The Silver Palate, offers a tangy, sweet, fruity complement to spicy curries.

Spicy Mango Chutney

MAKE ABOUT 2 CUPS

Depending on the sweetness of your mangos, you may need to adjust the sugar to taste. Mango chutney is a traditional condiment in Indian cooking and pairs well with simple grilled or roasted fish, poultry, and meats, such as Tandoori Chicken or Lamb (page 457).

SPICES

1	teaspoon dry mustard
1/8	teaspoon cayenne pepper
1/8	teaspoon ground cinnamon
	Pinch ground cloves

CHUTNEY

1	tablespoon unsalted butter
1	medium red onion, minced
	Salt
2	medium garlic cloves, minced or pressed through a garlic press (about 2 teaspoons)
1	tablespoon minced or grated fresh ginger
2	medium mangos, peeled, pitted, and chopped medium (see page 57)
1/4	cup packed light brown sugar, plus extra as needed (see note)
1	cup water
1/4	cup white vinegar
1/4	cup raisins
	Ground black pepper

1. Combine the spices in a small bowl and set aside. Melt the butter in a large saucepan over medium-high heat. Add the spices and sauté until fragrant, about 10 seconds. Stir in the onion and ½ teaspoon salt and cook until softened, 5 to 7 minutes.

2. Stir in the garlic and ginger until fragrant, about 30 seconds. Stir in the mangos and sugar and cook until the mangos release their liquid and the mixture thickens, about 10 minutes.

3. Stir in the water, vinegar, and raisins and simmer, stirring occasionally, until thickened, about 12 minutes.

4. Off the heat, season with salt, pepper, and sugar to taste. Cool to room temperature before serving, about 1 hour. (The chutney can be refrigerated in an airtight container for up to 4 days.)

SPICED RED LENTILS

Masoor Dal

RED LENTILS, ALSO SOLD UNDER THE INDIAN name *masoor dal*, are one of the most common legumes of India. The dishes made from lentils are also referred to simply as *dal*. Red lentils are mild and slightly nutty tasting and fade to a light mustard hue once cooked. They come both whole and split. The split variety cooks significantly faster and breaks down into a smooth puree within about 20 minutes (no soaking required), making them an ideal choice for a quick meal.

Dals are heavily spiced stews in which the lentils have broken down after cooking, creating a thick, coarse puree. Dals are a staple dish throughout most of India, particularly in the mountainous regions of northern India, where it is not uncommon to find some version of dal at every meal. Dal can be a meal on its own or can be served as an accompaniment to the main course—it can even be used as a spread for one of India's many flatbreads. We wanted our dal to be simple yet embody the complex flavors of Indian cuisine. So naturally, we started with the spices.

Not wanting to make our dal unbearably spicy, we sought out a basic blend of spices with heat as an afterthought. We settled on a combination of spices that included coriander, cumin, cinnamon, turmeric, cardamom, and finally, red pepper flakes. This offered a pleasing blend of deep and bright flavors that remained vibrant throughout the cooking process. We also tried adding garam masala—a blend of spices including coriander, cloves, cardamom, cumin, cinnamon, black pepper, and nutmeg—but found that this resulted in too many competing flavors.

Many of the recipes we researched called for adding the aromatics raw or skipping them altogether, relying entirely on spices and garnishes such as chutney for flavor. We felt this dish would benefit from the addition of onion, garlic, and ginger, but adding them to the dish raw overwhelmed the other flavors. We decided to first cook or "bloom" the spices in oil and then add the onion, garlic, and ginger before adding the lentils and liquid. Traditionally, additional spices are toasted in a separate pan with oil or ghee (clarified butter—see page 459 for more information) to make a mixture called *tarka* and then stirred into the lentils at the end of cooking to fortify the flavor of the finished dish. But our method of blooming the spices in oil boosted their flavor more easily without employing a second pan and additional fat.

Proper dal should have a porridge-like consistency, bordering on a puree. This consistency comes from cooking the lentils for the appropriate amount of time with the correct amount of water. This was easier said than done and it took us several tries to get the lentils to their ideal consistency while cooking off all the excess water in the pot. Whittling the water amount down gradually while keeping the amount of lentils the same, we finally settled on a 4 to 1 ratio of water to lentils. After a few more tweaks we added an extra ¼ cup of lentils to balance the texture.

For garnishes, we added cilantro for color and freshness and diced raw tomato for sweetness and acidity. The result was an authentic, well-balanced dal with both fragrant spice and buttery texture.

Spiced Red Lentils
Masoor Dal
SERVES 8 AS A SIDE DISH, OR 4 AS A VEGETARIAN MAIN COURSE

You cannot substitute brown lentils for the red lentils here; the red lentils have a very different texture. Serve with white rice and lemon wedges.

SPICES
½	teaspoon ground coriander
½	teaspoon ground cumin
½	teaspoon ground cinnamon
½	teaspoon ground turmeric
⅛	teaspoon ground cardamom
⅛	teaspoon red pepper flakes

LENTILS
1	tablespoon vegetable oil
1	medium onion, minced
4	medium garlic cloves, minced or pressed through a garlic press (about 4 teaspoons)
1½	teaspoons minced or grated fresh ginger
4	cups water
1¼	cups red lentils, rinsed and picked over
1	pound plum tomatoes (about 3 tomatoes), cored, seeded, and chopped medium
½	cup minced fresh cilantro leaves
2	tablespoons unsalted butter
	Salt and ground black pepper

1. Combine the spices in a small bowl and set aside. Heat the oil in a large saucepan over medium-high heat until shimmering. Add the spices and sauté until fragrant, about 10 seconds. Stir in the onion and cook until softened, 5 to 7 minutes. Stir in the garlic and ginger and cook until fragrant, about 30 seconds.

2. Stir in the water and lentils and bring to a boil. Reduce to a simmer and cook, uncovered, until the lentils are tender and resemble a coarse puree, 20 to 25 minutes. (At this point, the lentils can be refrigerated in an airtight container for up to 2 days; reheat over medium-low heat before continuing.)

3. Stir in the tomatoes, cilantro, and butter and season with salt and pepper to taste before serving.

➤ VARIATION
Red Lentils with Coconut Milk
The addition of coconut milk provides a lush, creamy texture and rich flavor; do not substitute light coconut milk here. You can freeze any leftover coconut milk.

Follow the recipe for Spiced Red Lentils, substituting 1 cup coconut milk for 1 cup of the water and omitting the butter.

RICE PILAF
Pulao

IN INDIA, AS IN MOST ASIAN COUNTRIES, rice plays a key role in the cuisine. In southern India, rice is the most widely consumed grain, compared to wheat in the North. Rice pilaf, or *pulao*, is long-grain rice that has been cooked in hot oil or butter before being simmered in hot liquid, typically either water or broth.

At its most basic, pilaf is a simple rice dish, made rich and flavorful from the sauté in fat and the addition of an aromatic such as onion or garlic. It can be served simply as is or made more elaborate with the addition of dried fruit, nuts, and spices. It can even be transformed into a main course with the addition of chicken or meat. We wanted to develop a basic recipe for foolproof pilaf that could easily be adapted to more elaborate preparations.

The logical first step in this process was to determine the best type of rice for pilaf. We immediately limited our testing to long-grain rice, since medium- and short-grain rice inherently produce a rather sticky, starchy product and we were looking for fluffy, separate grains.

Plain long-grain white rice worked well in our pilaf, but basmati rice, grown in the foothills of the Himalayas, was even better: Each grain was separate, long, and fluffy and the rice had a fresh, delicate fragrance. (That said, you can use plain long-grain rice if basmati is not available.)

Most sources indicate that the proper ratio of rice to liquid for long-grain white rice is 1 to 2, but many cooks use less water. After testing every possibility from equal amounts of water and rice to twice as much water as rice, we found that we got the best results using 1⅔ cups of water for every cup of rice. To make this easier to remember, as well as easier to measure, we increased the rice by half to 1½ cups and the liquid to 2½ cups.

With our rice to water ratio set, we were ready to test the traditional cooking method, which calls for rinsing the rice before cooking it. Most recipes declare this step to be essential to producing rice with distinct, separate grains that are light and fluffy. Rinsing the rice before cooking made a substantial difference, particularly with basmati rice. The resulting rice was less hard and more tender and it had a slightly shinier, smoother appearance than rice that hadn't been rinsed. To rinse the rice, you can either swish it around in a bowl of water, draining the water and repeating this process several times or rinse it in a fine-mesh strainer until the water runs clear.

We allowed the rice to steam for 10 minutes after removing it from the heat to ensure that the moisture was distributed throughout. We wondered if a longer or shorter steaming time would make much of a difference in the resulting pilaf. We made a few batches of pilaf, allowing it to steam for five minutes, 10 minutes, and 15 minutes. The pilaf that steamed for five minutes was heavy and wet. The batch that steamed for 15 minutes was the lightest and least watery. We also decided to try placing a clean kitchen towel between the pan and the lid right after we took the rice off the stove. We found this produced the best results of all, while reducing the steaming time to only 10 minutes. It seems that the towel (or two layers of paper towels) prevents condensation and absorbs the excess water in the pan during steaming, producing dryer, fluffier rice.

INGREDIENTS: Basmati Rice

Prized for its nutty flavor and perfume-like aroma, basmati rice is eaten worldwide in pilafs and biryanis and as an accompaniment to curries. Most Indian-grown rice comes from the Himalaya foothills, where the snow-flooded soil and humid climate offer ideal growing conditions. Choosing among the multitude of boxes, bags, and burlap sacks available today on supermarket shelves can be confusing. To find a truly great grain, we steamed seven brands, five from India and two domestic options. Matched against Indian imports, domestic brands Lundberg and Della suffered. They were less aromatic and the grains didn't elongate as much. Their overall texture was mushy, too. While all of the imported brands were acceptable, tasters overwhelmingly choose the longest sample—Tilda—as their favorite.

THE BEST BASMATI RICE

Indian-grown Tilda Pure Basmati Rice ($7.99 for 4 pounds) was tasters' top choice. It was praised for its "beautiful long grains," "slightly nutty" flavor, and especially "strong aroma."

We knew that sautéing the rice is essential for a light, nutty flavor and tender texture, but we were surprised to see that many Indian recipes called for as much as ¼ cup butter per cup of rice. We sautéed the rice in varying amounts of butter, from 1 to 4 tablespoons per 1½ cups rice. Three tablespoons was optimal. The rice was buttery and rich without being overwhelmingly so and each grain was shinier and more distinct than when cooked with less fat.

The addition of herbs, spices, and other flavorful ingredients is what gives pilaf its distinctive character. We found that dried spices and aromatics such as minced ginger, onion, and garlic are best sautéed briefly in the fat before the raw rice is added to the pan. Saffron and dried herbs are best added to the liquid as it heats up, while fresh herbs and toasted nuts should be added to the pilaf just before serving to maximize freshness, texture (in the case of nuts), and flavor. Dried fruits such as raisins, currants, or figs can be incorporated just before steaming the rice, which gives them enough time to heat through and plump up without becoming soggy.

EQUIPMENT: Nonstick Saucepans

In the test kitchen, small saucepans see plenty of action—we use them for making rice, heating milk, melting butter, or warming up soup. Because most of these tasks don't involve browning (and many involve sticky foods), we use nonstick 2-quart saucepans almost exclusively. Do pans that cost close to $100 offer significant performance, stick-resistance, or design advantages over models costing a quarter as much? We tested nine 2-quart nonstick saucepans to find out.

We designed our initial tests around the smaller, less complicated jobs for which these small saucepans are suited best, including steaming rice, scalding cream, and making pastry cream. The pastry cream test illustrated several design preferences—pouring hot cream from a saucepan is much neater if the pan from which you're pouring has either a spout or a rolled lip. And an ample diameter and sloped sidewalls make it easier to carry out the constant whisking necessary to prevent pastry cream from scorching. Also, saucepans often spend 30 minutes or more on the burner, so there's a clear advantage to handles that remain cool to the touch. All but three of the pans had hard thermal plastic or Santoprene (soft plastic) handles, which passed this test with no problem. Even the metal handles, which heated up alarmingly at the point of attachment, maintained a sufficiently comfortable temperature at the far end. Handles attached with rivets won points for their solid attachment to the pan, while pans with handles that were screwed on were downgraded (one screwed-on handle was loose from the get-go).

To measure evenness and speed of heat distribution, we sautéed chopped onions and cooked eggs in each pan. Weight, rather than materials (which were similar in all the pans tested), was the deciding factor. The onions were lightly and evenly colored in the heaviest pans. (In the past, we have often downgraded heavy skillets for being too slow to heat up and unwieldy, but a heavy saucepan is actually a good thing.)

Fresh from the box, all of the pans exhibited excellent stick resistance and it wasn't until we subjected them to an abuse test—leaving caramel to harden in the pans—that we noticed any difference. To remove the caramel, we tried bashing it with a wooden spoon and then whacked the pan upside down against the rim of a trash can with the hope that pieces of caramel would tumble out. If the caramel held fast after five tries, we then filled the pan with water, brought it to a boil, and melted it out. In only two pans, the Revere and the Anolon, did we have to resort to boiling. On the other hand, the Calphalon and the Swiss Diamond pans discharged the caramel with ease.

In the end, the performance differences were subtle—most of the pans will do a fine job of heating up soup or making rice. Design differences were more significant and the sturdy Calphalon pan—with its riveted handle, wide diameter, sloped sides, and superior nonstick coating—came out on top. The final factor, price, was the most decisive. The Calphalon pan costs just $30, a far cry from the second-place Swiss Diamond at $95.

THE BEST NONSTICK SAUCEPAN

The Calphalon Contemporary Nonstick 2½-Quart Shallow Saucepan with Lid ($29.99) is heavy, solid, and priced right.

Basic Rice Pilaf

Pulao

SERVES 4

To rinse the rice, you can either place it in a fine-mesh strainer and rinse under cool water or place it in a medium bowl and repeatedly fill the bowl with water while swishing the rice around, then carefully drain off the water; in either case, you must rinse until the water runs clear. A nonstick saucepan is crucial to prevent the wet rice from sticking to the pot; for the most evenly cooked rice, be sure to use a wide-bottomed saucepan with a tight-fitting lid.

2½	cups water
1½	teaspoons salt
	Pinch ground black pepper
3	tablespoons unsalted butter
1	small onion, minced
1½	cups basmati or other long-grain rice, rinsed (see note)

1. Bring the water to a boil, covered, in a small nonstick saucepan over medium-high heat. Off the heat, stir in the salt and pepper and cover to keep hot. Meanwhile, melt the butter in a large nonstick saucepan. Add the onion and cook until softened, 5 to 7 minutes.

2. Stir the rice into the onions and cook until the edges of the grains begin to turn translucent, about 3 minutes. Stir in the hot seasoned water and return to a boil. Reduce the heat to low, cover, and simmer until all the water is absorbed, 16 to 18 minutes.

STEAMING RICE

After the rice is cooked, cover the pan with a clean kitchen towel, replace the lid, and allow the pan to sit for 10 minutes.

3. Off the heat, remove the lid, place a clean, folded kitchen towel over the saucepan (see the illustration below), and replace the lid. Let stand for 10 minutes, then fluff the rice with a fork and serve.

➤ VARIATIONS

Spiced Rice Pilaf with Dates and Parsley
Follow the recipe for Basic Rice Pilaf, adding 2 minced garlic cloves, 2 teaspoons minced fresh ginger, ⅛ teaspoon ground cinnamon, and ⅛ teaspoon ground cardamom to the softened onion in step 2; cook until fragrant, about 30 seconds. After removing the rice from the heat in step 3, before covering with a towel, sprinkle ¼ cup chopped dates and 2 tablespoons minced fresh parsley leaves over the rice (do not mix in). Cover, let stand, and fluff as directed.

Saffron Rice Pilaf with Apricots and Almonds
Follow the recipe for Basic Rice Pilaf, adding ¼ teaspoon saffron threads, crumbled, to the softened onion in step 2. After removing the rice from the heat in step 3, before covering with a towel, sprinkle ¼ cup chopped apricots over the rice (do not mix in). Cover, let stand, and fluff as directed. Before serving, fold in ½ cup toasted slivered almonds.

SAFFRON CHICKEN AND RICE WITH YOGURT SAUCE

Murgh Biryani aur Raita

IN THE POPULAR INDIAN CHICKEN DISH *murgh biryani*, long-grain basmati rice takes center stage, enriched with butter, saffron, and a variety of fresh herbs and pungent spices. Pieces of tender chicken and browned onions are layered with the rice and baked until the flavors have mingled. This is India in a pot.

But it comes at a stiff price. Traditional biryani recipes are long in both ingredients and labor. The chicken is rubbed with spices and marinated before being browned; the rice is soaked, blanched, and mixed with a complex masala, or blend, of innumerable spices; the onions are deep-fried. Finally everything is layered into a cooking vessel and baked or steamed until the flavors have blended. In addition, most biryani recipes we tested were made greasy by the deep-fried onions and the rice had overcooked by the time the chicken was done. We set out to find a middle path between the extremes of dull simplicity and epicurean complexity.

We prepared a few classic biryani recipes to better acquaint ourselves with the dish, a task that required a full day in the test kitchen and produced a huge pile of dirty dishes. We made three timesaving discoveries. First, we learned that we could skip the step of marinating the chicken (too much time, too little flavor enhancement). Second, we could finish the rice in the oven, eliminating the need for constant monitoring on the stovetop. Third, it was possible to cook the onions and the chicken in the same Dutch oven, saving a pan. The streamlined recipe, in its working form, now consisted of browning the chicken, cooking the onions, parboiling the rice, and then steaming the layered biryani until done.

The best-tasting biryani from our recipe tests was made with an abundant layer of deep-fried onions, but they inevitably turned the dish greasy. Onions sautéed in a tablespoon of fat (oil or butter) failed to brown properly. More fat was clearly necessary, but how much could we add without turning the dish greasy? We started with ½ cup of fat for two sliced onions and reduced it 1 tablespoon at a time. In the end, 3 tablespoons proved sufficient. A combination of butter and rendered chicken fat prevailed over oil, adding more flavor and color. Garlic and ginger were added to the onions for extra punch, and mincing the garlic and grating the ginger intensified their flavor.

Tasters preferred dark meat chicken—it was more flavorful and juicy than white meat, which ended up dry. Bone-in thighs are the test kitchen favorite because they are so meaty. Having already eliminated marinating, we followed test kitchen protocol for braising chicken pieces. (Biryani is, in essence, a braise because it uses moist, low heat for cooking.) To eke out as much flavor as we could, we browned the chicken deeply, with the skin on for protection. Before layering the pieces with the rice, we stripped off the skin. With this last step, the greasiness issue was finally put to rest.

Biryani's subtle, delicate flavor and aroma are largely derived from the masala of whole spices blended into the rice. Before serving, we diligently fished out the spices from the rice, as tasters strongly objected to unexpectedly biting down on whole cardamom pods, but this nitpicky task grew tiresome. To save ourselves from fishing out cardamom pods and coriander seeds in our finished biryani, we opted for ground versions of these two spices. To keep the ground spices from tasting raw, we bloomed them, along with the whole spices, in the butter to both develop their flavor and infuse the butter. Tasters approved of ground cardamom and coriander, cinnamon stick, and whole cumin seeds. The cumin seeds added contrast to the soft, fluffy rice, as well as a burst of flavor. In the end, the only "fishing" we had to do was for two pieces of cinnamon stick, a reasonable task for the reward. Sweet, earthy, sharp, and musky, the spices paired well together.

Most of the recipes we found parboiled the rice before building the biryani. This was usually done by tossing the rice into a pot of boiling water and simmering for five minutes. In an effort to streamline this process, we prepared our rice in the same manner as our pilafs: we sautéed the rice in butter and spices until the edges of the grains began to turn translucent, about three minutes. Next, we added an equal amount of water to the rice, and allowed this mixture to simmer until all the water had evaporated, at which point we stirred in the currants, covered the pot, and set it aside until we were ready to layer our biryani. This process left the rice perfectly parcooked and well seasoned.

Saffron is mixed with the rice as both a coloring and flavoring agent. Any more than a pinch turned the rice Day-Glo orange and made it taste medicinal. To incorporate the saffron we used a technique that we found in our research. We bloomed the saffron in warm milk and swirled it on top of the rice layer. This left a visually appealing spiral design on top of the biryani, and when the rice was fluffed after cooking, gave a checkered appearance to the rice with specks of both yellow and white.

Tasters demanded a fair amount of heat to round out the flavor of the biryani. We added one jalapeño, along with some of its seeds for additional fire. A little sweetness from the currants (you could use raisins in a pinch) helped to temper the heat and accent the warm spices. Fresh cilantro sprinkled on just before serving gave the dish a shot of freshness, while a dollop of *raita*, a refreshing yogurt sauce, was the perfect accompaniment.

Saffron Chicken and Rice with Yogurt Sauce
Murgh Biryani aur Raita
SERVES 4 TO 6

We recommend using a medium or large Dutch oven. To rinse the rice, you can either place it in a fine-mesh strainer and rinse under cool water or place it in a medium bowl and repeatedly fill the bowl with water while swishing the rice around, then carefully drain off the water. In either case, you must rinse until the water runs clear. Adjust the spiciness of this dish by including the minced ribs and seeds from the jalapeño.

SPICES

1	cinnamon stick, broken in half
1	teaspoon ground coriander
1	teaspoon cumin seeds
⅛	teaspoon ground cardamom

BIRYANI

3	tablespoons unsalted butter
2	cups basmati rice, rinsed (see note)
	Salt and ground black pepper
2¾	cups water
¼	cup dried currants
8	bone-in, skin-on chicken thighs (about 3 pounds)
1	teaspoon vegetable oil, plus extra as needed
2	medium onions, halved and sliced thin
6	medium garlic cloves, minced or pressed through a garlic press (about 2 tablespoons)
1	tablespoon minced or grated fresh ginger
1	jalapeño chile, seeds and ribs removed, minced (see note)

½	teaspoon saffron threads, lightly crumbled
2	tablespoons milk, warmed
¼	cup minced fresh cilantro leaves
1	recipe Yogurt Sauce (recipe follows)

1. Adjust an oven rack to the lower-middle position and heat the oven to 350 degrees. Combine the spices in a small bowl and set aside. Melt the butter in a medium saucepan over medium-high heat. Add the spices and sauté until fragrant, about 10 seconds. Stir in the rice, 1 teaspoon salt, and ¼ teaspoon pepper and cook, stirring frequently, until the edges of the grains began to turn translucent, about 3 minutes. Stir in 2 cups of the water and cook, uncovered, until all the water has evaporated. Remove the rice from the heat, stir in the currants, cover, and set aside until needed.

2. Meanwhile, pat the chicken dry with paper towels and season with salt and pepper. Heat the oil in a medium Dutch oven over medium-high heat until just smoking. Brown the chicken well on both sides, 5 to 8 minutes per side, reducing the heat if the pan begins to scorch. Transfer the chicken to a plate, remove and discard the skin, and tent loosely with foil to keep warm.

3. Discard all but 3 tablespoons of the fat left in the pot (or add oil if needed). Add the onions and cook over medium heat, stirring often, until softened and dark brown, 10 to 12 minutes. Stir in the garlic, ginger, and jalapeño and cook until fragrant, about 30 seconds. Transfer the onion mixture to a bowl, season with salt to taste, and set aside.

4. Add the remaining ¾ cup water to the pot, scraping up the browned bits. Lay the chicken in the pot, skinned side up, and sprinkle the browned onions over the top. Pour the rice on top of the onions and smooth into an even layer with a rubber spatula (neither the onions nor chicken should be visible). Stir the saffron into the warm milk then pour the mixture over the rice in a spiral pattern.

5. Cover and bake until the rice is tender, about 45 minutes. Remove from the oven and let rest for 5 to 10 minutes. Fluff the rice with a fork, then portion the biryani into individual bowls, scooping from the bottom of the pot. Sprinkle the individual servings with cilantro and serve immediately with the yogurt sauce.

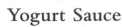

Yogurt Sauce

Raita

MAKES ABOUT I CUP

We prefer the flavor of whole milk yogurt here; however, low-fat or nonfat yogurt can be substituted.

- I cup plain whole milk yogurt
- 2 tablespoons minced fresh cilantro leaves
- 2 tablespoons minced fresh mint leaves
- I medium garlic clove, minced or pressed through a garlic press (about I teaspoon)
  Salt and ground black pepper

Combine all of the ingredients in a small bowl. Season with salt and pepper to taste and set aside to let the flavors meld, about 15 minutes. (The sauce can be refrigerated in an airtight container for up to 1 day; reseason before serving.)

FRESH CHEESE WITH SPINACH SAUCE

Saag Paneer

IN THE NORTHERN STATE OF PUNJAB, ONE of the most widely popular delicacies is fresh homemade cheese (*paneer*) with spinach sauce (*saag*). Making the cheese (which resembles a softer, less salty feta) is as simple as boiling milk. The spinach sauce is a mixture of pureed and coarsely chopped spinach with a buttery texture, redolent of garlic, ginger, cinnamon, and cumin. The cheese is added to the spinach sauce just before serving, and offers a mild counterpoint to the pungent sauce. Knowing that the simplest recipes can sometimes be the hardest to perfect, we approached this dish with some trepidation.

We began with the cheese, and all of our research turned up very similar and equally simple methods for making it. In short, boil milk, add an acid to form curds, strain the mixture through cheesecloth, and press. The main variation in these recipes was the type of acid used, usually lemon juice or distilled white vinegar. We tested both and found that they worked equally well, forming similar amounts of curds. The curds were then strained through cheesecloth, squeezed of as much liquid as possible, and finally pressed for about 30 minutes to form the finished cheese.

The cheese made with the lemon juice, not surprisingly, took on a strong but pleasant lemon flavor. While it was perfect on its own smothered in olive oil, its flavor was too prominent in our heavily spiced sauce. The cheese made with the vinegar tasted clean and fresh and didn't overwhelm the spinach sauce.

Many of the recipes we found prepared the cheese in one of three ways before adding it to the sauce. Some left the cheese curds unpressed and crumbled, others pressed the curds for 30 minutes then cubed the finished cheese, and still others fried the pressed cheese cubes. The method of preparation (unpressed, pressed, or pressed and fried) had no bearing on the flavor of the final product, but tasters disliked the way the unpressed, crumbled cheese disintegrated into the sauce. While the appearance of the fried cheese was the most attractive, frying made the cheese tough and there was no advantage to adding this step to the preparation of the dish. Tasters' top choice was actually the pressed, unfried cheese—they thought it absorbed more of the flavor from the sauce while retaining enough structure to remain distinct in the finished dish.

Moving along, we turned our attention to the spinach sauce. Based on our research, we developed a working recipe that began by blooming the spices in oil, then adding the aromatics, and finally adding the spinach, tomatoes, and liquid. A portion of this mixture was then pureed to develop a mostly smooth sauce that still retained some of the texture from the unpureed spinach and tomatoes. But before we could go any further, we first needed to determine which type of spinach to use.

We tested the three types available in most supermarkets: baby spinach, crinkly leaf spinach, and frozen spinach. When cooked, both varieties of

MAKING THE CHEESE FOR SAAG PANEER

1. Pour the curdled milk into the cheesecloth-lined colander and allow it to drain and cool for 10 minutes.

2. Pull the edges of the cheesecloth together to form a pouch and twist the pouch to squeeze out as much liquid as possible from the cheese curds.

3. Place the taut, twisted cheese pouch between 2 plates, and weigh down the top plate with a heavy Dutch oven. Set the cheese aside at room temperature until firm and set, about 30 minutes.

4. Unwrap the cheese and slice it into 1-inch strips. Slice the strips into 1-inch cubes.

fresh spinach initially took on a bright green hue that led us to believe we were on the right track. Although they did release significant amounts of liquid, we hoped this would play in our favor when it came time to puree a portion of the mixture. But after pureeing the fresh spinach in the blender, both the baby and crinkly leaf varieties developed an algae-like appearance and texture that tasters vehemently disliked. Further cooking only exacerbated the issue.

The frozen spinach, however, having been squeezed of all excess liquid in a clean kitchen towel prior to cooking, performed admirably. After it was pureed in the blender, there was none of the noticeable sliminess that was so problematic in the fresh spinach. Furthermore, it was a lot easier to work with 1¼ pounds of frozen spinach than an equal amount of fresh spinach, which required adding the spinach to the pan in batches and allowing it to cook down.

After having firmly established our spinach preference, we focused on the texture of the sauce. More precisely, this translated to how much of the sauce we needed to puree. We tried pureeing one quarter, one third, half, and finally, all of the sauce to find our ideal consistency. Pureeing the entire batch left a texturally boring sauce that was essentially too smooth. Pureeing one quarter of the sauce was hardly noticeable and half was slightly too much. Settling on pureeing one third of the sauce gave us the combination of textures we were looking for—not too smooth, not too coarse.

We tested whether using chicken or vegetable broths (or a combination of the two) in lieu of water would deepen the flavor of the dish. In the end, the spice-laden sauce made it all but impossible to tell whether the sauce contained broth, and we stuck with water.

Final adjustments to the dish entailed tweaking the spices to include garam masala, cumin, cinnamon, and cayenne. And to increase the richness of the sauce we added 2 tablespoons of butter to the blender when we pureed the spinach. This resulted in a final product that was a deep green concoction of heavily spiced spinach contrasted by soft, lightly salted cheese cubes.

Fresh Cheese with Spinach Sauce

Saag Paneer

SERVES 4 TO 6

We prefer the richer flavor of cheese made with whole milk; however, low-fat milk can be substituted. Do not substitute nonfat milk. When pressing the cheese in step 2, be sure to use two plates that nestle together nicely; do not invert the top plate, or use a bottom plate with a big rim that will get in the way of squeezing the cheese. Be sure to use a blender to puree the spinach in step 4; a food processor simply won't produce the same smooth creamy texture. Serve with Basic Rice Pilaf (page 447).

CHEESE
3	quarts whole milk
2¼	teaspoons salt
5	tablespoons distilled white vinegar

SPICES
1	teaspoon garam masala
½	teaspoon ground cumin
¼	teaspoon ground cinnamon
	Pinch cayenne pepper

SPINACH
2	tablespoons vegetable oil
1	medium onion, minced
	Salt
3	medium garlic cloves, minced or pressed through a garlic press (about 1 tablespoon)
1½	teaspoons minced or grated fresh ginger
2	(10-ounce) packages frozen spinach, thawed and squeezed dry
1	large tomato, cored, seeded, and chopped fine
3	cups water
2	tablespoons unsalted butter
	Ground black pepper

1. FOR THE CHEESE: Line a colander with a triple layer of cheesecloth and set in the sink. Bring the milk and salt to a boil in a large saucepan over medium-high heat. Stir in the vinegar, reduce the heat to low, and cook until the milk curdles, about

30 seconds. Following the illustrations on page 451, pour the milk mixture through the cheesecloth and let the curds drain for 10 minutes.

2. Pull the edges of the cheesecloth together to form a pouch and twist the pouch to squeeze out as much liquid as possible from the cheese curds

INGREDIENTS: Garam Masala

Though there are countless variations of garam masala, the warm flavors (*garam* means "warm" or "hot" and *masala* means "spice blend") dominating this Indian spice blend are consistent: coriander, black pepper, cumin, cardamom, and cinnamon are staples, while nutmeg, cloves, mace, fennel, and dried chiles frequently turn up as supporting players. Garam masala is commonly sprinkled on finished dishes, but we find this method results in harsh flavors. Instead, we prefer it bloomed in oil or butter at the outset of a dish.

Concocting this complex spice blend at home can add a great deal of time to recipe preparation—not to mention it can crowd your pantry with jar after jar of seldom-used ingredients, running up a hefty shopping tab in the process. In search of a good-tasting commercial garam masala, we tested a few of the top brands.

Tasters disliked the bitter and overwhelming flavors of Spice Islands and Zamouri garam masalas. Spice Barn garam masala was dubbed one-dimensional. Penzeys Punjabi Style garam masala combined the basic coriander-cardamom-cinnamon-pepper combination with a few exotic additions that tasters found warm, floral, and tangy.

But tasters' favorite was McCormick Gourmet Collection garam masala for its ability to both assimilate into dishes and also round out their acidic and sweet notes. Tasters also liked the slightly pungent hits of coriander and the subtle warmth of cardamom, cinnamon, and cloves. Widely available in supermarkets, McCormick won praise from tasters for adding a mellow, well-balanced aroma to most dishes.

THE BEST GARAM MASALA

Sticking with mostly core garam masala ingredients won this supermarket brand top ratings with tasters.

(see the illustration). Place the taut, twisted cheese pouch between 2 large plates and weigh down the top plate with a heavy Dutch oven. Set aside at room temperature until the cheese is firm and set, about 30 minutes. When the cheese is a firm block, cut it into 1-inch cubes. (At this point, the cheese can be refrigerated in an airtight container for up to 1 day.)

3. FOR THE SPICES AND SPINACH: Combine the garam masala, cumin, cinnamon, and cayenne in a small bowl. Heat the oil in a 12-inch nonstick skillet over medium-high heat until shimmering. Add the spices and toast until fragrant, about 10 seconds. Stir in the onion and ½ teaspoon salt and cook until softened, 5 to 7 minutes. Stir in the garlic and ginger and cook until fragrant, about 30 seconds. Stir in the spinach, tomato, and 2 cups of the water. Cover and cook until the tomatoes begin to break down, 5 to 7 minutes.

4. Transfer one-third of the spinach mixture, butter, and remaining 1 cup water to a blender and puree until smooth, 10 to 15 seconds. Return the pureed spinach to the pan and continue to simmer until the mixture is no longer watery, 5 to 7 minutes. Gently fold in the cheese cubes, season with salt and pepper to taste, and serve.

CHICKEN CURRY
Murgh Kari

THE TERM "CURRY" IS DERIVED FROM THE Tamil word *kari*, which simply means sauce or gravy. We tend to think of curry as a spiced yellow-colored meat and vegetable stew typically served over rice. But a curry can be most any type of stew, and as a result there are hundreds, perhaps thousands, of ways to make curry. We wanted to develop a recipe for yellow curry and set out to discover what separates good curry from bad curry while sticking as close to tradition as possible.

We began by gathering several different, seemingly authentic recipes from well-known Indian chefs. Variables included the types of spices used and whether they were whole or ground, the amounts of aromatics, whether the meat was seared or not, and whether the curry contained some

form of dairy, such as yogurt or sour cream (not truly authentic), or coconut milk instead.

While all the recipes had their strong points, none of them soared above the rest. One recipe had a ¼-inch film of oil on top (a sign of wealth in India); another left whole spices in the curry to be discovered with an unsuspecting bite. The curry made with sour cream was too rich, while the one made with yogurt didn't fare well either, resulting in curdled bits of dairy strewn throughout the curry. Coconut milk is a popular addition in southern Indian curries, but a few of the recipes called for so much of it that it overwhelmed the other elements of the curry, muting their flavors. So far we had more questions than answers.

We decided to focus first on what we consider to be the essence of curry, the combination of spices. Curries may include any number of spices and their selection is usually at the whim of the chef, who is in turn influenced by what is locally available. In India, there is no such thing as pre-mixed curry powder. Rather, most families purchase whole spices then toast and grind them to make personalized blends (called masalas). These spice blends are then used as a base, upon which more dish-specific spices can be added—this is as close to curry powder as it comes in India.

We found that several basic spices form the core of what we recognize as a traditional curry flavor. They include cumin, coriander, turmeric, cloves, cardamom, cinnamon, black pepper, and nutmeg. We decided to use preground spices for ease and started off with a heavy hand of ground cumin and coriander in equal amounts, then added a mere teaspoon of turmeric as it offers more color than flavor. Cloves, cardamom, cinnamon, black pepper, and nutmeg were added in varying amounts based on their intensity.

We cooked all of our spices in oil (a process known as "blooming") to develop their flavors and infuse the cooking oil. After several tests, and still confronted with countless options, we decided to try garam masala, a spice blend typically containing coriander, black pepper, cumin, cardamom, and cinnamon, and sometimes other "warm" spices such as nutmeg and clove. It worked great and simplified our process, though we still worked in additional spices for even more dimensions of flavor (and, in the case of turmeric, for the color it contributes).

Out of curiosity, we tested our favorite store-bought curry powder in place of our specialized spice blend. While store-bought curry powder has the advantage of being more convenient, we found its flavor to taste a bit muddy and stale compared to our homemade blend in this instance. It is OK in a pinch, but if we have a choice, we prefer our own blend here.

With our flavor base of spices in place, we moved on to the aromatics. Garlic and ginger are an integral part of all curries (and of Indian cuisine in general) and we found that using a healthy amount of both was crucial to a well-rounded curry flavor. A little fresh minced jalapeño also boosted the flavor and added some heat. Many of the curries we tested included some form of tomato product, be it fresh chopped tomatoes, tomato sauce, or tomato paste. We tried each of these on their own and in combination with one another. Fresh tomatoes by themselves added the acidity the curry needed, but didn't offer a very deep flavor. Tomato sauce offered an assertive tinny taste that some tasters felt was out of place. Tomato paste offered a sweet, roasted flavor when cooked with the onions. A combination of fresh tomatoes and tomato paste worked best. We added the tomato paste to the onion along with the garlic and ginger and stirred the fresh tomatoes in just before serving to preserve their texture.

As the curry was beginning to come together, we investigated whether it was essential to sear the chicken before it was simmered in the sauce—some recipes we found did this, while others did not. In a side-by-side test of chicken curry made with seared and unseared chicken, we found that it was nearly impossible to distinguish between them. The assertive flavors of the spices and colorful turmeric made searing unnecessary. Rather than searing, we found it beneficial to let the chicken and spices cook for a few minutes before adding the liquid—this allowed the flavor of the spices to penetrate the chicken more readily.

As for the chicken, we preferred chicken thighs to chicken breasts because they retain their moisture better, even if overcooked. Using boneless thighs was easier than using bone-in chicken and

we found they required just 15 to 20 minutes of simmering after adding the liquid in order to cook through and turn tender. We then removed them from the sauce and shredded the meat, stirring it back into the curry before serving. The shredded chicken not only looked far more appealing than cubes, but the shreds soaked up the sauce better.

As for the liquid component of the sauce, we were surprised to find that water did a fine job. Typically we would reach for chicken broth in a recipe like this, but given the complexity of our curry spices, chicken broth is simply unnecessary (as well as untraditional). Most authentic curry recipes we researched also include yogurt or coconut milk in with the water. In northern India, yogurt plays a key role not only in curries, but in chutneys, raitas, and drinks such as lassis. In the South, coconut milk takes the place of yogurt. Though we had trouble with both yogurt and coconut milk at the beginning of our testing, we found that if we added one of them at the end of cooking (to prevent curdling) and used less of it (so it didn't overwhelm the other flavors) it was the perfect finish to our curry. We liked the flavor of both, so we leave the decision up to you (we do prefer coconut milk in a vegetable curry variation on page 455, where its richer flavor is a welcome addition).

Finished with some green peas, a handful of minced cilantro, and a little butter to round out the sauce, our curry is as rich and flavorful as a traditional curry with the appeal and ease of a weeknight meal.

Chicken Curry
Murgh Kari
SERVES 4 TO 6

We like to use chicken thighs in this recipe but you can substitute 2 pounds of boneless, skinless chicken breasts; simmer the breasts as directed in step 2 until they reach 160 degrees, 10 to 15 minutes. We prefer the richer flavor of whole milk yogurt and regular coconut milk here; however, low-fat yogurt, nonfat yogurt, or light coconut milk can be substituted. Adjust the spiciness of this dish by including the minced ribs and seeds from the jalapeño. Serve with Basic Rice Pilaf (page 447) and any of the chutneys on pages 442–443.

SPICE

2½	teaspoons garam masala
1½	teaspoons ground cumin
1½	teaspoons ground coriander
1	teaspoon ground turmeric
½	teaspoon ground cinnamon
½	teaspoon mustard seeds
¼	teaspoon ground fennel
	Pinch cayenne pepper

CURRY

3	tablespoons vegetable oil
2	medium onions, minced
	Salt
6	medium garlic cloves, minced or pressed through a garlic press (about 2 tablespoons)
1	tablespoon minced or grated fresh ginger
1	jalapeño chile, seeds and ribs removed, minced (seeds reserved)
1	tablespoon tomato paste
2¼	pounds boneless, skinless chicken thighs, trimmed of excess fat
1	cup water
2	plum tomatoes, cored, seeded, and chopped fine (about 1 cup)
½	cup frozen peas, thawed
½	cup coconut milk or plain whole milk yogurt
¼	cup minced fresh cilantro leaves
2	tablespoons unsalted butter
	Ground black pepper

1. Combine the spices and set aside. Heat the oil in a large Dutch oven over medium heat until shimmering. Add the spices and sauté until fragrant, about 10 seconds. Stir in the onions and 1 teaspoon salt and cook, stirring constantly, until the onions are softened and lightly browned, 10 to 12 minutes. Stir in the garlic, ginger, jalapeño, and tomato paste and cook until fragrant, about 30 seconds.

2. Stir in the chicken to coat with the spices and cook, stirring often, until it is just opaque, about 4 minutes. Stir in the water and bring to a boil. Cover, reduce to a simmer, and cook until an instant-read thermometer inserted into the thickest part of the chicken registers 170 degrees, 15 to 20 minutes.

3. Transfer the chicken to a plate and shred into bite-sized pieces using two forks following the

illustration on page 69. Stir the tomatoes, peas, coconut milk, cilantro, and butter into the sauce until combined, then stir in the shredded chicken. Return the curry to medium heat and cook until the butter is melted and the sauce is hot, 1 to 2 minutes. Season with salt and pepper to taste and serve.

➤ VARIATIONS
Lamb Curry
You will need to buy 2¾ pounds leg of lamb in order to yield approximately 2¼ pounds of trimmed lamb for the curry.

Follow the recipe for Chicken Curry, substituting 2¼ pounds of boneless leg of lamb, trimmed and cut into 1 by 1½-inch chunks, for the chicken; cook in step 2 until the lamb is tender, about 45 minutes (do not remove the lamb from the curry or shred it). Stir in the tomatoes, peas, coconut milk, cilantro, and butter as directed in step 3 before serving.

Vegetable Curry
In this curry variation, we prefer the flavor and richness of coconut milk to yogurt.

Follow the recipe for Chicken Curry, omitting the chicken. Add 12 ounces red potatoes (2 to 3 medium), scrubbed and cut in ½-inch chunks, with the onions in step 1. Add 4 cups cauliflower florets, cut in 1-inch pieces (about ½ medium head), in place of the chicken in step 3; cook until just beginning to soften, about 4 minutes. Add 1 (15-ounce) can chickpeas, drained and rinsed, with the water in step 2; bring to a boil, cover, and simmer until the vegetables are tender, 7 to 11 minutes. Stir in the tomatoes, peas, coconut milk, cilantro, and butter as directed in step 3 before serving.

TANDOORI

TO MOST PEOPLE, TANDOORI CONJURES images of unnaturally red dyed chicken from local Indian restaurants. What they often don't realize is that the red dye has long since taken the place of a fiery coating of red pepper and that tandoori is not really a dish at all, but a cooking method. A tandoor oven is a beehive-shaped structure that cooks both meats and breads at a very high temperature in a very short time. The bottom of the tandoor contains a pile of red-hot coals that can crank the internal temperature of the tandoor in excess of 900 degrees. Meats, such as chicken and lamb, are skewered on long metal stakes that resemble thin-bladed swords. The tip of the skewer rests on the bottom of the tandoor and the heat circulates freely around the roasting meat.

Hoping to avoid the dry and flavorless meat that usually arrives when you order tandoori in many restaurants, we started out by testing a variety of recipes from noted Indian chefs. These recipes took us from the grill to the oven to the broiler and back again, trying to find a way to mimic the tandoor's searing heat and coal-roasted flavor. We used various spice rubs and marinades, but in the end, most of these recipes resulted in tough, overcooked meat that were either charred black or boiled-looking and wan. The marinades for most of these recipes, despite their laundry list of spices, yielded a flavor that was bland and chalky at best. Our goals were to replicate the intense heat of a tandoor oven at home, create a universal tandoori marinade base, and infuse our meat with some serious spice.

Focusing first on recreating a tandoor oven at home, the most logical place to begin our testing seemed to be the grill because it could best mimic the tandoor's intense coal-fired heat and flavor. We began our testing with bone-in chicken breasts (common tandoori fare) and a simple yogurt-based tandoori marinade. Right from the start, unfortunately, grilling posed a major problem. No matter how we stacked the coals, we had trouble preventing the marinade from burning on the outside before the chicken achieved the proper doneness on the inside. (Sure, a little char adds nice flavor, but too much overpowers the flavors of the spice and meat.) Also, we wanted to make this dish year-round, not just during barbecue season. So back into the kitchen we went.

Once inside, we headed straight for our oven and cranked up the broiler. Our initial tests proved the broiler to be almost as problematic as the grill. The bone-in chicken required several rack adjustments and flips in the oven to ensure even cooking and to avoid burning.

Growing increasingly frustrated, we tried our luck with a 500-degree oven. Adjusting the oven rack to the middle position, we started our chicken skin side up and waited for the results. This worked better, but again the heat proved too intense and the skin had begun to burn before the meat was cooked through. For the next round, we kept the oven at 500 degrees, but started the chicken skin side down, and flipped it over halfway through. Bingo! This prevented the skin from burning, but allowed it to achieve the slightly charred, crispy appearance we were looking for. Better yet, the meat was juicy and moist—nothing like the dried out, sawdust-like pieces of chicken from our local Indian takeout. We then decided to spoon on some extra marinade at the halfway point once we had flipped the chicken. This enhanced our crispy, golden crust and added the flavor of the marinade with each bite.

Although we had hoped for a universal cooking method, when we switched to a thinner cut of meat, lamb chops (another popular tandoori meat), we had to alter the cooking technique a little. After several tests, we concluded that cooking the chops in a 500-degree oven as we had done with the chicken was a great start, but because they cooked through so quickly, we had to finish them at an even higher heat to get the crisp edges and medium-rare interior we were after. So, we adjusted one rack to the middle position and the other directly beneath the broiler. Instead of continuing to roast the chops after flipping them halfway through, we slid them beneath the broiler. The broiler quickly gave the chops the slightly charred edges and crispy marinade crust we wanted without overcooking the meat.

With our cooking methods in place, we focused next on the flavor of the marinade—the vehicle for infusing the meat with flavor and spice. Most tandoori marinades use yogurt for its tang and also as a cool background for the pungent aromatics and spices. We used a generous amount of minced aromatics to flavor our marinade, but the pieces of garlic, ginger, and onion seemed to just float in the marinade without contributing much flavor. It was then that we decided to puree all the marinade ingredients in a blender. This simple step allowed for maximum flavor extraction from the aromatics, creating an intensely flavorful marinade.

Many of the marinade recipes we researched contained a liquid in the form of either water or oil.

We tried both and found it beneficial to add vegetable oil to the marinade for a few reasons. First, since the spices are oil soluble the oil in the marinade allowed them to bloom when heated. Next, the oil enriched the yogurt. And finally, the oil helped the exterior of the meat to crisp and brown. In terms of marinating time, we found it necessary to marinate the meat for at least 4 hours, and noted increasingly more flavor when the meat was allowed to sit in the marinade for up to 24 hours. Going longer than 24 hours didn't increase the flavor any, but turned the texture of the meat a bit mushy.

We hoped to use the same marinade for both the chicken and the lamb, but it quickly became obvious that the spices were more meat specific. Coriander, cumin, garam masala, nutmeg, cinnamon, and pepper worked well with both meats, but the chicken also benefited from the zing of lemon zest and earthiness of turmeric. The lamb's gaminess required tomato paste, extra garlic, and a heavy hand with the cumin and garam masala to bring it to life. At last, we had achieved what we had set out to accomplish; deeply flavored meat from a homemade "tandoor" that was not only juicy, but also had the slightly charred appearance of meat pulled directly from an authentic tandoor.

Tandoori Chicken
Tandoori Murgh
SERVES 4

Whole milk, low-fat, and nonfat yogurt all work equally well here. Serve with Basic Rice Pilaf (page 447), and Spicy Mango Chutney (page 443).

SPICES
- 1 tablespoon ground coriander
- 1 teaspoon ground cumin
- 1 teaspoon ground turmeric
- 1 teaspoon garam masala
- ½ teaspoon ground nutmeg
- ½ teaspoon ground cinnamon
- ¼ teaspoon ground black pepper

CHICKEN AND MARINADE
- 1 cup plain yogurt
- ¼ cup vegetable oil
- 1 medium onion, chopped coarse
- 5 medium garlic cloves, peeled
- 1 (2-inch) piece fresh ginger, peeled and chopped coarse
- 1 tablespoon grated zest from 1 lemon
- 2 teaspoons salt
- 4 bone-in, skin-on chicken breasts (10 to 12 ounces each)

1. Puree the spices, yogurt, oil, onion, garlic, ginger, lemon zest, and salt in a blender (or food processor) until smooth, about 30 seconds. Measure out ¼ cup of the mixture and refrigerate separately. Combine the remaining mixture with the chicken in a 1-gallon zipper-lock bag. Seal the bag, pressing out as much air as possible, and refrigerate for 4 hours or up to 24 hours, flipping the bag occasionally to ensure that the chicken marinates evenly.

2. Adjust an oven rack to the middle position and heat the oven to 500 degrees. Line a rimmed baking sheet with foil and set a wire rack on top. Remove the chicken breasts from the marinade and place them, skin side down, on the wire rack. Roast until an instant-read thermometer inserted into the thickest part of the chicken breasts registers 125 degrees, about 15 minutes.

3. Flip the chicken over, spread the ¼ cup reserved marinade evenly over the top, and continue to roast until an instant-read thermometer inserted into the thickest part of the breasts registers 160 degrees, 15 to 20 minutes longer. Remove the chicken from the oven and let rest for 5 minutes before serving.

Tandoori Lamb Chops
Tandoori Gosht
SERVES 4

Whole milk, low-fat, and nonfat yogurt all work equally well here. Since the lamb chops cook much faster than the chicken, it is necessary to broil them for the last few minutes to achieve the traditional charred flavor and appearance. We think lamb chops taste best when cooked to medium-rare; to cook them to a medium doneness, roast the chops to 105 to 110 degrees in step 2 (chops should register 135 to 140 degrees after broiling).

SPICES

1	tablespoon ground coriander
1	tablespoon ground cumin
1	tablespoon garam masala
½	teaspoon ground cloves
½	teaspoon ground nutmeg
½	teaspoon ground cinnamon
¼	teaspoon ground black pepper

LAMB AND MARINADE

1	cup plain yogurt
¼	cup vegetable oil
1	medium onion, chopped coarse
10	medium garlic cloves, peeled
1	(2-inch) piece fresh ginger, peeled and chopped coarse
3	tablespoons tomato paste
2	teaspoons salt
8	lamb loin chops

1. Puree the spices, yogurt, oil, onion, garlic, ginger, tomato paste, and salt in a blender (or food processor) until smooth, about 30 seconds. Measure out ¼ cup of the mixture and refrigerate separately. Combine the remaining mixture with the lamb in a 1-gallon zipper-lock bag. Seal the bag, pressing out as much air as possible, and refrigerate for 4 hours or up to 24 hours, flipping the bag occasionally to ensure that the lamb marinates evenly.

2. Adjust one oven rack to the middle position and a second oven rack 4½ inches from the broiler element and heat the oven to 500 degrees. Line a rimmed baking sheet with foil and set a wire rack on top. Remove the lamb chops from the marinade and place them on the wire rack. Roast until an instant-read thermometer inserted into the thickest part of the lamb chops registers 100 degrees, about 10 minutes.

3. Remove the lamb from the oven and turn the oven to broil. Flip the lamb chops over, spread the ¼ cup reserved marinade evenly over the top, and broil until spotty brown and an instant-read thermometer inserted into the chops registers 125 to 130 degrees for medium-rare, about 5 minutes. Remove the lamb chops from the oven and let rest for 5 minutes before serving.

CHICKEN TIKKA MASALA

AT ITS BEST, CHICKEN TIKKA MASALA CONSISTS of tender chunks of chicken marinated in yogurt and spices, which are then simmered in a rich, creamy tomato sauce. But all too often the chicken is either mushy or dry and the sauce unbearably rich and overspiced. The good news is that these problems are not impossible to overcome, and we set our sights on creating a foolproof recipe for chicken tikka masala that we could make any time of year.

Since we knew we wanted a four-season dish, we chose the broiler (not the grill) as our cooking medium, replacing the tandoor oven typically used in India. We began by analyzing the yogurt marinade for the chicken. The marinade is meant to tenderize the meat and infuse it with the essence of spices and aromatics. While overnight marinades did adequately flavor the chicken, they also made the texture too tender, bordering on mushy. Given enough time, the lactic acid in yogurt breaks down the protein strands in the meat. (This isn't as much the case with bone-in, skin-on chicken where the skin and bones protect the meat, but we had chosen to use boneless, skinless breasts, which are more susceptible to the acid in the yogurt.)

Using shorter marinating times, we embarked on a series of tests intended to improve the texture of the chicken, including marinating in heavily salted yogurt, lightly salted yogurt, watered-down yogurt, and in yogurt flavored with spices. Most of the chicken we produced still missed the mark. Two or three hours of marinating desiccated the outer layer of the chicken, while really short marinades didn't do much at all.

Cooking the boneless breasts whole and cutting them into pieces only after they were broiled was a step in the right direction. The larger pieces of chicken didn't dry out as quickly under the searing heat of the broiler. It also got rid of the fussy step of skewering raw, slippery chicken pieces. But the chicken still wasn't juicy enough.

We weren't having much luck with the yogurt marinade and were tempted to abandon it altogether. But yogurt is so fundamental to this recipe that excluding it felt like a mistake. Could we find a different way to use it? We considered salting, a technique we have used for steaks, roasts, chicken parts, and whole turkeys. Salt initially draws moisture out of protein; then, the reverse happens and the salt and moisture flow back in. What if we salted the chicken first, then dipped it in yogurt right before cooking?

We rubbed the chicken with a simple mixture of salt and everyday spices common in Indian cookery: coriander, cumin, and cayenne. We waited 30 minutes, which gave us time to prepare the masala sauce, then dunked the chicken in yogurt and broiled it. The result was the best tikka yet—nicely seasoned with spices and tender but not soft. In just half an hour's time, the salt rub had done its job of flavoring the chicken and keeping it moist and the yogurt mixture acted as a protective barrier, shielding the lean meat from the powerful heat of the broiler.

But we didn't stop there. To encourage gentle charring on the chicken, we fattened up the yogurt by adding two tablespoons of oil. We also took advantage of the yogurt's thick texture, mixing it with minced garlic and freshly grated ginger.

Having perfected the chicken, we shifted our focus to the sauce. Masala means spice mixture and the ingredients in a masala sauce depend largely on the whims of the cook. When the masala is to be served as part of chicken tikka masala, however, tomatoes and cream always form the base. Working with a mixture of sautéed aromatics (onions, ginger, garlic, and chiles) simmered with tomatoes (crushed tomatoes were favored over diced canned or fresh because of their smooth consistency) and cream, we tested combination after combination of spices. With plenty of winners and no real losers, we eventually settled on the simplest choice of all: commercial garam masala. Garam masala blends warm spices such as cardamom, black pepper, cinnamon, and coriander in one jar. To bloom

PANTRY SPOTLIGHT

GHEE

A staple ingredient of Indian cuisine, *ghee* is essentially clarified butter used for sautéing and finishing dishes. It is made by slowly melting unsalted butter (made from cow or buffalo milk) over low heat until the emulsion is broken. Once most of the water has evaporated and the milk solids have separated to the bottom of the pan, the layer of clear golden butterfat on top is the ghee. The ghee is poured off from the layer of milk solids and is ready for use. The purity of ghee is judged by the amount of remaining milk solids and water still present within the butterfat. Purer versions of ghee, those with fewer milk solids and a lower water content, can be stored at room temperature. (Pure ghee does not require refrigeration because it is the leftover milk solids and water that cause rancidity and those are no longer present.) Purity also influences the smoke point, with the purest versions of ghee having a smoke point as high as 485 degrees.

Contrary to popular belief, ghee is not the primary cooking fat used in India. Pure ghee (or *usli ghee*) is seldom used for daily cooking because it is expensive (its use is often considered a sign of wealth) and heavy on the palate. One exception to this rule can be found in the state of Punjab, where ghee continues to play a key role in the cuisine. However, in the rest of India usli ghee is typically reserved for special occasions, religious ceremonies, and even medicinal purposes.

Much of India commonly uses vegetable shortening rather than usli ghee— although it is still referred to as ghee—because it is lighter, cheaper, and perceived to be healthier than butter. Though similar in appearance and texture to ghee when cold, shortening has a much different flavor (its flavor is more neutral, like that of vegetable oil). Moreover, many Indians today use peanut, mustard, coconut, or sesame oils more often than ghee because of their widespread availability and clean flavor. The choice of oil is largely dependent on each particular region of India, and the use of these various oils have come to represent the food and flavors from those particular regions, much like usli ghee has come to represent the cuisine of Punjab.

Curious about ghee and its applications, we tried it in a number of recipes. We used it as a spread for our naan, we used it to sauté the spices and aromatics in our chicken curry, and we stirred it into our finished dal to add richness. When used in its raw form to spread on naan and to finish our dal, the ghee had a gamey flavor that some tasters objected to and we found butter to be a fine substitute. For sautéing, ghee behaved just like vegetable oil, shimmering when hot without sputtering the way butter does, and its flavor contribution was neutral. The bottom line? You could try using ghee for a totally authentic Punjab meal experience (you can find it at ethnic markets or online), but otherwise shortening or regular butter works fine.

the flavor of the garam masala, we sautéed it in oil along with the aromatics instead of adding it to the simmering sauce, as some recipes suggest. There was just one problem: Many commercially prepared masala sauces contain tartrazine, an artificial coloring, to give the sauce its characteristic hue. Without it, the spices lent our sauce an unappealing gray cast. A tablespoon of tomato paste easily restored a pleasant shade of red.

Most versions of chicken tikka masala call for a cup or more of cream, but tasters wanted us to scale back the amount. After experimenting with heavy cream, half-and-half, and even yogurt, we decided on ⅔ cup heavy cream, which was luxurious but not so rich that it was impossible to finish a whole serving.

At this point, our recipe was getting rave reviews, but we had the nagging feeling that something was missing. We scanned through a flavor checklist: Salt? No. Acidity? No. Heat? No. Sweetness? That was it. We stirred a teaspoon of sugar into the pot, then another. Our work was done, the sugar having successfully rounded out the flavors of the sauce. When we spooned the chicken over basmati rice and sprinkled it with fresh cilantro, we knew we had a dish worth staying home for.

Chicken Tikka Masala

SERVES 4 TO 6

This dish is best when prepared with whole milk yogurt, but low-fat yogurt can be substituted. For more heat, include the serrano ribs and seeds when mincing. Serve with Basic Rice Pilaf (page 447).

CHICKEN

1	teaspoon salt
½	teaspoon ground cumin
½	teaspoon ground coriander
¼	teaspoon cayenne pepper
4	boneless, skinless chicken breasts (5 to 6 ounces each)
1	cup plain whole milk yogurt (see note)
2	tablespoons vegetable oil
1	tablespoon minced or grated fresh ginger
2	medium garlic cloves, minced or pressed through a garlic press (about 2 teaspoons)

MASALA SAUCE

3	tablespoons vegetable oil
1	medium onion, minced
	Salt
2	medium garlic cloves, minced or pressed through a garlic press (about 2 teaspoons)
2	teaspoons minced or grated fresh ginger
1	serrano chile, ribs and seeds removed, chile minced
1	tablespoon garam masala
1	tablespoon tomato paste
1	(28-ounce) can crushed tomatoes
2	teaspoons sugar
⅔	cup heavy cream
¼	cup minced fresh cilantro leaves

1. FOR THE CHICKEN: Combine the salt, cumin, coriander, and cayenne in a small bowl. Pat the chicken dry with paper towels and sprinkle with the spice mixture, pressing gently so the mixture adheres. Place the chicken on a plate, cover with plastic wrap, and refrigerate for 30 to 60 minutes. In a large bowl, whisk together the yogurt, oil, ginger, and garlic; set aside.

2. FOR THE SAUCE: Heat the oil in a large Dutch oven over medium heat until shimmering. Add the onion and ¼ teaspoon salt and cook until softened and light golden, 5 to 7 minutes. Stir in the garlic, ginger, chile, garam masala, and tomato paste and cook until fragrant, about 30 seconds. Add the crushed tomatoes and sugar and bring to boil. Reduce the heat to medium-low, cover, and simmer for 15 minutes, stirring occasionally. Stir in the cream and return to a simmer. Remove the pan from the heat and cover to keep warm. (The sauce can be made ahead, refrigerated for up to 4 days in an airtight container, and gently reheated before adding the hot chicken.)

3. While the sauce simmers, adjust an oven rack to the upper-middle position (about 6 inches from the heating element) and heat the broiler. Line a rimmed baking sheet or broiler pan with aluminum foil and place a wire rack over the sheet. Using tongs, dip the chicken into the yogurt mixture (the chicken should be coated with a thick layer of yogurt) and arrange on the wire

rack. Discard the excess yogurt mixture. Broil the chicken until the thickest parts register 160 degrees on an instant-read thermometer and the exterior is lightly charred in spots, 10 to 18 minutes, flipping the chicken halfway through cooking.

4. Let the chicken rest 5 minutes, then cut into 1-inch chunks and stir into the warm sauce (do not simmer the chicken in the sauce). Stir in the cilantro, season with salt to taste, and serve.

CARDAMOM AND PISTACHIO ICE MILK

Kulfi

MILK PRODUCTS PLAY A PROMINENT ROLE IN a variety of sweets in India, and perhaps one of the most popular applications is the cardamom-spiced pistachio ice milk known as *kulfi*. Kulfi is often served on special occasions or during India's many religious holidays. It offers a cooling, sweet finish to heavily spiced meals and a welcome relief from the intense heat.

Kulfi recipes primarily fall into two categories: those that reduce fresh milk on the stove and those that utilize canned milk products such as sweetened condensed milk and/or evaporated milk. We tried both and found reducing fresh milk to be a long process resulting in the occasional messy boilover and yielding a less-than-spectacular flavor. Using canned products was easier—you simply stir all the ingredients together and freeze, while giving it the occasional stir—but the taste was slightly tinny and dull. We decided to take the path of using canned milk for its ease, but we had to improve the flavor.

We tested evaporated and sweetened condensed milk both on their own and in varying combinations with each other. Evaporated milk with the addition of sugar tasted metallic and the texture was unpleasantly laden with large ice crystals. Condensed milk by itself tasted cleaner and produced a creamy texture when frozen, but it also tasted a bit "cooked" and was unbearably sweet on its own. We tried mixing the evaporated and condensed milks together, but this didn't work any better and the resulting kulfi still lacked a clean, fresh flavor. Then it hit us: If a fresh milk flavor is what was missing, then couldn't we simply add some fresh milk? Mixing the sweetened condensed milk with some fresh milk (not reduced), we finally turned a corner and started producing kulfi with a lighter, cleaner, and less sweet flavor. After a few more rounds of testing, we found that a 2 to 1 ratio of fresh milk to sweetened condensed milk was perfect and produced a slightly sweet, rich, and clean flavor.

While small ice crystals are to be expected in kulfi, the addition of fresh milk created enormous ice crystals that were overwhelming and distracting. Adding sugar would help prevent these large crystals from forming, but we had already reached our saturation point for sweetness by using the sweetened condensed milk. Taking a cue from some fruit-based ice cream recipes we researched (fruit ice creams also have this very problem), we tried adding a dash of vodka—the alcohol lowers the freezing point of the mixture and helps to prevent the crystal formation (and vodka is flavorless). This was admittedly very untraditional, but to our delight the result was kulfi with fewer ice crystals and a smoother texture.

Up to this point, we had simply been whisking the ingredients together in a bowl then freezing the mixture until solid. At the beginning we faithfully stirred the mixture as it froze, but over the course of our testing, we dropped this detail because it became a hassle. We found out the hard way, however, that the stirring actually helped the mixture remain uniform as it froze. When we eliminated this step the mixture began to separate: the pistachios rose to the top, the cardamom sank to the bottom, and the milks separated slightly into layers. Could we achieve a uniform mixture without constant monitoring? Looking for another solution, we then tried blending all of the ingredients (except for the nuts) together in a blender. This quickly solved the majority of our separation problems. The sweetened milk and whole milk made an emulsion of sorts that evenly distributed the cardamom and remained uniform during freezing. We stirred the nuts in after the mixture was partially frozen, which kept them suspended evenly throughout the mixture.

Finally we adjusted the amount of cardamom to ¼ teaspoon and added a pinch of salt to bring the flavors to the foreground. When freezing the kulfi, we found it best to cover it to prevent ice crystals from forming on top. And leaving the kulfi at room temperature for five minutes prior to serving made scooping much easier.

Cardamom and Pistachio Ice Milk
Kulfi
MAKES ABOUT 1 QUART, SERVING 4 TO 6

The kulfi tastes best when made with whole milk; however, low-fat or nonfat milk can be substituted; if using a low-fat or nonfat milk, the kulfi will be a bit more icy and not as flavorful. Vodka is not a traditional ingredient in kulfi, but it prevents the milk from forming overly large ice crystals; there will, however, still be some small ice crystals in the final mixture; this is normal.

2½	cups whole milk
1	(14-ounce) can sweetened condensed milk
2	tablespoons vodka
¼	teaspoon ground cardamom
⅛	teaspoon salt
3	tablespoons chopped pistachio nuts

1. Blend the whole milk, sweetened condensed milk, vodka, cardamom, and salt together in a blender until thoroughly combined and emulsified, about 10 seconds. Pour the mixture into a 1-quart airtight plastic container. Press plastic wrap flush to the surface of the mixture, secure the container lid, and freeze until mostly frozen but stirrable, 4 to 5 hours.

2. Stir in the chopped pistachios, cover again with the plastic wrap and lid, and continue to freeze until solid, 4 to 5 hours longer or up to 1 week. Let the mixture sit at room temperature for a few minutes until softened, then scoop into individual bowls and serve.

MANGO AND YOGURT DRINK
Aam Lassi

WE'VE ALL BEEN THERE: YOU'VE TAKEN A bite of an insanely spicy dish, your mouth is on fire, and you find yourself chugging a glass of ice-cold water and waiting for relief—only to discover the burn continues on, unabated. A better bet is to take a cue from Indian cuisine, where spicy dishes are often accompanied by a *lassi*, a frothy, yogurt-based drink. In fact, yogurt is usually present in some form at every meal in India, as the fat in milk is able to disperse the capsaicin molecules that make chiles hot. (Water is ineffective because capsaicin is not water-soluble.)

Dairy is considered to be a perfect food in India and is even revered as holy. In a country where vegetables comprise much of the diet and many people do not eat meat, milk products are a key source of protein. Drinking dairy as a chilled beverage is a widespread practice, especially in the intense heat of the summer months.

There are two principal types of lassis: salty and sweet. Both are essentially yogurt thinned with water, a combination that is then mixed until frothy. The savory lassi is salted and spiced (most commonly with cumin but there are also lassis made with saffron, chile pepper, turmeric, and even garlic). The sweet version blends the yogurt with sugar or honey, fresh fruit, and essences such as rosewater. Most popular in both India and the U.S. is the mango lassi, a standard menu item in Indian restaurants worldwide.

And for good reason: mango is ubiquitous in Indian cuisine. The mango imparts a perfumed and slightly exotic taste to the plain yogurt. We chose to use honey over sugar to further sweeten the lassi, but we didn't need to use much since the mango naturally has a high sugar content. Some recipes we researched added a touch of lime juice to the lassi and we liked the way it brightened the mango flavor.

Mango and Yogurt Drink

Aam ki Lassi

SERVES 4

If the mangos are not very sweet, you may need to sweeten the drink with extra honey. Do not substitute frozen mangos or the drink will taste very flat. We prefer the flavor of whole milk yogurt here; however, low-fat or nonfat yogurt can be substituted. Place glasses in the freezer to chill before starting the recipe.

3	cups chopped fresh mango (from 2 to 3 mangos)
2	cups plain whole milk yogurt
1	cup ice water, about half water and half ice
2–4	teaspoons honey
2	teaspoons juice from 1 lime
⅛	teaspoon salt

Puree all of the ingredients together in a blender until there are no visible chunks of mango, about 1 minute. Strain the mixture through a fine-mesh strainer into a pitcher, pressing on the solids to extract as much liquid as possible; discard any solids left in the strainer. Serve in chilled glasses. (The mixture can be refrigerated for up to 4 hours; re blend before serving).

SPICED TEA WITH MILK

Masala Chai

IN INDIA, THE STREETS ARE PACKED WITH chai vendors who peddle this seductively spiced milk and tea concoction. Chai may be consumed any time of the day and makes an excellent accompaniment to dessert or can be served in lieu of dessert. Chai is the word for tea in India and what most westerners have come to recognize as chai is actually *masala chai*, a blend of tea, milk, sugar and spices such as cardamom, cinnamon, cloves, star anise, vanilla, black pepper, and ginger.

While there is no set recipe for chai, the tea is usually a strong, black loose-leaf variety. The milk, sugar, and spices take center stage and are combined together in a pot and simmered as quickly as five minutes or as long as 24 hours to marry the flavors. Jaggery, an unprocessed dark brown sugar redolent of caramel, is sometimes used in place of regular sugar as the sweetener, although it is not essential. The spices will vary with the region and individual tastes, and each family has their own signature blend of spices much as they do for curry. The ratio of spiced milk to tea can also vary greatly: some prefer chai made nearly entirely with milk, while others only add a drop—we found 1⅓ cups of milk to 3 cups of tea to be ideal.

Spiced Tea with Milk

Masala Chai

SERVES 4

We prefer the flavor of whole milk here; however, low-fat or nonfat milk can be substituted. Any type of generic supermarket black tea will work here. Depending on how sweet you like your chai, you will need to add between 1 and 2 tablespoons of sugar to the milk mixture in step 1.

1⅓	cups whole milk
1	cinnamon stick, broken in half
½	teaspoon vanilla extract
¼	teaspoon ground cardamom
¼	teaspoon whole black peppercorns
¼	teaspoon whole cloves
1–2	tablespoons sugar
4	bags black tea
3	cups boiling water

1. Simmer the milk, cinnamon, vanilla, cardamom, peppercorns, and cloves in a medium saucepan over medium-low heat until the milk is fragrant and flavorful, about 5 minutes. Off the heat, stir in 1 tablespoon of the sugar until dissolved, adding the remaining sugar to taste. Pour through a fine-mesh strainer, discarding the solids.

2. Meanwhile, steep each tea bag in a large mug with ¾ cup boiling water for about 5 minutes. Discard the tea bags and pour ⅓ cup of the spiced warm milk into each mug. Serve immediately.

INGREDIENTS: Supermarket Tea

While you can find black, green, and even white tea on supermarket shelves these days, it's all from the same plant, an evergreen called Camellia sinensis. The color and flavor differences come from the way the tea leaves are processed. We decided it was time to find out if the supermarket has the makings of a great cup of tea.

Because 87 percent of all tea drunk in America is black, we decided to focus our tasting on black teas. We bought the more "upscale" offerings distributed by national brands, all labeled simply black tea or English breakfast–type blends, a popular mix of black teas designed to stand up to the milk and sugar popular among the Brits. We chose loose tea when it was available and tea bags when it was not, including three teas that came in the new pyramid-shaped bags, which are touted as having more room for the tea to expand for better flavor. A panel of 20 tasters from our staff sampled 10 teas, both plain and with milk.

An ideal cup of black tea should taste fresh, with no stale overtones, and should not taste burnt, though a smoky or earthy flavor is acceptable. It should not be yeasty or sour. It should have a pleasing aroma, a bright color, and a crisp rather than heavy flavor, with some of the astringency tea professionals call "briskness." Black tea gets these characteristics from a number of factors, including where it is grown (cooler temperatures at higher elevations slow down the plant's growth and let it build more flavor), when it is picked (the often-prized "first flush" is the earliest), how it is picked (by hand is considered better—machines can be rough), and how it is processed.

When making black tea, processors let the harvested leaves wither for up to 24 hours, then roll or cut them. This breaks the cell walls and releases enzymes that oxidize to develop the tea's flavor and color—in the case of black tea, turning the leaves black. Then they heat (or "fire") the leaves to stop oxidation before drying them until they look like familiar dry tea. The leaves are then sold to tea companies, which generally blend tea from several sources, although really fine-quality leaves are often kept unblended as single-estate teas.

Our tasters began by assessing the tea samples' aroma, followed by complexity of flavor, astringency, and overall appeal. Tasters' scores for aroma most closely tracked with their overall ranking of the teas. Whenever the tea failed to deliver on that aromatic promise, however, our tasters downgraded it. Our tasters also preferred teas with smoother, less astringent profiles.

Surprisingly, when we tried the teas again with milk, the results were nearly the opposite. Tea gets its astringency from tannic substances called catechins. Tasted plain, the teas that tasters rated lowest for astringency and highest for complexity of flavor rose in the rankings. When milk was added, teas deemed too harsh became quite palatable, and those that were smoother but less robustly flavored sank in our tasters' estimation.

There's a chemical explanation for this: Proteins in the milk called caseins bind with the tea's catechins, taking the edge off the astringent effect on your palate. A little astringency is considered a good characteristic in a black tea. But too much turned off tasters, unless it was masked by milk.

Our favorite tea for drinking plain was Twinings English Breakfast Tea, which tasters found "floral, fragrant, and nicely balanced" and "not too strong" but packed "a lot of flavor." When combined with milk, tasters' favorite was Tazo Awake tea. It garnered comments such as "extremely smoky, with a strong, clean taste" and "great balance of flavor and intensity."

THE BEST SUPERMARKET TEA

Twinings English Breakfast Tea (left) was the favorite when tasted plain, while Tazo Awake (right) is our top choice when combined with milk.

12

SOUTHEAST ASIA

THAI-STYLE CHICKEN SOUP

Tom Kha Gai

ONE OF OUR FAVORITE WAYS TO BEGIN A meal at a Thai restaurant is with a bowl of *tom kha gai*, or the easier-to-pronounce translation: Thai chicken soup. It doesn't look like much—a creamy, pale broth laced with chicken slices, mushrooms, and cilantro—but what it lacks in looks it makes up for in flavor. Sweet and sour components balance the richness of lemon grass–and–lime-infused coconut milk, which, in turn, tempers a slow-building chili burn.

This classic Thai soup is relatively easy to make if you can find all of the proper ingredients, which not all of us can. Its complex flavor is largely derived from such exotica as galangal, kaffir lime leaves, and lemon grass. We'd be hard pressed to find most of these ingredients at our local market. Instead we aimed to make the most authentic version possible with widely available ingredients. We found a handful of "simplified" or "Americanized" Thai chicken soup recipes that, while largely informative regarding substitutions, mostly missed the mark. Each lacked the taut balancing of hot, sour, salty, and sweet components that makes Thai cooking so compelling. (Appropriately enough, that balance, in Thai, is called *yum*.) So, for the time being at least, we stuck with the classic recipes. We'd address substitutions once we knew how best to prepare the soup.

Variation in Thai chicken soup recipes tends to center on two basic components: broth and garnishes. Traditional recipes typically prepare the broth using one of two methods. The first involves poaching a whole chicken in water with aromatics, after which the broth is blended with coconut milk and further seasoned. The chicken is then shredded and stirred in with mushrooms. In the second approach, chicken broth and coconut milk are simmered with the aromatics, after which thin-sliced raw chicken and the remaining ingredients and seasonings are added. Both methods have their merits, but we much preferred the latter, which took half the effort and time without any apparent injury to flavor. The richness of the coconut milk and assertive seasonings added big flavor fast.

How long did the broth and aromatics need to simmer for the best results? We used broth ingredients from the best recipes we had tried—a blend of

---

INGREDIENTS: Coconut Milk

Coconut milk is not the thin liquid found inside the coconut itself; that is called coconut water. Coconut milk is a product made by steeping equal parts shredded coconut meat and either warm milk or water. The meat is pressed or mashed to release as much liquid as possible, the mixture is strained, and the result is coconut milk.

We tasted seven nationally available brands (five regular and two light) in coconut pudding, coconut rice, Thai-Style Chicken Soup, and curry. Among the five regular brands, tasters gravitated to those with more solid cream at the top of the can (most cans recommend shaking before opening to redistribute the solids). These brands also had a much stronger coconut flavor.

In the soup and curry, tasters preferred Chaokoh because of its exceptionally low sugar content (less than 1 gram per ⅓ cup). By comparison, brands with more than twice as much sugar (Ka-Me, Goya, Thai Kitchen) tasted "saccharine." In the sweet recipes, tasters gave velvety Ka-Me top votes for its "fruity" and "complex" flavor. In these recipes, the extra sugar was an advantage.

The light coconut milks we tasted were not nearly as creamy—a serious flaw in desserts but less so in soup. Of the two light brands tasted, we preferred the richer flavor of A Taste of Thai.

THE BEST COCONUT MILKS

Among the full-fat coconut milks, Ka-Me (left) is best suited for sweet recipes, while Chaokoh (center) is our favorite for soup. A Taste of Thai light coconut milk (right) was surprisingly good, especially in soup.

chicken broth, coconut milk, lemon grass, shallots, galangal, and cilantro. After sautéing the aromatics for a few minutes to bring out and deepen their flavors, we added the broth and noted that a scant 10 minutes of simmering proved perfect. Much longer and the broth tasted bitter and vegetal.

After preparing a few more batches with varying ratios of chicken broth and coconut milk, we settled on equal parts of each. Rich-tasting without being cloying, and definitely chicken-flavored, the blend was perfectly balanced. We also tried a technique we had come across in a couple of recipes. We added the coconut milk in two parts: half at the beginning and the remainder just before serving. What seemed fussy made a big difference, allowing the coconut flavor to come through clearly.

Now came the hard part: making substitutions. Most of the "simplified" recipes we tried or reviewed replaced the lemon grass with lemon zest, but we found the swap objectionable. Lemon zest—in conjunction with the sweet coconut milk—made for a broth with an odd, candy-like flavor. Dried lemon grass also failed to impress, as it lacked any of the depth of the fresh stuff. Luckily, we discovered lemon grass to be more readily available than we had assumed.

Galangal is a knotty, peppery-flavored rhizome distantly related to ginger, which most food writers suggest is the perfect substitute. While it wasn't perfect to us—ginger lacks the depth of flavor and piney finish of galangal—we decided it would do.

Kaffir lime leaves, the fresh or dried leaves from a potent variety of tropical lime, lend the broth a particularly floral, deep flavor and alluring aroma. Lime zest is the usual substitute, but one we felt lacked the intensity of the leaves. Once again, the substitute felt like a distant second.

This was a bad trend. Replacing the authentic ingredients was not working as well as we hoped and the soup didn't taste nearly as good as we expected. Perhaps authentic flavor really wasn't possible without the proper ingredients.

Then we found our magic bullet. After one taste test, a colleague suggested red curry paste, an ingredient we hadn't considered to that point. While it

is never added to traditional Thai chicken soup, the curry paste did include all the exotic ingredients for which we were trying so hard to find acceptable substitutions. We whisked a small spoonful of the paste into the soup in front of us and were struck by the surprising transformation from boring to—dare we say?—authentic.

Curry paste is usually added early on in cooking to mellow its potent flavor, but we found this flattened the flavor too much. Adding a dollop at the very end of cooking—whisked together with pungent fish sauce and tart lime juice—allowed the sharpness of the galangal, the fragrance of the kaffir lime leaves, and the bright heat of the chiles

PANTRY SPOTLIGHT

FISH SAUCE

Fish sauce is a salty, amber-colored liquid made from salted, fermented fish. It is used both as an ingredient and a condiment in Southeast Asia. It has a very concentrated flavor and, like anchovy paste, when used judiciously, it lends dishes a salty complexity that is impossible to replicate. Color correlates with flavor in fish sauce; the lighter the sauce, the lighter the flavor. However, with such a limited ingredient list—most brands contain some combination of fish extract, water, salt, and sugar—the differences between sauces are minimal. And because fish sauce is used in such small amounts, minute flavor differences get lost among the other flavors of a dish.

If you are a fan of fish sauce and use it often, you might want to make a special trip to an Asian market to buy a rich, dark sauce that is suitably pungent (we particularly like Tiparos fish sauce). In that case look for products with the labels *nuoc mam* (Vietnamese) or *nam pla* (Thai). Because most supermarkets don't carry a wide selection of fish sauce, we recommend buying whatever is available. That will most likely be Thai Kitchen, an Americanized brand found in most grocery stores, which was the lightest colored (and flavored) brand we tasted. Fish sauce will keep indefinitely without refrigeration.

467

to come through loud and clear. Out went the mediocre ginger and lime zest and in went 2 teaspoons of easy-to-find red curry paste.

With the broth tasting great, we could finally tackle the chicken and mushrooms. We initially thought that rich-tasting thigh meat would be the best choice to stand up to the full-flavored broth, but it was too fatty; boneless, skinless breast meat was better.

As for the mushrooms, oyster mushrooms are traditional but hard to find and expensive. Supermarket options like cremini, shiitake, and white mushrooms each had their merits, but the latter proved to be the closest match to the mild flavor and chewy texture of oyster mushrooms. Sliced thin and submerged in the broth, they quickly softened and absorbed the soup's flavors like a sponge.

A sprinkle of cilantro usually suffices as a finishing touch, but tasters wanted more. The clean, bright heat of thin-sliced Thai chiles and sharp bite of scallions did the trick. With twenty-odd minutes of cooking and a minimum of hands-on effort, we had Thai chicken soup that tasted every bit as good as that served at our local Thai restaurant.

Thai-Style Chicken Soup
Tom Kha Gai
SERVES 6 TO 8 AS AN APPETIZER,
OR 4 AS A MAIN COURSE

Although we prefer the richer, more complex flavor of regular coconut milk, light coconut milk can be substituted for one or both cans. Don't be tempted to use jarred or dried lemon grass—their flavor is characterless. For a spicier soup, add additional red curry paste to taste. Jarred Thai red curry paste is a great replacement for hard-to-find ingredients, as it contains many of the flavors commonly found in Southeast Asian cuisine (such as galangal and kaffir lime leaves) in a super-concentrated form.

1	teaspoon vegetable oil
3	stalks lemon grass, bottom 5 inches only, trimmed and sliced thin (see the illustrations below)
3	large shallots, chopped coarse
8	sprigs fresh cilantro, chopped coarse
3	tablespoons fish sauce
4	cups low-sodium chicken broth
2	(14-ounce) cans coconut milk
1	tablespoon sugar
½	pound white mushrooms, wiped clean, trimmed, and sliced ¼ inch thick
1	pound boneless, skinless chicken breasts (about 2 large breasts), halved lengthwise and sliced on the bias into ⅛-inch-thick pieces
3	tablespoons juice from 2 limes
2	teaspoons Thai red curry paste

GARNISH

½	cup loosely packed fresh cilantro leaves
2	fresh Thai, serrano, or jalapeño chiles, seeds and ribs removed, chiles sliced thin
2	scallions, sliced thin on the bias (see page 505)
1	lime, cut into wedges (for serving)

MINCING LEMON GRASS

1. Trim and discard all but the bottom 5 inches of the lemon grass stalk.

2. Remove the tough outer sheath from the trimmed lemon grass. If the lemon grass is particularly thick or tough, you may need to remove several layers to reveal the tender inner portion of the stalk.

3. Cut the trimmed and peeled lemon grass in half lengthwise, then slice it thin crosswise.

1. Heat the oil in a large saucepan over medium heat until just shimmering. Add the lemon grass, shallots, chopped cilantro sprigs, and 1 tablespoon of the fish sauce and cook, stirring frequently, until just softened but not browned, 2 to 5 minutes.

2. Stir in the chicken broth and 1 can of the coconut milk and bring to a simmer over high heat. Cover, reduce the heat to low, and simmer until the flavors have blended, about 10 minutes. Pour the broth through a fine-mesh strainer, discarding the solids in the strainer. (At this point, the soup can be refrigerated in an airtight container for up to 1 day.)

3. Return the strained soup to a clean saucepan and bring to a simmer over medium-high heat. Stir in the remaining can of coconut milk and the sugar and bring to a simmer. Reduce the heat to medium, add the mushrooms, and cook until just tender, 2 to 3 minutes. Add the chicken and cook, stirring constantly, until no longer pink, 1 to 3 minutes. Remove the soup from the heat.

4. Whisk the lime juice, curry paste, and remaining 2 tablespoons fish sauce together, then stir into the soup. Ladle the soup into individual bowls and garnish with the cilantro leaves, chiles, and scallions. Serve with the lime wedges.

VIETNAMESE RICE NOODLE SOUP WITH BEEF

Pho Bo

PHO (PRONOUNCED "FUH") IS PERHAPS THE best-recognized rice noodle soup from Southeast Asia. It begins with a stock made from beef bones, which is flavored with spices and sauces. The stock is rich but not heavy and is poured over wide rice noodles, meat (which can be anything from thinly sliced beef to chicken to meatballs), scallion slices, crisp bean sprouts, and an abundance of fresh herbs such as Thai basil and cilantro leaves. This mix of raw and cooked, hot and cold creates a unique and satisfying soup.

This soup relies heavily upon the quality of the broth, so we started there. But after some initial tests, we kept running into the inescapable fact that a full-flavored broth of this caliber (one that needs to simmer slowly for 5 hours or more) is impractical for most cooks today. Faced with this dilemma in the past, we have found it possible to punch up the otherwise mild flavor of store-bought chicken broth with extra aromatics to create a quick alternative.

We began to build our base by sautéing onions, garlic, and lemon grass, then adding chicken broth and some water and simmering the mixture briefly to allow the flavors to meld. This was a good start, but we thought we could further enhance our broth. Soy and fish sauces added much-needed body and depth of flavor. Soy sauce lent a meatiness that homemade beef stock would normally contribute, while fish sauce added just the right combination of salt and musky sweetness. Cloves and star anise are common components of this soup and tasters unanimously welcomed their addition. Lastly, we added a pinch of sugar, which balanced the salt and acidity from the sauces.

Satisfied with the broth, we turned our attention to the noodles. We found that boiled noodles had a tendency to turn mushy and—if left in the hot soup for any length of time—break apart. Ultimately, we settled on soaking the noodles in water that had been brought to a boil and then removed from the heat; the slightly cooler temperature did not overcook them. We drained the noodles when they had softened to the point that they were tender but still had a little chew and then let them finish cooking in the hot broth until they softened through.

We next looked at what meat to add and how it should be cooked. Beef filet, sirloin steak, tendons, tripe, meatballs, chicken, and chicken organs are all common additions, but we decided to focus on two meats that would be the simplest to prepare and find: thinly sliced beef and shredded chicken. Traditionally the beef is sliced paper thin and is added to the individual soup bowls raw (the idea is that it cooks directly in the broth). We had trouble getting the broth to cook the beef fully every time, so we opted for cooking the beef in the simmering broth before serving it. We tested a variety of steaks, and concluded that beef tenderloin—the authentic choice for this soup—was indeed the best because it was naturally lean (no bits of fat to turn rubbery in the soup) yet extremely tender and flavorful. As for the chicken, we chose to use boneless, skinless chicken breasts because they were so easy to poach in the broth then shred into bite-sized pieces. The finishing touch for this soup is a generous garnish of bean sprouts, fresh herbs, lime, and some sliced chile for heat.

PANTRY SPOTLIGHT

RICE NOODLES

In Southeast Asia and southern regions of China, a delicate pasta made from rice flour and water is used in an array of dishes including soups, stir-fries, and salads. Unlike other pasta, you don't want to boil these delicate noodles because they have a tendency to overcook very quickly, resulting in a mushy, sticky mess. Instead, it is best to bring a pot of water to a boil, then remove the pot from the heat and steep the noodles gently in the hot water.

Flat Rice Noodles come in several different widths from extra small to extra large. We use a medium width noodle, similar to linguine in size (about ¼ inch wide) for both the Vietnamese Rice Noodle Soups (see right) and Pad Thai (page 480).

Round Rice Noodles, also called *bun* or rice vermicelli, come in a variety of sizes, but we use the smallest size we can get our hands on in our Vietnamese Rice Noodle Salad (page 477) and Vietnamese Spring Rolls (page 473).

Vietnamese Rice Noodle Soup with Beef
Pho Bo
SERVES 4 AS A MAIN COURSE

To make slicing the steak easier, freeze it for 15 minutes. Be ready to serve the soup immediately after cooking the beef in step 3; if the beef sits in the hot broth for too long it will become tough. If you cannot find Thai basil, substitute regular basil.

BROTH
- 2 teaspoons vegetable oil
- 2 medium onions, minced
- 4 medium garlic cloves, minced or pressed through a garlic press (about 4 teaspoons)
- 1 stalk lemon grass, bottom 5 inches only, trimmed and sliced thin (see the illustrations on page 468)
- ⅓ cup fish sauce
- 8 cups low-sodium chicken broth
- 2 cups water
- 2 tablespoons soy sauce
- 2 tablespoons sugar
- 4 star anise pods
- 4 whole cloves

NOODLES, MEAT, AND GARNISH
- 8 ounces (¼-inch-wide) dried flat rice noodles (see left)
- 2 cups bean sprouts
- 1 cup loosely packed fresh Thai basil leaves (see note)
- 1 cup loosely packed fresh cilantro leaves
- 2 scallions, sliced thin on the bias (see page 505)
- 1 fresh Thai, serrano, or jalapeño chile, seeds and ribs removed, chile sliced thin
- 1 lime, cut into wedges (for serving)
- 12 ounces beef tenderloin (about 2 filets mignons), sliced in half lengthwise, then sliced crosswise into ¼-inch-thick pieces

1. FOR THE BROTH: Heat the oil in large saucepan over medium heat until just shimmering. Add

the onions, garlic, lemon grass, and 1 tablespoon of the fish sauce and cook, stirring frequently, until just softened but not browned, 2 to 5 minutes.

2. Stir in the remaining fish sauce, chicken broth, water, soy sauce, sugar, star anise, and cloves and bring to a simmer. Cover, reduce the heat to low, and simmer until the flavors have blended, about 10 minutes. Pour the broth through a fine-mesh strainer, discarding the solids in the strainer. (At this point, the soup can be refrigerated in an airtight container for up to 1 day.)

3. FOR THE NOODLES, MEAT, AND GARNISH: Bring 4 quarts of water to a boil in a large pot. Remove the boiling water from the heat, add the rice noodles, and let stand, stirring occasionally, until the noodles are tender but still chewy, about 10 minutes.

4. Drain the noodles, divide them evenly between 4 individual serving bowls, and top each with ½ cup of bean sprouts; set aside. Arrange the basil, cilantro, scallions, chile, and lime wedges attractively on a large serving platter; set aside.

5. Return the strained soup to a clean saucepan, bring to a simmer over medium-high heat, then reduce the heat to low. Add the beef and cook until no longer pink, about 1 minute (do not overcook). Remove the soup from the heat. Ladle the soup over the noodles and serve, passing the platter of garnishes separately.

➤ VARIATION

Vietnamese Rice Noodle Soup with Chicken

Follow the recipe for Vietnamese Rice Noodle Soup with Beef, substituting 12 ounces boneless, skinless chicken breasts (about 2 medium breasts) for the beef. Add the chicken breasts to the broth in step 2 with the all of the remaining broth ingredients and simmer as directed until the thickest part of the chicken breast registers 160 degrees on an instant-read thermometer, 10 to 15 minutes. Remove the breasts from the broth before straining and shred into bite-sized pieces using two forks (see the illustration on page 69). Return the shredded chicken to the strained broth and reheat for 1 to 2 minutes over medium heat before serving as directed in step 5.

FRESH SPRING ROLLS
Goi Cuon

THE FRESH SPRING ROLLS OF SOUTHERN Vietnam are made with translucent rice paper wrappers that have been softened in water and then filled with cool rice vermicelli, raw vegetables, shrimp, pork, and fragrant herbs. They offer a textural symphony (soft wrapper, firm noodles, and crunchy vegetables) as well as stark but appealing contrasts in flavor (mint, basil, cilantro, chiles, peanuts, and fish sauce). But fresh spring rolls are often disappointing, using gummy noodles, iceberg lettuce, soggy rice paper, shriveled herbs, and saccharine "peanut" sauces that taste not a whit like peanuts. Given that they require only a short list of fresh ingredients and minimal cooking, it occurred to us that we should be able to easily produce a four-star spring roll at home.

We began our investigation with the wrapper. Rice paper wrappers come out of the package hard and inedible and so must be soaked in water before use. It quickly became apparent that timing was crucial here. When soaked too long, the wrappers simply disintegrated; when soaked for just two or three seconds, the wrappers remained stiff.

Even with the correct soaking time, however, the wrappers are so delicate that they fall apart if simply placed on a kitchen counter for rolling. The trick,

---

PANTRY SPOTLIGHT

SPRING ROLL WRAPPERS

Made from a paste of rice flour and water that is stamped into bamboo mats and dried, rice paper wrappers are translucent, brittle, and delicate—meaning they can be difficult to work with. They are almost impossible to make at home, but can be purchased at Asian grocery stores, natural foods stores, and gourmet grocers. Make sure you look for all-rice wrappers, not the thin wrappers made with tapioca starch or the thick wheat flour wrappers.

ALL-RICE SPRING ROLL WRAPPERS

we discovered, is to use a damp kitchen towel, which supports the wrappers without sticking to them. We also found it best to make the rolls one at a time and to cover them with a second damp towel once finished to keep the wrappers moist and pliable.

With the wrappers taken care of, we turned to the filling, starting with the noodles. Thin vermicelli-style rice noodles are sometimes cooked just like American or Italian pasta, but after testing this against dropping the noodles into boiling water that had just been removed from the heat, we

ASSEMBLING THE SPRING ROLLS

1. Lay the herbs and cucumber on the wrapper, followed by the carrot mixture and noodles.

2. Fold a bottom 2-inch border of the wrapper up over the filling.

3. Fold the left, then the right edge of the wrapper over the filling.

4. Roll the filling to the top edge of the wrapper to form a tight cylinder.

preferred the latter method. However, we did note that the thickness ranges from brand to brand, which affects the cooking time. It's best to taste the noodles after 10 minutes to make sure they are tender.

Classically there are two main ingredients in these rolls, shrimp and pork. But we wanted to keep this recipe simple, so we chose to only use shrimp. We found that extra-large shrimp worked best and they had to be sliced down the back lengthwise in order to fit in these already bursting rolls.

As for the vegetables, carrot, daikon radish, and cucumber are the traditional accompaniments. Since daikon can be difficult to find, we eliminated it altogether. Carrots contributed a pleasantly sweet flavor and nice texture when grated. We tried grating cucumber as well but ended up with watery, soggy rolls. When sliced into matchstick-sized pieces, however, the cucumber added significant crunch without dampening the wrappers.

For the herbs, fragrant cilantro and mint sparkle when used in tandem and their frilly leaves are a visual bonus. We ran into trouble, though, when we inadvertently got a few whole large mint leaves in a single bite. The solution was twofold: tear large leaves into pieces before using and sprinkle them over the inner section of the rice paper before rolling (rather than piling them up, as most recipes suggest).

Despite our liberal dose of herbs, the rolls remained a little bland. We went back to our library of cookbooks and discovered spring roll recipes that included an acidic marinade for the vegetables and noodles that adds both flavor and moisture. The liquid ingredients for the marinade included a few typical Southeast Asian flavorings: lime juice, rice vinegar, and fish sauce (a pungent liquid made from fermented fish). We settled on a simple mixture based on fish sauce and lime juice. A teaspoon of sugar and some chopped fresh chiles balanced the acidity and gave the rolls a sweet-hot punch, while chopped peanuts added substance.

As for the dipping sauce, we began with a standard recipe for peanut sauce made with hoisin sauce (a common ingredient in Vietnamese-style peanut sauces), sugar, peanut butter, and water and tested a dozen variations. We decided to eliminate the sugar and cut back on the hoisin sauce, giving the peanut flavor center stage. Next we added garlic, chili sauce, and red pepper flakes to bring up the heat and tomato paste for color. The resulting sauce was gently sweet and spicy.

Now we finally had flavorful spring rolls that could be made easily and quickly at home. They are so good, in fact, that we won't be ordering them off a menu anytime soon.

Fresh Spring Rolls
Goi Cuon
MAKES 8 SPRING ROLLS

Adjust the spiciness of this dish by including the minced ribs and seeds from the chiles. We found it easiest to buy cooked shrimp for these rolls; you can cook your own shrimp if desired, but be sure to chill them thoroughly before using. Tear any large mint leaves into pieces before using.

3	ounces dried rice vermicelli (see page 470)
2½	tablespoons juice from 1 lime
1½	tablespoons fish sauce
1	teaspoon sugar
1	large carrot, peeled and grated on the large holes of a box grater
⅓	cup coarsely chopped roasted unsalted peanuts
2	fresh Thai, serrano, or jalapeño chiles, seeds and ribs removed, chiles minced
1	large cucumber, peeled, seeded, and sliced into 2-inch-long matchsticks
8	(8-inch) round rice paper wrappers (see page 471)
½	cup loosely packed fresh mint leaves, large leaves torn into pieces
½	cup loosely packed fresh cilantro leaves
4	large leaves red leaf or Boston lettuce, halved lengthwise and sliced thin
½	pound cooked extra-large shrimp (21 to 25 per pound), chilled and sliced in half lengthwise
1	recipe Hoisin-Peanut Dipping Sauce (recipe follows)

1. Bring 4 quarts of water to a boil in a large pot. Remove the boiling water from the heat, add the rice noodles, and let stand, stirring occasionally, until the noodles are tender, about 10 minutes. Drain the noodles and transfer them to a medium bowl.

2. Whisk the lime juice, fish sauce, and sugar together in a small bowl until the sugar dissolves. Toss 2 tablespoons of the lime juice mixture with the noodles. In a medium bowl, toss 1 more tablespoon of the lime juice mixture with the carrot, peanuts, and chiles. In a small bowl, toss the remaining 1 tablespoon lime juice mixture with the cucumber.

3. Spread a clean, damp kitchen towel on a work surface. Fill a 9-inch pie plate with 1 inch of room temperature water. Working with one rice paper wrapper at a time, immerse each wrapper in the water until just pliable, about 2 minutes, then lay the softened wrapper on the towel.

4. Scatter about 6 mint leaves and 6 cilantro leaves over the wrapper. Following the illustrations on page 472, arrange 5 cucumber sticks horizontally on the wrapper and top with 1 tablespoon of the carrot mixture, 2 tablespoons of the lettuce, 2½ tablespoons of the noodles, and 2 shrimp halves.

5. Wrap the spring roll following the illustrations on page 472, then transfer to a serving platter and cover with a second damp kitchen towel. Repeat with the remaining rice paper wrappers and filling ingredients. (The covered spring rolls can be refrigerated for up to 4 hours.) Serve with the hoisin-peanut dipping sauce.

Hoisin-Peanut Dipping Sauce
Tuong
MAKES ABOUT ¾ CUP

Adding the optional chili sauce will make the sauce a bit spicier. The sauce can be refrigerated in an airtight container for up to 3 days. Serve at room temperature.

¼	cup hoisin sauce
¼	cup creamy peanut butter
¼	cup water, plus extra as needed
2	tablespoons tomato paste
1	teaspoon Thai chili-garlic sauce, such as sriracha (optional, see note)
2	teaspoons vegetable oil
2	medium garlic cloves, minced or pressed through a garlic press (about 2 teaspoons)
1	teaspoon red pepper flakes

1. Whisk the hoisin, peanut butter, water, tomato paste, and chili sauce (if using) together in a small bowl and set aside. Cook the oil, garlic, and red pepper flakes in a small saucepan over medium heat until fragrant and sizzling, 1 to 2 minutes.

2. Stir in the peanut butter mixture, bring to a simmer, and then reduce the heat to medium-low and cook, stirring occasionally, until the flavors blend, about 3 minutes, adding more water as needed until the sauce has a ketchup-like consistency. Transfer to a bowl and cool to room temperature before serving.

INDONESIAN BEEF SATAY

Sate Sapi

SLENDER SLICES OF MARINATED BEEF WOVEN onto bamboo skewers and thrown briefly on the grill are popular Indonesian street food known as satay or sate. The meat has a sweet yet salty flavor, and the skewers are typically served as an appetizer, snack, or light main course alongside a spicy peanut sauce. When done correctly, the tender meat is easily pulled apart into small bites right off the skewer. All too often, however, the beef is tough and sliced so thickly it doesn't pull apart, leaving you with an ungainly mouthful of meat. The peanut sauce can be graceless with a glue-like consistency and muddy peanut flavor. Not only would finding the right cut of beef and slicing it correctly be the key to a tender satay, but we wondered how to make the marinade and accompanying peanut sauce.

Starting with the beef, we surveyed the local meat counter for possibilities. We skipped over the expensive cuts such as top loin, rib eye, and tenderloin and focused on the cheaper cuts more appropriate for marinating and skewering— sirloin, sirloin flap, round, skirt, flank, and blade steaks. Bringing these cheaper cuts back to the test kitchen, we immediately noted that slicing the raw beef into thin strips is a difficult task. To make things easier, we took to quickly pounding the sliced meat. Sliced, skewered, and cooked, these

various cheaper cuts of meat produced substantially different textures. Steaks from the round were the worst, with a tough, dry texture, followed closely by chewy sirloin, and stringy sirloin flap (a cut from the bottom sirloin). The blade steaks tasted great and were fairly tender, but their small size made it difficult to slice them into long, elegant strips. Both the skirt and flank steak were easy to slice and tasted best. Since skirt steak can be difficult to find and is a bit more expensive, flank steak is the best option.

We found that the key to tenderness hinges on slicing the meat perpendicular to its large, obvious grain (see the illustration below). Using a small, 2-pound flank steak, we could make about 40 skewers, enough for 12 to 18 people as an appetizer. Although satay is usually grilled, we found the broiler to be a simpler cooking method—and it allows you to enjoy satay any time of year. Cooked roughly six inches from the broiler element, these thinly sliced pieces of meat are done in only six to seven minutes.

Having found a tender cut of meat, we focused next on adding flavor with the marinade. Researching a variety of traditional Indonesian recipes, we noted that most were based on a combination of fish sauce, curry powder, fresh aromatics, coconut milk, and oil. This style of marinating without an acid is done to add flavor, rather than to tenderize the meat.

We began by testing various amounts of fish sauce. Although not much is used in the marinade, the fish sauce acts a little like a brine, resulting in moist meat. One tablespoon of fish sauce added just the right amount of salt and seasoning to the beef. When we tested higher amounts, tasters found

SLICING FLANK STEAK THIN FOR SATAY

Using a chef's knife, cut the partially frozen flank steak across the grain into ¼-inch-thick slices.

ARRANGING THE SKEWERS FOR THE BROILER

Using a narrow strip of aluminum foil, cover the exposed portion of each skewer to prevent burning. Secure the foil by crimping it tightly at the edges.

the flavor of the fish sauce overwhelmed the beef.

Next, we began adding flavors such as Asian chili sauce, sugar, and an array of fresh aromatics. We tested lemon grass, galangal, ginger, kaffir lime leaves, and coriander root, all of which added bright, fresh flavor, but some of which can be difficult to find. Our ingredient list was now becoming longer than we would like for such a simple dish, so instead we added red curry paste, which is readily available and included most of the aromatics we wanted to use. We also included turmeric, coriander, and cumin, which all appeared in virtually every satay recipe we came across. We tested different amounts of the dry spices; 1 teaspoon of each left a powdery texture, but ½ teaspoon of each added just the right amount of flavor. Garlic rounded out all of these flavors nicely. Sugar balanced the heat in the sauce, and we used light brown sugar, since it is the closest to palm sugar, the Indonesian sweetener of choice.

With the flavorings decided upon, we looked at the fat used in the marinade. Many recipes call for coconut milk, which not only complemented the flavor of the meat, but is fatty enough that we could eliminate oil as an ingredient. We also liked how the coconut milk marinade coated the beef, helping keep the flavorings on the meat instead of leaving them behind in the bowl. We tested marinating times and found that 30 minutes was long enough to give the beef good flavor, although the meat could be marinated for up to 24 hours.

Lastly, we focused on the peanut sauce. Using creamy peanut butter, we tried spicing it up using

a variety of flavorings. In the end, the same ingredients used in the marinade also tasted good in the peanut sauce—coconut milk, fish sauce, red curry paste, sugar, garlic, and minced cilantro. We also found that lime juice added a welcome burst of tart acidity. To keep the sauce from being too thick or pasty we simply thinned it with warm water. Pairing perfectly with the flavor of the marinated beef, the peanut sauce turns these beef skewers into an authentic satay.

Indonesian Beef Satay

Sate Sapi
SERVES 12 TO 18 AS AN APPETIZER, OR 8 TO 10 AS A MAIN COURSE

To make slicing the steak easier, freeze it for 15 minutes. Make sure to stir the coconut milk thoroughly to combine before measuring out the desired amount. Forty 6-inch-long wooden skewers are required for this recipe; if you only have 12-inch wooden or metal skewers, use just 20 skewers and stack two pieces of meat on each skewer.

1	(2-pound) flank steak
1	cup coconut milk
¼	cup water
2	tablespoons fish sauce
1	tablespoon light brown sugar
1	tablespoon Thai red curry paste
3	medium garlic cloves, minced or pressed through a garlic press (about 1 tablespoon)
½	teaspoon ground turmeric
½	teaspoon ground coriander
½	teaspoon ground cumin
1	recipe Peanut Dipping Sauce (recipe follows)

1. Following the illustration on page 474, slice the flank steak in half lengthwise, then crosswise on the bias into ¼-inch-thick pieces. Pound the slices of meat between 2 sheets of parchment to ⅛ inch thick.

2. Whisk the coconut milk, water, fish sauce, sugar, curry paste, garlic, turmeric, coriander, and cumin together in a medium bowl until the sugar dissolves. Stir in the meat, cover, and refrigerate for 30 minutes or up to 24 hours.

3. Weave the meat onto forty 6-inch-long

wooden skewers (1 piece per stick). Adjust an oven rack 6 inches from the broiler element and heat the broiler. Following the illustration on page 475, lay half of the skewers on a rimmed baking sheet and cover the skewer ends with foil. Broil the skewers until the meat is browned, 6 to 9 minutes, flipping the skewers over halfway through the cooking time. Transfer the cooked skewers to a large serving platter and broil the remaining skewers. Serve with the peanut dipping sauce.

Peanut Dipping Sauce
Soot Thua
MAKES 2 CUPS

We prefer the stronger, purer flavor of natural peanut butter here; however, any creamy peanut butter will work fine. Make sure to stir the coconut milk thoroughly to combine before measuring out the desired amount; light coconut milk can be substituted here. To make the sauce spicier, add additional red curry paste to taste. Jarred Thai red curry paste is a great replacement for hard-to-find ingredients, as it contains many of the flavors commonly found in Southeast Asian cuisine (such as galangal and kaffir lime leaves) in a super-concentrated form.

⅔	cup creamy peanut butter
½	cup coconut milk
¼	cup juice from 2 limes
3	tablespoons fish sauce
4	medium garlic cloves, minced or pressed through a garlic press (about 4 teaspoons)
1	teaspoon Thai red curry paste, plus extra to taste
½	teaspoon sugar, plus extra to taste
	Warm water, as needed
1	tablespoon minced fresh cilantro leaves

Blend all of the ingredients except the cilantro together in a blender until smooth. Blend in additional red curry paste and sugar to taste. (The sauce can be refrigerated in an airtight container for up to 3 days; bring to room temperature before serving.) Transfer the sauce to a bowl and add water until the sauce has a loose, heavy cream–like consistency. Sprinkle with the cilantro and serve.

VIETNAMESE RICE NOODLE SALAD
Bun

ONE OF OUR FAVORITE VIETNAMESE DISHES is *bun,* or rice noodle salad. Light yet satisfying, this multilayered salad is piled in a bowl with shredded lettuce at the bottom, followed by pickled carrots and cucumbers, fresh herbs, rice noodles, and grilled meat or seafood. It is garnished with a sprinkle of chopped roasted peanuts and dressed with *nuoc cham,* a sweet-tart and mildly spicy sauce. While it is often found in Vietnamese restaurants, it is relatively simple for home cooks to prepare. Most of the ingredients are meant to be served at room temperature and can be prepared ahead of time, leaving only the cooking of the meat for the last minute.

Starting with the protein, we found recipes made with shrimp, beef, and pork—and sometimes a combination of these. To keep this recipe simple we chose to just use pork in our recipe (though shrimp and beef would be great as well). We tested pork shoulder, chops, loin, and tenderloin. While the shoulder had a lot of flavor, it also had a lot of fat and tasters thought this cut was too gristly for the salad. The pork chops offered great flavor, but the meat was a little tough for this dish. The loin and the tenderloin were both winning options, but the tenderloin is our top pick—at about one pound, it provides just the right amount of meat for this recipe.

The pork is typically sliced thin, immersed in a salty-sweet marinade, and then broiled or grilled to achieve caramelized crispy-charred edges. The marinades we came across all consisted of the same basic combination of fish sauce, vegetable oil, and sugar. From there they deviated, with some also calling for soy sauce, Vietnamese-style caramel sauce (a simple sugar and water mixture that is cooked until just slightly bitter), and chili paste. Beginning with the sugar, we tested the caramel sauce, dark brown sugar, light brown sugar, and white sugar. Light brown and white sugar both failed to caramelize in the short time it took for the meat to cook. Tasters found no discernible difference between the caramel and dark brown sugar and liked both for their deep nutty flavors, so we opted for the less fussy addition of dark brown sugar. Next we tested fish sauce amounts and 2 tablespoons added just the right amount of saltiness to balance the sugar. Three tablespoons of oil was just enough to keep the lean tenderloin meat moist, without making it taste greasy.

The meat was ready, so we turned our attention to the salad dressing, called *nuoc cham*. It appears in a variety of Vietnamese dishes and can be used as a dipping sauce (such as for our Sizzling Saigon Crêpes on page 492) as well as a dressing. The fundamental ingredients are lime juice, fish sauce, sugar, garlic, and chiles, providing a careful balance of tart, sweet, salty, and spicy flavors. (A few recipes called for rice vinegar, but we preferred the citrus acidity of the lime juice.) Tasters continually requested more dressing, so we decided to use half of it to dress the salad and divided the other half into individual bowls so more sauce could be added as needed while eating.

This salad usually contains a mixture of pickled carrots and daikon radish, a combination that can be found in numerous Vietnamese dishes. Daikon radish can be difficult to find, so we left it out of our version. Because there are so many individual components to prepare in this salad, we opted to streamline this recipe by seasoning the carrots directly in the dressing. We also found the occasional recipe that called for pickling the cucumbers, a method we chose to use since it also ensured that the salad was well flavored. We simply combined the cucumbers with the carrots and let them marinate in the dressing.

The round rice noodles (called *bun*) used for this salad are also used in Vietnamese Spring Rolls (see page 473), so we already knew our preferred cooking technique was to drop them in boiling water that has just been removed from the heat. With that established, we realized that these noodles come in small, medium, large, and extra-large widths. After testing all four sizes, we settled upon the smallest as the best option for the salad—the dressing easily coated the thinner noodles and we got a more even ratio of noodles, meat, and vegetable in every bite.

Finally it was time to add the lettuce. We tried red and green leaf lettuce, Bibb lettuce, and iceberg. Tasters thought that the iceberg lettuce lacked flavor and got lost in the noodles. While the Bibb lettuce was an acceptable option, tasters preferred red or green leaf for the way it held the dressing and for its soft yet crunchy texture. In addition, an abundance of fresh herbs are added, usually mint, Thai basil, cilantro, and red perilla (a minty, citrusy herb). The last in the list is virtually impossible to find, unless you live near a Vietnamese grocery store. We focused on the first three herbs and liked a combination of all three in equal amounts—we settled on a generous ½ cup each.

While each component of this salad is typically layered into individual bowls, and served with the dressing on the side, we opted to toss it all in a large bowl to make the preparation simpler. It is a satisfying meal that you won't soon forget.

Vietnamese Rice Noodle Salad
Bun
SERVES 4 TO 6 AS A MAIN COURSE

To make slicing the pork easier, freeze it for 15 minutes. You can increase the spiciness of this dish by including the minced ribs and seeds from the chiles. We find the trio of fresh cilantro, basil, and mint essential for flavor in this salad; if you cannot find all three, increase the amount of the others to ¾ cup each. Or, if you cannot find Thai basil, substitute regular basil.

PORK

3	tablespoons vegetable oil
2	tablespoons fish sauce
2	tablespoons dark brown sugar
I	pork tenderloin (about I pound), trimmed and sliced crosswise into ⅛-inch-thick rounds

DRESSING

⅔	cup fish sauce
½	cup warm water
6	tablespoons juice from 3 limes
5	tablespoons sugar
3	fresh Thai, serrano, or jalapeño chiles, seeds and ribs removed, chiles minced (see note)
2	medium garlic cloves, minced or pressed through a garlic press (about 2 teaspoons)

SALAD

3   large carrots, peeled and grated on the large holes of a box grater (about 1½ cups)

1   large cucumber, peeled, seeded, and sliced into 2-inch-long matchsticks

¼   cup chopped unsalted roasted peanuts, plus extra for garnish

1   fresh Thai, serrano, or jalapeño chile, seeds and ribs removed, chile minced

8   ounces dried rice vermicelli (see page 470)

4   cups red or green leaf lettuce, thinly sliced

½   cup loosely packed fresh Thai basil leaves (see note)

½   cup loosely packed fresh cilantro leaves

½   cup loosely packed fresh mint leaves

1   recipe Fried Shallots (optional, page 482)

1. FOR THE PORK: Whisk the oil, fish sauce, and sugar together in a medium bowl until the sugar dissolves. Add the pork and toss to coat evenly. Cover and refrigerate for 30 minutes or up to 24 hours.

2. FOR THE DRESSING: Whisk all the ingredients together until the sugar dissolves and set aside.

3. FOR THE SALAD: Toss the carrots, cucumber, peanuts, and chile with ¼ cup of the dressing and set aside to marinate while cooking the noodles and pork.

4. Bring 4 quarts of water to a boil in a large pot. Off the heat, add the rice noodles and let stand, stirring occasionally, until tender, about 10 minutes. Drain the noodles and transfer them to a large bowl. Layer the carrot-cucumber mixture, lettuce, basil, cilantro, and mint on top of the noodles (do not toss), and set aside.

5. Adjust an oven rack 6 inches from the broiler element and heat the broiler. Line a broiler pan bottom with foil and top with a broiler pan top. Remove the pork from the marinade and spread it out over the broiler pan top. Broil the pork until golden on both sides with crisp edges, about 10 minutes, flipping the pork over halfway through the cooking time.

6. Pour half of the remaining dressing over the noodles, carrot-cucumber mixture, lettuce, and herbs and toss to combine. Divide the noodles evenly between 4 large individual serving bowls and top with the broiled pork. Sprinkle with additional peanuts and fried shallots (if desired) and serve, passing the remaining dressing separately.

PAD THAI

PAD THAI IS THE PERFECT REMEDY FOR A jaded palate. Hot, sweet, and pungent Thai flavors tangled in an un-Western jumble of textures awaken all of the senses that have grown weary of the usual grub. We have downed numerous platefuls of pad thai, many from an excellent Thai restaurant only a few blocks away from our test kitchen. What we noticed was that from one order to the next, pad thai prepared in the same reliable restaurant kitchen was inconsistent. If it was perfect, it was a symphony of flavors and textures. It balanced sweet, sour, and spicy and the tender, glutinous rice noodles ensnared curls of shrimp, crisp strands of bean sprouts, soft curds of fried egg, and sturdy bits of tofu. Sometimes, however, it tasted weak and flat, as if seasoned too timidly. At its worst, pad thai suffers from indiscriminate amounts of sugar and from noodles that are either slick and greasy or sticky, lifeless strands that glom onto one another.

We have become so enamored of pad thai and so tired of disappointment that we have attempted it several times in the test kitchen with only moderate success, and that we attribute to luck. The recipes were unclear, the ingredient lists daunting, and we stumbled through the steps only to produce dry, undercooked noodles and unbalanced flavors. Happily, though, our pad thai was loaded with plump, sweet shrimp and the flavors tasted clean and fresh. Our goal was to build on these positives and produce a consistently superlative pad thai.

Flat rice noodles, often called rice sticks, the type of noodles used in pad thai, are often only partially cooked, particularly when used in stir-fries. We found three different methods of preparing them: soaking them in room-temperature water, soaking them in hot tap water, and boiling them. We began with boiling and quickly realized that this was bad advice. Drained and waiting in the colander, the noodles glued themselves together. When we managed to stir-fry them, they wound up soggy and overdone. Noodles soaked in room-temperature water remained fairly stiff. After lengthy stir-frying, they eventually became tender, but longer cooking made this pad thai drier and stickier. Soaking the noodles in hot tap water for about 20 minutes was a little better, but the resulting noodles were still a bit stiff. We finally tried soaking the noodles in water that had been brought to a boil and then removed from the heat. They "softened," turning limp and pliant, but were not fully tender. Drained, they were loose and separate and they cooked through easily with stir-frying. The result? Noodles that were at once pleasantly tender and resilient.

Sweet, salty, sour, and spicy are the flavor characteristics of pad thai and none should dominate; they should coexist in harmony. Although the cooking time is short, the ingredient list isn't. Fish sauce supplies a salty-sweet pungency, sugar gives sweetness, the heat comes from ground chiles, vinegar provides acidity, and tamarind rounds out the dish with its fruity, earthy, sweet-tart molasses-tinged flavor. Garlic and sometimes shallots contribute their heady, robust flavors. Some recipes call for ketchup (sounded dubious but probably worth trying), and some require soy sauce.

With these ingredients in hand, we set off to find out which ones were key to success and how much of each to use to achieve balanced flavor. For 8 ounces of rice noodles, 3 tablespoons of fish sauce and the same amount of sugar were ideal. Three-quarters of a teaspoon of cayenne (many recipes call for Thai chiles, but for the sake of simplicity, we opted not to use them) brought a low, even heat—not a searing burn—and 1 tablespoon of rice vinegar (preferred in pad thai for its mild acidity and relatively complex fermented-grain flavor) greatly vivified the flavors.

Tasters liked the garlic at 1 tablespoon minced. Shallots had a surprising impact on flavor. Just one medium shallot produced a round, full sweetness

PANTRY SPOTLIGHT

TAMARIND

Sweet-tart, brownish red tamarind is a necessary ingredient for authentic pad thai as well as for a variety of other dishes such chutneys, sour orange curry, smoked fish, and coconut soup. Tamarind is commonly sold in paste (also called pulp) and in concentrate form. But don't fret if neither is available—you can still make a very good pad thai using lime juice and water. Here are your three options.

Tamarind Paste or Pulp

Tamarind paste, or pulp, is firm, sticky, and filled with seeds and fibers. We favored this product because it had the freshest, brightest flavor. To rehydrate the tamarind, soak it in boiling water until softened and mushy, 10 to 30 minutes (depending on the amount of tamarind). Mash the softened tamarind to break it up, then push it through a mesh strainer to remove the seeds and fibers and extract as much pulp as possible.

Tamarind Concentrate

Tamarind concentrate looks more like a scary pomade than a foodstuff. It's black, thick, shiny, and gooey. Its flavor approximates that of tamarind paste, but it tastes less fruity and more "cooked" and it colors the pad thai a shade too dark. To use in the pad thai recipe, mix 1 tablespoon with ⅔ cup hot water.

Lime Juice and Water Substitute

If tamarind is out of the question, combine ⅓ cup of lime juice and ⅓ cup of water and use it in its place; use light brown sugar instead of granulated to give the noodles some color and a faint molasses flavor. Because it will already contain a good hit of lime, do not serve this version of pad thai with lime wedges.

and depth of flavor. To coax the right character out of these two aromatics, we found that cooking them to the point of browning was critical; they tasted mellow, sweet, and mildly toasty.

Tamarind was the most enigmatic ingredient on our list. Tamarind is a fruit that grows as a round brown pod about five inches long and is often sold as a paste (a hard, flat brick) or as a sticky concentrate. (For more information, see page 479.) It is central—if not essential—to the unique flavor of pad thai. Tests showed that tamarind paste has a fresher, brighter, fruitier flavor than concentrate, which tasted dull by comparison. For those who cannot obtain either tamarind paste or concentrate, we worked out a formula of equal parts lime juice and water as a stand-in. This mixture produces a less interesting and less authentic dish, but we polished off several such platefuls with no qualms.

We tried a little ketchup, but its vinegary tomato flavor was out of place. As for soy sauce, even just a mere tablespoon was a big bully—its assertive flavor didn't play nicely with the others.

The other ingredients in pad thai are sautéed shrimp, scrambled eggs, chopped peanuts, bean sprouts, and scallions. For more textural intrigue and to achieve authentic pad thai flavor, dried shrimp and Thai salted preserved radish are optional but worthy embellishments (both sold in Asian grocery stores). Dried shrimp are sweet, salty, and intensely shrimpy and they add tiny bursts of incredible flavor. We used 2 tablespoons of the smallest dried shrimp we could find and chopped them up finer still, because tasters asked that their firm, chewy texture be mitigated. Thai salted preserved radish is brownish yellow in color, dry, and a bit wrinkled and it is sold in long sections (think daikon radish) folded into a flimsy plastic package. Two tablespoons of chopped salted radish added piquant, savory bits with a good crunch.

Oddly, after consuming dozens of servings of pad thai, we did not feel glutted. We were addicted. These days, if we order it in a restaurant, we prepare ourselves for disappointment. We've come to think that pad thai is best when made at home.

Pad Thai
SERVES 4

For an accurate measurement of boiling water, bring a full kettle of water to boil, then measure out the desired amount. Although this dish cooks very quickly, the ingredient list is long, and everything must be prepared and within easy reach at the stovetop when you begin cooking.

SAUCE

2	tablespoons tamarind paste plus ¾ cup boiling water or tamarind substitute (see page 479)
3	tablespoons fish sauce
3	tablespoons sugar
2	tablespoons vegetable oil
I	tablespoon rice vinegar
¾	teaspoon cayenne pepper

NOODLES, SHRIMP, AND GARNISH

8	ounces (¼-inch-wide) dried flat rice noodles (see page 470)
2	tablespoons vegetable oil
12	ounces medium shrimp (40 to 50 per pound), peeled and deveined (see page 363)
	Salt
I	medium shallot, minced
3	garlic cloves, minced or pressed through a garlic press (about I tablespoon)
2	large eggs, lightly beaten
I	tablespoon dried shrimp, chopped fine (optional)
2	tablespoons chopped Thai salted preserved radish (optional)
¼	cup chopped unsalted roasted peanuts, plus extra for garnish
3	cups bean sprouts (about 6 ounces)
5	scallions, green parts only, sliced thin on the bias (see page 505)
¼	cup loosely packed fresh cilantro leaves (optional)
I	lime, cut into wedges (for serving)

1. FOR THE SAUCE: Following the instructions on page 479, soak and rehydrate the tamarind paste in the boiling water until softened, about 10 minutes. Push the tamarind mixture through a fine-mesh strainer into a medium bowl to remove the seeds and fibers and extract as much pulp as possible. Stir in the remaining sauce ingredients and set aside.

2. FOR THE NOODLES, SHRIMP, AND GARNISH: Bring 4 quarts of water to a boil in a large pot. Remove the boiling water from the heat, add the rice noodles, and let stand, stirring occasionally, until the noodles are tender, about 10 minutes. Drain the noodles and set aside.

3. Heat 1 tablespoon of the oil in a 12-inch non-stick skillet over high heat until just smoking. Add the shrimp, sprinkle with ⅛ teaspoon salt, and cook, stirring occasionally, until the shrimp are opaque and browned around the edges, about 3 minutes. Transfer the shrimp to a plate and set aside.

4. Add the remaining tablespoon oil, shallot, garlic, and ⅛ teaspoon salt to the skillet, return to medium heat, and cook, stirring constantly, until light golden brown, about 1½ minutes. Stir in the eggs and cook, stirring constantly, until scrambled and barely moist, about 20 seconds.

5. Add the drained rice noodles, dried shrimp (if using), and salted radish (if using), and toss to combine. Add the sauce, increase the heat to high, and cook, tossing constantly, until the noodles are evenly coated, about 1 minute.

6. Add the cooked shrimp, peanuts, bean sprouts, and all but ¼ cup of the scallions and continue to cook, tossing constantly, until the noodles are tender, about 2½ minutes. (If not yet tender, add 2 tablespoons water to the skillet and continue to cook until tender.) Transfer the noodles to a serving platter, sprinkle with the reserved ¼ cup scallions, cilantro (if using) and additional peanuts. Serve immediately with the lime wedges.

➤ VARIATION

Pad Thai with Tofu

Tofu is a good and common addition to pad thai.

Add 4 ounces of extra-firm or pressed tofu, cut into ½-inch cubes (about 1 cup), to the skillet along with the cooked shrimp in step 6.

FRIED RICE
Nasi Goreng

IN INDONESIA AND MALAYSIA, FRIED RICE, or *nasi goreng*, is all about contrast of flavors (salty and sweet) and textures (raw and cooked). It is fried with a simple mixture of shallots, garlic, and chiles and served with a sprinkling of raw scallions, fried shallots, raw cucumber, and tomato slices. But the key to its flavor is a sweet soy sauce called kecap manis (pronounced "ketchup"—that's where the English word comes from). In Indonesia this dish is often eaten for breakfast with a fried egg on top or with satay (see page 475).

Fried rice was originally a way to use leftover rice. But since we don't usually have leftover rice on hand, we decided to experiment with making the dish from freshly cooked, still-warm rice. It was a disaster. The grains gelled together in large clumps and the whole dish was very wet. Freshly cooked rice that was then allowed to cool to room temperature fared much better. But we had the most success with rice that had been cooked and then chilled in the refrigerator overnight. The grains remained distinct and evenly coated with oil and the overall dish was much drier. Since this should be a simple dish, we didn't want to have to plan ahead to make it. Could we avoid the overnight refrigeration and still get good results? We spread the cooked rice on a baking sheet to cool it down to room temperature rapidly and

then fried the rice. The resulting fried rice was dry with minimal clumps, making this method a great option for cooks who want to make fried rice as quickly as possible from freshly cooked rice. (That said, leftover rice is still the best option.)

We tested various types of rice, including extra-long-, long-, medium-, and short-grain. (Don't try making fried rice with store-bought rice that has been precooked, parboiled, or converted. These processed rices become soggy and wet and the grains quickly begin to break down and disintegrate during frying.) Long-grain rice worked best and we chose to use jasmine rice since its fragrant flavor is similar to the rice commonly used in Indonesia and Malaysia. However, any long-grain rice will work.

Because there are very few ingredients in fried rice, it was particularly important that we found the right balance of flavors. This rice gets most of its flavor from the hefty amount of aromatics—a combination of cooked shallots and garlic, raw scallions, and fried shallots. The latter is a condiment that appears on tables and dishes across Southeast Asia. After testing various amounts we settled on four garlic cloves, four shallots, three fried shallots, and four scallions.

The odd thing about fried rice is that it's not truly fried. When food is fried, it is cooked in a large amount of fat, usually enough to cover the food. What we call fried rice is actually pan-fried or sautéed, which means it is cooked over relatively high heat in a much smaller amount of fat (in this case, oil). We needed to figure out exactly how much oil would be necessary and we knew that the pan we used would determine the amount. Because we wanted to make a large quantity of fried rice, we limited our testing to 12-inch skillets (nonstick and regular) and a 14-inch wok.

The wok held plenty of rice, but the sloped sides and small 6-inch bottom allowed only a small portion of the rice to cook at one time. The wok also required a great deal of oil. The rice on the bottom continually absorbed what was added. The flat surface of the skillet provided a larger cooking area and the rice sautéed more quickly and evenly. Choosing between regular and nonstick was easy.

The regular skillet required much more oil to keep the rice from sticking, making the dish greasy. We preferred the nonstick skillet for the lighter rice it produced.

Even using a nonstick pan, we found that a moderate amount of oil—nearly ¼ cup—was required to keep the rice grains separate. Too little oil caused the rice grains to clump together during sautéing.

Topped with a fried egg and a sprinkling of vegetables (fried shallots, scallions, and some thick

---

FRIED SHALLOTS

FRIED SHALLOTS ARE A POPULAR CONDIMENT across Southeast Asia. They are often homemade, but are also available for sale already fried. We purchased several brands from an Asian grocery and they varied from stale to rancid—none of them was good enough to eat. We decided that we needed to make our own, and keep it simple. They are a great addition to several dishes in this chapter, especially Indonesian Fried Rice (page 483).

Fried Shallots
MAKES 1 CUP

Be sure to remove the shallots from the skillet as they begin to turn golden; they will continue to brown and crisp as they cool.

½   cup vegetable oil
3   large shallots, peeled and sliced thin
     Salt

Cook the oil and shallots in a medium saucepan over high heat, stirring constantly, until the shallots are golden and crisp, about 8 minutes (they will still be soft; do not overcook). Using a slotted spoon, transfer the shallots to a paper towel–lined plate, season with salt, and let drain and turn crisp, about 5 minutes, before serving. (Once cooled, the fried shallots can be stored in an airtight container at room temperature for up to 3 days.)

slices of cucumbers and tomatoes for color and texture), we had a fried rice that was simple to prepare and full of flavor.

Indonesian Fried Rice
Nasi Goreng
SERVES 4

To rinse the rice, you can either place it in a fine-mesh strainer and rinse under cool water or place it in a medium bowl and repeatedly fill the bowl with water while swishing the rice around, then carefully drain off the water. In either case, you must rinse until the water runs clear. Adjust the spiciness of this dish by including the minced ribs and seeds from the chiles.

3⅓   cups water
2½   cups jasmine, basmati, or other long-grain
       white rice, rinsed (see note)
6   fresh Thai, serrano, or jalapeño chiles, seeds
       and ribs removed, chiles minced (see note)
4   large shallots, peeled and quartered
4   medium garlic cloves, peeled
6   tablespoons vegetable oil
¼   cup sweet soy sauce (see page 481), plus
       extra for serving
       Salt
1   medium cucumber, peeled, halved lengthwise,
       and sliced ½ inch thick
2   large plum tomatoes, cored and sliced into
       ½-inch-thick rounds
4   large eggs, cracked into 2 small bowls (2 eggs
       per bowl)
       Ground black pepper
4   medium scallions, sliced thin
1   recipe Fried Shallots (optional, see page 482)

1. Bring the water and rice to a boil in a large Dutch oven over high heat. Reduce the heat to low, cover, and cook until all the water has been absorbed, about 15 minutes. Remove the pot from the heat and let it sit, covered, until the rice is tender, about 15 minutes. Spread the cooked rice out over a baking sheet and let cool to room temperature, about 30 minutes. (The rice can be transferred to an airtight

container and refrigerated for up to 24 hours.)

2. Meanwhile, pulse the chiles, shallots, and garlic together in a food processor to a coarse paste, about 15 pulses, stopping to scrape down the sides of the bowl as needed; set aside.

3. Break up any large clumps of cooled rice with your fingers. Heat ¼ cup of the oil in a 12-inch nonstick skillet over medium heat until just shimmering. Add the processed chile mixture and cook until the shallots become translucent and the moisture evaporates, 3 to 5 minutes. Increase the heat to medium-high and add the rice, sweet soy sauce, and 1½ teaspoons salt. Cook, stirring constantly to break up any rice clumps, until the rice is heated through and evenly coated, about 5 minutes.

4. Portion the rice onto individual plates and garnish with the cucumber and tomatoes. Wipe the skillet clean with a wad of paper towels, add the remaining 2 tablespoons oil to the skillet, and return to medium-high heat until shimmering. Following the illustration on page 293, quickly add the eggs to the skillet. Season the eggs with salt and pepper, cover, and cook until the whites are set but the yolks are still runny, 2 to 3 minutes.

5. Uncover the eggs and remove from the heat. Carefully slide one egg over each plate of rice. Sprinkle with the scallions and fried shallots (if using) and serve.

Homemade Sweet Soy Sauce
Kecap Manis
MAKES ABOUT ½ CUP

½   cup sugar
¼   cup soy sauce
¼   cup water

Bring all of the ingredients to a simmer in a small saucepan over medium-high heat and cook, stirring often, until the sugar dissolves and the sauce has thickened to the consistency of syrup, about 5 minutes. (The sauce can be refrigerated in an airtight container for up to 1 month.)

THAI CURRY

Gaeng

LIKE MOST THAI FOOD, THAI CURRIES EMBRACE a delicate balance of tastes, textures, temperatures, and colors that come together to create a harmonious whole. Thai curries (basically any spicy stew is called a curry in Thailand) are considered signature dishes of this cuisine. They almost always contain coconut milk, which not only blends and carries flavors but also forms the base of the sauce. The balance is tilted toward aromatics, which are added in the form of a paste and usually consist of garlic, ginger, shallots, lemon grass, kaffir lime leaves, shrimp paste, and chiles. These curry pastes can be quite involved and may require an hour of preparation. The curries themselves come together rather quickly and gently simmer for a short amount of time.

In many recipes, curry paste is only used in small amounts so store-bought paste is a good option, but here it is the backbone of the dish and the difference in flavor is well worth the time and effort to prepare it from scratch. We set out to explore the two most common types of Thai curries: green curry and red curry. We wanted to understand the basic structure of these dishes and figure out ways to make them—and all their hard-to-find ingredients—accessible to the American home cook. In doing so, we would need to find substitutes for some ingredients, such as kaffir lime leaves and shrimp paste, which are not readily available in most American supermarkets.

Our work was divided into three neat areas: developing recipes for the pastes; cooking the pastes to draw out their flavor; and incorporating the protein into the curry. We started with the pastes.

Thai curry pastes are intensely flavored. They are used in stir-fries, soups, and sauces as well as curries. Traditionally, ingredients are pounded together in a mortar and pestle to form a smooth paste. Since this process can take up to an hour and requires a tool most American cooks don't own, we wanted to develop paste recipes that could be assembled by other means. We tested a blender and a food processor, but the lack of liquid in the curry paste presented a problem. The solution was to add some liquid. Once the liquid was added the blender became our preferred paste maker.

Focusing first on green curry, we noted that fresh green Thai chiles are the basis for most green curry pastes. These tiny chiles are less than an inch long and offer an intriguing balance of heat and floral flavors. They can be difficult to find so we tested several substitutions and found that serranos and jalapeños are the best candidates.

Shallots, garlic, and ginger are constants in most curry pastes. After testing various ratios, we concluded that green curry paste was best with high amounts of garlic as well as a generous dose of ginger to achieve the right balance of flavors.

Toasted and ground coriander seeds, as well as fresh coriander root, are other common additions to curry pastes. We found that cilantro leaves (the name commonly used for the leaves of the coriander plant) are too moist and floral to use as a substitute for the roots but that cilantro stems are fine. The stems are fairly dry and have a pungent, earthy flavor that's similar to the roots.

Lemon grass is an essential ingredient to Thai curry and we were happy to discover that it is relatively easy to find. We did find a substitute for galangal, a rhizome related to ginger that's both peppery and sour: A combination of fresh ginger and lime juice added the necessary hot and sour notes in this instance. We found that adding the lime juice directly to the finished curry rather than to the curry paste best preserves its flavor.

Kaffir lime leaves have a clean, floral aroma. Many tasters compare it with lemon verbena and we found that lime zest approximates this flavor.

Shrimp paste—a puree of salted, fermented shrimp and other seasonings—adds a salty, fishy note to Thai curry pastes. Since this ingredient is very hard to find, we searched for substitutes. Anchovy paste was a reasonable solution, but adding fish sauce directly to the curry is traditional and adds the same kind of subtle fishy flavor. (See page 467 for more information on fish sauce.)

With our green curry paste ingredients in order, we turned our attention to the red curry paste. Red curry paste relies on a similar assortment of ingredients as green curry paste, although dried red Thai chiles, rather than fresh, are used.

(Though dried red Thai chiles are traditional, japónes and de árbol chiles work well too.) The dried chiles are usually soaked in hot water until softened. We found that we could get more flavor out of the chiles if we toasted them and then tossed them in the blender dry instead of soaking (they rehydrate with the moisture in the blender). We found that pastes made with dried chiles alone seemed thin. A mixture of toasted dried chiles and fresh red jalapeños provided a more satisfying combination of flavor and body.

We were now satisfied with the base flavors for our green and red curry pastes, but we needed a liquid component to blend all the ingredients together to form a paste. In our research, we ran across three different liquids typically used: coconut milk, the thick coconut cream that floats to the top of cans of coconut milk, and oil. We added each one to a blender with the other curry ingredients to determine which would form the smoothest paste. The coconut milk subdued the potent flavors of the curry paste. Coconut cream, though flavorful, resulted in a separated final sauce. In addition, some tasters found it too rich in the finished dish. The paste made with oil was smooth and the oil didn't separate to the top of the finished sauce, nor did it compete with the other curry flavors. But we had to use a fair amount of oil to achieve a smooth paste. By adding some water, we were able to reduce the amount of oil to 2 tablespoons, resulting in a less greasy sauce. The flavors of the curry now came through strong and clear.

Moving on to the other components of the dish—the meat and vegetables—we decided to use chicken for our master recipe and offer beef and shrimp as variations. Common additions for vegetables include pea eggplant, breadfruit, bamboo shoots, young jackfruit, banana blossoms, and pumpkin tendrils. All except the bamboo shoots were difficult to find and none of us were keen on the addition of canned bamboo shoots. We had noted that it wasn't unusual to have a curry with only protein, especially with such a hefty amount of fresh herbs added at the end. Indeed, tasters liked the simplicity of the chicken-only curries.

With the meat decided upon, we looked at the cooking method. Adding water to the paste mixture (along with a little fish sauce and brown sugar) after it cooked was the best option. The water was flavored by the paste and the chicken, which was poached directly in the water. We tested cutting the chicken in different shapes, but tasters unanimously preferred shredded chicken. This was simple enough to achieve; we removed the chicken once it was fully cooked, and set it aside to cool before shredding it with two forks. Then we returned the chicken to the sauce, finishing it with coconut milk for a luxuriously smooth texture. Shrimp is a quick and easy substitute for the chicken, requiring just a few minutes of simmering time to cook through. And for our beef variation, we found blade steak to be our best option—it lends itself well to the cooking method, which is essentially a braise, and remains tender and flavorful.

Once the curry was finished, a final garnish of fresh Thai basil, cilantro, and lime juice completed the dish. Thai curries are saucy and hot and require a nice cushion of rice. Jasmine rice is the most traditional option, but regular long-grain rice works fine.

Green Thai Curry with Chicken

Gaeng Kheow Wan Gai

SERVES 4

We strongly prefer the flavor of Thai chiles here; however, serrano and jalapeño chiles are decent substitutes. Adjust the spiciness of this dish by including the minced ribs and seeds from the chiles. We like to use large chicken breasts here because they fit more easily into the skillet; if your chicken breasts are smaller, their cooking time will be shorter. If you can't find Thai basil leaves, substitute regular basil. Serve with Simple Steamed White Rice (page 516).

CURRY PASTE

⅓ cup water

12 fresh green Thai, serrano, or jalapeño chiles, seeds and ribs removed, chiles minced (see note)

8 medium garlic cloves, peeled

2 tablespoons minced cilantro stems

1 tablespoon minced or grated fresh ginger

2 teaspoons ground coriander

1 teaspoon ground cumin

2   stalks lemon grass, bottom 5 inches only, trimmed and sliced thin (see illustrations on page 468)
2   tablespoons grated zest from 3 limes
3   medium shallots, peeled and quartered
2   tablespoons vegetable oil
1   teaspoon salt

CHICKEN
1¼   cups water
2   tablespoons fish sauce
1   tablespoon light brown sugar
1½   pounds boneless, skinless chicken breasts (about 3 large breasts), trimmed
1   (14-ounce) can coconut milk
½   cup loosely packed fresh Thai basil leaves (see note)
½   cup loosely packed fresh cilantro leaves
2   tablespoons juice from 1 lime

1. FOR THE CURRY PASTE: Process all of the curry paste ingredients together in a blender to a fine paste, about 3 minutes, stopping to scrape down the sides of the bowl as needed.

2. FOR THE CHICKEN: Cook the curry paste in a 12-inch nonstick skillet over medium-high heat, stirring often, until the paste begins to sizzle and no longer smells raw, about 2 minutes. Stir in the water, fish sauce, and sugar to combine. Add the chicken and return to a simmer. Reduce the heat to medium-low, flip the chicken over, cover, and cook until the thickest part of the chicken breasts register 160 degrees on an instant-read thermometer, 15 to 20 minutes.

3. Transfer the breasts to a plate and let cool slightly. Meanwhile, stir the coconut milk into the skillet, return the sauce to a simmer over medium heat, and cook until the sauce is thick and creamy, about 8 minutes.

4. When the chicken is cool enough to handle, shred it into bite-sized pieces using 2 forks following the illustration on page 69. Return the shredded chicken to the skillet and continue to cook until the chicken is warmed through and coated nicely by the thickened sauce, about 2 minutes. Off the heat, stir in the basil, cilantro, and lime juice and serve.

➤ VARIATIONS
Green Thai Curry with Beef
To make slicing the steak easier, freeze it for 15 minutes.

Follow the recipe for Green Thai Curry with Chicken, substituting 1½ pounds beef blade steak, gristle and fat removed (see page 487), and sliced lengthwise into ½-inch-thick pieces, for the chicken. Increase the amount of water to 2 cups in step 2 and simmer the beef, covered, until tender, about 40 minutes. When the beef is tender, stir in the coconut milk and continue to simmer, uncovered, until the sauce is thick and creamy, about 10 minutes. Stir in the herbs and lime juice as directed in step 4.

Green Thai Curry with Shrimp
Follow the recipe for Green Thai Curry with Chicken, omitting the chicken. Add the coconut milk with the water in step 2 and simmer the sauce, uncovered, until creamy and thickened, about 10 minutes. Stir in 1 pound medium shrimp (40 to 50 per pound), peeled and deveined, and continue to simmer until the shrimp are fully cooked, about 5 minutes. Stir in the herbs and lime juice as directed in step 4.

Red Thai Curry with Chicken
Gaeng Ped Gai
SERVES 4

If you can't find fresh red jalapeño chiles, you can substitute green jalapeños but the color of the sauce will turn slightly muddy. For more information on toasting dried chiles, see page 37. We like to use large chicken breasts here because they fit more easily into the skillet; if your chicken breasts are smaller, their cooking time will be shorter. If you can't find Thai basil, substitute regular basil. Serve with Simple Steamed White Rice (page 516).

CURRY PASTE
8   dried red chiles, such as Thai, japónes, or de árbol
⅓   cup water
4   medium shallots, peeled and quartered
2   stalks lemon grass, bottom 5 inches only, trimmed and sliced thin (see the illustrations on page 468)

6   medium garlic cloves, peeled
1   medium red jalapeño chile, seeds and ribs
    removed (see note)
2   tablespoons minced cilantro stems
2   tablespoons vegetable oil
1   tablespoon grated zest from 1 lime
2   teaspoons ground coriander
1   teaspoon ground cumin
1   teaspoon minced or grated fresh ginger
1   teaspoon tomato paste
1   teaspoon salt

CHICKEN
1¼ cups water
2   tablespoons fish sauce
1   tablespoon light brown sugar
1½ pounds boneless, skinless chicken breasts
    (about 3 large breasts), trimmed
1   (14-ounce) can coconut milk
½   cup loosely packed fresh Thai basil leaves
    (see note)
½   cup loosely packed fresh cilantro leaves
2   tablespoons juice from 1 lime

1. FOR THE CURRY PASTE: Adjust an oven rack to the middle position and heat the oven to 350 degrees. Place the dry red chiles on a baking sheet and toast them in the oven until fragrant and puffed, about 5 minutes. Remove the chiles from the oven and let cool. When cool enough to handle, seed and stem the chiles, then break them into small pieces.

2. Blend the chile pieces with the remaining curry paste ingredients in a blender to a fine paste, about 3 minutes, stopping to scrape down the sides of the bowl as needed.

3. FOR THE CHICKEN: Cook the curry paste in a 12-inch nonstick skillet over medium-high heat, stirring often, until the paste begins to sizzle and no longer smells raw, about 2 minutes. Stir in the water, fish sauce, and sugar to combine. Add the chicken and return to a simmer. Reduce the heat to medium-low, flip the chicken over, cover, and cook until the thickest part of the chicken breasts register 160 degrees on an instant-read thermometer, 15 to 20 minutes.

4. Transfer the breasts to a plate and let cool slightly. Meanwhile, stir the coconut milk into the skillet, return the sauce to a simmer over medium heat, and cook until the sauce is thick and creamy, about 8 minutes.

5. When the chicken is cool enough to handle, shred it into bite-sized pieces using 2 forks following the illustration on page 69. Return the shredded chicken to the skillet and continue to cook until the chicken is warmed through and coated nicely by the thickened sauce, about 2 minutes. Off the heat, stir in the basil, cilantro, and lime juice and serve.

➤ VARIATIONS

Red Thai Curry with Beef
To make slicing the steak easier, freeze it for 15 minutes.

Follow the recipe for Red Thai Curry with Chicken, substituting 1½ pounds beef blade steak, gristle and fat removed (see below), and sliced lengthwise into ½-inch-thick pieces, for the chicken. Increase the amount of water to 2 cups in step 3 and simmer the beef, covered, until tender, about 40 minutes. When the beef is tender, stir in the coconut milk and continue to simmer until the sauce is thick and creamy, about 10 minutes. Stir in the herbs and lime juice as directed in step 5.

TRIMMING BLADE STEAKS

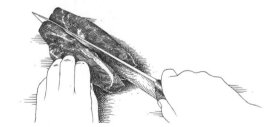

1. Halve each steak lengthwise, leaving the gristle on one half.

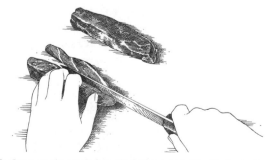

2. Cut away the gristle from the half to which it is still attached.

Red Thai Curry with Shrimp
Follow the recipe for Red Thai Curry with Chicken, omitting the chicken. Add the coconut milk with the water in step 3 and simmer the sauce, uncovered, until creamy and thickened, about 10 minutes. Stir in 1 pound medium shrimp (40 to 50 per pound), peeled and deveined, and continue to simmer until the shrimp are fully cooked, about 5 minutes. Stir in the herbs and lime juice as directed in step 5.

SPICY CHICKEN WITH BASIL

Gai Pad Bai Ga-Prow

CONSIDERED PEASANT FOOD IN THAILAND, *gai pad bai ga-prow* is a simple, flavorful, and satisfying meal. Similar to a stir-fry, this dish consists of spicy, quickly cooked ground chicken and lots of fragrant Thai basil, served over white rice and sometimes topped with a fried egg.

To start, we noted that ground chicken is sold in a variety of textures, from finely ground to coarsely processed. The finely ground chicken was easy to break into small, bite-sized pieces as it cooked. Coarsely ground chicken developed an unappetizing wormlike texture as it cooked. We recommend buying finely ground chicken if you can find it, but either way we found it best to smash the raw chicken with the back of a spoon before cooking to ensure that it is broken down into small pieces. We also wondered if mincing the ground chicken further in the food processor or processing whole chicken breasts would result in a better texture. The processed chicken breasts cooked into dry little morsels, while the advantage of the processed ground chicken was insignificant. We stuck with our smashed ground chicken and also made sure that we continued to break it into small pieces as it cooked.

Most recipes we researched called for similar flavorings, including fish sauce, lime juice, garlic, shallots, and chiles. Taking a cue from our curry pastes (see page 484) we decided to simplify the preparation of this dish by tossing the chiles, garlic,

and shallots in the food processor to mince. We then cooked this mixture until fragrant before adding the chicken.

This sauce is composed mostly of fish sauce and we found that ⅓ cup for 2 pounds of meat was ideal. The fish sauce enhances the flavor of the meat and is nicely tempered by a few tablespoons of sugar and 3 cups of fragrant Thai basil. While this dish traditionally doesn't have more than a drizzle of liquid, some tasters wanted a bit more sauce for their rice. When we raised the amount of fish sauce, the sauce became too salty and wasn't thick enough. To rectify this we went back to the original amount of fish sauce and supplemented it with ⅓ cup chicken stock, along with 1 teaspoon of cornstarch to thicken it. This gave us just enough sauce to flavor the rice without its flavor dominating the overall dish. We tried adding a fried egg as a finishing touch, but tasters felt this was unnecessary for such a simple dish. A dash of lime juice added just before serving was all it needed.

Spicy Chicken with Basil
Gai Pad Bai Ga-Prow
SERVES 4

Do not overcook the chicken or it will taste very dry. Most packages of ground chicken include both light and dark meat; if given the choice, use all dark meat because it is much more flavorful and less prone to drying out. Adjust the spiciness of this dish by including the minced ribs and seeds from the chiles. If you can't find Thai basil, substitute regular basil. Serve with Simple Steamed White Rice (page 516).

10	fresh Thai, serrano, or jalapeño chiles, seeds and ribs removed
8	medium garlic cloves, peeled
6	shallots, peeled
⅓	cup fish sauce
⅓	cup low-sodium chicken broth
3	tablespoons sugar
1	teaspoon cornstarch
2	pounds ground chicken (see note)
3	tablespoons vegetable oil
3	cups loosely packed fresh Thai basil leaves (see note)
3	tablespoons juice from 2 limes

1. Pulse the chiles, garlic, and shallots together in a food processor to a coarse paste, about 15 pulses, stopping to scrape down the sides of the bowl as needed; set aside. In a small bowl, whisk the fish sauce, chicken broth, sugar, and cornstarch together; set aside.

2. In a medium bowl, mash the ground chicken using the back of a spoon until smooth and no strand-like pieces of meat remain.

3. Heat the oil in a 12-inch nonstick skillet over medium-high heat until just shimmering. Add the processed chile mixture and cook until the shallots become translucent and the moisture evaporates, 3 to 5 minutes. Reduce the heat to medium, add the chicken, and cook, breaking up the meat with a wooden spoon, until it is no longer pink, about 7 minutes.

4. Sprinkle the basil leaves evenly over the chicken. Whisk the fish sauce mixture to recombine, then add it to the skillet and cook, stirring constantly, until the sauce has thickened, about 3 minutes. Stir in the lime juice, then transfer to a serving platter and serve.

Thai Chile Beef

Neua Pad Prik

BASED ON A SOPHISTICATED COMBINATION of four flavors—spicy, sweet, sour, and salty—Thai chile beef promises to be vastly more interesting than most everyday stir-fries. According to our recipe research, this simple transformation would be built on a foundation of just four ingredients: chiles, sugar, lime juice, and fish sauce.

We set out with high hopes, rounding up and testing cookbook recipes and even ordering Thai chile beef from three neighborhood restaurants. The net result of all this tasting and testing, however, was disappointment—with one notable exception. One "authentic" Thai recipe produced a wonderful dish. It contained no vegetables (restaurants frequently add vegetables to reduce the cost per serving) and the meat was sauced in a thick, complex, well-balanced chile jam. The problem?

For starters, the ingredient list, which contained dried prawns, shrimp paste, tamarind pulp, galangal, and palm sugar. And then there was the three-hour prep time, which involved deep-frying many of the ingredients separately. While we had tasted the ultimate Thai chile beef, we had to wonder how we could possibly re-create it for an American home kitchen.

We started with the key ingredient: the beef. We stirfried four easy-to-find cuts (filet, sirloin steak, strip steak, and blade steak) and compared them with our usual choice, flank steak.

The flank steak fared well, as expected. Mild filet, the choice in several recipes, could not stand up to the assertive Thai flavors. Sirloin and strip steaks both fared poorly because stir-fried meats tend to end up thoroughly cooked, making these cuts chewy and dry. The cheapest cut of all, the blade steak, was the surprise winner of the tasting. Generally, beef with the biggest flavor is tough, but blade steak is an exception. Cut from the chuck—the forequarter of the animal—this inexpensive, well-marbled cut delivered more than enough flavor to stand up to its spicy competition.

Salty, fermented fish sauce is a traditional ingredient in Thai chile beef—it seasons and tenderizes the meat. The fish sauce simulated the briny flavors of the dried shrimp and shrimp paste listed in the original recipe, but something was missing. We dug deeper into a few Thai cookbooks and discovered that white pepper is a key ingredient—and for good reason. It is deeply spicy and penetrating. We added a smidgen (a little goes a long way) to the marinade, along with citrusy coriander. This was a huge hit with tasters and substantially boosted the complexity and sophistication of the dish, even though the meat was marinated for a mere 15 minutes.

We also added some of the sweet element in this dish to the marinade as a strategy for developing extra caramelization on the beef. Palm sugar is the traditional sweetener used in Thai cooking, but we found light brown sugar to be a perfect substitute. A mere teaspoon was just the right amount; any more caused scorching.

Thai chiles are the classic choice for this recipe,

but they can be difficult to find. A taste test suggested that moderately hot serranos or milder jalapeños are the best stand-ins. (Insanely hot habanero chiles, tasting of tropical fruit, were admired by some but panned by most, who found the heat level punishing.)

After settling on the chiles, a new problem emerged: wild inconsistency in heat levels. Using a constant number of jalapeños, some stir-fries were flaming hot, while others didn't even send up sparks. We came up with a straightforward solution that can be used in any recipe calling for chiles. The trick is to use not one but two sources of heat, one of which is easily controlled (unlike fresh chiles). We tested cayenne and hot red pepper flakes and both produced likeable results, but the winner was Thai chili-garlic sauce, which provided a complex mix of flavors—spicy, toasty, and garlicky.

The last step in a stir-fry is to deglaze the hot pan with sauce ingredients. After many trials, we realized the importance of reintroducing every member of the Thai quartet at this stage. Adding fish sauce and brown sugar to the marinade boosted flavor, but the inclusion of both in the sauce really punched up the finished dish. For the sour component, both rice vinegar and tamarind paste fared better than lime juice—less acidity and more sweetness brought us closer to our goal of balanced flavors. We settled on rice vinegar because we usually keep it in our pantry.

The only remaining considerations were the fresh, raw ingredients added just before serving. Thai basil is traditional, contributing freshness and adding a cooling counterpoint to the chiles. We also added chopped peanuts for crunch. A squirt of fresh lime juice at the table was the final touch.

Thai Chile Beef
Neua Pad Prik
SERVES 4

To make slicing the steak easier, freeze it for 15 minutes. If you cannot find blade steak, substitute 1¾ pounds of flank steak; see the illustrations on page 516 for how to cut flank steak for a stir-fry. If you can't find Thai basil leaves, substitute regular basil. Serve with Simple Steamed White Rice (page 516).

SAUCE

2   tablespoons fish sauce
2   tablespoons rice vinegar
2   tablespoons water
1   tablespoon light brown sugar
1   tablespoon Thai chili-garlic sauce, such as sriracha (see page 561)

STIR-FRY

1   tablespoon fish sauce
1   teaspoon light brown sugar
¾   teaspoon ground coriander
⅛   teaspoon ground white pepper
2   pounds blade steaks, trimmed of gristle and fat (see page 487), and sliced crosswise on the bias into ¼-inch-thick pieces
3   medium garlic cloves, minced or pressed through a garlic press (about 1 tablespoon)
3   tablespoons vegetable oil
3   fresh Thai, serrano, or jalapeño chiles, halved lengthwise, seeded, and sliced crosswise ⅛ inch thick
3   medium shallots, trimmed of ends, peeled, quartered lengthwise, and layers separated
½   cup loosely packed fresh Thai basil leaves (see note)
½   cup loosely packed fresh cilantro leaves
⅓   cup coarsely chopped roasted unsalted peanuts
1   lime, cut into wedges (for serving)

1. FOR THE SAUCE: Whisk all of the ingredients together; set aside.

2. FOR THE STIR-FRY: Whisk the fish sauce, sugar, coriander, and pepper together in a small bowl. Add the beef, toss to coat, and let marinate for 10 minutes or up to 1 hour. In a separate bowl, mix the garlic with 1 teaspoon of the oil; set aside.

3. Heat 2 more teaspoons oil in a 12-inch non-stick skillet over high heat until just smoking. Add one-third of the beef, breaking up any clumps, then cook without stirring until well browned, about 2 minutes. Stir the meat and continue to cook until it is nearly cooked through, about 30 seconds. Transfer the beef to a medium bowl and repeat with 4 more teaspoons oil and the remaining beef in two batches; transfer to the bowl and set aside.

4. Add the remaining 2 teaspoons oil to the skillet and return to medium heat until shimmering. Add the chiles and shallots and cook, stirring frequently, until beginning to soften, about 3 minutes. Clear the center of the skillet, add the garlic mixture, and cook, mashing the mixture into the pan, until fragrant, 15 to 20 seconds. Stir the garlic mixture into the vegetables.

5. Add the fish sauce mixture to the skillet, increase the heat to high, and cook until slightly reduced and thickened, about 30 seconds. Stir in the beef with any accumulated juices and toss well to combine and coat with the sauce. Stir in half of the basil and cilantro, then transfer to a serving platter. Garnish individual servings with the peanuts and remaining herbs and serve with lime wedges.

SIZZLING SAIGON CRÊPES

Banh Xeo

NAMED FOR THE SOUND THESE CRÊPES MAKE when the batter is poured over a hot wok, sizzling Saigon crêpes could be described as Vietnamese paper-thin omelets. These crispy yellow crêpes, stuffed with shrimp, pork, and bean sprouts, are wrapped in lettuce and herbs and dipped in a sweet-tart dipping sauce. Originally a southern Vietnamese dish, this specialty is now found across the country. With recipes in hand, we headed to the kitchen with the hopes of finding a way to create this popular street food at home.

The batter is made with rice flour, but we found a few recipes that called for adding a bit of self-rising flour and all-purpose flour. We quickly discovered that crêpes made with self-rising and all-purpose flour were gummy and lacked the ultra-crisp texture we wanted. Using only rice flour was going to be key to achieving the proper texture.

The liquid component of the batter also played an important role in achieving a crisp crêpe. Most recipes called for a combination of coconut milk and water, but we also found recipes that used only water. We tested using only coconut milk,

only water, and a combination of the two. The all-coconut-milk crêpes had good flavor, but they were too greasy and barely crisp. The water-only crêpes were the crispest of all, almost cracker-like, but they tasted bland. A combination of the two was clearly the winner for both its subtle coconut flavor and its crisp exterior. After more testing we found the right balance of flavor and crispness with ½ cup coconut milk and 2 cups water.

These crêpes usually get their trademark yellow color from turmeric, but some recipes add curry powder instead of or in addition to the turmeric. We tested each spice alone as well as in combination. While the curry powder crêpes tasted nice on their own, tasters thought the curry's pungent flavor overpowered the dipping sauce. They also felt that it lacked the distinctive bright yellow color expected from these crêpes. Turmeric would flavor and color our batter.

Sizzling Saigon crêpes are filled with pork, shrimp, a sprinkling of scallions, and an abundance of bean sprouts. The meat is usually cooked right into the crêpe, and then the bean sprouts are piled in the center of the cooked crêpe. We chose large shrimp and, after a couple of tests, found that slicing them in half lengthwise helped to distribute them more evenly throughout the crêpe. For the pork we tested pork chops, loins, tenderloins, and ground pork. While all were suitable, we focused on the cuts that were available in small amounts: pork chops and ground pork. After tasting the two side by side we found that we preferred the ground pork because the small pieces got crisp and caramelized as they cooked. These crêpes are usually bursting with bean sprouts, but tasters felt that their presence was a bit overwhelming. With a nod to tradition we settled on a generous but manageable ½ cup per crêpe.

The next hurdle was determining how to fold the crêpes properly. These crêpes were so thin that they kept breaking under the weight of the meat cooked into them. None of the recipes we had come across during our research mentioned this problem, nor did any of them offer a special cooking method. Finally, after one particularly frustrating crêpe-folding test, a colleague suggested moving all of the meat to one side of the pan. The idea was brilliant and we placed all of the meat on the side of the pan closest to us before pouring the batter over it. This meant that the side of the crêpe we folded over the top of the bean sprouts was light and there was no meat to prevent an even seam.

Sliding the crêpes onto individual plates was the least risky way to get them from pan to plate without breaking them. We kept the finished crêpes warm in a 200-degree oven while we cooked the rest of them. Finished with a simple dipping sauce and lettuce, basil, and cilantro for garnish, they made a simple and satisfying meal. We found it best to give everyone their own bowl of sauce for dipping and then pass the lettuce and herbs around on a large serving platter.

Sizzling Saigon Crêpes
Banh Xeo
SERVES 6 AS A MAIN COURSE

Rice flour is available at some supermarkets, but can also be found in natural foods stores; you cannot substitute regular flour or cornstarch for the rice flour. Make sure to stir the coconut milk thoroughly to combine before measuring out the desired amount. Adjust the spiciness of this dish by including the minced ribs and seeds from the chiles. If you can't find Thai basil leaves, substitute regular basil.

DRESSING AND GARNISH

- ⅓ cup fish sauce
- ¼ cup warm water
- 3 tablespoons juice from 2 limes
- 2 tablespoons sugar
- 2 fresh Thai, serrano, or jalapeño chiles, seeds and ribs removed, chiles minced (see note)
- 1 medium garlic clove, minced or pressed through a garlic press (about 1 teaspoon)
- 2 heads red or green leaf lettuce, washed and dried, leaves separated and left whole
- 1 cup loosely packed fresh Thai basil leaves (see note)
- 1 cup loosely packed fresh cilantro leaves

CRÊPES

- 2 cups water
- 1¾ cups rice flour (see note)
- ½ cup coconut milk
- 4 medium scallions, sliced thin
- 1 teaspoon ground turmeric
- ½ teaspoon salt
- 5 tablespoons vegetable oil
- ½ pound ground pork
- 1 small onion, halved and sliced thin
- ½ pound large shrimp (31 to 40 per pound), peeled, deveined, and sliced in half lengthwise
- 3 cups bean sprouts

1. FOR THE DRESSING AND GARNISH: Whisk the fish sauce, water, lime juice, sugar, chiles, and garlic together in a small bowl until the sugar dissolves, then divide among 6 small dipping bowls and set aside. Arrange the lettuce, basil, and cilantro on a serving platter and set aside.

2. FOR THE CRÊPES: Adjust 2 oven racks to the upper- and lower-middle positions and heat the

PREPARING SIZZLING SAIGON CRÊPES

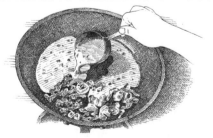

1. After quickly reheating the meat mixture, push it evenly over half of the skillet. Pour ½ cup of the batter into the skillet while swirling the pan gently to distribute it evenly over the pan bottom. Reduce the heat to medium and cook the crêpe until the edges pull away from the sides and are deep golden, about 2 minutes.

2. Once the crêpe is cooked, sprinkle ½ cup of the bean sprouts over the pork-shrimp side of the crêpe. Run a heatproof rubber spatula around the outer edge of the crêpe to loosen it from the pan, then gently fold the empty half of the crêpe over the bean sprouts.

oven to 200 degrees. Whisk the water, rice flour, coconut milk, scallions, turmeric, and salt together until uniform.

3. Heat 1 tablespoon oil in a 12-inch nonstick skillet over medium-high heat until shimmering. Add the pork and onion and cook until the pork is no longer pink and the onion is softened, 5 to 7 minutes. Add the shrimp and continue to cook until they curl and turn pink, about 2 minutes. Transfer the mixture to a bowl and set aside.

4. Wipe out the skillet with a wad of paper towels, add 2 more teaspoons oil, and return to medium-high heat until just smoking. Add ⅓ cup of the pork-shrimp mixture and let heat through, about 30 seconds. Following the illustrations on page 492, scrape the pork-shrimp mixture to one side of the skillet. Quickly stir the batter to recombine, then pour ½ cup of the batter into the skillet while swirling the pan gently to distribute it evenly over the pan bottom. Reduce the heat to medium and cook the crêpe until the edges pull away from the sides and are deep golden, about 2 minutes.

5. Sprinkle ½ cup of bean sprouts on top of the pork-shrimp side of the crêpe, then gently fold the opposite side of the crêpe over the sprouts. Slide the crêpe out of the skillet onto an individual serving plate and transfer to the oven to keep warm. Repeat five more times with the remaining 10 teaspoons oil, remaining batter, and remaining pork-shrimp mixture. Serve the crêpes with the individual bowls of sauce, passing the garnish platter separately. (To eat, slice off a wedge of the crêpe, wrap it in a lettuce leaf, and dip it into the sauce.)

CATFISH IN SALTY-SWEET CARAMEL SAUCE

Ca Kho To

ONE OF THE MOST POPULAR SOUTHERN Vietnamese "home style" dishes is catfish simmered in a caramel sauce (*ca kho to*). Vietnamese caramel sauce is a simple caramel made from a mixture of sugar and water that cooks just until it becomes slightly bitter, at which point more water is added to create a thin, caramel-flavored liquid. The combination of catfish and sweet, salty caramel sauce is uniquely satisfying. Every Vietnamese cookbook we looked at had a recipe for it and the variations in the recipes were truly intriguing.

To get our bearings, we chose three recipes that differed in both their ingredient lists and their method of cooking. They all used a caramel of some sort, as well as fish sauce, garlic, and scallions. But the similarities ended there. The type of caramel and the process of making it was one major variance. One recipe called for making the caramel separately, and then adding it to the rest of the sauce (which was composed mostly of fish sauce and oil). Only 2 tablespoons of this caramel were added to the finished sauce (which included 2 more tablespoons of sugar!) and, while we liked the overall flavor, this technique seemed too fussy. Another approach was to make the caramel directly in the skillet in which the fish and other sauce ingredients would cook. This method left us with crystallized sugar (constant stirring of the sugar and water mixture resulted in sugar that stuck to the sides of the pan) and a dry, overly salty sauce (too much of the liquid cooked off before the fish was done). The last recipe we tried used coconut soda (found in Asian markets) that eventually reduced to a syrupy caramel as it cooked the fish. This sauce was easy, but light in flavor and lacking in complexity.

While none of these sauces was perfect, we liked the idea of making the sauce right in the pan in which the fish would cook and we wondered if we could find a way to prevent the problems of hardened sugar and not enough sauce. The other major variation in these recipes was the cooking times; some recipes cooked the fish for as little as 10 minutes while others let it go for an astonishing two hours. Realizing that we wouldn't be able to take any shortcuts with this dish (i.e., the coconut soda), we instead decided to make a basic caramel directly in the skillet using water and sugar. We tested using dark brown sugar, light brown sugar, and white sugar. Both of the brown sugars left a cloyingly sweet aftertaste and lacked complexity. We thought white sugar was clean-tasting and gave us the nutty caramel flavor we sought. To prevent the sugar from crystallizing, we poured the water into the skillet first and then gently sprinkled the sugar evenly over the water. By evenly distributing the sugar we were able to eliminate the need to stir the mixture before it caramelized, which helped keep sugar from crystallizing on the sides of the skillet.

With our caramel in place, we turned to the other ingredients in the sauce. Garlic is a common addition and tasters liked a hefty five cloves. Vegetable oil and pork fatback are the two types of fat typically used in this dish; we chose vegetable oil because every cook is likely to have it on hand and its neutral flavor doesn't compete with the caramel. We mixed the garlic with the vegetable oil, then poured the mixture into the caramel to cook and release its flavors.

The remaining question was how much fish sauce to add. Knowing that a little goes a long way, and wanting to keep the careful balance of salty and sweet that is the hallmark of this dish, we tried amounts ranging from 2 tablespoons to ½ cup. After our first round of tasting, we settled on ¼ cup fish sauce as the perfect balance to the ⅓ cup of sugar in the caramel. Our sauce was just about finished, but we decided to add a good dose of black pepper to add the spicy dimension to the sauce that had captivated us in initial recipe tests.

Finally, we focused our attention on the catfish. All of the recipes we came across called for catfish steaks with the skin on, but these aren't available in most supermarkets, so we settled upon using the more readily available skinless catfish fillets. We had found a huge span of cooking times in the recipes we researched, so we decided to test the entire range. We cooked the fish for five minutes, 30 minutes, and two hours. Contrary to years of experience cooking fish in the test kitchen, the fish cooked for two hours, while a bit mealy, was still acceptable. The fish cooked for five minutes hadn't spent enough time in the pan to acquire the flavor of the sauce, but we found that a cooking time of 25 to 30 minutes was just long enough for the sauce to thicken and for the fish to absorb the sauce's complex flavors.

Served with just a sprinkling of cilantro leaves and scallions, this dish has quickly become a new favorite in the kitchen.

Catfish in Salty-Sweet Caramel Sauce
Ca Kho To
SERVES 4 TO 6

We particularly like the flavor of catfish here; however, any thin, medium-firm white fish fillets can be substituted. For an accurate measurement of boiling water, bring a full kettle of water to boil, then measure out the desired amount. Serve with Simple Steamed White Rice (page 516).

¼	cup vegetable oil
5	medium garlic cloves, minced or pressed through a garlic press (about 5 teaspoons)
¼	cup cold water
⅓	cup sugar
2	cups boiling water (see note)
¼	cup fish sauce
1½	teaspoons ground black pepper
2	pounds boneless, skinless catfish fillets (about 5 medium fillets), sliced crosswise into 2-inch-wide pieces
1	cup loosely packed fresh cilantro leaves
3	scallions, green parts only, sliced thin on the bias (see page 505)

1. Mix the oil and garlic together in a small bowl and set aside. Pour the ¼ cup cold water into a 12-inch nonstick skillet, then sprinkle the sugar evenly into the water. Cook the water-sugar mixture over medium heat, gently swirling the pan occasionally (do not stir), until the sugar melts and the mixture turns the color of maple syrup, about 10 minutes.

2. Stir in the garlic mixture and cook until fragrant, about 30 seconds. Off the heat, slowly whisk in the 2 cups boiling water (the sauce may bubble and sizzle slightly). Return the skillet to medium heat and stir in the fish sauce and pepper.

3. Lay the catfish fillets in the skillet (without overlapping), and turn to coat evenly with the sauce. Bring to a simmer, then reduce the heat to medium-low and cook, uncovered, until the fish is tender and the sauce has thickened to a thick, syrupy consistency, about 25 minutes.

4. Transfer the fish to a platter and pour the sauce over the top. Sprinkle with the cilantro and scallions and serve.

13
CHINA

PORK AND CABBAGE DUMPLINGS

Wor Tip

ROUND OR CRESCENT-SHAPED, BOILED OR pan-fried, Chinese dumplings (or potstickers) are a traditional Chinese food, essential during holidays in northern China. The filling may be sweet or savory, vegetarian or filled with meat and vegetables. The array of dumpling types and presentations is as vast as China itself.

The variety of dumplings offered in American dim sum restaurants is vast as well and among our favorites are potstickers. At their best, these dumplings are soft, savory pillows filled with tender ground meat and crunchy cabbage spiked with a pleasing hit of garlic, ginger, and soy. Unfortunately, the usual fare is nowhere near so glorious: dense, flavorless meatballs wrapped in a doughy blanket.

Despite such grim prospects, most cooks prefer rolling the dice at a restaurant to taking on what would seem to be a grueling project at home. As we surveyed dozens of authentic potsticker recipes, however, we were surprised to find out how straightforward most were: Mix ground pork, cabbage, and seasonings; spoon it all into dumpling wrappers; then steam and fry in a wok. But time logged in the test kitchen revealed that tough fillings, bland flavors, and bad wraps are not just the bane of busy restaurants. Could we make this recipe more foolproof?

First, we needed to lighten up the filling. Ground pork has a tendency to form a dense, solid mass when it's shaped and cooked, a phenomenon test kitchen staffers dubbed "the meatball effect." One bite into the dumpling and the small, dense "meatball" hidden inside would fall out onto the plate. Not very appetizing. The scallions and cabbage folded into the pork are meant to mitigate this problem by providing moisture and textural variety, but they just weren't doing the trick. We tried increasing the amount of cabbage. Tasters loved the looser consistency of the filling but complained that the cabbage flavor and texture were too dominant. Forgoing the raw cabbage we'd been using, we tried sautéing it briefly to mellow the sharp flavor, but tasters missed the crunch. We tried salting and draining the cabbage to get rid of excess moisture, a trick we often use in the test kitchen. This approach was a winner. After a 20-minute rest in the colander, the salted cabbage no longer dominated the filling, yet it still contributed a slightly bitter, crunchy edge. Tasters continued to complain that the filling still seemed a bit hard and dense. This time we borrowed a trick from meat loaf cookery and added lightly beaten egg whites to the pork and cabbage mixture. As the meat mixture cooked, the egg whites puffed up almost like a soufflé, making the otherwise compact ground meat filling light and tender.

A thick, doughy wrapper, often encountered in restaurant versions, was out, but the wrapper had to survive the cooking process, so it couldn't be paper-thin. Two ready-made versions are widely available (we were unwilling to make wrappers from scratch). Wonton wrappers—made with flour, egg, and salt—are a bit thin for this application. We found the better choice to be gyoza wrappers. Made without egg, they are sturdier and hold up better when pan-fried. Also, the more substantial texture seemed a better match for the flavorful filling.

So far, we had been spooning the filling into

CORE TECHNIQUE

ENSURING A TIDY DUMPLING

When making small, filled dumplings such as Pork and Cabbage Dumplings (page 498) or Pierogi (page 382), we noticed that any air left between the wrapper and filling can cause "ballooning" during cooking, as the wrapper puffs up and away from the filling. The result? A messy first bite and a pocket that can trap cooking water or oil inside the dumpling. Once we were mindful to press the air out of the filling before sealing the dough, our dumplings came out perfect every time.

the center of a round gyoza wrapper, folding it in half, then pressing the edges to seal. We placed the dumplings in a hot nonstick skillet seam side up to get a crisp, browned bottom, poured in some water, covered the pan, and let them steam until soft. Finally, we removed the cover to re-crisp the bottoms.

While mostly successful, this procedure did present a problem: The seam was drying out in the final stages of cooking. We increased the steaming time, but tasters still complained of toughness. The solution was easy. Instead of sautéing the dumplings standing straight up, we knocked them on their sides so that the seam would lie against the bottom of the pan. One side became crisp, while the rest of the dumpling remained pleasantly tender and chewy.

Placing 12 dumplings in a preheated skillet takes time and burns fingertips. By the time the last dumpling was in the pan, the first one was already browned, yielding an unevenly colored batch. The answer was to place the dumplings in a cold, lightly oiled skillet before turning on the burner—success. To cook the second batch, we took the pan off the heat, wiped it out with bunched-up paper towels, and started the process again.

A few of the potstickers were not holding their filling well after steaming. While steaming one batch, we peeked under the lid and saw some of the dumplings ballooning out like blowfish. When we removed the lid, they seemed to deflate back to normal, but a few still had an air bubble trapped inside that kept the interior of the wrapper from making contact with (and clinging to) the filling. As a result, one bite would send the filling crashing down onto the plate. The solution? More diligence in removing all the air while filling the wrappers. Trying several approaches, we came up with the best sequence: Fold the meat-filled wrapper into a half-moon, pinch the middle closed, then carefully seal the remaining edges while lightly pressing the filling to ensure that no air remains.

All these dumplings needed now was the right dipping sauce—not the heavy-handed kind demanded by dumplings with ho-hum flavor but a simple, bracing blend of soy sauce, rice vinegar, mirin (a sweet Japanese wine), and toasted sesame oil, with just a touch of chili oil to kick up the heat. Now they were not only light and flavorful but virtually foolproof as well.

FILLING THE DUMPLINGS

1. Place 1 rounded tablespoon of filling in the center of a gyoza wrapper.

2. After moistening the edge of the wrapper, fold it in half to make half-moon shape. (If using square wrappers, fold diagonally into a triangle. If using rectangular wrappers, fold in half lengthwise.)

3. With forefinger and thumb, pinch dumpling closed, pressing out any air pockets.

4. Place dumpling on its side and press gently to flatten bottom.

Pork and Cabbage Dumplings
Wor Tip
MAKES 24 DUMPLINGS, SERVING 6
AS A FIRST COURSE

We prefer to use gyoza wrappers. You can substitute wonton wrappers, but the cooking time in step 4 will be reduced from 10 minutes to 5 or 6 minutes and note that the yield will increase to 40 potstickers.

FILLING

3	cups minced napa cabbage leaves (about ½ medium head)
¾	teaspoon salt
¾	pound ground pork
4	scallions, minced (about 6 tablespoons)
2	egg whites, lightly beaten
4	teaspoons soy sauce
1½	teaspoons minced or grated fresh ginger
1	medium garlic clove, minced or pressed through a garlic press (about 1 teaspoon)
⅛	teaspoon ground black pepper

DUMPLINGS

24	round gyoza wrappers (see note)
2	tablespoons vegetable oil
1	cup water, plus extra for brushing
1	recipe Scallion Dipping Sauce (recipe follows)

1. FOR THE FILLING: Toss the cabbage with the salt in a colander set over a bowl and let stand until the cabbage begins to wilt, about 20 minutes. Press the cabbage gently with a rubber spatula to squeeze out any excess moisture, then transfer to a medium bowl. Add the remaining filling ingredients and mix thoroughly to combine. Cover with plastic wrap and refrigerate until the mixture is cold, at least 30 minutes or up to 24 hours.

2. FOR THE DUMPLINGS: Working with 4 wrappers at a time (keep the remaining wrappers covered with plastic wrap), follow the photos on page 497 to fill, seal, and shape the dumplings using a generous tablespoon of the chilled filling per dumpling. Transfer the dumplings to a baking sheet and repeat with the remaining wrappers and filling; you should have about 24 dumplings. (The dumplings can be wrapped tightly with plastic

wrap and refrigerated for up to 1 day or frozen for up to 1 month. Once frozen, the dumplings can be transferred to a zipper-lock bag to save space in the freezer; do not thaw before cooking.)

3. Line a large plate with a double layer of paper towels; set aside. Brush 1 tablespoon of the oil over the bottom of a 12-inch nonstick skillet and arrange half of the dumplings in the skillet, with a flat side facing down (overlapping just slightly if necessary). Place the skillet over medium-high heat and cook the dumplings, without moving, until golden brown on the bottom, about 5 minutes.

4. Reduce the heat to low, add ½ cup of the water, and cover immediately. Continue to cook, covered, until most of the water is absorbed and the wrappers are slightly translucent, about 10 minutes. Uncover the skillet, increase the heat to medium-high, and continue to cook, without stirring, until the dumpling bottoms are well browned and crisp, 3 to 4 minutes more. Slide the dumplings onto the paper towel–lined plate, browned side facing down, and let drain briefly. Transfer the dumplings to a serving platter and serve with the Scallion Dipping Sauce. Let the skillet cool until just warm, then wipe it clean with a wad of paper towels and repeat with the remaining dumplings, oil, and water.

Scallion Dipping Sauce
Zhan Jiang
MAKES ¾ CUP

Mirin is a Japanese sweet cooking wine found in most supermarkets (see page 547 more information); if you cannot find it, substitute 2 tablespoons dry white wine mixed with 1 teaspoon sugar.

¼	cup soy sauce
2	tablespoons rice vinegar
2	tablespoons mirin (see note)
2	tablespoons water
1	scallion, sliced thin on the bias (see page 505)
1	teaspoon chili oil (optional)
½	teaspoon toasted sesame oil

Combine all the ingredients in a serving bowl and serve. (The sauce can be refrigerated in a covered container for up to 6 hours.)

Scallion Pancakes

Cong You Bing

A TRULY GREAT SCALLION PANCAKE IS THIN— about ¼ inch thick—with multiple, paper-thin layers laced with scallions and just a hint of sesame. The exterior is golden brown and crisp, while the interior retains a soft chew. Unfortunately, this staple of Chinese takeout is often greasy, bland, and sadly lacking in scallion flavor. With bunches of scallions and recipes in hand, we headed into the test kitchen to develop an exemplary version of this addictive treat.

Scallion pancakes consist of a few simple ingredients—flour, water, scallions, and sometimes sesame oil. Scallion pancakes are more akin to a flatbread than a pancake and thus the ingredients, when mixed, form a soft dough rather than a pourable batter. It didn't take long to come up with flour and water amounts—1½ cups flour to ½ cup water—so we quickly turned to building flavor.

We wanted these pancakes to have a strong scallion flavor, unlike the bland versions we'd had in the past. We tested varying amounts of scallions until we finally settled on ½ cup (or 2 tablespoons of minced scallions for each of the four pancakes). Any more than this and the pancakes became difficult to roll. Some recipes we consulted contained herbs, such as parsley and cilantro, in addition to the scallions. Parsley was fine, but in terms of flavor, it didn't make much of an impact. Cilantro, on the other hand, infused the pancakes with its distinctive herbal flavor—and tasters were hooked.

Our last addition to these pancakes was sesame oil, a common ingredient in the more complex recipes found in our research. Most versions simply brushed the oil onto the pancake before rolling it out, but we felt adding it directly into the dough would be better. Unfortunately, it made the dough sticky and difficult to work with. So we simply brushed a thin layer directly onto the flattened pancake before sprinkling on the scallions and herbs.

At last, it was time to roll—a step that is crucial to the outcome of scallion pancakes. If rolled properly, not only are the scallions incorporated more

ROLLING AND FORMING SCALLION PANCAKES

1. Divide the dough into 4 equal pieces and keep covered with plastic wrap. Working with 1 piece of dough at a time, roll the dough into a 7-inch circle about ⅛ inch thick on a lightly floured work surface. Brush the round lightly with sesame oil, then sprinkle with 2 tablespoons of the scallions and 1½ teaspoons of the cilantro.

2. Roll the round into a tight cylinder, brushing away any clumps of flour that have stuck to the bottom of the dough.

3. Coil the cylinder into a tight round, tucking the end underneath.

4. Using a rolling pin, roll the round into a 5-inch pancake about ¼ inch thick, adding additional flour to the work surface as needed to prevent sticking.

evenly into the pancake, but the thin layers that remain from rolling the dough create the intricate layering of scallions and dough that define this dish. We knew from our research that just kneading the scallions into the dough then rolling it into a disk would form a heavy, dense pancake with no layers. Instead, we turned to the methods found in our library of Chinese cookbooks.

We started with the dough portioned into four balls and rested (the Chinese recipes were virtually identical to this point, so we followed suit). The most common method calls for rolling the pancake into a thin disk, then sprinkling the flavorings onto the dough and rolling it into a log. From there, the log is coiled around itself like a snake. Then the coiled patty is rolled (and flattened) into a pancake and ready to cook. While this method might sound fussy, we had mastered it by our second pancake. And with just a little effort, we were rewarded with tender layers and evenly incorporated scallions.

Finally, it was time to cook. Scallion pancakes are traditionally cooked in a generous amount of oil, but the grease factor was one of our chief complaints. We reduced the amount of oil down to just a couple of tablespoons, but by the time the fourth pancake was added to the pan, the others had soaked up all the oil and the resulting pancakes were soft, with little crispness. We increased the amount of oil at tablespoon increments until we settled on 4 tablespoons or ¼ cup. But to keep the "deep-fry" effect at bay, we split the 4 tablespoons between the pancakes, and cooked them one at a time with just 1 tablespoon of oil—enough to produce crispy scallion pancakes without the grease.

Scallion Pancakes
Cong You Bing
MAKES 4 PANCAKES, SERVING 4 TO 6

If serving these pancakes without the sauce, sprinkle with salt to taste before serving.

1½ cups unbleached all-purpose flour, plus extra for the work surface
1   teaspoon salt
½   cup water, at room temperature, plus extra if needed
¼   cup vegetable oil, plus extra for brushing
2   teaspoons toasted sesame oil
6   scallions, minced (about ½ cup)
2   tablespoons minced fresh cilantro leaves
1   recipe Scallion Dipping Sauce (optional, page 498)

1. Whisk the flour and salt together in a medium bowl. Add the ½ cup water and mix with a dinner fork until combined. (If there are any floury bits left in the bottom of the bowl, add additional water, 1 teaspoon at a time, until the dough comes together.) Turn the dough out onto a lightly floured work surface and knead until it is smooth and satiny, about 5 minutes, adding extra flour to the work surface or your hands as needed to prevent sticking. Transfer the dough to a clean bowl, brush with a thin layer of vegetable oil, and let it rest at room temperature for 30 minutes.

2. Divide the dough into 4 equal pieces and keep covered with plastic wrap. Working with 1 piece of dough at a time, roll into a 7-inch circle about ⅛ inch thick on a lightly floured work surface. Brush the dough round lightly with sesame oil, then sprinkle with 2 tablespoons of the scallions and 1½ teaspoons of the cilantro.

3. Following the illustrations on page 499, roll the dough into a cylinder, then coil the cylinder into a round tucking the tail end underneath. Then roll into a 5-inch pancake, about ¼ inch thick. Set aside and cover with plastic wrap while repeating with the remaining dough pieces.

4. Heat 1 tablespoon of the vegetable oil in a 12-inch nonstick skillet over medium heat until shimmering. Swirl the oil to coat the skillet, then add a dough round and cook until golden brown on both sides, 1½ to 2 minutes per side. Transfer the pancake to a cutting board, tent with foil, and repeat three more times with the remaining 3 tablespoons oil and remaining 3 dough rounds. Slice the cooked pancakes into wedges and serve with the Scallion Dipping Sauce, if desired.

HOT AND SOUR SOUP

Suan la Tang

THE HOT AND SOUR SOUP WE EAT IN CHINESE-American restaurants today isn't much different from the Sichuan original. Named for its potent peppery and vinegary flavors, the lightly thickened soup contains strips of pork, cubes of tofu, and wisps of egg. According to the cookbooks and Chinese cooking experts we consulted, hot and sour soup encapsulates the Taoist principle central to Chinese culture: *yin* and *yang*, the notion of balancing the universe's opposing yet complementary forces. In the kitchen, that means creating balanced dishes by strategically combining flavors, textures, colors, and temperatures—some yin, some yang.

Balancing universal forces we'd have to leave to the philosophers. (All we were after was a good soup.) But balancing flavors, textures, and temperatures? That was familiar territory. At the very least, we figured, the yin-yang principle left us some leeway to explore stand-ins for hard-to-find ingredients that show up in some authentic versions—for instance, mustard pickle, pig's-foot tendon, and dried sea cucumber—without sacrificing the spirit of authenticity. So armed with thoughts of yin, yang, and the inventory of our local supermarket, we headed to the test kitchen to work on a balanced and (philosophically) authentic take on hot and sour soup.

The heat in hot and sour soup traditionally comes not from fresh chiles but from ground white (or sometimes black) peppercorns. Unlike chiles, pepper delivers direct spiciness but doesn't leave a lingering burn in its wake. An all-black-pepper soup was sharp but one-dimensional; a half-black, half-white combination was an improvement. Better still was a version made with a full teaspoon of distinctive, penetrating white pepper. Nice, but we suspected that a second heat source might deliver yet another layer of complexity. Sure enough, chili oil—a bit unconventional for this recipe—supported the white-hot heat of the pepper, laying the groundwork for the opposing flavor of vinegar. This yin-yang balancing act was turning out easier than we'd anticipated.

Until the very next experiment, that is. Made from toasted rice, Chinese black vinegar (the traditional sour component) has an elusive flavor that almost defies description. Because it can be difficult to find, we needed to identify a substitute. Emboldened by the success of our first improvisation, we raided the test kitchen pantry and assembled 14 bottles of vinegar. Drop by drop, we confidently sniffed and tasted our way through the lineup, ultimately deciding that balsamic, cider, malt, rice, and red wine vinegar most closely resembled black vinegar. Next, we supplemented the vinegars, alone and in combination, with everything from angostura bitters to molasses to vermouth to Worcestershire sauce. A smidgen of this, a drizzle of that, and so it went. Sadly, every concoction was exceedingly harsh. To adhere to the yin-yang principle, we needed a substitute that would support, not outshine, the pepper.

Resting our weary palates, we reexamined the black vinegar label and noticed an acidity level of 1.18 percent. Most American vinegars measure in the 5 to 7 percent range, so we would have to use

SHOPPING NOTES:
Hot and Sour Soup

In Chinese cuisine, striking a delicate balance between contrasting elements is often more crucial than ingredient specifics. The sources of this soup's namesake elements, hot and sour, vary from recipe to authentic recipe, but we achieved the most satisfying balance when we combined white peppercorns with black vinegar.

White peppercorns (left) infuse our soup with heat. Chinese black vinegar (right) provides the hallmark sour element to our soup.

501

GETTING THE WISPED EGG JUST RIGHT

1. In order to achieve wispy, delicate ribbons of egg in the soup, you must first turn off the heat so that the surface of soup is calm. Then, using a soupspoon, drizzle thin streams of egg in a circular motion over the surface.

2. Let the eggs set in the soup off the heat for 1 minute, then briefly return the soup to a gentle boil to cook the eggs through. Once the soup reaches a gentle boil, remove it from the heat immediately to prevent the eggs from overcooking.

a lot less of our substitute vinegars. After several more rounds, we finally settled on a tablespoon each of dark, fruity balsamic and robust red wine vinegar as a workable substitute for 5 tablespoons of black vinegar. (That said, black vinegar is so distinctive that we recommend seeking it out.)

Now that we had carefully balanced the flavors of the soup, we turned our focus to texture. Cornstarch is the standard thickener, but a heavy hand resulted in a goopy gravy instead of a silky broth. We found that just 3 tablespoons yielded an agreeable, not-too-thick consistency that would gently support the other textures in the soup. To activate its thickening power, cornstarch is best added to the soup in the form of a cool slurry; the soup is then brought to a boil while being stirred constantly.

In addition to its role as thickener, cornstarch is believed by many Chinese cooks to play the part of meat (or protein) tenderizer. To test what seemed to us a dubious theory, we prepared two batches of soup, adding cornstarch to a simple soy sauce marinade for one julienned pork chop and omitting it in the marinade for another. The cornstarch-marinated pork was noticeably more tender. The cornstarch created a protective sheath that bought us the few extra minutes we needed to finish the soup without overcooking the pork.

After the pork is cooked and the soup thickened, beaten egg is drizzled in to create yet another complementary texture: fine, feathery shreds. The problem is if the egg doesn't set immediately, it can blend into the soup and muddy the appearance of the broth. Wanting to make this step foolproof, we tried mixing the egg with vinegar and cornstarch. The vinegar instantly coagulated the egg, whereas the cornstarch, once again, was the miracle worker: The cornstarch molecules stabilized the liquid proteins, preventing them from contracting excessively when they hit the hot liquid. The result? Lighter, softer eggs. (See "Tenderizing with Cornstarch" on the facing page.)

Spicy, bracing, pungent, tender, fluffy—this soup was already replete with pleasing balances of flavor and texture. But we weren't quite done yet. Almost all authentic hot and sour soup recipes start with reconstituted dried wood ear mushrooms and lily buds. Wood ear mushrooms, also known as tree ear or cloud ear, offer snappy texture but little else. We swapped in commonly available dried porcini and shiitake mushrooms, but their woodsy notes had a negative influence on the flavor equilibrium we'd worked so hard to achieve. Fresh, mild shiitake mushrooms were a better choice. Lily buds, or golden needles, are the dried buds of the tiger lily flower. Tangy, mildly crunchy canned bamboo shoots closely approximated the musky, sour flavor of lily buds and added textural variety (a crisp foil for the fluffy wisps of egg).

As for the tofu, we had one basic question: Must it be pressed? The answer was a simple yes. Sponge-like tofu is full of water, and weighting it beneath a heavy plate yielded firmer, cleaner-tasting cubes. Marinating was a mistake; an occasional bite of plain, mild (yin) tofu was a necessary respite in the mostly yang soup.

Many recipes call for passing potent toasted sesame oil at the table, but a generous pour overwhelmed the other flavors. We took a low-risk approach and added a measured amount to the marinade for the pork. A sprinkling of raw, crisp green scallions on the cooked soup symbolized a final embrace of the yin-yang philosophy.

Hot and Sour Soup

Suan la Tang

SERVES 6 TO 8

To make slicing the pork chop easier, freeze it for 15 minutes. The distinctive flavor of the Chinese black vinegar is important here (you can find it in Asian supermarkets); if you can't find it, substitute a mixture of 1 tablespoon red wine vinegar and 1 tablespoon balsamic vinegar. This soup is very spicy; for a less spicy soup, use the lower amount of chili oil or omit it altogether.

TOFU AND PORK

7 ounces (½ block) extra-firm tofu, drained

1 tablespoon soy sauce

1 teaspoon toasted sesame oil

1 teaspoon cornstarch

1 (½-inch thick) boneless, center-cut pork chop (about 6 ounces), trimmed and cut into ⅛-inch-thick matchsticks about 1 inch long

SOUP

6 cups low-sodium chicken broth

1 (5-ounce) can bamboo shoots, sliced into ⅛-inch-thick matchsticks (about 1 cup)

4 ounces fresh shiitake mushrooms, stemmed, wiped clean, caps sliced ¼ inch thick

5 tablespoons Chinese black vinegar (see note)

3 tablespoons soy sauce

3 tablespoons water

3 tablespoons cornstarch

1–2 teaspoons chili oil (see note)

1 teaspoon ground white pepper

EGG AND SCALLIONS

½ teaspoons cornstarch

1 teaspoon water

1 large egg

3 scallions, sliced thin on the bias (see page 505)

1. **FOR THE TOFU AND PORK:** Place the tofu in a pie plate, top with a heavy plate, and weigh down with 2 heavy cans. Set the tofu aside until it releases roughly ½ cup liquid, about 15 minutes. When drained, dice the tofu into ½-inch cubes and set aside. Meanwhile, whisk the soy sauce, sesame oil, and cornstarch together in a medium bowl, then stir in the pork to coat. Let the pork marinate for at least 10 minutes (but no more than 30 minutes).

2. **FOR THE SOUP:** Bring the broth to a simmer in a large saucepan over medium-low heat. Add the bamboo shoots and mushrooms and simmer until the mushrooms are just tender, about 5 minutes. Stir in the diced tofu and pork with its marinade and continue to simmer, stirring to separate any pieces of pork that stick together, until the pork is no longer pink, about 2 minutes.

3. Whisk the vinegar, soy sauce, water, cornstarch, chili oil, and pepper together to dissolve the cornstarch, then whisk into the soup. Continue to simmer the soup, stirring constantly, until it thickens and turns translucent, about 1 minute. Remove the soup from the heat (do not let the soup cool off).

CORE TECHNIQUE

TENDERIZING WITH CORNSTARCH

Most cooks keep a box of cornstarch on hand for a single purpose: thickening. So did we—until we noticed that cornstarch was working its magic in other ways as well. Predictably, adding cornstarch to our Hot and Sour Soup thickened it. What was surprising, however, were the two other uses we found for cornstarch. Adding just 1 teaspoon of cornstarch to the pork marinade of soy sauce and sesame oil caused the marinade to cling to and coat the meat during cooking, creating a protective sheath that slowed the inevitable rise in temperature that turns moist, tender pork into dry, chalky pork jerky. (This works with chicken as well; see Spicy Stir-Fried Chicken and Bok Choy with Hoisin Sauce on page 518.) And adding just ½ teaspoon of cornstarch to the egg that's drizzled into the soup at the end of cooking seemed to have a tenderizing effect. Cornstarch stabilizes liquid proteins when they're heated, staving off excessive shrinkage and contraction. So this last bit of cornstarch helped the eggs cook up lighter and softer.

4. FOR THE EGG AND SCALLIONS: Whisk the cornstarch and water together with a fork in a small bowl, then whisk in the egg until combined. Without stirring the soup, use a soupspoon to slowly drizzle very thin streams of the egg mixture into the hot soup in a circular motion. Let the soup continue to sit off heat for 1 minute. Briefly return the soup to a gentle boil over medium-high heat, then remove from the heat immediately. Gently stir the soup once to evenly distribute the egg, then ladle into individual bowls, sprinkle with the scallions, and serve.

SICHUAN GREEN BEANS

Ganbian Sijidou

AT ITS BEST, THE DISH CALLED SICHUAN green beans boasts wrinkly, sweet beans sprinkled with morsels of flavorful pork and coated in a pungent sauce—the flavors are hot, aromatic, and tangy all at the same time. Also referred to as twice-fried string beans, Sichuan green beans are traditionally deep-fried in peanut oil before being stir-fried with the other ingredients. The deep-frying makes these otherwise humdrum beans intensely sweet. But since deep-frying seems too fussy for such a simple dish of green beans, we wondered if we could replicate this dish minus the grease and mess.

We started our testing by first roasting the beans in a small amount of oil in a 450-degree oven until their skins shriveled and turned golden brown. But instead of a quick five-minute deep-fry, these beans took more than 20 minutes; plus, we had to dirty an additional pan to cook the pork and make the sauce.

Seeking something more streamlined, we tried our traditional stir-frying method, in a large skillet over high heat. This method was indeed quicker and more efficient, but the beans were more crisp than chewy and they weren't flavorful enough. For the next test, we cooked the beans a few minutes longer, until the skins began to shrivel. The beans were now slightly chewy (just like we wanted) and intensely flavorful. By letting the beans stir-fry longer than

usual, they had become charred in places, giving them a deeper, caramelized flavor that more than compensated for the fact that they were not deep-fried.

Once the beans were perfectly cooked, we continued to follow our stir-fry method and transferred them to a plate while we made the sauce. Authentic recipes rely on elusive ingredients such as Sichuan preserved mustard stems to produce the characteristic tang and modest heat. We tried substituting pickled ginger, and pickled jalapeños, but each flavor was too assertive. Fresh mustard was also too strong, but dry mustard added a nice, subtle tang. We tried different vinegars—both rice and white wine vinegar were too sharp, overpowering the other sauce flavors of soy, fresh ginger, and garlic. We found our answer in Chinese rice cooking wine (or dry sherry) plus a little sugar, which produced the right level of both acidity and sweetness.

This sauce now had the proper tang but still needed more heat. We tried fresh chiles and red pepper flakes. The pepper flakes had a straightforward punch, but we wanted a deeper heat as well. Tasters said black pepper was too mild and cayenne

---

PANTRY SPOTLIGHT

CHINESE GREEN BEANS

Long beans, also called yard-long or snake beans, are the traditional choice in Chinese stir-fries and other recipes, including Sichuan Green Beans. These thin, pliable pods can grow up to three feet long. They certainly look exotic, but are these specialty beans worth seeking out at an Asian market? We made a trip to Chinatown to find out. A few tests later, we found that older, thicker beans can be woody, so look for thin, very flexible beans. After cutting them down to size, we were surprised that even super-thin long beans required the same cooking time as thicker green beans. The long beans were chewier and less sweet than green beans, with a nice nutty flavor. If you find long beans, give them a try—even though our tasters were just as happy with plain old green beans from the supermarket.

too hot, but ground white pepper was perfect, adding aromatic warmth and a complex muskiness. A touch of cornstarch made the sauce cling to each bean, delivering more pungent flavor with each bite. Some chopped scallions and a drizzle of sesame oil were just right to finish this dish.

In restaurants, it is common to find chopped or shredded bits of Chinese barbecued pork mingling with the beans, but whipping up a batch of Char Siu (page 534) was out of the question for this quick stir-fry. We found that simple ground pork was a good substitute—no advance preparation (such as mincing or marinating in soy sauce) was necessary, as the pork absorbed the strong flavors of the sauce while adding a meaty richness to the dish.

Finally, we had Sichuan green beans with a crinkled, chewy texture and intriguing spicy tang, and no fuss.

Sichuan Green Beans

Ganbian Sijidou

SERVES 4 AS A SIDE DISH, OR
2 AS A MAIN COURSE

For information on Chinese long beans (the traditional choice in this recipe), see page 504. The cooking of this dish goes very quickly, so be sure to have all of the ingredients prepped before you start. Serve with Simple Steamed White Rice (page 516).

SAUCE

2 tablespoons water
2 tablespoons soy sauce
1 tablespoon Chinese rice cooking wine or dry sherry (see page 513)
1 teaspoon sugar
½ teaspoon cornstarch
¼ teaspoon ground white pepper
¼ teaspoon red pepper flakes
¼ teaspoon dry mustard

BEANS

2 tablespoons vegetable oil
1 pound Chinese long beans or green beans, trimmed and cut into 2-inch lengths
¼ pound ground pork

3 medium garlic cloves, minced or pressed through a garlic press (about 1 tablespoon)
1 tablespoon minced or grated fresh ginger
3 scallions, sliced thin on the bias (see below)
1 teaspoon toasted sesame oil

1. FOR THE SAUCE: Stir all of the ingredients together in a small bowl and set aside.

2. FOR THE BEANS: Heat the oil in a 12-inch nonstick skillet over high heat until just smoking. Add the beans and cook, stirring frequently, until the skins are shriveled and blackened in spots, 5 to 8 minutes (reduce the heat to medium-high if the beans darken too quickly). Transfer the beans to a large plate.

3. Add the pork to the skillet and cook over medium-high heat, breaking the meat into small pieces, until no longer pink, about 2 minutes. Stir in the garlic and ginger and cook until fragrant, about 30 seconds. Whisk the sauce to recombine, then add to the skillet and cook, tossing constantly, until the sauce is thickened, about 30 seconds. Remove the pan from the heat, stir in the scallions and sesame oil, and serve.

➤ VARIATION

Vegetarian Sichuan Green Beans with Mushrooms

Follow the recipe for Sichuan Green Beans, substituting 4 ounces shiitake mushrooms, stemmed and minced, for the pork; cook the mushrooms with 1 teaspoon of vegetable oil in the skillet over medium-high heat until softened, about 2 minutes, before adding the garlic and ginger in step 3.

SLICING SCALLIONS ON THE BIAS

Slicing the scallions on the bias makes for an attractive presentation. Simply hold the scallion at an angle, then slice the scallion thin.

NOT FAMILIAR WITH SICHUAN PEPPERCORNS? It's not surprising. From 1968 until 2005, these berries of a spiny shrub indigenous to the Sichuan province of China were banned from importation into the United States—it seems they were viewed as potential carriers of a tree disease that could have harmed our citrus crops. Now that they have returned, they are working their way back into authentic Sichuan dishes here in the United States.

Sichuan peppercorns are one of the ingredients of five-spice powder, a traditional Chinese spice blend. They have purplish-red husks and shiny black seeds. It is preferable to buy Sichuan peppercorns with the shiny black seeds removed as it's the reddish-brown husks that are used for their aromatic, gently floral fragrance and their telltale numbing effect on the tongue. One of their more common uses is mixed with salt and sprinkled over roasted meats.

Sichuan Peppercorn Salt
Jiu Yim

For plain toasted peppercorns, simply omit the five-spice powder and salt. Serve this garnishing salt at the table or sprinkle it over grilled or roasted meat before serving. We like to use kosher salt here because it is easier to sprinkle than table salt.

2   teaspoons Sichuan peppercorns
2   teaspoons five-spice powder
6   tablespoons kosher salt

Toast the peppercorns in a small skillet over medium heat, stirring frequently, until the peppercorns turn very dark and fragrant, about 3 minutes. Stir in the five-spice powder and toast for 30 seconds longer. Transfer the toasted spices to a bowl and let cool. When cool, grind to a coarse powder in a spice grinder, then toss with the salt and serve. (The salt can be stored in an airtight container at room temperature for up to 3 months.)

SESAME NOODLES WITH SHREDDED CHICKEN
Jisi Majiang Mian

MUCH LIKE A CHINESE FINGER TRAP THAT lures by appearing to be a toy, sesame noodles are not what they seem. You may think of them as merely a humble bowl of cold noodles, but don't be fooled—just one bite and you're hooked on these toothsome noodles with shreds of tender chicken, all tossed with fresh sesame sauce. And then you've got a real problem: Once you get the hankering, good versions of this dish can be hard to find. The cold noodles have a habit of turning gummy, the chicken often dries out, and the sauce is notorious for turning bland and pasty. We wanted a recipe that could not only quell a serious craving but could do it fast.

Though drawn to the softer texture of fresh Asian-style noodles, we conceded that dried spaghetti could serve as a second-string substitute. We tried using linguine (a favorite substitution in our other Asian noodle recipes), but tasters preferred the sturdier texture of spaghetti here. Regardless of what type of noodle we used, however, the trouble was that after being cooked and chilled, they gelled into a rubbery skein. After trying a number of ways to avoid this, we found it necessary to rinse the noodles under cold tap water directly after cooking. This not only cooled the hot noodles immediately but also washed away much of their sticky starch. To further forestall any clumping, we tossed the rinsed noodles with a little oil.

Boneless, skinless chicken breasts are quick to cook and easy to shred; the real question is how to cook them. The microwave seemed easy in theory, but we found the rate of cooking difficult to monitor—30 seconds meant the difference between overdone and underdone. Many recipes suggested poaching the chicken in water or broth, but this chicken had a washed-out flavor. Nor was roasting the answer; it caused the outer meat to dry out before the interior was fully cooked. Cooking under the broiler, however, worked perfectly. The chicken cooked through in minutes, retaining much of its moisture and flavor.

Most authentic sesame noodle recipes use Asian sesame paste (not to be confused with Middle Eastern tahini) and it is worth seeking out for its exotic, full sesame flavor. If you cannot find it, peanut butter makes an acceptable substitute. Tasters preferred chunky peanut butter over smooth, describing its flavor as fresh and more nutty. We had been making the sauce in a blender and realized that the chunky bits of peanuts were being freshly ground into the sauce, producing a cleaner, stronger flavor. We found the flavors of both fresh garlic and ginger necessary, along with soy sauce, rice vinegar, hot sauce, and brown sugar. We also ground some sesame seeds into the sauce for another hit of sesame flavor. To keep the sauce from being too thick or pasty we thinned it out with water.

We were almost there. To give the dish additional layers of flavor, we tossed the rinsed pasta with toasted sesame oil instead of a neutral oil and garnished the noodles with toasted sesame seeds. At last we had a bowl of sesame noodles and chicken we could savor.

Sesame Noodles with Shredded Chicken

Jisi Majiang Mian

SERVES 4 TO 6

Asian sesame paste, not to be confused with tahini (Middle Eastern–style sesame paste) can be found in the international aisle of well-stocked supermarkets or Asian markets. If you choose to use peanut butter instead of sesame paste, the test kitchen prefers the flavor and texture of chunky peanut butter in this recipe; in particular, conventional chunky peanut butter works well because it tends to be sweeter than natural or old-fashioned versions. For more information on Chinese noodles, see page 509.

SAUCE
- 5 tablespoons soy sauce
- 3 tablespoons sesame seeds, toasted (see page 135)
- ¼ cup Asian sesame paste or chunky peanut butter (see note)
- 2 tablespoons rice vinegar
- 2 tablespoons light brown sugar

- 1 tablespoon minced or grated fresh ginger
- 2 medium garlic cloves, minced or pressed through a garlic press (about 2 teaspoons)
- 1 teaspoon hot sauce
  Hot water

CHICKEN AND NOODLES
- 1½ pounds boneless, skinless chicken breasts (about 3 medium breasts), trimmed
- 1 tablespoon salt
- 1 pound fresh Chinese noodles or 12 ounces dried spaghetti
- 2 tablespoons toasted sesame oil
- 4 scallions, sliced thin on the bias (see page 505)
- 1 medium carrot, grated over the large holes of a box grater
- 2 tablespoons minced fresh cilantro leaves (optional)
- 1 tablespoon sesame seeds, toasted (see page 135)

1. FOR THE SAUCE: Blend the soy sauce, sesame seeds, sesame paste, vinegar, sugar, ginger, garlic, and hot sauce together in a blender until smooth, about 30 seconds. With the machine running, add hot water, 1 tablespoon at a time, until the sauce has the consistency of heavy cream (you should need about 5 tablespoons); set aside.

2. FOR THE CHICKEN AND NOODLES: Bring 6 quarts of water to a boil in a large pot for the noodles. Adjust an oven rack 6 inches from the broiler element and heat the broiler.

3. Set a slotted broiler pan top over a broiler pan bottom, spray the top with vegetable oil spray, and lay the chicken out over the top. Broil the chicken until lightly golden, 4 to 8 minutes. Flip the chicken over and continue to broil until the thickest part registers 160 degrees on an instant-read thermometer, 6 to 8 minutes longer. Transfer the chicken to a cutting board and let rest 5 minutes before shredding into bite-sized pieces using 2 forks (see the illustration on page 69).

4. While the chicken cooks, add the salt and noodles to the boiling water and cook, stirring constantly, until the noodles are tender, about 4 minutes for fresh or 10 minutes for the dried

spaghetti. Drain the noodles, rinse them under cold running water until cold, then toss them with the sesame oil.

5. Transfer the noodles to a large bowl, add the shredded chicken, sauce, scallions, carrot, and cilantro (if using) and toss to combine. Divide the mixture among individual bowls, sprinkle with the sesame seeds and serve.

➤ VARIATION

Sesame Noodles with Sweet Pepper and Cucumber

Follow the recipe for Sesame Noodles with Shredded Chicken, omitting the chicken, and adding 1 medium red bell pepper, cored, seeded, and sliced into ¼-inch wide strips and 1 medium cucumber, peeled, halved lengthwise, seeded, and sliced crosswise into ¼-inch-wide pieces, to the noodles with the sauce and other vegetables in step 5.

SPICY SICHUAN NOODLES

Dan Dan Mian

DAN DAN MIAN, OR SPICY SICHUAN NOODLES, is a dish that is both substantial and satisfying—a meal in a bowl. By all accounts it is street food in China, the equivalent of sausage and onions from a curbside cart in New York City. To make this dish, you top Chinese noodles with a rich, savory sauce—a mélange of browned ground pork, aromatic ginger and garlic, salty soy sauce, and nutty peanut butter in a chicken broth base. All this is set ablaze by the heat of chiles and finished with a sprinkling of sliced scallions and bean sprouts.

Since this recipe is absent from many Chinese restaurant menus, many of the test cooks didn't have much experience in sampling this dish, so we had to rely on our library of authentic Chinese cookbooks to find traditional versions of these spicy Sichuan noodles to taste. What we did find seemed a bit skimpy on the protein and garnish, but simply adding more to the mix would throw off the

delicate balance of flavors. We wanted a satisfying noodle-based dish substantial enough for a weeknight dinner and set out in search of just that.

The sauce for spicy Sichuan noodles is built simply. Ground pork, marinated briefly in soy sauce and Chinese rice cooking wine (or sherry), is browned either by sautéing it in a skillet with just a little oil or by deep-frying it in a cup or so of oil. The pork is then removed from the skillet, the oil drained off, and the ginger and garlic briefly cooked. Next the chicken broth is added, then peanut butter or sesame paste. In a simpler rendition, the ginger and garlic are omitted and the other sauce ingredients are simmered right in the skillet with the pork. In both versions, the mixture of pork and sauce is simply poured over noodles and served. We quickly determined that deep-frying the pork was not worth the trouble or waste of oil. Browning could be accomplished easily in only 1 tablespoon of oil.

Next we concluded that once the pork was browned, there was no need to remove it from the skillet. It was fine to build the sauce on top of it. Having decided on these two simplifications, we began weeding through the different ingredients called for in different recipes. We had one clear goal in mind—to create a rich, complex sauce in which the powerful flavors of garlic, ginger, and soy were well balanced. Fresh ginger and garlic spike the dish with aromatic piquancy, but in equal amounts their potencies vied for dominance and the pairing was not harmonious. Tasters voted garlic to the fore, relegating ginger to second position. Soy sauce brought a savory quality, while oyster sauce added a depth and sweetness that rounded out the flavors. Rice vinegar cut the richness of the sauce and livened things up.

Asian sesame paste (not the same as Middle Eastern tahini) is typically called for in spicy Sichuan noodle recipes, with peanut butter a recommended substitute. We first tried peanut butter because of its availability and it produced perfectly good results. Two tablespoons, the amount recommended in many recipes, was too little to contribute much flavor or to thicken the amount of chicken broth needed to coat a pound of cooked fresh noodles. We doubled the amount to 4 tablespoons, enough to add rich, nutty flavor and to adequately thicken the sauce. Any more and the sauce became intolerably rich as well as overly thick. We also preferred smooth peanut butter to chunky in this recipe.

Next we tried Asian sesame paste in place of peanut butter. Its flavor is mysterious, and it yields an intriguing sauce with an earthy, smoky flavor. If your supermarket carries Asian sesame paste or if an Asian grocer is nearby, we recommend seeking it out. The consistency varies from brand to brand—some are thin and pourable, like honey, while others are spreadable—so we found it necessary to compensate by making minor adjustments in the amount of chicken broth in the sauce. While you're shopping for sesame paste, look for Sichuan peppercorns (see page 506). These berries are from a prickly ash tree native to Asia and bring to the dish a woodsy flavor, with a hint of star anise.

Chinese grocery stores are stocked with a dizzying array of noodles, fresh as well as dried. A couple of recipes recommended fresh egg noodles, so we thought that this is where we would begin. In the refrigerator sections of the major Chinatown markets, the only fresh noodles we found that would qualify as egg noodles (because they listed eggs in their ingredient lists) were "wonton" noodles. Cooked and sauced, these noodles were clearly not right. They were far too delicate. As a result, they wilted under the weight of the sauce, clumped together into a ball, and ended up as listless as a pile of wet rags.

Back in the refrigerated-food aisle, we chose two more types of fresh noodles, lo mein and the descriptively named "plain noodles." We purchased from our local supermarket—for nearly twice the cost—a few packages of fresh "Asian-style noodles" in wide-cut and narrow-cut versions. Cooked, these three types of noodles were different from one another, but all were a better match for the sauce than the wonton noodles. The spaghetti-shaped lo mein didn't give the sauce much noodle surface to cling to and their very yielding texture was unremarkable. The plain noodles, shaped like fat, squared-off strands of spaghetti, were as soft and gummy as a piece of Bazooka; this pleased some

and annoyed others. The wide-cut supermarket noodles had good chew, too, but to a lesser degree. Their fettuccine-like shape was perfect for the sauce; the broad surfaces were easily sauced and could buoy up bits of pork.

Fresh noodles are not always an option, so we also looked into dried. We focused on flat noodles with a width between linguine and fettuccine. What was true of fresh noodles was also true of dried: the egg and the imitation egg noodles were too delicate for the sauce. Sturdier non-egg noodles, with their chewy and more substantial presence, were a superior match. In fact, for those

---

PANTRY SPOTLIGHT

FRESH CHINESE NOODLES

A key ingredient in Chinese cuisine, noodles come in many forms—fresh, dried, wheat, rice, cellophane, hand-pulled, or flash-fried. They're eaten hot, cold, boiled, steamed, stir-fried, and deep-fried. Many varieties of fresh Chinese noodles are available in local supermarkets, though the selection is vaster in an Asian market. Some noodles are cut thin (below left), while others are cut slightly wider (below right).

Their texture is a bit more starchy and chewy than dried noodles and their flavor is cleaner (less wheaty) than Italian pasta, making them an excellent match to potent, highly seasoned sauces such as Spicy Sichuan Noodles with Ground Pork (page 510), Sesame Noodles with Shredded Chicken (page 507), and Beef Lo Mein (page 511). You can substitute dried Italian pasta, such as linguine or spaghetti, but we think these fresh noodles—often called Chinese noodles or Asian-style noodles— are worth tracking down.

Fresh Chinese noodles cook quickly, usually for no more than 3 to 4 minutes in boiling water. Adding salt to the water is not always necessary—many Chinese noodle sauces are rich in soy sauce, which is high in sodium.

THIN   WIDE

who prefer noodles with a lesser "mush" quotient, dried noodles are better than fresh. And if neither fresh nor dried Asian noodles are available, dried linguine is an acceptable substitute. Most tasters polished off an entire bowl.

Common practice with Italian pasta is to toss the sauce with the cooked and drained pasta in the pot in which the pasta was cooked, giving the mix a little additional heat to help form a loose union. Noodles for dan dan mian, however, look and hold up better when simply divided among bowls, ladled with sauce, and then sprinkled with a garnish. It is then up to the diner to toss, swirl, and slurp down the noodles with chopsticks. . .or a fork.

Spicy Sichuan Noodles with Ground Pork

Dan Dan Mian

SERVES 4

If you are using Asian sesame paste that has a pourable rather than spreadable consistency, use only 1 cup of chicken broth. Because this sauce has a tendency to be on the salty side, we don't add any salt to the pasta cooking water. For more information on Chinese noodles, see page 509.

8	ounces ground pork
3	tablespoons soy sauce
2	tablespoons Chinese rice cooking wine or dry sherry
	Ground white pepper
2	tablespoons oyster sauce
¼	cup Asian sesame paste or smooth peanut butter
1	tablespoon rice vinegar
1–1¼	cups low-sodium chicken broth (see note)
1	tablespoon vegetable oil
6	medium garlic cloves, minced or pressed through a garlic press (about 2 tablespoons)
1	tablespoon minced or grated fresh ginger
¾	teaspoon red pepper flakes
1	tablespoon toasted sesame oil
1	pound fresh Chinese noodles or 12 ounces dried linguine

3	scallions, sliced thin on the bias (see page 505)
2	cups bean sprouts (optional)
1	tablespoon Sichuan peppercorns, toasted and ground (optional, see page 506)

1. Bring 6 quarts of water to a boil in a large pot for the noodles.

2. Meanwhile, toss the pork with 1 tablespoon of the soy sauce, rice wine, and a pinch of pepper to combine and set aside. In a separate bowl, whisk the remaining 2 tablespoons soy sauce, oyster sauce, sesame paste, vinegar, and a pinch of pepper together until smooth, then whisk in the chicken broth; set aside.

3. Heat the vegetable oil in 12-inch skillet over high heat until shimmering. Add the pork and cook, breaking up the meat with a wooden spoon, until the pork is in small well-browned bits, about 5 minutes. Stir in the garlic, ginger, and red pepper flakes and cook until fragrant, about 30 seconds. Stir in the chicken broth mixture, bring to a boil, then reduce to a simmer over medium-low heat and cook until slightly thickened, about 3 minutes. Off the heat, stir in the sesame oil; cover and set aside.

4. While the sauce simmers, stir the noodles into the boiling water and cook, stirring constantly, until the noodles are tender, about 4 minutes for fresh noodles or 10 minutes for dried linguine. Drain the noodles, divide them among individual bowls, then ladle a portion of the sauce over the top. Sprinkle with the scallions, bean sprouts (if using), and ground Sichuan peppercorns (if using) and serve.

➤ VARIATION

Spicy Sichuan Noodles with Dried Shiitake Mushrooms

Soak 8 small dried shiitake mushrooms in 1 cup boiling water until softened, 15 to 20 minutes; drain, reserving ½ cup soaking liquid. Trim and discard the stems, then slice the mushrooms ¼ inch thick and set aside. Follow the recipe for Spicy Sichuan Noodles with Ground Pork, substituting the reserved mushroom liquid for an equal amount of the chicken broth and stirring the sliced mushrooms into the sauce along with the sesame oil in step 3.

BEEF LO MEIN

BEEF LO MEIN IS A SIMPLE DISH—BASICALLY a beef stir-fry with boiled noodles. So why is this dish so often poorly executed? The lo mein served in many Chinese restaurants is frequently oily and uninteresting; the noodles are often a tasteless mass, and the sauce, a bland, muddy gravy. We wanted something different—flavorful strands of noodles mingled with thin slices of perfectly cooked beef coated in a light, tangy sauce.

Most lo mein recipes call for fresh Chinese egg noodles. Chinese noodles are more tender and chewier and absorb flavors more readily than fresh Italian pasta. Some fresh Chinese noodles contain eggs and some do not. We tried both styles and much preferred the noodles with eggs for their richer flavor. We moved on to examine cooking the noodles.

After cooking the noodles in plenty of boiling salted water, we rinsed and drained them with cold water and then immediately tossed them with a little bit of sesame oil to prevent clumping—the toasty oil also adds flavor. It's important to rinse the noodles, to not only wash away the excess starch (which causes the noodles to clump), but to also cool down the noodles so they don't overcook and become mushy.

We prefer flank steak in this dish, for its meaty chew and good beefy flavor. Before cooking, we slice it thinly across the grain. Freezing the steak for 15 minutes makes it easier to slice. Once cut into thin pieces, the steak only requires a quick two-minute sear. For vegetables, napa cabbage and bean sprouts give the lo mein freshness and crunch.

Next, we moved on to the sauce. Our thought was to generate the greatest flavor with the fewest ingredients. We also wanted to keep the sauce light and therefore an improvement on the goopy Chinese takeout sauces. Adding a little chicken broth to the sauce kept it from being too thick and gloppy. Soy sauce was another essential component. Oyster sauce also proved to be important. While not exactly a household staple (but easy to find in supermarkets), it was listed in most of the recipes we consulted. We found, and tasters agreed, that the oyster sauce gave the lo mein an appealing salty

richness and lush texture. And the best part about this sauce? It pairs well with lots of different proteins, making shrimp lo mein and chicken lo mein just a simple substitution away.

Beef Lo Mein

SERVES 4

To make slicing the flank steak easier, freeze it for 15 minutes; see page 516 for more information on slicing flank steak. For more information on Chinese noodles, see page 509.

¼	cup low-sodium chicken broth
3	tablespoons oyster sauce
3	tablespoon soy sauce
2	teaspoons cornstarch
2	medium garlic cloves, minced or pressed through a garlic press (about 2 teaspoons)
2	tablespoons plus 1 teaspoon vegetable oil
1	tablespoon salt
12	ounces fresh Chinese noodles or 8 ounces dried linguine
2	tablespoons toasted sesame oil
12	ounces flank steak, trimmed and sliced thin across the grain on the bias (see the illustration on page 516)
12	medium scallions, white and green parts separated, both parts sliced on the bias into 1-inch lengths
1	small head napa cabbage, sliced crosswise into ⅛ inch strips (about 4 cups)
1	cup bean sprouts

1. Bring 6 quarts of water to a boil in a large pot for the noodles.

2. Meanwhile, whisk the chicken broth, oyster sauce, soy sauce, and cornstarch together; set aside. In a separate bowl, mix the garlic with 1 teaspoon of the vegetable oil; set aside

3. Stir the salt and noodles into the boiling water and cook, stirring constantly, until the noodles are tender, about 4 minutes for fresh noodles or 10 minutes for dried linguine. Drain the noodles, rinse them under cold running water until cold, then toss with the sesame oil; set aside.

4. Heat 1 tablespoon of the vegetable oil in a 12-inch nonstick skillet over high heat until just smoking. Add the flank steak and cook until seared and almost cooked through, about 2 minutes. Transfer the steak to a clean bowl; set aside.

5. Add the remaining 1 tablespoon oil to the skillet and return to high heat until just smoking. Add the scallion whites and cook for 1 minute. Add the cabbage and cook until softened slightly, about 1 minute. Clear the center of the skillet, add the garlic mixture and cook, mashing the mixture into the pan, until fragrant, 15 to 20 seconds. Stir the garlic mixture into the vegetables.

6. Stir in the reserved noodles, beef with any accumulated juices, scallion greens, and sprouts. Whisk the chicken broth mixture to recombine, then add to the skillet and cook, tossing the noodles constantly, until the sauce is thickened and the noodles are heated through, about 1 minute; serve.

➤ VARIATIONS
Chicken Lo Mein
Coating the chicken with the cornstarch mixture is a technique called velveting, which makes the chicken more tender; see page 503 for more information.

Following the illustrations on page 516, slice 12 ounces trimmed, boneless, skinless chicken breast into thin slices. Toss the chicken with 2 tablespoons sesame oil, 1 tablespoon soy, 1 tablespoon Chinese rice cooking wine (or dry sherry), 1 tablespoon cornstarch, and 1 tablespoon all-purpose flour, until well coated. Follow the recipe for Beef Lo Mein, substituting the prepared chicken for the beef; cook as directed in step 4, until the chicken is lightly browned and cooked through, about 5 minutes.

Shrimp Lo Mein
While we prefer extra-large shrimp here, large or medium shrimp are fine too.

Follow the recipe for Beef Lo Mein, substituting 12 ounces extra-large shrimp (21 to 25 per pound), peeled and deveined, for the beef; cook as directed in step 4, until the shrimp are pink and curled, about 2 minutes.

STIR-FRIES

THE CHINESE INVENTED STIR-FRYING AS A means to conserve energy—the theory being the hotter the pan (or wok), the faster the cooking and the less energy used. To make the most of the heat being used, stir-fry recipes call for cooking in stages—items that take the longest to cook go into the pan first, followed in sequence until the last garnish is tossed in and the dish is served. With thousands of years to perfect this process, who were we to argue with the nuts and bolts? We set out to adapt this method of cooking to our home kitchens.

We began our testing with the protein—lean cuts of beef or pork, chicken breasts, shrimp, or tofu—typically the longest-cooking (and therefore first) element to go into a stir-fry. Unlike Americans who make meat the centerpiece of the meal, the Chinese incorporate meat into their diets in a less expensive and decidedly more healthful manner, by using meat (and other proteins such as fish and tofu) as a team player alongside vegetables. A stir-fry for four people generally calls for only ¾ pound protein to 1½ pounds prepared vegetables. This ratio keeps the stir-fry from becoming too heavy, providing a little bit of protein and lots of vegetables, although we upped the amount a bit to 1 pound of protein—just enough to satisfy any table of self-proclaimed carnivores.

The protein is cut into bite-sized pieces, which not only gives the illusion of more meat in the stir-fry, but also provides more surface area for absorbing flavors and for browning. The protein is marinated in a simple mixture of flavorful ingredients (we use soy sauce and Chinese rice cooking wine). The marinated protein is then cooked quickly over very high heat to maximize caramelization.

After the protein has been cooked, it is removed from the pan and bite-sized vegetables are added in batches. Because just a small volume of food is added at a time, the intense heat in the pan is maintained. Slow-cooking vegetables such as onions and mushrooms go into the pan first, followed by quicker-cooking items such as celery and snow peas. Leafy greens and herbs go in last.

For vegetables that won't soften even after several minutes of stir-frying, we add a bit of water to the pan and cover it to trap some steam. This method works especially well with broccoli and green beans. Once the vegetables are crisp-tender, the cover comes off so the excess water can evaporate.

We found that cooking times are affected by how the vegetables are prepared. For instance, sliced mushrooms cook more quickly than whole mushrooms. In many cases, we've found it necessary to remove cooked vegetables from the pan before adding the next batch. This is especially important if you are cooking a large volume of vegetables.

For maximum flavor without a lot of fat, we found that you need a generous amount of aromatics—minced garlic, ginger, and scallions. However, most recipes add these aromatics at the outset of the cooking process, when the pan is empty, or saturate them with as much as ¼ cup of oil, adding unnecessary fat and calories. Both approaches are big mistakes. By the time the stir-fry is done, the aromatics that have been added to the empty pan have burned and become harsh-tasting and the oil-sodden aromatics make for a greasy stir-fry.

Instead, we found it best to cook the aromatics after the vegetables. When the vegetables are done, we push them to the sides of the pan, add the aromatics mixed with just a little oil to the center, and cook until the aromatics are fragrant but not colored, about 45 seconds. The small amount of oil is important here because it keeps the aromatics from burning and becoming harsh-tasting. We then stir the fragrant aromatics into the vegetables. At this point, the seared beef, chicken, seafood, or tofu is returned to the pan along with the sauce to finish cooking or heat through.

To stir-fry properly, you need plenty of intense heat. The pan must be hot enough to caramelize sugars, deepen flavors, and evaporate unnecessary juices. All this must happen in minutes. Woks are round-bottomed because in China they traditionally rest in conical pits that contain the fire.

Unfortunately, what is practical in China makes no sense in the United States. A wok was not designed for stovetop cooking, where heat comes from the bottom only. On an American stove, the bottom of the wok gets hot, but the sides are only warm. A flat heat source requires a flat pan. Therefore, for stir-frying at home, we recommend a large skillet, 12 to 14 inches in diameter, with a nonstick coating. If you insist on using a wok for stir-frying, choose a flat-bottomed model. It won't have as much flat surface area as a skillet, but it will work better on an American stove than a conventional round-bottomed wok.

In this section, we have featured some of our favorite stir-fry combinations, utilizing lean cuts of beef and pork, chicken breasts, shrimp, and tofu and a wide range of vegetables, from classics like carrots, broccoli, and red bell peppers to Asian vegetables such as napa cabbage and bok choy. Note that the recipes in this section are designed to serve four as a main course with rice (see the Simple Steamed White Rice on page 516).

PANTRY SPOTLIGHT

CHINESE RICE COOKING WINE

Rice wine is a rich-flavored liquid that is made from fermented glutinous rice or millet. Aged for 10 years or more, rice wine is used both for drinking and cooking (the cooking rice wine has a lower alcohol content than the other). Technically, rice wine should be called rice "beer" since it's fermented from a grain and not a fruit.

Since ancient times, the most famous and highest quality rice wines have come from Shaoxing in the Zheijang province. Chinese rice cooking wine (not to be confused with mirin or sake) is also called yellow wine, Shao Hsing, or Shao Xing. It ranges in color from clear to amber and tastes slightly sweet and aromatic. It can be found in the international aisle of most supermarkets (or at specialty Asian markets) but dry sherry is a decent substitute.

Stir-Fried Beef and Broccoli with Oyster Sauce

SERVES 4

To make slicing the flank steak easier, freeze it for 15 minutes. Stir-fries cook quickly, so have everything prepped before you begin cooking. Serve with Simple Steamed White Rice (page 516).

SAUCE

5	tablespoons oyster sauce
2	tablespoons low-sodium chicken broth
1	tablespoon Chinese rice cooking wine or dry sherry
1	tablespoon light brown sugar
1	teaspoon toasted sesame oil
1	teaspoon cornstarch

STIR-FRY

1	pound flank steak, trimmed and sliced thin across the grain on the bias (see the illustration on page 516)
2	teaspoons soy sauce
2	teaspoons Chinese rice cooking wine or dry sherry
6	medium garlic cloves, minced or pressed through a garlic press (about 2 tablespoons)
1	tablespoon minced or grated fresh ginger
2	scallions, minced
2	tablespoons plus 1 teaspoon vegetable oil
1¼	pounds broccoli, florets and stems separated, florets cut into bite-sized pieces, stems trimmed, peeled, and sliced ⅛ inch thick
⅓	cup water
1	small red bell pepper, stemmed, seeded, and cut into matchsticks

1. For the sauce: Whisk all of the ingredients together; set aside.

2. For the stir-fry: Toss the beef with the soy sauce and rice wine in a small bowl and let marinate for 10 minutes or up to 1 hour. In a separate bowl, mix the garlic, ginger, scallions, and 1 teaspoon of the vegetable oil together; set aside.

3. Heat 1½ teaspoons vegetable oil in a 12-inch nonstick skillet over high heat until just smoking. Add half of the beef, break up any clumps, then cook without stirring until the meat is browned at the edges, about 1 minute. Stir the meat and continue to cook until it is nearly cooked through, about 1 minute longer. Transfer the beef to a medium bowl and repeat with 1½ teaspoons more vegetable oil and the remaining beef; transfer to the bowl, cover with foil, and set aside.

4. Add the remaining 1 tablespoon vegetable oil to the skillet and return to high heat until just smoking. Add the broccoli florets and stems and cook for 30 seconds. Add the water, cover, and reduce the heat to medium. Steam the broccoli until crisp-tender, about 2 minutes. Remove the lid, add the bell pepper and continue to cook until vegetables are crisp-tender, about 2 minutes.

5. Clear the center of the skillet, add the garlic mixture and cook, mashing the mixture into the pan, until fragrant, 15 to 20 seconds. Stir the garlic mixture into the vegetables.

6. Stir in the browned beef with any accumulated juices. Whisk the sauce to recombine, then add to the skillet and cook, tossing constantly, until the sauce is thickened, about 30 seconds. Transfer to a serving platter and serve.

PREPARING THE BROCCOLI

1. Place the head of broccoli upside down on a cutting board and with a large knife trim off the florets very close to their heads. Cut the florets into bite-sized pieces.

2. The stalks may also be trimmed and cooked. Stand each stalk up on the cutting board and square it off with a large knife. This will remove the outer ⅛-inch from the stalk, which is quite tough. Cut the trimmed stalk into ⅛-inch pieces.

Stir-Fried Pork, Scallions, and Bell Peppers with Hoisin Sauce

SERVES 4

To make slicing the pork easier, freeze it for 15 minutes. The scallions are used as a vegetable in this stir-fry, rather than simply as a garnish; you will need about 12 ounces of scallions. Stir-fries cook quickly, so have everything prepped before you begin cooking. Serve with Simple Steamed White Rice (page 516).

SAUCE

- ½ cup low-sodium chicken broth
- ¼ cup Chinese rice cooking wine or dry sherry
- 3 tablespoons hoisin sauce
- 1 tablespoon soy sauce
- 2 teaspoons cornstarch
- 1 teaspoon toasted sesame oil

STIR-FRY

- 1 pound pork tenderloin (about 1 medium tenderloin), trimmed and cut into thin strips (see page 516)
- 2 teaspoons soy sauce
- 2 teaspoons Chinese rice cooking wine or dry sherry
- 6 medium garlic cloves, minced or pressed through a garlic press (about 2 tablespoons)
- 1 tablespoon minced or grated fresh ginger
- ⅛ teaspoon red pepper flakes
- 2 tablespoons plus 1 teaspoon vegetable oil
- 12 medium scallions, white and green parts separated, both parts sliced on the bias into 1-inch lengths
- 2 medium red bell peppers, stemmed, seeded, and sliced into ¼-inch-wide strips

1. FOR THE SAUCE: Whisk all of the ingredients together; set aside.

2. FOR THE STIR-FRY: Toss the pork with the soy sauce and rice wine and let marinate for 10 minutes or up to 1 hour. In a separate bowl, combine the garlic, ginger, red pepper flakes and 1 teaspoon of the vegetable oil; set aside.

3. Heat 1½ teaspoons vegetable oil in a 12-inch nonstick skillet over high heat until just smoking.

Add half of the pork, break up any clumps, then cook without stirring until the meat is browned at the edges, about 1 minute. Stir the meat and continue to cook until it is nearly cooked through, about 1 minute longer. Transfer the pork to a medium bowl and repeat with 1½ teaspoons more vegetable oil and the remaining pork; transfer to the bowl, cover with foil, and set aside.

4. Add the remaining 1 tablespoon vegetable oil to the skillet and return to high heat until just smoking. Add the scallion whites and cook for 1 minute. Add the bell peppers and cook, stirring occasionally, until crisp-tender, 2 minutes.

5. Clear the center of the skillet, add the garlic mixture and cook, mashing the mixture into the pan, until fragrant, 15 to 20 seconds. Stir the garlic mixture into the vegetables.

6. Stir in the scallion greens and pork with any accumulated juices. Whisk the sauce to recombine, then add to the skillet and cook, tossing constantly, until the sauce is thickened, about 30 seconds. Transfer to a serving platter and serve.

EQUIPMENT:
Inexpensive Nonstick Skillets

Nothing takes the challenge out of cooking stir-fries and delicate foods like eggs better than a slick nonstick skillet. The downside is that the nonstick coating is easily damaged, so we find it best to buy inexpensive nonstick skillets. We tested nine 12-inch nonstick skillets ranging in price from $8.99 to $49.99. Our main criticisms focused on pan construction, because some of the pans turned out to be downright flimsy. However, the Cuisinart Chef's Classic Nonstick Hard Anodized Skillet ($41.95) was our favorite.

THE BEST NONSTICK SKILLET

The Cuisinart Chef's Classic Nonstick Hard Anodized 12-inch Skillet with Helper Handle offers the best combination of nonstick performance and solid construction.

Stir-Fry 101

Stir-fries are naturally quick cooking. The key is to have all your meat and vegetable prepped before you begin cooking. They should be cut into even pieces so they all cook at the same rate.

SLICING MEAT FOR STIR-FRIES

It is better to take five minutes and cut up your own meat rather than to buy packages labeled "for stir-fry," since this can be any type or cut of meat, merely cut into small pieces. The right type of meat makes all the difference between tender bites and pieces that resemble shoe leather. To make it easier to cut meat thin, place it in the freezer for 15 minutes.

BEEF

We like to use flank steak because is easy to find, relatively lean, and has a big beefy flavor that can stand up to the potent flavors in a stir-fry.

1. Place the partially frozen steak on a clean, dry work surface. Using a sharp chef's knife, slice the steak lengthwise into 2-inch-wide pieces..

2. Cut each 2-inch piece of flank steak against the grain into very thin slices.

CHICKEN

Boneless, skinless breasts work best for stir-fries and are easy to cut into ½-inch-wide strips. In the world of stir-frying, chicken requires a fairly long time to cook through and brown slightly—at least three or four minutes.

1. To produce uniform pieces of chicken, separate the tenderloins from the partially frozen boneless, skinless breasts. Center pieces need to be cut in half so they are approximately the same length as the end pieces.

2. Slice the breasts across the grain into ½-inch-wide strips that are 1½ to 2 inches long.

3. Cut tenderloins on the diagonal to produce pieces about the same size as the strips of breast meat.

PORK

Although some stir-fry recipes call for ground pork or thinly sliced boneless chops, we find that strips cut from a pork tenderloin are the most tender and flavorful option.

1. Place the partially frozen pork tenderloin on a clean, dry work surface. Using a sharp chef's knife, slice the pork crosswise into ¼-inch-thick medallions.

2. Slice each medallion into ¼-inch-wide strips.

SIMPLE STEAMED WHITE RICE

MAKES ABOUT 5 CUPS

To rinse the rice, you can either place it in a fine-mesh strainer and rinse under cool water or place it in a medium bowl and repeatedly fill the bowl with water while swishing the rice around, then carefully drain off the water.

2	cups long-grain or medium-grain white rice, rinsed
2½	cups water

1. Bring the rice and water to a boil in a large saucepan, then cover, reduce the heat to low, and cook until the water is just absorbed and there are small holes in the surface of the rice, about 10 minutes.

2. Remove the pot from the heat and let stand, covered, until the rice is tender, about 15 minutes longer. Serve.

STIR-FRYING STEP BY STEP

Here are the four key steps to making a stir-fry. (Be sure to use a 12-inch nonstick skillet and cook over high heat.)

1. Start by cooking the protein, but don't cook it through completely; instead, remove it from the pan when it is just shy of being done and cover with foil to keep warm. It will finish cooking with the sauce at the end.

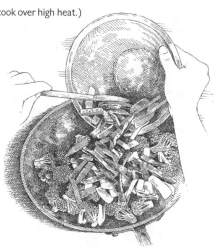

2. Next, cook the vegetables in batches, adding the tougher vegetables first and the more delicate vegetables later. This ensures that each vegetable will be perfectly cooked.

3. Push the vegetables to the edges of the skillet, clearing a spot in the middle. Add the garlic, ginger, and a little oil to the cleared spot and cook, mashing them into the hot pan using a wooden spoon until they are fragrant, about 30 seconds.

4. Return the cooked protein to the skillet, add the sauce, and toss to combine. Continue to cook until the sauce has thickened and the meat (if using) is fully cooked, 1 to 2 minutes.

ESSENTIAL TOOLS FOR STIR-FRYING SUCCESS

Stir-frying requires only a couple of pieces of basic equipment (you probably already own them). Woks are the traditional cooking vessel for stir-frying in China. Conically shaped, woks rest in cylindrical pits containing the fire. Flames lick the bottom and sides of the pan so that food cooks remarkably quickly. A wok, however, is not designed for stovetop cooking, where heat only comes from the bottom. Therefore, we prefer a 12- or 14-inch nonstick skillet for stir-frying. This pan requires a minimum of oil and prevents food from burning onto the surface as it stir-fries. We tested major brands of nonstick skillets (see page 515) and particularly liked pans that were sturdy, but not overly heavy, with a good nonstick performance.

Our second choice for stir-frying is a regular 12- or 14-inch traditional skillet. Without the nonstick coating, you will need to use slightly more oil. However, this pan will deliver satisfactory results. If you do not own a large skillet of any kind, do not substitute a smaller size. A 10-inch skillet is not large enough to accommodate all the ingredients in a stir-fry recipe for four. The ingredients will steam rather than stir-fry.

Chinese cooks use long-handled metal shovel-like spatulas to move food around woks. The same tool works well in a nonstick skillet, although to protect the pan's surface, you should use only plastic or wooden implements. We prefer a large shovel with a wide, thin blade and long, heat-resistant handle.

Spicy Stir-Fried Chicken and Bok Choy with Hoisin Sauce

SERVES 4

To make slicing the chicken easier, freeze it for 15 minutes. Stir-fries cook quickly, so have everything prepped before you begin cooking. Serve with Simple Steamed White Rice (page 516).

SAUCE

¼ cup hoisin sauce

1½ tablespoons soy sauce

1½ tablespoons Chinese rice cooking wine or dry sherry

1 tablespoon garlic-chili sauce, such as Sriracha

STIR-FRY

1 pound boneless, skinless chicken breasts (about 2 large breasts) trimmed and sliced thin (see page 516)

2 teaspoons soy sauce

2 teaspoons Chinese rice cooking wine or dry sherry

1 tablespoon cornstarch

1 tablespoon flour

2 tablespoons toasted sesame oil

3 medium garlic cloves, minced or pressed through a garlic press (about 1 tablespoon)

1 tablespoon minced or grated fresh ginger

2 scallions, minced

2 tablespoons plus 1 teaspoon vegetable oil

1 small head bok choy (about 1 pound), stalks and greens separated, stalks sliced crosswise into ¼-inch-wide pieces and greens cut into ½-inch-wide strips

1. FOR THE SAUCE: Whisk all of the ingredients together; set aside.

2. FOR THE STIR-FRY: Toss the chicken with the soy sauce, rice wine, cornstarch, flour, and sesame oil in a small bowl and let marinate for 10 minutes or up to 1 hour. In a separate bowl, mix the garlic, ginger, scallions, and 1 teaspoon of the vegetable oil; set aside.

3. Heat 1½ teaspoons vegetable oil in a 12-inch nonstick skillet over high heat until just smoking. Add half of the chicken, break up any clumps, then cook without stirring until the chicken is browned at the edges, about 3 minutes. Stir the chicken and continue to cook until the chicken is cooked through, about 3 minutes longer. Transfer the chicken to a medium bowl and repeat with 1½ teaspoons more vegetable oil and the remaining chicken; transfer to the bowl, cover with foil, and set aside.

4. Add the remaining 1 tablespoon vegetable oil to the skillet and return to high heat until just smoking. Add the bok choy stalks and cook for 1 minute. Clear the center of the skillet, add the garlic mixture and cook, mashing the mixture into the pan, until fragrant, 15 to 20 seconds. Stir the garlic mixture into the bok choy.

5. Stir in the bok choy greens and chicken with any accumulated juices. Whisk the sauce to recombine, then add to the skillet and cook, tossing constantly, until the sauce is thickened, about 30 seconds. Transfer to a serving platter and serve.

PREPARING BOK CHOY

1. Trim the bottom inch from the head of bok choy. Wash and dry the leaves and stalks. Cut the leafy green portion away from either side of the white stalk.

2. Cut each stalk in half lengthwise and then crosswise into ¼-inch-wide pieces.

3. Stack the leafy greens and then slice them crosswise into ½-inch-wide strips.

Stir-Fried Shrimp, Asparagus, and Carrots with Orange Sauce

SERVES 4

Use a vegetable peeler to peel strips of zest, but take care to avoid the bitter pith beneath the skin. If the asparagus spears are very thick, slice each stalk in half lengthwise before cutting them into 2-inch lengths. Stir-fries cook quickly, so have everything prepped before you begin cooking. Serve with Simple Steamed White Rice (page 516).

SAUCE

2	(2-inch-long) strips orange zest from 1 orange
½	cup juice from 2 oranges
¼	cup Chinese rice cooking wine or dry sherry
2	tablespoons soy sauce
1	tablespoon sugar
2	teaspoons cornstarch
1	teaspoon toasted sesame oil
½	teaspoon red pepper flakes

STIR-FRY

1	pound extra-large shrimp (21 to 25 per pound), peeled and deveined (see page 363)
2	teaspoons soy sauce
2	teaspoons Chinese rice cooking wine or dry sherry
3	medium garlic cloves, minced or pressed through a garlic press (about 1 tablespoon)
1	tablespoon minced or grated fresh ginger
2	scallions, minced
2	tablespoons plus 1 teaspoon vegetable oil
1	pound asparagus (about 1 bunch), tough ends trimmed and sliced on the bias into 2-inch lengths
2	carrots, peeled and cut into 2-inch-long matchsticks

1. FOR THE SAUCE: Whisk all of the ingredients together; set aside.

2. FOR THE STIR-FRY: Toss the shrimp with the soy sauce and rice wine in a small bowl and let marinate for 10 minutes or up to 1 hour. In a separate bowl, mix the garlic, ginger, scallions, and 1 teaspoon of the vegetable oil; set aside.

3. Heat 1½ teaspoons vegetable oil in a 12-inch nonstick skillet over high heat until just smoking. Add half of the shrimp and cook, without stirring, until the shrimp are browned at the edges, about 1 minute. Stir the shrimp and continue to cook until they are nearly cooked through, about 30 seconds longer. Transfer the shrimp to a medium bowl and repeat with 1½ teaspoons more vegetable oil and the remaining shrimp; transfer to the bowl, cover with foil, and set aside.

4. Add the remaining 1 tablespoon vegetable oil to the skillet and return to high heat until just smoking. Add the asparagus and carrots and cook until crisp-tender, 2 to 3 minutes. Clear the center of the skillet, add the garlic mixture and cook, mashing the mixture into the pan, until fragrant, 15 to 20 seconds. Stir the garlic mixture into the vegetables.

5. Stir in the shrimp with any accumulated juices. Whisk the sauce to recombine, then add it to the skillet and cook, tossing constantly, until the sauce has thickened, about 30 seconds. Transfer to a serving platter and serve.

CUTTING CARROTS INTO MATCHSTICKS

1. Start by slicing the carrot on the bias into rounds.

2. Fan the rounds and cut them into strips that measure about 2 inches long and ¼ inch thick.

Stir-Fried Tofu, Snow Peas, and Cabbage with Oyster Sauce
SERVES 4

Coating the tofu with cornstarch gives it a pleasant golden-brown crust. Instead of marinating the tofu in this recipe, we found glazing the cooked tofu in soy sauce, sugar and chicken broth gives this dish better flavor. See pages 516 and 517 for more information on stir-frying. Stir-fries cook quickly, so have everything prepped before you begin cooking. Serve with Simple Steamed White Rice (page 516).

SAUCE
I	cup low-sodium chicken or vegetable broth
3	tablespoons oyster sauce
I	tablespoon soy sauce
I	tablespoon cornstarch
2	teaspoons toasted sesame oil

STIR-FRY
2	tablespoons soy sauce
2	tablespoons sugar
¼	cup low-sodium chicken or vegetable broth
5	teaspoons minced or grated fresh ginger
3	medium garlic cloves, minced or pressed through a garlic press (about I tablespoon)
2	scallions, minced
¼	cup vegetable oil
⅓	cup cornstarch
I	(14-ounce) block extra-firm tofu, cut into 1-inch cubes
I	cup snow peas, strings removed
¼	cup water
I	pound green cabbage (about ½ medium head), cored and cut into 2-inch squares
I	tablespoon sesame seeds, toasted (optional)

1. FOR THE SAUCE: Whisk all of the ingredients together; set aside.

2. FOR THE STIR-FRY: Whisk the soy sauce, sugar, and broth together in a small bowl; set aside. In a separate bowl, mix the ginger, garlic, scallions, and 1 teaspoon of the vegetable oil together; set aside. Spread the cornstarch into a wide, shallow dish. Pat the tofu dry with paper towels, then coat all sides of the tofu evenly with the cornstarch and transfer to a plate.

3. Heat 1½ tablespoons more vegetable oil in 12-inch nonstick skillet over high heat until just smoking. Add half the tofu and cook, turning every few minutes, until all sides are crisp and browned, about 8 minutes. Transfer the tofu to a medium bowl and repeat with 1½ tablespoons more vegetable oil and the remaining tofu. Return all of the tofu to the skillet, add the soy mixture, and cook until the tofu is nicely glazed, 1 to 2 minutes. Transfer the glazed tofu to a plate, cover with foil, and set aside. Rinse and dry the skillet.

4. Add the remaining 2 teaspoons vegetable oil to the skillet and return to high heat until just smoking. Add the snow peas and cook until beginning to brown and soften, 1 to 2 minutes. Add the water, cover, and reduce the heat to medium. Steam the peas until crisp-tender, about 2 minutes. Remove the lid, add the cabbage, and continue to cook until cabbage is wilted, about 1 minute.

5. Clear the center of the skillet, add the ginger mixture and cook, mashing the mixture into the pan, until fragrant, 15 to 20 seconds. Stir the ginger mixture into the vegetables.

6. Return the tofu to the skillet. Whisk the sauce to recombine, then add to the skillet and cook, tossing constantly, until the sauce is thickened, about 30 seconds. Transfer to a platter, sprinkle with sesame seeds (if using) and serve.

STRINGING SNOW PEAS

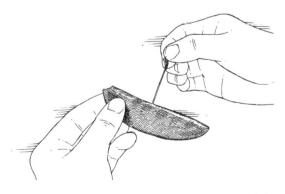

Snap off the tip of the snow pea and at the same time pull down along the flat side of the pod to remove the string.

INGREDIENTS: Soy Sauce

Most of us have rarely given soy sauce a second thought, using it as a kind of liquid salt. But this 2,500-year-old ingredient, brewed first in China and since the seventh century in Japan, can offer nearly as much variety, complexity, and flavor as wine or olive oil and it deserves serious consideration.

At its most basic, soy sauce is a fermented liquid made from soybeans and wheat. Soybeans contribute a strong, pungent taste, while wheat lends sweetness. Tamari is a type of soy sauce traditionally made with all soybeans and no wheat— though, confusingly, many tamaris do contain a little wheat. As a result, tamari has a more pungent flavor than soy sauce. Similarly, stronger, earthier Chinese soy sauce tends to be made with a lower proportion of wheat than the sweeter, lighter Japanese soy sauce.

All soy sauce begins with whole soybeans or defatted soy meal cooked and mixed with roasted grain, usually wheat (but sometimes barley or rice). This bean and grain mixture is inoculated with a mold called *koji* and left for a few days to allow the mold to grow and spread. Then salt water and yeast are added to form a mash called *moromi*. And here comes the biggest difference in quality levels of soy sauce: The mash is fermented for anywhere from two days to four years. The brown liquid that is extruded from the mash is soy sauce, which is usually filtered, pasteurized, and bottled.

We tasted a variety of the most commonly found soy sauces, including both tamari and regular soy sauce, from Japan, China, and the United States. Each was tasted three times: first plain, then with warm rice, and finally cooked in a teriyaki sauce with ginger, garlic, and mirin and brushed over broiled chicken thighs.

Since we prefer simplicity in the test kitchen, we were hoping one clear winner would emerge from our tasting. No such luck. Our tasters liked one type of soy sauce for plain, uncooked applications and an entirely different one for cooked dishes. Our results clearly underscored the fact that there's no "one-size-fits-all" soy sauce.

In the plain tasting, Ohsawa Nama Shoyu (a traditionally brewed import from Japan) came out on top. With 720 milligrams per tablespoon, it has the lowest sodium level of the 12 brands we tasted. When the sauces were drizzled over warm rice and cooked into a teriyaki glaze, our tasters preferred a mass-produced Chinese brand, Lee Kum Kee Tabletop Soy Sauce, which has the highest sodium level of the lineup, at 1,200 milligrams per tablespoon. Ohsawa Nama Shoyu was described as having a "sweet," "delicate," even "floral" taste, while tasters dubbed Lee Kum Kee "salty," "malty," and "delicious."

THE BEST SOY SAUCE

LEE KUM KEE TABLETOP SOY SAUCE
This Chinese brand won rice and teriyaki tastings. With rice, its flavor was described as "salty, sweet, roasted, pleasant," and "fruity," with a "great aroma." Cooked in teriyaki, it was "salty, malty, and delicious," with "good depth" and "balance." Contains more sodium than other brands tested.

OHSAWA NAMA SHOYU ORGANIC UNPASTEURIZED SOY SAUCE
This Japanese brand won the plain tasting, with its flavor described as "clean," "caramel," and "rich and nuanced." A few tasters called it "sweet and dimensional," even "floral," with one adding that it was "lighter in style and flavor than others." Contains less sodium than other brands tested.

KUNG PAO SHRIMP

KUNG PAO, THE CLASSIC SICHUAN STIR-FRY of meat or shellfish with peanuts and chiles in a rich brown sauce is now a Chinese restaurant standard, although its origins date back to 19th-century central-western China in the Sichuan province. While most of the original versions of this dish we found use chicken, we've found more modern versions of kung pao dishes that use beef, seafood, tofu, or just vegetables, and shrimp is a popular variation.

Unfortunately, the kung paos we sampled in half a dozen well-reputed restaurants were hopeless. The first one was dismal, with tough, tiny little shrimp drenched in a quart of pale, greasy, bland sauce, and things just got worse from there.

Like most stir-fries, kung pao cooks quickly, so it is well suited for a weeknight meal. Moreover, we thought that by carefully examining the key cooking issues—the type and preparation of both the shrimp and the nuts along with the composition and texture

SHOPPING NOTES: Chiles

Without spicy chile heat, it's not kung pao. The recipes we consulted, however, offered little agreement about the best source of that heat. So we hit the supermarket up the street and picked up the most oft-repeated contenders, including whole dried chiles (the traditional choice), red pepper flakes, fresh chiles, chili oil, and two popular and widely available Asian chili sauces, *sambal* and *Sriracha*. Thus outfitted to heat things up, we returned to the test kitchen and conducted a side-by-side kung pao tasting.

The exact formula for sambal, a chunky chili-garlic paste, varies from maker to maker. Ours was seasoned with salt, sugar, and rice vinegar. Smoother Sriracha is a popular Thai chili sauce and ours was seasoned with salt, sugar, garlic, and fish extract. Both sambal and Sriracha are common Asian table condiments, but tasters gave them a thumbs-down in the kung pao because they lacked depth and tended to taste too salty. Chili oil was also passed by because the one we used, actually a chile-flavored sesame oil, was judged too mild and it made the sauce a bit greasy. The fresh chiles—jalapeños, to be exact—provided sharp heat, but the tasters did not appreciate the distinct green, vegetal notes. Red pepper flakes provided a bright, direct heat that was utterly acceptable, but the tasters' favorite by a long shot was the whole dried chiles, which infused the kung pao with a round, even spiciness that offered a deep, toasty, almost smoky dimension as well.

This finding, of course, begged the question of whether one particular type of dried chile would be best, as there are many varieties. With our sights set on relatively small chiles (large chiles simply looked wrong in the dish), we returned to the market and gathered six varieties, including an unnamed Asian specimen from the bulk bin, Japones, arbol, guajillo, Costeño, and cascabel. Tasters strained to detect distinctions between them in the kung pao. We concluded that any small whole dried red chiles will do quite nicely.

SMALL WHOLE DRIED RED CHILES
We tested various sources of heat in developing Kung Pao Shrimp and found that whole dried chiles infused the dish not just with heat, but with spicy, complex flavor as well.

of the sauce—we could come up with something akin to what the Chinese cook at home.

Most Chinese stir-fries go heavy on the vegetables, but kung pao dishes are different. The quantity of vegetables is limited, with the emphasis instead on the shrimp and the nuts. The restaurant versions we tried often included green pepper, and some added bamboo shoots, carrots, celery, scallions, and zucchini. We worked our way through these choices and more and settled on a modest amount of red pepper for sweetness and scallion for freshness, bite, and color. kung pao needs nothing else from the vegetable kingdom.

Taking a step up the food chain, we looked at the shrimp next. While some recipes call for small or medium shrimp, we felt that larger shrimp made a more satisfying kung pao, and large shrimp were easier to peel, too. After checking out jumbo, extra-large, and large, we selected extra-large (21 to 25 per pound) for their combination of succulence and generous appearance. (See page 524 to learn how shrimp are sized.)

The best way to prepare the shrimp was a matter of some debate. Traditionally, they are coated with egg white, cornstarch, and seasonings, and then fried in a generous quantity of oil. The idea here is to create a softly crisp coating that will help the sauce adhere. Though this method does have its supporters, we are not among them, for two reasons. First, the egg coating tended to cook up in unattractive clumps, which would later float about in the dish, and second, the two to three cups of oil required to deep-fry seemed both cumbersome and wasteful. Dealing with all that oil, from measuring it out to disposing of it later, edged the dish out of the realm of simple weeknight cooking. It would be much better, we felt, to quickly stir-fry the shrimp in a film of oil and to thicken the sauce slightly to help it coat the shrimp.

The nuts help define kung pao. In most of the restaurant dishes we tried, the flavor of the nuts was underdeveloped, so they acted more as a garnish than a key element. In contrast, we wanted to better integrate the nuts into the dish and to deepen their flavor. One move accomplished both goals. Whereas most recipes add the nuts near the end of the cooking time, we stir-fried them right along with the shrimp at the beginning. This way, they toasted briefly in the pan, intensifying in flavor, which they then contributed to the sauce. Most kung pao recipes rely on either peanuts or cashews, and we appreciated the former for their savory flavor and crisp texture. By comparison, cashews seemed both sweet and a little soft.

Luckily for us, the test kitchen has conducted extensive investigations into stir-frying technique, so we knew that a wide, heavy skillet, preheated until the oil smokes, is a better mate with the flat American stovetop burner than a deeply curved wok. With all that heat, though, it would be easy to overcook, and therefore toughen, the shrimp and to burn the aromatic garlic and ginger that are part of the sauce. Two simple tricks helped us to avoid both problems. First, we learned not to cook shrimp all the way through at first because they would finish cooking in the sauce later; an initial stay in the pan of just under two minutes was ideal. Second, while most stir-fry recipes add garlic and ginger near the beginning, we prefer to add them near the end of cooking to prevent burning and preserve their fresh flavors.

When it came to the sauce, we pictured it deep brown, syrupy in texture, and glistening, with balanced elements of sweet, savory, salty, garlicky, and hot. We tried both chicken broth and water as a base and preferred the broth for the savory underpinning it provided. For a bit of sweetness we added sugar in amounts from 1 tablespoon down to 1 teaspoon, but even a mere teaspoon was overkill. Instead, we chose to add the classic Asian trio of hoisin sauce, oyster sauce, and sesame oil, all available (separately) in the supermarket and all good sources of color, flavor depth, and subtle sweetness. An ample supply of garlic—three cloves—gave the sauce authority and ginger and rice vinegar added brightness. We liked Chinese black rice vinegar (also called Chinkiang vinegar) even better because it was more complex—smoky, salty, plum-like, and slightly sweet. Cornstarch is the thickener of choice for Asian sauces and 1½ teaspoons reliably gelled the sauce to a soft, glazy, shrimp-coating consistency.

For heat, we unanimously chose whole dried chiles, which are traditional for this dish (although red pepper flakes work well also). We altered the technique with which they are generally used, however, by stir-frying them with the shrimp and peanuts at the beginning of the cooking. This extra bit of pan time toasted the chiles, deepening their flavor noticeably.

Sichuan peppercorns are the other defining flavor in authentic kung pao dishes, as we discovered from our cursory research on this dish, but we had trouble finding recipes that use them. Curious, we dug a bit deeper to find that from 1968 to 2005, it was illegal to bring Sichuan peppercorns into the U.S. (they are carriers of a tree disease that can potentially harm citrus crops). Since they're now available (mostly at Asian markets and specialty spice purveyors), we tested different amounts and were amazed to realize that some recipes include handfuls of this potent spice. We found that 1 teaspoon, crushed and added with the peanuts and chiles to bloom in the hot pan, was just the right amount to tingle our palates and give this kung pao shrimp the authenticity it demanded.

Kung Pao Shrimp
SERVES 4

You can substitute plain rice vinegar for the black rice vinegar (available in Asian markets), but we prefer the latter for its fruity, salty complexity. Don't eat the whole chiles in the final dish; if you can't find small dried red chiles, substitute 1 teaspoon dried red pepper flakes. For more information on Sichuan peppercorns, see page 506. Serve with Simple Steamed White Rice (page 516).

SAUCE

¾	cup low-sodium chicken broth
I	tablespoon oyster sauce
I	tablespoon hoisin sauce
2	teaspoons black rice vinegar or plain rice vinegar
2	teaspoons toasted sesame oil
I½	teaspoons cornstarch

STIR-FRY

1   pound extra-large shrimp (21 to 25 per
    pound), peeled and deveined (see page 363)

2   teaspoons soy sauce

2   teaspoons Chinese rice cooking wine or
    dry sherry

3   medium garlic cloves, minced or pressed
    through a garlic press (about 1 tablespoon)

1   teaspoons minced or grated fresh ginger

2   scallions, minced

2   tablespoons plus 1 teaspoon vegetable oil

6   small whole dried red chiles (each about 2
    inches long)

½   cup roasted unsalted peanuts

1   medium red bell pepper, stemmed, seeded
    and cut into ½-inch pieces

1   teaspoon Sichuan peppercorns, crushed

1. FOR THE SAUCE: Whisk all of the ingredients together; set aside.

2. FOR THE STIR-FRY: Toss the shrimp with the soy sauce and rice wine in a small bowl and let marinate for 10 minutes, or up to 1 hour. In a separate bowl, mix together the garlic, ginger, scallions, and 1 teaspoon of the vegetable oil; set aside. In a third bowl, crumble half of the chiles coarsely, then toss with the remaining whole chiles and peanuts; set aside.

3. Heat 1½ teaspoons vegetable oil in a 12-inch nonstick skillet over high heat until just smoking. Add half of the shrimp and cook, without stirring, until the shrimp are browned at the edges, about 1 minute. Stir in the chiles and peanuts and cook until the shrimp are almost completely opaque and the peanuts have darkened slightly, about 30 seconds longer. Transfer the mixture to a medium bowl and repeat with 1½ teaspoons more vegetable oil and the remaining shrimp; transfer to the bowl and set aside.

4. Add the remaining 1 tablespoon vegetable oil to the skillet and return to high heat until just smoking. Add the red bell pepper and Sichuan peppercorns and cook until the bell pepper is slightly softened and the peppercorns are fragrant, about 1 minute.

5. Clear the center of the skillet, add the garlic mixture and cook, mashing the mixture into the pan, until fragrant, 15 to 20 seconds. Stir the garlic mixture into the peppers. Stir in the shrimp mixture with any accumulated juices. Whisk the sauce to recombine, then add to the skillet and cook, tossing constantly, until the sauce is thickened, about 30 seconds. Transfer to a platter and serve.

SIZING SHRIMP

Shrimp are sold by size (small, medium, large, and so on) as well as by the number needed to make 1 pound, usually given in a range. Choosing shrimp by the numerical rating is more accurate than choosing by a size label, which varies from store to store. Here's how the two systems line up, with shrimp shown in actual sizes. For information on buying frozen shrimp, see page 361.

SMALL	MEDIUM	LARGE	EXTRA-LARGE
51 to 60 per pound	41 to 50 per pound	31 to 40 per pound	21 to 25 per pound

CRISPY TOFU WITH SWEET CHILI SAUCE

Tianla Cuipi Doufu

FRESH BEAN CURD, OR TOFU, IS A NATURAL candidate for both pan-frying and for pairing with a sweet chili sauce. The crispy coating is a good foil for the creamy, mild tofu interior and the bracing and bright sweet chili sauce enlivens tofu's mild flavor and texture, making this a popular dish in China. We set out to create our own version of this satisfying vegetarian entrée.

We started our testing with the tofu. Based on our past test kitchen experience where we found extra-firm tofu to be the best type to stir-fry, we felt certain this would also be the case with the crispy tofu. We coated and pan-fried extra-firm, firm, medium-firm, and soft tofus and tasted them side by side and were surprised to hear tasters say that the extra-firm tofu was their least favorite of the bunch. In fact, tasters unanimously preferred the medium-firm and soft tofus for their creamy, custard-like texture. Because we were using a softer tofu, we decided not to press the tofu under a weighted plate to expel excess moisture as we had with our past stir-fry recipes, as we didn't want the tofu to lose its shape. Instead we simply cut the tofu into planks and then placed it on multiple layers of paper towels to drain. Once the drained tofu was encased in a coating, a little excess water only helped the tofu stay moist. Note, because softer tofu is more fragile it should be handled gently so that it holds it shape.

Next we tested the coating. Again we turned to our past experience with tofu in stir-fries. We had good luck in the past with a pure cornstarch coating, as it helps the sauce adhere to the tofu pieces. We started our testing there; the cornstarch yielded a thin, crispy coating that barely browned, but held up well in the pan. Because the tofu isn't tossed in the sauce, but served alongside it, we felt we could be a bit more adventurous with the coating. After all, we weren't looking for the sauce to adhere to the tofu, we just wanted the flavors and textures to work well together.

In our library of authentic Chinese cookbooks, we had stumbled across a couple of recipes where cornmeal is added to the coating. We started with ½ cup cornmeal mixed with ½ cup cornstarch but found that to be too heavy on the cornmeal—tasters complained of a gritty texture. We cut back to ¼ cup cornmeal with ¾ cup cornstarch, which proved just the right combination. This tofu had a crispy, golden coating with a creamy interior.

Up to this point we'd been cutting the tofu blocks into planks about 1 inch thick, but tasters started to complain that they wanted more coating. Cutting each plank in half to make "fingers" quickly solved the problem. Now we had a greater coating to tofu ratio that everyone thought gave the right balance of crispy to creamy.

Finally, we turned our attention to the sauce. A classic pairing with tofu is a sweet chili sauce. While most people in China simply buy this condiment because of its availability in most markets, we opted to come up with a recipe. A little research showed that this sauce consists of five simple ingredients simmered together in a saucepan. We started with equal parts sugar, water, and rice vinegar. To that we added just enough heat with 2 teaspoons of chile

---

PANTRY SPOTLIGHT

TOFU

Popular across Asia, tofu is made from the curds of soy milk. Although freshly made tofu is common across the Pacific, in the U.S., tofu is typically sold in blocks packed in water and found in the refrigerated section of supermarkets. You can find tofu in a variety of textures, such as silken, soft, medium-firm, firm, and extra-firm. We prefer the latter two in stir-frying because the tofu holds its shape well while being moved around a hot pan. In recipes where the contrast of a crunchy crust to a creamy interior is desired, such as Crispy Tofu with Sweet Chili Sauce (page 526), medium-firm or soft tofu is best.

Like dairy products, tofu is perishable and should be kept well chilled to maximize its shelf life. We prefer to use it within a few days of opening. If you want to keep an open package of tofu fresh for several days, cover the tofu with fresh water and store it in the refrigerator in an airtight container, changing the water daily. Any hint of sourness means the tofu is past its prime.

paste and the same amount of cornstarch to thicken the sauce. It was a good start, but tasters complained that it was too sweet and not hot enough. By cutting the sugar down to 3 tablespoons and increasing the chili paste to 1 tablespoon, we had just the right balance for this sweet chili sauce. Now we just had to stack up our crispy tofu on a plate, pour some sauce over the pieces, and start eating.

Crispy Tofu with Sweet Chili Sauce
Tianla Cuipi Doufu
SERVES 4 AS A FIRST COURSE, OR
2 AS A MAIN COURSE

We prefer the softer, creamier texture of medium-firm or soft tofu here; firm or extra-firm tofu will also work, however, they will taste drier. Be sure to handle the tofu gently and thoroughly pat it dry before seasoning and coating.

SAUCE
- 3 tablespoons sugar
- ¼ cup water
- ¼ cup rice vinegar
- 2 teaspoons cornstarch
- 1 tablespoon Indonesian chile paste, such as sambal oelek (see page 561)

TOFU
- 1 (14-ounce) block medium-firm or soft tofu (see note), sliced crosswise into 1-inch-thick slabs, each slab sliced into two 1-inch-wide fingers
- ¾ cup cornstarch
- ¼ cup cornmeal
  Salt and ground black pepper
- ¾ cup vegetable oil

1. FOR THE SAUCE: Whisk all of the ingredients together in a small saucepan and cook over medium-high heat, whisking constantly, until the sauce is hot and thickened, about 4 minutes. Cover and set aside to keep warm.

2. FOR THE TOFU: Meanwhile, spread the tofu out over several layers of paper towels and let sit for 20 minutes to drain slightly. While the tofu drains, adjust an oven rack to the middle position, place a paper towel–lined plate on the rack, and heat the oven to 200 degrees.

3. Place a wire rack over a baking sheet and set aside. Toss the cornstarch and cornmeal together in a wide, shallow dish. Season the tofu with salt and pepper. Working with a few pieces of tofu at a time, coat them thoroughly with the cornstarch mixture, pressing on the coating to adhere, then transfer to the wire rack.

4. Heat the oil in a 12-inch nonstick skillet over medium-high heat until shimmering. Carefully lay half of the tofu in the skillet and cook, turning the pieces occasionally with a spatula, until crisp and lightly golden on all sides, about 4 minutes. Using a spatula, gently lift the tofu from the oil, letting any excess oil drip back into the pan, and transfer to the prepared plate in the oven. Repeat with the remaining tofu pieces and let them drain briefly on the prepared plate before serving with the warm sauce.

CRISPY WEST LAKE FISH
Xihu Cuyu

WEST LAKE IS A FRESH WATER LAKE LOCATED in central Hangzhou in eastern China that has been famous for its exquisite beauty for more than a thousand years. The source of inspiration for many famous poets and artists, West Lake has also inspired various dishes, including West Lake fish, a whole freshwater fish, either poached or fried, and served with a spicy sweet and sour sauce. We've had a couple of versions of West Lake fish at our local Chinese restaurant and were very impressed. Gently poached or crisply fried, a white fish, often catfish, is presented to the table still whole, looking as though it's swimming across the plate, yet it falls easily into ready-to-eat portions with barely an effort. Theatrics aside, the sweet, moist flesh of the fish pairs perfectly with the sweet and sour sauce that defines this dish. We set out to see if we could create a home version.

While West Lake fish is traditionally cooked and served whole, we wanted an easier approach to this dish, so off the bat we decided to use fish fillets. Traditional recipes are divided into two camps when it comes to the cooking method: poached and pan-fried. Poaching the fillets was a bit tricky as they had a tendency to fall apart during cooking. The poached fillets also tasted uninteresting when compared to the pan-fried version with its golden, crisp crust, so we settled on pan-fried. Many of the pan-fried recipes we found dredged the fish in cornstarch before cooking to give it an extra-crisp coating and we thought that this was a good idea. There is no need to coat the fish with egg or oil before coating with the cornstarch, because the natural moisture within the fish provides a tacky texture to which a thin, even coating of cornstarch can stick. We encourage this by salting the fish and letting it sit for a few minutes before coating with cornstarch. For more information on this technique see page 170.

With our cooking method in order, it was time to address the sauce. We started with the sweet and sour elements, namely sugar and vinegar. Many of the recipes we consulted recommend Chinese red vinegar, but we found this product difficult to find and decided on red wine vinegar as a viable substitute. An equal amount of sugar brought the right balance to this sauce. We stumbled across an interesting recipe in our research where the sugar is caramelized first with the aromatics (garlic and ginger) before the liquid ingredients are added. We tested it and tasters were sold. The caramelized sugar mixture added a depth of flavor that was clearly missing in previous versions of the sauce. We also found that fresh red chiles benefited from this caramelization. One chile was enough to give our sauce a bit of fire, while the bright red color lent the dish a fresh appearance.

Sweet and sour sauces always include soy sauce—it adds a necessary saltiness and savory element to this dish. But other similar sauces use as much soy sauce as they do vinegar or sugar. In this case, the soy was far too overpowering for the fish and we ultimately brought it all the way down to 1 tablespoon, or one-third of the sweet or sour element for the right balance of flavors. A modest amount of rice wine rounded out the potent acid and sweet elements of the sauce, and a cup of water took this sweet and sour sauce from too intense to just right.

Finally, our sauce was in harmony with the fish—except that the sauce was thin and watery. We added just 1 tablespoon of cornstarch to thicken this sauce to the right consistency, so that it clung to the crispy, tender fish.

Crispy West Lake Fish
Xihu Cuyu
SERVES 4

You can use either skinless or skin-on fillets here; most tasters liked the crisp texture of the cooked skin. Any thin, medium-firm white fish fillets can be substituted for the catfish, including haddock, tilapia, flounder, snapper, trout, orange roughy, tilefish, and arctic char. Keep the sauce and the fish separate until ready to serve to help preserve the crisp exterior of the fish.

SAUCE
- 1 tablespoon minced or grated fresh ginger
- 2 medium garlic cloves, minced or pressed through a garlic press (about 2 teaspoons)
- 1 small Thai red, serrano, or red or green jalapeño chile, stemmed, seeded, and chopped coarse
- 3 tablespoons sugar
- 1 cup water
- 3 tablespoons red wine vinegar
- 1 tablespoon soy sauce
- 1 tablespoon Chinese rice cooking wine or dry sherry
- 1 tablespoon cornstarch
- 3 scallions, sliced thin

FISH
- 4 catfish fillets (about 6 ounces each)
  Salt and ground black pepper
- 3 tablespoons cornstarch
- ¼ cup vegetable oil

1. FOR THE SAUCE: Combine the ginger, garlic, chile, and sugar together in a small heavy-bottomed saucepan and cook over medium-high heat until the sugar melts and turns golden brown, 5 to 7 minutes. Whisk the water, vinegar, soy sauce, rice wine, and cornstarch together, then carefully whisk into the saucepan—the sugar mixture will

be extremely hot. Continue to simmer, stirring constantly, until the sauce is thickened, 2 to 4 minutes. Cover and set aside off the heat.

2. FOR THE FISH: Adjust the oven racks to the lower- and upper-middle positions, set 4 heatproof dinner plates on the racks, and heat the oven to 200 degrees. Pat the fish dry with paper towels and season both sides with salt and pepper; let stand until the fillets are glistening with moisture, about 5 minutes.

3. Spread the cornstarch into a wide, shallow dish. Coat both sides of the fillets with cornstarch, shake off the excess, and lay in a single layer on a baking sheet. Heat 2 tablespoons of the oil in a 12-inch nonstick skillet over high heat until shimmering. Carefully place 2 fillets in the skillet, skin side down, and immediately reduce the heat to medium-high. Cook, without moving the fish, until the edges of the fillets are opaque and the bottom is golden and crisp, about 4½ minutes.

4. Following the illustration on page 170, use 2 spatulas to gently flip the fillets, then continue to cook on the second side until the thickest part of the fillet easily separates into flakes when a toothpick is inserted, about 3 minutes longer. Transfer each of the fillets to a heated dinner plate

in the oven. Wipe out the skillet and repeat with the remaining 2 tablespoons oil and the remaining fillets; transfer each fillet to a plate in oven. (The fish can be held in the oven for up to 10 minutes before continuing.)

5. Return the sauce to a brief simmer over medium-high heat. Stir in the scallions, then pour the sauce over the fish and serve immediately.

RED-COOKED CHICKEN
Hongshaoji

RED-COOKED CHICKEN—PIECES OF CHICKEN gently simmered in dark soy sauce, rice wine, ginger, scallions, and star anise until stained a deep mahogany—is as dramatic as it is delicious. A soothing dish akin to comfort food, red-cooked chicken is also often referred to as a "rice-sending dish" because the sauce is said to stimulate the appetite for rice.

Red cooking is a Chinese cooking technique that is also called Chinese stewing, red stewing, or red braising and is linked to Shanghai and other parts of eastern China that are known for the premium quality of their soy sauce and rice wine. We were lucky enough to stumble across this dish at our local Chinese restaurant and knew we wanted this in our repertoire of Chinese recipes. So with some recipes in hand we headed to the test kitchen to try to replicate red-cooked chicken.

We've braised a lot of chicken in the test kitchen, and whether it contains wine, broth, or soy sauce, there are some similarities. All braises start by browning the chicken to yield a fond that enriches the braising liquid, then aromatics are added, followed by the braising liquid. Finally, it all simmers together until the meat is fall-apart tender. The tricky part for us was that we were unfamiliar with using dark soy sauce—the defining ingredient in red-cooked dishes—as part of the braise. Different than the soy sauce we see in supermarkets, dark soy sauce is a darker, slightly thicker soy sauce that is aged longer and contains added molasses to give it its distinctive appearance and slightly bitter flavor.

PANTRY SPOTLIGHT

DARK SOY SAUCE

There are many different kinds of soy sauce, but most of them fit into two categories: light and dark. Light soy sauce (aka regular soy sauce), the kind most commonly used, is the thinner and saltier of the two and is used as a condiment as much as it's used in cooking. For more information on light soy sauce and our recommended brands, see page 521. Dark soy sauce, on the other hand, is used exclusively in cooking. It is less salty, a bit sweet, darker in color, and thicker due to a longer brewing process and the addition of molasses. It adds a fruity richness and dark brown color to dishes, such as Red-Cooked Chicken (page 529). Look for dark soy sauce in Asian markets and some well-stocked supermarkets.

Our inexperience showed in the earliest versions, which are now referred to as the red-cooked clunkers. But the memory of the restaurant version propelled us back into the test kitchen to get it right.

As with any braise, this dish begins with the meat. We tried using a whole bird cut into manageable pieces, but found the extra work unnecessary and ultimately decided on chicken pieces. Dark meat is the most forgiving part of the bird when braising, as it's difficult to overcook, but white meat also works well in this braise as long as it's removed from the pot when it reaches 160 degrees (otherwise it dries out).

Our next, and most challenging, focus was the sauce. Once the chicken was browned, we added our sauce ingredients—equal amounts of dark soy sauce and chicken broth formed the base of the sauce. Chinese rice cooking wine or dry sherry (we found either one works well in this dish) added a little acid and a generous 3 tablespoons of sesame oil rounded out the flavors. Unfortunately, the resulting sauce was thinner and more bitter than we wanted. Simply decreasing the chicken broth from ½ cup to ⅓ cup helped remedy that problem, but not enough. With the slightly bitter quality of the dark soy sauce, the flavor of the sauce was still not quite right—we would need something to counter the bitterness. Sugar was our most likely savior, and after trying granulated, light brown, and dark brown, we found that 3 tablespoons of light brown sugar added enough rich sweetness to bring this sauce back into balance.

Next we turned our attention to aromatics. Ginger and garlic are typically used in recipes for red-cooked dishes and a generous 2 tablespoons of each was perfect. Spices traditional to the flavor of this dish are star anise and five-spice powder. We found that three pieces of star anise added a delicate licorice flavor to the sauce, while the five-spice powder made the sauce a bit gritty. Instead, we singled out one of the spices in five-spice powder—Sichuan peppercorns—adding just 1 teaspoon to the mix for its alluring heat.

With our recipe for red-cooked chicken near completion, we headed back into the kitchen for one last test. In our early research we had come across a few recipes that included hard-cooked eggs alongside the chicken. Although tasters weren't sold on the idea, just one test changed their minds. The eggs, which are hard-cooked first, cooled, and then peeled, are added to the braise with the browned chicken. In the finished dish, the outsides of the eggs are stained a deep mahogany, yet the interiors remain snowy white and bright yellow. But it was the combination of the rich, earthy eggs alongside the moist, meaty chicken that had everyone sold. This simple extra step turned this Chinese classic into a new test kitchen favorite.

Red-Cooked Chicken
Hongshaoji
SERVES 4

Dark soy sauce gives this dish its characteristic red color and deep, earthy flavor; you can substitute regular soy sauce but the dish will be lighter in color and less flavorful. If you use both chicken breasts and legs, we recommend cutting the breast pieces in half so that each person can have some white meat and some dark meat. The breasts and thighs do not cook at the same time; if using both, note that the breast pieces are added partway through the cooking time. Serve with Simple Steamed White Rice (page 516).

4   pounds bone-in, skin-on chicken pieces (thighs, drumsticks, and/or split breasts cut in half)
2   tablespoons vegetable oil, plus extra as needed
2   tablespoons minced or grated fresh ginger
6   medium garlic cloves, minced or pressed through a garlic press (about 2 tablespoons)
1   teaspoon Sichuan peppercorns (see page 506)
3   star anise
⅓   cup low-sodium chicken broth
½   cup dark soy sauce (see page 528)
¼   cup Chinese rice cooking wine or dry sherry
3   tablespoons toasted sesame oil
3   tablespoons light brown sugar
4   hard cooked eggs, peeled (see page 63)

1. Pat the chicken dry with paper towels. Heat the oil in a large Dutch oven over medium-high heat until shimmering. Brown half of the chicken on both sides, 5 to 8 minutes per side, reducing

the heat if the pan begins to scorch. Transfer the chicken to a plate, leaving the fat in the pot. Return the pot with the fat to medium-high heat and repeat with the remaining chicken; transfer the chicken to the plate.

2. Pour off all but 1 tablespoon of the fat in the pot (or add vegetable oil if needed); add the ginger, garlic, Sichuan peppercorns, and star anise and cook over medium heat until fragrant, about 30 seconds. Stir in the chicken broth, soy sauce, rice wine, sesame oil, and brown sugar, scraping up any browned bits.

3. Nestle the hard-cooked eggs and chicken, along with any accumulated juices, into the pot and bring to a simmer. Cover, turn the heat to medium-low, and simmer until the chicken is fully cooked and tender, about 1 hour for the thighs and drumsticks, or 20 minutes for the breasts (160 degrees on an instant-read thermometer), turning the chicken and eggs over halfway through cooking to ensure even cooking (and coloring). (If using both types of chicken, simmer the thighs and drumsticks for 40 minutes before adding the breasts.)

4. Transfer the chicken and eggs to a serving dish, tent loosely with foil, and let rest while finishing the sauce. Pour the sauce into a fat separator and let it sit until the fat has risen to the top, about 5 minutes. Once separated, pour the defatted broth over the chicken and eggs, and serve.

SWEET AND SOUR PORK RIBS

Tangcu Paigu

RICH, MEATY PORK RIBS BATHED IN A TANGY sweet and sour sauce is a Chinese favorite. However, order this dish in a Chinese restaurant in the U.S., and you're often met with ribs covered in a sticky sweet glaze more akin to candy than dinner fare. So where did this dish take a turn for the worse? We headed to the test kitchen to recreate a rib dish that harkens back to a time when the sweet and sour sauce was used to cook and gently flavor the pork, not coat it with a sticky shellac.

We started with the ribs (both spare- and baby back), and right off the bat preferred the baby back ribs because they are smaller and fit more easily in a braising pot. We also quickly learned that you have to shop carefully. Unfortunately, labeling of pork ribs can be confusing. Some slabs are labeled "baby back ribs," while other seemingly identical ribs are labeled "loin back ribs." After a bit of detective work, we learned that the only difference is weight. Both types of ribs are taken from the upper portion of a young hog's rib cage near the backbone and should have 11 to 13 bones. A slab (or rack) of loin back ribs generally comes from a larger pig and weighs more than 1¾ pounds; a slab of ribs weighing less is referred to as baby back ribs, although most restaurants don't follow this rule, using the term "baby back" no matter what they've got because it sounds better. During testing, we came to prefer loin back ribs because they are meatier.

There is one other shopping issue to consider. Beware of racks with bare bone peeking through the meat (along the center of the bones). This means that the butcher took off more meat than necessary, robbing you and your guests of full, meaty portions. Once you've purchased the ribs, there remains the question of whether the skin-like membrane located on the "bone side" of the ribs should be left on during cooking. One theory holds that it prevents flavor from penetrating the meat, while some rib experts say that removing it robs the ribs of flavor and moisture. We found that the skin did not interfere with flavor; in fact, it helped to keep the ribs intact.

At last, it was time to start cooking. We turned our attention first to the cooking method, employing a basic sweet and sour braising liquid to do our testing. The best way to cook baby back ribs is to slow cook them with moist heat. This allows time for the meat to become fall-off-the-bone tender and for the generous amount of fat to render away from the meat and bone. We wanted enough sauce at the end of cooking to be able to generously coats the ribs before serving.

With most braises, we brown the meat first, before adding the liquid, but we wondered if this step was necessary. The benefits of browning the meat first are a richer-tasting sauce as well as the rendering of some of the fat. The benefit of omitting the browning step is the time and mess it saves. Seeing the pros and cons of each, we settled it over a side-by-side taste test and went with the method where the ribs are browned first, because the flavor is simply much better.

Up to this point we had been cutting the racks into single ribs before braising them, as was suggested in a recipe we found for a similar dish. We tried braising the racks whole in a roasting pan covered with foil, as this seemed like a more streamlined method. Unfortunately, the rate at which the braising liquid evaporated depended on how tight the foil was, and sometimes the ribs burned to the bottom of the pan—it was just too unpredictable. If we added enough water to keep the braise from burning, the resulting sauce was too watery. We decided to stick with the most reliable method of braising, which was in a large pot with a tight fitting lid. Once the meat was cooked, we noticed the sauce was really greasy from all the fat rendered while cooking. A simple solution was to remove the ribs from the sauce, pour the liquid into a fat separator, and wait a minute or two until the fat had risen to the top so we could pour off the defatted sauce.

Next we had to determine the ratio of sweet and sour elements in the sauce. We started with ½ cup each of red wine vinegar, soy sauce, and sugar, then added to that some rice wine to balance the flavors. Tasters felt the sauce was too sweet while the vinegar was just a background note. The sauce was also too intense—this braise would benefit from some additional water. For the next batch, we reduced the sugar to ⅓ cup, leaving everything else the same, and we added ½ cup of water. This was a big improvement, and the flavors were starting to fall into place, but the sweet and sour balance was still not right. Just one additional tablespoon of vinegar did the trick. Moving from regular sugar to brown sugar helped to deepen the flavor of the sauce, as did a little garlic and ginger.

Finally, it was time to finish the sauce. Once the ribs are cooked, they rest on a serving platter while the generous amount of rendered fat rises to the top of the sauce. It was at this point some tasters felt the defatted sauce should go directly onto the ribs while others wanted the sauce to go back into the pan to be thickened with cornstarch. The thickened sauce had a nice glossy sheen and clung to the ribs, but the texture became a little sticky and too reminiscent of the Chinese restaurant disasters we'd experienced. We went with the simpler method—as soon as the sauce was defatted, it was poured over the ribs and we started eating.

PANTRY SPOTLIGHT

IDENTIFYING PORK RIBS

There are three basic types of pork rib racks: baby back ribs, spareribs, and St. Louis–style ribs. Baby back ribs (sometimes called back ribs or loin back ribs), despite the name "baby," are cut from the back of an adult pig. The ribs are smaller and the meat is considered to be more delicate, tender, and prone to drying out—making them the perfect candidate for a moist cooking method such as a braise. Spareribs are cut closer to the belly, are a little tougher, and have a bit more fat—making them perfect for long, dry-heat cooking methods such as barbecue. St. Louis–style spareribs are simply spareribs that have been trimmed down a bit more—they are often confused with baby back ribs because they have been trimmed and thus look smaller, but should be treated just like spareribs.

BABY BACK RIBS

SPARERIBS

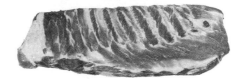

ST. LOUIS–STYLE RIBS

Sweet and Sour Pork Ribs
Tangcu Paigu
SERVES 4

Note that baby back and loin back ribs are the same type of rib—although loin back come from larger pigs and are thus a bit meatier. Either works well in this recipe. We usually braise meats in the oven, but because these ribs are stirred frequently during cooking, we prefer to cook them on top of the stove. Serve with Simple Steamed White Rice (page 516).

2	tablespoons vegetable oil
2	racks loin back or baby back ribs (about 4 pounds total), cut into individual ribs
3	medium garlic cloves, minced or pressed through a garlic press (about 1 tablespoon)
1	tablespoon minced or grated fresh ginger
½	cup plus 1 tablespoon red wine vinegar
½	cup soy sauce
½	cup water
⅓	cup packed light or dark brown sugar
3	tablespoons Chinese rice cooking wine or dry sherry (see page 513)

1. Heat the oil in a large Dutch oven over medium-high heat until just smoking. Brown a third of the ribs on several sides, about 6 minutes, reducing the heat if the pot begins to scorch. Transfer the ribs to a plate and repeat twice more with the remaining ribs using the fat left in the pot.

2. Add the garlic and ginger to the fat in the pot, turn the heat to medium, and cook until fragrant, about 30 seconds. Stir in the vinegar, soy sauce, water, sugar, and rice wine, scraping up the browned bits. Bring to a simmer, stirring to dissolve the sugar.

3. Return all of the browned ribs to the pot. Cover, reduce the heat to medium-low, and cook until the ribs are tender and the meat easily pulls away from bone, 1¾ to 2¼ hours, using tongs to rearrange the ribs every 30 minutes, so that they're moistened with the braising liquid. (The liquid should be simmering very gently; adjust the heat as necessary.)

4. Transfer the ribs to a serving platter and tent with foil to keep warm. Strain the sauce into a fat separator and let sit until the fat has risen to the top, about 4 minutes (you should have about 1½ cups of defatted sauce). Gently pour the defatted sauce over the ribs and serve.

CHINESE BARBECUED PORK
Char Siu

THERE WAS A TIME IN CHINA WHEN MOST households did not have ovens, so it was typical to buy Chinese barbecued pork or *char siu* in the same Chinese markets where you bought your roasted duck and salt-roasted chicken. The leftovers got recycled into other dishes until it was time to go back to the market. But ovens are commonplace in homes now, and Chinese barbecued pork, with its ruby-red color, deeply browned and crusty edges, and sticky glazed exterior, is so good, we wondered if we could replicate this classic Chinese dish at home. After all, isn't it just barbecued meat?

Unlike American barbecue, where large cuts are cooked with smoke on outdoor cookers until they achieve a fall-apart tenderness, Chinese barbecued meats are usually cut into strips and cooked in an oven. Once the exterior is slightly charred, the meat is brushed with honey and cooked until a lacquered glaze forms. It's like having barbecue with almost all crust. Sounds simple enough.

There was just one hook—actually, more like eight hooks. Traditional recipes call for cutting the meat into thin strips and hanging the strips on metal rods that go inside refrigerator-sized ovens. The idea is that the heat can attack the meat from all sides and create a thick crust. We tried fabricating S-shaped hooks out of metal hangers and suspending the meat from the top rack of a test kitchen oven, but our forearms were soon covered with battle scars caused by our failed attempts to rescue dangling pieces of meat before they fell onto the floor of the oven. No meat—no matter how delicious—is worth second-degree burns. We needed to develop a cooking method suited to a home oven.

Traditional recipes cut pork butt into long

strips. When we cut the meat into thicker steaks, it was much too fatty and tough. We concluded that cutting the meat into strips is a must, as it helps render fat during the relatively short cooking time. We tried using country-style ribs, because they are already cut into strips, but found that they tasted more dry and chewy than strips cut from a pork butt. Working with a boneless pork butt, we cut the pork in half lengthwise and then into eight long strips—removing some of the hard fat between the individual muscles. We marinated the meat in a classic mixture of light and dark soy sauces, Chinese rice wine, hoisin sauce, spices, and either fermented red bean curd or red food coloring (red foods are seen as bringing good fortune in Chinese cuisine).

Suspending the meat from hooks was out, but what if we placed the strips of meat on a rack set over a baking sheet? Wouldn't an all-over crust form? We ran a series of tests with oven temperatures ranging from 350 to 500 degrees. The pork roasted in the cooler ovens remained moist and was less fatty, but it never achieved the characteristic browning and intense flavor; the meat cooked in the hotter ovens browned beautifully, but it was still too tough, with pockets of unrendered fat. Choosing the middle road (roasting at 425 degrees) didn't work, so we were left with one option—cooking the meat at a low temperature to render the fat and then cranking up the heat to develop a burnished crust.

For our next tests, we lost the rack and placed the strips of meat on a big sheet of aluminum foil, poured the marinade over the top, and then tightly sealed the foil. After two hours, we opened the foil packet and browned the pork under the broiler. All the fat had been rendered, but the meat reminded tasters of slightly charred pot roast—it simply fell apart at the approach of a fork. Like all good barbecue, char siu needs to have some chew to it.

We returned to cooking the meat on a rack set over a baking sheet, but this time we covered the pan with foil. After an hour at 300 degrees, we removed the foil and turned the oven to broil. The meat had a better crust, but it was still too soft. Eventually, we discovered that covering the meat for only 20 minutes during the initial hour of cooking was all that we needed to render excess fat and keep the meat tender. We then removed the foil and continued to cook the meat until a thick crust formed. A final blast of heat from the broiler produced a thick, slightly charred crust, and the meat was now tender but chewy.

All the pork needed was a final adjustment of flavor in the marinade and glaze. First, we needed to tinker with the traditional marinade ingredients—light and dark soy sauces, rice wine, red fermented bean curd, hoisin sauce, and five-spice powder. In the end, tasters were happy with just regular soy sauce. The red bean curd was just too hard to find. Instead, we boosted the flavor of the marinade with ginger, garlic, toasted sesame oil, and white pepper.

Marinades are all about flavor penetration, but how long does that take? After four hours, the meat

PREPARING PORK FOR CHAR SIU

Pork butts are usually about 4 inches thick. If using a pork butt that is thinner than 4 inches, cut it into six pieces instead of eight.

1. Cut the roast in half lengthwise.

2. Turn each half on the cut side and slice lengthwise into 4 equal pieces.

3. Trim the excess hard, waxy fat, leaving some fat to render while cooking.

had soaked up the potent flavors of the marinade. Times in excess of four hours caused the meat to become too salty. But four hours was a long time to wait. Could we speed up this process? Pricking the meat with a fork before marinating enhanced the penetration of the marinade so much that just 30 minutes was sufficient.

To achieve a lacquered appearance, char siu requires the application of a honey glaze during the last few minutes of cooking. To achieve the traditional red color, we supplemented the honey with ketchup. We simmered honey and ketchup (along with some reserved marinade) to give it a syrupy consistency. We had finally replicated one of our favorite Chinese dishes at home.

Chinese Barbecued Pork

Char Siu

SERVES 6

If you don't have a wire rack that fits inside a rimmed baking sheet, substitute a broiler pan, although the meat may not darken as much. Do not use a drawer broiler in step 5 because the heat source will be too close to the meat and will burn the glaze. Instead, increase the oven temperature in step 5 to 500 degrees and cook the pork for 8 to 12 minutes before glazing, then about 6 to 8 minutes once the glaze has been applied (on both sides). Serve with Simple Steamed White Rice (page 516).

1	(4-pound) boneless pork butt, cut into 8 strips and trimmed of excess fat (see the illustrations on page 533)
½	cup sugar
½	cup soy sauce
6	tablespoons hoisin sauce
¼	cup Chinese rice cooking wine or dry sherry
2	tablespoons minced or grated fresh ginger
2	medium garlic cloves, minced or pressed through a garlic press (about 2 teaspoons)
1	tablespoon toasted sesame oil
1	teaspoon five-spice powder
¼	teaspoon ground white pepper
¼	cup ketchup
⅓	cup honey

1. Using a fork, prick the pork 10 to 12 times on each side, and place in a large zipper-lock bag. Whisk the sugar, soy sauce, hoisin sauce, rice wine, ginger, garlic, sesame oil, five-spice powder and pepper together in a medium bowl. Measure out ½ cup of the marinade and reserve separately. Pour the remaining marinade into the bag with the pork. Seal the bag, pressing out as much air as possible, and refrigerate for 30 minutes or up to 4 hours, flipping the bag occasionally to ensure that the pork marinates evenly.

2. While the meat marinates, combine the ketchup and honey with the reserved ½ cup marinade in a small saucepan and cook over medium heat, whisking occasionally, until syrupy and measures about 1 cup, 4 to 6 minutes.

3. Adjust an oven rack to the middle position and heat the oven to 300 degrees. Line a rimmed baking sheet with aluminum foil, set a wire rack on the sheet, and spray the rack with vegetable oil spray.

4. Remove the pork from the marinade, letting any excess drip off, and place on the wire rack. Pour ¼ cup of water into the bottom of the pan. Cover the pan with heavy-duty aluminum foil, crimping the edges tightly to seal. Roast the pork for 20 minutes. Remove the foil and continue to roast the pork until the edges begin to brown, 40 to 45 minutes.

5. Turn the oven to broil and broil the pork, leaving it on the same oven rack, until evenly browned, 7 to 9 minutes. Being careful of the hot juices in the pan bottom, remove the pan from the oven, brush the pork with half of the glaze, then continue to broil until the meat is deep a mahogany color, 3 to 5 minutes.

6. Using tongs, flip the meat over and continue to broil until the second side is evenly browned, 7 to 9 minutes. Being careful of the hot juices in the pan bottom, remove the pan from the oven, brush the pork with the remaining glaze, then continue to broil until the meat is a deep mahogany color, 3 to 5 minutes. Remove the pork from the oven and let cool for at least 10 minutes, before cutting the meat into thin strips and serving.

INGREDIENTS: Hoisin Sauce

Hoisin sauce is a thick, reddish brown mixture of soybeans, sugar, vinegar, garlic, and chiles used in many classic Chinese dishes, including Chinese Barbecued Pork (page 534) and Kung Pao Shrimp (page 523). Spoonfuls of six hoisin sauces and forkfuls of our hoisin-basted barbecued pork indicated that no two brands of this staple condiment are identical; in fact, they vary dramatically in flavor, consistency, and even color—from gloppy and sweet, like plum sauce, to grainy and spicy, like Asian chili paste.

According to our tasters, the perfect hoisin sauce balances sweet, salty, pungent, and spicy elements so that no one flavor dominates. Kikkoman came closest to this ideal, with tasters praising its initial "burn," which mellowed into a harmonious blend of sweet and aromatic flavors. Two other brands also fared well in our tasting. Koon Chun was described as "fruity" (if a bit grainy) and Lee Kum Kee was deemed "plummy" but salty.

THE BEST HOISIN SAUCE

Kikkoman's Hoisin Sauce won praise for its balance of sweetness and salinity.

BRAISED BEEF SHORT RIBS WITH BLACK BEAN SAUCE

Chizhi Paigu

BEEF SHORT RIBS AND BLACK BEAN SAUCE (made with fermented black beans) are a classic combination in Chinese cookery and it's no wonder—the rich, meaty short ribs are perfectly suited to the musky, salty beans. Marrying these two flavors together seemed as easy as taking our favorite braised short rib recipe and tossing in some of these beans but, one batch of overly salty, inedible short ribs later, we learned not everything is as it seems. Our inexperience with using fermented black beans had never been so evident. We headed into the test kitchen to find how to get this dish right.

Our first challenge was to find out more about fermented black beans. After a shopping trip and time logged in the library, we found that these small black preserved soybeans are commonly used in conjunction with garlic as a seasoning. They also are said to heighten the flavor of beef, chicken, and pork. Because they are quite pungent and salty, fermented black beans should be rinsed and soaked before cooking—and they should be used sparingly. Although not readily available in all supermarkets, they are easy to find in Asian markets.

Beef short ribs, on the other hand, are often hard to miss in the supermarket meat case, as they're rather intimidating hunks of meat and bone. But braise them and they become tender and succulent. Douse the braised ribs with a velvety sauce and they are as satisfying as beef stew. Unfortunately, all of this comes at a price: short ribs are outrageously fatty. The first challenge is to get them to give up their fat.

The first step in most braises is browning the meat, which, in the case of short ribs, presents an opportunity to render some of the fat. We tried browning both on the stovetop and in the oven and found both work well to render some of the fat. The major inconvenience of oven browning is deglazing the roasting pan on the stovetop, which makes a burner-worthy roasting pan a prerequisite. Instead we opted for browning on the stovetop. True, we needed to brown the ribs in two batches, but we didn't see this as much of an inconvenience. With our browning method down, we moved on

---

PANTRY SPOTLIGHT

FERMENTED BLACK BEANS

Also called salted or dried black beans, fermented black beans are not the black beans found in Mexico. They are actually soybeans that have been dried and fermented with garlic, salt, and other spices. It is important to rinse and soak the beans before using them or they may impart too much of a salty flavor to a dish. Fermented black beans are used sparingly and will last for months in an airtight container in the refrigerator.

to building our black bean sauce.

Because the flavor of the fermented beans is so strong, we didn't have to look further than water for a braising liquid. Still, since we often braise meats in chicken broth, we thought we'd give that a try too. Tasting the sauces side by side, we couldn't detect much difference, so we stayed with the water in a nod to authentic Chinese preparation.

We next turned our attention to enhancing the flavor of the sauce. We tried soy sauce, common in many recipes found in our research. Soy sauce adds not only flavor to the sauce, but color as well. We tested various amounts and found that a mere 2 tablespoons was enough to heighten the flavor of the braise. At this point, we felt that the braising liquid could use a bit of brightness and rice wine did the job admirably. If the braising liquid were to transform itself into the sauce we were after, it would need some thickening. In Chinese dishes we consider cornstarch the go-to ingredient for thickening sauces, but for argument's sake we tested flour as well. The former was added in the form of a slurry at the end of cooking after the ribs had been removed from the pot. The sauce thickened in a matter of minutes.

As they braise, the browned short ribs continue to release fat, which means that the braising liquid must be defatted before it can be served. We found the easiest technique was to use a fat separator and to use it before the sauce was thickened. Once poured over the ribs, the lush, flavorful sauce clung perfectly to the meaty ribs—tasters grabbed plenty of napkins before digging in.

Braised Short Ribs with Black Bean Sauce

Chizhi Paigu

SERVES 8

Fermented black beans can be found in some well-stocked supermarkets and Asian markets. For more information on these beans, see page 535. Because the braising liquid doesn't cover all of the ribs in the pot, be sure to move the ribs around during the cooking to ensure even doneness and flavor. This recipe can be easily halved to serve four; the cooking times will remain the same. Serve with Simple Steamed White Rice (page 516).

6 tablespoons fermented black beans, rinsed
2 tablespoon soy sauce
2 tablespoons Chinese rice cooking wine or dry sherry
4 medium garlic cloves, minced or pressed through a garlic press (about 4 teaspoons)
8 English-style beef short ribs, bone-in (10 to 12 ounces each), trimmed of excess fat and silver skin
   Ground black pepper
2 tablespoons vegetable oil
6 cups water
2 tablespoons cornstarch

1. Adjust an oven rack to the middle position and heat the oven to 300 degrees. Soak the fermented black beans in 2 cups of warm water to reduce their saltiness, about 20 minutes. Drain the beans, then toss with the soy sauce, rice wine, and garlic; set aside.

2. Meanwhile, pat the ribs dry with paper towels and season with pepper. Heat the oil in a large Dutch oven over medium-high heat until just smoking. Add half the ribs and brown all sides, 7 to 10 minutes, reducing the heat if the pot begins to scorch. Transfer the ribs to a plate and repeat with the remaining ribs.

3. Pour off all of the fat left in the pot, add the black bean mixture, and cook over medium heat, scraping up any browned bits, until most of the liquid has cooked off, about 1 minute. Return the ribs to the pot and add 5¾ cups of the water. Bring to a simmer then cover and transfer to the oven. Cook until the meat is tender, 2 to 2½ hours, rearranging the ribs halfway through the cooking time so that all the ribs become moistened with the braising liquid.

4. Transfer the ribs to a serving platter and tent loosely with foil. Pour the braising liquid into a fat separator and set aside to settle, about 4 minutes. Pour the defatted sauce back into the pot and return to a simmer over medium-high heat. Whisk the cornstarch with the remaining ¼ cup water to dissolve, then whisk into the sauce. Continue to simmer the sauce, whisking constantly, until thickened, about 4 minutes. Pour some sauce over the ribs, reserving the rest to serve at the table.

14
JAPAN AND KOREA

COLD SOBA NOODLE SALAD

Zaru Soba

SOBA NOODLES, MADE WITH BUCKWHEAT, can be served hot or cold, with hot soba more widespread in the winter and cold soba more predominant in the summer months. Hot soba noodles are served in a light broth with various toppings such as shrimp tempura, sliced daikon, and fermented soybeans, commonly referred to as black beans (for more information, see page 535). Cold soba noodles are traditionally served on a bamboo tray (which allows excess cooking water to drip away as the noodles are eaten), accompanied by a dipping sauce. Using chopsticks, diners dip the noodles a few at a time into the soy-based sauce, which is usually seasoned with dashi (a seafood broth), ginger, and wasabi. Open to interpretation, cold soba noodle dishes offer a delicate balance of key Japanese flavors as a refreshing light lunch or side dish. But eating noodles in this manner is undoubtedly a very foreign concept to the Western world. The required chopstick skills alone are enough to make your head spin. With this in mind, we took the liberty of creating a chilled soba noodle salad and transforming the dipping sauce into a dressing to pull the whole thing together for a fork-friendly dish.

Like other noodles, soba noodles require an ample amount of water for cooking. The consequence of too little water is a slimy mixture of badly disintegrated noodles. We achieved best results by cooking the noodles in at least 4 quarts of salted water. When the noodles were just tender, we found it best to quickly rinse them under cold running water. It's important not to skip this step, as simply draining the buckwheat noodles and spreading them on a baking sheet (the test kitchen method for prepping noodles for Italian pasta salads) resulted in gummy noodles that overcooked from the residual heat.

After the noodles were sufficiently cooled, we tossed them with 1 tablespoon of vegetable oil to prevent them from sticking together as they sat in the colander. For the dressing, we wanted to simulate the flavors of a traditional dipping sauce, which sometimes relies on a subtle sea flavor in combination with soy sauce, mirin, and wasabi. Some dipping sauces utilize dashi, a seafood broth made from kombu (dried kelp), bonito flakes (dried, smoked fish flakes), and water. But making dashi added steps to our recipe that we thought were unnecessary. Instead we experimented with adding a few of the dashi ingredients to our dressing.

We began by building a simple dressing for our salad using the following traditional elements: soy sauce, mirin, ginger, and wasabi. We compared this dressing to one made with dashi. Tasters liked our simple dressing, but felt that the clean, salty fish flavor from the dashi-based dressing added an exciting dimension that was lacking in our soy-based version. We wondered if we could add the flavor of the sea through the salad's garnishes. Seaweed, such as wakame or nori, is often used to garnish this salad and we realized that it would be essential here. We chose nori for its accessibility—it can be found in the international aisle of most well-stocked supermarkets, whereas wakame is sold exclusively through Asian markets. We toasted the nori (to increase its flavor) and cut it into strips before adding it to the dressed noodles. We also found that using scissors to cut the nori strips was much easier than using a knife. Some tasters, however, were not completely satisfied and felt the salad needed more of a flavor boost. Those who craved a taste of the sea liked dried bonito flakes added to the dressing. However, their smoky fish flavor is somewhat potent, so we made them optional.

Moving along, we tasted the remaining ingredients for our salad. We sampled daikon, pickled daikon, and red radishes and eventually settled on red radishes. Availability was an obvious factor, but tasters also thought their peppery flavor worked well with our dressing and their bright red skin lent some vibrant color to the dish. Scallions rounded out our soba noodle salad. While not exactly identical to what you might find in Japan, our salad definitely captures the flavors of this Japanese staple, and you don't need superlative chopstick skills to enjoy it.

Cold Soba Noodle Salad
Zaru Soba
SERVES 6

To give this salad more heat, add additional wasabi paste to taste. Bonito flakes, which we list as optional, are dried fish flakes found in Asian and natural foods markets; they add a distinct, smoky flavor to this dish, but their potent flavor may not be to everyone's liking.

1	tablespoon salt
14	ounces dried soba noodles (see page 541)
1	tablespoon vegetable oil
¼	cup soy sauce
3	tablespoons mirin
½	teaspoon sugar
½	teaspoon minced or grated fresh ginger
¼	teaspoon wasabi powder or paste
4	large red radishes, grated on the large holes of a box grater
3	medium scallions, sliced thin on the bias (see page 505)
1	(8 by 2½-inch) piece nori (about one-third of an 8-inch square sheet), toasted (see right)
¼	cup bonito flakes, optional (see note)

1. Bring 4 quarts of water to a boil in a large pot. Stir in the salt and noodles and cook, stirring occasionally, until tender, about 4 minutes. Drain the noodles and rinse them under cold running water until cooled. Transfer the noodles to a large bowl, toss with the oil, and set aside.

2. Whisk the soy sauce, mirin, sugar, ginger, and wasabi together in a small bowl, then pour over the noodles. (At this point, the noodles can be tossed to coat and refrigerated in a covered container for up to 1 day; add the vegetables and garnishes just before serving and toss again.) Add the radishes and scallions and toss until well combined. Portion the noodles into individual serving bowls, sprinkle with the nori and bonito flakes (if using), and serve.

PANTRY SPOTLIGHT

JAPANESE SEAWEED

Seaweed has long played a role in the cuisine of Japan. It is used to flavor stocks and soups, as a garnish for rice and noodle dishes, and as a key ingredient for *maki*, commonly referred to as rolled sushi. Throughout our recipe research, three main types of seaweed reappeared time and again: nori, kombu, and wakame.

Nori is the Japanese word for seaweed and is the only variety used for maki (rolled sushi). It is also used as a garnish for rice or noodles. Nori is available plain, seasoned with a mixture of soy sauce, sugar, and spices, or seasoned with sesame oil and salt (Korean-style). Nori is often toasted before being added to a dish to release its flavor and to make it more pliable for rolling sushi. To toast nori, heat a large dry skillet over medium-high heat. Place the nori sheet in the skillet and toast on one side until the color turns from emerald to light green in spots and the edges of the sheet begin to curl slightly, 10 to 20 seconds. Flip the nori over and repeat.

Kombu is a key ingredient in dashi, a broth essential to Japanese cuisine. When purchasing kombu, take note of the chalky, white powder on the exterior. This is an indication of the glutamic acid content and translates to increased flavor. Kombu is primarily sold in dried whole sheets that are quite thick. It is often simmered in soups or broths to impart flavor and the softened kombu can then be eaten as part of the meal.

Wakame is a traditional garnish in miso soup and many Japanese salads. It is available dried in thin sheets, shreds (or flakes), or fresh-salted. Both dried and fresh varieties are used to flavor soups or made into salads. Dried wakame must be rehydrated in cold water for at least 3 to 5 minutes before using, while fresh-salted wakame should be rinsed briefly to remove the excess salt, then soaked in cold water for 1 to 2 minutes.

RAMEN SOUP

Ramen

INSTANT RAMEN NOODLES HAVE THE REPUTATION of being a mainstay on college campuses across the country. Ramen is the go-to meal for many college students, who sometimes even forgo the troublesome task of boiling the noodles and instead eat them raw like giant, wavy potato chips. However, in Japan, ramen (or ramen soup) is a much more serious endeavor, with ramen shops on almost every street corner, where the noodles are served in a variety of broths. Our favorite among these is a rich, meaty broth made from long-simmered pork bones, called *tonkotsu*. Tonkotsu ramen is commonly garnished with thinly sliced pieces of tender pork, scallions, and toasted sesame seeds. We set out to duplicate this hearty bowl of noodles in our test kitchen with the goal of keeping it accessible to the home cook, but without compromising flavor. Good ramen starts with a great broth, so we began there.

The pork broth starts with pounds of meaty bones, so off the bat we sought out a more practical alternative method. We've had good results with store-bought chicken broth, so we decided to use that as a base and looked for ways to boost its meaty flavor. We looked at several cuts of pork, noting that we wanted one cut to provide both flavor for the broth and meat for the garnish. For testing purposes, we chose boneless shoulder (also called pork butt), pork tenderloin, bone-in ribs, and boneless country-style ribs.

To start, we cut the shoulder, tenderloin, and boneless ribs into 1-inch chunks and placed them into their respective pots with an onion and 2 quarts of chicken broth. The bone-in ribs were separated from one another to increase their surface area and added to another pot.

After an hour, we gathered around for a tasting. The pork butt came across as too ham-like while the tenderloin offered little in the flavor department, and the bone-in ribs made the broth excessively greasy. The boneless country-style ribs passed muster, delivering a strong meaty flavor without coming across as too "gamey." Overall, however, tasters still commented that the finished broth needed a stronger, more complex meat flavor to win their approval. So back to the stove we went to try and eke out more flavor from our pork ribs.

Again, we started by cutting the meat into 1-inch chunks, but then transferred them to the food processor and pulsed them until coarsely ground. This increased the surface area of the meat, allowing more pork flavor to infuse the broth. Our next move was to thoroughly brown the meat before adding the chicken broth. The browned meat and browned bits in the pot (called fond) gave our broth a solid base of flavor and, once simmered in the broth, mimicked a long, slow cooking process. At this point, we revisited our cooking time of 1 hour and found that by browning the meat before adding the broth, we were able to reduce the simmering time to 40 minutes.

To give the broth a sweet and smoky flavor we incorporated a small amount of red miso paste (a salty, savory fermented bean paste; see page 544 for more information). The finished broth was strained and now its deep flavor could fool even some of our more experienced tasters. Our broth was coming together and the addition of garlic and ginger rounded it out nicely.

With our broth in place, we turned our attention to the meat garnish. Boneless country-style ribs come in a long rectangular shape that is ideal for slicing into bite-sized pieces. To help with getting the slices as thin as possible, we put the meat in the freezer to firm up for 20 minutes while we prepared our broth. Initially we experimented with marinating our meat in soy sauce, mirin, and sesame oil, but we found that the amount of flavor that the marinade provided was negated when the meat was added to the broth. Instead, after our broth had been strained, we added the soy sauce, mirin, and sesame oil along with the sliced pork and allowed the meat to steep for 3 minutes. This technique resulted in flavorful meat that was also extremely tender.

When it came to the noodles, we were admittedly a little hesitant to use the dried ramen noodles that flood grocery store shelves. For comparison, we sought out dried ramen from an Asian market (although they seemed indistinguishable from their supermarket counterpart), along with high-end *chuka soba* noodles (noodles made from all wheat flour or a combination of wheat and buckwheat flours) and fresh Chinese egg noodles. Chuka soba noodles were much thinner and, frankly, didn't have as much flavor as the more common dried ramen noodles. Part of the reason may be that dried ramen noodles are actually fried as part of the drying process. This frying instills a richer flavor, which in our tests gave them a slight advantage over fresh noodles.

In the end, each soupy bowl of noodles needed little more than some thinly sliced scallions and a sprinkling of toasted sesame seeds. The finished product was a rich, meaty concoction that elevates a college staple to a true Japanese treat.

PANTRY SPOTLIGHT

JAPANESE NOODLES

Noodles play an important role in Japanese cuisine and their consumption varies with each region. Most noodles in Japan are made from wheat, buckwheat, mung beans, or potato starch, or some combination thereof, and not from rice flour as is common in China and other Asian countries. Vendors dot the streets of Japan offering steaming bowls of noodle soup in the winter (the trademark loud slurp is actually a method for cooling hot noodles as they pass the lips) and chilled noodles with dipping sauces in the summer.

Ramen noodles were introduced to Japan by China and India in the seventeenth century, but the Japanese have taken ramen noodles to another level and made them distinctly their own. Ramen noodles are traditionally made from wheat flour and eggs, but many instant varieties replace eggs with chemical additives and yellow food coloring. Fresh ramen noodles labeled *chuka soba* and *shina soba* can be found in Asian markets.

Udon noodles are made with all-purpose flour, water, and salt. The result is a highly elastic dough that yields thick, chewy noodles. Udon dough was originally kneaded by placing it between two towels and stepping on it. Today, machines do much of the work. Udon noodles can be purchased both fresh and dried. Common udon preparations include *tempura udon* (a hot noodle soup usually topped with tempura shrimp or vegetables) and *nabeyaki udon* (udon noodles cooked with broth in an earthenware pot and topped with a soft cooked egg). Udon noodles can also be served cold with a dipping sauce in much the same way as soba noodles. In fact, many of the vendors that sell soba noodles also sell udon.

Soba noodles possess a rich, nutty flavor and delicate texture. With their high nutrient content, soba noodles can easily be considered "health food." They get their unusual flavor from buckwheat flour. However, buckwheat flour contains no gluten so a binder, usually wheat, is added to give the noodles structure and hold them together during cooking. The Japanese agricultural department requires that all noodles labeled as soba contain a minimum of 30 percent buckwheat flour and the higher the percentage of buckwheat flour, the higher the price. Soba noodles are traditionally served chilled with a dipping sauce.

Somen noodles are made from high-gluten wheat flour and the dough is stretched rather than cut. They are only sold in their dry form and it is believed that their flavor improves after aging over 1 to 2 years. Somen are eaten in much the same way as soba noodles, accompanied by a dipping sauce. Some restaurants serve what it known as "floating somen" where the noodles are placed in a bamboo flume filled with cold running water. This flume circulates throughout the restaurant passing by diners' tables and the noodles are skillfully plucked out with chopsticks.

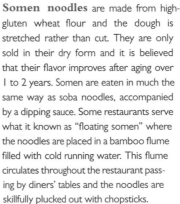

Ramen Soup

Ramen

SERVES 4

To make processing and slicing the pork easier, freeze it for 15 minutes. Supermarket ramen works well here; just be sure to discard the flavoring packet. Dried ramen noodles (the kind sold without a dusty packet of flavoring) can be found at Asian markets. If you can't find miso paste, you can simply omit it but the soup will have a less complex flavor. Be ready to serve the soup immediately after cooking the pork in step 4; if the pork sits in the hot broth for too long it will turn tough.

BROTH

1½	pounds boneless, country-style pork ribs
1	tablespoon vegetable oil
1	medium onion, chopped medium
6	medium garlic cloves, smashed and peeled
1	(1-inch) piece fresh ginger, peeled, sliced into ¼-inch-thick coins, and smashed
8	cups low-sodium chicken broth

SOUP

4	(3-ounce) packages ramen noodles, flavoring packets discarded
	Salt
3	tablespoons red miso paste (see page 544)
2	tablespoons soy sauce
1	tablespoon mirin
½	teaspoon toasted sesame oil
2	scallions, sliced thin on the bias (see page 505)
1	tablespoon sesame seeds, toasted

1. FOR THE BROTH: Slice ½ pound of the pork ribs crosswise into ⅛-inch-thick slices; cover and refrigerate until needed. Cut the remaining 1 pound pork ribs into 1-inch chunks, then process in a food processor to a coarse chopped texture, about 10 pulses.

2. Heat the oil in a large Dutch oven over medium heat until shimmering. Add the chopped pork and cook, breaking up the meat with a wooden spoon, until well browned, about 10 minutes. Stir in the onion, garlic, and ginger and cook until softened, about 2 minutes. Stir in the chicken broth, partially cover, bring to a simmer and cook until the broth is flavorful, about 40 minutes. Pour the broth through a fine-mesh strainer, discarding the solids in the strainer. (The broth can be refrigerated in an airtight container for up to 1 day.)

3. FOR THE SOUP: Bring 4 quarts of water to a boil in a large pot. Add the ramen noodles and 1 tablespoon salt and cook until just tender, about 2 minutes. Drain the noodles and divide them evenly between 4 individual serving bowls.

4. Return the strained broth to a clean saucepan and bring to a simmer over medium-high heat. Whisk ½ cup of the hot broth into the miso until dissolved and smooth, then whisk the miso mixture into the saucepan. Stir in the soy sauce, mirin, sesame oil, and sliced pork. Cover, remove the saucepan from the heat, and let sit until the pork is cooked through, about 3 minutes (do not overcook). Season with salt to taste. Ladle the soup into individual bowls, garnish with the scallions and sesame seeds, and serve.

MISO SOUP

Miso Shiru

MISO SOUP, MADE WITH FERMENTED BEAN paste, is a Japanese restaurant standard. Order anything—except a soupy main dish—and some steaming, cloudy miso soup in a faux lacquered bowl is set down in front of you in a portion just large enough to whet your appetite. Miso soup is common in Japanese households, too, where it is considered a comfort food, akin to our chicken soup.

Served in a restaurant, miso soup is rarely judged, but it doesn't take a connoisseur to appreciate its subtleties and finer points. Bad miso soup is immediately identifiable as salty and hollow, with a one-dimensional flavor that is sometimes compensated for with MSG. This sort of institutional miso soup often begins with an instant broth and ends in a salt explosion on the palate, with no redeeming qualities or interesting flavors. Good miso soup is alive with layers of sweet, smoky, briny, earthy flavors. The flavors linger and evolve in the mouth and the soup is a pleasure to sip.

Just as chicken noodle soup has a base of chicken stock, miso soup is made with a seafood broth called *dashi*. A basic dashi is made from a simple combination of water, kombu (kelp), and dried bonito flakes (bonito is a type of fish). Miso is added to the strained dashi, and, with the addition of tofu or seaweed and a sprinkling of scallions, the soup is complete. Esoteric ingredients do not mean that miso soup is unapproachable for the American home cook. All the ingredients can likely be purchased in just a single trip to an Asian grocer, well-stocked supermarket, or natural foods store.

With only two ingredients (excluding water) each component in dashi serves an important function. Kombu gives dashi saltiness, a bit of sweetness, and a briny ocean essence. It also gives the dashi a little body. Kombu is sold in dried sheets—several to a package—and the sheets are naturally dusted with glutamic acid, a desirable whitish powder that adds flavor. Bonito flakes give dashi smokiness and a savory fishy quality. They are available in shavings of different sizes. Fine flakes are usually sold in small packets; they are sprinkled over foods and intended to be used as a garnish or condiment. Larger flakes are sold in bigger pillowy bags and are used primarily for making dashi.

Generally, dashi is a simple broth to prepare. Kombu and cold water are brought to a simmer, the kombu is removed, then the bonito flakes are added and cooked or steeped until the dashi is infused with their flavor. The details of the traditional process for making this broth found in several Japanese books seem overcomplicated. They often include wiping the kombu with a damp cloth before simmering and adding about ½ cup of cold water along with the bonito flakes, returning the liquid to a boil, and then straining immediately. Side-by-side tests could not give credence to these steps. The step of wiping the kombu did not significantly benefit the dashi, and there was no apparent advantage to adding cold water along with the bonito flakes. We

opted instead to use the kombu straight out of the package and merely steep the bonito flakes in the liquid off the heat for three to five minutes. Any longer and the smokiness and fishiness became overpowering.

After straining the dashi, miso is added to make miso soup. There are numerous kinds of miso, though for miso soup shiromiso (white miso) is the type commonly used. We tried other types of miso and found that our tasters preferred white miso. (For more information on types of miso, see page 544.) We tested different amounts of white miso per cup of dashi and found that 2 tablespoons per cup produced the right amount of salty, savory flavor.

Miso is a thick paste and is not easily dispersed in the dashi. We found it best to thin the miso with a small amount of dashi before adding it to the pot. Most recipes and books indicate that the dashi should be boiling or simmering before the thinned-out miso is added, to minimize the amount of time the miso is exposed to heat, which weakens its flavor. Our testing bore this out. We made three batches of miso soup. In the first batch, the soup was made according to the advised method of bringing the dashi to a simmer, then adding the miso; in the second, the miso was put into the dashi and brought to a simmer so as to give the miso prolonged heat exposure; and the third was made in the same manner as the first batch but was allowed to simmer for about two minutes. Indeed there were flavor differences. Soups two and three suffered from the prolonged heat. The miso seemed to have lost some of its delicate flavor and subtle nuances. This time tradition won out.

Miso soup is not complete without some tofu or wakame (seaweed) or both in the bottom of the bowl. Adding these ingredients directly to the pot seemed the obvious thing to do, but we preferred to portion out the ingredients in individual bowls. This way, the delicate tofu does not get mangled during ladling and the wakame that settles flat on the floor of the pot can be more evenly distributed. A sprinkling of sliced scallions and out goes the call *itadaki-masu*, the Japanese equivalent of "bon appétit."

Miso Soup

Miso Shiru

SERVES 8 TO 10

This recipe can easily be halved. The dashi (broth) is best made just before making the soup, though it can be made ahead, cooled, and refrigerated in an airtight container for up to 2 days. Once the miso has been stirred into the simmering dashi, serve the soup immediately.

DASHI

2   quarts water
2   (4-inch) pieces kombu (see page 539)
2   cups loosely packed bonito flakes

SOUP

1   tablespoon wakame flakes or four 6-inch strips wakame (see page 539)
8   ounces silken tofu, cut into ½-inch cubes
1   cup white miso
3   scallions, sliced thin on the bias (see page 505)

1. FOR THE DASHI: Bring the water and kombu to a boil in a large saucepan over medium heat. When the water is boiling, remove the saucepan from the heat and discard the kombu. Stir in the bonito flakes, cover, and let steep until the broth is flavorful, about 5 minutes. Pour the broth through a fine-mesh strainer, discarding the solids in the strainer. (The dashi can be refrigerated in an airtight container for up to 1 day.)

2. FOR THE SOUP: Cover the wakame with cold water and set aside until softened, about 15 minutes, then drain. Portion the softened wakame and tofu between 4 individual serving bowls; set aside.

3. Return the strained dashi to a clean saucepan and bring to a simmer over medium-high heat. Whisk ½ cup of the hot dashi into the miso until dissolved and smooth, then whisk the miso mixture into the saucepan. Return the soup to a brief simmer, then remove immediately from the heat. Ladle the soup into the individual bowls, garnish with the scallions, and serve.

PANTRY SPOTLIGHT

MISO

Miso is the Japanese word for "bean paste." Commonly found in Asian—most notably Japanese—cuisines, miso is a fermented paste of soybeans and rice, barley, or rye. Miso paste is incredibly versatile, suitable for use in soups, braises, dressings, and sauces as well as for topping grilled foods. This salty, deep-flavored paste ranges in strength and color from a mild, pale yellow (referred to as white) to stronger-flavored red or brownish-black, depending on the fermentation method and ingredients. Avoid miso labeled "light," as this is an American low-sodium product whose flavor pales in comparison to the real thing. Miso can be found in well-stocked grocery stores and Japanese or Asian markets. It will keep for up to a year in the refrigerator.

MISO-GLAZED SALMON

Sake Misoyaki

ORIGINALLY A METHOD OF PRESERVATION before refrigeration, miso-marinated fish has long been a part of Japanese cuisine. And its salty-sweet flavor has made it a popular addition to restaurant menus worldwide. Misoyaki is most commonly an oily fish such as salmon, black cod, or mackerel that has been marinated in a blend of white miso paste, sugar, and rice wine for up to 3 days. (Miso is a fermented bean paste with salty, rich, savory flavor; see above for more information) The miso and sugar essentially cure the fish, with the miso lending saltiness and the sugar sweetness. After an extensive marinade, the fish is then grilled or broiled to produce a dark brown crust and a candy-like coating of nutty miso flavor. The texture of the fish becomes firm and pleasantly chewy—worlds away from light and flaky. We set out to create our own version of misoyaki. Determined to get to the bottom of this centuries-old technique-turned-recipe, we headed into the kitchen to create fish that had a pleasant balance of both salty and sweet, as well as the firmness that only comes from days of curing. But could we do it without leaving the fish in the marinade for three days—the typical time cited in recipes uncovered in our research?

To start, we chose salmon for its high fat content and widespread availability. But before we invested the time marinating the fish we needed to hammer out our marinade. After reviewing several recipes from Japanese cookbooks, we built a simple recipe of white miso, sugar, and sake. Whisking all the marinade ingredients together, we submerged our salmon fillets in the mixture for an hour, then cooked and tasted.

The results were disappointing. The salmon was more sweet than salty and the flavor was largely unbalanced. We thought about decreasing the sugar and increasing the miso to boost the saltiness. But upon closer inspection, we noticed that there were two problems with our initial recipe. First off, we had inadvertently purchased "light" miso from a local natural foods market. Light miso is an American product that is meant as a low-sodium substitute to authentic miso. It just tastes like salt, without the maltiness and nuttiness of authentic Japanese miso. The next issue stemmed from the viscosity of the marinade. About the consistency of heavy cream, it just wasn't thick enough to cling to the fish and have much of an impact.

Going back into the kitchen with the right miso (purchased from an Asian market), we tweaked amounts of all the ingredients to yield a thicker marinade. The results? Fish with a wonderful salty, sweet flavor. We next turned our attention to the marinade time.

We began testing the marinade times in one-hour increments up to 12 hours, and then skipped to one day, two days, and three days (the traditional marinating time found in our research). But as we tested these traditional two- and three-day marinating times, we felt that this was just not practical. Instead we decided to focus on two marinating times. One, a minimum duration for marinating the fish—long enough to flavor the fish adequately and second, a modified traditional marinade for when you want to take the time to impart more flavor.

Salmon that was cured for only one hour had little marinade flavor. While the crust of the fish was very flavorful, the interior was largely bland. Our testing eventually led us to a minimum marinade time of five hours. This was enough to flavor the interior of the salmon and firm it up as well. And for a longer marinade time, 24 hours or one day produced fish with deep, slightly sweet flavor and tasters loved the way the fish firmed up once cooked.

Creating some flavorful caramelization on the flesh of the fish was a key goal, so we focused right away on high-heat cooking. Grilling was doomed from the start. Thanks to the high sugar content of our marinade, the fish stuck to the grill and broke apart when we tried to flip it.

We next tried roasting, but this method resulted in pale fish that tasted dry. Broiling was the next step up in heat and here we met with success. The salmon browned nicely under the intense broiler heat and, as a result, also developed better flavor. Best of all, the fish didn't dry out, but remained juicy and moist.

Miso-Glazed Salmon
Sake Misoyaki
SERVES 4

Although we prefer the flavor of white miso here, you can substitute brown, red, barley, or brown rice miso, but do not substitute "light" miso; its flavor is too mild for this dish. When removing the salmon from the marinade, do not wipe away any excess marinade clinging to the fish; the excess marinade will turn to a sweet-salty crust during cooking. If portions of the salmon begin to burn while cooking, shield those areas from the heat with aluminum foil. Cod or mackerel can be substituted for the salmon.

1	cup white miso (see note)
1	cup sugar
½	cup sake
4	(8-ounce) center-cut salmon fillets

1. Whisk the miso, sugar, and sake together in a medium bowl to dissolve the sugar and miso (the mixture will be quite thick). Gently lay the salmon in a 1-gallon zipper-lock bag and pour the marinade into the bag. Seal the bag, pressing out as much air as possible, and refrigerate for at least 5 hours and up to 24 hours, flipping the bag occasionally to ensure that the fish marinates evenly. (Do not overmarinate.)

2. Adjust an oven rack 6 inches from the broiler element and heat the broiler. Line a broiler pan

bottom with foil and top with a slotted broiler pan top. Remove the fish from the marinade, lay on the broiler pan top skin side down and spoon 1 tablespoon of the marinade out of the bag over each fillet; discard the remaining marinade.

3. Broil the salmon until nicely browned and the flesh is opaque and flakes apart when gently prodded with a paring knife, 6 to 9 minutes. Transfer the salmon to a platter and serve.

CHICKEN TERIYAKI

WHEN THE FISH ISN'T SO FRESH AND THE soba's just so-so, you can usually count on chicken teriyaki as a reliable standby at most Japanese restaurants. But with so many lackluster Americanized adaptations out there—including everything from skewered chicken chunks shellacked in a corn-syrupy sauce to overmarinated, preformed chicken breast patties—what is the real deal? Traditionally, chicken teriyaki is pan-fried, grilled, or broiled, with the sauce added during the last stages of cooking. In fact, the Japanese term *teriyaki* can be translated as *teri*, meaning "shine" or "luster"—referring to the glossy sauce—and *yaki*, meaning "to broil." Tired of food-court chicken teriyaki wanna-bes, we were determined to develop a simple but authentic recipe.

In Japan, the chicken is most often served off the bone and cut into thin strips. The sauce itself—unlike most bottled versions—consists of just three basic ingredients: soy sauce, sugar, and either mirin (a sweet Japanese rice wine) or sake.

The half-dozen test recipes we assembled were, for the most part, disappointing. The most promising recipes had one thing in common: The skin was left on. Despite minor complaints about the sauce being too watery, tasters seemed to like a marinated and broiled version best, followed by one in which the chicken was pan-fried and simmered in sauce during the final minutes of cooking. While the skin kept the meat tender and moist, it also had a major flaw: its chewing-gum-like texture. We had

to come up with a way to keep the skin crisp, even with the addition of sauce. A skillet or broiler—or perhaps a tag-team effort employing both—would be integral to getting us there.

Although chicken thighs were clearly preferred by tasters over chicken breasts, we couldn't give up on the ubiquitous boneless, skinless variety just yet, as they're so popular and convenient. But in subsequent tests, whether the chicken breasts were seared and broiled, solely broiled, marinated, or left plain and sauced at the end, they always ended up unappealingly dry, bland, and even a little rubbery around the edges compared with the thigh meat. The deeper, meatier taste of the thighs stood up nicely to the salty profile of the teriyaki sauce, while the breast meat acted as not much more than a one-dimensional backdrop, contributing little flavor of its own.

With the thighs now an established standard, the questions of bone-in or bone-out, skin-on or skin-off, begged to be answered. The skin seemed to create a protective barrier against the heat source, keeping the meat moist, so it would have to be left on. Because most skin-on chicken thighs are sold with the bone attached, we would have to bone them ourselves if we wanted to serve the meat in easy-to-eat strips. Even with a sharp paring knife and a straightforward technique, it took kitchen novices a few tries before they felt completely comfortable with the procedure. But the effort was well worth it. Not only did boning the chicken thighs allow the meat to cook faster, it also made cutting the pieces of hot chicken into strips much easier (and less messy). If you want to skip the knife work, you can cook and serve the chicken with the bone in, but the presentation is not nearly as nice and everyone will have to work harder at the table.

Because most of the recipes we came across in our research called for marinating the meat to infuse it with as much flavor as possible, all of our initial efforts began with this step. But whether we pricked the skin with a fork or slashed it with a knife, marinating the thighs in the teriyaki sauce caused the skin to become unattractively flabby. A combination of searing the thighs and then finishing them under the broiler yielded the most promising results, but once the meat received its final dredge in a reduced portion of the marinade (which we now referred to as a sauce) to get that shiny glaze, the skin always slipped back into sogginess.

Exhausted at the thought of having to refine a long-winded process of boning, marinating, searing, reducing, and broiling that didn't seem to work, we solicited the advice of our colleagues in the test kitchen. One suggested browning unmarinated thighs skin side down in a 12-inch skillet, weighting them with a Dutch oven, followed by simmering them skin side up in the reducing sauce. Frustrated and covered in splotches of chicken grease, we turned to another colleague, who suggested something so simple, so obvious, that we wondered why we hadn't thought of it sooner. "Why not just broil the chicken without marinating it and spoon the sauce on at the end?" she asked. We had gotten so caught up with trying to infuse the meat with flavor that we had all but forgotten a main technique of traditional teriyaki: applying the sauce at the end.

After playing musical racks with the oven broiler to get the thighs up to the requisite 175-degree temperature without burning the skin or leaving it pale and fatty, we found that placing the rack in the middle (about 8 inches from the heat source) provided the most consistent level of browning and crispness for the lightly salted-and-peppered thighs. On the middle rack, the skin turned almost as crispy as a potato chip, but there were still some spots where the fat didn't render completely. To remedy this problem, we slashed the skin, which allowed the heat to penetrate more easily, and tucked the exposed edges of meat underneath the skin while smoothing out the tops, which reduced the occurrence of dips and bumps where small pockets of fat had gotten trapped.

With the chicken taken care of, it was time to concentrate on the sauce. Bottled teriyaki was uniformly rejected in favor of a homemade sauce, which took just five minutes to prepare. Working with various amounts of soy sauce, sugar, and mirin (which tasters preferred to sake), we achieved the best balance of sweetness and saltiness with ½ cup each of soy sauce and sugar and 2 tablespoons of mirin, which added a slightly sweet wine flavor. Getting the right glaze consistency (neither as thick as molasses nor as thin as water) was difficult. No matter how carefully we watched the sauce simmer, it either was too thin or became tacky while the soy sauce burned, producing what one person called a "strangely bologna-like" flavor. A minimal amount of cornstarch (2 teaspoons) quickly solved this problem. Although the sauce was now clean and balanced, it needed more depth, which was achieved through the addition of some grated ginger and minced garlic. With at-once crisp and moist, sweet and salty glazed chicken now available at home, we would never have to eat food-court teriyaki again.

With chicken teriyaki down, it didn't take long to develop a beef version. But rather than broiling the steaks (as we did for the chicken), we found that pan-searing creating a better crust, without overcooking the meat.

PANTRY SPOTLIGHT

MIRIN

Mirin is a tawny, sweetened Japanese rice wine that is used in many Japanese recipes, such as marinades, teriyaki sauce, and various glazes where it adds sheen and luster to foods.

Mirin comes in two varieties: Hon mirin, which is brewed in the traditional method using glutinous rice, malted rice, and distilled alcohol and requires over a year to brew and mature, and aji mirin which is simply sake fortified with sugar to mimic the flavor and syrupy consistency of hon mirin. Hon mirin is more expensive and difficult to find while aji mirin is more widely available.

To replace 2 tablespoons of this sweet Japanese rice wine in a recipe, substitute an equal amount of white wine or sake plus 1 teaspoon of sugar.

Chicken Teriyaki

SERVES 4 TO 6

If you prefer not to bone the chicken thighs, simply trim the thighs of excess skin and fat and broil as directed, adjusting the oven rack 12 inches from the broiler element and increasing the broiling time to 20 to 26 minutes. This recipe was developed to work in an in-oven broiler, not the drawer-type broiler typical of older gas ovens. Serve with Simple Steamed White Rice (page 516).

8	bone-in, skin-on chicken thighs (about 5 ounces each), trimmed, boned, and skin slashed (see the illustrations below)
	Ground black pepper
½	cup soy sauce
½	cup sugar
2	tablespoons mirin (see page 547)
2	teaspoons cornstarch
I	medium garlic clove, minced or pressed through a garlic press (about I teaspoon)
½	teaspoon minced or grated fresh ginger

1. Adjust an oven rack about 8 inches from the broiler element and heat the broiler. Line a broiler pan bottom with foil and top with a slotted broiler pan top. Season the chicken with pepper and lay it skin side up on the broiler pan top. Tuck any exposed meat under the skin and lightly flatten the thighs to be evenly thick following illustration 6 below.

2. Broil the chicken until the skin is crisp and golden brown and the thickest parts of the thighs register 175 degrees on an instant-read thermometer, 8 to 14 minutes, rotating the pan halfway through the cooking time for even browning.

3. Meanwhile, whisk the soy sauce, sugar, mirin, cornstarch, garlic, and ginger together in a medium bowl to dissolve the cornstarch. Pour the mixture into a small saucepan, bring to a simmer over medium-high heat, then reduce the heat to low and cook, stirring occasionally, until the sauce is a thick, syrupy glaze and measures about ¾ cup, about 5 minutes. Transfer the sauce to a small bowl, cover, and set aside.

4. Transfer the chicken to a cutting board and let rest for about 3 minutes. Slice the chicken into ½-inch-wide strips, then transfer the chicken to a platter. Drizzle about half of the sauce over the top and serve, passing the remaining sauce separately.

PREPARING CHICKEN THIGHS FOR TERIYAKI

1. After trimming the excess skin and fat (leave enough skin to cover the meat), cut a slit along the white line of fat from one joint to the other joint to expose the bone.

2. Using the tip of a knife, cut/scrape the meat from the bone at both joints.

3. Slip the knife under the bone to separate the meat completely from the bone.

4. Discard the bone. Trim any remaining cartilage from the thigh.

5. Cut three diagonal slashes in the skin. Do not cut into the meat.

6. Tuck the meat under the skin and lightly flatten the thigh to an even thickness.

➤ VARIATION
Beef Teriyaki
SERVES 4

Note that these steaks are best cooked to medium-rare or medium. When cooked to rare, they are too chewy.

2	boneless shell sirloin steaks (top butt), 1¼ inches thick or whole flap meat steaks (about 1 pound each)
	Ground black pepper
2	tablespoons vegetable oil
½	cup soy sauce
½	cup sugar
2	tablespoons mirin
2	teaspoons cornstarch
1	medium garlic clove, minced or pressed through a garlic press (about 1 teaspoon)
½	teaspoon minced or grated fresh ginger

1. Pat the steaks dry with paper towels and season with pepper. Heat the oil in a 12-inch skillet over medium-high heat until just smoking. Lay the steaks in the skillet and cook, without moving the steaks, until well browned, about 2 minutes.

2. Flip the steaks over, reduce the heat to medium, and continue to cook until well browned on the second side and the internal temperature registers 125 degrees on an instant-read thermometer for medium-rare (about 5 minutes) or 130 degrees for medium (about 6 minutes).

3. Transfer the steaks to a large plate, tent loosely with foil, and let rest until the internal temperature registers 130 degrees for medium-rare or 135 degrees for medium, 12 to 15 minutes.

4. While the steaks rest, whisk the soy sauce, sugar, mirin, cornstarch, garlic, and ginger together in a medium bowl to dissolve the cornstarch. Pour the mixture into the skillet and bring to a simmer over medium-high heat, scraping up any browned bits. Reduce the heat to low and cook, stirring occasionally, until the sauce is a thick, syrupy glaze and measures about ¾ cup, about 5 minutes. Transfer the sauce to a small bowl, cover, and set aside.

5. Slice the steak against the grain on the bias into ¼-inch-thick pieces and arrange on a serving platter. Drizzle about half of the sauce over the top and serve, passing the remaining sauce separately.

JAPANESE-STYLE BREADED PORK CUTLETS

Tonkatsu

IN JAPAN, CRISP, FRIED PORK CUTLETS CALLED *tonkatsu* are popular fare. Seasoned simply with crunchy Japanese panko bread crumbs, salt, and pepper, these thin pork cutlets offer a substantial and flavorful bite, especially when served with their signature tangy sauce which includes ketchup and Worcestershire sauce. At their best, the cutlets are tender and the breading crisp, light, and golden. But when things go wrong, the result is tough disks of meat shrouded in a greasy, pale crust. We aimed to develop a superlative rendition of this Japanese favorite.

Testing started with the basics: the pork itself. The two suitable cuts of pork we found in the supermarket, boneless loin chops and tenderloin, were also the two cuts cited most consistently in the recipes we researched. We tried both, but because the meat is meant to have some chew, tasters favored boneless loin chops, because they had more flavor than the tenderloin.

The next issue was thickness. When the cutlets were too thick, the breading overbrowned by the time the interior cooked through; when too thin, the meat was done long before the breading had taken on enough color. We ended up preferring chops pounded to a ¼ inch thickness. They were thick enough to offer some chew and a cushion against overcooking as the crust developed to a deep, even golden brown. Pounding the chops both increased the diameter of the cutlets so they looked more attractive and further tenderized them.

As we often do in the test kitchen, we tried brining the cutlets—soaking them in a solution of water, salt, and sugar—to impart more moisture and flavor. After several tests and considerable debate, we decided to skip this step since it did not significantly improve the texture of the meat (pork loin is relatively tender and supple unless overcooked). Liberally seasoning the cutlets with salt and pepper was a much easier way to add flavor. This was an essential step, as experiments with seasoning only the breading were far less effective.

While many classic Japanese recipes call for panko (extra-crunchy dried bread crumbs), we experimented with several other options to start. We tried a coating made from fresh bread crumbs (made by grinding high-quality white sandwich bread in the food processor), regular dried bread crumbs, crushed crackers, and a cornmeal-flour combination. The fresh bread crumbs lacked crunch, the dried crumbs were stale, the crackers pasty, and the cornmeal-flour combination yielded a gritty coating. Only the panko crust satisfied tasters with a light, crisp texture. Dipping the cutlets into beaten egg and oil acted as glue between the meat and crumbs, and a sheer dusting of cornstarch

INGREDIENTS: Panko Bread Crumbs

The incredibly light, shatteringly crisp texture of panko is a far cry from the dusty, fine dry bread crumbs familiar to most cooks in the U.S. The crumbs of panko are larger than standard issue bread crumbs and thoroughly dried. Some brands of panko contain oil and some do not. As panko has become more popular in the U.S., more brands have made their way to grocery store shelves.

To see if there really is a difference between brands, we picked up four samples—Wel-Pac, Dynasty, Kikkoman, and Ian's—at Boston-area supermarkets and tested them with our tonkatsu recipe. Each brand worked fine for this application, but with slightly different textural qualities. While the Wel-Pac, Dynasty, and Kikkoman brands possessed a delicate crispness, the oil-free Ian's (purchased from a large natural foods market) provided a much more substantial crunch. In the end, if a super-crunchy—rather than delicate and crisp— texture is what you're aiming for, choose Ian's. Otherwise, brand doesn't really matter.

THE BEST PANKO BREAD CRUMBS

If you're looking for crumbs with substantial crunch, tasters deemed Ian's brand of panko the crunchiest of the bunch.

applied to the meat just beforehand encouraged the egg to cling, which prevented patches of crust from falling off the cooked cutlets. We also let the breaded pork cutlets sit a few minutes to allow the breading to dry slightly. This further ensured that the crust would stay put during pan-frying.

Cooking the cutlets is where things can easily go awry. Using the right amount of oil is essential, as is heating it until it's hot. We tried cooking a batch of four cutlets in just 4 tablespoons of oil, and the result—poor, splotchy browning—confirmed our hunch that using enough oil is critical. To develop their hallmark golden, crunchy crust, the cutlets must be pan-fried in oil that reaches roughly halfway up their sides, about ½ cup oil for each batch of two cutlets.

Heat, or lack thereof, is another problem that most cooks encounter when pan-frying. When we failed to heat the oil enough before adding the cutlets to the skillet, several problems arose. First, the breading absorbed too much oil, so the finished cutlets were greasy. Second, the breading took too long to brown properly, and that extended stay in the pan caused the meat to toughen slightly. These pitfalls are avoided easily enough, though, if the oil is hot enough for the cutlets to sizzle briskly upon entering the pan and to then continue cooking at a moderate pace that allows the breading to brown evenly without burning at the edges. We found that the pan must be preheated over medium-high heat until the oil starts to shimmer—about 2½ minutes. (The time may vary depending on your particular pan and stovetop.) Taking care not to overcrowd the skillet with more than two cutlets per batch, we tested cooking times and learned that 2½ minutes per side browned the breading to a gorgeous golden hue without overcooking the meat within.

So if you don't skimp on either the oil or the heat, you can produce beautifully browned pork cutlets that are crisp on the outside and tender and juicy on the inside. These pork cutlets are usually served cut in strips with tonkatsu sauce. This sauce is sold bottled in Japan, but it can be easily made with pantry staples—simply stir together ketchup, Worcestershire sauce, soy sauce, and dry mustard, then drizzle over the hot, crunchy cutlets.

Japanese-Style Breaded Pork Cutlets

Tonkatsu

SERVES 4

Tonkatsu sauce can also be purchased at Japanese markets; however, you probably have all the ingredients to make it from scratch in your pantry. These cutlets also make an excellent filling for sandwiches.

TONKATSU SAUCE

½   cup ketchup
2   tablespoons Worcestershire sauce
2   teaspoons soy sauce
½   teaspoon dry mustard powder dissolved in 1 teaspoon water

PORK

½   cup cornstarch
2   large eggs
1   cup plus 1 tablespoon vegetable oil
3   cups panko (see page 550)
4   boneless center-cut pork loin chops (about 6 ounces each), trimmed of excess fat and pounded ¼ inch thick
    Salt and ground black pepper

1. FOR THE TONKATSU SAUCE: Whisk all of the ingredients together in a small bowl; set aside.

2. FOR THE PORK: Adjust an oven rack to the lower-middle position, place a rimmed baking sheet lined with a wire rack on the oven rack, and heat the oven to 200 degrees. Spread the cornstarch in a wide, shallow dish. Beat the eggs with 1 tablespoon of the oil in a second wide, shallow dish. Spread the panko in a third wide, shallow dish.

3. Pat the pork dry with paper towels and season with salt and pepper. Working with one piece of pork at a time, coat the cutlets thoroughly with the cornstarch, shaking off any excess. Using tongs, dip the pork in the egg mixture to coat, allowing the excess to drip back into the dish. Coat the pork with the bread crumbs, pressing the crumbs to adhere. Place the breaded cutlets in a single layer on a separate wire rack set over a baking sheet and repeat with the remaining pork. Let the pork sit until the coating is dry, about 5 minutes.

4. Heat ½ cup more of the oil in a 12-inch nonstick skillet over medium-high heat until shimmering. Lay 2 cutlets in the skillet and fry until deep golden brown and crisp on the first side, gently pressing on the cutlets with a spatula to ensure even browning, about 2½ minutes. Using tongs, flip the cutlets over, reduce the heat to medium, and continue to cook until the meat feels firm when pressed gently and the second side is deep golden brown and crisp, about 2½ minutes longer. Transfer the cutlets to the rack on the baking sheet in the oven.

5. Discard the oil in the skillet and wipe the skillet clean using tongs and a large wad of paper towels. Repeat step 4 with the remaining ½ cup of oil and remaining 2 cutlets. Slice the cutlets into ¾-inch-wide strips, transfer to a serving platter, drizzle with the sauce, and serve.

KOREAN FRIED CHICKEN

Yang-nyum Tong Dak

FRIED CHICKEN HAS, UNTIL RECENTLY, always been considered a Western delicacy. But in recent years as Western culture migrates east so too has its penchant for fast food and with it, fried chicken. The Koreans, however, have completely transformed the thick-crusted fried chicken of the American South into chicken with a paper-thin, crisp coating—each piece painted with a tangy saucy glaze.

While fried foods play only a minimal role in the Korean diet, we wanted to find out what all the hype was about. Korean-style fried chicken is purportedly twice-fried to give it its super-crispy skin. Twice-frying involves frying the chicken pieces for an initial period, typically 3 to 5 minutes, removing the chicken from the oil and allowing it to rest for about 5 to 7 minutes, then returning it to the oil to finish cooking. We were curious to see how well this technique actually worked so we built a recipe from existing information gathered from Korean cookbooks and headed into the test kitchen.

To begin, we tested twice-fried chicken against our conventional fried chicken. For these initial tests we left off any coating so we could fully judge the results of the frying method. The twice-fried chicken had an initial fry time of 5 minutes, followed by a 5-minute rest, and concluded with a 3- to 5-minute fry until the chicken was cooked. The conventional fried chicken was fried straight through for 8 to 10 minutes until cooked.

After tasting both versions side by side it was clear that the twice-fried method resulted in a crispier, thinner-skinned chicken. But why does twice-frying yield crisper chicken? We consulted our science editor for the answer.

To explain, our science editor began with the problem of traditional fried chicken. Hold a piece of crisp Southern fried chicken in your hand and peel back the crisp breading. What do you find underneath? Flabby skin. Skin is composed of 50 percent water, 40 percent fat, and the remaining 10 percent is connective tissue and other matter. During the process of frying the chicken, the meat cooks and the moisture in the skin begins to evaporate and the fat begins to melt, or render. But by the time the chicken is cooked through, there is still a significant amount of water remaining in the skin, as well as fat. In order to crisp the skin, one could continue to fry the chicken, but then the meat would overcook and the skin would start to burn. Twice-frying, however, slows down the cooking process to allow for more moisture to evaporate and more fat to render. Here's how it works: In the first fry, the meat begins to cook and the moisture in the skin—specifically the outer layer of the skin—begins to evaporate and the fat begins to render. The chicken is then removed from the oil and rested, which brings down the temperature of both the meat and the skin. This resting period serves two purposes: first, it allows time for more moisture to evaporate from the skin, and second, it helps prevent the meat from overcooking. In the second fry the relatively dry outer layer of skin can quickly become very hot and crisp, while retaining moisture within the deepest layers of skin and the meat. During this process more fat is rendered, providing an ultra-thin crisp skin. With a clear explanation of the twice-frying process, we moved on to determining the best coating for the chicken.

Many of the recipes we found called for dusting the chicken with cornstarch before frying, while other recipes took it a step further and dipped their chicken into a thin mixture of cornstarch and water or into a batter of eggs, cornstarch, and water. We tested our fried chicken with all three techniques. The chicken that was coated with only cornstarch fried up crisper than without the coating, gaining a golden brown color. But the skin was only moderately crisp and the cornstarch seemed to weigh the skin down in some spots. The two batter tests yielded lackluster results, as both slid immediately off the chicken when it hit the hot oil. It was clear that we needed to prepare the surface of the chicken in a manner that would allow the batter to stick. The solution was coating the chicken pieces with a thin layer of cornstarch before dipping them into the batter.

Now that the batter was adhering to the chicken, we tried our test again. The egg batter turned into a heavy, dense crust. The cornstarch and water batter, however, yielded chicken with a light, crisp, and beautifully golden crust. This was unlike any fried chicken we'd ever eaten.

With our chicken fried, we shifted our attention to our sauces. Proper Korean fried chicken is coated very lightly with a pungent sauce. But before you think along the lines of Buffalo wings, think again. The coating is very light, not a thick slather. The two most popular Korean fried chicken sauces are a sweet soy-garlic sauce and a spicy chili sauce. We made our sweet soy-garlic sauce by combining sugar, soy sauce, water, and garlic in a saucepan and reducing it to a glaze. We balanced the sauce with a splash of rice wine vinegar and a shot of hot sauce. The chili sauce was also quite simple, composed of ketchup, sugar, chili-garlic sauce, and a touch of lemon juice. Once the chicken was fried, we tossed it lightly with the sauce until coated and sprinkled it with sliced scallions and minced cilantro. Tasters grabbed plenty of napkins before stepping up to enjoy this fried chicken feast.

Korean Fried Chicken

Yang-nyum Tong Dak

SERVES 4

The chicken must be fried in two batches. To make the best use of your time, batter the second batch of chicken while the first batch is resting. If using both light and dark meat (breasts and thighs or drumsticks) we suggest dividing them into separate batches since the dark meat requires a few extra minutes to cook through on the second fry in step 5.

3	quarts vegetable oil
1½	cups cornstarch
3½	pounds bone-in, skin-on chicken pieces (split breasts cut in half, drumsticks, and/or thighs)
	Salt and ground black pepper
1	cup water
1	recipe Sweet Soy-Garlic Sauce or Tomato Chili-Garlic Sauce (recipes follow)
2	scallions, sliced thin on the bias (see page 505)
1	tablespoon minced fresh cilantro leaves

1. Adjust an oven rack to the middle position and heat the oven to 200 degrees. Measure 2 inches of oil into a large Dutch oven and heat over medium-high heat to 350 degrees. (Use an instant-read thermometer that registers high temperatures or clip a candy/deep-fat thermometer onto the side of the pan.) Line 2 rimmed baking sheets with wire racks; set aside.

2. Sift ½ cup of the cornstarch into a wide, shallow dish. Set a large mesh strainer over a large bowl. Pat the chicken dry with paper towels and season with salt and pepper. Working with several pieces of chicken at a time, coat the chicken thoroughly with the cornstarch, then transfer to the strainer and shake vigorously to remove all but a thin coating of cornstarch. Transfer the chicken to one of the wire racks.

3. Whisk the remaining 1 cup cornstarch, water, and 1 teaspoon salt together in a large bowl to form a smooth batter. When the oil is hot, finish coating the chicken by adding half of the chicken to the batter and turn to coat well. Using tongs, remove the chicken the batter, one piece at a time, allowing any excess batter to drip back into the bowl, and add to the hot oil.

4. Fry the chicken, stirring to prevent the pieces from sticking together and adjusting the heat as necessary to maintain an oil temperature of 350 degrees, until the chicken begins to crisp, turn slightly golden, and registers about 90 degrees on the thermometer, about 5 minutes. Transfer the fried chicken to the second prepared wire rack, and set aside for 5 to 6 minutes. Batter and fry the remaining chicken during this time.

5. Line a baking sheet with several layers of paper towels, and return the oil to 350 degrees (if necessary) over medium-high heat. Return the first batch of fried chicken to the oil and continue to fry until the exterior is very crisp, deep golden brown, and an instant-read thermometer inserted into the center of the chicken registers about 160 degrees for breasts, or 175 degrees for thigh or drumsticks, 3 to 6 minutes. Transfer the chicken to the paper towel–lined baking sheet to drain, and keep warm in a 200 degree oven. Repeat with the second batch; let the second batch drain for about 1 minute. (The unsauced fried chicken wings can be held for up to an hour in a 200-degree oven.)

6. Transfer all the chicken to a large bowl, drizzle with the sauce, and gently toss until evenly coated. Transfer the chicken to a platter, sprinkle with the scallions and cilantro, and serve.

➤ VARIATION

Korean Fried Chicken Wings

Follow the recipe for Korean Fried Chicken, substituting 3½ pounds chicken wings, separated into sections, wingtips discarded, for the chicken pieces; fry in 2 batches as directed in steps 4 and 5 (the cooking times will be about the same).

Sweet Soy-Garlic Sauce

MAKES ABOUT ⅔ CUP

To make the sauce spicier, stir in additional chili-garlic sauce to taste.

½	cup sugar
¼	cup soy sauce
¼	cup water
3	medium garlic cloves, minced or pressed through a garlic press (about 1 tablespoon)

1   tablespoon rice vinegar

1   teaspoon Thai chili-garlic sauce, such as
     sriracha (see page 561)

Simmer all of the ingredients together in a small saucepan over medium heat until syrupy, about 5 minutes. Let cool to room temperature before serving. (The sauce can be refrigerated in an airtight container for up to 1 day.)

Tomato Chili-Garlic Sauce

MAKES ABOUT ⅔ CUP

To make the sauce spicier, stir in additional chili-garlic sauce to taste.

5   tablespoons sugar

¼   cup ketchup

1   tablespoon Thai chili-garlic sauce, such as
     sriracha (see page 561)

1   teaspoon juice from 1 lemon

Whisk the sugar, ketchup, chili sauce, and lemon juice together and let sit to blend the flavors, about 15 minutes, before serving. (The sauce can be refrigerated in an airtight container for up to 1 day.)

KOREAN GRILLED SHORT RIBS

Kalbi

KOREANS TAKE THEIR GRILLED BEEF AS seriously as Americans do their burgers and steaks. Although the preparations are worlds apart, both are highly seasoned with the barbecued flavor of the grill. While Americans might argue about the best fat percentage for hamburgers or if hot dogs should be all-beef or pork, Koreans debate the merits of various cuts of beef—the most prized being *kalbi*, or beef short ribs.

Kalbi is a dish of thinly sliced beef shortribs marinated in a sweet soy mixture with garlic, scallions, and pears. It is often eaten wrapped in lettuce leaves, sort of like a taco. Restaurants known as "kalbi houses" offer this Korean staple, and diners cook their short ribs on a hot grill in the center of the table. The result: crusty, browned meat slices with a barbecued char that are nonetheless tender. Knowing that short ribs take hours of braising to become tenderized, we wondered how the Koreans accomplished this in a matter of minutes. If we could figure this out, we would have something

GETTING ENGLISH-STYLE RIBS READY TO GRILL

1. Remove the meat from the bone, positioning a chef's knife as close as possible to the bone.

2. Trim the excess hard fat and silver skin from both sides of the meat.

3. Slice the meat at an angle into 4 to 5 pieces ranging from ½ to ¾ inch thick.

4. Place plastic wrap over the meat and pound into even ¼-inch-thick pieces.

other than hamburgers and hot dogs to throw on the grill when we got home from work.

When we grilled big short ribs from the supermarket, they were barely chewable and overly fatty, despite the "great for grilling" sticker. We quickly realized that how the ribs are butchered is essential to the success of this dish. Most short ribs sold in supermarkets are cut English style—a single rib bone with a thick piece of meat attached to it. Korean short ribs are cut in the opposite direction, across the bones, or flanken-style. Naturally, our first thought was to try flanken-style ribs. However, the markets that do sell them cut the ribs ½ to 1 inch thick—much too big to work in a quick Korean barbecue recipe. We eventually got the butcher to use a band saw to slice flanken-style ribs ¼ inch thick, like in Korean restaurants, but it was clear that our recipe would have to start with widely available English-style ribs.

We first tried removing the meat from the bone and butterflying it—cutting it nearly in half widthwise and opening it like a book. While better than the whole grilled ribs, it was still tough. We suspected that slicing the meat into more uniform pieces might be the answer. We angled the knife against the meat and fabricated four slices from each rib. These pieces were large and chunky, but a quick pounding evened them out. On the grill, they looked much like a thinner, boneless version of the Asian cut. What's more, we didn't have to worry about removing bones before wrapping them up in lettuce like a Korean taco.

Although the beef looked the part, it was still tough and chewy. Clearly, the secret to authentic Korean barbecued ribs was more than just proper butchering. The right marinade was critical, too. We lined up the ingredients for inspection: soy sauce, sugar, rice vinegar, garlic, and scallions. In previous test kitchen work, we have discovered that soy acts as a brine and helps tenderize meat, so we figured we were on the right track. For more flavor we added sesame oil and ginger. But surprisingly, the texture didn't change. Surely, upping the amount of vinegar would do the trick. No. More vinegar made the meat even tougher and imparted an unpleasant sour flavor.

We had one more series of tests to run. Many kalbi recipes add pureed pear to the marinade, claiming it acts as a tenderizer. Pineapple and papaya are well known for their tenderizing properties, but we had never heard of using pear. When we added pureed pear to our marinade, tasters unanimously thought the ribs were more tender. So maybe pear *is* a secret tenderizer? To test this hypothesis, we tried marinating the ribs with pear alone, but the result, once again, was tough meat. Simple deduction told us that one of the ingredients in the marinade was working with the pear.

Conversations with food scientists taught us that the acidity in pears helps speed up the work of proteases, tenderizing compounds found in soy sauce. The rice vinegar does the same thing, only more so, which is why the pear-only marinade

SHOPPING NOTES: Short Ribs

English-Style ribs contain a single bone, about 4 to 5 inches long. Look for ribs that have at least 1 inch of meat above the bone.

Flanken-Style have been cut across the ribs and contains 2 to 3 oval-shaped cross sections of bone. These ribs can be difficult to find in the supermarket.

Korean-Style ribs, the authentic choice, are sold only in Asian markets and require no butchering. The same as flanken-style ribs but cut much thinner, usually about ¼ inch thick.

didn't have much effect on the meat. But rice vinegar can't do it alone, which is why increasing the vinegar in the marinade made the meat taste sour. Besides acidity, pears add sweetness and a fruity flavor that complements the beefy char. The pear might have a modest role as a tenderizer, but it plays an important part in the flavor development.

Now to the grill. To replicate the hot indoor restaurant grills that char the meat without making shoe leather, we tried banking the hot coals to one side of a kettle-style grill, creating what the test kitchen refers to as a modified two-level fire. This created the more intense heat that we needed to get a quick char without making the meat tough. Keeping the hot coals on one side also allowed us to move the meat to the cooler side when flare-ups occurred. With the marinade flavor and grilling technique perfected, we could now add short ribs to our shopping list, alongside the hot dogs and beef patties. And pears, too.

Charcoal-Grilled Korean Short Ribs

Kalbi

SERVES 4 TO 6

Buy English-style short ribs that have at least 1 inch of meat on top of the bone; avoid ribs that have little meat or large bones. Two and a half pounds Korean-style beef short ribs, sliced no more than ¼ inch thick, can be substituted for the English-style, with the following modifications: Skip step 1 and trim the ribs thoroughly of excess fat—these ribs are fattier than English-style. Marinate and grill the rubs as directed, reducing the amount of charcoal (if using) to 3 quarts and watch for flare-ups. Traditionally, these ribs are wrapped in a lettuce leaf and eaten like a taco, however they also can be served over Simple Steamed White Rice (page 516).

5	pounds English-style beef short ribs (about 6 to 8 ribs, see page 555)
1	medium ripe pear, peeled, halved, cored, and chopped coarse
½	cup soy sauce
6	tablespoons sugar
2	tablespoons toasted sesame oil

6	medium garlic cloves, minced or pressed through a garlic press (about 2 tablespoons)
4	teaspoons minced or grated fresh ginger
1	tablespoon rice vinegar
3	scallions, sliced thin
	Vegetable oil, for grilling
	Kimchi, for serving (see page 558)
	Gochujang, for serving (optional, see page 561)

1. Following the illustrations on page 554, remove the bone from each short rib, trim the meat of excess fat and silver skin, then slice each on the bias in 4 to 5 pieces ranging from ½ to ¾ inch thick. Cover the meat with plastic wrap and pound into even, ¼-inch-thick pieces.

2. Process the pear, soy sauce, sugar, sesame oil, garlic, ginger, and vinegar in a food processor until smooth, about 30 seconds, scraping down the sides of the bowl as needed. Transfer the mixture to a medium bowl and stir in the scallions.

3. Spread one-third of the marinade in a 13 by 9-inch pan (or similarly sized dish). Arrange half of the meat in the dish in a single layer. Pour half of the remaining marinade over the meat, followed by the remaining meat and marinade. Wrap the dish with plastic wrap, and refrigerate for 4 hours and up to 12 hours, turning the meat once or twice to ensure that it marinates evenly. (Do not overmarinate.)

4. Light a large chimney starter two-thirds full of charcoal (about 4 quarts) and allow to burn until all the charcoal is covered with a layer of fine gray ash. Build a hot fire by spreading the coals over just two-thirds of the grill bottom (confining the coals to a smaller space makes for a hotter fire). Set the cooking grate in place, cover the grill with the lid, and let the grate heat up, about 5 minutes. The grill is ready when the coals are hot; you can hold your hand 5 inches above the cooking grate for just 2 seconds. Scrape the cooking grate clean with a grill brush and wipe with a wad of oil-soaked paper towels, holding the towels with tongs.

5. Remove the half of the meat from the marinade, lay directly over the hot coals, and grill, turning 3 or 4 times, until well browned on both sides, 7 to 12 minutes. (If flare-ups occur, move the

meat to the cooler side of the grill until the flames die down.) Move the first batch of meat to the cooler side of grill and repeat the browning with the second batch.

6. Transfer the second batch of meat to a serving platter. Return the first batch of meat to the hot side of the grill, heat through for 30 seconds, then transfer to a platter. Serve with kimchi and gochujang (if using).

➤ VARIATION
Gas-Grilled Korean Short Ribs
In order to maximize the heat on a gas grill, keep all burners on high and remain vigilant about flare-ups, spraying flames with water from a squirt bottle if necessary. Note that the cooking time on a gas grill will be slightly longer than times on a charcoal grill.

Follow the recipe for Charcoal-Grilled Korean Short Ribs through step 3. Heat the grill with all the burners set to high, and the lid down, until very hot, about 15 minutes. Scrape the cooking grate clean with a grill brush and wipe with a wad of oil-soaked paper towels, holding the towels with tongs. Continue with the recipe from step 5, cooking the meat in 2 batches with the lid down for 10 to 14 minutes per batch.

KOREAN RICE BOWL WITH BEEF, VEGETABLES, AND FRIED EGG

Bibimbap

RICE IS ALL BUT GUARANTEED AT EVERY Korean meal. Perhaps the most popular way to enjoy rice is in *bibimbap*—tender-chewy short-grain rice heaped into bowls and topped with an array of sautéed vegetables, beef, and a fried egg. Just before serving, this steaming bowl of rice is drizzled with sesame oil, and the egg yolk is broken and stirred throughout the mixture giving credit to bibimbap's literal translation of "mixed rice."

Recipes for bibimbap can vary dramatically. Some rely heavily on leftovers while others use all freshly made components. Whatever path is chosen, the technique is largely the same: all the ingredients are sautéed separately to retain individual textures and flavors, and then these ingredients are spooned into separate portions on top of the rice. We set out to develop our own version of this dish, but first we started with the rice.

Throughout Korea, short-grain rice is grown by nearly half of all farmers. And while cooking a pot of rice seem like a simple task, there is more to it than meets the eye. Short-grain rice, we found, requires a completely different cooking technique than the long-grain rice that we most commonly use in the test kitchen (as in our Basic Rice Pilaf on page 447).

Our first short-grain rice tests revolved around determining the right proportion of water to rice. Long-grain rice requires about 1½ cups of water for every cup of rice; however, short-grain rice requires a bit more liquid in order for it to soften correctly. Yet if you add too much liquid to short-grain rice, it takes on a creamy, risotto-like texture. Testing a variety of water to rice ratios, we found a 1 to 1 ratio of water to rice to be ideal.

Rinsing the rice, as we do with our pilaf, is also crucial when cooking short-grain rice. Rinsing rids the rice of excess starch that coats the individual grains. If the rice is not rinsed, the cooked rice is likely to have a gluey consistency.

Researching various short-grain rice cooking methods exposed a number of techniques, including the simple approach of bringing the water to a boil, adding the rice, and cooking it through. This straightforward method was fairly disastrous, producing lots of blown-out rice grains and a thick layer of sticky, charred rice coating the bottom of the pot. A more complicated method—adding the rice to boiling water to boil for one minute, reducing the heat for five minutes, increasing the heat for 10 seconds, then finally removing the pot from the heat altogether to finish cooking through—worked well, but did cooking rice really need to be so complicated? We decided to see if we could streamline this method.

Rather than adding the rice to boiling water, we tried bringing the rice and water to a boil together, then reducing the heat to a gentle simmer until the rice was tender. This more gentle approach proved better (we no longer had a burnt bottom), but the rice still turned out overly sticky and gummy.

We then tried this approach again, but instead of cooking the rice through at a gentle simmer, we removed the pot from the heat after just a few minutes of simmering. We let the rice finish cooking, covered, off the heat. This very gentle, three-step cooking technique finally yielded the rice we were looking for—delicately textured, fluffy grains. A trick we learned along the way is to leave the pot uncovered when bringing the water and rice to the initial boil so you can see when the rice starts to simmer, and then cover the pot for rest of the process to help the rice cook evenly. As for timing, we found seven minutes of simmering followed by 15 minutes of off-heat steaming to be ideal. Finally, we had produced rice with consistently tender rice and could focus on the toppings.

Since our research uncovered dozens of combinations of toppings, we picked our favorites, starting with beef and shiitake mushrooms. We cooked the beef and shiitakes together in a hot nonstick skillet. As the beef began to release its liquid, the mushrooms immediately soaked it up, keeping the pan dry and allowing the beef to caramelize. When done, we transferred the beef and shiitakes to a warm platter in a 200-degree oven while we prepared the rest of the ingredients.

Sautéed spinach with garlic was another favorite topping choice, not only for its emerald green color, but also its contrasting texture and cooling flavor. Using the same skillet, we added more oil, toasted the garlic for a moment, sautéed the spinach until wilted, and transferred it to the platter in the oven.

Carrots, cucumbers, and mung bean sprouts were also plentiful in many recipes. Remembering that we still had to fry the eggs, we were beginning to feel like we were approaching the limits of what could actually be sautéed in a reasonable amount of time. Reviewing our options, a fellow test cook recommended pickling the remaining vegetables. This not only saved our skillet for another use, but it also offered a crisp, bright flavor to our bibimbap—and was also authentic, since bibimbap is often served with kimchi (pickled vegetables). For our pickled carrots, cucumbers, and bean sprouts, we simply grabbed a bottle of seasoned rice vinegar and tossed some with the vegetables. After 30 minutes the vegetables were well-seasoned and crisp-tender.

At this point we portioned the hot rice among four bowls and arranged each component individually on the rice—the beef and shiitakes in one spot, the spinach and garlic in another, the pickled vegetables in a third, and so on. We slipped the assembled dishes into the oven to keep them warm while we turned to the final component—the eggs. Fried eggs are an essential topper for bibimbap. The soft, runny egg yolk is broken and stirred throughout the rice and among the meat and vegetables just before it is eaten. This adds a level of richness to this otherwise very lean dish. Again reusing our already hot skillet we added four cracked eggs, reduced the heat to low, and covered the skillet until the whites were cooked through and tender and the yolks were hot but still runny. The eggs slid easily out of our nonstick skillet and topped each bowl of rice with a bright yellow dot. We then gave the dish a final flourish with a drizzle of rich, nutty sesame oil. Some tasters immediately dug in, while others went the traditional route and added *gochujang* (a spicy bean paste made from soybeans), kimchi, and yet more sesame oil.

PANTRY SPOTLIGHT

KIMCHI

Kimchi is a pickled vegetable condiment found at nearly every meal in Korea. It is also a common ingredient in many Korean stews and fried rice dishes.

The type of kimchi available depends on the seasonality of ingredients and the region. There are more than 100 different varieties of kimchi; however, the most popular variety consists primarily of napa cabbage, scallions, garlic, and ground chiles in brine (salted water). It is packed in jars, where it is allowed to ferment and build its spicy and pungent flavor. Paired with Kalbi (page 556), it's an unbeatable flavor combination.

Korean Rice Bowl with Beef, Vegetables, and Fried Egg

Bibimbap

SERVES 4

You can substitute sushi rice for the short-grain rice; if using medium- or long-grain rice, increase the amount of water to 3 cups and simmer until the grains are tender, 18 to 20 minutes, before letting the rice sit off the heat in step 2. Regular rice vinegar can be substituted for the seasoned rice vinegar. Serve with kimchi (see page 558) and gochujang (see page 561).

PICKLED VEGETABLES

2 cups bean sprouts

1 medium carrot, peeled and grated on the large holes of a box grater

1 medium cucumber, peeled, halved lengthwise, seeded, and sliced ¼ inch thick

1 cup seasoned rice vinegar

RICE

2 cups short-grain white rice (see note)

2 cups water

BEEF, SPINACH, AND EGGS

5 ounces blade steak, trimmed and cut into ¼-inch-thick slices (see page 487)

1 tablespoon soy sauce

3 tablespoons vegetable oil

8 ounces shiitake mushrooms, wiped clean, stemmed, and sliced thin

3 medium garlic cloves, minced or pressed through a garlic press (about 1 tablespoon)

1 (10-ounce) bag baby spinach
Salt and ground black pepper

4 large eggs, cracked into 2 small bowls (2 eggs per bowl)

1 tablespoon toasted sesame oil

1. FOR THE PICKLED VEGETABLES: Toss the sprouts, carrot, cucumber, and vinegar together in a medium bowl to combine. Press lightly on the vegetables to submerge in the vinegar as much as possible, then cover with plastic wrap and refrigerate for 30 minutes, or up to 24 hours. Drain the vegetable from the vinegar and set aside.

2. FOR THE RICE: Meanwhile, bring the rice and water to a boil in a medium saucepan over high heat, then cover, reduce the heat to low, and cook for 7 minutes. Remove the rice from the heat, and let sit, covered, until tender, about 15 minutes.

3. FOR THE BEEF, SPINACH, AND EGGS: Adjust an oven rack to the lower-middle position, place 4 ovensafe serving bowls on the rack, and heat the oven to 200 degrees. Toss the beef and soy sauce together in a medium bowl.

4. Heat 1 tablespoon of the vegetable oil in a 12-inch nonstick skillet over medium-high heat until just smoking. Add the beef and shiitakes and cook until the beef is cooked through and the mushrooms are soft, about 3 minutes. Transfer the mixture to a platter and keep warm in the oven next to the bowls.

5. Add 1 more tablespoon vegetable oil and the garlic to the skillet and return to medium-high heat until the garlic is sizzling and fragrant, about 30 seconds. Stir in the spinach and cook, tossing constantly, until wilted, about 1 minute. Season with salt and pepper to taste and spoon onto the platter in a separate pile next to the beef in the oven.

6. Portion the cooked rice into the warm serving bowls, top with the beef, mushrooms, and spinach, and return to the oven to keep warm while cooking the eggs.

7. Wipe the skillet clean with a wad of paper towels, add the remaining tablespoon oil to the skillet, and return to medium-high heat until shimmering. Following the illustration on page 293, quickly add the eggs to the skillet. Season the eggs with salt and pepper, cover, and cook until the whites are set but the yolks are still runny, 2 to 3 minutes.

8. Uncover the eggs and remove from the heat. Remove the bowls of rice from the oven and slide one egg on top of each bowl. Drizzle the sesame oil over the eggs, add the pickled vegetables, and serve immediately.

Stone Pot–Style Korean Mixed Rice

In the city of Jeonju in South Korea, bibimbap is served in a hot stone bowl that turns the bottom layer of rice into a crispy, golden crust. Here's how to replicate the roasted flavor and crunchy texture of the rice using a skillet.

Follow the recipe for Korean Rice Bowl with Beef, Vegetables, and Fried Egg, returning the skillet to medium-high heat after transferring the cooked spinach to the platter with the beef in step 5. Brush the skillet evenly with 1 teaspoon vegetable oil, then gently pack the cooked rice into an even layer in the skillet and cook until the bottom of the rice is toasted and brown, about 6 minutes. Remove the skillet from the heat and portion the rice into the warm bowls as directed in step 6.

SWEET POTATO NOODLES WITH BEEF AND VEGETABLES

Japchae

JAPCHAE IS A NOODLE DISH POPULAR DURING holidays and special occasions in Korea. And if you've ever been to a Korean restaurant, you've probably seen it on the menu. What sets this Korean favorite apart from other noodle dishes are the noodles themselves. The sweet potato noodles, called *dangmyeon*, fall into a class called cellophane noodles; the name is derived from their translucent appearance when cooked. (Other cellophane noodles are made from mung beans.) Sweet potato noodles are somewhat thick and have a soft but chewy texture. In addition to the noodles, the dish usually consists of an array of stir-fried meat (usually beef) and vegetables and sometimes strips of a flat egg omelet, all tossed with a dressing rich in soy sauce and sesame oil. We set out to create our own version of this intriguing dish.

We began with the noodles. Sweet potato noodles are sold dry, packaged in foot-long bundles,

which stretch to about 3 feet in length once cooked—not exactly manageable for eating. And unlike other Asian noodles or Italian pasta, these noodles are unbreakable in their dry state. Before we figured out how to cut them down to size, however, we determined the best way to cook them. These noodles require an ample amount of water for cooking. It is important to cook them long enough so that they're softened but still chewy and elastic. Overcooking, we learned, turns these noodles slimy. We found that about 10 minutes in salted boiling water was long enough to yield perfect noodles.

By their nature, sweet potato noodles are very sticky and simply tossing the hot noodles with oil would not prevent them from sticking to one another. Instead, we found it necessary to thoroughly rinse the drained noodles in cold water. This was enough to wash away the excess starch while we cut them into manageable lengths with kitchen scissors. It's not an exact method but it works: Simply lift rinsed bundles of noodles from the colander and cut approximate 6-inch lengths. (We did try cutting the noodles on a cutting board, but this was a messy affair, to say the least.) Next, we tossed the cut noodles in a bowl with 1 tablespoon of sesame oil.

With our noodles set, we turned our attention to our sauce. Many recipes called for a sweet-salty mixture of ingredients. Korean rice wine called *cheongju* is a key ingredient. Chinese rice wine (*shaoxing*) is similar. Tasters tried both rice wines and found little difference. We also made the sauce with sherry, which tasters thought was just fine. The other sauce elements include sugar for further sweetness, soy sauce for saltiness and depth, and sesame oil, which adds richness and brings all the flavors into balance.

With our cooked noodles and sauce at the ready, we next needed to prepare the dish's other elements, the meat and vegetables. Beef is traditional and we chose blade steak, as we've had success stir-frying this cut in the past. We also chose the most common and popular vegetables found in recipes for this dish—shiitake mushrooms, carrots, and spinach. We began by borrowing 2 tablespoons of our sauce to season the beef just prior to cooking. We stir-fried the beef along with the shiitakes—the shiitakes soaked up any liquid exuded by the beef, allowing the beef to sear instead of steam in its own juices. We then transferred the beef and mushrooms to the waiting bowl of noodles.

Next, we cut the carrot into thin matchsticks and sautéed them with the garlic and spinach. We also transferred this mixture to the bowl of noodles. With the skillet clear, we cooked a quick flat omelet, then sliced it into thin strips and added it to the noodles as well. Once everything was in the bowl, we added the remaining sauce, and tossed it all together. The combination of flavors and textures is well worth the effort.

Sweet Potato Noodles with Beef and Vegetables
Japchae
SERVES 4

If you cannot find sweet potato noodles, mung bean noodles, often labeled "cellophane noodles," are sold in many well-stocked supermarkets and are an acceptable substitute. But note that mung bean noodles are much thinner than sweet potato noodles and therefore will cook in less time, so follow the package instructions for cooking.

NOODLES
- 1 tablespoon salt
- 12 ounces sweet potato noodles (see note)
- 1 tablespoon toasted sesame oil

SAUCE
- ¼ cup Chinese rice cooking wine or dry sherry
- ¼ cup soy sauce
- 3 tablespoons sugar
- 2 tablespoons toasted sesame oil

BEEF AND VEGETABLES
- 8 ounces blade steak, (see page 487) trimmed and cut into ¼-inch-thick slices following the illustration on page 487
- 3 tablespoons vegetable oil
- 8 ounces shiitake mushrooms, wiped clean, stemmed, and sliced thin
- 1 medium carrot, peeled and cut into matchsticks (see the illustrations on page 519)
- 3 medium garlic cloves, minced or pressed through a garlic press (about 1 tablespoon)
- 1 (10-ounce) bag baby spinach
- 2 large eggs, lightly beaten
- 2 scallions, sliced thin on the bias (see page 505)
- 2 tablespoons sesame seeds, toasted
  Salt and ground black pepper

PANTRY SPOTLIGHT

ASIAN CHILE PRODUCTS

There are a variety of chili-based sauces and pastes on the market and all are used to add a little heat to your Asian dishes. But how do you know what you're buying? Here's your guide to the basic styles that are available on American supermarket shelves.

Sriracha, also called Thai chili-garlic sauce, is the generic name for a Southeast Asian hot sauce from Thailand. It is named after the seaside town Si Racha, where it was first produced in small batches as a local product. It is made from sun-ripened chile peppers, vinegar, garlic, sugar, and salt. It has a consistency like slightly chunky ketchup—you might also see it labeled Asian chile sauce.

Sambal oelek or *sambal ulek*, also called Indonesian chile paste, is one of many varieties of Sambal, a spicy, red condiment used in Indonesia, Malaysia, Singapore and Sri Lanka—and is one of the more recognizable chile pastes found on supermarket shelves. It is made from a variety of peppers, although chile peppers are the most common, as well as sugar, salt, and sometimes garlic and vinegar.

Gochujang, also called Korean spicy bean paste, is a condiment that is dark red in color, with a smooth, paste-like consistency and a rich, spicy flavor. It is made from glutinous rice powder mixed with powdered fermented soybeans, red chili powder, and salt. Sometimes a bit of sweetener is added, such as sugar, syrup, or honey.

Hot chili oil is an infused oil consisting of a mildly flavored oil like canola or soybean and crushed dried hot chiles. It is used as a seasoning, in place of a chile paste or sauce when you want the heat of the chile, but no additional flavors.

1. FOR THE NOODLES: Bring 4 quarts of water to a boil in a large pot. Stir in the salt and noodles and cook, stirring occasionally, until tender but slightly chewy, about 10 minutes. Drain the noodles and rinse them under cold running water until cool. While lifting bunches of noodles in one hand, use kitchen scissors to cut the noodles into lengths of about 6 inches. Transfer the noodles to a very large bowl and toss with the oil; set aside.

2. FOR THE SAUCE: Whisk all of the ingredients together in a small bowl to dissolve the sugar.

3. FOR THE BEEF AND VEGETABLES: Toss the beef with 2 tablespoons of the sauce. Heat 1 tablespoon of the vegetable oil in a 12-inch nonstick skillet over medium-high heat until just smoking. Add the beef and shiitakes and cook until the beef is cooked through and the mushrooms are soft, about 3 minutes. Transfer the mixture to the bowl with the noodles.

4. Add 1 more tablespoon of the vegetable oil to the skillet and return over medium-high heat until shimmering. Add the carrot and cook until softened slightly, about 30 seconds. Stir in the garlic and cook until fragrant, about 30 seconds. Stir in the spinach and cook, tossing constantly, until wilted, about 1 minute. Transfer the mixture to the bowl with the noodles and beef.

5. Add the remaining 1 tablespoon oil to the skillet and return to low heat until shimmering. Add the eggs and cook, using a heatproof spatula to pull the set edges of the eggs toward the center, tilting the pan so any uncooked egg runs to the pan's edges. Turn the cooked egg pancake out onto a cutting board, and slice into 2-inch-long matchsticks. Transfer the eggs to the bowl with the noodles, beef, and vegetables. Pour the remaining sauce over the top and toss to combine. Sprinkle with the scallions and sesame seeds and season with salt and pepper to taste; serve.

PANTRY SPOTLIGHT

TOASTED SESAME OIL

Toasted, or dark, sesame oil, which has a deep amber color, is primarily used for seasoning because of its intense, nutty flavor. (Raw sesame oil, which is very mild and light in color, is used mostly for cooking.) Toasted sesame oil is frequently used to finish dishes all over Asia. Toasted sesame oil will turn rancid if not used within a few months. It is also particularly prone to damage from heat and light, so it should be purchased only in tinted glass and stored in the refrigerator.

PREPARING AN EGG PANCAKE

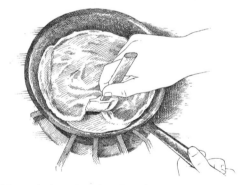

Pull the cooked eggs from the edges of the pan toward the center, tilting the pan so any uncooked egg runs to the pan's edges.

INDEX